CW09485247

AA

HOTELS AND RESTAURANTS IN BRITAIN

Consultant Editor: I M Tyers, FHCIMA, FTS, MCFA
Editor: Michael Buttler
Designers: Andrew Haughton, Ashley Tilleard, Gary Crook
Gazetteer: Compiled by the Publications Research Unit of the Automobile Association
Maps: Prepared by the Cartographic Services Unit of the Automobile Association
Design concept: Michael Preedy MSIAD
Cover Picture: Feathers Hotel, Ludlow

Head of Advertisement Sales: Christopher Heard Tel 0256 20123 (ext 2020)
Advertisement Production: Karen Weeks Tel 0256 20123 (ext 3525)
Advertisement Sales Representatives:
London, East Anglia, East Midlands, Melanie Mackenzie-Aird Tel 0494 40208
Central Southern and South East England, Edward May Tel 0256 20123 (ext 3524) or 0256 67568
South West, West, West Midlands, Bryan Thompson Tel 027580 3296
Wales, North of England, Scotland, Arthur Williams Tel 0222 60267

Filmset by: Tradespools Ltd, Frome, Somerset
Printed and bound by: Chorley and Pickersgill Ltd, Leeds

The contents of this book are believed correct at the time of printing. Nevertheless, the Publisher can accept no responsibility for errors or omissions or for changes in the details given. While every effort is made by the Publisher to ensure that the information appearing in advertisements is correct, no responsibility can be accepted for inaccuracies.

ISBN 0 86145 187 2

Published by The Automobile Association, Fanum House, Basingstoke, Hampshire RG21 2EA

Contents

Introduction

The 1984 edition of HOTELS AND RESTAURANTS IN BRITAIN is the fullest and best ever. We provide more detailed information about more hotels and restaurants than in previous years, with improved descriptions of most of them. Red star hotels are, as usual, described in considerable detail and this year we also provide more detail and extended descriptions of those hotels that received all three merit awards (***H***, ***B*** and ***L***) for the quality of their hospitality, bedrooms and public areas.

An important feature of the book this year is that it contains the results of a major AA survey into what the public really think of Britain's hotels – as opposed to what other so-called 'experts' say. Read about these fascinating findings on page 7.

Another of our themes this year is spotting new talent and new enterprises. We have been following the careers of a number of young chefs who are showing great promise, and on page 33 we pick the Top Ten of them as ***Star Chefs of Tomorrow***. We have also been looking for the Best Newcomer – that is the best hotel appearing in the guide for the first time this year. We have found ten superb, newly-appointed hotels, and awarded the finest of them the accolade of ***Best Newcomer***. In addition we have also announced the Regional Winners of this contest, and all the results, illustrated in colour, can be found in the article on page 17.

Our analysis of trends in the hotel and restaurant industry reflects the fact that we are still in a time of economic difficulty for Britain's hotels and restaurants. Only by providing good quality service and looking for ways of attracting custom will the hotelier continue to survive and, hopefully, prosper. Our survey on page 7 shows some areas of hotel operation that need watching. We have also found it disappointing that porterage seems to be getting more and more difficult to obtain.

Finally we would like to thank our readers for all the comments and suggestions about the book we receive, and we are also grateful to the hoteliers and restaurateurs who willingly co-operate in providing the information contained in the gazetteer.

Money-off Vouchers

Save £5 by using the money-off vouchers opposite. Each voucher, worth £1, entitles you to money off your hotel or restaurant bill at many of the establishments in this book. The full list of hotels and restaurants which are prepared to accept the voucher is given on page 693. In addition, each establishment's entry in the gazetteer contains the symbol VS if vouchers are accepted there.

The conditions of use of the vouchers, printed on the reverse side, are as follows:

* *A copy of **AA Hotels and Restaurants in Britain 1984** must be produced with the voucher.*

* *Only one voucher per person or party accepted.*

* *Not redeemable for cash. No change given.*

* *The voucher will not be valid after 31st December, 1984.*

* *Use of the voucher is restricted to when payment is made before leaving the hotel or restaurant premises.*

* *The voucher will only be accepted against hotel accommodation at full tariff rates or to restaurant bills over £5 excluding VAT and any service charge.*

The Voucher worth
£1
May be redeemed in accordance with the conditions overleaf at any of the 1,562 establishments listed on pages 693 et seq. of AA Hotels and Restaurants 1984 against a restaurant or hotel bill.
The Voucher worth
£1
May be redeemed in accordance with the conditions overleaf at any of the 1,562 establishments listed on pages 693 et seq. of AA Hotels and Restaurants 1984 against a restaurant or hotel bill.
The Voucher worth
£1
May be redeemed in accordance with the conditions overleaf at any of the 1,562 establishments listed on pages 693 et seq. of AA Hotels and Restaurants 1984 against a restaurant or hotel bill.
The Voucher worth
£1
May be redeemed in accordance with the conditions overleaf at any of the 1,562 establishments listed on pages 693 et seq. of AA Hotels and Restaurants 1984 against a restaurant or hotel bill.
The Voucher worth
£1
May be redeemed in accordance with the conditions overleaf at any of the 1,562 establishments listed on pages 693 et seq. of AA Hotels and Restaurants 1984 against a restaurant or hotel bill.

Conditions

A copy of AA Hotels and Restaurants in Britain 1984 must be produced with this voucher.

Only one voucher per person or party accepted.

Not redeemable for cash. No change given.

The voucher will not be valid after 31st December, 1984.

Use of the voucher is restricted to when payment is made before leaving the hotel or restaurant premises.

The voucher will only be accepted against hotel accommodation at full tariff rates or to restaurant bills over £5 excluding VAT and any service charge.

Conditions

A copy of AA Hotels and Restaurants in Britain 1984 must be produced with this voucher.

Only one voucher per person or party accepted.

Not redeemable for cash. No change given.

The voucher will not be valid after 31st December, 1984.

Use of the voucher is restricted to when payment is made before leaving the hotel or restaurant premises.

The voucher will only be accepted against hotel accommodation at full tariff rates or to restaurant bills over £5 excluding VAT and any service charge.

Conditions

A copy of AA Hotels and Restaurants in Britain 1984 must be produced with this voucher.

Only one voucher per person or party accepted.

Not redeemable for cash. No change given.

The voucher will not be valid after 31st December, 1984.

Use of the voucher is restricted to when payment is made before leaving the hotel or restaurant premises.

The voucher will only be accepted against hotel accommodation at full tariff rates or to restaurant bills over £5 excluding VAT and any service charge.

Conditions

A copy of AA Hotels and Restaurants in Britain 1984 must be produced with this voucher.

Only one voucher per person or party accepted.

Not redeemable for cash. No change given.

The voucher will not be valid after 31st December, 1984.

Use of the voucher is restricted to when payment is made before leaving the hotel or restaurant premises.

The voucher will only be accepted against hotel accommodation at full tariff rates or to restaurant bills over £5 excluding VAT and any service charge.

Conditions

A copy of AA Hotels and Restaurants in Britain 1984 must be produced with this voucher.

Only one voucher per person or party accepted.

Not redeemable for cash. No change given.

The voucher will not be valid after 31st December, 1984.

Use of the voucher is restricted to when payment is made before leaving the hotel or restaurant premises.

The voucher will only be accepted against hotel accommodation at full tariff rates or to restaurant bills over £5 excluding VAT and any service charge.

Britain's Hotels– An AA Hotel and Restaurant Guide Investigation

During 1983 the AA conducted an important survey of public attitudes towards, and usage of, hotels and other forms of accommodation in Britain including guesthouses, inns, farmhouses and campsites. Over 2,500 people, covering a complete cross-section of the community, were interviewed, almost a quarter of whom had been hotel users during the previous twelve months. Many aspects of their experience of hotels were analysed, and they were also asked about specific hotel operations and how successful some of these were. We looked at a number of aspects of hotel life that are popularly supposed to be unsatisfactory, and found that several of these were myths that could be soundly demolished by our findings. We also found some comments and results that caused us great concern and these also are discussed here.

This is by no means the first survey of its type carried out by the AA. The structure of our inspection team, and the inspectors' criteria for judging hotel standards, are based on regular feedback from our members and from market surveys. These keep us in touch with public tastes and requirements and, when we make our assessments, we balance them against our detailed knowledge of how hotels work. As public tastes change, so we reflect them in modification of our own requirements.

Cause for Complaint?

We know very well that a large number of hoteliers are friendly and hospitable people, for whom no aspect of their guests' comfort is too much trouble. The results of this AA investigation, however, showed that there were a number of instances where hoteliers could have been more helpful.

One of the most significant findings of this investigation was that, of all those who had stayed in hotels, one in four had, at some time, been obliged to complain about one aspect or another of their hotel. The detailed nature of these complaints was not discussed in the survey but the AA's own statistics are shown in the box on page 8.

Moreover, the investigation found that an alarmingly large number of people were dissatisfied with the way their complaint was handled. Nearly one third of those who complained felt that their grievance had been handled indifferently, poorly, that they had been fobbed off, or even that nothing was done. And a higher proportion still, 41%, did not know the outcome of their complaint. These people, perhaps, made their complaint at the end of their stay, and were not able to find out what was done about it. All this is not to deny, of course, that 39% were satisfied with the way their complaints were dealt with.

This seems to be a serious criticism of hotel managements. Certainly, there are many good hoteliers who are anxious to correct difficulties as soon as possible; yet clearly, many people feel there is room for improvement. Also, any guest who is dissatisfied can help resolve the situation by the attitude he adopts. There is a right and a wrong way to complain and we give our advice on how to do so in the panel opposite.

We shall be watching this subject closely during the coming year and have included a report form in the book to help us do this. We hope that everyone who stays in a hotel will use this form to let us know of their experience. We are interested in the good things as well as the problems and disappointments and we look forward to hearing your comments.

Some Myths Debunked

There were several further surprises in the results of our investigation. A number of criticisms of particular aspects of Britain's hotels have been made in recent years, and we have investigated to what extent hotel users agree with them.

Myth 1. Hotels offer poor value for money. There has been a great deal of publicity about how expensive British hotels are. We found that 78% of hotel users thought that the price they paid reflected good value for money, while 90% had a good idea in advance of what the cost of their room would be.

Myth 2. Hotel breakfasts are poor quality. There was little agreement with this myth. 89% of the sample found the quality of the food at breakfast was good, and 82% praised the service.

Myth 3. British hotels are unwelcoming. We found little support for this assertion. 85% agreed that they were made to feel welcome on arrival at the hotel. Our inspectors report that there is still some room for improvement in the hospitality at the reception desk, but it is pleasing that so many people felt they received a good welcome.

The AA Complaints File

The AA receives correspondence from members who have complaints against particular hotels, and records are kept about the aspects of the hotel operation complained about. The general categories into which these complaints fall are shown in the diagram below.

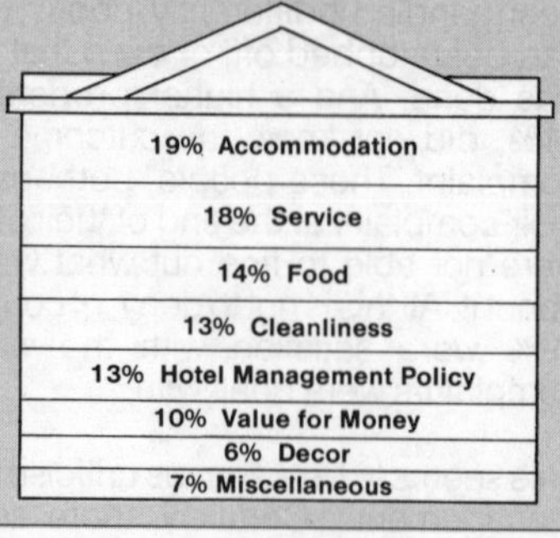

19% Accommodation
18% Service
14% Food
13% Cleanliness
13% Hotel Management Policy
10% Value for Money
6% Decor
7% Miscellaneous

Each category includes a wide variety of different individual topics of complaint, and, while the total number of these letters received by the AA has been dropping in recent years, the general pattern of complaints has remained broadly constant.

Page 691 contains a report form for use by all readers of this book. We should be very pleased to receive as many reports as possible about the hotels in this book with details of shortcomings, if any, and also commendations where appropriate.

How to make a complaint

Everyone with a legitimate complaint, in our opinion, is entitled to a fair hearing from the hotelier and reassurance as to what can be done about it. Points to remember are:

***Be reasonable.** The more reasonable the tone adopted when making the complaint the better the chance of getting something done; lost tempers are seldom the best way to resolve a dispute.

***Make your complaint promptly on the spot.** This should provide an opportunity for the hotelier to correct matters. Leaving the matter for a period of time can make it difficult or impossible to receive satisfaction.

*Only if a personal approach fails, write to the nearest AA Regional Office.

Problem areas

Overall, the results of our investigation show a high level of satisfaction with Britain's hotels. There were however, two problem areas highlighted. They were:

Problem 1 – the difficulty in controlling the temperature of the bedroom (34% commented on this).

Problem 2 – the difficulty in obtaining light refreshments outside regular meal times (23% commented on this).

Our team of inspectors studied the systems used for bedroom temperature control in over two hundred hotels of all types. They found considerable variation in the amount of control a guest could exercise over the bedroom temperature and several cases where the heating was not on when it should have been. The AA classification system imposes different requirements for different star ratings, but this is clearly an area we shall need to review. Nearly a quarter of hotel users said they found it difficult to obtain light refreshments outside regular meal times. Although the AA classification requirements vary according to the star rating of the hotel, we appreciate that the change in public eating habits during the past decade or so, together with the reduction in importance of the traditional hotel restaurant in many locations, have had their effect. Both we and hoteliers, therefore, must take account of the increasingly diverse needs of the hotel user relating to meal times and the nature of the refreshments provided.

Satisfactions

The generally high level of satisfaction with Britain's hotels shown by this investigation is gratifying, but allows us no room for complacency. The problem of dealing with complaints is a serious one that we shall be watching during the coming year, with the help of our readers.

Hotel and Restaurant Classification

This guide aims to provide, in an easily understood form as much up-to-date information as possible about AA inspected hotels and restaurants in Britain. Classifications are decided on a purely objective basis, as distinct from accolades such as red stars, rosettes and other subjective awards, which reflect personal opinions. The AA system of appointing hotels began in 1908. Over the years, standards have been adapted to take into account current trends in hotel construction and operation, and the changing requirements of members.

The Inspectors

Much of the inspectors' work consists of routine re-examination of premises, furniture, equipment and facilities. Life for them is by no means one long round of food, wine and luxury living. Inspectors are drawn from hotel and catering industries and from experienced staff within the Association. This creates a balance between qualified men and women with specialised knowledge of the industries on the one hand, and those with an expert appreciation of members' needs on the other. Regular courses serve to keep their knowledge abreast of the times, and consultants are available in each region to assist the inspectors in providing informed and unbiased reports upon which the Committees can base their decisions. Additional information from members – who themselves form a nation-wide inspectorate – is also greatly valued.

Hotels

Application for recognition and appointment is made to the AA by the proprietors. An inspector then visits the hotel unannounced, stays overnight and takes every opportunity of testing as many services as possible. Having settled his bill in the morning, he introduces himself and makes a thorough inspection of the entire premises. At subsequent discussions with the management he will draw attention to any points which may affect the classification. Once granted recognition and given a rating, the hotel is subject to annual inspection to ensure that standards are maintained. If the hotel changes hands, it is automatically deleted until the new proprietor applies for recognition and the hotel has been reassessed. Current applications and possible reclassifications or deletions are considered regularly by the Hotel Appointment Committee. This Committee also keeps the Association's general policy of classification under review.

Basic requirements for appointed hotels are: bedrooms with hot and cold water; adequate bath and lavatory arrangements; service of all meals (with a choice of main dishes) to residents. Full details of the principal requirements for each classification are printed in the leaflet HH5 ***Hotels and the Automobile Association*** available from the Hotels Department, AA Regional Headquarters (addresses in ***Members' Handbook***).

Black stars denote hotels offering traditional service in traditional accommodation. The majority of AA-appointed hotels are in this category.

★ Good hotels and inns, generally of small scale and with acceptable facilities and furnishings.

★★ Hotels offering a higher standard of accommodation, with some private bathrooms/showers; lavatories on all floors; wider choice of food.

★★★ Well-appointed hotels; a good proportion of bedrooms with private bathrooms/showers.

★★★★ Exceptionally well-appointed hotels offering high standards of comfort and service, the majority of bedrooms having private bathrooms/showers.

★★★★★ Luxury hotels offering the highest international standards.

Note: Hotels often satisfy ***some*** of the requirements for a higher classification than that awarded. In provincial 5 star hotels some of the services are provided on a more informal and restricted basis.

☆ White Stars indicate establishments high in amenities but which have deliberately limited services, designed and operated to cater mainly for short stay guests.

- 🏠 Denotes an AA Country House hotel, where a relaxed, informal atmosphere prevails. Some of the facilities may differ from those at urban hotels of the same classification.
- ○ Hotels due to open during the currency of this guide which had not been inspected at the time of going to press.

Red Star Hotels ★

Red Stars were introduced in 1975 and indicate the hotels that AA inspectors consider to be of outstanding merit within their classification. In each of them it is hoped you will find a warm welcome and a high standard of hospitality. Red Stars are awarded only after a great deal of consideration, and a change of management or ownership is likely to result in the award being carefully reviewed. In the whole of Great Britain there are only 51 Red Star hotels (see list on page 705 for locations). They are highlighted in the gazetteer by a special panel containing detailed description and a photograph, as well as the standard information. Look out for red stars and the words 'a red star hotel' on those familiar, yellow, AA hotel signs.

Merit Symbols

The black (and white) star awards for hotels are based upon an objective assessment by the AA inspector, in accordance with a carefully laid down set of criteria. In many cases, however, there are particular aspects of a hotel that are very good and better than that implied by the star classification awarded to that hotel. In order to highlight these more subjective assessments a system of merit symbols was introduced in 1982. Three symbols are used, printed in red in the gazetteer. A hotel may qualify for one or more of these awards. See page 705 for a quick reference list of all these hotels. Hotels which are considered of outstanding merit in all respects within their star category are awarded Red Stars.

The three symbols are:

- ***H*** Hospitality, friendliness and service well above the average for hotels similarly classified.
- ***B*** Bedrooms significantly better than those to be expected within the star classification.
- ***L*** Lounges, bars and public areas significantly above the standard implied by the star classification.

Restaurants

Restaurant classifications are assessed differently from those for hotels. For the most part, the approach is made by the Association rather than the proprietor. AA inspectors seek out new restaurants and visit them anonymously. Subsequently they report to the Restaurant Committee who, if they consider the cuisine to be of a high enough standard, award 'crossed knives and forks' to denote the physical amenities.

The basic requirements for the recommendation of any restaurant are a high standard of cuisine, prompt and courteous service, pleasant atmosphere and value for money.

- X Modest but good restaurant
- XX Restaurant offering a higher standard of comfort than above
- XXX Well-appointed restaurant
- XXXX Exceptionally well-appointed restaurant
- XXXXX Luxury restaurant

Rosettes

The Association introduced the first subjective award system in 1955. It was felt that an accolade should be awarded to hotels and restaurants where our inspectors considered the food was of a particularly high standard. A quick reference list appears on page 705.

- ❀ Hotel or restaurant where the cuisine is considered to be of a higher standard than is expected in an establishment within its classification.
- ❀❀ Hotel or restaurant offering very much above the average food irrespective of classification.
- ❀❀❀ Hotel or restaurant offering outstanding food, irrespective of classification.

We have superb hotels from Land's End to John O'Groats. (Except Land's End and John O'Groats.)

GRIMSBY
LIVER...
ST ANNES
ABERDEEN
GATWICK
BEXLEY
SWINDON
YEOVIL
WALSALL
PRESTON
LEEDS
STOW
HULL
LUTON
BASILDON
MAIDENHEAD
SOUTHSEA
BRISTOL
EXETER
DERBY
ABERDEEN
COVENTRY
GLOUCESTER
CARDIFF

A Crest Hotel's just the place to relax, especially after a long drive.

And fortunately, there are lots of them.

Fifty-four, to be exact. Ideally situated throughout the UK near places of interest and motorway networks.

All with one thing in common:

The same high standard of comfort and service you've come to expect from Crest.

What may be an unexpected bonus is this. If you take advantage of our special Family Weekend Plan, you could end up with some extra spending money.

By getting a double room for the price of a single and free accommodation for children under 14.

So why not give us a ring at one of the numbers below. Because no matter where you're planning on going, you don't have to go without a Crest Hotel.

Crest Hotels

Reservation numbers, from south to north

London (01) 903 6422, **Birmingham** (021) 6434428 **Coventry** (0203) 611813, **Manchester** (061) 834 1300 **Preston** (0772) 52682, **Glasgow** (041) 211 223.

How to use this book

Annexes

The number of bedrooms available in an annexe is shown in the gazetteer entry provided they are at least of the same standard as those in the rest of the hotel. Facilities may not be the same as in the main building, however, and it is advisable to check the nature of the accommodation and the tariff before making a reservation. In some hotels accommodation is only available in an annexe.

Children

Hotels listed accommodate children of all ages unless a minimum age is given but it does not necessarily follow that they are able to provide special facilities. If you have very young children, enquire into the arrangements (such as the provision of cots and high chairs) and whether reductions are made for children, before reserving accommodation. Establishments which do have special facilities for children are indicated by the symbol ♣. All the following amenities will be found at these establishments: 'baby-sitting service or baby intercom system, playroom or playground, laundry facilities, drying and ironing facilities, cots and high chairs, and special meals. Some hotels offer free accommodation provided children share their parents' room.

Club licences

Note that at hotels which have registered clubs, club membership cannot take effect – nor can drink be bought – until forty-eight hours after joining.

Coaches

Some of the gazetteer entries include a no-coaches symbol ⛟. This information has been compiled and published in good faith from the details supplied to the AA by the establishment concerned. If, however, the establishment is an inn at law, it has certain well-defined obligations to travellers. This would be a matter for the customer to take up with either the proprietor or the licensing authorities of the area.

Company-owned hotels

In some entries, the name of the group operating the hotel follows the address. A key to the abbreviations used may be found on page 59. Before its name is shown in the guide a company must own at least five AA appointed hotels, or a hotel must be affiliated to one of the following marketing consortia: Best Western, ExecHotels, Inter-Hotels, Minotels or Prestige.

Complaints

Members who wish to complain about food, services or facilities are urged to do so promptly on the spot, since this should provide an opportunity for the hotelier or restaurateur to correct matters. If a personal approach fails, members should inform the AA regional office nearest to the establishment concerned.

Credit cards

The numbered boxes below indicate the credit cards which the hotels and restaurants accept.

1 Access/Euro
2 American Express
3 Barclays Visa
4 Carte Blanche
5 Diners

It is advisable to check when booking to ensure that the cards are still accepted.

Disabled persons

If the wheelchair symbol ♿ is shown in a hotel's entry it means that a disabled person can be accommodated. This information has been supplied to the AA by the hotel proprietor, but it is advisable to check with the hotel concerned before making reservations. Details more relevant to disabled persons may be obtained from the *AA Guide for the Disabled Traveller*, (1983 edition) available from AA offices, free to members, £1.50 to non-members. Members with any form of disability should notify proprietors, so that appropriate arrangements can be made to minimise difficulties, particularly in the event of an emergency.

Dogs

Hotels that do not allow dogs into bedrooms are indicated by a symbol ★ but other establishments may impose restrictions as to the size of dogs permitted, and the rooms into which they may be taken. Hotels which may not normally accept dogs may allow guide dogs. The conditions under which pets are accepted should be confirmed with the management when bookings are being made. Generally dogs are not allowed in the dining room.

Dress

Some hotels and restaurants do not permit guests to enter the dining-room or restaurant in informal or unconventional dress.

Fire precautions

So far as we can discover every hotel in Great Britain listed in this publication has applied for and not been refused a fire certificate. Remember that the Fire Precautions Act does not apply to the Channel Islands, or the Isle of Man, which exercise their own rules with regard to fire precautions for hotels.

Gazetteer

The gazetteer is listed in strict alphabetical town order throughout, including the London section.

In the restaurant entry, the '*bedrooms available*' phrase is for information only, and does not infer that they have been inspected by the AA.

When establishments' names are shown in ***italics*** the particulars have not been confirmed by the management.

The order is red stars, then black or white by alphabetical listing under each classification in descending star order. Hotels precede restaurants. (See also page 60.)

Licence to sell alcohol

All hotels and restaurants listed are licensed for the sale and consumption of intoxicating liquor unless otherwise stated.

Licensing – children and young persons on licensed premises

England Children under 14 are not allowed in bars (including any place exclusively or mainly used for the sale and consumption of intoxicating liquor) during permitted hours (unless they are children of the licence-holder, or are resident but not employed in the premises or are passing through the bar to or from some other part of the building which is not a bar and to or from which there is no other convenient access). When a bar is usually set apart for the service of table meals and is not used for the sale of intoxicating liquor except for consumption by persons having table meals as an ancillary to the meal this prohibition does not apply. In licensed premises, alcoholic drinks may not be sold to, or purchased by, persons under the age of 18; neither may such persons consume intoxicating liquor in a bar. 16–18-year-olds may purchase beer, porter, cider or perry for consumption with a meal in a part of the premises (not a bar) usually set apart for the service of meals.

Basically similar laws apply in Wales and Scotland but more details, together with information pertaining to the Channel Islands, Isle of Man and Isles of Scilly, may be found in the leaflet, HH20 (see *Licensing hours*).

Licensing hours

The general licensing hours, subject to modification by the Justices, permitted in public houses are as follows:

England 11.00–15.00hrs and 17.30–22.30hrs on weekdays (23.00hrs in London and certain other places), 12.00–14.00hrs and 19.00–22.30hrs on Sundays, Christmas Day, and Good Friday.

Wales As above except that there is no Sunday opening in the following 'dry' districts (June 1978):
Ceredigion (old administrative county of Cardiganshire); and Dwyfor (parts of old county of Caernarfonshire).

Scotland 11.00–14.30hrs & 17.00–23.00 on seven days a week; some still close at 22.00hrs or 22.30hrs on Mondays to Thursdays. Many do not open on Sundays depending on the area.

Channel Islands, Isle of Man & Isles of Scilly Licensing hours in these areas are complex and details may be obtained from leaflet HH20 *The Law about Licensing Hours & Children/ Young Persons on Licensed Premises* available from AA offices.

Licensed hotels and restaurants The general position is that separate rules apply to these premises. But, with exceptions, the permitted hours are as above with extensions in certain circumstances. Hotel residents may be served intoxicating liquor at any time but special rules govern their guests.

NB *Contents of the above two main sections have been compiled by the AA on the information available to it, as part of its service to members, and the contents are believed correct as at March 1983. However it should be noted that laws can change.*

Meals

The terms quoted are for full English breakfast unless otherwise stated. (An English breakfast is a cooked meal usually of three courses, including items like cereals with milk, eggs and bacon, and toast with butter and marmalade.)

All four- and five-star hotels serve *morning coffee*. Many one- and two-star hotels provide only limited lunch facilities and non-residents may be refused service. In awarding stars, the Association has taken each such case on its merits. Some hotels also find it uneconomical to serve *afternoon tea* but this is normally available at all four- and five-star hotels and at most three-star hotels to residents. In some parts of Britain, particularly in Scotland, *high tea* (*ie* a savoury dish followed by bread and butter, scones, cake, etc) is sometimes served instead of dinner which may, however, be available on request. The last time at which high tea or dinner may be ordered on weekdays is shown, but this may be varied at weekends. On Sundays some hotels serve the main meal at midday and provide only a cold supper in the evening. Some hotels serve meals only between stated hours and the dining room is closed at other times.

Morning coffee and afternoon tea

The ✿ symbol in the gazetteer entry means that morning coffee is served to chance callers.
If the symbol ☕ appears it means that afternoon tea is served to chance callers. This can vary from a pot of tea to a full tea with light refreshments.

Night porter

All four- and five-black star hotels have night porters on duty. Other hotels employing a night porter are shown in the gazetteer by ☾.

Prices

Inflation, variations in the rate of VAT and many other factors may influence tariffs in the coming year so you should always ascertain the current prices before making a booking. Those given in this book have been provided by hoteliers and restaurateurs in good faith and must be accepted as indications rather than firm estimates. Where proprietors have not provided information about 1984 prices you are requested to make enquiries direct. Bed and breakfast terms – which include a full English breakfast (see *Meals*, page 14) unless otherwise stated – are quoted in the guide. These show minimum and maximum prices for one and two persons, but charges may vary according to the time of year. Where a Continental breakfast is included in the price quoted, this is stated in the gazetteer. Some hotels charge for bed, breakfast and dinner whether dinner is taken or not. Many hotels, particularly in short-season holiday areas, accept period bookings only at full-board rate. Prices are inclusive of VAT and service where applicable.

Minimum and maximum table d'hôte prices are given for main meals served in hotel dining-rooms and restaurants. Where an à la carte menu is available, the average price of a three-course dinner and lunch is shown. In cases where establishments offer both types of menu, table d'hôte prices are the only ones given, but with an indication that à la carte is also available. All prices should include cover charge. The price of wine quoted is that of the cheapest full bottle (*ie* 70cl). (See also *Reservations* below on this page.)

Private facilities in rooms

Where rooms have *en suite* bath or shower and WC the number precedes the appropriate symbol or symbols. Where both symbols appear together rooms generally offer both bath and shower.

Reservations, Deposits, Cancellations, and Payment of Bills

Book as early as possible, particularly if accommodation is required during a holiday period (beginning of July to end of September plus Public Holidays, and during the ski-ing season in some parts of Scotland). Some hotels, particularly in large towns and holiday centres, ask for a deposit, and some also ask for full payment in advance, especially for one-night bookings taken from chance callers. Not all hotels take advance bookings for bed and breakfast for only one or two nights, and some will not accept reservations from midweek.

Once the booking has been confirmed do notify the hotel straightaway if you are in any doubt about whether you can keep to the arrangements you have made. If the hotel cannot re-let your accommodation you may be liable to pay about two-thirds of the price you would have paid had you stayed there (your deposit will count towards this payment). Please note that in Britain it is accepted that a legally binding contract has been made as soon as a hotel has accepted your booking, either in writing or on the telephone. Illness is not accepted as a release from this contract. For these reasons you are advised to effect insurance cover, *eg AA Travelsure*, against a possible cancellation.

Most hotels will accept cheques in payment of accounts only if notice is given and some form of identification (preferably a cheque card) is produced. Travellers' cheques issued by the leading banks and agencies are accepted by many hotels, but not all. If a hotel accepts credit or charge cards, this is indicated in the relevant gazetteer entry.

The hotel industry's Voluntary Code of Booking Practice was introduced in June 1977 and the AA encourages its use in appropriate establishments. Its prime object is to ensure that the customer is clear about the precise services and facilities he is buying, and what price he will have to pay, before he commits himself to a contractually binding agreement. The guest should be handed a card at the time of registration stipulating the total obligatory charge. The Tourism (Sleeping Accommodation Price Display) Order 1977 compels hotels, motels, guesthouses, farmhouses, inns and self-catering accommodation with four or more letting bedrooms to display in entrance halls the minimum and maximum prices charged for each category of room. This order complements the Voluntary Code of Booking Practice.

Restricted service

Some hotels whilst remaining open operate a restricted service during the less busy months. This is indicated by the prefix RS. RS Nov–Mar, for example, indicates that a restricted service is operated from November to March. This may take the form of a reduction in meals served or accommodation available, or in some cases both.

Tea and coffee in bedrooms

The symbol ® means that tea and coffee making facilities are available in bedrooms, although they may only be available on request; so please check when booking. The nature of these facilities will vary from hotel to hotel.

Telephone calls

Many hotels impose a surcharge for calls made through the switchboard. Always ascertain full details before making the call. A public telephone is usually available in the hotel hallway or foyer.

Telephone numbers

Unless otherwise stated, the **telephone exchange** is that of the town under which the establishment is listed. Where the exchange for a particular establishment is not that of the town under which it appears, the name of the exchange is given after the telephone symbol ☏ and before the dialling code and number. In some areas telephone numbers are likely to be changed by the telephone authorities during the currency of this publication. In case of difficulty, check with the operator.

Television

If the gazetteer entry shows 'CTV' or 'TV' this indicates that either colour or monochrome television is available in a lounge. The entry may also show the number of guests' bedrooms with 'CTV' or 'TV' available. This can be in the form of televisions permanently fixed or available on request from the hotel management. In all cases these points should be checked when making a reservation.

Telex numbers

When making a hotel reservation by telex it is advisable to specify which hotel you wish to book with as some hotels (particularly those in groups) use a central telex service.

Value Added Tax

In the United Kingdom and the Isle of Man, VAT is payable on both basic prices and any service. The symbol S% in the gazetteer indicates that the inclusive prices shown reflect any separate accounting for service made by the establishment. VAT does not apply in the Channel Islands. With this exception, prices quoted in the gazetteer are inclusive of VAT.

Vegetarian

Where the symbol **V** appears in the gazetteer entry the proprietor has indicated that a choice of vegetarian dishes are available. However it is advisable to check with the establishment before booking.

Best Newcomer

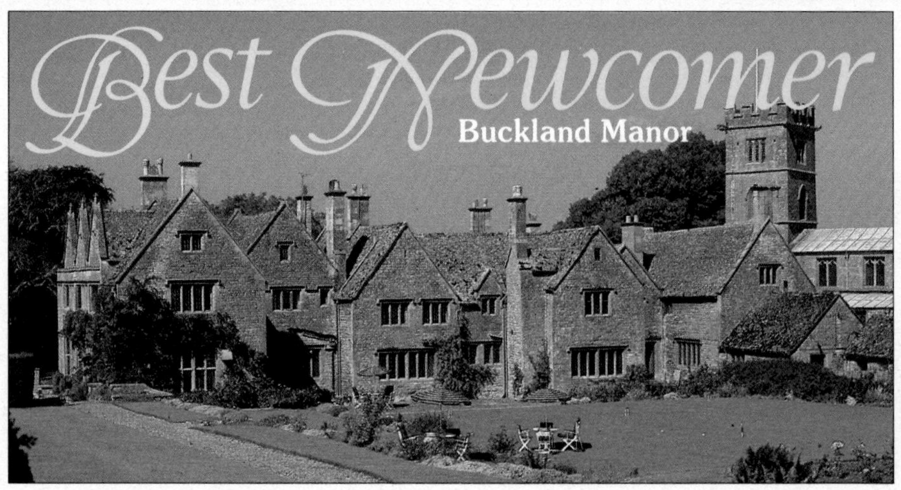
Best Newcomer
Buckland Manor

Every year new hotels open and, on receiving AA appointment, are featured in this guide. This year we have looked at all the new ventures to come our way and have picked the best of them all for this feature. As it happens none of them is brand new, or a purpose-built hotel; all are conversions of older houses into comfortable, relaxing, and frequently elegant, hotels. None of them has appeared in an AA guide before, and several have been open only a short time. In these days of economic hardship and depression it is heartening to find imaginative, optimistic ventures getting off the ground, usually thanks to the devotion and energy of enthusiastic individuals.
The results of our search to find the Best Newcomers are:

Best in Britain and Winner for

South West England
Buckland Manor
Buckland
Gloucestershire

South East England
Oakley Court Hotel
Water Oakley
Windsor
Berkshire

Midlands
Congham Hall
Grimston
Kings Lynn
Norfolk

Northern England
Devonshire Arms Hotel
Bolton Abbey
North Yorkshire

Wales
Celtic Manor Hotel
Newport
Gwent

Scotland
Balcraig House
Scone
Tayside

Runners up

Arisaig House
Arisaig
Highland

Netherfield Place
Battle
East Sussex

Ardsheal House
Kentallen of Appin
Highland

Hob Green Hotel
Markington
Harrogate
North Yorkshire

BUCKLAND MANOR, BUCKLAND, GLOUCESTERSHIRE

THE TINY, ALMOST PERFECT HAMLET of Buckland is tucked away at the end of a no-through-road beneath the Cotswold Hills, and only a stone's throw from the over-crowded, over-commercialised showpiece village of Broadway. It is an oasis of peace amid a bustling tourist area, and is the setting for a fine hotel, Buckland Manor.

There is no mistaking this grand, golden-stone manor house as you drive into Buckland village. Beside the church (almost joined on to it, apparently) is a graceful, gabled house that has obviously been part of the village since earliest times. Old and historic it certainly is, but this house is now a beautiful and hospitable hotel that offers every comfort with attentive, friendly service, superb haute-cuisine food, relaxing gardens, a wide range of amenities and a wonderful, natural setting. It opened in May 1982, and appears in the AA guide for the first time this year.

The hotel has eleven fine bedrooms, all with deep pile carpets, en-suite bathrooms, some with separate shower as well as bath, television (all colour with remote control and Video) and direct dial telephones. Those thoughtful extra touches, that distinguish the caring host include bathrobes, hair dryers, and attractive soap and bath gel, as well as welcoming extras such as fresh flowers, bowls of fruit and Malvern water in the bedrooms. Two of the bedrooms have antique four poster beds, and one, the Garden Room, has its own door leading to part of the front gardens. Every comfort is to hand in the bedrooms and the suites, and an unusual feature is that all the bathrooms are fed with spring water from the manor's own spring.

Adrienne and Barry Berman began to create this country house hotel in March 1982, when they first moved in. In an amazing nine weeks they had converted a tired, rather damp old mansion into this comfortable, welcoming hotel. They had to completely renovate all the bedrooms, installing the bathrooms and fitting them with all modern comforts. They had to design and build the kitchen, and bring mains water and gas to it, install a new central heating system, a fire alarm system with smoke and heat detectors, and they also needed to put the gardens into shape. That all this work was completed in so short a time is a credit to their energy and determination, and also to all the craftsmen who worked with them. Staying in the house today, it is impossible to believe that the atmosphere has not always been so relaxed and comfortable.

The earliest days of the manor go back to at least 600AD when it was mentioned in the records of Gloucester Abbey who received it as a gift from one of the rulers of Mercia, a certain King Kynred. At the time of the Domesday Book, the estate was reckoned to be worth £9. The church next-door is a most interesting building and dates from the 13th century, when the original manor house, part of which is retained in the fabric of the hotel, was built. Only recently, some unique ceiling paintings were uncovered in the church, and these are so unusual as to be of national importance.

The house itself stayed in the keeping of Gloucester Abbey until the Dissolution, when it passed to the Gresham family. They exchanged it for property in Yorkshire and it subsequently passed to the Thynne family whose relation Colonel Bernard Granville, lived in the house with his family from 1715. Both the Thynnes and Colonel Granville have memorials in the church. A daughter of the Granvilles was Mrs Delany, who became famous for her interest in botany. One of the many books in the hotel is one about this lady, *Mrs Delany, Her Life and Her Flowers* by Ruth Hayden, which contains interesting references to the house in earlier days, and also an old engraving of it.

Today's visitor can, if he wishes, bask in these historic echoes, or, alternatively, he could explore the sweet-smelling spacious gardens. At the upper extreme, there are some most attractive water gardens, with a feast of unusual wild flowers, many of them protected species. As well as these, there is a host of exotic imported plants, bamboos and ornamental shrubs which have been preserved through the years by one of the previous owners of the manor. They all remain to delight those who stroll through the gardens.

For the more energetic there is tennis or swimming in the heated pool, and for the langourous, a round on the putting green or croquet on the excellent lawn might appeal or perhaps a gentle journey in the pony and trap to some of the nearby attractions such as Broadway. Riding is also available for those who enjoy it.

After a day's activity out of doors, there is plenty of incentive to relax inside the house. Adrienne and Barry Berman are impeccable hosts, and endeavour to provide every comfort. Dinner itself is a splendid experience master-minded by Chef de Cuisine Robert Elsmore, who came here after working with Anton Mosimann at the Dorchester, London. All the food is well prepared using produce from local suppliers wherever possible, the Vale of Evesham which is so close, and the gardens of the hotel, where the herbs and many of the vegetables are grown.

One item we particularly liked was the granité, an iced mixture of red wine and fruit syrups that makes a refreshing end (or interlude) to the meal. There is a sound wine list, and Barry Berman is obviously an

enthusiastic advocate of its virtues. The fresh cafétière coffee and petits fours make a fitting conclusion to the meal.

A fine setting, good food, and an interesting and comfortable house go nearly all the way to making an excellent hotel, but they would not gel without the essential lubricant of attentive and caring hosts. Adrienne and Barry Berman have not worked in the hotel industry before opening this hotel, but they show how important is their caring interest in their guests' comfort, food, wine and welfare.

Everyone who stays here will have been looked after extremely well and will feel that they have been most welcome guests in a beautiful house.

OAKLEY COURT HOTEL, WATER OAKLEY, WINDSOR, BERKSHIRE

A FANTASTIC VICTORIAN GOTHIC BUILDING with turrets, castellations and ornamented pinnacles reaching to the sky, Oakley Court was originally built in 1859. After 1965, it lay empty for nearly twenty years and during this time Bray Studios saw it as a superb and atmospheric location, when over two hundred films were made at the house. Some of the more famous ones were 'Half a Sixpence', 'The Rocky Horrow Show' and the St Trinians series. But perhaps most appropriately, the largest number of films were the Dracula films in the Hammer House of Horror series. Today, though, there are no frights in store for guests at this most comfortable of hotels. It is in a beautiful riverside setting, elegantly and comfortably furnished and with friendly, most attentive service.

The work of converting the old house to a luxury hotel was started in 1979 when it was acquired by the Celebrated Country Hotels Group. Two new bedroom wings were added at Oakley Court, and the bedroom suites in the main house were fully restored and modernised.

As much as possible of the original plastering was restored, and this is particularly effective in the White Lounge. A very attractive and popular room is the Billiard Room, where the 300 year old table has been beautifully restored.

As befits a luxury hotel, all the bedrooms are very comfortable indeed and well equipped. There are four luxury suites in the house itself and they all have views of the river. One even has a secret compartment that used to go down to the cellars. The hidden door still works but access to the cellars has been closed off. The rooms in the annexes are also large and have views of either the river or the extensive gardens.

The food in the large dining room is always most enjoyable. It is prepared by Paul Magson, who came here from the Hyde Park Hotel, London. He combines the best ideas from both classical and nouvelle cuisine, and also specialises in Taste of England dishes. There is an elegantly furnished bar and very comfortable lounge, drawing room and library with a very wide selection of books. Great care has been lavished on all aspects of the decor and furnishings and the effect is luxurious and comfortable.

The general manager is Mr Hester who came here from the Grand Hotel at Torquay. He and the very pleasant staff provide an excellent standard of service that makes the guest feel really cossetted, one of the most essential aspects of an enjoyable hotel stay.

BALCRAIG HOUSE, SCONE, TAYSIDE

THIS LARGE, STONE, VICTORIAN HOUSE IN enormous grounds was built in 1872, and came on to the market in 1980. Michael and Kitty Pearl bought it and by the end of 1981 had decided to open it as a hotel. The first eight months of 1982 were devoted to hectic restoration work with great care being exercised to ensure that all the craftsmanship was of the highest possible standard. Michael Pearl was very interested in antiques and paintings and he was able to see that the house was decorated and furnished in exquisite taste. There are beautiful pictures and fine pieces of furniture wherever you look, particularly in the library and the drawing room.

At this fine hotel, the food is particularly carefully prepared. There is a very interesting farm and market garden surrounding the hotel where as much as possible is produced for the table. Sixty varieties of herbs are grown here in probably the most extensive herb garden of any hotel in Scotland. A wide variety of vegetables and fruits are also grown, including the new variety of Tayberry as well as melons, peppers, and red, green and yellow gooseberries. The farm provides most of the poultry and meat for the table, from the carefully prepared and splendid gamecock to guinea fowl, quails and the recently purchased wild boar. The pedigree Aberdeen Angus herd has a prize bull which was champion at the famous Perth Bull Sales.

With such excellent produce so imaginatively prepared, chef Malcolm Smith provides a regularly changing, enjoyable menu. Michael Pearl looks after the wine list which is a very extensive, catholic list featuring over 300 wines from all over the world. It is particularly strong on clarets, and the specially constructed wine cellar holds around 5,000 bottles.

All the bedrooms are particularly attractive and each one is different. One has a four poster bed, the others have individual and unusual brass beds. Special care has been lavished on the bathrooms which have twin washbasins which were specially made in different shades of marble, and each bathroom has its own beautiful mural specially created by Sally Anderson.

Every detail of this perfectly furnished hotel has been carefully thought out from scratch by Michael and Kitty Pearl, a couple with no previous experience of hotel keeping. Its beauty and its relaxing atmosphere are a tribute to their energy and judgement.

Celtic Manor

CELTIC MANOR, NEWPORT, GWENT

THIS GOOD, CAREFULLY RESTORED HOTEL WAS converted from a Victorian and Edwardian house standing high above the M4 motorway just outside Newport in South Wales. The house was originally built in 1865 for Thomas Powell, but he was murdered and eaten by cannibals in Abyssinia three years later. After belonging to a series of local coal barons, it subsequently became a maternity hospital and for sixty years until the late 1970s faithfully looked after around 60,000 babies. Then it was closed because of a Local Authority cut-back and it remained empty for the next four years. Celtic Inns acquired it in 1981, and they set about an extensive programme of renovation and improvement, opening the present hotel in April 1982.

From the rooms in the original house, seventeen bedrooms have been created, two of them with four-poster beds and all of them with en-suite bathrooms. The original matron's office and sitting room have been converted into the à la carte restaurant, Hedleys. This is a lovely room with two very attractive stained glass windows. One of these represents the Christening of the first Prince of Wales, and in the evening they take on a magical aspect when they are floodlit from the back. The chef is David Hill and he presents a popular, varied menu. The other restaurant is the Patio, which is a modern glass and steel extension to the side of the original house. This is kept well cooled and has splendid views over the M4 motorway. A less extensive grill menu is available in this restaurant.

The Lounge Bar has been splendidly reconstructed from the original drawing room which had previously fallen into a worse state of decay than any other in the house. It is a light and popular room, situated at the foot of the fine sweeping Edwardian wooden staircase. Another bar has been created in the cellar and uses brickwork decor to create an authentic relaxing atmosphere.

The modernisation of this unusual old house has been tastefully and skilfully done. Every modern comfort has been provided and the most interesting aspects of the old house have been retained. Appropriately, several of the staff were born here in the days when it was a maternity hospital and they ensure a continuity of life here. This is a newly opened hotel and there are ambitious plans to expand it and to increase the range of facilities it offers. It is in an attractive area of South Wales, and provides excellent facilities for the tourist and businessman alike.

CONGHAM HALL, GRIMSTON, KINGS LYNN, NORFOLK

THIS 18TH CENTURY MANOR HOUSE WAS bought by Christine and Trevor Forecast in April 1982 from Lady Meriel Howarth and they spent six months converting it to a luxury country house hotel. They employed the talents of Donald Warren of Herts Interiors to turn their ideas into reality. He has created a thoroughly tasteful interior with some clever and attractive colour schemes. Light yellow forms a unifying theme for the hall and drawing room while the beautiful dining room is pink and lily with trailing plants giving a garden atmosphere.

The Chef, John McGeever is very much part of the team behind the hotel. He is a very promising young chef with plenty of ideas for making food interesting and enjoyable. He is a member of the Society of Master Chefs and is particularly keen to use and explore local produce. One of his dishes is red mullet served with pickled samphire, the samphire being a Norfolk delicacy, rather like asparagus, that grows particularly well on the East Anglia salt marshes. He is very interested in the fish recipes that were devised in the Cromer area, and he gets his oysters from Cromer and Blakeney. Most of the herbs and the more unusual and exotic vegetables and fruits are grown in the hotel gardens, and John McGeever has been known to keep the crayfish in the hotel stream. Dinner is served as an eight course meal with each dish modest and satisfying. The wine list includes selections from many countries and is reasonably priced.

There are nine bedrooms in the house, including two most attractive suites. One of them has a four poster bed and they all have very good and nicely decorated bathrooms with electronic showers. Heating in the bedrooms can be controlled to suit individual requirements via a centralised computer controlled system at the reception desk. Every room has a hair dryer and a wide range of small toiletries. For those who like to completely relax in a Jacuzzi, there is a special, individual spa bath available.

The house is set in forty-four acres of rambling parkland. There is a heated outdoor swimming pool, tennis court and the hotel owns the local cricket pitch. Among the outbuildings are stables and loose boxes, so that riding on your own horse can easily be enjoyed. In this peaceful setting with so many facilities to hand, it is impossible not to relax, and the Forecasts make every effort to help their guests do just that. As they say, they aim to provide 'a bit of magic and a lot of relaxation'.

DEVONSHIRE ARMS HOTEL, BOLTON ABBEY, NORTH YORKSHIRE

THE HOTEL IS SITUATED IN BEAUTIFUL Wharfedale in the Yorkshire Dales National Park. It is part of the Bolton Abbey Estate, the family estate of the Duke of Devonshire, and was taken over by the Trustees of the Chatsworth Settlement in 1980, when it was decided to completely restore and enlarge the original coaching inn into a comfortable hotel. A leading part in the planning and restoration work was played by the Duchess of Devonshire herself and the result has been a uniquely personal stamp on this very tasteful and elegant hotel, which re-opened in June 1982.

Reminders of the links with the Devonshire family are everywhere. The carpets throughout the hotel were specially designed to incorporate the Devonshire crest and the superbly woven carpet in the Restaurant is most attractive. Striking colour schemes have been used to create individual identities in several rooms, particularly the Restaurant, and the Yellow Room with its fascinating set of engravings. Indeed items from Chatsworth fill much of the hotel and there are many fine antiques and fascinating pictures. One of the most unusual pictures recently acquired for the hotel, is of the Craven Heifer. This was an enormous beast kept on the Devonshire Estate at Bolton, and the Duchess has challenged anyone to produce records of a larger animal.

There are nine bedrooms in the original building, superbly furnished with antiques and paintings. Two of them have four poster beds which were specially made by the craftsmen on the Chatsworth Estate. In the new wing are a further twenty-nine bedrooms, which are all large and airy, and very well equipped. Some of them overlook the quadrangle lawn and some the local cricket ground.

The food is prepared by the French Chef, Jean Michel Gaufré who came to the hotel from Eastwell Manor. The menu includes English and French dishes, blending nouvelle cuisine ideas with more traditional cuisine. Local game is available in season and there is always a good supply of fish. The wine list is compiled with great care by the Marquess of Hartington.

Set in glorious countryside there is plenty to do here, especially for the sportsman. There are five miles of fishing in the River Wharfe on the estate and the river is well stocked with trout and grayling. The estate also has some of the best shooting and the hotel is particularly popular with shooting parties.

RUNNERS UP

As well as the six hotels nominated as Regional Winners and National Winner in our search to find the Best Newcomers, we also highly commend a further four which our inspectors felt were excellent hotels, newly-appointed and appearing in the 1984 guide for the first time.

ARISAIG HOUSE

Arisaig, Highland

A VERY ATTRACTIVE VICTORIAN STONE HOUSE in large and beautiful gardens has been most tastefully converted into an elegant country house hotel. All the rooms are large and comfortably furnished and the spacious, bedrooms all have superb outlooks, most of them across the gardens to Loch nan Uamh. The hotel is run by the Smither and Wilkinson families. The son-in-law, David Wilkinson used to be a Michelin inspector and the food he cooks is of the highest quality with interesting and imaginative menus for the set dinners. A popular room in the house is the huge billiard room on the top floor and there is croquet on one of the south-facing lawns. Altogether a beautiful, comfortable and relaxing hotel with the accent on comfort and personal service.

NETHERFIELD PLACE *Battle, East Sussex*

AMID THE QUIET COUNTRY LANES OF East Sussex is the luxury, Georgian style hotel, Netherfield Place. The house itself was built in 1924 in a gracious, traditional manner. It is set in thirty acres of park-like gardens that include many rare shrubs (some from the Himalayas), collected by one of the previous owners. The house itself is elegant and spacious with a splendid panelled dining room. All the bedrooms are very comfortably furnished with exquisite carpets and antique furniture, and a special attraction of each room is its unusual lights. Its comfortable, elegant rooms and the fine food make this a splendid country hotel.

AMERICAN EXPRESS
DATES *
* NOT VALID IF CAN
©AMEX

ARDSHEAL HOUSE

Kentallen of Appin
Highland

ALTHOUGH THIS HOTEL HAS BEEN OPEN FOR several years, it appears in our guide for the first time this year. An American couple, Jane and Robert Taylor bought the house in 1976 and, after considerable improvements and renovation, opened it in 1977. The house itself dates from 1760, but there was an earlier house here that was destroyed during the 1745 uprising. The house is full of character, homely and very much lived in, with the Taylors providing friendly and helpful but never obtrusive hospitality and very good food. Its setting is absolutely superb with bedrooms at the back of the house having breathtaking views along the whole length of Loch Linnhe.

HOB GREEN HOTEL

Markington
Harrogate
North Yorkshire

SET IN WELL OVER 800 ACRES OF ROLLING Yorkshire countryside is a very pleasant country house that has been converted to a fine hotel. It is not large, having only eleven bedrooms, but they have each been individually furnished with great care and are very well appointed. The very pleasant reception rooms include the drawing room with some good antique furniture and a charming sun lounge with light, summery colours and cane furniture. The manager, Peter Cawardine, also does the cooking and the menu is based on classical French cuisine, using English produce, including vegetables, fruit and herbs grown in the hotel gardens. This is a very elegantly furnished hotel in a most relaxing setting.

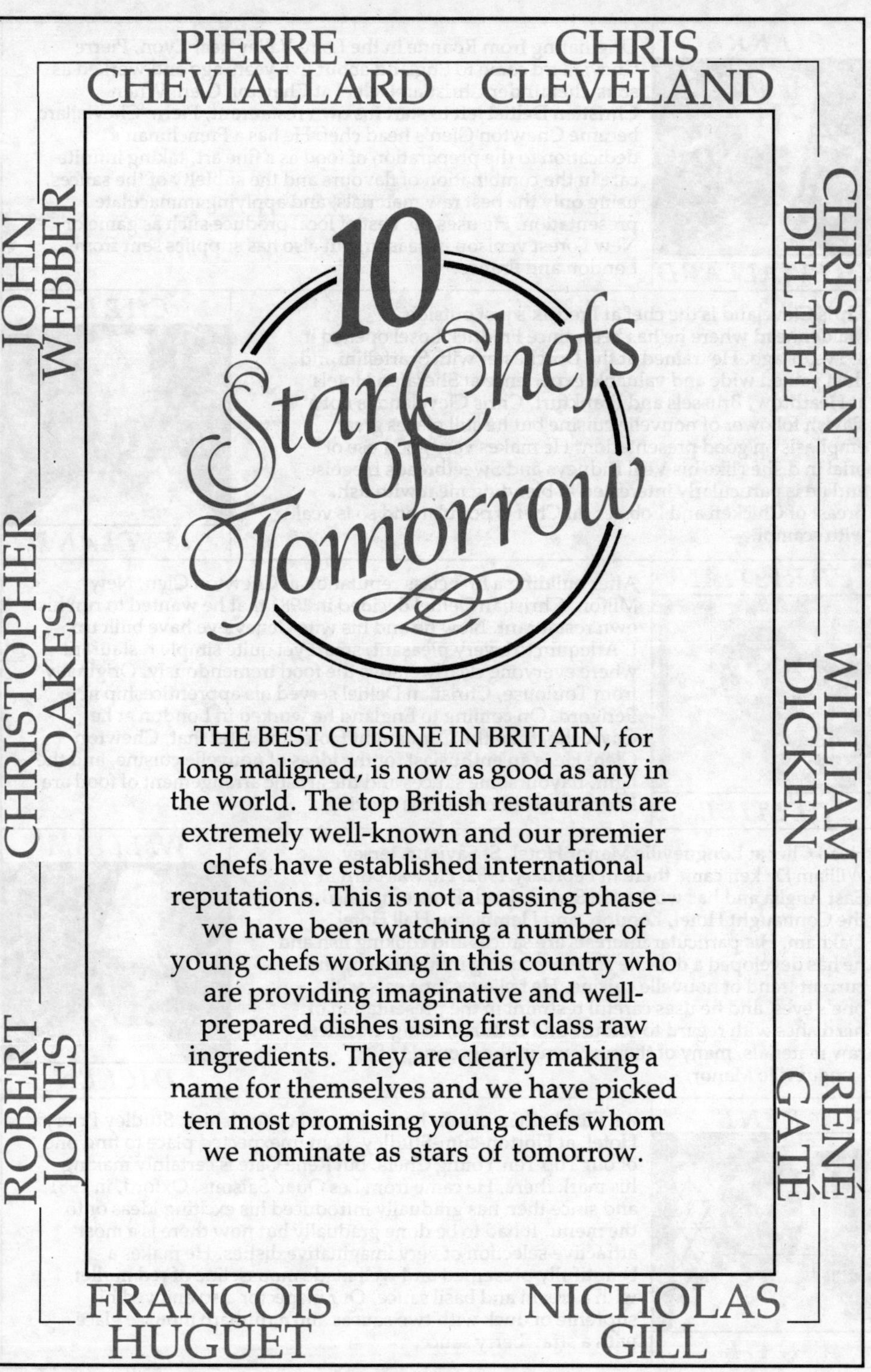
PIERRE CHEVIALLARD
CHRIS CLEVELAND
CHRISTIAN DELTEIL
WILLIAM DICKEN
RENÉ GATÉ
NICHOLAS GILL
FRANÇOIS HUGUET
ROBERT JONES
CHRISTOPHER OAKES
JOHN WEBBER

10 Star Chefs of Tomorrow

THE BEST CUISINE IN BRITAIN, for long maligned, is now as good as any in the world. The top British restaurants are extremely well-known and our premier chefs have established international reputations. This is not a passing phase – we have been watching a number of young chefs working in this country who are providing imaginative and well-prepared dishes using first class raw ingredients. They are clearly making a name for themselves and we have picked ten most promising young chefs whom we nominate as stars of tomorrow.

PIERRE CHEVIALLARD

Originating from Roanne in the Loire Valley near Lyon, Pierre Cheviallard came to England about five years ago and worked as sous-chef under Christian Deltiel at Chewton Glen. When Christian Deltiel left to start his own restaurant, Pierre Cheviallard became Chewton Glen's head chef. He has a Frenchman's dedication to the preparation of food as a fine art, taking infinite care in the combination of flavours and the subtelty of the sauces, using only the best raw materials, and applying immaculate presentation. He uses the best of local produce such as game or New Forest venison in season, but also has supplies sent from London and France.

CHRIS CLEVELAND

Chris Cleveland is the chef at Fredrik's just outside Maidenhead where he has been since Fredrick Losel opened it, 4½ years ago. He trained at the Dorchester with Scarfellini and then gained wide and valuable experience at Sheraton Hotels at Heathrow, Brussels and Frankfurt. Chris Cleveland is not a slavish follower of nouvelle cuisine but he still places great emphasis on good presentation. He makes very good use of offal in dishes like his Veal Kidneys and Sweetbreads Liegoise and he is particularly interested in blending meat with fish. Breast of Chicken and Lobster du Chef is popular and so is veal with scampi.

CHRISTIAN DELTIEL

After building a first class reputation at Chewton Glen, New Milton, Christian Deltiel decided in 1981 that he wanted to run his own restaurant. Now he and his wife Geneviève have built up L'Arlequin to a very pleasant, smart yet quite simple restaurant where everyone clearly enjoys the food tremendously. Originally from Toulouse, Christian Deltiel served his apprenticeship in Perigord. On coming to England he worked in London at Le Gavroche, then the Connaught Hotel and after that, Chewton Glen. He is an enthusiast for the ideas of nouvelle cuisine, and the light, flavoursome sauces and the artistic arrangement of food are important elements of his cooking.

WILLIAM DICKEN

Head Chef at Longueville Manor Hotel, St Saviour, Jersey, William Dicken came there in February 1982. He was born in East Anglia and has worked in Switzerland, France and also at the Connaught Hotel, London, and Hambleton Hall Hotel, Oakham. His particular interests are sauces and cooking fish and he has developed a delicate style of cooking influenced by the current trend of nouvelle cuisine. He believes 'one eats with one's eyes' and he uses careful restraint in the presentation of his dishes with regard to colours and textures, using the finest raw materials, many of them grown in the grounds of Longueville Manor.

RENÉ GATÉ

An Elizabethan manor house in rural Oxfordshire, Studley Priory Hotel, at Horton-cum-Studley, is an unexpected place to find one of our Top Ten Young Chefs, but René Gaté is certainly making his mark there. He came from Les Quat' Saisons, Oxford, in 1981, and since then has gradually introduced his exciting ideas onto the menu. It had to be done gradually but now there is a most attractive selection of very imaginative dishes. He makes a beautifully presented and well made mousseline of red mullet, with a cream and basil sauce. Our inspector also enjoyed his supreme of duck with two sauces and a rhubarb mousse glacé with a strawberry sauce.

NICHOLAS GILL

Nick Gill has been Head Chef at Hambleton Hall, Oakham, from the time it opened in 1980. Since then it has gained many accolades including AA Red Stars, and an AA Rosette. Before he came here Nick Gill was working at Maxim's in Paris, where he was the first British Chef de Partie. He trained at the Westminster Hotel School in London and worked at Walton's, The Savoy and Park Lane Hotel in London before going to Paris. Nick Gill was impressed by nouvelle cuisine in France and at Hambleton Hall he presents basically English dishes in a four course dinner where each course is very light and the whole meal is a special experience made up of a variety of different tastes.

FRANÇOIS HUGUET

In the magical building of Inverlochy Castle near Fort William works a young Frenchman whom we have picked as one of the Top Ten Young Chefs in Britain. He is now in his second season at the hotel and the dinner menu is a very well balanced meal of five courses with a selection of alternative dishes. François Huguet comes from Chartres and has worked with the Roux Brothers at Le Gavroche and Le Poulbot in London. He was working in the San Francisco Restaurant at the Düsseldorf Hilton when Mrs Hobbs enticed him to work at Inverlochy Castle and he provides technically faultless cuisine in a superb Highland setting.

ROBERT JONES

The West of England is gaining a reputation as a centre of gastronomic excellence, and Robert Jones at Ston Easton Park is one of the reasons for this reputation. Though he admires the lightness and attractiveness of nouvelle cuisine, his emphasis here is on simple food, very well prepared. He is keen on very light starters, such as a mousse of smoked salmon and lumpfish or quenelles of pike with spinach and saffron. Typical main courses include duck breast with pink and green peppercorns, lamb, salmon and veal fillet. Robert Jones is a Yorkshireman who has worked at the Savoy and the Connaught Hotels in London before moving to Ston Easton.

CHRISTOPHER OAKES

Like many of Britain's younger chefs, Christopher Oakes, head chef at The Castle Hotel, Taunton, is an exponent of nouvelle cuisine with its emphasis on simplicity, the use of fresh ingredients and light sauces. He had previously worked at Le Talbooth, Dedham and The Pier, Harwich, as well as the Post Hotel in Davos. He came to The Castle in early 1983 and has found the opportunity to try out his own ideas by using local produce and a basis of English tradition to put his own stamp on nouvelle cuisine methods. Some of his dishes are deceptively simple, others are more complicated and even exotic in their combinations of flavours.

JOHN WEBBER

One of our inspectors said he had 'the best meal he has ever eaten' at Gidleigh Park, Chagford, where John Webber is Head Chef. He has been there since 1980, before which he was Sous-Chef at the Dorchester Hotel, London, under Anton Mosimann. He has enabled Gidleigh Park to earn Rosettes from the AA and is a founder member of 'Country Chefs Seven', a group of top young British Chefs. His style of cooking follows the ideas of nouvelle cuisine, though he dislikes its occasional faddiness. His re-discovery and modern adaptation of classic dishes uses excellent, fresh ingredients. Vegetables are served on a separate plate and are crisply cooked al dente.

Guidance for overseas visitors to Britain on how to use this book

But de ce livret

Le but de ce livret est de fournir, sous une forme simple, autant de renseignements à jour que possible, renseignements concernant des hôtels et des restaurants sélectionnés. Les symboles et les abréviations, qui sont expliqués à l'intérieur de la couverture, servent à faire de cette section un répertoire compact mais cependant complet. Des explications concernant le classement et le système de recommandation AA ainsi que des notes sur le répertoire, suivent.

Table des Matières

Notre système de classement

Les étoiles décernées aux hôtels et les couteaux et fourchettes des restaurants sont basés sur le degré de confort, la gamme des installations et le standard du service fourni. Le classement est fait selon des critères précis (cf.page 37). Les accolades telles qu'étoiles rouges, rosettes et récompenses reflètent une opinion subjective.

Hôtels

Les propriétaires de l'hôtel font la demande d'agréement auprès de l'AA. Un inspecteur visite l'hôtel sans se faire annoncer, passe la nuit et cherche à tester autant de services que possible. Après paiement de sa note le matin, il se présente et fait une inspection complète des lieux. Dans les discussions qui suivent avec la direction, il attirera l'attention sur tout point qui peut avoir un effet sur le classement. Une fois agréé et quand une catégorie lui a été désignée, l'établissement sera inspecté une fois par an pour s'assurer que le niveau est maintenu. Si l'hôtel change de propriétaires, il est automatiquement rayé de la liste jusqu'à ce que les nouveaux propriétaires fassent une demande et que l'hôtel soit jugé.

Classement des Hôtels

Pour qu'un hôtel soit agréé par l'AA, il faut qu'il offre le minimum suivant: chambres avec eau chaude et froide; installations adéquates de bain et W.C.; service des repas (avec choix de menu pour le plat principal) à tous les résidents.

★	Auberges et hôtels de bonne qualité, souvent de petite taille et avec installations et mobilier de bon niveau.
★★	Hôtels offrant un niveau plus élevé de logement, avec chambres avec salle de bain ou douche; W.C. à tous les étages; choix plus important de repas.
★★★	Hôtels bien installés; bonne proportion de chambres avec salle de bain ou douche.
★★★★	Hôtels particulièrement bien installés offrant un haut standard de confort et de service, la plupart des chambres offrant salle de bain ou douche.
★★★★★	Hôtels de luxe offrant les standards internationaux les plus élevés.
★	Les étoiles noires désignent les hôtels qui offrent un service traditionnel dans un cadre traditionnel. La plupart des hôtels agréés par l'AA font partie de cette catégorie.
☆	Les étoiles blanches indiquent les hôtels qui offrent de nombreuses installations mais dont les services sont délibérément limités; ils

servent principalement aux courts séjours.

★ Les étoiles rouges indiquent les hôtels qui sont de qualité exceptionnelle au sein de leur catégorie.

♣ Indique un Hôtel de Campagne AA, où l'ambiance est amicale et détendue. Certaines des installations peuvent être différentes de celles que l'on trouve dans des hôtels urbains de la même catégorie.

○ Hôtels qui doivent ouvrir prochainement et qui n'ont pas été inspectés au moment de la mise sous presse.

N.B. Les hôtels remplissent souvent certaines des conditions qui leur permettraient d'être classées dans la catégorie supérieure.

Symboles de mérites spéciaux

H Bon accueil amical et service bien au dessus de la moyenne des hôtels de la même catégorie.

B Chambres souvent meilsures que celles des hôtels de la même catégorie.

L Salons, bars et endroits communs meilleurs que ceux de la même catégorie d'étoiles.

Hôtels à étoiles rouges

Les étoiles rouges indiquent les hôtels qui ont été reconnus être les meilleurs de leur catégorie, par les inspecteurs de l'AA. On espère que vous y recevrez un accueil chaleureux et que les installations seront d'un niveau élevé. Les étoiles rouges ne sont décernées qu'après de longues considérations et quand il y a changement de propriétaires, la catégorie est sérieusement réétudiée. Il n'y a que 51 hôtels à étoile rouge dans toute la Grande-Bretagne. (cf. la liste rapide à la page 705 pour les situer). Ils reçoivent une mention spéciale dans la liste du répertoire au moyen d'une photo en noir et blanc dans un panneau rouge, accompagnée d'une description en plus des renseignements habituels. Sur la route, vous pourrez reconnaître ces hôtels car leur catégorie est indiquée par une étoile rouge (au lieu de l'étoile noire habituelle) sur le panonceau jaune de l'AA.

Classement des Restaurants

Le classement des restaurants se fait d'une façon différente. Les inspecteurs AA recherchent les nouveaux restaurants et les visitent de façon anonyme. Ils font ensuite leur rapport au Restaurant Committee qui, si le restaurant est d'assez bon niveau, décerne les "fourchettes et couteaux croisés" pour montrer le standard du restaurant. Chaque restaurant d'hôtel de Londres particulièrement intéressant, est jugé indépendamment de l'hôtel.

Les conditions de base pour qu'un restaurant soit agréé sont un haut niveau de cuisine, un service prompt et courtois, une ambiance agréable et des prix intéressants.

✕ Restaurant modeste mais bon

✕✕ Restaurant offrant un meilleur niveau de confort que ci-dessus

✕✕✕ Bon restaurant

✕✕✕✕ Restaurant particulièrement bon

✕✕✕✕✕ Restaurant de luxe

A la rubrique restaurant, la phrase "chambres disponibles" n'implique pas qu'elles aient été visitées par l'AA.

Cuisine

❀ Hôtel ou restaurant où la cuisine est de meilleur niveau que dans la plupart des établissements de la même catégorie.

❀❀ Hôtel ou restaurant offrant des repas meilleurs que la moyenne quelle que soit la catégorie.

❀❀❀ Hôtel ou restaurant offrant des repas exceptionnels, quelle que soit la catégorie.

Rosettes

Les rosettes sont décernées aux hôtels et aux restaurants que nos inspecteurs considèrent être de très haut niveau en ce qui concerne les repas.

En plus des symboles

Prix

Il est prudent de toujours vérifier les prix avant de réserver car il est possible qu'ils changent pendant que ce guide est en circulation. L'inflation, les changements possibles du taux de la T.V.A. (VAT) peuvent influencer les prix au cours de l'année. Les prix publiés nous ont été fournis par les hôteliers et les restaurateurs en toute bonne foi mais ils doivent être considérés comme une indication plutôt que comme un prix ferme. Dans le cas où des prix 1984 ne sont pas indiqués, il vous faudra demander le renseignement directement.

Les prix de Bed-and-Breakfast sont indiqués dans ce guide. Ils précisent les prix minimum et maximum pour une et deux personnes mais les tarifs peuvent changer selon l'époque de l'année. Le terme "petit déjeuner" signifie habituellement "petit déjeuner complet à l'anglaise" (voir note sur les repas page 39); si le petit déjeuner est plus léger, à la française, ceci est indiqué dans le répertoire.

Certains hôtels font payer la chambre, le petit déjeuner et le dîner que ce repas soit pris ou non. Les prix s'entendent tout compris, T.V.A. et service le cas échéant.

Les prix minimum et maximum du menu fixe sont indiqués pour les repas principaux servis dans les salles à manger des hôtels et les restaurants. Si il est possible de commander à la carte, nous avons indiqué le prix moyen d'un repas comportant trois plats, déjeuner ou dîner. Si un établissement offre les deux possibilités, seuls les prix du menu fixe apparaissent mais il est mentionné que la carte est disponible. Tous les prix doivent comprendre le couvert. Le prix du vin indiqué s'entend pour une bouteille du vin le meilleur marché.

Comment faire votre réservation

Réservez dès que possible surtout si vous voulez prendre vos vacances entre le début juillet et la fin septembre.

Cependant, dès que la réservation a été confirmée, prévenez l'hôtel si vous pensez que vous ne pourrez venir à la date indiquée. Il est important de le faire car si l'hôtel ne peut relouer votre chambre, vous pourrez avoir à payer les deux-tiers du prix que vous auriez payé si vous étiez venu. (Vos arrhes seront incluses dans le montant de ce paiement).

Veuillez noter qu'en Grande-Bretagne, que ce soit au téléphone ou par écrit, il est considéré que vous êtes engagé légalement dès que l'hôtel a accepté votre réservation. La maladie ne constitue pas une excuse vous permettant de vous dégager. Pour toutes ces raisons, il est prudent de contracter une assurance en cas d'annulation.

Certains hôtels demandent le règlement total à l'avance, surtout si aucune réservation n'a été effectuée et que le client ne compte séjourner qu'une seule nuit. Certains hôtels n'acceptent des réservations de longue durée (une semaine ou plus) qu'au prix de la pension complète; d'autres n'acceptent pas de réservations qui commencent en milieu de semaine. Des réservations à l'avance pour la chambre et le petit déjeuner seulement sont souvent impossibles à effectuer.

Affichage des prix

Tous les hôtels, les motels, les pensions de famille, les auberges et les locations de Grande-Bretagne offrant au moins quatre chambres doivent, de par la loi, afficher les tarifs minimum et maximum pour la nuit. Ces prix doivent être mis bien en évidence à l'entrée ou à la réception. Les prix cités doivent comprendre le service le cas échéant et si le service n'est pas facturé, ceci doit être précisé. Il faut aussi préciser si ces prix comprennent la T.V.A. (VAT); si non, elle doit être indiquée séparément. Si les repas sont fournis avec le logement, ceci doit aussi être précisé.

Ceci est recommandé par le Code de Conduite Volontaire de l'Industrie Hôtelière que l'AA s'efforce d'encourager. Son but est d'assurer que le client a connaissance des services précis et des installations qu'il va recevoir, combien il va payer avant qu'il n'effectue sa réservation et ne s'engage à respecter un contrat (cf. paragraphe "Comment faire votre réservation" ci-dessus.) Au moment de son arrivée, il doit lui être remis une carte comportant le prix total qu'il aura à payer.

Règlement

La plupart des hôtels acceptent les chèques, en règlement de votre note si vous les en avez prévenus et si vous présentez une carte bancaire de préférence à toute autre façon de justifier de votre identité. Bien des hôtels acceptent les chèques de voyage émis par les grandes banques et les agences mais il est préférable de s'en assurer à l'avance. Dans le cas d'hôtels qui acceptent les cartes de crédit, les cartes concernées sont indiquées dans les entrées du répertoire. (cf. Abréviations et Symboles).

Repas

Les termes pour le petit déjeuner s'entendent pour un repas complet à l'anglaise sauf indication contraire. (Un petit déjeuner à l'anglaise est un repas chaud comportant environ trois plats, habituellement oeufs au bacon et céréales et lait). Tous les hôtels à quatre et cinq étoiles servent le café à onze heures du matin. Beaucoup d'hôtels à une et deux étoiles offrent maintenant des possibilités limitées pour déjeuner et il est possible qu'ils ne servent les repas qu'aux pensionnaires.

En décernant ses étoiles, l'Assocation a pris tous ces cas en considération. Certains hôtels trouvent aussi qu'il n'est pas rentable de servir le thé l'après-midi; celui-ci est souvent servi aux résidents uniquement. Dans certaines régions de Grande-Bretagne, (en particulier en Ecosse) 'high tea' (un plat salé suivi de tartines, de scones, gâteaux etc) est parfois servi à la place du dîner. Il est parfois possible de se faire servir à diner. L'heure limite à laquelle on peut commander le 'high tea' ou le dîner est indiquée pour les jours de semaine mais c'est souvent plus souple aux weekends. Le dimanche, certains hôtels servent le repas principal le midi et ne servent que des assiettes anglaises le soir. Il est possible que des hôtels ne servent les repas qu'entre certaines heures.

Plaintes

Si vous pensez que les repas, le service ou les installations ne sont pas satisfaisants, il est préférable de vous plaindre directement auprès de la direction pour que le personnel essaie de vous satisfaire. Si vous n'obtenez toujours pas satisfaction, informez l'office régional de l'AA le plus proche de l'hôtel.

Chiens

Les visiteurs ne doivent pas importer d'animaux de quelque sorte que ce soit en Grande-Bretagne sauf s'ils sont prêts à laisser leur animal en longue période d'isolement. Dû à la menace permanente que représente la rage, les peines encourues sont extrêmement sévères.

Installations dans les chambres

Un nombre devant le symbole bain ⇜, ou douche ⋒ indique le nombre de chambres qui offrent ces installations dans des pièces contigües. Il est recommandé de vérifier au moment de la réservation pour vous assurer que vos désirs sont satisfaits.

Hôtels qui servent des boissons alcoolisées

Tous les hôtels et les restaurants de la liste ont une patente leur permettant de vendre des boissons alcoolisées sauf avis contraire.

La loi interdit aux enfants de moins de 14 ans d'entrer dans les bars où de l'alcool est servi et consommé. Cependant, ceci ne s'applique pas aux endroits où les boissons ne sont servies qu'avec des repas.

Un bar avec patente ne peut vendre d'alcool à des personnes de moins de 18 ans; ces jeunes ne peuvent pas non plus consommer d'alcool dans ces bars. Entre 16 et 18 ans, il est possible d'acheter de la bière, du porter, du cidre ou du poiré pour consommer avec un repas dans un endroit souvent réservé aux repas. Des lois semblables sont en vigueur en Ecosse et au Pays de Galles.

Voir page 14 pour les heures d'ouverture.

Comment utiliser le répertoire

La liste du répertoire présente les établissements sous le nom de la ville dans laquelle ils sont situés en Grande-Bretagne. Le classement est fait par ordre alphabétique.

Après chaque nom de ville, le nom de la région ou comté apparait. N'oubliez pas qu'il s'agit d'un comté ou d'une région administrative et que celle-ci ne fait pas nécessairement partie de l'adresse. Dans le cas de régions d'Ecosse ou d'îles, l'ancien nom du comté suit en italiques.

Il est possible que quelques cartes ou plans de ville ne soient pas accompagnés d'un texte. Ceci est dû au fait qu'ils doivent être fournis avant que les dernières retouches ne soient faites au répertoire.

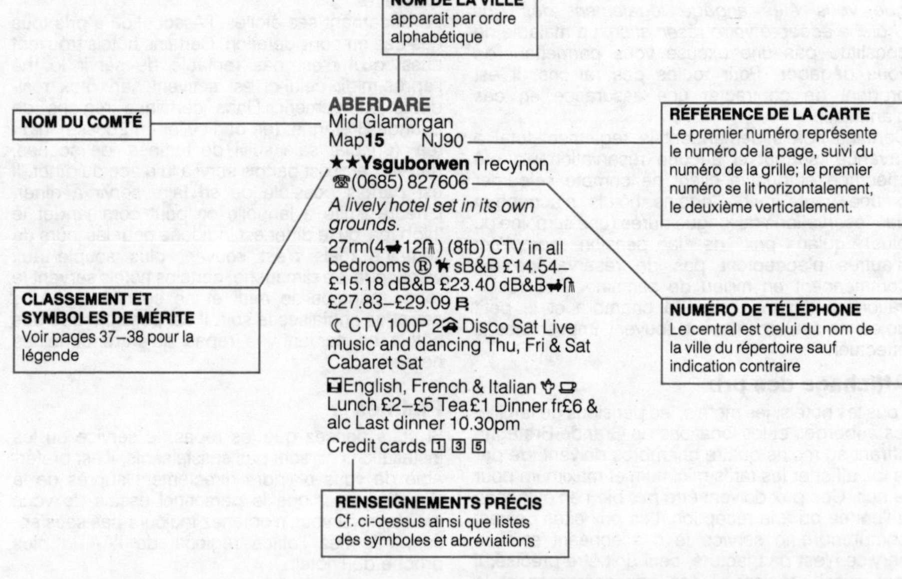
NOM DE LA VILLE
apparait par ordre alphabétique
NOM DU COMTÉ
ABERDARE
Mid Glamorgan
Map**15** NJ90
★★**Ysguborwen** Trecynon
☎(0685) 827606
A lively hotel set in its own grounds.
27rm(4→12⋒) (8fb) CTV in all bedrooms ® ★ sB&B £14.54–£15.18 dB&B £23.40 dB&B→⋒ £27.83–£29.09
☾ CTV 100P 2 Disco Sat Live music and dancing Thu, Fri & Sat Cabaret Sat
English, French & Italian
Lunch £2–£5 Tea £1 Dinner fr£6 & alc Last dinner 10.30pm
Credit cards 1 3 5
RÉFÉRENCE DE LA CARTE
Le premier numéro représente le numéro de la page, suivi du numéro de la grille; le premier numéro se lit horizontalement, le deuxième verticalement.
CLASSEMENT ET SYMBOLES DE MÉRITE
Voir pages 37–38 pour la légende
NUMÉRO DE TÉLÉPHONE
Le central est celui du nom de la ville du répertoire sauf indication contraire
RENSEIGNEMENTS PRÉCIS
Cf. ci-dessus ainsi que listes des symboles et abréviations

Tall, Dark and Handsome...

NEW EDITION £3.25 Net UK
LARGE AREA PAGE AND MAP SIZE
AA
LARGE 4 MILES TO 1 INCH SCALE
BIG ROAD ATLAS OF BRITAIN
INDEX FOR 25,000 PLACE NAMES
LONDON STREET PLANS
PARKS AND SANDY BEACHES
INDEX TO PLACES OF INTEREST
OVER 8,000 PLACES OF INTEREST
SUPERBLY DETAILED TOWN PLANS

don't be without one.

Size: 15⅛ x 11¼. Map scale 4 miles to 1". Contains London Street Plans, detailed town plans. Index for 25,000 place-names and to 8,000 places of interest.

Please visit your local AA Centre . . .

ABERDEEN BASINGSTOKE BEDFORD BELFAST BIRMINGHAM BOURNEMOUTH BRADFORD BRIGHTON BRISTOL CAMBRIDGE CARDIFF CHEADLE HULME CHELMSFORD CHESTER COLCHESTER COVENTRY CROYDON DERBY DOVER DUBLIN DUNDEE EALING EDINBURGH ERSKINE EXETER GLASGOW GUILDFORD HALESOWEN HANLEY IPSWICH ISLE OF MAN JERSEY LEEDS LEICESTER LIVERPOOL HULL LONDON: Leicester Square, The City, Hammersmith, LUTON MAIDSTONE MANCHESTER MIDDLESBROUGH NEWCASTLE-UPON-TYNE NEW MALDEN NORTHAMPTON NORWICH NOTTINGHAM OXFORD PLYMOUTH READING ROMFORD SHEFFIELD SLOUGH SOUTHAMPTON STANMORE SWANSEA SWINDON TRURO TWICKENHAM WOLVERHAMPTON YORK

Über dieses Buch

Der vorliegende Führer ist dazu gedacht, in einer dem Leser leicht verständlichen Form möglichst viele neue Informationen über ausgewählte Hotels und Restaurants zu bieten. Der Gebrauch von Symbolen und Abkürzungen, deren Entschlüsselung Sie auf der Innenseite des Bucheinbandes finden, trägt dazu bei, diese Informationen in knapper Verzeichnisform zu präsentieren. Erläuterungen zur Klassifizierung durch den AA und dessen Empfehlungssystem sowie Anmerkungen zum Ortsverzeichnis schließen sich an.

Inhalt

Unser Klassifizierungssystem

Die Vergabe von 'Sternen' an Hotels und von 'gekreuzten Messer und Gabel' – Einstufungen an Restaurants orientiert sich am Umfang des Komforts, der Einrichtungen und dem Standard des Services, die geboten werden. Die Klassifizierung erfolgt auf Grund spezifischer Kriterien (siehe S.42). Auszeichnungen wie ein roter Stern, eine Rosette und Auszeichnungen für besondere Verdienste sind Ausdruck subjektiver Meinungen.

Hotels

Der Antrag auf Anerkennung und Empfehlung erfolgt durch den Besitzer beim AA. Ein Inspektor besucht dann ohne Voranmeldung das Hotel, übernachtet dort und nimmt jede sich bietende Gelegenheit wahr, möglichst viele Dienstleistungen zu testen. Nach Bezahlung seiner Rechnung am nächsten Morgen stellt er sich dann vor und besichtigt eingehend das gesamte Gebäude. In einem anschließenden Gespräch mit der Hotelleitung gibt er Hinweise auf alles, was die Klassifizierung beeinträchtigen könnte. Ist das Hotel dann schließlich anerkannt und hat es seine Einstufung erhalten, dann wird es jedes Jahr einer neuen Inspektion unterzogen, um die Einhaltung des Standards zu gewährleisten. Wechselt das Hotel den Besitzer, dann wird es automatisch aus der Liste entfernt, bis der neue Besitzer um Empfehlung nachsucht und das Hotel erneut einer Prüfung unterzogen worden ist.

Hotelklassifikation

Zu den Grundvoraussetzungen des AA gehören: Zimmer mit kalt und warm Wasser, ausreichende Bad- und Toiletteneinrichtungen, das Servieren von allen Mahlzeiten an Hotelgäste (mit einer Auswahl an Gerichten für den Hauptgang).

★	Gute Hotels und Gasthöfe, im allgemeinen von kleiner Größe und mit annehmbaren Einrichtungen und Ausstattungen.
★★	Hotels, die einen höheren Unterbringungsstandard bieten, mit einigen privaten Bädern/ Duschen, Toiletten auf jedem Flur und einer breiteren Auswahl an Gerichten.
★★★	Gut ausgestattete Hotels mit einem Großteil Zimmern mit eigenem Bad/ Dusche.
★★★★	Außerordentlich gut ausgestattete Hotels, die einen hohen Standard an Komfort und Bedienung bieten und dessen Räume mehrheitlich über ein eigenes Bad/Dusche verfügen.
★★★★★	Luxushotels mit dem höchstmöglichen internationalen Standard.
★	Schwarze Sterne kennzeichnen Hotels, die einen traditionellen Service in traditioneller Unterkunft bieten. Die meisten der vom AA empfohlenen Hotels befinden sich in dieser Kategorie.
☆	Weiße Sterne kennzeichnen Unternehmen mit besonders vielen Einrichtungen, doch mit absichtlich begrenzten Dienstleistungen, die hauptsächlich für Kurzverweiler ausgelegt und betrieben werden.

★ Rote Sterne stehen für Hotels, die innerhalb ihrer Klasse als besonders herausragend gelten.

♣ Kennzeichnet ein Landgut-Hotel des AA, in welchem eine entspannte Atmosphäre herrscht. Es ist möglich, daß sich einige der Einrichtungen von denen in Stadthotels der gleichen Klasse unterscheiden.

○ Hotel wird während der Laufzeit dieses Führers eröffnet und konnte vor Redaktionsschluß nicht geprüft werden.

Hinweis: Die Hotels genügen oftmals den Ansprüchen für eine höhere Klasse als jene, in die sie eingestuft sind.

Verdienst-Symbole

H Kennzeichnet Gastfreundschaft, Freundlichkeit und Service weit über dem Durchschnitt ähnlich eingestufter Hotels.

B Kennzeichnet Zimmer, die wesentlich besser sind, als in dieser Sterne-Einstufung zu erwarten ist.

L Kennzeichnet Aufenthaltsräume, Bars und öffentliche Räume, die qualitativ weit über dem von der Sterne-Einstufung angedeuteten Standard liegen.

Rote-Stern-Hotels

Die roten Sterne kennzeichnen Hotels, die von den AA-Inspektoren als die besten ihrer Art empfohlen werden. Man hofft, daß Sie in allen einen herzlichen Empfang und ein hohes Maß an Gastfreundlichkeit erfahren. Rote Sterne werden nur nach eingehender Überlegung vergeben, und ein Wechsel in der Hotelleitung führt nahezu immer zu einer erneuten Prüfung der Auszeichnung. Es gibt in ganz Großbritannien nur 51 Hotels mit roten Sternen (siehe Nachschlageliste auf S.705 für Ortsangaben). Im Ortsverzeichnis werden sie durch ein Schwarzweißphoto auf einem roten Feld und zusätzlich einer Beschreibung zu den üblichen Angaben hervorgehoben. Diese Hotels sind von der Straße aus erkennbar, da ihre Klassifizierung durch rote Sterne (anstatt der üblichen schwarzen Sterne) auf dem gelben AA-Schild gekennzeichnet ist.

Restaurantklassifikation

Die Klassifizierung von Restaurants geschieht auf andere Weise. Die AA-Inspektoren suchen neue Restaurants aus und besuchen diese, ohne sich erkennen zu geben. Sie erstatten dann dem Restaurant-Ausschuß Bericht, und dieser vergibt zur Kennzeichnung der jeweiligen Gegebenheiten 'gekreuzte Messer und Gabeln', wenn man der Meinung ist, daß der Standard hoch genug ist. In London wird jedes Hotelrestaurant unabhängig von seinem Mutterhotel nach besonderen Verdiensten eingestuft.

Die Grundvoraussetzungen für die Empfehlung eines Restaurants sind ein hoher Standard der Küche, prompte und höfliche Bedienung, eine angenehme Atmosphäre und eine angemessene Preisrelation.

× Bescheidenes, aber gutes Restaurant

×× Restaurant mit einem im Vergleich zur obigen Kategorie höheren Maß an Komfort

××× Gut ausgestattetes Restaurant

×××× Außergewöhnlich gut ausgestattetes Restaurant

××××× Luxus-Restaurant

Der Zusatz 'Zimmer vorhanden' beim Restaurant-Eintrag bedeutet nicht, daß diese vom AA inspiziert worden sind.

Küche

❀ Hotel oder Restaurant, dessen Küche einem höheren Standard entspricht, als in einem Unternehmen dieser Gruppe zu erwarten wäre.

❀❀ Hotel oder Restaurant, das ungeachtet der Klassifizierung ein wesentlich über dem Durchschnitt liegendes Essen bietet.

❀❀❀ Hotel oder Restaurant, das ungeachtet der Klassifizierung ein hervorragendes Essen bietet.

Rosetten

Rosetten werden den Hotels oder Restaurants zuerkannt, deren Essen nach Meinung unserer Inspektoren einem besonders hohen Standard entspricht.

Zusätzliche Hinweise zu den Symbolen

Preise

Prüfen Sie immer vor Ihrer Buchung die Preise nach, da diese während der Laufzeit dieses Führers wahrscheinlich schwanken werden. Die Auswirkungen der Inflation, mögliche Veränderungen im Mehrwertssteuersatz (VAT) können im kommenden Jahr die Preise beeinflussen. Die veröffentlichten Preise beruhen auf Angaben der Hoteliers und Restauranthalter, die in gutem Glauben gemacht wurden. Sie sollten diese jedoch eher als annähernde denn als feste Preisangaben betrachten. Ist vom Unternehmen kein Preis für 1984 angegeben worden, dann richten Sie bitte Ihre Anfrage direkt an dieses.
Es werden in diesem Führer die Preise für Zimmer mit Übernachtung genannt. Es handelt sich dabei um Mindest- und Höchstpreise für ein oder zwei Personen, doch können diese je nach Jahreszeit schwanken. Frühstück gilt im allgemeinen als englisches Frühstück (siehe Anmerkung über

Mahlzeiten auf S.44); es wird im Ortsverzeichnis angegeben, wenn ein leichteres, kontinentales Frühstück serviert wird.
Manche Hotels berechnen Übernachtung, Frühstück und Abendessen, auch wenn Sie letzteres nicht einnehmen. Die Preise schließen VAT (MWSt) und gegebenenfalls die Bedienung ein.
Es werden die Mindest- und Höchstpreise für das Tagesmenü für alle im Hotel – Speisesaal oder Restaurants – servierten Hauptmahlzeiten angegeben. Wo man à la carte essen kann, wird der Durchschnittspreis für ein dreigängiges Mittag- und Abendessen genannt. Bietet das Unternehmen beides, dann wird nur der Tagesmenüpreis angegeben, aber darauf hingewiesen, daß auch à la carte gegessen werden kann. Alle Preise sollten das Gedeck enthalten. Der für Wein genannte Preis gilt für die billigste 0,7l-Flasche.

Buchung Ihrer Unterkunft

Buchen Sie so früh wie möglich, vor allem wenn Ihr Urlaub in der Zeit von Anfang Juli bis Ende September geplant ist.
Wenn Sie jedoch nach Erhalt einer Buchungsbestätigung Zweifel bekommen, ob Sie sich an die gemachten Vereinbarungen halten können, dann teilen Sie dies dem Hotel umgehend mit. Dies ist auch in Ihrem eigenen Interesse, denn wenn das Hotel Ihre Unterkunft nicht weitervermieten kann, sind Sie möglicherweise zur Zahlung von zwei Dritteln des Preises Ihres geplanten Aufenthaltes verpflichtet. (Ihre Anzahlung wird auf diese Zahlung angerechnet). Bitte beachten Sie, daß man in Großbritannien davon ausgeht, daß ein rechtlich bindender Vetrag geschlossen worden ist, sobald ein Hotel Ihre Buchung schriftlich oder telefonisch angenommen hat. Krankheit wird nicht als Grund zur Entlassung aus dieser Vertragsverpflichtung akzeptiert. Es sei Ihnen daher geraten, zur Deckung einer eventuellen Stornierung eine Versicherung abzuschließen.
Einige Hotels verlangen eine volle Zahlung im voraus, vor allem wenn keine Vorausbuchung vorgenommen wurde und der Gast nur eine Nacht bleibt. Viele Hotels nehmen Buchungen für ganze Zeiträume (z.B. eine Woche oder länger) nur zum Vollpensionstarif an. Andere wiederum akzeptieren keine Buchungen von der Wochenmitte an. Bei Zimmer mit Frühstück (Bed and Breakfast) werden oft keine Vorausbuchungen angenommen.

Aushang der Hotelpreise

Alle Hotels, Motels, Pensionen und Gasthäuser sowie Selbstversorgerunterkünfte in Großbritannien mit vier oder mehr Zimmern zur Miete sind verpflichtet, die Mindest- und Höchstpreise für Übernachtung auszuhängen. Der Aushang dieser Preise muß an einer deutlich sichtbaren Stelle im Eingang oder im Empfangsraum angebracht sein. Die Angaben sollten die Bedienung einschließen, wenn eine solche erhoben wird, andernfalls muß ersichtlich sein, daß kein solcher Zuschlag erhoben wird. Auch sollte angegeben sein, ob diese Preise VAT (Value Added Tax = Mehrwertsteuer) enthalten oder nicht. Wird diese nicht auf den Preis aufgeschlagen, so muß sie getrennt ausgewiesen werden. Wenn Mahlzeiten im Unterkunftspreis eingeschlossen sind, muß auch das kenntlich gemacht werden.
Diese Vorschrift wird weiter vervollständigt durch den freiwilligen Kodex für die Buchungspraxis der Hotelindustrie, für dessen Verbreitung sich der AA einsetzt. Sein Zweck ist es, sicherzustellen, daß der Kunde sich voll über die von ihm erworbenen Dienstleistungen und Einrichtungen im klaren ist und wieviel er dafür bezahlen muß, bevor er seine Buchung macht und sich damit vertraglich bindet (siehe Buchung Ihrer Unterkunft weiter oben). Wenn er sich als Gast einschreibt, sollte er eine Karte mit dem gesamten Tarif einschließlich des Gesamtbetrages erhalten, den er zu zahlen hat.

Zahlungsform

Die meisten Hotels akzeptieren eine Zahlung per Scheck nur dann, wenn Sie ihnen dies im voraus mitgeteilt haben und den Scheck mit irgendeiner Legitimation, vorzugsweise einer Scheckkarte, belegen können. Viele Hotels nehmen Reiseschecks führender Banken und Agenturen an, doch sollten Sie sich davon vorher vergewissern. Akzeptiert ein Hotel Kreditkarten, dann werden die wichtigsten davon in der Verzeichniseintragung aufgezählt. (Siehe Abkürzungen und Symbole.)

Mahlzeiten

Sofern nichts anderes angegeben ist, gehört ein volles englisches Frühstück zur Übernachtung. (Ein englisches Frühstück ist eine warme Mahlzeit mit ungefähr drei Gängen, wozu im allgemeinen Eier mit Speck und Getreideflocken mit Milch gehören).
Alle Vier- und Fünf-Sterne-Hotels servieren Kaffee am Morgen. Viele Ein- oder Zwei-Sterne-Hotels bieten nur begrenzte Möglichkeiten zur Einnahme eines Mittagessens, und es kann sein, daß nur Hausgästen serviert wird.
Bei der Vergabe der Sterne hat der AA von Fall zu Fall entschieden. Manche Hotels halten es auch nicht für wirtschaftlich, Nachmittagstee zu servieren. In einigen Teilen Großbritanniens (insbesondere in Schottland) pflegt man häufig anstatt eines Abendessens einen sogenannten 'High Tea' (eine herzhafte Mahlzeit, gefolgt von Brot, Butter, Scones, Kuchen usw.) zu servieren. Es ist jedoch möglich, daß ein Abendessen auf Anfrage erhältlich ist.
Es wird der letzte Zeitpunkt angegeben, bis zu welchem man an Wochentagen den High Tea oder das Abendessen bestellen kann, am Wochenende gibt es eventuell etwas mehr Spielraum. Manche Hotels servieren die Hauptmahlzeit am Sonntag zur Mittagszeit und nur ein kaltes Essen am Abend. Es ist außerdem möglich, daß die Hotels Mahlzeiten nur zu festen Zeiten servieren.

Beschwerden

Sind Sie mit dem Essen, der Bedienung oder den Einrichtungen nicht zufrieden, dann beschweren Sie sich am besten direkt bei dem jeweiligen Unternehmen, so daß das Personal versuchen kann, Ihren Wünschen entgegenzukommen. Haben Sie dann noch immer Anlaß zur Beschwerde, dann informieren Sie bitte das dem Unternehmen am nächsten gelegene regionale AA-Büro.

Hunde

Besucher sollten keinerlei Art von Haustieren nach Großbritannien mitbringen, sofern sie nicht bereit sind, die Tiere in eine längere Quarantäne zu geben. Wegen der anhaltenden Tollwutgefahr sind die Strafen für Zuwiderhandlungen gegen die Vorschriften sehr empfindlich.

Private Einrichtungen beim Zimmer

Eine Zahl vor den Symbolen für Bad ⇥, oder Dusche ⋒ gibt die Anzahl der Zimmer an, die mit eigenen Einrichtungen versehen sind. Es empfiehlt sich, bei der Buchung nachzuprüfen, ob Ihren Wünschen in dieser Hinsicht entgegengekommen wird.

Hotel mit Ausschanklizenz

Alle aufgeführten Hotels haben eine Lizenz für den Verkauf und Ausschank von Alkohol, sofern nichts anderes angegeben ist.
Gemäß den Schankgesetzen ist es Kindern unter 14 Jahren nicht erlaubt, während der Zeit, in der Alkohol ausgeschenkt und genossen wird, eine Bar zu betreten. Dies trifft jedoch nicht auf Bars zu, in denen alkoholische Getränke nur zu den Mahlzeiten serviert werden.
In Lokalen mit Schankerlaubnis dürfen alkoholische Getränke an Personen unter 18 Jahren weder verkauft, noch von diesen gekauft werden. Auch ist es diesen Personen nicht erlaubt, in einer Bar Alkohol zu sich zu nehmen. 16 bis 18jährige dürfen Bier, Porter, Apfelwein oder Birnenmost in Verbindung mit einer Mahlzeit kaufen, wenn diese in einem speziell für diesen Zweck bereitgestellten Raum des Lokals eingenommen wird. In Wales und Schottland sind ähnliche Gesetze in Kraft. Siehe S.14 für die Ausschankzeiten.

Zur Benutzung des Ortsverzeichnisses

Die Eintragungen sind im Ortsverzeichnis unter dem Namen der Stadt in Großbritannien aufgelistet, in welcher sie liegen. Die Auflistung erfolgt in alphabetischer Reihenfolge der Städtenamen.
Auf den Ortsnamen folgt immer die Grafschaft oder die Region. Denken Sie daran, daß es sich hier um die verwaltende Grafschaft oder Region handeln kann, nicht unbedingt um einen Teil der richtigen Postanschrift. Bei den schottischen Regionen oder Inseln folgt der alte Grafschaftsname in Kursivdruck.
Es ist durchaus möglich, daß es einige Karten- oder Städteeintragungen ohne Begleittext gibt. Der Grund hierfür ist, daß diese abgeschlossen werden müssen, ehe die letzte Fassung des Verzeichnistextes zusammengestellt wird.

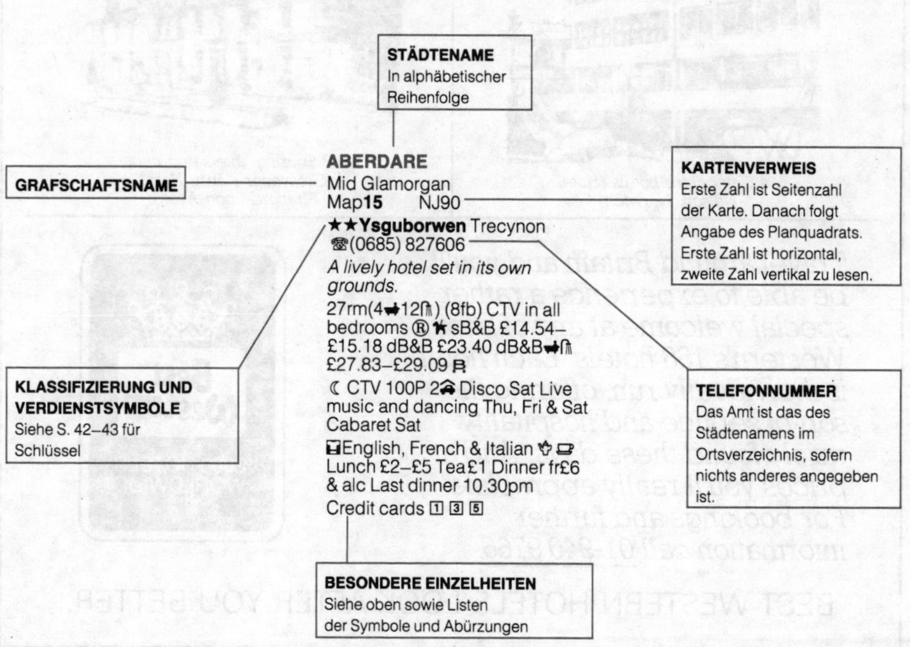
STÄDTENAME
In alphäbetischer Reihenfolge
GRAFSCHAFTSNAME
ABERDARE
Mid Glamorgan
Map15 NJ90
KARTENVERWEIS
Erste Zahl ist Seitenzahl der Karte. Danach folgt Angabe des Planquadrats. Erste Zahl ist horizontal, zweite Zahl vertikal zu lesen.
★★Ysguborwen Trecynon
☎(0685) 827606
A lively hotel set in its own grounds.
27rm(4⇥12⋒) (8fb) CTV in all bedrooms ® ★ sB&B £14.54–£15.18 dB&B £23.40 dB&B⇥⋒ £27.83–£29.09
☾ CTV 100P 2 Disco Sat Live music and dancing Thu, Fri & Sat Cabaret Sat
English, French & Italian Lunch £2–£5 Tea£1 Dinner fr£6 & alc Last dinner 10.30pm
Credit cards 1 3 5
TELEFONNUMMER
Das Amt ist das des Städtenamens im Ortsverzeichnis, sofern nichts anderes angegeben ist.
KLASSIFIZIERUNG UND VERDIENSTSYMBOLE
Siehe S. 42–43 für Schlüssel
BESONDERE EINZELHEITEN
Siehe oben sowie Listen der Symbole und Abürzungen

drive
AND TRAIL
AA

Eat your heart out

SWEET TROLLY
drive
D.I.Y.
REPAIR
FEATURE
NOEL
FORD

Every car connoisseur should sample *DRIVE&TRAIL's* menu. It changes every month, with something to everyone's taste. We carve cars into spicey road tests served up by the AA's experts, followed by the cream of camping and campsite reviews. And our main course of consumer protection stories is so fresh you'll be sure to come back for another helping. It's enough to make the other magazines eat their hearts out. So put more *DRIVE* in your diet with a regular order – 12 copies by post direct from the AA for £12.95. Better still, use the special subscription form in *DRIVE&TRAIL* and we'll give you *FREE* the popular *AA Touring Map of Great Britain,* worth £1.50. Or your could qualify for a *FREE Big Road Atlas* worth £3.25. Whichever gift you choose, we've got plenty for you to get your teeth into during 1984.

Che cos'è questa guida

Questa guida vuole fornire, in modo facile e chiaro, informazioni per quanto possibile aggiornate su alberghi e ristoranti attentamente selezionati. L'uso di segni convenzionali e di abbreviazioni, la cui spiegazione si trova sul retro della copertina, rende possibile tutto ciò in modo conciso. Seguono le spiegazioni del sistema di classificazione e di segnalazione AA e annotazioni sulla guida.

Indice

Il sistema di classificazione

Il conferimento di 'stelle' ad alberghi, e di 'forchetta e coltello incrociati' a ristoranti, si basa sul grado di comfort, sulla gamma delle attrezzature e sulla qualità del servizio. Le classificazioni vengono stabilite in base a criteri precisi (vedi pag. 48). Particolari segni convenzionali di apprezzamento e di merito, come stelle rosse, rosette e riconoscimenti, riflettono opinioni soggettive.

Alberghi

I proprietari si rivolgono alla AA per essere riconosciuti e segnalati. Un ispettore visita quindi l'albergo senza preavviso, vi passa una notte e coglie ogni occasione per sperimentare il maggior numero possibile di servizi. Dopo aver pagato il conto la mattina seguente, si presenta e ispeziona accuratamente tutto l'esercizio. Successivamente parla con il gestore, puntualizzando qualsiasi aspetto possa influire sulla classificazione. Una volta conferito il riconoscimento e stabilita la categoria, gli alberghi vengono ispezionati annualmente per garantire che il livello standard sia mantenuto. Se l'esercizio cambia gestione, viene automaticamente cancellato fino a quando il nuovo proprietario non faccia domanda e l'albergo non venga nuovamente ispezionato.

Classificazione degli alberghi

I requisiti fondamentali degli alberghi segnalati dalla AA sono: camere con acqua calda e fredda; bagni e servizi adeguati; servizio ristorante per tutti i pasti per i clienti (con scelta di piatti principali).

★	Buoni alberghi e locande, generalmente piccoli, con attrezzature e arredamento discreti.
★★	Alberghi che offrono un tipo di sistemazione migliore, con alcuni bagni o doccie privati; WC su tutti i piani; una scelta più ampia di piatti.
★★★	Alberghi ben attrezzati; buona parte delle stanze con bagno o doccia.
★★★★	Alberghi ottimamente attrezzati. Servizio e comfort di alto livello. La maggior parte delle stanze ha bagno o doccia.
★★★★★	Alberghi di lusso di alto livello internazionale.
★	Le stelle nere indicano alberghi che offrono servizio e sistemazione tradizionali. La maggior parte degli alberghi segnalati dalla AA rientrano in questa categoria.
☆	Le stelle bianche indicano alberghi con molte comodità, ma con servizi volutamente ridotti, gestiti principalmente ad uso di clienti di passaggio.
★	Le stelle rosse indicano alberghi da considerarsi di eccezionale qualità all'interno della loro categoria.
[simbolo]	Indica una AA Country House Hotel, dove regna un'atmosfera informale e tranquilla. Alcune attrezzature possono essere diverse da quelle di alberghi di città della stessa categoria.
○	Alberghi che saranno aperti durante il periodo di validità della guida e non ancora ispezionati al momento della stampa.
Nota:	Gli alberghi spesso soddisfano alcuni requisiti per classificazioni superiori a quella attribuita.

Simboli convenzionali di merito

H Indica ospitalità, accoglienza cordiale e servizio superiore alla media di alberghi della stessa categoria.

B Indica camere decisamente migliori di quelle che si trovano in alberghi della stessa categoria.

L Indica la presenza di sale, bar e altri spazi aperti al pubblico, decisamente superiori al livello indicato dal numero di stelle.

Alberghi a stelle rosse

Stelle rosse indicano quegli alberghi che gli ispettori della AA raccomandano come i migliori del loro genere. In ciascuno di essi si dovrebbe trovare una accoglienza cordiale e ospitalità di alto livello. Le stelle rosse vengono attribuite solo dopo attenta considerazione e, un cambiamento di gestione, può portare ad un'attenta revisione della classificazione. In tutta la Gran Bretagna ci sono solo 51 alberghi a stelle rosse (vedi la lista di rapida consultazione a pag. 705 per l'ubicazione). Sono messi in risalto nelle liste della Guida per mezzo di fotografie in bianco e nero su riquadro rosso, accompagnate da descrizione oltre alle consuete informazioni. Durante il viaggio, questi alberghi si possono riconoscere poichè indicati da stelle rosse (invece delle solite stelle nere) sull'insegna gialla della AA.

Classificazione dei Ristoranti

Le classificazioni dei ristoranti vengono fatte in modo diverso. Ispettori della AA vanno alla ricerca di nuovi ristoranti e vi si recano in incognito. Fanno poi un resoconto al Comitato Ristoranti e, se il ristorante viene giudicato all'altezza, gli viene conferito il segno convenzionale di 'forchette e coltelli incrociati' per indicarne la qualità. I ristoranti degli alberghi londinesi vengono classificati indipendentemente dall'albergo di cui fanno parte.
Requisiti fondamentali per la segnalazione di un ristorante sono ottima cucina, servizio efficiente e cortese, atmosfera piacevole, prezzi equi.

✕ Ristorante modesto ma buono.
✕✕ Ristorante che offre maggior comfort del precedente.
✕✕✕ Ristorante molto confortevole.
✕✕✕✕ Ristorante di gran comfort.
✕✕✕✕✕ Ristorante di lusso.

Nella voce ristorante, la frase 'dispone di camere' non implica che siano state ispezionate dalla AA.

Cucina

❀ Albergo o ristorante la cui cucina è di livello superiore a quello di un esercizio della stessa categoria.

❀❀ Albergo o ristorante che offre una cucina di gran lunga superiore alla media, indipendentemente dalla classificazione.

❀❀❀ Albergo o ristorante che offre una cucina eccezionale, indipendentemente dalla classificazione.

Rosette

Rosette vengono assegnate ad alberghi e ristoranti in cui, secondo i nostri ispettori, la cucina è di livello particolarmente alto.

Avvertenze

Prezzi

Si dovrebbero sempre controllare i prezzi prima di prenotare perché possono variare durante il periodo di validità di questa guida. Le conseguenze dell'inflazione, possibili variazioni dell'IVA, possono influire sui prezzi del prossimo anno. I prezzi pubblicati sono stati indicati da albergatori e ristoratori in buona fede, ma devono essere considerati come indicazioni piuttosto che come prezzi stabili. Nel caso in cui i proprietari non abbiano indicato i prezzi del 1984, si consiglia di chiedere informazioni direttamente.
Nella guida vengono citati prezzi che si riferiscono a camera e prima colazione. Questi indicano il prezzo minimo e massimo per una o due persone, ma le tariffe possono variare a seconda del periodo dell'anno. Normalmente colazione indica colazione all'inglese (vedi nota sui pasti, pag. 50); nella guida vengono indicati gli alberghi in cui si serve una prima colazione più leggera, Continentale.
Alcuni alberghi fanno pagare camera, prima colazione e cena anche se la cena non viene consumata. I prezzi comprendono l'IVA e il servizio quando dovuto.
Vengono indicati prezzi minimi e massimi per pasti principali 'table d'hote' nelle sale da pranzo degli alberghi e nei ristoranti. Dove c'è un menù à la carte, viene indicato il prezzo medio di un pranzo o cena di tre portate. Nei casi in cui ci siano tutti e due i tipi di menù, vengono dati solo i prezzi 'table d'hote', ma con l'indicazione che è disponibile anche il menù à la carte. Tutti i prezzi dovrebbero comprendere il coperto. Il prezzo del vino segnato è quello del vino meno costoso in bottiglia.

Prenotazioni

Bisogna prenotare il più presto possibile, specialmente se si va in vacanza dall'inizio di luglio alla fine di settembre.
Comunque, una volta confermata la prenotazione, è necessario far sapere immediatamente all'albergo l'eventuale cancellazione della prenotazione. E' nell'interesse del cliente farlo, poiché se l'albergo non può più affittare la camera prenotata, è probabile che il cliente debba pagare circa i due terzi della tariffa. (Il deposito concorrerà in parte al pagamento). *Si fa notare che in Gran Bretagna la conferma di prenotazione da parte di un albergo, o per iscritto o telefonicamente, è considerata un*

contratto legalmente vincolante. Le malattie non esonerano da questo contratto. Per questo motivo è consigliabile assicurarsi contro possibili rinunce. Alcuni alberghi richiedono il pagamento completo in anticipo, particolarmente se non è stata fatta alcuna prenotazione e se l'eventuale ospite si ferma per una sola notte. Molti alberghi accettano prenotazioni per un certo periodo (una settimana o più) soltanto a pensione completa; altri non accettano prenotazioni da metà settimana in poi. Spesso non vengono accettate prenotazioni soltanto per camera e prima colazione.

Indicazione dei prezzi

Tutti gli alberghi, motel, pensioni, locande e residence in Gran Bretagna che abbiano quattro o più stanze, devono esporre i prezzi minimi e massimi per una notte. Questi prezzi devono essere esposti in modo ben visibile nella Hall o alla ricezione. I prezzi segnati dovrebbero comprendere il servizio e deve essere specificato se il servizio non è compreso. Dovrebbe inoltre essere indicato se i prezzi comprendono anche l'IVA: se l'IVA non è inclusa, deve essere indicata separatamente. Deve inoltre essere specificato se la tariffa comprende anche i pasti.
Queste disposizioni fanno parte del Codice Volontario delle Prenotazioni Alberghiere che la AA si sforza in ogni modo di incoraggiare. Esso si prefigge di assicurare che il cliente sappia chiaramente quali servizi e quali attrezzature avrà, quanto pagherà prima di prenotare e di impegnarsi in un accordo contrattualmente vincolante (Vedi sopra, *Prenotazioni*). Al momento della firma del registro degli ospiti, al cliente dovrebbe essere consegnato un foglio con la tariffa completa e l'ammontare totale che dovrà pagare.

Pagamento

La maggior parte degli alberghi accetta assegni a pagamento del conto solo se il cliente ha preavvisato e se l'assegno è accompagnato da un documento di identificazione, preferibilmente una cheque card. Molti alberghi accettano travellers' cheques emessi dalle principali banche, ma è meglio assicurarsene in anticipo. La guida indica le principali carte di credito accettate dagli alberghi. (Vedi Abbreviazioni e Segni Convenzionali).

Pasti

I prezzi indicati si riferiscono alla colazione all'inglese, a meno che non sia diversamente specificato. (La prima colazione all'inglese è di circa tre portate, generalmente con uova e pancetta, e cereali con latte).
Tutti gli alberghi a quattro e cinque stelle servono il 'morning coffee'. Ora molti alberghi a una e due stelle offrono semplici seconde colazioni e, a volte, solo per gli ospiti residenti.
Nel conferire le stelle, l'Association ha valutato ciascun esercizio individualmente. Alcuni alberghi ritengono anti-economico servire il tè del pomeriggio; spesso riservato solo ai residenti. In alcune parti della Gran Bretagna (specialmente in Scozia) invece della vera e propria cena, viene talvolta servito 'high tea', costituito da un piatto appetitoso con pane e burro, scones, dolce ecc. La cena può comunque essere servita su richiesta. E' indicato fino a che ora è possibile ordinare 'high tea' o la cena durante i giorni feriali, ma ci può essere maggiore elasticità durante il fine settimana. Alcuni alberghi di domenica servono il pasto principale a mezzogiorno, e una cena fredda alla sera. E' probabile che gli alberghi possano servire i pasti solo nelle ore stabilite.

Reclami

Se rilevate che la cucina, il servizio o le attrezzature non sono soddisfacenti, conviene reclamare direttamente con la Direzione dell'esercizio, in modo che il personale possa rimediare. Se nonostante ciò, non siete ancora soddisfatti, informate l'agenzia AA più vicina all'esercizio in questione.

Cani

I turisti non devono portare animali di nessun genere in Gran Bretagna, a meno che non siano preparati a lasciarli in quarantena. Data la continua minaccia costituita dalla rabbia, le sanzioni per i trasgressori sono estremamente severe.

Attrezzature delle camere

Un numero di fronte ai simboli bagno ➡, o doccia ⋔ indica il numero delle camere dotate di tali servizi. Nel fare una prenotazione, è consigliabile accertarsi che tutto corrisponda alle vostre esigenze.

Alberghi autorizzati alla vendita di alcolici

Tutti gli alberghi e ristoranti elencati sono autorizzati alla vendita e consumo di alcolici, a meno che non sia diversamente specificato.
Le leggi sugli alcolici proibiscono ai minori di 14 anni di entrare nei locali in cui si servono o si consumano alcolici. Questo divieto non riguarda comunque i locali in cui gli alcolici sono serviti solo con i pasti.
Nei locali autorizzati alla vendita di alcolici, questi non possono essere venduti ai minori di 18 anni, che non possono neppure consumare alcolici nel bar. I minori dai 16 ai 18 anni possono acquistare birra, birra scura, sidro di pere e mele da prendere durante un pasto, in una parte dell'esercizio generalmente adibita a sala da pranzo. Leggi fondamentalmente uguali sono in vigore nel Galles e in Scozia.
Vedi pag. 14 per le ore in cui è permessa la vendita e il consumo di alcolici.

Come usare la guida

Le voci sono elencate sotto il nome della città in cui si trovano. Le città sono elencate in ordine alfabetico.
Al nome di ciascuna località, segue quello della contea o regione. E'da ricordate che la contea o regione amministrativa non fanno necessariamente parte del corretto indirizzo postale. Nelle regioni o isole della Scozia, l'antico nome della contea è stampato in corsivo.
Ci possono essere alcune voci che si riferiscono a piante di città, non corredate da spiegazioni. Ciò è dovuto al mancato completamento prima della correzione finale della guida.

IL NOME DELLA CITTÀ APPARE in ordine alfabetico

NOME DELLA CONTEA

ABERDARE
Mid Glamorgan
Map**15** NJ90
★★**Ysguborwen** Trecynon
☎(0685) 827606
A lively hotel set in its own grounds.
27rm(4⇌12⋒) (8fb) CTV in all bedrooms Ⓡ ★ sB&B £14.54–£15.18 dB&B £23.40 dB&B⇌⋒ £27.83–£29.09 ⊟
☾ CTV 100P 2⌂ Disco Sat Live music and dancing Thu, Fri & Sat Cabaret Sat
English, French & Italian ✿ ☕ Lunch £2–£5 Tea £1 Dinner fr£6 & alc Last dinner 10.30pm
Credit cards 1 3 5

RIFERIMENTI ALLE PIANTE Il primo numero si riferisce alla pagina della pianta. I numeri che seguono si riferiscono rispettivamente alla posizione orizzontale e verticale.

NUMERO DI TELEFONO
Il prefisso è quello della città citata nella guida, a meno che non sia diversamente specificato.

CLASSIFICAZIONE E SIMBOLI DI MERITO
Vedi pp. 48–49 per la spiegazione

DETTAGLI PARTICOLARI
Vedere sopra l'Elenco dei Simboli e delle Abbreviazioni

Acerca de este libro

El propósito de esta guía es el de proveer, en una manera fácilmente comprensible para el lector, la mayor información actualizada posible acerca de hoteles y restaurantes seleccionados. El uso de símbolos y abreviaturas, cuyas claves se presentan en el interior de las tapas de este libro, hace posible ofrecer tanta información dentro de una breve sección de gacetero. Las explicaciones para las clasificaciones de la AA y sistema de recomendación y notas del gacetero siguen a continuación.

Indice

Nuestro sistema de clasificación

Se otorgan 'estrellas' y 'tenedor y cuchillo' en calidad de clasificación a hoteles y restaurantes respectivamente, basándose en el grado de confort, la extensión de las facilidades y el nivel de servicio ofrecidos. Las clasificaciones se deciden partiendo de criterios específicos (ver p. 52). Recomendaciones tales como estrellas rojas, rosetas y premios al mérito reflejan opiniones subjetivas.

Hoteles

Los propietarios de los establecimientos solicitan a la AA ser reconocidos e incluidos en su registro. Un inspector visita entonces el hotel sin previo aviso, permanece en él una noche y hace uso de todas las oportunidades posibles para comprobar la eficacia de los servicios. Después de abonar su cuenta por la mañana, se presenta en su calidad de inspector y realiza una inspección detallada de todo el establecimiento. En conversaciones subsecuentes con la administración, indicará cualquier punto que pueda afectar la clasificación. Una vez que se les ha reconocido y se les ha adjudicado una clasificación, los hoteles son inspeccionados anualmente para asegurarse que se mantiene el mismo nivel. Si el hotel cambia de propietario, es automáticamente eliminado hasta que el nuevo propietario presente una solicitud de reconocimiento y el hotel haya sido reevaluado.

Clasificación de hoteles

Los requerimientos básicos para los hoteles recomendados por la AA son: habitaciones con agua fría y caliente; disposición adecuada de baño y lavabo; servicio de comidas (desayuno, almuerzo y cena, con selección de platos) para los residentes.

- ★ Buenos hoteles y posadas, generalmente en escala pequeña y con facilidades y comodidades aceptables.
- ★★ Hoteles que ofrecen un nivel más elevado de alojamiento, con algunos baños/duchas privados; lavabos en todos los pisos; selección más amplia de comida.
- ★★★ Hoteles bien equipados; una buena proporción de habitaciones con baño/ducha privado.
- ★★★★ Hoteles excepcionalmente bien equipados, que ofrecen un alto nivel de confort y servicio; la mayoría de sus habitaciones cuenta con baño/ducha privado.
- ★★★★★ Hoteles de lujo, que ofrecen el más alto nivel internacional.
- ★ Las estrellas negras denotan a los hoteles que ofrecen servicio tradicional en alojamiento tradicional. La mayoría de los hoteles seleccionados por la AA están en esta categoría.
- ☆ Las estrellas blancas indican establecimientos con muchas comodidades pero con servicios deliberadamente limitados, planeados y operados para atender principalmente a huéspedes de estancia breve.
- ★ Las estrellas rojas denotan hoteles considerados de excepcional mérito dentro de su clasificación.
- Denota un AA Country House Hotel (en una casa de campo), de ambiente cálido y reposado. Algunas de las facilidades peuden ser diferentes a aquellas de hoteles urbanos dentro de la misma clasificación.

○ Hoteles a ser inaugurados durante la vigencia de esta guía, que no han sido inspecionados en el momento de ir a la imprenta.

Nota: Los hoteles a menudo satisfacen algunos de los requerimientos para una clasificación más elevada de aquella que se les otorga.

Símbolos de mérito

H Denota hospitalidad, amabilidad y servicio muy por encima de lo corriente para hoteles de clasificación similar.

B Denota habitaciones considerablemente mejores que las normales dentro de esa clasificación.

L Denota salones, bares y zonas públicas marcadamente por sobre el nivel implicado por la clasificación de estrellas.

Hoteles de estrellas rojas

Las estrellas rojas indican los hoteles que los inspectores de la AA han recomendado como lo mejor dentro de su clase. Se espera que en cada uno de ellos usted encontrará una cálida bienvenida y un alto nivel de hospitalidad. Las estrellas rojas se otorgan sólo después de muchas consideraciones, y un cambio de administración resultará posiblemente en una cuidadosa revisión de su mérito. En toda Gran Bretaña existen solamente 51 hoteles de estrellas rojas (ver la lista de referencia rápida en la página 705 para situaciones). Están señalados en las listas del gacetero por medio de una fotografía en blanco y negro en un panel rojo, acompañado por una descripción, además de la información corriente. En el camino, podrá distinguir estos hoteles porque su nivel está indicado por estrellas rojas (en lugar de las negras corrientes) sobre el signo amarillo de la AA.

Clasificación de restaurantes

En la clasificación de restaurantes se procede de manera diferente. Los inspectores de la AA buscan nuevos restaurantes y los visitan anónimamente. Seguidamente informan al Comité de Restaurantes quien, si se considera que el restaurante es de un nivel lo suficientemente alto, le otorga el galardón de 'Cuchillos y tenedores', para denotar las amenidades. Todos los restaurantes de hoteles de mérito particular en Londres son clasificados independientemente del hotel al que pertenecen.
Los requerimientos básicos para la recomendación de cualquier restaurante son el alto nivel de la cocina, servicio pronto y cortés, ambiente agradable y precios adecuados.

X Restaurante modesto pero bueno
XX Restaurante que ofrece un nivel de confort superior al de más arriba
XXX Restaurante bien establecido
XXXX Restaurante bien establecido y equipado
XXXXX Restaurante de lujo

En la información sobre un restaurante, la frase 'bedrooms available' (see dispone de alojamiento) no implica que las habitaciones han sido inspeccionadas por la AA.

Cocina

❁ Hotel o restaurante donde la cocina es considerada de un nivel más alto que el ordinario en un establecimiento dentro de su clasificación.

❁❁ Hotel o restaurante que ofrece comida muy por encima de lo corriente, irrespectivamente de la clasificación.

❁❁❁ Hotel o restaurante que ofrece comida sobresaliente, irrespectivamente de su clasificación.

Rosetas

Se otorgan rosetas a hoteles y restaurantes donde nuestros inspectores consideran que la comida es de un nivel especialmente alto.

Símbolos: Información suplementaria

Precios

Deberá siempre confirmar los precios antes de reservar, ya que pueden variar durante la vigencia de esta guía. Los efectos de la inflación, las posibles variaciones en el porcentaje del Impuesto al Valor Añadido (VAT), pueden tener influencia en los precios del siguiente año. Los precios publicados han sido suministrados por los dueños de hoteles y restaurantes, y deberán ser aceptados como indicaciones y no precios establecidos. Donde los propietarios no han facilitado los precios para 1984, sírvase solicitar información directamente.
Se mencionan también en la guía las tarifas para 'bed and breakfast' (habitación y desayuno). Estas indican los precios mínimos y máximos para una y dos personas, pero estos pueden variar de acuerdo a la temporada. El desayuno significa normalmente desayuno inglés completo (ver nota sobre comidas, p.54); donde se ofrece un desayuno continental, más ligero, se indica en el gacetero. Algunos hoteles cobran habitación, desayuno y cena, se coma o no esta última. Los precios incluyen el VAT y el servicio cuando es aplicable.
Los precios mínimos y máximos de menú fijo se indican para las comidas principales servidas en los comedores y restaurantes de los hoteles. Donde existe un menú a la carta, se indica el precio promedio de un almuerzo y cena de tres platos. En los casos en que los establecimientos ofrecen los dos tipos de menú, se mencionan

solamente los precios menú fijo, indicándose que también se sirve a la carta. Todos los precios deben incluir el cubierto. El precio del vino es el de la botella más económica.

Reservas de alojamiento

Reserve con la mayor anticipación posible, especialmente si sus vacaciones son entre el principio de julio y el fin de setiembre.

Una vez que ha sido confirmada la reserva, notifique al hotel inmediatamente si piensa que no podrá ocupar el alojamiento en la fecha prevista. Esto es en su propio interés, pues si el hotel no puede ocupar el alojamiento reservado por usted, podrá exigirle el pago de dos tercios del precio que hubiera pagado en caso de ocuparlo. (Su depósito será parte de este pago). *Sírvase notar que en Gran Bretaña se acepta que se ha hecho un contrato legalmente obligatorio en el momento en que el hotel acepta la reserva, ya sea por escrito o por teléfono.* No se acepta una enfermedad como causa para rescindir el contrato. Por estas razones le aconsejamos sacar un seguro contra una posible cancelación.

Exhibición de tarifas hoteleras

Todos los hoteles, moteles, casas de huéspedes, posadas y alojamiento sin servicio en Gran Bretaña, con cuatro o más habitaciones para alquilar, deben exhibir noticias indicando los precios mínimos y máximos por una noche. Estos precios deberán exhibirse en un sitio prominente a la entrada o en la zona de recepción. Los precios indicados deberán incluir el servicio, cuando existe este cargo, y deberá indicarse claramente cuando no se cobra. También debe indicarse si los precios incluyen el VAT (Impuesto al Valor Añadido) o no: si no se ha añadido al precio deberá indicarse separadamente. Se deberá mencionar igualmente si se ofrecen comidas con el alojamiento. Esta orden se complementa con el Código Voluntario para la práctica de reservas de la industria hotelera, que la AA hace todo lo posible por alentar. Su propósito es el de asegurarse que el cliente tiene una idea clara de los servicios y facilidades que está comprando, y cuánto pagará por ellos, antes de efectuar la reserva y entrar en un contrato de calidad obligatoria (ver *Reservas de alojamiento,* más arriba). Cuando se registra como huésped deberá entregársele una tarjeta con la tarifa completa, incluyendo el costo total que deberá abonar.

Pago

La mayoría de los hoteles aceptan cheques en pago de cuentas sólo si se les ha notificado previamente, y si respalda el cheque con alguna forma de identificación, preferentemente una tarjeta bancaria. Muchos hoteles aceptan cheques de viajero emitidos por los principales bancos y agencias, pero es conveniente confirmarlo. Donde los hoteles aceptan tarjetas de crédito, aquellas concernientes están numeradas en la información del gacetero. (ver Abreviaturas y símbolos).

Comidas

Los términos cotizados son desayuno inglés completo, a menos que se indique lo contrario, (un desayuno inglés es una comida caliente de tres platos aproximadamente, incluyendo generalmente huevos y tocino, y cereales con leche).

Todos los hoteles de cuatro y cinco estrellas sirven café por la mañana. Muchos de los hoteles de una y dos estrellas ofrecen ahora un servicio limitado de almuerzo, quizás sólo para residentes.

Al otorgar las estrellas, la Asociación considera cada caso por sus méritos. Algunos hoteles encuentran desventaja económica en servir el té de la tarde, que a menudo se sirve sólo a los residentes. En algunas partes de Gran Bretaña (especialmente en Escocia) se sirve a veces, en lugar de la cena, el llamado 'high tea', que consiste en un plato acompañado de pan y mantequilla, scones, torta, etc. La cena puede, sin embargo, servirse a pedido. Se indica la hora hasta la que puede servirse el té tardío o la cena en días de semana, pero en fines de semana pueden prolongarse estos horarios. Los domingos algunos hoteles sirven la comida principal al mediodía, ofreciendo sólo una cena fría por la noche. Los hoteles podrán servir comidas sólo entre las horas establecidas.

Quejas

Si no está usted satisfecho con la comida, los servicios o las facilidades, lo mejor es presentar una queja directamente al establecimiento concerniente, de manera que el personal podrá tratar de obviar la causa de su queja. Si aún no está usted satisfecho, sírvase informar a la oficina regional de la AA más próxima al establecimiento en cuestión.

Perros

Los visitantes no deberán traer consigo a Gran Bretaña ningún tipo de animal doméstico, a menos que estén dispuestos a someterlos a una prolongada cuarentena. Debido a la continua amenaza de la rabia, las sanciones por ignorar el reglamento son extremadamente severas.

Facilidades privadas en las habitaciones

Un número junto al símbolo del baño ➔ o ducha ⋒ indica el número de habitaciones que cuentan con estas facilidades. Se recomienda verificar, al hacer la reserva, que sus requerimientos sean satisfechos.

Hoteles con licencia para servir bebidas alcohólicas

Todos los hoteles y restaurantes mencionados poseen licencia para servir bebidas alcohólicas, a menos que se indique lo contrario. Las leyes prohiben a los niños menores de 14 años la entrada a los bares mientras se sirve y se consume alcohol. No obstante, esta prohibición no es aplicable en los bares donde la bebida se sirve solamente acompañando las comidas.

En los establecimientos con licencia las bebidas alcohólicas no deberán venderse, o ser compradas, por personas menores de 18 años; tampoco podrán tales personas beber alcohol

en un bar. Las personas de 16 a 18 años podrán comprar cerveza, cerveza oscura, sidra o sidra de peras, para consumir con una comida en una parte del establecimiento normalmente destinado al servicio de comidas. Leyes similares se aplican en Gales y Escocia.
Ver p. 14 para Horas de licencia.

Cómo utilizar el gacetero

La información sobre los distintos establecimientos aparece en el gacetero bajo el nombre de las problaciones británicas donde están situados. Las poblaciones se dan en orden alfabético.
Después del nombre de cada sitio, se indica el condado o la región. Recuerde que este es el condado o región administrativa, y no necesariamente la dirección postal correcta. Con las regiones e islas escocesas, el viejo nombre del condado sigue en letra itálica.
Puede haber algunos pocos títulos de mapas o mapas urbanos sin referencia en el texto. Esto se debe a que estos deben ser completados antes de efectuar las correcciones definitivas en el texto del gacetero.

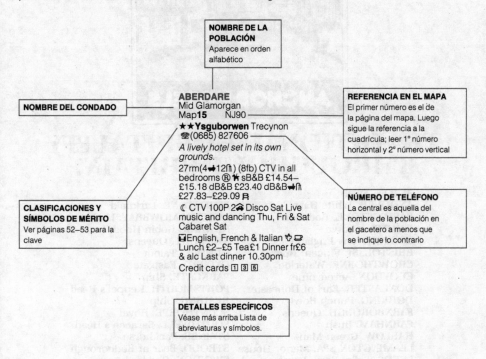

NOMBRE DE LA POBLACIÓN
Aparece en orden alfabético

NOMBRE DEL CONDADO

REFERENCIA EN EL MAPA
El primer número es el de la página del mapa. Luego sigue la referencia a la cuadrícula; leer 1° número horizontal y 2° número vertical

ABERDARE
Mid Glamorgan
Map**15** NJ90
★★**Ysguborwen** Trecynon
☎(0685) 827606
A lively hotel set in its own grounds.
27rm(4⇌12⋒) (8fb) CTV in all bedrooms Ⓡ ★ sB&B £14.54–£15.18 dB&B £23.40 dB&B⇌⋒ £27.83–£29.09 ⊟
☾ CTV 100P 2⌂ Disco Sat Live music and dancing Thu, Fri & Sat Cabaret Sat
English, French & Italian
Lunch £2–£5 Tea £1 Dinner fr£6 & alc Last dinner 10.30pm
Credit cards 1 3 5

CLASIFICACIONES Y SÍMBOLOS DE MÉRITO
Ver páginas 52–53 para la clave

NÚMERO DE TELÉFONO
La central es aquella del nombre de la población en el gacetero a menos que se indique lo contrario

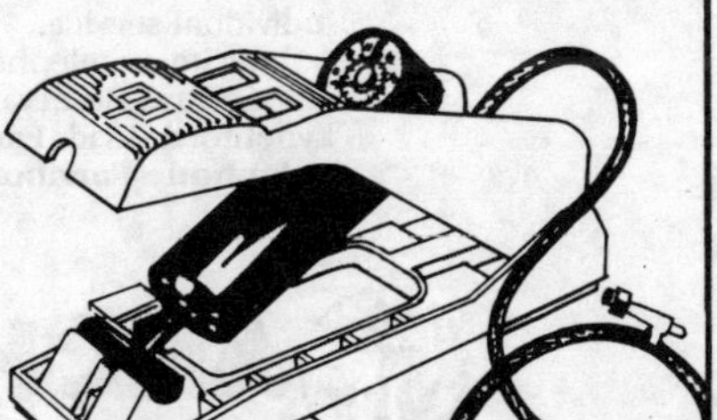

DETALLES ESPECÍFICOS
Véase más arriba Lista de abreviaturas y símbolos.

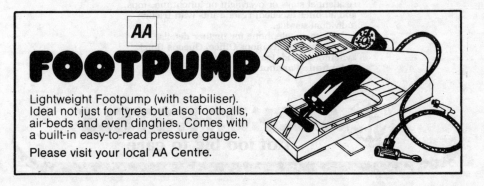

ANCHOR HOTELS

ANCHOR HOTELS
not too big to care

LONDON TO EDINBURGH, BRISTOL TO LEEDS AND BOURNEMOUTH TO DOWNTOWN ULLAPOOL!

As a lesson in geography, this map shows where some of our major towns and cities are, together with a few scenic places too.

As a lesson in where to find the best hotels it's more useful, because it tells you where to find Ladbroke Hotels.

And to save you counting up all our little 'L's', there are 32 of them.

Unfortunately our map isn't able to show that all our rooms have a private bathroom, colour TV, radio and tea and coffee tray. But we're working on it!

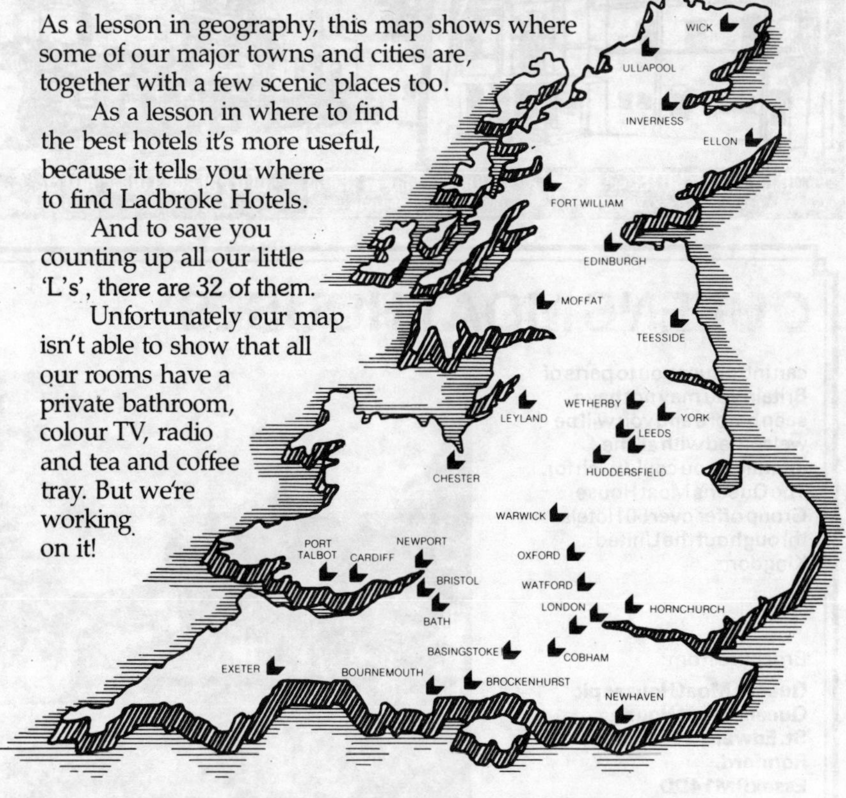

WICK
ULLAPOOL
INVERNESS
ELLON
FORT WILLIAM
EDINBURGH
MOFFAT
TEESSIDE
LEYLAND
WETHERBY
YORK
LEEDS
HUDDERSFIELD
CHESTER
WARWICK
PORT TALBOT
CARDIFF
NEWPORT
BRISTOL
BATH
OXFORD
WATFORD
LONDON
HORNCHURCH
BASINGSTOKE
COBHAM
EXETER
BOURNEMOUTH
BROCKENHURST
NEWHAVEN

Ladbroke Hotels

Central reservations: **LONDON 01-734 6000 Telex 897618**
LEEDS (0532) 872717 Telex 556324 EDINBURGH 031-343 3111 Telex 727979

Hotel groups

Key to abbreviations and central reservation telephone numbers (where applicable)

Special corporate rates are available at hotel companies marked with an *, through the facilities of business travel accounts with the AA Business Travel Service.

Bookings may be made via the AA Travel Agencies shown below

Company	Abbreviations	Telephone
Allied Hotels (Scotland)	Allied Scotland	01-836 0471
Anchor Hotels & Taverns Ltd	Anchor	Farnborough (Hants) 517517
Ansells Brewery Co Ltd	Ansells	
Berni Inns Ltd	Berni	
Best Western	Best Western	01-940 9766
Charrington & Co	Charrington	01-790 1860
Comfort Hotels International	Comfort	01-221 2626
Commonwealth Holiday Inns of Canada Ltd	Commonwealth	01-722 7755
*Crest Hotels Ltd	Crest	01-903 6422
De Vere Hotels Ltd	De Vere	01-404 0991
Embassy Hotels	Embassy	01-584 8222
ExecHotels	Exec	01-289 2168 Barry 740069
Forest Dale Hotel Group	Forest Dale	
Forum Hotels	Forum	01-930 7722
Frederic Robinson Ltd	Frederic Robinson	
Great British Hotels (Anchor, GW and Swallow Groups). See details under Anchor, Greenall Whitley and Swallow		
Greenall Whitley Hotels Ltd	Greenall Whitley	0925 35471
*Holiday Inn International		01-722 7755
Home Brewery Co Ltd	Home Brewery	
Hotel Representative Incorporated for Berkeley, Claridges, Connaught, Savoy, Hyde Park, London; Royal Crescent, Bath, Avon; Lygon Arms, Broadway, Worcs; Grosvenor, Chester; Chewton Glen, New Milton, Hants		01-583 3050
Ind Coope (Alloa Brewery Co Ltd)	Ind Coope (Alloa)	
Inter-Continental Hotels	Inter-Continental	01-491 7181
Inter-Hotels	Inter-Hotels	01-373 3241
Kingsmead Hotels Ltd	Kingsmead	Reading 302925
*Ladbroke Hotels Ltd	Ladbroke	01-734 6000
Minotels Ltd	Minotels	Brighton 731908
*Mount Charlotte Hotels Ltd	Mount Charlotte	Leeds 444866
The North Hotels	North	01-589 1212
Paten & Co Ltd	Paten	
Percy R Brend (Hotels) Ltd	Brend	Bognor Regis 826222
Porter Group	Porter	
*Prestige Hotels	Prestige	01-734 4267
Prince of Wales Hotels Ltd	Prince of Wales	Southport 314331/37700
Queens Moat House Ltd	Queens	
Rank Hotels Ltd	Rank	01-262 2893
*Reo Stakis Organisation	Stakis	01-930 0342 & 041-221 4343
Saxon Inn Motor Hotels Ltd	Saxon Inn	
Scottish Highland Hotels	Scottish Highland	041-332 6538
Scottish & Newcastle Breweries Ltd	Scottish & Newcastle	Newcastle upon Tyne 21073
*Swallow Hotels Ltd	Swallow	Sunderland 77424
*Thistle Hotels (Scottish & Newcastle Breweries)	Thistle	01-937 8033
Travco Hotels Ltd	Travco	
Trusthouse Forte Hotels Ltd	Trusthouse Forte	01-567 3444
Wessex Taverns Ltd	Wessex Taverns	
Whitbread Wessex (Retail)	Whitbread	
Whitbread West Pennines Ltd	Whitbread West Pennines	
Wolverhampton & Dudley Breweries Ltd	Wolverhampton & Dudley	Wolverhampton 711811

Automobile Association

Bookings for hotels belonging to groups marked* can be made through AA Travel Agencies. The telephone numbers of the principal ones are given below. For a full list of AA Travel Agencies consult the *AA Members' Handbook* or PO Yellow Pages.

Birmingham	021-643 3373	Glasgow	041-204 0911
Bristol	Bristol 290992	London (City)	01-623 4152
Cheadle Hulme	061-485 8551	London (West End)	01-930 2462

Hours Mon–Fri 9am–5pm; Sat 9am–12.30pm. Closed Sun.

How to Use the Gazetteer

Sample entry The entry is fictitious

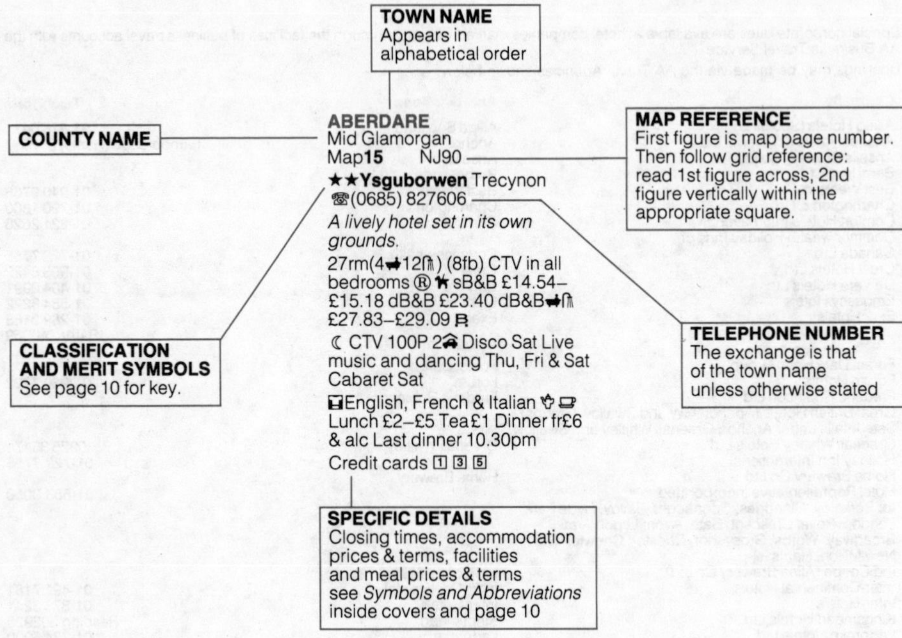

TOWN NAME
Appears in alphabetical order
COUNTY NAME
ABERDARE
Mid Glamorgan
Map**15** NJ90
★★**Ysguborwen** Trecynon
☎(0685) 827606
A lively hotel set in its own grounds.
27rm(4⇌12⋒) (8fb) CTV in all bedrooms ® ★ sB&B £14.54–£15.18 dB&B £23.40 dB&B⇌⋒ £27.83–£29.09 B
☾ CTV 100P 2⌂ Disco Sat Live music and dancing Thu, Fri & Sat Cabaret Sat
English, French & Italian Lunch £2–£5 Tea £1 Dinner fr£6 & alc Last dinner 10.30pm
Credit cards 1 3 5
MAP REFERENCE
First figure is map page number. Then follow grid reference: read 1st figure across, 2nd figure vertically within the appropriate square.
CLASSIFICATION AND MERIT SYMBOLS
See page 10 for key.
TELEPHONE NUMBER
The exchange is that of the town name unless otherwise stated
SPECIFIC DETAILS
Closing times, accommodation prices & terms, facilities and meal prices & terms see *Symbols and Abbreviations* inside covers and page 10

Additional information

After each placename, the county, region or island area, is given. Remember that this is the administrative county, or region, and not necessarily a part of the correct postal address. With Scottish regions or islands, the old county name follows in italics.

There may well be a few map or town plan entries unsupported by text. This is because these have to be completed before final amendments are made to the gazetteer.

For details of alternative accommodation, see *AA Guesthouses, Farmhouses and Inns in Britain.*

Key to town plans

Roads with restricted access

Churches

Tourist Information centre

AA Service centre

Car parking

Hotel & restaurant

Red star hotel

Built-up area (shown on London plans only)

Distance to hotels from edge of plan

DERBY 9m Mileage to town from edge of plan

Gazetteer

The gazetteer gives locations and details of AA-appointed hotels and AA-recommended restaurants, listed in alphabetical order of placenames throughout Great Britain, Channel Islands and Isle of Man. Details for islands are shown under individual placenames but the gazetteer text also gives appropriate cross-references. A useful first point of reference is to consult the location maps which show where AA-appointed establishments are situated.
NB *There is no map for Isles of Scilly*

ABBERLEY
Hereford & Worcester
Map **7** SO76

ABERDARON
Gwynedd
Map **6** SH12

★★Ty Newydd ☎(075886) 207
Three storey hotel in centre of Aberdaron, with direct access to the beach.
14rm(8→1⋒) (2fb) CTV in all bedrooms ★sB&B£14.75–£15.75 sB&B→⋒£15.75–£16.75 dB&B£24.50–£26.50 dB&B→⋒£26.50–£28.50
Continental breakfast B
CTV 8P
Mainly grills ♥ Bar lunch £3.25–£5.75&alc Dinner £6.95–£8.95 Wine £5.25 Last dinner 9pm

★★★

❀★★★ELMS, ABBERLEY
(on A443) (Prestige)
☎Great Witley (029921) 666
Telex no 337105

Despite the change of ownership of this hotel, Miss Mooney still manages it with a great deal of success. The same standards of hospitality and service are maintained and if anything, we find the service a little more polished. This is a lovely Queen Anne building standing in its own grounds with a most attractive garden which also provides vegetables and herbs for the kitchen. They are put to good use by the chef, the talented Murdo Macssween, who meets the skill of the exacting menus with aplomb. The only weaknesses we have found are the puddings which could be a little better to meet the standards of the rest of the meal. The extensive breakfast menu is not without a good deal of interest either. The interior is elegantly and comfortably furnished with some antiques. There are three sitting rooms and the Library bar has fine mahogany bookcases; clearly there is plenty of space to relax in front of cheerful open fires. Bedrooms are

also in keeping and all sorts of thoughtful touches are provided, such as bathgowns, wall safes, trouser pressers and direct dial telephones as well as a miniature of sherry, fresh fruit and a selection of toiletries. Our members report most favourably on this hotel and think it a near perfect example of an English country house.
18→⋒ Annexe 9→⋒ (1fb) 1 CTV in all bedrooms ★sB&B→⋒£35 dB&B→⋒£55 B
100P 10 ✽ xmas
V ♥ Lunch £8.50&alc Tea £3 Dinner £15&alc Wine £6.50 Last dinner 9pm
Credit cards 1 2 3 4 VS

ABBOTS SALFORD
Warwickshire
Map **4** SP05

★★★Salford Hall
☎Evesham (0386) 870561
An historic but lively hotel, often busy with banquets and coach parties.
10rm(6→) (1fb) ® sB&B fr£15 sB&B→ fr£16 dB&B fr£28 dB&B→ fr£30 B
CTV 200P ✽ xmas
V ♥ Lunch fr£5alc Tea 70p Dinner fr£7&alc Wine £4.50 Last dinner 9.30pm
Credit cards 1 2 3 5

ABERDEEN
Grampian *Aberdeenshire*
Map **15** NJ90
See plan See also Aberdeen Airport

☆☆☆☆ **B Holiday Inn Bucksburn** Old Meldrum Rd, Bucksburn (3m N A947) (Holiday Inns) ☎(0224) 713911 Telex no 73108 Plan **9** *C8*
Hotel with a modern external appearance and pleasant, comfortable interior.
99→⋒ (45fb) CTV in all bedrooms ® ✱sB&B→⋒£47.95 dB&B→⋒£59.68 B
Lift ☾ # 150P 6 CFA (heated) *xmas*
International V ♥ ✱Lunch £5.50–£7.50&alc Tea £1.75 High Tea £5–£7.50 Dinner £6.50–£8.50&alc Wine £4.95 Last dinner 10.30pm
Credit cards 1 2 3 4 5 VS

☆☆☆☆ **B Skean Dhu Altens** Souter Head Rd, Altens (3m S off A956) ☎(0224) 877000 Telex no 739631 Plan **15** *E1*
Modern hotel complex situated on south side of city.
221→⋒ (70fb) CTV in all bedrooms ® sB→⋒£38.95 (room only) dB→⋒£44.95 (room only) B
Lift ☾ # 300P CFA (heated) billiards
V ♥ ✱Lunch £2.50–£6.50&alc Tea 55p–£1 Dinner £2.50–£7.50&alc Wine £5.70 Last dinner 9.45pm
Credit cards 1 2 3 4 5

☆☆☆ **Amatola** 448 Gt Western Rd ☎(0224) 38724 Telex no 739443 Plan **2** *A2*
Modern hotel complex situated on ring road one mile from city centre.
54rm(36→18⋒) CTV in all bedrooms ® ★✱sB&B→⋒£37.50 dB&B→⋒£47.50 B
☾ 120P 40 Live music and dancing Fri & Sat *xmas*
♥ ✱Lunch £5.50&alc Tea 65p&alc Dinner £7.50&alc Wine £6 Last dinner 10pm
Credit cards 1 2 3 5

★★★Caledonian Thistle 10 Union Ter (Thistle) ☎(0224) 640233 Telex no 73758 Plan **3** *D5*
81rm(71→10⋒) CTV in all bedrooms ® ✱sB→⋒£39–£45 (room only) dB→⋒£42–£50 (room only) B
Lift ☾ 35P 100
European. ✱Lunch £5.25 Dinner £8.75&alc Last dinner 9.30pm
Credit cards 1 2 3 4 5 VS

★★★*Imperial* Stirling St (Swallow) ☎(0224) 29101 Telex no 73365 Plan **10** *D4*
RS Xmas & New Year
Commercial hotel in quiet city centre location, popular with oil men.
103rm(10→90⋒) CTV in all bedrooms ® ★B
Lift ☾ disco wkly live music and dancing 6 nights wkly
English & French ♥ Last dinner 10pm
Credit cards 1 2 3 4 5

☆☆☆ **B Stakis Royal Darroch** Cults (3m SW A93) (Stakis) ☎(0224) 868811 Plan **14** *A2*
67→ CTV in all bedrooms ® ✱sB&B→£35 dB&B→£40
Lift ☾ 200P
English & French V ♥ Last dinner 10pm
Credit cards 1 2 3 5 VS

Aberdeen

1 Atlantis Sea Food ✕
2 Amatola ☆☆☆
3 Caledonian Thistle ☆☆☆
4 Dee Motel ☆☆
5 Dickens ✕✕
6 Gerard's ✕✕
7 Gloucester ★★
8 Gordon ★★
9 Holiday Inn Bucksburn ☆☆☆☆
10 Imperial ★★★
11 Light of Bengal ✕
12 Pinocchio ✕✕
13 Poldino's ✕
14 Stakis Royal Darroch ☆☆☆
15 Skean Dhu Altens ☆☆☆☆
16 Tree Tops Crest ★★★

★★★**Tree Tops Crest** 161 Springfield Rd (Crest) ☎(0224) 33377 Telex no 73794 Plan **16** *A2*

Modern hotel in its own landscaped grounds on the outskirts of the city centre.

108rm(82🛁21🚿) CTV in all bedrooms Ⓡ ✱sB fr£24.50 (room only) sB🛁🚿 fr£36 (room only) dB fr£36 (room only) dB🛁🚿 fr£42 (room only) ⊟

Lift ☾ ⁄ 300P CFA ✽

📺 International 🍴 ☕ ✱ Bar lunch £2.50–£3.95 Tea 75p–£1.50 Dinner £8.25–£8.95&alc Wine £6.95 Last dinner 10pm

Credit cards ① ② ③ ④ ⑤ **VS**

☆☆**Dee Motel** Garthdee Rd (Comfort) ☎(0224) 321474 Telex no 73212 Plan **4** *A1*

Popular and friendly hotel set in a convenient location on the outskirts of the city.

Annexe: 75rm(31🛁44🚿) CTV in all bedrooms Ⓡ ✱sB&B🛁🚿 fr£23 dB&B🛁🚿 fr£29.50 Continental breakfast

☾ 150P CFA Live music and dancing Tues, Wed, Thu, Sat & Sun *xmas*

🍴 ☕ Bar lunch fr£2.50&alc Tea fr£1&alc Dinner fr£4.75&alc Wine £3.95 Last dinner 9.45pm

Credit cards ① ② ③ ④ ⑤ **VS**

See advert on page 64

★★**Gloucester** 102 Union St (Allied) ☎(0224) 641095 Telex no 76357 Plan **7** *D5*

71rm (36🛁35🚿) (10fb) CTV in all bedrooms Ⓡ ✱sB&B🛁🚿 £30 dB&B🛁🚿 £40 ⊟

Lift ☾ CTV 🅿 *xmas*

🍴 ☕ Last dinner 9pm

Credit cards ① ② ③ ④ ⑤

★★**Gordon** Wellington Rd (Ind Coope) ☎(0224) 873012 Plan **8** *E1*

26rm(3🛁13🚿) CTV in all bedrooms Ⓡ sB&B fr£17.50 sB&B🛁🚿 fr£21.50 dB&B fr£26.50 dB&B🛁🚿 fr£33 ⊟

☾ 100P *xmas*

📺 Mainly grills **V** 🍴 ☕ Lunch £2.95–£6.95&alc Tea 60p–£1 Dinner £3.60–£8.50&alc Wine £3.50 Last dinner 9.30pm

Credit cards ① ② ③ ⑤

See advert on page 64

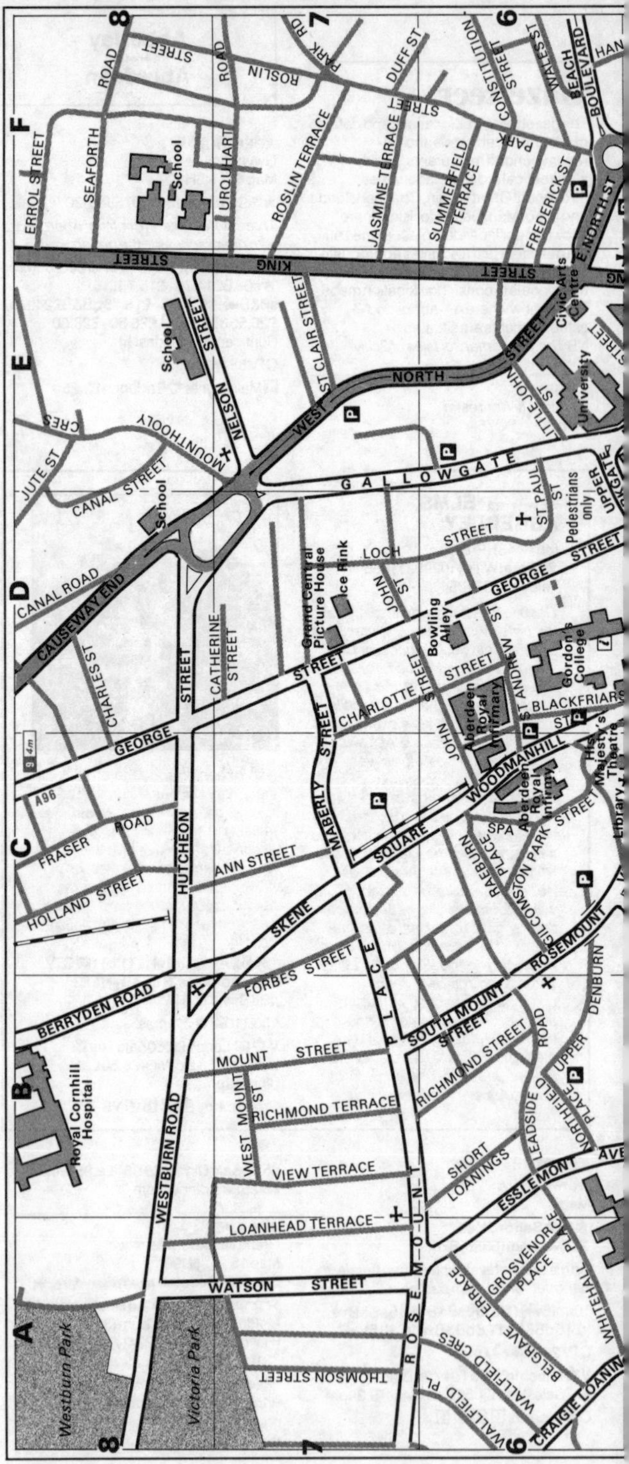

Aberdeen
Mercat Cross
Tolbooth
Town House
Justice Market
ABC Cinema
Harbour Offices
Provost Ross's House
Municipal Buildings
Pedestrians only
Green Market
Queen's Cinema
James Dun's House
Union Terrace Gdns
Music Hall
Palace Ballroom
P.O.
St Mary of Assumption Cathedral
Capitol Cinema
Bon Accord Swimming Pool
Odeon Cinema
Christ's College
Queen's Cross Maternity Home
Nellfield Cemetery
Fonthill Maternity Home
Ferry Terminal for Shetland
Fish Market
Goods Station
Bus Station
Railway Station
Victoria Bridge
River Dee
School
UNION STREET
MARKET STREET
GUILD STREET
COLLEGE STREET
SOUTH COLLEGE STREET
BRIDGE STREET
UNION TERRACE
DENBURN ROAD
BELMONT STREET
BACK WYND
UNION BR
THE GREEN
RENNIE'S WYND
CARMELITE ST
STIRLING ST
EXCHANGE ST
MARKET ST
ST NICHOLAS STREET
TRINITY QUAY
REGENT QUAY
VIRGINIA ST
MARISCHAL ST
MEARNS ST
JAMES ST
CASTLE TERR.
CASTLE ST
SHIP ROW
JAMIESON'S QUAY
COMMERCIAL QUAY
REGENT RD
ALBERT QUAY
NORTH ESPLANADE EAST
NORTH ESPLANADE WEST
SOUTH ESPLANADE EAST
SOUTH ESPLANADE WEST
VICTORIA BRIDGE
VICTORIA ROAD
SINCLAIR ROAD
CROMBIE ROAD
CROMBIE PL
GLENBERVIE ROAD
GRAMPIAN ROAD
WALKER ROAD
MENZIES ROAD
OSCAR ROAD
RIVERSIDE DRIVE
A956
STELL ROAD
PALMERSTON ROAD
PALMERSTON RD
RAIK ROAD
POYNERNOOK ROAD
RUSSEL ROAD
OLD FORD RD
CROWN TERRACE
CROWN STREET
WINDMILL BRAE
DIAMOND STREET
GOLDEN SQ.
SILVER STREET
SKENE TERRACE
CRIMON PLACE
HUNTLY STREET
SUMMER STREET
UNION ROW
CHAPEL STREET
ROSE STREET
THISTLE STREET
VICTORIA STREET
SKENE STREET
WAVERLEY PLACE
ALBERT STREET
ALBERT TERRACE
CARDEN PLACE
ALBYN PLACE
ALFORD PL.
DEE STREET
DEE PLACE
LANGSTANE PLACE
BON-ACCORD STREET
BON-ACCORD CRESCENT
JUSTICEMILL LANE
UNION GLEN
HARDGATE
SPRINGBANK TERRACE
SPRINGBANK ST
AFFLECK ST
WELLINGTON PLACE
WILLOWBANK ROAD
UNION GROVE
ASHVALE PLACE
HOLBURN STREET
GT WESTERN ROAD
A93
HOWBURN PLACE
NELLFIELD PLACE
HOLBURN ROAD
BROOMHILL ROAD
BALMORAL PL
BALMORAL ROAD
BLOOMFIELD ROAD
A9103
SOUTHERN ROAD
FONTHILL ROAD
FONTHILL TERRACE
WHINHILL ROAD
ALBURY ROAD
ALBURY PLACE
CALEDONIAN PLACE
FERRYHILL TERRACE
FERRYHILL ROAD
FERRYHILL PLACE
MILLBURN ST
BANK STREET
PROSPECT TERRACE
STH SOUTH CROWN STREET
DEVANHA GDNS
POLMUIR ROAD
SYCAMORE PLACE
DEEMONT ROAD

✕✕**Dickens** 347 Union St ☎(0224) 20318 Plan **5** *C4*

An unusual Chinese restaurant with bright modern décor and International cuisine.

International 90 seats ✱Lunch £3.50–£4&alc Dinner £12alc Wine £4.90 Last dinner 11pm

S% Credit cards 1 2 3 4 5

✕✕**Gerard's** 50 Chapel St ☎(0224) 571782 Plan **6** *B4*

Closed Sun

French **V** 85 seats ✱Lunch £3.60–£3.95&alc Dinner £12–£15alc Wine £6.10 Last dinner 11pm 20P

S% Credit cards 1 2 3 4 5

✕✕**Pinocchio** 58–60 Justice Mill Ln ☎(0224) 24599 Plan **12** *B4*

Closed Sun

Italian **V** 70 seats ✱Lunch £5.50alc Dinner £7.50alc Wine £5.60 Last dinner 11pm

Credit cards 1 2 3 5

✕**Atlantis Sea Food** 145 Crown St ☎(0224) 51403 Plan **1** *D3*

Closed Sun

American & French **V** 38 seats Lunch £15alc Dinner £20alc Wine £6 Last dinner 10pm 8P

Credit cards 1 2 3 5

✕**Light of Bengal** 13 Rose St ☎(0224) 644963 Plan **11** *B4*

European, Bengali, Indian & Persian 125 seats ✱Lunch £4.50–£7.50&alc Dinner £4.50–£7.50&alc Last dinner 11.30pm

Credit cards 1 2 3 5 **VS**

✕**Poldino's** 7 Little Belmont St ☎(0224) 647777 Plan **13** *D5*

A modern Italian restaurant in quiet back street near the city centre.

Closed Sun, Xmas Day & New Years Day

Italian **V** 70 seats Lunch £3.75&alc Dinner £9.70alc Wine £5.30 Last dinner 10.45pm

Credit cards 1 2 3 5

ABERDEEN AIRPORT
Grampian *Aberdeenshire*
Map **15** NJ81

☆☆☆☆**Holiday Inn Aberdeen Airport** Riverview Dr, Farburn, Dyce (Commonwealth) ☎Aberdeen (0224) 770011 Telex no 739651

154 (68fb) CTV in all bedrooms sB&B fr£44 (room only) dB&B fr£50 (room only)

☾ #200P CFA ✽ (heated) sauna bath Disco 5 nights wkly Live music and dancing 5 nights wkly Cabaret 5 nights wkly ♿

International **V** Lunch £9.95&alc Tea £3.50 Dinner £10&alc Wine £4.95 Last dinner 11pm

S% Credit cards 1 2 3 4 5

☆☆☆☆ **B** **Skean Dhu Hotel** Argyll Rd (adjacent to main entrance 1m N of A96) ☎Aberdeen (0224) 725252 Telex no 739239

Hotel with restaurant overlooking the enclosed courtyard which houses the swimming pool.

148 (48fb) CTV in all bedrooms ® sB £38.95 (room only) dB £44.95 (room only)

☾ #250P CFA (heated)

V ✱Bar lunch £1.30–£5.20 Tea 55p–£1 Dinner £3–£7.50&alc Last dinner 9.45pm

Credit cards 1 2 3 4 5

☆☆☆**Skean Dhu Dyce** Farburn Ter, Dyce (off A947) ☎Aberdeen (0224) 723101 Telex no 73473

A comfortable and modern hotel that is busy and popular.

222 (82fb) CTV in all bedrooms ® sB £35.95 (room only) dB £39.95 (room only)

☾ #250P CFA squash

V ✱Lunch £10alc Dinner £2.50–

World Hotel Reservations

£7.50&alc Wine£5.70 Last dinner 9.45pm
Credit cards 1 2 3 4 5 **VS**

ABERDOUR
Fife *Fife*
Map **11** NT18

★★**Woodside** High St ☎(0383) 860328
Closed Xmas & New Year
Busy hotel with cocktail bar decorated in stained glass and panelling from the old Orient liner Orantes.
12rm(2⇌4⋒) (1fb) CTV in 12 bedrooms TV in 4 bedrooms sB&B£16.50 sB&B⇌⋒£21.50 dB&B£33 dB&B⇌⋒£36
CTV 25P ✽
International Lunch fr£7.85&alc Tea fr£1.25 High Tea fr£4&alc Dinner fr£7.85&alc Wine£5.95 Last dinner 9pm
Credit cards 1 2 3 5

★**Fairways** Manse St ☎(0383) 860478
10rm (2fb) sB&B£13.50 dB&B£24 B
CTV 12P
Continental Bar lunch £2.60–£3.15 Dinner fr£4.90&alc Wine£4.80 Last dinner 9pm
Credit cards 1 2 3 5 **VS**

ABERDOVEY
Gwynedd
Map **6** SN69

★★★ *BL* **Plas Penhelig** (Inter-Hotels) ☎(065472) 676
Closed Jan & Feb
Edwardian holiday hotel, set high over Aberdovey with well tended gardens and delightful oak panelled central hall.
12rm(11⇌1⋒) (3fb) CTV available in bedrooms ✱sB&B⇌⋒£18–£21.85 dB&B⇌⋒£30–£37 B
CTV 50P ✽ (hard) nc6
French **V** ✱Lunch £5.50 Tea 75p Dinner £8.50–£10 Wine£4.40 Last dinner 9pm
Credit cards 1 2 3

★★★**Trefeddian** ☎(065472) 213
Closed 15 Oct–3 Apr
An impressive detached hotel standing in own grounds, 1m from Aberdovey.
46rm(35⇌3⋒) (4fb) TV available in bedrooms sB&B£11.30 sB&B⇌⋒£17.30–£18.30 dB&B£22.60 dB&B⇌⋒£34.60–£36.60
Lift CTV 28P 17 ✽ (heated) (hard)
V Lunch £2.50–£5.10 Tea £1 Dinner £7.70–£7.90 Wine£4.30 Last dinner 8.30pm
S% Credit card 1 **VS**

★**Harbour** 17 Glandovey Ter ☎(065472) 250
Victorian, family run holiday hotel in centre of resort.
7rm(2⇌4⋒) (1fb) CTV available in bedrooms Ⓡ✱sB&B£9.50–£12 sB&B⇌⋒£9.50–£12 dB&B£19–£24 dB&B⇌⋒£19–£24 B
CTV
✱Lunch £1.50–£4.50 Dinner £3.50–£4.50 Wine£2.75 Last dinner 8.30pm
Credit cards 1 3 **VS**

ABERFELDY
Tayside *Perthshire*
Map **14** NN84

★★***Palace*** ☎(0887) 20359
Closed Nov–Mar
Large coloured-stone Victorian building in market town by River Tay.
18rm(1⇌2⋒) Annexe: 7rm B
CTV 30P ✽ Live music and dancing 3 nights wkly
Last dinner 8.30pm
See advert on page 66

★★**Weem** Weem (1m NW B846) (Inter-Hotels) ☎(0887) 20381
A friendly roadside inn, full of character and with an interesting history.
12rm(4⇌) (2fb) Ⓡ sB&B£8–£12 sB&B⇌£9–£13 dB&B£16–£24 dB&B⇌£18–£26 B
CTV 20P ✽ →

Aberfeldy — Aberporth

V♔☕Lunch £5–£6 Tea 50p–£1 Dinner £7–£9 Wine £3.50 Last dinner 8.45pm

Credit card 3

★**Station** Dunkeld St ☎(0887) 20372

8rm (2fb) Ⓡ ✦ sB&B£9 dB&B£16

CTV 20P Live music and dancing nightly (high season) *xmas*

♔☕Bar lunch £1–£2.50 High Tea £2.50–£3 Dinner £5.75–£6.50 Last dinner 9pm

Credit card 3

✕***Ailean Chraggan*** Weem (1m NW B846) ☎(0887) 20346

Closed Nov–Mar

Scottish, English & French 45 seats Last dinner 8.30pm 40P bedrooms available

ABERFOYLE
Central *Perthshire*
Map **11** NN50

★★★**Forest Hills Hotel** Kinlochard (3m W on B829) ☎Kinlochard (08777) 277

Beautiful location within well landscaped grounds in the centre of a luxury development.

14rm (10⇌) (1fb) CTV in all bedrooms Ⓡ sB&B£10–£20 sB&B⇌£10–£20 dB&B£15–£40 dB&B⇌£15–£40 B

☾ CTV 50P ✽ (heated) (hard) Live music and dancing 4 nights wkly *xmas*

British & French V♔☕Lunch £3.75–£5.85&alc Tea £1.50–£3.50 High Tea £4.50–£6.50 Dinner £7.95&alc Wine £4.25 Last dinner 9pm

Credit cards 1 2 3 5 VS

ABERGAVENNY
Gwent
Map **3** SO21

★★★**Angel** Cross St (Trusthouse Forte) ☎(0873) 7121

Comfortable town centre hotel of great character.

29⇌ (3fb) CTV in all bedrooms Ⓡ sB&B⇌£35.50 dB&B⇌£49.50 B

27P *xmas*

♔☕Last dinner 10pm

Credit cards 1 2 3 4 5

★★***B*Llanwenarth Arms** Brecon Rd ☎(0873) 810550

Friendly hotel and restaurant with spectacular views of the River Usk.

Annexe: 18⇌ CTV in all bedrooms Ⓡ ✦ 60P

VS

ABERGELE
Clwyd
Map **6** SH97

★★**Kinmel Manor** St Georges Rd ☎(0745) 822014

Detached Georgian hotel, with modern extension, set in its own grounds.

22rm (19⇌2) CTV in all bedrooms Ⓡ sB&B£19.50 sB&B⇌£21.50 dB&B⇌£32 B

CTV 60P ✽ (heated) *xmas*

French V♔☕Lunch £5.50&alc Tea 75p Dinner £7.50&alc Last dinner 10.15pm

S% Credit cards 1 2 3 5

ABERLADY
Lothian *East Lothian*
Map **12** NT47

★★**Kilspindie House** Main St ☎(08757) 319

White-painted stone building with crow stepped gables and a recent extension to one side.

13rm (5⇌) Ⓡ sB&B£10–£13 sB&B⇌£12–£17 dB&B£20–£22 dB&B⇌£22–£26 B

CTV 40P 3 Live music and dancing Sat

V♔Lunch fr£4.25 High Tea £3.25–£5 Dinner fr£6.50&alc Wine £3.80 Last dinner 9pm

Credit cards 1 3

ABERLOUR (Charlestown of Aberlour)
Grampian *Banffshire*
Map **15** NJ24

★★**Aberlour** High St ☎(03405) 287

Centrally situated three-storey hotel.

18rm (14⇌1) Ⓡ sB&B£12.65 sB&B⇌£13.90–£14.75 dB&B⇌£23.90–£24.90

CTV 20P 9

♔☕✽Lunch £3.25&alc Tea fr60p High Tea £2.45–£4.90 Dinner £6.90–£7.50 Wine £4.10 Last dinner 9pm

VS

★**Lour** The Square ☎(03405) 224

Traditional stone Victorian hotel in the centre of this busy Speyside village.

9rm (2⇌) Ⓡ sB&B£10.65 dB&B£18.50 dB&B⇌£20.50

CTV 10P 7 billiards

Mainly grills Lunch £3.45–£4.50 High Tea £2.45–£4.95 Dinner £7.50–£8.50 Wine £3.90 Last dinner 8pm

ABERMULE
Powys
Map **7** SO19

★★***Dolforwyn Hall*** ☎(068686) 221

Closed Xmas

An elegant Georgian façade fronts this 15th-century manor house set above the A483.

7rm (3⇌4) CTV in all bedrooms Ⓡ B

70P ✽

English & French ♔☕Last dinner 9.45pm

ABERPORTH
Dyfed
Map **2** SN25

★★★**Hotel Penrallt** ☎(0239) 810227

Closed Xmas & New Year

A comfortable country hotel with modern facilities and spacious bedrooms.

17rm (13⇌4) (4fb) CTV in all bedrooms Ⓡ sB&B⇌£23 dB&B⇌£33 B

CTV 100P ✽ (hard)

♔☕Bar lunch fr£2 Tea fr£1.50 Dinner fr£6.50&alc Wine £4 Last dinner 9pm

Credit cards 1 3 5

★★**Highcliffe** ☎(0239) 810534

A proprietor run hotel in an elevated position, 200 yards from two sandy beaches.

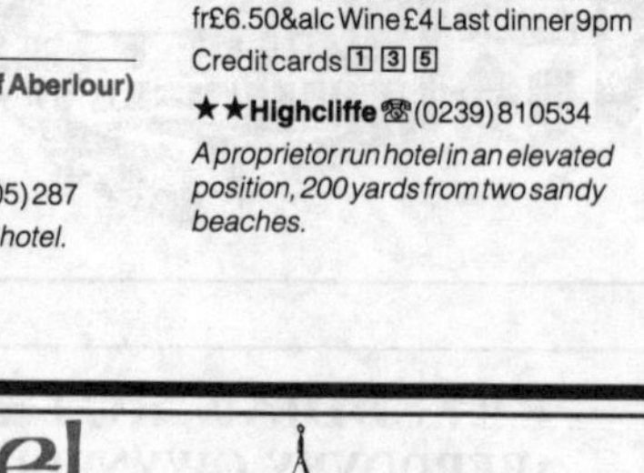

6 Annexe: 6 (3fb) TV in all bedrooms Ⓡ sB&B £18–£21 dB&B £28–£31 B
CTV 16P *xmas*
V Lunch £6.50&alc Tea £1.50 High Tea £3 Dinner fr £6.50&alc Wine £3.90 Last dinner 9.30pm
Credit cards 1 3

★★**Morlan Motel** ☎(0239) 810611
Closed Nov–Feb
Small motel with self-catering units also available.
39rm (15 14) (8fb) CTV in all bedrooms Ⓡ sB&B £15–£16.20 dB&B £24.50–£26.40 B
46P 6

Lunch £5.50–£6&alc Tea 50p–75p&alc Dinner £6&alc Wine £2.80 Last dinner 9pm
Credit cards 1 2 3 5

ABERSOCH
Gwynedd
Map **6** SH32

★★★**Abersoch Harbour** (Best Western) ☎(075881) 2406
Closed Nov–Feb
Prominent detached holiday hotel with small garden.
9rm (5 1) Annexe: 7rm (3 2) (2fb) CTV in all bedrooms sB&B £17–£23 sB&B £18–£24 dB&B £34–£46 dB&B £36–£48 B
70P ✽
French V Bar lunch 90p–£3.60&alc Tea £1.40 Dinner £9.50&alc Wine £5.60 Last dinner 9.30pm
Credit cards 1 2 3 5 **VS**

❀★★★ *HL* **Porth Tocyn** Bwlch Tocyn ☎(075881) 2966
Closed Nov–Etr (except Xmas & New Year)

→

Abersoch

(Rosette awarded for dinner only)
A cottage style country house situated in a quiet position within its own gardens with lovely views over Cardigan Bay to Snowdonia.

16 (3fb) CTV available in bedrooms ® *sB&B £19.70–£25.20 dB&B £31.50–£47

CTV P (heated) (hard) *xmas*

English & French Lunch £1–£5.50 Tea 80p–£1.20 High Tea £2–£4 Dinner £8.50–£12.50 Wine £5 Last dinner 9.30pm

Credit cards 1 2 **VS**

★★**Deucoch** (Inter-Hotels) ☎(075881) 2680

A comfortable, well appointed family holiday hotel in peaceful setting.

10rm(3 6) (1fb) CTV in all bedrooms ® sB&B £13.50–£17 sB&B £17.50–£21 dB&B £27–£34

50P

Bar lunch fr£2 Dinner fr£7&alc Wine £3 Last dinner 9.30pm

Credit cards 1 2 3 5

★★**Y-Neigwl** Lon Sarn Bach ☎(075881) 2363

Closed Nov, 3wks Dec, Jan & Feb. RS Mar

A small, personally run hotel, close to shops and beaches.

8rm(2 1) Annexe: 4rm (2fb) TV available in bedrooms ® sB&B £10.50–£12.50 sB&B £12.50–£14.50 dB&B £21–£25 dB&B £23–£27

CTV 30P 3 Live music and dancing *xmas*

V Lunch £4.25&alc Wine £4.25 Last dinner 9.30pm

★★**Riverside** ☎(075881) 2419
Closed Nov–Mar
A Victorian house with a modern extension, located in the centre of the village.
14rm(6⇌2⋔)(3fb) ✱ sB&B£15–£17 sB&B⇌⋔£17–£19 dB&B£30–£34 dB&B⇌⋔£34–£38
CTV 25P ⛟ ▭(heated)
◧Cosmopolitan ♆ ☕ Bar lunch £1.20–£5 Tea £1–£1.20 High Tea £2.50–£3.50 Dinner £9–£11 Wine £5 Last dinner 8.30pm
Credit card 3

★★**White House** ☎(075881) 2136
Closed Nov–Feb
RS Mar–May & Oct
16rm(9⇌)(4fb) CTV in all bedrooms ® sB&B£11.50 sB&B⇌£16.10 dB&B£28.76 dB&B⇌£32.20
CTV 100P ⛟ ✽ disco 3nights wkly ⌂
◧English & French ♆ Bar lunch £1.30–£2.20 Dinner £7–£12&alc Wine £3.80 Last dinner 9.30pm
Credit cards 1 2 3 5

ABERYSTWYTH
Dyfed
Map **6** SN58
★★★ ♔ ***Conrah*** Ffosrhydygaled, Chancery ☎(0970) 617941
Georgian style country mansion, with mountain views.
13rm(10⇌) CTV in all bedrooms ® ✱ B
Lift CTV 40P ✽ ⩫(heated) sauna bath nc5yrs
◧Welsh & Continental **V** ♆ ☕ Last dinner 9pm
Credit cards 1 2 3 5

★★**Belle Vue Royal** Marine Ter (Best Western) ☎(0970) 617558
Impressive Victorian hotel on the promenade adjacent to shops.
40rm(11⇌)(6fb) CTV in 15 bedrooms Ⓡ sB&B£12.50–£14 sB&B⇌£15.50–£18 dB&B£24–£26 dB&B⇌£26–£29 Ɓ
☾ CTV 5P 8
V Lunch £4 Dinner £6.25&alc Last dinner 8.30pm
Credit cards 1 2 3 4 5 VS

★★**Cambrian** Alexandra Rd ☎(0970) 612446
Four storey hotel in mock Tudor style opposite railway station.
12rm
CTV
Last dinner 8pm

★★**Groves** 42–46 North Pde (Minotel) ☎(0970) 617623
Closed 23 Dec–6 Jan
Comfortable, friendly hotel offering high quality home cooking.
12rm(5⇌7⋒)(1fb) CTV in all bedrooms Ⓡ ✻sB&B⇌⋒fr£16.50 dB&B⇌⋒fr£26.50 Ɓ
8P nc3yrs
Welsh & French V ✻Lunch £5.75–£7.25 Dinner £6.25alc Wine £4.10 Last dinner 8.30pm
Credit cards 1 2 3

★★**Seabank** Victoria Ter ☎(0970) 617617
Small, friendly hotel on the promenade
21rm(10⇌4⋒)(5fb) CTV in all bedrooms Ⓡ sB&B£13.25 sB&B⇌⋒£16 dB&B£21 dB&B⇌⋒£25.50 Ɓ
Lift
French V Lunch £4.60–£6.10 Tea 50p–60p Dinner £5.52–£8.12 Wine £3.80 Last dinner 8pm
Credit cards 1 2 3 5 VS

ABINGDON
Oxfordshire
Map **4** SU49

★★ *B* **Upper Reaches** Thames St (Trusthouse Forte) ☎(0235) 22311
Converted Abbey corn mill in country surroundings.
20⇌ CTV in all bedrooms Ⓡ sB&B⇌£38 dB&B⇌£62.50 Ɓ
90P *xmas*
Last dinner 10pm
Credit cards 1 2 3 4 5

ABOYNE
Grampian *Aberdeenshire*
Map **15** NO59

★★**Balnacoil House** ☎(0339) 2252
Large hotel standing in its own grounds on the banks of the River Dee.
11rm(3⇌1⋒) CTV available in bedrooms Ⓡ sB&B£16 sB&B⇌⋒£17 dB&B£29 dB&B⇌⋒£31 Ɓ
CTV P 2

Lunch fr£4 Tea fr£1 High Tea fr£4.50 Dinner fr£7.50 Wine £3.50 Last dinner 9pm
Credit card 5

★★ ***HB*** **Birse Lodge** ☎(0339) 2253
Closed mid Oct–late Mar
Personally run hotel set in its own grounds, popular with shooting parties and anglers.
12rm(11⇌1⋒) Annexe 4⇌ sB&B£15 sB&B⇌⋒£16 dB&B⇌⋒£32
CTV 30P
Bar Lunch from £1.60 Tea £1.20 Dinner £9.50 Wine £4.40 Last dinner 8.30pm
Credit cards 2 5

★★**Huntley Arms** ☎(0339) 2101
Friendly, traditional hotel close to the field where the Aboyne Games are played.
42rm(13⇌5⋒)(3fb) Ⓡ ✻sB&B£11.50–£14.50 sB&B⇌⋒£15.50–£16.50 dB&B£29–£32 dB&B⇌⋒£29–£32
Continental breakfast Ɓ
☾ CTV 120P 3 billiards sauna bath *xmas*
International V ✻Lunch £7&alc Dinner £9.50&alc Wine £3.35 Last dinner 9.30pm
Credit cards 1 2 3 VS

★**Charleston** ☎(0339) 2475
Small, converted private house, just off the main road, overlooking an open field.
7rm(2fb) ✻sB&B£9.25 dB&B£18.50
CTV 20P Live music and dancing Sat
V ✻Lunch £3.20–£6.65&alc Tea £1.30–£2 High Tea £2.95–£4.40 Dinner £5.50–£8&alc Wine £3.65 Last dinner 7.30pm

ABRIDGE
Essex
Map **5** TQ49

✕✕✕ ***Roding*** Market Pl ☎Theydon Bois (037881) 3030
Closed Sun
Good quality cooking and professional service are found in this 15th-century beamed restaurant.
French V 80 seats Last dinner 11pm 6P
Credit cards 1 2 3 5

ACHNASHEEN
Highland *Ross & Cromarty*
Map **14** NH15

★★ ***H*** **Ledgowan Lodge** (Best Western) ☎(044588) 252 Telex no 8814912
Closed Oct–Etr
A red sandstone former shooting lodge standing in its own grounds amidst tall pines.
18rm(9⇌1⋒)(4fb) Ⓡ sB&B£17.75–£19 sB&B⇌⋒£19.95–£21 dB&B£27.50–£32 dB&B⇌⋒£31.90–£36 Ɓ
30P

Lunch £4–£6 Tea 75p–£1.25 Dinner £8.25–£9.50&alc Wine £4 Last dinner 9pm
Credit cards 1 2 3 4 5 VS

ADLINGTON
Lancashire
Map **7** SD61

★**Gladmar** Railway Rd ☎(0257) 480398
Closed Xmas & New Year
13rm(9⋒)(2fb) CTV in 11 bedrooms Ⓡ sB&B£20 sB&B⋒£22 dB&B£27 dB&B⋒£28
CTV 24P
V Lunch £3 Tea £1 Dinner £6.50–£8.50&alc Wine £4.44 Last dinner 8.30pm

AIRDRIE
Strathclyde *Lanarkshire*
Map **11** NS76

★★**Tudor** Alexander St (Ind Coope) ☎(02364) 64144
White painted hotel with extensive car parking.
21rm(10⇌) CTV in all bedrooms Ⓡ sB&B£21.45 sB&B⇌£25.85 dB&B£29.70 dB&B⇌£37.95 Ɓ
☾ 100P
European Lunch £7.50alc Dinner £7.50alc Wine £4.50 Last dinner 9.30pm
Credit cards 1 2 3 5

✕✕**Postillion** 8–10 Anderson St ☎(02364) 67525
Attractive restaurant housed in Staging Post Hotel, located in town centre.
Closed 1–2 Jan
Lunch not served Sat
European & French V 60 seats Lunch £4.25&alc Dinner £10alc Wine £4.60 Last dinner 9.30pm bedrooms available
Credit cards 1 2 3 5

ALBRIGHTON
(nr Wolverhampton) Shropshire
Map **7** SJ80

✕✕✕ ***Lea Manor*** Holyhead Rd ☎(090722) 3266
English & French 60 seats Last dinner 10pm P bedrooms available Live music and dancing Thu–Sun Cabaret Sat
Credit card 3

ALCESTER
Warwickshire
Map **4** SP05

☆☆ ***Cherrytrees*** Stratford Rd ☎(0789) 762505
These cedarwood chalet units are set just off the main road and have ample car parking space.
Annexe: 22rm(16⇌6⋒) CTV in all bedrooms Ⓡ Ɓ
22P
V Last dinner 9.30pm
Credit cards 1 3

✕**Rossini** 50 Birmingham Rd ☎(0789) 762764

Closed Sun

English, French & Italian 40 seats Lunch £5.50 Dinner £8–£9alc Wine £4.50 Last dinner 10.30pm 14P

Credit cards 1 2 3 5

ALDBOROUGH
Norfolk
Map **9** TG13

XX Old Red Lion Cromer (0263) 761451

Modernised 16th-century Inn set on the edge of the village green.

Closed Mon, 14–28 Feb & 17–31 Oct
Dinner not served Sun

English & French 34 seats * Lunch £6.95&alc Dinner £11.50alc Wine £4.60 Last dinner 9pm 20P

ALDBOURNE
Wiltshire
Map **4** SU27

XX Raffles The Green Marlborough (0672) 40700

Closed Mon Dinner not served Sun

Continental 36 seats Lunch £7.50alc Dinner £10alc Wine £4.50 Last dinner 10.30pm

Credit cards 1 2 3 5 **VS**

ALDBROUGH
(nr Hull) Humberside
Map **8** TA23

XX *George & Dragon* (04017) 230

Dinner not served Sun

International 45 seats Last dinner 10pm 30P

Credit cards 1 3

ALDEBURGH
Suffolk
Map **5** TM45

★★★ Brudenell The Parade (Trusthouse Forte) (072885) 2071

47 (3fb) CTV in all bedrooms Ⓡ sB&B £32.50

Lift CTV 14P 6 *xmas*

Last dinner 9pm

Credit cards 1 2 3 4 5

★★★ Wentworth Sea Front (072885) 2312
Closed Jan

33rm(19 1) CTV in 33 bedrooms sB&B£18.55–£20.75 sB&B £20.75–£26 dB&B£33–£40 dB&B £37–£50.50

16P

English & French Lunch £5.50–£6.25 Tea 70p Dinner £7.75–£8.25&alc Wine £4.25 Last dinner 8.45pm

Credit card 5 **VS**

★★★ White Lion Market Cross Pl (072885) 2720

34rm(28 2) (1fb) CTV in 2 bedrooms Ⓡ sB&B£22 sB&B £26.95 dB&B £49.50

Lift CTV 12P *xmas*

V Lunch £6&alc Tea 50p Dinner £8.25&alc Wine £4.07 Last dinner 8.45pm

Credit cards 1 2 3 5

See advert on page 72

★★ *Uplands* Victoria Rd (072885) 2420
Closed Feb

Two storey period house with its own grounds, on main approach road.

13rm(2) Annexe: 7rm(5) CTV in 6 bedrooms Ⓡ

CTV 18P

Last dinner 9pm

Credit cards 1 2 3

ALDERLEY EDGE
Cheshire
Map **7** SJ87

★★★ De Trafford Arms London Rd (Greenall Whitley) (0625) 583881
Telex no 629462
RS Public Hols (B&B only)

Commercial hotel with modern bedrooms on the southern approach to the village.

37rm(32 5) (2fb) CTV in all bedrooms

→

Ⓡ sB&B £29–£30 dB&B £39–£40

Lift # CTV 52P

English & French V Bar lunch £1.60–£1.75 Dinner fr£7 Wine £5 Last dinner 10pm

Credit cards 1 2 3 5

✕**Olivers Bistro** 47 London Rd ☎(0625) 583942

Closed Sun

Lunch not served

French V 70 seats ✻Dinner £7.95&alc Wine £4.60 Last dinner 9.45pm

Live music Fri

S% Credit cards 1 3

ALDERSHOT
Hampshire
Map **4** SU84

✕***Johnnie Gurkhas*** 54 Station Rd ☎(0252) 27736

Nepalese V 35 seats Last dinner 11.30pm

Credit cards 1 2 3 5

ALFOLD
Surrey
Map **4** TQ03

✕✕**Chez Jean** Alfold Crossways (on A281) ☎Loxwood (0403) 752357

Cottage-style restaurant and free house with skilful and fresh cooking.

Closed Mon (except Public Hols) Dinner not served Sun

French 52 seats Lunch £6–£6.50&alc Dinner £8–£8.75&alc Wine £5.50 Last dinner 10pm 75P

Credit cards 1 2 3 5

ALFRISTON
East Sussex
Map **5** TQ50

★★★*L* **Star Inn** (Trusthouse Forte) ☎(0323) 870495

13th-century inn with comfortable lounges and modernised bedrooms.

33 CTV in all bedrooms Ⓡ sB&B £36 dB&B £55.50

36P *xmas*

Last dinner 9pm

Credit cards 1 2 3 4 5

✕**Moonraker's** High St ☎(0323) 870472

Closed Sun, Mon & 17 Jan–11 Feb Lunch not served

International 36 seats Dinner £10.40 Wine £4.30 Last dinner 9.15pm

ALLENDALE
Northumberland
Map **12** NY85

★★ **Ashleigh** ☎(043483) 351

An impressive country house set in its own grounds.

12rm (4fb)

sB&B fr£11 dB&B fr£17

CTV P Disco wkds

English & Italian Lunch £4–£5 Dinner £4.50–£5.50 Wine £5 Last dinner 10pm

Credit card 3

ALLENHEADS
Northumberland
Map **12** NY84

★ ***Allenheads Inn*** ☎(043485) 200

Closed 20 Dec–6 Jan

Simple country inn with old world atmosphere, personally run by proprietor.

10rm (1)

TV 25P Live music Sat nc3yrs

Last dinner 7pm

Credit cards 1 3

ALLERTHORPE
Humberside
Map **8** SE74

✕**Plough Inn** ☎Pocklington (07592) 2349

Dinner not served Mon

V 40 seats ✻Lunch £4–£5.50 Dinner £4–£7.50 Wine £4.85 Last dinner 10pm 40P

ALMONDBANK
Tayside *Perthshire*
Map **11** NO02

XX ***Huntingtower Country*** Crieff Rd (off A85) ☎(073883) 241 Perth plan **3**

Dinner not served Sun

French 50 seats Last dinner 9.30pm 40P

Credit cards 1 2 3 4 5

ALNMOUTH
Northumberland
Map **12** NU21

★★**Schooner** Northumberland St ☎(0665) 830216

Modest tourist and commercial hotel, in the centre of the village, close to the sea.

22rm (4fb) ® sB&B£11.50–£15 dB&B£22.50–£29 B

CTV 40P ✽ squash *xmas*

V Lunch £3.20–£4&alc Dinner £5.50–£7&alc Wine £3.50 Last dinner 10pm

Credit cards 1 2 3 5 **VS**

★**Saddle** 24–25 Northumberland St (Minotel) ☎(0665) 830476

A cosy, family hotel in the village centre, close to the sea.

9rm (4 5) CTV in all bedrooms ® sB&B £13–£20 dB&B £26–£30 B

2P

International V Lunch £3–£5 Tea £1–£2.50 High Tea £2.50–£5 Dinner £5.50–£10&alc Wine £5 Last dinner 9pm

Credit cards 1 3 5 **VS**

ALNWICK
Northumberland
Map **12** NU11

★★★**White Swan** Bondgate Within (Swallow) ☎(0665) 602109 Telex no 53168

A warm welcome awaits guests at this old hotel with modern amenities.

41rm (40) (5fb) CTV in all bedrooms ® sB&B£19–£26 sB&B £19–£26 dB&B £29–£40 B

CTV 30P Live music and dancing mthly *xmas*

Lunch £4.50–£5.50&alc Tea £1.30–£3 High Tea £2.50–£4 Dinner £7–£8&alc Wine £4.80 Last dinner 9pm

Credit cards 1 2 3 4 5 **VS**

★★**Hotspur** Bondgate Without ☎(0665) 602924
Closed Xmas Day

Historic coaching inn with good comfortable restaurant.

28rm (17 1) (1fb) sB fr£15 sB fr£17 dB fr£29 dB fr£32

CTV 22P

V ✻ Lunch fr£4 Dinner fr£7 Last dinner 9pm

Credit cards 1 3

ALRESFORD
Hampshire
Map **4** SU53

X**O'Rourkes** Pound Hill ☎(096273) 2293

Closed Sun Lunch not served

French 55 seats ✻ Dinner £14alc Last dinner 10pm

S%

ALSTON
Cumbria
Map **12** NY74

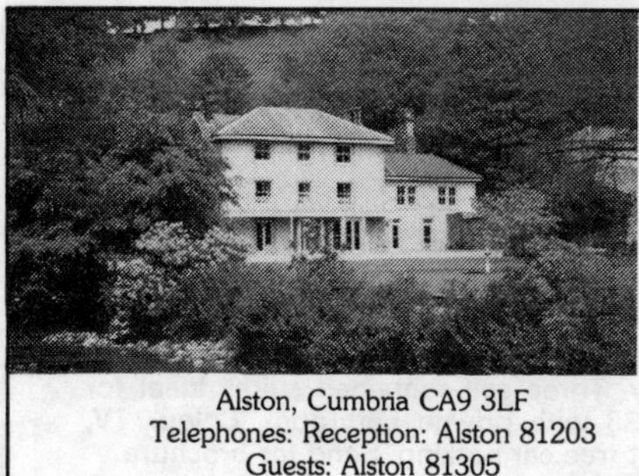

★★ *HL* **Lovelady Shield Country House** ☎(0498) 81203

Closed Nov–Jan
RS Feb

A delightful hotel offering attractive accommodation, personally supervised by the proprietors.

11rm (7 4) sB&B £17 dB&B £34 B

CTV 20P ✽ (hard)

English & Continental Tea fr60p Dinner fr£10 Wine £3.75 Last dinner 8pm

Credit cards 2 5 **VS**

★★**Lowbyer Manor** ☎(0498) 81230
Closed Nov–Apr →

Converted 18th-century manor house with courtyard, and a cellar restaurant.

7rm(3⇌1⋒) Annexe: 4⇌ Ⓡ ★ sB&B⇌⋒ £19 dB&B£28 dB&B⇌⋒ £31.50 B

CTV 12P ✽

English & French Lunch £4 Dinner £7.50&alc Wine £4.95 Last dinner 8.15pm

VS

★**Hillcrest** ☎(0498) 81251

A small, friendly hotel under the personal supervision of the resident proprietors.

11rm (2fb) ★ sB&B£12.50–£13 dB&B£23–£24 B

CTV 20P 3 ✽ *xmas*

Lunch £4.50–£5 Tea 40p High Tea £2–£5 Dinner £6.50–£7 Wine £4.10 Last dinner 8pm

★**Victoria** Front St ☎(0498) 81269

A family run hotel in the market place with a friendly and informal atmosphere.

7rm (2fb) sB&B£8.50–£9.50 dB&B£17–£18 B

CTV 1

Mainly Grills V Lunch £2.75–£8&alc Tea 35p–80p&alc High Tea £2.50&alc Dinner £2.75–£8&alc Wine £3.40 Last dinner 10pm

Credit cards 2 3 4 5

ALTON
Hampshire
Map **4** SU73

☆☆☆**Swan** High St (Anchor) ☎(0420) 83777 Telex no 858875

Attractive 16th-century former coaching inn, historically associated with the Civil War battle.

38rm(33⇌5⋒) 1 CTV in all bedrooms Ⓡ sB&B⇌⋒ £34.10 dB&B⇌⋒ £44 B

60P CFA

Lunch £5.50&alc High Tea fr40p Dinner £5.50&alc Last dinner 9.15pm

Credit cards 1 2 3 5 **VS**

★★ *H* **Grange** 17 London Rd, Holybourne ☎(0420) 86565

Small hotel with well equipped bedrooms, good English home-cooking, and friendly service and atmosphere.

15rm(9⇌4⋒) CTV in all bedrooms Ⓡ ✻sB&B£23.10–£28.60 sB&B⇌⋒ £23.10–£28.60 dB&B⇌⋒ £31.90–£38.50

☾ 40P ✽

V ✻Lunch £5.45–£6.55&alc Tea fr65p High Tea £1.50–£2.50 Dinner £5.45–£6.55&alc Wine £3.85 Last dinner 9.15pm

S% Credit cards 1 2 3 5

✕✕**Leathern Bottle** 16 Amery St ☎(0420) 88988

Closed Sun & Mon Lunch not served Sat

English & French V 50 seats Lunch £8.50alc Dinner £10.50alc Wine £4.30 Last dinner 9.30pm

S% Credit cards 1 2 3 5 **VS**

ALTON
Staffordshire
Map **7** SK04

✕✕**Wild Duck Inn** New Rd ☎Oakamoor (0538) 702218

Closed Mon Dinner not served Sun

English & Continental 80 seats Lunch £1.40–£8.50&alc Dinner £3.95–£9.95&alc Wine £4.75 Last dinner 9.15pm 80P bedrooms available Live music Wed–Sat

Credit cards 2 3 5

ALTRINCHAM
Gt Manchester
Map **7** SJ78

☆☆☆**Ashley** Ashley Rd, Hale (Greenall Whitley) ☎061-928 3794 Telex no 629462

Modern hotel above shopping parade.

49rm (48⇌1⋒) CTV in all bedrooms Ⓡ sB&B⇌⋒ £29.70–£30.70 dB&B⇌⋒ £39.60–£40.60 B

Lift ☾ CFA Disco Tue

English & French V Lunch £5.20&alc Tea fr60p Dinner £6.50&alc Wine £4.80 Last dinner 10pm

S% Credit cards 1 2 3 5

★★★ *H* **Bowdon** Langham Rd, Bowdon ☎061-928 7121 Telex no 668208

This hotel is situated in quiet semi-rural surroundings close to some lovely Cheshire countryside.

41rm(38⇌) CTV in all bedrooms sB&B£16–£23 sB&B⇌£19.50–£29 dB&B£24–£36 dB&B⇌£29–£43 B

☾ CTV 150P CFA Live music and dancing Sat

English & French Lunch £7–£8&alc Dinner £7–£8&alc Wine £4.75 Last dinner 10pm

Credit cards 1 2 3 5 **VS**

☆☆☆**Cresta Court** Church St (Best Western) ☎061-928 8017 Telex no 667242

139⇌⋒ (1fb) CTV in all bedrooms Ⓡ ✻sB&B⇌⋒ £28 dB&B⇌⋒ £38 B

Lift ☾ CFA ♿

Credit cards 1 2 3 5

★★**George & Dragon** Manchester Rd (Greenall Whitley) ☎061-928 9933 Telex no 629462

RS 1–7 Jan

50rm(33⇌⋒) (1fb) CTV in all bedrooms Ⓡ sB&B⇌⋒ £29–£30 dB&B⇌⋒ £39–£40 B

Lift ☾ 65P

Lunch £6.75–£7.95&alc Tea 50p–£1.20&alc Dinner £6.75–£7.95&alc Wine £5.65 Last dinner 10pm

Credit cards 1 2 3 5 **VS**

☆☆**Pelican** Manchester Rd (Greenall Whitley) ☎061-962 7414 Telex no 629462

Black and white inn with modern motel block added.

50⋒ CTV in all bedrooms Ⓡ sB&B⋒ £28.50–£29.50 dB&B⋒ £37–£38 B

☾ 150P *xmas*

V Bar lunch fr£2 Tea fr55p Dinner fr£7 Wine £5.25 Last dinner 9.30pm

Credit cards 1 2 3 5

✕✕✕ ***Le Bon Viveur*** Wood Ln, Timperley (2m E A560) ☎061-980 5299
Lunch not served Sat Dinner not served Sun
French 54 seats Last dinner 10pm
Credit cards 2 3 5

✕✕ ***Evergreen*** 169-171 Ashley Rd, Hale ☎061-928 1222
Lunch not served
Cantonese 76 seats Last dinner 10pm 25P

✕✕ **Hilal** 351 Stockport Rd, Timperley (2m E A560) ☎061-980 4090
Closed Xmas
Indian **V** 70 Seats Lunch £3.50–£4.50&alc Dinner £5.50–£7&alc Wine £3.60 Last dinner 11.30pm 20P
Credit cards 1 3

At **Bucklow Hill** (4m SW on A556)
☆☆☆ **Swan** (Greenall Whitley) ☎Bucklow Hill (0565) 830295
74rm(44→30⋒) 200P

ALVELEY
Shropshire
Map **7** SO78

✕✕ **Mill** Birds Green ☎Quatt (0746) 780437
Closed Mon Dinner not served Sun
English, French & Italian **V** 90 seats Lunch £3–£4.50&alc Dinner £4.50–£6.50&alc Wine £4.50 Last dinner 10.30pm 150P bedrooms available
S% Credit cards 1 2 3 4 5 **VS**

ALVESTON
Avon
Map **3** ST68

☆☆☆ **Post House** Thornbury Rd (Trusthouse Forte) ☎Thornbury (0454) 412521 Telex no 444753
Convenient for M4/M5, this Tudor inn has been extended and modernised.
75→ (50fb) CTV in all bedrooms Ⓡ sB&B→£43 dB&B→£56.50 Ɓ
☾ 200P CFA ✽ ⩱ (heated) *xmas*
Last dinner 10.15pm
Credit cards 1 2 3 4 5

★★ **Alveston House** ☎Thornbury (0454) 415050 Telex no 449683
Georgian building, comfortable and friendly, with a new restaurant and secluded garden.
15rm(6→9⋒) Annexe: 2rm(1→1⋒) (2fb) CTV in all bedrooms Ⓡ sB&B→⋒£24.50 dB&B→⋒£34 Ɓ
45P CFA ✽ *xmas*
English & Continental Lunch £5.50&alc Tea 75p–£1.50 Dinner £5.50&alc Wine £4.75 Last dinner 9.30pm
Credit cards 1 3 **VS**

ALYTH
Tayside *Perthshire*
Map **15** NO24

★★★ ***Lands of Loyal*** Loyal Rd ☎(08283) 2481
Closed Xmas & New Year
Originally built by William Ogilvy in 1850, this building stands on elevated ground with fine views over Strathmore.
14rm(7→⋒) 1 Ɓ
CTV 15P 4 ✽ ⩱
English & French Last dinner 9.30pm
Credit cards 2 5

AMBERGATE
Derbyshire
Map **8** SK35

★ **Hurt Arms** ☎(077385) 2006
A detached, stone-built commercial inn, standing on the A6.
6rm (2fb) sB&B£11 dB&B£20
CTV 100P
Lunch £4.60 Tea £1 High Tea £4.60 Dinner £6 Wine £4.20 Last dinner 7.30pm

AMBERLEY
Gloucestershire
Map **3** SO80

★★ *H* **Amberley Inn** (Best Western) ☎(045387) 2565
A warm and comfortable inn offering a superb view and situation.
10rm(7→) Annexe: 5→ Ⓡ sB&B£19 sB&B→£26–£32 dB&B£32 dB&B→£35–£40 Ɓ
CTV 20P ✽ *xmas*
Lunch £4.50–£6.50&alc Tea 65p Dinner £8&alc Wine £4.30 Last dinner 9.30pm
S% Credit cards 1 2 3

AMBLESIDE
Cumbria
Map **7** NY30

See also **Elterwater** and **Langdale, Great**
(Ambleside telephone numbers are liable to change during the currency of this guide)

❀★★★ *HBL* **Rothay Manor** Rothay Br ☎(09663) 3605
Closed last 3wks Jan
(Rosette awarded for dinner only.)
Mrs Bronwen Nixon, her two sons and dedicated staff run this elegant Regency country house on the edge of Ambleside. Its hospitality and service make a visit here rather special. The highest standard of food is served at the five course dinners in the candle-lit dining room. Bedrooms are comfortable and very well appointed, many with balconies overlooking the gardens.
14→ (5fb) CTV in all bedrooms sB&B→£37–£38 dB&B→£54–£59 Ɓ
30P ✽ *xmas*
English & Continental **V** Lunch £5–£7 Tea £2.50–£3 Dinner £14.50–£15 Wine £4.70 Last dinner 9pm
Credit cards 1 2 3 5 **VS**

★★★ **Waterhead** Lake Rd (Best Western) ☎(09663) 2566 Telex no 69273
Occupies a fine position overlooking the lake and mountains at Waterhead Bay.
30rm(15→15⋒) (6fb) CTV in all bedrooms Ⓡ sB&B→⋒£16.60–£22 dB&B→⋒£33.20–£44 Ɓ
50P ✽ Live music and dancing Sat (Oct–Mar) *xmas*
English & French **V** Lunch £2.50–£4.50 Tea £1.50 Dinner £9&alc Wine £3.50 Last dinner 8.30pm
S% Credit cards 1 2 3 5 **VS**

★★ ***Glen Rothay*** Rydal ☎(09663) 2524
RS Dec–Feb
Friendly hotel where the cooking is imaginative and the bedrooms charming.
11rm(4⇌7⋒) 2▣ Ⓡ ⊞
CTV 40P ⊕ ✽ ♪
V ✿ Last dinner 7.30pm
Credit cards ① ② ③ ⑤

★★ ***HBL*** **Kirkstone Foot Country House** Kirkstone Pass Rd ☎(09663) 2232
Closed 11 Nov–Mar
A charming country house hotel dating back to the 17th century and set in secluded gardens at the foot of Kirkstone Pass. The bedrooms are attractively decorated and comfortably furnished. The hotel has a reputation for good traditional English cooking and Mr and Mrs Bateman provide a relaxed, friendly and comfortable atmosphere.
12⇌ (3fb) CTV available in bedrooms Ⓡ
✻sB&B⇌£20–£21.50 (incl dinner)
dB&B⇌£40–£43 (incl dinner)
30P ⊕ ✽
V ✿ Dinner £9.50 Wine £3.50 Last dinner 8.30pm
S% Credit cards ① ② ③ ④ ⑤

★★ **Regent** Waterhead (1m S A591)
☎(09663) 2254
Closed Jan
11rm(5⇌4⋒) (2fb) 1▣ CTV in all bedrooms Ⓡ sB&B£16.50–£20
sB&B⇌⋒£20–£25 dB&B£40–£45
dB&B⇌⋒£42–£47 ⊞
40P ⊕ Live music and dancing Fri & Sat *xmas*
▣ English, French & Italian V ✿ ☐ Bar lunch £1.95–£5alc Tea fr£2.50 Dinner £8.50–£10&alc Wine £3.95 Last dinner 10.30pm
Credit cards ① ② ③ ⑤ **VS**

★★ **Royal Yachtsman** Lake Rd
☎(09663) 2244
Dates from 1656, but has a modernised interior. Situated in the centre of Ambleside, which is in the heart of the National Park.
40rm(3⇌) (5fb) CTV in 10 bedrooms Ⓡ
✻sB&B£14 sB&B⇌£14 dB&B£28
dB&B⇌£35 ⊞
☾ CTV P billiards Disco Fri & Sat Live music and dancing Fri & Sat Cabaret Fri & Sat *xmas*
✿ ☐ Wine £3.40 Last dinner 5.30pm
Credit cards ① ② ③ ⑤

★★ **Skelwith Bridge** Skelwith Bridge (2½m W A593) ☎(09663) 2115
Originally a 17th-century inn, situated in woodlands near the the Langdale Valley.
19rm(8⇌) Annexe: 5⇌ (2fb) Ⓡ
sB&B£12–£18.50 sB&B⇌£13.50–£20
dB&B£24–£37 dB&B⇌£27–£40 ⊞
CTV 60P ⊕ ✽ *xmas*
▣ English & French. V ✿ Lunch £4.95–£5.50 Dinner £8–£8.75 Wine £4.50 Last dinner 8.45pm
S% Credit cards ① ③ **VS**

★★ **Vale View** Lake Rd (Minotels)
☎(09663) 3192
Closed Nov–Mar
An old established hotel, in the process of being modernised, yet retaining its original character.
20rm(9⇌2⋒) (3fb) sB&B£11.75–£12.50
sB&B⇌⋒£15.75–£16.50 dB&B£22.50–£24 dB&B⇌⋒£26.50–£28 ⊞
CTV 9P
▣ English & Continental ✿ Bar Lunch £3.30alc Dinner £7 Wine £2.50 Last dinner 8pm
S% Credit cards ① ③ **VS**

★★ ***L*** **Wateredge** Waterhead ☎(09663) 2332
Closed mid Nov–mid Feb
Originally two 17th-century cottages with later additions. The lawns extend to the edge of the lake.
20rm(9⇌2⋒) (1fb) Ⓡ sB&B£15–£20
dB&B£25–£36 dB&B⇌⋒£32–£46 ⊞
CTV 25P ✽

French Tea £1.20 Dinner £10.90–£11.90 Wine £3.90 Last dinner 8pm
Credit cards 1 3

★**Fisherbeck** Old Lake Rd (09663) 3215
RS Jan & Feb
16rm(12) (5fb) CTV in 4 bedrooms ® sB&B£13–£16 sB&B£14–£17 dB&B£22–£24 dB&B£24–£28
CTV 24P *xmas*
V Bar lunch £3&alc Dinner fr£6.50&alc Wine £3.60 Last dinner 8pm
Credit card 1

★**HL Nanny Brow Country House** Clappersgate (09663) 2036
Closed New Year
Peaceful, secluded hotel, personally supervised by the proprietors.
13rm(7 1) (2fb) CTV in all bedrooms ® sB&B£11.25–£14.50 sB&B £14.25–£17.50 dB&B£22.50–£29 dB&B £28.50–£35
13P *xmas*
English & French **V** Lunch £4.50–£5.50 Dinner £7.50–£8.50&alc Wine £2.80 Last dinner 8pm
Credit cards 1 3 **VS**

★**White Lion** (09663) 3140
Closed 1 wk Xmas
A 17th-century country inn situated in the centre of the village.
12rm (2fb) sB&B fr£13.75 dB&B fr£27
CTV 24P 8 nc4yrs
Lunch fr£6 Tea fr£1.50 Dinner fr£7 Wine £5 Last dinner 7.45pm
VS

AMERSHAM
Buckinghamshire
Map **4** SU99

★★**Crown** High St (Trusthouse Forte) (02403) 21541
The accent is on comfort in this interesting Elizabethan inn with its wood panelling, inglenooks and wall paintings.
19rm(6) CTV in all bedrooms ® sB&B£33.50 sB&B£39 dB&B£50 dB&B£55.50
51P *xmas*
Last dinner 10pm
Credit cards 1 2 3 4 5

XX**Kings Arms** High St (02403) 6333
Closed Mon Dinner not served Sun
English & French **V** 30 seats Lunch £9alc Dinner £10.50alc Wine £4.15 Last dinner 10pm 25P
Credit cards 1 2 3 5 **VS**

X**Lam's Garden** 131 Station Rd (02403) 5505
Peking **V** 40 seats *Lunch £1.80–£5&alc Dinner £5.50–£10&alc Wine £5.30 Last dinner 11.15pm
Credit cards 1 3 5 **VS**

AMESBURY
Wiltshire
Map **4** SU14

★★**Antrobus Arms** Church St (0980) 23163
20rm(12) (1fb) CTV in all bedrooms ® *sB&B£18.50 sB&B£23.25 dB&B£28.50 dB&B£33.50
60P 6
English & French Lunch £6 Tea £1 Dinner £8.25 Last dinner 10pm
Credit cards 1 2 3 5

AMLWCH
Gwynedd
Map **6** SH49

★★***Dinorben Arms*** Dinorben Sq (0407) 830358
Two-storey former coaching house set in the centre of the town.
15 CTV available in bedrooms
CTV 60P
Last dinner 8.30pm
Credit cards 2 3

★★**Trecastell** Bull Bay (Frederic Robinson) (0407) 830651
This hotel in the centre of the town used to be a coaching house.
12rm(8 2) (3fb) ® sB&B£14–£16 dB&B£24–£28
CTV 80P
V Lunch £4.75–£6.50 Tea 60p–£1.50 Dinner £6.50–£8&alc Wine £3.50 Last dinner 9pm
Credit cards 1 2 3

AMMANFORD
Dyfed
Map **2** SN61

★★**B Mill at Glynhir** Llandybie (3m NE off A483) (0269) 850672
Closed Dec & Jan RS Nov & Feb
Small country hotel, originally a 17th century mill.
6rm(3 3) Annexe: 2rm(1 1) (3fb) CTV in all bedrooms ® sB&B£20 dB&B£40
12P (heated) nc11yrs
British & Continental Lunch £5–£7&alc Dinner £9.50&alc Wine £4.25 Last dinner 9.30pm
VS

AMPFIELD
Hampshire
Map **4** SU32

☆☆☆**Potters Heron** (Whitbread) Chandler's Ford (04215) 66611
Well appointed hotel incorporating popular pub and grill restaurant.
42 CTV in all bedrooms ® sB&B fr£35 dB&B fr£45
120P CFA

English & French Lunch fr£5.50&alc Dinner fr£7.50&alc Wine £4.75 Last dinner 10pm
Credit cards 1 2 3 5

AMPTHILL
Bedfordshire
Map **4** TL03

X***Kings Arms*** Kings Arms Yard, off Church St (0525) 404303
17th-century building with a small courtyard, and featuring a low-beamed first floor dining room.
Closed Mon Lunch not served Sat Dinner not served Sun
French **V** 45 seats Last dinner 10pm
12P
Credit cards 1 2 3 5

ANDOVER
Hampshire
Map **4** SU34

★★**White Hart** Bridge St (Anchor) (0264) 52266
Historic 16th-century former coaching inn, situated near several prehistoric sites and ancient crossroads.
21rm(18 3) CTV in all bedrooms ® *sB&B£31 dB&B£40
16P
English & French **V** Lunch £6.50–£8.50alc Dinner £6.50–£8.50alc Wine £4.50 Last dinner 9.45pm
Credit cards 1 2 3 4 5

ANDREAS
Isle of Man
Map **6** SC49

XX**Grosvenor** Kirk Andreas (062488) 576
Closed Tues, Oct & Xmas Day
Dinner not served Sun
International 50 seats *Lunch £5&alc Dinner £10alc Wine £4.25 Last dinner 9pm
80P
S% Credit card 1

ANGMERING-ON-SEA
West Sussex
Map **4** TQ00

★★**South Strand** South Strand Rustington (09062) 5086
Small, friendly, family-run hotel with simple accommodation.
15rm(3) (2fb) *sB&B£14 dB&B£28 dB&B£32
CTV 30P
*Lunch £7–£10 Tea fr50p High Tea £3 Dinner £7–£10 Wine £3.25 Last dinner 8pm

ANNAN
Dumfries & Galloway *Dumfriesshire*
Map **11** NY16

★★**Queensberry Arms** (Osprey) (04612) 2024
Whitewashed, two-storey building in the

→

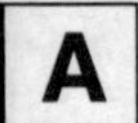

centre of the town, 10 miles from the English border.

26rm(5⇌)(2fb) CTV in all bedrooms ® *sB&B£17 sB&B⇌£20 dB&B£28 dB&B⇌£34 B

35P 6🚗✽ Live music and dancing most wknds *xmas*

Scottish, English, French & Italian ✽Lunch fr£3.50&alc Tea 55p–£1.20 High Tea £3–£5.85 Dinner £6.50&alc Wine £3.80 Last dinner 9pm

Credit cards 1 2 3 4 5 VS

★**Corner House** High St (Mount Charlotte) ☎(04612) 2754

Town centre hotel popular with coach parties.

31rm(1🚿)(3fb) sB&B£12.50 dB&B£17.50 B

60P Live music and dancing twice wkly

Lunch £2.50–£3 Dinner ££3.50–£4&alc Wine £4.75 Last dinner 8pm

Credit cards 1 3

ANSTRUTHER
Fife *Fife*
Map **12** NO50

★★★**Craws Nest** Bankwell Rd ☎(0333) 310691 Telex no 727396

A resort hotel in this small, East Fife fishing village.

31⇌(5fb) CTV in all bedrooms ® sB&B⇌£19–£20 dB&B⇌£36–£38 B

☾ ## 150P sauna bath Live music and dancing wkly *xmas*

V Lunch fr£5 Tea fr60p High Tea £3–£5.60 Dinner £8–£9.25 Wine £4.75 Last dinner 9pm

Credit cards 1 2 3 4 5

★★**Smugglers Inn** High St ☎(0333) 310506

The original inn dates back to 1300, and was a noted tavern in the days of Queen Anne.

9rm(1⇌5🚿) sB&B£14–15 sB&B⇌🚿£15–£16 dB&B£28–£30 dB&B⇌🚿£30–£32

CTV 16P

V Lunch £5–£6.50&alc Dinner £7&alc

Wine £2.20 Last dinner 9.30pm

Credit cards 1 2 3 4 5

❀✕✕**Cellar** 24 East Green ☎(0333) 310378

Seafood restaurant, with original stone work and beams and many objets d'art.

Closed 1wk May, 1wk Nov & Xmas

Lunch not served Sun–Thu

Reservations advisable especially in winter

French 30 seats ✽Lunch £6alc Dinner £11.50–£15.50 Wine £4.50 Last dinner 9pm

Credit card 3

APPLEBY
Cumbria
Map **12** NY62

★★★**Appleby Manor** Roman Rd ☎(0930) 51571 Telex no 64100

Closed 15 Dec–15 Jan

A pink sandstone Victorian country house standing in its own extensive grounds.

10rm(7⇌)(2fb) CTV in 5 bedrooms ® sB&B£17 sB&B⇌£19.50–£20.50 dB&B£25 dB&B⇌£29.34 B

CTV 40P 7🚗✽ ♿

English & French Lunch £9alc Tea 75palc Dinner £9alc Wine £4.50 Last dinner 9pm

Credit cards 1 3 VS

★★**Royal Oak Inn** Bongate ☎(0930) 51463

A 14th-century coaching inn lying in the Eden Valley.

8rm CTV in 4 bedrooms sB&B£12.50 dB&B£25

9P 4🚗

Mainly grills **V** Lunch £2.50–£4.95&alc Dinner £7.50&alc Wine £3.10 Last dinner 9.30pm

★★**Tufton Arms** Market Sq ☎(0930) 51593

19rm(14⇌)(1fb) CTV available in bedrooms sB&B£15 sB&B⇌£16.50 dB&B£28 dB&B⇌£30.50 B

CTV 30P 6🚗 *xmas*

✽Lunch £4 Tea 55p High Tea £2.50–£3.50 Dinner £6.50–£7.75&alc Wine £3.50 Last dinner 8.30pm

Credit cards 1 3 VS

★***Courtfield*** Bongate ☎(0930) 51394

A small, homely establishment, set in three acres of gardens on the outskirts of the town.

10rm Annexe: 6rm ® B

CTV 33P 2🚗✽ billiards

V Last dinner 7.45pm

Credit cards 1 3

★**White Hart** Boroughgate ☎(0930) 51598 RS Dec–Feb (no accommodation)

This 18th-century, small, modernised hotel is situated in the town centre.

8rm(2fb) sB&B£9.50 dB&B£19

CTV 4P

V Lunch £6alc Dinner £6.50alc Wine £3.20 Last dinner 9pm

APPLEDORE
Devon
Map **2** SS43

★★***Seagate*** The Quay ☎Bideford (02372) 2589

Closed Xmas

A pleasant, busy inn with most convivial atmosphere, overlooking the estuary.

9rm(2⇌) B

CTV 20P

Last dinner 9.30pm

ARBROATH
Tayside *Angus*
Map **12** NO64

★★**Hotel Seaforth** Dundee Rd ☎(0241) 72232

20rm(10⇌) CTV in all bedrooms ® *sB&B£15 sB&B⇌£20 dB&B£27 dB&B⇌£30 B

CTV 150P Live music and dancing Fri & Sat *xmas*

✽Lunch £3&alc Tea 65p&alc Dinner £5.65&alc Wine £4.50 Last dinner 9pm

Credit cards 1 2 3 5

★**Towerbank** James St ☎(0241) 75987
7rm (3fb) Ⓡ sB&B£12 dB&B£18 Ⓑ
CTV 12P 🚫
🍽English & French **V** ♔ ☕ Lunch £1.40–£3.10&alc Tea 50p High Tea £3.75–£4 Dinner £5.50–£6.10&alc Wine £4.55 Last dinner 10.15pm
Credit card ①

✕✕**Carriage Room** Meadowbank Inn, Montrose Rd ☎(0241) 75844
Closed Sun Lunch not served Sat Dinner not served Mon
🍽French **V** 55 seats ✱Lunch £4–£6.50&alc High Tea £3.50–£4.50 Dinner £9.25&alc Wine £4.75 Last dinner 10pm 75P Live music and dancing Thu & Sat
Credit cards ② ⑤

ARCHIRONDEL
Jersey, Channel Islands
Map **16**

★★*B* **Les Arches** Archirondel Bay ☎Jersey (0534) 53839 Telex no 4192085
An attractive holiday hotel, with modern bedrooms and good bars, overlooking the sea.
53rm (35🛁19🚿) CTV available in bedrooms sB&B🛁🚿£15–£20.25 dB&B🛁🚿£30–£40.50
☾ CTV 120P CFA 🚫 ✽ ⛆(heated) Disco 6 nights wkly Cabaret wkly in season *xmas*
🍽English & Continental ♔ ☕ Lunch £5–£20 Tea 60p–£1.50 Dinner £6.50–£25 Wine £2.50 Last dinner 8.30pm
Credit cards ① ③ ④

ARDELVE
Highland *Ross & Cromarty*
Map **14** NG82

★*HL* **Loch Duich** ☎Dornie (059985) 213 Telex no 75605
Closed Xmas & New Year
A delightful and friendly little hotel with a reputation for its hospitality and food.
18rm
⚡CTV 40P 1🏠 🚫 ✽
♔ ☕ Last dinner 9pm
Credit cards ① ③ **VS**

ARDEN
Strathclyde *Dunbartonshire*
Map **10** NS38

★★★*B* **Lomond Castle** (Best Western) ☎(038985) 681
Hotel, chalet and leisure complex on banks of Loch Lomond.
21rm (16🛁5🚿) (2fb) CTV in all bedrooms Ⓡ sB&B🛁£35 dB&B🛁£45 Ⓑ
☾ 300P ✽ ⛆(heated) 🎾(hard) ⛵ sauna bath 🏠 *xmas*
🍽Scottish, English & French ♔ ☕ Lunch £6.50&alc Tea £1alc Dinner £6.50–£11• Wine £6.50 Last dinner 10pm
Credit cards ① ② ③ ④ ⑤ **VS**

ARDENTINNY
Strathclyde *Argyllshire*
Map **10** NS18

★★*H* **Ardentinny** (Inter-Hotels/ ExecHotel) ☎(036981) 209 Telex no 777205
Closed Dec–Feb RS Nov & Mar (wknds only)
Good food and friendly service commend this historic hotel in a beautiful mountain setting.
11rm (5🛁6🚿) (1fb) Ⓡ sB&B🛁🚿£15.50–£17.50 dB&B🛁🚿£28–£32 Ⓑ
CTV 20P 🚫 ✽ 🏠
🍽Scottish & French ♔ ☕ Lunch £4alc Tea £1alc Dinner £8–£10 Wine £4 Last dinner 9.30pm
Credit cards ① ② ③

ARDEONAIG
Central *Perthshire*
Map **11** NN63

★★**Ardeonaig** South Loch Tayside ☎Killin (05672) 400
Closed Nov–Feb RS Mar
14rm (9🛁5🚿) (3fb) Ⓡ sB&B🛁🚿£14–£17.50 dB&B🛁🚿£18–£35 Ⓑ
CTV 40P 🚫 ✽ ⛵
🍽Scottish, English & Continental ♔ ☕ Bar lunch fr£1 Dinner fr£10.50 Wine £4.54 Last dinner 9pm
S% **VS**

ARDFERN
Strathclyde *Argyllshire*
Map **10** NM80

★**Galley of Lorne** ☎Barbreck (08525) 284
Closed Xmas Day
A drover's inn during the 16th century, it is particularly popular with yachtsmen today.
10rm (2🛁) Ⓡ dB&B£12–£24 dB&B🛁🚿£16–£28 Ⓑ
CTV 40P ✽
🍽International **V** ♔ ☕ Bar lunch £2.50–£3alc Tea 50p alc High Tea £2–£3 Dinner £6.50–£7.50 Wine £3.50 Last dinner 9.30pm
Credit cards ① ② ⑤ **VS**

ARDLUI
Strathclyde *Dunbartonshire*
Map **10** NN31

★★**Ardlui** ☎Inveruglas (03014) 243
A large, white-painted house whose gardens run down to shores of Loch Lomond.
11rm (1🛁) (5fb) sB&B£13–£14.50 dB&B£23–£25.50 dB&B🛁£26–£28.60
CTV 50P ✽ Live music and dancing 5 nights wkly
V ♔ ☕ Bar lunch £3alc Tea 50p Dinner £6alc Wine £4.20 Last dinner 8.30pm

ARDUAINE
Strathclyde *Argyllshire*
Map **10** NM80

★★★*HL* **Loch Melfort** ☎Kilmelford (08522) 233
Closed mid Oct–19 Apr
Spectacular views are a feature of this popular hotel with its chalet extension.
6rm (3🛁) Annexe: 20🛁 CTV in 1 bedroom Ⓡ sB&B£16–£25 sB&B🛁£19–£30 dB&B£38 dB&B🛁£50 Continental breakfast
CTV 50P 🚫 ✽ 🏠
V ♔ ☕ ✱Bar lunch £4.50alc Dinner £10.50alc Wine £4.15 Last dinner 8.30pm
Credit card ①

ARDVASAR
Isle of Skye, Highland *Inverness-shire*
Map **13** NG60

★★**Ardvasar** ☎(04714) 223
Former coaching inn with modern extension located near the shore overlooking Mallaig.
12rm (4🛁) Ⓡ ✱sB&B£10–£12 sB&B🛁£12–£14 dB&B£20–£27 dB&B🛁£24–£32 Ⓑ
CTV 30P ✽ ⛵
♔ ☕ ✱Lunch fr£3&alc Tea £1.25&alc Dinner £6 Wine £4.15 Last dinner 8.45pm

ARINAGOUR
Isle of Coll, Strathclyde *Argyllshire*
Map **13** NM26

★**Isle of Coll** ☎Coll (08793) 334
Pleasant family atmosphere in this 1720 island inn.
9rm (2fb) CTV available in bedrooms Ⓡ sB&B£13.60–£17 dB&B£24.80–£31 Ⓑ
CTV 30P ✽ sauna bath Live music nightly
♔ ☕ Lunch £7.50 Tea £1.50 Dinner £9 Wine £3.50 Last dinner 9.30pm
Credit cards ① ⑤ **VS**

ARISAIG
Highland *Inverness-shire*
Map **13** NM68

❀★★★🏰*HBL* **Arisaig House** Beasdale (3m E A830) ☎(06875) 622
Closed Nov–mid Mar
(*Rosette awarded for dinner only*)
A magnificent stone mansion set in 20 acres of beautiful gardens leading down to the sea. The rooms are furnished in soft, pastel colours enlivened by water colours and flowers. The dining room is well appointed and the set dinner, in the modern style is delicious. Bedrooms are spacious and attractive. (See p. 28.)
16🛁 (2fb) CTV in all bedrooms ★ ✱sB&B£18.50 sB&B🛁£20.50–£47.70 dB&B🛁£59–£85.40 Ⓑ
20P 🚫 ✽ billiards nc10yrs
🍽English & French ♔ ☕ Lunch £6–£8 Tea fr75p Dinner fr£14.50 Wine £5 Last dinner 8.30pm
Credit cards ① ② ③ ⑤
See advert on page 80

ARMATHWAITE
Cumbria
Map **12** NY54
★ ***Duke's Head Inn*** ☎(06992) 226
An old world village inn, situated in the centre of Armathwaite, with large garden, aviaries and a fish pool.
8rm
TV ✽
Last dinner 8pm

ARMITAGE
(nr Rugeley) Staffordshire
Map **7** SK01
✕✕ **Old Farmhouse** ☎(0543) 490353
Interesting selection of well cooked dishes at sensible prices.
Closed Sun, Mon, Spring Bank Hol wk, 2 wks Jul–Aug, 24 Dec–5 Jan & Public Hols
V 100 seats ✻Lunch £4.75–£8.50 Dinner £7.90–£11.35 Wine £3.95 Last dinner 9.30pm 60P
Credit cards 1 2 5

ARRAN, ISLE OF
Strathclyde *Bute*
Map **10**
See **Blackwaterfoot, Kilmory, Lamlash** and **Whiting Bay.**

ARUNDEL
West Sussex
Map **4** TQ00

★★★ **Norfolk Arms** High St (Forest Dale) ☎(0903) 882101 Telex no 47439
An 18th-century coaching inn with a central arch and also featuring an ornate staircase.
21rm(19➡) Annexe: 13➡ 4 CTV in all bedrooms Ⓡ sB&B➡£25–£27.50 dB&B➡£34–£38
24P 12 *xmas*
V Lunch £4.95–£5.65 Tea fr 50p Dinner £7.95–£9.50 Wine £4.35 Last dinner 10pm
Credit cards 1 2 3 5 **VS**

ASCOT
Berkshire
Map **4** SU96
☆☆☆☆ **Berystede** Bagshot Rd, Sunninghill (Trusthouse Forte) ☎(0990) 23311 Telex no 847707
Efficient, well-appointed conference hotel.
90rm(85➡5⋒) CTV in all bedrooms Ⓡ sB&B➡£45.50 dB&B➡£59
Lift ☾ 140P 6 CFA ✽ (heated)
xmas
Last dinner 10pm
Credit cards 1 2 3 4 5

ASHBURTON
Devon
Map **3** SX77
★★ **Dartmoor Motel** (A38/B3357) ☎(0364) 52232
RS Xmas Day
Touring and business hotel, situated close to A38.
8rm(6➡2⋒) Annexe: 14➡ (8fb) CTV in 3 bedrooms TV in 19 bedrooms Ⓡ sB&B➡⋒£19.85–£21.85 dB&B➡⋒£24.85–£28.85
50P 2 ✽
Mainly grills Lunch £3.50–£4.50&alc Tea fr £1 Dinner £3.50–£4.50&alc Wine £2.80 Last dinner 9.15pm
Credit cards 1 2 3 5 **VS**

★★ H **Holne Chase** (Inter-Hotels) ☎Poundsgate (03643) 471
An attractive period house in a magnificent setting with most impressive views.
12rm(5➡3⋒) Annexe: 3rm(2➡) (1fb) Ⓡ ✻sB&B£16 sB&B➡⋒£21–£26 dB&B£29 dB&B➡⋒£29–£35
CTV 20P 3 ✽ ♿
V ✻Lunch £5.75&alc Tea 50p–£1.50 Dinner £6.50–£9.50 Wine £4 Last dinner 8.30pm
Credit cards 1 2 3 5

★ **Tugela House** 68 East St ☎(0364) 52206

6rm(2➡)CTV in 1 bedroom
*sB&B£10.50 dB&B£21 dB&B➡£25
CTV 3P
Last dinner 9.30pm

ASHBY-DE-LA-ZOUCH
Leicestershire
Map **8** SK31

★★★**Royal Crest** Station Rd (Crest) ☎(0530) 412833
This large Regency building beside the A453 is conveniently close to the town centre.
31rm(25➡6⋔)CTV in all bedrooms ®
*sB➡⋔ fr£31 (room only) dB➡⋔ fr£40 (room only) B
☾ 250P ✽
International V *Lunch £5.10–£6.50&alc Tea 50p Dinner £6.50–£8.25&alc Last dinner 9.15pm
Credit cards 1 2 3 4 5

✕**La Zouch** 2 Kilwardby St ☎(0530) 412536
Simple bistro near town centre.
Closed Mon Dinner not served Sun
46 seats Lunch £2–£4&alc Dinner £9alc Wine £3.90 Last dinner 10pm
Credit cards 1 2 3 5

ASHFORD
Kent
Map **5** TR04

★★★★ *BL* **Eastwell Manor** Eastwell Park (3m N A251) (Prestige) ☎(0233) 35751 Telex no 966281
Attractive country house with beautifully decorated interior standing in 3,000 acres of rolling pastureland.
21➡⋔ CTV in all bedrooms
sB&B➡⋔£35–£55 dB&B➡⋔£55–£70
Lift ☾ 60P 15 ✽ (hard) billiards
xmas
French V Lunch £9&alc Tea £2–£4.50 Dinner £20alc Wine £6.50 Last dinner 9.30pm
Credit cards 1 2 3 5 VS

★★★**Spearpoint** Canterbury Rd, Kennington (Exec Hotel) ☎(0233) 36863 Telex no 965853
Set in 5 acres of parkland, hotel also features Du Vert Galant Restaurant.
37rm(30➡4⋔)(2fb) CTV in all bedrooms ® sB&B£18.50 sB&B➡⋔£28.50 dB&B➡⋔£38.50 B
☾ CFA 60P ✽
French V Lunch £7.50alc Tea 65p&alc Dinner £9alc Wine £4.25 Last dinner 9.45pm
S% Credit cards 1 2 3 5

ASHFORD
Surrey
London plan **5** A2 (page **422**)

✕✕**Terrazza** 45 Church St ☎(07842) 44887 Heathrow plan **13** *D1*
Closed Sun Lunch not served Sat
Continental V 70 seats Lunch fr£7.50&alc Dinner £7.50&alc Wine £5.80 Last dinner 11pm Live music 1st Mon of month
S% Credit cards 1 2 3 5 VS

ASHINGTON
West Sussex
Map **4** TQ11

★★*H* ***Mill House*** Mill Ln (off A29) (Minotel) ☎(0903) 892426
10rm(1⋔)CTV in 7 bedrooms
CTV 10P ✽
Last dinner 9.30pm
Credit cards 2 3 4 5

ASHLEY HEATH
Dorset
Map **4** SU10

★★***Struan*** Horton Rd ☎Ringwood (04254) 3553
White painted hotel in pleasantly wooded residential area.
10rm(5⋔)®
CTV 70P ✽ U sauna bath →

English & French Last dinner 10pm
Credit cards 1 2 3 5

ASHTEAD
Surrey
Map **4** TQ15
✕**Snooty Fox** 21 The Street
☎(03722) 76606
Modern restaurant with friendly service.
Closed Sun & 1–5 Jan
Lunch not served Sat
English & French Unlicensed 32 seats Lunch £8.50&alc Dinner £8.50&alc Wine £4.80 Last dinner 10pm bedrooms available
S% Credit card 4

ASHTON-UNDER-LYNE
Gt Manchester
Map **7** SJ99
★★**York House** York Pl, off Richmond St ☎061-330 5899
Closed Boxing Day
Large hotel near town centre with Victorian style restaurant.
17rm(4) (1fb) CTV in all bedrooms ® sB&B£15.30 sB&B£21.50 dB&B£28 dB&B£30.70
☾ 26P
English & French **V** Lunch £5.50alc Dinner £5.50alc Wine £3.95 Last dinner 9.30pm
Credit cards 1 2 5 **VS**

ASKHAM
Cumbria
Map **12** NY52
★★***Queens Head*** ☎Hackthorpe (09312) 225
Attractive old village inn with exposed beams in lounge and bars.
6rm
CTV 30P *xmas*
V Last dinner 7.30pm

ASTON CLINTON
Buckinghamshire
Map **4** SP81
★★★**Bell**
See Red Star panel.

ATHERSTONE
Warwickshire
Map **4** SP39
★**Old Red Lion** ☎(08277) 3156
Closed Xmas
A busy and centrally situated inn, that is popular with the locals.
10rm(4) CTV in 4 bedrooms ® *sB&B£13.50 sB&B£18.50 dB&B£20.50 dB&B£26
CTV 20P 5
V *Lunch £4.25&alc Tea 55p Dinner £4.25&alc Wine £3.55 Last dinner 9.45pm
Credit cards 1 2 3

AUCHENCAIRN
Dumfries & Galloway *Kirkcudbrightshire*
Map **11** NX75
★★★**Balcary Bay** ☎(055664) 217
12rm(5 2) (2fb) 2 sB&B£25 sB&B £26 dB&B£50 dB&B £52
CTV 75P billiards
French **V** Bar lunch fr£2.50&alc Tea fr£1.50 High Tea fr£4 Dinner fr£5alc Wine £4.50 Last dinner 9.30pm
Credit cards 1 2 3 4 5

★★★**BELL, ASTON CLINTON**
☎Aylesbury (0296) 630252
Telex no 826715

Originally a 17th century coaching inn, the Bell has been developed over the years into a comfortable hotel with a first class restaurant. Most of the accommodation is across the way in a converted brewery with a cobbled courtyard adorned with flowering plants in season. Like those in the main building, the rooms are comfortably furnished, often with antiques and have comfortable sitting areas. They are also well equipped with mini-bars, direct dial telephone, and bath robes. Above average room service is provided under what could be difficult conditions.
Perhaps its great claim to fame is the restaurant. It has continually held our rosette award since its inception and deservedly so. Jack Dick, the chef, has been there for some years and cooks very well indeed. Latterly he has been influenced by the modern school but the daily dish carved from the heated trolley still persists. No-one must forget the long and comprehensive wine list! It is

something of a hobby for Michael Harris and certainly provides something for everyone at not unreasonable prices. They can be bought retail as can other delicacies at the hotel shop.
The owners, the Harris family, can be proud of the deserved popularity of their hotel with our members.
21 2 CTV in all bedrooms
*sB&B fr£39.30 dB&B fr£52.90 Continental breakfast
250P
English & French *Lunch £14alc Tea £2alc Dinner £15alc Wine £4.20 Last dinner 9.45pm
S% Credit cards 1 3

AUCHTERARDER
Tayside *Perthshire*
Map **11** NN91

★★★★★*L* **Gleneagles** (Prestige) ☎(07646) 2231 Telex no 76105
Impressive French château-style hotel with comprehensive sporting facilities.
206 (17fb) CTV in all bedrooms *sB&B £45–£55 dB&B £75–£95
Lift ☾ 300P CFA (heated) (hard & grass) squash billiards sauna bath Live music and dancing nightly *xmas*
International V Lunch £14.50 Tea £4.75 High Tea £6.50 Dinner £15.50&alc Wine £5.50 Last dinner 11pm
Credit cards 1 2 3 4 5

★**Crown** 112/114 High St ☎(07646) 2375
13rm ®sB&B £11.50–£12.65 dB&B £20–£23
CTV P *xmas*
Lunch £2–£3.50 High Tea £2.95–£3.45 Dinner £7 Wine £2.90 Last dinner 8.30pm
Credit cards 1 5

AUCHTERHOUSE
Tayside *Forfarshire*
Map **11** NO33

★★★*HB* **Old Mansion House** ☎(082626) 366
Closed 1–8 Jan
A most comfortable hotel steeped in history, dating to the 16th century.
6rm (5 1) (2fb) 1 CTV in all bedrooms ® sB&B £32–£35 dB&B £40–£44
50P 1 (heated) (grass) squash
Scottish & French V Lunch £6.25–£6.50&alc Dinner £14alc Wine £4.95 Last dinner 9.30pm
Credit cards 1 2 3 5

AUDENSHAW
Gt Manchester
Map **7** SJ99

★**Trough House** 103 Manchester Rd ☎061-370 1574
RS Sat
A simple, commercial hotel situated on A635.
10rm Annexe: 15rm (1) ® sB&B £13.95 dB&B £25.30 dB&B £26.50
CTV 80P
V Lunch £3.25–£4.20&alc Tea 50p High Tea £1.75–£2.50 Dinner fr £4.20&alc Wine £3.65 Last dinner 9pm

AULTBEA
Highland *Ross & Cromarty*
Map **14** NG88

★★***Drumchork Lodge*** (Inter Hotels) ☎(044582) 242
Stone building with extension, overlooking Loch Ewe.
14rm (4) Annexe 4 ®
CTV 50P sauna bath
English & Continental Last dinner 8.30pm
Credit cards 1 2 3 5 **VS**

★**Aultbea** ☎(044582) 201
Closed Nov–Mar
9rm (1) (1fb) ® sB&B fr £12 sB&B fr £15 dB&B fr £24 dB&B fr £27
CTV 25P
Cosmopolitan V Bar lunch fr £3 Tea fr 50p High Tea fr £3 Dinner fr £7.50 Wine £2.65 Last dinner 8pm
Credit cards 1 3

AUSTWICK
North Yorkshire
Map **7** SD76

★**Traddock** ☎Clapham (04685) 224
Closed Oct–19 Apr
A Georgian country house of stone construction in own grounds on edge of village.
12rm (7) ®
CTV 12P nc5
Last dinner 7.30pm

AVIEMORE
Highland *Inverness-shire*
Map **14** NH81

☆☆☆☆**Stakis Coylumbridge** (Stakis) ☎(0479) 810661 Telex no 75272
This is the closest hotel to the Cairngorm ski slopes, 8 miles away, and is set amidst woodland and heather.
133 CTV in 130 bedrooms ® *sB&B £32 dB&B £42
☾ 80P CFA (heated) sauna bath Disco nightly (except Tue) Live music and dancing Fri & Sat *xmas*
English & French V Last dinner 9.45pm
Credit cards 1 2 3 5 **VS**

☆☆☆**Badenoch** (Osprey) ☎(0479) 810261
Conveniently situated in the Aviemore Centre and offering a choice of budget or normal accommodation.
81rm (61) CTV in 61 bedrooms ® *sB&B £14 sB&B £26 dB&B £26 dB&B £36
Lift ☾ # CTV 100P CFA (heated) disco 3 nights wkly *xmas*
Scottish, English & French Lunch £4 Tea 75p High Tea £3–£4.50 Dinner £8&alc Wine £4.10 Last dinner 9.30pm
Credit cards 1 2 3 4 5 **VS**

☆☆☆**Post House** Aviemore Centre (Trusthouse Forte) ☎(0479) 810771
Modern hotel, at the rear of the Aviemore Centre, is close to the dry ski-slope and convenient for the other facilities of the centre.
103 (46fb) CTV in all bedrooms ® sB&B £34.50 dB&B £52.50
Lift ☾ 140P *xmas*
Last dinner 10pm
Credit cards 1 2 3 4 5

☆☆☆**Strathspey Thistle** (Thistle) ☎(0479) 810681 Telex 75213
The front facing bedrooms offer the best views of the valley and mountains in the area. Close to all the centre's facilities.
89 (19fb) CTV in all bedrooms ® *dB&B £39.50–£45
Lift ☾ CTV 150P CFA sauna bath Live music and dancing Nov–Apr *xmas*
European Lunch £5 Dinner £7.25 Last dinner 8.45pm
Credit cards 1 2 3 4 5 **VS**

★★**Cairngorm** (Best Western) ☎(0479) 810233
Granite building on the main road, oppsoite the railway station, and adjacent to the Aviemore Centre.
24rm (12 6) (4fb) ® *sB&B fr £12 sB&B fr £13 dB&B fr £24 dB&B fr £28
☾ CTV 25P *xmas*
V Bar lunch fr £3 Tea 50p High Tea £5 Dinner £7 Wine £4 Last dinner 8.30pm
Credit cards 1 2 3 5

★★*H* ***Lynwilg*** Loch Alvie ☎(0479) 810207
18th-century coaching inn with cosy log fires and relaxing atmosphere.
12rm (2)
CTV 40P *xmas*
International V Last dinner 9pm
Credit cards 2 3

★★**Red McGregor** Main Rd ☎(0479) 810256
Modern small hotel in Swedish design on main road in centre of village.
16rm (10) CTV in all bedrooms ®
CTV 20P Live music and dancing nightly (summer) Fri, Sat & Sun (winter)
Mainly grills Last dinner 10.30pm
Credit cards 1 3 5

✕✕**Winking Owl** ☎(0479) 810646
Friendly, family-run restaurant and bar in converted cottage.
Closed Sun & Nov–10 Dec
60 seats Bar lunch £1.50–£3.75 Dinner £7.30–£9&alc Wine £4.20 Last dinner 9.15pm 50P
Credit cards 1 2 3 5

AVON
Hampshire
Map **4** SZ19

★★**Tyrells Ford Country House** (4m S of Ringwood on B3347) ☎Bransgore (0425) 72646
Small country house with galleried panelled rooms and coal fires, offering warm hospitality and good home cooking.
13rm (6 7) CTV in all bedrooms ® *sB&B £17.50 dB&B £35 →

Lift 100P 4🚗⊘✽⌂ *xmas*
V♧☕✱Lunch £4&alc Tea £1&alc Dinner £8&alc Wine £4.25 Last dinner 10pm
Credit cards [1] [2] [3] [5]

AXMINSTER
Devon
Map **3** SY29

★★★**Koppers** Kilmington ☎(0297) 32074
11rm(4➡7⋔)(2fb)Ⓡ⊘
✱sB&B➡⋔£19.50–£24.50 dB&B➡⋔ fr£32 B
CTV 40P⊘✽ nc7yrs *xmas*
▤English & French V♧☕✱Lunch £3.75alc Tea 65p–£1.20 Dinner £6.90&alc Wine £3.83 Last dinner 9pm
Credit cards [1] [2] [3] [5]

★★***Cedars*** Silver St ☎(0297) 32304
Converted 18th-century house near the town centre.
15rm(1➡)
CTV
♧☕

★★**Woodbury Park Country House** Woodbury Cross
☎(0297) 33010
8rm(5➡1⋔)(2fb)⊘sB&B£10–£12 sB&B£12–£14 dB&B£20–£24 dB&B➡⋔£24–£28 B
CTV 50P⊘✽⩦(heated) sauna bath *xmas*
♧Lunch fr£4.25 Tea fr35p Dinner £4.25&alc Wine £3.75 Last dinner 9.30pm
Credit cards [1] [2] [3] [5]

AYLESBURY
Buckinghamshire
Map **4** SP81

★★**Bell** Market Sq (Trusthouse Forte)
☎(0296) 89835
Old coaching house, situated in the centre of this market town.
17rm(16➡1⋔) CTV in all bedrooms Ⓡ sB&B➡⋔£35.50 dB&B➡⋔£49.50 B
⊘ *xmas*
♧Last dinner 9.30pm
Credit cards [1] [2] [3] [4] [5]

✕**Pebbles** Pebble Ln ☎(0296) 86622
Closed Sun
▤English & French 30 seats ✱Lunch £4.50 Dinner £8.30&alc Wine £5.15 Last dinner 10.30pm
Credit card [1]

AYLESFORD
Kent
Map **5** TQ75

✕✕**Hengist** 7–9 High St ☎Maidstone (0622) 79273
Traditional country fare in a cosy 16th-century setting.
Closed Mon & 1st 2 wks Jan
Lunch not served Sat
Dinner not served Sun
70 seats Lunch £16alc Dinner £16alc Wine £4.70 Last dinner 9.30pm ⊘
S% Credit cards [1] [2] [3] [5]

AYR
Strathclyde *Ayrshire*
Map **10** NS32 **See plan**

★★★**Belleisle** Belleisle Park ☎(0292) 42331 Telex no 777546 Plan **3** *B1*
Extensive stone mansion, set in a large public park to the south of the town.
17rm(6➡5⋔)(3fb) 1▭ CTV in all bedrooms Ⓡ sB&B➡⋔£24–£25.50 dB&B£31–£32.50 dB&B➡⋔£35–£37 B
☾ CTV 200P✽⚑18 *xmas*
▤British & French ♧☕Lunch £3–£4&alc Tea 95p–£1.50 High Tea £3–£4 Dinner £7.50–£8.50&alc Wine £4.25 Last dinner 9.30pm
Credit cards [1] [2] [3] [5] **VS**

☆☆☆**Caledonian** Dalblair Rd (Allied (Scotland))
☎(0292) 69331 Telex no 76357 Plan **5** *C2*
122rm(61➡61⋔) CTV in all bedrooms ✱sB&B➡⋔£29.50 dB&B➡⋔£45 B
Lift ☾ 100P CFA billiards sauna bath *xmas*
♧☕Last dinner 9.30pm
Credit cards [1] [2] [3] [4] [5]

★★★*H* **Pickwick** 19 Racecourse Rd
☎(0292) 60111 Plan **14** *B1*
Stone mansion, dating from 1890, in residential area and popular for its value for money and good food.
15rm(10➡5⋔)(4fb) 1▭ CTV in all bedrooms Ⓡ⊘✱sB&B➡⋔£20 dB&B➡⋔£32 B
☾ 100P⊘✽
▤French V♧✱Bar lunch £5alc High Tea £4alc Dinner £8alc Wine £4.90 Last dinner 9.30pm
Credit card [3]

★★★**Savoy Park** Racecourse Rd
☎(0292) 266112 Plan **16** *B1*
Red sandstone building standing in 3 acres of grounds.
17rm(13➡4⋔)(4fb) CTV in all bedrooms Ⓡ✱sB&B➡⋔£20 dB&B➡⋔£35–£37 B
☾ 80P⊘⌂ *xmas*
▤Scottish & French V♧☕✱Lunch fr£3.50&alc High Tea fr£3.50&alc Dinner fr£9&alc Last dinner 8.30pm
Credit cards [1] [2] [3]

★★★**Stakis Ayr** (*formerly Station Hotel*) Burns Statue Sq (Stakis) ☎(0292) 263268 Telex no 778704 Plan **17** *D1*
A traditional style hotel, adjoining the station, providing modern facilities and services.
74➡ CTV in all bedrooms Ⓡ✱sB&B➡ £28 dB&B➡£36 B
Lift ☾ 50P Disco Fri, Sat & Sun Live music and dancing Fri & Sat *xmas*
▤English & French ♧☕Last dinner 10pm
Credit cards [1] [2] [3] [5] **VS**

★★**Ayrshire and Galloway** 1 Killoch Pl
☎(0292) 262626 Plan **1** *C1*
White town centre inn with simple rooms and attractive bars.
25rm(8➡)(3fb) CTV in 8 bedrooms sB&B£12–£14 sB&B➡£16–£20 dB&B£22–£24 dB&B➡£26–£30
CTV 20P
Lunch fr£4&alc High Tea £3.50–£4.50&alc Dinner £6.50&alc Wine £4.75 Last dinner 9pm

★★**Balgarth** Dunure Rd, Alloway (2m S A719) (Inter-Hotels) ☎Alloway (0292) 42441 Plan **2** *B1*
15rm(4➡7⋔)(2fb) CTV in all bedrooms Ⓡ sB&B£14 sB&B➡⋔£18 dB&B£26 dB&B➡⋔£32 B
CTV 80P✽⌂ *xmas*
▤Scottish & French V♧☕✱Lunch £1.75–£4.35&alc Tea fr60p&alc High Tea £2.85–£5.25 Dinner fr£6&alc Wine £4.50 Last dinner 9.30pm
Credit cards [1] [2] [3]

★★**Burns Monument** Alloway (2m S on B7024) ☎Alloway (0292) 42466 Plan **4** *C1*
A modernised roadside inn, retaining an 'old world' character overlooking Burns Monument and the Brig O'Doon.
9rm(6➡1⋔)(1fb)Ⓡ⊘sB&B£12–£14 sB&B➡⋔£14–£18 dB&B£20–£22 dB&B➡⋔£22–£26
CTV 12P✽🐟
♧Bar lunch fr£3.50&alc Dinner £7.50&alc Wine £5.25 Last dinner 10pm

★★**Elms Court** 21 Miller Rd ☎(0292) 264191 Plan **7** *C1*
20rm(11➡⋔)(4fb) CTV in all bedrooms Ⓡ sB&B£12.50–£14 sB&B➡⋔£13.50–£14.50 dB&B£24–£26 dB&B➡⋔£27–£28
☾ 50P⊘ Live music & dancing twice wkly *xmas*
▤English & French V♧☕Lunch £3.50–£4.50&alc Tea £1&alc High Tea £3.10–£5&alc Dinner £6.50–£7.50&alc Wine £3.50 Last dinner 9.30pm
Credit cards [1] [2] [3] [5]

★★**Gartferry** 44 Racecourse Rd
☎(0292) 262768 Plan **10** *B1*
18th-century hotel with attractive lounge, cellar bar and compact bedrooms.
15rm(2➡5⋔)(2fb) CTV in all bedrooms Ⓡ✱sB&B£10–£14 sB&B➡⋔£13–£18 dB&B£20–£25 dB&B➡⋔£26–£30 B
CTV 100P Cabaret seasonal
♧☕✱Bar lunch £1.50–£4.50 Tea fr55p High Tea £1.75–£4.25 Dinner £7.50&alc Wine £4 Last dinner 10pm
Credit cards [1] [2] [3] [5]
See advert on page 86

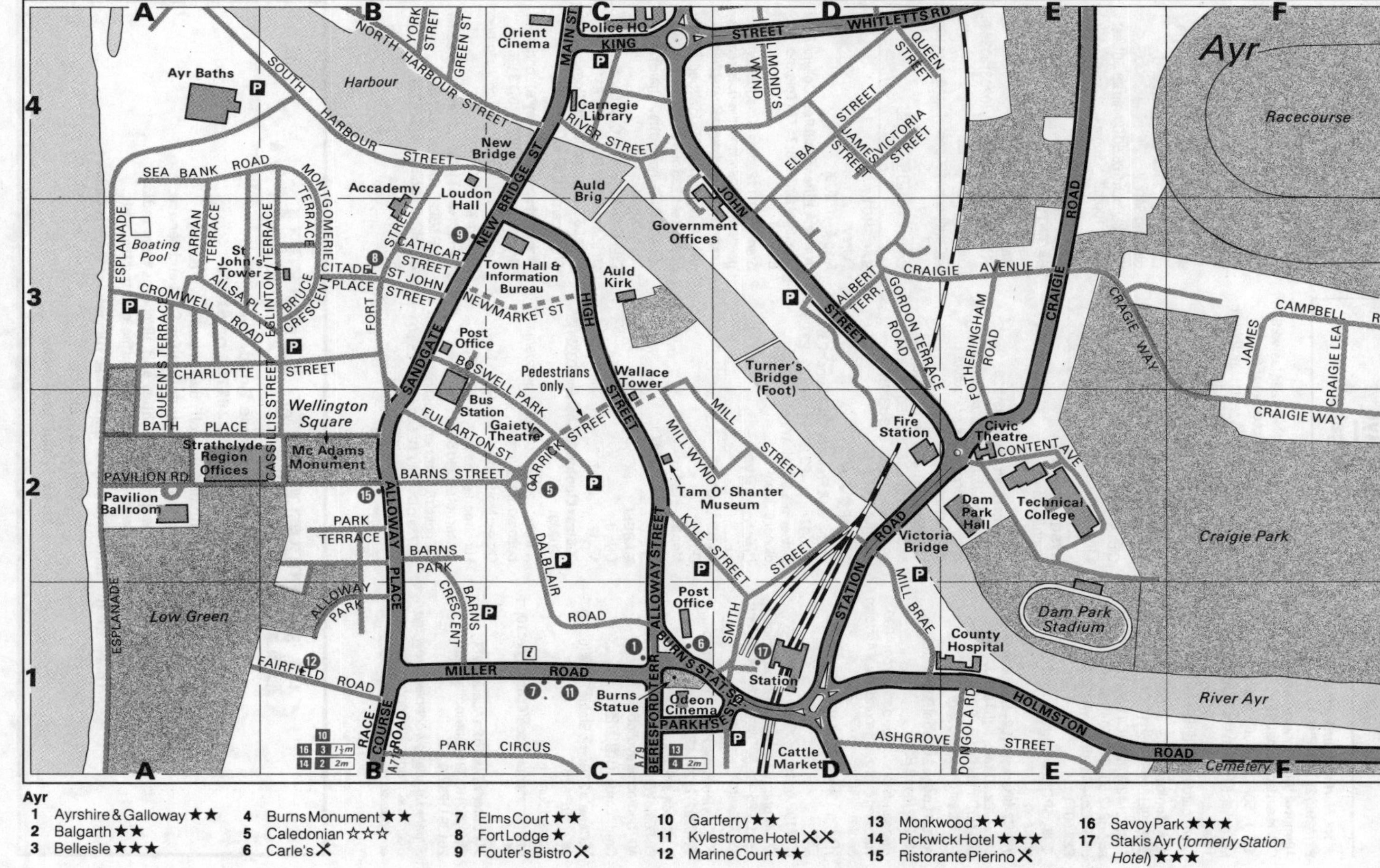
Ayr
Racecourse
Harbour
Ayr Baths
New Bridge
Auld Brig
Accademy
Loudon Hall
Town Hall & Information Bureau
Auld Kirk
Government Offices
Orient Cinema
Police HQ
Carnegie Library
Post Office
Bus Station
Gaiety Theatre
Pedestrians only
Wallace Tower
Turner's Bridge (Foot)
Tam O' Shanter Museum
Fire Station
Civic Theatre
Technical College
Dam Park Hall
Victoria Bridge
Dam Park Stadium
County Hospital
Craigie Park
River Ayr
Cemetery
Station
Cattle Market
Odeon Cinema
Burns Statue
Wellington Square
Mc Adams Monument
Strathclyde Region Offices
Pavilion Ballroom
Low Green
Boating Pool
St John's Tower
A

Ayr

1 Ayrshire & Galloway ★★	4 Burns Monument ★★	7 Elms Court ★★	10 Gartferry ★★	13 Monkwood ★★	16 Savoy Park ★★★
2 Balgarth ★★	5 Caledonian ☆☆☆	8 Fort Lodge ★	11 Kylestrome Hotel ✕✕	14 Pickwick Hotel ★★★	17 Stakis Ayr (*formerly Station Hotel*) ★★★
3 Belleisle ★★★	6 Carle's ✕	9 Fouter's Bistro ✕	12 Marine Court ★★	15 Ristorante Pierino ✕	

★★*L* ***Marine Court*** Fairfield Rd ☎(0292) 267461 Plan **12** *B1*

18rm(8⇌10⋒) Annexe: 9rm(5⇌4⋒) 1▭ CTV in all bedrooms Ⓡ ⛿

☾ CTV 50P Live music and dancing Sat

▣English & French ♁ ▭ Last dinner 10pm

Credit cards ① ② ③ ⑤

★★**Monkwood** 33–35 Carrick Rd ☎(0292) 60952 Plan **13** *C1*

11rm(2⇌2⋒) (2fb) CTV in all bedrooms sB&B£12.50–£13.50 sB&B⇌⋒£15–£16 dB&B£20–£21 dB&B⇌⋒£22.50–£23.50 ⛿

☾ ## 35P Disco Wed Cabaret Tue & Thu *xmas*

V ♁ ▭ ✻Bar lunch £2–£3.50&alc Tea £1.50–£2.50&alc High Tea £3.40–£6&alc Dinner £4.95–£7.10&alc Wine £4.25 Last dinner 9.30pm

★**Fort Lodge** 2 Citadel Pl ☎(0292) 265232 Plan **8** *B3*

Red sandstone lodge dating from 1880 standing in its own grounds near Ayr town centre.

7⋒ (2fb) ✻ sB&B£14–£17 dB&B£26–£32

CTV 10P *xmas*

♁ ▭ Lunch £3.50alc Tea 75palc High Tea £3.25–£5.50 Dinner £6–£8.50 Wine £3.60 Last dinner 8pm

✕✕**Kylestrome Hotel** 11 Miller Rd ☎(0292) 262474 Plan **11** *C1*

V 100 seats ✻Lunch £5alc Dinner £8.50alc Wine £4.50 Last dinner 10pm 40P bedrooms available

Credit cards ① ② ③ ⑤

✕**Carle's** 27 Burns Statue Sq ☎(0292) 262740 Plan **6** *C1*

Closed Sun

▣International 70 seats Last dinner 10pm ⚑

✕**Fouter's Bistro** 2a Academy St ☎(0292) 61391 (Due to change to 261391) Plan **9** *B3*

Situated in a narrow cobbled street, the Bistro's authentic atmosphere is emphasised by the old stone floor.

Closed Mon, Xmas, New Year, last wk Sep & 1st wk Oct Lunch not served Sun

▣French & Italian **V** 42 seats Lunch £5alc Dinner £11alc Wine £5.65 Last dinner 10.30pm ⚑

Credit cards ① ② ③ ④ ⑤ **VS**

✕**Ristorante Pierino** 1A Alloway Pl ☎(0292) 69087 Plan **15** *B2*

Closed Sun

▣Italian 40 seats

AYSGARTH

North Yorkshire
Map **7** SE08

★**Palmer Flatt** ☎(09693) 228

A stone built inn, converted from a pilgrim's hospice, set in beautiful Wensleydale.

11rm(2⇌1⋒) (2fb) 1▭ CTV in 8 bedrooms Ⓡ sB&B£11.50–£12.50 sB&B⇌⋒£12.50–£13 dB&B£24 dB&B⇌£26 ⛿

CTV 10P ✽ ♪ ⌂

▣English & French **V** ♁ ▭ Lunch £3.15–£4.50 Tea £1–£3.25 High Tea £2–£3.25 Dinner fr£5.95&alc Wine £4.50 Last dinner 8.30pm

Credit card ⑤ **VS**

BABBACOMBE

Devon
Map **3** SX96

See under Torquay

BABELL

Clwyd
Map **7** SJ17

✕**Black Lion Inn** ☎Caerwys (0352) 720239

A 16th-century country inn, with a small beamed dining room.

Closed Mon, 1st wk Feb & 1st wk Nov

Lunch not served Sat
Dinner not served Sun

▣English & Continental 64 seats Lunch £5.75alc Dinner £12.50alc Wine £5.50 Last dinner 10pm 80P

S% Credit card ② **VS**

BACKFORD CROSS

Cheshire
Map **7** SJ37

☆☆☆**Ladbroke** (& Conference centre) Backford Cross Roundabout (A41/A5117) (Ladbroke) ☎Chester (0244) 851551 Telex no 61552

122⇌⋒ (9fb) CTV in all bedrooms Ⓡ ✻sB⇌⋒£34 dB⇌⋒£44 (room only) ⛿

Lift ☾ 150P CFA ♪ Live music and dancing Sat

♁ ▭ ✻Lunch fr£6.50 Dinner £8.50 Last dinner 10pm

Credit cards ① ② ③ ⑤

BAGINTON

Warwickshire
Map **4** SP37

✕✕***Old Mill*** ☎Coventry (0203) 303588

Lunch not served Sat

▣Continental 120 seats Last dinner 10pm 500P

Credit cards ① ② ③ ④ ⑤

BAGSHOT

Surrey
Map **4** SU96

★★★★**Pennyhill Park** College Ride (Prestige) ☎(0276) 71774 Telex no 858334

Standing in 112 acres of magnificent gardens and parkland, this hotel retains its former country house atmosphere.

18⇌ Annexe: 17⇌ CTV in all bedrooms Ⓡ ✻ sB⇌fr£35 dB⇌fr£54 (room only) ⛿

☾ 250P ✽ ⛆(heated) ⛳ 🎾(hard) ♪ U sauna bath ⌂ *xmas*

▣English & French **V** ♁ ▭ Lunch £9.95&alc Tea £1alc Dinner £11.95&alc Wine £6.50 Last dinner 10.30pm

Credit cards ① ② ③ ④ ⑤ **VS**

★★**Cricketers (Henekey's)** London Rd (Trusthouse Forte) ☎(0276) 73196

A popular inn, with the local cricket ground at the rear.

26rm(11⇌1⋒) (8fb) CTV in all bedrooms Ⓡ sB&B£26 sB&B⇌⋒£29.50 dB&B£36.50 dB&B⇌⋒£41 ⛿

50P ✽ ⌂ *xmas*

Mainly grills Last dinner 10.30pm
Credit cards 1 2 3 4 5 VS

XX **Sultans Pleasure** 13 London Rd, Bagshot Bypass ☎(0276) 75114
Family run Turkish restaurant, featuring authentic charcoal grilled kebabs and Sasliks.
Closed Sun & Mon Lunch not served
Turkish 60 seats *Dinner £12alc Wine £5.70 Last dinner 10.30pm

BAINBRIDGE
North Yorkshire
Map **7** SD99
★★**Rose & Crown** Village Green ☎Wensleydale (0969) 50225
Original 15th-century inn, featuring an open fireplace and many old beams.
13rm(6) CTV in all bedrooms Ⓡ sB&B£14.50 dB&B£29 dB&B£34
60P *xmas*
English & Continental V Bar lunch 70p–£4 Dinner £8.50–£11.50 Wine £4.50 Last dinner 9pm
Credit cards 1 3

BAKEWELL
Derbyshire
Map **8** SK26
★★★***Rutland Arms*** The Square ☎(062981) 2812
Large early 19th-century, stone built inn located in the town centre.
33 CTV in all bedrooms Ⓡ
60P
French
Credit cards 1 2 3 4 5

★***H*** **Milford House** Mill St ☎(062981) 2130
Closed Jan RS Nov, Dec & Feb
A fine Georgian house in a peaceful situation, less than 400yds from the town centre.
11rm(5) (1fb) *sB&B£13.50 dB&B£25.30 dB&B£27.60
CTV 10P 9 nc8yrs
Lunch *£6.30–£6.60 Dinner £6.60–£7.25 Wine £3.50 Last dinner 7.30pm

BALA
Gwynedd
Map **6** SH93
★★**Bala Lakeside Motel** (1m S on B4403 Llangower rd) ☎(0678) 520344
Closed Feb & Xmas
RS Nov–19 Apr
Regency hunting lodge with motel block at the rear, situated 1m from Bala.
Annexe: 14 Ⓡ *sB&B£16.10–£18.40 dB&B£26.45–£29.90
40P 10
V *Lunch £6alc Tea £1.15alc High Tea £1.15alc Dinner £6.50alc Wine £4.20 Last dinner 8.30pm
S% Credit cards 1 3

★★***Plas Coch*** High St ☎(0678) 520309
Closed Xmas Day
RS Nov–Mar (B&B only)
Three-storey Victorian building located in Bala's main street.
9rm(1)
CTV 10P
Last dinner 8.30pm
Credit cards 1 2 3

★★**White Lion Royal** High St (Greenall Whitley) ☎(0678) 520314 Telex no 629462
Closed Xmas
A former coaching inn, now a holiday hotel in the main street.
22rm(21 1) (2fb) Ⓡ sB&B£20.90–£21.90 dB&B£27.50–£28.50
CTV 40P
French V Lunch £4.50–£5 Tea £1–£1.50 High Tea £2–£2.50 Dinner £6–£7.50 Wine £4.75 Last dinner 8.30pm
S% Credit cards 1 2 3 5

BALLACHULISH
Highland *Argyllshire*
Map **14** NN05
See also **North Ballachulish**
★★★**Ballachulish** (Inter-Hotel) ☎(08552) 239
Closed Dec–Feb
35rm(17 9) (2fb) CTV available in bedrooms Ⓡ
CTV 20P
V Lunch £3.50–£6.50&alc Tea £1.20–£2 High Tea £3.50–£5.50&alc Dinner £7.50–£9&alc Wine £3.90 Last dinner 8.30pm
Credit cards 1 2 3 4 5 VS

BALLATER
Grampian *Aberdeenshire*
Map **15** NO39
★★***H*** **Craigard** 3 Abergeldie Rd ☎(0338) 55445
Closed Nov–Mar
A friendly, proprietor run hotel, standing on the edge of the golf course.
15rm(8 3) (3fb) Ⓡ *sB&B£10–£15.50 sB&B£12–£15.50 dB&B£20–£31 dB&B£20–£35
CTV 22P
V *Bar lunch £2.60–£3.65 Tea 60p Dinner £7 Wine £3.20 Last dinner 8pm
S% Credit cards 1 2 3 5
See advert on page 88

CLOSED

★★***HL*** **Darroch Learg** ☎(0338) 55443
Closed Nov–Feb
A friendly and very comfortable hotel commanding fine views.
15rm(14 1) Annexe: 8rm(2 1) (2fb) CTV in 5 bedrooms Ⓡ sB&B£10.50–£13 sB&B£12.50–£16 dB&B£21–£26 dB&B£25–£32
CTV 25P
V Lunch £2–£4&alc Tea 75p–£1.75 High Tea £3.50 Dinner £7.50 Wine £3 Last dinner 8.30pm
See advert on page 88

BALLOCH
Strathclyde *Dunbartonshire*
Map **10** NS38
★★**Balloch** (Ind Coope) ☎Alexandria (0389) 52579
Attractive small hotel in the town centre right on the banks of the River Leven.
13rm(6) (3fb) 1 Ⓡ *sB&B fr£15.68

→

sB&B⇌fr£19.53 dB&B fr£25.30
dB&B⇌fr£31.35 Ⓑ
CTV 30P
Scottish & European Lunch £3.75 Tea £1 High Tea £3.50alc Dinner £7.50alc Wine £3.50 Last dinner 8pm
Credit cards 1 2 3 5

BALMACARA
Highland *Ross & Cromarty*
Map **14** NG82
★★*HL* **Balmacara** (Minotel)
☎(059986) 283 Telex no 75605
Closed 30 Dec–7 Jan

Family run roadside hotel with fine views across Loch Alsh towards Skye.
29rm(25⇌4⋒)(3fb) sB&B⇌⋒£15–£18.50 dB&B⇌⋒£30–£36 Ⓑ
CTV 40P
Lunch £3–£4.50 Tea 75p High Tea £2–£3 Dinner fr£8.50 Wine £5.50 Last dinner 9pm
Credit cards 1 3

BAMBURGH
Northumberland
Map **12** NU13
★★**Lord Crewe Arms** Front St
☎(06684) 243
Closed Nov–19 Apr
26rm(12⇌)(2fb) CTV in 12 bedrooms sB&B£16–£17.50 sB&B⇌£21–£22.50 dB&B£27–£29 dB&B⇌£32–£34 Ⓑ
CTV 34P nc5yrs
English & French V Lunch £3alc Tea 50palc High Tea £2alc Dinner £7.50–£8 Wine £4.25 Last dinner 8.30pm

See advert on page 90

★★Victoria Front St ☎(06684) 431
25rm(16➡1⋒)(3fb) CTV available in bedrooms Ⓡ sB&B£12–£14.70 sB&B➡⋒£14.70–£17 dB&B£20–£27.30 dB&B➡⋒£29.40–£34
CTV 25P 6🚘 *xmas*
V ♈ Lunch £4–£5&alc High Tea £3–£3.25 Dinner £7.50–£8&alc Wine £4.50 Last dinner 8pm
Credit cards 1 2 3 5 **VS**

★Sunningdale ☎(06684) 334
Closed Nov–Feb
18rm(6➡)(3fb) sB&B£10–£13.80 sB&B➡£11.50–£16.10 dB&B£20–£23 dB&B➡£23–£29.90 Ḃ
CTV 16P 🚫
♈ Bar lunch £1.80–£4 Dinner £5.75–£6.90&alc Wine £3.60 Last dinner 7.30pm
VS

BAMPTON
Devon
Map **3** SS92

★★*Bark House* Oakford Br (2½m W A396) ☎Oakford (03985) 236
Closed 22 Nov–6 Dec & 28 Dec–10 Jan
Small and comfortable, cottage style hotel, with most congenial atmosphere.
6rm(2➡2⋒) Continental breakfast Ḃ
16P *xmas*
♈ ☕ Last dinner 9.30pm
Credit cards 1 2 3 5

★*White Horse* Fore St ☎(0398) 31245
Closed Xmas Day
RS Oct–Mar
Friendly hotel, once an old coaching inn, which has modest accommodation.
10rm Ḃ
CTV 8P billiards 🏠
♈ ☕ Last dinner 9.30pm

BANAVIE
Highland *Inverness-shire*
Map **14** NN17

★★*HL* Moorings (3m from Fort William on A830) ☎Corpach (03977) 550
Closed Dec–Feb
Family run modern hotel with Jacobean style dining room.
14rm(4➡1⋒) Ⓡ ✱ sB&B£9–£15 sB&B➡£14–£20 dB&B£18–£24 dB&B➡⋒£24–£32 Ḃ
CTV 25P 🚫 ✽
V ♈ ☕ Lunch £3.75–£7.50 Tea £1.50–£3 Dinner £8.75–£14 Last dinner 8.30pm
VS

BANBURY
Oxfordshire
Map **4** SP44

★★★★Whately Hall Banbury Cross (Trusthouse Forte) ☎(0295) 3451 Telex no 837149
A 17th-century stone building with a modern wing, set in two acres of gardens.
72rm(63➡9⋒) CTV in all bedrooms Ⓡ sB&B➡⋒£40 dB&B➡⋒£53 Ḃ
Lift ☾ 80P CFA *xmas*
♈ ☕ Last dinner 9.30pm
Credit cards 1 2 3 4 5

★★★Banbury Moat House 27–29 Oxford Rd (Queens Moat) ☎(0295) 59361
RS 24 Dec–1 Jan
This hotel features modern, well-equipped bedrooms, with spacious bathrooms, and more traditional public rooms.
30rm(29➡1⋒)(1fb) CTV in all bedrooms Ⓡ sB&B➡⋒£22–£32 dB&B⋒£40 Ḃ
☾ 30P CFA
▣ International V ♈ Lunch £6.25&alc Dinner £8.25&alc Wine £4.50 Last dinner 10pm
Credit cards 1 2 3 5 **VS**

B

BANCHORY
Grampian *Kincardineshire*
Map **15** NO69

★★★ BANCHORY LODGE, BANCHORY

☎(03302) 2625
Closed 13 Dec–29 Jan

This transformation by Mr & Mrs Jaffray of a run down Georgian building into a welcoming country house hotel never fails to please our members. It is not one of those slickly smart examples, but with its two sitting rooms (one with television) and the Cobblehough bar, a restful atmosphere exists, helped by the good natured friendliness of the staff. There are open fires, lots of fresh flowers which add to the atmosphere, as do the largely fishing clientele. Perhaps because of the irregular hours and informality, our members say how relaxed it all is. Banchory Lodge is situated in its own grounds just outside the town, and the River Dee flows past the bottom of the garden where leaping salmon can sometimes be seen. The hotel has its own fishing rights. They keep a good table of country house type cooking featuring local produce, and it is served by pleasant

waitresses. As we have said in the past, the Jaffrays are to be congratulated on creating a characterful hotel.

27rm(22⇌1⋒)(10fb) 2⊟ CTV in 8 bedrooms TV in 7 bedrooms Ⓡ *sB&B£23–£25.30 sB&B⇌⋒£24–£26.30 dB&B£35–£40 dB&B⇌⋒£35–£40

CTV 50P 3⌂✽ ♩ sauna bath ⌂

V ♡ ⊐ Lunch £4.50–£6.50 Tea £2.25alc Dinner £9.50–£10.95 Last dinner 9.30pm

Credit cards 1 2 3 VS

★★★ Raemoir ☎(03302) 2622
18rm(14⇌) Annexe: 6rm(4⇌2⋒)(5fb) CTV available in bedrooms TV in 1 bedroom sB&B£24.50 sB&B⇌⋒£25.30 dB&B⇌⋒£37.95–£50.60 ⊟

⁄ CTV 200P 10⌂⌂✽⌂ *xmas*

⊟ International V ♡ ⊐ Bar lunch £1–£2.50&alc Tea 80p High Tea £4.50 Dinner £11.50 Wine £4.55 Last dinner 9.30pm

Credit cards 1 2 5

★★★ Tor-na-Coille ☎(03302) 2242
A white, granite house, standing in its own wooded gardens, above the A93.
25rm(15⇌10⋒)(1fb) CTV in all bedrooms Ⓡ *sB&B⇌⋒£17.50–£23.50 dB&B⇌⋒£35 ⊟

Lift CTV 60P ✽ squash ⌂

♡ ⊐ *Lunch £3.75–£7 Tea 70p–£1.20 Dinner £9&alc Wine £5.50 Last dinner 9.45pm

Credit cards 1 2 3 4 5 VS

★★ *Burnett Arms* ☎(03302) 2545
Rough cast and granite fronted building in the main street of this pleasant, Deeside town.
17rm(4⇌6⋒) CTV available in bedrooms ⊟
CTV 40P 4⌂⌂

⊟ Scottish & European ♡ ⊐
Credit cards 3 5 VS

BANFF
Grampian *Banffshire*
Map **15** NJ66

☆☆☆ Banff Springs Golden Knowes Rd ☎(02612) 2881
A modern hotel, west of the town set on a hillside with good views over Moray Firth.
30rm(25⇌5⋒)(4fb) CTV in all bedrooms Ⓡ ✶ *sB&B⇌⋒£22 dB&B⇌⋒£34 ⊟
☾ 250P ⌂
⊟ Scottish & French V ♡ ⊐ *Bar lunch £2.07–£3.27 Tea £1.70 Dinner £6–£7&alc Wine £3.70 Last dinner 9pm
Credit cards 1 2 3 5

★★ *HL* The County High St ☎(02612) 5353
RS Sun
An elegant, Georgian mansion behind weeping ash trees, set in an elevated position overlooking the Bay.
6⇌1⊟ CTV in all bedrooms sB&B⇌£26–£29 dB&B⇌£42–£49 ⊟
15P ⌂ nc 10yrs *xmas*
⊟ International ♡ Lunch £5.50alc Dinner £13.95–£14.95 Wine £5.10 Last dinner 9.30pm
S% VS

★ Dounemount ☎Macduff (0261) 32262 RS Nov–Apr
This attractive house is attached to the farm and is located on a quiet country lane between Banff and Macduff.
8rm(2⋒)(2fb) CTV in all bedrooms Ⓡ ✶ *sB&B fr£10.75 sB&B⋒ fr£11.75 dB&B fr£19.50 dB&B⋒£20.75
CTV 30P 2⌂⌂✽ U snooker Live music and dancing wknds ⌂
V *Bar lunch £1–£3 Dinner £6.25–£8alc Wine £3.75 Last dinner 9pm

★ *B Fife Lodge* Sandyhill Rd ☎(02612) 2436
Homely and attractive small country hotel where open fires are lit in the public rooms in cold weather.
6rm(3⇌3⋒) CTV in all bedrooms Ⓡ 200P ✽ ⌂
V Last dinner 9pm

BANGOR
Gwynedd
Map **6** SH57

★★★**British** High St ☎(0248) 364911
Three-storey, commercial/tourist hotel located beside a busy road ½m from the town centre.
53 (3fb) CTV available in bedrooms Ⓡ sB&B £15–£16 dB&B £30–£32
Lift ☾ CTV 50P 2 CFA *xmas*
V Lunch £2.75–£3.50&alc Dinner £4.75–£5.50&alc Wine £3.20 Last dinner 9pm
Credit cards 1 3 **VS**

★★***Railway*** High St ☎(0248) 362158
Large, tourist hotel ½m from the town centre and next to the railway station.
20rm(16) TV in 10 bedrooms Ⓡ
☾ CTV 20P 6
Last dinner 10pm
Credit cards 1 3 5

★★***H Telford*** Holyhead Rd ☎(0248) 352543
Closed 25 & 26 Dec
Small family run hotel with superb views of the Menai Strait, the Menai Bridge and Anglesey.
9rm(3)
CTV 15P
International Last dinner 9.30pm
Credit cards 1 3

★★***L Ty-Uchaf*** Tal-y-Bont (2m E off A55) ☎(0248) 352219
Closed 20 Dec–19 Jan
Converted farmhouse set between the main road and the railway line.
10rm(7 3) Ⓡ
CTV 30P
Last dinner 9pm
Credit cards 1 3 **VS**

BARBON
Cumbria
Map **7** SD68

★★***Barbon Inn*** ☎(046836) 233
10rm 1 CTV in 6 bedrooms
12P 4
International Last dinner 9pm
Credit cards 2 3 5

BARDON MILL
Northumberland
Map **12** NY76

★**Bowes** ☎(04984) 237
A roadside hotel on the A69.
6rm (2fb) *sB&B £7.47 dB&B £14.95
CTV 6P
V Lunch £2.25–£4.50&alc Dinner £2.25–£4.50&alc Wine £2.20 Last dinner 8.30pm
VS

★**Vallum Lodge** Military Rd, Twice Brewed ☎(04984) 248
7rm sB&B £9.50–£11 dB&B £19–£22
CTV 25P
Mainly grills Lunch £2.60–£3.75&alc Tea 40p–£2 Dinner £3.75–£5.50&alc Wine £3.20 Last dinner 7.30pm
VS

BARDSEY
North Yorkshire
Map **8** SE34

✕✕**Bingley Arms** Church Ln ☎Collingham Bridge (0937) 72462
One of Englands oldest inns, mentioned in the Domesday Book.
Closed Mon Lunch not served Sat Dinner not served Sun
English & Continental 80 seats *Lunch fr£4.50&alc Dinner £9.50alc Wine £4.40 Last dinner 9.30pm 60P
Credit card 3

BARFORD
Warwickshire
Map **4** SP26

★★***Glebe*** Church St ☎(0926) 624218
A Georgian country inn situated in one acre of gardens. →

14rm(7→3⋒) ® ✈
CTV 40P ✽
Last dinner 9.45pm
Credit cards 1 2 3 5

BARFORD ST MARTIN
Wiltshire
Map **4** SU03
✕✕**Michels** ☎Salisbury (0722) 742240
Well appointed restaurant with good Nouvelle-style cuisine. (Lunch by reservations only)
Closed Sun
French 25 seats ✻Dinner £12.50alc Wine £4.50 Last dinner 9.30pm 10P bedrooms available
Credit cards 3 5

BAR HILL
Cambridgeshire
Map **5** TL36
☆☆☆☆**Cunard Cambridgeshire** ☎Crafts Hill (0954) 80555 Telex no 817141
100→⋒ CTV in all bedrooms ®
✻sB&B→⋒£39.75–£42
dB&B→⋒£52.50–£55.40 B
(200P CFA ✽ (heated) (hard) squash sauna bath Live music and dancing Sat *xmas*
International Lunch £9.25–£9.95&alc Tea 85p–90p High Tea £4.25–£4.60 Dinner £9.25–£9.95&alc Last dinner 10pm
Credit cards 1 2 3 4 5 **VS**

BARLEY
Lancashire
Map **7** SD84
✕✕***Barley Mow*** ☎Nelson (0282) 64293
Closed Mon Lunch not served Tue & Sat
36 seats Last dinner 10pm 12P

BARMOUTH
Gwynedd
Map **6** SH61
★★**Cors Y Gedol** High St (ExecHotel) ☎(0341) 280402
An impressive holiday hotel in the town centre, ½m from the beach.
25rm(11→) (20fb) CTV in all bedrooms ®
sB&B£16.75–£19.50 sB&B→⋒£25.50
dB&B£31.50–£36.50 dB&B→⋒£42.50 B
Lift CTV 20P sauna bath *xmas*
English & French **V** Lunch £6.50 Tea 65p High Tea £4 Dinner £3.85–£8.75&alc Wine £3.25 Last dinner 9.30pm
S% Credit cards 1 3

★★**Lion** High St ☎(0341) 280324
Tourist holiday hotel near the town centre and ½m from the beach.
14rm (1fb) sB&B£10.10 dB&B£20
CTV nc3yrs
English & French **V** Lunch 85p–£1.95 Dinner £4.95–£7.25&alc Wine £2.90 Last dinner 8pm
VS

★★**Plas Mynach** Llanaber Rd ☎(0341) 280252
A stone building set in wooded grounds and situated 1m from the shops and ¾m from the beach.
13rm(7→) (4fb) 1 CTV in 5 bedrooms
sB&B£9.77 sB&B→£11.77 dB&B£19.54
dB&B→£23.54
CTV 20P ✽
V Lunch £5.75&alc Tea 70p Dinner £5.75&alc Wine £4.50 Last dinner 7.45pm
Credit card 3 **VS**

★★**Royal** King Edward St (Minotel) ☎(0341) 280383 Closed Nov–24 Mar
Occupying a corner position in the town centre, this hotel is ¾m from the beach.
16rm(2→12⋒) (2fb) CTV in 5 bedrooms ® ✈ sB&B→⋒£16.95 dB&B£27.30
dB&B→⋒£32.55
CTV 25P
V Lunch £5.50–£6.50&alc Tea 60p Dinner £5.50–£6.50&alc Wine £2.80 Last dinner 4pm
Credit cards 1 3 **VS**

★**Marwyn** 21 Marine Pde ☎(0341) 280185 Closed Dec & Jan
Victorian terrace hotel on Promenade.
7rm(3→4⋒) (1fb) 1 CTV in all bedrooms ✈ sB&B→⋒£12–£20
dB&B→⋒£24–£35 B
CTV 2 Cabaret Mon nc7yrs
Lunch £4–£5 Tea £1–£1.50 Dinner £6–£7.75&alc Wine £4 Last dinner 9.30pm
Credit cards 1 3 **VS**

★**Min-y-Mor** Promenade ☎(0341) 280555
A detached hotel, situated on the promenade, 1m from the town centre.
50rm(6→5⋒) (5fb) ✈ sB&B£9.50–£12.50 sB&B→⋒£11.50–£14.50
dB&B£30–£35 dB&B→⋒£34–£39
CTV 50P ✽
Lunch £2.30–£3.40 Tea 90p Dinner £5.50 Wine £3.40 Last dinner 7.30pm
Credit cards 1 3

★**Ty'r Craig Castle** Llanaber Rd ☎(0341) 280470
Closed Nov–Mar
Built in the style of a small mock castle, it is set high up overlooking the coastline.
12rm(2→1⋒) (3fb) CTV in 3 bedrooms TV in 4 bedrooms ✈ sB&B£11.50–£13.50
dB&B£20–£24 dB&B→⋒£26–£30 B
15P ✽
Welsh, English & French Lunch £6&alc Tea £1 Dinner £6&alc Wine £4 Last dinner 8pm

BARNARD CASTLE
Co Durham
Map **12** NZ01
★★**King's Head** 12–14 Market Pl ☎Teesdale (0833) 38356
19→ (1fb) CTV in all bedrooms ® ✈
sB&B→£22.50 dB&B→£31
CTV 30P 10
English & French **V** ✻Bar lunch £1.95–£4 Dinner £7.50&alc Wine £2.90 Last dinner 9pm
Credit cards 1 2 3 5 **VS**

BARNBY MOOR
Nottinghamshire
Map **8** SK68
★★★**Ye Olde Bell** (Trusthouse Forte) ☎Retford (0777) 705121
An original 17th-century posting house whose guests have included Queen Victoria and Queen Maud of Norway.
55rm(44→) (1fb) CTV in all bedrooms ®
sB&B£33.50 sB&B→£36 dB&B£46
dB&B→£50 B
(250P CFA ✽ *xmas*
Last dinner 9.30pm
Credit cards 1 2 3 4 5

BARNHAM BROOM
Norfolk
Map **5** TG00
★★★**Barnham Broom Golf & Country Club** (Best Western) ☎(060545) 393
35→ (6fb) CTV in all bedrooms ®
sB&B→£31–£34 dB&B→£38.50–£41.50 B
(CTV 200P CFA ✽ (heated) (hard) squash billiards sauna bath Disco twice mthly Live music and dancing twice mthly *xmas*
V Lunch £4.50–£5.50&alc Tea 40p–50p Dinner £7.50–£8.50&alc Wine £4.50 Last dinner 9.30pm
Credit cards 1 2 3 5

BARNSDALE BAR
South Yorkshire
Map **8** SE51
☆☆☆**TraveLodge** (Trusthouse Forte) ☎Pontefract (0977) 620711 Telex no 557457
72→ CTV in all bedrooms ® sB&B→£25
dB&B→£35.50 Continental breakfast B
(350P
Mainly grills
Credit cards 1 2 3 4 5

BARNSLEY
South Yorkshire
Map **8** SE30
★★★**Ardsley House** Doncaster Rd, Ardsley (Best Western) ☎(0226) 89401 Telex no 547762
63→ (6fb) 3 CTV in all bedrooms ®
sB&B→£30 dB&B→£42 B
(250P ✽ billiards Live music and dancing Fri
English & French **V** Lunch fr£6.50

Tea fr75p Dinner fr£7.50&alc Wine £4.75 Last dinner 10.30pm

Credit cards 1 2 3 5 **VS**

★★ *B* **Queens** Regent St (Anchor) ☎(0226) 84192 Telex no 858875

A three-storey, stone built Victorian hotel, located next to the railway station.

37⇌(3fb) CTV in all bedrooms Ⓡ
*sB&B⇌ fr£28.50 dB&B⇌ fr£36 B

☾ ⚡ CFA

V ✿ ▭ *Lunch £3&alc Tea 55p–£1.50 High Tea £3 Dinner £5.50alc Wine £4.50 Last dinner 10pm

Credit cards 1 2 3 4 5

★ **Royal** Church St (Anchor) ☎(0226) 203658 Telex no 858875

Comfortable, well-appointed hotel with spacious lounge bars and restaurant featuring local dishes.

17rm(1⇌)(1fb) CTV in all bedrooms sB&B£21 sB&B⇌£28.50 dB&B£31 dB&B⇌£35 B

CTV 🚗

V ✿ ▭ Lunch £3.25–£4.75 Tea 45p–£1.50 Dinner £5.80 Wine £4.50 Last dinner 9.30pm

Credit cards 1 2 3 4 5

✕✕ **Brooklands** Barnsley Rd, Dodworth (2m W A628 close to M1 Junct 37) ☎(0226) 6364

Closed Xmas

▣ English, French, German & Italian 110 seats Lunch £4.20 Dinner £9.50alc Wine £2.58 Last dinner 9.30pm 300P bedrooms available

Credit cards 1 2 5

BARNSTAPLE
Devon
Map **2** SS53

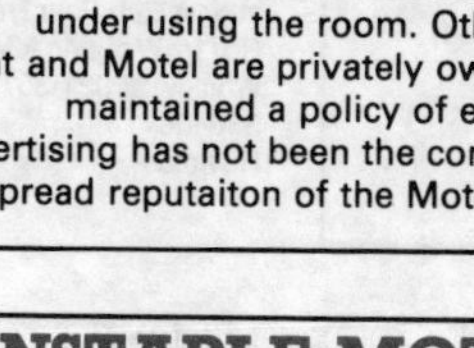

☆☆☆ ***Barnstaple Motel*** Braunton Rd →

☎(0271) 76221 RS Xmas
A modern, purpose-built tourist hotel in a quiet setting.
60⇨ CTV in 30 bedrooms TV in 40 bedrooms
☾ CTV 100P 32🏠 (heated)
English & French ✿ Last dinner 10pm
Credit cards 1 2 3 5

★★★**Imperial** Taw Vale Pde (Trusthouse Forte) ☎(0271) 45861
All modern facilities are found in this centrally situated hotel.

56rm(55⇨1⋔) CTV in all bedrooms ® sB&B⇨⋔£33.50 dB&B⇨⋔£49 B
Lift ☾ 80P
✿ Last dinner 8.45pm
Credit cards 1 2 3 4 5

☆☆☆**North Devon Motel** Taw Vale (Brend) ☎(0271) 72166
A small hotel with modern amenities, and a restaurant on the first floor.

26⇨ CTV in all bedrooms
*sB&B⇨£19.30 dB&B⇨£30.36
☾ CTV 50P
English & French ✿ *Lunch £5.25&alc Dinner fr£7.25&alc Wine £4.15 Last dinner 9.30pm
S% Credit cards 1 2 3 5

★★**Royal & Fortescue** Boutport St (Brend) ☎(0271) 42289
Named after King Edward VII, then Prince of Wales, who was a guest here.
64rm(16⇨3⋔) CTV in 15 bedrooms
*sB&B£14.23 sB&B⇨⋔ fr£18.65 dB&B fr£27.83 dB&B⇨⋔ fr£32.26 B
Lift ☾ CTV 25P 6🏠 *xmas*
English & French ✿ *Lunch £2.25–£3.75 Tea 42p Dinner fr£6.04&alc Wine £4.25 Last dinner 9pm
Credit cards 1 2 3 5

★★

★★**DOWNREW HOUSE, BARNSTAPLE**
(off unclass rd 1½m SE Bishop's Tawton A377) ☎(0271) 42497
Open mid Mar–Oct
RS Nov & part Dec

Situated a few miles out of Barnstaple and reached via its own 15 hole approach golf course, this mainly Queen Anne gentleman's residence is the home as well as the business of Desmond and Aleta Ainsworth. With the help of Heather Rowles – who arrived here for a holiday 16 years ago and has remained ever since – they offer warm hospitality.
Unusually, children are well provided for, and the well kept and attractive garden contains a heated swimming pool.
Bedrooms are comfortably furnished and equipped with radio and television. Some are in an annexe which also has a games room and a TV room. The public rooms in the main building comprise a tiny but intimate little bar, a card room and a comfortable drawing room with log fire. There is also the bright dining room that is the concern of Mrs Ainsworth. She produces a high standard of country house type cooking for the four course dinner menu and a small à la carte menu which must be ordered in advance. Another good feature of the catering is the wide choice of packed lunches available. Service is by cheerful young girls.
Our members are always delighted with this hotel and in particular commend the good natured service and value for money.

7⇨ Annexe: 7⇨ CTV in all bedrooms ®(in Annexe) ★*sB&B⇨£25.59–£32.78 (incl. dinner) dB&B⇨£51.18–£65.56 (incl. dinner)
14P ✿ (heated) (hard) billiards nc7yrs
English & French *Dinner £11.21 Wine £4 Last dinner 8.30pm
VS

✕✕✕**Lynwood House** Bishop's Tawton Rd ☎(0271) 43695
Closed Sun, 25, 26, 31 Dec & 1 Jan Lunch not served
English & Continental **V** 20 seats *Dinner £12alc Wine £4.25 Last dinner 9.30pm 24P
Credit cards 1 2 3 5

BARNT GREEN
Hereford & Worcester
Map **7** SP07

✕✕**Barnt Green Inn** Kendal End Rd ☎021-445 4949
Closed Mon Lunch not served Sat Dinner not served Sun
English & French 100 seats Lunch £5.95–£7.95&alc Dinner £7.95–£9.25&alc Wine £5.25 Last dinner 10pm 150P
Credit cards 1 3 4 5 **VS**

BARR, GREAT
West Midlands
Map **7** SP09

★★★**Barr** Pear Tree Drive, off Newton Rd (1m W of junc A34/A4041) (Greenall Whitley) ☎021-357 1141 Telex no 336406
RS Xmas

A smoothly run commercial hotel.
111⇌⋒ CTV in all bedrooms ® ★ sB&B⇌⋒ £29.50–£30.50 dB&B⇌ £39–£40 ⊟
☾ 250P Live music and dancing Sat
European ♡ ☕ Lunch £5.50&alc Tea fr50p Dinner £6&alc Wine £5 Last dinner 10pm (9pm Fri & 7.45pm Sun)
Credit cards 1 2 3 5

☆☆☆**Post House** Chapel Ln (at junc M6/A34) (Trusthouse Forte) ☎021-357 7444 Telex no 338497
204⋒ CTV in all bedrooms ® sB&B⇌ £38.50 dB&B⇌ £51 ⊟
☾ 280P CFA ≋ (heated)
♡ ☕ Last dinner 10pm
Credit cards 1 2 3 4 5

BARRA, ISLE OF
Western Isles *Inverness-shire*
Map **13**
See Tangusdale

BARRHEAD
Strathclyde *Renfrewshire*
Map **11** NS45
✿★★**Dalmeny Park** Lochlibo Rd ☎041-881 9211
19th-century house with gardens, on the edge of town, with open fires and Georgian-style function suite.
20rm(10⋒) (2fb) CTV in all bedrooms ® sB&B fr£24.50 sB&B⋒ fr£28.50 dB&B fr£30.50 dB&B⋒ fr£34.50 ⊟
☾ CTV 100P ✽ ⌂
French V ♡ ☕ Lunch fr£6.25&alc Tea fr75p Dinner fr£8.75&alc Wine £3 Last dinner 10pm
Credit cards 1 2 3 5 **VS**

BARRINGTONS, THE
(nr Burford) Gloucestershire
Map **4** SP21
★★★**Inn for all Seasons** (3m W of Burford on A40) ☎Windrush (04514) 324
Closed 25 Dec–4 Jan
9⇌⋒ CTV in all bedrooms ® ★ sB&B⇌⋒ £24–£27.50 dB&B⇌⋒ £37.50–£40 ⊟
18P ✽ nc10yrs
♡ Lunch £3–£7.25 Tea £1–£1.50 Dinner £5–£6.95&alc Wine £4.25 Last dinner 9.30pm
Credit card 2

BARROW-IN-FURNESS
Cumbria
Map **7** SD16
★★★**Victoria Park** Victoria Rd (Whitbread West Pennines) ☎(0229) 21159
Closed 24–26 & 31 Dec, & 1 Jan
An extensively-modernised Victorian building, situated just off the A590 on the approach to the town.
44rm(22⇌1⋒) CTV in all bedrooms ® ★ sB&B £20.90 sB&B⇌⋒ £26.40 dB&B £28.60 dB&B⇌⋒ £35.20 ⊟
☾ CTV 60P
English & Continental V ♡ Lunch £5&alc Dinner £7.50&alc Wine £4.45 Last dinner 9.30pm
Credit cards 1 3

★★**White House** Abbey Rd ☎(0229) 27303
A Falstaff tavern on the A590, main approach road to the town centre.
29rm(2⇌) CTV in all bedrooms ® sB&B £18.50 sB&B⇌ £22 dB&B £24 dB&B⇌ 28 ⊟
☾ 60P 20⌂
English & French V ♡ ☕ Lunch £4&alc Tea 50p High Tea fr£2 Dinner £6.95&alc Last dinner 9.30pm
Credit cards 1 2 3 4 5

BARRY
South Glamorgan
Map **3** ST16
★★★**Hotel International** Port Rd, Rhoose (2½m W A4226) ☎(0446) 710787
→

This modern hotel, adjacent to Cardiff (Wales) Airport, has compact rooms with good facilities.

32 (1fb) CTV in all bedrooms ® sB&B £26.95 dB&B £32.95

250P CFA Disco 3 nights wkly Live music and dancing 2 nights wkly

V Lunch £2.50–£4.75&alc Tea 50p–60p High Tea £1.95–£4.95 Dinner £2.50–£4.95&alc Wine £3.90 Last dinner 10.45pm

Credit cards 1 2 3 5

★★★**Mount Sorrel** Porthkerry Rd (Exec Hotel) (0446) 740069

Comfortable, small hotel overlooking the town.

33rm (20 13) Annexe: 4 (3fb) CTV in all bedrooms sB&B £22.50–£25 dB&B £30–£33

CTV 17P Live music and dancing Sat

Welsh, English & French V Lunch £2.20–£4.50&alc Dinner £7.25–£7.75&alc Wine £4.10 Last dinner 9.45pm

Credit cards 1 2 3 4 5 VS

★★★**Water's Edge** The Knap (0446) 733392

A modern hotel, with small well-equipped rooms, overlooking Porthkerry Bay.

37 (1fb) CTV in all bedrooms sB&B £22–£27 dB&B £36–£40

Lift CTV 200P Disco Fri Live music and dancing Sat & Sun *xmas*

English & French V Lunch £6.25–£7&alc Tea 60p–90p High Tea £2.50–£3 Dinner £6.25–£7&alc Wine £5.50 Last dinner 10pm

Credit cards 1 2 3 4 5

BARTLE
Lancashire
Map **7** SD43

★★★***Bartle Hall*** Lea Ln Preston (0772) 690506

11 2 CTV in all bedrooms ®

CTV 100P 2 (heated) (hard)

International Last dinner 9.30pm

Credit cards 1 2 3

BARTON
Lancashire
Map **7** SD53

★★★**Barton Grange** Garstang Rd (Best Western) Preston (0772) 862551 Telex no 67392

An extended and modernised hotel set in a garden centre complex.

60rm (53 7) (11fb) CTV in all bedrooms ® sB&B fr£18.50 sB&B fr£28.50 dB&B fr£28 dB&B fr£38

Lift CTV 200P CFA (heated) (hard) billiards Live music and dancing Sat *xmas*

English & French V *Lunch £5.50 Dinner fr£7&alc Wine £4.75 Last dinner 9.15pm

Credit cards 1 2 3 4 5 VS

BASILDON
Essex
Map **5** TQ78

☆☆☆**Crest** Cranes Farm Rd (Crest) (0268) 3955 Telex no 995141

Closed Xmas

Well equipped modern hotel with popular bar and restaurant.

116 CTV in all bedrooms ® *sB fr£34 dB fr£42 (room only)

Lift 175P CFA *xmas*

International V *Lunch fr£6.95&alc Dinner fr£8.25&alc Wine £5.95 Last dinner 10pm

Credit cards 1 2 3 4 5 VS

BASINGSTOKE
Hampshire
Map **4** SU65

☆☆☆**Crest** Grove Rd (Crest) (0256) 68181 Telex no 858501

86 CTV in all bedrooms ® *sB fr£37 dB fr£44 (room only)

140P CFA Live music Fri & Sat

International V *Lunch £8.80alc

Dinner £10.15alc Wine £5.95 Last dinner 9.45pm

S% Credit cards 1 2 3 4 5 **VS**

☆☆☆**Ladbroke** (& Conferencentre) Aldermaston Rbt, Ringway North (A339) (Ladbroke) ☎(0256) 20212 Telex no 858223

Popular commercial motel with good bedrooms and small restaurant.

82🛁 (8fb) CTV in all bedrooms ® ✱sB🛁£36 dB🛁£42.50 (room only) B

Lift ☾ 200P CFA

V Last dinner 9.45pm

Credit cards 1 2 3 5

★★**Red Lion** London St (Anchor) ☎(0256) 28525 Telex no 859504

An early 17th-century three storey inn with a beamed interior and a modern extension.

64rm(26🛁38🚿) (4fb) CTV in all bedrooms ® ✱sB&B🛁🚿£36 dB&B🛁🚿£42 B

Lift ☾ 65P

V ✱Lunch £5.85–£11 Tea £1.10 High Tea £1.10–£3.50 Dinner £5.85–£11 Wine £4.50 Last dinner 10.30pm

Credit cards 1 2 3 4 5

BASLOW
Derbyshire
Map **8** SK27

★★★***BL*** **Cavendish** ☎(024688) 2311

13🛁🚿 (5fb) CTV in all bedrooms ® ✱sB🛁🚿£35 dB🛁🚿£45 (room only) B

50P

V Lunch £6.95–£8.95&alc Tea 80p Dinner £6.95–£8.95&alc Last dinner 10pm

Credit cards 2 3

BASSENTHWAITE
Cumbria
Map **11** NY23

★★★★**Armathwaite Hall** ☎Bassenthwaite Lake (059681) 551

37rm(29🛁8🚿) (3fb) 1 CTV in all bedrooms ✱sB&B🛁🚿£25–£30 dB&B🛁🚿£36–£55 B

Lift ☾ 100P 6 (heated) (hard) squash billiards sauna bath Live music and dancing Sat in winter *xmas*

International **V** Lunch fr£6.50&alc Tea fr£2.50 Dinner fr£10&alc Wine £5 Last dinner 9.30pm

Credit cards 1 2 3 5

★★★**Castle Inn** ☎Bassenthwaite Lake (059681) 401
Closed 7–22 Nov & 20–29 Dec

21🛁🚿 (2fb) 1 CTV in all bedrooms sB&B🛁🚿£26.75 dB&B🛁🚿£35.50 B

☾ 100P (heated) (grass) sauna bath Live music and dancing Sat

V Lunch fr£5.75 Tea fr70p Dinner fr£8.50 Wine £4.95 Last dinner 8.30pm

Credit cards 1 2 3 5

★★***HL*** **Overwater Hall** Ireby (2m N of Bassenthwaite) ☎Bassenthwaite Lake (059681) 566 Closed 24 Dec–20 Feb

A building of architectural and historic interest, once owned by the Cumbrian family of Gilbanks as far back as 1780.

13rm(9🛁) (2fb) 2 CTV in all bedrooms sB&B fr£17 sB&B🛁 fr£19 dB&B fr£24 dB&B🛁 fr£28 B

P

English & Continental Bar lunch fr£1.50 Tea fr75p Dinner fr£8.95 Wine £3.45 Last dinner 8.30pm

Credit cards 1 3

★★***L*** **Pheasant Inn** ☎Bassenthwaite Lake (059681) 234
Closed Xmas Day

A coaching inn of character, situated off the A66, below Thornthwaite Forest.

20rm(11🛁1🚿) ® sB&B£19 sB&B🛁🚿£20 dB&B£38 dB&B🛁🚿£40 B

80P

V Lunch £5.50 Tea £2–£2.30 Dinner £9 Wine £3.45 Last dinner 8.15pm

S%

See advert on page 99

BATH
Avon
Map **3** ST76

★★★★**Francis** Queen Sq (Trusthouse Forte) ☎(0225) 24257 Telex no 449162 Plan **2** *C3*

Comfortable accommodation and an elegant restaurant are found in this Georgian-style hotel.

90🛁 CTV in all bedrooms ® sB&B🛁£45.50 dB&B🛁£61.50 B

Lift ☾ 72P CFA *xmas*

Last dinner 9.30pm

Credit cards 1 2 3 4 5

☆☆☆☆**Ladbroke Beaufort** (& Conferencentre) Walcot St (Ladbroke) ☎(0225) 63411 Telex no 449519 Plan **4** *C4*

Modern business hotel in the city centre with comfortable bedrooms. Chargeable basement car park.

123🛁 CTV in all bedrooms ® ✱sB🛁🚿£37 dB🛁🚿£47 (room only) B

Lift ☾ CFA

✱Lunch fr£6.50 Dinner fr£8.50 Last dinner 9.30pm

Credit cards 1 2 3 5

See advert on page 99

★★★★***HBL*** ***Royal Crescent*** 16 Royal Crescent (Prestige) ☎(0225) 319090 Telex no 444251 Plan **11** *A4*

A luxurious hotel, meticulously restored with decorations and furnishings of the highest standard. An 18th century Palladian villa in the grounds is being restored to provide further bedrooms. Service is quietly efficient and each guest is well looked after.

29rm(27🛁) 6 CTV in all bedrooms B

Lift ☾ 12P 2

French **V** Last dinner 10pm

Credit cards 1 2 3 4 5

★★★***Combe Grove*** Monkton Combe (1½m S on Exeter light traffic road A367 and turn off at Brass Knocker Hill) ☎(0225) 834644 Not on plan

12rm(3🛁6🚿) CTV in all bedrooms ® B →

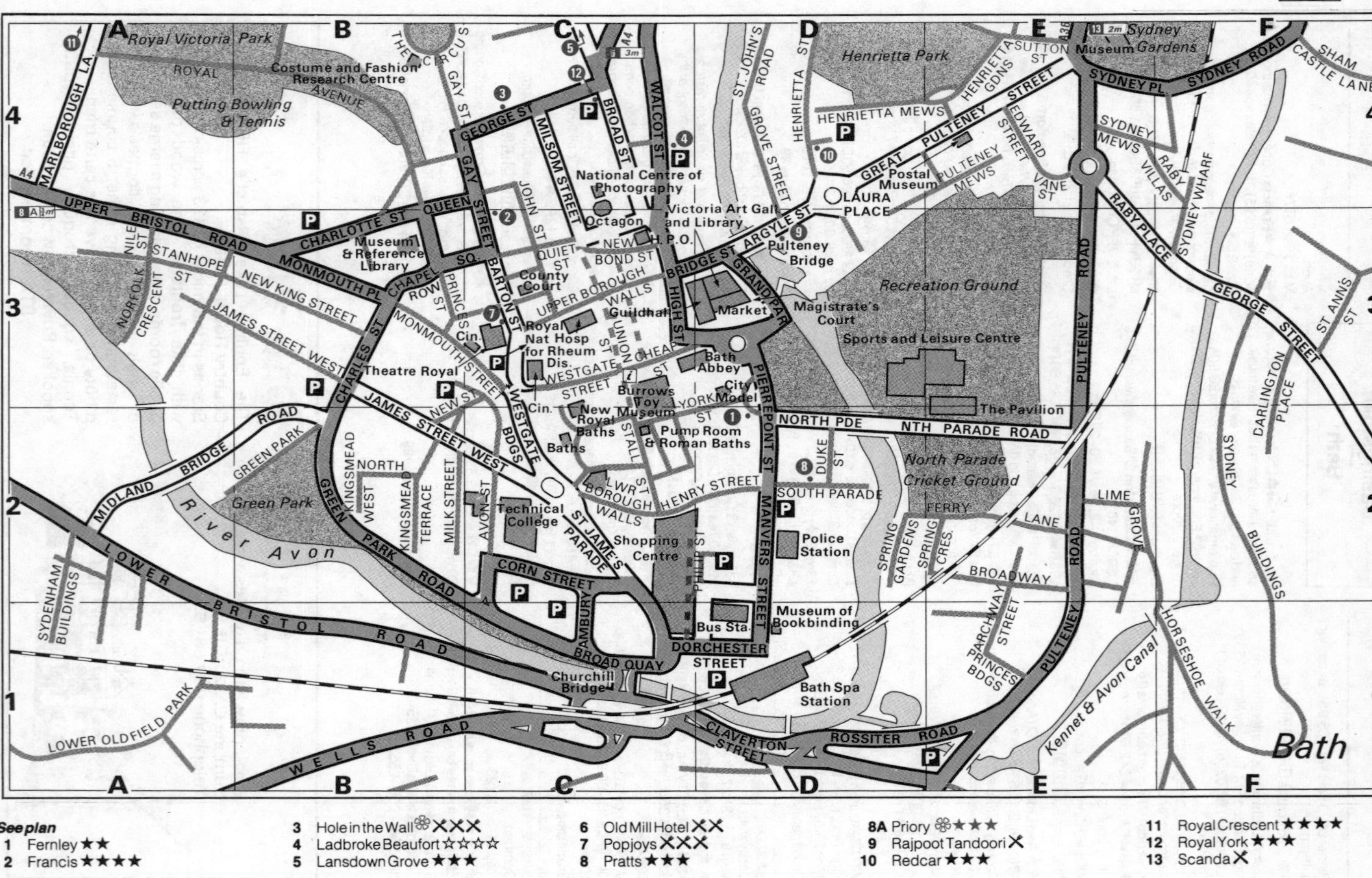
Bath
Royal Victoria Park
Costume and Fashion Research Centre
Royal Avenue
Putting Bowling & Tennis
The Circus
Gay St
George St
Milsom Street
Broad St
Walcot St
National Centre of Photography
Octagon
Victoria Art Gall and Library
H.P.O.
Henrietta Park
Henrietta Mews
Henrietta St
St. John's Road
Grove Street
Great Pulteney Street
Postal Museum
Pulteney Mews
Laura Place
Edward Street
Vane St
Henrietta Gdns
Sutton St
Sydney Museum
Sydney Gardens
Sydney Pl
Sydney Road
Sham Castle Lane
Sydney Mews
Raby Villas
Sydney Wharf
Raby Place
George Street
St Anns St
Darlington Place
Sydney Buildings
Marlborough La.
Upper Bristol Road
Charlotte St
Queen Sq.
John St
Quiet St
New Bond St
Museum & Reference Library
Nile St
Stanhope St
Norfolk Crescent
New King Street
Monmouth Pl
Chapel Row
Princes St
Barton St
County Court
Upper Borough Walls
Bridge St
Argyle St
Pulteney Bridge
Grand Par
Market
Guildhall
Union St
High St
Magistrate's Court
Recreation Ground
Sports and Leisure Centre
The Pavilion
James Street West
Monmouth Street
Cin.
Royal Nat Hosp for Rheum Dis.
Theatre Royal
Westgate Street
Cheap St
Bath Abbey
City Model
Burrows Toy Museum
York St
New Royal Baths
Pump Room & Roman Baths
Baths
Stall St
Pierrepont St
North Pde
Nth Parade Road
North Parade Cricket Ground
Charles St
New St
Westgate Bdgs
Road
Green Park
Bridge
Midland
Kingsmead West
Kingsmead North
Kingsmead Terrace
Milk Street
Avon St
Technical College
Lwr Borough Walls
Henry Street
Duke St
South Parade
St James's Parade
Shopping Centre
Philip St
Manvers Street
Police Station
Green Park Road
River Avon
Lower Bristol Road
Sydenham Buildings
Corn Street
Ambury
Broad Quay
Bus Sta.
Dorchester Street
Museum of Bookbinding
Churchill Bridge
Bath Spa Station
Spring Gardens
Spring Cres.
Ferry Lane
Broadway
Archway Street
Princes Bdgs
Pulteney Road
Lime Grove
Horseshoe Walk
Kennet & Avon Canal
Lower Oldfield Park
Wells Road
Claverton Street
Rossiter Road
A4
A36
A
B
C
D
E
F
1
2
3
4

See plan

1 Fernley ★★
2 Francis ★★★★
3 Hole in the Wall ❀ ✕✕✕
4 Ladbroke Beaufort ☆☆☆☆
5 Lansdown Grove ★★★
6 Old Mill Hotel ✕✕
7 Popjoys ✕✕✕
8 Pratts ★★★
8A Priory ❀ ★★★
9 Rajpoot Tandoori ✕
10 Redcar ★★★
11 Royal Crescent ★★★★
12 Royal York ★★★
13 Scanda ✕

150P ⛟ ✽

☐ English & French **V** ✿ ☐ Last dinner 9.45pm

Credit cards 1 5

See advert on page 99

★★★**Lansdown Grove** Lansdown Rd (Best Western) ☎(0225) 315891 Plan **5** *C4*

Privately owned Georgian mansion with pretty gardens and good views of Bath.

41rm(35⇀3⋔) (3fb) CTV in all bedrooms Ⓡ sB&B£21.95 sB&B⇀⋔£29.50 dB&B£33.50 dB&B⇀⋔£43 B

Lift ☾ CTV 26P 9⛟ CFA ✽ ☐ ♿

☐ English, French, Italian **V** ✿ ☐ ✽ Lunch £5 Tea 80p Dinner £8&alc Wine £4.30 Last dinner 9.30pm (9pm Sundays)

Credit cards 1 2 3 5

★★★**Pratts** South Pde (Forest Dale) ☎(0225) 60441 Telex no 47439 Plan **8** *D2*

Converted Georgian house dating from 1743, make up this city centre tourist hotel.

47⇀ (5fb) CTV in all bedrooms Ⓡ sB&B⇀£24.50–£26.75 dB&B⇀£36–£38

Lift ☾ Live music and dancing Sat (winter season) *xmas*

V ✿ ☐ Bar lunch £2.50–£4.25 Tea 50p Dinner £7.95–£9.50 Wine £4.35 Last dinner 10pm

Credit cards 1 2 3 5 **VS**

★★★**Redcar** Henrietta St (Kingsmead) ☎(0225) 60231 Telex no 849768 Ref 101 Plan **10** *D4*

A city centre hotel forming part of a Georgian terrace.

31rm(22⇀4⋔) CTV in all bedrooms Ⓡ sB&B fr£24.50 sB&B⇀⋔ fr£30 dB&B fr£37 dB&B⇀⋔ fr£43.50 B

☾ 15P CFA *xmas*

☐ English & French **V** ✿ ☐ Lunch £6.75&alc Tea 65p Dinner £6.75&alc Wine £5.25 Last dinner 9.45pm

Credit cards 1 2 3 5

★★★**Royal York** George St ☎(0225) 61541 Telex no 23241 Plan **12** *D4*

A stone built hotel, popular during the coaching era, once visited by Queen Victoria.

53rm(41⇀) 1☐ CTV in all bedrooms Ⓡ sB&B£21 sB&B⇀£28.50 dB&B£33 dB&B⇀£43.50 B

Lift ☾ 6⛟ CFA

V ✿ ☐ ✽ Lunch fr£4.25&alc Tea fr55p Dinner fr£6.75&alc Wine £4.25 Last dinner 9.15pm

S% Credit cards 1 2 3 5

★★**Fernley** North Pde ☎(0225) 61603 Plan **1** *D2*

✿★★★**PRIORY, BATH**

Weston Rd ☎(0225) 331922 Telex no 44612 Plan **8A** *A3*

Closed 1–9 Jan

(Rosette awarded for dinner only)

After a distinguished career in hotel management, John Donnithorne, bought this interesting hotel five years ago. About a mile away from Bath Abbey on the outskirts of the town, it is a Victorian Gothic villa in two acres of gardens (where tea can be served in summer) and provides a tranquil atmosphere where the tourist or businessman can relax. There is an intimate bar and an elegant drawing room with gentle colour schemes, comfortable seating and an open fire. Antique furniture and lovely flower arrangements add to its charm. Chef Michael Collom goes from strength to strength and many of his dishes share the elegance of the decor. He is influenced by the modern school of cooking, but not entirely so. He provides set meals priced according to the main course chosen and the well balanced. Individual dishes demonstrate his choice of fresh seasonal foods and the flavouring and seasoning of them is just right. Puddings are light, often with clean fruity flavours that complement the rest of the meal. The

extensive wine list is well chosen and deserves special mention. The individually decorated bedrooms are very well done and the year has seen further improvements, with a number of them having been refurbished to even higher standards than before: With friendly, solicitous staff, you are assured of a pleasant stay here.

15rm(14⇀1⋔) 1☐ CTV in all bedrooms ☐ sB&B⇀⋔£40 dB&B⇀⋔£72 Continental breakfast B

20P ⛟ ✽ ☐ (heated) nc10yrs *xmas*

☐ French ✿ ☐ Lunch fr£10 Dinner fr£15.50 Wine £5.30 Last dinner 9.30pm

S% Credit cards 1 2 3 4

A 19th-century stone and brick building in the city centre, opposite Parade Gardens.

47rm(27⇀) CTV in all bedrooms Ⓡ ☐ sB&B£21 sB&B⇀£31 dB&B£33 dB&B⇀£42 B

Lift ☐ Live music and dancing 4 nights wkly

✿ ☐ Lunch £2.50–£7 Tea fr80p Dinner £6.50alc Wine £3.50 Last dinner 10pm

Credit cards 1 3

✿XXX **Hole in the Wall** 16 George St ☎(0225) 25242 Plan **3** *C4*

Good quality raw materials are prepared with skill and flair in this city-centre restaurant.

Closed Sun & 3 wks Xmas

☐ French **V** 50 seats Lunch £15&alc Dinner £15&alc Wine £6.25 Last dinner 10pm ☐ bedrooms available

S% Credit cards 1 2 3 4 5

XXX **Popjoys** Beau Nash House, Sawclose ☎(0225) 60494 Plan **7** *C3*

Closed Sun

☐ English & French 40 seats Dinner £7–£8&alc Wine £3.90 Last dinner 11pm ☐

Credit cards 1 2 3 4 5

XX **Old Mill Hotel** Tollbridge Rd, Batheaston (3m NE on A4, Chippenham road) ☎(0225) 858476 Plan **6** *C4*

☐ Continental **V** 85 seats Lunch £5.95–£6.50&alc Dinner £7.90–£8.70&alc Wine £4.65 Last dinner 9.30pm 30P bedrooms available

Credit cards 1 2 5 **VS**

XX **Rajpoot Tandoori** 4 Argyle St ☎(0225) 66833 Plan **9** *D3*

Closed Mon (Jan–May)

☐ Indian **V** 60 seats Lunch £5–£8&alc Dinner £5.50–£18&alc Wine £4.50 Last dinner 11.30pm ☐

S% Credit cards 1 2 3 5 **VS**

X **Scanda** Bathampton ☎(0225) 62539 Plan **13** *E4*

A self-service, Norwegian restaurant.

☐ Scandinavian 120 seats ✽ Lunch fr£4.60 Dinner fr£9.78&alc Wine £4.95 Last dinner 10pm 300P Disco Fri & Sat

Credit cards 1 3

BATHGATE

Lothian *West Lothian*
Map **11** NS96

☆☆☆**Golden Circle** (Swallow) ☎(0506) 53771 Telex no 53168

A custom-built hotel, lying off the A7066 to the south of the town.

69⇀ CTV in all bedrooms Ⓡ sB&B⇀£22–£30 dB&B⇀£31–£40 B

Lift ☾ 100P

V Lunch £4–£7 Dinner £6.50–£8.50&alc Wine £5 Last dinner 9.45pm

Credit cards 1 2 3 5

XXX ***Balbairdie*** Bloomfield Pl ☎(0506) 55448 →

B

THE LANSDOWN GROVE HOTEL BATH BA1 5EH AVON

TELEPHONE: (0225) 315891/2/3

A distinctly individual hotel for all seasons. Fully licensed with every comfort and friendly efficient service. Majority of bedrooms with private bathrooms, all with telephone, radio and television. Delightful Restaurant offering good food and fine wines.

Cocktail Bar.
Charming gardens with shady lawns.
Excellent facilities for Seminars, Banquets, Wedding Receptions, Cocktail Parties, Private Dances and Meetings.
Hot and Cold Help Yourself Lunch daily.
Ample car parking and garage.
Illustrated brochure and tariff sent upon application.

AA★★★

A member of Best Western
Fine independently owned hotels throughout the World.

Rudloe Park Hotel

LEAFY LANE, CORSHAM, WILTSHIRE SN13 0PA

TELEPHONE HAWTHORN (0225) 810555

A 19th Century peaceful Country House Hotel set in 3½ acres of beautiful gardens with extensive views to and beyond the Georgian City of Bath (6 miles). Luxuriously appointed bedrooms all with bathroom ensuite. Telephone, colour television, tea and coffee. A four poster suite for your honeymoon or that special occasion. The elegant restaurant, which offers an extensive a La Carte menu and is open everyday, overlooks the lawn where one may relax or play croquet. Our lounge bars offer a good value selection of bar food. We are on the main A4 equidistant from Bath and Chippenham.

Food and Hotel Guides

Limpley Stoke Hotel

Lower Limpley Stoke, near Bath

This Georgian 'Consort' Country House Hotel which was enlarged and first opened in 1860, is delightfully situated in the celebrated Valley of the Avon, 5 miles South of Bath.
"The scenery here is superb and is classed amongst the most lovely and romantic in the West of England."
Restaurant, Lounge, TV Lounge, tea/coffee makers. Open all the Year. Attractive Bargain Breaks. Private Parking.

Telephone: Limpley Stoke (022 122) 3333

See gazetteer entry under Limpley Stoke.

An attractive first floor restaurant, situated in a renovated stone building in one of the lanes in the town centre.

Closed Sun

▣Scottish & French 40 seats Last dinner 10pm

Credit cards 1 2 3 5

BATTLE
East Sussex
Map **5** TQ71

★★★ *BL* **Netherfield Place** Netherfield (3m NW B2096) ☎(04246) 4455

A tastefully appointed country house hotel with good food, an elegant panelled restaurant and superb gardens. *(See p. 28.)*

11➡⋔(1fb) 1▣CTV in all bedrooms ★ sB&B➡⋔£25 dB&B➡⋔£44–£65

30P 2⌂ ✽ *xmas*

▣International **V** Lunch £12.50&alc Dinner £12.50&alc Wine £6 Last dinner 10pm

Credit cards 1 2 3 5

★★**George** High St ☎(04246) 4466

Comfortable coaching inn featuring Parliament Clock in restaurant.

22rm(20➡2⋔)(3fb) 1▣CTV in 2 bedrooms TV in 20 bedrooms Ⓡ sB&B➡⋔£15.57–£19.65 dB&B➡⋔£22.76–£28.30 ⊟

62P 5⌂

✿ ☐ Lunch £6.95&alc Tea 75p Dinner £6.95–£7.45&alc Wine £4.95 Last dinner 9.30pm

S% Credit cards 1 2 3 5

★**Nonsuch** 27 High St ☎(04246) 2255

8rm(2➡)(1fb) CTV in 2 bedrooms sB&B fr£14.50 sB&B➡ fr£17.25 dB&B fr£22 dB&B➡ fr£27.50 ⊟

CTV 2P 2⌂ *xmas*

▣English & French **V** ✿ ☐ Lunch £5–£6&alc Tea 75p Dinner £6.25–£7.25&alc Wine £5 Last dinner 9.30pm

Credit cards 1 2 3 5

BAUGHTON
Hereford & Worcester
Map **3** SO84

✕✕**Gay Dog Inn** ☎Upton-upon-Severn (06846) 2706

Closed Mon Lunch not served Tue–Sat Dinner not served Sun

36 seats Lunch £5-£5.40 Dinner £7alc Wine £3.90 Last dinner 9.30pm 50P

BAWTRY
South Yorkshire
Map **8** SK69

★★★**Crown** High St (Anchor) ☎Doncaster (0302) 710341 Telex no 547089

An interesting old coaching inn, now modernised, and standing in the old Market Place on the Great North Road.

57➡(4fb) CTV in all bedrooms Ⓡ ✻sB&B➡£19.50-£33.50 dB&B➡£27–£41 ⊟

☾ CTV 40P CFA ⌂ *xmas*

V ✿ ☐ ✻Lunch £4.85–£5.50 Tea fr40p Dinner fr£7.50 Wine £4.50 Last dinner 9.45pm

Credit cards 1 2 3 4 5 **VS**

BAYCLIFF
Cumbria
Map **7** SD27

★★***Fishermans Arms*** ☎Bardsea (022988) 387 Closed 24–27 Dec

A comfortable hotel on the coast road.

12rm(3➡3⋔) Ⓡ ★

CTV 60P

V ✿

S% Credit card 1

BAYHORSE
Lancashire
Map **7** SD45

★**Foxholes** ☎Forton (0524) 791237

10rm(1➡)(3fb) ★ sB&B£10.50 dB&B£17.75 dB&B➡£23

CTV 50P ✽

✿ Lunch fr£3.50 Dinner £9.50alc Wine £3.25 Last dinner 9pm

BEACHLEY
Gloucestershire
Map **3** ST59

★★**Old Ferry** ☎Chepstow (02912) 2474

Closed 24–26 Dec

This hotel is located next to the old Ferry landing, in the shadow of the Severn Bridge.

16rm(4➡1⋔)(2fb) CTV available in bedrooms sB&B£16.35 sB&B➡£20.35 dB&B£27.70 dB&B➡£31.70 ⊟

CTV 100P ✽ Live music and dancing Sat

▣English & French **V** ✿ ☐ Lunch fr£4.25 Tea 65p Dinner £2.35–£4.50&alc Wine £2.50 Last dinner 9.30pm

Credit cards 1 2 3 5 **VS**

BEACONSFIELD
Buckinghamshire
Map **4** SU99

☆☆☆☆**Bellhouse** (2m E A40) (DeVere) ☎Gerrards Cross (0753) 887211 Telex no 848719

Busy hotel with tastefully appointed bedrooms.

120➡ CTV in all bedrooms ✻sB&B➡£34.50 dB&B➡£44.70 ⊟

Lift ☾ 750P CFA ✽ Live music and dancing Fri & Sat *xmas*

▣English & French **V** ✿ ☐ ✻Lunch £6.55&alc Dinner £7.10&alc Wine £5.50 Last dinner 10pm

Credit cards 1 2 3 5

☆☆**Crest** Aylesbury End (Crest) ☎(04946) 71211

This holiday hotel has a well appointed bar.

13rm Annexe: 28➡ CTV in all bedrooms Ⓡ ✻sB fr£23 sB➡ fr£33 dB fr£30 dB➡ fr£43 (room only) ⊟

☾ ⚟ 100P

▣International ✿ ✻Bar lunch £3.10–£7.75 Dinner £6.70–£12&alc Wine £5.95 Last dinner 9.30pm

Credit cards 1 2 3 4 5 **VS**

✕***China Diner*** 7 The Highway, Station Rd ☎(04946) 3345

Closed Xmas

▣Pekinese & Szechuan 56 seats Last dinner 11.30pm ⚑

Credit cards 1 2 3 5

✕**Jasmine** 15a Penn Rd ☎(04946) 5335

Modern, well-appointed Chinese restaurant.

▣Cantonese 100 seats Last dinner 2.15am 80P

Credit cards 1 2 3 5

BEAMINSTER
Dorset
Map **3** ST40

✕**Nevitt's Eating House** 57 Hogshill St ☎Dorchester (0308) 862600

Closed Mon Lunch not served Tue–Sat Dinner not served Sun

▣English & Continental **V** 30 seats ✻Lunch £5 Dinner £10alc Wine £4.25 Last dinner 10pm 12P

BEARSDEN
Strathclyde *Dunbartonshire*
Map **11** NS57

☆☆**Stakis Burnbrae** Milngavie Rd (Stakis) ☎041-942 5951 Telex no 778704

A custom-built, modern hotel, set back from the A81 on the outskirts of the town.

16rm(13➡) CTV in all bedrooms Ⓡ ✻sB&B➡ fr£30 dB&B➡ fr£38 ⊟

☾ 100P

▣English & French ✿ ☐ Last dinner 10.30pm

Credit cards 1 2 3 5 **VS**

✕✕**La Bavarde** 9 New Kirk Rd ☎041-942 2202

Closed Sun, Mon, last 3wks Jul & 2wks Xmas

50 seats Lunch £3.50 Dinner £9 Wine £4.90 Last dinner 9.30pm ⚑

Credit cards 1 2 3 5

✕**Ristorante da Riccardo** 130 Drymen Rd ☎041-943 0960

An attractive little restaurant and delicatessen, with a modern frontage, in the centre of the town.

Closed Mon Lunch not served Sun

▣Italian **V** 40 seats ✻Lunch £2.95&alc Dinner £10&alc Wine £4.10 Last dinner 10.15pm

Live music Thu

Credit cards 1 2

BEATTOCK
Dumfries & Galloway *Dumfriesshire*
Map **11** NT00

★★**Auchen Castle** (Inter-Hotels/Execotel)
☎(06833) 407 Telex no 777205
Closed Dec–Jan

This hotel was built in 1849 for the W. Younger family, and is set in extensive grounds.

18rm(13➡2⋔) Annexe: 10⋔ (7fb) CTV in all bedrooms Ⓡ sB&B➡⋔£22 dB&B➡⋔£30–£36 Ｂ
CTV P 2 Live music and dancing Sat (Oct–Mar)
Scottish, English & French V Bar lunch 75p–£3 Tea 65p Dinner £7–£9 Wine £4.60 Last dinner 9pm
S% Credit cards 1 2 3 4 5

★★**Beattock House** ☎(06833) 403

This is a converted mansion, dating from 1812, that stands in 6½ acres of grounds.

7rm(2⋔) (2fb) Ⓡ sB&B fr£13.50 sB&B⋔ fr£13.50 dB&B fr£27 dB&B⋔ fr£27 Ｂ
CTV 30P *xmas*
V Lunch fr£4.75 Tea fr£2 High Tea fr£3.85 Dinner fr£7.10&alc Wine £4.70 Last dinner 9.30pm

★★***Old Brig Inn*** ☎(06833) 401

Comfortable, modernised coaching inn.

8rm(1⋔) Ⓡ Ｂ
20P
Last dinner 8.30pm
Credit cards 2 3 5 VS

BEAULIEU
Hampshire
Map **4** SU30

★★★*L* **Montagu Arms** ☎(0590) 612324
Gabled and creeper-clad building of mellow local brick.
26➡(2fb) 6⊟ CTV in all bedrooms sB&B➡£28.50–£32.50 dB&B➡£39.50–£47.50 B
☾ 100P 12🚗✽ *xmas*
▣English & French V ♈ ☕ Lunch £6.35 Tea £1.25 High Tea fr£4.50 Dinner £10.75&alc Wine £5.95 Last dinner 10pm
Credit cards 1 2 3 4
See advert on page 103

BEAULY
Highland *Inverness-shire*
Map **14** NH54
★★**Priory** The Square (Minotel) ☎(0463) 782309
A modernised hotel situated in the town square.
12rm(6➡⋒)(1fb) Ⓡ ✻ sB&B£10.75–£15.75 sB&B➡⋒£11.75–£16.75 dB&B£17.50–£24 dB&B➡⋒£18.50–£25 B
CTV Disco Fri Live music and dancing Sat & Sun Cabaret Sat & Sun
▣Mainly grills V ♈ ☕ Bar lunch £1.20–£3.50&alc Tea fr40p Dinner £6–£8&alc Wine £3 Last dinner 9pm
Credit cards 1 2 3 5 VS

BEAUMARIS
Gwynedd
Map **6** SH67
★★*H* **Bishopsgate House** 54 Castle St ☎(0248) 810302
Closed Nov–mid Apr
11rm(7⋒) CTV in 11 bedrooms Ⓡ sB&B£12.75–£13.75 sB&B⋒£13.75–£14.75 dB&B£20.30–£22.60 dB&B⋒£22.60–£24.50
12P nc5yrs
♈ Lunch fr£4.50 Dinner £6.50–£7.50&alc Wine £4.25 Last dinner 9pm
Credit cards 1 3

★★**Bulkeley Arms** Castle St ☎(0248) 810415
Looking over the Menai Straits, this three-storey, stone, scheduled building is close to the local shops.
42rm(18➡)(2fb) 1⊟ CTV in all bedrooms Ⓡ sB&B£15.50–£18 sB&B➡£18–£22 dB&B£31–£36 dB&B➡£36–£44 B
Lift 30P Live music and dancing wkly *xmas*
▣English & French ♈ ☕ Lunch £5–£10&alc Tea 70p–£1 High Tea £1.50–£3 Dinner £7.50–£10&alc Wine £4.25 Last dinner 9pm
Credit cards 1 2 3 5 VS

★★**Henllys Hall** ☎(0248) 810412
Rural surroundings provide a peaceful setting for this former monastery.
25rm(18➡7⋒)(4fb) 3⊟ CTV in all bedrooms Ⓡ sB&B➡⋒£15–£17 B
Lift 100P ✽ ⊡(heated) 🎾 sauna bath ⌂ *xmas*
▣International V ♈ ☕ Bar lunch 90p–£2 Tea £1–£1.20 High Tea £2–£2.50 Dinner £7&alc Wine £4 Last dinner 10pm
Credit cards 1 2 3 5 VS

✕***Hobson's Choice*** 13–13A Castle St ☎(0248) 810323
A double-fronted restaurant in the centre of Beaumaris.
▣International V 75 seats Last dinner 10pm 🚭
Credit card 1

BEAUMONT
Jersey, Channel Islands
Map **16**
★★**Hotel L'Hermitage** ☎Jersey (0534) 33314 Telex no 4192170 Closed end Oct–mid Mar
Tourist hotel with the bedrooms surrounding swimming pool and gardens.
109rm(96➡13⋒)(9fb) CTV in all bedrooms Ⓡ ✱ sB&B➡⋒£11–£15 dB&B➡⋒£22–£30
☾ 100P 🚫✽ ⊡(heated) ≈(heated) sauna bath Disco wkly Live music and dancing wkly Cabaret wkly nc14yrs
▣English & French ♈ ☕ Lunch £3 Tea 30p Dinner £4 Wine £2.50 Last dinner 8pm
Credit card 1

BECCLES
Suffolk
Map **5** TM49
★★**Waveney House** Puddingmoor ☎(0502) 712270
A flint-faced 16th-century house, alongside the River Waveney, visited by boats.
13rm(11➡)(3fb) 1⊟ CTV in all bedrooms Ⓡ sB&B£23–£27 sB&B➡£25–£28 dB&B£39.50–£43 dB&B➡£39.50–£43 B
50P ✽ ♩ nc2yrs
▣International V ♈ ☕ Lunch £5.50–£6&alc Tea 80p–£1.50 High Tea £4–£4.50 Dinner £5–£7&alc Wine £4.50 Last dinner 9.30pm
Credit cards 1 2 3 5

BECKENHAM
Gt London
plan **5** D5 (page 420)
✕✕**Le Bon Bec** 189A High St ☎01-650 0593
Closed Sun Lunch not served Sat
▣French V 75 seats Lunch £8.40 Dinner £8.40&alc Wine £4.80 Last dinner 11pm 🚭🚭
S% Credit cards 1 2 3 4 5

BEDALE
North Yorkshire
Map **8** SE28
☆☆☆**Motel Leeming** (1m NE junct A1/A684) ☎(0677) 23611
40➡(4fb) CTV in all bedrooms sB&B➡£21 dB&B£28 B
☾ 100P 20🚗✽
▣English & Continental ♈ ☕ Lunch £3.25–£4&alc Tea 50p–£1.50&alc High Tea £1.95–£4.50&alc Dinner £6.95&alc Wine £3.95 Last dinner 9.45pm
Credit cards 1 2 3 5

BEDDGELERT
Gwynedd
Map **6** SH54
★★★**Royal Goat** ☎(076686) 224
An impressive, three-storey tourist hotel, situated ¾m from Gelert's Grave.
25rm(21➡1⋒)(4fb) Ⓡ dB&B➡£27.50–£34
CTV 100P ♩ Live music & dancing Sat
▣English & Welsh V ♈ ☕ ✻ Lunch fr£5–£5.50 Tea fr65p–£1.10 Dinner fr£7.50–£8&alc Last dinner 8.30pm
Credit cards 1 2 3 5

★⛪*H* **Bryn Eglwys** Railbridge ☎(076686) 210
A detached Georgian house in its own grounds, about ½m from the village.
10rm(2fb) sB&B£11–£13 dB&B£22–£26 B
CTV 20P 🚫✽ ⌂ *xmas*
♈ ☕ Lunch fr£6.25 Tea £1 Dinner £6.25&alc Wine £3.60 Last dinner 9.30pm
VS

★**Tanronen** (Frederic Robinson) ☎(076686) 3471
A two storey tourist hotel, in the centre of the village.
9rm ✱ ✻ sB&B£11 dB&B£22 B
CTV 12P 3🚗 *xmas*
♈ ☕ ✻ Lunch £3.50 Tea £1.15 Dinner £6.25 Last dinner 9pm
Credit card 1

BEDFORD
Bedfordshire
Map **4** TL04
★★★**Bedford Moat House** St Marys St (Queens Moat) ☎(0234) 55131 Telex no 825243
Closed Xmas
117➡⋒ CTV in all bedrooms Ⓡ ✱ sB&B➡⋒£20–£35 dB&B➡⋒£27–£50 B
Lift ☾ CTV 45P CFA sauna bath Live music and dancing Sat
♈ Lunch fr£4.50&alc Dinner fr£6.75&alc Wine £5 Last dinner 9.45pm
Credit cards 1 2 3 5

★★★**Woodlands Manor** Green Ln, Clapham (2m N A6) ☎(0234) 63281 Telex no 825007
Closed 1wk Xmas–New Year & 1st 2wks Aug
Three and a half acres of gardens and woodlands surround this converted manor house.

18rm(5🛁13🚿)CTV in all bedrooms ★ sB&B🛁🚿£36–£40 dB&B🛁🚿£48–£71 B

☾ 200P 🚗 ✽ nc7yrs

🍴English & French ♆ ☕ Lunch £9.75–£12&alc Tea 80p Dinner £9.75–£12&alc Wine £6.70 Last dinner 9pm

Credit cards 1 2 3

★★**Bedford Swan** The Embankment (Paten) ☎(0234) 46565

A late 18th-century hotel, with a new extension, situated in an attractive riverside position.

102rm(84🛁)(3fb) 2⊟ CTV in 84 bedrooms Ⓡ ✻sB&B🛁£26.45 dB&B🛁£36.80 B

☾ CTV 70P CFA *xmas*

🍴English & French V ♆ ☕ ✻Lunch fr£4.75–£6.25&alc Tea fr60p Dinner fr£4.75–£6.25&alc Wine £3.45 Last dinner 9.30pm

Credit cards 1 2 3 5

★★**De Parys** De Parys Av (Exec Hotels) ☎(0234) 52121

Closed 26 Dec–2 Jan

This hotel is reputed to have been built on the site of the hospital and rectory of St John, founded in 1118 by Robert de Parys.

34rm(6🛁9🚿)(1fb) CTV in all bedrooms Ⓡ sB&B£21 sB&B🛁🚿£28 dB&B£32 dB&B🛁🚿£37.50 B

18P ✽

V ♆ ☕ Bar lunch £1–£3.50 Tea 50p Dinner £6&alc Wine £4 Last dinner 9pm

Credit cards 1 2 3 5

BEELEY
Derbyshire
Map **8** SK26

✕✕**Devonshire Arms** ☎ Darley Dale (062983) 3259

A stone-built, beamed village inn with an attractive, modern restaurant extension.

Closed Mon Dinner not served Sun

50 seats ✻Lunch £3–£5 Dinner £7.85 Wine £4.05 Last dinner 9.45pm 100P

Credit card 1 **VS**

BEER
Devon
Map **3** SY28

★★**Dolphin** Fore St ☎ Seaton (0297) 20068

A two-storey, former coaching inn.

23rm (4fb) CTV in 6 bedrooms Ⓡ sB&B£10–£12.50 dB&B£15–£23

CTV 60P 🏠 *xmas*

🍴Mainly grills ♆ Lunch £5–£6alc Dinner £6.50&alc Wine £4.20 Last dinner 9pm

Credit cards 1 3

BEESTON
Cheshire
Map **7** SJ55

☆☆☆**Wild Boar Inn** (Embassy) ☎ Bunbury (0829) 260309 Telex no 61455

Closed 27–29 Dec

Annexe: 30🛁 CTV in all bedrooms Ⓡ sB&B🛁 fr£29.25 dB&B🛁 fr£40.50 B

100P 🚗

🍴French V ♆ Lunch fr£8.80&alc Dinner £13alc Wine £6 Last dinner 10pm

S% Credit cards 1 2 3 5

BEETHAM
Cumbria
Map **7** SD47

★**Wheatsheaf** ☎ Milnthorpe (04482) 2123

An attractive village inn, with oak beams, close to lakeland.

8rm(2🛁)(1fb) CTV in 3 bedrooms Ⓡ ✻sB&B£13.50 sB&B🛁£15 dB&B£21.50 dB&B🛁£26.50

CTV 78P 6🏠 ⚲

V ♆ ✻Lunch £2.75–£3.75 Dinner £6.75&alc Wine £3 Last dinner 8.30pm

Credit card 3

BELBROUGHTON
Hereford & Worcester
Map **7** SO97

✕✕***Bell Inn*** Bell End ☎(0562) 730232

→

B

Lunch not served Sat Dinner not served Sun

⊟French **V** 60seats Last dinner 10pm 120P

Credit cards 1 2 3 5

✕✕ ***Four Winds*** Hollies Hill ☎(0562) 730332

Closed Mon Lunch not served Sat Dinner not served Sun

68seats Last dinner 9.30pm

BELFORD
Northumberland
Map **12** NU13

★★**Blue Bell** (Swallow) ☎(06683) 543
Telex no 77424

Attractive ivy-clad building with comfortable well-appointed bedrooms.

15rm(8➡)(1fb) 1⊟ CTV in all bedrooms Ⓡ sB&B£20–£22 sB&B➡£25–£28 dB&B£33–£35 dB&B➡£38–£40 ⊟

CTV 40P 2⌂✽ ℘ *xmas*

V✿⊒ Lunch £5 Tea £1.25 High Tea £3.85 Dinner £7.50–£10.25 Wine £4.75 Last dinner 9pm

Credit cards 1 2 3 5

BELLINGHAM
Northumberland
Map **12** NY88

★★**Riverdale Hall** ☎(0660) 20254

12rm(8➡3⋔)(4fb) 4⊟ CTV in 12 bedrooms Ⓡ sB&B£11–£13 sB&B➡⋔£15–£18 dB&B£23–£28 dB&B➡⋔£29–£35 ⊟

⋕ CTV 60P ✽ ⊡(heated) ♩ Disco twice wkly Live music and dancing mthly Cabaret mthly *xmas*

⊟English & Scandinavian **V**✿⊒ Lunch £4–£5&alc Tea 45p Dinner £7.50–£9 Wine £3.90 Last dinner 9.30pm

VS

BELLSHILL
Strathclyde *Lanarkshire*
Map **11** NS76

★**Hattonrigg** Hattonrigg Rd (Scottish & Newcastle) ☎(0698) 748488

A small, commercial hotel.

8rm(4➡) CTV in all bedrooms Ⓡ sB&B fr£16 sB&B➡fr£17 dB&B➡fr£32 ⊟

70P Disco wkly Live music and dancing wkly Cabaret wkly nc5yrs

✿Lunch £3&alc Dinner £7alc Wine £4 Last dinner 9pm

Credit cards 1 2 3 4 5

BELPER
Derbyshire
Map **8** SK34

✕✕**Remy's** 84 Bridge St ☎(077382) 2246

Closed Sun, Mon, Public hols, 1 wk Jul & 2wks Aug

⊟French 25 seats Lunch £9.75alc Dinner £12alc Wine £5.80 Last dinner 9.30pm

S% Credit cards 2 5

BEMBRIDGE
Isle of Wight
Map **4** SZ68

★★**Birdham** 1 Steyne Rd ☎(098387) 2875

Small comfortable inn with good cuisine.

14rm(12➡)(5fb) CTV in all bedrooms sB&B£11.50 sB&B➡£14.37 dB&B£23 dB&B➡£28.75

★★**HIGHBURY, BEMBRIDGE**

Lane End ☎(098387) 2838 Closed 23–28 Dec & 1st 3 wks Oct

A favourite with our members, this little hotel has been described by many as honest and unpretentious. And so it is! Tony and Francis Cobb, the owners, with just a few friendly staff provide warm and good natured hospitality that is very much appreciated. It is an Edwardian villa with a small garden, on the outskirts of the village. It has a small swimming pool, as well as a sauna and solarium. Leading off the hall is the Edwardian dining room, spotlessly clean and brightly shining with polished copperware. Here you can sample the honestly cooked food from the reasonably priced set menu or the à la carte which is augmented by daily dishes that often include fresh, locally caught fish.
Opposite the dining room is an intimate little bar and a small sitting room. The latter, and a quieter sitting room on the first floor, are furnished in Victorian style and suitably decorated with pictures and bric a brac. The bedrooms are prettily decorated, comfortable and thoughtfully provided with many little extras to contribute to your comfort. A relaxed atmosphere prevails and the hotel is a useful one for both businessmen and holiday makers.

9rm(5➡3⋔)(2fb) 1⊟ TV in all bedrooms sB&B fr£16.50 sB&B➡⋔ fr£23 dB&B➡⋔£34.50–£36.50 ⊟

12P⇌✽ ⊡(heated) sauna bath

⊟Cosmopolitan **V**✿⊒ Lunch £5–£5.50&alc Tea 95p Dinner £8.50&alc Wine £4.70 Last dinner 10pm

S% Credit cards 1 2 3 5 **VS**

☾ ⚡ CTV 120P ✽ Live music and dancing twice wkly *xmas*

▣ English & French V ✿ Lunch £2.90–£4.25&alc Dinner £4.60–£6.60&alc Wine £3.50 Last dinner 9.45pm

Credit card ②

★★ **BL** ***Elm Country*** ☎ (098387) 2248

Closed Nov–Feb

Quiet family house with attractive garden and friendly atmosphere.

12rm (10➡ 2⋒) CTV in all bedrooms Ⓡ

☾ 60P ✽

▣ Cosmopolitan ✿ ☐ Last dinner 9.30pm

BENLLECH BAY

Gwynedd

Map **6** SH58

★★ **Bay Court** Beach Rd ☎ Tynygongl (0248) 852573

This holiday hotel is convenient for the beach.

18rm (2➡ 1⋒) Annexe: 4➡ (3fb) Ⓡ ✽ sB&B£12.50–£14.50 sB&B➡⋒ £15–£17 dB&B£25–£29 dB&B➡⋒ £30–£34 B

☾ CTV 65P billiards Live music and dancing Fri & Sat

▣ Welsh & English V ✿ Lunch £3.50alc Dinner £5.50&alc Wine £4 Last dinner 8.30pm

Credit cards ① ③ **VS**

★★ **Glanrafon** ☎ Tynygongl (0248) 852364

Closed Nov–Apr

A detached, Victorian holiday hotel, with gardens, and fine coastal views.

20rm (10➡) sB&B£12 sB&B➡ £13.25 dB&B£24 dB&B➡ £26.50 B

CTV 70P ✽

V ✿ ☐ Bar lunch fr£1.50 Tea fr£1 Dinner fr£5 Wine £2.75 Last dinner 9pm

Credit cards ① ③ **VS**

BERKELEY

Gloucestershire

Map **3** ST69

★★ ***Berkeley Arms*** ☎ Dursley (0453) 810291

A central, wide arch forms the entrance to this 18th-century red brick building.

13rm

CTV 30P 4

✿ ☐ Last dinner 8.30pm

Credit cards ① ③

BERKELEY ROAD

Gloucestershire

Map **3** SP70

★★ **B** ***Prince of Wales*** ☎ Dursley (0453) 810474

This inn, dating from 1850, offers comfort and character with busy bars and restaurant.

9rm (7➡⋒) CTV in all bedrooms Ⓡ B

40P 3 ✽ Live music and dancing Sat

▣ English & French V ✿ ☐ Last dinner 9.30pm

Credit cards ① ② ③ ⑤ **VS**

BERKHAMSTED

Hertfordshire

Map **4** SP90

★ **Swan** High St ☎ (04427) 71451

14rm (5➡) 1 TV in all bedrooms Ⓡ sB&B£22–£25 sB&B➡ £24–£28 dB&B£31–£35 dB&B➡ £35–£38 B

CTV 14P 2 sauna bath

▣ English & French ✿ ☐ Lunch £1.75–£8&alc Tea 75p Dinner £8&alc Wine £3.75 Last dinner 10pm

S% Credit cards ① ③

BERKSWELL

West Midlands

Map **4** SP27

✕✕ **Bear Inn** ☎ (0676) 33202

This historic inn dates from the 15th-century.

Lunch not served Sat

Dinner not served Sun

▣ English & French 75 seats Lunch £6.50–£9 Dinner £7.50–£9 Last dinner 10pm 200P

Credit cards ① ② ③ ⑤

BERWICK-UPON-TWEED

Northumberland

Map **12** NT95

★★★ **Turret House** Etal Rd, Tweedmouth ☎ (0289) 307344

Elegant hotel in its own grounds with tastefully decorated open plan bar, dining room and lounge.

10rm (7➡) (1fb) CTV in all bedrooms sB&B£22 sB&B➡ £26 dB&B£32 dB&B➡ £37 B

CTV 100P ✽

V ✿ ☐ Lunch £3.65–£4.20 Tea 45p–60p Dinner £9.25 Wine £5.50 Last dinner 9.30pm

Credit cards ① ② ③ ⑤ **VS**

★★ ***Castle*** Castle Gate ☎ (0289) 306471

A terraced hotel, situated on the main route through the town.

16rm CTV in 1 bedroom TV in 3 bedrooms Ⓡ

CTV

V ✿ ☐ Last dinner 9.30pm

Credit cards ① ③ **VS**

★★ **King's Arms** Hide Hill (Inter-Hotel) ☎ (0289) 307454 Telex no 8811232

This impressive, stone-built hotel, makes up the greater part of the terrace on Hide Hill.

39rm (19➡ 1⋒) (3fb) 1 CTV in all bedrooms sB&B£17–£19.50 sB&B➡⋒ £21–£23.50 dB&B£30–£34 dB&B➡⋒ £35–£39 B

☾ CTV ✽ *xmas*

V ✿ ☐ Lunch £4.50 Tea 60p High Tea £4 Dinner £7.50&alc Wine £4 Last dinner 9.30pm

Credit cards ① ② ③ ⑤ **VS**

★★ **Ravensholme** 32–36 Ravensdowne ☎ (0289) 307170

Bright and cheerful personally run hotel with comfortable accommodation.

14rm (8➡ 1⋒) (3fb) CTV in 14 bedrooms Ⓡ sB&B£12–£13 sB&B➡⋒ £14–£15 dB&B£24–£26 dB&B➡⋒ £28–£30 B

CTV

▣ English & French V ✿ ☐ →

*Lunch £4.25 Tea 40p–£1.25 High Tea £1.50–£4.75 Dinner £6.95&alc Last dinner 9.30pm

Credit cards 1 2 3

★ ***Queens Head*** Sandgate ☎(0289) 307852

Charming, character hotel with cosy lounge and bar, and large bedrooms.

6rm Ⓡ

CTV

Mainly grills V Last dinner 10pm

Credit cards 1 2 3

BETWS-Y-COED
Gwynedd
Map **6** SH75

★★★**Royal Oak** Holyhead Rd ☎(06902) 219

An impressive, stone, three-storey hotel in the centre of the village.

21 Annexe: 10 (5fb) CTV in all bedrooms sB&B £30 dB&B £40 B

200P

International V Lunch £4 Tea 50p–£1.50 Dinner £9 Wine £4.75 Last dinner 9pm

Credit cards 1 2 3 5

★★**Craig-y-Dderwen Country House** (Minotel) ☎(06902) 293

21rm (10 5) Annexe: 1 (6fb) CTV in all bedrooms Ⓡ sB&B £12–£16 sB&B £13.50–£17.50 dB&B £24–£32 dB&B £27–£35 B

50P

Welsh & French V Lunch fr £5.50&alc Tea £2–£3.50 High Tea £3–£4 Dinner £7.50&alc Wine £3.80 Last dinner 8.30pm

Credit cards 1 2 3 4 5 VS

★★**Park Hill** Llanrwst Rd ☎(06902) 540

Closed Jan

Victorian house set in its own gardens.
11rm(6🛁2🚿)(1fb) CTV in 1 bedroom Ⓡ sB&B£13–£16 dB&B🛁🚿 fr£28 B
CTV 12P 🚗 ✽ nc6yrs *xmas*
♈ ☕ Bar lunch £2.50–£3.50 Tea fr75p Dinner fr£6.50 Wine £4 Last dinner 7.30pm
Credit cards 1 2 3 VS

☆☆**Waterloo Motel** (Exec Hotel) ☎(06902) 411
Closed Xmas
Annexe: 28rm(27🛁1🚿)(2fb) CTV in 5 bedrooms Ⓡ sB&B🛁🚿 £13.50–£18.50 dB&B🛁🚿 £24–£34 B
CTV 150P ✽ ♪ ⌂
🍴 International V ♈ Bar lunch £1.25–£6 Dinner £5.75–£6.75&alc Wine £4.40 Last dinner 10pm
Credit cards 1 2 3 4 5

★***Fairy Glen*** ☎(06902) 269
17th-century hotel by the river near Fairy Glen beauty spot. It is family run with a homely atmosphere.
10rm(5🛁) Ⓡ B
13P 🚗
🍴 Welsh & Continental V ♈ ☕ Last dinner 7.30pm
Credit card 2 VS

BEVERLEY
Humberside
Map **8** TA03

★★★**Beverley Arms** North Bar Within (Trusthouse Forte) ☎ Hull (0482) 869241 Telex no 527568
A converted and modernised Georgian building, located in the town centre.
61🛁 CTV in all bedrooms Ⓡ sB&B🛁£39 dB&B🛁£55 B
Lift ☾ 70P *xmas*
♈ ☕ Last dinner 10pm
Credit cards 1 2 3 4 5

★★★**Tickton Grange** Tickton (3m NE on A1035) ☎ Leven (0401) 43666
This family-owned, Georgian country house is set in 3½ acres of gardens.
12rm(5🛁7🚿)(1fb) CTV in all bedrooms Ⓡ *sB&B🛁🚿 £33 dB&B🛁🚿 £44 B
65P ✽ ⌂
🍴 English & French V ♈ ☕ Lunch £5–£10&alc Tea 75p–£1.50 High Tea £1.50–£2.50 Dinner £6.50–£14 Wine £5.50 Last dinner 9.30pm
Credit cards 1 2 3 VS

★★**Lairgate** 30–34 Lairgate ☎ Hull (0482) 882141
A three-storey, Georgian building, situated near to the town centre.
20rm(8🛁2🚿)(2fb) CTV in all bedrooms Ⓡ *sB&B£18 sB&B🛁🚿 £20 dB&B£28 dB&B🛁🚿 £31 B
CTV 20P
🍴 English & French V ♈ ☕ *Lunch £4 Tea £1 High Tea £3 Dinner £7&alc Wine £4.50 Last dinner 9.30pm
Credit cards 1 3

BEWDLEY
Hereford & Worcester
Map **7** SO77

★★***Black Boy*** Kidderminster Rd ☎(0299) 402119 Closed Xmas Day
An extended and modernised 16th-century inn, near the River Severn.
17rm(5🛁8🚿) Annexe: 8rm(2🛁) TV in 12 bedrooms B
40P 🚗 ✽
V ♈ ☕ Last dinner 9.30pm
Credit cards 1 2 3

✕✕**Bailiffs House** 68 High St ☎(0299) 402691
Closed Mon Lunch not served Tue–Sat Dinner not served Sun
40 seats Lunch £6.95 Dinner £13.50 Wine £4.95 Last dinner 9.30pm ♪
Credit cards 1 3

BEXHILL-ON-SEA
East Sussex
Map **5** TQ70

★**Southlands Court** Hastings Rd ☎(0424) 210628 →

Quiet, old fashioned hotel with good, simple cooking.

28rm(8→10⋒)(2fb) CTV available in bedrooms Ⓡ sB&B£11 sB&B→⋒£12.90 dB&B£22.30 dB&B→⋒£27 B

CTV 12P 5 ✽ *xmas*

Lunch £3.50alc Tea fr60p High Tea £1.50 Dinner £4 Wine £3.50 Last dinner 7pm

BEXLEY
Gt London
Map **5** TQ47

☆☆☆**Crest** Southwold Rd (Crest)
☎Crayford (0322) 526900 Telex no 8956539

78→ CTV in all bedrooms Ⓡ ✱sB→fr£34 dB→fr£44 (room only) B

Lift ☾ 130P ✽ ♿

International V Lunch fr£7.25&alc Dinner fr£8.50&alc Wine £5.25 Last dinner 9.45pm

Credit cards 1 2 3 4 5

BIBURY
Gloucestershire
Map **4** SP10

★★★*L* **Swan** ☎(028574) 204

Cotswold stone inn with riverside gardens. Sitting rooms are comfortable and the atmosphere is charming.

23rm(22→1⋒) CTV in all bedrooms sB&B→⋒ fr£23.50 dB&B→⋒ fr£39.50 B

CTV 20P 4 ✽ ♩ *xmas*

International V Lunch fr£7.75 Tea fr75p Dinner fr£11.25 Wine £4.50 Last dinner 8.30pm

Credit cards 1 3

★★*L* **Bibury Court** ☎(028574) 337

Delightfully informal country house hotel in a beautiful setting.

16rm sB&B fr£18 dB&B fr£29 Continental breakfast B

CTV 200P ✽ ♩ U

V Dinner £9–£10 Wine £3.95 Last dinner 8.45pm

Credit cards 1 2 3 5

BICKLEIGH
(nr Tiverton) Devon
Map **3** SS90

★★***Fisherman's Cot*** ☎(08845) 237

A picturesque, thatched building on the bank of the river Exe.

6rm(3→) Annexe: 13rm(7→6⋒) CTV in all bedrooms Ⓡ

☾ 150P ✽ ♩

V Last dinner 9pm

Credit cards 1 2 3

BIDDENDEN
Kent
Map **5** TQ83

✕✕**Ye Maydes** ☎(0580) 291306

Skilful and imaginative cooking is found in this medieval half-timbered house.

Closed Sun & Mon

English & French 58 seats ✱Lunch £2.99–£4.90 Dinner £11.50alc Wine £4.50 Last dinner 9.15pm

Credit card 1 **VS**

BIDEFORD
Devon
Map **2** SS42

★★★**Durrant House** ☎(02372) 2361

A Georgian building with a modern extension, set on the Northam road.

50→⋒ Annexe: 8→⋒ CTV available in bedrooms Ⓡ sB&B→⋒£25.30 dB&B→⋒£34–£37 B

☾ CTV 140P CFA ✽ (heated) billiards sauna bath Live music and dancing Fri & Sat

English, French & Italian V Lunch £2.50–£10 High Tea £1.50 Dinner £7.50 Wine £3.50 Last dinner 9.30pm

Credit cards 1 2 3 5

★★**Riversford** Limers Ln (Inter-Hotels) ☎(02372) 4239 Closed Dec–Jan

A comfortable holiday hotel with slipway and moorings, set in a secluded position.
17rm(14⇌)(10fb) 2⊟ CTV in all bedrooms ® sB&B£12.35 sB&B⇌£19.60 dB&B£24.70 dB&B⇌⋔£31.20–£33.90 ⊟
☾ CTV 20P 2⌂ ✽ ⌂
⊟ English & Continental ⚘ ☐ Lunch £4.45&alc Tea 65p Dinner £6.95&alc Wine £4.25 Last dinner 8pm
Credit cards 2 3 5 **VS**

★★**Royal** ☎ Barnstaple St (Brend) ☎ (02372) 2005
A traditional hotel, situated at the eastern end of the bridge.
33rm(13⇌) CTV in 13 bedrooms ✻ sB&B fr£12.65 sB&B⇌ fr£16.10 dB&B fr£23 dB&B⇌ fr£29.90 ⊟
CTV 30P 3⌂ *xmas*
⚘ ☐ Bar lunch fr£1.25 Dinner £5.46–£6.50 Wine £3.50 Last dinner 8.30pm
Credit cards 1 2 3 5

★★**Yeoldon House** Durrant Ln, Northam ☎ (02372) 4400
Closed 24 Dec–10 Jan
A comfortable, well-appointed hotel, in a peaceful situation, that enjoys fine views over Torridge.
10rm(8⇌2⋔)(3fb) 1⊟ CTV in all bedrooms ✻ sB&B⇌⋔£25.75–£27.50 dB&B⇌⋔£42–£45 ⊟
20P ⌂ ✽ ⌂
⊟ English & Continental ⚘ ☐ Bar lunch £1–£5 Tea 70p–£1.25 Dinner £8.25–£9 Wine £3.95 Last dinner 8.30pm
S% Credit cards 1 2 3 5 **VS**

★**Rosskerry** Orchard Hill ☎ (02372) 2872 RS Nov–Feb
A small, secluded hotel in two acres of grounds.
10rm(4⇌)(3fb) ✻ sB&B£9.25–£10.50 sB&B⇌£10.75–£12 dB&B£18.50–£21 dB&B⇌£21.50–£24
CTV 20P ⌂ ✽
⚘ Bar lunch 55p–£1.15 Dinner fr£4.25 Wine £3.60 Last dinner 7.30pm
Credit cards 1 3 **VS**

BIDFORD-ON-AVON
Warwickshire
Map **4** SP05
★★**White Lion** High St ☎ (0789) 773309
15rm(1⇌7⋔) 1⊟ CTV in 13 bedrooms ® sB&B fr£15.50 sB&B⇌⋔ fr£18.50 dB&B fr£27 dB&B⇌⋔ fr£29 ⊟
CTV 15P  *xmas*
V ⚘ ☐ Bar lunch £3.50–£4.50 Tea 85p Dinner £8.45 Wine £4.25 Last dinner 9pm
Credit card 2

BIGBURY-ON-SEA
Devon
Map **3** SX64
★**Henley** ☎ (054881) 240
Closed Oct–mid May
There are superb views of Bigbury Bay from this small country-house, set in its own grounds.
9rm(6⇌1⋔)(1fb) ® sB&B£11 sB&B⇌£12 dB&B£22 dB&B⇌£24
CTV 10P ⌂ ✽ nc3
⚘ Lunch £3.50alc Dinner £5alc Wine £3 Last dinner 7.30pm
VS

BIGGLESWADE
Bedfordshire
Map **4** TL14
★**Crown** High St ☎ (0767) 312228
RS Xmas
A small hotel with modest accommodation in the town centre.
17rm (2fb) sB&B fr£15 dB&B fr£19
CTV 21P
⚘ Bar lunch 90p–£3.50 Dinner £6.50–£7.50 Wine £3.20 Last dinner 8.30pm
VS
See advert on page 112

BILBROOK
Somerset
Map **3** ST04

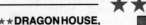

★★**DRAGON HOUSE, BILBROOK**
☎Washford (0984) 40215
CLosed Nov
RS Dec–Feb (except Xmas when fully open)

Built in 1704 of mellow stone, this hotel stands in 2½ acres of the most pleasing gardens. The interior is full of beams and character with its galleried hall with lantern above, and impressive, large fireplaces. The sitting room with its log fire is cosy and comfortable as is the little bar. There are some nice pieces of country furniture which is particularly suited to the style of this charming little place. The owners, Tony and Valerie Wright, play their part in contributing to the relaxed air. Mr Wright looks after the front of the house while his wife looks after the catering to very good effect. She keeps a good table and fine raw materials are freshly cooked to provide interesting and enjoyable meals. They are served by cheerful girls. There is also a pine decorated bistro type restaurant where lighter dishes are available. Although situated at the side of the

road, those rooms affected by noise are double glazed. All the rooms are individually decorated – one with an impressive half tester bed – and some have televisions; all are comfortable. It is a tribute to the Wrights that so many of our members comment that to stay here is as relaxing as staying with friends.

9rm(4⇌2⋒) Annexe: 2⇌1⋒ CTV in 5 bedrooms ® ⊞

25P ✽ U

English & French Last dinner 9.15pm

Credit cards 1 2 3 5

★*Bilbrook Lawns* ☎Washford (0984) 40331 Closed 24 Dec–Feb

This comfortable, well appointed Georgian house offers a friendly atmosphere and good food.

7rm(1⇌1⋒) Annexe: 3rm(1⇌) TV in all bedrooms ® ⊞

14P ✽ nc5

English & French Last dinner 6pm

VS

BILDESTON
Suffolk
Map **5** TL94

✕*Bow Window* ☎(0449) 740748
Closed Sun & Mon Lunch not served
English & French 50 seats Last dinner 9.30pm
Credit cards 1 2 3

BILLESLEY
Warwickshire
Map **4** SP15

★★★*BL* **Billesley Manor** ☎Stratford-upon-Avon (0789) 763737

Antiques of all kinds fill this very comfortable, converted manor house.

28⇌ 4 CTV in all bedrooms ★
sB&B⇌£35 dB&B⇌£45 ⊞
☾ 80P ✽ (heated) (hard) sauna bath *xmas*

French Lunch £8.50–£9.50&alc Tea £1–£1.50 Dinner £12.50–£16&alc Wine £6.75 Last dinner 9pm
Credit cards 1 2 3

BILLINGTON
Lancashire
Map **7** SD73

✕✕✕**Foxfields** Whalley Rd ☎Whalley (025482) 2556
Closed Mon & Public hols
Lunch not served Sat
French 60 seats Lunch £7.25&alc Dinner £13.50alc Wine £5.50 Last dinner 9.30pm 65P
Credit cards 1 2 3

BINGLEY
West Yorkshire
Map **7** SE13

★★★**Bankfield** Bradford Rd (Embassy)
☎Bradford (0274) 567123
RS Public holidays

A 19th-century house, with modern bedroom extensions, overlooking the River Aire.

72⇌⋒ CTV in all bedrooms ®
sB&B⇌⋒£25.50–£30.50
dB&B⇌⋒£32–£39.50 (room only) ⊞
☾ 250P 30 CFA ✽ Live music and dancing Sat (Oct–May) *xmas*
V ✱Lunch fr£6.70 Dinner fr£6.70 Wine £4.50 Last dinner 9.15pm
Credit cards 1 2 3 4 5

BIRKENHEAD
Merseyside
Map **7** SJ38

★★★*B* **Bowler Hat** 2 Talbot Rd, Oxton (Porter) ☎051-652 4931 Telex no 837921

29⇌ (3fb) CTV in all bedrooms ®
sB&B⇌£19.25–£37.40 dB&B⇌£26.40–£47.30 Continental breakfast ⊞
☾ 30P CFA ✽ *xmas*
English & French **V** Lunch fr£8.75&alc Dinner £10.45&alc Last dinner 10pm
S% Credit cards 1 2 3 5 **VS**

★★H **Riverhill** Talbot Rd, Oxton ☎051-652 4847

This hotel is set in its own grounds, in a residential area.

10rm(5⇌2⋒) CTV in all bedrooms ® ✶ sB&B£15 sB&B⇌⋒£20 dB&B£30 dB&B⇌⋒£35

25P ✽

Lunch £4.45–£5.50 Tea fr65p High Tea fr£3.50 Dinner £4.95–£6&alc Wine £4 Last dinner 9pm

Credit card 1 2 3 5 **VS**

★★ **Woodside** Chester St (Whitbread West Pennines) ☎051-647 4121

This public house has modern bedrooms, and is located by the river, near the Mersey Ferry.

27rm(5⇌6⋒) ® ✶ sB&B£12.25 sB&B⇌⋒£13.75 dB&B£22.80 dB&B⇌⋒£24

☾ CTV 60P

V ✻Lunch £5&alc Dinner £5.50&alc Wine £3.10 Last dinner 9pm

S% Credit cards 1 2 3

BIRMINGHAM
W Midlands
Map **7** SP08
See plan

See also Birmingham Airport and Birmingham (National Exhibition Centre)

★★★★ **Albany** Smallbrook, Queensway (Trusthouse Forte) ☎021-643 8171 Telex no 337031
Central plan **1** *D3*

An impressive, modern, thirteen-storey building with extensive views over the city.

254⇌ CTV in all bedrooms ® sB&B⇌£46.50 dB&B⇌£62.50 B →

B

Birmingham Central

1 Albany ★★★★
2 Le Biarritz ✕✕
3 Birmingham International ☆☆☆
4 La Capanna ✕✕
5 Chung Ying ✕✕
6 Grand ★★★
7 New World ✕✕
8 Holiday Inn ☆☆☆☆
9 House of Mr Chan ✕✕
10 Lorenzo's ✕✕
11 Maharaja ✕
12 Midland ★★★★
13 New Happy Gathering ✕✕
14 New Imperial ★★
15 Radjoot ❀✕✕
16 Royal Angus Thistle ★★★

Lift ☾ # CFA ⊡ (heated) squash billiards sauna bath

♆ ▭ Last dinner 11pm

Credit cards 1 2 3 4 5

☆☆☆☆ ***B* Holiday Inn** Holliday St (Holiday Inns) ☎021-643 2766 Telex no337272 Central plan **8** *B3*

This modern building, with bright interior dècor, overlooks the city centre.

304⇌⋒ (270fb) CTV in all bedrooms sB⇌⋒ £46 dB⇌⋒ £51.75 (room only) ₿

Lift ☾ ⊡ (heated) sauna bath Cabaret Mon–Thu *xmas*

▣ English & French ♆ ▭ Lunch £7.95&alc Tea fr£1.30 Dinner fr£8.95&alc Wine £5.95 Last dinner 10.30pm

Credit cards 1 2 3 4 5 **VS**

★★★★ ***Midland*** New St ☎021-643 2601 Telex no338419 Central plan **12** *D4*

A traditional hotel in the busy city centre.

114rm(106⇌⋒) CTV in all bedrooms ® ₿

Lift ☾ CTV CFA Live music and dancing Sat in winter

▣ English & French **V** ♆ ▭ Last dinner 10pm

Credit cards 1 2 3 5

See advert on page 113

❀★★★★ ***B* Plough & Harrow** Hagley Rd, Edgbaston (Crest) ☎021-454 4111 Telex no338074 District plan **30** Closed Xmas

This traditional-style hotel, has modern bedrooms and provides interesting cuisine.

44⇌ CTV in all bedrooms ® ✭ ✻ sB⇌ fr£49.50 dB⇌ fr£57 (room only)

Lift ☾ ⅟ P ⊞ sauna bath

▣ English & French **V** ♆ ▭ ✻ Lunch £13.50–£19.75&alc Dinner £13.50–£19.75&alc Wine £6.95 Last dinner 10.30pm

Credit cards 1 2 3 4 5 **VS**

See advert on page 118

☆☆☆☆ **Strathallan Thistle** 225 Hagley Rd, Edgbaston (Thistle) ☎021-455 9777 Telex no336680 District plan **33** →

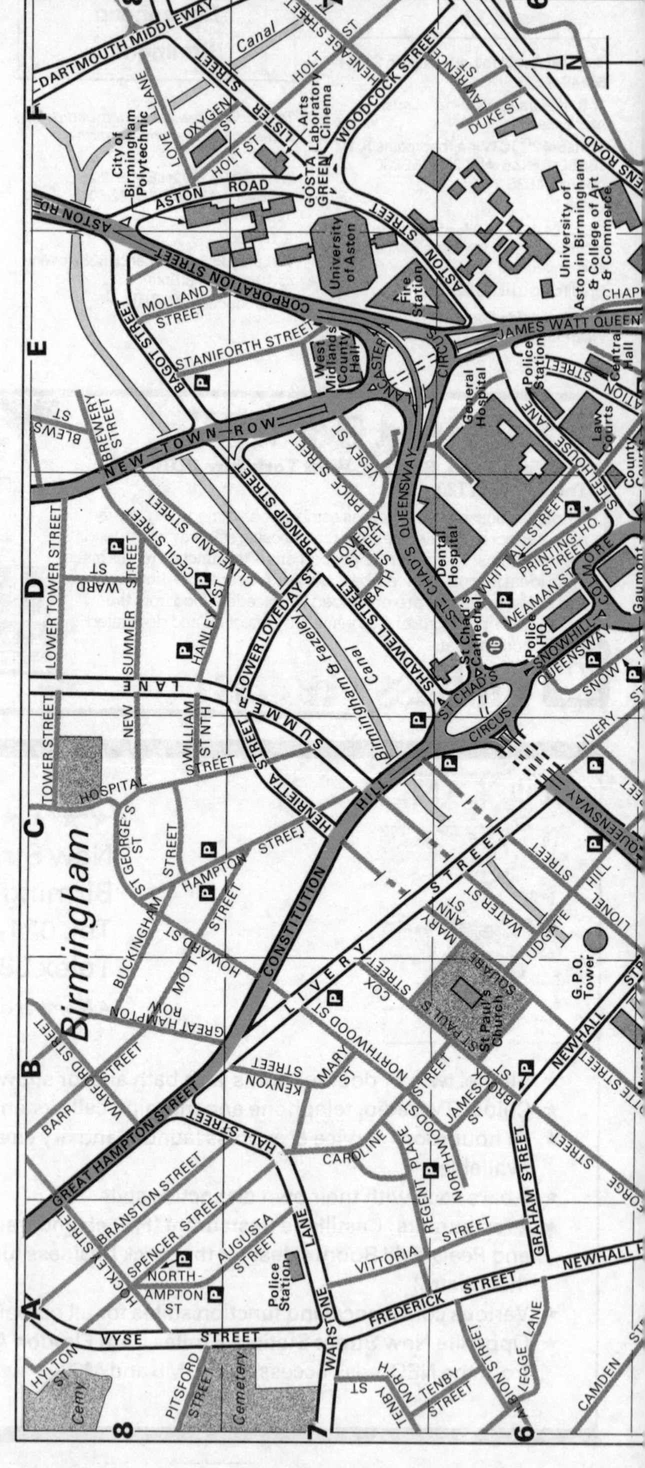

Birmingham
DARTMOUTH MIDDLEWAY
Canal
LOVE LANE
OXYGEN ST
HOLT ST
LISTER STREET
HENEAGE STREET
WOODCOCK STREET
DUKE ST
ASTON ROAD
ASTON RD
City of Birmingham Polytechnic
Arts Laboratory Cinema
GOSTA GREEN
University of Aston
University of Aston in Birmingham & College of Art & Commerce
CORPORATION STREET
ASTON STREET
Fire Station
MOLLAND STREET
BAGOT STREET
STANIFORTH STREET
West Midlands County Hall
JAMES WATT QUEENSWAY
Police Station
General Hospital
Law Courts
Central Hall
NEW TOWN ROW
BLEWS ST
BREWERY STREET
PRINCIP STREET
PRICE STREET
VESEY ST
ST CHAD'S QUEENSWAY
Dental Hospital
LOWER TOWER STREET
SUMMER STREET
WARD ST
CECIL STREET
LOWER LOVEDAY ST
SHADWELL STREET
Birmingham & Fazeley Canal
St Chad's Cathedral
WEAMAN ST
PRINTING HO. STREET
SNOW HILL QUEENSWAY
Police HQ
LANE
NEW SUMMER STREET
TOWER STREET
HOSPITAL
WILLIAM ST NTH
SUMMER ROW
HENRIETTA STREET
ST CHAD'S CIRCUS
LIVERY ST
ST GEORGE'S ST
HAMPTON STREET
CONSTITUTION HILL
LIVERY STREET
WATER ST
ANN ST
MARY ST
LUDGATE HILL
LIONEL
G.P.O. Tower
BUCKINGHAM ST
HOWARD ST
MOTT STREET
GREAT HAMPTON ROW
COX STREET
ST PAUL'S SQUARE
St Paul's Church
NORTHWOOD ST
KENYON STREET
BARR STREET
WARSTONE STREET
GREAT HAMPTON STREET
HALL STREET
CAROLINE
JAMES ST
NEWHALL ST
GRAHAM STREET
BRANSTON STREET
SPENCER STREET
AUGUSTA STREET
HOCKLEY STREET
NORTHAMPTON ST
Police Station
VITTORIA STREET
FREDERICK STREET
NEWHALL HILL
VYSE STREET
HYLTON ST
Cemy
Cemetery
PITSFORD STREET
WARSTONE LANE
TENBY ST
TENBY STREET NORTH
ALBION STREET
LEGGE LANE
CAMDEN
A B C D E F
6 7 8

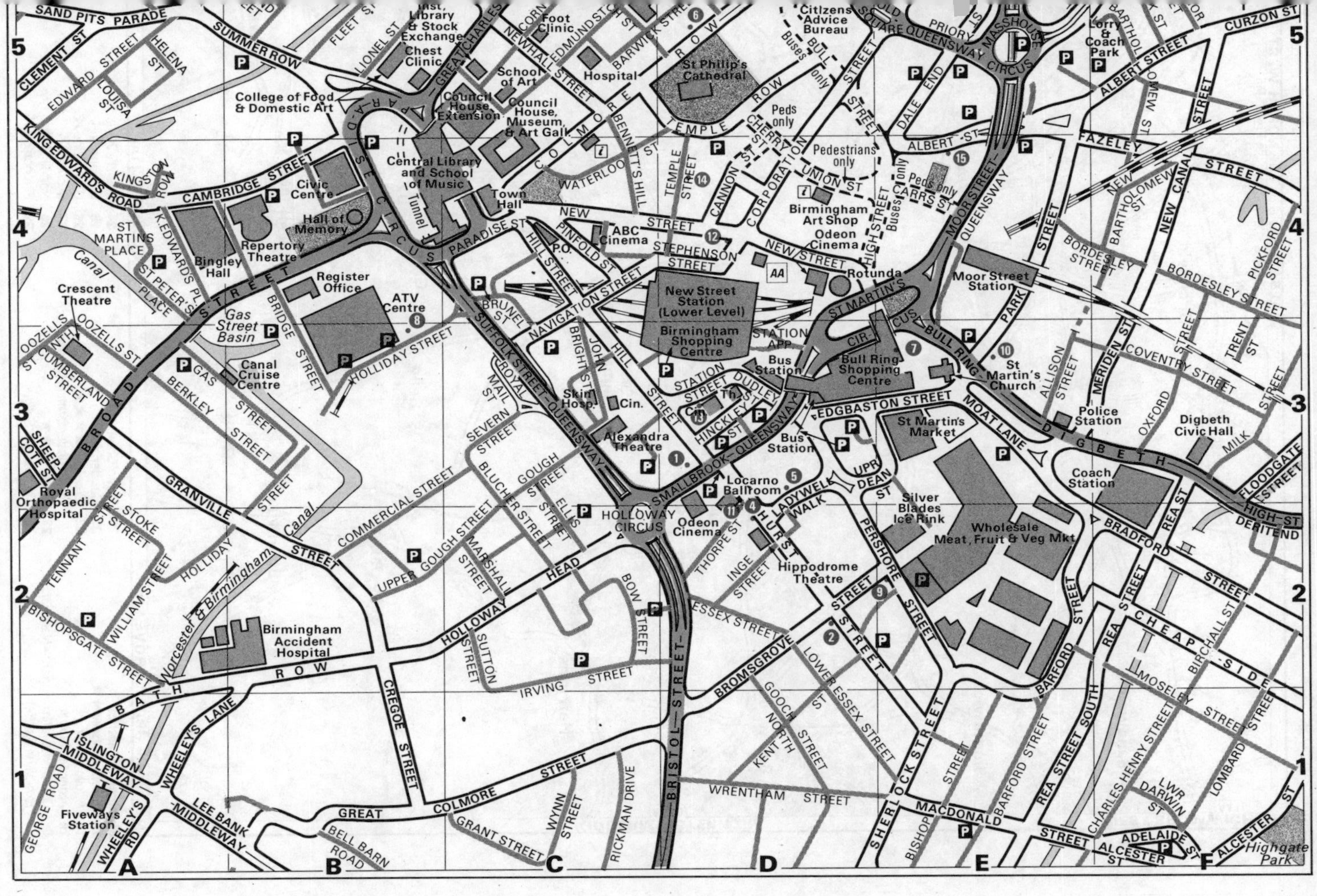

Moor Street Station
New Street Station (Lower Level)
Birmingham Shopping Centre
Bull Ring Shopping Centre
St Martin's Church
St Martin's Market
Wholesale Meat, Fruit & Veg Mkt
Coach Station
Police Station
Digbeth Civic Hall
Silver Blades Ice Rink
Hippodrome Theatre
Locarno Ballroom
Odeon Cinema
Alexandra Theatre
Skin Hosp.
Rotunda
Birmingham Art Shop
Citizens Advice Bureau
St Philip's Cathedral
Hospital
Foot Clinic
School of Art
Council House, Museum & Art Gal.
Council House Extension
Town Hall
Central Library and School of Music
Chest Clinic
Library & Stock Exchange
ABC Cinema
ATV Centre
Register Office
Hall of Memory
Civic Centre
Repertory Theatre
Bingley Hall
College of Food & Domestic Art
Canal Cruise Centre
Gas Street Basin
Crescent Theatre
Royal Orthopaedic Hospital
Birmingham Accident Hospital
Fiveways Station
Highgate Park
Lorry & Coach Park
Tunnel
Canal
Worcester & Birmingham Canal
QUEENSWAY
SMALLBROOK QUEENSWAY
SUFFOLK STREET QUEENSWAY
MOOR STREET QUEENSWAY
MASSHOUSE CIRCUS
PARADISE CIRCUS
HOLLOWAY CIRCUS
ST MARTIN'S CIRCUS
BULL RING
DIGBETH
MOAT LANE
EDGBASTON STREET
PERSHORE STREET
BRISTOL STREET
BROMSGROVE STREET
HOLLOWAY HEAD
BROAD STREET
CORPORATION STREET
NEW STREET
COLMORE ROW
BULL STREET
NEW CANAL STREET
PARK STREET
BORDESLEY STREET
CHEAPSIDE
REA STREET
BARFORD STREET
SHERLOCK STREET
GRANVILLE STREET
BATH ROW
LEE BANK MIDDLEWAY
ISLINGTON MIDDLEWAY
KING EDWARDS ROAD
SUMMER ROW
SAND PITS PARADE
CAMBRIDGE STREET
GREAT CHARLES
CREGOE STREET
COMMERCIAL STREET
HURST ST
ESSEX STREET
LOWER ESSEX STREET

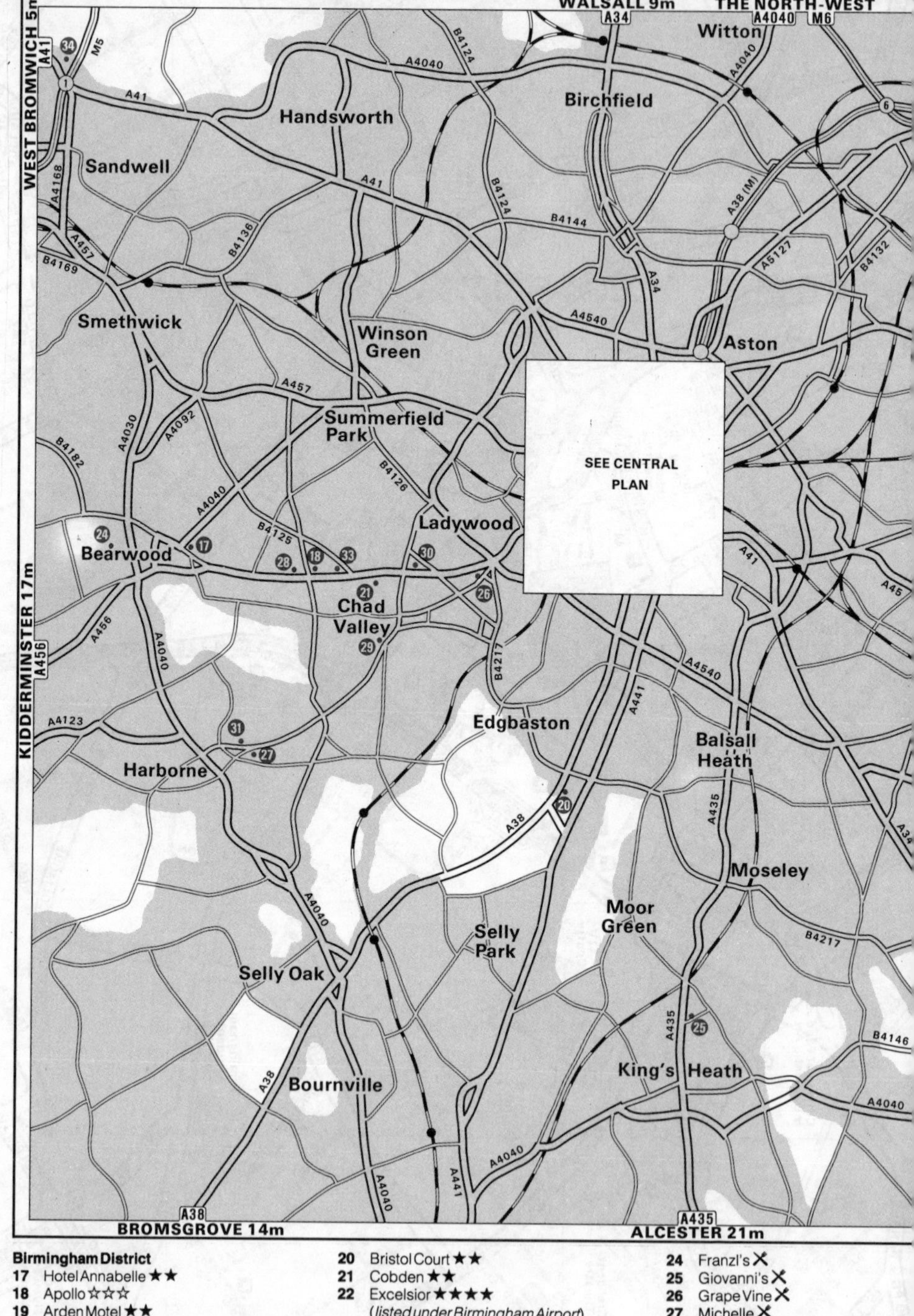
WALSALL 9m
THE NORTH-WEST
A34
A4040
M6
WEST BROMWICH 5m
A41
KIDDERMINSTER 17m
A456
BROMSGROVE 14m
A38
ALCESTER 21m
A435
Witton
Birchfield
Handsworth
Sandwell
Smethwick
Winson Green
Aston
Summerfield Park
SEE CENTRAL PLAN
Ladywood
Bearwood
Chad Valley
Edgbaston
Balsall Heath
Harborne
Moseley
Moor Green
Selly Park
Selly Oak
Bournville
King's Heath

Birmingham District

17 Hotel Annabelle ★★
18 Apollo ☆☆☆
19 Arden Motel ★★
(*listed under Birmingham – National Exhibition Centre*)
20 Bristol Court ★★
21 Cobden ★★
22 Excelsior ★★★★
(*listed under Birmingham Airport*)
23 Flemings ★★
(*listed under Solihull*)
24 Franzl's ✕
25 Giovanni's ✕
26 Grape Vine ✕
27 Michelle ✕
28 Norfolk ★★
29 Pinocchio's ✕

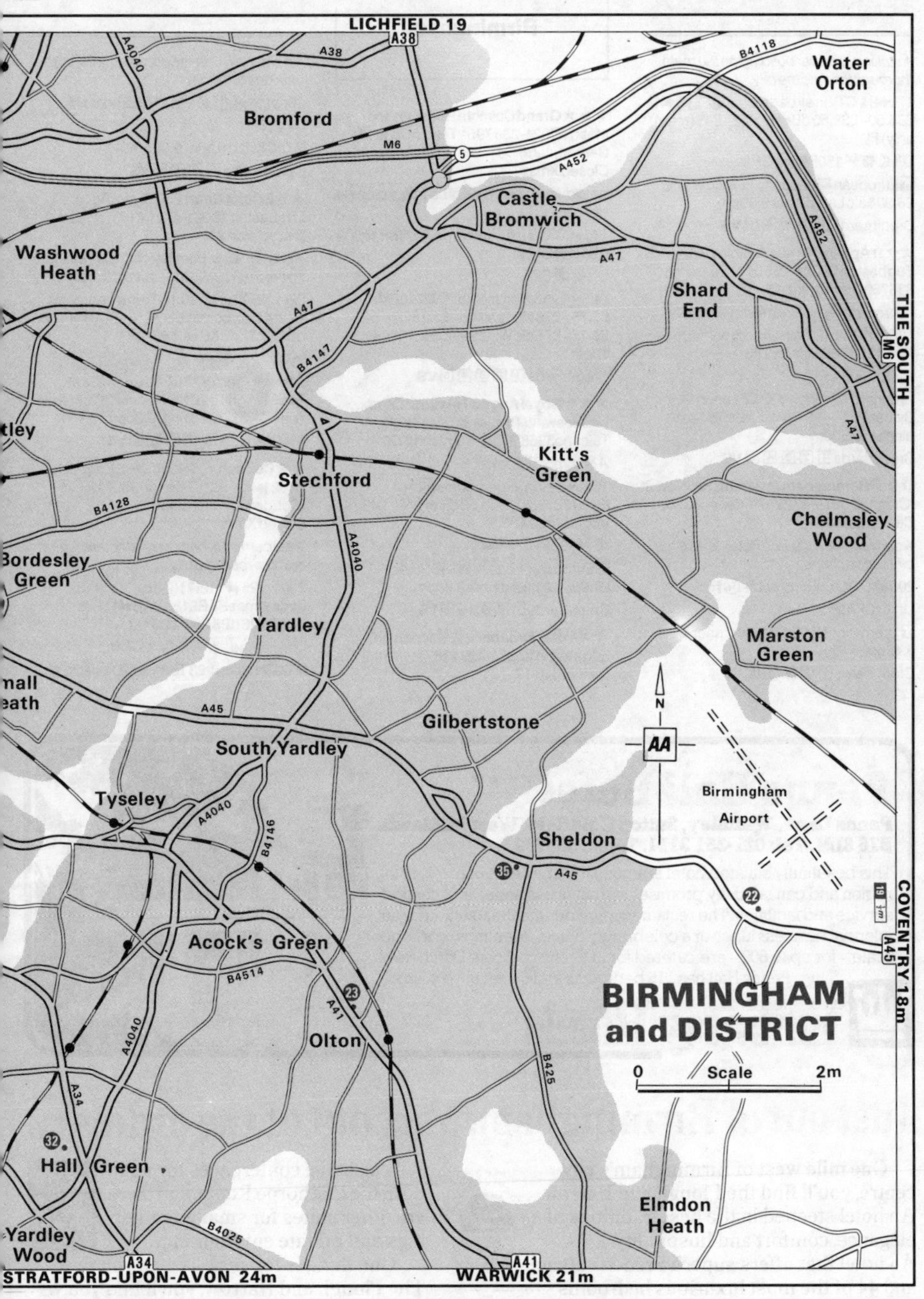

LICHFIELD 19
A38
A4040
Bromford
M6
5
A452
B4118
Water Orton
Castle Bromwich
Washwood Heath
A47
Shard End
THE SOUTH
B4147
tley
Stechford
Kitt's Green
B4128
A4040
Chelmsley Wood
Bordesley Green
Yardley
Marston Green
mall eath
A45
Gilbertstone
N
AA
South Yardley
Birmingham Airport
Tyseley
A4040
B4146
Sheldon
35
A45
22
19
COVENTRY 18m
A45
Acock's Green
B4514
23
A41
BIRMINGHAM and DISTRICT
A4040
Olton
0
Scale
2m
B425
A34
32
Hall Green
Elmdon Heath
Yardley Wood
B4025
A34
A41
STRATFORD-UPON-AVON 24m
WARWICK 21m

30 Plough & Harrow ❀★★★★
31 Le Provençal ✕
32 Skittles ✕
33 Strathallan Thistle ☆☆☆☆
34 West Bromwich Moat House ☆☆☆
(listed under West Bromwich)
35 Wheatsheaf ★★

A striking, circular building on the main thoroughfare into the city.

170 CTV in all bedrooms Ⓡ ✱sB £35.50–£38.50 dB £42–£45 (room only) B

Lift ☾ # 150P 93 CFA

European ✱Lunch £6&alc Dinner £8.50&alc Last dinner 9.30pm

Credit cards 1 2 3 4 5 VS

☆☆☆**Apollo** 243–247 Hagley Rd, Edgbaston ☎021-455 0271 Telex no 336759 District plan **18**

A three-storey hotel on the main road.

126 (7fb) CTV in all bedrooms Ⓡ sB £37 dB £49 B

Lift ☾ 130P CFA

English & French V Lunch fr£9 Dinner £7.50–£9.70 Wine £4.75 Last dinner 10.30pm

Credit cards 1 2 3 4 5 VS

☆☆☆***Birmingham International*** New St (Crest) ☎021-643 2747 Telex no 338331 Central plan **3** *D4*

A conveniently situated hotel, above the city centre shops.

200 CTV in all bedrooms Ⓡ B

Lift ☾ CFA

International V Last dinner 9.45pm

Credit cards 1 2 3 4 5

★★★**Grand** Colmore Row (Queens Moat) ☎021-236 7951 Telex no 338174 Central plan **6** *D5*
Closed Xmas

An old, traditional type of building, close to city centre.

145 CTV in all bedrooms Ⓡ sB&B £39 dB&B £48 B

Lift ☾ CFA

English & Continental Lunch £6.75–£7&alc Tea 75p–£1.75 Dinner £6.75–£7&alc Wine £5.40 Last dinner 10pm

Credit cards 1 2 3 4 5 VS

★★★**Royal Angus Thistle** St Chads, Queensway (Thistle) ☎021-236 4211 Telex no 336889 Central plan **16** *D6*

A busy hotel, above the central car park.

139 CTV in all bedrooms Ⓡ ✱sB £33.50–£36.50 dB £40–£43 (room only) B

☾ 700 CFA

European ✱Lunch £6.85 Dinner £7.90&alc Last dinner 9.30pm

Credit cards 1 2 3 4 5 VS

★★***Hotel Annabelle*** 19 Sandon Rd, Edgbaston ☎021-429 1182 District plan **17**

A personally-managed, small hotel on the outskirts of the city.

16rm (11 4) TV in all bedrooms B CTV 18P

V Last dinner 9.30pm

Credit cards 1 2 4 5 VS

★★**Bristol Court** 250 Bristol Rd, Edgbaston ☎021-472 0413 District plan **20**

A comfortable, commercial hotel, located on the ring road to the south of the city.

32rm (3 10) (2fb) CTV in 4 bedrooms TV in 4 bedrooms sB&B £18 sB&B £20 dB&B £32 dB&B £36 B

CTV 25P 3

Mainly grills V ✱Lunch £3&alc Tea £1 High Tea £1.50 Dinner fr£3.75&alc Wine £4.25 Last dinner 9.30pm

S% Credit cards 1 2 3 5 VS

★★**Cobden** 166 Hagley Rd, Edgbaston ☎021-454 6621 Telex no 339715 (Cobden) District plan **21**
Closed Xmas

A modernised, commercial hotel situated on main road into city.

210rm (25 112) (24fb) CTV in 137 bedrooms sB&B £13 sB&B £26 dB&B £26 dB&B £37 B

Unlicensed Lift ☾ CTV 130P

V Lunch fr£3 Tea fr70p Dinner fr£6

→

Last dinner 8.45pm
S% Credit cards 1 2 3

★★**New Imperial** Temple St
☎021-643 6751 Telex no 57515 Central plan **14** *D4*
97rm(9⇌)(2fb) CTV in all bedrooms ® sB&B£19.60–£21.80 sB&B⇌£25.40–£28.20 dB&B£30.10–£33.45 dB&B⇌£37.60–£41.80 B
Lift ☾ CTV *xmas*
Lunch £4 Tea 60p Dinner £6.50 Wine £3.59 Last dinner 9.30pm
Credit cards 1 2 3 5 **VS**

★★**Norfolk** 257/267 Hagley Rd, Edgbaston ☎021-454 8071 Telex no 339715 (Norfolk) District plan **28**
Closed Xmas
A large, modernised hotel on busy road into city.
180rm(32⇌56⋒)(8fb) CTV in 88 bedrooms sB&B£13 sB&B⇌⋒£24.50 dB&B£26 dB&B⇌⋒£35 B
Unlicensed Lift ☾ CTV 130P ✽ ♿
V Lunch fr£3 Tea fr70p Dinner fr£6 Last dinner 8.45pm (7.45pm Sat & Sun)
Credit cards 1 2 3

★★**Wheatsheaf** Coventry Rd, Sheldon (Ansells) ☎021-743 2021 District plan **35**
100rm(84⋒) CTV in all bedrooms ® sB&B fr£23.75 sB&B⋒ fr£28.75 dB&B⋒ fr£34.25 B
☾ CTV 120P
Lunch fr£6&alc Dinner fr£6.50&alc Wine £3.90 Last dinner 10pm
Credit cards 1 2 3 **VS**

✕✕***Le Biarritz*** 148/9 Bromsgrove St
☎021-622 1989 Central plan **2** *D2*
Closed Sun & Public hols Lunch not served Sat
French 50 seats Last dinner 10.30pm
Credit cards 1 2 3 5

✕✕***La Capanna*** Hurst St
☎021-622 2287 Central plan **4** *D2*
Closed Sun & Bank hol Mons
Italian **V** 60 seats Last dinner 11.15pm 12P
Credit cards 1 2 3 4 5

✕✕**Chung Ying** 16/18 Wrottesley St
☎021-622 5669 Central plan **5** *D3*
Cantonese 250 seats Lunch £5&alc Dinner £7&alc Wine £4.50 Last dinner 11.45pm 10P
S% Credit cards 1 2 3 5

✕✕***House of Mr Chan*** 167 Bromsgrove St ☎021-643 1725 Central plan **9** *E2*
Cantonese 85 seats
Credit cards 1 2 5

✕✕**Lorenzo's** Park St ☎021-643 0541 Central plan **10** *E3*
Closed Sun & Public hols
Lunch not served Sat
Dinner not served Mon
Italian 60 seats Lunch £5.50&alc Dinner £13.50alc Wine £4.30 Last dinner 11pm
S% Credit cards 1 2 3 5

✕✕***New Happy Gathering*** 43–45 Station St ☎021-643 5247 Central plan **13** *D3*
Closed Xmas
Cantonese 100 seats Last dinner 11.45pm
Credit cards 2 5

✕✕***New World*** 308 Bull Ring Centre, Small Brook Ringway
☎021-643 0033 Central plan **7** *E3*
Cantonese 150 seats Last dinner 11pm
Credit cards 2 3 5

✕✕**Rajdoot** 12–22 Albert St
☎021-643 8805 Central plan **15** *E4*
Lunch not served Sun & Public hols
Indian **V** 80 seats

✕**Franzl's** 151 Milcote Rd, Bearwood (3½m W off A4123) ☎021-429 7920 District plan **24**
Closed Sun, Mon & Aug Lunch not served
Austrian 32 seats ✻Dinner £10alc Wine £5.10 Last dinner 10.30pm
Credit cards 1 3

✕***Giovanni's*** 27 Poplar Rd, King's Heath
☎021-443 2391 District plan **25**
Closed Sun, Mon, last 2wks Feb & Jul
English & Italian. 52 seats Last dinner 10.30pm
Credit cards 1 2 3 5

✕**Grapevine** 2–3 Edgbaston Shopping Centre, Five Ways ☎021-454 0672 District plan **26**
Closed Sun
Vegetarian/Wholefood Unlicensed 75 seats ✻Lunch £3alc Dinner £6.75alc Last dinner 9pm 100P
S% Credit cards 1 3

✕**Maharaja** 23–25 Hurst St
☎021-622 2641 Central plan **11** *D2*
Closed Sun
North Indian **V** 65 seats ✻Lunch £3.80alc Dinner £7alc Wine £3.95 Last dinner 11.30pm
Credit cards 1 2 3 5

✕**Michelle** 182–184 High St, Harborne (4m W off A456) ☎021-426 4133 District plan **27**
Closed Sun
French **V** 80 seats ✻Lunch £2.65–£7.80&alc Dinner £6.96–£7.80&alc Wine £4.80 Last dinner 10pm

✕**Pinocchio's** 8 Chad Sq, Edgbaston
☎021-454 8672 District plan **29**
Closed Sun
Italian 45 seats ✻Lunch £3.75–£4.90&alc Dinner £9.50alc Wine £4.40 Last dinner 10.30pm 40P

✕**Le Provençal** 1 Albany Rd, Harborne (4m W off A456) ☎021-426 2444 District plan **31**
Closed Sun, Xmas & Public hols Lunch not served Sat & Mon
French 50 seats Lunch £4&alc Dinner £8alc Wine £5.30 Last dinner 10pm
Credit cards 1 3 5

✕**Skittles** 1347 Stratford Rd, Hall Green
☎021-777 3185 District plan **32**
Closed Mon, Boxing day–2 Jan & 1st 2wks Jul
Lunch not served Sat
Dinner not served Sun
English & French 42 seats ✻Lunch

£2.85–£5.15&alc Dinner £7.50&alc Wine £4.50 Last dinner 10pm 4P

Credit cards 1 2 3 5

✕La Villa Biançа 1036 Stratford Rd, Monkspath, Shirley (6m S A34) ☎021-744 7232 Not on plan

Closed Mon

Lunch not served Sat

English & Italian 47 seats *Lunch £3.15&alc Dinner £6.30alc Wine £4.15 Last dinner 11.30pm 30P

Credit cards 1 2 3 5

At **Barr, Great**

★★★**Barr** Pear Tree Dr, off Newton Rd (1m W junc A34/A4041) (Greenall Whitley) ☎021-357 1141 Not on plan

111 250P

☆☆☆**Post House** Chapel Ln (At junc M6/A34) (Trusthouse Forte) ☎021-357 7444 Not on plan

204 280P

BIRMINGHAM AIRPORT

W Midlands

Map **7** SP18

★★★★**Excelsior** Coventry Rd, Elmdon (Trusthouse Forte) ☎021-743 8141 Telex no 338005 Birmingham District plan **22**

This luxurious building is conveniently situated at the entrance to Birmingham Airport.

141 CTV in all bedrooms Ⓡ sB&B£40.50 dB&B£55

☾ # 200P CFA

Last dinner 10.15pm

Credit cards 1 2 3 4 5

BIRMINGHAM (NATIONAL EXHIBITION CENTRE)

West Midlands

Map **7** SP18

★★***Arden Motel*** Coventry Rd, Bickenhill Village, Solihull (A45) ☎Hampton-in-Arden (067 55) 3221 Birmingham District plan **19**

46 CTV in all bedrooms Ⓡ

Lift ☾ CTV 150P CFA

Credit cards 1 2 3 **VS**

BISHOP AUCKLAND

Co Durham

Map **8** NZ22

★★**Binchester Hall** ☎(0388) 604646

Busy commercial hotel in pleasant rural setting.

21rm(2 8) (1fb) sB&B£11 sB&B £15 dB&B£20 dB&B £22

CTV 150P Disco twice wkly

English & French **V** Lunch £2.50alc Dinner £5alc Wine £3.20 Last dinner 9.30pm

VS

★★***Kings Arms*** 36 Market Pl ☎(0388) 661296 Closed Xmas & New Year

A rambling, former coaching inn, overlooking the market square.

14rm(13 1) CTV in all bedrooms Ⓡ

9P

English & Continental **V** Last dinner 9pm

Credit cards 1 2 3 5

★★***HB Park Head*** New Coundon (1m N on A688) ☎(0388) 661727

Comfortable, modernised hotel with attractive bars and good food.

12rm(10 2) Annexe: 6rm CTV in all bedrooms Ⓡ

English & French **V** Last dinner 10.30pm

Credit cards 1 2 3 5

★★**Queens Head** Market Pl ☎(0388) 603477

10rm(1 1) CTV in all bedrooms Ⓡ *sB&B fr£12 sB&B fr£14.50 dB&B fr£18 dB&B fr£20

45P

*Lunch fr£2&alc Dinner fr£5.50&alc Wine £3.25 Last dinner 9.30pm

Credit cards 1 2 3

★***Grand*** Holdforth Crest, Southchurch Rd ☎(0388) 661610

5 CTV in all bedrooms

CTV 70P

Mainly grills **V** Last dinner 10pm

Credit cards 1 3

BISHOPBRIGGS

Strathclyde *Lanarkshire*

Map **11** NS67

✕✕**Iram Tandoori** 4 Woodhill Rd ☎041-772 1073

Tandoori barbecue cooking is the speciality of this modern restaurant.

Lunch not served Sat & Sun

Indian 75 seats Dinner £3.50–£4.50 Wine £2.95 Last dinner 11.30pm 50P

Credit cards 1 2 3 5

BISHOP'S LYDEARD

Somerset

Map **3** ST12

✕**Rose Cottage Inn** ☎(0823) 432394

Closed Sun, Mon, 1st 2wks Nov & 2wks from 24 Dec

English & French **V** 35 seats *Lunch £5alc Dinner £9alc Wine £5.90 Last dinner 9.30pm 20P

BISHOP'S STORTFORD

Hertfordshire

Map **5** TL42

★★★***Foxley*** Foxley Dr, Stansted Rd ☎(0279) 53977 Closed 1wk after Xmas

Traditional country-style hotel on town outskirts.

9 Annexe: 2rm(1) CTV in 9 bedrooms TV in 2 bedrooms

CTV 30P

English & French Last dinner 9.30pm

Credit cards 1 3

★**Brook House** Northgate End ☎(0279) 57892

24rm(10 12) (4fb) CTV in all bedrooms *sB&B£17.50 sB&B £18.50 dB&B £24

CTV 28P 4

English & French **V** *Lunch £5–£8&alc Tea fr£1.25 Dinner £6–£10&alc Wine £3.75 Last dinner 9pm

BLACKBECK

Cumbria

Map **11** NY00

★★***Blackbeck Inn*** ☎Beckermet (094684) 661

Closed Xmas day

A converted Georgian farmhouse with one and a half acres of paddock.

22rm(20 2) 1 CTV in all bedrooms Ⓡ

CTV 100P

Mainly grills **V** Last dinner 9.30pm

Credit cards 1 2 3

BLACKBURN

Lancashire

Map **7** SD62

★★★***Saxon Inn*** Preston New Rd (Saxon Inn) ☎(0254) 64441

RS Xmas–New Year

95 CTV in all bedrooms Ⓡ sB&B £29.25 dB&B £41.50

Lift ☾ 250P CFA (heated) Live music and dancing Fri & Sat

English & French **V** Lunch £5.50&alc Tea fr£1.50 Dinner fr£6–£6.50&alc Wine £5.90 Last dinner 10.15pm

Credit cards 1 2 3 5 **VS**

See advert on page 122

★★**Millstone** Church Ln, Mellor (3m NW) ☎Mellor (025481) 3333

15rm(5 9) (1fb) CTV in all bedrooms Ⓡ sB&B £13.50–£24.95 dB&B £24.50–£36

35P

English, French & Italian **V** Bar lunch £2.50alc Tea £1.25alc Dinner £6.95&alc Wine £3.95 Last dinner 9.45pm

Credit cards 1 2 3 5

★★**Witton Bank** Spring Ln ☎(0254) 61598 RS Xmas wk (B&B only)

16rm(4 1) (3fb) Ⓡ sB&B£13.80 sB&B £17.25 dB&B£23 dB&B £25.30

CTV 25P

V Lunch fr£4.10 Tea 50p Dinner fr£4.10 Wine £3.85 Last dinner 8pm

BLACKPOOL
Lancashire
Map **7** SD33

☆☆☆☆**Pembroke** North Promenade ☎(0253) 23434 Telex no 677469

Large modern sea front hotel with spacious rooms and swimming pool.

205➡ (6fb) CTV in all bedrooms Ⓡ sB&B➡£27–£32.50 dB&B➡£39.60–£47 Ᵽ

Lift ☾ CTV 300P ▭(heated) Disco 5 nights wkly Live music and dancing wkly Cabaret wkly *xmas*

English & French ✿ ▭ Lunch £5.75 Tea £1.95&alc Dinner £6.75&alc Wine £4.75 Last dinner 10pm

Credit cards 1 2 3 4 5

★★★**New Clifton** Talbot Sq (Prince of Wales) ☎(0253) 21481 Telex no 67415

A large four-storey building on the promenade overlooking the North Pier.

78rm(77➡1⋔) (3fb) CTV in all bedrooms Ⓡ✱sB&B➡⋔£27 dB&B➡⋔£41 Ᵽ

Lift ☾ ⁄ CFA Disco Thu, Fri & Sat Live music and dancing Thu, Fri & Sat *xmas*

English & Italian V ✿ ▭ ✱Lunch £5&alc Tea 85palc Dinner £5alc Wine £3.60 Last dinner 11pm

Credit cards 1 2 3 5 **VS**

★★★**Savoy** North Shore, Queens Prom ☎(0253) 52561 Telex no 67570

Large, impressive sea-front hotel.

128rm(96➡19⋔) (16fb) CTV in all bedrooms Ⓡ sB&B£16–£20 sB&B➡⋔£17–£21 dB&B£32–£40 dB&B➡⋔£34–£42 Ᵽ

Lift ☾ CTV 40P CFA Live music and dancing Sat (& 5 nights in season) Cabaret 4 nights wkly in season *xmas*

English & French ✿ Lunch £4.25–£6 Dinner £6.50–£9&alc Wine £4 Last dinner 11.30pm

Credit cards 1 2 3 5 **VS**

★★**Carlton** North Prom ☎(0253) 28966 Closed Xmas wk

Sea front hotel with a gabled roof and modern frontage.

58rm(33➡5⋔) (5fb) CTV in all bedrooms Ⓡ sB&B£10–£18 sB&B➡⋔£12–£24 dB&B£30–£38 dB&B➡⋔£35–£45 Ᵽ

Lift ☾ 50P Live music and dancing Sat

English & French V ✿ ▭ Bar lunch £1.50–£3.50 Tea 50p–£1.20 Dinner £5.75–£6.50&alc Wine £2.95 Last dinner 8.45pm

Credit cards 1 2 3 5

★★**Chequers** 24 Queens Prom ☎(0253) 56431 Telex no 67570 (Ref AA122)
Closed 1–14 Jan

This hotel is situated on the north shore sea front.

46rm(41➡5⋔) (9fb) CTV in all bedrooms Ⓡ sB&B➡⋔£20.50–£22.60 dB&B➡⋔£33–£36.40 Ᵽ

Lift ☾ CTV 17P 3⌂ ⌂ *xmas*

English & French ✿ ▭ Bar lunch 70p–£3 Tea 50p–£1 Dinner £6 Wine £3.30 Last dinner 7.45pm

Credit cards 1 2 3 5 **VS**

★★**Claremont** 270 North Prom ☎(0253) 293122

A large well-furnished sea front hotel.

145➡ (60fb) CTV in all bedrooms Ⓡ ✱sB➡£10.75–£11.25 dB➡£21.50–£22.50 (room only) Ᵽ

Lift ☾ ⌗ 80P CFA Disco nightly Live music and dancing in season *xmas*

English & French ✿ ▭ ✱Lunch fr90p Tea fr30p Dinner fr£6.25 Wine £3.40 Last dinner 8pm

Credit cards 1 2 3 **VS**

★★**Cliffs** Queens Prom ☎(0253) 52388

168rm(82➡) (12fb) CTV in all bedrooms Ⓡ sB&B£10.50–£15 sB&B➡£13.50–£18 dB&B£21–£30 dB&B➡£27–£36 Ᵽ

Lift ☾ CTV 70P billiards Live music and dancing nightly (in season) Cabaret Sun *xmas*

English & French ✿ ▭ Lunch £3.25–£3.75 Tea 50p Dinner £6.50–£7&alc Wine

£3.95 Last dinner 10pm
Credit cards 1 2 3 VS

★★**Gables Balmoral** Balmoral Rd ☎(0253) 45432
A commercial and tourist hotel with modern bedrooms situated close to the pleasure beach.
70rm(62⇌8⋒) (20fb) 1 CTV in 24 bedrooms sB&B⇌⋒£16.50–£18 dB&B⇌⋒£29–£33 B
☾ CTV 4P CFA sauna bath *xmas*
Lunch fr£3.75 Tea fr65p High Tea fr£1.75 Dinner £6alc Wine £3.80 Last dinner 9.30pm
Credit cards 1 2 3 5 VS

★★***Headlands*** New South Prom ☎(0253) 41179 Closed 12–30 Nov
A pleasant family hotel, situated on the south shore sea front.
54rm(13⇌) B
Lift CTV 38P 8
Last dinner 8pm

★**Kimberley** New South Prom ☎(0253) 41184 Closed 2–15 Jan
A family hotel with modern furnishings, located on the sea front.
56rm(27⇌2⋒) (14fb) CTV in 3 bedrooms sB&B fr£10.75 sB&B⇌⋒ fr£11.75 dB&B fr£21.50 dB&B⇌⋒ fr£23.50
Lift ☾ CTV 20P *xmas*

V Lunch fr£3.25 Tea fr40p Dinner fr£3.95 Wine £3.40 Last dinner 7.30pm
Credit cards 1 3 VS

★**Revill's** North Prom ☎(0253) 25768
A tall sea-front hotel close to the town centre.
53rm(8⇌) (7fb) Ⓡ sB&B£10.35–£11.50 sB&B⇌£12.65–£13.80 dB&B£20.70–£23 dB&B⇌£25.30–£27.60 B
Lift ☾ CTV 15P billiards *xmas*
Tea 45p Dinner £5–£6 Wine £4 Last dinner 7.30pm
Credit cards 1 3 VS

BLACKWATERFOOT
Isle of Arran, Strathclyde *Bute*
Map **10** NR92

★★***Kinloch*** (Inter-Hotels) ☎Shiskine (077086) 286
A two-storey hotel with a modern extension, standing on the coast overlooking Kilbrannan Sound.
55rm(25⇌) CTV available in bedrooms Ⓡ B
CTV 50P CFA (heated) squash sauna bath
Last dinner 8pm
Credit cards 2 3

BLACKWOOD
Gwent
Map **3** ST19

★★★**Maes Manor** ☎(0495) 224551
A converted country house standing in its own grounds.
10rm(7⇌) Annexe: 16rm(10⇌) (2fb) CTV available in bedrooms Ⓡ sB&B£24 sB&B⇌£26 dB&B£35.50 dB&B⇌£37.50 B
☾ 200P Disco Thu Live music and dancing Sat Cabaret Sat
Welsh, English & French V Lunch £4–£7&alc Tea £1.25–£2.50 Dinner £4–£7&alc Wine £4.50 Last dinner 9.30pm
Credit cards 1 2 3 5 VS

BLAGDON
Avon
Map **3** ST55

★★★**Mendip** ☎(0761) 62688
A modern split-level building, set on a hill overlooking the lake.
50rm(37⇌13⋒) (2fb) CTV in all bedrooms sB&B⇌⋒ fr£23 dB&B⇌⋒ fr£34 B
CTV 200P CFA
Lunch fr£6.35&alc Tea fr£1.75 Dinner fr£8.65&alc Wine £4.50 Last dinner 9.30pm
Credit cards 1 2 3 5

BLAIR ATHOLL
Tayside *Perthshire*
Map **14** NN86

★★**Atholl Arms** ☎(079681) 205
A large greystone roadside hotel, built and furnished in traditional Scottish style.
29rm(8→1⋒)(2fb) 1⊟ sB&B£10.50–£11 sB&B→⋒£12–£12.50 dB&B£21–£22 dB&B→⋒£24–£25 ⊟
CTV 30P 2⌂ ✽
Scottish & French ♀ ⊟ Bar lunch £1.40–£3 Tea 70p–£1 Dinner £7–£7.25&alc Wine £3.20 Last dinner 8.30pm
Credit cards 1 3 5

BLAIRGOWRIE
Tayside *Perthshire*
Map **15** NO14

★★**Angus** ☎(0250) 2838 Telex no 76526
Busy town centre hotel with its own sporting facilities.
82→(2fb) CTV in all bedrooms Ⓡ sB&B→£14–£18 dB&B→£28–£36 ⊟
Lift CFA ⊡(heated) squash billiards sauna bath Disco wkly in season Live music and dancing wkly in season Cabaret wkly in season *xmas*
V ♀ ⊟ Lunch £5 Tea 80p High Tea fr£1.25 Dinner £7.50 Wine £3.25 Last dinner 8.30pm
Credit cards 1 2 3

✿★★ *H* **Kinloch House** ☎Essendy (025084) 237
(Rosette awarded for dinner only)
9rm(5→2⋒)(1fb) 3⊟ Ⓡ sB&B£15.50 sB&B→⋒£18 dB&B£29 dB&B→⋒£33
CTV 50P ✽
V ♀ ⊟ Bar lunch £2.10–£4.60 Tea £1 Dinner £9.50&alc Wine £3.95 Last dinner 9.15pm
Credit cards 1 2 5

★★**Rosemount Golf** Golf Course Rd, Rosemount ☎(0250) 2604
A friendly, family run hotel set in its own spacious grounds close to Rosemount Golf Course.
12rm(7→5⋒)(2fb) TV in all bedrooms Ⓡ sB&B→⋒£11 dB&B→⋒£22
TV 70P ✽
V ♀ ⊟ Lunch £3.50alc Tea £1alc High Tea £3.50alc Dinner £5alc Wine £2.95 Last dinner 10pm
VS

★**Golf View** Perth Rd, Rosemount ☎(0250) 2895
This cosy little hotel is popular with golfers and skiers.
6rm(3→1⋒)(1fb) CTV in 3 bedrooms TV in 4 bedrooms Ⓡ sB&B£12 dB&B£21 dB&B→⋒£26–£28 ⊟
CTV 70P
Scottish & International V Lunch £3.50 High Tea £2.50–£6 Dinner £4–£7.95 Wine £3.50 Last dinner 9.30pm
Credit cards 1 2 3 5 VS

BLAIRLOGIE
Central *Stirlingshire*
Map **11** NS89

✕✕**Blairlogie House Hotel** ☎Alva (0259) 61441
A warm and friendly house standing in its own tidy grounds.
Dinner not served Sun
Scottish & French V 50 seats Lunch £6&alc Tea £1 Dinner £8–£13&alc Wine £5.40 Last dinner 9.30pm 40P bedrooms available
Credit cards 1 3 VS

BLAKENEY
Gloucestershire
Map **3** SO60

★**Old Severn Bridge** Etloe (2m S on north bank of River Severn) ☎Dean (0594) 42454
8rm(2→) CTV in 6 bedrooms Ⓡ sB&B£11.50 sB&B→£13.50 dB&B£21 dB&B→£25 ⊟
40P ✽
V ♀ ⊟ Lunch £3.50–£5&alc Tea 50p–£1

Dinner £5&alc Last dinner 10pm

Credit cards 1 2 3 5 VS

BLAKENEY
Norfolk
Map **9** TG04

★★★**Blakeney** Quayside (Best Western) ☎Cley (0263) 740797

41rm(24⇌2⋒) Annexe: 13⇌(6fb) CTV in all bedrooms Ⓡ sB&B£17–£22 sB&B⇌⋒£19–£29 dB&B£32–£44 dB&B⇌⋒£36–£46 B

☾ CTV CFA ✽ (heated) sauna bath *xmas* ♿

V ♉ Bar lunch £1.50–£4.15 Tea £1 Dinner £8.20&alc Wine £4.60 Last dinner 9.30pm

Credit cards 1 2 3 5

★★**Manor** ☎Cley (0263) 740376 Closed 12–25 Nov & Xmas wk

8⇌(1fb) CTV in all bedrooms Ⓡ sB&B⇌£21.88 dB&B⇌£37.95–£41.25 B

60P ✽

V ♉ Lunch £5 Tea £1.50 High Tea £1.75 Dinner £7 Wine £3.50 Last dinner 8.45pm

S%

BLANCHLAND
Northumberland
Map **12** NY95

★★**Lord Crewe Arms** (Swallow) ☎(043475) 251 Telex no 53168 RS Jan–Feb

Once part of a medieval monastery, this is now a friendly village inn.

5rm(3⇌2⋒) Annexe 12rm(5⇌) 1 Ⓡ sB&B£16–£20 sB&B⇌⋒£20–£24 dB&B£28–£33 dB&B⇌⋒£32–£38 B

CTV 15P ✽ *xmas*

♉ Lunch £5.50–£5.75 Tea 50p Dinner £8.50 Wine £4.75 Last dinner 9.15pm

Credit cards 1 2 3 5 VS

BLANDFORD FORUM
Dorset
Map **3** ST80

★★★**Crown** 1 West St ☎(0258) 56626

A Georgian building in the centre of town near to the shops, yet with rural views on one side across the river.

28rm(27⇌1⋒) 1 CTV in all bedrooms Ⓡ sB&B⇌⋒£22–£28 dB&B⇌⋒£34–£45 B

60P 4 *xmas*

English & French V ♉ Lunch fr£5.50&alc Tea fr60p Dinner fr£8&alc Wine £4.75 Last dinner 9pm

Credit cards 1 2 3 5

★★***Anvil*** Pimperne (2m NE A354) ☎(0258) 53431 Closed Boxing Day

Thatched cottage-style hotel with beamed ceilings and a pleasant garden.

8rm(4⇌2⋒)

CTV 35P ✽ (heated)

V ♉ Last dinner 10.30pm

Credit cards 1 2 3 5

✕✕**La Belle Alliance** Portman Lodge, Whitecliff Mill St ☎(0258) 52842

Closed Sun Lunch not served

French V 25 seats Dinner £10alc Wine £4.20 Last dinner 10pm 8P bedrooms available

Credit cards 1 5

BLEADNEY
Somerset
Map **3** ST44

✕**Stradlings** ☎Wells (0749) 73576

Closed Mon Lunch not served Tue–Sat

English & French 46 seats ✱ Lunch fr£3.75 Dinner £8alc Wine £4.20 Last dinner 9.30pm 50P

Credit cards 1 3 VS

BLEADON
Avon
Map **3** ST35

✕***La Casita*** Bridgwater St ☎(0934) 812326

English & French 50 seats Last dinner 10pm 40P

Credit cards 1 2 3 5

BLICKLING
Norfolk
Map **9** TG12

✕**Buckinghamshire Arms Hotel** ☎Aylsham (026373) 2133

A country inn adjoining Blickling Hall.

French V 45 seats Dinner £10alc Wine £5 Last dinner 9.30pm 100P bedrooms available

Credit cards 1 2 3 5 VS

BLOCKLEY
Gloucestershire
Map **4** SP13

❀★★**Lower Brook House** ☎(0386) 700286 Closed 16–31 Jan

(Rosette awarded for dinner only)

A charming small cottage style hotel, with comfortable, pretty bedrooms.

8rm(5⇌1⋒) (1fb) CTV available in bedrooms Ⓡ sB&B£31–£32 sB&B⇌⋒£32.50–£34 dB&B£63–£66 dB&B⇌⋒£65–£68 (incl. dinner) B

10P ✽ *xmas*

English & French V ♉ Lunch £5alc Dinner £12.50alc Wine £5 Last dinner 9.30pm

Credit card 1

BLOFIELD
Norfolk
Map **5** TG30

✕✕**La Locanda** Fox Ln ☎Norwich (0603) 713787

Closed Sun, Public hols & 2wks annual holiday Lunch not served Sat

Italian 45 seats Lunch fr£4.85&alc Dinner £10alc Wine £5.75 Last dinner 11pm 20P

Credit cards 1 2 3 5

BLOXHAM
Oxfordshire
Map **4** SP43

★★**Olde School** Church St (Minotel) ☎Banbury (0295) 720369

One-time village school with small, well-equipped bedrooms and professional restaurant. →

11rm(4➡7⚐)CTV available in all bedrooms ® ✱ sB&B£13–£30 sB&B➡⚐£13–£30 dB&B➡⚐£20–£46 B

CTV 50P ⌂

V ♁ ☐ Lunch £4.80–£9.50&alc Tea £1–£1.50 High Tea £2–£4 Dinner £5.50–£7.50&alc Wine £4.70 Last dinner 10pm

Credit cards 1 2 3 5 **VS**

BLUE ANCHOR
Somerset
Map **3** ST04

★**Langbury** ☎ Dunster (064382) 375
Closed last 2wks Oct

A small holiday hotel with its own garden, overlooking the bay.

9rm(3⚐)(2fb) sB&B£9 sB&B⚐£12 dB&B£18 dB&B⚐£21 B

CTV 9P ✱ ✿ ≋ (unheated)

♁ Bar lunch fr£1.50 Dinner £5.50–£6 Wine £3.50 Last dinner 7.30pm

BLUNDELLSANDS
Merseyside
Map **7** SJ39

★★★**Blundellsands** Serpentine (Whitbread West Pennines)
☎ 051-924 6515 Liverpool plan **2** *B8*

An Edwardian red brick building situated in a quiet suburban area.

44rm(24➡4⚐)(1fb) CTV in all bedrooms sB&B£21 sB&B➡⚐£24 dB&B£34 dB&B➡⚐£39 B

Lift ☾ CTV 200P ✱ Disco Mon

V ♁ ☐ Lunch £6.50&alc Tea 75p Dinner £7.50&alc Wine £4 Last dinner 9pm

S% Credit cards 1 2 3 5

BLYTH
Nottinghamshire
Map **8** SK68

★★***Fourways*** ☎ (090976) 235

12rm sB&B£18 dB&B£25 B

CTV 60P 2⌂ ✿ Live music and dancing Sat

☐ English & French. V ♁ ☐ Last dinner 9.30pm

Credit cards 1 2 3 4 **VS**

✗✗**Charnwood at Blyth** Oldcotes Rd ☎ (090976) 610
Closed Mon

☐ International **V** 70 seats ✱ Lunch £4.25–£7.50&alc Dinner £7.50–£9.50&alc Wine £4.30 Last dinner 10pm 80P Disco Sat & Sun

Credit cards 1 2 3 5

BOAT OF GARTEN
Highland *Inverness-shire*
Map **14** NH91

★★★**Boat** (Inter-Hotel) ☎ (047983) 258
Closed Nov & Dec

A village centre hotel standing beside the Strathspey Railway Station, overlooking golf course and close to River Spey.

36rm(25➡9⚐)(3fb) CTV in all bedrooms ® sB&B£13.25–£18 sB&B➡⚐£14.75–£19.50 dB&B£26.50–£36 dB&B➡⚐£29.50–£39 B

30P CFA ✿ ⌂ *xmas*

V ♁ ☐ Lunch £5–£6&alc Tea 75p Dinner £8–£9.50 Wine £3.83 Last dinner 9pm

Credit cards 1 2 3 5

★★**Craigard** Kinchurdy Rd ☎ (047983) 206

This late-Victorian shooting lodge was converted to a hotel in 1931. It is set in 2½ acres of grounds with direct access to the golf course.

22rm(7➡1⚐)(5fb) sB&B£12–£15 dB&B£24–£30 dB&B➡⚐£26–£32 B

CTV 30P 4⌂ ✱ ✿ ⌂ *xmas*

V ♁ Bar lunch £1.50–£3.50 Dinner £7.50–£8.50 Last dinner 8pm

Credit cards 1 2 3 5 **VS**

BODELWYDDAN
Clwyd
Map **6** SJ07

✗✗***Faenol Fawr Manor*** ☎ Rhuddlan (0745) 590784

Impressive manor house set in its own grounds.

V 60 seats Last dinner 9.30pm 300P bedrooms available ✗ Disco Tue & Thu–Sat Live music and dancing Tue & Thu–Sat Cabaret Tue & Thu–Sat

Credit cards 1 2

BODINNICK
Cornwall
Map **2** SX15

★**Old Ferry Inn** ☎ Polruan (072687) 237

A comfortably appointed historic inn with commanding views, beside the River Fowey. Sailing available.

13rm(5➡)(1fb) 1 ☐ sB&B£15.50 sB&B➡£17 dB&B£31 dB&B➡£34

CTV 10P 4⌂ ✱

☐ English & French **V** ♁ Bar lunch 50p–£1.25 High Tea £3 Dinner fr£9&alc Wine £2.65 Last dinner 9.15pm

BODMIN
Cornwall
Map **2** SX06

See also Helland Bridge

★★**Allegro** 50 Higher Bore St ☎ (0208) 3480

A small, modern, comfortable hotel located in the centre of Bodmin.

12rm(2➡) TV in 9 bedrooms ✱ sB&B£12–£15 sB&B➡£18–£20 dB&B£22–£26 dB&B➡£27–£32

CTV 36P ✿

☐ Mainly grills **V** ♁ ☐ Lunch fr£3.50 Tea fr50p Dinner £8alc Wine £4.50 Last dinner 10pm

Credit cards 1 3 **VS**

★★**Westberry** Rhind St ☎ (0208) 2772
Closed Xmas & New Year

20rm(5➡)(2fb) CTV in 7 bedrooms sB&B fr£14 sB&B➡fr£19.50 dB&B fr£21 dB&B➡fr£27 B

CTV 24P

♁ ☐ Lunch £2–£4&alc Tea £1–£1.25 Dinner £6.50–£9.50 Wine £4 Last dinner 8pm

Credit cards 1 3

BOGNOR REGIS
West Sussex
Map **4** SZ99

★★★*B* **Royal Norfolk** The Esplanade (Best Western) ☎(0243) 826222 Telex no 837921

Splendid Regency building facing the sea with 3 acres of lawns and gardens.

53rm(38⇌1⋒)(7fb) 2⊟ CTV in all bedrooms ® sB&B fr£21.50 sB&B⇌ fr£35 dB&B fr£33.50 dB&B⇌ fr£47 B

Lift ☾ 150P 4⌂ CFA ✽ ≈(heated) ⚲(hard) Live music & dancing Sat ⌂ *xmas*

English & French V ♡ ☕ Lunch fr£6.50&alc Dinner fr£7.50&alc Wine £5.65 Last dinner 9.30pm

Credit cards 1 2 3 4 5 **VS**

★★**Clarehaven** Wessex Av ☎(0243) 823265

Victorian terraced building with balconies overlooking the sea.

28rm(4⇌2⋒) Annexe: 6rm sB&B£13.50–£18.50 sB&B⇌⋒£20–£25 dB&B£27–£37 dB&B⇌⋒£30.50–£40.50 B

CTV 12P Live music and dancing Fri ⌂ *xmas*

V ♡ ☕ Lunch £3.80–£5&alc Tea 50p–£1.75 Dinner £4.50–£5.50&alc Wine £3.95 Last dinner 8pm

Credit cards 1 2 3

★★**Royal** The Esplanade ☎(0243) 864665

Privately owned family hotel with an informal friendly atmosphere.

30rm(2⇌4⋒)(4fb) CTV in 18 bedrooms sB&B£12.65–£13.95 sB&B⇌⋒£17.50–£18.50 dB&B£25.30–£27.90 dB&B⇌⋒£35–£37 B

☾ CTV 6P *xmas*

English & Italian V ♡ ☕ *Lunch £2.95–£3.60 Tea 65p–£2 Dinner £3.95–£4.60 Wine £4.95 Last dinner 10pm

Credit cards 1 2 3 5 **VS**

★**Black Mill House** Princess Av ☎(0243) 821945

Quiet, friendly hotel near marine gardens.

22rm(6⇌2⋒) Annexe: 4rm (5fb) sB&B£12–£17 sB&B⇌⋒£18.50–£23.50 dB&B£22–£34 dB&B⇌⋒£25.50–£37.50 B

CTV 12P ⌂ *xmas*

V ♡ ☕ Lunch £3.50–£4.50 Tea 40p–50p Dinner £4.50–£5.50 Last dinner 7.30pm

Credit cards 1 2 3

★*H* **Lyndhurst** Selsey Av ☎(0243) 822308

Simple, modern, comfortable hotel with friendly personal service.

8rm (2fb) CTV available in bedrooms ✱ sB&B£10–£14 dB&B£20–£28 B

CTV 3P ✽ ⌂ *xmas*

BOLLINGTON
Cheshire
Map **7** SJ97

★★★**Belgrade** Jackson Ln ☎(0625) 73246 Telex no 667217

A stone built hotel within its own grounds and with a modern extension.

62⇌ (1fb) CTV in all bedrooms ® ✱ *sB&B⇌£26.50 dB&B⇌£32

☾ 250P CFA

♡ ☕ Tea £1–£1.50 Dinner £8.50&alc Wine £3.65 Last dinner 10.30pm

Credit cards 1 2 3 5 **VS**

BOLTON
Gt Manchester
Map **7** SD70

☆☆☆**Crest** Beaumont Rd (Crest) ☎(0204) 651511 Telex no 635527

A modern hotel situated on the Bolton ring road close to the M61.

100⇌ CTV in all bedrooms ® *sB⇌ fr£34 dB⇌ fr£44 (room only) B

☾ ⚡ 153P CFA

International V ♡ *Lunch £3.90–£5.75&alc Tea 65p–£1.50 High Tea £2– →

£6.50 Dinner fr£7.75&alc Wine £4.95 Last dinner 10pm

Credit cards 1 2 3 4 5 VS

★★★ B **Egerton House** Egerton (3m N A666) ☎(0204) 57171 Closed 1 Jan RS 23–31 Dec

25🛁 CTV in all bedrooms sB&B🛁£34.15 dB&B🛁£43.01 B

50P ✽

International V Lunch £6&alc Dinner £10alc Wine £4.50 Last dinner 9.30pm

Credit cards 1 2 5

★★★ **Last Drop** Hospital Rd, Bromley Cross (3m N off B6472) ☎(0204) 591131 Telex no 635322 Closed 26 Dec

This modern hotel is set within a newly-built village complex, created out of former farm buildings.

62🛁 Annexe: 7🛁 2 CTV in all bedrooms ® ✱sB&B🛁£18.50–£31 dB&B🛁£29.50–£40 B

☾ CTV 450P CFA ✽ Live music and dancing Sat

International V Lunch £5–£6&alc Tea £1.50–£3 Dinner £8–£12alc Last dinner 10.15pm

Credit cards 1 2 3 5

★★★ **Pack Horse** Bradshawgate, Nelson Sq (Greenall Whitley) ☎(0204) 27261 Telex no 635168 Closed 24 Dec–1 Jan

A modern commercial hotel situated in the town centre.

78rm (71🛁 5🚿) CTV in all bedrooms ® sB&B🛁🚿£32.50–£33.50 dB&B🛁🚿£42–£43 B

Lift ☾ CFA ♿

V Lunch £6–£7 Tea 50p–£1.50 Dinner £7.50–£8.50 Wine £4.90 Last dinner 10pm

Credit cards 1 2 3 5 VS

BOLTON ABBEY

North Yorkshire

Map 7 SE05

★★★ L **Devonshire Arms** ☎(075671) 441 Telex no 51218

Finely restored and enlarged coaching inn whose elegant mirrored restaurant features a high standard of cuisine. Friendly willing service and modern facilities. Winner, Best Newcomer, North England, page 27.

38🛁🚿 2 CTV in all bedrooms ® sB&B🛁🚿£43.50 dB&B🛁🚿£52 B

☾ CTV 100P ✽ xmas

French ✱Lunch £7.50alc Tea 75p–£1.95alc Dinner £15alc Wine £5.50 Last dinner 9.30pm

Credit cards 1 2 3 5

BOLTON-BY-BOWLAND

Lancashire

Map 7 SD74

✕ **Copy Nook** ☎(02007) 205

Dinner not served Mon

43 seats Lunch £4.25–£7.50 Dinner £4.25–£7.50 Wine £4.50 Last dinner 9.15pm 50P bedrooms available

Credit card 5

BONAR BRIDGE

Highland *Sutherland*

Map 14 NH69

★★ ***Bridge*** (Minotel) ☎Ardgay (08632) 204

Closed 1 Jan

Two-storey stone house situated on the main road, with views of Kyle of Sutherland.

16rm (4🛁 2🚿) CTV in all bedrooms ® B

20P

Last dinner 8pm

Credit cards 1 2 3 5

★★ **Caledonian** Dornoch Rd ☎Ardgay (08632) 214

7rm (6🛁🚿) Annexe: 8rm (4🛁🚿) ® sB&B£9.50–£11.50 sB&B🛁🚿£10.50–£12.50 dB&B£19–£21 dB&B🛁🚿£21–£23 B

CTV 20P ✽ Live music and dancing Sat

V Lunch £2.50–£3.50&alc Tea 50p–60p High Tea £3.75–£4.75&alc Dinner £6.75–£9&alc Wine £2.75 Last dinner 8pm

Credit cards 1 2 3 5

BONNYRIGG

Lothian *Midlothian*

Map 11 NT36

★★★★ ***HBL* Dalhousie Castle** (Prestige) ☎Gorebridge (0875) 20153 Telex no 72380

A 12th-century castle in 1000 acres offers gracious living and ancient splendour under the guidance of Mr and Mrs Saint Claire. The many public rooms are spacious and interesting, the Dungeon restaurant is a delight and bedrooms are elegant with modern features. Service is friendly and personal, while morning tea arrives with a fresh carnation.

24🛁🚿 (6fb) 1 CTV in all bedrooms ✱sB&B🛁🚿£47.50–£49.50 dB&B🛁🚿£62–£72 B

☾ 100P CFA ✽ sauna bath xmas

Scottish & French Lunch £15alc Tea £4 Dinner £17.50alc Last dinner 10pm

Credit cards 1 2 3 5 VS

BONTDDU

Gwynedd

Map 6 SH61

★★★ ***HL* Bontddu Hall** ☎(034149) 661

Closed Nov–Feb

Built in the country house style, with 2½ acres of grounds this hotel overlooks the Mawddach Estuary.

16rm (12🛁 4🚿) Annexe: 8🛁 (10fb) CTV in all bedrooms sB&B🛁🚿£16.50–£21.50 dB&B🛁🚿£37–£49 B

50P ✽ nc3yrs

International Lunch £3.95 Tea £1 Dinner £10.50 Wine £4.45 Last dinner 9pm

Credit cards 1 2 3 5 VS

BOOTLE

Merseyside

Map 7 SJ39

★★★ **Park** Park Lane West, Netherton (off A5036 1m SW of junc M57/M58/A59) (Greenall Whitley) ☎051-525 7555 Telex no 629772 Liverpool plan 11 *D8*

60rm(21➡39⋔) CTV in all bedrooms Ⓡ sB&B➡⋔£28.50–£29.50 dB&B➡⋔£39–£40 ⊟
Lift ☾ 200P 2⌂ CFA ♿
V ♧ ☕ Lunch fr£5.50 Dinner fr£5.50 Wine £4.75 Last dinner 9.30pm
Credit cards 1 2 3 5 **VS**

BOREHAM STREET
East Sussex
Map **5** TQ61

★★★**White Friars** (Best Western) ☎Herstmonceux (0323) 832355
Comfortable welcoming ivy-clad hotel in four acres of grounds.
12rm(8➡) Annexe: 9➡ (1fb) 1⊞ CTV in all bedrooms Ⓡ sB&B£18 sB&B➡£22 dB&B£31.50 dB&B➡£38 ⊟
50P ✽ *xmas*
⊟ International ♧ ✱ Lunch £6.50&alc Dinner £8.95alc Wine £4.50 Last dinner 9.15pm
S% Credit cards 1 2 3 5

✕✕**Smuggler's Wheel** ☎Herstmonceux (0323) 832293
Closed Mon
⊟ Italian **V** 60 seats Lunch £6–£6.50&alc Dinner £11alc Wine £4.85 Last dinner 9.30pm 20P
S% Credit cards 1 2 3 5

BOREHAMWOOD
Hertfordshire
Map **4** TQ19

☆☆☆**Elstree Moat House** Barnet bypass (Queens Moat) ☎01-953 1622
A pleasant, thatched hotel.
60➡ (8fb) CTV in all bedrooms Ⓡ ✱sB&B➡£33 dB&B➡£41 ⊟
☾ 400P CFA ✽ ⌒ (heated)
V ♧ ☕ ✱ Lunch £6.75&alc Tea 65p Dinner £6.75&alc Wine £4.50 Last dinner 9.45pm
Credit cards 1 2 3 4 5

★***Grosvenor*** 148 Shenley Rd ☎01-953 3175 Closed Xmas
Hotel has modest accommodation but well-run restaurant.
24rm Annexe: 6rm Ⓡ ⊟
CTV 12P 3⌂
⊟ English, Austrian & French **V** Last dinner 10pm
Credit cards 1 3 5

BORGUE
Dumfries & Galloway *Kircudbrightshire*
Map **11** NX64

★★♣**Senwick House** Brighouse Bay ☎(05577) 236
9rm(4➡) (1fb) CTV in all bedrooms Ⓡ sB&B£11–£13 sB&B➡£13–£14.50 dB&B£23–£26 dB&B➡£26–£29 ⊟
CTV 30P ⌂ ✽ ℘(hard) Disco Fri Live music and dancing Sat *xmas*
V ♧ Lunch fr£4.50 Tea fr40p High Tea £1–£5 Dinner £8 Wine £4 Last dinner 9pm
Credit card 5

BOROUGHBRIDGE
N Yorkshire
Map **8** SE36

★★★***HBL*** **Crown** Horsefair ☎(09012) 2328
This former coaching inn has been totally reconstructed and refurbished to an extremely high standard. The public rooms are delightful and the bedrooms very well appointed. Warmth and hospitality help recreate the atmosphere of more leisurely days.
43rm(42➡1⋔) (5fb) CTV in all bedrooms Ⓡ sB&B➡⋔£27.50 dB&B➡⋔£34.50 ⊟
Lift ☾ 50P sauna bath Disco mthly *xmas* ♿
⊟ International **V** ♧ ☕ Lunch £6.95&alc Tea 75p High Tea £4.75 Dinner £8.25&alc Wine £5.65 Last dinner 9.15pm
Credit cards 1 2 3 5 **VS**

★★★**Three Arrows** Horsefair (Embassy) ☎(09012) 2245
A Victorian country mansion standing in its own grounds.

→

17rm(16➡1⋒)(4fb) CTV in all bedrooms ® sB➡⋒ fr£27 dB➡⋒ fr£38.50 (room only) ⊟
70P ✽ *xmas*
V ♡ ☐ ✱Lunch fr£5.60 Dinner fr£6.50 Wine £4.30 Last dinner 9pm
S% Credit cards 1 2 3 5

BORROWASH
Derbyshire
Map **8** SK43

✕✕Wilmot Arms ☎ Derby (0332) 672222

Restaurant is in converted stable block next to 17th century inn.

Closed Sun Lunch not served Sat
⊟ Continental. **V** 58 seats Lunch fr£5&alc Dinner fr£8.50&alc Wine £5.59 Last dinner 9.50pm 60P bedrooms available
Credit cards 1 2 3 5 **VS**

BORROWDALE
Cumbria
Map **11** NY21
See also Grange (in-Borrowdale), Rosthwaite and Keswick

★★★*B* Mary Mount ☎ (059684) 223
Telex no 64305 (Lodore Swiss)
Closed 20 Nov–26 Dec

Close to Lodore Beck, the hotel stands in its own gardens and woodland on the banks of Derwent Water. (The recreational facilities at the nearby sister hotel 'Lodore Swiss' are available for use by residents of the Mary Mount.)

9➡ Annexe: 6➡ (2fb) CTV in all bedrooms ® (annexe only) ✱ sB&B➡ fr£25 dB&B➡ fr£38
30P 🚗 ✽ ⌂
⊟ International **V** ♡ ☐ Bar lunch £2.50alc Tea fr70p Dinner fr£8.50 Wine £4.50 Last dinner 8.30pm

★★*HBL* Borrowdale ☎ (059684) 224
Closed Xmas & Jan

A charming Lakeland hotel in majestic mountain scenery at the entrance to Borrowdale valley. Gunter and Jean Fidmure provide a warm, personal welcome in this traditional, comfortable and peaceful hotel. Dinner is the highlight of the day with English and Continental cuisine. Bar lunches are also very good.

35rm(32➡3⋒)(5fb) 5⊟ CTV in all bedrooms sB&B➡⋒ £14.05–£19.55 dB&B➡⋒ £27.10–£38.10
100P 🚗 ✽ ⌂
⊟ English & Continental **V** ♡ ☐ Lunch £5.80 Dinner £8.95 Wine £3.70 Last dinner 8.15pm

BOSCASTLE
Cornwall
Map **2** SX09

★★Bottreaux House ☎ (08405) 231

Small, comfortable hotel at the top of this picturesque harbour village.

11rm(2➡4⋒)(2fb) TV in 9 bedrooms ® sB&B£10.50 sB&B➡⋒ £12.50 dB&B£21 dB&B➡⋒ £25 ⊟
CTV 11P 🚗
⊟ English & French ♡ ☐ Lunch £6&alc Tea fr50p Dinner £6&alc Wine £3.30 Last dinner 9.30pm
Credit cards 1 3

★★Riverside The Harbour ☎ (08405) 216

This small, comfortable hotel and restaurant has a warm friendly atmosphere. It is located opposite the harbour.

11rm(6→3⋒)®sB&B£10sB&B→⋒£12 dB&B£24 dB&B→⋒£24
CTV *xmas*
English & French V Lunch £4alc Tea £1alc Dinner £7.70alc Wine £3.65 Last dinner 10.30pm
Credit card 1

★★**Valency House** Boscastle Harbour ☎(08405) 288
Closed end Nov–mid Mar
A small listed building of great character, with pleasant tea gardens, overlooking the harbour.
6rm® sB&B£10 dB&B£20
6P nc12yrs
French V Lunch £1–£2.60 Tea £1–£1.10 Dinner £5–£9&alc Wine £5 Last dinner 9pm
Credit card 2

BOSHAM
West Sussex
Map **4** SU80

★★*B* **Millstream** Bosham Ln (Best Western) ☎(0243) 573234
Small picturesque hotel with good service and comfortable bedrooms.
22rm(19→) CTV in 20 bedrooms ® sB&B£22 sB&B→£25 dB&B£40 dB&B→£42
CTV 40P *xmas*
English & French V Lunch £7.50&alc Tea 70p–£2.50 Dinner £9&alc Wine £4.80 Last dinner 10pm
Credit cards 1 2 3 5 **VS**

BOSTON
Lincolnshire
Map **8** TF34

★★**Burton House** Wainfleet Rd ☎(0205) 62307
A comfortable, well appointed establishment at junction of A52 and A16.
6rm(2→) CTV in all bedrooms ® *sB&B fr£16 sB&B→ fr£20 dB&B fr£22 dB&B→ fr£25
100P
International Wine £3.35 Last dinner 9pm

★★**New England** Wide Bargate (Anchor) ☎(0205) 65255 Closed 25–26 Dec
25→(1fb) CTV in all bedrooms ® *sB&B→£29.50 dB&B→£39.50
V *Lunch £4.95–£7 Dinner £5.35–£8 Wine £4.50 Last dinner 10pm
Credit cards 1 2 3 5

BOTALLACK
Cornwall
Map **2** SW33

✕✕**Count House** ☎Penzance (0736) 788588
Ruins of former Cornish mine workings house this character restaurant.
Closed Mon & Tue Lunch not served Wed–Sat Dinner not served Sun
European 36 seats *Lunch £5.60 Dinner £12alc Wine £4.40 Last dinner 9.45pm 25P
Credit cards 1 2 3 4 5 **VS**

BOTESDALE
Suffolk
Map **5** TM07

✕✕**Crown Hill House** ☎Diss (0379) 898369
Lunch not served
English & French 24 seats Dinner £9 Wine £4.50 Last dinner 9pm 6P bedrooms available
S% Credit cards 1 2 3 5 **VS**

BOTHWELL
Strathclyde *Lanarkshire*
Map **11** NS75

★★*B* **Silvertrees** Silverwells Cres ☎(0698) 852311
This is a large house in a quiet residential position, whose interior is a tasteful blend of old and modern.
7→⋒ Annexe: 17→⋒ CTV in 19 bedrooms ® (annexe only)
sB&B→⋒£25.50–£26.50 dB&B→⋒£29–£30
100P3
V Lunch £5&alc High Tea £4.50 Dinner £6.50&alc Wine £4.80 Last dinner 9pm
Credit cards 1 2 3 5

BOTLEY
Hampshire
Map **4** SU51

✕***Cobbett's*** 13 The Square ☎(04892) 2068
Closed Sun, Public hols, 2wks summer & 2wks winter Lunch not served Sat & Mon
French V 45 seats Lunch £8.50&alc Dinner £15.50alc Wine £4.60 Last dinner 9.30pm 20P
Credit cards 1 3

BOTTOM HOUSE
Staffordshire
Map **7** SK05

✕**Forge** Ashbourne Rd ☎Onecote (05388) 249
Dinner not served Mon
English & French V 50 seats *Lunch £1.50–£4.60&alc Dinner £6–£9&alc Wine £5.40 Last dinner 10pm 150P

BOULEY BAY
Jersey, Channel Islands
Map **16**

★★★★*HL* **Water's Edge** ☎Jersey (0534) 62777 Telex no 4191462
Closed Nov–Mar
A well-appointed, modernised, holiday hotel, in a quiet, rocky bay.
57rm(52→5⋒)(1fb) CTV in all bedrooms *sB&B→⋒ £21–£31 dB&B→⋒ £42–£62
Lift 25P CFA (heated) sauna bath Live music and dancing 6 nights wkly
English & French V *Lunch fr£6.60&alc Tea £1.10–£3.30 High Tea fr£3.30 Dinner £8.80&alc Wine £3.50 Last dinner 9.45pm
S% Credit cards 1 2 3 5 **VS**

Bournemouth & Boscombe

BOURNEMOUTH & BOSCOMBE
Dorset
Map **4** SZ09
Telephone exchange 'Bournemouth'
For town plans see Key Map or page 134 for Central Plan, page 138 for Boscombe & Southbourne plan, or page 138 for Westbourne & Branksome plan.
For additional hotels see **Christchurch** and **Poole**

★★★★★*L* **Royal Bath** Bath Rd (De Vere) ☎(0202)25555 Telex no 41375 Central plan **31** *E2*
Large elegant hotel with gymnasium and casino. Bedrooms are of high standard and service is prompt and courteous.
133⇌ 1⊟ CTV in all bedrooms ★ *sB&B⇌£36.75 dB&B⇌£63 ⊟
Lift ☾ CFA 120⌂✽ ⩩ (heated) (in summer) sauna bath Live music and dancing Sat ⌂ *xmas*
⊟International V ♆ ⊒ *Lunch fr£7.35&alc Tea £2.65 Dinner fr£10.50&alc Wine £5.50 Last dinner 10pm
S% Credit cards 1 2 3 4 5

★★★★**East Cliff Court** East Overcliff Dr ☎(0202)24545 Central plan **15** *F3*
Fine sea views enjoyed from this well maintained clifftop hotel.
72rm(69⇌3⋒) CTV in all bedrooms sB&B⇌⋒£23–£28 dB&B⇌⋒£42.90–£58.30 ⊟
Lift ☾ 100P CFA ⩩ (heated) sauna bath Live music and dancing 2 nights wkly ⌂ *xmas*
⊟English, French & Polish V ♆ ⊒ Lunch fr£6.50 Tea fr75p Dinner fr£8.75 Wine £4.25 Last dinner 9.30pm
Credit cards 1 2 3 5

★★★★**Highcliff** West Cliff, St Michael's Rd (Best Western) ☎(0202)27702 Telex no 417153 Central plan **19** *C1*
This hotel is situated close to the cliff lift, and has an imposing frontage with fine sea views.
99rm(77⇌18⋒)(39fb) CTV in all bedrooms ® sB&B£24–£30 sB&B⇌⋒£25–£31 dB&B£40–£54 dB&B⇌⋒£42–£56 ⊟
Lift ☾ 80P CFA✽ ⩩ ⟟(hard) sauna bath disco 6 nights wkly Live music and dancing wkly ⌂ *xmas*
V ♆ ⊒ Lunch £3.75–£5.50&alc Tea 70p–£1.50 High Tea £3–£4 Dinner £8.50–£9&alc Wine £4.50 Last dinner 9pm
Credit cards 1 2 3 5 **VS**

★★★★**Marsham Court** Russell Cotes Rd (De Vere) ☎(0202)22111 Telex no 22121 Central plan **21** *E2*
Rough cast colour wash hotel, located on East Cliff near the pier and town centre.
89rm(80⇌9⋒) CTV in all bedrooms ★ *sB&B⇌⋒£26.25 dB&B⇌⋒£42 ⊟
Lift ☾ 40P 36⌂ CFA✽ ⩩ (heated) (in summer) billiards disco Tue, Thu & Sat (in summer) Live music and dancing Tue, Thu & Sat (in summer) *xmas*
♆ ⊒ *Lunch £6.60&alc Tea £2.60 Dinner £8&alc Wine £5.50 Last dinner 9.30pm
S% Credit cards 1 2 3 4 5

★★★★**Palace Court** Westover Rd ☎(0202)27681 Telex no 418451 Central plan **26** *D2*
A balconied building of architectural interest, centrally located near the shops and opposite the Pavilion.
108⇌(4fb) CTV in all bedrooms ® *sB&B⇌fr£30 dB&B fr£49 ⊟
Lift ☾ CFA 200⌂ sauna bath ⌂ *xmas*
⊟English, French & Italian ♆ ⊒ *Lunch fr£7.50&alc Dinner fr£8.50&alc Wine £4.75 Last dinner 9pm
Credit cards 1 2 3 5

★★★**Anglo-Swiss** Gervis Rd, East Cliff ☎(0202)24794 Telex no 418261 Central plan **1** *F4*
A large hotel in an avenue of pine trees with formal service. (Use of hotel group's indoor sports centre, 1 mile from hotel.)
64rm(43⇌1⋒)(14fb) CTV in all bedrooms ® sB&B£14–£21 sB&B⇌⋒£16–£23 dB&B£28–£42 dB&B⇌⋒£32–£46 ⊟

Lift ☾ 65P CFA ✽ (heated in season) Disco 3 nights wkly (in season) Live music and dancing wkly (in season) *xmas*

French **V** Bar lunch fr£1.50 Tea fr£1.50 Dinner fr£7 Wine £4.25 Last dinner 8.30pm

Credit cards 1 2 3 5 **VS**

★★★ ***Angus*** Bath Rd ☎(0202) 26420 Central plan **2** *E3*

A brick, colour wash hotel near to shops, pier and entertainments, situated off the main road, close to Lansdowne.

48rm(37 4) CTV in all bedrooms

Lift ☾ 50P CFA

English & French **V** Last dinner 10pm

Credit cards 1 2 3 5

★★★ ***H Burley Court*** Bath Rd ☎(0202) 22824 Central plan **4** *E3* Closed 31 Dec–14 Jan

Attentive staff provide a relaxing atmosphere in this family run hotel.

42rm(30 1) CTV in 31 bedrooms TV in 11 bedrooms

Lift ☾ CTV 40P (heated)

English & French Last dinner 8.30pm

Credit cards 1 3

See advert on page 135

★★★ **Cecil** Parsonage Rd, Bath Hill ☎(0202) 293336 Telex no 418261 Central plan **5** *E3*

Centrally situated red brick hotel, within walking distance of the shops, theatre and pier. (Use of hotel group's indoor sports centre, 1m from hotel.)

(27) (3fb) CTV in all bedrooms ® sB&B £15–£23.50 dB&B £30–£47

Lift 25P Live music and dancing twice wkly *xmas*

French **V** Lunch fr£4.30 Tea fr£1.50 Dinner fr£7 Wine £4.25 Last dinner 9.30pm

Credit cards 1 2 3 5

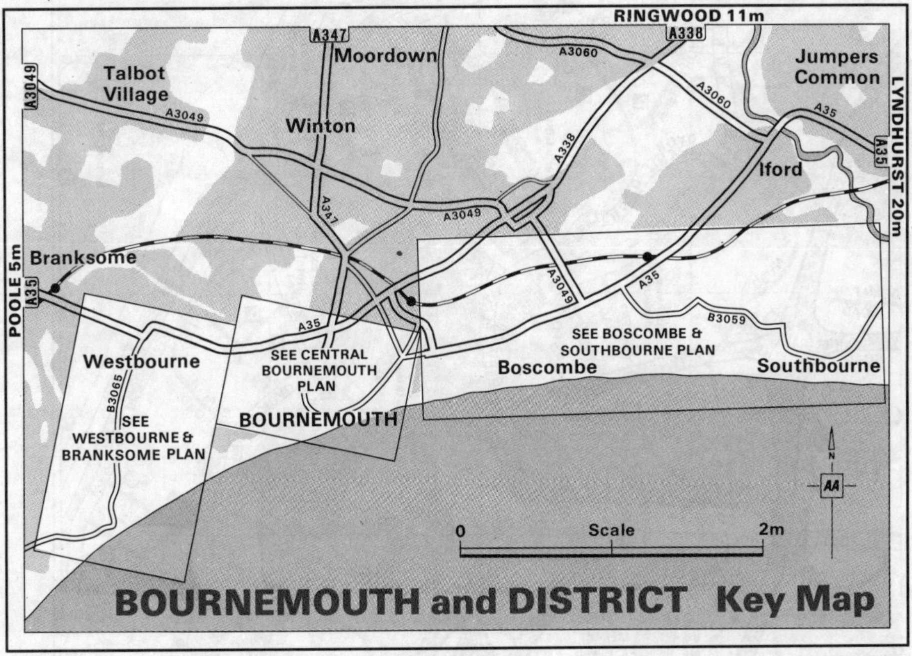

RINGWOOD 11m
A347
A338
Moordown
A3060
Jumpers Common
A3049
Talbot Village
A3049
Winton
A3060
A35
A338
LYNDHURST 20m
A35
Iford
A347
A3049
Branksome
POOLE 5m
A35
A3049
A35
B3059
A35
SEE BOSCOMBE & SOUTHBOURNE PLAN
SEE CENTRAL BOURNEMOUTH PLAN
Westbourne
Boscombe
Southbourne
B3065
BOURNEMOUTH
SEE WESTBOURNE & BRANKSOME PLAN
N
AA
0 Scale 2m

BOURNEMOUTH and DISTRICT Key Map

B

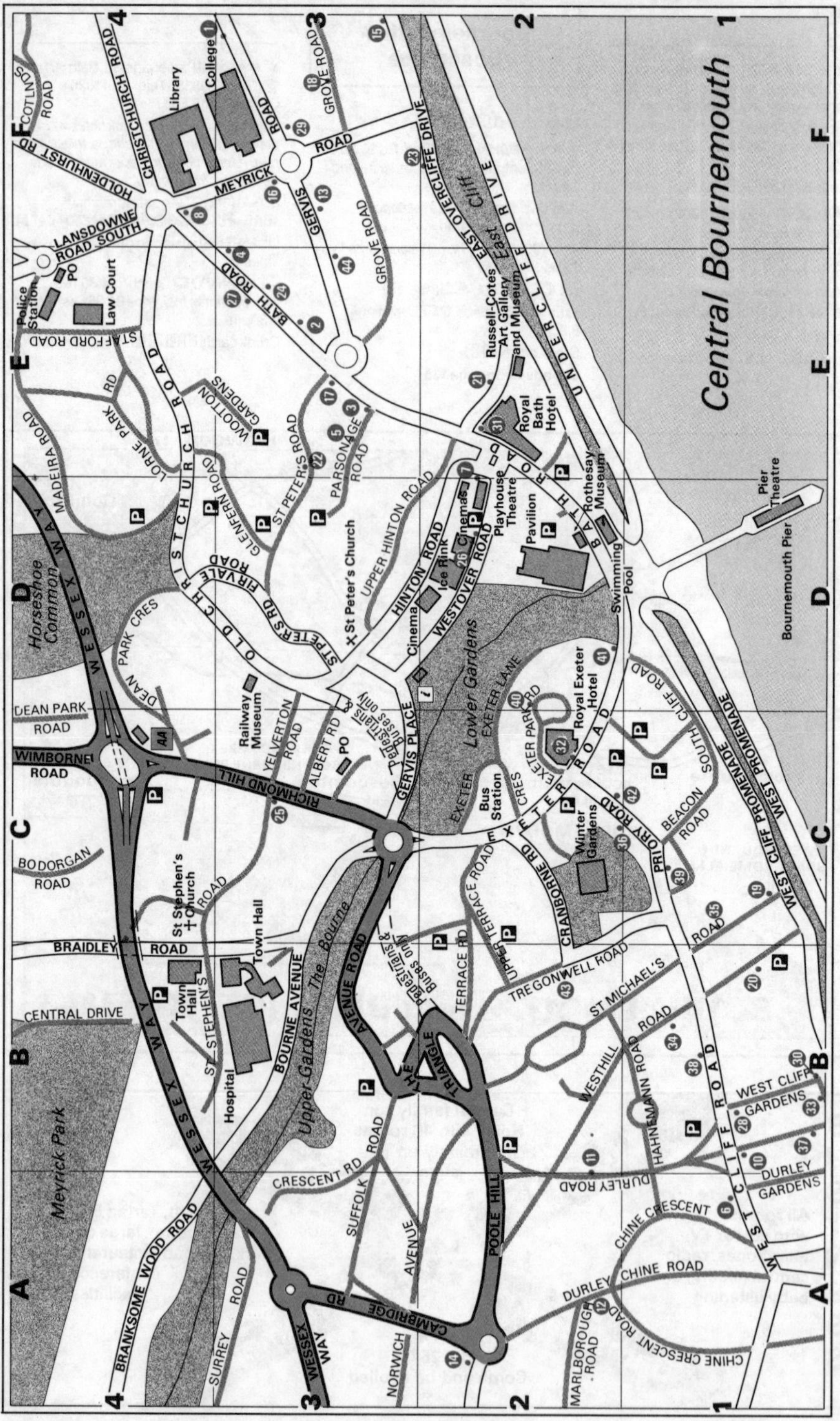

Central Bournemouth

Bournemouth & Boscombe

Bournemouth Central
1 Anglo-Swiss ★★★
2 Angus ★★★
3 Belvedere ★★
4 Burley Court ★★★
5 Cecil ★★★
6 Cliff Court ★
7 County ★★
8 Crest ☆☆☆
10 Durley Dean ★★★
11 Durley Grange ★★
12 Durley Hall ★★★
13 Durlston Court ★★★
14 East Anglia ★★★
15 East Cliff Court ★★★★
16 Embassy ★★★
17 Grosvenor ★★★
18 Heathlands ★★★
19 Highcliff ★★★★
20 Ladbroke Savoy ★★★
21 Marsham Court ★★★★
22 Melford Hall ★★★
23 Miramar ★★★
24 New Somerset ★★
25 Norfolk ★★★
26 Palace Court ★★★★
La Taverna ✕✕
27 Pavillion ★★★
28 Pinehurst ★★
29 Queens ★★★
30 Hotel Riviera (Westcliff Gdns) ★★
31 Royal Bath ★★★★★
32 Royal Exeter ★★
33 St George ★★
34 Sun Court ★★
35 Tralee ★★
36 Trouville ★★★
37 Ullswater ★
38 Wessex ★★★
39 West Cliff Hall ★★
40 Whitehall ★★
41 White Hermitage ★★★
42 Winterbourne ★★
43 Winter Gardens ★★
44 Woodcroft Tower ★★

★★★**Chesterwood** East Overcliff Dr ☎(0202) 28057 Boscombe & Southbourne plan **51** *A1* Closed Jan–Feb

A detached hotel on the East Cliff, offering uninterrupted sea views.

51rm(33➡9⋔)(15fb) CTV in all bedrooms sB&B£14–£18.85 sB&B➡⋔£15–£19.85 dB&B£26–£35.70 dB&B➡⋔ fr£28 Ƀ

Lift ☾ 30P 8♠✽ ⩧(heated) Live music and dancing 3 nights wkly in season Cabaret Xmas & Etr only *xmas*

V♡☐ Lunch fr£5 Tea fr50p Dinner fr£6.25 Wine £3.60 Last dinner 8pm

Credit cards 1 3 5

See advert on page 136

★★★**Chine** Boscombe Spa Rd, Boscombe ☎(0202) 36234 Boscombe & Southbourne plan **52** *B1*

A Victorian, gable and tile building with a modern extension and good views.

108rm(73➡1⋔)(15fb) CTV in 50 bedrooms Ⓡ ✱ sB&B£14–£21 sB&B➡£15.50–£22.50 dB&B£28–£42 dB&B➡£31–£45 Ƀ

Lift ☾ ⊁ CTV 100P 5♠ CFA ✽ ⩧ & ⩧(heated) sauna bath disco twice wkly Live music and dancing wkly ⌂ *xmas*

▣International V♡☐ Lunch fr£5.50 Tea fr50p Dinner fr£6.50 Wine £3 Last dinner 8.30pm

★★★**Cliff End** Manor Rd, East Cliff ☎(0202) 309711 Boscombe & Southbourne plan **53** *B1*

Modernised hotel with new wing extension offering traditional services and pleasant lounges.

40rm(35➡5⋔)(20fb) CTV in all bedrooms Ⓡ ✱sB&B➡⋔£18.50–£20.50 dB&B➡⋔£37–£41 Ƀ

Lift ☾ 40P CFA ⩧(heated) ⅋(hard) Live music and dancing wkly ⌂ *xmas*

▣English & French V♡☐ ✱Lunch fr£5.50 Tea fr50p Dinner fr£6.95 Wine £3.90 Last dinner 8.30pm

VS

★★★*H* **Cliffeside** East Overcliff Dr ☎(0202) 25724 Boscombe & Southbourne plan **54** *A1*

This hotel on the East Cliff has a sun terrace overlooking swimming pools and panoramic views.

64rm(40➡10⋔)(6fb) CTV in all bedrooms ✱ sB&B£17.50–£23.50 sB&B➡⋔£19.50–£25.50 dB&B£29–£37 dB&B➡⋔£33–£42 Ƀ

Lift ☾ CTV 50P CFA ⩧(heated) Live music and dancing twice wkly Cabaret twice wkly ⌂ *xmas*

V♡☐ Lunch fr£5.50 Tea 95p Dinner £6.50 Wine £4 Last dinner 8.15pm

Credit cards 1 3

See advert on page 136

★★★**Hotel Courtlands** 16 Boscombe Spa Rd, East Cliff ☎(0202) 302442 Boscombe & Southbourne plan **57** *B1*

Large hotel with modern extension and well equipped bedrooms.

48rm(24➡6⋔)(13fb) CTV in all bedrooms Ⓡ sB&B➡£16–£20.90 dB&B£32–£41.80 dB&B➡£32–£41.80 Ƀ

Lift ☾ 60P CFA ✽ ⩧(heated) Live music and dancing 6 nights wkly in season ⌂ *xmas* ♿

▣English & French ♡☐ Lunch fr£5 High Tea fr£2.50 Dinner fr£6.80 Wine £4.20 Last dinner 8.30pm

Credit cards 1 2 3 5 **VS**

☆☆☆**Crest** Lansdowne (Crest) ☎(0202) 23262 Telex no 41232 Central plan **8** *F4*

A modern, purpose-built hotel of an interesting, circular design.

102➡ CTV in all bedrooms Ⓡ ✱sB➡£29–£34 dB➡ fr£46 (room only) Ƀ

Lift ☾ ⊁ 78♠ CFA

▣International ♡☐ ✱Lunch £3.95–£7.05&alc Tea 55p–£1.45 High Tea £1.25–£5.85 Dinner £4.95–£8.25&alc Wine £5.95 Last dinner 9.45pm

Credit cards 1 2 3 4 5 **VS**

★★★**Durley Dean** West Cliff Rd ☎(0202) 27711 Central plan **10** *B1*

Large holiday hotel with good entertainment facilities.

110rm(80➡6⋔)(14fb) Ⓡ sB&B£15.50–£17.50 sB&B➡⋔£18–£20 dB&B£30–£34 dB&B➡⋔£35–£39 Ƀ →

B

Lift ☾ CTV 35P CFA ⛱ (heated) billiards Live music and dancing 7 nights wkly nc3yrs *xmas*
♔ ⊒ Lunch £5 Tea 45p Dinner £6&alc Wine £3.80 Last dinner 10pm
VS

★★★**Durley Hall** Durley Chine Rd ☎(0202) 766886 Central plan **12** *AZ*
An imposing hotel in its own grounds set back off a quiet road.
74rm(47→5⋒) Annexe: 10rm(8→1⋒) (25fb) CTV in all bedrooms sB&B£14–£18 sB&B→⋒£17–£22 dB&B£28–£36 dB&B→⋒£34–£44 B̶

Lift ☾ ⊞ 250P CFA ✱ ⛱ (heated) Disco twice wkly Live music and dancing 5 nights wkly ⌂ *xmas*
V ♔ ⊒ Lunch £4.50 Tea 75p Dinner £6.50–£8.25 Wine £4.25 Last dinner 8.30pm
Credit cards 1 2 3 5

★★★**Durlston Court** Gervis Rd, East Cliff ☎(0202) 291488 Telex no 418261 Central plan **13** *F3*
Large hotel with spacious lounge and bar, and modern bedroom facilities. (Use of hotel group's indoor sports-centre, 1 mile from hotel.)
63rm(38→1⋒) CTV in all bedrooms ® sB&B£14–£21 sB&B→£16–£23 dB&B£28–£42 dB&B→£32–£46 B̶
Lift ☾ 40P CFA ⛱ (heated in season) Disco 3 nights wkly Live music and dancing wkly in season ⌂ *xmas* ♿
▣ French **V** ♔ ⊒ Bar lunch fr£1.50 Tea fr£1.50 Dinner £7 Wine £4.25 Last dinner 8.30pm
Credit cards 1 2 3 5 **VS**

★★★**East Anglia** 6 Poole Rd ☎(0202) 765163 Central plan **14** *A2*

Bournemouth & Boscombe

Owned by the same family for twenty-seven years, this hotel is conveniently situated for the town centre.

49rm(40⇌9⋒) Annexe: 23rm(14⇌1⋒) (10fb) CTV in all bedrooms Ⓡ ✱ sB&B£14.50–£20 sB&B⇌⋒£16.50–£22 dB&B£23–£28 dB&B⇌⋒£27–£39 B

Lift ☾ 80P CFA ⩯ (heated) sauna bath *xmas*

Lunch £3.40–£6.20 Tea 60p–80p Dinner £7–£7.50 Wine £4 Last dinner 8.30pm

Credit cards 1 2 3 5

★★★ ***Embassy*** Meyrick Rd ☎ (0202) 20751 Central plan **16** *F3*

Comfortable, traditional style hotel near cliff top.

40rm(37⇌7⋒) CTV in 40 bedrooms Ⓡ B

Lift ☾ CTV 50P CFA ⩯ (heated) disco wkly Live music and dancing wkly

International Last dinner 8.30pm

Credit cards 1 2 3 5 **VS**

★★★ **Grosvenor** Bath Rd, East Cliff, ☎ (0202) 28858 Central plan **17** *E3*

Well equipped bedrooms, nicely furnished lounges and personal service are found in this pleasant central hotel.

38rm(31⇌3⋒) (8fb) CTV in all bedrooms Ⓡ sB&B£13.50–£17 sB&B⇌⋒£15.50–£19 dB&B£27–£34 dB&B⇌⋒£31–£38 B

Lift ☾ CTV 35P Live music and dancing wkly ♿ *xmas*

Lunch £3.60 Tea 50p–£1.75 Dinner £6.50 Wine £3.75 Last dinner 8pm

Credit cards 1 2 3 5 **VS**

★★★ **Hazelwood** Christchurch Rd, East Cliff ☎ (0202) 21367 Boscombe & Southbourne plan **61** *A1* Closed Jan

58rm(29⇌9⋒) (5fb) ✱sB&B£14.95–£15.52 sB&B⇌⋒£17.25–£18.40 dB&B£29.90–£31.04 dB&B⇌⋒£34.50–£36.80 B

→

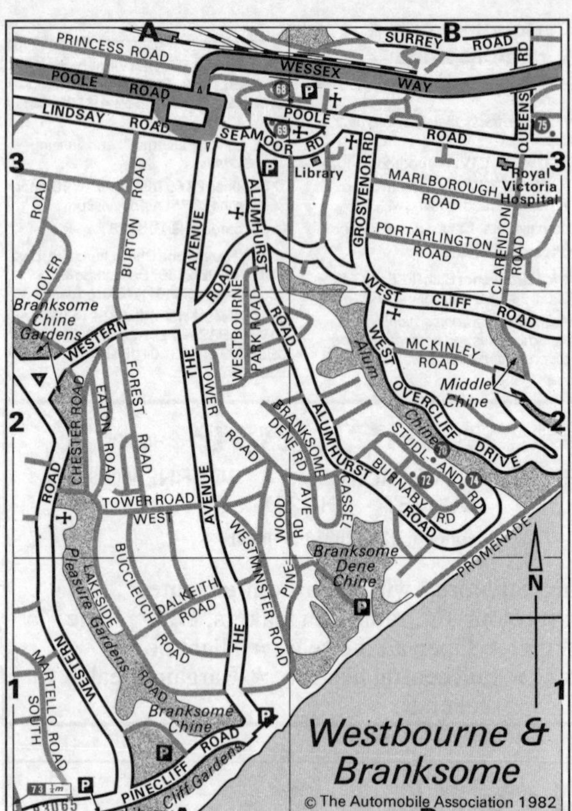
Westbourne & Branksome
© The Automobile Association 1982
PRINCESS ROAD
POOLE ROAD
LINDSAY ROAD
WESSEX WAY
SURREY ROAD
SEAMOOR RD
POOLE ROAD
Library
Royal Victoria Hospital
MARLBOROUGH ROAD
PORTARLINGTON ROAD
WEST CLIFF ROAD
MC KINLEY ROAD
Middle Chine
WEST OVERCLIFF DRIVE
Alum Chine
Branksome Chine Gardens
WESTERN ROAD
THE AVENUE
Branksome Dene Chine
PROMENADE
Branksome Chine
Pleasure Gardens
PINECLIFF ROAD
Clift Gardens
B3065
Library

Westbourne & Branksome

68 Cadogan ★★
70 Chinehurst ★★
72 Riviera (Burnaby Rd) ★★
73 Sea Witch ★★
(listed under Poole)
74 Studland Dene ★★
75 Wellington ★

Lift ☾ CTV 40P ✽ ⛵ (heated) Live music and dancing Fri & Sat Cabaret Sat ⌂ *xmas*

▣ English & French **V** ♧ ☐ ✻ Lunch fr£4.50 Tea 60p Dinner fr£8.05 Wine £4.02 Last dinner 8.30pm

Credit cards 1 2 3 5

★★★ **Heathlands** Grove Rd, East Cliff (Inter Hotels) ☎ (0202) 23336 Telex no 418261 Central plan **18** *F3*

Large modern hotel in its own grounds near East Cliff. (Use of hotel group's indoor sports centre, 1 mile from hotel.)

120rm (104⇌ 1⫛) (13fb) CTV in all bedrooms Ⓡ sB&B£15–£22 sB&B⇌⫛ £17–£24 dB&B£28–£42 dB&B⇌⫛ £32–£46 B

Lift ☾ 80P ✽ CFA ⛵ (heated in season) Disco twice wkly Live music and dancing twice wkly in season ⌂ *xmas* ♿

▣ French **V** ♧ ☐ Bar lunch fr£1.50 Tea fr£1.50 Dinner fr£7 Wine £4.25 Last dinner 8.30pm

Credit cards 1 2 3 4 5 **VS**

★★★ **Ladbroke Savoy** West Hill Rd, West Cliff (Ladbroke) ☎ (0202) 294241 Central plan **20** *B1*

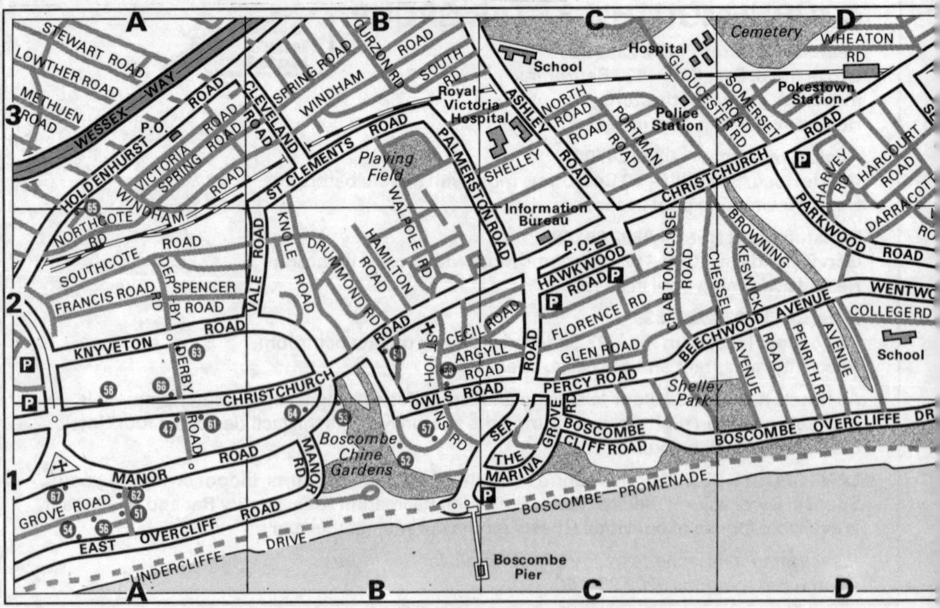

A cliff-top hotel, having balconies, spacious sun terraces and sea views.

88rm(80→) CTV in all bedrooms ® *sB&B→ fr£28 dB&B→ fr£46 B

Lift ☾ 45P 4🚗 CFA ≈ (heated) ⌂ *xmas*

♔ ☕ *Lunch fr£6.50 Dinner fr£8.50 Last dinner 9pm

Credit cards 1 2 3 4 5

★★★**B Langtry Manor** 26 Derby Rd, East Cliff ☎(0202) 23887 Boscombe & Southbourne plan **63** *A2*

19rm(15→4⋔) 3⊟ CTV in all bedrooms ✦ *sB&B→⋔ £24–£28 dB&B→⋔ £36–£42 B

30P ⊕ nc2yrs *xmas*

V ♔ ☕ *Lunch fr£5.50 Tea fr£1 High Tea fr£4 Dinner fr£7.75&alc Wine £4.95 Last dinner 8.30pm

Credit cards 1 2 3 5 **VS**

★★★**Melford Hall** St Peters Rd ☎(0202) 21516 Central plan **22** *E3*

This hotel with a sun deck, stands in its own grounds. It is centrally located yet enjoys a quiet setting.

63rm(56→1⋔) CTV in 56 bedrooms *sB&B£12.65–£17.05 sB&B→£15.20–£19 dB&B£25.30–£34.10 dB&B→£30.40–£38.10 B

Lift ☾ 55P ✿ Live music and dancing wkly Cabaret wkly in season ⌂ *xmas*

V ♔ ☕ *Lunch £5.70–£6 Dinner £6.95–£8.20 Wine £4.42 Last dinner 8pm S%

★★★**Miramar Hotel** Grove Road ☎(0202) 26581 Central plan **23** *F3*

Warm, comfortable, traditional hotel where many rooms have fine sea views.

42rm(30→5⋔) (4fb) CTV in all bedrooms sB&B£16.68–£19.55 sB&B→⋔ £21.85–£24.73 dB&B£33.36–£39.10 dB&B→⋔ £36.80–£46 B

Lift ☾ CTV 30P 6🚗 ⊕ ✿ *xmas*

V ♔ ☕ Lunch fr£5.75 Tea 70p Dinner fr£8.05 Wine £4 Last dinner 8pm

★★★**Norfolk** Richmond Hill ☎(0202) 21521 Central plan **25** *C3*

65rm(40→) (17fb) CTV in all bedrooms ® ✦ sB&B£14–£21 sB&B→£15.50–£22.50 dB&B£28–£42 dB&B→£31–£45

Lift ☾ ⊁ 100P Live music and dancing Sat *xmas*

▣ English & International V ♔ ☕ Lunch fr£5.50 Tea 75p Dinner fr£6.50 Wine £3.50 Last dinner 8.30pm

Credit cards 1 3 5

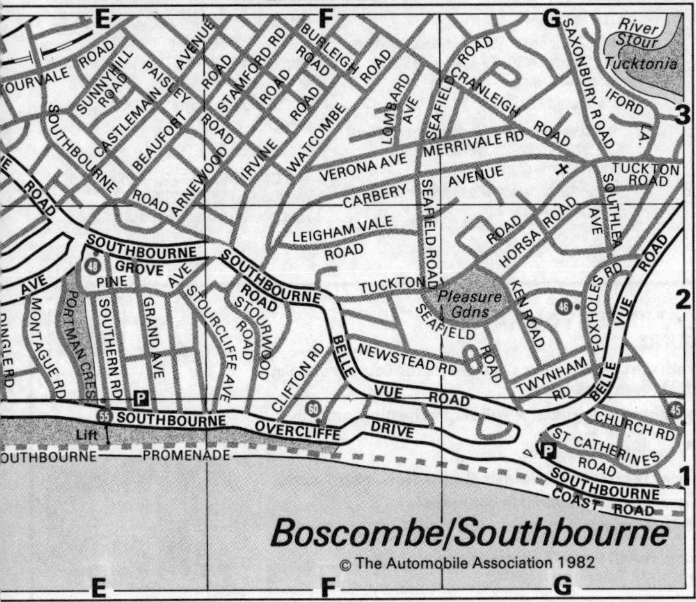

E
F
G
3
2
1
River Stour
Tucktonia
Pleasure Gdns
Southbourne Road
Southbourne Grove
Tuckton Road
Belle Vue Road
Southbourne Overcliffe Drive
Southbourne Coast Road
Southbourne Promenade
Lift
Boscombe/Southbourne
© The Automobile Association 1982

Boscombe & Southbourne

45 Albany ★★
46 Avonmore ★★
47 Avon Royal ★★
48 Boote's ✕✕
50 Brummell Touring ★★
51 Chesterwood ★★★
52 Chine ★★★
53 Cliffe End ★★★
54 Cliffside ★★★
55 Commodore ★★
56 Cottonwood ★★
57 Hotel Courtlands ★★★
58 Elstead ★★
59 Fircroft ★★
60 Grange ★★
61 Hazelwood ★★★
62 Hinton Firs ★★
63 Langtry Manor ★★★
64 Manor House ★★
65 Trattoria San Marco ✕
66 Tree Tops ★
67 Yenton ★★

Bournemouth & Boscombe

★★★ ***H*****Pavilion** Bath Rd (Best Western) ☎(0202) 291266 Central plan **27** *E3*

A comfortable building with a modern lounge overlooking front lawns, putting green and gardens.

47rm(33⇌6⋒)(8fb) CTV in all bedrooms sB&B£17–£18 sB&B⇌⋒£21.50–£22.50 dB&B£27–£29 dB&B⇌⋒£36–£38 B

Lift ☾ CTV 30P CFA

English & French Lunch £5.50–£6&alc Tea 80p–£1 Dinner £7.50–£8&alc Last dinner 8.30pm

Credit cards 1 2 3 5

★★★ **Queens** Meyrick Rd, East Cliff ☎(0202) 24415 Central plan **29** *F3*

Large modern hotel with spacious rooms.

116rm(80⇌1⋒)(16fb) CTV in all bedrooms ® sB&B£16–£20.50 sB&B⇌£18–£23.60 dB&B£28–£35.70 dB&B⇌£32–£42 B

Lift ☾ 50P 10 CFA *xmas*

Lunch fr£6&alc Dinner fr£7&alc Wine £4.75 Last dinner 8.15pm

Credit cards 1 2 3 5 **VS**

★★★ **Trouville** Priory Rd ☎(0202) 22262 Central plan **36** *C2*

Closed Jan & Feb

Centrally situated hotel, adjoining Winter Gardens.

80rm(70⇌)(20fb) CTV in all bedrooms sB&B£17–£21 sB&B⇌£20–£24 dB&B⇌£34–£42

Lift ☾ 70P 5 Live music and dancing Sun in season *xmas*

Tea 45p–75palc Dinner £10alc Wine £4.70 Last dinner 8.30pm

S%

★★★ **Wessex** West Cliff Rd (Travco) ☎(0202) 21911 Central plan **38** *B1*

Large Victorian building situated on the West Cliff within walking distance of shops and seafront.

97rm(57⇌18⋒)(10fb) CTV in all bedrooms ® sB&B£18 sB&B⇌⋒£21 dB&B£29 dB&B⇌⋒£32 B

Lift ☾ 200P CFA (heated) billiards sauna bath Disco wkly Live music and dancing 3 nights wkly *xmas*

British & French **V** Lunch fr£5 Tea £1 Dinner fr£6 Wine £3.95 Last dinner 8.30pm

Credit cards 1 2 4 5

★★★ **White Hermitage** Exeter Rd ☎(0202) 27363 Central plan **41** *D2*

Central hotel by lower pleasure gardens, overlooking pier.

85rm(64⇌6⋒)(18fb) CTV in all bedrooms ® *sB&B£16–£21.50 sB&B⇌£19–£26 dB&B£28–£38 dB&B⇌£34–£44 B

Lift ☾ 60P CFA sauna bath Live music and dancing wkly *xmas*

*Lunch £5.50–£6&alc Tea 80p–90p Dinner £6.50–£7.50&alc Last dinner 8.30pm

Credit cards 1 2 3 5

★★ ***Albany*** Warren Edge Rd, Southbourne ☎(0202) 428151 Boscombe & Southbourne plan **45** *G1*

22⇌⋒ CTV available in bedrooms B

Lift CTV 20P Disco 6 nights wkly Live music and dancing wkly Cabaret wkly nc3yrs

English & French Last dinner 7.45pm

Credit cards 1 2 3 4 5

★★ **Avonmore** Foxholes Rd, Southbourne ☎(0202) 428639 Boscombe & Southbourne plan **46** *G2*

Small, quiet hotel with neat bedrooms.

15rm(5⇌)(4fb) sB&B£6.50–£10.50 sB&B⇌£10.50–£16 dB&B£13–£20 dB&B⇌£17–£24 B

CTV 10P

V Lunch £2.50–£3.75&alc Tea 60p–85p Dinner £4.50–£7&alc Wine £3.50 Last dinner 9pm

Credit cards 1 3 **VS**

★★ **Avon Royal** 45 Christchurch Rd East Cliff ☎(0202) 292800 Boscombe & Southbourne plan **47** *A1*

Attractive hotel with pleasant garden and personal service.

21rm(5⇌4⋒)(2fb) ® sB&B£11–£13.50 sB&B⇌⋒£12.50–£15 dB&B£20–£23 dB&B⇌⋒£23–£26 B

CTV 25P Disco wkly Live music and dancing wkly *xmas*

Bar lunch £1.50–£2.90 Tea fr80p Dinner fr£4.50 Wine £3.80 Last dinner 8.30pm

Credit card 1

★★ **Belvedere** Bath Rd ☎(0202) 21080 Central plan **3** *E3*

Colourwashed hotel in central position.

28rm(13⇌5⋒)(5fb) CTV in 8 bedrooms ® sB&B£13.50–£17 sB&B⇌⋒£16.50–£20 dB&B£24–£30 dB&B⇌⋒£30–£36 B

Lift CTV 21P *xmas*

English & Continental Bar lunch £3.50alc Tea 60p–£1.30 Dinner £5.50–£6.50&alc Wine £4.20 Last dinner 8.30pm

Credit cards 1 2 3 5

★★ **Brummells Touring** 2 Boscombe Spa Rd, Christchurch Rd ☎(0202) 33252 Boscombe & Southbourne plan **50** *B2*

Small family run holiday hotel offering seasonal entertainment and home cooking.

23rm(3⇌9⋒)(17fb) *sB&B£12–£16 sB&B⇌⋒£13.50–£18.50 dB&B£20–£26 dB&B⇌⋒£23–£29 B

☾ CTV 23P billiards Disco nightly Live music and dancing 3 nights wkly Cabaret wkly *xmas*

*Lunch £2.50–£4.50 Dinner £5 Wine £4 Last dinner 7.30pm

★★ ***Cadogan*** 8 Poole Rd ☎(0202) 763006 Westbourne & Branksome plan **68** *A3*

Set back off main Poole road, this is a gabled building with a new wing.

50rm(21⇌6⋒) 1 CTV in 13 bedrooms B

Lift CTV 60P nc5yrs

V

Credit cards 1 3

★★ **Chinehurst** 18–20 Studland Rd, Westbourne ☎(0202) 764583 Westbourne & Branksome plan **70** *B2*

Close to the sea front, this hotel is located in quiet, residential Alum Chine.

29rm(18➡5⋒)(10fb) CTV in 12 bedrooms ✻sB&B£12.50–£16.50 sB&B➡⋒£14–£18 dB&B£23–£30 dB&B➡⋒£26–£33 B

CTV 22P Disco twice wkly nc3yrs *xmas*

V ☕ ✻Lunch £3.25&alc Tea 55p High Tea £1.25–£2 Dinner £5.25–£6&alc Last dinner 8pm

Credit cards 1 2 3 5 **VS**

★★**Commodore** Overcliff Dr, Southbourne (Whitbread Wessex) ☎(0202) 423150 Boscombe & Southbourne plan **55** *E1* Closed Nov–Mar

A cliff top hotel with fine views.

18rm Ⓡ ✻ sB&B fr£15.50 dB&B fr£30

Lift CTV 12P

Bar lunch fr£2.50 Dinner fr£6.50 Wine £4.75 Last dinner 8.30pm

Credit cards 1 2 3

★★***Cottonwood*** Grove Rd, East Cliff ☎(0202) 23183 Boscombe & Southbourne plan **56** *A1*

A colour washed, brick building, surrounded by well kept lawns and gardens, in the East Cliff area overlooking the sea.

30rm(15➡4⋒) CTV in all bedrooms B

Lift 80P ✽ billiards Live music and dancing twice wkly

Bournemouth & Boscombe

☕ Last dinner 8pm

Credit card 3

★★**County** Westover Rd ☎(0202) 22385 Central plan **7** *E2* Closed Jan

Conveniently located hotel with friendly efficient service.

55rm(28➡3⋒)(15fb) CTV in all bedrooms Ⓡ sB&B£13–£20 dB&B£24–£34 dB&B➡⋒£28–£40 B

Lift ☾ CTV Live music and dancing twice wkly. Cabaret wkly *xmas*

English & Continental **V** ☕ Lunch fr£5 Tea fr£1 Dinner fr£6.50 Wine £4.50 Last dinner 8pm

Credit cards 1 2 3 **VS**

★★***Durley Grange*** 6 Durley Rd, West Cliff ☎(0202) 24473 Central plan **11** *B2* Closed Jan–mid Feb

Within short walking distance of Durley Chine this hotel is also near the town centre.

50rm(19➡6⋒) CTV in 19 bedrooms Ⓡ B

Lift CTV Cabaret twice wkly nc3yrs

Last dinner 7.30pm

Credit cards 1 3 **VS**

see advert on page 142

★★**Elstead** 12–14 Knyveton Rd ☎(0202) 22829 Boscombe & Southbourne plan **58** *A2*

Closed Oct–Mar

60rm(22➡5⋒)(9fb) CTV in 7 bedrooms sB&B£11–£14 sB&B➡⋒£12.75–£15.75 dB&B£22–£24.50 dB&B➡⋒£25.50–£28 B

Lift ☾ CTV 40P 8 Live music and dancing twice wkly

☕ Bar lunch £2–£4 Tea fr35p Dinner £5–£7 Wine £3.60 Last dinner 8pm

Credit card 1

★★**Fircroft** 4 Owls Rd, Boscombe ☎(0202) 309771 Boscombe & Southbourne plan **59** *B2*

A large. Victorian building with modern extensions, set in its own grounds.

49rm(43➡6⋒)(18fb) CTV in all bedrooms sB&B➡⋒£13.50–£18 dB&B➡⋒£27–£36 B

☾ CTV 50P CFA squash Disco wkly Live music and dancing twice wkly *xmas*

☕ Bar lunch £1–£3&alc Tea fr60p Dinner £5–£6 Wine £3.90 Last dinner 8pm

Credit cards 1 3 **VS**

★★**Grange** Overcliff Dr, Southbourne ☎(0202) 424228 Boscombe & Southbourne plan **60** *F1*

The frontage of this cliff-top hotel has been recently modernised.

30rm(15➡1⋒)(6fb) CTV in 6 bedrooms TV in 18 bedrooms Ⓡ sB&B£9.78–£12 →

B

sB&B→fi£11.28–£13.50 dB&B£19–£23 dB&B→fi£22.54–£24 ₿
Lift ⅋ CTV 55P ✽ ⌂ *xmas*
English & Italian ♡ ☐ Lunch £3–£4&alc Tea 50p–£1&alc High Tea £2–£4 Dinner £3–£5&alc Wine £4.50 Last dinner 9.30pm
VS

★★***L*** **Hinton Firs** Manor Rd (Exec Hotel) ☎(0202) 25409 Boscombe & Southbourne plan **62** *A1*
Attentive service and well furnished lounges make this an attractive, relaxing hotel.
50rm(28→) Annexe:6→ (20fb) CTV in all bedrooms Ⓡ sB&B£12.60 dB&B£22 dB&B→£26.75 ₿
Lift ☾ CTV 40P (heated) Disco wkly in season Live music and dancing twice wkly in season *xmas*
♡ ☐ Lunch £5–£6 Dinner £6 Wine £4 Last dinner 8pm
S%

★★**Manor House** Manor Rd, East Cliff ☎(0202) 36669 Boscombe & Southbourne plan **64** *B1*
Attractive hotel with pleasant garden offering personal attention by resident owner.
27rm(6→2fi) (12fb) TV in 4 bedrooms Ⓡ sB&B£8–£11.50 dB&B£16–£23 dB&B→fi£18–£25 ₿

Bournemouth & Boscombe

CTV 30P ✽ Disco wkly Cabaret wkly *xmas*
V ♡ ☐ Lunch £3–£5 Tea 50p–80p Dinner £4–£6 Wine £4 Last dinner 8pm
Credit cards 1 2 **VS**

★★**New Somerset** Bath Rd ☎(0202) 21983 Central plan **24** *E3*
A red brick, villa-type hotel, located on the main road opposite the town centre, shops and pier.
38rm(7→1fi) (6fb) CTV available in bedrooms Ⓡ sB&B£11–£12.50 sB&B→fi£12.25–£13.75 dB&B£22–£25 dB&B→fi£24.50–£27.50 ₿
Lift ☾ CTV 20P ✽ *xmas* ♿
♡ ☐ Lunch £3.45–£4.50 Tea 40p–60p High Tea £1.50–£2.50 Dinner £5.20–£6 Wine £4.30 Last dinner 8pm
Credit cards 1 3

★★**Pinehurst** West Cliff Gdns ☎(0202) 26218 Central plan **28** *B1*
Closed Jan
Situated on the West Cliff, near to Pine Lawns and Durley Chine.
75rm(33→20fi) (11fb) CTV in 53 bedrooms Ⓡ sB&B£11.50–£13 sB&B→£13.50–£15 dB&B£22–£25 dB&B→£26–£29 ₿
Lift ☾ CTV 44P Disco wkly Live music and dancing three times wkly *xmas*

♡ ☐ Tea fr 40p Dinner fr £5.60 Wine £4 Last dinner 8.30pm
Credit card 1 **VS**

★★**Riviera Burnaby Rd**, Alum Chine ☎(0202) 763653 Westbourne & Branksome plan **72** *B2*
Closed 3–31 Jan
64rm(37→15fi) Annexe:9rm(3→6fi) (25fb) CTV in all bedrooms sB&B£13.50–£24.09 sB&B→fi£15.50–£26.09 dB&B£27–£48.18 dB&B→fi£31–£52.18 ₿
Lift 80P & (heated) sauna bath Live music and dancing 7 nights wkly *xmas*
English, French, Italian ♡ ☐ ✻ Lunch fr £3.75 Dinner fr £6.90 Wine £5 Last dinner 8pm

★★**Hotel Riviera West Cliff Gdns** ☎(0202) 22845 Central plan **30** *B1*
Closed Nov–Mar
The terrace and some bedrooms of this modern hotel have sea views.
35rm(10→) CTV in all bedrooms sB&B£10.35–£13.23 dB&B£20.70–£26.46 dB&B→£24–£29.90 ₿
Lift ☾ 24P ⌂ *xmas*
♡ ☐ Lunch £2.50–£3.50 Tea 40p Dinner £3.50–£5 Wine £3.05 Last dinner 7.30pm

★★**Royal Exeter** Exeter Rd (Berni) ☎(0202) 20566 Central plan **32** *C2*

38rm(23➡9⋒)(2fb) CTV available in bedrooms ® ✈ sB&B£13–£17 sB&B➡⋒£14–£19 dB&B£21–£29 dB&B➡⋒£24.50–£33 🅱

Lift ☾ ## CTV 50P Disco Mon–Sat

🅱 Mainly grills V ♡ Lunch £5alc Dinner £6.50alc Wine £3.96 Last dinner 10.30pm

Credit cards 1 2 3 5

★★**St George** Sea Front, West Cliff Gdns ☎(0202) 26075 Central plan **33** *B1*
Closed 31 Oct–mid Apr

22rm(13➡5⋒)(4fb) CTV in all bedrooms ® sB&B£9–£13.50 sB&B➡⋒£10.50–£14.50 dB&B£19–£27 dB&B➡⋒£22–£34 🅱

CTV 5P nc5yrs

♡ ☐ Lunch £3–£4 Tea 45p Dinner £5–£6 Wine £3.25 Last dinner 7.45pm

Credit cards 1 2 3 5

★★**Studland Dene** Studland Rd, Alum Chine ☎(0202) 765445 Westbourne & Branksome plan **74** *B2*

Corner sited hotel, nestling into Alum Chine with good sea views.

30rm(10➡6⋒)(7fb) CTV in all bedrooms ✱sB&B£12.50–£16.50 sB&B➡⋒£14.50–£18.50 dB&B£25–£33 dB&B➡⋒£29–£37

10P 🚗 *xmas*

🅱 English & French V ♡ ☐ ✱Lunch £2.60–£5.30 Tea 25p–50p Last dinner 7.15pm

★★**Sun Court** West Hill Rd ☎(0202) 21343 Central plan **34** *B1*
RS May–Oct

Situated in the West Cliff area, within short walking distance of Cliff Lawns and town centre.

36rm(15➡16⋒)(8fb) CTV in all bedrooms ® sB&B£13–£19 sB&B➡⋒£15.50–£21.50 dB&B£24–£36 dB&B➡⋒£29–£42 🅱

Lift CTV 26P *xmas*

♡ ☐ Lunch £4 Tea 44p High Tea £1.25–£2 Dinner £4.50–£6&alc Wine £4 Last dinner 8pm

Credit cards 1 2 3 5 **VS**

★★*L* **Tralee** West Hill Rd, West Cliff ☎(0202) 26246 Central plan **35** *C1*

Large mellow hotel with spacious accommodation, plus pool, sauna and games room.

100rm(33➡2⋒)(20fb) CTV available in bedrooms ® sB&B£15–£18 sB&B➡⋒£19–£22 dB&B£30–£36 dB&B➡⋒£38–£44 🅱

Lift ☾ ⚟ CTV 40P CFA ⊡(heated) sauna bath Live music and dancing nightly (summer); 4 nights wkly (winter) ⛳ *xmas*

♡ ☐ Lunch £4.50 Tea 75p Dinner £5 Last dinner 8pm

Credit cards 1 2 3 4 5 **VS**

See advert on page 144

★★**West Cliff Hall** 14 Priory Rd ☎(0202) 22669 Central plan **39** *C1*
Closed Nov–Mar

Detached stucco exterior with mansard roof, adjacent to cliff top and close to town centre.

49rm(12➡7⋒) CTV in all bedrooms ® ✱sB&B£9.50–£15.50 sB&B➡⋒£11.50–£17.50 dB&B£17–£29 dB&B➡⋒£21–£33 🅱

Lift CTV 34P *xmas*

♡ ☐ ✱Bar lunch 60p–£1.50&alc Tea 40p&alc Dinner £4&alc Wine £4 Last dinner 8pm

Credit cards 1 2 3

★★**Whitehall** Exeter Park Rd ☎(0202) 24682 Central plan **40** *D2*
Closed Nov–Feb

47rm(22➡)(5fb) CTV in all bedrooms ® sB&Bfr£12.75–£16.75 sB&B➡£14.25–£18.25 dB&B£25.50–£33.50 dB&B➡£28.50–£36.50 🅱

Lift ☾ CTV 25P

♡ ☐ Lunch fr£3.75 Tea fr50p Dinner £5.50 Last dinner 7.30pm

Credit cards 1 2 3 5

★★**Winterbourne** Priory Rd ☎(0202) 24927 Central plan **42** *C1* →

In an elevated position, with views across the town centre, and also some sea views.

41rm(32⇌9⋒)(10fb) CTV in all bedrooms sB&B£11.50–£18.50 sB&B⇌⋒£13.25–£21.50 dB&B£19–£30 dB&B⇌⋒£22–£40 ₽

Lift 32P 2🚗✽ (heated) Disco twice wkly xmas

Bar lunch 60p–£6&alc Tea 45p–£1&alc High Tea £1–£5&alc Dinner £7.10&alc Wine £3.80 Last dinner 8pm

Credit cards 1 3 **VS**

★★**Winter Gardens** 32 Tregonwell Rd, West Cliff ☎(0202) 25769 Central plan **43** *B2*

Early 19th-century building, with public rooms overlooking well-kept gardens.

40rm(16⇌)(10fb) CTV in 16 bedrooms sB&B£11.38–£15.52 sB&B⇌£12.54–£18.28 dB&B£22.76–£31.04 dB&B⇌£25.08–£36.56 ₽

Unlicensed Lift ☾ CTV 24P 2🚗 *xmas*

V Lunch £4.02&alc Tea 50p Dinner £5.17&alc Last dinner 8pm

Credit cards 1 3 **VS**

★★**Woodcroft Tower** Gervis Rd, East Cliff ☎(0202) 28202 Central plan **44** *E3*

Standing in its own grounds, a convenient walking distance from shops, pier and the sea front.

43rm(17⇌2⋒)(4fb) CTV in 19 bedrooms sB&B£11.50–£14.95 sB&B⇌£13.80–£17.25 dB&B£23–£29.90 dB&B⇌£27.60–£34.50 ₽

Lift ☾ CTV 30P 6🚗✽ Live music and dancing twice wkly in season *xmas*

Lunch fr£3.75 Tea fr60p Dinner fr£5.18 Wine £3.60 Last dinner 8pm

Credit cards 1 2

★★**Yenton** 5–7 Gervis Rd, East Cliff ☎(0202) 22752 Boscombe & Southbourne plan **67** *A1*

A detached, brick and rough stone hotel with neat lawns and gardens, situated in a tree lined road.

22rm(8⇌7⋒) Annexe: 9rm(4⇌5⋒) CTV in all bedrooms Ⓡ ★ sB&B£10–£19 sB&B⇌⋒£11.50–£20.50 dB&B£20–£38 dB&B⇌⋒£23–£41 ₽

CTV 25P ✽ Cabaret twice wkly *xmas*

V Lunch £4–£5 Tea 60p–£1.60 Dinner £5.95–£6.95 Wine £3.95 Last dinner 8.30pm

Credit card 1 2 3 **VS**

★**Cliff Court** 15 West Cliff Rd ☎(0202) 25994 Central plan **6** *A1* Closed 6 Nov–24 Dec, Jan & Feb

43rm(16⇌14⋒)(7fb) CTV available in bedrooms on request Ⓡ sB&B£10–£13 sB&B⇌⋒£11.50–£14.50 dB&B£20–£26 dB&B⇌⋒£23–£29 ₽

Lift CTV 30P

✻Bar lunch £2.75–£3.75 Tea fr50p Dinner £4.75–£5.25 Wine £4.10 Last dinner 7.30pm

Credit card 3

★**Tree Tops** 50–52 Christchurch Rd ☎(0202) 23157 Boscombe & Southbourne plan **66** *A2*

A large hotel on the main road between the town centre and Boscombe.

58rm(17⇌1⋒)(18fb) CTV available in 1 bedroom TV available in bedrooms Ⓡ sB&B£9.77–£12.65 sB&B⇌⋒£14.68–£16.10 dB&B£19.55–£25.30 dB&B⇌⋒£23–£28.75

Lift CTV 40P Disco wkly Live music and dancing twice wkly

V Wine £3.50

Credit card 1

★**Ullswater** West Cliff Gdns ☎(0202) 25181 Central plan **37** *B1* Closed Jan–mid Feb

Red brick hotel near cliff top, with friendly service.

47rm(4⇌4⋒)(10fb) CTV in 8 bedrooms sB&B£13–£17 sB&B⇌⋒£15.50–£19.50 dB&B£26–£34 dB&B⇌⋒£31–£39 ₽

Lift CTV 15P billiards *xmas*

Lunch £3.80–£4.80 Tea £1 Dinner £6.60 Wine £3.55 Last dinner 6.45pm

VS

★**Wellington** 10 Poole Rd, West Cliff ☎(0202) 768407 Westbourne & Branksome plan **75** *B3*
Closed Nov RS Jan & Feb
There is a warm welcome from the resident owners of this Victorian hotel.
27rm(5🛁2⋒)(7fb) CTV in 10 bedrooms sB&B£10–£13.50 dB&B£20–£27 dB&B🛁⋒£23–£30 B
Lift CTV 30P Disco wkly *xmas*
V Bar lunch 75p–£2 Tea fr25p Dinner £3.50–£6 Wine £2.99 Last dinner 7.30pm
Credit card 3

✕✕**Boote's** 31 Southbourne Grove ☎(0202) 421240 Boscombe & Southbourne plan **48** *E2*
Closed Sun 1wk May & 1wk Nov
Lunch not served Mon
International **V** 32 seats Lunch £4.85alc Dinner £8.65alc Wine £4.25 Last dinner 11pm
Credit cards 1 2 3 5 **VS**

✕✕**La Taverna** Westover Rd ☎(0202) 27681 Central plan **26** *D2*
Closed Sun
Italian 50 seats ✻Lunch £7.50&alc Dinner fr£8.50&alc Wine £4.80 Last dinner 10.45pm bedrooms available
Credit cards 1 2 3 5 **VS**

✕**Trattoria San Marco** 148 Holdenhurst Rd ☎(0202) 21132 Boscombe & Southbourne plan **65** *A3*
Small Italian restaurant with warm atmosphere. Autographed photographs of personalities cover the walls.
Closed Mon & Xmas Dinner not served Sun
International 40 seats ✻Lunch £8–£12alc Dinner £12–£15alc Last dinner 11pm 18P
Credit cards 1 2 3 4 5

BOURTON-ON-THE-WATER

Gloucester
Map **4** SP12

★★★ ***Old Manse*** ☎(0451) 20642
Attractive 18th-century Cotswold-stone house near River Windrush.
8🛁 CTV in all bedrooms B
CTV 20P Live music and dancing wkly Cabaret wkly nc12yrs
English & French **V** Last dinner 9.30pm
Credit cards 1 3 5

★★**Chester House Hotel & Motel** Victoria St (Minotel) ☎(0451) 20286
Closed Xmas & Jan
Some of the rooms are in a converted row of Cotswold stone cottages, the rest are in the hotel.
12rm(2🛁3⋒) Annexe: 10🛁(11fb) CTV in all bedrooms Ⓡ ✻sB&B fr£16.50 sB&B🛁⋒ fr£19 dB&B fr£24.40 dB&B🛁⋒ fr£29.60 B
22P
Mainly grills ✻Lunch £4.10alc Dinner £6.60alc Wine £4.95 Last dinner 8.30pm
Credit cards 1 2 3 5
See advert on page 146

★★**Old New Inn** High St ☎(0451) 20467
Closed Xmas
Part 18th-century building with intriguing model village in the garden.
18rm sB&B fr£14.50 dB&B fr£29 dB&B🛁 fr£31 B
CTV 25P 9
Lunch £3–£4.50 Dinner £7.50–£8.50 Wine £3.50 Last dinner 8.15pm
S% Credit cards 1 3

✕**Rose Tree** Riverside ☎(0451) 20635
Closed Mon Lunch not served winter Dinner not served Sun
This cottage style restaurant has sound cooking and extensive wine list.
French 28 seats Lunch £9.50alc Dinner £15alc Wine £4.95 Last dinner 9.30pm
Credit cards 1 2 3

B

BOVEY TRACEY
Devon
Map **3** SX87

★★**Blenheim** Brimley Rd ☎(0626) 832422
Early 20th-century small holiday hotel set in two acres of gardens on the edge of the village.
8rm(1⋒)(1fb)Ⓡ sB&B£11.35–£12.50 sB&B⋒£12.25–£13.50 dB&B£22.70–£25 B
CTV 8P 1 ✽
English, Brazilian & Portuguese Lunch £4–£4.30 Tea 90p Dinner £6.90–£7.50 Wine £2.90 Last dinner 8.30pm
VS

★★*L* **Coombe Cross** Coombe Cross (Inter-Hotels) ☎(0626) 832476
Closed 23 Dec–19 Feb
Comfortable and well appointed traditional country hotel, personally run by the owners.
23rm(17➡)(1fb) CTV available in bedrooms Ⓡ sB&B£13–£13.75 sB&B➡£15.25–£16 dB&B£26–£27.50 dB&B➡£30.50–£32
CTV 20P ✽
V Lunch £3.25–£4 Tea 80p–£1.20 Dinner £7–£7.50 Wine £4.50 Last dinner 8.30pm
Credit cards 2 3

★★**Edgemoor** Haytor Rd ☎(0626) 832466
Family run rural hotel with spacious reception rooms and open fires.
18rm(9➡)(3fb) *sB&B£15.25 dB&B£27.75 dB&B➡£31 B
CTV 50P 2 ✽ *xmas*
English & Continental **V** *Bar lunch fr£1.50 Tea fr65p High Tea fr£1.75 Dinner fr£7.50&alc Wine £3.25 Last dinner 8.30pm
Credit cards 1 2 3 5 **VS**

★★*HBL* **Prestbury Country House** Brimley Ln ☎(0626) 833246 Closed Nov–Feb
John and Barbara Steventon provide a warm relaxed atmosphere at this charming, quiet hotel. It is furnished with fine pictures, china and antiques and is very comfortable. Bedrooms are thoughtfully prepared and the food, cooked by both Mr and Mrs Steventon, is most enjoyable.
9rm(5➡2⋒) sB&B£16.50–£18.50 sB&B➡⋒£16.50–£18.50 dB&B➡⋒£33–£37
CTV 12P ✽ nc12yrs
English & French Bar lunch £2–£3.50 Tea £1–£2 Dinner £8–£10 Wine £4 Last dinner 8pm
Credit cards 1 2 3 5 **VS**

★*L* **Redacre** Challabrooke Ln ☎(0626) 833289
7rm CTV 8P ✽

BOWES
Co Durham
Map **12** NY91

★★**Ancient Unicorn** ☎Teesdale (0833) 28321
Old world bars and lounge contrast with modern well-appointed bedrooms built around the courtyard.
Annexe: 11rm(4➡7⋒)(3fb) CTV in 11 bedrooms Ⓡ sB&B➡⋒£16.50–£18 dB&B➡⋒£25–£26.50 B
CTV 40P *xmas*
English & French **V** Lunch £4.50–£6.50&alc Tea £1.50–£2&alc High Tea £3.50–£4.50&alc Dinner £7.50–£8.50&alc Wine £4.60 Last dinner 10pm
Credit cards 1 2 3 5

BOWMORE
Isle of Islay, Strathclyde *Argyll*
Map **10** NR35

★★**Lochside** Shore St ☎(049 681) 244
Good food and views of the bay can be enjoyed from this hotel.

7rm(2⇌)CTV in all bedrooms ®
sB&B£18–£19 dB&B£34–£36
dB&B⇌£38–£40
CTV
V ✿ ☕ *Lunch £3.50alc Tea 60p High Tea £2alc Dinner £8alc Wine £3.50 Last dinner 9.30pm
Credit cards 1 2 3

BOWNESS-ON-WINDERMERE
Cumbria
Map **7** SD49
Hotels are listed under Windermere

BRACKLEY HATCH
Northamptonshire
Map **4** SP64
★**Green Man Inn** ☎Syresham (02805) 209
Traditional old inn situated on the A43 near the Silverstone Circuit.
8rm(2⇌) ® ★ *sB&B£16.50 dB&B£27.50 dB&B⇌£33
CTV 40P 3
International ✿ *Lunch £10alc Dinner £12.50alc Wine £5 Last dinner 9pm
Credit cards 1 2 3 5

BRADFORD
W Yorkshire
Map **7** SE13
☆☆☆☆**Stakis Norfolk Gardens** Hall Ings (Stakis) ☎(0274) 34733 Telex no 517573
123⇌ CTV in all bedrooms ®
*sB&B⇌£35 dB&B⇌£40 B
Lift ☾ Disco Fri & Sat *xmas*
English & French ✿ ☕ Last dinner 10.30pm
Credit cards 1 2 3 5 **VS**

☆☆☆**Novotel Bradford** Merrydale Rd (3m S adjacent to M606) ☎(0274) 683683 Telex no 517312
Modern, multi-storey hotel standing close to the motorway.
136⇌ CTV in all bedrooms
*sB&B⇌£29.90 dB&B⇌£37.75 B
Lift ☾ ## 140P ✿ (heated) billiards

Continental V ✿ ☕ *Lunch £6.50alc Tea 70p Dinner £6.50alc Wine £6 Last dinner mdnt
Credit cards 1 2 3 4 5 **VS**

★★★**Victoria** Bridge St (Trusthouse Forte) ☎(0274) 728706 Telex no 517456
Architecturally interesting hotel with tall elegant reception rooms, comfortable bedrooms and self-service carvery.
59rm(38⇌6) CTV in all bedrooms ®
sB&B£30.50 sB&B⇌£36.50 dB&B£42
dB&B⇌£50 B
Lift ☾ 40P CFA
Mainly grills ✿ Last dinner 10pm
Credit cards 1 2 3 4 5

★**Dubrovnik** 3 Oak Av ☎(0274) 43511
Graceful Victorian building, former wool merchants house standing in own grounds.
14rm
30P *xmas*
✿ Last dinner 10pm
Credit card 3

BRADWORTHY
Devon
Map **2** SS31
★ *HB* **Lake Villa** ☎(040924) 342
19th-century part converted farmhouse and Victorian house on the edge of the Moor, ¼m from the village.
8rm(2⇌3) 3 TV in 6 bedrooms ® ★
sB&B£14–£17 sB&B⇌£15–£18
dB&B£26–£32 dB&B⇌£28–£34 B
CTV 10P ✿ (hard) billiards nc8yrs *xmas*
V ✿ ☕ Lunch £6.50–£7.50 Tea fr50p Dinner £8.50–£10 Wine £6.25 Last dinner 9pm **VS**

BRAE
Shetland
Map **16** HU36
★★★ *HBL* **Busta House** ☎(080622) 506
Closed mid Dec–mid Jan
Dating from the 16th century, this listed historic building is said to be the oldest continuously inhabited house on Shetland. It overlooks its own harbour and has been carefully modernised while retaining a country house atmosphere.
21rm(13⇌8) CTV in all bedrooms ®
sB&B⇌£25–£40 dB&B⇌£25–£50 B
☾ 30P ✿
V ✿ ☕ Lunch £6.15 Tea £1 Dinner £12.50 Wine £4.60 Last dinner 9.30pm
VS

BRAEMAR
Grampian *Aberdeenshire*
Map **15** NO19
★★★**Invercauld Arms** ☎(03383) 605 Telex no 739169
Closed Nov–30 Dec
A large stone-built, early Victorian building on the outskirts of the village with some historic associations.
55rm(39⇌) (5fb) ® sB&B£10–£14
sB&B⇌£14–£20 dB&B£20–£28
dB&B⇌£28–£54
Lift CTV 50P
✿ ☕ Lunch £6.50&alc Tea £1 Dinner £10&alc Wine £4.50 Last dinner 8.30pm
Credit cards 1 2 3 5 **VS**

BRAINTREE
Essex
Map **5** TL72
★★ *B* **White Hart (Henekey's)** Bocking End (Trusthouse Forte) ☎(0376) 21401
Ancient inn with a modern exterior, retaining 16th-century ceiling beams and wall timbers.
36rm(31⇌) (4fb) CTV in all bedrooms ®
sB&B£26 sB&B⇌£29.50 dB&B⇌£41 B
☾ 54P *xmas*
Mainly grills ✿ Last dinner 10pm
Credit cards 1 2 3 4 5

✕**Braintree Chinese** 3 Rayne Rd ☎(0376) 24319
Large cheerful restaurant offering sound authentic Chinese cuisine.
Chinese 78 seats *Lunch £10alc Dinner £10alc Wine £4 Last dinner →

11.30pm
S% Credit cards 2 3 5

BRAITHWAITE
Cumbria
Map **11** NY22

★★★**Ivy House** ☎(059682) 338
Closed Nov–mid Mar
A 17th-century house with a Georgian wing added in 1790, quietly situated in the centre of the village.
8rm(5→2⋔) 2 CTV in 6 bedrooms TV in 2 bedrooms Ⓡ sB&B£14 sB&B→⋔£14 dB&B£28 dB&B→⋔£30
9P nc10yrs
English & French Tea £1 Dinner £8.95 Wine £3.75 Last dinner 7.30pm
Credit cards 1 3 5 **VS**

★★***Middle Ruddings*** ☎(059682) 436
Closed Dec & Jan (except Xmas & New Year)
16rm(7→1⋔) TV in 8 bedrooms Ⓡ
CTV 18P 1
English & Continental **V** Last dinner 8.15pm

BRAMHALL
Gt Manchester
Map **7** SJ88

☆☆☆**Bramhall Moat House** Bramhall Lane South (Queens Moat) ☎061-439 8116 Closed 24 Dec–2 Jan
A modern well-furnished hotel in a pleasant area.
40→⋔ CTV in all bedrooms Ⓡ sB&B→⋔£30–£32 dB&B→⋔£41.50–£43
Lift ☾ # 132P CFA
International Bar lunch £2–£6 Tea 75p–80p Dinner £7.50–£8&alc Wine £4.50 Last dinner 10pm
Credit cards 1 2 3 5

BRAMHOPE
W Yorkshire
Map **8** SE24

☆☆☆**Post House** Leeds Rd (Trusthouse Forte) ☎Leeds (0532) 842911 Telex no 556367
A multi-storey, modern hotel situated on the outskirts of Leeds.
120→ CTV in all bedrooms Ⓡ sB&B→£43 dB&B→£55
Lift ☾ 220P CFA *xmas*
Last dinner 10.15pm
Credit cards 1 2 3 4 5

BRAMPTON
Cambridgeshire
Map **4** TL27

☆☆☆**Brampton** (junc A1/A604) (Kingsmead) ☎Huntingdon (0480) 810434
17→ CTV in all bedrooms Ⓡ
*sB&B→£31.50 dB&B→£42
Lift ☾ 250P 16 Disco Fri *xmas*
V *Lunch £6.50&alc Dinner £6.50&alc Wine £5.25 Last dinner 10pm
Credit cards 1 2 3 4 5

BRAMPTON
Cumbria
Map **12** NY56

★★**Howard Arms** Front St ☎(06977) 2357
Tastefully modernised 17th-century coaching inn situated in the centre of the old Market Place.
11rm(2⇌9⋔) CTV in all bedrooms sB&B⇌⋔£14.50 dB&B⇌⋔£26–£27
CTV 20P
V ✿ ☕ Lunch fr£2.10 Tea 40p–£1.80 Dinner £2.20–£5.50 Wine £4.70 Last dinner 8.45pm
Credit cards 1 2 3 **VS**

★★**New Bridge** Lanercost (2½m NE on unclass road) ☎(06977) 2224
This hotel stands in its own grounds and on the River Irthing.
6rm(2⇌1⋔) Annexe: 2rm(1⇌1⋔)(1fb) sB&B£15–£16.50 sB&B⇌⋔£18–£19.50 dB&B£28–£30.50 dB&B⇌⋔£32–£35 B
CTV 30P ✱
International ✿ ☕ Bar lunch £3.50alc Tea 50p Dinner £7.50alc Wine £4 Last dinner 8.30pm

❀★★**Tarn End** Talkin Tarn (2½m S off B6413) ☎(069 77) 2340
Closed Oct & Xmas Day
7rm
CTV 100P ✱ nc14yrs
English & French ✿ ☕ Last dinner 8.45pm
Credit card 1

BRANDON
Suffolk
Map **5** TL78
★**Great Eastern** Bridge St ☎Thetford (0842) 810229
Small family-run hotel, near the railway station.
12rm (2fb) TV in 4 bedrooms ® ✱sB&B fr£12 dB&B fr£19.50
CTV 20P 3
Mainly grills V ✿ ☕ ✱Lunch fr£3&alc Tea fr£1.50 Dinner fr£9&alc Wine £3.85 Last dinner 8.15pm

BRANDON
Warwickshire
Map **4** SP47
★★★**Brandon Hall** Main St (Trusthouse Forte) ☎Coventry (0203) 542571 Telex no 31472
A recently modernised commercial hotel situated in wooded grounds.
68rm(44⇌) CTV in all bedrooms ® sB&B£26 sB&B⇌£36.50 dB&B£40 dB&B⇌£51 B
☾ 250P CFA ✱ squash *xmas*
✿ ☕ Last dinner 9.30pm
Credit cards 1 2 3 4 5

BRANKSOME
Dorset
See **Poole**

BRANSCOMBE
Devon
Map **3** SY18
✕**Masons Arms** ☎(029 780) 300
A country inn with a restaurant, in this small village not far from the beach.
English & French **V** 44 seats Lunch £5 Tea fr40p High Tea £1–£2.50 Dinner £8–£12 Wine £4.15 Last dinner 9pm 30P bedrooms available

BRANSGORE
Hampshire
Map **4** SZ19
★★★ *H Harrow Lodge Country House* Lyndhurst Rd ☎(0425) 72064
Secluded Victorian house in 14 acres, where Mrs Shutler's cooking matches the quality of the friendly service.
12⇌ CTV in all bedrooms B
32P 2 ✱ nc7yrs
English & French **V** ✿ Last dinner 9.30pm
Credit card 5 **VS**
See advert on page 150

BRANSTON
Lincolnshire
Map **8** TF06
★★**Moor Lodge** (Exec Hotel) ☎Lincoln (0522) 791366
Early 20th-century house with numerous additions including Spanish and Swiss bars.
34rm(13⇌3⋔)(4fb) CTV in all bedrooms ® sB&B fr£19 sB&B⇌⋔ fr£21 dB&B fr£33 dB&B⇌⋔ fr£36 B
150P *xmas* ♿
English & Continental **V** ✿ Lunch £4.25–£5&alc Dinner £6–£6.50&alc Wine £5 Last dinner 9.15pm
Credit cards 1 2 3 5 **VS**

BRAY
Berkshire
Map **4** SU97
✕✕ ***Hind's Head*** ☎Maidenhead (0628) 26151
125 seats Last dinner 10pm P
Credit cards 1 2 3 5

BRECHFA
Dyfed
Map **2** SN53
✕✕ ***Ty Mawr Country House Hotel*** ☎(026789) 332
Attractive small hotel and restaurant.
Closed Sun (except for residents)
V 55 seats Last dinner 9.30pm 60P bedrooms available
Credit cards 3 **VS**

BRECHIN
Tayside *Angus*
Map **15** NO56
★★**Northern** Clerk St ☎(03562) 2156
Closed Xmas, 1 & 2 Jan →

❀❀❀✕✕✕✕**WATERSIDE, BRAY**
Ferry Rd ☎Maidenhead (0628) 20691
Closed Mon, 26 Dec–25 Jan & Public Hols
Lunch not served Tues in summer & Sun Nov–Etr
At its best, this restaurant under the direction of Michel Roux is probably unsurpassed in Britain. Its setting on the bank of the River Thames is charming, the decor of the beautifully appointed rooms are elegantly garden-like and the service by emaculately attired Frenchmen anticipates your every need. It all makes for a remarkable ambience in which to enjoy Michel Roux's superb cooking.
At luncheon there is a good value set meal as well as the normal à la carte together with the 'Menu Exceptionelle' (minimum two people). The dishes are presented with the greatest artistry; more to the point they taste even better than they look. Michel Roux is that rare individual, someone who knows how to eat, as well as how to cook inventively. However recherché the combinations of ingredients in a dish may seem, they are always in balance and in perfect taste, demonstrating his innate skill and panache. It is difficult to single out any particular strong point but surely his way with fish is perfect.
Some people criticise the temperature of the items – the reasons are explained on the menu – and others the lack of vegetables, but really, you can forget the usual British eating habits when eating here; from beginning to end the whole meal is perfectly balanced and an occasion to be enjoyed as a unique experience that can leave you breathless with admiration.
As you would expect the wine list of some 230 items dating back to 1921 is also superb, featuring wines that are among the best of their kind and age. Neither food nor the wines are cheap but as so many of our members tell us, they would prefer to eat here once a month than almost anywhere else once a week.
French 70 seats Lunch £18.50&alc Dinner £33alc Wine £11 Last dinner 10pm 20P
S% Credit cards 1 2 3 4 5

Homely, commercial hotel in the town centre.

19rm(5➡12⋔)(1fb) CTV in 7 bedrooms ✻sB&B£12.50 sB&B➡⋔£15–£17 dB&B£25 dB&B➡⋔£25

CTV 26P 2🚗 billiards

✿✻Lunch £4 High Tea £2–£5 Dinner £5.50–£6 Wine £2.50
Last dinner 8.30pm

Credit cards 2 3 5

BRECON
Powys
Map **3** SO02

★★***Castle of Brecon*** The Avenue ☎(0874) 2551

32rm(12➡13⋔) Annexe: 12rm 1▭ CTV in 12 bedrooms TV in 20 bedrooms Ⓡ

CTV 70P ✽ ⌂

▣English & French **V** ▭ ✿ Last dinner 9pm

Credit cards 1 2 3 5

★**Lansdowne** The Watton ☎(0874) 3321
Closed mid Nov–Feb

Small comfortable hotel of character with friendly personal service.

12rm(1➡1⋔)(3fb) 1▭ Ⓡ sB&B£10.50–£11 dB&B£17–£18 dB&B➡⋔£22–£25 B

CTV ✗

▣English & French ✿ ▭ Lunch fr£3.95 Tea fr65p High Tea fr£1.60 Dinner fr£4 Wine £3.70 Last dinner 8.30pm

Credit cards 1 3 **VS**

BRENDON
Devon
Map **3** SS74

★★**Stag Hunters Inn** ☎(05987) 222
Closed Jan–mid Apr

Pleasant, privately owned inn, in this valley village in the heart of Exmoor.

22rm(5➡)(2fb) 2▭ Ⓡ sB&B£14 dB&B£26 dB&B➡£30–£32 Continental breakfast B

CTV 50P ✽ *xmas*

▣English & French **V** ✿ ▭ Bar lunch 80p–£4.50 Tea fr45p Dinner fr£7 Wine £4.75
Last dinner 8.30pm

BRENT KNOLL
Somerset
Map **3** ST35

★**Battleborough Grange** Bristol Rd ☎(0278) 760208

Informal but pleasant country house near M5.

11rm(1➡5⋔)(2fb) 1▭ CTV available in bedrooms Ⓡ ✝ sB&B£11.50–£12.50 sB&B➡⋔£12–£15 dB&B£23–£25 dB&B➡⋔£25–£30 B

CTV 35P ✽ nc3yrs

▣English & French ✿ ▭ Lunch £3.50–£5.50 Tea £1–£1.70 Dinner £4.50–£5.50&alc Wine £3.50 Last dinner 9.30pm

Credit cards 1 2 3

★⌂**Woodlands** Hill Ln ☎(0278) 760232
Closed Dec–Feb

10rm(5⋔)(3fb) ✝✻sB&B£8.50–£9.50 sB&B⋔£9.50–£10.50 dB&B£23–£28 dB&B⋔£25–£30 B

CTV 28P ✽ ⛆(heated)

Wine £4.50

Credit card 3

BRENTWOOD
Essex
Map **5** TQ59

★★★★**Brentwood Moat House** (Queens Moat) ☎(0277) 225252 Telex no 995182 RS Public hols

The building dates back to 1520 and was the home of Catherine of Aragon.

39rm(34➡⋔)(4fb) 1▭ CTV in all bedrooms sB&B£28.25 sB&B➡⋔£40.75 dB&B£42 dB&B➡⋔£52.50 B

☾ 100P billiards ⌂

▣French & Italian **V** ✿ ▭ Lunch £10–£15alc Tea £3alc High Tea £3alc Dinner

£10–£15alc Wine£5.25 Last dinner 10pm
S% Credit cards 1 2 3 4 5

☆☆☆**Post House** Brook St (Trusthouse Forte) ☎(0277) 210888 Telex no 995379
Modern hotel with buttery and formal restaurant.
120⇌ (67fb) CTV in all bedrooms ®
sB&B⇌£43 dB&B⇌£55 B
Lift ☾ 148P ⛆ (heated) CFA
♈ ☐ Last dinner 10pm
Credit cards 1 2 3 4 5

BRIDESTOWE
Devon
Map **2** SX58
✕**White Hart Inn** ☎(083 786) 318
It is advisable to make table reservations.
20 seats Dinner £9alc Wine £4.50 Last dinner 9.30pm 20P bedrooms available
Credit cards 1 3 5 **VS**

BRIDGEFORD, GREAT
Staffordshire
Map **7** SJ82
✕✕**Worston Mill** Worston (1m NW off A5013) ☎Seighford (078575) 710
Closed Sun Lunch not served Sat & Public hols
▣European 60 seats ✱Lunch £5.75&alc Dinner fr£5.75&alc Wine £3.50 Last dinner 9.30pm 250P
Credit cards 1 2 3 5

BRIDGEND
Mid Glamorgan
Map **3** SS97
☆☆☆*B* **Heronston** Ewenny (2m S B4265) (Inter-Hotel) ☎(0656) 68811
Small modern hotel offering comfortable bedrooms and friendly service.
20⇌⋔ (1fb) CTV in all bedrooms ® ✱
✱sB&B⇌⋔£33 dB&B⇌⋔£48 B
☾ 80P CFA ⇌ ▭ (heated) sauna bath
Live music and dancing twice wkly *xmas*
♈ ☐ ✱Lunch fr£10alc Tea fr50p Dinner £6.50–£8.50&alc Wine £3.75 Last dinner 9.50pm
Credit cards 1 2 3 5

✕✕✕**Coed y Mwstwr Hotel** Coychurch (3m E of Bridgend: 1m NE of Coychurch) ☎Pencoed (0656) 860621
Well appointed country house restaurant.
Closed 25 & 26 Dec
Lunch not served Sat
Dinner not served Sun
▣English & Continental 65 seats Lunch £3–£10.95&alc Dinner £10.95&alc Wine £5.25 Last dinner 10pm 50P bedrooms available
Live music Fri & Sat
Credit cards 1 2 3 5
See advert on page 152

BRIDGE OF ALLAN
Central *Stirlingshire*
Map **11** NS79
★★★**Royal** Henderson St (Best Western) ☎(0786) 832284
Large building, dating from 1836, standing on the main road in the centre of the town.
32rm(14⇌) (3fb) CTV in 14 bedrooms
sB&B fr£19 sB&B⇌⋔ fr£24 dB&B fr£35 dB&B⇌⋔ fr£42 B
Lift ☾ CTV 60P
▣Scottish & French ♈ ☐ Lunch fr£4.50&alc Tea fr60p Dinner £8.&alc Wine £4.95 Last dinner 8.45pm
Credit cards 1 2 3 5

BRIDGE OF CALLY
Tayside *Perthshire*
Map **15** NO15
❀★*HBL* **Bridge of Cally** ☎(025 086) 231
Closed Nov
(Rosette awarded for dinner only.)
A white hotel nestling cosily in the centre of the village, it is run by Mr and Mrs Innes. They work hard to provide high standards and a warm atmosphere.
9rm(3⇌3⋔) (1fb) sB&B£13.50–£15 dB&B£22–£24 dB&B⇌⋔£24–£26 B
CTV 40P ⇌ ✽ ⌒ →

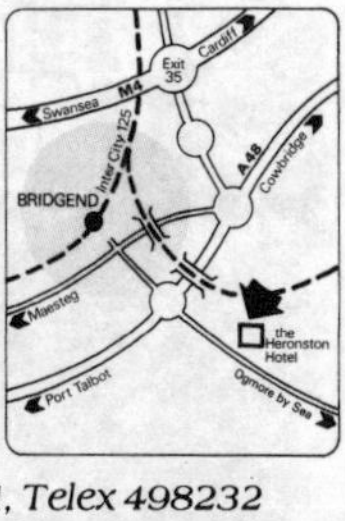

V ♔ ☐ Lunch £2.90–£4.80 Tea £1 Dinner £7.95 Wine £4.10 Last dinner 8.30pm
Credit cards 1 3 **VS**

BRIDGE OF EARN
Tayside *Perthshire*
Map **11** NO11

★★ ***Moncrieffe Arms*** ☎(073881) 2931
Personally managed attractive hotel, located 3 miles south of Perth.
13rm(4⇌1⋒) ⋿
CTV 80P 2⌂ ⇋ ✽
French ♔ Last dinner 9pm
Credit cards 1 2 3 4 5 **VS**

BRIDGNORTH
Shropshire
Map **7** SO79

★★ **Falcon** St John Street, Lowtown ☎(07462) 3134
16rm(3⇌) CTV in 3 bedrooms sB&B£20 sB&B⇌£24 dB&B⇌£31
CTV 200P *xmas*
English & Continental V ♔ ☐ Lunch £5.50–£6.50&alc Tea 70p–£1.30 High Tea £1.60–£3.50 Dinner £6–£7.50&alc Wine £4.95 Last dinner 9.30pm
Credit cards 1 2 3 4 5 **VS**

✕✕✕ **Rib Room** 84 High St, North Gate ☎(07462) 3640
Dinner not served Sun
English & French 42 seats Lunch £4.40 Tea £3 Dinner £12alc Wine £4.25 Last dinner 9.30pm
Credit cards 1 2 3 5

BRIDGWATER
Somerset
Map **3** ST33

★★ *L* **Royal Clarence** Cornhill ☎(0278) 55196
Built in the early 1820s as a coaching inn, this hotel stands in the centre of Bridgwater.
27rm(7⇌8⋒) (1fb) CTV in 24 bedrooms TV in 3 bedrooms Ⓡ sB&B£21 sB&B⇌⋒£23–£26.65 dB&B£27.90 dB&B⇌⋒£32.90–£34.90 ⋿
☾ 26P 8⌂ *xmas*
English & French V ♔ ☐ ✽ Lunch £5.50&alc Dinner £8alc Last dinner 9.15pm
S% Credit cards 1 4 5 **VS**

✕ **Old Vicarage** 45–49 St Mary Street ☎(0278) 58891
Closed Sun
English & French V 60 seats Lunch £4.35–£10.20&alc Dinner £5.35–£11.20&alc Wine £3.75 Last dinner 10.30pm 8P bedrooms available Live music Fri
Credit cards 1 2 3 **VS**

BRIDLINGTON
Humberside
Map **8** TA16

★★★ **Expanse** North Marine Dr ☎(0262) 75347
50rm(32⇌2⋒) (2fb) CTV in all bedrooms ✽ sB&B£16.50–£18 sB&B⇌⋒£17.50–£21 dB&B£31.25–£33 dB&B⇌⋒£32.50–£36 ⋿
Lift ☾ 12P 15⌂ ⇋ ⌂ *xmas*
English & Continental ♔ ☐ ✽ Lunch £4.25 Tea 55p–£1.50 Dinner fr£6.50 Wine £3.95 Last dinner 8.30pm
Credit cards 1 2 3 5 **VS**

★★ **Monarch** South Marine Dr ☎(0262) 74447 Closed Nov–Mar
43rm(23⇌1⋒) (6fb) CTV available in 6 bedrooms ✽ sB&B£15–£16 sB&B⇌£19.50–£20.50 dB&B£27–£29 dB&B⇌£32–£34 ⋿
Lift ☾ CTV 10P 6⌂ ⇋ ⌂
English & French ♔ ☐ Lunch £3.95–£4.40&alc Tea 55p Dinner £6.50–£6.75&alc Wine £3.70 Last dinner 9pm
Credit cards 1 3

XX**Old Cooperage** High St ☎(0262) 75190

Small, elegant restaurant with comfortable lounge bar.

Closed Mon Lunch not served Sat

Continental **V** 35 seats *Lunch £2.75&alc Dinner £7.95alc Wine £4.50 Last dinner 9.30pm

Credit cards 1 3

BRIDPORT

Dorset

Map **3** SY49

★★★**Haddon House** West Bay (2m S off B3157 Weymouth rd) ☎(0308) 23626

13rm(11➡2fi) CTV in all bedrooms ® sB&B➡fi fr£18.50 dB&B➡fi fr£27.50 B

50P 4

Lunch fr£4.75 Dinner fr£6.25 Wine £4.25 Last dinner 8.30pm

Credit cards 1 2 3 **VS**

★★**Eype's Mouth** Eype (2m SW) ☎(0308) 23300

An extended hotel, situated in a quiet secluded valley facing the sea.

20rm(10➡1fi)(5fb) ® sB&B£14 sB&B➡fi £16 dB&B£28 dB&B➡fi £32 B

CTV 60P Live music and dancing Sat *xmas*

Lunch £3.85 Tea 65p Dinner £4.40 Wine £3.85 Last dinner 8.30pm

S% Credit cards 1 2 3 5

★★***Greyhound*** East St ☎(0308) 22944

14rm(3➡) B

CTV 12 Disco wkly Live music and dancing wkly →

English & French Last dinner 9.30pm
Credit cards 1 3

★★ **West Mead** West Rd ☎(0308) 22609
Mellow stone manor house in its own grounds with comfortable lounges and well-appointed bedrooms.
26rm(19) ⌫
☾ CTV 100P (hard) Live music and dancing Sat & Sun
Credit cards 1 5

★ **Bridport Arms** West Bay (2m S off B3157 Weymouth rd) ☎(0308) 22994
Colour-washed, stone, cottage-style hotel, next to the harbour and West Bay beach.
8rm(1 5) Annexe: 5rm (3fb) Ⓡ sB&B£8–£9.50 sB&B £10–£11 dB&B£16–£19 dB&B £20–£22 ⌫
CTV 20P 4
English, French & Italian ✻ Bar lunch 70p–£2.70 Dinner £4.50–£5.50&alc Last dinner 8.30pm

★ **Bull** 34 East St ☎(0308) 22878
Coaching inn on the main road in the centre of the town.
21rm(2) (2fb) sB&B£10–£11.50 sB&B £13.50–£15.50 dB&B£19.50–£21.50 dB&B £22.50–£24.50 ⌫
CTV 40P 2 billiards
English & French Lunch £4.75–£11 Tea 75p Dinner £4.75–£11&alc Wine £4.25 Last dinner 9.15pm
Credit cards 1 3

★ **Little Wych Country House** Burton Rd ☎(0308) 23490
RS 20 Dec–Jan
6rm (2fb) 1 CTV available in bedrooms Ⓡ sB&B£15 dB&B£30 ⌫
CTV 10P 1 (hard) sauna bath nc3yrs
V Dinner £7&alc Wine £5.10 Last dinner 8.30pm

✕ **Bistro Lautrec** 53 East St ☎(0308) 56549
Closed Sun & 1st 2wks Nov Lunch not served Sat
English & French 35 seats ✻ Lunch £2.50alc Dinner £6.30alc Wine £4 Last dinner 10pm

BRIGHTLINGSEA
Essex
Map **5** TM01

✕✕ **Jacobe's Hall** High St ☎(020630) 2113
An historic, timbered, sea-food restaurant, complete with lobster tanks and offering personal service.
Closed Tue Dinner not served Sun
English & French 40 seats Lunch £13alc Dinner £13alc Wine £4.15 Last dinner 9.30pm 45P
Credit cards 1 2 3 5 **VS**

BRIGHTON & HOVE
East Sussex
Map **4** TQ30
See plan
See also Rottingdean

★★★★ **Dudley** Lansdowne Place, Hove (Trusthouse Forte) ☎(0273) 736266 Telex no 87537 Not on plan
79 CTV in all bedrooms Ⓡ sB&B £45.50 dB&B £64.50 ⌫
Lift ☾ CTV 30P 18 CFA *xmas*
Last dinner 9.45pm
Credit cards 1 2 3 4 5

★★★★ **Grand** Kings Rd (DeVere) ☎(0273) 26301 Telex no 877410
Plan **4** *B1*
Spacious, eight-storey hotel with wrought iron balconies and colonnaded entrance.
178 1 CTV in all bedrooms ✻ sB&B £34.65 dB&B £58.80 ⌫
Lift ☾ CFA Live music and dancing Sat *xmas*

English & French Lunch £7.35&alc Tea £2.60 Dinner £8.40&alc Wine £5.50 Last dinner 9.30pm

S% Credit cards 1 2 3 4 5

★★★ **Alexandra** 42 Brunswick Ter, Hove (Exechotels) ☎(0273) 202722 Telex no 877159 (Alexandra) Not on plan

60rm(58 2) (2fb) CTV in all bedrooms ® *sB&B £28.50 dB&B £42.75

Lift ☾ CTV CFA *xmas*

English & French Lunch £5.50&alc Dinner £7.50&alc Wine £4.75 Last dinner 9.30pm

S% Credit cards 1 2 3 5 **VS**

★★★ ***B*** **Courtlands** The Drive, Hove ☎(0273) 731055 Telex no 87574 Not on plan

57rm(44 6) Annexe: 5 (1fb) CTV in all bedrooms ® (annexe only) sB&B £18.50–£20 sB&B £29.50–£32.50 dB&B £26–£30 dB&B £37.50–£42.50

Lift ☾ CTV 26P 6 CFA *xmas*

International Lunch £6.50–£7.50&alc Tea 75p–£90p Dinner £8.50–£9.50&alc Wine £4.25 Last dinner 9.30pm

Credit cards 1 2 3 5

★★★ **Old Ship** King's Rd ☎(0273) 29001 Telex no 877101 Plan **7** *C1*

This hotel's history can be traced back to 1559.

153rm(147 6) 1 CTV in all bedrooms ® *sB&B £35–£40 dB&B £49.50–£55

Lift ☾ 80 CFA Live music and dancing Sat *xmas*

English, French & Italian **V** *Lunch £3.50alc Tea £1alc High Tea £1.80alc Dinner £8&alc

Credit cards 1 2 3 5 **VS**

★★★ **Royal Albion** Old Steine (Prince of Wales) ☎(0273) 29202 Telex no 878277 Plan **9** *D1*

Modernised hotel with comfortable bedrooms and a spacious lounge.

114 (4fb) CTV in all bedrooms ® *sB&B £35 dB&B £48

Lift ☾ 9 *xmas*

International **V** *Lunch £5.50 Tea 65p Dinner £7.50&alc Wine £4.65 Last dinner 9pm

Credit cards 1 2 3 5 **VS**

★★★ **Sackville** 189 Kingsway, Hove (Best Western) ☎(0273) 736292 Telex no 877830 Not on plan

Traditional hotel on sea front with modern facilities.

48rm(46 2) Annexe: 2 1 CTV in all bedrooms ® sB&B £32–£41 dB&B £44–£59.50

Lift ☾ 10 *xmas*

V Lunch £3.85–£6.95 Tea 95p–£2.25 High Tea £3.50–£5.50 Dinner £6–£8.95 Last dinner 9pm

Credit cards 1 2 3 5 **VS**

★★ **Hotel Curzon** Cavendish Pl (Trusthouse Forte) ☎(0273) 25788 Plan **2** *A1*

45rm(10 2) CTV in all bedrooms ® sB&B £28 sB&B £32 dB&B £43 dB&B £49.50

Lift ☾ 16P *xmas*

Last dinner 8.45pm

Credit cards 1 2 3 4 5

★★ **Granville** 125 King's Rd ☎(0273) 26722 Plan **5** *B1*
Closed Xmas

A small, privately owned hotel with an attractive lounge and good food.

14rm(4 7) 2 CTV in all bedrooms sB&B £15.50–£17.05 sB&B £23.50–£25.85 dB&B £29.50–£32.45 dB&B £33.50–£36.85

English & French **V** Lunch fr£5.50&alc Dinner fr£9.95&alc Wine £4.50 Last dinner 10.30pm

S% Credit cards 1 2 3 5 **VS**

See advert on page 157

B

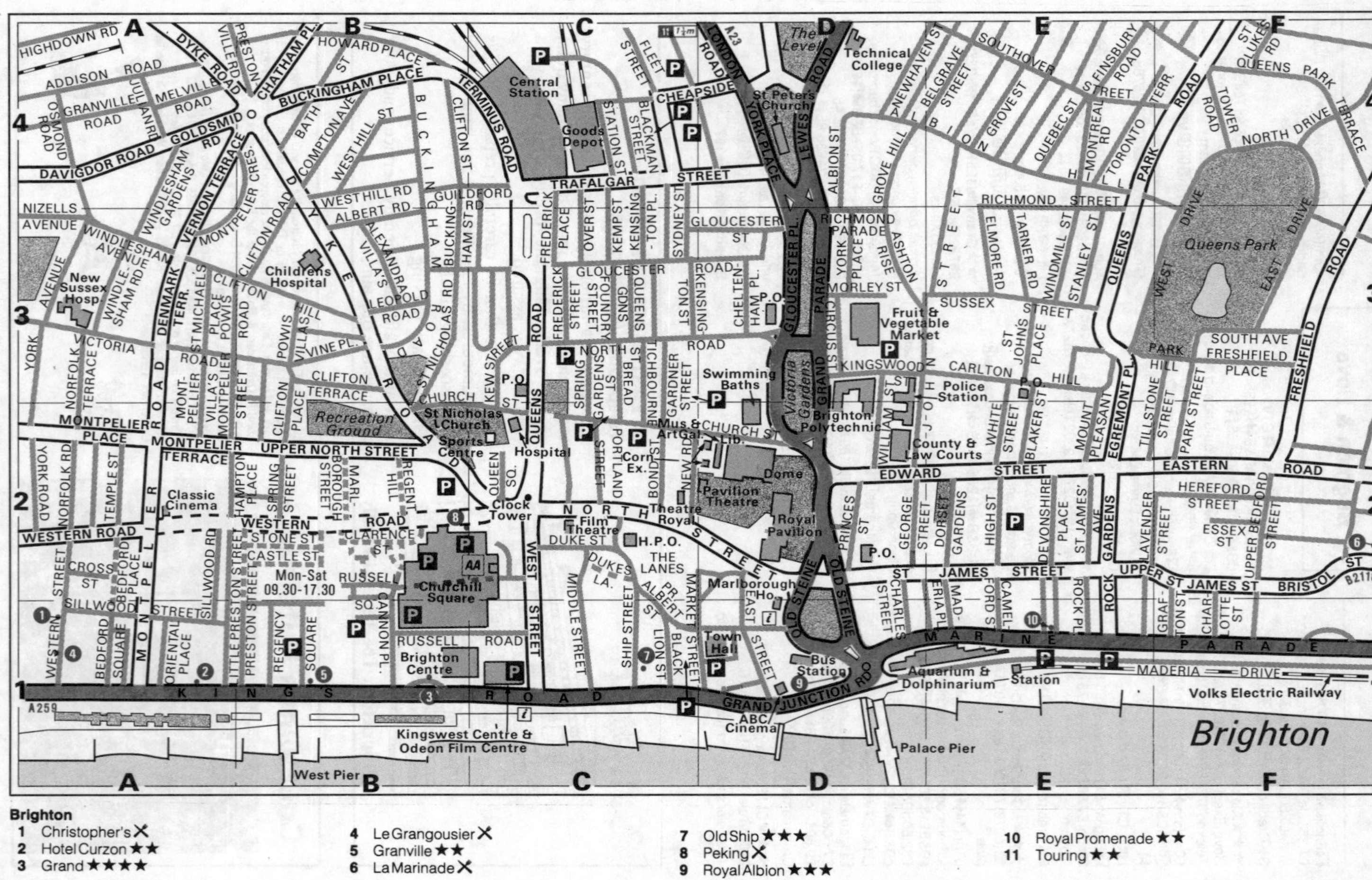

Brighton
Volks Electric Railway
Palace Pier
West Pier
Aquarium & Dolphinarium
Queens Park
The Level
Victoria Gardens
Royal Pavilion
Dome
Pavilion Theatre
Theatre Royal
Churchill Square
Brighton Centre
Kingswest Centre & Odeon Film Centre
Central Station
Goods Depot
Clock Tower
Recreation Ground
Childrens Hospital
New Sussex Hosp.
Technical College
Brighton Polytechnic
Fruit & Vegetable Market
Police Station
County & Law Courts
Swimming Baths
Town Hall
Bus Station
ABC Cinema
Classic Cinema
Film Theatre
St Peters Church
St Nicholas Church
Sports Centre
Hospital
Mus & Art Gal. Lib.
Corn Ex.
H.P.O.
The Lanes
Marlborough Ho.
Mon-Sat 09.30-17.30
Kings Road
Grand Junction Rd
Marine Parade
Maderia Drive
Old Steine
North Street
West Street
Western Road
Queens Road
Dyke Road
London Road
York Place
Lewes Road
Edward Street
Eastern Road
St James Street
Trafalgar Street
Terminus Road
Gloucester Pl.
Grand Parade
Montpelier Road
Upper North Street
Queens Park Road
Freshfield Road
Richmond Street

Brighton
1 Christopher's ✕
2 Hotel Curzon ★★
3 Grand ★★★★
4 Le Grangousier ✕
5 Granville ★★
6 La Marinade ✕
7 Old Ship ★★★
8 Peking ✕
9 Royal Albion ★★★
10 Royal Promenade ★★
11 Touring ★★

★★**Langfords** Third Av, Hove ☎(0273) 738222 Not on plan
Busy commercial hotel set in a quiet residential area.
69rm(24➡25⋒)(3fb) CTV in all bedrooms sB&B£18 sB&B➡⋒£22.50 dB&B£29.50 dB&B➡⋒£35 B
Lift ☾ CTV ✗ CFA ✽ *xmas*
V ♧ ☐ Lunch £5.50–£7.50 Dinner £5.50–£7.50 Wine £4.75 Last dinner £10pm
S% Credit cards [1] [2] [3] [4] [5]

★★***Royal Promenade*** 3–5 Percival Ter, Marine Pde ☎(0273) 697376 Plan **10** *E1*
Quiet, commercial hotel.
40➡ CTV in all bedrooms B
Lift ☾ ⊁ CTV 10P
▪ International ♧ ☐ Last dinner 9pm
Credit cards [1] [2] [3] [4]

★★**St Catherine's Lodge** Kingsway, Hove (Inter-Hotel) ☎(0273) 778181 Telex no 877073 Not on plan
55rm(36➡)(4fb) CTV in 40 bedrooms TV in 15 bedrooms sB&B£18–£20 sB&B➡£22–£26 dB&B£30–£34 dB&B➡£36–£40 B
Lift ☾ CTV 4P 5⌂ CFA ✽ ⌂ *xmas*
V ♧ ☐ Lunch £4.50–£5&alc Tea 70p–90p Dinner £6.60–£7.50&alc Wine £4.50 Last dinner 9pm

S% Credit cards [1] [2] [3] [5] **VS**

★★**Preston Continental** 216 Preston Rd ☎(0273) 507853 Telex no 877247 Plan **11** *C4*
Large, private house, converted and modernised.
25rm(1➡8⋒) CTV in all bedrooms B
41P
♧ Last dinner 9pm
Credit cards [1] [2] [3]

XXX**Eaton** Eaton Gdns, Hove ☎(0273) 738921 Not on plan
Spacious restaurant with attractive lounge bar.
Closed Xmas day & Good Fri
Dinner not served Sun
▪ International **V** 90 seats Lunch £8–£8.50&alc Dinner £9.50–£11&alc Wine £5.75 Last dinner 9.45pm 30P
Credit cards [1] [2] [3] [5]

X***Christopher's*** 24 Western St ☎(0273) 775048 Plan **1** *A1*
Closed Wed & last 2wks Mar & Oct, Xmas & New Year Lunch not served
▪ French 22 seats Last dinner 10.30pm ✗
Credit cards [1] [2]

X**Le Grandgousier** 15 Western St ☎(0273) 772005 Plan **4** *A1*
Small restaurant with country-style cooking and friendly service.
Closed Sun & 23 Dec–3 Jan
Lunch not served Sat
▪ French 42 seats Lunch £8.15–£11 Dinner £8.15–£11 Last dinner 9.30pm ✗
S% Credit card [2] **VS**

X**Lawrence** 40 Waterloo St, Hove ☎(0273) 772922 Not on plan
Small friendly well appointed restaurant.
Closed Sun
Lunch not served
▪ French **V** 20 seats Dinner £10–£12 Wine £4.15 Last dinner 10.30pm ✗
S% Credit cards [1] [2] [3]

X**La Marinade** 77 St George's Rd, Kemptown ☎(0273) 600992 Plan **6** *F2*
Closed Sun & 25 Dec–5 Jan
▪ French 26 seats Lunch £3.50 Dinner £8alc Wine £3.25 Last dinner 10.30pm ✗
S% Credit cards [1] [2] [3] [4] [5] **VS**

X***Peking*** 9 Western Rd, Hove ☎(0273) 722090 Plan **8** *B2*
Well appointed restaurant in busy area.
Closed 25 & 26 Dec
▪ Chinese 40 seats Last dinner 11.30pm
Credit cards [1] [2] [3]

✕**Vogue** 57 Holland Rd, Hove ☎(0273) 775066 Not on plan

Dinner not served Sun & Mon

French 32 seats ✻Lunch £3.70–£4.15&alc Dinner £5.70–£6.15&alc Wine £4.60 Last dinner 10pm

Credit cards 1 2 3 VS

BRISTOL
Avon
Map **3** ST57
See plan

☆☆☆☆**Crest** Filton Rd, Hambrook (6m NE off A4174) (Crest) ☎(0272) 564242 Telex no 449376 Plan **3** *F5*

Well appointed, comfortable, modern hotel near M4/M5 interchange.

151➡ CTV in all bedrooms Ⓡ ✻sB➡ fr£38 dB➡ fr£46 (room only) Ⓑ

Lift ☾ 250P CFA Live music and dancing Sat

International ✻Lunch £8.25&alc Tea 65p Dinner £8.95&alc Wine £6.25 Last dinner 9.45pm

Credit cards 1 2 3 4 5 VS

★★★★*B* **Grand** Broad St (Mount Charlotte) ☎(0272) 291645 Telex no 449889 Plan **5** *D3*

A comfortable, traditional, city-centre hotel, recently extensively refurbished.

179rm (162➡17⋒) CTV in all bedrooms Ⓡ sB&B➡⋒ £40 dB&B➡⋒ £50 Ⓑ

Lift ☾ 20P CFA Live music and dancing Sat

International Lunch £5.55–£6&alc Dinner £8–£8.50&alc Wine £5.75 Last dinner 10.30pm

Credit cards 1 2 3 5 VS

☆☆☆☆**Holiday Inn** Lower Castle St (Commonwealth) ☎(0272) 294281 Telex →

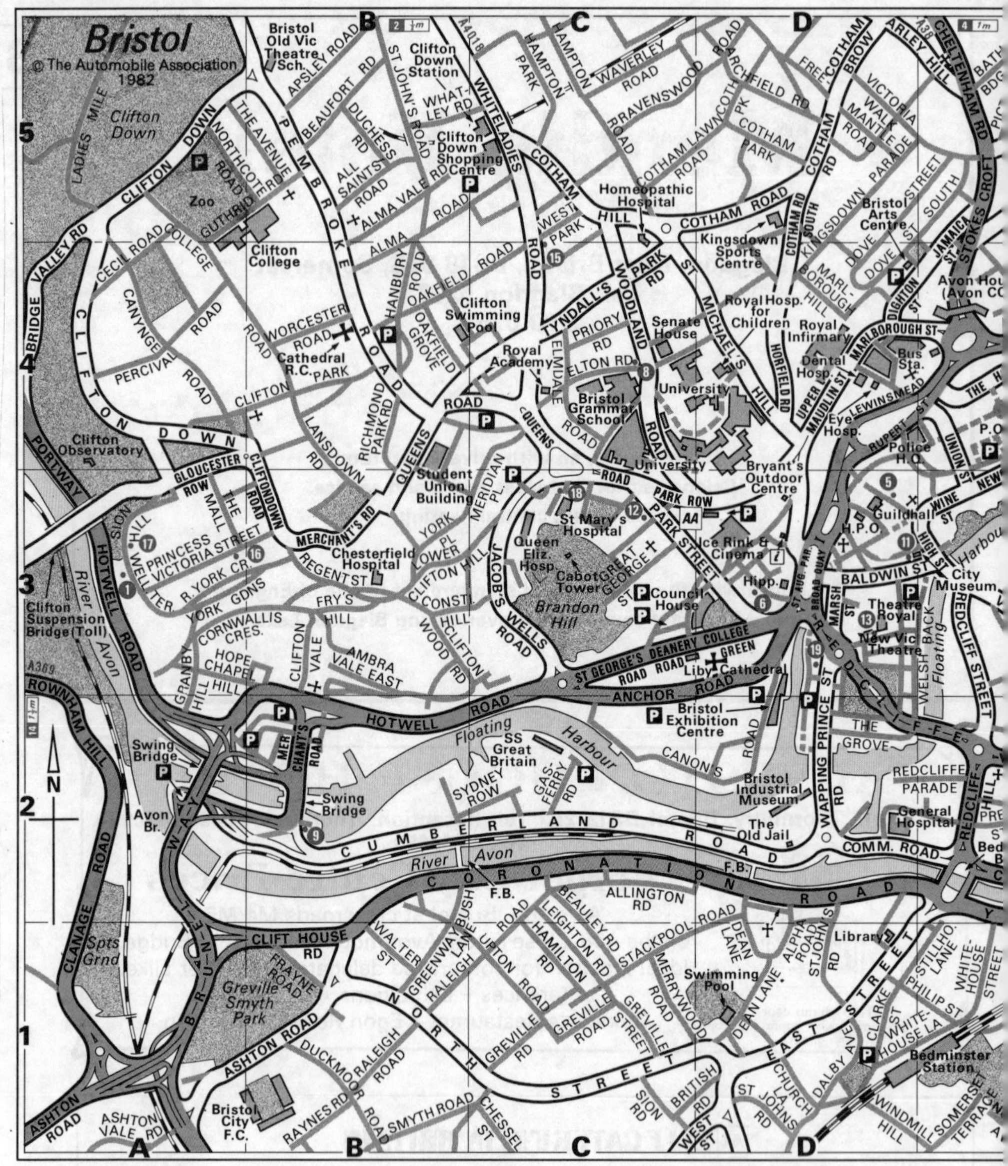
Bristol
© The Automobile Association 1982
Clifton Down
Zoo
Clifton College
Cathedral R.C.
Clifton Observatory
Clifton Suspension Bridge (Toll)
River Avon
Bristol Old Vic Theatre Sch.
Clifton Down Station
Clifton Down Shopping Centre
Clifton Swimming Pool
Royal Academy
Bristol Grammar School
Homeopathic Hospital
Kingsdown Sports Centre
Senate House
University
Royal Hosp. for Children
Royal Infirmary
Dental Hosp.
Eye Hosp.
Bristol Arts Centre
Bus Sta.
Police H.Q.
Guildhall
H.P.O.
Student Union Building
St Mary's Hospital
Queen Eliz. Hosp.
Cabot Tower
Brandon Hill
Council House
Ice Rink & Cinema
Bryant's Outdoor Centre
Hipp.
Chesterfield Hospital
Theatre Royal
New Vic Theatre
City Museum
Liby
Cathedral
Bristol Exhibition Centre
Floating Harbour
SS Great Britain
Swing Bridge
Avon Br.
Bristol Industrial Museum
The Old Jail
General Hospital
Library
Swimming Pool
Greville Smyth Park
Spts Grnd
Bristol City F.C.
Bedminster Station
Hotwell Road
Cumberland Road
Coronation Road
Clifton Down
Whiteladies Road
Park Street
Pembroke Road
Queens Road
Jacob's Wells Road
North Street
East Street
Ashton Road
Clanage Road
Rownham Hill
Portway
Brunel Way
Redcliffe Parade
Anchor Road
St George's Road
Baldwin St
Wapping Rd
Cotham Road
Cotham Hill
St Michael's Hill
Park Row
A
B
C
D
1
2
3
4
5
N

Bristol

1 Avon Gorge ★★★
2 Comptons ✕
3 Crest ☆☆☆☆
4 Ganges ✕
5 Grand ★★★★
6 Harveys ✕✕✕✕
7 Hawthorn's ★★
8 Holiday Inn ☆☆☆☆
9 Howards ✕
10 Ladbroke Dragonara ★★★★
11 Marco's ✕✕
12 Rajdoot ✕✕
13 Raj Tandoori ✕
14 Redwood Lodge ☆☆☆

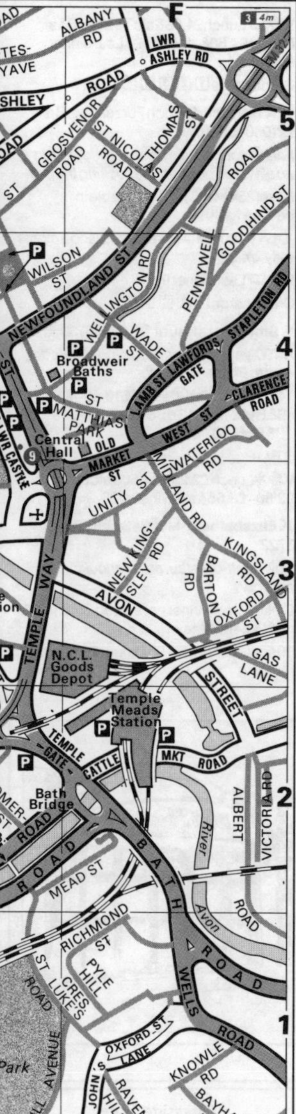
ALBANY RD
LWR ASHLEY RD
ASHLEY
GROSVENOR ROAD
ST NICOLAS ROAD
THOMAS ST
WILSON ST
NEWFOUNDLAND ST
WELLINGTON RD
PENNYWELL
GOODHIND ST
STAPLETON RD
WADE ST
LAMB ST
LAWFORDS GATE
CLARENCE ROAD
Broadweir Baths
ST MATTHIAS PARK
Central Hall
OLD MARKET ST
WEST ST
WATERLOO RD
LWR CASTLE
UNITY ST
MIDLAND RD
NEW KINGSLEY RD
BARTON RD
KINGSLAND RD
OXFORD ST
TEMPLE WAY
AVON
N.C.L. Goods Depot
GAS LANE
STREET
Temple Meads Station
TEMPLE GATE
CATTLE MKT ROAD
Bath Bridge
ALBERT
VICTORIA RD
River Avon
BATH ROAD
MEAD ST
RICHMOND ST
PYLE HILL
ST LUKE'S CRES.
ROAD
WELLS ROAD
OXFORD ST
LANE
KNOWLE RD
ST JOHN'S
RAVEN-HILL RD
BAYHAM RD
HILL AVENUE
Park
F
5
4
3
2
1

15 Restaurant de Gourmet ✕✕
16 Rossi's Ristoranti ✕
17 St Vincent Rocks ★★
18 Tearles ✕✕
19 Unicorn ☆☆☆☆

Bristol

no 449720 Plan **8** *E4*
Very modern hotel in the city centre, overlooking Castle Green, and adjacent to a multi-storey car park.
284➡⋒ (141fb) CTV in all bedrooms sB➡⋒ fr£41.40 dB➡⋒ fr£51.75 (room only) B
Lift ☾ # CFA (heated) sauna ♿
Continental V ♧ ☐ *Lunch £9.95–£11.95 Dinner fr£8.95&alc Wine £6.25 Last dinner 10.45pm
Credit cards 1 2 3 4 5

☆☆☆☆ *L* **Ladbroke Dragonara** Redcliffe Way (Ladbroke) ☎(0272) 20044 Telex no 449240 Plan **10** *E2*
Modern, comfortable hotel with unusual restaurant set in former Bristol glass kiln.
210➡⋒ CTV in all bedrooms ® *sB➡⋒ fr£37 dB➡⋒ fr£47 (room only) B
Lift ☾ CTV 160P 8 CFA ✽ Live music and dancing Mon–Sat Cabaret Mon–Sat
V ♧ ☐ Last dinner 10.30pm
Credit cards 1 2 3 5 **VS**
See advert on page 158

☆☆☆☆ **Unicorn** Prince St (Rank) ☎(0272) 294811 Telex no 44315 Plan **19** *D3*
Modern city centre hotel with its own multi-storey car park.
193➡⋒ CTV in all bedrooms ® sB&B➡⋒ fr£35 dB&B➡⋒ fr£52 B
Lift ☾ 400P CFA Live music Fri & Sat
International V ♧ ☐ *Lunch £5.25&alc Tea 80p High Tea £1.30 Dinner £7.25&alc Wine £4.75 Last dinner 10pm
Credit cards 1 2 3 4 5

★★★ **Avon Gorge** Sion Hill, Clifton (Mount Charlotte) ☎(0272) 738955 Telex no 444237 Plan **1** *A3*
Traditional hotel with terrace, bar and restaurant, overlooking Avon Gorge and Brunel's suspension bridge.
76rm (64➡9⋒) (5fb) CTV in all bedrooms sB&B➡⋒ £32 dB&B➡⋒ £41 B
Lift ☾ CFA Live music and dancing 6 nights wkly
V ♧ ☐ Lunch £5.90alc Dinner £6.70alc Wine £5.50 Last dinner 10pm
Credit cards 1 2 3 4 5 **VS**
See advert on page 158

☆☆☆ **Redwood Lodge** Beggar Bush Ln, Failand (2m W of Clifton Bridge on B3129) ☎Long Ashton (027580) 3901 Telex no 449205 Plan **14** *A2*
Comfortable, new hotel on the rural outskirts of the city with extensive sporting facilities.
72➡ CTV in all bedrooms ® ★ sB&B➡ £32 dB&B➡ £40 B
☾ CTV 150P CFA ✽ & (heated) (hard) squash billiards sauna bath Disco Thu & Sat wkly Live music and dancing Sat Cabaret Sat
International ♧ ☐ Lunch £5.95 Tea fr40p Dinner £7.75&alc Wine £4.95 Last dinner 9.45pm
Credit cards 1 2 3 5 **VS**

★★ ***Hawthorn's*** Woodland Rd, Clifton (Berni) ☎(0272) 738432 Telex no 44220 Plan **7** *C4* Closed Xmas
Lively city-centre hotel with grill restaurant.
155rm (55➡⋒) 1 CTV available in bedrooms ® ★ B
Lift ☾ 80P ✽
Mainly grills ♧ ☐ Last dinner 10pm
Credit cards 1 2 3 5

★★ **St Vincent's Rocks** Sion Hill, Clifton (Anchor) ☎(0272) 739251 Plan **17** *A3*
46➡ (3fb) CTV in all bedrooms ® sB&B➡ fr£33 dB&B➡ fr£41 B
☾ CTV 20P CFA *xmas*
English, French & Italian V ♧ ☐ *Lunch fr£6.50 Dinner fr£7.50 Wine £4.80 Last dinner 9.30pm
Credit cards 1 2 3 4 5

✕✕✕✕ ***Harveys*** 12 Denmark St ☎(0272) 277665 Plan **6** *D3*
Well appointed cellar restaurant.
Closed Sun Lunch not served Sat
French 120 seats Last dinner 11.15pm Live music Sat
Credit cards 1 2 3 5

✕✕ **Marco's** 59 Baldwin St ☎(0272) 24869 Plan **11** *D3*
Good value Italian restaurant.
Closed Sun Lunch not served Sat
French & Italian V 90 seats Lunch £8alc Dinner £8alc Wine £4.50 Last dinner 11.15pm
Credit cards 1 2 3 5

✕✕ **Rajdoot** 83 Park St ☎(0272) 28033 Plan **12** *C3*
Atmospheric Indian restaurant.
Closed Xmas & Boxing Day Lunch not served Sun & Public hols
Indian V 56 seats *Lunch £4–£9.20 Dinner £4.50–£9.20&alc Wine £4.80 Last dinner 11.30pm
S% Credit cards 1 2 3 4 5

✕✕ **Restaurant du Gourmet** 43 Whiteladies Rd ☎(0272) 736230 Plan **15** *C4*
Consistent French restaurant with sound cooking and relaxed, informal service.
Closed Sun & Mon Lunch not served Sat
French 80 seats *Lunch £12–£15alc Dinner £12–£15alc Wine £5.05 Last dinner 11.15pm
Credit cards 1 2 3 4 5

✕✕ **Tearles** 2 Upper Byron Pl, The Triangle, Clifton ☎(0272) 28314 Plan **18** *C3*
Reservations only Bank holiday Mon.
Closed Sun Lunch not served Sat & Mon →

English & French 30 seats Last dinner 10pm
Credit cards 1 2 3 5

✕**Compton's** 52 Upper Belgrave Rd, Clifton ☎(0272) 733515 Plan **2** *B5*
Closed Sun Lunch not served Sat Dinner not served Mon
English & French 32 seats Lunch £9alc Dinner £9alc Wine £5 Last dinner 10.30pm
Credit cards 1 3 5

✕**Ganges** 368 Gloucester Rd, Horfield ☎(0272) 45234 Plan **4** *E5*
Intimate restaurant with sound Indian cooking.
Indian **V** 42 seats Lunch £1.95–£3.60&alc Dinner £4.25–£9.50&alc Wine £3.95 Last dinner 11.30pm
Credit cards 1 2 3 5

✕**Howard's** 1a Avon Cres, Hotwells ☎(0272) 22921 Plan **9** *B2*
Informal bistro with relaxed service.
Closed Mon Lunch not served
English & French **V** 65 seats Dinner £7–£8alc Wine £4.50 Last dinner 11pm P Live music Fri & Sat

✕**Raj Tandoori** 35 King St ☎(0272) 291132 Plan **13** *D3*
Adjacent to the city's Theatre Royal.
Indian **V** 90 seats Lunch fr £2&alc Dinner £6alc Wine £3.80 Last dinner mdnt
Credit cards 1 2 3 5

✕**Rossi's Ristoranti** 35 Princess Victoria St ☎(0272) 730049 Plan **16** *B3*
Well-appointed, small restaurant in Clifton village.
Closed Public hols
Lunch not served Sat
International 42 seats Lunch £8alc Dinner £8alc Wine £4.90 Last dinner 11pm
Credit cards 1 2 3 4 5

BRIXHAM
Devon
Map **3** SX95

★★★**Quayside** King St (Inter-Hotels) ☎(08045) 55751 Telex no 42962
Modernised old quayside inn overlooking the harbour, catering for both tourist and commercial trade.
32rm(22→3⋔)(6fb) 2 CTV in all bedrooms ® sB&B £19–£22 sB&B→⋔ £21–£24 dB&B £32.50–£39 dB&B→⋔ £36.50–£47 B
☾ 37P Live music and dancing 3 nights wkly *xmas*
V Lunch £4.85&alc Tea £2.50&alc Dinner £7.50&alc Wine £5 Last dinner 9.30pm
Credit cards 1 2 3 4 5

★★***Northcliffe*** North Furzenham Rd ☎(08045) 2751
Family hotel situated outside the town in an elevated position overlooking the sea.
60rm(25→19⋔) CTV available in bedrooms ® B
☾ CTV 100P ❋ (heated) Disco 3 nights wkly *xmas*
V Last dinner 9pm
Credit cards 1 2 3 5

★**Smugglers Haunt** ☎(08045) 3050
A 400-year-old stone-built inn situated next to Brixham harbour.
14rm(4→)(2fb) ® sB&B £10.50–£11 sB&B→ £12–£13 dB&B £17.50–£19 dB&B→ £20–£22
CTV 1P
V ✱ Lunch £2.25–£4.50&alc Dinner £2.50–£8.95&alc Wine £4.35

✕**Elizabethan** 8 Middle St ☎(08045) 3722
Bow fronted restaurant overlooking harbour.
Closed Mon Dinner not served Sun, Tue & mid Oct–mid May
30 seats Lunch £3–£5 Dinner £7.50alc

Wine £4.25 Last dinner 9.30pm

Credit cards 2 5

BROADFORD
Isle of Skye, Highland *Inverness-shire*
Map **13** NG62

★★**Broadford** (Best Western) ☎(04712) 204 Closed 16 Oct–Mar

An original inn, dating from 1611, that has been considerably altered and extended.

19rm(3🛁6⋒) Annexe: 9rm(2🛁7⋒) (3fb) Ⓡ sB&B£16.50–£17.50 sB&B🛁⋒£20.50–£21.50 dB&B£31–£33 dB&B🛁⋒£35–£37 Ⓑ

CTV 30P ✽

Bar lunch £2.60–£4 Dinner £7.50–£8.50 Wine £3.60 Last dinner 9pm

Credit cards 1 3

BROAD HAVEN
Dyfed
Map **2** SM81

★**Rosehill Country** Portfield Gate (3m NE off B4341) ☎(043783) 304

10rm (1fb) CTV available in bedrooms ✻sB&B£10 dB&B£20 Ⓑ

CTV 30P ✽ Disco Fri & Sat

V ✻Bar lunch £1–£2.25 Tea 60p High Tea £1.50 Dinner £8.15alc Wine £5 Last dinner 9.30pm

Credit cards 1 3 **VS**

BROADSTAIRS
Kent
Map **5** TR36

★★**Castlemere** Western Esp (Exec Hotel) ☎Thanet (0843) 61566

37rm(26🛁4⋒) Annexe: 4rm(2🛁) (6fb) CTV in all bedrooms sB&B£14.95–£18 sB&B🛁⋒£18.45–£21.70 dB&B£26.90–£33 dB&B🛁⋒£33.90–£40.40 Ⓑ

CTV 30P 2 ✽

English & French Bar lunch £1.60 Tea 90p Dinner £8.80 Wine £3.95 Last dinner 7.45pm

S% Credit cards 1 3 **VS**

BROADWAY
Hereford & Worcester
Map **4** SP03
See also Buckland

★★★*H* **Broadway** The Green ☎(0386) 852401

A 16th-century coaching house with modern extensions, situated in the town centre.

13rm(10🛁1⋒) Annexe: 10rm(8🛁) (2fb) 1 CTV in 22 bedrooms TV in 2 bedrooms Ⓡ sB&B£18–£20 sB&B🛁⋒£21–£24 dB&B£36–£40 dB&B🛁⋒£38–£46 Ⓑ

30P ✽ *xmas*

★★★★**LYGON ARMS, BROADWAY**

☎(0386) 852255 Telex no 338260

This is a charming hotel in a beautiful showpiece village. Under the direction of Douglas Barrington, with the help of his Managing Director, Kirk Ritchie, the hotel has become something of an attraction in its own right. Most of it is around 400 years old with some features dating to the 15th century, and it is a romantic, many gabled old Cotswold stone house. The series of cosy sitting rooms retain many of their original structural features and are appropriately furnished with antiques and artefacts of the period, mixed with some modern pieces from the Russell workshops nearby. With open fires and comfortable seating contributing to one's comfort, no wonder it is so popular with overseas visitors. The Great Hall is used for dining in the summer and is very impressive with its new and striking décor. Bedrooms, too, are well furnished, also with different pièces of old furniture, and are superbly equipped with everything you could wish for, including a welcoming glass of sherry.

There is an intimate bar and across the way is a Wine Bar, but guests would be foolish to miss the meals in

the main restaurant. Shaun Hill continues to improve and his cooking in the modern style pleases our members very much. There is also a table d'hôte lunch in traditional style but the à la carte shows him at his best. The refined cooking with delicate sauces is quite delicious. Mr Barrington is to be congratulated on this well run hotel.

67rm(63🛁⋒) (7fb) 3 CTV in all bedrooms sB&B🛁⋒£40 dB&B🛁⋒£66–£95 Continental breakfast Ⓑ

☾ CTV 200P CFA 5 ✽ (hard) *xmas*

Lunch £7.50&alc Tea £2.50 Dinner £14&alc Wine £5.25 Last dinner 9.30pm

Credit cards 1 2 3 4 5

See advert on page 164

English & French V ✻Lunch £6.50alc Tea 80p–£1.50 Dinner £8.50&alc Wine £4.85 Last dinner 9pm

Credit cards 1 2 3 5 **VS**

★★★*HB* **Dormy House** Willersey Hill (2m E off A44) ☎(0386) 852711 Telex no 338571

A former 17th-century farmhouse offering comfortable accommodation in a traditional Cotswold setting.

26🛁 Annexe: 24🛁 2 CTV available in bedrooms (in main building) ✻sB&B🛁£25 dB&B🛁£50 Ⓑ

☾ 70P CFA ✽ *xmas*

English & French V ✻Lunch £8.25&alc Tea 1.20 High Tea £1.85–£5 Dinner £10.75&alc Wine £4.95

Credit cards 1 2 3 4 5

See advert on page 164

★★*HB* **Collin House** Collin Ln ☎(0386) 858354 Closed 25 & 26 Dec

Delightful, friendly, family-run hotel on the outskirts of Broadway.

7rm(5🛁1⋒) 2 ✻sB&B£22 sB&B🛁⋒£22 dB&B£40–£44 dB&B🛁⋒£40–£44 Ⓑ

CTV 30P ✽ nc8yrs

V ✻Bar lunch £1.50–£6 Dinner £9.50–£11.50 Wine £4.25 Last dinner 9pm

Credit cards 1 3

✕✕✕ ***Hunter's Lodge*** High St ☎(0386) 853247

Closed Mon & 2–26 Jan Dinner not served Sun

English & French V 64 seats Last dinner 9.45pm 20P

Credit cards 1 2 3 5

BROCKDISH
Norfolk
Map **5** TM27

✕✕ **Sherriff House** ☎Hoxne (037975) 316

A period cottage where the quoted prices include aperitif, first course, main course, cheese, sweet, coffee and half bottle of wine. It is necessary to make table reservations.

Closed Wed

24 seats ✻Lunch fr£5.75&alc Dinner fr£5.75&alc Wine £4.31 Last dinner 9pm P

Credit card 1

BROCKENHURST
Hampshire
Map **4** SU20

★★★**Carey's Manor Motor** Lyndhurst Rd ☎Lymington (0590) 23551 Telex no 47442

Comfortable hotel with modern bedrooms and popular 'Jugged Hare' bar.

57🛁⋒ 2 CTV in all bedrooms Ⓡ sB&B🛁£29.75–£33.75 dB&B🛁£39.90–£47.90 Ⓑ

☾ 200P ✽ Live music and dancing Fri & Sat *xmas* →

B

⊟English & French V Lunch £6.95–£7.95&alc Dinner £9.95–£10.95&alc Wine £5.90 Last dinner 10pm

Credit cards 1 2 3 4 VS

★★★**Forest Park** Rhinefield Rd (Forest Dale) ☎Lymington (0590) 22095 Telex no 477802

Half-timbered hotel, formerly a vicarage, overlooking the forest.

38rm(36⇌)(2fb) CTV in all bedrooms ® sB&B fr£25 sB&B⇌ fr£25 dB&B fr£34 dB&B⇌ fr£34

50P ✽ ≈(heated) ℘(hard) ∪ sauna bath Live music and dancing Sat ⌂ *xmas*

V♡ Lunch £5.25–£5.75 Tea 50p Dinner £7.95–£9.25 Wine £4.35 Last dinner 10pm

Credit cards 1 2 3 5 VS

★★★**Ladbroke Balmer Lawn** Lyndhurst Rd (Ladbroke) ☎Lymington (0590) 23116

Commercial hotel with good facilities, located on the edge of the New Forest.

60rm(50⇌4⋔)(2fb) CTV in all bedrooms ®✱sB&B⇌⋔ fr£30 dB&B⇌⋔ fr£45 B

Lift ☾ 70P 3⌂ CFA ✽ ≈(heated) ℘ squash ⌂ *xmas*

V♡ ✱Lunch fr£6.50 Dinner fr£8.50 Last dinner 8.45pm

Credit cards 1 2 3 4 5 VS

★★**Cloud** Meerut Rd ☎Lymington (0590) 22165 Closed 3 wks Jan

From this hotel there are uninterrupted views of the New Forest.

19rm(2fb) CTV available in bedrooms sB&B£16.50–£19.25 dB&B£33–£38.50 B

☾ CTV 20P 3⌂ *xmas*

♆☕ Lunch fr£5 Tea 51p High Tea fr£3 Dinner fr£8 Wine £3.10 Last dinner 8pm
VS

★★**Watersplash** The Rise ☎Lymington (0590) 22344
Set in pleasant gardens and offering modest accommodation with generally modern furnishings.
26rm (14➡2⫚) (5fb) sB&B£17–£19 sB&B➡⫚£20–£22 dB&B£32–£36 dB&B➡⫚£38–£42 ℞
CTV 30P 4 ✿ ≗ (heated) *xmas*
♆☕ Lunch £4.50–£5.50 Tea 60p–£1 High Tea £2–£3.50 Dinner £7.50–£8 Wine £4.30 Last dinner 8pm
Credit cards 1 3

BROME
Suffolk
Map **5** TM17

☆☆**Brome Grange Motel** (on A140) ☎Eye (0379) 870456
Cottage style roadside inn that has been converted from a farmhouse; modern rooms have been built in the courtyard.
2⫚ Annexe: 20➡ (2fb) CTV in all bedrooms ® sB&B➡⫚ £21–£22.50 dB&B➡⫚ £31.50–£33 ℞
CTV 100P ✿ *xmas*
V ♆☕ Lunch £4.95&alc Tea 60p–£1 Dinner £6.35&alc Wine £3.95 Last dinner 9.45pm
Credit cards 1 2 3 5 **VS**

★★**Oaksmere** ☎Eye (0379) 870326
Enchanting Tudor/Victorian country house in 20 acres of parkland with fine topiary gardens.
5rm (4⫚) CTV in all bedrooms ®
*sB&B⫚ £27 dB&B⫚ £29–£38.50 ℞
80P
International ♆☕

BROMLEY
Gt London
Plan **5** F2 (page 423)

★★★***Bromley Court*** Bromley Hill ☎01-464 5011 Telex no 896310
Modernised commercial hotel with informal atmosphere and good lounges.
130➡ CTV in all bedrooms ® ℞
Lift ☾ CTV 100P CFA ✿ Live music and dancing Sat
English & Continental **V** ♆☕ Last dinner 9.45pm
Credit cards 1 2 3 5

✕**Capisano's** 9 Simpsons Rd ☎01-464 8036
Closed Sun, Mon, Public hols, last 2 wks Aug & 1st wk Sep
Italian 65 seats *Lunch fr£6.50&alc Dinner £12alc Wine £5.60 Last dinner 11pm
Credit cards 1 2 3

✕**Peking Diner** 71 Burnt Ash Ln ☎01-464 7911
Fashionable restaurant specialising in authentic regional Chinese cuisine.
Chinese *Lunch £10alc Dinner £10alc Wine £4.50

BROMPTON-BY-SAWDON
N Yorkshire
Map **8** SE98

✿✕**Brompton Forge** ☎Scarborough (0723) 85409
Closed Mon & Feb Lunch not served Tue Dinner not served Sun
English & French **V** 40 seats Last dinner 9pm P

BROMSGROVE
Hereford & Worcester
Map **7** SO97

★★★**Perry Hall** Kidderminster Rd (Embassy) ☎(0527) 31976
Closed Xmas Day evening
The former home of poet A E Houseman, the hotel has added modern extensions. It is popular with businessmen.
55rm (37➡18⫚) CTV in all bedrooms ® sB➡⫚ fr£31 dB➡⫚ £30.50–£36 (room only) ℞

→

☾ 85P CFA Live music Sun
🍴English & French V ♧ ☕ Lunch £6.20 Dinner £7.65&alc Wine £4.50 Last dinner 9.45pm
Credit cards 1 2 3 4 5

❀ ✕✕✕ **Grafton Manor** Grafton Ln ☎(0527) 31525
Historic manor house featuring well cooked fresh food.
Closed Mon Lunch not served Tue–Sat Dinner not served Sun
🍴French **V** 50 seats ✱ Lunch £8.50 Dinner £13.75 Wine £4.50 Last dinner 9pm 55P bedrooms available
Credit cards 1 2 3 5 **VS**

BROMYARD
Hereford & Worcester
Map **3** SO65

✕ **Old Penny** High St ☎(0885) 83227
Small restaurant with good, reasonably priced food.
Closed Mon, Tue, 1st wk Oct & 2nd wk Jan Dinner not served Sun
🍴International 34 seats Lunch fr£4.20 Dinner fr£8.50 Wine £4 Last dinner 9pm
Credit cards 1 3

BROOK (nr Cadnam)
Hampshire
Map **4** SU21

★★ **Bell Inn** ☎ Southampton (0703) 812214
Pleasant inn adjoining two golf courses on the edge of the New Forest.
12rm(9⇌)(2fb) CTV in all bedrooms ® sB&B fr£21 sB&B⇌ fr£23 dB&B⇌ fr£46
100P ✽ 18
♧ Lunch £6.50&alc Dinner £8.95&alc Wine £3.65 Last dinner 9.30pm
Credit cards 1 2 3 5

BRORA
Highland *Sutherland*
Map **14** NC90

★★ **Royal Marine** Golf Rd ☎(04082) 252
Closed 1st wk Jan
11rm(4⋔)(3fb) TV available in bedrooms ® ✱ sB&B£12–£14.50 sB&B⋔ £14–£16.50 dB&B£24–£29 dB&B⋔ £28–£33
CTV 41P 8🚗 ✽
V ♧ ☕ ✱ Bar lunch £2.45–£8.10 Tea 65p–£1.75 High Tea £3.25 Dinner £7.50 Wine £3.45 Last dinner 8.45pm
Credit card 1

BROUGHTON
Borders *Peeblesshire*
Map **11** NT13

★★ *H* **Greenmantle** ☎(08994) 302
RS 10 Jan–Feb
6rm(1⇌2⋔)(1fb) CTV in all bedrooms ® sB&B£14.50–£16.50 sB&B⇌⋔ £16.50–£19.50 dB&B£21–£25 dB&B⇌⋔ £22.50–£30 B
CTV 50P ✽
🍴English & French V ♧ ☕ Bar lunch 90p–£3.50 Tea £1.70–£2.10 High Tea £3.50–£5.50 Dinner £7–£9&alc Wine £4.60
Last dinner 9pm
Credit cards 1 2 3 5 **VS**

BROUGHTON-IN-FURNESS
Cumbria
Map **7** SD28

★★ ***Eccle Riggs*** Foxfield Rd (Minotel) ☎(06576) 398
A Victorian, stone-built house in gardens and woodland.
13rm(4⇌) B
CTV 100P ✽ (heated)
♧ Last dinner 8.30pm
Credit cards 1 3

★ ***Old King's Head*** Station Rd ☎(06576) 293 Closed 24 Dec–2 Jan
Old, white-washed village inn with oak beams, old prints and horse brasses.
9rm sB&B£8.50
20P 4🚗
V ♧ Last dinner 8pm

BROWNHILLS
West Midlands
Map **7** SK00
★★***Rising Sun*** Chester Road North (Junc A5/A452) ☎(0543) 375687
A friendly family-run, cottage-style inn.
9rm
CTV 200P ❀
English & Italian Last dinner 10pm
Credit card 3

BRUTON
Somerset
Map **3** ST63
✕**Clogs** 95 High St ☎(074981) 2255
Closed Mon Lunch not served Tue–Sat Dinner not served Sun
Dutch & Indonesian 18 seats ✱Lunch £5.50alc Dinner £8–£12alc Wine £4.20 Last dinner 10.15pm
VS

BUCKDEN
Cambridgeshire
Map **4** TL16
★★***George*** High St ☎Huntingdon (0480) 810304
Closed Xmas Day
Former-coaching inn dating from the 16th century, with a small garden.
12rm(4)
CTV 40P 4 ❀
Last dinner 8pm
Credit cards 1 3

BUCKDEN
North Yorkshire
Map **7** SD97
★**Buck Inn** ☎Kettlewell (075676) 227
10rm (2fb) TV in all bedrooms ®
✱sB&B£10–£13 dB&B£20–£28
CTV 40P *xmas*
English & Continental V Bar lunch £1–£5 Tea fr40p Dinner £7&alc Wine £4.20 Last dinner 9.15pm
S% Credit cards 1 2 3 5

BUCKFASTLEIGH
Devon
Map **3** SX76
★**Bossell House** Plymouth Rd ☎(0364) 43294
Closed 25 & 26 Dec
Comfortable family holiday hotel with country house atmosphere.
11rm(1 1) (4fb) ® sB&B£10–£11.50 sB&B £11.50–£13 dB&B£20–£23 dB&B £21.50–£24.50
CTV 30P ❀ (hard)
English & French V ✱Lunch £5.60&alc Dinner £5.60&alc Wine £4.95 Last dinner 9pm
VS

BUCKHURST HILL
Essex London plan **5** F5 (page 421)
★★**Roebuck** High Rd (Trusthouse Forte) ☎01-505 4636
Large, gabled building in Epping Forest, smartly modernised with willing, cheerful service.
23 CTV in all bedrooms ® sB&B £39 dB&B £52
45P *xmas*
Last dinner 9.30pm
Credit cards 1 2 3 4 5

BUCKIE
Grampian *Banffshire*
Map **15** NJ46
★★***Cluny*** High St ☎(0542) 32922
Closed 1 & 2 Jan
Victorian building on a corner site in the main square with views out to sea.
10rm(8 2) Annexe: 6rm(3 1) CTV in 14 bedrooms TV in 2 bedrooms ®
30P
V Last dinner 9pm
Credit cards 1 2 3 5

★★***St Andrews*** St. Andrews Sq ☎(0542) 31227
15rm(3 1) CTV in 4 bedrooms TV in 1 bedroom sB&B£10.75–£11.25
CTV 12P 6 billiards disco 3 nights wkly Live music and dancing wkly Cabaret wkly
V Last dinner 7pm
S% Credit cards 1 3

BUCKINGHAM
Buckinghamshire
Map **4** SP63
★★**White Hart** Market Sq (Trusthouse Forte) ☎(02802) 2131
18th-century traditional hotel with comfortable modernised bedrooms.
19rm(16 3) (2fb) CTV in all bedrooms ® sB&B £35.50 dB&B £49.50
30P *xmas*
Last dinner 9.30pm
Credit cards 1 2 3 4 5

BUCKLAND (nr Broadway)
Gloucestershire
Map **4** SP03
❀★★★♛***HBL* Buckland Manor**
☎Broadway (0386) 852626
A large, Cotswold stone manor house nestles idyllically in this tiny Gloucestershire village. Adrienne and Barry Berman have converted this house into a splendid country house hotel that has been awarded AA Best Newcomer *(see p. 17).* *It has beautifully appointed bedrooms, first-class food and superb gardens.*
11 (1fb) 2 CTV in all bedrooms
✱sB&B £49.50–£52.50 dB&B £62.50–£85
30P ❀ (heated) (hard) nc12yrs *xmas*
International V ✱Lunch £14alc Tea £1alc Dinner £14alc Wine £4.50 Last dinner 9pm
Credit cards 1 2 3 5

BUCKLAND IN THE MOOR
Devon
Map **3** SX77
★★♛**Buckland Hall** ☎Ashburton (0364) 52679
Closed Nov–mid Apr
Comfortably-appointed, personally run hotel in a superb situation offering fine views.
6rm(5 1) ® sB&B £14–£18 dB&B £28–£36
CTV 20P ❀ nc6yrs
English & French Dinner £6–£8&alc Wine £4 Last dinner 8pm
VS

BUCKLERS HARD
Hampshire
Map **4** SU40
★★**Master Builders House**
☎(059063) 253
Overlooking Beaulieu River and countryside, once the home of Henry Adams, the 18th-century shipbuilder.
6rm (4) Annexe: 17 1 CTV in all bedrooms ® sB&B£15 sB&B £22 dB&B£37 dB&B £37
80P ❀ Live music and dancing Thu *xmas*
English & French Lunch fr£5.5&alc Dinner £7alc Wine £4.95 Last dinner 9.45pm
Credit cards 1 2 3 4 5

BUCKLOW HILL
Cheshire
Map **7** SJ78
☆☆☆**Swan** (Greenall Whitley) ☎(0565) 830295 Telex no 666911
Once a monastery that provided sanctuary during the Civil War.
74rm(44 30) (9fb) 3 CTV in all bedrooms ® sB&B £32.50–£33.50 dB&B £45–£46
☾ 200P Disco Sat
French V Lunch £5.50&alc Dinner £9.50–£11.50&alc Wine £5.60 Last dinner 9.45pm
Credit cards 1 2 3 5 **VS**

BUDE
Cornwall
Map **2** SS20
See plan
★★★**Grenville** Belle Vue (Mount Charlotte) ☎(0288) 2121 Plan **7** *C4*
Closed Oct–May
Castle-like family hotel set in its own grounds, with towers and a modern extension.
71rm(49 2) CTV in 20 bedrooms sB&B£18.50–£19 sB&B £20–£21 dB&B£28–£30 dB&B £30–£32 →

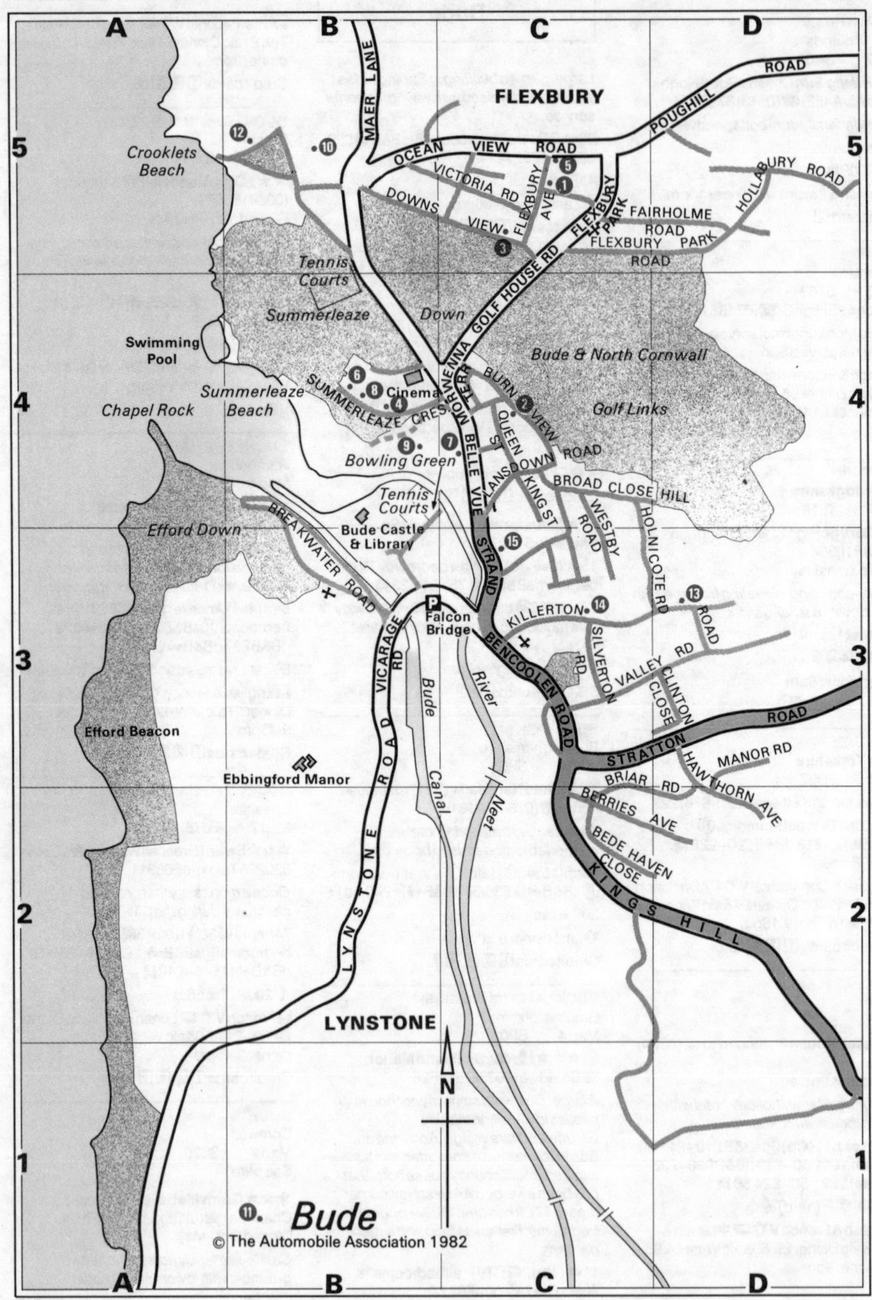
A
B
C
D
5
4
3
2
1
FLEXBURY
POUGHILL ROAD
MAER LANE
OCEAN VIEW ROAD
VICTORIA RD
DOWNS VIEW
FLEXBURY AVE
FLEXBURY PARK
FAIRHOLME ROAD
FLEXBURY PARK ROAD
HOLLABURY ROAD
Crooklets Beach
Tennis Courts
Summerleaze Down
GOLF HOUSE RD
MORWENNA TERR
Swimming Pool
Bude & North Cornwall Golf Links
Cinema
SUMMERLEAZE CRES
BURN VIEW
Summerleaze Beach
Chapel Rock
QUEEN ST
BELLE VUE
Bowling Green
LANSDOWN ROAD
BROAD CLOSE HILL
KING ST
WESTBY ROAD
HOLNICOTE RD
Tennis Courts
Efford Down
BREAKWATER ROAD
Bude Castle & Library
STRAND
Falcon Bridge
KILLERTON
ROAD
SILVERTON RD
VALLEY RD
CLINTON CLOSE
BENCOOLEN ROAD
VICARAGE RD
Bude Canal
River Neet
STRATTON ROAD
MANOR RD
Efford Beacon
Ebbingford Manor
BRIAR RD
BERRIES AVE
HAWTHORN AVE
BEDE HAVEN CLOSE
KINGS HILL
LYNSTONE ROAD
LYNSTONE
N
Bude
© The Automobile Association 1982

Bude

1 Bude Haven ★
2 Burn Court ★★
3 Camelot ★
4 Edgcumbe ★
5 Flexbury Lodge ★
6 Florida ★
7 Grenville ★★★
8 Grosvenor ★★
9 Hartland ★★★
10 Maer Lodge ★
11 Meva Gwin ★
12 Penarvor ★
13 Penwethers ★
14 St Margaret's ★★
15 Strand ★★★

Lift ☾ CTV 70P ✽ ⛵ (heated) billiards Live music and dancing 4 nights wkly ⌂

♆ ▭ Lunch £5–£5.50 Dinner £7.50–£8 Wine £4.90 Last dinner 9pm

Credit cards 1 2 3 5

★★★ ***Hartland*** Hartland Ter (Exec Hotel) ☎(0288) 2509 Plan **9** *B4*
Closed Nov–Mar

Comfortable, family-owned hotel, occupying a favourable position overlooking the sandy beach.

30rm(21⇌4⋒) 3▭ TV in 24 bedrooms
Lift 30P ✽ ⛵ (heated) Live music and dancing 3 nights wkly ⌂ *xmas*

▭ International ♆ ▭ Last dinner 8.30pm

★★★ **Strand** The Strand (Trusthouse Forte) ☎(0288) 3222 Plan **15** *C3*

Modern, well appointed commercial and family hotel by the River Neet estuary.

40rm(37⇌3⋒) (2fb) CTV in all bedrooms Ⓡ sB&B⇌⋒ £33.50 dB&B £52.50 ₿

Lift ☾ 40P CFA *xmas*

♆ ▭ Last dinner 9pm

Credit cards 1 2 3 4 5

★★ H ***Burn Court*** Burn View ☎(0288) 2872 Plan **2** *C4*

Comfortable, well-established, modern hotel on the edge of the golf course.

34rm(6⇌16⋒) TV available in bedrooms ★₿

CTV 12P nc8yrs

Last dinner 8pm

★★ ***Grosvenor*** Summerleaze Cres ☎(0288) 2062 Plan **8** *B4*

Small, terraced, comfortable hotel, 300 yards from Summerleaze Beach.

14rm(2⇌4⋒) TV available in bedrooms Ⓡ ₿

CTV 5P 1⌂

♆ ▭ Last dinner 8pm

★★ **St Margaret's** Killerton Rd ☎(0288) 2252 Plan **14** *C3*

Small comfortable hotel close to the town centre.

10rm(4⇌) (2fb) Ⓡ sB&B £10.50–£11 sB&B⇌ £12.50–£13 dB&B £18–£20 dB&B⇌ £20–£24 ₿

CTV 12P nc3yrs *xmas*

▭ English & Continental ♆ ▭ Lunch £2.50–£3.95&alc Tea 55p–£2 Dinner £4.50–£4.95&alc Wine £3.95 Last dinner 9pm

Credit cards 1 3 **VS**

★ **Bude Haven** Flexbury Av ☎(0288) 2305 Plan **1** *C5*

Comfortable, small, detached, privately-owned hotel within walking distance of Crooklets Beach.

11rm(2⇌2⋒) (3fb) Ⓡ sB&B £10.50–£11.50 sB&B⇌⋒ £12.50–£13.50 dB&B £21–£23 dB&B⇌⋒ £25–£27 ₿

CTV 8P ⛟ *xmas*

▭ English & Continental

Credit cards 1 3

★ **Camelot** Downs View ☎(0288) 2361 Plan **3** *C5*

The welcome would be fit for King Arthur at this comfortable hotel near Crooklets Beach.

14rm(2⇌5⋒) (4fb) Ⓡ sB&B £10.50–£12 sB&B⇌⋒ £12.50–£14 dB&B £21–£24 dB&B⇌⋒ £23–£26 ₿

CTV 10P ⛟ ✽ ⌂ *xmas*

V ♆ ▭ Bar lunch £1.20–£2.20 Tea fr 65p Dinner £6.95–£7.95 Wine £3.30 Last dinner 7.30pm

Credit cards 1 3 **VS**

★ **Edgcumbe** Summerleaze Cres ☎(0288) 2314 Plan **4** *B4*

Closed Oct–Feb

15rm(4⋒) (6fb) Ⓡ sB&B £9.20 dB&B £18.40 dB&B⋒ £21.90 ₿

CTV 11P ⛟

V ♆ ▭ ✱ Lunch £3.75 Tea 50p Dinner £4.60 Wine £3.75 Last dinner 6.30pm

★ **Flexbury Lodge** Ocean View Rd ☎(0288) 3227 Plan **5** *C5*

Small, detached, family-run hotel close to the beach and golf course.

→

16rm(5fb) ✱sB&B£9.50–£10.50 dB&B£19–£21 B
CTV 9P ❀ billiards ⌂ *xmas*
V ☕ Lunch £2.50–£6 Tea 50p–£1.50 Dinner £3.95–£6 Wine £3.75 Last dinner 9.30pm
VS

★**Florida** 17–18 Summerleaze Cres ☎(0288) 2451 Plan **6** *B4*
Closed Nov–Feb
Comfortable, small, terraced hotel near Summerleaze Beach and the town centre.
19rm(6⋔)(7fb) Ⓡ sB&B£9.50–£12.65 sB&B⋔£11.22–£14.37 dB&B£19–£25.30 dB&B⋔£22.44–£28.74 B
CTV 10P
V ☕ Lunch £3 Tea 75p Dinner £4–£5 Wine £3.50 Last dinner 7.30pm

★**Maer Lodge** Crooklets Beach ☎(0288) 3306 Plan **10** *B5*
Closed 20 Oct–19 Apr
Detached, family holiday hotel close to Crooklets Beach.
24rm(2➡3⋔)(7fb) CTV available in bedrooms sB&B£6–£12 dB&B£10–£24 dB&B➡⋔£24–£28 B
CTV 30P ❀ ⌂
☕ Lunch fr£3.50 Tea fr30p Dinner fr£5.50 Wine £3.25 Last dinner 7.15pm
Credit cards 1 3

★**Meva Gwin** Upton ☎(0288) 2347 Plan **11** *B1*
Family holiday in an isolated position on the cliff road to Widemouth Bay.
19rm(4➡1⋔)(7fb) Ⓡ sB&B£6.25–£7.50 dB&B£13–£15 dB&B➡⋔£14.50–£16.50 B
CTV 45P nc3yrs
☕ Lunch £3–£5 Tea £1–£1.50 High Tea £2–£3 Dinner £3–£5 Wine £3.50 Last dinner 7.30pm

★*L* ***Penarvor*** Crooklets Beach ☎(0288) 2036 Plan **12** *B5*
RS end Oct–Mar (open wknds only)
Owner-run hotel and restaurant only yards from Bude's famous surfing beach.
15rm(4➡⋔) TV in all bedrooms Ⓡ
17P 3 ❀
☕
Credit card 3 **VS**

★**Penwethers** Killerton Rd ☎(0288) 2504 Plan **13** *D3*
Closed Xmas
Detached hotel situated in a residential area close to the town centre.
8rm(4fb) TV in 1 bedroom sB&B£8.50 dB&B£17
CTV 8P ⌂
V ☕ Lunch fr£2.25 Tea fr50p High Tea fr£2 Dinner fr£4.50 Last dinner 9pm

BUDLEIGH SALTERTON
Devon
Map **3** SY08

★★***Long Range*** Vales Rd ☎(03954) 3321 Closed mid Oct–mid Mar
Small attractive hotel in quiet residential area.
10rm(1➡⋔)
Unlicensed CTV 8P 2 nc4yrs
☕ Last dinner 8pm

BUILTH WELLS
Powys
Map **3** SO05

★★ *H* **Caer Beris Manor** Garth Rd ☎(0982) 552601
Originally a private manor house of Tudor styled elegance once owned by Lord Swansea. Situated high above the banks of the Irfon River.
14rm(4➡) B
CTV 30P ❀ ⌂
☕ Last dinner 9.30pm
Credit cards 1 2 3 4 5

★**Lion** 2 Broad St ☎(0982) 553670
Character stone built inn in heart of town overlooking River Wye.
17rm(7➡2⋔)
CTV 8P
☕ Last dinner 9pm

★**Pencerrig Country House** Llanewedd ☎(0982) 553226
27rm(10➡)(1fb) CTV in 5 bedrooms TV in 4 bedrooms Ⓡ sB&B£7–£14 sB&B➡£15 dB&B£14–£25 dB&B➡£30 B
CTV 60P ❀ ⌂ *xmas*
Welsh, English, French & Italian V ☕ Lunch £4&alc Tea fr50p High Tea fr£1 Dinner £6&alc Wine £3 Last dinner 9.30pm
Credit cards 1 2 3 5

BULPHAN
Essex
Map **5** TQ68

☆☆**Ye Olde Plough House Motel** Brentwood Rd ☎Grays Thurrock (0375) 891592
Modern chalets contrast with the central building here which is a 14th-century Essex yeoman's house.
Annexe: 65rm(47➡18⋔)(12fb) CTV in all bedrooms Ⓡ sB&B➡⋔£24.50–£29.50 dB&B➡⋔£36.80 B
☾ ## CTV 150P CFA ❀ (heated) (hard) ⌂
English & French ☕ Lunch £6.25&alc Tea 45p Dinner £6.25&alc Wine £5 Last dinner 10pm
S% Credit cards 1 2 3 4 5

BUNGAY
Suffolk
Map **5** TM38

✕✕**Brownes** 20 Earshaw St ☎(0986) 2545
Closed 3wks Nov Lunch not served
V 36 seats Dinner £12–£15.20 Wine £4.50
Credit cards 1 3

BUNWELL
Norfolk
Map **5** TM19

★★ *BL* **Bunwell Manor** (Minotel) ☎(095389) 317
Former manor house dating back to the 16th century set in three acres of grounds.
11rm(4➡3⋔)(1fb) CTV in 5 bedrooms TV in 2 bedrooms Ⓡ sB&B£15–£16 sB&B➡⋔£16–£17 dB&B£24–£25 dB&B➡⋔£26–£28 B
CTV 30P ❀ ⌂

▣English & French V♆▭ Lunch £4.50–£6 Tea 55p–65p Dinner £7–£8 Wine £3.95 Last dinner 9pm

Credit cards 1 2 3

BURFORD
Oxfordshire
Map **4** SP21

★★**Golden Pheasant** High St ☎(099382) 3223

Small friendly hotel with attractive comfortable lounges.

12rm(4⇀8⋔) 2▤ CTV in all bedrooms ®
✻sB&B⇀⋔£26–£28 dB&B⇀⋔£32–£36 Ɓ

16P *xmas*

▣English & French V♆▭✻Bar lunch £3–£9.50 Dinner £7.50–£12.50 Wine £4.80 Last dinner 9.30pm

Credit cards 1 2 3 4 5

★ ***Winter's Tale*** (on A40) ☎(099382) 3176

Small, unpretentious hotel.

6rm(3⇀2⋔) CTV in 3 bedrooms TV in 3 bedrooms ✶Ɓ

CTV 30P Live music and dancing Sat Cabaret Sat *xmas*

♆▭ Last dinner 9.30pm

Credit cards 1 2 3 5

BURGHFIELD
Berkshire
Map **4** SU66

✕✕**Knights Farm** ☎Reading (0734) 52366

Closed Sun, Mon, 24 Dec–2 Jan & last 3wks Aug Lunch not served Sat

V 45 seats Lunch £10.50 Dinner £12.75 Wine £5.25 Last dinner 9pm 30P

S% Credit cards 1 2 3 5

BURGH HEATH
Surrey
Map **4** TQ25

☆☆***B*Pickard Motor** Brighton Rd (Best Western) ☎(07373) 57222 Telex no 929908 Gatwick plan **16A**

Hotel has well-equipped bedrooms and Happy Eater restaurant.

44⇀⋔(20fb) CTV in all bedrooms ®
✻sB&B⇀⋔£30–£35 dB&B⇀⋔£40–£46 Ɓ

☾ 150P CFA✽

♆▭ Lunch £4.50alc Tea £1.50alc High Tea £3alc Dinner £5alc Wine £4.60 Last dinner 10pm

Credit cards 1 2 3 5 **VS**

BURLEY
Hampshire
Map **4** SU20

★★★**Burley Manor** (Forest Dale) ☎(04253) 3314 Telex no 477802

Country manor house surrounded by lawns, gardens and parkland.

22⇀(1fb) 1▤ CTV in all bedrooms ®
sB&B⇀fr£25 dB&B⇀fr£34

50P✽ ≈(heated) ♩Ս⌂ *xmas*

V♆▭ Bar lunch £1.75–£3.25 Dinner £7.95–£9.25 Wine £4.35 Last dinner 10pm

Credit cards 1 2 3 5 **VS**

★★**Moorhill** ☎(04253) 3285

Victorian country house in three acres of lawns and wooded grounds.

24rm(19⇀5⋔) (Annexe: 3rm) (6fb) 1▤ CTV available in 6 bedrooms ®
✻sB&B£19–£21 sB&B⇀⋔£21–£23 dB&B£32–£35 dB&B⇀⋔£37–£40 Ɓ

CTV 40P 4⌂✽ ▭(heated) sauna⌂ *xmas*

▣English & French V♆▭✻Lunch £3–£6 Tea 65p High Tea £2 Dinner £6.50&alc Last dinner 9pm

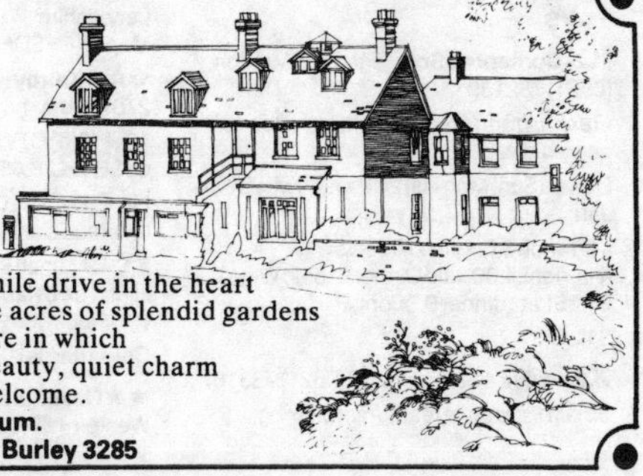

Credit cards 1 2 3 5 **VS**

★**Tree House** The Cross ☎(04253) 3448

Closed Dec–Feb

Attractive, informal and friendly small hotel, situated in the heart of the New Forest.

8rm(4⋔) (4fb) CTV in all bedrooms ®✶
sB&B£13.50–£16.95 sB&B⋔£15.95–£16.95 dB&B£23–£29.90 dB&B⋔£23–£29.90 Ɓ

→

12P 🚗 nc3yrs

✿ 🖵 Lunch £2.25–£5.90 Tea £1 Dinner £6.50 Wine £4 Last dinner 7.30pm

Credit cards 1 2 3

✕✕White Buck Bisterne Cl ☎(04253) 2264

Attractive, Regency-style hotel restaurant.

French 60 seats Lunch £3.50–£5.50&alc Dinner £8–£11&alc Wine £3.20 Last dinner 10pm 150P bedrooms available

Credit cards 1 2 3 4 5 **VS**

BURN BRIDGE (nr Harrogate)
N Yorks
Map **8** SE35

✕✕Roman Court ☎Harrogate (0423) 879933

Closed Sun & 14 Aug–5 Sep Lunch not served

English, French & Italian 70 seats Dinner £10.25 Wine £4.50 Last dinner 10.30pm 30P

S% Credit card 1

BURNHAM MARKET
Norfolk
Map **9** TF84

❀ **✕Fishes** Market Pl ☎(032873) 588

On the ground floor of a converted period building, overlooking the Market Place.

Closed Mon (in winter)
Dinner not served Sun (in winter)

V 48 seats Last dinner 9.30pm P

Credit cards 1 2 3 5

BURNHAM-ON-CROUCH
Essex
Map **5** TQ99

★Ye Olde White Harte The Quay ☎Maldon (0621) 782106
Closed 25 & 26 Dec

Welcoming old coaching inn with comfortable bedrooms overlooking estuary.

11rm(3➡) Annexe:4rm (2fb) ✱sB&B£12.65 sB&B➡£16.50 dB&B£21.45 dB&B➡£24.75 B

CTV 12P 🚗

V ✿ ✱Lunch £4.75–£8&alc Dinner fr£5&alc Wine £3.50 Last dinner 9pm

S% **VS**

✕✕Contented Sole High St ☎Maldon (0621) 782139

Fresh fish and French dishes impeccably served here.

Closed Sun, Mon last 2wks Jul, 4wks Dec–Jan

French & English 70 seats ✱Lunch £4.30&alc Dinner £15alc Wine £4.25 Last dinner 9.30pm

S%

✕Boozles 4 Station Rd ☎(0621) 783167

Small bistro style restaurant offering traditional British fare together with some less usual dishes.

Closed Mon Dinner not served Sun

26 seats ✱Lunch £8alc Dinner £8alc Wine £4.50 Last dinner 10pm

Credit cards 1 3

BURNHAM-ON-SEA
Somerset
Map **3** ST34

★★Dunstan House 8–10 Love Ln ☎(0278) 784343

Attractive Georgian house with additions. The hotel is family run with friendly atmosphere and good food.

10rm(2➡2⋒) (1fb) CTV in all bedrooms Ⓡ sB&B£12 sB&B➡⋒£13 dB&B£22 dB&B➡⋒£24 B

25P 🚗 ✽

English & French **V** ✿ 🖵 Lunch £1.75–£3&alc Tea fr50p Dinner £3–£6&alc Wine £4.25 Last dinner 10pm

Credit cards 1 2 3 5

★★Royal Clarence The Esplanade (Minotel) ☎(0278) 783138

A privately owned and run Georgian house on the sea front with modern facilities.

15rm(5➡) (2fb) CTV in all bedrooms Ⓡ sB&B£11.50–£12.50 dB&B£21–£22 dB&B➡£22–£23 B

☾ CTV 15P

V ✿ 🖵 Lunch fr£3.50&alc Dinner £4–£4.50&alc Wine £3.90 Last dinner 8.30pm

Credit cards 1 3 5 **VS**

★Richmond 32 Berrow Rd ☎(0278) 782984

Personally-run small hotel with good home cooking.

12rm(4➡2⋒) (4fb) CTV in 2 bedrooms TV in 1 bedroom sB&B£8.50 sB&B➡⋒£10.50 dB&B£16 dB&B➡⋒£20

CTV 8P 🚗 nc5yrs

V ✿ 🖵 Lunch £3 Tea 75p Dinner fr£5 Wine £3.50 Last dinner 8pm

Credit cards 1 3

BURNLEY
Lancashire
Map **7** SD83

☆☆☆Keirby Keirby Walk ☎(0282) 27611 Telex no 63119

49➡ (8fb) CTV in all bedrooms Ⓡ sB&B➡£28.65 dB&B➡£36.15 B

Lift ☾ ## CTV 200P 11 🏠 Disco twice wkly Live music and dancing twice wkly

V ✿ 🖵 Lunch £1.25–£4.45 Tea fr55p High Tea £1.25–£4.45 Dinner £6.25–£10&alc Wine £5.25 Last dinner 9.45pm

Credit cards 1 2 3 5

★★Rosehill House Rosehill Av (Best Western) ☎(0282) 53931

Large, attractive, stone-built house in elevated grounds yet close to the town centre.

20rm(10➡10⋒) (1fb) CTV in all bedrooms Ⓡ sB&B➡⋒£23–£25 dB&B➡⋒£32–£35 B

☾ 60P ✽ 🏠

International **V** ✿ 🖵 Lunch £3.95&alc Tea 70p–80p Dinner £5.95–£8.95&alc Wine £5.50

Last dinner 9.30pm

Credit cards 1 3 **VS**

BURNSALL
N Yorkshire
Map **7** SE06

★★Fell ☎(075672) 209
Closed Jan & Feb

Detached stone building in an elevated position overlooking the River Wharfe.

16rm(8➡1⋒) (4fb) Ⓡ ✱ sB&B£15–£21 dB&B£22–£26 dB&B➡⋒£25–£32 B

CTV 60P ✽

English & Continental **V** ✿ Lunch £4alc Dinner £7.50&alc Wine £4.50 Last dinner 9pm

Credit cards 1 3

★★Red Lion ☎(075672) 204

An old-world, stone-built inn on the banks of the River Wharfe in the centre of the village.

12rm(2➡2⋒) CTV in 4 bedrooms Ⓡ B

CTV 40P

Last dinner 8.45pm

BURPHAM
West Sussex
Map **4** TQ00

★Burpham Country Old Down ☎Arundel (0903) 882160

7rm Ⓡ ✱ sB&B£15–£19 dB&B£28–£35 B

CTV 12P 🚗 ✽ nc5yrs *xmas*

✿ 🖵 Lunch £4.80–£6 Tea fr65p Dinner £8&alc Wine £4.50 Last dinner 9pm

Credit cards 1 3 **VS**

BURRINGTON
Devon
Map **2** SS61

★★★ Northcote Manor (2m NW of village towards Portsmouth Arms Station & A377) (Best Western) ☎High Bickington (0769) 60501
Closed 28 Nov–26 Feb

An 18th century building of great character where modern facilities are combined with traditional comfort.

12rm(10➡) CTV in all bedrooms ✱ sB&B£20–£22 sB&B➡£20–£22 dB&B£40–£44 dB&B➡£40–£44 B

20P 🚗 ✽ *xmas*

✿ 🖵 Lunch £4–£4.50 Tea 50p–60p Dinner £9–£9.50&alc Wine £4.40 Last dinner 8.30pm

Credit cards 1 2 3 5 **VS**

BURTON BRADSTOCK
Dorset
Map **3** SY48

★★**Burton Cliff** Cliff Rd ☎(0308) 897205
Closed 3 Jan–Feb
RS 2 Mar–23 Mar & 9 Nov–2 Jan
Gabled villa with new extensions, located on the clifftop where it has unrivalled views.
14rm(3➡)(3fb) Ⓡ sB&B£11.50–£13 sB&B➡£14–£16 dB&B£23–£26 dB&B➡£28–£32 ₿
CTV 60P ⛟ Live music and dancing Fri, Sat & Sun (Aug) *xmas*
V ♈ ☕ Lunch £3.75–£5.50 Tea 85p–£1.30 Dinner £5.50&alc Wine £3.90 Last dinner 9.30pm
VS

BURTON UPON TRENT
Staffordshire
Map **8** SK22

★★★**Riverside** Warren Ln, Branston ☎(0283) 63117
23rm(21➡) CTV in all bedrooms sB&B£25 sB&B➡£25 dB&B£35 dB&B➡£35
☾ 250P ⛟ ❀ ♪
🂠English & French ♈ ☕ Lunch £6.50–£6.75&alc Dinner £7.25–£7.50&alc Wine £4.95 Last dinner 10pm
Credit cards 1 3

★★*HB* **Brookhouse Inn** Brookside, Rolleston-on-Dove (2½m N off A50) (Exec Hotel) ☎(0283) 814188
Closed Xmas & New Year
A William and Mary period farmhouse with meticulous red brick façade set in peaceful surroundings.
8➡ Annexe: 8rm(7➡1⋔) CTV in 16 bedrooms Ⓡ ✱ sB&B➡⋔£28 dB&B➡⋔£35 ₿
50P ⛟ nc10yrs
♈ ✻ Lunch £4.75&alc Dinner £11&alc Wine £4.55 Last dinner 9.30pm
Credit cards 1 2 3 5

BURY
Gt Manchester
Map **7** SD81

★**Woolfield House** Wash Ln ☎061-764 7048
Large functional, partially modernised hotel with resident proprietor.
13rm TV in all bedrooms ✻ sB&B£12.65 dB&B£21.85
CTV 30P
♈ ☕ ✻ Lunch fr£4.25 Tea fr40p Dinner fr£6.55&alc Wine £3.90 Last dinner 8.45pm

❀ ✕✕**Normandie**, Birtle (3m NE off Rochdale rd B6222) ☎061-764 3869
Sophisticated decor and a high standard of French cuisine characterise this remote restaurant.
Closed Sun Lunch not served Sat
🂠French 70 seats Lunch £10–£14&alc Dinner £14–£17&alc Wine £6.50 Last dinner 9.30pm 60P
S% Credit cards 1 2 3 5 **VS**

BURY ST EDMUNDS
Suffolk
Map **5** TL86

★★★*BL* **Angel** Angel Hill ☎(0284) 3926 Telex no 81630
Traditional hotel with the deserved reputation of being one of East Anglia's best.
43rm(38➡1⋔) 4▤ CTV in all bedrooms sB&B fr£26 sB&B➡⋔ fr£39 dB&B fr£39 dB&B➡⋔ fr£50 ₿
☾ 20P 6🏠 CFA *xmas*
V ♈ ☕ Lunch £10alc Tea 45p&alc Dinner £16alc Wine £6 Last dinner 9.45pm
Credit cards 1 2 3 5

★★*Everards* Cornhill ☎(0284) 5384
A modernised, Georgian inn.
16rm(4➡) CTV in all bedrooms Ⓡ ₿
CTV 14P 4🏠
🂠English & French ♈ Last dinner 9.30pm
Credit cards 1 3

★★**Suffolk** 38 The Buttermarket (Trusthouse Forte) ☎(0284) 3995
41rm(13➡) CTV in all bedrooms Ⓡ sB&B£30.50 sB&B➡£33 dB&B£40.50 dB&B➡£49.50 ₿
☾ 16🏠 *xmas*
♈ Last dinner 9.30pm
Credit cards 1 2 3 4 5

BUSHEY
Hertfordshire
Map **4** TQ19

☆☆☆**Ladbroke** (& Conference centre) Elton Way, Watford Bypass (A41) (Ladbroke) ☎Watford (0923) 35881 Telex no 923422
175➡⋔ (7fb) CTV in all bedrooms Ⓡ ✻sB➡⋔£36 dB➡⋔£46 (room only) ₿
Lift ☾ 400P CFA ❀ Live music and dancing Sat Cabaret Sat
🂠French ♈ ☕ ✻ Lunch fr£6.50 Dinner fr£8.50 Last dinner 10pm
Credit cards 1 2 3 5

☆☆**Spider's Web Motel** Watford Bypass ☎01-950 6211 Telex no 268048
Convenient, modern, motor hotel
104➡ (4fb) CTV in all bedrooms Ⓡ ✻sB&B➡£17–£30 dB&B➡£22–£35 ₿
☾ CTV 300P CFA ❀ ⛆(heated) billiards sauna bath Disco Tue & Sat 🏠
🂠Mainly grills **V** ♈ ☕ ✻ Lunch £6.50&alc Tea 50p Dinner £6.50&alc Last dinner 9.30pm
Credit cards 1 2 3 4 5 **VS**

BUTE, ISLE OF
Strathclyde *Bute*
Map **10**
See Rothesay

BUTTERMERE
Cumbria
Map **11** NY11

★★**Bridge** ☎(059 685) 252
Closed Dec–Jan
20rm(15➡5⋔) (2fb) Ⓡ sB&B➡⋔£15 dB&B➡⋔£30–£32 ₿
30P 2🏠 ⛟
🂠English & French **V** ♈ Bar lunch £2–£5 Dinner £9 Wine £3.75 Last dinner 8.30pm
S% **VS**

BUXTON
Derbyshire
Map **7** SK07

★★★**Leewood** 13 Manchester Rd (A5002) (Best Western) ☎(0298) 3002
A large Georgian house standing in its own grounds, overlooking the cricket ground.
40rm(28→12⋒) (2fb) CTV in all bedrooms sB&B→⋒£23–£27 dB&B→⋒£34–£38 B
Lift ☾ 50P CFA ✽
English & French V ♧ ▭ Bar lunch £2–£6.50 Tea 70p Dinner £7–£8.60&alc Wine £4.50 Last dinner 9pm
Credit cards 1 2 3 5 **VS**

★★★**Palace** Palace Rd ☎(0298) 2001
Stately stone building, built around 1870, having stylish public rooms with delicate plasterwork.
120→ (6fb) CTV in all bedrooms sB&B→£28 dB&B→£39 B
Lift ☾ 200P CFA ✽ ▭ (heated) billiards sauna bath Live music and dancing wkly *xmas*
English & French ♧ ▭ Lunch £5.75–£6.50&alc Tea £1.50–£3 High Tea £2–£3.50 Dinner £6.75–£7.50&alc Wine £4.75 Last dinner 9pm
Credit cards 1 2 3 5

★★**Buckingham** 1 Burlington Rd ☎(0298) 3439
30rm(4→13⋒) (8fb) CTV in 24 bedrooms ★✻sB&B fr£13 sB&B→⋒ fr£19 dB&B fr£22 dB&B→⋒ fr£28 B
Lift CTV 30P ♣ ♪ billiards *xmas*
♧ ▭ ✻Lunch £4.50 Tea fr65p Dinner £6.95&alc Wine £4.25 Last dinner 9.30pm
Credit cards 1 2 3 5

★★**Grove** Grove Pde (Frederic Robinson) ☎(0298) 3804
A one-time coaching inn situated above a row of shops in the town centre.
22rm (7fb) Ⓡ ★✻sB&B£10–£11 dB&B£20 B
CTV ▶ *xmas*
English & French ♧ ▭ ✻Lunch £3.50–£5.50 Tea 40p–£1 High Tea £1.50–£3.50 Dinner £7.50–£10 Wine £3.95 Last dinner 9.30pm
Credit cards 1 2 3

★★***Sandringham*** Broad Walk ☎(0298) 3430 Closed 24 Dec–1 Jan
39rm(7→5⋒) CTV available in bedrooms Ⓡ B
CTV 12P
♧ ▭ Last dinner 8.15pm
Credit card 3

★**Hartington** Broad Walk ☎(0298) 2638 Closed Xmas RS Nov–Mar
Stone-built house overlooking the Pavilion gardens and a small lake.
17rm(3→2⋒) (3fb) CTV in 3 bedrooms ★ sB&B fr£11 sB&B→⋒ fr£15 dB&B fr£20 dB&B→⋒ fr£25 B
CTV 15P 1⌂ ♿
V Dinner £5–£5.50 Wine £3.50 Last dinner 8pm

✕**Nathaniels** 35 High St ☎(0298) 78388
18th century former bakery, excellent food served amidst the Victoriana.
Closed Mon (except Bank hols) & 1 Jan Dinner not served Sun
English, Continental & Oriental **V** 50 seats Lunch £4.50&alc Dinner £8.50–£15&alc Wine £3.95 Last dinner 10.30pm ▶
Credit cards 1 2 3 5

CADNAM
Hampshire
Map **4** SU21

✕✕***Le Chanteclerc*** Romsey Rd ☎(042 127) 3271
Mainly French restaurant also offers locally-caught fresh fish.
Closed Sun, Mon, 1st 2wks Aug & 1st 2wks Jan Lunch not served Sat
French **V** 50 seats Last dinner 10pm 30P
Credit cards 1 3

CAERNARFON
Gwynedd
Map **6** SH46

★★★**Royal** ☎(0286) 3184
Closed Xmas & New Year
Stone, former coaching inn with modern bedroom extension, situated close to the shops.
58rm(54→4⋔) TV in all bedrooms ® sB&B→⋔£20–£25 dB&B→⋔£38–£42 B
Lift ☾ CTV 200P Disco wkly ♿
Lunch £5–£5.75&alc Tea 60p–£2 Dinner £6.75–£10&alc Wine £4.20 Last dinner 9.30pm
Credit cards 1 2 3 4

★**Menai Bank** North Rd ☎(0286) 3297
Tourist and commercial hotel on the main road to Bangor with comfortable lounge and lovely views over the Menai Strait.
16rm(1→2⋔) (2fb) ® sB&B£10–£12 sB&B→⋔£13.50–£15 dB&B£18–£20 dB&B→⋔£21–£23 B
CTV 12P
Lunch £2.50–£3.50&alc Dinner £4.25–£4.50&alc Wine £3.50 Last dinner 7.30pm
Credit card 1

★***Muriau Park*** South Rd ☎(0286) 4647
Closed Xmas
Country style hotel with historic oak table.
6rm B
CTV 10P
Welsh, English & Spanish Last dinner 8.45pm

★***Plas Bowman*** 5 High St ☎(0286) 5555
This is a 13th-century house situated in a quiet street.
8rm TV in all bedrooms ® B
CTV
V Last dinner 9.30pm

At **Llanwnda** (4m S on A487/A499)

☆☆☆ ***B*Stables** (Inter-Hotels) ☎(0286) 830711
Annexe: 12→ 60P

CAERPHILLY
Mid Glamorgan
Map **3** ST18

☆☆ ***Griffin Inn Motel*** Rudry (3m E on unclass rd) ☎(0222) 883396
Closed Xmas
A character inn, with well-equipped motel rooms, in a rural setting.
20→ CTV in all bedrooms ®
200P (heated) Live music and dancing Sat
Last dinner 10pm
Credit cards 1 2 3 5

CAERSWS
Powys
Map **6** SO09

★★**Maesmawr Hall** (Inter-Hotels/Minotels) ☎(068 684) 255
A 16th-century, half-timbered, listed manor house in wooded grounds.
14rm(5→3⋔) Annexe: 6rm(4→2⋔) (5fb) CTV in all bedrooms ® sB&B£24–££26.80 sB&B→⋔£26.50–£29.30 dB&B£38.50–£43 dB&B→⋔£43.50–£48 B
CTV 100P 2 Disco Sat Live music and dancing Sat *xmas* ♿
V Lunch fr£5.75&alc Tea £1.75 High Tea £4.60 Dinner fr£8&alc Wine £3.85 Last dinner 9.30pm
Credit cards 1 2 3 4 5 **VS**
See advert on page 176

CALDBECK
Cumbria
Map **11** NY33

✕**Parkend** Parkend (1m W of village) ☎(06998) 442
Closed Mon (except Bank hols)
V 28 seats ✻Lunch £2.80–£9.95 Tea £1.50–£2.50 Dinner £12.50 Wine £4.50 Last dinner 9pm 20P
Credit card 1

CALLANDER
Central *Perthshire*
Map **11** NN60

★★★ ***BL*Roman Camp** ☎(0877) 30003
Closed mid Dec–Jan
Dating from 1625 reminiscent of a miniature château with small towers in 20 acres of gardens bordering the River Teith. The hotel tastefully decorated and furnished.
11rm(9→2⋔) CTV in all bedrooms ® ✻sB&B→⋔£25 dB&B→⋔ fr£42 B
20P
V ✻Lunch fr£4&alc Dinner £11.50 Wine £4.70 Last dinner 9pm

★***HL*Bridgend House** Bridgend ☎(0877) 30130
7rm(5→⋔) (1fb) 1 CTV in 3 bedrooms TV in 2 bedrooms ✻sB&B£12–£16 sB&B→⋔£16 dB&B£16 dB&B→⋔£24 B
40P 1 *xmas*
International **V** Lunch £1.95–£6.90 Tea £1.50 High Tea £2.50&alc Dinner £7alc Wine £3.65 Last dinner 9.30pm
Credit cards 1 2 3 5

★***BL*Lubnaig** Leny Feus (off A84) ☎(0877) 30376
Closed Nov–Mar RS Apr
Gabled, stone-built house in large lawned garden, in the village used as Tannochbrae for 'Dr Finlay's Casebook'.
8⋔ Annexe: 2⋔ (2fb) TV available on request ® sB&B⋔£10.30–£15.90 dB&B⋔£20.60–£27.80 B
CTV 14P nc7yrs
V Bar lunch £1.50–£3.50 Dinner £4.50–£10 Wine £3.50 Last dinner 7pm
Credit card 5 **VS**
See advert on page 176

★**Pinewood** Leny Rd, Strathyre Rd ☎(0877) 30111 Closed mid Oct–mid Apr
Unpretentious, tourist hotel in a quiet location set back from the main road.
16rm(2→) (3fb) sB&B£9.49–£10.12 dB&B£18.98–£20.24 dB&B→£22.78–£24.04 B
CTV 30P ♿
V Lunch £3.75 Tea 50p–60p Dinner £5.69–£6.33 Wine £4.60 Last dinner 8.30pm

★ ***Waverley*** Main St ☏(0877) 30245
Privately owned, unpretentious hotel.
13rm ® ₽
CTV Live music and dancing twice wkly
Last dinner 9pm
Credit cards 1 3

CALNE
Wiltshire
Map **3** ST97
★★ ***Lansdowne Strand*** The Strand (Exec Hotel) ☏(0249) 812488 Closed Xmas
Well established hotel with attractive bars and restaurant.
15rm (7 1) CTV in 7 bedrooms ® ₽
CTV 20P
Mainly grills **V** Last dinner 10pm
Credit cards 1 2 3 5

CALSTOCK
Cornwall
Map **2** SX46
✕**Boot Inn** ☏Tavistock (0822) 832331
Country inn with intimate wood-panelled dining room.
Lunch not served (except Sun)
50 seats ✱Lunch £4.45 Dinner £8alc Wine £4.50 Last dinner 9.30pm 6P bedrooms available
Credit cards 1 2 3 5 **VS**

CALVERHALL
Shropshire
Map **7** SJ63
✕**Old Jack Inn** ☏(094 876) 235
Closed Sun & Mon
70 seats ✱Lunch £1.35–£2.75 Dinner £10alc Wine £4.20 Last dinner 9.30pm bedrooms available
Credit cards 1 3

C

CAMBERLEY
Surrey
Map **4** SU86

★★★**Frimley Hall** Portsmouth Rd (Trusthouse Forte) ☎(0276) 28321 Telex no 858446
Fine Victorian house in 4 acres of grounds with good food and modern bedroom extension.
66rm(63⇌3⋒) CTV in all bedrooms ® sB&B⇌⋒£39 dB&B⇌⋒£55.50 B
☾ CTV 200P CFA ✽ *xmas*
♉ Last dinner 9.45pm
Credit cards 1 2 3 4 5

CAMBRIDGE
Cambridgeshire
Map **5** TL45

★★★★**Garden House** Granta Pl, off Mill Ln (Prestige) ☎(0223) 63421 Telex no 81463
Modern hotel, set in three acres of riverside gardens, close to the city centre.
117⇌⋒ (6fb) CTV in all bedrooms ★ sB&B⇌⋒£38 dB&B⇌⋒£52 Continental breakfast B
Lift ☾ 200P CFA ✽ ♩ Live music and dancing Sat *xmas*
English & Continental ♉ Lunch £8.95–£11.20&alc Tea £2.50 Dinner £8.95–£11.50&alc Wine £5.45 Last dinner 9.30pm
Credit cards 1 2 3 5 **VS**

★★★★**University Arms** Regent St (Inter-Hotels) ☎(0223) 351241 Telex no 817311
Traditional, family-owned hotel with spacious public rooms, modernised bedrooms, convenient for the city centre.
115⇌ CTV in all bedrooms sB&B⇌£28.50 dB&B⇌£42 B
Lift ☾ 75P CFA Live music and dancing Sat (Oct–Mar) ♿
English & Continental **V** ♉ Lunch fr£6.20&alc Tea fr£2 Dinner £7.50&alc Wine £3.90 Last dinner 9.45pm
S% Credit cards 1 2 3 5

★★★**Gonville** Gonville Pl ☎(0223) 66611 Closed Xmas
62⇌ (6fb) CTV in all bedrooms ® sB&B⇌£28.50 dB&B⇌£42 B
Lift ☾ CTV 100P CFA
English & French ♉ Lunch £5.95&alc Tea 50p Dinner £7.95&alc Last dinner 8.45pm (Sat 9.45)
Credit cards 1 2 3

★★**Arundel House** 53 Chesterton Rd ☎(0223) 67701 Closed 25 Dec–1 Jan
58rm(17⇌17⋒) Annexe: 6rm(5⇌1⋒) (6fb) CTV in all bedrooms ® sB&B£14.10–£18.75 sB&B⇌⋒£18.85–£27.15 dB&B£30.40–£32.90 dB&B⇌⋒£31.90–£37.80 Continental breakfast B
☾ 40P
English & French **V** ♉ Lunch £5.25&alc Tea fr50p Dinner £6.85&alc Wine £4.25 Last dinner 10pm
Credit cards 1 2 3 **VS**

★★**Blue Boar** Trinity St (Trusthouse Forte) ☎(0223) 63121
Friendly, traditional, city centre hotel in a good position for exploring the area.
48rm(11⇌) CTV in all bedrooms ® sB&B£28 dB&B£44 dB&B⇌£52 B
☾ *xmas*
♉ Last dinner 9.30pm
Credit cards 1 2 3 4 5

✕**Peking** 21 Burleigh St ☎(0223) 354755
Closed 25 & 26 Dec
Pekinese **V** 62 seats ✻Lunch £2–£3&alc Dinner £5–£10&alc Wine £3.50 Last dinner 10.30pm P
S%

At **Bar Hill** (6m W on A604)
☆☆☆☆**Cunard Cambridgeshire** ☎Crafts Hill (0954) 80555
100⇌ 200P

CAMPBELTOWN
Strathclyde *Argyllshire*
Map **10** NR72

C

★★ ***Ardshiel*** Kilkerran Rd ☎(0586) 2133
Closed weekends Oct–Mar
14rm
Lift CTV 10P
Last dinner 8pm
Credit cards 1 3

CANNICH
Highland *Inverness-shire*
Map **14** NH33

★★ **Glen Affric** ☎(04565) 214
Closed mid Oct–Etr
A family run, roadside hotel situated amidst magnificent Highland scenery in a popular fishing area.
23rm(5)(2fb) sB&B£9.75 sB&B£10.75 dB&B£19.50 dB&B£21.50
CTV 30P
V Bar lunch fr£1.50 Tea fr£85p High Tea fr£3 Dinner fr£5.50 Wine £4 Last dinner 7pm
S%

CANNOCK
Staffordshire
Map **7** SJ91

☆☆☆ **Roman Way** Watling St, Hatherton (on A5) (ExecHotels) ☎(05435) 72121
A large, modern hotel complex on the A5.
Annexe: 24rm(20 4)(4fb) CTV in all bedrooms Ⓡ sB&B £27.50 dB&B £37
200P Live music and dancing Fri Cabaret Mon & Tue
International **V** Lunch £6&alc Tea fr50p Dinner fr£6&alc Wine £4.75 Last dinner 10pm
Credit cards 1 2 3 5 **VS**
See advert on page 182

★★ ***Hollies*** Hollies Av ☎(05435) 3151
Closed Xmas wk
6rm CTV in 6 bedrooms
CTV 150P 6 Disco Fri & Sat Live music and dancing twice mthly Cabaret twice mthly
English & Italian **V** Last dinner 9.30pm
Credit cards 1 2 3 5 **VS**

CANONBIE
Dumfries & Galloway *Dumfriesshire*
Map **11** NY37

★★ **Cross Keys** ☎(05415) 382
Roadside coaching inn, overlooking the River Esk, with attractive dining room and lounge with open fire.
10rm(4)(1fb) Ⓡ sB&B£12.50–£16.50 sB&B£16.50 dB&B£25 dB&B£28.75
CTV 12P
Scottish & French **V** Bar lunch £1.25–£2.95 High Tea £1.95–£6.95&alc Dinner £1.95–£6.95&alc Wine £4.50 Last dinner 9pm
Credit cards 1 2 3 5

✕ **Riverside Inn** ☎(05415) 295
(Rosette awarded for dinner only.)
Closed Sun & 2wks Jan Lunch not served
36 seats Dinner £10.25alc Wine £3.55 Last dinner 8.30pm 25P bedrooms available
VS

CANTERBURY
Kent
Map **5** TR15

★★★ **Chaucer** Ivy Ln (Trusthouse Forte) ☎(0227) 64427 Telex no 965096
Very comfortable hotel with sound cooking and efficient service.
51rm(30 2) CTV in all bedrooms Ⓡ sB&B£29.50 sB&B £35.50 dB&B£44 dB&B £51.50
42P CFA
Last dinner 9.30pm
Credit cards 1 2 3 4 5

★★★ **County** High St (Best Western) ☎(0227) 66266 Telex no 965076
Large hotel with well-equipped bedrooms, restaurant and coffee shop.

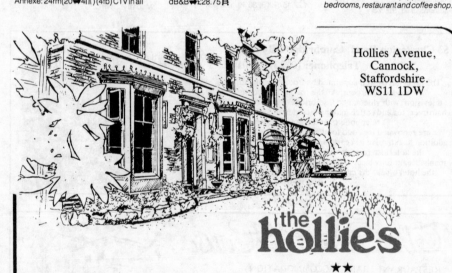

74➡⋒ (3fb) CTV in all bedrooms Ⓡ ✱ sB&B➡⋒ £33 dB&B➡⋒ £47.50 B̶

Lift ☾ 50P 25🚗 *xmas*

🍴British & French V ☆ ☕ ✱ Lunch £5.95&alc Tea 85p Dinner £8.95&alc Wine £5.75 Last dinner 10pm

Credit cards 1 2 3 5

★★★**Slatters** St Margarets Street (Queens Moat) ☎(0227) 63271 Telex no 966227

Friendly modern hotel with well-equipped, older style bedrooms.

32rm(23➡) (2fb) CTV in all bedrooms Ⓡ sB&B£21 sB&B➡£29.50 dB&B£32 dB&B➡£39.50 B̶

Lift ☾ 30P *xmas*

🍴English & French V ☆ Lunch fr£3.75&alc Dinner fr£5.95&alc Wine £4.70 Last dinner 9pm

Credit cards 1 2 3 4 5 VS

★★**Falstaff** St Dunstans Street (Whitbread Fremlins/Minotel) ☎(0227) 62138

An ancient timbered inn with modern bedrooms.

10rm(3➡1⋒) Annexe: 6➡ 1⋒ TV in all bedrooms Ⓡ ✱ sB&B fr£16.50 sB&B➡⋒ fr£16.50 dB&B fr£26.50 dB&B➡⋒ £31–£36 B̶

20P *xmas*

☆ ☕ Lunch £4.25 Dinner £9alc Wine £4.50 Last dinner 9.30pm

Credit cards 1 2 3

CAPEL CURIG
Gwynedd
Map **6** SH75

★★**Bryn Tyrch** ☎(06904) 223

Two-storey hotel beside the A5, with good views. It is well situated for climbers and walkers.

15rm(3➡) (1fb) Ⓡ sB&B£10.75–£11.75 sB&B➡£11.75–£12.75 dB&B£21.50–£23.50 dB&B➡£23.50–£25.50 B̶

CTV 30P 2🚗 ✽

V ☆ Bar lunch £2–£3.70 High Tea £1.50–£2.50 Dinner £6–£8.25 Wine £3.15 Last dinner 9pm

Credit cards 1 2 3 5

★★**Ty'n-y-Coed** ☎(06904) 231

13➡ (2fb) CTV available in bedrooms Ⓡ sB&B➡ fr£14 dB&B➡ fr£23 B̶

CTV 80P ✽

V ☆ ☕ Lunch £5.50alc Tea £1.20alc Dinner fr£7&alc Wine £5 Last dinner 10pm

Credit cards 1 2 3 VS

CARBIS BAY
Cornwall
Map **2** SW53

See St Ives, Cornwall

CARDIFF
South Glamorgan
Map **3** ST17

See plan See also St Mellons

☆☆☆☆**Inn on the Avenue** Circle Way East, Llanedeyrn ☎(0222) 732520 Telex no 497582 Plan **6** *F4*

Modern hotel situated in its own grounds 6m from Cardiff, just off the A48.

150➡⋒ (10fb) CTV in all bedrooms Ⓡ sB&B➡⋒ £36 dB&B➡⋒ £48 B̶

Lift ☾ CTV 300P CFA ✽ (heated) sauna bath Live music and dancing Sat *xmas*

🍴Welsh, English & French ☆ ☕ Lunch £7.50&alc Tea 60p–£2.75 Dinner £8.50&alc Wine £4.85 Last dinner 11pm

Credit cards 1 2 3 4 5 VS

See advert on page 181

★★★★ *B* **Park** Park Pl (Mount Charlotte) ☎(0222) 23471 Telex no 497195 Plan **7** *E3*

Comfortable, city centre hotel offering a choice of restaurants, the Caernarvon or the Theatre.

108➡ CTV in all bedrooms sB&B➡£40 dB&B➡£48 B̶ →

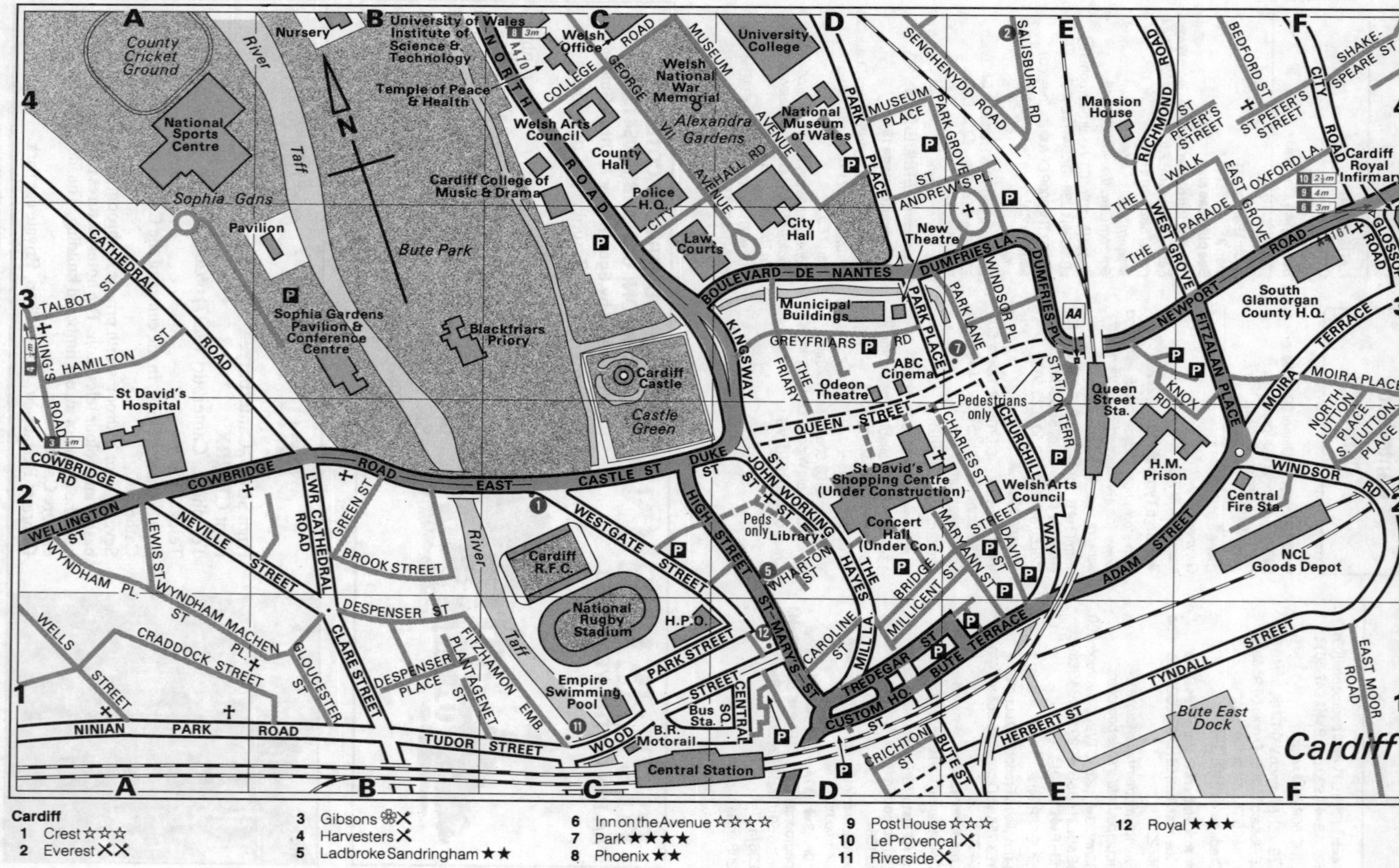
C
Cardiff
County Cricket Ground
National Sports Centre
Sophia Gdns
Pavilion
Sophia Gardens Pavilion & Conference Centre
River Taff
Nursery
Bute Park
Blackfriars Priory
University of Wales Institute of Science & Technology
Temple of Peace & Health
Cardiff College of Music & Drama
Welsh Office
Welsh Arts Council
County Hall
Police H.Q.
Law Courts
City Hall
Welsh National War Memorial
Alexandra Gardens
University College
National Museum of Wales
Cardiff Castle
Castle Green
Municipal Buildings
New Theatre
ABC Cinema
Odeon Theatre
Pedestrians only
Peds only
Library
St David's Shopping Centre (Under Construction)
Concert Hall (Under Con.)
Welsh Arts Council
Queen Street Sta.
H.M. Prison
Central Fire Sta.
NCL Goods Depot
South Glamorgan County H.Q.
Cardiff Royal Infirmary
Mansion House
St David's Hospital
Cardiff R.F.C.
National Rugby Stadium
H.P.O.
Empire Swimming Pool
Bus Sta.
B.R. Motorail
Central Station
Bute East Dock
NORTH ROAD
A470
BOULEVARD DE NANTES
KINGSWAY
CASTLE ST
DUKE ST
HIGH STREET
ST MARY'S ST
QUEEN STREET
CHURCHILL WAY
STATION TERR
NEWPORT ROAD
A4161
FITZALAN PLACE
ADAM STREET
BUTE TERRACE
TYNDALL STREET
EAST MOOR ROAD
COWBRIDGE ROAD EAST
WELLINGTON ST
CATHEDRAL ROAD
TUDOR STREET
NINIAN PARK ROAD
WESTGATE STREET
PARK PLACE
MUSEUM AVENUE
CITY ROAD
RICHMOND ROAD
THE WEST GROVE
SENGHENYDD ROAD
SALISBURY RD
Cardiff
1 Crest ☆☆☆
2 Everest ✕✕
3 Gibsons ✕
4 Harvesters ✕
5 Ladbroke Sandringham ★★
6 Inn on the Avenue ☆☆☆☆
7 Park ★★★★
8 Phoenix ★★
9 Post House ☆☆☆
10 Le Provençal ✕
11 Riverside ✕
12 Royal ★★★

Lift ☾ 80P CFA Live music and dancing wkly ♿

English, Welsh & French V Lunch £5.50–£6&alc Dinner £6.50–£7&alc Wine £5.75 Last dinner 11pm

Credit cards 1 2 3 4 5 **VS**

☆☆☆**Crest** Westgate St (Crest) ☎(0222) 388681 Telex no 497258 Plan **1** *C2*

Modern, comfortable, city-centre hotel.

160➡ CTV in all bedrooms Ⓡ ✱sB➡ fr£34 dB➡ fr£44 (room only) B

Lift ☾ 75P CFA

Mainly grills ✱Bar lunch £1.35–£6.10 Tea fr55p Dinner fr£8.50&alc Wine £5.25 Last dinner 9.45pm

Credit cards 1 2 3 4 5 **VS**

☆☆☆**Post House** Pentwyn Rd, Pentwyn (Trusthouse Forte) ☎(0222) 731212 Telex no 497633 Plan **9** *F4*

Modern hotel situated just off the A48, about six miles from the city centre.

150➡ (60fb) CTV in all bedrooms Ⓡ sB&B➡ £38.50 dB&B➡ £51 B

Lift ☾ 210P CFA

Last dinner 10.15pm

Credit cards 1 2 3 4 5

★★★**Royal** St Mary's Street (Embassy) ☎(0222) 23321 Plan **12** *D1*

Traditional Victorian hotel in the city centre.

67rm(31➡5⋒) CTV in all bedrooms Ⓡ sB£24.25 sB➡⋒ £35.75 dB£37 dB➡⋒ £42 (room only) B

Lift ☾ CFA

V ✱Lunch fr£6.50 Tea fr£1 Dinner fr£6.50 Wine £4.70 Last dinner 10pm

Credit cards 1 2 3 4 5

C

★★**Ladbroke Sandringham** St Mary's Street (Ladbroke) ☎(0222) 32161 Plan **5** *D2*

Company owned commercial hotel in the city centre.

28rm(8⇌) (4fb) CTV in all bedrooms ® sB&B⇌£12.50–£25 dB&B⇌£19–£35 ₽

☾ CTV ⚑ *xmas*

Mainly grills **V** ♡ ☕ Lunch £4.50alc Tea fr50p Dinner £4.50alc Wine £3.15 Last dinner 11.30pm

Credit cards 1 2 3 5

★★**Phoenix** 199–201 Fidlas Rd, Llanishan (Minotel) ☎(0222) 764615 Plan **8** *C4*

Privately owned hotel with business clientele.

25rm(4⇌16⋒) CTV in all bedrooms ®

*sB&B⇌⋒£18.70 dB&B£21.70 dB&B⇌⋒£27.70 ₽

Lift ☾ CTV 50P

V ♡ *Lunch £4.15alc Dinner fr£5&alc Wine £3.95 Last dinner 10pm

Credit cards 1 2 3 4 5

✕✕**Everest** 43–45 Salisbury Rd, Cathays ☎(0222) 374881 Plan **2** *E4*

Indian **V** 120 seats Lunch £4.95–£6&alc Dinner £5.50–£6&alc Wine £4.30 Last dinner 11.30pm

S% Credit cards 1 2 3 5

❀✕**Gibsons** Romilly Cres ☎(0222) 41264 Plan **3** *A2*

Imaginative menus here often feature regional dishes.

Closed Sun Public hols & 1 wk Xmas

French 38 seats Last dinner 10pm ⚑

Credit cards 1 2 3 5

✕***Harvesters*** 5 Pontcanna St ☎(0222) 32616 Plan **4** *A3*

Imperial, Bistro-style restaurant.
Closed Sun & 2 wks Aug Lunch not served
V 38 seats Last dinner 11.30pm
Credit cards 1 3

XLe Provençal 779 Newport Rd (0222) 78262 Plan **10** *F4*
Closed Sun & Mon Lunch not served Sat
French **V** 65 seats *Lunch £3.60&alc Dinner £7.50alc Wine £3.90
Last dinner 10pm P
Credit cards 1 2 3 5 **VS**

XRiverside 44 Tudor St (0222) 372163 Plan **11** *C1*
A Cantonese restaurant, among the best of its kind in Wales.
Closed Xmas Day
Cantonese 140 seats *Lunch £6alc Dinner £6alc Wine £3.80 Last dinner 11.30pm
S% Credit cards 1 2 3 5 **VS**

CARDIGAN
Dyfed
Map **2** SN14
See also Gwbert-on-Sea

★***Angel*** St Mary Street (0239) 612561
Closed 24–26 Dec
Small character inn, originally St John's Hospice in 1231.
11rm

CTV 8P 4
Last dinner 7.30pm

XXRhyd-Garn-Wen Croft (3m SW on A487) (0239) 612742
Lunch not served
V 12 seats Dinner £9.50 Wine £3.75 Last dinner 9.30pm 16P bedrooms available

CARFRAEMILL
Borders *Berwickshire*
Map **12** NT55

★★**Carfraemill** Oxton (05785) 200
A traditional road-side hotel, just off the A68.
10rm(2)(1fb) CTV in 2 bedrooms Ⓡ *sB&B£8–£12.50 sB&B£9.50–£14.50 dB&B£19–£25 dB&B£23–£29
#CTV 60P Live music and dancing mthly *xmas*
V *Lunch £5 Tea £1.65 High Tea £3.15–£4.50 Dinner £7 Last dinner 9pm
Credit card 3

CARLISLE
Cumbria
Map **12** NY45

☆☆☆**Crest** Kingstown (junc 44/M6) (Crest) (0228) 31201 Telex no 64201
A modern building next to the motorway.
100 CTV in all bedrooms Ⓡ *sB fr£34 dB fr£43 (room only)
200P CFA
International **V** *Lunch £3.85–£6.40&alc Tea 60p Dinner £8.50&alc Wine £4.80 Last dinner 10pm
Credit cards 1 2 3 4 5 **VS**

★★★**Crown & Mitre** English St (Comfort) (0228) 25491 Telex no 64183
Conveniently situated close to both the cathedral and the castle.
78rm(72 5) Annexe: 18 CTV in all bedrooms Ⓡ *sB&B fr£25.25 dB&B fr£35.75 Continental breakfast
Lift CTV 25P 25 CFA
Mainly grills *Lunch fr£5&alc Dinner fr£5&alc Wine £3.95
Last dinner 10pm
Credit cards 1 2 3 4 5 **VS**

★★★**Cumbrian Thistle** Court Sq (Thistle) (0228) 31951 Telex no 64287
Spacious comfortable hotel with modernised bedrooms adjoining railway station.
70rm(66 4)(3fb) CTV in all bedrooms Ⓡ *sB £29–£31 dB £35–£40 (room only)
Lift CTV 50P 30 CFA
European *Lunch £2.75&alc Dinner £6.75&alc Last dinner 9.30pm
Credit cards 1 2 3 4 5 **VS**

C

★★★**Swallow Hilltop** London Rd (Swallow) ☎(0228) 29255 Telex no 64292

115rm(98⇌4⋒) (4fb) CTV in all bedrooms Ⓡ sB&B£22–£26 sB&B⇌⋒£27–£35 dB&B£32–£35 dB&B⇌⋒£37–£45 B

Lift ☾ CTV 500P CFA ✽ Disco Tue Live music and dancing Sat Cabaret mthly *xmas*

V ♧ ☕ Lunch £5.25–£6&alc Tea 55p–70p Dinner £7–£7.75&alc Wine £4.75 Last dinner 9.45pm

Credit cards 1 2 3 5

★★**Central** Victoria Viaduct (Greenall Whitley) ☎(0228) 20256

This hotel stands on Carlisle's old city walls.

84rm(18⇌2⋒) CTV in all bedrooms sB&B£13.50 sB&B⇌⋒£15.50 dB&B£21.50 dB&B⇌⋒£24 B

Lift ☾ CTV 25P

V ♧ ☕ Lunch £3.50 Tea 75p High Tea £3 Dinner £6.25&alc Wine £2.75 Last dinner 9pm

S% Credit cards 1 2 3 5

★★**Pinegrove** 262 London Rd ☎(0228) 24828

Comfortable hotel with hospitable proprietor.

20rm(8⇌) (6fb) CTV in all bedrooms sB&B£13.80 sB&B⇌£18.40 dB&B£20.70 dB&B⇌£27.60

CTV 40P ✽ Live music and dancing Sun

▣ English & French ♧ ☕ Lunch £3–£7&alc Tea £1.50 Dinner £3.50–£9 Wine £4 Last dinner 8.30pm

Credit cards 1 3

★**Cumbria Park** 32 Scotland Rd ☎(0228) 22887

Comfortable accommodation and friendly service.

35rm(25⇌) 1▣ Ⓡ ★

CTV 30P

Last dinner 7.30pm

Credit cards 1 3

★**Vallum House** Burgh Rd ☎(0228) 21860

10rm (2fb) CTV in 2 bedrooms TV in 8 bedrooms Ⓡ sB&B£17.33 dB&B£27.53

TV 20P ⛟ ✽

V ♧ ☕ Lunch £3.50–£4.50 Tea £1 High Tea £3.50–£4 Dinner £5.75 Last dinner 9.30pm

Credit cards 1 3 5

CARMARTHEN
Dyfed
Map **2** SN42

★★★**Ivy Bush Royal** Spilman St (Trusthouse Forte) ☎(0267) 235111 Telex no 48520

A popular hotel with businessmen, it is also well situated for touring in West Wales.

88rm(72⇌10⋒) (4fb) CTV in all bedrooms Ⓡ sB&B⇌⋒£31.50 dB&B⇌⋒£45 B

Lift ☾ CTV 63P 3⌂ CFA ✽ sauna bath *xmas*

♧ ☕ Last dinner 9pm

Credit cards 1 2 3 4 5

CARMUNNOCK
Strathclyde *Lanarkshire*
Map **11** NS55

✕**Cool Jade** 107 Waterside Rd ☎041-644 2544

Closed 2–4 Feb Lunch not served Sat & Sun

▣ Cantonese & Malaysian 72 seats Lunch fr£3.50&alc Dinner £3.50–£15&alc Wine £5.50 Last dinner 11.30pm 20P

Credit cards 1 2 3

CARNFORTH
Lancashire
Map **7** SD47

★★**Royal Station** Market Pl ☎(0524) 732033

Town centre public house, situated close to the railway station.

12rm (4fb) CTV in all bedrooms Ⓡ ✱sB&B fr£11.50 dB&B fr£21 B

CTV 6P 10⌂

▣ English, French & Italian V ♧ ✱Lunch fr£4.25&alc High Tea fr£1.50&alc Dinner fr£5.50&alc Wine £3 Last dinner 8pm

Credit cards 2 3 5 VS

CARNOUSTIE
Tayside *Angus*
Map **12** NO53

★★**Carlogie House** ☎(0241) 53185

Closed 1–3 Jan

11rm(1⇌10⋒) (1fb) CTV in all bedrooms Ⓡ ★ sB&B⇌⋒ fr£20 dB&B⇌⋒ fr£35 B

CTV ✽ ⌂

▣ Scottish & French V ♧ ☕ Lunch fr£5&alc Tea fr75p High Tea fr£3.50 Dinner fr£7.50&alc Wine £5.50 Last dinner 9.30pm

Credit cards 1 2 3 5 VS

★★***Earlston*** Church St ☎(0241) 52352

A stone building, standing back from the main road at the northern end of town.

21rm(2⇌5⋒) B

CTV 60P ⛟ Live music and dancing twice wkly *xmas*

V ♧ ☕ Last dinner 9.15pm

Credit cards 1 2 3 5

★★**Glencoe** Links Pde ☎(0241) 53273

Three-storey, stone house with modern extensions overlooking the sea and the golf course.

10rm(2⇌5⋒) (2fb) CTV in all bedrooms sB&B£12.65–£13.65 dB&B⇌⋒ £28–£30

CTV 10P ⛟

▣ Scottish & French V ♧ ☕ Bar lunch £3alc Tea 60p alc High Tea £3.30alc Dinner £6alc Wine £5 Last dinner 9pm

S% Credit cards 1 2 3 5 VS

★**Station** ☎(0241) 52447

Small, friendly, town centre hotel.

9rm(3⋒) (1fb) sB&B£9 dB&B£18 dB&B⋒£25 B

CTV 12P Disco Fri & Sat Live music and dancing Sat *xmas*

V ♧ ☕ Lunch £2.50–£4 Tea 35p High Tea £2.75–£4 Dinner £5–£6&alc Wine £3.50 Last dinner 9.30pm

Credit cards 1 2 3

CARRADALE
Strathclyde *Argyllshire*
Map **10** NR83

★★***Carradale*** ☎(05833) 223

Pleasant holiday hotel standing in its own gardens, next to the golf course and overlooking Kilbrannan Sound.

15rm(1⇌2⋒) Annexe: 6rm(3⋒) B

CTV 25P ✽ ▶ squash sauna bath ⌂ *xmas*

V ♧ ☕ Last dinner 8.45pm

CARRBRIDGE
Highland *Inverness-shire*
Map **14** NH92

✕**Landmark** ☎(047984) 613

Closed Nov–Mar

120 seats Lunch £1.75alc Tea £1alc High Tea £2.50alc Dinner £5.60alc Wine £4 Last dinner 8.30pm 100P

Credit cards 1 2 3

CARTMEL
Cumbria
Map **7** SD37

★★*B* **Aynsome Manor** (1m N on unclass rd) ☎(044854) 276 Closed 2–23 Jan

Lovely old manor house set in the Vale of Cartmel, only a short distance from the village.

13rm(9⇌1⋒) Annexe: 2⋒ (2fb) 1▣ CTV in 1 bedroom sB&B£15 sB&B⇌⋒£17 dB&B£30 dB&B⇌⋒£34 B

CTV 20P ⛟ ✽ *xmas*

V ♧ ☕ Lunch fr£5.95 Dinner fr£9.30 Wine £3.75 Last dinner 8.30pm

Credit cards 1 2 3 VS

★★***Grammar*** ☎(044854) 367

Closed Jan

Converted school-house, now a comfortable hotel overlooking the racecourse.

11⇌ CTV in 4 bedrooms Ⓡ B

⊁ TV 40P ✽

♧ Last dinner 9pm

VS

★**Priory** The Square ☎(044854) 267

Closed mid Nov–mid Mar

Delightful small hotel, family owned and run, located in the town square.

9rm(5⇌) (3fb) Ⓡ sB&B£12–£14

sB&B⇌£13–£15 dB&B£24–£28 dB&B⇌£26–£30 Ḃ
CTV 7P
English & French Lunch £4.95 Tea 85p Dinner £7.50–£8.50 Wine £3.35 Last dinner 8pm
Credit card 1

CASTERTON
Cumbria
Map **7** SD67
★★**Pheasant Inn** ☎ Kirkby Lonsdale (0468) 71230 Closed Xmas Day
Village inn with newly appointed restaurant and bedrooms.
6rm(5⇌1⋔)(1fb) 1 CTV in all bedrooms ® sB&B⇌⋔£13 dB&B⇌⋔£25 Ḃ
CTV 60P ✽
Lunch £5.75 Tea Dinner £9 Wine £2 Last dinner 9pm

CASTLE ASHBY
Northamptonshire
Map **4** SP85
✕✕**Falcon** ☎ Yardley Hastings (060 129) 200
English & French **V** 70 seats Lunch £6.50alc Tea £1.50alc High Tea £2.95alc Dinner £9.95alc Last dinner 10pm 10P bedrooms available
Credit cards 1 2 3 5

CASTLE CARY
Somerset
Map **3** ST63
★★*B* **George** High St ☎ (0963) 50761 Closed Xmas
17rm(15⇌2⋔) 1 CTV in all bedrooms ✽sB&B⇌ fr£22.42 dB&B⇌ fr£32.79 Ḃ
12P
English & French **V** ✽Lunch £2.50alc Tea 35p High Tea £1.50alc Dinner £10alc Wine £3.95 Last dinner 9.30pm
Credit cards 1 2 3 5

CASTLE COMBE
Wiltshire
Map **3** ST87
★★★ *L* **Manor House** (Best Western) ☎ (0249) 782206 Telex no 44220
A 14th-century house, with 26 acres of parkland in wooded valley. It is tastefully furnished and comfortably appointed.
13rm(10⇌3⋔) Annexe: 20⇌ (3fb) 2 CTV in all bedrooms ✽sB&B⇌⋔£30 dB&B⇌⋔£63 Ḃ
☾ 100P ✽ (heated) (hard) xmas
International **V** ✽Lunch fr£6.50&alc Tea 70p–£1.60 Dinner fr£11.50&alc Wine £5.20 Last dinner 9pm
Credit cards 1 2 3 5
See advert on page 186

★★**Castle** ☎ (0249) 782461
RS Xmas Day
A 13th-century inn built from Cotswold stone with mellow oak beams.
9rm(3⇌1⋔) ® sB&B£25 sB&B⇌⋔£25 dB&B£32 dB&B⇌⋔£40 Ḃ
CTV 12P nc5yrs
English & French **V** Bar lunch 90p–£4.25 Tea £1 Dinner £10.75&alc Wine £4.25 Last dinner 9pm

CASTLE DONINGTON
Leicestershire
Map **8** SK42
★★★**Priest House Inn** Kings Mills (2m W unclass) (Inter-Hotel) ☎ Derby (0332) 810649 Telex no 841995
Annexe: 14rm(4⇌10⋔)(1fb) CTV in all bedrooms ® sB&B⇌⋔£24.20–£26.50 dB&B⇌⋔£36–£38 Ḃ
150P ✽ Live music and dancing Wed *xmas*
V Lunch £4.95–£5.75&alc Tea £1.50–£1.95 Dinner £6.25–£7.15&alc Wine £5.25 Last dinner 10pm
Credit cards 1 2 3 5 **VS**
See advert on page 186

★★**Donington Manor** ☎ Derby (0332) 810253 Closed 27–31 Dec
Restored and modernised Regency posting house and coaching inn, catering mainly for the commercial trade.
35rm(33⇌) Annexe: 3rm(1⇌)(2fb) 3 CTV in all bedrooms ® sB&B£22 sB&B⇌£25 dB&B£30 dB&B⇌£35
☾ 50P Live music and dancing Sat
English & French Lunch fr£5&alc Dinner fr£6&alc Wine £4.25 Last dinner 9.15pm
S% Credit cards 1 2 3 5

CASTLE DOUGLAS
Dumfries & Galloway *Kirkcudbrightshire*
Map **11** NX76
★★**Imperial** King St ☎ (0556) 2086
Neat, homely hotel in main street.
14rm(3⋔) sB&B£12–£14 dB&B£24–£28 dB&B⋔£28–£30
CTV 15P 9
V Bar lunch £1.50–£3.20&alc Tea £1.25–£1.75 High Tea £2.25–£5&alc Wine £4.50 Last high tea 7pm
Credit cards 1 3 **VS**

★★**King's Arms** St Andrew's Street ☎ (0556) 2626
Modernised coaching inn, standing on corner site in this thriving market town.
15rm(4⇌2⋔)(1fb) sB&B£12–£15 sB&B⇌⋔£17–£19 dB&B£24–£30 dB&B⇌⋔£34–£38 Ḃ
CTV 17P
French **V** Lunch £4–£4.50 High Tea £4–£6 Dinner £9–£9.50 Wine £3.50 Last dinner 8pm
Credit cards 2 3 5 **VS**

★**Merrick** 193 King St ☎ (0556) 2173
Friendly hotel which forms upper storeys of main street building.
6rm(2fb) ® ✽sB&B£8–£9 dB&B£16–£17 Ḃ
CTV 6P
V Lunch £3–£4&alc High Tea £3–£4&alc Dinner £4–£5&alc Wine £4 Last dinner 8pm

CASTLETON
Gwent
Map **3** ST28
☆☆☆**Ladbroke Wentloog Castle** (Ladbroke) ☎ (0633) 680591 →

Well appointed, modern hotel convenient for businessmen using M4.

55⇌⋔ (2fb) CTV in all bedrooms ® sB&B⇌⋔ £15–£32 dB&B⇌⋔ £22–£41 ₿

☾ 75P ✽ sauna bath Live music and dancing Fri & Sat *xmas*

International V ♈ ⊒ Lunch fr£6.50&alc Tea fr£1.75 Dinner fr£6.50&alc Wine £3.75 Last dinner 10.30pm

Credit cards 1 2 3 5

CASTLETON
North Yorkshire
Map **8** NZ60

★★**Moorlands** ☎(02876) 206
Closed Nov–19 Apr

Country house on the edge of the village, with views across the Esk Valley.

10rm(1⇌5⋔) (1fb) sB&B£12 dB&B⇌⋔ £24–£26

CTV 20P

♈ Bar lunch 80p–£4.50 Dinner £7.50–£8.50&alc Wine £4.25 Last dinner 8.30pm

VS

CASTLETOWN
Isle of Man
Map **6** SC26

★★★**Golf Links** Fort Island ☎(0624) 822201 Telex no 627636
Closed 11 Oct–15 Apr

At southerly extreme of island, surrounded by golf course.

75rm(50⇌25⋔) Annexe: 5⇌ (15fb) CTV in 40 bedrooms sB&B⇌⋔ £22–£23.20 dB&B⇌⋔ £41.50–£43.50

CTV 80P CFA ✽ (heated) ▶18 (hard) billiards

French V ♈ ⊒ Lunch £5.90 Tea £1.65

Dinner £7.25&alc Wine £4.40 Last dinner 9.15pm

S% Credit cards 1 2 3

CÂTEL (Castel)
Guernsey, Channel Islands
Map **16**

★★**Hotel Hougue du Pommier** Hougue du Pommier Rd ☎ Guernsey (0481) 56531

44rm(12→18⋒)(13fb) CTV in all bedrooms ® ✱

✽ ⛆(heated) ▶18 *xmas*

♆ ☕

Credit cards 1 3

See advert on page 188

CATTERICK BRIDGE
North Yorkshire
Map **8** SE29

★★**Bridge House** ☎ Richmond (0748) 818331

17rm(4→)(2fb) CTV in 4 bedrooms ® sB&B£15 sB&B→£20 dB&B£24 dB&B→£27.50 B

CTV 74P ✽ ♪

♆ ☕ Lunch £4.95–£5.95 Dinner £6.50–£7.50&alc Wine £5.10 Last dinner 9.45pm

Credit cards 1 2 3 5 **VS**

CAVENDISH
Suffolk
Map **5** TL84

✕✕**Alfonso** ☎ Glemsford (0787) 280372

Continental **V** 50 seats Lunch £7.50–£8.50&alc Tea £1.60 Wine £5 Last dinner 10pm 50P bedrooms available

Credit cards 2 5

CAWSAND
Cornwall
Map **2** SX45

★★ *L* ***Criterion*** Garrett St ☎ Plymouth (0752) 822244 Closed 3 Oct–Mar

Small family-run hotel at the water's edge, in the village centre.

8rm(2⋒) Annexe: 3⋒

Lift CTV ♪

English & French **V** ♆ ☕ Last dinner 7.30pm

Credit card 3

★★★

✽★★★ **GIDLEIGH PARK, CHAGFORD**

☎ (06473) 2225

Don't be put off by the hair raising two mile drive from Chagford along a narrow potholed lane to reach this charming country house. For a pedestrian however, it is quite another matter, because to walk this pretty route is to appreciate the charm of Gidleigh Park. All who come learn to enjoy the calm and serenity, the loudest noise outside being the tumbling River North Teign.
Inside, the loquacious American proprietor, Mr Paul Henderson, is much in evidence and he is always solicitous of one's needs. Indeed, his dedication and enthusiasm is not only infectious but adds unusually to the charm of this elegant, spacious, comfortable house. His courteous and willing staff all add to the atmosphere of well-being by their low key, good natured approach and discreet manner. There are wood panelled public rooms with antiques and fresh flowers, and an elegant dining room which is all well maintained as are the comfortable bedrooms.
In the kitchen the chef, John Webber offers a fixed price menu at dinner and the fresh ingredients used are first class, and sauces are honest and well made. Interesting as the food is, however, it is the wine list that catches the eye. Naturally Mr Henderson

enthusiastically encourages American wines by offering a wide variety of good quality examples. Happily this is not at the expense of French wines where his serious and knowledgeable approach is much in evidence. Many fine wines are available and what a pleasure it is to record the wide availability of half bottles, so often neglected by other restaurants. Overall, a delightful and comfortable place to stay which is much appreciated by our members, who have always enjoyed it very much.

12→ CTV in all bedrooms sB&B→£57.50–£86.25 dB&B→£63.25–£97.75 Continental breakfast B

25P ✽ ♪ nc8yrs *xmas*

♆ ☕ Lunch £22alc Tea £1.70alc Dinner £25.30alc Wine £8.60 Last dinner 9pm

CERNE ABBAS
Dorset
Map **3** ST60

✕✕**Old Market House** 25 Long St ☎ (03003) 680

Closed Mon & Jan (except Fri & Sat) Dinner not served Sun

English & French 48 seats Lunch £6alc Dinner £9.75alc Wine £5 Last dinner 9.30pm

Credit cards 1 2 3 4 5

CHADLINGTON
Oxfordshire
Map **4** SP32

★★**Chadlington House** (Minotels) ☎ (060876) 437

Closed Jan–12 Feb

Gabled residence standing in its own grounds with views of the Evenlode Valley.

10rm(2→4⋒)(2fb) 1 CTV in 2 bedrooms ® ✱ sB&B£10–£13.50 sB&B→⋒£15–£17.50 dB&B£20–£26 dB&B→⋒£27–£32 B

CTV 20P 2 ✽

English & French ♆ ☕ Tea 50p Dinner £6.50–£8&alc Wine £3.95 Last dinner 8pm

Credit card 3

CHAGFORD
Devon
Map **3** SX78

★★★ *HB* **Great Tree** Sandy Park (2½m N on A382) ☎ (06473) 2491 Closed 27 Dec–Jan

A 19th century hunting lodge set in 20 acres of grounds with splendid views of the Dartmoor tors.

14→⋒ Annexe: 1→⋒ (2fb) CTV in all bedrooms ® sB&B→⋒£24.15–£26.45 dB&B→⋒£46–£52.90 B

⊬ 20P 3 ✽ *xmas*

V ♆ ☕ Lunch £4.50–£6.50 Tea £1.20–£2.50 Dinner £9.50&alc Wine £3.95 Last dinner 9pm

Credit cards 1 2 3 5 **VS**

★★★ *HL* **Mill End** Sandy Park (2m N on A382) ☎ (06473) 2282

Closed 18–28 Dec RS Nov–Mar

Carefully converted from an old water mill this hotel has well kept grounds set in lovely countryside.

16rm(13→2⋒)(2fb) CTV in all bedrooms sB&B£14–£22 sB&B→⋒£15.50–£28 dB&B£28.50–£38 dB&B→⋒£31.50–£47

17P 4 ✽ ♪

English & French ♆ ☕ Lunch £7–£8 Tea £1–£3 Dinner £11–£12 Wine £4.75 Last dinner 9pm

S% Credit cards 1 2 3 5

✽★★★ *H* **Teignworthy** Frenchbeer (2m S on unclass road to Thornworthy) ☎ (06473) 3355

Charming stone house in lovely setting →

with superb views where the owners provide a welcoming atmosphere.

6⇒ Annexe: 3⇒ CTV in all bedrooms Ⓡ ✱sB&B⇒£31.50 dB&B⇒£53 Ᵽ

15P 2 ⇏ ✽ (grass) sauna bath nc14yrs *xmas*

English & French Lunch £14alc Tea fr£1.50 Dinner £15 Wine £4.50 Last dinner 9.30pm

S% **VS**

★★ ***Moor Park*** Lower St ☎(06473) 2202

Privately owned and run, this holiday and touring hotel is situated close to the centre of Chagford.

20rm(4⇒) Ᵽ

CTV 40P ✽

English & French **V** Last dinner 9pm

Credit cards 1 2

★★ **Three Crowns** ☎(06473) 3444

A 13th-century stone inn with busy bars, situated in the village.

7rm(4⇒2⋔) 2 ✱sB&B£12–£13 dB&B£24–£26 dB&B⇒⋔£26–£30

CTV 20P 1 Live music and dancing Sat *xmas*

V ✱Lunch £5–£7 High Tea £10alc Dinner £7–£10 Wine £4.15 Last dinner 9.30pm

Credit cards 1 2 3 4 5 **VS**

★ ***BL*** **Easton Court** Easton Cross (1½m E A382) ☎(06473) 3469

Charming, small, 15th-century country house with beams and log fires.

8rm(3⇒5⋔) CTV available in bedrooms sB&B⇒⋔£13–£18 dB&B⇒⋔£26–£36 Ᵽ

10P ⇏ nc10yrs *xmas*

English & French Bar lunch £1–£4 Tea 75p Dinner £10.50–£12 Wine £4.95 Last dinner 8.30pm

Credit cards 1 2 3 5 **VS**

CHALFORD
Gloucestershire
Map **3** SO80

★★ ***H*** **Springfield House** (on A419) ☎Brimscombe (0453) 883555
Closed Jan

A comfortable small hotel offering personal service and well prepared meals.

7rm(5⇒) (1fb) 1 CTV in 5 bedrooms Ⓡ ✱sB&B£15 sB&B⇒£22 dB&B£25 dB&B⇒£35 Ᵽ

20P ⇏ ✽

✱Lunch fr£5.50 Tea fr75p Dinner £7.75&alc Wine £4.75 Last dinner 9pm

Credit cards 2 3 5

CHANNEL ISLANDS
Map **16**
Information is shown under individual placenames. Refer first to Guernsey, Jersey and Sark for details

CHARD
Somerset
Map **3** ST30

★★ **George** Fore St ☎(04606) 3413
RS Xmas night (no restaurant)

Former 16th-century coaching inn situated in the town centre.

21rm(6⇒) (2fb) CTV in 2 bedrooms TV in 13 bedrooms Ⓡ sB&B£13.50 sB&B⇒£19.50 dB&B£21 dB&B⇒£26 Ᵽ

CTV P sauna bath Cabaret wknd

English & French **V** ✱Bar lunch £3.50alc Dinner £6alc Wine £3.85 Last dinner 10.30pm

Credit cards 1 2 3 5

CHARLECOTE
Warwickshire
Map **4** SP25

☆☆☆ **Charlecote Pheasant Country** ☎Stratford upon Avon (0789) 840649
Stratford upon Avon plan **4** *C2*

A 17th-century farmhouse in a quiet hamlet has been tastefully modernised to form this hotel.

Annexe: 15rm(4➡11⋒)(4fb) 4▣ CTV in all bedrooms ® sB&B➡⋒ £22 dB&B➡⋒ £30 ₿

130P ✽ (hard) sauna bath xmas

V ♡ ☐ Lunch £5.70&alc Tea £1 Dinner £6.70&alc Wine £4.20 Last dinner 9.45pm

Credit card 1 2 3 **VS**

CHARLWOOD
Surrey
Map **4** TQ24
Hotels are listed under Gatwick Airport

CHARMOUTH
Dorset
Map **3** SY39

★★**Charmouth House** ☎(0297) 60319

10rm(1➡)(1fb) ® sB&B £12 dB&B £24 dB&B➡ £27 ₿

CTV 30P ✽ (heated) sauna bath *xmas*

♡ Lunch £12alc Dinner £12alc Wine £5.50 Last dinner 10pm

Credit cards 1 3

★★**Fernhill** ☎(0297) 60492
Closed mid Nov–Feb

Large house in 13 acres of grounds, adjacent to the golf course and overlooking the English Channel.

15rm(5➡3⋒)(7fb) ® sB&B £15–£18.50 dB&B £30–£37 dB&B➡⋒ £33.20–£40.20 ₿

CTV 60P ✽ (heated) squash

English & Continental V ♡ Bar lunch £3.50 Dinner £8.25–£9.85&alc Wine £4 Last dinner 8.45pm

Credit card 3

★★**Queen's Arms** The Street ☎(0297) 60339 Closed Xmas

Rendered, colour-washed hotel, once visited by Catherine of Aragon, Charles II and Edward VII.

11rm(5➡4⋒)(1fb) 1▣ ® sB&B £13.50–£15.75 sB&B➡⋒ £13.50–£15.75 dB&B £27–£31.50 dB&B➡⋒ £27–£31.50 ₿

CTV 25P ✽ nc4yrs

English & French ♡ Bar lunch £3.50alc Dinner £7.50&alc Wine £3.60 Last dinner 8.30

Credit card 2

★**Sea Horse** Higher Sea Ln ☎(0297) 60414 Closed Nov–Mar

An 18th-century house standing in one acre of grounds, with a secluded walled garden and views of sea and the hills.

8rm Annexe: 2rm(3fb) ✻ sB&B £8.50–£9.50 dB&B £17–£19 ₿

CTV 14P ✽ *xmas*

♡ ☐ ✻ Bar lunch 75p–£2 Tea 50p Dinner £5 Wine £3.40

CHARNOCK RICHARD
Lancashire
Map **7** SD51

☆☆**Hunters Lodge Motel** ☎Coppull (0257) 793011

21rm(2➡19⋒) CTV in all bedrooms ® ✻ sB&B➡⋒ £16–£22 dB&B➡⋒ £19.50–£31 ₿

100P CFA Live music and dancing Fri

English, French & Italian ♡ ✻ Lunch fr£4.50&alc High Tea fr£4.50 Dinner fr£6.95&alc Wine £5.70 Last dinner 10pm

Credit cards 1 2 3 5 **VS**

CHARNOCK RICHARD
(M6 Motorway Service Area) Lancashire
Map **7** SD51

☆☆☆**TraveLodge** Mill Ln (Trusthouse Forte) ☎Coppull (0257) 791746 Telex no 67315

The restaurant is situated in the adjacent service area and provides mainly grills.

108➡ CTV in all bedrooms ® sB&B➡ £24 dB&B➡ £33.50 Continental breakfast ₿

120P

♡

Credit cards 1 2 3 4 5

CHEADLE HULME
Gt Manchester
Map **7** SJ88

✕**Cheshire Tandoori** 9 The Precinct ☎061-485 4942

Colourful restaurant featuring delicately spiced dishes.

Lunch not served Sun

Indian 40 seats Lunch £3.10–£7.95&alc Dinner £5.95–£7.95&alc Wine £4.50 Last dinner 10.45pm 100P

Credit cards 1 2 3 5 **VS**

CHEDINGTON
Dorset
Map **3** ST40

★★★**Chedington Court** ☎Corscombe (093 589) 265

Lovely Jacobean-style country house in splendid grounds. Rooms are large and comfortable, food is carefully prepared and the atmosphere is relaxed.

8➡ 1▣ CTV in all bedrooms ® sB&B➡⋒ £28.60–£31.90 dB&B➡⋒ £46.20–£52.80 ₿

20P 1 ✽ billiards

English & French Dinner £13 Wine £3.80 Last dinner 9pm

S% Credit card 2 **VS**

CHELMSFORD
Essex
Map **5** TL70

★★★**South Lodge** 196 New London Rd (Best Western) ☎(0245) 64564 Telex no 99452

Busy hotel with compact, well equipped bedrooms.

25rm(24➡1⋒) Annexe: 16➡⋒ (3fb) CTV in all bedrooms ® ✻ sB&B➡⋒ £28–£31.50 dB&B➡⋒ £36–£38.80

Continental breakfast ₿

☾ 50P ✽

French V ♡ ☐ ✻ Lunch £6.32&alc Dinner £7.15&alc Last dinner 9.15pm

S% Credit cards 1 2 3 5

★★**County** Rainsford Rd ☎(0245) 266911
Closed 27–30 Dec

Busy commercial hotel with modern bedrooms.

34rm(17➡7⋒) Annexe: 23rm(7➡)(2fb) CTV in 31 bedrooms ® sB&B £19.50 sB&B➡⋒ £25.75 dB&B £33 dB&B➡⋒ £41.50

☾ CTV 70P

English & French V ♡ ☐ Lunch £5alc Tea 50p alc Dinner £6&alc

Credit cards 1 2 3 5

CHELTENHAM
Gloucestershire
Map **3** SO92
See also Cleeve Hill

☆☆☆☆**Golden Valley Thistle** Gloucester Rd (Thistle) ☎(0242) 32691 Telex no 43410

Modern well appointed hotel with extensive conference facilities.

103➡⋒ CTV in all bedrooms ® ✻ sB➡⋒ £36–£39 dB➡⋒ £46–£49 (room only) ₿

Lift ☾ 279P CFA ✽

European ♡ ☐ ✻ Lunch £6.75&alc Dinner £8.95&alc Last dinner 9.30pm

Credit cards 1 2 3 4 5 **VS**

★★★★**Queen's** The Promenade (Trusthouse Forte) ☎(0242) 514724 Telex no 43381

A comfortable, traditional style hotel, impressively situated overlooking gardens.

77➡ (7fb) CTV in all bedrooms ® sB&B➡ £45.50 dB&B➡ £61.50 ₿

Lift ☾ 32P CFA *xmas*

♡ ☐ Last dinner 10.30pm

Credit cards 1 2 3 4 5

★★★**Carlton** Parabola Rd ☎(0242) 514453

Traditional hotel with well equipped bedrooms, situated near the town centre.

49➡ CTV in all bedrooms ® sB&B➡⋒ £28.50 dB&B➡ £39.50 ₿

Lift ☾ 20P CFA *xmas*

V ♡ ☐ Lunch £5.75&alc Tea 52palc Dinner £7.50&alc Wine £3.75 Last dinner 9pm

Credit cards 1 2 3 5

See advert on page 191

★★★ **Hotel De La Bere** Southam (3m NE A46) (Best Western) ☎(0242) 37771 Telex no 43232 (ref DLB)
Closed 27 Dec–5 Jan

22rm(21➡1⋒) Annexe: 11rm(10➡1⋒) (2fb) 6▣ CTV in all bedrooms ® sB&B➡⋒ £25.50–£29.75 →

dB&B→ƒ £37–£51 Continental breakfast ⊞

☾ 250P CFA ✽ ⛵ (heated in summer) ⚲(hard) squash sauna bath Disco 3 nights wkly *xmas*

⊟French ✿ ☐ Lunch £5.25 Tea 45p&alc Dinner £11&alc Wine £5.35 Last dinner 9.45pm

Credit cards 1 2 3 5 **VS**

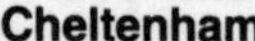

Cheltenham

★★★**Lilleybrook Aparthotel** Cirencester Rd, Charlton Kings ☎(0242) 25861 Telex no 43581

Comfortable hotel overlooking a lake and the golf course, with facilities for health and fitness enthusiasts.

40rm(23→17ƒ)(3fb) CTV in all bedrooms ★ sB&B→ƒ £37 dB&B→ƒ £45 Continental breakfast ⊞

☾ 200P ⛟ CFA ✽ sauna bath Live music and dancing alternate Sat

⊟English & French ✿ ☐ Lunch fr£7.50 Tea fr75p High Tea fr£1.95 Dinner fr£8.50 Wine £5.25 Last dinner 9.30pm

Credit cards 1 2 3 5 **VS**

★★★

❀★★★ **GREENWAY, CHELTENHAM**

Shurdington ☎(0242) 862352 Telex no 437216

Closed 28 Dec–10 Jan

This delightful Cotswold country house, set in 37 acres of grounds and gardens, under the personal supervision of Tony and Maryan Elliott, appears well established now and is certainly worthy of our Red Star award. The house takes its name from the 4,000 year old walkway which runs beside the hotel up to the Cotswolds. This old road, the Green Way, was the original drovers road through the lowlands which were then marsh and forest inhabited by wild animals. Such dangers are no longer present, but now guests can return from their explorations to find a warm welcome and the tranquil atmosphere of a real home, for that is what the Greenway offers. Ground floor rooms are elegant and spacious, yet truly comfortable with roaring log fires in season and access to the formal gardens in summer. The Elliotts boast their own herb garden which receives keen attention to ensure that interesting and fresh ingredients find their way to the kitchen. The meals are served in a very attractive panelled dining room which lends itself to the enjoyment of the small but well chosen menu in a romantic candlelit atmosphere. Upstairs the bedrooms are

individually decorated and furnished with antiques. They have achieved a fine compromise in offering the best of both worlds, by providing modern-day creature comforts to complement the character of the old rooms. The Elliotts genuine hospitality is obvious and their staff are inspired by them to provide traditional services in a friendly manner. This together with the tranquil surroundings promote the hotel as an ideal home and an excellent base for either the businessman or the tourist to travel from.

12→ 1⊟ CTV in all bedrooms ★ sB&B→ £45–£55 dB&B→ £65–£75 ⊞

35P ⛟ ✽ nc7yrs *xmas*

V Lunch £11 Dinner £16 Wine £5.60 Last dinner 9.30pm

S% Credit cards 1 2 3 5

★★★*B* **Wyastone** Parabola Rd (Exec Hotel) ☎(0242) 22659

A comfortable, small proprietor-run hotel.

13rm(5→8ƒ)(1fb) 1⊟ CTV in all bedrooms Ⓡ ★ sB&B→ƒ £30 dB&B→ƒ £42.50–£44 ⊞

18P 1🚗 ⛟ ✽

⊟Continental **V** ✿ ☐ Lunch fr£6&alc Tea fr£3 High Tea fr£6alc Dinner fr£7.50&alc Wine £4.30 Last dinner 10pm

S% Credit cards 1 2 3 5 **VS**

See advert on page 192

★★**George** St George's Rd ☎(0242) 35751

Traditional-style town hotel offering good value meals.

39rm(22→4ƒ)(4fb) CTV in all bedrooms Ⓡ sB&B £18.50 sB&B→ƒ £24 dB&B £28.50 dB&B→ƒ £33 ⊞

☾ CTV 18P 4🚗 *xmas*

⊟English & Continental **V** ✿ ☐ Lunch £3.95&alc Tea 70p Dinner £6.50–£9&alc Wine £5 Last dinner 9.45pm

Credit cards 1 2 3 4 5

★★**Lansdown** Lansdown Rd (Wessex Taverns) ☎(0242) 22700

Detached Regency building on edge of town centre with small garden and friendly atmosphere.

13rm(8→5ƒ)(1fb) CTV in all bedrooms Ⓡ ★ sB&B→ƒ £25 dB&B→ƒ £36 ⊞

30P ✽ nc8yrs

⊟English & French **V** ✿ ✱ Lunch £4.70–5.95&alc Dinner £5.95&alc Wine £3.20 Last dinner 10pm

Credit cards 1 2 3 5

★★**Prestbury House** The Burgage, Prestbury (2m NE A46) →

C

C

☎(0242) 29533 Closed Xmas wk, New Year, Etr & Public hols

Good food is a feature of this proprietor-run hotel.

10rm(6⇌) (2fb) CTV in 9 bedrooms ® ✽sB&B£24.66 sB&B⇌£24.66 dB&B£35.42 dB&B⇌£35.42

40P 🚗 ✽

V ✽Lunch £9.15–£13.38 Dinner £9.85–£12&alc Wine £4.50 Last dinner 9pm

★ ***Royal Ascot*** Western Rd ☎(0242) 513640

Quiet hotel supervised by the proprietors.

10rm(1⇌)

CTV 20P 🚗

English & French Last dinner 9.30pm

Credit card 3

✕✕✕ **Cleeveway House** Bishop's Cleeve (3m N A435) ☎Bishop's Cleeve (024267) 2585

This well-appointed country house restaurant makes commendable use of game, fish and raw materials in season.

Closed 1 wk after Xmas & Public hols

Lunch not served Mon Dinner not served Sun

English & French **V** 38 seats Lunch £10alc Dinner £10alc Wine £4.60 Last dinner 9.45pm 25P bedrooms available

Credit card 1

✕ **Mister Tsang** 63 Winchcombe St ☎(0242) 38727

Small Cantonese restaurant that is a perfect introduction to Cantonese cooking, a subject on which the proprietor is always pleased to advise.

Closed Sun & between 1st & 3rd wk Jan

Lunch not served Mon

Chinese V 44 seats *Lunch £1.55–£1.95&alc Dinner £3.30–£4.50&alc Wine £4.25 Last dinner 11.30pm

Credit cards 1 2 3 5

✕**Rajvooj Tandoori** 1 Albion St ☎(0242) 24288

Indian 49 seats Last dinner 11.30pm 20P

S% Credit cards 1 2 3 5

CHENIES
Buckinghamshire
Map **4** TQ09

★★★**Bedford Arms Thistle** (Thistle) ☎Chorleywood (09278) 3301 Telex no 893939

Small country hotel with nice bedrooms, an attractive restaurant, good food and some unusual drinks.

10 CTV in all bedrooms *sB £39–£42 dB £49.50–£52 (room only) B

80P *xmas*

European *Lunch £14.45alc Dinner £16.75alc Last dinner 9.30pm

Credit cards 1 2 3 4 5 VS

CHEPSTOW
Gwent
Map **3** ST59

★★**Beaufort** Beaufort Sq ☎(02912) 5074 Telex no 498280

17th century hotel with a welcoming atmosphere.

12rm(2) (3fb) sB&B£18–£25 sB&B£20–£25 dB&B£27–£33 dB&B£30–£35 B

CTV 12P

International V Lunch £5.50–£6.50&alc Dinner £5.50–£6.50&alc Wine £3.80 Last dinner 9.30pm

Credit cards 1 2 3 5

★★*H* Castle View 16 Bridge St ☎(02912) 70349 Telex no 498280
Comfortable small hotel with good home produced cooking.
8rm(7→1⋒)(4fb) CTV in all bedrooms ® sB&B→⋒£21–£23.50 dB&B→⋒£33–£37 B
xmas
V ✿ ✻Lunch £6.70alc Dinner £7.50alc Wine £4.20 Last dinner 9pm
Credit cards 1 3 **VS**

★★George Moor St (Trusthouse Forte) ☎(02912) 2365
Small friendly hotel with comfortable bedrooms.
20rm(5→1⋒)(3fb) CTV in all bedrooms ® sB&B£30.50 sB&B→⋒£33 dB&B£40.50 dB&B→⋒£46 B
25P
✿ Last dinner 9.30pm
Credit cards 1 2 3 4 5

CHESTER
Cheshire
Map **7** SJ46

☆☆☆Abbots Well Whitchurch Rd, Christleton (Embassy) ☎(0244) 332121 Telex no. 61561
Well appointed, modern hotel, situated on the A41 south of Chester.
127→(5fb) CTV in all bedrooms ® sB→£31.50 dB→£42.75 (room only) B
☾ ### 250P CFA ✽
English & French ✿ ✻Lunch fr£6.10&alc Tea 55p Dinner fr£7.50&alc Last dinner 10pm
Credit cards 1 2 3 5

★★★Blossoms St John Street (Prince of Wales) ☎(0244) 23186 Telex 61113
Large and elegant city centre hotel which is over 300 years old.
70rm(52→18⋒)(2fb) CTV in all bedrooms ® ✻sB&B→⋒£33 dB&B→⋒£44 B
Lift ☾ CFA
English & French V ✿ ✻Lunch £3.95–£4.70&alc Tea fr50p Dinner £6.20–£6.70&alc Wine £4.20 Last dinner 9.30pm
Credit cards 1 2 3 4 5

★★★Mollington Banastre Parkgate Rd (A540) (Best Western) ☎Great Mollington (0244) 851471 Telex 61686
Mid-Victorian mansion in 8½ acres of grounds.
48→(5fb) 3 CTV in all bedrooms sB&B→£35–£38 dB&B→£44–£48 B
Lift ☾ CTV 200P CFA ✽ (grass) sauna bath Live music and dancing Wed & Sun
English & French V ✿ Lunch £10alc Tea £2alc Dinner £10–£12&alc Wine £7 Last dinner 9.30pm
Credit cards 1 2 3

★★★Plantation Inn Liverpool Rd (Comfort) ☎(0244) 374100 Telex 61263 Closed Xmas–New Year
Large hotel in its own grounds with modern extension.
85→⋒(4fb) CTV in all bedrooms ® sB&B→⋒£22.50–£28.50 dB&B→⋒£37.50–£40 B
CTV 120P ✽ Disco & Live music and dancing Mon–Sat ♿
English & French V ✿ Lunch £4.25–£5.50 Tea £1.25 High Tea £3.50–£4.25

★★★★GROSVENOR, CHESTER
Eastgate St (Prestige) ☎(0244) 24024 Telex 61240 Closed Xmas
Modern traffic management in this ancient city may make it hard to find this half timbered hotel if you travel by car but, once you have arrived, everything is made easy by the spontaneous service readily provided at this elegant town centre hotel. The internal scale of the hotel is impressive with a balanced blend of antique and modern fittings, and lots of facilities, all combined with first class service from uniformed courteous staff. Although there is a lift, you will be tempted to use the imposing oak and pine grand staircase with its Georgian crystal chandelier. The bedrooms are pleasantly decorated and comfortable; a special mention should be made of the efficient room service. There are two bars and two restaurants offering different types of food as well as a comfortable sitting area. As we have said before, it is good to see a hotel reflecting the life of the town in a traditional way. The restaurant has a clean-cut style, elegant and pleasing, serving very decent food from the French Menu.

We do not have many Red Star hotels in cities because they so often lack the character and hospitality required by this accolade, but here the atmosphere is such that, for the member who needs to stay in the fine city of Chester, it is a worthy member of our Red Star list.
98→⋒(6fb) 1 CTV in all bedrooms sB→⋒ fr£38.50 dB→⋒ fr£55 (room only) B
Lift ☾ P Live music and dancing Sat (in winter) CFA
International V ✿ Lunch fr£6.50&alc Tea £1.25–£2.75 Dinner fr£10&alc Wine £6.80 Last dinner 10pm
Credit cards 1 2 3 4 5 **VS**

Dinner £5.75–£6.75&alc Wine £4.10 Last dinner 11.30pm

Credit cards ① ② ③ ④ ⑤ VS

☆☆☆**Post House** Wrexham Rd (Trusthouse Forte) ☎(0244) 674111 Telex no 61450

Modern hotel with spacious well-appointed bedrooms.

62➡ (2fb) CTV in all bedrooms Ⓡ sB&B➡£37.50 dB&B➡£50 B

☾ 250P CFA ✽ *xmas*

Last dinner 9.45pm

Credit cards ① ② ③ ④ ⑤

★★★**Queen** City Rd (Trusthouse Forte) ☎(0244) 28341 Telex no 617101

A mid-Victorian building next to the railway station and near the town centre.

91➡ (11fb) CTV in all bedrooms Ⓡ sB&B➡£36.50 dB&B➡£52.50 B

Lift ☾ 130P ✽ *xmas*

Last dinner 9.15pm

Credit cards ① ② ③ ④ ⑤

★★***Oaklands*** Hoole Rd (Scottish & Newcastle) ☎(0244) 22156

Victorian building with modern extensions, one mile from the centre.

18rm(10➡⋒) CTV in all bedrooms Ⓡ

CTV 70P ✽

English & French

Last dinner 9.15pm

Credit cards ① ② ③ ④ ⑤

★★**Rowton Hall** Whitchurch Rd, Rowton (2m SE A41) ☎(0244) 335262

Closed 28–30 Dec

Ivy-clad country house in its own pleasant grounds, 2m from the city centre.

27rm(2➡25⋒) (3fb) 2 CTV in all bedrooms Ⓡ sB&B£19 sB&B➡⋒£22–£24 dB&B£30 dB&B➡⋒£35–£38 B

☾ CTV 120P 6 ✽ sauna bath Live music and dancing Sat (Oct–Apr)

V Lunch £5.25 Dinner £6.75 Wine £4.95 Last dinner 9.30pm

Credit cards ① ② ③ ⑤ VS

★***Dene*** Hoole Rd ☎(0244) 21165

Large house with a modern extension, situated on the A56 one mile from the city.

40rm(14➡2⋒) Ⓡ B

CTV 52P 3

Last dinner 8pm

★**Ye Olde Kings Head** 48–50 Lower Bridge St (Greenall Whitley) ☎(0244) 24855 RS Xmas & New Year

Black & White Cheshire inn (circa 1520) with beams and plenty of character.

11rm (1fb) CTV in 1 bedroom Ⓡ sB&B£13.20–£18.70 dB&B£19.80–£24 B

CTV 3P 6

English & French V Lunch fr£3.50 Tea 50p High Tea £2–£3 Dinner £4.50–£5.50 Wine £4.60 Last dinner 8.45pm

S% Credit cards ① ② ③ ⑤

✕✕**Courtyard** St Werburgh Street ☎(0244) 21447

Closed Sun & Public hols

English & French 100 seats ✱Lunch £2–£5&alc Tea 80p–£1.80 High Tea £1.50–£4 Dinner £6.95&alc Wine £4.65 Last dinner 10pm Disco Fri & Sat

Credit cards ① ③ VS

At **Backford Cross** (5m NW on A41)

☆☆☆**Ladbroke** (& Conference centre) Backford Cross Rbt (A41/A5117) (Ladbroke) ☎(0244) 851551

122➡⋒ 150P

CHESTERFIELD
Derbyshire
Map **8** SK37

★★★**Chesterfield** Malkin St (Best Western) ☎(0246) 71141

Four-storey, Victorian 'railway' hotel, near the station and town centre.

64rm(52➡) (4fb) CTV in all bedrooms Ⓡ ✱sB&B£19.50 sB&B➡£28 dB&B➡£38 B

Lift ☾ CTV 65P 10 CFA *xmas*

V Lunch £4.45&alc Tea 60–90p →

C

Dinner £6.95&alc Wine £4.50 Last dinner 10pm
Credit cards 1 2 3 4

★★**Portland** West Bars (Anchor) ☎(0246) 34502 Telex no 858875 Closed Boxing Day

Two-storey, half-timbered, gabled hotel in the town centre.

23rm(11→3⋒) (3fb) CTV in all bedrooms ® sB&B£20.50 sB&B→⋒£28.50 dB&B£31.50 dB&B→⋒£37.50 ℞

☾ 30P Live music Mon & Tue

Mainly grills V ♡ Lunch £4.40–£6.50 Dinner £5.45–£6.95&alc Wine £4.50 Last dinner 9.30pm

Credit cards 1 2 3 4 5

✕ ***Old Spinner*** Sheffield Rd, Sheepbridge ☎(0246) 450550

Closed Sun & Public hols Lunch not served Sat Dinner not served Mon

English & French 60 seats Last dinner 10pm 100P

Credit cards 1 3 5

CHESTERFORD, GREAT
Essex
Map **5** TL54

★★**H** ***Crown House*** ☎Saffron Walden (0799) 30515

A small, historical building, that also offers well-equipped, modern annexe accommodation.

14rm(8→4⋒) CTV in all bedrooms ℞ CTV 30P ♿

English & French V ♡

Credit cards 1 3

CHESTER-LE-STREET
Co Durham
Map **12** NZ25

★★★**Lumley Castle** Lumley Castle ☎(0385) 885326

Closed Xmas & New Year RS Sun

8rm(7→1⋒) Annexe: 42rm(33→9⋒) (12fb) 5 CTV in all bedrooms ® *sB&B→⋒£22–£34.50 dB&B→⋒£32–£43 ℞

☾ 200P CFA ✽ (heated) billiards sauna bath

English & French V ♡ Lunch £6.95–£7.50&alc Tea fr70p Dinner fr£8.75 Wine £4.80 Last dinner 10pm

Credit cards 1 2 3 5

★★***Lambton Arms*** Front St (Scottish & Newcastle) ☎(0385) 883265

A high street public house with comfortable accommodation.

10rm CTV in all bedrooms ® ★ ℞ 36P

♡ Last dinner 9pm

Credit cards 1 3

CHESTERTON
Oxfordshire
Map **4** SP52

✕ **Woods Farm House** ☎Bicester (08692) 41444

Closed Bank Hol Mons & New Years Day Lunch not served Sat Dinner not served Sun

V 40 seats Lunch £1.10–£10.70 Dinner £8.75–£13.85 Wine £4.30 Last dinner 9.30pm 25P

Credit cards 1 2 3 5

CHICHESTER
West Sussex
Map **4** SU80

★★★**Chichester Lodge** Westhampnett ☎(0243) 786351 Telex no 869210 RS Xmas

A modern motel-style hotel situated on the A27.

43→ (9fb) CTV in all bedrooms ® sB&B→£31.50 dB&B→£42.50 ℞

☾ 100P 10 ✽ CFA Live music and dancing Sat (Oct–Feb)

French V ♡ Lunch £6&alc Tea £1–£2 Dinner fr£8&alc Wine £5.25 Last dinner 9.30pm

Credit cards 1 2 3

★★★**Dolphin & Anchor** West St (Trusthouse Forte) ☎(0243) 785121

This hotel opposite the cathedral

combines two ancient inns and has elegant décor.

54rm(49⇌5⋔)(5fb) CTV in all bedrooms ®sB&B⇌£39 dB&B⇌£54.50 B

☾ CFA 16P *xmas*

♆☐ Last dinner 10.30pm

Credit cards 1 2 3 4 5

✕✕Christopher's 149 St Pancras ☎(0243) 788724

Simple restaurant with elegant bar and spicy French food.

Closed Sun, Mon & Xmas wk

▣French 36 seats ✻Lunch £4.10–£5.60&alc Dinner £4.10–£5.60&alc Wine £3.95 Last dinner 10pm ⁋

Credit cards 1 2 3 5

CHICKERELL
Dorset
Map **3** SY68

✕Turks Head Inn 6 East St ☎Weymouth (0305) 783093

Closed Mon Dinner not served Sun

50 seats Lunch £3.25–£4.25 Dinner £5.50–£6.50alc Wine £3.85 Last dinner 9pm 50P bedrooms available

Credit cards 1 3

CHIDDINGFOLD
Surrey
Map **4** SU93

✕✕✕Crown Inn ☎Wormley (042879) 2255

Traditional dishes and a short imaginative French menu are skilfully cooked in this beautiful timbered medieval restaurant.

Closed Mon

▣French 48 seats ✻Lunch £12.50&alc Tea £1.25 Dinner £12.50&alc Wine £5.90 Last dinner 10pm 5P bedrooms available

Credit card 1 2 3 5 **VS**

CHIDDINGSTONE
Kent
Map **5** TQ44

✕Castle Inn ☎Penshurst (0892) 870247

Closed Tue & Jan Lunch not served Wed

V 36 seats ✻Lunch £7–£15 Dinner £12.50–£15 Wine £4.50 Last dinner 9.30pm ⁋

S% Credit cards 1 2 3 5 **VS**

CHIDEOCK
Dorset
Map **3** SY49

★Clock House ☎(029 789) 423

Ancient, thatched, cottage-style hotel on the main road, in the village centre.

3rm Annexe: 3rm(1⇌) ®sB&B£9.90–£10.90 sB&B⇌£16.50–£18 dB&B£19.80–£22 dB&B⇌£22–£25

CTV 30P squash

V ♆Bar lunch £3alc Dinner £7.50alc Wine £4.25 Last dinner 10pm

S% Credit cards 1 3 **VS**

CHILGROVE
West Sussex
Map **4** SU81

❀ **✕✕White Horse Inn** ☎East Marden (024 359) 219

Well cooked and presented English and French food plus outstanding wine list.

Closed Sun, Mon, Jan–Feb (3wks) & Oct–Nov (2wks)

▣English & French **V** 60 seats Lunch £2.75–£5.75&alc Dinner £15alc Wine £4.95 Last dinner 9.30pm 200P

S% Credit cards 1 2 3 4 5 **VS**

CHILLINGTON
Devon
Map **3** SX74

★★Oddicombe House ☎Frogmore (054 853) 234

Closed Jan–Mar RS Nov–Dec

Standing in three acres of grounds with views of the surrounding countryside.

8rm(5⇌) Annexe: 2rm (2fb) ® ✻sB&B£12.50–£15 sB&B⇌£14–£16.50 dB&B£25–£30 dB&B⇌£28–£33

CTV 16P ✻

▣International ♆☐ ✻Lunch £4–£6 Tea 60p–£1.60 Dinner £7&alc Wine £4 Last dinner 8.45pm

VS

CHILTON POLDEN
Somerset
Map **3** ST34

✕Wilton Farm House 9 Goose Ln ☎(0278) 722134

Closed Sun & Mon (except Public hols) Lunch not served

▣English & Continental **V** 24 seats ✻Dinner £7.75–£8.50&alc Wine £4.50 Last dinner 10pm 7P

Credit cards 3 5 **VS**

CHIPPENHAM
Wiltshire
Map **3** ST97

★★Angel Market Pl (Norfolk Capital) ☎(0249) 652615 Telex 23241

Building dates from 1770 and has studio style bedrooms in modern block to the rear.

12rm Annexe: 41⇌ CTV in all bedrooms ®sB&B£18 sB&B⇌£24.50 dB&B£28 dB&B⇌£35.50 B

☾ 60P

✻Lunch £6.50alc Tea fr70p Dinner £6.50alc Wine £4.20 Last dinner 10pm

S% Credit cards 1 2 3 5

★★Bear 11 Market Pl ☎(0249) 653272

Attractive, Bath stone, Gothic-style hotel with a portico, situated in the town centre.

8rm(1⇌1⋔)(1fb) sB&B£13.20–£14.30 dB&B£26.40–£28.60 dB&B⇌⋔£33

CTV 5

V ♆ ✻Lunch fr£5&alc Dinner fr£5&alc Last dinner 8.45pm

S% Credit cards 1 3

CHIPPERFIELD
Hertfordshire
Map **4** TL00

★★Two Brewers Inn The Common (Trusthouse Forte) ☎King's Langley (09277) 65266

20⇌ CTV in all bedrooms ®sB&B⇌£39 dB&B⇌£55.50 B

25P *xmas*

♆☐ Last dinner 10pm

Credit cards 1 2 3 4 5

C

CHIPPING CAMPDEN
Gloucestershire
Map **4** SP13

★★**Cotswold House** The Square
☎Evesham (0386) 840330
Closed 25–30 Dec

A traditional hotel on The Square.

18rm(10⇌1⋒) Annexe: 7rm (2fb) sB&B£12.50–£20.90 sB&B⇌⋒£14–£25.70 dB&B£25.50–£33.90 dB&B⇌⋒£28–£42 Continental breakfast served in season B

12P 6 ✽ nc6yrs

English & French V Lunch £5.50–£9 Tea 70p–75p Dinner £8.50–£9 Wine £3.50 Last dinner 9pm

Credit card 1

❀★★**King's Arms** The Square
☎Evesham (0386) 840256

(Rosette awarded for dinner only.) Comfortable small hotel whose interesting menus and sound cooking are particularly recommended.

14rm(2⇌) sB&B£16.69 dB&B£33.49 dB&B⇌£41.74 B

50P ✽

English & French Bar lunch 70p–£2.95 Tea 40p Dinner £10.94–£12 Wine £4.05 Last dinner 9pm

Credit cards 1 2 3 5

★★**Noel Arms** (ExecHotel) ☎Evesham (0386) 840317

Comfortable 14th-century inn with an open courtyard and a bowling green to the rear.

19rm(12⇌1⋒) (1fb) 2 sB&B£21.25–£23.25 sB&B⇌⋒£22.85–£24.85 dB&B£27–£29 dB&B⇌⋒£35.50–£37.50 B

CTV 70P *xmas*

V Lunch £5.50–£6.50&alc High Tea £4–£5 Dinner £7.50–£8.50&alc Wine £5.35 Last dinner 9pm

Credit card 1

CHIPPING NORTON
Oxfordshire
Map **4** SP32

★★**Crown & Cushion** High St (Inter-Hotels) ☎(0608) 2533 Telex no 837955
RS Sun

Old world 15th-century hotel with comfortable bedrooms.

12rm(6⇌6⋒) (3fb) CTV in 6 bedrooms TV in 6 bedrooms ✻sB&B£14.50–£16 sB&B⇌⋒£19.50 dB&B£29–£32 dB&B⇌⋒£39 B

CTV 12P 4 sauna bath *xmas*

English & French Lunch £6&alc Dinner £6&alc Wine £4.20 Last dinner 9pm

Credit cards 2 5 VS

★★**White Hart** High St (Trusthouse Forte) ☎(0608) 2572

Comfortable hotel with attractive lounge and bar, both with log fires.

12rm(1⇌) Annexe: 10rm(5⇌) 1 CTV in all bedrooms Ⓡ sB&B£30.50 sB&B⇌£33 dB&B£40.50 dB&B⇌£46.50 B

CTV 16P ♿ *xmas*

Last dinner 9.45pm

Credit cards 1 2 3 4 5

✕**La Madonette** 7 Horsefair ☎(0608) 2320

Closed Sun & Mon Lunch not served

French 30 seats ✻Dinner £10alc Wine £6.25 Last dinner 9.30pm

Credit cards 1 3 5

CHIPPING SODBURY
Avon
Map **3** ST78

✕***Le Cordon Bleu*** 66 Rounceval St
☎(0454) 318041
Closed Sun

English, French & Italian 90 seats Last dinner 11pm 25P

Credit cards 3 5

CHIRNSIDE
Borders *Berwickshire*
Map **12** NT85

★★**Chirnside Country House**
☎(089 081) 219

Closed 25 & 26 Dec
Early Victorian country mansion with extensive grounds and a walled garden.
15rm (3fb) sB&B£11.50–£12.50 dB&B£23–£25 B
Lift CTV 20P ✽
Scottish & Continental Lunch fr£4.95 Tea fr50p High Tea fr£3.50 Dinner fr£8 Wine £3.70 Last dinner 8.45pm
Credit cards 1 2 3 5 **VS**

CHOLLERFORD
Northumberland
Map **12** NY97
★★★**George** Humshaugh (Swallow) ☎Humshaugh (043481) 611
Ivy-clad hotel with a modern bedroom wing and riverside gardens.
54 1 CTV in 27 bedrooms TV in 27 bedrooms Ⓡ ✱sB&B £24.75–£27.50 dB&B £36–£40.60 B
100P ✽ (heated) sauna bath Live music and dancing Sat xmas
V ✱Lunch £6 Tea £2 Dinner fr£8&alc Wine £4.75 Last dinner 9pm
Credit cards 1 2 3 5

CHRISTCHURCH
Dorset
Map **4** SZ19
★★★**Avonmouth** Mudeford (2m E off B3059) (Trusthouse Forte) ☎(0202) 483434
23 Annexe: 14 CTV in all bedrooms Ⓡ sB&B £34.50 dB&B £58.50 B
☾ 66P ✽ (heated) *xmas*
Last dinner 8.45pm
Credit cards 1 2 3 4 5

★★★**King's Arms Crest** Castle St (Crest) ☎(0202) 484117
Mellow, brick-built hotel with coloured portico and a wrought iron balcony, overlooking the castle ruins.
26rm (22 4) Annexe: 6rm (4 2) CTV in all bedrooms Ⓡ ✱sB fr£28 dB fr£39 (room only) B
Lift ☾ 80P CFA ✽ Live music Fri & Sat *xmas*
International **V** ✱Lunch fr£7.25&alc Dinner £7.25–£9.50&alc Wine £5.25 Last dinner 10pm
Credit cards 1 2 3 4 5 **VS**

★★**Fishermans Haunt** Salisbury Rd, Winkton (2½m N on B3347) ☎(0202) 484071 RS Xmas Day
Attractive 17th century country house with good food, attentive service and comfortable bedrooms.
4rm (2 2) Annexe: 9rm (5 2) (3fb) 2 CTV in 13 bedrooms Ⓡ sB&B£14.50 sB&B £16 dB&B£27.50
dB&B £31 B
CTV 150P
Lunch £3–£4.50 Tea 65p–£1.50 Dinner £9–£11.50&alc Wine £3.85 Last dinner 10pm
Credit cards 1 2 3 5 **VS**

★★**Waterford Lodge** Bure Ln, Friars Cliff, Mudeford (2m E off B30591) ☎Highcliffe (04252) 72948
Detached, red brick hotel with pleasant rear garden, within walking distance of beach.
21rm (11) (2fb) CTV in 10 bedrooms sB&B£13.80 sB&B £16.70–£19 dB&B£27.60 dB&B £33.35 B
CTV 25P ✽ *xmas*
V Lunch fr£4.60 Tea fr£1.15 High Tea £2.60 Dinner fr£5.75 Wine £3.80 Last dinner 7pm
Credit cards 1 3 **VS**

✕**Splinters** 12 Church St ☎(0202) 483454
Small, intimate bistro in town centre.
Closed Sun & 25 & 26 Dec
Lunch not served
French **V** 36 seats ✱Dinner £12alc Wine £4.60 Last dinner 10.30pm
Credit card 2

C

CHUDLEIGH
Devon
Map **3** SX87

✕***Highwayman's Haunt*** Old Exeter Rd ☎(0626) 853250
Just off the A35, this restaurant has been converted from three former farm cottages.
80 seats Last dinner 9.30pm 60P

CHURCH STOKE
Powys
Map **7** SO29

★★**Mellington Hall** ☎(05885) 456
Closed Nov & Feb
Impressive, Victorian stone country house set in parkland at the end of a long drive.
10rm(5➡) TV in 3 bedrooms Ⓡ
*sB&B£12.65 sB&B➡£14.40 dB&B£22 dB&B➡£25
CTV 100P ✽ *xmas*
♈☐ *Lunch £2.50–£5.50 Tea 60p–£1.50 Dinner £3.10–£6.30 Wine £4.25 Last dinner 9pm

CHURCH STRETTON
Shropshire
Map **7** SO49

★★★**Long Mynd** Cunnery Rd (Minotels) ☎(0694) 722244
Four-storey building with stone terraces and 24 acres of high, wooded grounds.
51rm(34➡3⋒) (5fb) CTV in all bedrooms Ⓡ sB&B£20–£22 sB&B➡⋒£23–£25 dB&B£28–£31 dB&B➡⋒£34–£37 B
Lift 150P 5🚗✽ ≈(heated) sauna bath Disco Sat ⛳ *xmas* ♿
▣English & French **V**♈☐ Lunch £5–£6&alc Tea 75p High Tea £2.50–£3.50 Dinner £6–£7&alc Wine £4.50 Last dinner 9.30pm
Credit cards 1 2 3 5

★★★**Stretton Hall** All Stretton ☎(0694) 723224
12rm(8➡) (2fb) CTV in all bedrooms Ⓡ sB&B£13.50–£15 sB&B➡£14.50–£16.50 dB&B£21–£23 dB&B➡£26–£28 B
75P ✽ ≈(heated) *xmas*
V♈☐ Lunch £4.25–£4.50&alc Tea 40p High Tea £1.25–£1.50 Dinner £5.25–£5.50&alc Wine £5.25 Last dinner 6pm
Credit cards 1 2 3 5 **VS**

★★**Sandford** Watling St South ☎(0694) 722131
25rm(6➡2⋒) (2fb) CTV in 1 bedroom TV in 1 bedroom Ⓡ sB&B fr£14 sB&B➡⋒ fr£15.50 dB&B fr£24 dB&B➡⋒ fr£27 B
CTV 30P ✽ billiards *xmas*
▣Continental **V**♈☐ *Lunch fr£3.75&alc Tea fr55p High Tea fr£1.40 Dinner fr£4.75&alc Wine £3.40 Last dinner 9.30pm
Credit cards 1 3

CHURSTON FERRERS
Devon
Map **3** SX95

★★★***Broadsands Links*** Bascombe Rd ☎(0803) 842360
Large, detached hotel built in 1935 with fine views of Torbay; there is a private path to the beach.
26➡⋒ CTV in bedrooms on request Ⓡ ✱ B
☾ 60P 5🚗✽ billiards Live music and dancing wkly nc12yrs
▣English & French **V**♈☐ Last dinner 9.30pm
Credit card 3

CHURT
Surrey
Map **4** SU83

★★★L **Frensham Pond** ☎Frensham (025 125) 3175 Telex no 858610
Professional family-run hotel, offering high standards of service, skilful cooking and comfortable well equipped bedrooms.
7➡ Annexe: 12➡ (2fb) CTV in all bedrooms Ⓡ sB&B➡£34–£38 dB&B➡£44–£48 B

☾ 100P 🚗 ✽ ♪ Live music and dancing Sat *xmas*

V ♆ ✽ Lunch fr£7.75&alc Dinner fr£8.75&alc Wine £5.25 Last dinner 9.30pm

Credit cards 1 2 3 5

★★**Pride of the Valley Inn** ☎ Hindhead (042873) 5799

Quietly situated, traditional hotel, with comfortable bedrooms.

10rm(8➡1⋒) CTV in all bedrooms ® sB&B➡⋒ £35.50 dB&B➡⋒ £54.50 Ɓ

50P ✽ *xmas*

♆ ▭ Last dinner 10pm

Credit cards 1 2 3 4 5

CIRENCESTER
Gloucestershire
Map **4** SP00
See also Ewen

★★★★ $_H$**King's Head** Market Pl (Best Western) ☎ (0285) 3322 Telex no 43470
Closed 27–29 Dec

A 14th-century inn situated in the town centre offering traditional service particularly to the commercial and conference trade.

70➡ (4fb) 2 ▭ CTV in all bedrooms sB&B➡ £33 dB&B➡ £44 Ɓ

Lift ☾ 25P CFA *xmas*

V ♆ ▭ Lunch £6.35–£6.55&alc Tea £2alc Dinner £8.50–£8.75&alc Wine £6 Last dinner 9.30pm

Credit cards 1 2 3 4 5 **VS**

★★★ $_L$**Stratton House** Gloucester Rd (A417) ☎ (0285) 61761

Elegant and traditional hotel with country house atmosphere, set in attractive walled gardens.

→

C

26rm(18➡1⋒)(2fb) CTV available in bedrooms ® sB&B£22.50 sB&B➡⋒£25.50 dB&B£35 dB&B➡⋒£39.50 B
CTV ✽ xmas
English & French V Lunch £5.95&alc Tea 75p Dinner £7.50–£7.95&alc Wine £4.55 Last dinner 9.45pm
Credit cards 1 2 3 5 VS

★★ ***Corinium Court*** Gloucester St ☎(0285) 4499
A traditional, small, proprietor-run hotel.
8rm(4➡3⋒) B
CTV 40P ✽
English & French Last dinner 9.30pm
Credit cards 1 2 3 4 5 VS

★★ **Fleece** Market Pl ☎(0285) 2680
Comfortable, small, company-owned hotel.
19➡(4fb) 1 CTV in all bedrooms ® ✽sB➡£33.25 dB➡£42.50 room only B
30P
English & French V ✽Lunch £5.95–£10.45 Tea 60p–£3.45 Dinner £7.95–£11.45 Wine £5.10 Last dinner 10pm
Credit cards 1 2 3 4 5

XX **Centurion Rooms** Watermoor Rd ☎(0285) 2933
Closed Sun & 25–27 Dec Dinner not served Tue
English & French 40 seats Lunch £1.50–£5.50&alc Dinner £8.50alc Wine £4.95 Last dinner 10pm
Credit cards 1 2 3 5

CLACHAN-SEIL
Strathclyde *Argyllshire*
Map **10** NM71

★ **Willowburn** (Inter-Hotel) ☎Balvicar (08523) 276 Closed Nov
Rosette awarded for dinner only. Small hotel with informal, hospitable atmosphere.
6rm(1➡2⋒)(1fb) ® ✽sB&B£17.60 dB&B£29.15 dB&B➡⋒£31.35 B
CTV 25P ✽
English & French ✽Bar lunch 60p–£5 Dinner £8.50alc Wine £3.30 Last dinner 8.30pm
S% Credit cards 1 2 3 5 VS

CLACTON-ON-SEA
Essex
Map **5** TM11

★★ **King's Cliff** King's Pde, Holland on Sea ☎(0255) 812343
Sea front hotel with spacious lounges and reasonable bedrooms.
13rm(1➡)(4fb) ® sB&B£13.75–£15.95 sB&B➡£18.15–£20.35 dB&B£27.50–£31.90 dB&B➡£31.90–£36.30
CTV 70P 5 ✽ Live music and dancing Sat Cabaret Sat *xmas*
V Lunch £3.95–£4.50&alc Tea 55p Dinner £4.50–£5.50&alc Wine £3.90 Last dinner 9pm
VS

CLAPHAM
North Yorkshire
Map **7** SD76

X **Goat Gap** ☎Ingleton (0468) 41230
40 seats Lunch £1–£7alc High Tea £1–£7alc Dinner £8.75–£9.75&alc Wine £4.50 Last dinner 10pm 100P

CLARE
Suffolk
Map **5** TL74

★★ ***Bell*** ☎(078 727) 7741
20rm(12➡1⋒) 4 CTV in 12 bedrooms ®
CTV 16P
Last dinner 9.30pm
Credit cards 1 2 3 5

CLAVERING
Essex
Map **5** TL43

✕Cricketer's ☎(079985) 442
Classification awarded for dinner only.

V 50 seats Lunch £2–£6 Dinner £9.40alc Wine £3.80 Last dinner 10pm 20P

Credit cards 1 2 3 **VS**

CLAWTON
Devon
Map **2** SX39

★★ *HL* **Court Barn Country House** ☎North Tamerton (040927) 219
RS 2wks Dec & 2wks Jan
Attractive, small, holiday hotel with friendly atmosphere in a peaceful, country setting.

8rm(4→2⋒) (3fb) sB&B£12.25–£16.85 sB&B→⋒£15.50–£19 dB&B£23.50–£33.50 dB&B→⋒£26.50–£37 B

CTV 12P *xmas*

Wine £3.95 Last dinner 7.45pm

VS

CLAYTON-LE-WOODS
Lancashire
Map **7** SD52

★★★ **Pines** ☎Preston (0772) 38551
Telex no 677584
Closed 25–26 Dec
A well-furnished, late Victorian house with modern extensions,

25→ CTV in all bedrooms Ⓡ sB&B→£20.24–£30.36 dB&B→£26–£32.89 B

☾ 120P squash Disco Fri

English & French Lunch £5&alc Dinner £8.50alc Wine £3.65 Last dinner 9.30pm

S% Credit cards 1 2 3 5

CLEARWELL
Gloucestershire
Map **3** SO50

✕Wyndham Arms ☎Dean (0594) 33666
This village-centre restaurant is in an old 14th-century building.

Closed Mon & last 2wks Oct

International **V** 50 seats Lunch £4.55&alc Dinner £11.50alc Wine £3.75 Last dinner 10pm 30P bedrooms available

Credit cards 1 2 3 4 5

CLEETHORPES
Humberside
Map **8** TA30

★★★ **Kingsway** Kingsway ☎(0472) 601122 Closed 25 & 26 Dec
Charming and comfortable, three-storeyed, hotel, overlooking the sea.

53rm(46→) CTV in all bedrooms sB&B£23 sB&B→£30–£32 dB&B£31 dB&B→£39.50–£40.50 B

Lift ☾ 30P 20

Lunch £6.50 Dinner £7.50&alc Wine £4.95 Last dinner 9pm

S% Credit cards 1 2 3 5

★★ ***Lifeboat*** 40–43 Kingsway ☎(0472) 697272
Overlooks the sea on the south side of town.

28rm(5⋒) TV in 6 bedrooms Ⓡ B
☾ CTV 55P *xmas*

Mainly grills Last dinner 9.30pm

Credit cards 1 3

CLEEVE HILL
Gloucestershire
Map **3** SO92

★★ *B* **Rising Sun** (Trophy Taverns) ☎Bishops Cleeve (024 267) 2002
Closed Xmas Day
Small, comfortable hotel overlooking the Cotswold countryside to the Malverns.

13rm(4→9⋒) (2fb) CTV in all bedrooms Ⓡ *sB&B→⋒£25 dB&B→⋒£34 B
60P

Mainly grills *Lunch £5.50alc Dinner £5.50alc Wine £3.85 Last dinner 10.30pm

Credit cards 1 2 3 5

❀✕✕✕ **Malvern View** ☎Bishops Cleeve (024 267) 2017
(Rosette awarded for dinner only.) Elegant restaurant with high standard of cuisine.

Closed Sun & 3wks Xmas
Lunch not served

English & French **V** 45 seats Dinner £12–£12.50 Wine £5.50 Last dinner 9.30pm 20P bedrooms available

S% **VS**

See advert on page 204

CLEISH
Tayside *Kinross-shire*
Map **11** NT09

✕✕Nivingston House ☎Cleish Hills (05775) 216

Scottish & French **V** 60 seats Lunch £8.50 Tea £2.75 Dinner £12.50 Wine £6.75 Last dinner 9.30pm 60P bedrooms available

Credit cards 1 2 3 5 **VS**

See advert on page 204

CLEOBURY MORTIMER
Shropshire
Map **7** SO67

★★ **Redfern Hotel** (formerly Old Lion Inn) (Minotel) ☎(0299) 270395 Telex no 335176

5rm(2→3⋒) Annexe: 6rm(3→3⋒) (6fb) 1 CTV in all bedrooms Ⓡ sB&B→⋒£19.50 dB&B→⋒£29 B

20P billiards

English & French **V** Lunch £4alc Dinner £6.75alc Wine £4
Last dinner 9.30pm

S% Credit cards 1 2 3 5 **VS**

CLEVEDON
Avon
Map **3** ST47

★★★ ***Walton Park*** Wellington Ter. ☎(0272) 874253
Imposing hotel in its own grounds, overlooking the Bristol Channel, and offering good views.

37rm(19→3⋒) CTV in all bedrooms Ⓡ B
Lift 40P 20 *xmas*

Last dinner 8.30pm

Credit cards 1 3 5

CLIFTONVILLE
Kent
see **Margate**

CLIMPING
West Sussex
Map **4** TQ00
★★★ **BL Bailiffscourt**
☎Littlehampton (09064) 23511
Closed 3 Jan–mid Feb
Architecturally unique, this hotel has pleasant, informal staff and beautifully appointed bedrooms.
8➡ Annexe: 10➡ 7☐ CTV in all bedrooms sB&B➡⋔ £35–£36 dB&B➡⋔ £50–£65
60P ✽ ⛆ (heated) (hard) sauna bath nc12yrs *xmas*
Lunch £8.75–£10.25&alc Tea 65p–£1.25 Dinner £12.50–£15.25 Wine £6
Last dinner 10pm
Credit cards 1 2 3 5

CLITHEROE
Lancashire
Map **7** SD74
★★ ***Roefield*** Edisford Bridge (Exec Hotel) ☎(0200) 22010
Large Georgian house with modern extension set on the banks of the River Ribble.
22➡ 3☐ CTV in all bedrooms
46P CFA ✽ billiards sauna bath Disco twice wkly
English & French
Last dinner 8.45pm
Credit cards 1 2 3 5 **VS**

CLOVA
Tayside *Angus*
Map **15** NO37
★★ **Ogilvy Arms** Glen Clova (Clova Village) ☎(05755) 222

Located at the end of a beautiful glen, this hotel is popular with walkers and hikers.

7rm(4➡)(3fb) TV in 3 bedrooms Ⓡ sB&B£11–£13 sB&B➡£12–£14 dB&B£22–£26 dB&B➡£24–£28 B

CTV 20P

V Bar lunch £1.10–£3 Tea £1.20 High Tea £3.50 Dinner £9 Wine £4.50 Last dinner 9.30pm

★★ **HB Rottal Lodge** Glen Clova (3m SE on B955 on east bank of river) ☎(05755) 224

Closed mid Nov–Apr

A former Victorian shooting lodge set in its own grounds.

12rm(6➡1⋒) Ⓡ *sB&B fr£25.73 sB&B➡⋒ fr£25.73 dB&B fr£49.45 dB&B➡⋒ fr£49.45 B

CTV 10P ✽

Lunch fr£4.60 Tea fr£1.27 Dinner £9.49–£10.93 Wine £3.49 Last dinner 8.15pm

CLUMBER PARK
Nottinghamshire
Map **8** SK67

✕✕ **Normanton Inn** ☎Worksop (0909) 475769

Roadhouse inn with rustic brickwork, thought to be a converted manor house.

Dinner not served Sun

English & French **V** 48 seats *Lunch £5.95–£6.50&alc Dinner £4.65–£5.85&alc Wine £4.50 Last dinner 9.45pm 150P

Credit cards 1 2 3 **VS**

COATBRIDGE
Strathclyde *Lanarkshire*
Map **11** NS76

★★★ **Coatbridge** Glasgow Rd ☎(0236) 24392

Modern hotel with old-world style bar and restaurant.

24rm(22➡⋒) CTV in all bedrooms Ⓡ sB&B➡⋒ £29.50 dB&B➡⋒ £37.50 B

☾ CTV 100P Disco Sun

Scottish & French **V** Lunch fr£3.25&alc Dinner £8.50&alc Wine £3.95 Last dinner 9.30pm

Credit cards 1 2 3 5

COATHAM MUNDEVILLE
Co Durham
Map **8** NZ22

★★★ *L* **Hall Garth** ☎Aycliffe (0325) 313333

Closed 24 Dec–2 Jan RS Sun

Rambling, Georgian house in 56 acres of park and woodland, one mile from A1 (M) and three miles from the centre of Darlington.

10rm(8➡2⋒) Annexe: 9rm(2➡7⋒) 4 CTV in all bedrooms Ⓡ sB&B➡⋒ £28–£30 dB&B➡ £43–£47 Continental breakfast B

60P ✽ (heated) sauna bath

English & French **V** Lunch £6.25–£8.25 Dinner £10.75alc Wine £4.50 Last dinner 9.15pm

VS

COBHAM
Surrey
Map **4** TQ16

☆☆☆ **Ladbroke Seven Hills** (& Conference centre) Seven Hills Rd (Ladbroke) ☎(09326) 4471 Telex no 929196

Situated in 23 acres of parkland.

92➡(6fb) CTV in all bedrooms Ⓡ *sB➡£38.50 dB➡£48.50 (room only) B

Lift ☾ 300P CFA ✽ squash sauna bath Live music and dancing Fri & Sat

English & French **V** *Lunch fr£6.50 Dinner fr£8.50

Credit cards 1 2 3 4 5

COCKERMOUTH
Cumbria
Map **11** NY13

★★★ **Broughton Craggs** Great Broughton ☎(0900) 824400

Mid 19th-century manor house, comfortably modernised.

10➡(2fb) 1 CTV in all bedrooms sB&B➡£20 dB&B➡£28 B

☾ 60P ✽

Lunch £5&alc Tea £1.50 Dinner £8&alc Wine £4.25 Last dinner 9.30pm

S% Credit cards 1 2 3 5

★★★ **Trout** Crown St ☎(0900) 823591

Closed Xmas Day

Modernised but retaining its 18th-century character, the Trout has private frontage to the River Derwent, with fishing rights.

16rm(11➡4⋒) CTV in all bedrooms Ⓡ sB&B£19 sB&B➡⋒ £21 dB&B£30 dB&B➡⋒ £31 B

☾ 75P ✽

English & Italian **V** Lunch £5.50&alc Dinner £9&alc Wine £5 Last dinner 9.30pm

Credit card 3

★★ ***Globe*** Main St ☎(0900) 822126

This hotel is situated close to the lakes and forms an ideal touring base.

32rm(7➡) Ⓡ B

CTV 15 Disco Tue

International **V** Last dinner 9.30pm

Credit cards 1 2 3 5 **VS**

★★ **Wordsworth** Main St ☎(0900) 822757

Formerly a coaching inn, dating back to the early 17th-century.

18rm(4➡)(2fb) 2 CTV in 5 bedrooms TV in 13 bedrooms sB&B£15.53 sB&B➡⋒ £20.41 dB&B£23 dB&B➡⋒ £29.90 B

CTV 20P 6

V Bar lunch £2.80–£5.85 Tea 70p Dinner £6.90&alc Wine £4.85 Last dinner 9pm

Credit cards 1 3 **VS**

✕ **Old Court House** Main St ☎(0900) 823871

Closed Sun & Xmas Day

Continental 35 seats *Lunch £2.50alc Dinner £8 Wine £4.30 Last dinner 9pm

C

COGGESHALL
Essex
Map **5** TL82

★★★ *H* **White Hart** ☎(0376)61654
Closed Aug & 27 Dec–3 Jan
Hospitable coaching inn with modern bedrooms and good restaurant.
24rm(18→6⋒)(1fb) CTV in all bedrooms sB&B→⋒£28 dB&B→⋒£40
CTV 20P 6
English & French V Lunch £15alc Dinner £15&alc Wine £5.75 Last dinner 10pm
Credit cards 1 2 3 4 5

COLBOST
Isle of Skye, Highland *Inverness-shire*
Map **13** NG24

✕ **Three Chimneys** ☎Glendale (047081) 258
Closed Sun (except Jul & Aug) & 16 Oct–31 Mar
Scottish V 35 seats ✻Lunch £4alc Dinner £7.50alc Wine £3.10 Last dinner 8.30pm 15P

COLCHESTER
Essex
Map **5** TL92

★★ **Kings Ford Park** Layer-de-la-Haye (2½m S B1026) ☎(0206) 34301 Telex no 987562
Comfortable Regency house in woodland park with some modernised bedrooms.
15rm(11→3⋒)(2fb) 1 CTV in all bedrooms sB&B£17.50 sB&B→⋒£21.50 dB&B→⋒£27.50 B
CTV 100P ✽ Live music and dancing Sat *xmas*
English, French & Italian Lunch £6&alc Dinner £6&alc Wine £4.50 Last dinner 9.30pm
Credit cards 1 2 3 5

★★ **Red Lion (Henekeys)** High St (Trusthouse Forte) ☎(0206) 577986
20rm(15→) CTV in all bedrooms ® sB&B£26 sB&B→£29.50 dB&B£36.50 dB&B→£41 B
CTV *xmas*
Mainly grills Last dinner 10pm
Credit cards 1 2 3 4 5

★★ **Rose & Crown** East Gates ☎(0206) 866677
An historic hotel, with some small bedrooms, complemented by a professional and well run restaurant.
14rm(4→⋒) Annexe: 14→⋒ (1fb) 1 CTV in all bedrooms sB&B£21.50 sB&B→⋒£23.50 dB&B£27.50 dB&B→⋒£29.50–£32.50 B
☾ CTV 80P
English & French V Lunch fr£5.75&alc Tea £1 Dinner fr£9 Wine £4.95 Last dinner 10pm
Credit cards 1 2 3 5 **VS**

✕✕ **Wm Scragg's** 2 North Hill ☎(0206) 41111
Cosy character restaurant specialising in fresh fish.
Closed Sun
45 seats Lunch £7&alc Dinner £7&alc Wine £3.95 Last dinner 10.30pm
S% Credit cards 1 2 3 **VS**

At **Marks Tey** (5½m SW on A12)
☆☆☆ **Marks Tey** London Rd (Paten) ☎(0206) 210001
106→ 160P

COLDSTREAM
Borders *Berwickshire*
Map **12** NT83

★ **Majicado** 71 High St ☎(0890) 2112
Converted sandstone house dating from 1860, close to the River Tweed.
7rm (1fb) sB&B£10 dB&B£20
CTV
Lunch £4.20–£5.50alc High Tea £1.50–£5 Dinner £4.75–£9&alc Wine £2.75
Last dinner 8.30pm

COLEFORD
Gloucestershire
Map **3** SO51

★★ ***Bells Hotel & Golf Club*** Lords Hill ☎Dean (0594) 32583 Closed Xmas day
Popular golf club and hotel with modern accommodation.
25→® B
CTV 200P ✽ (hard) Disco Sat Live music and dancing Sat
Last dinner 11.30pm
Credit cards 1 3

★★ **Speech House** Forest of Dean (Trusthouse Forte) ☎Cinderford (0594) 22607
Comfortable hotel built in 1676 as a court house for the Verderers of the Forest of Dean.
14rm(3→)(2fb) 3 CTV in all bedrooms ® sB&B£33 sB&B→£35.50 dB&B£43 dB&B→£49 B
40P ✽ *xmas*
Last dinner 9.30pm
Credit cards 1 2 3 4 5

★ *H* **Lambsquay** ☎Dean (0594) 33127
Peacefully situated, attractive Georgian house, offering high quality, home-produced cooking.
10rm(5→) 1 CTV in all bedrooms ® sB&B£15–£20 sB&B→£20–£30 dB&B£28–£36 dB&B→£38–£42 B
30P ✽ nc11yrs
International V Lunch £4.50–£6.50&alc Dinner £5.50–£6.50&alc Wine £4.70 Last dinner 7.30pm
VS

COLERNE
Wiltshire
Map **3** ST87

✕ **Vineyard** ☎Box (0225) 742491
Ivy-clad, stone building. Where the slopes of an earlier vineyard now form part of a walled garden at the rear.
Closed Sun & Public hols
English & French 68 seats ✻Lunch £5–£7.50&alc Dinner £6.50–£7.50&alc Wine £3.50 Last dinner 9.30pm 28P
Credit cards 1 2 3 4 5

COLESHILL
Warwickshire
Map **4** SP28

★★**Swan** High St (Ansells) ☎(0675) 62212
Fully-modernised hotel popular with business people.
34rm(23⋔) CTV in all bedrooms Ⓡ sB&B fr£24.75 sB&B⋔ fr£29.95 dB&B fr£30.25 dB&B⋔ fr£35.75
CTV 120P
Lunch fr£4.75&alc Dinner fr£4.75&alc Wine £3.90 Last dinner 10pm
Credit cards 1 2 3 **VS**

COLL, ISLE OF
Strathclyde *Argyllshire*
Map **13**
See **Arinagour**

COLLIN
Dumfries & Galloway *Dumfriesshire*
Map **11** NY07

★★★**Rockhall** ☎(038 775) 427
A converted 17th-century tower house standing in an elevated position.
9rm(4⇌1⋔) (2fb) CTV in 5 bedrooms Ⓡ sB&B£16 sB&B⇌⋔£21 dB&B£25 dB&B⇌⋔ fr£29
CTV 100P ✽ Live music and dancing Sat
International **V** Bar lunch £4alc Tea £1.50alc Dinner £8alc Wine £4.20 Last dinner 9pm
Credit cards 1 2 3 5

COLONSAY, ISLE OF
Strathclyde *Argyllshire*
Map **10**
See **Scalasaig**

COLWALL
Hereford & Worcester
Map **3** SO74

★★**Colwall Park** (Inter-Hotel) ☎(0684) 40206
6rm(5⇌1⋔) (2fb) CTV in all bedrooms Ⓡ sB&B⇌⋔£23.50 dB&B⇌⋔£35
40P ✽
V Lunch £4.50–£7.50 Tea fr £1.50 High Tea fr £4.75 Dinner £7.50–£9 Wine £4.25 Last dinner 9pm
Credit cards 1 3

COLWYN BAY
Clwyd
Map **6** SH87
See plan

★★★**Hopeside** Prince's Dr ☎(0492) 33244 Telex no 61254 Plan **4** *B2*
Closed 22 Dec–5 Jan
Detached holiday and tourist hotel near shops and beach.
19rm(13⇌6⋔) (6fb) CTV in all bedrooms Ⓡ sB&B⇌⋔£23 dB&B⇌⋔£40
25P nc6yrs
V Lunch £5.25&alc Tea £2.25 Dinner £7.25&alc Wine £2.50 Last dinner 9pm
Credit cards 1 2 3 5

★★★*HL* **Norfolk House** Prince's Dr ☎(0492) 31757 Telex no 61254 Plan **8** *B2*
Closed 23 Dec–7 Jan
Modernised holiday and commercial hotel with Mexican food table in basement lounge bar.
33rm(16⇌17⋔) (3fb) CTV in all bedrooms Ⓡ sB&B⇌⋔£25.50–£26.50 dB&B⇌⋔£38–£39.50
Lift ☾ 40P ✽
Bar lunch 95p–£6 Tea 50p–£1.25 Dinner £8.25–£8.75&alc Wine £4.65 Last dinner 9pm
Credit cards 1 2 3 5 **VS**

★★★**Rhos Abbey** 111 Rhos Promenade (Inter-Hotel) ☎(0492) 46601 Plan **10** *A4*
Large building on the seafront, within walking distance of the village.
32rm(20⇌12⋔) (4fb) CTV in all bedrooms Ⓡ ✻sB&B⇌⋔£24.50 dB&B⇌⋔£39
Lift ☾ 80P squash Disco twice wkly Live music and dancing wkly Cabaret wkly *xmas*
Welsh, English, French ✻Lunch £4&alc Tea 75p Dinner £6.50&alc Wine £4.10 Last dinner 9.30pm
Credit cards 1 2 5

✿☆☆☆*H* **Hotel 70°** Penmaenhead ☎(0492) 516555 Telex no 61362 Plan **5** *C1*
Closed 23 Dec–2 Jan
(*Rosette awarded for dinner only.*)
Modern, comfortable, personally run hotel on cliff side overlooking sea.
44⇌ CTV in all bedrooms Ⓡ sB⇌£28–£35 dB⇌£35–£47
☾ 200P CFA Live music and dancing Sat
International **V** Lunch £6.95–£7.95&alc Tea £1.50alc Dinner £7.95–£11.95&alc Wine £5 Last dinner 9.30pm
Credit cards 1 2 3 4 5 **VS**
See advert on page 208

★★**Ashmount** College Av, Rhos-on-Sea ☎(0492) 45479 Plan **1** *A4*
Detached holiday hotel in a quiet residential area.
14rm(4⇌10⋔) (3fb) CTV in all bedrooms Ⓡ sB&B⇌⋔ fr£14 dB&B⇌⋔ fr£24
10P *xmas*
V Bar lunch 90p–£2&alc Tea fr 70p High Tea fr £1 Dinner fr £5.50 Wine £3.60 Last dinner 8pm
Credit cards 1 3 **VS**
See advert on page 208

★★**Lyndale** 410 Abergele Rd, Old Colwyn ☎(0492) 517878 Plan **6** *C1*
Detached, Edwardian building on A55 near to Old Colwyn shops.
14rm(6⇌8⋔) (4fb) CTV in all bedrooms Ⓡ sB&B⇌⋔£15 dB&B⇌⋔£26
CTV 20P *xmas*
English & French **V** Lunch fr £3.95 Tea fr £1.50 Dinner fr £5.50 Wine £3.75 Last dinner 9.30pm
Credit cards 1 3 **VS**
See advert on page 208

★**Clevedon** Hawarden Rd ☎(0492) 2368 Plan **2** *B2*
Victorian, semi-detached house near the shops and ½m from the beach.
15rm Ⓡ sB&B£7.50–£8 dB&B£15–£16
CTV 8P *xmas* →

C

HOTEL 70°

PENMAENHEAD
COLWYN BAY
CLWYD
N. WALES

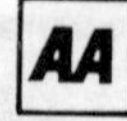

AA

☆☆☆

70° 70°
RESTAURANT
BARS
HOTEL

Here is a unique hotel nestling on the limestone cliffs overlooking the entire bay of Colwyn, with breathtaking views both by day and by night. Privately owned and open all year round the hotel is situated on the A55 Coast Road and incorporates every modern facility for the holiday-maker and businessman. All bedrooms are luxuriously complete with bathrooms, direct dial telephone, radio and colour TV. Two super bars, French Restaurant (live entertainment & dancing) and ample parking. Weekend breaks & golf mid-week breaks are available throughout the year. If you're looking for a luxury hotel with a difference, write today for the illustrated colour brochure and tariff to the resident proprietor,

Mr. M. L. SEXTON

Telex: 61362 **Telephone: Colwyn Bay (0492) 516555** **Telegrams: Bestotel**

The Lyndale Hotel & Restaurant

Lyndale Hotel & Restaurant

Abergele Road, Colwyn Bay, North Wales
Telephone: (0492) 517878 **AA ★★**

Situated on the main Chester Road (A55) overlooking the Bay of Colwyn. Our modern bedrooms are all en suite and contain colour televisions, radios, intercoms, tea making facilities and baby listening units. Enjoy excellent cuisine in our splendid restaurant where there is an extensive choice of menu's including table d'hôte and à la carte, containing many of our Chefs speciality dishes.

THE HOTEL
Ashmount

★★

Rhos-on-Sea · Colwyn Bay · North Wales
Telephone: Colwyn Bay (0492) 45479 *(Office)* 44582 *(Guests)*
College Avenue · Rhos-on-Sea · Clwyd LL28 4NT

Ashmount is a detached luxury two star Hotel where quality, elegance and service really matter. All 14 bedrooms have Private bathrooms, central heating, colour television, radio, tea and coffee making facilities.
Ashmount is 125yds from the beach and ideal for touring North Wales, many Golf courses nearby, parking on premises.
Special weekend and mid week offers available. Open all Year including Christmas.
Bed and Breakfast, per night inc. VAT from £12.00.
Dinner, bed and breakfast, per night inc VAT from £17.50.
Reductions for weekly bookings.

V ✿ ☕ ✱ Dinner £3.50 Wine £3.95 Last dinner 7.30pm

Credit cards 1 3

★**Edelweiss** Lawson Rd ☎(0492) 2314 Plan **3** *C1*

Detached Victorian house set in its own grounds, ½m from the beach.

30rm(7🛁4🚿)(5fb) sB&B fr£12.50 sB&B🛁🚿 fr£13.65 dB&B fr£25 dB&B🛁🚿 fr£27.30 B̶

CTV 25P ✿ 🏠

🍴English, Welsh & Continental V ✿ ☕ Lunch fr£3.25 Tea fr£1.25 High Tea fr£1.45 Dinner fr£4.50 Wine £4.65 Last dinner 8pm

VS

★**Marine** West Prom ☎(0492) 30295 Plan **7** *B2*

Closed mid Nov–Mar

Personally run holiday hotel overlooking the sea with colourful terraced garden.

15rm(7🚿)(3fb) TV available Ⓡ ✱sB&B£9.60–£10.60 sB&B🚿£10.60–£11.60 dB&B£17.20–£19.20

Colwyn Bay

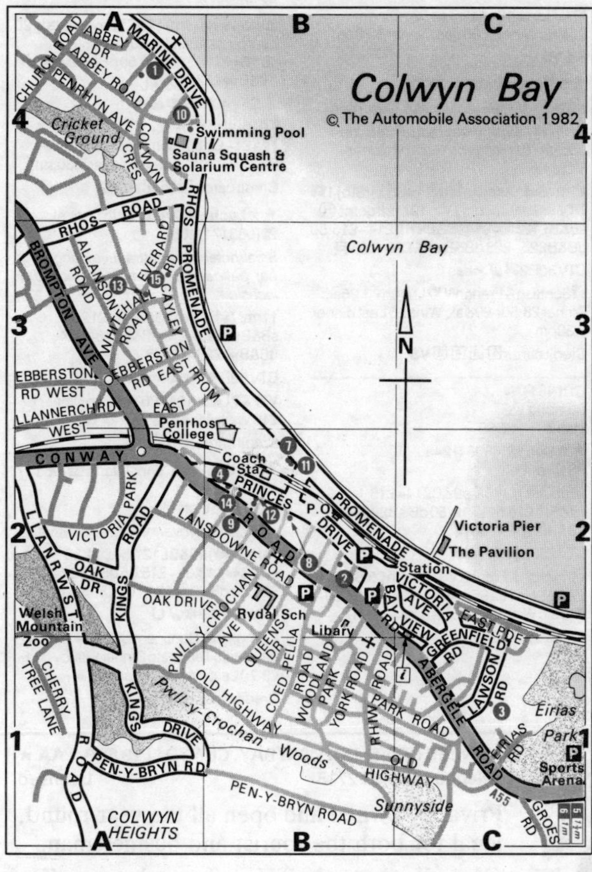

Colwyn Bay
© The Automobile Association 1982
Colwyn Bay
Swimming Pool
Sauna Squash & Solarium Centre
Cricket Ground
Penrhos College
Coach Sta
Victoria Pier
The Pavilion
Station
Rydal Sch
Library
Welsh Mountain Zoo
Eirias Park
Sports Arena
Sunnyside
Pwll-y-Crochan Woods
COLWYN HEIGHTS
MARINE DRIVE
PROMENADE
CONWAY
PRINCES DRIVE
PEN-Y-BRYN RD
PEN-Y-BRYN ROAD
OLD HIGHWAY
ABERGELE ROAD
A55

Colwyn Bay

1 Ashmount ★★
2 Clevedon ★
3 Edelweiss ★
4 Hopeside ★★★
5 Hotel 70° ✿☆☆☆
6 Lyndale ★★
7 Marine ★
8 Norfolk House ★★★
9 Raynham ★
10 Rhos Abbey ★★★
11 St Enoch's ★
12 St Margaret's ★
13 Stanton House ★
14 West Point ★
15 Whitehall ★

dB&B🚿£19.20–£20 B̶

CTV 12P

V ✿ ☕ ✱ Lunch £3 Tea 30p Dinner £4 Wine £3.45 Last dinner 7.30pm

Credit card 2 **VS**

★**Raynham** Ellesmere Rd ☎(0492) 30738 Plan **9** *B2*

Closed one wk Oct

Comfortable, personally run hotel in central position.

9rm(3fb) Ⓡ sB&B£7.50 dB&B£15 B̶

CTV 4P 🚗

✿ ☕ Bar lunch 60p–£2 Dinner £3.45–£6.50 Wine £3.85 Last dinner 7pm

Credit card 1 **VS**

★*L* ***St Enoch's*** Promenade ☎(0492) 2031 Plan **11** *B2*

Family-run with excellent collection of Welsh baronial memorabilia, knights retreat bar and replica Silver Jubilee Queen Elizabeth chair.

23rm(7🛁) CTV in 5 bedrooms B̶

CTV 6P

✿ ☕ Last dinner 7pm

★**St Margaret's** Prince's Dr ☎(0492) 2718 Plan **12** *B2*

Late-Victorian hotel occupying a corner position, ½ mile from the shops and beach.

14rm(1🛁1🚿)(3fb) TV in all bedrooms Ⓡ sB&B£10.25 sB&B🛁🚿£12.25 dB&B£20.50 dB&B🛁🚿£22.25 B̶

CTV 10P

✿ ☕ Lunch £2 Tea 55p High Tea £2–£3 Dinner £5 Wine £4.95 Last dinner 7.30pm

Credit cards 1 3

See advert on page 210

★**Stanton House** Whitehall Rd, Rhos on Sea ☎(0492) 44363 Plan **13** *A3*

11rm(3🛁)(3fb) CTV in 3 bedrooms TV in 1 bedroom Ⓡ sB&B£9.50–£9.95 sB&B🛁£11.50–£11.95 dB&B£18–£18.50 dB&B🛁£20–£20.50 B̶

CTV 6P *xmas*

Wine £3.50 Last dinner 7.15pm

Credit card 1

★***West Point*** 102 Conway Rd (Minotel) ☎(0492) 30331 Plan **14** *B2*

Closed 3 wks Oct

Late-Victorian hotel on the main A55

13rm TV available in bedrooms B̶

CTV 12P 🏠

✿ ☕ Last dinner 6.45pm

Credit cards 1 3 4 **VS**

★**Whitehall** Cayley Prom, Rhos-on-Sea ☎(0492) 47296 Plan **15** *A3*

Closed Nov–Mar

Family run hotel close to the beach.

14rm(6🚿)(3fb) CTV in 8 bedrooms Ⓡ sB&B£9.50–£10.50 sB&B🚿£12.50–£13.75 dB&B£19–£21 dB&B🚿£22–£24 B̶

CTV 6P nc3yrs →

C

V Bar lunch £1.50–£3 Dinner £5.50 Wine £3.50 Last dinner 7pm
VS

COLYTON
Devon
Map **3** SY29

XX Old Bakehouse ☎(0297) 52518
A former bakehouse, dating from the 17th century
Lunch not served Dinner not served Sun
28 seats ✱Dinner £10alc Wine £3.95 Last dinner 9.30pm 10P bedrooms available
VS

COMBEINTEIGNHEAD
Devon
Map **3** SX97

★★ Netherton House ☎ Shaldon (062687) 3251
Closed mid Nov–mid Dec & mid Jan–mid Feb
10rm(5⇌1⋒) CTV available in bedrooms Ⓡ✱sB&B£15 dB&B£30 dB&B⇌⋒£39 ⎘
30P ✱ (heated) nc10yrs *xmas*
✱Bar lunch fr£1 Tea fr75p Dinner fr£8.95&alc Wine £3.75 Last dinner 8pm
Credit cards 1 3

COMBE MARTIN
Devon
Map **2** SS54

★ *Britannia* Moory Meadow, Seaside ☎(027188) 2294 Closed Xmas
Neat, clean, quiet hotel with good sea fish meals.
10rm
CTV 14P 2
Last dinner 7.30pm
VS

★ Delve's ☎(027188) 3428
RS Jan & Feb
A Victorian-style house situated on the main Ilfracombe to Minehead road.
14rm(1⇌10⋒)(3fb) sB&B£9.95–£10.50 sB&B⇌⋒£9.95–£10.50 dB&B£19.50–£21 dB&B⇌⋒£19.50–£21
CTV 20P

Lunch £4–£5.50 Tea 50p Dinner £5.50 Wine £3 Last dinner 8pm
VS

COMRIE
Tayside *Perthshire*
Map **11** NN72

★★ Comrie Drummond St ☎(0764) 70239
RS Nov–Etr
10rm(1⇌5⋒) Annexe: 2⇌ Ⓡ sB&B£10 sB&B⇌⋒£13.95 dB&B£20 dB&B⇌⋒£27.90
CTV 24P nc5yrs
Lunch £4&alc Tea 80p Dinner £8&alc Wine £2.80 Last dinner 8.30pm
S% **VS**

★★ Royal ☎(0764) 70200
RS Nov–Mar except Xmas & New Year
Built in 1765, the hotel has prints in the cocktail bar recalling visits by Queen Victoria.
11rm(6⇌) Annexe: 5rm(4⇌1⋒)(3fb) 1 CTV in 6 bedrooms TV in 10 bedrooms Ⓡ sB&B£12.50–£14 sB&B⇌⋒£14–£15.50 dB&B£25–£28 dB&B⇌⋒£28–£31 ⎘
CTV 30P 2 *xmas*
Scottish & French **V** Lunch £3.25alc Dinner £8.50–£9&alc Wine £5 Last dinner 9.30pm
Credit cards 1 3 4 5 **VS**

CONISTON
Cumbria
Map **7** SD39

★★ Sun ☎(09664) 248
RS Dec–Feb
10rm(4⋒)(3fb) ✱sB&B£14–£15 sB&B⋒£16.50–£18.50 dB&B£28–£30 dB&B⋒£32–£36 ⎘
CTV 25P 4 ✱
English & French **V** Lunch £5.50–£7.50&alc Tea 95p–£1.50 Dinner £7.50–£8&alc Wine £4.75 Last dinner 8pm
Credit cards 1 3

★ Black Bull Yewdale Rd ☎(09664) 335
Old world village inn dating back to the 16th century.
7rm(3fb) CTV in one bedroom TV in one bedroom ✱sB&B£12 dB&B£21.85 ⎘
CTV 8P 2
English & French **V** ✱Bar lunch fr£3 Tea fr45p High Tea fr£3 Dinner fr£6.50 Wine £3 Last dinner 8pm

CONNEL
Strathclyde *Argyllshire*
Map **10** NM93

★★ Falls of Lora ☎(063171) 483
RS Xmas & New Year
Large Victorian hotel with modern extension.
30rm(19⇌)(4fb) 1 CTV available in 20 bedrooms sB&B£9.50–£19.50 sB&B⇌£17.50–£26.50 dB&B£25–£29 dB&B⇌£23–£53 ⎘
☾ CTV 40P ✱
Scottish & French **V** Lunch £4.50 Tea £1–£2.50 High Tea £4.50 Dinner £7.75 Wine £4.75 Last dinner 9.30pm
Credit cards 1 2 3 5 **VS**

★★ Lochnell Arms North Connel ☎(063171) 408
Small hotel with an attractive lounge and bar, patio and gardens extending to the lochside.
11rm(7⇌)(3fb) sB&B£9–£12 sB&B⇌£10–£13 dB&B£18–£24 dB&B⇌£20–£26 ⎘
CTV 50P ✱ *xmas*
V Lunch £4–£6 Tea 50p Dinner £7–£10 Wine £4.60 Last dinner 10pm
Credit cards 1 2 3 5

★★ L Ossians Connel North ☎(063171) 322
Closed 15 Oct–Mar
Modern hotel overlooking Loch Etive.
14rm(4⇌) sB&B£12.35–£14.35 sB&B⇌£13.35–£15.35 dB&B£24.70–£28.70 dB&B⇌£26.70–£30.70
CTV 50P ✱ U
English & Continental **V** Lunch £2–£3alc Tea £1alc Dinner £8alc Wine £3.70 Last dinner 8.30pm
Credit cards 2 3

CONSTANTINE BAY
Cornwall
Map **2** SW87
★★★*HL* **Treglos** ☎Padstow (0841) 520727 Closed 7 Nov–22 Mar
Attractive hotel with views over rocky coastline and golfing facilities nearby.
44⇌ (5fb) CTV in all bedrooms sB&B⇌£20–£28 dB&B⇌£40–£56 B
CTV Lift ☾ 50P 10 CFA ✽ (heated)
English & French V ♡ Lunch £6.50&alc Tea £1–£1.50 Dinner £9&alc Wine £3.40 Last dinner 9.30pm

CONTIN
Highland *Ross & Cromarty*
Map **14** NH45
★★**Craigdarroch Lodge** Craigdarroch Dr ☎Strathpeffer (09972) 265
19rm (9⇌2⋔) (2fb) ® sB&B£13.50 sB&B⇌⋔£15.50 dB&B£27 dB&B⇌⋔£31 B
CTV 20P ✽ (hard) billiards *xmas*
Scottish & Continental V ♡ Lunch £6 Tea 50p Dinner £9&alc Wine £3.80 Last dinner 8.30pm
VS

CONWY
Gwynedd
Map **6** SH77
★★★**Sychnant Pass** Sychnant Pass Rd ☎(049263) 6868 Telex no 61155 Closed Jan
10rm (8⇌2⋔) (2fb) CTV in all bedrooms ® ✱sB&B⇌⋔£15–£18 dB&B⇌⋔£24–£35 B
CTV 40P ✽ U sauna bath *xmas*
International V ♡ ✱Lunch £5.50–£6.50 Tea 80p–£1.90 Dinner £7.30–£10&alc Wine £3.95 Last dinner 10pm
Credit cards 1 2 3
★★**Castle** High St (Trusthouse Forte) ☎(049263) 2324
25 (2fb) CTV in all bedrooms ® sB&B⇌£33 dB&B⇌£49.50 B
30P *xmas*
♡ Last dinner 9.15pm
Credit cards 1 2 3 4 5
★**Castle Bank** Mount Pleasant ☎(049263) 3888
Closed 25 & 26 Dec
RS Dec–Feb
Victorian stone house standing in its own gardens, next to the castle walls.
9rm (8⋔) (3fb) CTV in all bedrooms ® sB&B£10.50–£11 sB&B⇌£10.50–£11 dB&B£24 dB&B⋔£24 B
CTV 12P
International V ♡ ✱Lunch £3.75–£4.25 Dinner £6.50&alc Wine £3.50 Last dinner 8.30pm
VS
See advert on page 212

COODEN BEACH
East Sussex
Map **5** TQ70
★★★**Cooden Beach** Cooden Sea Rd ☎(04243) 2281 Telex no 95489
34rm (29⇌5⋔) (5fb) CTV in all bedrooms sB&B£23–£25 sB&B⇌⋔£25–£29 dB&B£40–£45 dB&B⇌⋔£45–£49.50 B
☾ CTV 120P 10 ✽ (heated) *xmas*
French ♡ ✱Lunch £6.50&alc Tea 40p–60p Dinner £8.95&alc Last dinner 9.30pm
Credit cards 1 2 3 5

COOKHAM
Berkshire
Map **4** SU88
✕✕✕***Bel & The Dragon*** High St ☎Bourne End (06285) 21263
Historic beamed restaurant overlooking attractive garden.
English & Continental. 125 seats Last dinner 10.30pm 10P
✕**Le Radier** 19–21 Station Hill Pde ☎Bourne End (06285) 25775 →

Closed Sun, Mon, 3 wks end Aug/Sep
Lunch not served Tue–Sat
French 25 seats ✱Dinner £8.80&alc
Wine £5.50

COPTHORNE
West Sussex
Map **4** TQ33
Hotels are listed under **Gatwick Airport**

CORBIÈRE
Jersey, Channel Islands
Map **16**

✕✕✕**Sea Crest Hotel Restaurant** Petit Port ☎Jersey (0534) 42687
Attractive hotel restaurant specialising in fresh fish and Italian dishes.
English, French & Italian **V** 55 seats
Lunch £10alc Dinner £12alc Wine £2.95
Last dinner 10pm 50P bedrooms available
Credit cards 1 3 4

CORBRIDGE
Northumberland
Map **12** NY96

★★**Angel Inn** Main St (Scottish & Newcastle) ☎(043471) 2119
Attractive old coaching inn with comfortable bedrooms and a wealth of mahogany panelling.
6rm CTV in all bedrooms Ⓡ sB&B£15
dB&B£19.80
30P
English & Continental **V** Bar lunch £1.50–£2.25 Dinner £6alc Wine £3.70
Last dinner 10pm
Credit cards 1 2 3 5

★**Riverside** Main St ☎(043471) 2942
10rm(1) (2fb) ✱sB&B£13 sB&B£15 dB&B£19.50 dB&B£22 B
CTV 6P
Tea 45p Dinner £4.95–£7.95 Wine £4.50 Last dinner 9.30pm

✕✕**Ramblers Country House** (½m SE on A68) ☎(043471) 2424
German cuisine is a feature of this elegant country house restaurant.
Closed Sun & Mon Lunch not served
English & German **V** 70 seats ✱Dinner £12alc Wine £3.95 Last dinner 9.30pm
30P
Credit cards 1 3 5

CORBY
Northamptonshire
Map **4** SP88

★★★**Grosvenor** George St ☎(05363) 3441 Telex no 312517
Purpose-built, multi-storey building near the town centre.
42rm(24 18) CTV in all bedrooms Ⓡ sB&B fr£24.50 dB&B £29.50 B
Lift ☾ 40P CFA Disco 3 nights wkly Live music and dancing wkly
British & French **V** Lunch £2.75&alc Tea 55p Dinner £5.75–£6.95&alc Wine £4.55 Last dinner 10pm
Credit cards 1 2 3 5 **VS**

CORNHILL-ON-TWEED
Northumberland
Map **12** NT83

★★★*L* **Tillmouth Park** (Exec Hotels) ☎Coldstream (0890) 2255
Stately country mansion with most bedrooms furnished with antique pieces.
16rm(6 1) Annexe: 1 (2fb) 1 sB&B£18.50–£28 sB&B £25–£28 dB&B£29–£48 dB&B £43–£48 B
CTV 50P 2✽ *xmas*
Lunch £6.50 Dinner £8.50 Wine £4.75
Last dinner 8.45pm
Credit cards 1 2 3 5 **VS**

★★**Collingwood Arms** ☎Coldstream (0890) 2424
Closed Xmas Day
Informal traditional country inn with modern accommodation.
17rm(5 2) (2fb) 1 CTV in 5

bedrooms TV in 1 bedroom Ⓡ sB&B£15.50–£16 sB&B £17.50–£18.50 dB&B£24.50–£27 dB&B £24.50–£27 B
CTV 54P 3 ✽ ♿
V Lunch £2.50–£6.50&alc Tea fr45p&alc High Tea £2–£3.50&alc Dinner fr£7.50&alc Wine £3.60 Last dinner 9.30pm
Credit cards 1 3

CORSE LAWN
Hereford & Worcester
Map **3** SO83

✽XXX**Corse Lawn House** ☎Tirley (045278) 479
Good family-run restaurant.
Closed Mon Dinner not served Sun
French 45 seats ✱Lunch fr£8.50&alc Dinner fr£11.75&alc Wine £3.80 Last dinner 10pm 50P bedrooms available
Credit cards 1 2 3 5

CORSHAM
Wiltshire
Map **3** ST86

★★★ *B* **Rudloe Park** Leafy Ln ☎Hawthorn (0225) 810555
8 (3fb) 1 CTV in all bedrooms Ⓡ sB&B £31.63 dB&B £51.75
60P 2 ✽ Live music and dancing Sat *xmas*
International V Lunch £8.50alc Tea 60palc High Tea £6alc Dinner £9.50alc Wine £6.05 Last dinner 10pm
S% Credit cards 1 2 5 **VS**

★★ ***Methuen Arms*** High St ☎(0249) 714867
Stone building with portico, set in attractive grounds in the town centre.
23rm(11 5) CTV in 14 bedrooms Ⓡ B
CTV 85P ✽
Last dinner 9.30pm
Credit cards 1 3 5 **VS**

☆☆**Stagecoach** Park Ln, Pickwick ☎(0249) 713162 Telex no 449752
Modern hotel with studio-style bedrooms and attractive bar.
21rm(20 1) (10fb) CTV in all bedrooms Ⓡ sB £22.50–£24.75 dB £33.50–£36.25 B
☾ CTV 36P CFA ✽ *xmas*
English & French V Lunch £5.25–£5.75 Tea 65p&alc High Tea £3alc Dinner £5.25–£6.25&alc Wine £3.95 Last dinner 9.30pm
Credit cards 1 2 3 5 **VS**

XX**Weavers Loft** High St ☎(0249) 713982
Dinner not served Sun
English & Continental V Dinner £9.75alc Wine £5.15
Credit card 1 3 **VS**

COSSINGTON
Leicestershire
Map **8** SK61

XX**Cossington Mill** ☎Sileby (050981) 2205
Converted old mill in rural surroundings, close to the Rivers Wreake and Soar.
English & French V 60 seats Lunch £4.25&alc Dinner £6.30–£9.25&alc Wine £4.75 Last dinner 11pm 100P
Credit cards 1 2 3 **VS**

COTTINGHAM
Northamptonshire
Map **4** SP89

XX**Hunting Lodge** ☎Rockingham (0536) 771370
Closed 25 & 26 Dec
Lunch not served Sat
V 60 seats ✱Lunch £7.50&alc Dinner £7.50&alc Wine £5 Last dinner 10pm 100P
Credit cards 1 2 3 5 **VS**

COVE
Strathclyde *Dunbartonshire*
Map **10** NS28

★★ *HB* ***Knockderry*** ☎Kilcreggan (043684) 2283
13rm(5) B
CTV 50P ✽
Last dinner 8.30pm
Credit cards 1 2 3 5

COVENHAM
Lincolnshire
Map **9** TF39

XX**Mill House** ☎Fulstow (050786) 652
Closed Sun Lunch not served (Bar meals only)
V 36 seats ✱Dinner fr£8.25&alc Last dinner 10pm 50P
Credit cards 1 2 3 **VS**

COVENTRY
West Midlands
Map **4** SP37

☆☆☆☆**Crest** Hinckley Rd, Walsgrave (junc 2 M6) (Crest) ☎(0203) 613261 Telex no 311292
Modern hotel close to Junction 2 of the M6.
160 CTV in all bedrooms Ⓡ ✱sB fr£34 dB fr£43 (room only) B
Lift ☾ 250P CFA Disco Sat in summer ♿
International ✱Lunch £6.95&alc Tea 60p High Tea £3.50 Dinner £8.95&alc Wine £4.95 Last dinner 9.45pm
Credit cards 1 2 3 4 5 **VS**

★★★★**De Vere** Cathedral Sq (DeVere) ☎(0203) 51851 Telex no 31380
215 CTV in all bedrooms ✱sB £37.80 dB £51.45 (room only) B
Lift ☾ CFA Live music and dancing Sat ♿
English & French ✱Lunch £4&alc Dinner £12.60alc Wine £5.50 Last dinner 10.30pm
S% Credit cards 1 2 3 5

★★★★**Hotel Leofric** Broadgate (Embassy) ☎(0203) 21371 Telex no 311193
Closed 25–27 Dec
91 CTV in all bedrooms Ⓡ sB £37 dB fr£45 (room only) B
Lift ☾ CFA
International V Lunch fr£6.70 Dinner fr£6.70 Wine £4.70 Last dinner 10pm
Credit cards 1 2 3 4 5

★★★**Allesley** Allesley Village ☎(0203) 403272
Closed Xmas Day
A fully-modernised, commercial hotel.
24rm(14⇌2⋒) Annexe: 13rm CTV in 33 bedrooms Ⓡ ✻sB&B£17.08–£18.97 sB&B⇌£25.93 dB&B£30.36 dB&B⇌£36.05 Ɓ
☾ CTV 350P Disco Tue & Wed Live music and dancing Thu–Sat
V♁▭✻Lunch £4.83–£6.56 Dinner £5.40–£7.46 Wine £4.90 Last dinner 10.30pm
Credit cards 1 2 3 4 5

★★★*B* **Chace Crest** London Rd, Willenhall (Crest) ☎(0203) 303398 Telex no 311993
68⇌ CTV in all bedrooms Ⓡ ✻sB⇌ fr£32 dB⇌ fr£40 (room only) Ɓ
☾ ⅍ 150P ✽
▣ International V✻Lunch £3–£7 Tea fr50p Dinner £6–£8&alc Last dinner 9.45pm
Credit cards 1 2 3 4 5 VS

☆☆☆**Novotel Coventry** Wilsons Ln (A444/M6 junc 3) ☎(0203) 365000 Telex no 31545
Modern well equipped motel.
99⇌⋒ (99fb) CTV in all bedrooms sB&B⇌⋒ £31.90 dB&B⇌⋒ £41 Ɓ
Lift ☾ ⌗ 160P CFA ✽ ⩦ (heated) squash billiards sauna bath Disco Fri & Sat ♘ ♿
V♁▭✻Lunch £7.55–£9.50&alc Tea 65p Dinner £7.55–£9.50 Wine £5.85 Last dinner mdnt
Credit cards 1 2 3 5 VS

☆☆☆**Post House** Rye Hill, Allesley (Trusthouse Forte) ☎(0203) 402151 Telex no 31427
196⇌ (52fb) CTV in all bedrooms Ⓡ sB&B⇌ £39.50 dB&B⇌ £52 Ɓ
Lift ☾ ⌗ 297P CFA
♁▭ Last dinner 10.15pm
Credit cards 1 2 3 4 5

★★★**Royal Court** Tamworth Rd, Keresley (3m NW on B4098) ☎Keresley (020333) 4171 Telex 312549
Closed Xmas Day
99rm(78⇌12⋒)(12fb) CTV in all bedrooms Ⓡ ★✻sB&B£21.56 sB&B⇌⋒ £25.74 dB&B£30.61 dB&B⇌⋒ £36.18 Ɓ
Lift ☾ CTV 400P ✽ ⌕(hard) Disco Wed–Sat Live music and dancing Sat
V♁✻Lunch £6.50&alc Dinner £7.06–£7.41&alc Wine £4.95 Last dinner 10.30pm
S% Credit cards 1 2 3 5

★★**Beechwood** Sandpits Ln, Keresley (3m NW on B4098) ☎Keresley (020333) 4243
Commercial hotel, situated in a quiet rural area.
26rm(1⇌18⋒)(2fb) CTV in all bedrooms sB&B£17.71–£20.36 sB&B⇌⋒ £20.24–£23.27 dB&B£25.30–£29.09 dB&B⇌⋒ £30.36–£34.91 Ɓ
☾ 160P ✽
▣ English, French & Italian V♁▭ Lunch £6.50–£7.50 Tea £1–£3 Dinner £6.50–£9.50 Wine £4.39 Last dinner 10pm
Credit cards 1 2 3 VS

✕✕ ***Grandstand*** Coventry City FC, King Richard St, Highfield ☎(0203) 27053
Closed Sat & Sun
▣ English & French 120 seats 200P
Credit cards 1 2 3 5

COWBRIDGE
South Glamorgan
Map **3** SS97

★★**Bear** High St ☎(04463) 4814
15th century coaching inn with a modern bedroom wing.
21rm(18⇌) Annexe: 10⇌ (2fb) 1 ⊟ CTV in all bedrooms Ⓡ sB&B fr£19 sB&B⇌ £23 dB&B⇌ £29 Ɓ
CTV 40P
▣ French ♁✻Lunch £3.35–£6.50&alc Dinner £5.95&alc Wine £4.75

Last dinner 9.45pm
Credit cards 1 3

COWES
Isle of Wight
Map **4** SZ49
See also Whippingham

★★★**Holmwood** Egypt Point ☎(0983) 292508
Closed Xmas
Superbly situated hotel, overlooking the Solent.
19rm(6→7⋔) CTV in 10 bedrooms Ⓡ sB&B£18.50 sB&B→⋔£25.25 dB&B£38.25 dB&B→⋔£41.62
CTV 12P
International V Lunch fr£7 Tea fr50p Dinner fr£9 Wine £5 Last dinner 9.30pm
Credit cards 1 2 3 5
See advert on page 216

COWFOLD
West Sussex
Map **4** TQ22

✕**St Peter Cottage** ☎(040386) 324
Closed Mon, last 2 wks Jan & last 2 wks Jun Dinner not served
63 seats ✱Lunch £4.55–£5&alc Tea £1.45–£1.90 High Tea £2–£3 Wine £4.20 Last high tea 5.25pm
Credit cards 1 3 **VS**

COXWOLD
North Yorkshire
Map **8** SE57

✕✕***Fauconberg Arms*** ☎(03476) 214
Attractive 17th-century inn in a picturesque village.
→

C

COWES Isle of Wight

Tel 292508 and 295831

A typical scene from the hotel

THE HOLMWOOD HOTEL

with the famous Flying Dutchman Restaurant

In a magnificent position on the sea front near Egypt Point, Cowes, the Holmwood Hotel provides luxury, comfort, good food and wine, and the relaxed and friendly atmosphere expected of every first class hotel – with the additional bonus of unrivalled panoramic views of yachting in the Solent throughout the year. The world's largest ocean liners pass close by the hotel.
Under the personal supervision of Kate and John Hobart.
Open all year round. Spring and Winter Breaks available.

Padmore House

HOTEL and RESTAURANT

BEATRICE AVE., WHIPPINGHAM, COWES
Tel: (0983) 293210

Combines the charm of an English Country House with a reputation for excellent food and wines unsurpassed on this lovely island.
Set in five acres of tranquil grounds overlooking the beautiful Medina Valley.
Close to main ferry terminals with ample parking space.
All rooms have colour TV, telephone, central heating, and most have private facilities.
Open all year, log fires in winter. Brochures on request. Special week-end breaks all year.

AA ★★

Closed Mon, 1 wk Feb & 2 wks Oct
Dinner not served Sun
60 seats Last dinner 9.30pm P bedrooms available

CRACKINGTON HAVEN
Cornwall
Map **2** SX19
★★**Coombe Barton** ☎ St Gennys (08403) 345
Closed Nov–Feb
Comfortable residence, part 18th-century, set right by the sea.
10rm(3→)(1fb)Ⓡ sB&B£12.75–£13.75 dB&B£22.50–£24.50 dB&B→£25.50–£28 B
CTV 60P
Bar lunch £3.25 Dinner £7.50–£8.50&alc Wine £4.50 Last dinner 9.30pm
VS

★**Crackington Manor** ☎ St Gennys (08403) 397
Closed Jan–Feb
Friendly hotel in National Trust headland.
16rm(7→1⋔)(4fb) sB&B£12.60–£14.40 sB&B→⋔ fr£14.95 dB&B£20.70–£25.30 dB&B→⋔ £22.45–£27.60 B
CTV 25P ✽ (heated) billiards sauna bath
English, French & Italian V Bar lunch 85p–£2 Tea 60p–£1.20 High Tea £2.50–£3.50 Dinner £7.50 Wine £3.50 Last dinner 9pm
Credit cards 1 2 3

CRAFTHOLE
Cornwall
Map **2** SX35
★H **Whitsand Bay** Portwrinkle ☎ St Germans (0503) 30276
Closed Nov–mid Mar →

Unusual, family run character hotel with fine views and golf course.
30rm(26)Ⓡ sB&B£10–£14 sB&B£12–£14 dB&B£16.40–£20.40 dB&B£20.30–£24.30 B
CTV 50P sauna bath
Lunch £3.30–£3.50 Tea 75p–85p Dinner fr£6.75 Wine £3.50 Last dinner 8.30pm
S% **VS**

CRAIGELLACHIE
Grampian *Banffshire*
Map **15** NJ24
★★★**Craigellachie** (03404) 204
Closed Jan–Feb RS Oct–Dec
32rm(23 2)(2fb)Ⓡ sB&B£18 sB&B£19 dB&B£34 dB&B£45
CTV 70P
V Lunch £3.40alc Tea 45p High Tea £5–£7 Dinner £7&alc Wine £4.20 Last dinner 9pm
S% 1 3

CRAIGHOUSE
Isle of Jura, Strathclyde *Argyllshire*
Map **10** NR56
★★ *L* **Jura** Jura (049682) 243
Situated beside a small bay, across road from distillary and the only hotel on the island.
18rm(3)(1fb)Ⓡ *sB&B£15 sB&B£16.50 dB&B£30 dB&B£33
CTV 15P 10
*Lunch £4.50 Dinner £8 Wine £3.75 Last dinner 8.30pm
S% Credit cards 1 2 3 5

CRAIL
Fife
Map **12** NO60
★**Croma** Nethergate (03335) 239
Closed Nov–Mar
Small, well maintained, family hotel with a garden at the rear, situated in a quiet, residential area.
10rm(4 2)(2fb) CTV in 4 bedrooms Ⓡ sB&B£7.50–£10 sB&B£8.50–£11 dB&B£15–£20 dB&B£17–£22 B
CTV

V Lunch £5–£6 Tea fr£1.50 High Tea £3–£3.50 Dinner £5.50–£6.50 Wine £5 Last dinner 10pm
VS

★***Marine*** Nethergate (03335) 207
Small family hotel with garden extending to waters edge.
12rm
CTV nc6yrs
Last dinner 8.30pm

CRANBROOK
Kent
Map **5** TQ73
★★ *BL* **Kennel Holt** (0580) 712032
Fine Elizabethan manor house, set in delightful English gardens.
7rm(4) 1 CTV in 7 bedrooms *sB&B£21 sB&B£21 dB&B£42 dB&B£46–50 B
30P *xmas*
French *Lunch fr£3 Dinner fr£8 Wine £3.95 Last dinner 8pm
S% **VS**

★★**Willesley** (0580) 713555
Closed 1st wk Feb
A well run, friendly hotel, part of which dates from the 14th century, with modern, well equipped bedrooms.
16(1fb) CTV in all bedrooms Ⓡ sB&B£26–£27.50 dB&B£35–£38 B
CTV 50P *xmas*
English & Continental **V** Lunch £5.45–£5.95 Dinner £7.95–£8.45&alc Wine £4.50
Last dinner 9.30pm
S% Credit cards 1 2 3 4 5 **VS**

★**George** Stone St (0580) 713348
9rm
CTV P2
French Last dinner 9.30pm

CRANTOCK
Cornwall
Map **2** SW76
★★***Crantock Bay*** West Pentire (0637) 830229 Closed Nov–Mar

Family hotel in its own grounds, with views over cliff and coastline.
31rm(18)Ⓡ
CTV 35P Live music and dancing wkly
Last dinner 8pm

★★**Fairbank** West Pentire Rd (0637) 830424 Closed 2nd wk Oct–Mar
Small, friendly, family hotel in a quiet village, commanding views over the nearby coastline.
29rm(4 16)(3fb) 1 CTV available in bedrooms Ⓡ sB&B£12.50–13.50 sB&B£14.50–£16 dB&B£25–£27 dB&B£29–£32 B
CTV 40P Live music Wed
V Bar lunch 75p–£3.50 Tea 60p–£2 High Tea £1.50–£4 Dinner £6.50–£8.50 Wine £4.10 Last dinner 7.15pm
Credit cards 1 3 5 **VS**

CRATHORNE
North Yorkshire
Map **8** NZ40
★★★★ *L* **Crathorne Hall**
Stokesley (0642) 700398
Reputed to be one of the last Stately Houses, built 1906, it stands in 15 acres of grounds.
31rm(24 7)(4fb) 1 CTV in all bedrooms Ⓡ sB&B£30–£38.50 dB&B£40–£50.50 B
CTV 100P billiards *xmas*
French **V** Lunch £6.25–£6.90&alc Tea 70p Dinner £9.50&alc Wine £5.75 Last dinner 10pm
Credit cards 1 2 3 5 **VS**

CRAWLEY
Hampshire
Map **4** SU43
✕***Fox & Hounds*** Sparsholt (096272) 285
In a beautiful village setting, the Fox & Hounds offers sound French and English cuisine.
Closed Mon & Xmas
Dinner not served Sun
30 seats 34P

CRAWLEY
West Sussex
Map **4** TQ23
Hotels are listed under Gatwick Airport

CREDITON
Devon
Map **3** SS80

★★**Coombe House Country** Coleford (2m NW of A377) (Minotels) ☎Copplestone (03634) 487 Telex no 42551

Elegant Georgian country house with fine restaurant, spacious rooms and 800 year old cellar.

12rm(10➡1⋒) (3fb) Ⓡ sB&B£14 sB&B➡⋒£17 dB&B£22 dB&B➡⋒£24–28 Ɓ

CTV 60P ✽ ⛀(heated) ℘(hard)

⊟English & French **V** ♆ Bar lunch £3.50alc Dinner £7alc Wine £4.30 Last dinner 9.30pm
Credit cards 1 3 **VS**

CRESSAGE
Shropshire
Map **7** SJ50

✕**Old Hall** ☎(095 289) 298

Closed Mon Dinner not served Sun

⊟English & French **V** 55 seats Lunch £8alc Dinner £8alc Wine £4.50 Last dinner 9.15pm 40P bedrooms available

S% Credit cards 1 3 5

CREWE
Cheshire
Map **7** SJ75

★★★**Crewe Arms** Nantwich Rd (Embassy) ☎(0270) 213204
Closed Xmas & New Year

Large modern hotel next to the railway station.

35rm(31➡4⋒) (1fb) CTV in all bedrooms Ⓡ sB&B➡⋒£28 dB&B➡⋒£36 Ɓ

☾ CTV 250P CFA

⊟English & French ♆ ⊒ Bar lunch £1.25–£2 Tea 55p Dinner fr£6.50&alc Wine £4.55 Last dinner 9.30pm

Credit cards 1 2 3 4 5

CREWKERNE
Somerset
Map **3** ST40

★★*HB* **Old Parsonage** Barn St ☎(0460) 73516
RS Xmas & New Year

4rm(1➡) Annexe: 7rm(3➡2⋒) CTV in all bedrooms Ⓡ sB&B£15–£15.50 sB&B➡⋒£17.50 dB&B£26.50 dB&B➡⋒£32 Ɓ

CTV 12P ✽ nc12yrs

Lunch £4.50–£5.50 Dinner £6–£7.50&alc Wine £3.95 Last dinner 9pm

Credit cards 1 2 3 5

CRICCIETH
Gwynedd
Map **6** SH43

★★★**Bron Eifion** ☎(076671) 2385

Country house with magnificent panelled hall and gallery and well tended gardens.

19rm(13➡4⋒) Annexe: 5rm CTV available in bedrooms ✻sB&B £26.50–£28.50 incl dinner sB&B➡⋒£29.50–£32.50 incl dinner dB&B£53–£65 incl dinner dB&B➡⋒£66–£73 incl lunch & dinner Ɓ

☾ CTV 100P ✽ nc3yrs

⊟English & Continental **V** ♆ ⊒ ✻Lunch £5.50–£6 Tea fr50p Dinner £10 Wine £5 Last dinner 9pm

S%

★★***George IV*** ☎(076671) 2168

Late-Victorian, holiday/tourist hotel in Criccieth main street.

40rm(5➡2⋒) Ⓡ

Lift CTV 60P ✽

V ♆ ⊒ Last dinner 9pm

Credit cards 1 3 **VS**

★★**Lion** Y Maes ☎(076671) 2460

Detached hotel, set back from the main road in the centre of town, ½ mile from the beach.

40rm(12➡2⋒) (4fb) TV in all bedrooms Ⓡ sB&B£11–£14.50 sB&B➡⋒£12.50–£16.80 sB&B£22–£27 dB&B➡⋒£25–£30 Ɓ

Lift ☾ CTV 20P 12⌂ Live music and dancing 3 nights wkly

V ♆ ⊒ Lunch £3.50 Tea fr45p Dinner £6.50 Wine £3.99 Last dinner 8.15pm

Credit cards 1 2 3 5

★★**Parciau Mawr** High St ☎(076671) 2368 Closed Oct–Feb

Country house, built in 1907, set in its own grounds which include a 300-year-old barn.

7rm(2➡) Annexe: 6⋒ (4fb) CTV in all bedrooms Ⓡ ★ sB&B£14–£15 sB&B➡⋒£17.50–£19 dB&B£28–£30 dB&B➡⋒£31.50–£34 Ɓ

30P ✽ nc5yrs

⊟English & French Dinner £6.50&alc Wine £3.80 Last dinner 8pm

Credit cards 1 3

★★**Plas Gwyn** Pentrefelin (1m NE A497) ☎(076671) 2559

Detached, Victorian hotel situated 1 mile from Criccieth.

16rm(5⋒) (6fb) CTV in 12 bedrooms Ⓡ sB&B£13–£15 sB&B⋒£13–£15 dB&B£26–£30 dB&B⋒£26–£30 Ɓ

CTV 40P 4⌂ Disco wkly

⊟English & Continental **V** ♆ ⊒ Lunch £4–£6&alc Dinner £5.50–£10.50&alc Wine £4.65 Last dinner 8.30pm

Credit cards 1 3 **VS**

★★**Plas Isa** Porthmadog Rd ☎(076671) 2443

12➡⋒ CTV in all bedrooms Ⓡ ★ sB&B➡⋒£16–£19.50 dB&B➡⋒£32–£39 Ɓ

☾ CTV 25P ✽ Live music and dancing Fri & Sat Cabaret Fri & Sat *xmas*

⊟British, French & Italian **V** ♆ ⊒ Bar lunch £1.20–£4.20 Tea 45p–60p Dinner £3.50–£5.75&alc Wine £4.50 Last dinner 10pm

Credit cards 1 2 3 5

★**Abereistedd** West Pde ☎(076671) 2710 Closed Oct–Mar

Detached Victorian hotel in corner position at end of promenade, ½ mile from shops.

14rm(3⋒) (3fb) Ⓡ sB&B£9.50–£10.50 dB&B£19–£21 dB&B⋒£22–£24

CTV 8P 2⌂ nc2yrs →

Bar lunch £1–£3 Tea fr60p Dinner £4.25–£6 Wine £4 Last dinner 7.30pm

★ ***Bron Aber*** Pwllheli Rd ☎(076671) 2539
Semi-detached, Victorian, holiday hotel alongside the A497, and ¼ mile from the beach and shops.
10rm TV available in bedrooms CTV 8P
Last dinner 7.30pm
Credit card 1

★ **Caerwylan** ☎(076671) 2547
Closed Nov–mid Apr
Semi-detached, Victorian hotel on the sea front.
31rm(5) (5fb) sB&B fr£8 sB&B fr£10.50 dB&B fr16 dB&B fr£21
Lift CTV 9P 14
Lunch fr£3.50 Tea fr65p Dinner fr£4.50 Wine £4 Last dinner 7.30pm
VS

★ ***Henfaes*** Porthmadog Rd ☎(076671) 2396 Closed mid Nov–mid Apr
Semi-detached, Victorian hotel beside the A497.
11rm(10) TV in all bedrooms
CTV 10 5P
Last dinner 7.30pm

CRICK
Northamptonshire
Map **4** SP57
☆☆☆☆ **Post House** (Trusthouse Forte) ☎(0788) 822101 Telex no 311107
96 CTV in all bedrooms Ⓡ sB&B £42 dB&B £54 B
☾ 150P CFA
Last dinner 10.30pm
S% Credit cards 1 2 3 4 5

CRICKHOWELL
Powys
Map **3** SO21
★★***H*** **Bear** ☎(0873) 810408
Traditional, inn-style, hotel.
12rm(3 6) (2fb) CTV in 1 bedroom Ⓡ sB&B £15.52–£17.25 sB&B £21.85 dB&B £23 dB&B £28.75 B
CTV 24P 2

Bar lunch £3.75–£6.90 Dinner £10alc Wine £4.25 Last dinner 9pm
Credit cards 1 3

★★***HL*** **Gliffaes** ☎Bwlch (0874) 730371
Closed Jan–mid Mar
Comfortable hotel in beautiful location offering good country cooking
19rm(16 1) (3fb) Ⓡ sB&B £16.75 sB&B £20 dB&B £33.50 dB&B £40 B
CTV 30P (hard) billiards
V Lunch £5.80 Tea £2 Dinner £8 Wine £4.50 Last dinner 9pm
S% Credit cards 1 2 3

CRICKLADE
Wiltshire
Map **4** SU19
★★ **White Hart** High St ☎Swindon (0793) 750206
RS 31 Dec–4 Jan
Mellow stone and rough cast, gabled, hotel in the centre of the town.
18rm (2fb) TV in all bedrooms Ⓡ *sB&B £16 dB&B £24 B
CTV 30P 6 Live music and dancing Thu
English, French & Italian V
*Lunch £5.95&alc Dinner £5.95&alc Wine £4.50 Last dinner 10pm
Credit cards 1 2 3 4 5

★ **Vale Inn** High St ☎Swindon (0793) 750223
Brick-built hotel with ornamental shutters and secluded rear patio, located in the centre of the town.
9rm(5 1) CTV in 5 bedrooms Ⓡ sB&B £15 sB&B £20 dB&B £21 dB&B £25
CTV 50P
International Bar lunch £1–£5 Tea £1 Dinner £2.50–£6 Wine £4 Last dinner 9.15pm

CRIEFF
Tayside *Perthshire*
Map **11** NN82
★★***B*** ***Murraypark*** Connaught Ter ☎(0764) 3731
This hotel is in a quiet residential area, with fine views across to the Ochil Hills.
15rm(10) CTV in 2 bedrooms
CTV 50P
Scottish & French Last dinner 9.15pm
Credit cards 1 5 VS

★ **George** King St ☎(0764) 2089
26rm(4) (2fb) Ⓡ sB&B £9.50–£11 dB&B £19–£22 dB&B £24–£28
CTV 26P billiards *xmas*
V Lunch fr£4 Tea fr40p High Tea fr£3.25 Dinner fr£6.50 Last dinner 9pm
VS

★***B*** **Gwydyr House** Comrie Rd ☎(0764) 3277
Closed Nov–Mar
Former private mansion, overlooking MacRosty Park on the west side of Crieff.
10rm (4fb) Ⓡ sB&B £8.75–£10 dB&B £17.50–£20
CTV 15P
British & French Bar lunch £2.50–£6 Dinner £6.25&alc Wine £5.15 Last dinner 8pm
VS

★ ***Star*** East High St ☎(0764) 2632
10rm(1) B
CTV 20P sauna bath Live music and dancing Mon
Welsh & French Last dinner 9pm
Credit cards 1 2 5 VS

CRINAN
Strathclyde *Argyllshire*
Map **10** NR79
★★★***L*** **Crinan** ☎(054683) 235
Closed Nov–mid Mar
Spectacular scenery makes a superb location for this tastefully refurbished hotel.
22rm(20 2) (1fb) *sB&B £24–£26.50 dB&B £39–£41.50

dB&B→⋒£41.50–£44 Continental breakfast

Lift CTV 30P ✽

V ♧ ▭ Lunch £12alc Tea £1alc High Tea £3.50alc Dinner £12.50–£17.50 Wine £4.95 Last dinner 9.30pm

Credit cards 1 2 5

CROCKETFORD
Dumfries & Galloway *Kirkcudbrightshire*
Map **11** NX87

★★*H* **Galloway Arms** Stranraer Rd (Minotels) ☎(055669) 240 Closed Feb

A traditional, family-run hotel with attractive cottage restaurant.

13rm(9→) (2fb) CTV in all bedrooms Ⓡ sB&B£15–£17 sB&B→⋒£17–£19 dB&B£30–£34 dB&B→⋒£34–£38 B

CTV 30P ✽ ⌂ *xmas*

▣ Scottish & French V ♧ ▭ Lunch £4.50–£6.50&alc Tea £1.75–£2 High Tea £3–£4 Dinner £8.50–£10&alc Wine £4 Last dinner 10pm

Credit cards 1 3 **VS**

★ **Lochview Motel** ☎(055669) 281 Closed 26 Dec & New Years Day

Bungalow style motel/restaurant on main road by Loch. Comfortable bedrooms.

7⋒ CTV in all bedrooms Ⓡ ★ sB&B⋒£12 dB&B⋒£18

60P ♪

♧ ▭ Lunch £3–£3.50 Tea £1.30 High Tea £3–£4 Dinner £6–£8 Wine £3.60 Last dinner 10pm

Credit cards 1 3

CROFTAMIE
Strathclyde *Dunbartonshire*
Map **11** NS48

✕ **Red House Grill** ☎Drymen (0360) 60358

Closed Mon & Feb

Small restaurant in redstone cottage.

Lunch not served

48 seats Dinner £7.50alc Wine £4.50 Last dinner 9.30pm 30P

CROMARTY
Highland *Ross & Cromarty*
Map **14** NH76

★★*H* **Royal** Marine Ter ☎(03817) 217

11rm(4→) (2fb) TV available in bedrooms Ⓡ ✻ sB&B£8.50–£12.50 dB&B£17–£22 dB&B→£22–£26 B

CTV 20P 10⌂ ✽ ⌂ *xmas*

V ♧ ▭ Lunch £3–£4 Tea 85p–£1.50 High Tea £3–£4 Dinner £7–£8.50 Wine £3.40 Last dinner 8.30pm

CROMER
Norfolk
Map **9** TG24

★★★ **Colne House** (Mount Charlotte) ☎(0263) 512013

Originally the home of Lord Boxton, now extended and providing various children's facilities.

30rm(19→) sB&B£18.50–£19 sB&B→£20–£21 dB&B£28–£30 dB&B→£30–£32 B

☾ CTV 70P ✽ ⌂ (heated) ⌕ (hard) Live music and dancing twice wkly ⌂

♧ ▭ Lunch £5–£5.50 Dinner £7.50–£7.75 Wine £4.85 Last dinner 9pm

Credit cards 1 2 3

★★ **Cliftonville** Runton Rd (Inter-Hotel) ☎(0263) 512543

Imposing, Victorian building with spacious lounges overlooking the sea.

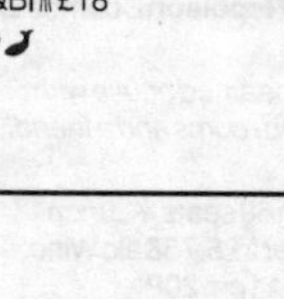

46rm(9→4⋒) (4fb) CTV in 7 bedrooms TV in 2 bedrooms Ⓡ sB&B fr£13 sB&B→⋒ fr£16 dB&B fr£26 dB&B→⋒ fr£29 B

Lift ☾ CTV 20P 3⌂ billiards Live music and dancing twice wkly *xmas*

V ♧ ▭ ✻ Lunch fr£4.50 Tea fr40p High Tea fr£1.50 Dinner fr£7 Wine £4.20 Last dinner 9pm

Credit cards 1 2 3 5

★★ **Hotel de Paris** Sea Front ☎(0263) 513141

→

55rm(31➡2⋒)(12fb) CTV in 45 bedrooms TV in 2 bedrooms sB&B£16.50 sB&B➡⋒£20 dB&B£31 dB&B➡⋒£35 B
Lift ☾ CTV CFA Live music and dancing wkly *xmas*
V ♈ ☐ Lunch £5.50 Tea £1.50 Dinner fr£7.50&alc Wine £3.50 Last dinner 9pm
Credit cards 1 2 3 4 5 **VS**

★**West Parade** Runton Rd ☎(0263) 512443 Closed mid Oct–May except Xmas & Etr
30rm(4fb) Ⓡ sB&B£11–£11.50 dB&B£22–£23 B
CTV 26P *xmas*
♈ ☐ ✱Lunch £3.50 Tea 35p Dinner £5.75 Wine £4.50 Last dinner 7.45pm
VS

CROOKLANDS
Cumbria
Map **7** SD58

★★★ ***Crooklands*** (Best Western) ☎(04487) 432 Telex no 61686
This 400-year-old inn has modern bedrooms and its restaurant forms part of a converted barn.
15➡ CTV in all bedrooms Ⓡ B
☾ 120P ✽ ♩ Disco Sat Cabaret Fri ⌂
▣English, American & French V ♈ Last dinner 10pm
Credit cards 1 2 3 **VS**

CROSBY-ON-EDEN
Cumbria
Map **12** NY45

★★★**Newby Grange** ☎(022873) 645
20➡⋒ (4fb) CTV in all bedrooms sB&B➡⋒£20 dB&B➡⋒£28.50 B
☾ CTV 200P ✽ Disco twice wkly
▣International V ♈ ☐ Lunch £4.75&alc Tea 90p High Tea £3 Dinner £7&alc Wine £2.35 Last dinner 10.30pm
Credit card 1

★★ *H* **Crosby Lodge** ☎(022873) 618 Closed 24 Dec–21 Jan RS Sun
9rm(5➡2⋒) Annexe: 2➡⋒ (2fb) 1 ▭ CTV available in bedrooms sB&B£26.50 sB&B➡⋒£29 dB&B£40 dB&B➡⋒£45 B
CTV 40P ✽
▣English & Continental ♈ Lunch £8–11&alc Dinner £11.25–£13.25&alc Wine £4.50 Last dinner 9pm
Credit cards 2 5

CROSSMICHAEL
Dumfries & Galloway *Kirkcudbrightshire*
Map **11** NX76

★★ **Culgruff House** ☎(055667) 230
Baronial mansion set in secluded, wooded grounds in the heart of farming land high above the village.
17rm(1➡)(2fb) sB&B£12.65 dB&B£23 dB&B➡£27.60 B
CTV 50P 8 ✽

V ♈ ☐ Lunch £5&alc Tea 60p–£2&alc High Tea £3.60&alc Dinner £8&alc Wine £4.50 Last dinner 8pm
Credit cards 1 2 3

CROSSWAY GREEN
Hereford & Worcester
Map **7** SO86

★**Mitre Oak** ☎Hartlebury (0299) 250352
Large building, with carved wooden fireplace in the restaurant.
7rm CTV 1 bedroom Ⓡ ★ ✱sB&B £11.50 dB&B £23
CTV 100P ✽ Live music and dancing Wed–Sun ⌂
▣English & French ♈ ✱Lunch £2.50&alc High Tea £2.50 Dinner £6.50&alc Wine £5 Last dinner 9.15pm
Credit cards 1 2 3 4 5

CROSTHWAITE
Cumbria
Map **7** SD49

★★★**Damson Dene Country** Lythe Valley (A5074) ☎(04488) 227
22rm(10➡12⋒)(4fb) CTV in all bedrooms Ⓡ
✱sB&B➡⋒£17.50 dB&B➡⋒£35 B
☾ 100P ✽ ⛆ sauna bath ⌂ *xmas*
V ♈ ✱Lunch fr£4.50&alc High Tea fr£3.10&alc Dinner fr£6&alc Wine £3.70 Last dinner 9pm
Credit cards 1 3

CROWBOROUGH
East Sussex
Map **5** TQ53

★★★**Crest** Beacon Rd ☎(08926) 2772 Closed 24 & 25 Dec
Small comfortable hotel situated on main coastal road and popular with locals.
30rm(13➡8⋒)(2fb) CTV in all bedrooms Ⓡ sB&B£17.60 sB&B➡⋒£25.30 dB&B£29.70 dB&B➡⋒£38.50 B
Lift ☾ 85P
▣English & French ♈ Lunch £6.05–£6.60&alc Dinner £6.85–£7.70&alc Wine £4
Last dinner 8.30pm
S% Credit cards 1 2 3 5

CROWTHORNE
Berkshire
Map **4** SU86

☆☆☆**Waterloo** Dukes Ride (Anchor) ☎(0344) 777711 Telex No. 848139
Modern facilities and friendly service are found in this basically Victorian building.
54rm(32➡22⋒)(3fb) 1 ▭ CTV in all bedrooms Ⓡ sB&B➡⋒fr£37 dB&B➡⋒fr£41 B
☾ 120P ✽
▣International V ♈ ☐ Lunch £2.75–£6.75&alc Tea 50p Dinner fr£7.50&alc Wine £4.75 Last dinner 10pm
Credit cards 1 2 3 5

CROYDON
Greater London plan **5** D1 (page 421)
See also Sanderstead

☆☆☆**Aerodrome** Purley Way (Anchor) ☎01-688 5185 Telex no 893814
Three-storey hotel with a large modern extension at one side, close to the main Brighton road.
85rm(84➡1⋒)(1fb) CTV in all bedrooms Ⓡ ✱sB&B➡⋒£36 dB&B➡⋒£41 B
☾ # 90P CFA
V ♈ ☐ ✱Lunch £4–£7&alc Tea 60p High Tea 95p Dinner £4–£7&alc Wine £4.50 Last dinner 10pm
Credit cards 1 2 3 4 5

★ ***Briarley*** 8–10 Outram Rd ☎01-654 1000 Telex no 943763 (Crocom G)
Small but very comfortable and well equipped friendly hotel.
19rm(8➡3⋒) 1 ▭ CTV in all bedrooms Ⓡ B
CTV 9P
V ♈ ☐
Last dinner 10pm
Credit cards 1 2 3 5

✕✕✕**Château Napoleon** Coombe Ln ☎01-686 1244
Secluded Tudor beamed house with delightful panelled rooms and a friendly atmosphere
▣French & Italian 60 seats ✱Lunch fr£6.75&alc Dinner fr£8.75&alc Wine £5.35 Last dinner 11pm 20P
Credit cards 1 2 3 5

✕**Tung Kum** 205–207 High St ☎01-688 0748
Spacious Chinese restaurant with good selection of dishes and delightful wall length mural.
▣Cantonese 80 seats ✱Lunch fr£8alc Dinner fr£8alc Wine £5 Last dinner 11pm
S% Credit cards 1 2 3 5

CRUDWELL
Wiltshire
Map **3** ST99

★**Mayfield House** ☎(06667) 409
Closed 25 Dec–6 Jan
21rm(8➡)(1fb) CTV in 8 bedrooms Ⓡ sB&B£12.75 sB&B➡£16 dB&B£23 dB&B➡£28 B
CTV 50P ✽
▣English & French V ♈ ☐ Lunch £3–£5 Tea 50p–£1.25 Dinner fr£5.95–£8&alc Wine £4.40
Last dinner 9pm
Credit card 3 **VS**

CRUGYBAR
Dyfed
Map **2** SN63

★★ *H* **Glanrannel Park** ☎Talley (05583) 230 Closed Nov–Mar

A country home overlooking a small lake in 23 acres of grounds.
8rm(5⇌)(2fb) sB&B fr£12.50 sB&B⇌ fr £12.50 dB&B fr£25 dB&B⇌ fr£25
CTV 40P 3 ✽
Bar lunch fr£1.50 Tea 40p–£1.10 High Tea £1.50–£3 Dinner £6.50–£8.50 Wine £3.50 Last dinner 8.30pm

CUCKFIELD
West Sussex
Map **4** TQ32

★★★*B* **Ockendon Manor** Ockendon Ln ☎Haywards Heath (0444) 416111 Telex no 87677
10rm(9⇌1⋒) 1 CTV in all bedrooms ® ✽sB&B⇌⋒ £28.50 dB&B⇌⋒ £50 Continental breakfast
☾ 30P 3 *xmas*
Last dinner 9.45pm
Credit cards 1 2 3 4 5

★★ **Hilton Park** ☎Haywards Heath (0444) 454555
Family run country house with fine gardens overlooking South Downs
14rm(5⇌2⋒)(5fb) CTV in 9 bedrooms TV in 1 bedroom ® sB&B£20–£23 sB&B⇌⋒ £24–£27 dB&B£32–£34 dB&B⇌⋒ £36
CTV 50P 2 ✽ *xmas*
English, Scottish & French V Tea

fr75p High Tea fr£1.50 Dinner fr£8 Wine £6 Last dinner 8pm
Credit cards 1 2 3 5

CULLEN
Grampian *Banffshire*
Map **15** NJ56

★★★*L* ***Seafield Arms*** Seafield St (Best Western) ☎(0542) 40791
Modernised, coaching inn, built in 1822 by the Earl of Seafield.
25rm(17⇌) CTV in all bedrooms ®
CTV 30P
V Last dinner 9.30pm
Credit cards 1 2 3 4 5

★★ **Cullen Bay** ☎(0542) 40432
Closed Jan
18rm(4⇌6⋒)(1fb) CTV in 4 bedrooms ® sB&B£13–£14 sB&B⇌⋒ £15–£16 dB&B£30 dB&B⇌⋒ £30
CTV 150P 4 ✽ billiards
Lunch £3 High Tea £3 Dinner £5.50&alc Wine £3 Last dinner 8.30pm
Credit cards 2 3 5

CULLINGWORTH
West Yorkshire
Map **7** SE03

★★★*B* **Five Flags** Manywells Heights (near juct A629/B6429) ☎Bradford (0274) 834188
27⇌(11fb) CTV in all bedrooms ✽sB&B⇌ fr£31 dB&B⇌ fr£39
☾ CTV 120P
English, French, Greek & Italian V ✽Lunch fr£4.75&alc Dinner fr£6.95&alc Wine £5.75 Last dinner 10pm
Credit cards 1 2 3 4

CUMBERNAULD
Strathclyde *Dunbartonshire*
Map **11** NS77

✕ **Neelam Tandoori** Dalshannon Farm, Condorral ☎(02367) 20648
Closed 1 Jan Lunch not served Sun
European & Indian V 75 seats Lunch £2.25–£2.35&alc Dinner £5–£6&alc Wine £5.75 Last dinner 11.30pm 3P
Credit card 3 5

CUMNOCK
Strathclyde *Ayrshire*
Map **11** NS51

★★ **Royal** 1 Glaisnock St ☎(0290) 20822
Red sandstone, two-storey hotel, dating from 1850 standing on the main road in the town centre.
12rm(1fb) CTV in 3 bedrooms TV in 1 bedroom sB&B£12.50 dB&B£25
CTV 8P 2

→

V ♔ ☕ Lunch £3.50–£4.50 Tea £1.30–£1.80 High Tea £3.50–£4.50 Dinner £6.50–£7.50 Wine £4.70 Last dinner 9pm

Credit card 1

CUMNOR
Oxfordshire
Map **4** SP40

✕✕**Bear and Ragged Staff** ☎(0865) 862329

Imaginative French and English cuisine is served in this Cotswold stone inn

Closed Mon Dinner not served Sun

English & French **V** 32 seats Lunch £8.75&alc Dinner £8.75&alc Wine £4.45 Last dinner 10pm 50P

Credit cards 1 2 3 5 **VS**

CUPAR
Fife
Map **11** NO31

✕**Ostlers Close** 25 Bonnygate ☎(0334) 55574

Small cottage style restaurant.

Closed Sun, Mon, 25–26 Dec & 1–2 Jan

Scottish & French **V** 32 seats Lunch £5.50alc Dinner £10alc Wine £4.75 Last dinner 9.30pm ⁄ **VS**

CWMBRAN
Gwent
Map **3** ST29

★★★**Hotel Commodore** Mill Ln, Llanyravon ☎(06333) 4091

60rm(47⇛11⋒)(2fb) CTV in all bedrooms ✻sB&B£14–£16 sB&B⇛⋒£25–£27.50 dB&B⇛⋒£35 B

Lift ☾ CTV 200P 6 ⌂ CFA ✽ Disco 5 nights wkly Live music and dancing twice wkly Cabaret twice wkly ♫ *xmas*

English & French **V** ♔ ☕ Lunch fr£3.50&alc Tea fr65p High Tea fr£2 Dinner £5–£6.50&alc Wine £3.65 Last dinner 10pm

Credit cards 1 2 3 5

DALRY
Dumfries & Galloway *Kirkcudbrightshire*
Map **11** NX68

★★**Lochinvar** ☎(06443) 210

Traditional ivy clad hotel with good cooking.

15rm(3⇛) sB&B£11.95 dB&B£23.90 dB&B⇛£28.90

⁄ CTV 35P 3 ⌂ ✽

V ♔ ✻Lunch fr£6 Dinner fr£7 Wine £1.75 Last dinner 7.30pm

VS

DALSTON
Cumbria
Map **11** NY35

★★★**Dalston Hall** Dalston Rd (Best Western) ☎Carlisle (0228) 710271

18rm(12⇛1⋒)(4fb) 4 CTV in all bedrooms Ⓡ sB&B£19 sB&B⇛⋒£26 dB&B£36 dB&B⇛⋒£40 B

150P ✽ ♫ Live music and dancing Fri & Sat ♫ *xmas*

♔ ☕ Bar lunch £1.25–£4.95&alc Tea £1–£1.50 Dinner £8.25&alc Wine £4.75 Last dinner 9.30pm

Credit cards 1 2 3 4 5 **VS**

DALTON
North Yorkshire
Map **12** NZ10

✕**Travellers Rest** ☎Teesdale (0833) 21225

Small country inn with cosy dining room.

Closed Sun, Xmas Day & New Year's Day

24 seats ✻Dinner £9alc Wine £4.50 Last dinner 9pm 30P

Credit card 1

DALWHINNIE
Highland *Inverness-shire*
Map **14** NN68

★★**Loch Ericht** (Minotel) ☎(05282) 257

RS Nov–Jan

Situated in Scotland's highest village, this modern hotel has an unusual and attractive design.

27⇛⋒(4fb) Ⓡ sB&B⇛⋒£12.75–£14.75 dB&B⇛⋒£19–22.50 B

CTV 70P ✽ Disco Sat Live music and dancing Fri & Sat

V Lunch £2.25–£6.50 Tea 90p–£1.50 High Tea £2.25–£4.50 Dinner £5–£7.75 Wine £3.10 Last dinner 9pm

Credit cards 1 2 3 5 VS

DARESBURY
Cheshire
Map **7** SJ58

★★★**Lord Daresbury** Chester Rd (Greenall Whitley) ☎ Warrington (0925) 67331 Telex no 629330
RS 24 Dec–1 Jan

141 (7fb) CTV in all bedrooms Ⓡ sB&B £34–£35 dB&B £45–£46 B

Lift ☾ 300P CFA ✽ Disco Sat

English & French Lunch £7.50 Tea 50p–60p Dinner £7.50 Wine £5.50 Last dinner 10.30pm

Credit cards 1 2 3 5 VS

DARLINGTON
Co Durham
Map **8** NZ21

☆☆☆☆ ***Blackwell Grange Moat House*** Blackwell Grange (Queens Moat) ☎ (0325) 60111 Telex no 587272

Converted 17th-century mansion in 15 acres of wooded parkland with a golf course.

96 1 CTV in all bedrooms Ⓡ B

Lift ☾ ## 300P 2 CFA ✽ (hard) Live music and dancing wkly Cabaret wkly

English & French V Last dinner 9.45pm

Credit cards 1 2 3 4 5

★★★**Kings Head** Priestgate (Swallow) ☎ (0325) 67612 Telex no 53168

Victorian, four-storey hotel, set in the town centre.

86 (7fb) 1 CTV in all bedrooms Ⓡ *sB&B £19–£28 dB&B £30–£36 B

Lift ☾ CTV 20P 6 CFA

English & French V *Bar lunch 45p–£1.80 Tea 45p Dinner 6.95&alc Wine 4.50 Last dinner 9.30pm

Credit cards 1 2 3 4 5 VS

★★**Coachman** Victoria Rd ☎ (0325) 286116
Closed Xmas

Recently renovated and modernised 19th-century building with comfortable bedrooms and attractive public areas.

25rm 1 (3fb) CTV in all bedrooms Ⓡ *sB&B £15.50–£18.50 dB&B £24–£28.50

☾ 12P 4

Lunch £4.95–£7.35&alc Tea 50p Dinner £5.50–£7.35 Wine £3.75 Last dinner 9pm

Credit cards 1 3

✕✕ ***Bishop's House*** 38 Coniscliffe Rd ☎ (0325) 286666

Closed Sun, Public hols & 25 Dec–5 Jan Lunch not served Sat

French 28 seats Last dinner 9.30pm

Credit cards 1 2 3

DARTMOUTH
Devon
Map **3** SX85

★★★**Dart Marina** Sandquay (Trusthouse Forte) ☎ (08043) 2580

Comfortable, modernised hotel on the quayside with fine views of the River Dart.

37rm (26) CTV in all bedrooms Ⓡ sB&B £27 sB&B £34.50 dB&B £39 dB&B £53.50 B

xmas

Last dinner 9pm

Credit cards 1 2 3 4 5

★★ ***Royal Castle*** 11 The Quay (Anchor) ☎ (08043) 2397 Telex no 858875

Coaching inn, dating from 1639, with views of River Dart.

20rm (9) 2 CTV in all bedrooms Ⓡ B
CTV

V Last dinner 8.45pm

Credit cards 1 2 3 4 5 VS

★**Royle House** Mount Boone ☎ (08043) 3649

Georgian house in its own grounds in an elevated position overlooking the town.

9rm (8) (2fb) Ⓡ sB&B fr£21–£25 sB&B fr£21–£25 dB&B £38–£45 dB&B fr£42–£50 B

CTV 15P ✽ sauna bath *xmas*

Bar lunch £5alc Tea £1.25alc Dinner fr£5.95&alc Wine £3.95 Last dinner 9pm

Credit cards 1 3 5 VS

✕✕ **Carved Angel** 2 South Embankment ☎ (08043) 2465

Good menu and excellent wine list in this pleasant waterfront restaurant

Closed Mon & Jan Lunch not served Tue Dinner not served Sun

European V 35 seats *Lunch £14alc Dinner £16alc Wine £7 Last dinner 10pm

S% Credit cards 1 2 3 5

DARWEN
Lancashire
Map **7** SD62

★★★**Whitehall** Springbank, Whitehall ☎ (0254) 71595

18rm (14) (1fb) CTV in 18 bedrooms Ⓡ sB&B fr£16.50 sB&B fr£26 dB&B fr£35 B

CTV 60P ✽ (heated) sauna bath Disco Fri & Sat

English & French V Lunch fr£5&alc Tea fr50p High Tea fr£3.75 Dinner fr£7.50&alc Wine £4.40 Last dinner 9.45pm

Credit cards 1 3 5 VS

★**Millstone** The Circus ☎ (0254) 72588

Tall, sandstone, public house in the town centre.

9rm sB&B £9.86 dB&B £19.72

CTV

Lunch £3.20alc Tea £2alc Dinner £6alc Wine £2.92 Last dinner 9pm

Credit cards 1 3

✕**Le Bifteck** 1 Belgrave Cottage, Belgrave Rd ☎ (0254) 76927

Lunch not served Sat →

English & French V 60seats *Lunch £4.25–4.50&alc Dinner £8.10&alc Wine £5.25 Last dinner 10pm 40P
Credit cards 1 3

DAVIOT
Highland *Inverness-shire*
Map **14** NH73

★★*H* **Meallmore Lodge** ☎(046385) 206
Charming family run traditional hotel with spacious rooms and comfortable lounges.
11rm(3) ® *£10.50–£14.50 sB&B£12.50–£16.50 dB&B £21–£29 dB&B£25–£33
CTV 70P 3
V Lunch £4&alc Tea £1.45&alc Dinner £6.50&alc Wine £3.35 Last Dinner 9pm
Credit cards 1 2 3 5

DAWLISH
Devon
Map **3** SX97

★★★ **Langstone Cliff** Dawlish Warren (1½m NE off A379 Exeter road) (ExecHotels) ☎(0626) 865155
RS Nov–Mar except Xmas & New Year
Modern, family hotel set in 12 acres of grounds.
71rm(57) (64fb) CTV in all bedrooms sB&B£15–£18.50 sB&B£17.50–£20.50 dB&B£30–£37 dB&B£35–£41
Lift CTV 200P CFA (heated) (heated) billiards Disco twice wkly Live music and dancing twice wkly *xmas*
International V Lunch £4.50 Tea 50p Dinner £7.50 Wine £4 Last dinner 8.30pm
Credit cards 1 2 3 5 **VS**

★★ **Charlton House** Exeter Rd ☎(0626) 863260
RS Nov–Feb
Commercial and tourist hotel, set in an elevated position on the edge of the town.
22rm(14 2) (6fb) CTV in 14 bedrooms TV in 8 bedrooms sB&B£10.50–£13.50 sB&B£11.50–£15.25 dB&B£21–£27.50 dB&B£24–£30.50
CTV 40P (heated) sauna bath Disco wkly Live music and dancing wkly *xmas*
English & French V Lunch £4–£4.75&alc Tea 30p–45p Dinner £6.75–£7.25&alc Wine £4.70 Last dinner 8.30pm
Credit cards 1 2 3 4 5 **VS**

DEDDINGTON
Oxfordshire
Map **4** SP43

★★ **Holcombe** High St (Best Western) ☎(0869) 38274 Telex no 826717
Comfortable well equipped bedrooms with service and cooking well above average.
12rm(7 2) (1fb) CTV in 10 bedrooms ® sB&B£18 sB&B£28 dB&B£26 dB&B£35
CTV 20P 1 *xmas*
French V Lunch fr£10&alc Tea fr75p High Tea fr£1.50 Dinner fr£10&alc Wine £5.50 Last dinner 9.30pm
Credit cards 1 2 3 5 **VS**

DEDHAM
Essex
Map **5** TM03

★★*B* **Dedham Vale** Stratford Rd ☎Colchester (0206) 322273
Closed Xmas
Modernised Regency house with attractive lawns, featuring the Terrace restaurant with its huge, moulded, glass roof.
6 (1fb) CTV in all bedrooms sB&B£30–£35 dB&B£45–£50 Continental breakfast
75P
V Lunch £14.50alc Dinner £14.50alc Last dinner 10pm
S% Credit cards 1 2 3 5 **VS**

❀XXX**Le Talbooth** ☎Colchester (0206) 323150

Flemish weavers' 16th-century, timbered cottage, in a delightful setting on the banks of the River Stour.

English & French **V** 80 seats Lunch £10.25&alc Dinner £16alc Wine £5.55 Last dinner 9.30pm 50P

S% Credit cards 1 2 3 4 5 **VS**

★★★

❀★★★**MAISON TALBOOTH, DEDHAM**

Stratford Rd ☎Colchester (0206) 322367

(Rosette awarded for XXX Le Talbooth Restaurant.)

This establishment has two parts, a charmingly furnished hotel with stylish decor, and Le Talbooth, a restaurant in its own right, about half a mile away nestling on the bank of the River Stour. Transport can be provided between the two parts. The hotel derives from a 16th century weaver's house and although it has been extended it still retains such picturesque features as gables and beams. Sam Chalmers is the chef and provides a variety of interesting dishes cooked with more than average skill which well deserve our rosette.

Because of the distance between the two parts breakfast is served in your room. The bedrooms are elegantly furnished and decorated with antique furniture and are spacious enough to make them part sitting rooms; flowers, comfortable chairs, occasional tables, remote control TV, mini bar and fruit are all welcome facilities. Some of the bathrooms are splendidly luxurious and provide almost everything you can think of including bath sheets. There is nothing lacking that would contribute to your creature comforts here. On the ground floor, there are two

sitting rooms, one with a grand piano, both decorated in the same exquisite taste as the bedrooms. Services of the hotel are provided by friendly young girls and their attention contributes to your stay in no small measure. Gerald Milson, the owner, is the prime mover in forming an Association of British Country Hotels called 'Pride of Britain'. If they all reach the high standards that are provided here our members will no doubt welcome them.

10rm(9➡1⋔)(2fb) CTV in all bedrooms ✱ sB&B➡⋔£46.75–£63.25 dB&B➡⋔£60.50–£88 Continental breakfast

15P ✱

English & French **V** Lunch £9.75–£10.75&alc Tea £2.70 Dinner £22alc Wine £4.50 Last dinner 9.30pm

Credit cards 1 2 3 4 5 **VS**

DEGANWY
Gwynedd
Map **6** SH77

★★**Bryn Cregin** Ty Mawr Rd ☎(0492) 83402

Set in its own grounds in a quiet position just off the main road.

17rm(11➡6⋔) CTV in all bedrooms sB&B➡⋔£13–£18 dB&B➡⋔£18–£32 B

30P ✱ Live music and dancing Sat

V Bar lunch £2.50–£3.50&alc Tea 75p–£1.50 Dinner £6.50&alc Wine £3.75 Last dinner 10pm

Credit cards 1 2 3

★★**Deganwy Castle** Station Rd ☎(0492) 83358

From this hotel there are fine views across the Conwy estuary to Conwy Castle and the mountains of Snowdonia.

32rm(12➡)(4fb) CTV in 12 bedrooms ✱sB&B£10–£15 sB&B➡£14–£17 dB&B£20–£30 dB&B➡£28–£34 B

100P CTV ✱ *xmas*

✱Lunch £4.95 Tea 60p Dinner £7.50 Wine £3.75 Last dinner 9.15pm

Credit cards 1 2 3

DELABOLE
Cornwall
Map **2** SX08

★★**Poldark Inn** Treligga Downs ☎Camelford (0840) 212565

Modern, comfortable and rural hotel and restaurant.

11rm(6➡)(1fb) CTV in all bedrooms Ⓡ ✱ sB&B£8–£12 dB&B£16–£24 dB&B➡£18–£26

70P Disco wkly Live music and dancing 2 nights wkly Cabaret 2 nights wkly nc10yrs *xmas*

English & French **V** Lunch £4–£6 Dinner £5.50–£6&alc Wine £3.62 Last dinner 9.30pm

Credit cards 1 2 3

DENBIGH
Clwyd
Map **6** SJ06

★★**Bull** Hall Sq ☎(074571) 2582

This former coaching inn is a tourist and commercial hotel in the centre of the town.

13rm(1➡⋔)(4fb) sB&B£13.75 sB&B➡⋔£14.75 dB&B£26.50 →

dB&B➡⋒£27.50 Ɓ
CTV 12P
⊟Mainly grills V✿☕Lunch £4.50–£6&alc Tea £1.50–£1.75 High Tea £2.50–£3.50 Dinner £4.50–£6&alc Wine £4.50 Last dinner 9.30pm
Credit cards 1 2 3 VS

D

DENTON
Gt Manchester
Map **7** SJ99

★★★**Old Rectory** Meadow Ln, Haughton Green ☎061-336 7516 Telex no 668615
Closed 25 Dec–1 Jan RS Sun & Public hols
Modern, family-run hotel, with good home cooking.
26➡ CTV in all bedrooms ℝ✶ sB&B➡£27 dB&B➡£37 Ɓ
✗CTV 60P ✽
⊟International V Lunch £8alc Dinner £9alc Wine £4 Last dinner 9pm

DERBY
Derbyshire
Map **8** SK33

★★★**Crest** Pasture Hill, Littleover (Crest) ☎(0332) 514933 Telex no 377081
Large house with modern extension.
66➡ CTV in all bedrooms ℝ*sB➡fr£34 (room only) dB➡fr£44 (room only) Ɓ
☾✗200P✽
⊟International V✿*Lunch £2.50–£5.95 Dinner £8.50–£9 Wine £5.25 Last dinner 10pm
Credit cards 1 2 3 4 5 VS

★★★**Midland** Midland Rd ☎(0332) 45894
Britain's oldest railway hotel, built in 1854 and situated next to the railway station.
63rm(34➡) (2fb) CTV in all bedrooms sB&B£22 sB&B➡£34 dB&B£35 dB&B➡£41 Ɓ
☾ CTV 40P 10🚗 CFA✽
✿☕Lunch £5.50 Tea 85p Dinner £7.50–£9 Wine £4.30 Last dinner 10pm
Credit cards 1 2 3 4 5

★★★**Pennine** Macklin St (Greenall Whitley) ☎(0332) 41741 Telex no 377545
RS 24–30 Dec
Five-storey modern hotel, offering views over the city centre.
100rm(55➡45⋒) CTV in all bedrooms ℝ sB&B➡⋒£31–£32 dB&B➡⋒£39–£40 Ɓ
Lift ☾ CFA
V✿☕Bar lunch £1.25–£4.50&alc Tea 60p–£2.50 Dinner £7.25&alc Wine £5 Last dinner 9.45pm
Credit cards 1 2 3 5 VS

★★*H* **Clarendon** Midland Rd ☎(0332) 365235
Late-Victorian, predominantly commercial hotel, close to the railway station.
52rm(13➡) (1fb) CTV in 13 bedrooms ℝ *sB&B£14.95 sB&B➡£25.50 dB&B£21 dB&B➡£29.50 Ɓ
☾ CTV 60P
⊟English, Austrian & French ✿ *Lunch £1.95–£5 Tea 60p Dinner £6.50 Wine £3.35 Last dinner 10.30pm
Credit cards 1 2 3 5

★★*H* **Gables** 119 London Rd ☎(0332) 40633
Closed Xmas & New Year
Predominantly commercial hotel, close to the railway station and town centre.
56rm(4➡16⋒) (3fb) CTV in 20 bedrooms sB&B£14.50 sB&B➡⋒£22 dB&B£22 dB&B➡⋒£30
☾ CTV 60P
✿Lunch £5.50alc Tea fr55p Dinner £5.50alc Wine £4.50 Last dinner 9.45pm

★★**International** 288 Burton Rd ☎(0332) 369321
Large, modernised, Victorian house on the main Burton road.
44➡⋒ (4fb) CTV in all bedrooms ℝ sB&B➡⋒£33 dB&B➡⋒£42 Ɓ
Lift ☾ 60P Disco Sat
⊟International V✿☕Lunch £5 Tea £2.15 High Tea £4 Dinner £6.50–£8.50&alc Wine £4.50 Last dinner 10pm
Credit cards 1 2 3 5 VS

★★*Mackworth* Ashbourne Rd, Mackworth (3m NW A52) ☎Kirk Langley (033 124) 324
Large roadside inn on the A52, situated 3 miles north of the city centre.
14➡ CTV in all bedrooms ℝ✶ Ɓ
60P✽ Live music and dancing wkly
✿☕Last dinner 10pm
Credit cards 1 2 3 5

★**Howard** Friar Gate ☎(0332) 43455
RS Sun (B&B only)
20rm(1➡1⋒) (3fb) *sB&B£11–£14 sB&B➡⋒ fr£14 dB&B£15.50–£18 dB&B➡⋒ fr£18 Ɓ
CTV 60P Disco Mon–Sat
⊟French V✿*Dinner £4–£5.50&alc Wine £3.75 Last dinner 10.30pm
Credit cards 2 5

✕✕*Cathedral* 22 Iron Gate ☎(0332) 368732
Upstairs restaurant opposite Cathedral.
Lunch not served Sat
⊟English, French & Italian 50 seats Last dinner 10pm P Live music Sat
Credit cards 1 2 3 5

✕✕**Golden Pheasant** Shelton Lock ☎(0332) 700112
Dinner not served Sun
⊟English & Continental V 85 seats Lunch £4.80–£5.25&alc Dinner £6.50–£7.50&alc Wine £5.35 Last dinner 10pm
30P Live music Tue/Disco Sat
Credit cards 1 2 3 5

✕*San Remo* 5 Sadler Gate ☎(0332) 41752
Small, simple Italian restaurant.
Closed Sun, last wk Jul, 1st 2wks Aug & Public hols Dinner not served Mon
⊟English & Italian 45 seats
Last dinner 10pm
Credit card 5

DEREHAM (EAST)
Norfolk
Map **9** TF91

★★★**Phoenix** Church St (Trusthouse Forte) ☎(0362) 2276
28rm(17➡) (1fb) CTV in all bedrooms ℝ sB&B £30.50 sB&B➡£33 dB&B£43 dB&B➡£49.50 Ɓ
40P *xmas*
✿Last dinner 9.30pm
Credit cards 1 2 3 4 5

★★**King's Head** Norwich St ☎(0362) 3842
Small 17th-century modernised inn with a walled garden.
10rm(4➡2⋒) Annexe: 5rm(2➡3⋒) (2fb) CTV in all bedrooms ℝ sB&B fr£19 sB&B➡⋒ fr£21 dB&B fr£27 dB&B➡⋒ fr£30 Ɓ
CTV 30P 3🚗 (grass)
⊟English & French V✿Lunch fr£5 Dinner fr£6 Wine £4 Last dinner 9pm
Credit cards 1 2 3

DERSINGHAM
Norfolk
Map **9** TF62

★**Feathers** (Charrington) ☎(0485) 40207
Victorian building standing in three acres of grounds on the edge of the Sandringham estate.
6rm CTV in all bedrooms ℝ✶ sB&B£13.50 dB&B£20
50P✽ nc14yrs
V✿Lunch £2.95–£3.95&alc Dinner £3.95&alc Wine £4.60 Last dinner 9.30pm
Credit cards 1 3 5

DEVIZES
Wiltshire
Map **4** SU06

★★**Bear** Market Pl ☎(0380) 2444
16th-century coaching hotel with traditional comfort and good menu.
26rm(14➡) (5fb) 1🛏 CTV in all bedrooms ℝ sB&B£22 sB&B➡£25 dB&B£30 dB&B➡£34 Ɓ
CTV 30P Live music and dancing Wed
⊟English & French ✿☕Lunch £6–£8&alc Tea 35p–£3 Dinner £7.50–£10.50&alc Wine £5.25 Last dinner 9.45pm
Credit cards 1 2 3 4

DINGWALL
Highland *Ross & Cromarty*
Map **14** NH55

★★**Royal** High St ☎(0349) 62130
Recently renovated commercial hotel on a corner site in the town centre.
15rm(7⇌2⋒)(1fb) CTV in all bedrooms ®*sB&B£12–£15 sB&B⇌⋒£15–£18 dB&B£23–£27 dB&B⇌⋒£27–£30 B
CTV 26P Live music and dancing twice wkly Cabaret wkly *xmas*
V ♡ ☐ Lunch £5.25–£8.50 Tea £1–£1.50 High Tea £2.95–£8.50alc Dinner £4.50–£6&alc Wine £3.50 Last dinner 10pm
Credit cards 1 3 5 **VS**

DINNINGTON
South Yorkshire
Map **8** SK58

✕✕**Deans** Falcon Sq ☎(0909) 562455
Lunch not served Sat Dinner not served Sun
75 seats *Lunch £4.50&alc Dinner £10alc Wine £3.45 16P bedrooms available Cabaret Sun lunch
Credit cards 1 2 3 5

DIRLETON
Lothian *East Lothian*
Map **12** NT58

★★★*HB* **Open Arms** ☎(062085) 241 Telex no 727887
Small select hotel with good food in a picturesque setting by the village green.
7rm(6⇌1⋒) CTV in all bedrooms *sB&B⇌⋒£35.20 dB&B⇌⋒£48 B
40P ✽ *xmas*
♡ ☐ *Lunch fr£5.75 Tea fr£1.50 Dinner fr£10.75 Wine £4.50 Last dinner 10pm
S% Credit cards 1 2 3 5 **VS**

DISLEY
Cheshire
Map **7** SJ98

★★★**Moorside** Mudhurst Ln, Higher Disley (Best Western) ☎(06632) 4151 Telex no 665170 RS Xmas Day
Modern hotel standing on the edge of Lyme Park with good views.
25rm(21⇌4⋒)(3fb) CTV in all bedrooms ®*sB&B⇌⋒£25 dB&B⇌⋒£35 B
☾ # 250P CFA ✽ Live music and dancing twice wkly
French V ♡ ☐ *Lunch £5.75–£12.50&alc Dinner £9.50&alc Wine £5.75 Last dinner 10pm
Credit cards 1 2 3 5

✕✕***Copperfield*** 49 Buxton Old Rd ☎(06632) 4333
Lunch not served
70 seats Last dinner 10pm

DISS
Norfolk
Map **5** TM18

✕✕**Salisbury House** 84 Victoria Rd ☎(0379) 4738
Comfortably furnished restaurant with interesting menu
Closed Sun, Mon, Xmas & New Year, 1wk Spring & 1wk Autumn Lunch not served
25 seats Dinner £14 Wine £5.60 Last dinner 9.30pm 10P bedrooms available

DITTON PRIORS
Shropshire
Map **7** SO68

✕✕**Howard Arms** ☎(074634) 200
Closed Mon & mid-Aug–mid Sep Lunch not served Tue–Sat Dinner not served Sun
English & French **V** 36 seats *Lunch £7–£7.75 Dinner £11–£16 Wine £5.40 Last dinner 9.30pm 60P bedrooms available

DODDISCOMBSLEIGH
Devon
Map **3** SX88

✕**Nobody Inn** ☎Christow (0647) 52394
Closed Sun, Mon (except Public Hols) & Xmas Day Lunch not served
English & Continental 50 seats Dinner £8alc Wine £3 Last dinner 9.30pm 50P bedrooms available
Credit cards 1 3 **VS**

DOLGELLAU
Gwynedd
Map **6** SH71

★★**Dolserau Hall** ☎(0341) 422522
Country house in its own rural surroundings, 1 mile from Dolgellau.
12rm(9⇌1⋒)(3fb) ® sB&B£10 sB&B⇌⋒£10 dB&B£20 dB&B⇌⋒£20 B
Lift CTV 100P ✽ Disco wkly *xmas* ♿
V ♡ Lunch £3–£4.50 Dinner £7–£8&alc Wine £4 Last dinner 9pm

★★***Golden Lion Royal*** Lion St ☎(0341) 422579 Closed Xmas
Ivy-clad regency coaching inn with pleasant garden. Lounge has large stone fireplace.
18rm(9⇌) Annexe: 4⇌5 CTV in 13 bedrooms ® B
CTV
♡ ☐ Last dinner 9pm
Credit cards 1 2 3

★★**Royal Ship** (Frederic Robinson) ☎(0341) 422209
Commercial and tourist hotel in the town centre, dating back to the 18th century.
25rm(7⇌)(1fb) ®*sB&B£10–£12 sB&B⇌£14–£15 dB&B£20–£24 dB&B⇌£28–£30 B
Lift CTV 8P 3 *xmas* ♿
♡ ☐ *Lunch £4 Tea £1.30 Dinner £7.50 Last dinner 9pm
Credit card 1

DOLWYDDELAN
Gwynedd
Map **6** SH75

★★★**Plas Hall** Pont-y-Pant ☎(06906) 206 Telex no 61467
Victorian slate house, nestling in a quiet valley with the river below.
17rm(16⇌1⋒)(2fb) 1 CTV in all bedrooms ® sB&B⇌⋒£15–£22 dB&B⇌⋒£26–£36 B
50P ✽ ♿
Welsh & French **V** ♡ ☐ Lunch £5.50&alc Tea £1.50–£3.50 Dinner £6.90&alc Wine £3.50 Last dinner 9.30pm
Credit cards 1 2 3 5 **VS**

D

★★**Elen's Castle** ☎(06906) 207 Closed Oct–Mar
18th-century coach house with spectacular views across the Lledr Valley.
10rm(2➡2⋒)(2fb) 1▭ CTV TV available in bedrooms Ⓡ sB&B£9.75–£10.70 dB&B£19.50–£21.40 dB&B➡⋒£22.50–£24.40
CTV 40P 2 ✽
V ♡ ▭ Lunch fr£1.30 Tea fr60p Dinner fr£5.40 Wine £3.90 Last dinner 8pm

DONCASTER
South Yorkshire
Map **8** SE50
See also Rossington
★★★**Danum** High St (Swallow) ☎(0302) 62261 Telex no 53168
Town centre hotel recently refurbished to provide modern accommodation and an attractive first floor restaurant.
72rm(45➡7⋒)(2fb) CTV in all bedrooms Ⓡ ✻sB&B£15–£23 sB&B➡⋒£18.50–£34 dB&B£19–£31.50 dB&B➡⋒£25–£40 B
Lift ☾ 60P 20 CFA
English & French V ♡ ▭ ✻Lunch £6–£6.50&alc Tea £1.50–£2&alc Dinner £7.50–£8&alc Wine £4.50 Last dinner 9.30pm
S% Credit cards 1 2 3 4 5

★★★**Earl of Doncaster** Bennetthorpe ☎(0302) 61371 Telex no 547923
Four-storey hotel of contemporary design near the town centre.
53rm(51➡2⋒)(1fb) CTV in all bedrooms Ⓡ ✻sB&B➡⋒£33.50 dB&B➡⋒£41 B
Lift ☾ 50P CFA
V ♡ ▭ ✻Lunch £6.50&alc Tea 55p Dinner £6.50&alc Wine £4.50 Last dinner 9.45pm
Credit cards 1 2 3 4 5

★★★**Punch's** Bawtry Rd, Bessacarr (Embassy) ☎(0302) 535235
Two-storey, brick building on the southern outskirts of town.
25rm(15➡)(3fb) CTV in all bedrooms Ⓡ sB&B£23.50 sB&B➡£34.50 dB&B£31 dB&B➡£41.50 B
☾ 150P ✽
V ♡ ▭ Lunch £6.70&alc Tea 55p Dinner £6.70&alc Wine £4.50 Last dinner 9.15pm
S% Credit cards 1 2 3 4 5

★★*B* **Regent** Regent Sq ☎(0302) 64180
RS Xmas & Public Hols
Victorian town houses have been converted into this conveniently situated hotel.
34rm(11➡13⋒)(2fb) 1▭ CTV in all bedrooms Ⓡ ✻sB&B➡⋒ fr£25 dB&B➡⋒ fr£34 B
Lift ☾ 25P sauna bath Disco Fri & Sat *xmas*
English & French V ♡ ▭ ✻Lunch fr £2.20 Tea fr£1 High Tea fr£2.50 Dinner fr£5.50&alc Wine £4.95 Last dinner 10pm
Credit cards 1 2 3 5 VS

DONNINGTON
Shropshire
Map **7** SJ71
See under Telford

DONYATT
Somerset
Map **3** ST31
✕✕ ***Thatcher's Pond*** ☎Ilminster (04605) 3210
Mellow, stone, thatched Somerset long-house on the A358, offering for lunch and dinner a good Continental cold table.
Closed Mon & 24 Dec–Jan
26 seats Last dinner 9pm P

DORCHESTER
Dorset
Map **3** SY69
★★★**King's Arms** (Exec Hotel) ☎(0305) 65353
An 18th-century inn with bow windows over the pillared porch.
27rm(16➡)(3fb) 2▭ CTV in all bedrooms Ⓡ ✻sB&B£17.50 sB&B➡£24 dB&B£32 dB&B➡£37.50–£40.50 B
☾ CTV 35P 4
V ♡ ▭ ✻Lunch fr£5&alc Tea 50p Dinner £8–£9.10 Wine £3.25 Last dinner 8.45pm
Credit cards 1 2 3 VS

DORCHESTER-ON-THAMES
Oxfordshire
Map **4** SU59
★★★*L* **White Hart** High St ☎Oxford (0865) 340074
Attractive, modernised 18th-century coaching inn, with well-appointed bedrooms.
16➡⋒ 1▭ CTV in all bedrooms Ⓡ sB&B➡⋒£36.80 dB&B➡⋒£40 B
☾ CTV 40P
English & French ♡ ✻Lunch £8.95&alc Dinner £12.50alc Wine £6.50 Last dinner 9.30pm
S% Credit cards 1 2 3 4 5

DORKING
Surrey
Map **4** TQ14
★★★★*L* **Burford Bridge** Burford Bridge, Box Hill (2m NE A24) (Trusthouse Forte) ☎(0306) 884561 Telex no 859507 Gatwick plan **2**
52➡ CTV in all bedrooms Ⓡ sB&B➡£47 dB&B➡£68.50 B
☾ 80P CFA ✽ (heated) sauna bath *xmas*
♡ ▭ Last dinner 9.30pm
Credit cards 1 2 3 4 5

☆☆☆**Punch Bowl Motor** Reigate Rd (Anchor) ☎(0306) 889335 Telex no 858875 Gatwick plan **18**
Overlooking Box Hill, this old pub has modern bedroom annexe.
Annexe: 29➡(6fb) CTV in all bedrooms Ⓡ ✻sB&B➡⋒£32 dB&B➡⋒£39 B
☾ 150P ✽ *xmas*
V ♡ Lunch £5.35–£8.20&alc Dinner £5.35–£8.20&alc Wine £4.50 Last dinner 9.30pm
Credit cards 1 2 3 4 5 VS

★★★ **White Horse** High St (Trusthouse Forte) ☎(0306) 881138
Comfortable traditional coaching inn with well appointed bedrooms in modern extension.
38rm(35⇌3⋒) Annexe: 32⇌ CTV in all bedrooms ® sB&B⇌⋒ £39 dB&B⇌⋒ £54.50 B
☾ 73P ⩧ (heated) *xmas*
♔ ☐ Last dinner 9.15pm
Credit cards 1 2 3 4 5

✕ **River Kwai** 274–276 High St ☎(0306) 889053
Closed Mon
🅸 Thai **V** 40 seats ✻ Lunch £5alc Dinner £8alc Wine £5.80 Last dinner 11pm
Credit cards 1 3 5

DORNOCH
Highland *Sutherland*
Map **14** NH78

★★ **Burghfield House** ☎(0862) 810212
Closed 16 Oct–Mar
Scottish, baronial-style, turreted mansion standing in 5½ acres of tree-studded grounds.
16rm(4⇌) Annexe: 31rm(4⇌) (13fb) sB&B £13.20–£15.40 sB&B⇌ £14.20–£16.40 dB&B £26.40–£30.80 dB&B⇌ £28.40–£32.80 B
CTV 100P ✽ Disco twice wkly
🅸 International **V** ♔ Lunch £4.50–£5 Tea 55p–65p Dinner £8.80–£9 Last dinner 9pm
Credit cards 1 2 3 5 **VS**

★★ **Dornoch Castle** Castle St ☎(0862) 810216 Closed mid Oct–Mar
The former seat of the Bishops of Caithness, this hotel is situated in the centre of the town overlooking Dornoch Firth.
20rm(11⇌) (3fb) ® sB&B £13–£15 sB&B⇌ £15.50–£17.50 dB&B £23–£27 dB&B⇌ £25.50–£29.50
Lift CTV 14P 1
♔ ☐ Lunch £3.50alc Tea 60p–£1.20 Dinner £8.75–£9.75 Wine £3.40 Last dinner 9.30pm
Credit cards 1 3 **VS**

DORRIDGE
West Midlands
Map **7** SP17

★★ *B* **Forest** Station Approach ☎Knowle (05645) 2120
RS Sun
12rm(10⇌) (2fb) CTV in all bedrooms ® ✻ sB&B⇌ £20.90 dB&B⇌ £28.05
110P
🅸 English & French **V** ♔ ☐ ✻ Lunch fr£4 Tea fr50p High Tea fr£1 Dinner £5 Wine £3.75 Last dinner 10pm
Credit cards 1 2 5

DOUGLAS
Isle of Man
Map **6** SC37

★ ***Woodbourne*** Alexander Dr ☎(0624) 21766 Closed Nov–Mar
Friendly, comfortable public house in residential area.
12rm
CTV nc 15yrs
♔ Last dinner 9.30pm
VS

✕✕✕ ***Boncomptie's*** King Edward Rd, Onchan ☎(0624) 5626
Closed Sun Lunch not served Sat
🅸 Continental **V** 85 seats Last dinner 9.30pm P
Credit cards 1 2 5 **VS**

DOUNE
Central *Perthshire*
Map **11** NN70

✕ **Broughton's** (2½m S on A873) ☎(078684) 897
Closed Sun & Mon
🅸 International 30 seats ✻ Lunch fr£4.85 Dinner fr£9.25 Wine £4.25 Last dinner 10pm 10P
Credit cards 1 5

DOVER
Kent
Map **5** TR34

☆☆☆☆ **Holiday Inn** Townwall St (Holiday Inns) ☎(0304) 203270 Telex no 96458
Well-equipped hotel with limited restaurant facilities.
83⇌⋒ (33fb) CTV in all bedrooms sB⇌⋒ £38.75–£41.25 dB⇌⋒ £51.50–£58.75 (room only) B
Lift ☾ ## 8P CFA (heated)
🅸 English & French ♔ ☐ Lunch £5.95&alc Tea £1–£2.15 High Tea fr£4.10 Dinner £7.75–£8.75&alc Wine £5.25 Last dinner 10.30pm
Credit cards 1 2 3 4 5

☆☆☆ *H* **Dover Motel** Whitfield (3m NW junc A2/A256) ☎(0304) 821222 Telex no 965866
Friendly, hospitable motel with modern, well equipped bedrooms.
67⇌⋒ (47fb) CTV in all bedrooms sB⇌⋒ £32.95–£37.95 dB⇌⋒ £44.90–£47.90 (room only) B
☾ 75P ✽ ♿
🅸 English & French ♔ ☐ Lunch £4.95–£5.55&alc Tea £1.50 Dinner £7.95&alc Wine £4.95 Last dinner 10.45pm
Credit cards 1 2 3 5

★★★ **White Cliffs** Esplanade ☎(0304) 203633 Telex no 965422
Closed Xmas
Its sea front setting provides splendid views of the activity in Dover harbour.
63rm(25⇌2⋒) (6fb) CTV in 15 bedrooms TV in 23 bedrooms sB&B £17.50–£18.50 sB&B⇌⋒ £20–£21 dB&B £29–£30 dB&B⇌⋒ £33–£34 B
Lift ☾ CTV 25
♔ ☐ ✻ Lunch £4.25–£5.50&alc Tea fr95p Dinner £5.50–£6.50&alc Wine £4.50 Last dinner 9.15pm
Credit cards 1 2 3 5 **VS**
See advert on page 232

★★ **Cliffe Court** 25–26 Marine Pde ☎(0304) 211001
A friendly and well managed hotel adjacent to the Eastern Docks.
23rm(7⇌) Annexe: 1⋒ CTV in all bedrooms ✻ sB&B £14–£15 dB&B £24–£26 dB&B⇌⋒ £28 →

☾ CTV P ⌂

🍴International V ♈ ☕ ✻ Lunch £4.25&alc Tea 35p&alc High Tea £2.25&alc Dinner £4.50&alc Wine £3.75 Last dinner 9.30pm

Credit cards 1 2 3 4 5

D

DOWNDERRY
Cornwall
Map **2** SX35

★★**Wide Sea** ☎(05035) 240
Closed Nov–Mar

Small hotel whose commanding position gives it wide panoramic coastal views.

32rm(5 🛁) (4fb) sB&B£9–£10 dB&B£18–£20 dB&B 🛁 £20–£22 B

☾ CTV 30P 4 🚗 ✻ billiards ⌂

♈ ☕ Lunch £2.50–£3.50 Tea 50p–60p Dinner £6–£8 Wine £3.75 Last dinner 8.30pm

Credit card 3

DOWNHAM MARKET
Norfolk
Map **5** TF60

★**Crown** Bridge St ☎(0366) 382322

10rm(4 🛁 3 🚿) CTV in 7 bedrooms ★ sB&B£13 sB&B 🛁 🚿 £17 dB&B£22 dB&B 🛁 🚿 £27 B

CTV 50P 🚗 nc14yrs

🍴Mainly grills V ♈ ☕ Lunch £2.40–£5.80 Tea £1.20–£2.40 Dinner £5.60–£7.20&alc Wine £3.40 Last dinner 10pm

Credit cards 2 3 5

DOWN THOMAS
Devon
Map **2** SX55

★★ **Langdon Court** ☎Plymouth (0752) 862358

Modernised Elizabethan mansion on an unclassified road between Wembury and Down Thomas.

14 🛁 (2fb) CTV in all bedrooms ® sB&B 🛁 £22.50 dB&B 🛁 £33 B

40P 🚗 ✻ nc5yrs

🍴English & French V ♈ Bar lunch £6.50alc Dinner £8.50alc Wine £3.65 Last dinner 9.30pm

Credit cards 1 2 4 5 **VS**

DOWNTON
Wiltshire
Map **4** SU12

★***Bull*** ☎(0725) 20374

A 300-year-old coaching inn, with fishing rights on the River Avon.

4rm(1 🛁) Annexe: 7rm(4 🛁) 2 📺 ® TV 40P 4 🚗 ✻ 🎣

V ♈ ☕ Last dinner 8.45pm

Credit cards 1 2 5

DRAKES BROUGHTON
Hereford & Worcester
Map **3** SO94

✕✕✕ ***Plough & Harrow*** ☎Worcester (0905) 840259

Closed Mon Dinner not served Sun

🍴International **V** 60 seats Last dinner 9.30pm 60P

Credit cards 1 2 3 5

DRAYCOTT
Derbyshire
Map **8** SK43

★★★*HL* ***Tudor Court*** Gypsy Ln (Best Western) ☎(03317) 4581

Recently built hotel with a mock Tudor façade, standing in 8¼ acres of grounds.

30 🛁 CTV in all bedrooms ® B

☾ 250P ✻ Live music and dancing twice wkly

🍴French ♈ ☕ Last dinner 11.30pm

Credit cards 1 2 3 4 **VS**

DRIFFIELD, GREAT
Humberside
Map **8** TA05

★★★*B* **Bell** 46 Market Pl ☎(0377) 46661

An old coaching inn set in the centre of town.

14 🛁 1 📺 CTV available in bedrooms ★ sB&B 🛁 fr£23 dB&B 🛁 fr£25.50 B

⚡ 50P squash billiards Disco Fri nc12yrs

V ♈ Lunch fr£4.50 Dinner £7.50alc Wine £3.80 Last dinner 9.30pm

Credit cards 1 2 3 5

★★ **Wold House** Nafferton (3m E A166) ☎(0377) 44242

Georgian style country house with country views.

14rm(3 🛁 3 🚿) Annexe: 1 🚿 (3fb) CTV available in bedrooms sB&B£17.50 sB&B 🛁 🚿 £19 dB&B£27 dB&B 🛁 🚿 £30 B

CTV 40P 3 🚗 ✻ ⛱ (heated) billiards

V ♈ ☕ Lunch £5 Tea 60p High Tea £4 Dinner £7.20 Wine £3 Last dinner 8.30pm

DROITWICH
Hereford & Worcester
Map **3** SO86

★★★★*H* **Château Impney** ☎(0905) 774411 Telex no 336673 Closed Xmas

An authentic copy of a French château built during the 19th century and set in some 70 acres of parkland.

67rm(64 🛁 3 🚿) (8fb) 1 📺 CTV in 67 bedrooms sB 🛁 🚿 fr£44.95 (room only) dB 🛁 🚿 fr£49.95 (room only) B

Lift ☾ CTV 600P CFA ✻ 🎾

🍴English & French V ♈ ☕ Lunch £6.99&alc Tea 95p Dinner £8.99&alc Wine £6.45 Last dinner 10pm

Credit cards 1 2 3 5 **VS**

★★★★ **Raven** St Andrews Street ☎(0905) 772224 Telex no 336673 Closed Xmas

Large, central hotel with many conference facilities.

55 🛁 (7fb) CTV in all bedrooms sB 🛁 🚿 fr£34.95 (room only) dB 🛁 🚿 fr£39.95 (room only) B

Lift ☾ CTV 200P CFA

🍴English & French V ♈ ☕ Lunch £6.99&alc Tea 95p&alc High Tea £4.25 Dinner £8.99&alc Wine £6.45 Last dinner 10pm

Credit cards 1 2 3 5 **VS**

★**St Andrew's House** Worcester Rd ☎(0905) 773202

25rm(16 🛁) (5fb) CTV in all bedrooms ® sB&B£15.75 sB&B 🛁 £20.25 dB&B£28 dB&B 🛁 £32 B

75P ✽

V Lunch £4.60–£5&alc Dinner £5.85–£6&alc Wine £3 Last dinner 10.30pm

Credit cards [1] [2] [3] [5]

DRONFIELD
Derbyshire
Map **8** SK37

★★ *B* **Manor** 10 High St ☎ (0246) 413971
Closed Public hols RS Sun
A converted Georgian building in the centre of this ancient hamlet.

10rm(1→9) CTV in all bedrooms Ⓡ ✽sB&B→ £19.80–£21.50 dB&B→ £25.30–£27.50

CTV 40P Live music and dancing Fri

English & French ✽Lunch £4.25&alc Dinner £6.50&alc Wine £4.25 Last dinner 9.45pm

Credit cards [1] [3]

DROXFORD
Hampshire
Map **4** SU61

✕ ***White Horse Inn*** ☎ (04897) 490
Popular, friendly pub, with good bar snacks and a small separate restaurant offering good, home-made plain cooking.

Closed Mon Lunch not served Mon–Sat Dinner not served Sun

28 seats Last dinner 9pm 20P bedrooms available

DRUMNADROCHIT
Highland *Inverness-shire*
Map **14** NH53

★★ **Drumnadrochit** ☎ (04562) 218
Closed Nov–mid Mar
Large stone-built building on the site of a 16th-century inn.

24rm(1→) Ⓡ sB&B £12–£15 sB&B £12.50–£14.50 dB&B £24–£30 dB&B→ £26.50–£32.50

CTV 70P ✽

Scottish & Continental Lunch £4.50–£5.50&alc Tea 50p Dinner £7–£8.50&alc Wine £3.95 Last dinner 9.40pm

Credit cards [3] [5]

★★ *HBL* **Polmally House** Milton ☎ (04562) 343
Closed 12 Dec–Jan & 22 Oct–15 Nov RS Feb–27 Mar & 16 Nov–11 Dec
This Edwardian country house hotel is situated near Glen Urquhart and Loch Ness. It has 20 acres of grounds that include a swimming pool and tennis court. Individual touches are evident throughout both in the public areas and in the bedrooms. The new owners who took over in early 1983 certainly make one feel welcome.

11rm(5→)(3fb) 1 sB&B £18.50 dB&B £37 dB&B→ £40

25P ✽ (hard)

Continental Lunch £3.15–£3.95 Dinner £8alc Wine £4 Last dinner 9.30pm

Credit cards [1] [2] [3] [5] **VS**

★ **Benleva** ☎ (04562) 288

6rm(4)(3fb) Ⓡ ✽sB&B £7.50 dB&B £15 dB&B £17 Continental breakfast

CTV P billiards Live music and dancing wknds

✽Bar Lunch fr£2.75 Tea fr£1.20 Dinner fr£6.50 Wine £4 Last dinner 9.30pm

Credit card [3]

DRYBRIDGE
Grampian *Banffshire*
Map **15** NJ46

✕✕ **Old Monastery** (1m E off Deskford road) ☎ Buckie (0542) 32660
(Rosette awarded for dinner only.)
Closed Sun, Mon, 2wks Jan, 2wks Oct & Xmas

Scottish & French 36 seats Lunch £5.30alc Dinner £9alc Wine £4.60 Last dinner 9pm 15P

DRYBURGH
Borders *Berwickshire*
Map **12** NT53

★★★ *L* **Dryburgh Abbey** (Best Western) ☎ St Boswells (0835) 22261
Telex no 727396 (att Dryburgh)
This turreted mansion, dating from 1848, stands in 11 acres of parkland on the banks of the River Tweed.

27rm(13→)(1fb) 3 Ⓡ sB&B £21.80 sB&B→ £25.10 dB&B £38.50 dB&B→ £48.20–£57.50

CTV 100P 3 ✽ *xmas*

V ✽Lunch £7alc Tea £2.25alc Dinner fr£9.75 Wine £3.75 Last dinner 8.30pm

S% Credit cards [1] [2] [3] [5]

DRYMEN
Central *Stirlingshire*
Map **11** NS48

★★★ **Buchanan Arms** (Scottish Highland) ☎ (0360) 60588 Telex no 778215
Modernised 18th-century coaching inn situated in the centre of this small village.

35→(2fb) CTV in all bedrooms Ⓡ ✽sB&B £17.75 sB&B→ £21.45–£31 dB&B £36.90 dB&B→ £50

70P ✽ *xmas*

International V ✽Lunch fr£5.95&alc Tea fr£1.80 Dinner fr£9.45&alc Wine £4.85 Last dinner 9.30pm

Credit cards [1] [2] [3] [4] [5] **VS**

DUDLEY
West Midlands
Map **7** SO99

★★ ***Station*** Birmingham Rd (Wolverhampton & Dudley) ☎ (0384) 53418

29rm(11→) CTV in all bedrooms Ⓡ Lift CTV 100P

Last dinner 9pm

Credit cards [1] [3] **VS**

★ ***Ward Arms*** Birmingham Rd (Wolverhampton & Dudley) ☎ (0384) 52723

13rm Ⓡ

CTV 100P

Last dinner 8pm

Credit cards [1] [3] **VS**

DULNAIN BRIDGE
Highland *Morayshire*
Map **14** NH92

★★ *H* **Muckrach Lodge** ☎ (047985) 257
(Rosette awarded for dinner only.)
Formerly a shooting lodge, now a family-run hotel, Muckrach Lodge stands in 10 acres of grounds.

9rm(4→) TV & CTV available in bedrooms sB&B £13–£14 sB&B→ £15–£17 dB&B £27–£28 dB&B→ £30–£32

50P 4 ✽

Scottish & European **V** Bar lunch £3.50alc Dinner £10.50alc Wine £6 Last dinner 8.15pm

★★ *HBL* **Skye of Curr** ☎ (047985) 345
A popular base for the Spey Valley, this small, charming hotel is set in well maintained grounds. The wood panelled receptional hall lounge is very welcoming and the individually decorated bedrooms are spacious and spotlessly clean, with fine views of the Cairngorms.

9rm(1→)(3fb) Ⓡ ✽sB&B £13.50–£15.50 dB&B £27 dB&B→ £30

CTV 20P ✽

V ✽Lunch £4.50 Dinner £8.50alc Wine £3.55 Last dinner 8pm

Credit cards [1] [2] [3] [5]

DULVERTON
Somerset
Map **3** SS92

★★★ *HL* **Carnarvon Arms** Brushford (2m S on B3222) ☎ (0398) 23302
Traditional sporting hotel with its own shooting and fishing facilities.

27rm(19→) Ⓡ ✽sB&B £10–£16 sB&B→ £11–£18 dB&B £18–£30 dB&B→ £20–£32.50 Continental breakfast

CTV 50P ✽ (heated) (hard) billiards

V ✽Lunch £3.55–£8 Tea 75p Dinner £8.50–£12 Wine £4.25 Last dinner 8.30pm

★★⚑*H* ***Three Acres*** Brushford (2m S on B3222) ☎(0398) 23426
Closed Nov–Apr
Standing in extensive grounds with views of the Barle and Exe Valleys.
7rm(2⇌) ®
⊬ CTV 8P ⊞ ✽ nc8yrs
▣English & French ♧ ⊒ Last dinner 7.45pm

DUMFRIES
Dumfries & Galloway *Dumfriesshire*
Map **11** NX97

★★★**Station** 49 Lovers Walk ☎(0387) 54316
Victorian, sandstone building situated close to the railway station.
30rm(24⇌6⋒) (1fb) CTV in all bedrooms ® sB&B⇌⋒£24 dB&B⇌⋒£30 ꞗ
Lift ☾ CTV 60P Live music Sat
♧ ⊒ ✻Bar lunch 70p–£4 Tea 70p Dinner £6.50–£7.50 Wine £4.75 Last dinner 9.30pm
Credit cards ① ② ③ ⑤ **VS**

★**Dalston** 5 Laurieknowe ☎(0387) 54422
Closed Xmas & New Year
7rm (1fb) sB&B£9.50 dB&B£19
CTV 17P ⊞
♧ ⊒ Lunch fr£3.50 Tea fr60p High Tea £4.50alc Dinner fr£5.50 Wine £4.50 Last dinner 7.30pm

★**Moreig** 67 Annan Rd ☎(0387) 55524
A small, informal commercial hotel with homely atmosphere, situated on the A75 on eastern outskirts of town.
8rm(1⋒) (4fb) ✻sB&B£9.50 dB&B£19 dB&B⋒£23
☾ CTV 50P
▣Mainly grills ♧ ⊒ ✻Lunch £2.55–£2.65 Tea £2 High Tea £3.40–£7.25 Dinner £5.60–£9.20&alc Wine £3.60 Last dinner 7.30pm

★***Skyline*** 123 Irish St ☎(0387) 62416
Closed New Year's Day
6rm(2⇌⋒) CTV available on request ★ ꞗ
CTV 20P ⊞
Last dinner 8pm

★**Swan at Kingholm** Kingholm Quay ☎(0387) 53756
Small inn-style hotel near River Nith.
9rm sB&B£11.50 dB&B£20
CTV 40P ✽
V ♧ ✻Bar lunch £2.20–£4 High Tea £2.95–£5.50 Wine £3.20 Last high tea 7.30pm
Credit card ①

★**Winston** Rae St ☎(0387) 54433
RS 24 Dec–3 Jan
Red sandstone house standing in a residential area near the railway station and shops.
14rm (4fb) ✻sB&B fr£9.20 dB&B fr£18.40
CTV 6P
♧ ✻Lunch fr£3.50 Dinner £4.50 Last dinner 7.30pm

✕✕**Bruno's** Balmoral Rd ☎(0387) 55757
Closed Tue Lunch not served
Cosy atmosphere in the two separate eating areas.
▣British & Italian **V** 70 seats Dinner £7–£15&alc Wine £5 Last dinner 10pm P

DUNBAR
Lothian *East Lothian*
Map **12** NT67

★★*H* **Bayswell** Bayswell Park ☎(0368) 62225
12rm(8⇌1⋒) (2fb) CTV in all bedrooms ® sB&B£18–£24 sB&B⇌⋒£21–£27 dB&B£26–£30 dB&B⇌⋒£30–£36 ꞗ
20P ⊞ ✽
♧ Lunch £4–£9.50&alc Dinner £7.50–£12&alc Wine £4.75 Last dinner 8pm
Credit cards ① ③

DUNBLANE
Central *Perthshire*
Map **11** NN70

★★★**Stakis Dunblane Hydro** (Stakis) ☎(0786) 822551 Telex no 778704
Imposing, well modernised, 19th-century building where the atmosphere is always relaxed.
126⇌ CTV in all bedrooms ® ✻sB&B⇌ fr£31 dB&B⇌ fr£42 ꞗ
Lift ☾ 300P CFA ✽ ⊡(heated) ⚲ sauna bath Live music and dancing Mon–Sat (in season) ♿
▣English & French ♧ ⊒ Last dinner 9.30pm
Credit cards ① ② ③ ⑤ **VS**

DUNDEE
Tayside *Angus*
Map **11** NO33

★★★**Angus Thistle** 10 Marketgait (Thistle) ☎(0382) 26874 Telex no 76456
Modern hotel with attractive restaurant and cocktail bar and offering alternatives of pub meals or coffee shop snacks.
58rm(55⇌⋒) CTV in all bedrooms ® ✻sB⇌⋒£32–£40 (room only) dB⇌⋒£38–£44 (room only) ꞗ
Lift ☾ ⌗ ⊬ 18P CFA Live music and dancing Sat ♿
▣European ⊒ ✻Lunch £3.50–£5.50&alc Dinner £8&alc Last dinner 9.30pm
Credit cards ① ② ③ ④ ⑤ **VS**

☆☆☆**Invercarse** 371 Perth Rd, Ninewells ☎(0382) 69231 Telex no 76608
Extended private house, standing in its own grounds.
27rm(7⇌20⋒) (1fb) CTV in all bedrooms ® ✻sB&B⇌⋒£33.75 dB&B⇌⋒£39.50 ꞗ
☾ ⊬ 200P ✽
▣Scottish & French **V** ♧ ⊒ ✻Lunch £4.80–£5.50&alc Tea 60p High Tea £3.50–£5 Dinner £7–£7.70&alc Wine £5.35 Last dinner 9.45pm
Credit cards ① ② ③ ⑤ **VS**

☆☆☆**Swallow** Kingsway West, Invergowrie (3½m W off A972 Dundee Ring Road) (Swallow) ☎(0382) 641122 Telex no 53168
Closed 25–26 Dec & 1–2 Jan
69⇌⋒ (6fb) 2⊟ CTV in all bedrooms ®

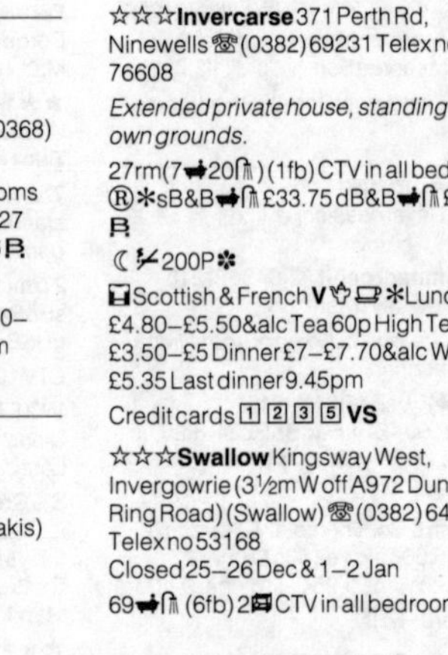

*sB&B🛁⛆£18.50–£34.50 dB&B🛁⛆£30–£48 B

☾ 90P ✽ (heated) sauna bath ♿

International V ☕ *Lunch £3.35–£4.25&alc Tea 50p–£2 Dinner £7.20–£7.65&alc Wine £4.75 Last dinner 9.45pm

Credit cards 1 2 3 5

★★**Queen's** 160 Nethergate ☎(0382) 22515

Friendly, traditional, hotel popular with businessmen.

56rm(11🛁1⛆)(2fb) CTV in all bedrooms Ⓡ sB£20 (room only) sB🛁⛆£26 (room only) dB£26 (room only) dB🛁⛆£33 (room only) B

Lift ☾ 40P

V ☕ Lunch £4.50–£6.50&alc Tea 65p–95p High Tea £4.50 Dinner £7.50 Wine £4.80 Last dinner 10pm

Credit cards 1 2 3 4 5

★★**Tay** Whitehall Cres ☎(0382) 21641 Telex no 57515

Large, commercial hotel close to the city's railway station.

87rm(30🛁)(3fb) CTV in all bedrooms Ⓡ sB&B£19.60–£21.80 sB&B🛁£25.40–£28.20 dB&B£30.10–£33.45 dB&B🛁£37.60–£41.80 B

Lift ☾ CFA ♿ *xmas*

☕ Lunch £4 Tea 60p Dinner £6.50 Wine £3.50 Last dinner 9.30pm

Credit cards 1 2 3 5

★★**Tay Park** Broughty Ferry (3m E A930) ☎(0382) 78924

Fine country mansion, in its own terraced grounds and commanding magnificent views of the River Tay estuary.

12rm(4🛁3⛆)(1fb) CTV in all bedrooms Ⓡ sB&B fr£18.15 sB&B🛁⛆ fr£19.15 dB&B fr£26 dB&B🛁⛆ fr£37 B

☾ 100P ✽

International V ☕ Lunch £5.60 Tea £1.40 High Tea fr£3.20 Dinner fr£7.80&alc Wine £4.80 Last dinner 9.30pm

Credit cards 1 2 3

DUNDONNELL

Highland *Ross & Cromarty*
Map **14** NH08

★★**Dundonnell** (Inter-Hotels/Minotel) ☎(085483) 204

Closed Nov–Mar

A comfortable, family run hotel standing close to Little Loch Broom.

24rm🛁⛆ (4fb) CTV in all bedrooms Ⓡ sB&B🛁⛆£17.50–£21 dB&B🛁⛆£30–£35

CTV 60P

☕ Lunch £4–£6 Tea fr£1.50 Dinner £8.50–£9.50 Wine £4.50 Last dinner 8.15pm

Credit cards 1 2 3 **VS**

DUNFERMLINE

Fife
Map **11** NT08

★★★ *B* **Keavil House** Crossford (2m W A994) ☎(0383) 736258 Telex no 728227

32rm(28🛁4⛆)(2fb) CTV in all bedrooms Ⓡ sB&B🛁⛆£20–£26 dB&B🛁⛆£34–£40 B

CTV 70P ✽

Scottish & French V ☕ Lunch £7.50alc Tea 50p–£2.50 High Tea £3.50–£6.50 Dinner fr£10 Wine £4 Last dinner 9pm

Credit cards 1 3

☆☆☆**King Malcolm Thistle** Queensferry Rd, Wester Pitcorthie (Thistle) ☎(0383) 722611 Telex no 727721

Modern low hotel built in a residential area on the outskirts of the town.

48🛁⛆ CTV in all bedrooms Ⓡ *sB🛁⛆£31–£38 (room only) dB🛁⛆£38–£43 (room only) B

☾ CTV 60P ✽

European ☕ *Lunch £4.95&alc Dinner £8.50alc Last dinner 9pm

Credit cards 1 2 3 4 5 **VS**

★★★**Pitfirrane Arms** Main St, Crossford (½m W A994) ☎(0383) 736132 Telex no 727709

Former coaching inn restored and greatly extended to provide modern standards.

31rm(20🛁11⛆) CTV in all bedrooms Ⓡ *sB&B🛁⛆ fr£22 dB&B🛁⛆ fr£36 B

☾ CTV 80P (grass) Live music and dancing Wed

☕ *Lunch £4.50&alc Tea 60p Dinner £8&alc Wine £3.25 Last dinner 9.15pm

Credit cards 1 2

★★**Brucefield** Woodmill Rd ☎(0383) 722199

Converted, Victorian mansion dating from 1845 and standing in its own grounds.

9rm(6🛁)(2fb) TV in 4 bedrooms sB&B£11.50 sB&B🛁£14.50 dB&B£20 dB&B🛁£27

CTV 60P

☕ Lunch fr£4.03 Tea fr£1.50 High Tea fr£4.03 Dinner fr£6.33 Wine £5 Last dinner 8pm

Credit card 1 **VS**

★★**City** 18 Bridge St ☎(0383) 722538

City centre hotel of considerable age standing on the main road in the shopping centre.

17rm(9🛁1⛆)(2fb) Ⓡ sB&B£15 sB&B🛁£17.50 dB&B£23.50 dB&B🛁£25 B

☾ CTV 35P

V ☕ Lunch £3.50 Tea £1.40 High Tea £2.90–£5.35 Dinner £7.50&alc Wine £3.45 Last dinner 9pm

Credit card 1

DUNHOLME

Lincolnshire
Map **8** TF07

☆☆**Four Seasons** Scothern Ln ☎Welton (0673) 60108

Restaurant/entertainment centre with a separate block of modern bedrooms, in rural area.

12rm(8🛁4⛆)(1fb) CTV in all bedrooms Ⓡ sB&B🛁⛆£20 dB&B🛁⛆£30 B

200P ✽

V ☕ Lunch £6.50alc Dinner £6.50&alc Wine £4.50 Last dinner 10pm

Credit cards 1 3

DUNKELD
Tayside *Perthshire*
Map **11** NO04

★★★ *L* ***Dunkeld House*** ☎(03502) 243
Impressive though relaxed country house standing in over 100 acres of magnificent woodland by the River Tay.
31rm(24 1) CTV in all bedrooms Ⓡ 100P 7 ✽ (hard) xmas
French Last dinner 9pm

★★ **Atholl Arms** Bridgehead (Minotels) ☎(03502) 219
Closed Xmas Day
Corner sited hotel overlooking the River Tay.
20rm(4) sB&B£11 sB&B£28 dB&B£22 dB&B£32 B
CTV 17P 2 ✽
Bar lunch £4alc Tea £1.50 Dinner £7.50&alc Wine £4.50 Last dinner 9pm
Credit cards 1 2 3 5 **VS**

★ **Taybank** Tay Ter ☎(03502) 340
Closed Nov–Feb
Modest, but friendly, country inn.
6rm (1fb) sB&B£11–£14 dB&B£22–£28
CTV 20P ✽
Bar lunch £1.10–£2.70 Dinner £6.50–£8 Wine £2.30 Last dinner 8pm

DUNMOW, GREAT
Essex
Map **5** TL62

★★ *L* **Saracen's Head** High St (Trusthouse Forte) ☎(0371) 3901
An 18th-century inn, with traces of the previous 17th-century building, facing the market square.
24 CTV in all bedrooms Ⓡ sB&B£39 dB&B£54.50 B
P xmas
Last dinner 10pm
Credit cards 1 2 3 4 5

✕✕ **Starr** Market Pl ☎(0371) 4321
(Rosette awarded for dinner only.)
A most attractive restaurant, quietly and efficiently serving good quality English and French cuisine.
Closed Mon, Aug & 2wks Xmas
Lunch not served Tue–Sat Dinner not served Sun
English & French **V** 50 seats Lunch £12 Dinner £17–£20alc Wine £6.25 Last dinner 9.30pm 20P
Credit cards 1 2 3 5 **VS**

DUNNET
Highland *Caithness*
Map **15** ND27

★★ **Northern Sands** ☎Barrock (084 785) 270
11rm(2 1) sB&B£11 sB&B£12 dB&B£22 dB&B£24
CTV 60P Live music and dancing Sat
Scottish & Italian **V** Bar lunch £1–£4.50 Tea 70p–£1.50 Dinner £6.50alc Last dinner 8.45pm

DUNOON
Strathclyde *Argyllshire*
Map **10** NS17

★★ **Abbeyhill** Dhailling Rd (Minotel) ☎(0369) 2204
Named after an old folly resembling an abbey, the hotel stands on a hillside, and has a tidy garden and excellent views.
15rm(8 7) (2fb) CTV in all bedrooms Ⓡ sB&B£20 dB&B£35
40P ✽
Lunch £1–£3 Tea 75p Dinner £7&alc Wine £4.75 Last dinner 8.30pm
Credit card 3

★★ **Argyll** ☎(0369) 2059
In central position overlooking the pier and offering modest accommodation at economical prices.
30rm(6) (4fb) CTV in all bedrooms Ⓡ sB&B fr£9.50 sB&B fr£11.20 dB&B fr£19 dB&B fr£22.40 B
Lunch fr£3.20 Tea fr40p High Tea fr£3.20 Dinner fr£6.50
Last dinner 8pm
Credit card 1 **VS**

★★ **Enmore** Marine Pde, Kirn ☎(0369) 2230
Closed Dec–mid Apr
16rm(5 2) (2fb) CTV available in bedrooms Ⓡ sB&B£16.50 dB&B£33 dB&B£40 B
CTV 15P ✽ squash
Scottish & French Lunch £2–£4 Tea fr£2 High Tea fr£5 Dinner fr£10 Wine £2.75 Last dinner 8.30pm
Credit card 4

★★ *BL* **Firpark** Ardnadam (3m N A815) ☎Sandbank (036985) 210
A small, well appointed hotel with wood panelled drawing room and individually decorated bedrooms, at Lanzaretto Point by the Holy Loch.
6rm(2 2) CTV in all bedrooms Ⓡ sB&B£15 sB&B£16.50–£19.75 dB&B£25–£27.50 dB&B£30–£35 B
CTV 40P ✽
French **V** Lunch £5.75alc Tea 75palc Dinner £9.50–£12alc Wine £4.75 Last dinner 9pm
Credit card 3

★★ ***Royal Marine*** Sea Front, Hunters Quay (2m N A815) ☎(0369) 3001
A substantial, stone building with a mock-Tudor frontage.
34rm(2) Annexe: 10rm(9) CTV in 15 bedrooms B
CTV 40P ✽ billiards Disco Fri & Sat
Last dinner 9pm
S% Credit cards 1 3 **VS**

DUNSTABLE
Bedfordshire
Map **4** TL02

★★★ ***Old Palace Lodge*** Church St ☎(0582) 62201 Closed Boxing Day
A roadside, ivy-clad building, that was part of the original Dunstable Palace.
16rm(14) 2
CTV 74P ✽ xmas
V Last dinner 10pm
Credit cards 1 2 3 5 **VS**

★★**Highwayman** London Rd ☎(0582) 61999
Closed Xmas
Modest commercial hotel.
26rm(14⇌12⋒) CTV in all bedrooms Ⓡ
✱sB&B⇌⋒£18.50 dB&B⇌⋒£28 B
☾ # 50P
Dinner £5.40alc Last dinner 9pm
Credit cards 1 2 3 5

DUNSTER
Somerset
Map **3** SS94
★★★*H* **Luttrell Arms** High St (Trusthouse Forte) ☎(064382) 555
This traditional, holiday and touring hotel of character, has modern amenities, and dates from the 14th century.
21⇌ 4 CTV in all bedrooms Ⓡ
sB&B⇌£35.50 dB&B⇌£52.50 B
2 ✽ *xmas*
Last dinner 9.30pm
Credit cards 1 2 3 4 5

★★*HL* **Exmoor House** West St ☎(064382) 268
Closed Jan
Small, comfortable hotel in the town.
6rm(1⇌3⋒) (1fb) CTV in 3 bedrooms
sB&B£15 sB&B⇌⋒£17 dB&B£26 dB&B⇌⋒£30 B
☾ CTV ✽ *xmas*
English & French **V** Lunch £3.50&alc Tea £1 Dinner £8&alc Wine £3.95
Last dinner 9pm
Credit cards 1 2 3 5 **VS**

DUNTOCHER
Strathclyde *Dunbartonshire*
Map **11** NS47
★★**Maltings** Dumbarton Rd ☎(0389) 75371
Small modern hotel with distillery theme in bars.
28⇌ (2fb) CTV in all bedrooms Ⓡ
sB&B⇌£18 dB&B⇌£27 B
☾ CTV 200P ✽ Live music and dancing twice wkly Cabaret twice wkly *xmas*
Scottish, English, French & Italian **V** ✱Lunch £3–£5&alc Tea £1.50–£2.50 High Tea £2–£3 Dinner £6–£10&alc Wine £4.75 Last dinner 10pm
Credit cards 1 2 3 4 5

DUNTULM
Isle of Skye, Highland *Inverness-shire*
Map **13** NG47
★*L* ***Duntulm Castle*** ☎(047052) 213
Closed mid Oct–mid Apr RS mid Apr–end Apr
Attractive, family run hotel situated close to secluded bay overlooking castle ruins.
15rm(2⇌) Annexe: 13rm(3⇌2⋒) B
TV 40P
Scottish **V**
Last dinner 8.30pm
VS

DUNVEGAN
Isle of Skye, Highland *Inverness-shire*
Map **13** NG24
★★***Dunvegan*** ☎(047022) 202 Closed Nov–Mar
6rm Ⓡ
CTV 60P ✽ Live music and dancing Cabaret
Last dinner 9pm
Credit cards 1 2 3

DURHAM
Co Durham
Map **12** NZ24
★★★★**Royal County** Old Elvet (Swallow) ☎(0385) 66821 Telex no 538238
Overlooking the river, this historic hotel has a Georgian façade and a new bedroom wing.
119rm(118⇌1⋒) (11fb) 1 CTV in all bedrooms Ⓡ ✱sB&B⇌⋒£33 dB&B⇌⋒£45 B
Lift ☾ 120P CFA sauna bath ♿
French **V** ✱Lunch £5.75&alc Tea 90p High Tea £2.50 Dinner £8&alc Wine £4.75 Last dinner 10.15pm
S% Credit cards 1 2 3 4 5

★★★***Bowburn Hall*** Bowburn (3m SE junc A177/A1(M)) ☎(0385) 770311
Standing in own grounds, hotel has well-appointed bedrooms and most attractive dining room and lounge.
20rm(16⇌⋒) CTV in all bedrooms B
50P ✽
English & French Last dinner 9.30pm
Credit cards 1 2 3 4 5

☆☆☆**Bridge** Croxdale (2¼m S off A167) ☎(0385) 780524 Telex no 538156
Modern chalet accommodation is to be found in the courtyard behind the original inn, which houses the restaurant and bar.
Annexe: 46⇌ CTV in all bedrooms Ⓡ
✱sB&B⇌£14–£23 dB&B⇌£25–£29.50 B
☾ 60P
✱Lunch £4.50–£5.50 Tea £1–£1.75 Dinner £6.50–£7.50&alc Wine £4.95 Last dinner 9.45pm
Credit cards 1 2 3 5

★★★**Ramside Hall** Belmont (3m NE A690) ☎(0385) 65282 Telex no 537681
Converted country house with spacious, comfortable bars and set in 80 acres of parkland.
11rm(5⇌) CTV in all bedrooms sB&B£21 sB&B⇌£23 dB&B£30 dB&B⇌£32
CTV 500P ✽ Disco Mon Live music and dancing Sun, Wed, Thu & Fri *xmas*
English & French Lunch £5.50 Tea 40p Dinner £7.75–£9 Last dinner 9.30pm
Credit cards 1 2 3 5

★★★**Three Tuns** New Elvet (Swallow) ☎(0385) 64326
51⇌⋒ (4fb) 1 CTV in all bedrooms Ⓡ
✱sB&B⇌⋒£28.50 dB&B⇌⋒£36.50 B
☾ 35P CFA
✱Lunch fr£5 Tea fr55p High Tea fr£1.75 Dinner fr£6.95 Wine £4.50 Last dinner 9.30pm
Credit cards 1 2 3 4 5

✕**Squire Trelawny** 80 Front St, Sherburn Village (3m E off A181) ☎(0385) 720613
Closed Sun & Mon Lunch not served
English & French 30 seats ✱Dinner £9alc Wine £4.10 Last dinner 9.45pm
Credit cards 1 2 3 5

✕***Travellers Rest*** 72 Claypath ☎(0385) 65370
A quaint, old world inn with an intimate first floor restaurant.
Closed Sun Lunch not served
French 46 seats Last dinner 9.30pm
Credit cards 1 2 3 5

DUROR
Highland *Argyllshire*
Map **14** NM95
★★*L* **Stewart** (Best Western) ☎(063174) 268 Telex no 778866 Closed Nov–Mar
29rm(21⇌) (6fb) TV in 2 bedrooms Ⓡ
sB&B⇌£19–£27.50 dB&B⇌£27–£44
Continental breakfast B
CTV 50P ✽ Live music wkly
V Bar lunch fr£1.50 Tea fr50p Dinner £10.25 Wine £4.40 Last dinner 8.30pm
Credit cards 1 2 3 5 **VS**

DYKE
Lincolnshire
Map **8** TF12
★***Wishing Well*** ☎Bourne (07782) 2970
Closed Xmas
Quiet, country inn on the edge of the Fens.
8rm(2⋒) TV in 1 bedroom
CTV 50P
Mainly grills Last dinner 10.30pm

EAGLESHAM
Strathclyde *Renfrewshire*
Map **11** NS55
★★**Eglinton Arms** Gilmour St (Scottish & Newcastle) ☎(03553) 2631
Attractive and popular inn in centre of picturesque village.
13⇌ CTV in all bedrooms Ⓡ
sB&B⇌£26.50 dB&B⇌£34 B
☾ 50P Disco Sun Live music and dancing Mon
French **V** Lunch £1.75–£5 Dinner fr£6.90&alc Wine £4.20 Last dinner 9.30pm
Credit cards 1 2 3 5

✕✕**Pepper Pot**, Cross Keys Inn ☎(03553) 2002
Attractive first floor restaurant facing village green.
Closed Sun, Xmas Day & New Years Day
Scottish & French **V** 70 seats ✻Lunch fr£6.30&alc
Dinner £12alc Wine £4.85 Last dinner 10pm 30P
Credit cards 1 3

EARLS COLNE
Essex
Map **5** TL82
✕**Drapers House** High St ☎(07875) 2484
Closed Mon Lunch not served Sat Dinner not served Sun
International **V** 60 seats ✻Lunch £4.25&alc Dinner £7&alc Wine £3.80 Last dinner 9pm 14P
Credit cards 1 2 3 5

EARL SHILTON
Leicestershire
Map **4** SP49
★***Fernleigh*** 32 Wood St ☎(0455) 47011
Closed 26–31 Dec
12rm(1→11⋒) CTV in all bedrooms Ⓡ
12P
English & French **V** Last dinner 9.30pm
Credit cards 1 3

EASINGWOLD
North Yorkshire
Map **8** SE56
★★**George** Market Pl ☎(0347) 21698
Closed Xmas Day
A former coaching inn.
18rm(1→2⋒) (1fb) CTV in all bedrooms Ⓡ sB&B→⋒ fr£14 dB&B→⋒ fr£24 B
Lunch fr£4 Tea fr£1.95 Dinner £6.50 Last dinner 9.30pm
Credit card 3

EASTBOURNE
East Sussex
Map **5** TV69
See plan
★★★★★**Grand** King Edwards Pde (DeVere) ☎(0323) 22611 Telex no 87332
Plan **7** *D1*
Large and impressive Victorian sea front hotel.
178→ CTV in all bedrooms
✻sB&B→£36.75 dB&B→£63 B
Lift ☾ 100P CFA ✻ (heated) in summer billiards Live music and dancing Wed, Fri & Sat Cabaret Wed (in summer) *xmas*
International **V** ✻Lunch £10.50&alc Tea £2.60 Dinner £12.60&alc Wine £5.50 Last dinner 9.30pm
Credit cards 1 2 3 4 5

★★★★**Cavendish** Grand Pde (De Vere) ☎(0323) 27401 Telex no 87579
Plan **2** *D1*
Luxury hotel in fine position, popular for conferences and holidays.
115→ CTV in all bedrooms
✻sB&B→£35.70 dB&B→£60 B
Lift ☾ 40P CFA Live music and dancing Sat Cabaret Wed (in summer) *xmas*
French ✻Lunch £9.45&alc Tea £2.65 Dinner £11&alc Wine £5.50 Last dinner 9.30pm
Credit cards 1 2 3 4 5

★★★★*H* **Queens** Marine Pde (DeVere) ☎(0323) 22822 Telex no 877736
Plan **16** *D2*
Imposing, late-Victorian, six-storey building, situated on an island site facing the sea.
108→ CTV in all bedrooms
✻sB&B→£27.30 dB&B→£48.30 B
Lift ☾ 90P CFA billiards Live music and dancing Wed & Sat (Jun–Sep) Cabaret Wed (Jun–Sep) *xmas*
English & French ✻Lunch £8.40&alc Tea £2.60 Dinner £10&alc
Wine £5.50 Last dinner 8.30pm
Credit cards 1 2 3 4 5

★★★**Chatsworth** Grand Pde ☎(0323) 30327 Plan **3** *D1*
Closed Jan & Feb RS Nov, Dec (except Xmas) & Mar
Four-storey building with sun terrace overlooking the sea, situated between the pier and the bandstand.
45rm(14→31⋒) (1fb) CTV in all bedrooms sB&B→⋒£18.40–£20.70 dB&B→⋒£36.80–£41.40 B
Lift ☾ CTV CFA *xmas*
Lunch fr£5.60 Tea fr60p Dinner fr£6.90 Last dinner 8pm
Credit card 1 **VS**

★★★**Cumberland** Grand Pde ☎(0323) 30342 Plan **4** *D1*
Nicely appointed hotel with enclosed sun terrace and sea views.
71rm(65→6⋒) (2fb) CTV in all bedrooms sB&B→⋒£19–£24 dB&B→⋒£36–£42 B
Lift ☾ CTV CFA Live music and dancing 6 nights wkly in summer *xmas*
English & French ✻Lunch £4.03 Dinner £6.33 Wine £3 Last dinner 8.15pm

★★★*L* **Imperial** Devonshire Pl ☎(0323) 20525 Plan **8** *D1*
Comfortable and comprehensively equipped hotel with conference facilities.
115rm(66→2⋒) (1fb) CTV in all bedrooms sB&B fr£19 sB&B→⋒ fr£22 dB&B fr£34 dB&B→⋒ fr£40 B
Lift ☾ 12P CFA Live music and dancing twice wkly *xmas*
English & Continental Lunch fr£6 Tea fr60p Dinner fr£7 Wine £4 Last dinner 7.45pm
Credit cards 1 2 3 5 **VS**

★★★*L* **Lansdowne** King Edward's Pde (Best Western) ☎(0323) 25174
Plan **10** *D1*
Closed 1–19 Jan
Comfortable hospitable hotel facing sea. →

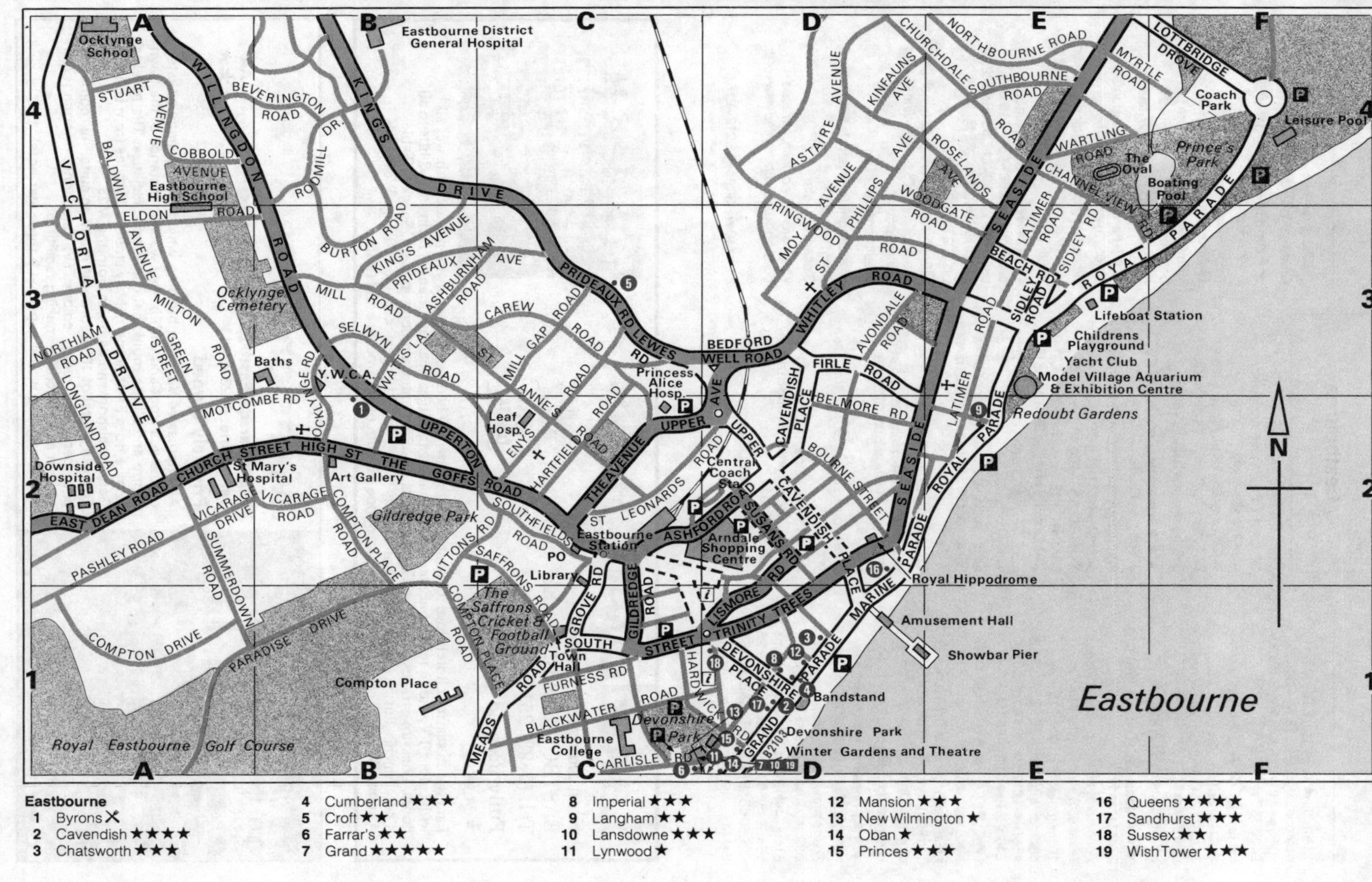
Eastbourne
Eastbourne District General Hospital
Ocklynge School
Eastbourne High School
Ocklynge Cemetery
Baths
Y.W.C.A.
St Mary's Hospital
Art Gallery
Downside Hospital
Gildredge Park
Leaf Hosp.
Princess Alice Hosp.
Central Coach Sta.
Eastbourne Station
Arndale Shopping Centre
PO
Library
The Saffrons Cricket & Football Ground
Town Hall
Compton Place
Eastbourne College
Devonshire Park
Royal Eastbourne Golf Course
Royal Hippodrome
Amusement Hall
Showbar Pier
Bandstand
Devonshire Park
Winter Gardens and Theatre
Lifeboat Station
Childrens Playground
Yacht Club
Model Village Aquarium & Exhibition Centre
Redoubt Gardens
Coach Park
Leisure Pool
Prince's Park
The Oval
Boating Pool
N

Eastbourne

1 Byrons ✕
2 Cavendish ★★★★
3 Chatsworth ★★★
4 Cumberland ★★★
5 Croft ★★
6 Farrar's ★★
7 Grand ★★★★★
8 Imperial ★★★
9 Langham ★★
10 Lansdowne ★★★
11 Lynwood ★
12 Mansion ★★★
13 New Wilmington ★
14 Oban ★
15 Princes ★★★
16 Queens ★★★★
17 Sandhurst ★★★
18 Sussex ★★
19 Wish Tower ★★★

E

E

137rm(68→12⋒)(5fb) CTV in all bedrooms Ⓡ sB&B£15.50–£22.25 sB&B→⋒£17.50–£25.25 dB&B£31–£40 dB&B→⋒£35–£46.50 Ḃ

Lift ☾ ⅟ CTV 20⌂ CFA billiards *xmas*

♆ ☕ Lunch fr£5.50&alc Tea fr65p High Tea fr£3.25 Dinner fr£7&alc Wine £4.25 Last dinner 8.30pm

S% Credit cards 1 3 **VS**

★★★**Mansion** Grand Pde ☎(0323) 27411 Plan **12** *D1*

Four-storey building, with enclosed sun terrace, overlooking the sea.

103rm(60→2⋒)(10fb) CTV in all bedrooms Ⓡ ✱ sB&B£15.50–£23.50 sB&B→⋒£17.50–£25.50 dB&B£30–£46 dB&B→⋒£34–£50 Ḃ

Lift ☾ ₱ CFA Live music and dancing twice wkly *xmas*

▣ English & French **V** ♆ ☕ Lunch £4.75 Tea 95p Dinner £5.75 Wine £4.50 Last dinner 8.30pm

Credit cards 1 2 3 5 **VS**

★★★**Princes** Lascelles Ter (Inter-Hotel) ☎(0323) 22056 Plan **15** *D1*

Four-storey, late Victorian, terraced building, just off the sea-front.

51rm(34→)(5fb) CTV in all bedrooms Ⓡ sB&B£15.50–£17.50 sB&B→£19.25–£21.50 dB&B£29–£33 dB&B→£36.50–£41 Ḃ

Lift ☾ CTV ₱ CFA Live music and dancing wkly *xmas*

♆ ☕ Lunch £5alc Tea 70palc Dinner £7.50alc Wine £4 Last dinner 8.30pm

S% Credit cards 1 2 3 **VS**

★★★**Sandhurst** Grand Pde ☎(0323) 27868 Plan **17** *D1*

Well-appointed hotel overlooking the sea.

64rm(26→6⋒)(2fb) CTV in all bedrooms ✻sB&B£15.53–£20.13 sB&B→⋒£16.68–£22.43 dB&B£31.06–£40.26 dB&B→⋒£33.36–£44.86 Ḃ

Lift ☾ CFA ⇎ Live music and dancing wkly ⌂ *xmas*

▣ International **V** ♆ ☕ ✻Lunch £5 Tea 95p Dinner £6.50 Wine £3.80 Last dinner 8.30pm

Credit cards 2 5 **VS**

★★★**Wish Tower** King Edward's Pde (Trusthouse Forte) ☎(0323) 22676 Plan **19** *D1*

Three houses converted to form this sea front hotel.

74rm(40→) CTV in all bedrooms Ⓡ sB&B£25 sB&B→£31.50 dB&B£42 dB&B→£49 Ḃ

Lift ☾ CTV 3⌂ ⇎ CFA *xmas*

♆ ☕ Last dinner 8.30pm

Credit cards 1 2 3 4 5

★★*Croft* 18 Prideaux Rd ☎(0323) 642291 Plan **5** *C3*

Mock Tudor house with modern bedrooms and delightful restaurant.

10rm(8→) CTV in 1 bedroom TV in 7 bedrooms

CTV P ⇎ ✽ ≈(heated) ⚲(hard)

★★*H* **Farrar's** 3–5 Wilmington Gdns ☎(0323) 23737 Plan **6** *C1*

White, five-storey, late Victorian building with a modern entrance, situated just off the sea front.

44rm(24→6⋒)(21fb) CTV in 30 bedrooms sB&B£14.50–£16.50 sB&B→⋒£15.50–£17.50 dB&B£29–£33 dB&B→⋒£31–£35 Ḃ

Lift ☾ CTV 26P *xmas*

▣ English & French **V** ♆ ☕ Lunch £4&alc Tea 45p Dinner £5.50–£6 Wine £3 Last dinner 8pm

Credit cards 1 2 3

★★**Langham** Royal Pde ☎(0323) 31451 Plan **9** *E2*

Closed Nov–Mar

Three-storey, Victorian, terraced building, with uninterrupted views of the sea.

84rm(40→)(3fb) sB&B£12–£16

sB&B🛁£14.50–£24 dB&B£24–£36 dB&B🛁£26–£40 Ⓑ

Lift ☾ CTV 3⌂ Live music and dancing twice wkly Cabaret wkly

V ♧ ☕ Lunch £5 Tea fr60p Dinner £6.50 Wine £3.05 Last dinner 7.30pm

★★**Sussex** Cornfield Ter ☎(0323) 27681 Plan **18** *D1*

A predominantly commercial hotel with a garden style restaurant.

32rm (4fb) TV in all bedrooms ★ sB&B£15.50–£16.50 dB&B£23–£24 Ⓑ

Lift ☾ CTV ⚑ *xmas*

▣ English V ✻ Lunch £3.95&alc Dinner £3.95&alc Wine £4.40 Last dinner 8.30pm

Credit cards 1 2 3 4 5

★**Lynwood** 31–39 Jevington Gdns ☎(0323) 23982 Plan **11** *D1*

Family run hotel with comfortable lounges and well equipped bedrooms.

76rm (22🛁 1🚿) (4fb) CTV in 26 bedrooms sB&B£13.75–£19.50 sB&B🛁🚿£15.50–£21.50 dB&B£27.50–£39 dB&B🛁🚿£31–£43 Ⓑ

Lift ☾ CTV 5P 4⌂ nc2yrs *xmas*

♧ ☕ Lunch £4.50 Tea 60p Dinner £6.50 Wine £3.95 Last dinner 7.45pm

Credit card 1

★**New Wilmington** 25 Compton St ☎(0323) 21219 Plan **13** *D1*

Closed Nov–Feb (except Xmas)

Friendly family run hotel.

30rm (13🛁 5🚿) (4fb) Ⓡ

Lift CTV ⚑

VS

E

E

★***Oban*** King Edward's Pde ☎(0323) 31581 Plan **14** *D1*
Closed Nov–Mar
Family run sea front hotel close to theatres and shops.
28➡⋒®Ⓑ
Lift ☾ CTV
V Last dinner 7pm

✕**Byrons** 6 Crown St, Old Town ☎(0323) 20171 Plan **1** *B2*
Restaurant with a romantic French air complementing the cuisine.
French 20 seats ✻Lunch £10.50alc Dinner £10.50alc Wine £5.25 Last dinner 10.30pm
S% Credit cards 3 5

EAST CHINNOCK
Somerset
Map **3** ST41
★**Barrows Country House** Weston St ☎West Coker (093586) 2390
Closed 25 Dec–1 Jan
Attractive, peaceful house in quiet situation and with friendly atmosphere.
6rm sB&B£9.25 dB&B£18.50
CTV 6P ✻ nc5yrs
Lunch £2 Dinner £4.50&alc Wine £3.90 Last dinner 5pm

EAST GRINSTEAD
West Sussex
Map **5** TQ33
★★★**Felbridge Hotel and Health Club** London Rd ☎(0342) 26992 Telex no 95156 Gatwick plan **6A**
Well appointed comfortable hotel with adjacent health and leisure club.
48➡⋒ (10fb) 3 CTV in all bedrooms ®
sB&B➡⋒£28 dB&B➡⋒£32–£45 Ⓑ
☾ 600P CFA ✻ (heated) billiards sauna bath Roller disco 3 nights wkly
English & French ✻Lunch £6.25–£6.50 Tea fr£1 Dinner £7.50–£9&alc Wine £5 Last dinner 9pm
S% Credit cards 1 2 3 4 5

EAST HADDON
Northamptonshire
Map **4** SP66
✕✕***Buckby Lion*** ☎(060 125) 393
Closed Mon Dinner not served Sun
English & French 80 seats Last dinner 10pm 100P Disco Fri
Credit cards 1 2 3

★★★

★★★GRAVETYE MANOR, EAST GRINSTEAD
(3m SW off unclass road joining B2110 & B2028) ☎Sharpthorne (0342) 810567 Telex no 957239
Gatwick plan **14**

A great favourite with our inspectors, our members and other guides, some say this is the very nicest country house hotel in England. The creation of Mr Peter Herbert, he has developed this lovely hotel over the years to a very high standard indeed. His staff are helpful and friendly; qualities which help to form the uniquely relaxed atmosphere which prevails here. Naturally, his efforts have been aided by the magnificent Elizabethian mansion and its superb gardens designed by William Robertson, and lovingly maintained by Mr Herbert. There is also a lake and the whole place is set in 1,000 acres of rolling Sussex countryside, yet this idyllic place is within 30 miles of London!
The interior is filled with the aroma of blazing log fires, and the sitting rooms are appropriately and comfortably furnished with antiques, fresh flowers and lots of magazines. The ambience here, however, has to be experienced to be believed. The bedrooms, named after English trees, are well done, with cheerful soft furnishings and comfortable furniture as well as good quality accessories and other thoughtful little touches. There is a club bar (automatic membership for residents) and it is pleasant to enjoy a drink here while choosing a meal from the à la carte menu. The chef, Allan Garth, cooks in the modern style and thoroughly deserves our rosette. The menu is quite extensive and fine produce is used. His standards are high and continue to improve so we hope we shall be able to justify two rosettes next year! All in all a complete hotel in which it is a great experience to stay.
14rm (12➡2⋒) 1 CTV in all bedrooms sB➡⋒£44–£55 dB➡⋒£55–£107 (room only)
30P ✻ nc7yrs
English & French Lunch £20alc Tea £1.05 Dinner £20alc Wine £6.20 Last dinner 9.30pm

EAST HORSLEY
Surrey
Map **4** TQ05
★★★**Thatchers** Epsom Rd (Best Western) ☎(04865) 4291 Telex no 265933
Set in 4 acres, this hotel has modern bedrooms and imaginative cooking.
30➡ 2 CTV in all bedrooms ®
sB&B➡£37 dB&B➡£52.50–£59 Ⓑ
☾ 120P ✻ (heated) Live music and dancing Sat *xmas*

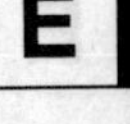

▣International V🍷☕Lunch £6.50&alc Tea £1.50–£2.50 Dinner £9&alc Wine £5.95 Last dinner 9.30pm
Credit cards 1 2 3 5

EAST KILBRIDE
Strathclyde *Lanarkshire*
Map **11** NS65

☆☆☆**Bruce** Cornwall St (Swallow) ☎(03552) 29771 Telex no 778428
This modern, custom-built, hotel forms part of the New Town complex.
84🛁🚿 (6fb) CTV in all bedrooms ® sB&B🛁🚿 fr£36 dB&B🛁🚿 fr£46 B
Lift ☾ ##25 CFA Disco Sun
V🍷☕Lunch fr£4&alc Dinner fr£7&alc Wine £5 Last dinner 9.45pm
Credit cards 1 2 3 4 5

☆☆☆**Stuart Thistle** Cornwall Way (Thistle) ☎(03552) 21161 Telex no 778504
Modern hotel in town centre.
30rm(26🛁4🚿) CTV in all bedrooms ® ✻sB🛁🚿 £30–£35 dB🛁🚿 £32–£38 (room only) B
Lift ☾ ⊘CTV ⊘
▣European ✻Lunch £6.50alc Dinner £7.25&alc Last dinner 9.15pm
Credit cards 1 2 3 4 5 VS

EASTLEIGH
Hampshire
Map **4** SU41

☆☆☆**Crest** Leigh Rd, Passfield Av (Crest) ☎(0703) 619700
Attractive modern hotel with friendly service and choice of restaurants.
120🛁 CTV in all bedrooms ® ✻sB🛁 fr£36 (room only) dB🛁 fr£45 (room only) B
Lift ☾ ⊘P
▣International V🍷☕✻Lunch £5.50–£7&alc Tea 75p–95p High Tea £2.50–£4 Dinner £7–£9.50&alc Wine £6.50 Last dinner 9.30pm
Credit cards 1 2 3 4 5 VS

EAST MOLESEY
Surrey London plan **5** *B1* (page 420)

✕✕**Lantern** 20 Bridge Rd ☎01-979 1531
Tastefully decorated restaurant with conservatory, run by chef-patron and his wife.
Closed Sun, last 3wks Aug & Public hols Lunch not served
▣French 50 seats ✻Dinner £8.95–£12.50&alc Wine £4.75 Last dinner 11pm ⊘
S% Credit cards 1 2 3 5

✕**Le Chien Qui Fume** 107 Walton Rd ☎01-979 7150
Closed Sun, Mon & Public hols
▣French 50 seats Lunch £5&alc Dinner £10.50alc Wine £5 Last dinner 11pm ⊘
Credit cards 1 2 3 5

EAST PORTLEMOUTH
Devon
Map **3** SX73

★★**Gara Rock** ☎Salcombe (054884) 2342
RS Nov–Mar
Converted coastguard cottages with superb sea views and pleasant gardens.
24rm(7🛁6🚿) (8fb) ✻sB&B £15–£18.50 dB&B £17–£18 dB&B🛁🚿 £17–£20 B
CTV 100P ⊘ ✽ ≈ (heated) 🎾(hard) Disco wkly
▣International V🍷☕✻Bar lunch £2.10–£4.95 Tea 45p–£1.50 Dinner £10.50&alc Wine £4.90 Last dinner 8.30pm
Credit cards 1 3

EAST PRESTON
West Sussex
Map **4** TQ00

★**Three Crowns** 101 Sea Rd ☎Rustington (09062) 4074
Pub hotel with comfortable bedrooms and specialising in grill meals.
10rm (2fb) ® sB&B £9.50 dB&B £19 B
CTV 60P
▣Mainly grills 🍷Lunch £3.50–£4.50&alc Dinner £3.50–£4.50&alc Wine £2.60 Last dinner 9pm
Credit card 3

✕✕**Old Forge** The Street ☎Rustington (09062) 2040
Restaurant retains Victorian character from when it was the home of E. Hardy the water colourist.
Closed Mon Dinner not served Sun
▣English & French V 75 seats ✻Lunch £4.50–£5.15&alc Dinner £10alc Wine £4.50 Last dinner 10pm 24P
S% Credit cards 1 2 3 4 5

EASTWOOD
Nottinghamshire
Map **8** SK44

★**Sun Inn** ☎Langley Mill (07737) 2940
17rm sB&B £12 dB&B £24 B
CTV 50P ✽
▣English & Italian V🍷☕Lunch £3–£4.50&alc Tea £1.20&alc Dinner £4–£7.50 Wine £2.90 Last dinner 7.30pm

EATHORPE
Warwicks
Map **4** SP36

★★**Eathorpe Park** Fosse Way ☎Marton (0926) 632245 Closed Xmas night
Large, early-Victorian building situated amid eleven acres of woodland.
9rm(1🛁4🚿) (1fb) sB&B £19.25 sB&B🛁🚿 £21.25 dB&B £29.50 dB&B🛁🚿 £32.50 B
⊘CTV 200P ✽ Live music and dancing one Sat per month

🍷Lunch £4.95&alc Dinner £8.50alc Wine £3.95 Last dinner 9.45pm
Credit cards 1 2 3

EDDLESTON
Borders *Peeblesshire*
Map **11** NT24

✕✕**Horse Shoe Inn** ☎(07213) 225
Attractive country restaurant also renowned for bar meals.
▣Scottish & French V 60 seats ✻Lunch £4.25–£8.95&alc Dinner £6.95–£13.95&alc Wine £5.40 Last dinner 10pm 50P
Credit cards 1 2 3 5

EDENHALL
Cumbria
Map **12** NY53

★★**Edenhall** ☎Langwathby (076881) 454
The hotel dining room, with its large expanse of windows, offers fine views of the garden.
31🛁🚿 ⊘ sB&B🛁🚿 £13.20 dB&B🛁🚿 £25 B
CTV 60P 3 ⊘ ✽ *xmas*
V🍷☕Lunch £3.75&alc Tea 65p–£1.50 High Tea fr£3.60 Dinner £6.50&alc Last dinner 9pm
Credit cards 1 2 3 5

EDINBURGH
Lothian *Midlothian*
Map **11** NT27
See plan

★★★★*L* **Caledonian** Princes St ☎031-225 2433 Telex no 72179 Central plan **8** *B4*
262rm(217🛁36🚿) (9fb) CTV in all bedrooms sB🛁🚿 £35–£49 dB🛁🚿 £48–£70 (room only) B
Lift ☾ 100P CFA Live music and dancing nightly *xmas* ♿
▣International 🍷☕Lunch £8–£15 Tea £3.50 Dinner £8&alc Wine £5.50 Last dinner 11pm
Credit cards 1 2 3 4 5

★★★★**George** George St (Forum) ☎031-225 1251 Telex no 72570 Central plan **15A** *D5*
Tastefully modernised, traditional hotel with a magnificent dining room and elegant French restaurant.
196🛁 CTV available in bedrooms ® sB&B🛁 £33–£45 dB&B🛁 £46–£62
Lift ☾ 24P CFA *xmas*
▣British & French V🍷☕Lunch £8.40–£8.75 Tea £2.50 Dinner £8.40&alc Wine £5.75 Last dinner 10pm
Credit cards 1 2 3 4 5

☆☆☆☆**Ladbroke Dragonara** Bells Mills, Belford Rd (Ladbroke) ☎031-332 2545 Telex no 727979 Central plan **22** *A5*
Modern hotel, built on the site of an old →

E

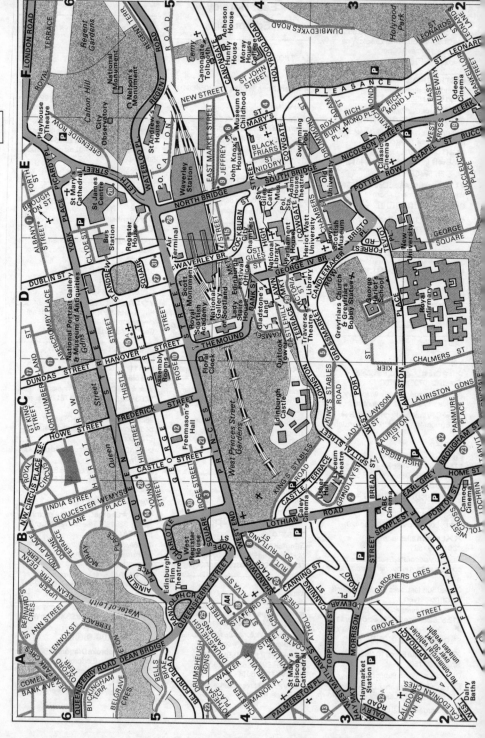

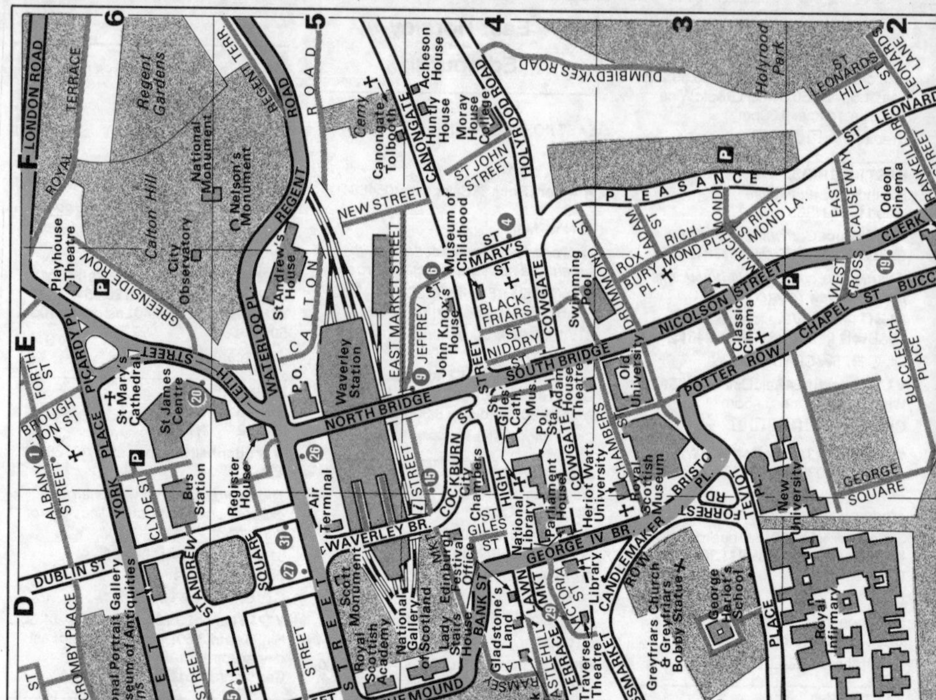

Edinburgh Central
1 Albany ★★
2 Alcove ✕
3 Alp-Horn ✕✕
4 L'Auberge ✕✕
5 Beehive ✕✕
6 Blacks ✕✕
7 Bruntsfield ★★★
8 Caledonian ★★★★
9 Carlton ★★★
10 Casa Española ✕
11 Le Caveau ✕
12 Chumleys ✕✕
13 Clarendon ★★
14 Denzier's ✕✕
15 Doric Tavern ✕
15A George ★★★★
16 Handsel ✕✕
17 Howard ★★★
18 Howtowdie ✕✕
19 Kalpna ✕
20 King James Thistle ☆☆☆
21 Kobe's ✕✕
22 Ladbroke Dragonara ☆☆☆
23 Lafayette ✕
24 Nimmo's ✕
25 No 10 ✕✕
26 North British ★★★★
27 Old Waverley ★★★
28 Ristorante Cosmo ✕✕✕
29 Ristorante Milano ✕✕
30 Roxburghe ★★★
31 St Andrew ★★
32 Shamiana ❀✕
32A Verandah Tandoori ✕

mill, and incorporating one of the original buildings.

146🛁🚿 (3fb) CTV in all bedrooms ® sB🛁🚿 fr£43 dB🛁🚿 fr£60 (room only) ▣

Lift ☾ 89P 3🚗 CFA

🍴International ☕ Last dinner 10.30pm

Credit cards [1] [2] [3] [5]

See advert on page 246

★★★★**North British** Princes St ☎031-556 2414 Telex no 72332 Central plan **26** *E5*

193rm(171🛁) (13fb) CTV in all bedrooms *sB🛁£29.50–£33 dB🛁£42.50–£50 (room only) ▣

Lift ☾ 🎵 Cabaret 6 nights wkly (summer) *xmas*

🍴International ☕ Lunch £8alc Tea £3.50 Dinner fr£8&alc Wine £5.50 Last dinner 10pm

Credit cards [1] [2] [3] [4] [5]

☆☆☆☆**Royal Scot** 111 Glasgow Rd (Swallow) ☎031-334 9191 Telex no 727197 District plan **51**

251🛁🚿 (58fb) CTV in all bedrooms ® sB&B🛁🚿£18.70–£42 dB&B🛁🚿£27.50–£55 ▣

Lift ☾ 🏊(heated) 300P CFA sauna bath 🌬 *xmas*

🍴English & French **V** ☕ Lunch £6.95–£7.95 Dinner £7.95–£12alc Wine £4.75 Last dinner 10.30pm

S% Credit cards [1] [2] [3] [4] [5]

★★★***Albany*** 39–43 Albany St (Best Western) ☎031-556 0397 Central plan **1** *E6*

The restored Georgian façade is a feature of this 'new-town' hotel – 5 minutes from Princes Street.

22rm(16🛁6🚿) CTV in all bedrooms ☾

☕ Last dinner 10pm

Credit cards [1] [2] [3] [5]

★★★**Barnton Thistle** Queensferry Rd, Barnton (Thistle) ☎031-339 1144 Telex no 727928 District plan **33**

Traditional building which has been modernised and extended.

50rm(27🛁23🚿) CTV in all bedrooms ® *sB🛁🚿£34–£38 dB🛁🚿£40–£45 (room only) ▣

Lift ☾ 🚭 150P CFA Live music and dancing Sat & Sun Cabaret Sun *xmas*

🍴European ☕ *Lunch £5.95&alc Dinner £7.95&alc Last dinner 9.30pm

Credit cards [1] [2] [3] [4] [5] **VS**

★★★**Braid Hills** 134 Braid Rd, Braid Hills (2½m S A702) ☎031-447 8888 District plan **34**

Old established hotel, standing in its own grounds and offering fine views of the city.

60rm(35🛁3🚿) (9fb) CTV in 35 bedrooms ® sB&B£15.50–£21 sB&B🛁🚿£19.50–£28 dB&B£22–£30 dB&B🛁🚿£39–£45 ▣

☾ CTV 30P ❀

V ☕ Lunch £4.75–£5.50&alc Dinner £6.50–£7.50&alc Wine £4 Last dinner 8.45pm

Credit cards [1] [2] [3] [5]

★★★**Bruntsfield** 69–74 Bruntsfield Pl (Best Western) ☎031-229 1393 Telex no 727897 Central plan **7** *B1*

Formerly a traditional hotel, it is undergoing a steady programme of upgrading and modernisation.

54rm(33🛁1🚿) (6fb) CTV available in bedrooms ® sB&B£20–£22 sB&B🛁🚿£26–£28 dB&B£28–£32 dB&B🛁🚿£35–£46 ▣

Lift ☾ CTV 25P CFA

🍴British & French **V** ☕ Lunch £5.50 Dinner £8&alc Wine £5.40 Last dinner 9.45pm

Credit cards [1] [2] [3] [5] **VS**

See advert on page 246

★★★**Carlton** North Bridge (Scottish Highland) ☎031-556 7277 Telex no 778215 Central plan **9** *E4*

Large, Gothic building, carefully modernised, with the dining room and comfortable cocktail lounge retaining the traditional theme.

98🛁 (4fb) CTV in all rooms ® sB&B🛁£31 dB&B🛁£52 ▣

Lift ☾ 🎵 CFA

🍴British & French **V** ☕ Lunch fr£5.50 Tea fr£1 High Tea fr£5 Dinner fr£7.60 Wine £5 Last dinner 9.30pm

Credit cards [1] [2] [3] [4] [5]

☆☆☆**Crest** Queensferry Rd (Crest) ☎031-332 2442 Telex no 72541 District plan **37**

Modern hotel, situated 1m from city centre on the main road from Edinburgh to the Forth Road Bridge.

120rm(60🛁60🚿) CTV in all bedrooms ® *sB🛁🚿 fr£35 (room only) dB🛁🚿 fr£43 (room only) ▣

Lift ☾ 🚭 CFA 120P

🍴International **V** ☕ *Lunch £4.85–£6.75&alc Dinner £5.25–£7.95&alc Wine £4.80 Last dinner 9.45pm

Credit cards [1] [2] [3] [4] [5] **VS**

★★★*L* **Donmaree** 21 Mayfield Gdns ☎031-667 3641 District plan **38**

Late-Victorian, stone mansion dating from 1869 and furnished in keeping with the period.

9rm(6🛁3🚿) (2fb) *sB&B🛁🚿£26.45 dB&B🛁🚿£40.25

☾ 🐕 CTV 6P

🍴French **V** ☕ *Lunch £6.05&alc Tea £1 Dinner £14&alc Wine £4.85 Last dinner 10pm

S% Credit cards [1] [2] [3] [4] [5] **VS**

E

BRUNTSFIELD HOTEL

★★★**Ellersly House** Ellersly Rd (Allied (Scotland)) ☎031-337 6888 Telex no 76357 District plan **39**

Former private mansion, now extended, west of the city centre close to the A8.

52⇛⋒ (3fb) CTV in all bedrooms Ⓡ *sB&B⇛⋒£31 dB&B⇛⋒£46 B

Lift ☾ 40P ✽ Live music and dancing Fri–Sun Cabaret Fri–Sun *xmas*

♆☐ Last dinner 9.30pm

Credit cards 1 2 3 4 5

★★★*L* **Howard** Great King St ☎031-557 3500 Telex no 727887 Central plan **17** *C6*

Relaxing club-like atmosphere in this small hotel in Georgian newtown area.

25rm(7⇛15⋒) (3fb) CTV in all bedrooms Ⓡ sB&B⇛⋒£30 dB&B⇛⋒£44 B

Lift ☾ CTV 15P ⇎ CFA ⌂ *xmas*

V ♆☐ Lunch £5.60–£6.30 Tea £1 Dinner fr£10.25&alc Wine £4.50 Last dinner 9.30pm

Credit cards 1 2 3 4 5

☆☆☆**King James Thistle** 107 St James Centre (Thistle) ☎031-556 0111 Telex no 727200 Central plan **20** *E6*

Modern hotel in shopping centre development.

162rm(117⇛45⋒) CTV in all bedrooms Ⓡ *sB⇛⋒£35–£40 dB⇛⋒£45–£52 (room only) B

Lift ☾ ⚡ 15P CFA

▣European ♆☐ Lunch £5–£9&alc Dinner £7.50–£9&alc Last dinner 9.30pm

Credit cards 1 2 3 4 5 **VS**

★★★**Old Waverley** Princes St (Scottish Highland) ☎031-556 4648 Telex no 778215 Central plan **27** *D5*

Traditional hotel whose front rooms have fine views of the gardens and Edinburgh Castle.

66rm(53⇛13⋒) (3fb) CTV in all bedrooms Ⓡ sB&B⇛⋒£30 dB&B⇛⋒£50 B

Lift ☾ CFA *xmas*

▣Scottish, English, French & Italian **V** ♆☐ Lunch £5.75–£7.50&alc Dinner £8.50&alc Wine £4.50 Last dinner 8.45pm

Credit cards 1 2 3 5

★★★**Oratava** 41–43 Craigmillar Park ☎031-667 9484 Telex no 727401 District plan **48**

54⇛ (3fb) CTV in all bedrooms

Lift ☾ P CFA *xmas*

V ♆ Lunch £2.45–£4.10 Dinner £7.40&alc Last dinner 9.30pm

S% Credit cards 1 2 3 5 **VS**

☆☆☆**Post House** Corstorphine Rd (Trusthouse Forte) ☎031-334 8221 Telex no 727103 District plan **49**

Large hotel with good views across city.

208⇛ (96fb) CTV in all bedrooms Ⓡ sB&B⇛£42.50 dB&B⇛£56 B

Lift ☾ 158P CFA

♆☐ Last dinner 10.15pm

Credit cards 1 2 3 4 5

★★★*HBL* **Roxburghe** Charlotte Sq (Best Western) ☎031-225 3921 Telex no 727054 Central plan **30** *B5*

Situated in one of Edinburgh's most elegant squares, this traditional hotel was designed by Robert Adam. The atmosphere is much like a private club, but there is a popular cocktail bar and two restaurants. Several bedrooms are elegant and very spacious, and all are thoughtfully furnished and decorated.

72rm(49⇛13⋒) CTV in all bedrooms Ⓡ sB&B£30–£36 sB&B⇛⋒£36–£42 dB&B⇛⋒£42.50–£70 Continental breakfast B

Lift ☾ CFA ⚡

▣International **V** ♆☐ Lunch fr£6.50&alc Tea fr£1.50 High Tea £5alc Dinner fr£8.50&alc Wine £4.95 Last dinner 10pm

Credit cards 1 2 3 4 5

★★**Clarendon** Grosvenor St (Scottish Highland) ☎031-337 7033 Telex no →

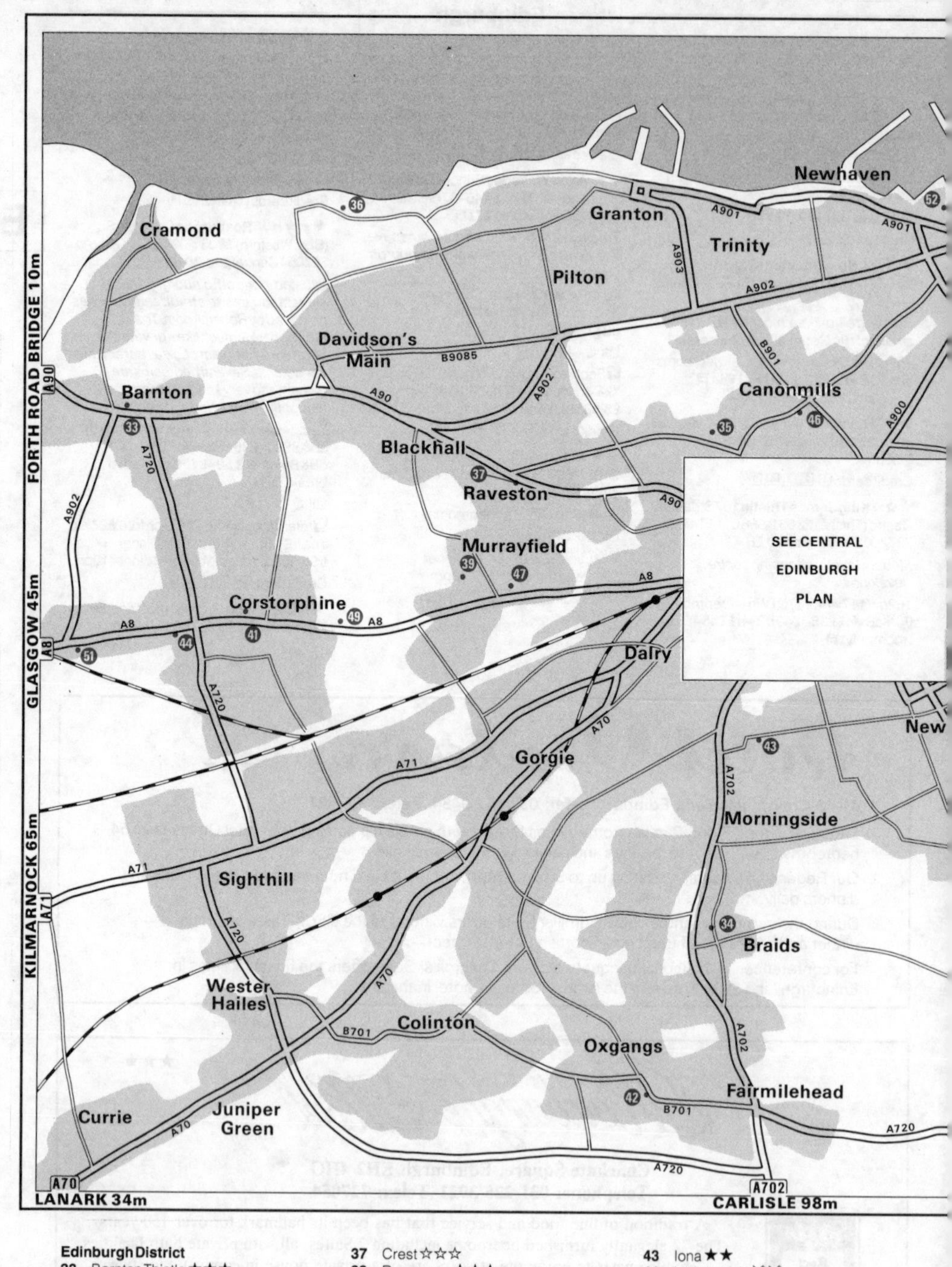
Newhaven
Granton
Trinity
Cramond
Pilton
Davidson's Main
Barnton
Canonmills
Blackhall
Raveston
Murrayfield
Corstorphine
Dalry
Gorgie
Morningside
Sighthill
Braids
Wester Hailes
Colinton
Oxgangs
Fairmilehead
Currie
Juniper Green
New
SEE CENTRAL EDINBURGH PLAN
FORTH ROAD BRIDGE 10m
GLASGOW 45m
KILMARNOCK 65m
LANARK 34m
CARLISLE 98m
A90
A8
A71
A70
A702
A720
A902
A901
A903
A900
B9085
B901
B701

Edinburgh District

33	Barnton Thistle ★★★	37	Crest ☆☆☆	43	Iona ★★
34	Braid Hills ★★★	38	Donmaree ★★★	44	Lightbody's ✕✕
35	Chez Julie ✕	39	Ellersly House ★★★	46	Mermans ✕
36	Stakis Commodore ☆☆	41	Harp ★★	47	Murrayfield ★★
		42	Hunters Tryst ✕✕	48	Oratava ★★★

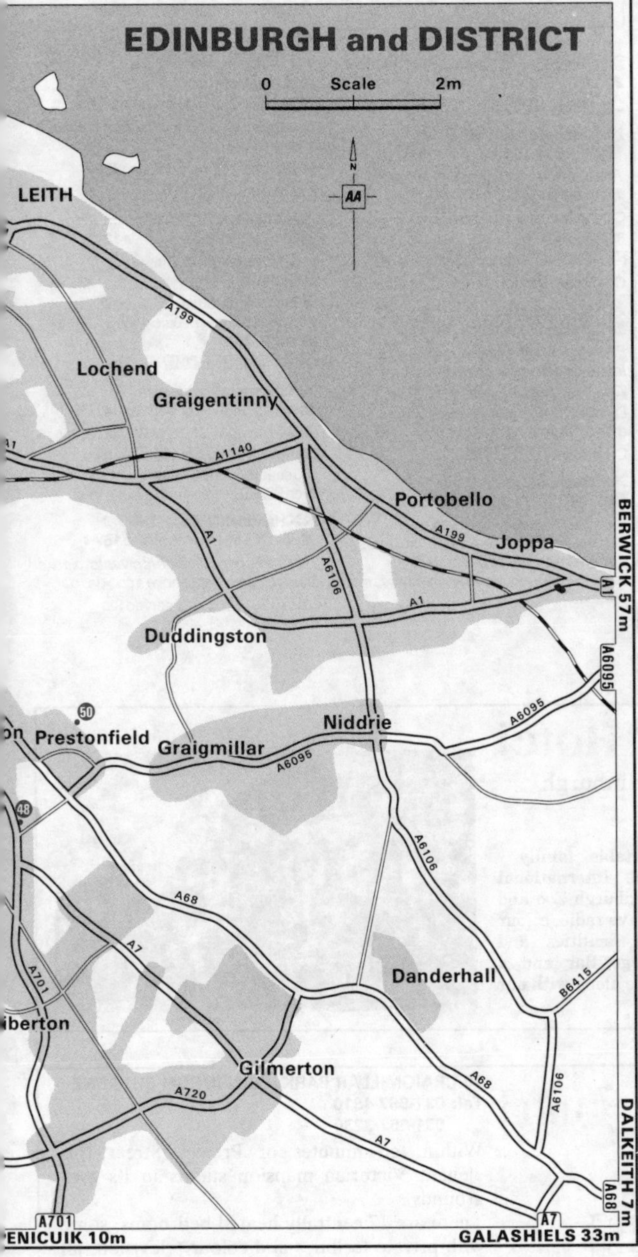
EDINBURGH and DISTRICT
0 Scale 2m
N
AA
LEITH
A199
Lochend
Graigentinny
A1140
Portobello
A199
Joppa
A1
A6106
A1
BERWICK 57m
A1
Duddingston
A6095
50
Prestonfield
Graigmillar
Niddrie
A6095
A6095
48
A6106
A68
A7
A701
Danderhall
B6415
iberton
Gilmerton
A68
A6106
A720
A7
DALKEITH 7m
A68
A701
A7
PENICUIK 10m
GALASHIELS 33m

49 Post House ☆☆☆
50 Prestonfield House ✕✕✕✕
51 Royal Scot ☆☆☆☆
52 Skippers ✕
53 Suffolk Hall ★★

778215 Central plan **13** *A3*
Closed Nov–Mar
A spacious, tourist hotel.
55rm(34➡19⋒)(5fb) CTV in all bedrooms Ⓡ ✱sB&B➡⋒ £28 dB&B➡£46 ⎘
Lift ☾ CTV
⊟ International **V** Lunch £3–£5.50alc Tea fr50p Dinner £5.50–£8.25 Wine £3.95 Last dinner 8.30pm
Credit cards 1 2 3 4 5

★★***Harp*** St John's Rd, Corstorphine (3½m W on A8) (Osprey) ☎031-334 4750 District plan **41**
Commercial, suburban hotel with compact bedrooms.
20rm(1➡7⋒) CTV in 8 bedrooms Ⓡ ⎘
☾ CTV 40P
♈ Last dinner 9pm
Credit cards 1 2 3 4 5 **VS**

★★**Iona** Strathearn Pl ☎031-447 6264 District plan **43**
Small commercial/tourist hotel in a quiet residential area. The dinner menu offers exceptional value.
21rm(2➡2⋒)(2fb) Ⓡ sB&B fr£17 sB&B➡⋒ fr£18 dB&B fr£31 dB&B➡⋒ fr£35
CTV 20P ⊄ ✽
V ♈ Lunch fr£4.50 High Tea fr£4.50 Dinner fr£7&alc Wine £4.50 Last dinner 8.30pm
VS

★★**Murrayfield** 18 Corstorphine Rd (Ind Coope) ☎031-337 1844 District plan **47**
22rm(7➡) CTV in all bedrooms Ⓡ ✱sB&B fr£21 sB&B➡ fr£23.50 dB&B fr£31 dB&B➡ fr£33.50 ⎘
☾ CTV 40P
V ♈ ⊑ ✱Lunch fr£3.75 Tea fr90p Dinner fr£6.25 Last dinner 9.30pm
Credit cards 1 2 3 5 **VS**
See advert on page 250

★★**St Andrew** 8–10 South St Andrew Street ☎031-556 8774 Central plan **31** *D5*
A traditional city-centre hotel just off Princes Street.
40rm(9⋒)(3fb) CTV in 9 bedrooms Ⓡ sB&B £15–£17 sB&B⋒ £18–£20 dB&B £30–£36 dB&B⋒ £36–£38 ⎘
Lift ☾ CTV ⊅ *xmas*
⊟ Scottish & French ♈ ⊑ ✱Lunch £3.75–£4.50 Tea £1 Dinner £5 Wine £3 Last dinner 8.45pm
Credit cards 1 2 3 4

☆☆**Stakis Commodore** West Marine Dr, Cramond Foreshore (Stakis) ☎031-336 1700 Telex no 778704 District plan **36**
Set in parkland overlooking Firth of Forth, hotel has a restaurant specialising mainly in steaks.
49➡ CTV in all bedrooms Ⓡ ✱sB&B➡ fr£30 dB&B➡ fr£40 ⎘
Lift ☾ 150P CFA *xmas*
♈ ⊑ Last dinner 10pm
Credit cards 1 2 3 5 **VS**

E

★★**Suffolk Hall** 10 Craigmillar Park (Minotel) ☎031-667 4810 District plan **53**

Family run tourist/commercial hotel in residential suburb close to students halls of residence.

13rm(2⇌3⋒) Annexe: 4rm CTV in 8 bedrooms Ⓡ ✱ sB&B£15 sB&B⇌⋒£17 dB&B£22 dB&B⇌⋒£30 B

CTV 15P

✱ Bar lunch £2alc Dinner £6 Last dinner 10pm

Credit cards 1 2 3 4

✕✕✕✕**Prestonfield House** Priestfield Rd ☎031-667 8000 District plan **50**

A 17th-century house in twenty-three acres of grounds, with sheep grazing and peacocks displaying.

British & French **V** 800 seats Lunch £10–£20&alc Dinner £12–£25&alc Wine £4.75 Last dinner 9.30pm 300P bedrooms available

Credit cards 1 2 3 4 5

✕✕✕***Ristorante Cosmo*** 58A North Castle St ☎031-226 6743 Central plan **28** *B5*

Seafood and pasta are the specialities of this long established restaurant.

Closed Sun & Mon Lunch not served Sat

Italian **V** 60 seats Last dinner 10.15pm

Credit cards 1 3 4

✕✕***Alp-Horn*** 167 Rose St ☎031-225 4787 Central plan **3** *B5*

There is a touch of Alpine atmosphere at this cheerful restaurant.

Closed Sun, Mon, 3wks mid-Sep, 2wks after Xmas

Swiss **V** 46 seats Last dinner 10pm

Credit card 1

✕✕**L'Auberge** 56 St Mary's St ☎031-556 5888 Central plan **4** *F4*

Friendly French restaurant with interesting menu specialising in fish.

French **V** 40 seats Lunch £3.75&alc Dinner £10–£15alc Wine £4.95 Last dinner 10pm

Credit cards 1 2 3 **VS**

✕✕**Beehive** Grassmarket ☎031-225 7171 Central plan **5** *D3*

Salad buffet to accompany the main course, and a wide selection of mustards are features of this superior steak restaurant. The lounge bar specialises in real ales.

Closed Sun Lunch not served Sat

Mainly grills 45 seats

Credit cards 1 2 3 4 5

✕✕***Blacks*** 15 Jeffrey St ☎031-557 2537 Central plan **6** *E4*

Quality British cooking in tasteful colonial style setting.

50 seats Last dinner 10.30pm

Credit cards 1 2 3 5

✕✕**Chumleys** 72 Rose St, North Ln ☎031-225 3106 Central plan **12** *C5*

Lunch not served Sat Dinner not served Mon

International 30 seats Lunch £5.50–£6.50&alc Dinner £10alc Wine £4.50 Last dinner 10.30pm

Credit cards 1 2 3 5

✕✕**Denzlers** 80 Queen St ☎031-226 5467 Central plan **14** *B5*

Closed Sun, 25–27 Dec & 31 Dec–3 Jan

Scottish, French, Italian & Swiss **V** 130 seats Lunch £6.14alc Dinner £8.14alc Wine £3.95 Last dinner 10.30pm

✕✕**Handsel** 22 Stafford St ☎031-225 5521 Central plan **16** *A4*

Tasteful Regency theme is given to this first floor restaurant above a cocktail bar.

Closed Sun Lunch not served Sat

Scottish & French **V** 48 seats ✻Lunch £4.95&alc Dinner £10alc Wine £5 Last dinner 10pm

Credit cards 1 2 3 4 5 **VS**

✕✕**Howtowdie** 27a Stafford St ☎031-225 6291 Central plan **18** *A4*

Closed Sun

Scottish & French **V** 50 seats Lunch £10.50alc Dinner £20alc Wine £5.90 Last dinner 11pm

Credit cards 1 2 3 4 5

✕✕**Hunters Tryst** Oxgangs Rd ☎031-445 3132 District plan **42**

Modernised, former coaching inn.

Closed Sun & Mon

International 60 seats Lunch fr£3.90&alc Dinner £6&alc Wine £4.15 Last dinner 10pm 50P

Credit cards 1 2 3 4 5

✕✕***Kobe's*** 15a Castle St ☎031-225 5869 Central plan **21** *C5*

Basement restaurant, offering an unexpected country house atmosphere and environment.

Closed Sun, Xmas, 1–3 Jan & local Public hols Lunch not served Sat

50 seats

Credit cards 1 2 3 4 5

✕✕**Lightbodys** 23 Glasgow Rd ☎031-334 2300 District plan **44**

Cheerful restaurant with friendly service.

Closed Sun

International 54 seats Lunch fr£4.75&alc Dinner £10.50alc Wine £4.50 Last dinner 10pm 12P

Credit cards 1 2 3 5

✕✕**No 10** 10 Melville Pl ☎031-226 3579 Central plan **25** *A5*

British premiers adorn the walls of this basement restaurant.

Closed Sun Lunch not served Sat

34 seats Wine £4.15 Last dinner 10.30pm

✕✕**Ristorante Milano** 7 Victoria St ☎031-226 5260 Central plan **29** *D4*

Restaurant with Italian influenced decor, and semi-arched ceiling.

Closed Sun

Italian **V** 65 seats Lunch £10–£15alc Dinner £18alc Wine £5 Last dinner 11pm

S% Credit cards 1 2 3 4 5

✕**Alcove** 44 Grindley St ☎031-229 4554 Central plan **2** *B3*

European & Indian **V** 34 seats Lunch fr£1.95&alc Dinner £7.50alc Wine £4.50 Last dinner 11.45pm

Credit cards 1 2 3 5

✕***Casa Española*** 61–65 Rose St ☎031-225 5979 Central plan **10** *C5*

Bullfighting is the theme in this compact Spanish restaurant which serves highly seasoned food.

Continental 80 seats Last dinner 10.30pm 40P bedrooms available

Credit cards 1 3

✕**Le Caveau** 13B Dundas St ☎031-556 5707 Central plan **11** *C6*

Modestly appointed cellar restaurant

Closed 1st 2wks Jul

French **V** 50 seats ✻Lunch £8alc Dinner £10alc Wine £4.70 Last dinner 10pm

✕**Chez Julie** 110 Raeburn Place ☎031-332 2827 District plan **35**

Small, friendly bistro style restaurant.

Closed Sun Dinner not served Mon

French **V** 38 seats ✻Lunch £2.10–£3.50&alc Dinner £6.60alc Wine £3.50 Last dinner 10pm

✕***Doric Tavern*** 15/16 Market St ☎031-225 1084 Central plan **15** *E4*

Compact, traditional restaurant.

Closed Sun

Scottish & French 46 seats Last dinner 9.30pm

E

✕**Kalpna** 2–3 St Patrick Sq
☎031-667 9890 Central plan **19** *F2*
Closed Sun
▣Indian **V** 66 seats Lunch £1.50–£3&alc Dinner £3.95–£6&alc Wine £4.25 Last dinner 11pm ⊘⊁
S% Credit cards 1 3 **VS**

✕***Lafayette*** 22 Brougham Pl
☎031-229 0869 Central plan **23** *C2*
Closed Sun
▣French 28 seats Last dinner 10.15pm ⊘

✕**Mermans** 8–10 Eyre Pl
☎031-556 1177 District plan **46**
Unpretentious façade hides this simple, modern speciality fish and seafood restaurant.
Closed Sun, Xmas, New Year & Public hols Lunch not served
▣British & French 26 seats Wine £4.75 Last dinner 10.15pm P⊁
S% Credit cards 1 2 3 5

✕**Nimmo's** 101 Shandwick Pl
☎031-229 6119 Central plan **24** *B4*
Friendly lounge bar, wine bar and bistro complex.
Closed Sun Lunch not served Sat
▣International **V** 40 seats ✻Lunch £6.25alc Dinner £8.50alc Wine £4.85 Last dinner 10.15pm
Credit cards 1 2 3 4 5

❀✕**Shamiana** 14 Brougham St ☎031-229 2265 Central plan **32** *C2*
Small compact Indian restaurant, neatly decorated.
Closed Sun, Xmas Day & New Years Day Lunch not served
▣Indian & Kashmiri **V** 42 seats Dinner £8alc Last dinner 11pm ⊘
S% Credit cards 1 2 3 4 5 **VS**

✕**Skippers** 1a Dock Pl, Leith
☎031-554 1018 District plan **52**
Closed Sun & mid Sep–early Oct
▣French 38 seats ✻Lunch £5.50alc Dinner £7.50–£10alc Wine £4 Last dinner 9.30pm

✕**Verandah Tandoori** 17 Dalry Rd
☎031-337 5828 Central plan **32A** *A3*
▣Bangladeshi & North Indian **V** 44 seats ✻Lunch £7.90–£10alc Dinner £7.90–£10alc Wine £4.40 Last dinner 11.45pm ⊘
Credit cards 1 2 3 5

At **Musselburgh** (6m E A198)

☆☆**Drummore** North Berwick Rd
☎031-665 2302
47⇥⋒ 150P

★**Pittencrieff** 59–60 Linkfield Rd
☎031-665 2104
24rm (2⋒)

EDZELL
Tayside *Angus*
Map **15** NO56

★★★**Glenesk** High St ☎(03564) 319
Closed 1 & 2 Jan
Popular golfing hotel with access to the neighbouring course.
24rm (9⇥4⋒) (2fb) CTV in all bedrooms Ⓡ sB&B fr£19 sB&B⇥⋒ fr£22 dB&B fr£38 dB&B⇥⋒ fr£44 ⊟
150P 8⌂✻ ♩ billiards ⌂
V♧☐ Lunch fr£4.50 Tea fr£1.50 Dinner fr£8.50 Last dinner 9.45pm
Credit cards 2 5

★★**Central** ☎(03564) 218
A small, three-storey hotel, standing in a quiet street.
19rm (3⇥11⋒) (2fb) CTV in 11 bedrooms TV in 1 bedroom sB&B £10 sB&B⇥⋒ £16 dB&B £20 dB&B⇥⋒ £28 ⊟
CTV 70P 2⌂ billiards
V♧☐ Lunch £2.75 Tea fr60p–£1.25 High Tea £2.50–£3.75 Dinner £5–£6.50&alc Wine £4.60 Last dinner 8.30pm
Credit cards 2 3 **VS**

★★*B* **Panmure Arms** High St ☎(03564) 420 Telex no 76534
Attractive, mock-Tudor hotel, situated in a quiet village on the edge of the Highlands.
16rm (5⇥11⋒) (6fb) 1⊞ CTV in all bedrooms ✻sB&B⇥⋒ fr£21 dB&B⇥⋒ £36 ⊟
☾⊁30P ▭(heated) ♩ squash billiards sauna bath Live music and dancing 3 nights wkly ⌂ *xmas*
V♧☐ Lunch £7.50 Tea 75p High Tea £3.50 Dinner £7.50 Wine £3.90 Last dinner 9pm
Credit cards 1 2 3 5

EGGESFORD
Devon
Map **3** SS61

★★**Fox & Hounds** ☎Chulmleigh (0769) 80345 Closed Xmas RS Oct–Feb
Privately-owned fishing hotel in its own grounds.
10rm (4⇥) Annexe: 2⇥ Ⓡ 1⊞ sB&B £11–£18 dB&B £18–£22 dB&B⇥ £12–£36 ⊟
CTV P 6⌂⊞✻ ♩ Live music and dancing Tue & Sat nc 10yrs
♧☐ Bar lunch £2–£6 Tea 50p–£2 Dinner £6 Wine £3.90 Last dinner 9.30pm

EGHAM
Surrey
Map **4** TQ07

☆☆☆☆**Runnymede** ☎(0784) 36171 Telex no 934900 Heathrow plan **10** *A1*
Large modern hotel beside the Thames, offering good range of services and facilities.
90⇥⋒ (9fb) CTV in all bedrooms Ⓡ ✻sB&B⇥⋒ £20–£34.50 dB&B⇥⋒ £40–£45 Continental breakfast ⊟
Lift ☾ 200P✻ ⚑ ♩ Disco Fri & Sat *xmas*
▣English & French **V**♧☐ ✻Lunch £7&alc Tea 60p Dinner £8.25&alc Wine £5.45 Last dinner 9.45pm
Credit cards 1 2 3 5 **VS**

EGLWYSFACH
Dyfed
Map **6** SN69

★★★♠**Ynyshir Hall** ☎Glandyfi (065 474) 209 Closed first 2 wks Feb
Comfortable manor house set amidst gardens next to RSPB bird sanctuary.
11rm (6⇥1⋒) 1⊞ Ⓡ sB&B fr£33 (incl

dinner) sB&B⇌fr£36.50 (incl dinner) dB&B fr£66 dB&B⇌fr£73 (incl dinner) ₿

⅟ 20P ✽ *xmas*

English & French V Dinner fr£15 Last dinner 9.30pm

Credit cards 1 2 3 5 VS

ELCOT
Berkshire
Map **4** SU36

★★*B* **Elcot Park** (1m N of A4) (Best Western) ☎ Kintbury (0488) 58100

Hotel with countryside views and tastefully furnished, well-equipped bedrooms.

22rm (18⇌2⋒) (1fb) 2 CTV in all bedrooms Ⓡ *sB&B£25 sB&B⇌⋒£34–£45 dB&B£34 dB&B⇌⋒£43–£65 ₿

200P 4 ✽ *xmas*

English & French *Lunch fr£6.50 Tea fr65p High Tea fr£2.25 Dinner £8.95&alc Wine £5 Last dinner 9.30pm

Credit cards 1 2 3 5

ELGIN
Grampian *Morayshire*
Map **15** NJ26

☆☆☆ **Eight Acres** Sheriffmill ☎ (0343) 3077

45rm (21⇌20⋒) (1fb) CTV in 21 bedrooms TV in 24 bedrooms sB&B fr£17.50 sB&B⇌⋒ fr£22.85 dB&B⇌⋒ fr£35 ₿

CTV 200P CFA ✽ billiards *xmas*

Scottish, French & Italian V Lunch fr£4.55 Tea fr80p Dinner £6.50–£8 Wine £3 Last dinner 9pm

Credit cards 1 2 3 5 VS

★★ ***Laichmoray*** Station Rd ☎ (0343) 2558 Closed New Year's Day

Friendly, commercial hotel, opposite the goods station.

23rm ₿

CTV 65P

V

Last dinner 9pm

Credit cards 1 3 5

★ **St Leonards** Duff Av ☎ (0343) 7350

Closed New Years Day

Conversion from a private residence standing in grounds in a residential area of the town.

17rm (6⇌2⋒) (2fb) CTV in 4 bedrooms TV in 1 bedroom Ⓡ sB&B£13–£15 sB&B⇌⋒£16–£18 dB&B£22–£25 dB&B⇌⋒£28–£30 ₿

CTV 60P

Scottish & French V Lunch £4–£5 Tea £1–£1.50 High Tea £2.50–£5.50 Dinner £6–£8 Wine £3.75 Last dinner 8.30pm

S% Credit cards 1 3

✕✕ **Enrico's** 15 Grey Friars St ☎ (0343) 2849

Closed Sun

Italian 56 seats *Lunch fr£2.75 Dinner £8alc Last dinner 9.30pm

Credit cards 1 2 3 5 VS

ELIE
Fife
Map **12** NO40

★★*HL* **Golf** Bank St ☎ (0333) 330209

Closed Nov–Jan

21rm (6⇌4⋒) (4fb) Ⓡ sB&B£13.45–£16.45 sB&B⇌⋒£14.80–£17.95 dB&B£26.90–£32.90 dB&B⇌⋒£29.60–£35.90 ₿

CTV 50P ✽

Lunch £3.25–£3.65 Tea £1.50–£1.65 High Tea £3.30–£3.65 Dinner £7.50–£8.25&alc Wine £5 Last dinner 9pm

Credit cards 1 3

ELLESMERE
Shropshire
Map **7** SJ33

★ ***Black Lion*** Scotland St ☎ (069171) 2418

6rm →

CTV 20P 4
Last dinner 9.45pm
Credit card 1

★**Red Lion** Church St ☎(069171) 2632
Closed Xmas
8rm sB&B fr£9 dB&B fr£17
CTV 15P Disco Fri Live music and dancing Sat
Bar lunch £2.50–£4 Dinner £4.50–£7.50 Wine £3.65 Last dinner 5.30pm

ELLON
Grampian *Aberdeenshire*
Map **15** NJ93

☆☆☆**Ladbroke** (Ladbroke) ☎(0358) 20666 Telex no 739200
Closed Xmas
33 (11fb) CTV in all bedrooms Ⓡ *sB fr£30 dB fr£40 (room only)
(150P CFA
V Lunch fr£6.50 Dinner fr£8.50 Last dinner 9.30pm
Credit cards 1 2 3 5

★***Buchan*** ☎(0358) 20208
17rm (1 16) CTV in 1 bedroom TV in 5 bedrooms
CTV 60P Disco twice wkly Live music and dancing wkly
V Last dinner 6.30pm

★**New Inn** Market St ☎(0358) 20425
12rm (2 4) (2fb) CTV in 7 bedrooms *sB&B £9.50 sB&B £12 dB&B £19 dB&B £24
CTV 63P
V *Lunch £2.75 Tea fr75p High Tea fr£2.75 Last High Tea 7pm
S% Credit cards 1 2 3 5

ELTERWATER
Cumbria
Map **7** NY30

★**Britannia Inn** ☎Langdale (09667) 210
Closed Xmas RS Nov–Feb
Personally-managed, modest country inn with old world atmosphere.
10rm (1fb) Ⓡ sB&B £14–£14.50
dB&B £28–£29
Bar lunch £3.60alc Dinner £9.90–£10.50 Wine £4.75 Last dinner 7pm

★***Eltermere*** (on unclass road between A593 & B5343) ☎Langdale (09667) 207
Closed Nov–Etr
Charming peaceful old mansion, standing in its own grounds.
16rm
20P 4 nc5yrs
Last dinner 7.30pm

ELY
Cambridgeshire
Map **5** TL58

Old Fire Engine House 25 St Mary's Street ☎(0353) 2582
Ely's horse-drawn fire engine is on show in the garden of this restaurant.
Closed 2wks Xmas & Public hols Dinner not served Sun
36 seats Lunch £6.80alc Tea 90p–£1.50alc Dinner £8alc Wine £3.80 Last dinner 9pm 8P

EMBLETON
Northumberland
Map **12** NU22

★★**Dunstanburgh Castle** ☎(066576) 203
A quaint village inn in the heart of the Northumberland countryside, near to the sea.
17rm (9) (3fb) Ⓡ *sB&B £11.25 sB&B £13.25 dB&B fr£22.50 dB&B fr£26.50
CTV 20P 2
English & French *Lunch fr£3.95&alc Tea fr£1.75 Dinner fr£7.50 Last dinner 7.45pm

EMSWORTH
Hampshire
Map **4** SU70

★★**Brookfield** Havant Rd ☎(02434) 3363
Friendly, well-run hotel with good bedrooms but limited lunch facilities.
17rm (10 7) CTV in all bedrooms sB&B £24 dB&B £32
CTV 100P
French **V** Lunch £7alc Dinner £7alc Wine £3.70 Last dinner 9.30pm
Credit cards 1 2 3 5

ENFIELD
Greater London
Map **4** TQ39

★★★**Royal Chace** The Ridgeway ☎01-366 6500 Telex no 266628
Very busy commercial and conference hotel with tasteful restaurant and well equipped bedrooms.
90rm (62 28) (3fb) 6 CTV in all bedrooms Ⓡ sB&B fr£30 dB&B fr£44
(300P CFA
International **V** Lunch £3&alc Dinner fr£5&alc Wine £5.15 Last dinner 10pm
Credit cards 1 2 3 5

★★***Holtwhites*** Chase Side ☎01-363 0124 Telex no 299670
Small, privately owned hotel with friendly atmosphere.
28rm (15 18) CTV in all bedrooms
CTV 20P nc4yrs
V Last dinner 9pm
Credit cards 1 2 3 5

XX***Norfolk*** 80 London Rd ☎01-363 0979
Closed Sun, 1st 3wks Aug Lunch not served Sat Dinner not served Mon
English & Continental 80 seats Last dinner 10pm P
Credit cards 1 2 3 5

ENGLEFIELD GREEN
Surrey
Map **4** SU97

XXX**Bailiwick** ☎Egham (0784) 32223
Dinner not served Sun
French 70 seats *Lunch £13alc Dinner £13alc Wine £5.25 Last dinner 9.30pm 10P
Credit cards 1 2 3 5

EPPING
Essex
Map **5** TL40

☆☆☆**Post House** High Rd, Bell Common (Trusthouse Forte) ☎ (0378) 73137 Telex no 81617
Hotel offers variety of types of bedroom and good restaurant.
82🛁 (20fb) CTV in all bedrooms ® sB&B🛁£42.50 dB&B🛁£54 Ɓ
☾ 95P CFA *xmas*
♔☕ Last dinner 10.15pm
Credit cards 1 2 3 4 5

EPSOM
Surrey
Map **4** TQ26

★★**Drift Bridge** Reigate Rd (Charrington) ☎ Burgh Heath (07373) 52163
Modest roadside hotel with extensive bar facilities and modern bedrooms.
25rm(14🛁) (2fb) CTV in 24 bedrooms ® sB&B£17–£23.50 sB&B🛁£19.50–£31 dB&B£23–£30 dB&B🛁£27–£36 Ɓ
CTV 80P 8🚗 billiards
V ♔ Lunch fr£5.70 Dinner fr£5.70 Wine £4.15 Last dinner 9.45pm
Credit cards 1 2 3 5

At **Burgh Heath** (3m SE on A217)

☆☆*B* **Pickard Motor** Brighton Rd ☎ Burgh Heath (07373) 57222
44🛁🚿 150P

ERBISTOCK
Clwyd
Map **7** SJ34

✕***Boat inn*** ☎ Bangor-on-Dee (0978) 780143
▤International **V** 56 seats Last dinner 9.15pm 70P
Credit cards 1 2 3 5

ERMINGTON
Devon
Map **2** SX65

★★*HB* **Ermewood House** ☎ Modbury (0548) 830741 Closed 23 Dec–3 Jan
Friendly, country house style hotel, catering for the tourist and commercial trade.
9rm(6🛁3🚿) (1fb) CTV in all bedrooms ® sB&B🛁🚿£21–£24 dB&B🛁🚿£38–£44 Ɓ
15P 🐕 ✽
▤English & Continental ♔☕ Bar lunch £3.20alc Tea fr£1.25 Dinner fr£7 Wine £3.95 Last dinner 9.30pm
Credit cards 1 2 3 5 **VS**

ERSKINE
Strathclyde *Renfrewshire*
Map **11** NS47

☆☆☆☆**Crest Hotel Erskine Bridge** North Barr, Inchinnan (Crest) ☎ 041-812 0123 Telex no 777713
Closed Xmas wk
Purpose built hotel on the banks of the Clyde near Erskine Bridge.
200🛁 CTV in all bedrooms ® ✻ sB🛁 fr£36 (room only) dB🛁 fr£43 (room only) Ɓ
Lift ☾ 🚭 350P CFA Live music and dancing Sat ♿
▤International **V** ♔☕ ✻ Lunch £7.30&alc Tea 60p Dinner £8.60&alc Wine £6.95 Last dinner 10pm
Credit cards 1 2 3 4 5 **VS**

ESHER
Surrey London plan **5** B1 (page 420)

★**Haven** Portsmouth Rd (1m NE of Scilly Isles rbt on A307) (Minotels) ☎ 01-398 0023
Small commercial suburban hotel, with homely atmosphere and fresh table d'hôte food.
17rm(2🚿) Annexe: 4rm(2🛁2🚿) (4fb) CTV in 6 bedrooms ® ✻ £16.25 sB&B🛁🚿£21.50 dB&B£25 dB&B🛁🚿£31
CTV 20P 1🚗 🐕 🅿
▤International ♔☕ ✻ Bar lunch 50p–£1.50&alc Tea 25p–£1.50 Dinner £5.25–£7.25 Wine £3.50 Last dinner 8pm
Credit cards 1 2 3 4 5 **VS**

✕✕**Good Earth** 14–16 High St ☎ (0372) 62489
Modern Chinese restaurant specialising in regional cuisine.
▤Cantonese & Pekinese **V** 90 seats Lunch £8.50–£14.50&alc Dinner £8.50–£14.50&alc Wine £4.60 Last dinner 11pm
🚭
S% Credit cards 1 2 3 5

✕✕**Restaurant Le Pierrot** 63 High St ☎ (0372) 63191
Comfortable well appointed French restaurant featuring enterprising and imaginative cooking.
Closed Sun Lunch not served Sat
▤French 36 seats ✻ Lunch fr£6 Dinner fr£7.50&alc Wine £4.75 Last dinner 11pm
Credit cards 1 2 3 5

✕**Shapla** 34 High St ☎ (0372) 67285
A small modern well appointed Tandoori featuring authentic speciality cooking.
▤Indian 40 seats ✻ Lunch fr£14.50&alc Dinner fr£14.50&alc Wine £4.30 Last dinner 11.30pm
S% Credit cards 1 3

ESKDALE
Cumbria
Map **7** SD19

★★**Bower House Inn** ☎ (09403) 244
Delightful old inn nestling in the Eskdale Valley.
6rm Annexe: 8🛁 (1fb) CTV in 8 bedrooms ® 🐕 ✻ sB&B£15.50 sB&B🛁£17.50 dB&B£22 dB&B🛁£24 Ɓ
60P *xmas*
♔☕ ✻ Bar lunch £2.50–£3.50 Tea 50p–£1 Dinner £8.50 Wine £4.25 Last dinner 9pm

ESKDALEMUIR
Dumfries & Galloway *Dumfriesshire*
Map **11** N29

★★*H* **Hart Manor** ☎ (05414) 217
Situated in the upper reaches of the Border Esk valley, this small but nicely appointed friendly hotel offers an ideal setting. →

7rm(5⋒)®✻sB&B£12.50 sB&B⋒£13.50 dB&B£23 dB&B⋒£25
CTV ✿ ♩
✻Bar lunch £3alc Dinner £8&alc Wine £3.55 Last dinner 9pm
Credit card 3

ETON
Berkshire
Map **4** SU97
✕✕Antico 42 High St ☎Windsor (07535) 63977
Historic Italian restaurant with authentic cuisine.
Closed Sun Lunch not served Sat
Italian 70 seats Lunch £12.50alc Dinner £14alc Wine £4.20 Last dinner 11pm 6P
S% Credit cards 1 2 3 5

ETTINGTON
Warwickshire
Map **4** SP24
❀★★ *HB* **Chase Country House** Banbury Rd ☎Stratford-upon-Avon (0789) 740000
Closed 24 Dec–22 Jan
(Rosette awarded for dinner only.)
Quiet, country hotel situated in extensive grounds, with a very popular restaurant.
11rm(10⇌1⋒) (2fb) CTV in all bedrooms ® sB&B⇌⋒£21–£30 dB&B⇌⋒£35–£45
50P ✿ nc8yrs
Lunch £7.50–£9.50 Dinner £10–£15 Wine £5.05 Last dinner 9pm
Credit cards 1 2 3

ETTRICKBRIDGE
Borders *Selkirkshire*
Map **11** NT32
★★ **Ettrickshaws** Seakirk (1m W off B7009) ☎(07505) 229
Closed Jan RS Nov, Dec & Feb
Homely, Victorian country mansion close to the River Ettrick in the Ettrick Valley.
6rm(5⇌) (1fb) CTV in all bedrooms ® sB&B⇌£13–£17 dB&B⇌£22–£28
12P ✿ ♩ nc9yrs

English, Arabic, Chinese, French & Indian Bar lunch £2–£5 Dinner £7–£8&alc Wine £5 Last dinner 9pm
S% Credit cards 1 2 3 5 **VS**

EVANTON
Highland *Ross & Cromarty*
Map **14** NH66
★★ **Novar Arms** ☎(0349) 830210
Homely, informal, commercial hotel in a small village.
10rm sB&B£10 dB&B£20
CTV 30P
Mainly grills ✻Bar lunch 90p–£2.55 Tea 60p–£1 High Tea £5.50alc Wine £3.60 Last High Tea 8pm
Credit card 3

EVERCREECH
Somerset
Map **3** ST63
★★ **Glen** Queens Rd ☎(0749) 830369
Closed Xmas
An hospitable country house with an attractive garden.
14rm(6⇌) Annexe: 4rm (2fb) ® sB&B£13 sB&B⇌£16 dB&B£24 dB&B⇌£28
CTV 60P ✿
Lunch £5&alc Tea £1 Dinner £5&alc Last dinner 10pm
Credit cards 1 2 3 5

EVESHAM
Hereford & Worcester
Map **4** SP04
★★★ **Evesham Hotel** Coopers Ln, off Waterside ☎(0386) 49111 Telex no 339342
This hotel is situated in a quiet lane not far from the centre of Evesham.
34rm(28⇌5⋒) CTV in all bedrooms ® ✻sB&B£27.50 sB&B⇌⋒£33.50 dB&B£40 dB&B⇌⋒£48
45P ✿ *xmas*
International **V** Lunch £4.80–£7.80 Tea 60p Dinner £10.75alc Wine £4.70 Last dinner 9.30pm
S% Credit cards 1 2 3 5 **VS**

★★ **Northwick Arms** Waterside ☎(0386) 6109 Closed Xmas
Family-run hotel close to the town centre standing opposite the River Avon.
21rm(2⇌1⋒) Annexe: 1⇌ (4fb) ® ✻sB&B£12–£16 sB&B⇌⋒£18–£22 dB&B£20–£25 dB&B⇌⋒£30–£35
CTV 100P Live music and dancing Thu
V ✻Lunch £4alc Dinner £5alc Last dinner 9.30pm
Credit cards 1 3

★ **Park View** Waterside ☎(0386) 2639
Closed 24 Dec–2 Jan
Small hotel, close to the town and River Avon.
29rm (2fb) sB&B£10.75–£12.25 dB&B£21.50–£24
CTV 50P
Bar lunch 65p Tea 45p Dinner £5–£5.75 Wine £3.30 Last dinner 7pm
Credit cards 1 3

EWEN
(nr Cirencester) Gloucestershire
Map **4** SU09
★★★ ***Wild Duck Inn*** ☎Kemble (028577) 310
Cosy village inn with popular restaurant and pretty bedrooms.
7⇌⋒ CTV in all bedrooms ®
50P ✿ Live music and dancing Tue & Sun
English & French
Last dinner 9.50pm
Credit cards 1 5

EXETER
Devon
Map **3** SX99
See plan
★★★ *H* **Buckerell Lodge Crest** Topsham Rd (Crest) ☎(0392) 52451 Plan 1 *C1*
This house, dating from the 12th century, has now been converted to a hotel.
56⇌ CTV in all bedrooms ® →

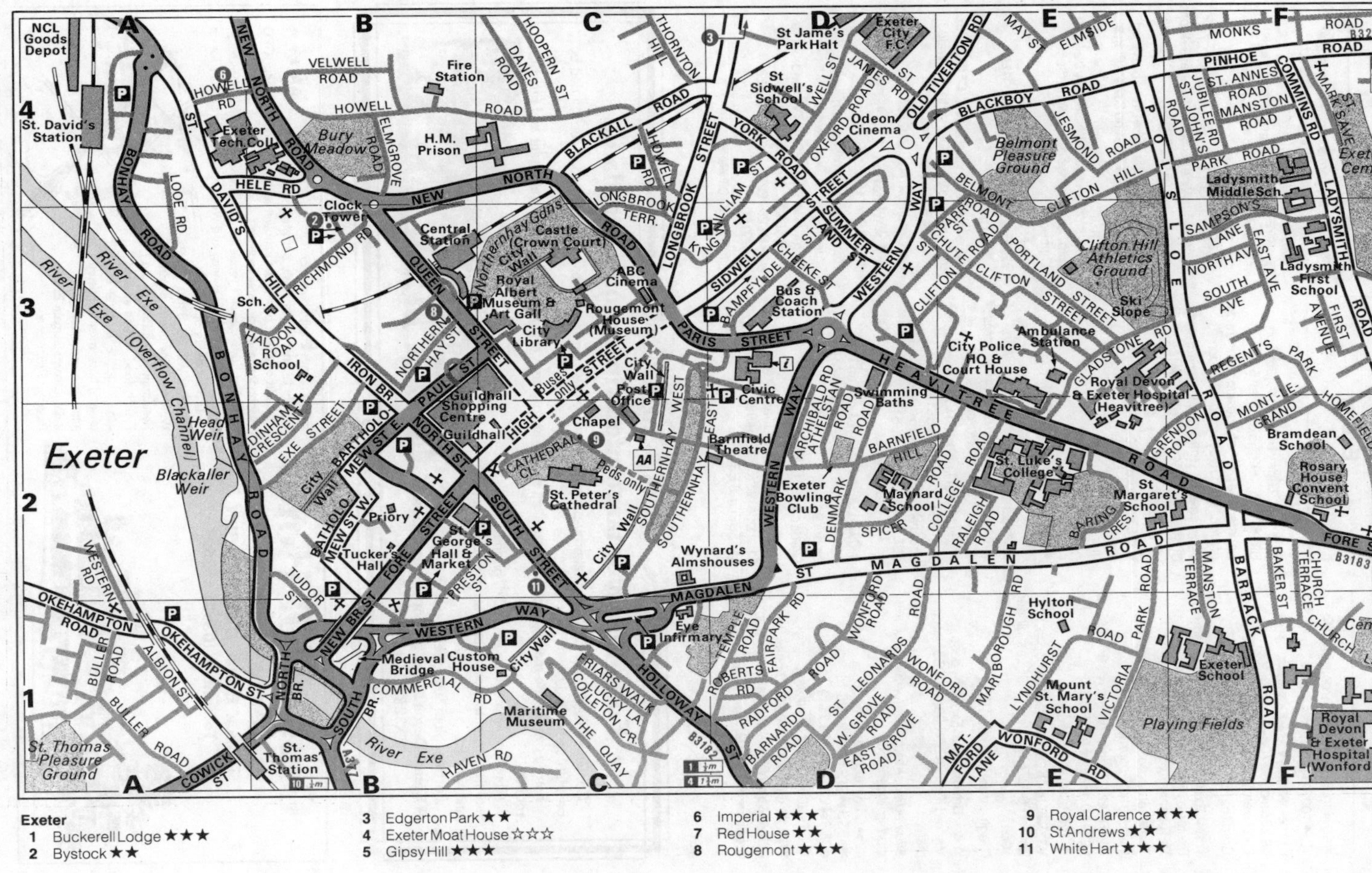
Exeter
NCL Goods Depot
St. David's Station
River Exe
River Exe (Overflow Channel)
Head Weir
Blackaller Weir
BONHAY ROAD
NEW NORTH ROAD
ST. DAVID'S HILL
Exeter Tech. Coll.
Bury Meadow
Clock Tower
H.M. Prison
Fire Station
Central Station
QUEEN STREET
Royal Albert Museum & Art Gall
Castle (Crown Court)
Northernhay Gdns
Rougemont House (Museum)
City Library
ABC Cinema
Guildhall Shopping Centre
Guildhall
HIGH STREET
St. Peter's Cathedral
Chapel
Post Office
City Wall
SOUTHERNHAY
Wynard's Almshouses
Barnfield Theatre
Civic Centre
PARIS STREET
Bus & Coach Station
SIDWELL STREET
HEAVITREE ROAD
WESTERN WAY
MAGDALEN ROAD
Eye Infirmary
HOLLOWAY ST
Maritime Museum
Medieval Bridge
Custom House
THE QUAY
COMMERCIAL RD
St. George's Hall & Market
Tucker's Hall
Priory
FORE STREET
SOUTH STREET
St. Thomas Station
St. Thomas Pleasure Ground
OKEHAMPTON ROAD
COWICK ST
St Sidwell's School
St Jame's Park Halt
Exeter City F.C.
Odeon Cinema
Belmont Pleasure Ground
Clifton Hill Athletics Ground
Ski Slope
City Police HQ & Court House
Ambulance Station
Swimming Baths
Royal Devon & Exeter Hospital (Heavitree)
St. Luke's College
St Margaret's School
Maynard School
Exeter Bowling Club
Hylton School
Mount St. Mary's School
Exeter School
Playing Fields
Royal Devon & Exeter Hospital (Wonford)
Bramdean School
Rosary House Convent School
Ladysmith Middle Sch.
Ladysmith First School
POLSLOE ROAD
BARRACK ROAD
BLACKBOY ROAD
PINHOE ROAD
LADYSMITH ROAD
Exeter Cemy
WONFORD ROAD

Exeter

1 Buckerell Lodge ★★★
2 Bystock ★★
3 Edgerton Park ★★
4 Exeter Moat House ☆☆☆
5 Gipsy Hill ★★★
6 Imperial ★★★
7 Red House ★★
8 Rougemont ★★★
9 Royal Clarence ★★★
10 St Andrews ★★
11 White Hart ★★★

E

E

✱sB⇒ fr£32 dB⇒ fr£42 (room only) B̶
☾ ⅍ 100P ✽ Live music Sat ♿
▣ International V ♔ ☕ ✱Lunch £8.25&alc Tea 70p–£3.75 Dinner £9.25&alc Wine £6.25 Last dinner 9.45pm
Credit cards 1 2 3 4 5 VS

☆☆☆ **Exeter Moat House** Topsham Rd, Exeter-by-Pass (Queens Moat) ☎ Topsham (039287) 5441 Plan **4** *C1*
The hotel bedrooms here are detached from the reception and public rooms.
44⇒ (1fb) CTV in all bedrooms Ⓡ sB&B⇒ fr£29.50 dB&B⇒ fr£38.50 B̶
☾ 120P CFA ✽ *xmas* ♿
V ♔ ☕ Lunch £5–£6&alc Tea 60p–£1.50 Dinner £6–£7&alc Wine £4.95 Last dinner 10pm
Credit cards 1 2 3 4 5

☆☆☆ **Devon Motel** Exeter bypass, Matford (Brend) ☎ (0392) 59268 Not on plan
Situated close to the Exeter-by-Pass, with modern extensions.
42⇒ CTV in all bedrooms Ⓡ ✱sB&B⇒ £19.55–£21.28 dB&B⇒ £25.30–£28.75 B̶
☾ CTV 200P CFA ✽ ⌂ *xmas*
♔ ☕ ✱Lunch £2.25–£5.50 Dinner fr£5.46&alc Wine £4.95 Last dinner 9pm
Credit cards 1 2 3 5

★★★*BL* **Gipsy Hill** Pinhoe (3m E on B3181) ☎ (0392) 65252 Plan **5** *F2*
Located in a peaceful position on the edge of the city, with well-appointed rooms.
19rm (18⇒ 1⋒) (2fb) CTV in all bedrooms Ⓡ ✗ sB&B⇒⋒ £26.50 dB&B⇒⋒ £37 B̶
☾ 45P ⛟ ✽
V ♔ ☕ Lunch £4.50–£5&alc Tea 75p Dinner £8–£8.50&alc Wine £3.90 Last dinner 9pm
Credit cards 1 2 3

★★★ **Imperial** St David's ☎ (0392) 211811 Plan **6** *A4*
Built as a mansion during Queen Anne period, this hotel is situated in five acres of spacious, sheltered grounds.
25rm (19⇒ 2⋒) (1fb) CTV in 20 bedrooms TV in 2 bedrooms sB&B£15–£17 sB&B⇒⋒ £22.50–£25 dB&B£25–£28 dB&B⇒⋒ £32.50–£35 B̶
☾ CTV 70P 3 ⌂ ✽ ⌂
V ♔ ☕ Lunch £4.95–£7.45 Tea 70p–£2.50 Dinner £6.50–£10 Wine £4 Last dinner 9pm
Credit cards 1 2 3 5 VS

★★★ **Rougemont** Queen St (Mount Charlotte) ☎ (0392) 54982 Telex no 42455 Plan **8** *B3*
Recently modernised hotel in a central position, catering for the tourist and commercial trade.
63rm (59⇒ 4⋒) CTV in all bedrooms sB&B⇒⋒ £27 dB&B⇒⋒ £37 B̶
Lift ☾ 35P CFA
V ♔ ☕ Lunch £5.50–6&alc Dinner £7–£7.50&alc Wine £5.50 Last dinner 9.45pm
Credit cards 1 2 3 5 VS

★★★ **Royal Clarence** Cathedral Yard ☎ (0392) 58464 Telex no 23241 (Plan **9** *C2*
Four-storey, white 18th-century building with bay windows overlooking the Cathedral.
60⇒ CTV in all bedrooms Ⓡ sB&B⇒ £29.50 dB&B⇒ £44.50 B̶
Lift ☾ CFA ♿
▣ English & Continental V ♔ ☕ ✱Lunch fr£5&alc Tea £3.25 Dinner fr£6.50&alc Wine £4.50 Last dinner 9.30pm
S% Credit cards 1 2 3 5

★★★ **White Hart** 65 South St ☎ (0392) 79897 Plan **11** *C2* RS Xmas
Comfortable, former coaching inn, standing in the town centre.
63rm (31⇒ 18⋒) (2fb) CTV in bedrooms ✗ sB&B£17 sB&B⇒⋒ £21.50–£24.50 dB&B£26–£28.50 dB&B⇒⋒ £35–£36.50 B̶
Lift ☾ CTV 70P ⛟

♔☕ Lunch £4.50&alc Dinner £7alc Wine £4.10 Last dinner 9.30pm

Credit cards 1 2 3 5

★★**Bystock** Bystock Ter ☎(0392) 72709 Plan **2** *B3*

Gabled, terraced hotel in residential/business square.

25rm(4➡2⋔) CTV in 10 bedrooms ✱sB&B£11.50–£12.50 sB&B➡⋔£14–£15 dB&B£20–£22 dB&B➡⋔£24–£26

CTV 🚗

▣English & French **V**♔☕✱Lunch £3–£4.50alc Tea 40p Dinner £4–£5.50&alc Wine £3 Last dinner 9.45pm

Credit cards 1 3

★★**Edgerton Park** 84 Pennsylvania Rd ☎(0392) 74029 Plan **3** *D4*

Red brick hotel in university area of city.

17rm(5➡12⋔)(3fb)Ⓡ sB&B➡⋔£16–£18 dB&B➡⋔£28–£31 Ⓑ

CTV 60P 🚗✽ nc5

▣English & French **V**♔ Lunch £2.95–£10&alc Dinner £2.95–£10&alc Wine £3.80 Last dinner 9pm

Credit cards 1 3 **VS**

★★**Red House** 2 Whipton Village Rd ☎(0392) 56104 Plan **7** *F4*

Modern hotel in suburban location, short distance from town.

14rm(3➡4⋔)(4fb) CTV in all bedrooms Ⓡ sB&B£10–£13.50 sB&B➡⋔£13.50–£16 dB&B➡⋔£22–£27 Ⓑ

40P nc5yrs

▣English & French **V**♔✱Lunch £4.60alc Dinner £6.65alc Wine £3.50 Last dinner 9pm

Credit cards 1 2 3 5 **VS**

★★**St Andrews** 28 Alphington Rd ☎(0392) 76784 Plan **10** *B1*
Closed Xmas

16rm(6➡)(1fb) CTV in all bedrooms Ⓡ sB&B£18–£21.50 sB&B➡£21–£25 dB&B£26–£31 dB&B➡£33–£39.50 Ⓑ

CTV 20P 🚗

♔ Bar lunch £3–£5 Tea fr85p Dinner £6.50–£9.20 Wine £3.67 Last dinner 8pm

Credit cards 1 2 3

★★♜**Trood Country House** Little Silver Ln, Alphington (from M5 junc 30 S for 3m on A379 following Okehampton signs) ☎(0392) 75839 Not on plan

Detached Georgian house in extensive grounds in a quiet location, three miles from the city centre.

10rm(6➡)1▣ CTV in 7 bedrooms ✱sB&B£14 sB&B➡£18 dB&B£24 dB&B➡£30 Ⓑ

⅍40P✽

▣English & French **V**♔☕✱Lunch £5–£6 Tea 45p–£1.50 High Tea £1.50–£2 Dinner £7–£15alc Wine £3.75 Last dinner 9.30pm

S% Credit cards 1 3 **VS**

At **Kennford** (6m SW on A38)

☆☆☆**Ladbroke** (on A38) (Ladbroke) ☎Exeter (0392) 832121 Not on plan

61➡⋔ 300P

See advert on page 260

★★*B* **Fairwinds** ☎Exeter (0392) 832911 Not on plan

7rm(3➡2⋔) 9P

EXFORD
Somerset
Map **3** SS83

★★*B* ***Crown*** (Inter-Hotels) ☎(064383) 554

Comfortable, modernised 17th-century inn.

18➡ CTV in all bedrooms Ⓡ Ⓑ 40P✽ U nc12yrs

▣English & French **V**♔☕ Last dinner 9.30pm

Credit cards 1 2 3 5 **VS**

See advert on page 260

Exmouth

EXMOUTH
Devon
Map **3** SY08

★★★**Devoncourt** Douglas Av
☎(03952) 72277
This hotel is set in four acres of sub-tropical grounds, overlooking the sea.
61⇌ sB&B⇌£16.10–£18.97 dB&B⇌£32.20–£37.94 B
Lift ☾ CTV 60P 10 CFA ✽ ≋(heated) (hard) *xmas* ♿
English & French **V** Lunch £4&alc Tea 60p Dinner £5.20&alc Wine £4.42 Last dinner 9.30pm

E

★★★**Imperial** The Esplanade (Trusthouse Forte) ☎(03952) 74761
Stands in four acres of gardens, facing south.
58⇌ Annexe: 3⇌ (11fb) CTV in all bedrooms Ⓡ sB&B⇌£33.50 dB&B⇌£56.50 B
Lift ☾ 55P CFA ✽ ≋heated (hard) sauna bath *xmas*
Last dinner 9pm
Credit cards 1 2 3 4 5

★★★**Royal Beacon** The Beacon
☎(03952) 4886
Originally a Georgian posting house, this hotel has a Regency style dining room.
35rm(32⇌) (3fb) CTV in all bedrooms Ⓡ sB&B fr£15 sB&B⇌fr£17.50 B
Lift CTV 25P 10 CFA billiards Live music and dancing Sat *xmas*
English & French **V** Lunch fr£3.50 Tea fr£1.50 High Tea fr£1.50 Dinner fr£6.50 Wine £3.95 Last dinner 9pm
Credit cards 1 2 3 4 5 **VS**

★★**Barn** Foxholes Hill, off Marine Drive (03952) 74411 (Due to change to 274411)
Friendly hotel with garden, set in an elevated position, that gives it pleasant sea views.
11rm(8 1) (4fb) CTV in 1 bedroom TV in 4 bedrooms ® *sB&B £15.50–£16.50 dB&B £31–£33 B
CTV 30P 3 (grass) *xmas*
V *Lunch £8&alc Tea £1alc High Tea £1.50alc Dinner £8alc Wine £4 Last dinner 8pm
VS

★★***Cavendish*** 11 Morton Cres, The Esplanade (03952) 72528
Closed Nov–Mar (except Xmas)
Terraced hotel situated on the sea front with fine views and short distance to shops.
64rm(27)
Lift CTV 25P Disco wkly Live music and dancing 5 nights wkly
Last dinner 8pm
Credit card 3

★★**Grand** Morton Cres, The Esplanade (03952) 3278
89rm(52) CTV in 15 bedrooms TV in 74 bedrooms ® sB&B £14–£20 sB&B £20–£25 dB&B £28–£35 dB&B £35–£40 B
Lift 40P CFA billiards Live music and dancing 3 nights wkly *xmas*
V Lunch £3.50–£4.50&alc Dinner £5.50&alc Wine £4.30 Last dinner 7.30pm

★★**Manor** The Beacon (03952) 72549
RS Nov–May
Terraced hotel in central location, overlooking park.
40rm(35 5) (6fb) CTV in all bedrooms sB&B £15.52–£17.82 dB&B £31.04–£35.64 B
Lift 10P 3 Live music and dancing 3 nights wkly *xmas*
V Lunch £3.75&alc Tea fr50p Dinner £5.75&alc Wine £3.85 Last dinner 8pm
Credit cards 1 3

FADMOOR
North Yorkshire
Map **8** SE68
Plough Inn Kirkbymoorside (0751) 31515
Closed Sun, Mon & 1wk in Feb
Lunch not served
English & French 24 seats *Dinner £7.40–£8.10 Last dinner 8.30pm P
S%

FAIRBOURNE
Gwynedd
Map **6** SH61
★★**Springfield** Beach Rd (0341) 250378
Modern hotel, situated ¼ mile from the beach, catering mainly for the holiday trade.
18rm(4) (2fb) ® *sB&B £12.50 dB&B £25 dB&B £27 B
CTV 100P
English, Welsh, French & Italian V
*Lunch £4.50 Tea £2 Dinner fr£5.50&alc Wine £3.95 Last dinner 9.15pm

★**Brackenhurst** (0341) 250226
Closed Nov–Apr
Country house whose high position affords good views over the Mawddach Estuary.
10rm(1 1) (2fb) sB&B fr£10.90 dB&B fr£21.80 dB&B fr£23.30
CTV 15P
English & French Lunch fr£3.50 Tea fr45p Dinner fr£6.50 Wine £3.95 Last dinner 8.30pm
Credit cards 1 3

FAIRFORD
Gloucestershire
Map **4** SP10
★★★**Bull** Market Pl Cirencester (0285) 712535
Traditional-style hotel situated in the market square.
19rm(14) 1 CTV in all bedrooms ® sB&B £18 sB&B £23.50 dB&B £28.50 dB&B £34.50 B
CTV 50P 11 Live music and dancing Thu Cabaret Thu & Sat
English, French & Italian V Lunch £7.50alc Tea 50palc High Tea £1.95alc Dinner £7.50alc Wine £2.95 Last dinner 9.30pm
Credit cards 1 2 3 5

★***HB*** **Hyperion** London St Cirencester (0285) 712349
A comfortable, privately-run hotel, offering sound home cooking.
23rm(20) (2fb) CTV in all bedrooms sB&B £14.50 sB&B £19.15 dB&B £23.75 dB&B £33.50 B
CTV 50P *xmas*
English & French Bar lunch fr£1 Tea 50p Dinner fr£7.35 Last dinner 8.15pm
Credit cards 1 2 3 5 **VS**

FAIRY CROSS
Devon
Map **2** SS42
★★★***Portledge*** (off A39) Horns Cross (02375) 262 Closed Jan & Feb
26rm(18) CTV in 1 bedroom
CTV 100P CFA (heated) (hard) nc5yrs
English & Continental Last dinner 9pm
Credit card 3

FALFIELD
Avon
Map **3** ST69
★★**Park** (0454) 260550
Colour-washed, gabled building standing in its own grounds, in a pleasant rural setting.
10rm(4 2) (2fb) CTV in all bedrooms sB fr£20 sB fr£25 dB fr£30 dB fr£33.50 (room only) B
100P Live music and dancing in winter *xmas*
Continental V Lunch fr£8.50&alc Dinner fr£10.50&alc Last dinner 10pm
Credit cards 1 2 3 4 5

FALKIRK
Central *Stirlingshire*
Map **11** NS87
☆☆☆**Stakis Park** Arnot Hill, Camelon Rd (Stakis) (0324) 28331 Telex no 778704
55 CTV in all bedrooms ® *sB&B fr£31 dB&B fr£39 B
Lift 100P CFA
English & French Last dinner 10pm
Credit cards 1 2 3 5 **VS**

Pierre's 140 Graham's Rd (0324) 35843
Closed Xmas Day, 1–12 Jan, 1st 3 wks Jul & Local hols
French 35 seats Lunch £3.90–£5.20&alc Dinner £8.45–£8.85&alc Wine £4.40 Last dinner 9.30pm
Credit cards 1 2 3 5 **VS**

FALMOUTH
Cornwall
Map **2** SW83
See plan
★★★**Bay** Cliff Rd (0326) 312094 Telex no 45262 Plan **1** *D1* Closed Nov–Mar
Large, traditional hotel on the sea front, overlooking Gyllynvrase beach, yet close to the town centre.
36 (2fb) CTV in all bedrooms ® sB&B £19.50–£24.50 dB&B £39–£49 B
Lift 50P 3 billiards sauna bath
English & French V Lunch £5.50 Tea 60p–£1.50 Dinner £8.50 Wine £4.50 Last dinner 8.30pm
Credit cards 1 2 3 5

★★★**Falmouth** (0326) 312671 Telex no 45262 Plan **5** *D2* Closed Xmas wk
Comfortable, large, modernised hotel in its own grounds on the sea front.
73 (12fb) CTV in all bedrooms ® sB&B £19.50–£30 dB&B £39–£60 B
Lift 100P 30 CFA (heated) billiards sauna bath Disco wkly
English & French Lunch £5.50 Tea 60p–£1.50 Dinner £8.50&alc Wine £4.50 Last dinner 10pm
Credit cards 1 2 3 5

Falmouth

F

★★★**Greenbank** Harbourside
☎(0326) 312440 Telex no 45240 Plan **6** *C3*
Closed 24 Dec–2 Jan
Comfortable, well appointed hotel with friendly relaxed atmosphere.
40rm(35🛁5🚿)(6fb) CTV in all bedrooms
Ⓡ sB&B🛁🚿£24–£26
dB&B🛁🚿£40.50–£44.50 B
Lift ☾ 30P 30🚗
🍴English & French **V**☕☕✻Lunch fr£4.50 Tea fr£1.25 High Tea £2.50 Dinner fr£9 Wine £3.95 Last dinner 10pm
Credit cards 1 2 3 5

★★★**Green Lawns** Western Ter
☎(0326) 312734 Telex no 45169 Plan **7** *B2*
Closed wk Xmas
Built in 1920 in the style of a French château, the hotel has 1½ acres of terraced lawns.
27rm(19🛁4🚿) Annexe: 5rm(1🛁1🚿) (5fb) CTV in all bedrooms Ⓡ
sB&B£12.65–£23 sB&B🛁🚿£20.12–£23
dB&B£18.40–£37 dB&B🛁🚿£25.30–£37 B
☾ ✈60P CFA ✻ 🎾 squash Live music and dancing Sat
🍴English & French **V**☕☕Lunch £1.85–£5&alc Tea fr60p High Tea fr£1 Dinner £7.50&alc Wine £4.60 Last dinner 9pm
Credit cards 1 2 3 4 5 **VS**

★★★**Gyllyngdune** Melvill Rd ☎(0326) 312978 Plan **8** *C1*
Old Georgian manor house situated in two acres of beautiful gardens overlooking the bay.
35rm(30🛁1🚿)(3fb) 3🛏 CTV in all bedrooms ✻sB&B£14.50–£16.50
sB&B🛁🚿£14.50–£16.50 dB&B£29–£33 dB&B🛁🚿£29–£33
☾ 16P 3🚗 ✻ ⛱(heated) billiards sauna bath *xmas*
🍴English & Continental ☕☕✻Lunch £4 Tea 50p–£1.30 Dinner £7&alc Wine £3.50 Last dinner 9pm
Credit cards 1 2 3 5

★★★🏠*HB* **Penmere Manor** Mongleath Rd (Best Western) ☎(0326) 314545 Plan **13** *A1*
Closed 19 Dec–3 Jan
Attractive, comfortable, family-owned Georgian mansion with views across Falmouth Bay.
24🛁3🚿 Annexe: 2🛁 CTV in all bedrooms
Ⓡ sB&B🛁🚿£20.50 dB&B🛁🚿£41 B
40P 🚫 ✻ ⛱(heated)
☕☕Bar lunch 70p–£3.50 Tea 65p Dinner £7.50 Wine £5 Last dinner 8.30pm
Credit cards 1 2 3 5 **VS**

★★★**Royal Duchy** Cliff Rd (Brend)
☎(0326) 313042 Plan **15** *D1*
Large, traditional-style, hotel on the sea front.
38rm(24🛁) CTV available in bedrooms
sB&B£13.23–£14.38 sB&B🛁£16.68–£18.40 dB&B£24.15–£27.60 dB&B🛁 31.60–£34.50 B
Lift ☾ CTV 55P 12🚗 ✻ 🏠 *xmas*
☕☕✻Lunch fr£4.60 Dinner fr£6.90&alc Last dinner 9pm
Credit cards 1 2 3 5
See advert on page 264

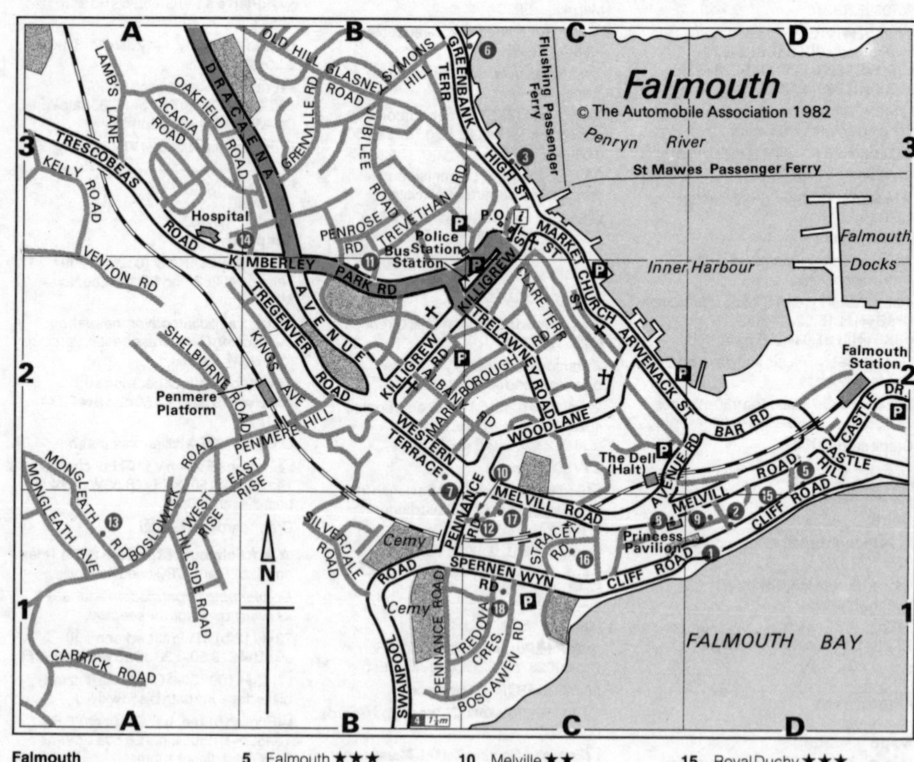

Falmouth
© The Automobile Association 1982
A
B
C
D
1
2
3
Penryn River
St Mawes Passenger Ferry
Flushing Passenger Ferry
Inner Harbour
Falmouth Docks
Falmouth Station
FALMOUTH BAY
Hospital
Police Station
Bus Station
P.O.
Penmere Platform
The Dell (Halt)
Princess Pavilion
Cemy
Cemy
N
LAMB'S LANE
OAKFIELD ROAD
ACACIA ROAD
DRACAENA AVENUE
OLD HILL
GLASNEY ROAD
SYMONS HILL
GREENBANK TERR
GRENVILLE RD
JUBILEE ROAD
TREVETHAN RD
PENROSE RD
HIGH ST
MARKET ST
CHURCH ST
ARWENACK ST
KILLIGREW ST
CLARE TERR
TRELAWNEY ROAD
TRESCOBEAS ROAD
KELLY ROAD
VENTON RD
KIMBERLEY PARK RD
TREGENVER ROAD
KINGS AVE
SHELBURNE ROAD
PENMERE HILL
KILLIGREW
ALBANY
MARLBOROUGH RD
WESTERN TERRACE
WOODLANE
BAR RD
AVENUE RD
CASTLE DR
CASTLE HILL
MELVILL ROAD
CLIFF ROAD
PENNANCE RD
STRACEY RD
SPERNEN WYN RD
SILVERDALE ROAD
SWANPOOL ROAD
PENNANCE ROAD
TREDOVA CRES.
BOSCAWEN RD
MONGLEATH RD
MONGLEATH AVE
BOSLOWICK ROAD
WEST RISE
EAST RISE
PENMERE ROAD
HILLSIDE ROAD
CARRICK ROAD

Falmouth

1 Bay★★★
2 Carthion★★
3 Continental ✕
4 Crill House★★
5 Falmouth★★★
6 Greenbank★★★
7 Green Lawns★★★
8 Gyllyngdune★★★
9 Lerryn★★
10 Melville★★
11 Park Grove★★
12 Pendower★★
13 Penmere Manor★★★🏠
14 Rosslyn★★
15 Royal Duchy★★★
16 Hotel St Michaels★★★
17 Somerdale★★
18 Suncourt★

GREEN LAWNS HOTEL

WESTERN TERRACE, FALMOUTH, CORNWALL, TR11 4QJ
Telephone: (0326) 312734 Telex: G Lawns G45169

The Green Lawns stands in 1½ acres of delightful gardens in a position which commands extensive and magnificent views of the bay and surrounding countryside. Falmouth is the centre of the 'Cornish Riviera' and Green Lawns was designed and furnished to enable visitors to enjoy the subtropical climate in inexpensive comfort. Our Garras Restaurant has acquired a high reputation for English and French cuisine.

Send for Brochure and Tariff.

The Gyllyngdune Manor Hotel

AA ★★★

Melville Road, Falmouth, Cornwall TR11 4AR

Telephones: (0326) Management: 312978 Guests: 311479

Old Georgian manor house, romantically situated in two acres of beautiful gardens, overlooking the Bay and Estuary. Guaranteed away from traffic, but within ten minutes' walk of the town centre. Very large car park, covered space if required. Luxury indoor heated swimming pool, games room, Sauna and Solarium. Golf at Falmouth Golf Club. 95% rooms en-suite and coloured TV. Every comfort with personal attention the primary consideration. Gourmet cuisine, table d'hôte, à la carte our speciality and highly recommended.

★★★
Penmere
Manor
Hotel
Best
Western

MONGLEATH ROAD,
FALMOUTH

Tel: Falmouth (0326) 314545

A FINE GEORGIAN MANSION SET IN SECLUDED GARDENS AND WOODLAND OF 5 ACRES WITH VIEWS OF FALMOUTH BAY.

29 attractive bedrooms with private bathroom en suite, radio, colour TV, PO telephone, tea and coffee making facilities; 3 resident's lounges, lounge bar and cellar games room; full central heating. Large heated swimming pool.

The hotel is personally run by Mr & Mrs David Pope and family; meals are prepared and supervised by Mrs Rachel Pope and her daughter Elizabeth, with a variety of menus to make each visit to the dining room something to look forward to.

★★★*H* **Hotel St Michaels** Cliff Rd ☎(0326) 312707 Telex no 45540 Plan **16** *D1*

Situated in four acres of prize-winning gardens that slope down to the beach. This hotel has fine views of the Cornish riviera coastline.

60rm(36⇌24⋒) Annexe: 9⇌⋒ (18fb) CTV in all bedrooms Ⓡ sB&B⇌⋒ £19.50–£26 dB&B⇌⋒ £35–£48 B

☾ CFA ✽ (heated) sauna bath *xmas*

English, French & Italian Lunch £4.50 Tea 55–60p High Tea £5 Dinner £9–£9.50&alc Wine £4.05 Last dinner 10.30pm

Credit cards 1 2 3 5 **VS**

★★*HL* **Carthion** Cliff Rd ☎(0326) 313669 Plan **2** *D1*

Closed Dec–28 Feb

Comfortable, family owned hotel, with fine views over Falmouth Bay.

14rm(8⇌1⋒) (3fb) CTV available in bedrooms sB&B £9.75–£16.30 dB&B £17.85–£31 dB&B⇌⋒ £21–£33.60 B

CTV 18P ✽

French **V** Bar lunch £2.10–£3.50 Tea 40p–£1 Dinner £7&alc Wine £3.30 Last dinner 4.30pm

Credit cards 1 2 3 5 **VS**

★★*B* **Crill House** Golden Bank (3m W on unclass rd) ☎(0326) 312994 Plan **4** *B1*

Closed mid Oct–mid Mar

Small, comfortable, friendly hotel in a peaceful rural location.

11rm(10⇌1⋒) (3fb) Ⓡ ✻ sB&B⇌⋒ £13–£21 dB&B⇌⋒ £26–£42

CTV 22P 1 ✽ (heated)

F

English & Continental Bar lunch 40p–£3.25 Tea 60p–£1.10 Dinner fr£6&alc Wine £3.75 Last dinner 8pm

Credit cards 1 3 **VS**

★★**Lerryn** De Pass Rd (0326) 312489 Plan **9** *D1*
Closed 14 Oct–mid Apr
Small hotel in quiet position near sea front.
20rm(9 7) (3fb) CTV in all bedrooms Ⓡ sB&B£9–£11 sB&B £10–£13.50 dB&B£17–£20 dB&B £18.50–£23 B
13P nc5yrs
V Bar lunch £1–£2.50 Tea £1–£1.50 Dinner £5–£6.50&alc Wine £2 Last dinner 8pm

★★***Melville*** Sea View Rd (0326) 312134 Plan **10** *C2*
Closed Nov
Three-storey, family hotel in an elevated position within pleasant grounds and gardens.
21rm(8) B
CTV 30P 10 Disco wkly
Last dinner 8pm
Credit cards 1 2 3 **VS**

★★**Park Grove** Kimberley Park Rd (0326) 313276 Plan **11** *B2*
Closed Nov–Feb
Friendly, comfortable, family hotel opposite the park and gardens.
17rm(9) (4fb) Ⓡ sB&B 9.50–£12 sB&B £11.50–£14 dB&B£19–£24 dB&B £23–£28
CTV 20P
V Lunch £3–£4 Tea £1–£2 Dinner £5.50–£6.50 Wine £3.90 Last dinner 7.30pm
Credit cards 1 3 **VS**

★★**Pendower** Sea View Rd (0326) 312108 Plan **12** *C1*
Closed Dec–Feb
Family, holiday hotel in its own small grounds.
29rm(12 6) Ⓡ sB&B£12.75–£13.85 sB&B £14–£15.50 dB&B£23.50–£26 dB&B £26–£29 B
20P (heated) sauna bath
Wine £4 Last dinner 8pm
Credit cards 1 3 **VS**

★★**Rosslyn** Kimberley Park Rd (0326) 312699 Plan **14** *A3*
Closed Nov–Feb
Located in one acre of gardens and grounds in an elevated position.
25rm(5 10) (5fb) Ⓡ sB&B£11–£12.50 sB&B £12–£13.50 dB&B£22–£25 dB&B £30–£35 B
CTV 30P Live music and dancing 3 nights wkly
Bar lunch £1.35–£1.98 Tea £1 Dinner £4.50–£6 Wine £3.80 Last dinner 8pm

★★**Somerdale** Sea View Rd (Minotel) (0326) 312566 Plan **17** *C1*
Small, comfortable, friendly, family hotel close to the beaches.
18rm(10 2) Annexe: 1 (4fb) CTV in all bedrooms Ⓡ sB&B£15.53 sB&B £17.54 dB&B£31.06 dB&B £35.08 B
13P *xmas*
V Lunch £3 Tea 75p Dinner £6.75–£10.25 Wine £4.25 Last dinner 9pm
Credit cards 1 2 3 5 **VS**
See advert on page 266

★**Suncourt** Boscowen Rd (0326) 312886 Plan **18** *C1*
Small, pleasantly situated hotel overlooking the bay, and in a quiet position near to the beach.
14rm(3) (1fb) sB&B£7.25–£9.66 dB&B£14.50–£19.32 dB&B £19.32–£28.98
CTV 12P
Lunch £5 Dinner £6.50 Wine £3.25 Last dinner 6.30pm
VS

✕**Continental** 29 High St (0326) 313003 Plan **3** *C3*
Closed Sun Lunch not served Sat →

F

Continental 45 seats *Lunch £5alc Dinner £11alc Wine £5 Last dinner 10pm

Credit cards 3 5

FAREHAM
Hampshire
Map **4** SU50

★★**Red Lion** East St (Whitbread Wessex) ☎(0329) 239611
Well-appointed coaching inn with excellent bedrooms.
33 (2fb) CTV in all bedrooms ® sB&B fr£29 dB&B fr£42
CTV 100P
Lunch £6alc Dinner £7.50alc Wine £4.75 Last dinner 10pm
Credit cards 1 2 3 5

FARINGDON
Oxfordshire
Map **4** SU29

★★***Bell*** Market Pl (Exec Hotel) ☎(0367) 20534
RS Xmas
Traditional coaching inn with comfortable bedrooms.
11rm(3) CTV in 2 bedrooms TV in 1 bedroom
CTV 11P 3
V Last dinner 9.30pm
Credit cards 1 2 3 5

★***Salutation*** Market Pl ☎(0367) 20536
Small family run hotel with modest accommodation.
7rm Annexe: 1 ®
TV 3P 2 nc10yrs
English & French Last dinner 8.45pm

FARNBOROUGH
Hampshire
Map **4** SU85

☆☆☆**Queens** Lynchford Rd (Anchor) ☎(0252) 545051 Telex no 858875
84rm(79) (2fb) CTV in all bedrooms ® *sB&B£19.50 sB&B £35.50 dB&B£24 dB&B £42
200P CFA
V *Lunch £5.50-£8.70&alc Dinner £5.50-£8.70&alc Wine £4.50 Last dinner 9.15pm
Credit cards 1 2 3 4 5

FARNHAM
Surrey
Map **4** SU84

★★★L **Bush** The Borough (Anchor) ☎(0252) 715237 Telex no 858764
This town-centre hotel used to be a coaching inn.
73rm(55 2) CTV in all bedrooms ® *sB&B fr£22.50 sB&B fr£35.50 dB&B fr£34 dB&B fr£42
60P CFA *xmas*
V *Lunch £10.50alc Tea 45palc High Tea £1.25alc Dinner £10.50alc Wine £4.50 Last dinner 10.30pm
Credit cards 1 2 3 4 5

★★**Bishops Table** 27 West St (Best Western) ☎(0252) 715545
Town centre hotel with some modern and some sumptuous bedrooms and choice of restaurants.
16rm(10 4) (1fb) 1 CTV in all bedrooms ® sB&B£25 sB&B £27 dB&B £37
Continental V *Lunch £7&alc Tea 55p–£1.25 Dinner £7&alc Wine £4.60 Last dinner 9.30pm
S% Credit cards 1 2 3 5

★★**Trevena House** Alton Rd ☎(0252) 716908
Closed 24 Dec–8 Jan
Hotel has comfortable, smart bedrooms; restaurant provides snack lunches and well-cooked dinners.
20rm(15 2) (3fb) CTV in all bedrooms ® sB&B£17 sB&B £17–£29 dB&B£22 dB&B £29–£38
40P (heated) (hard) sauna bath
French Tea £1.50alc Dinner £11alc Wine £5 Last dinner 9.15pm
S% Credit cards 1 2 3 5 **VS**

✕✕**Viceroy** 23 East St ☎(0252) 710949
Elegant, Indian restaurant.
Closed Sun, 25 & 26 Dec
Indian & Pakistan **V** 55 seats Lunch £6–£8alc Dinner £6–£8alc Wine £4.60 Last dinner 11.30pm
Credit cards 1 2 3 4 5

✕***Gibbons*** Castle St ☎(0252) 714721
Closed Mon, 25 Dec–early Jan, except 31 Dec (dinner only) Dinner not served Sun
French 62 seats Last dinner 11pm
Credit cards 1 2 3 5

FARNSFIELD
Nottinghamshire
Map **8** SK65

✕✕***White Post Inn*** ☎Mansfield (0623) 882215
Dinner not served Sun
120 seats Last dinner 10pm 200P bedrooms available Live music Fri & Sat
Credit cards 1 2 3

FARRINGTON GURNEY
Avon
Map **3** ST55

✕✕**Old Parsonage** Main St ☎Temple Cloud (0761) 52211
Closed Mon & 3wks staff hols Dinner not served Sun
English & French 26 seats Lunch £15alc Dinner £15alc Wine £4 Last dinner 9.30pm 100P bedrooms available

FAUGH
Cumbria
Map **12** NY55

★★★B **String of Horses Inn** ☎Hayton (022870) 297
13rm(8 5) 2 CTV in all bedrooms ® sB&B £28.50–£32 dB&B £36–£54
CTV 50P (heated) sauna bath
English & French **V** Lunch £7alc Dinner £6.25–£9.75&alc Wine £4.50 Last dinner 10.30pm
Credit cards 1 2 3 4 5 **VS**

F

FAVERSHAM
Kent
Map **5** TR06
❀✕✕**Read's** Painters Forstal ☎(0795) 535344
Smart but friendly restaurant with sound French cuisine.
Closed Sun
French 36 seats ✱Lunch fr£6.50&alc Dinner £12alc Wine £4.44 Last dinner 10pm 36P
Credit cards 2 3 5 **VS**

FEARNAN
Tayside *Perthshire*
Map **11** NN74
★**Tigh-an-Loan** ☎Kenmore (08873) 249
Closed Oct–19 Apr
Cosy, personally-run hotel overlooking Loch Tay.
10rm (2fb) sB&B fr£10.50 dB&B fr£21
CTV 25P ✱
Bar lunch £2.50alc Tea 50palc Dinner £6.50alc Wine £3 Last dinner 7.30pm

FELIXSTOWE
Suffolk
Map **5** TM33
★★★★**Orwell Moat House** Hamilton Rd (Queens Moat) ☎(0394) 285511
The service is friendly and hospitable at this traditional hotel.
65rm (50⇌10⋒) CTV in all bedrooms sB fr£27 sB⇌⋒ fr£34 dB fr£42 dB⇌⋒ fr£48 (room only) 🅱
Lift ☾ 150P 10 CFA ✱ Live music and dancing Sat
V Lunch fr£6.50 Tea fr£1.50 Dinner fr£7.95 Wine £4.95 Last dinner 9.45pm
Credit cards 1 2 3 5 **VS**

★★**North Sea** Sea Front ☎(0394) 282103
25rm (10⇌2⋒) (3fb) TV in all bedrooms ® sB&B£20 sB&B⇌⋒ £23 dB&B£27 dB&B⇌⋒ £30 🅱
☾ CTV 10P
English & French **V** Lunch £5.25&alc Dinner £6.25&alc Wine £5.60 Last dinner 9.30pm
Credit cards 1 3 **VS**

★***Cavendish*** Sea Front ☎(0394) 282696
Closed Xmas
Three-storey, family-run hotel at the southern end of the promenade.
13rm
Lift CTV 50P
Last dinner 8pm

FELSTED
Essex
Map **5** TL62
✕✕**Boote House** ☎Gt Dunmow (0371) 820279
Imaginative dishes are skilfully cooked and efficiently served.
Closed Tue & 2wks Aug Lunch not served Mon–Sat Dinner not served Tue
French 75 seats Lunch £6.25 Dinner £10–£15 Wine £4.95 Last dinner 9.30pm P
Credit cards 1 2 3 5

FENNY BENTLEY
Derbyshire
Map **7** SK14
★★**Bentley Brook Inn** ☎Thorpe Cloud (033529) 278
Detached gabled house on the edge of the Peak National Park.
8rm (3⇌) (1fb) CTV in all bedrooms ® sB&B£15 sB&B⇌£18 dB&B£24 dB&B⇌£28 🅱
CTV 60P ✱ Live music and dancing Sat *xmas*
Lunch £4–£6.50 Dinner £5–£6.50&alc Last dinner 9.30pm
Credit card 1

FENNY BRIDGES
Devon
Map **3** SY19
★***Fenny Bridges*** ☎Honiton (0404) 850218
An inn-style small hotel in own grounds beside A30.
6rm CTV 50P 1 ✱
Last dinner 9.30pm
Credit cards 1 3

FERMAIN BAY
Guernsey, Channel Islands
Map **16**
★★★**Le Chalet** ☎Guernsey (0481) 35716
Closed Nov–Apr
43rm (35⇌7⋒) Annexe: 7⇌ CTV in all bedrooms sB&B⇌⋒ £15.95–£18.15 dB&B⇌⋒ £27.50–£34.10
30P ✱
English, Austrian & French Lunch £3.50–£5&alc Dinner £5–£5.50&alc Wine £2.50
Credit cards 1 2 3 4 5

★★**La Favorita** ☎Guernsey (0481) 35666
Closed Nov–Mar
30rm (28⇌2⋒) (4fb) CTV in all bedrooms ® sB&B⇌⋒ £14–£18.50 dB&B⇌⋒ £28–£37 🅱
30P ✱ Live music and dancing wkly
V ✱Lunch fr£4 Tea 50palc Dinner £4.20alc Wine £2.32 Last dinner 8pm
Credit card 3

FERNDOWN
Dorset
Map **4** SU00
★★★★**Dormy** New Rd (DeVere) ☎(0202) 872121 Telex no 418301
Attractive hotel with well-appointed bedrooms, some in individual bungalows in hotels extensive grounds.
62⇌ Annexe: 28⇌ CTV in all bedrooms ✱sB&B⇌£29 dB&B⇌£52.50 🅱
Lift ☾ CTV 120P 2 CFA ✱ (heated) in summer (grass) Live music and dancing Sat *xmas*
English & French ✱Lunch £7.35&alc Tea £2.60 Dinner £8.40&alc Wine £5.50 Last dinner 9.30pm
S% Credit cards 1 2 3 4 5
See advert on page 268

☆☆**Coach House Motel** Tricketts Cross (junc A31/A348) ☎(0202) 871222
Modern hotel where all bedrooms are sited in individual units.
44⋔ CTV in all bedrooms Ⓡ sB⋔ £19 dB⋔ £26.50 (room only) B
120P 20 CFA
Lunch £6.50&alc Dinner £6.50&alc Wine £4.25 Last dinner 10pm
Credit cards 1 2 3 5 **VS**

FILEY
North Yorkshire
Map **8** TA18
★★★**White Lodge** The Crescent ☎Scarborough (0723) 514771
A three-storey 'villa'-type, converted residence overlooking the bay.
23rm(16⇌2⋔) (2fb) CTV in all bedrooms Ⓡ sB&B£14–£16 sB&B⇌⋔ £16.40–£18.40 dB&B£30.20–£32.20 dB&B⇌⋔ £34.80–£36.80 B
Lift ☾ 10P *xmas*
English, French & Italian **V** Lunch £5–£6 Tea 60p Dinner £8–£9 Wine £5 Last dinner 7.45pm
Credit cards 1 3

★★**Hylands** The Crescent (Minotel) ☎Scarborough (0723) 512091
Conversion of fine Georgian terraced houses, overlooking the bay.
47rm(9⇌9⋔) (4fb) sB&B£12–£13 sB&B⇌⋔ £13.25–£14.25 dB&B£24–£26 dB&B⇌⋔ £26.50–£28.50 B
Lift ☾ CTV Disco 4 nights wkly Live music 3 nights wkly Cabaret wkly
Lunch £3.50 Tea 50p High Tea £1.75–£3.75 Dinner £6–£6.50 Wine £3.75 Last dinner 8pm
Credit card 1 3

XX ***Victoria Court*** The Crescent ☎Scarborough (0723) 513237
Dinner not served Sun–Tue
English & French **V** 40 seats Last dinner 10pm

FINDON
West Sussex
Map **4** TQ10
★**Village House** The Square ☎(090671) 3350
Homely hotel with equestrian theme in bar.
9rm (1fb) Ⓡ sB&B£12.50–£13.50 dB&B£20–£22
CTV 10P
Lunch £4.50–£5.50 Tea fr£1 Dinner £5.50&alc Last dinner 9.30pm
Credit cards 1 2 3 5

X ***Darlings Bistro*** The Square ☎(090671) 3817
Closed Sun
French 16 seats Last dinner 9pm P
Credit cards 1 2 3 5

FISHGUARD
Dyfed
Map **2** SM93
★★★**Fishguard Bay** Goodwick ☎(0348) 873571
Impressive building, surrounded by woodland and overlooking the bay.
62rm(27⇌2⋔) (6fb) 1 CTV in 8 bedrooms *sB&B£18 sB&B⇌⋔ £20 dB&B£30 dB&B⇌⋔ £32.50 B
Lift ☾ CTV 50P CFA (heated) billiards *xmas*
English & French **V** *Lunch £5.50 Tea 80p Dinner £6.75&alc Wine £3.75 Last dinner 9.30pm
Credit cards 1 2 3 5 **VS**

★★**Cartref** High St (Minotel) ☎(0348) 872430
Comfortable hotel situated in the town centre.
14rm(2⇌4⋔) sB&B£12.50 sB&B⇌⋔ £15.50 dB&B£21 dB&B⇌⋔ £25 B
CTV 15P 2 nc7yrs *xmas*

Lunch £4 Dinner fr£6 Wine £3.80 Last dinner 8pm

Credit cards 1 3

★ ***Manor House*** Main St ☎(0348) 873260

Closed Oct

Small, pleasant, terraced Georgian house in the town centre, with views of the harbour from the garden.

8rm CTV 1 bedroom Ⓡ

CTV P

Last dinner 9pm

VS

FITTLEWORTH
West Sussex
Map **4** TQ01

★★**Swan** ☎(079882) 429

A 13th-century coaching inn with oak beams and a unique collection of painted panels in the dining room.

8rm(1) (1fb) 2 Ⓡ *sB&B£16 dB&B£28–£34

CTV 30P *xmas*

V *Lunch £5.25&alc Tea 50p–£1 High Tea £2 Dinner £9alc Wine £3,70 Last dinner 9.30pm

S% Credit cards 1 2 3 5 **VS**

FLAMBOROUGH
Humberside
Map **8** TA26

★★*B* **Timoneer Country Manor** South Sea Rd ☎Bridlington (0262) 850219

10 CTV in all bedrooms Ⓡ sB&B £15.50–£19.50 dB&B £29–£33

150P 20 Disco Sat

English & French **V** Lunch £4.75–£5.65&alc Dinner £6.55&alc Wine £3.80 Last dinner 10pm

Credit cards 1 2 3 4 5 **VS**

FLEET
Dorset
Map **3** SY68

★★ **Moonfleet Manor** ☎Weymouth (0305) 786948

Manor house set in a secluded location alongside Chesil Beach, which has associations with the smuggling novel 'Moonfleet'.

39rm(22 4) (13fb) 1 CTV in 12 bedrooms Ⓡ sB&B£9.50–£16 sB&B £16–£24 dB&B£19–£38 dB&B £32–£42

CTV 200P (heated) (hard) squash billiards sauna bath Disco twice wkly in summer Live music and dancing twice wkly in summer *xmas*

V Bar lunch fr£1.95 Dinner fr£6.50 Wine £3.50 Last dinner 9pm

Credit cards 1 2 3 5 **VS**

FLEET
Hampshire
Map **4** SU85

★★★**Lismoyne** Church Rd ☎(02514) 28555

Victorian hotel with variety of bedrooms and popular restaurant.

29 3 CTV in all bedrooms Ⓡ sB&B£20 sB&B £28–£32 dB&B£30 dB&B £38

☾ 80P Live music and dancing Sat

English & French **V** Lunch fr£5.35&alc Tea fr50p Dinner fr£6.35&alc Wine £4.55 Last dinner 9.30pm

Credit cards 1 2 3 5 **VS**

FLEETWOOD
Lancashire
Map **7** SD34

★★★**North Euston** The Esplanade ☎(03917) 6525

Mid-Victorian, crescent-shaped building overlooking the sea.

62rm(29 4) (6fb) CTV in all bedrooms Ⓡ sB&B£17 sB&B £18.50 dB&B£29 dB&B £31

Lift ☾ 65P Disco 3 nights wkly *xmas*

Lunch £4.25&alc Dinner £6.75&alc Wine £4.80 Last dinner 9.30pm

Credit cards 1 2 3 5

FLICHITY
Highland *Inverness-shire*
Map **14** NH62

✕**Grouse & Trout** ☎Farr (08083) 314

Attractive cottage restaurant with bar and craft shop.

Closed Mon

English, Scottish & French 50 seats *Lunch 80p–£4&alc Tea 65p&alc Dinner £10alc Wine £3.95 Last dinner 10pm 60P

Credit cards 1 2 3 5 **VS**

FLITTON
Bedfordshire
Map **4** TL03

✕**White Hart Inn** ☎Silsoe (0525) 60403

Pretty pub, specialising in fresh fish dishes.

Closed Sun

V 50 seats Lunch £6.75–£10.75 Dinner £6.75–£10.75 Wine £5.20 Last dinner 9.30pm 24P

Credit cards 1 2 3 5

FOCHABERS
Grampian *Morayshire*
Map **15** NJ35

★★**Gordon Arms** ☎(0343) 820508

12rm(6) Annexe: 2rm(1 1) CTV in all bedrooms Ⓡ sB&B£18–£20 sB&B £22–£25 dB&B£28–£30 dB&B £35–£38

CTV 50P

Lunch £3.50–£4.50 Tea £1.20–£1.50 High Tea £3.50–£4.50 Dinner £7–£9&alc Wine £4.50 Last dinner 9pm

Credit cards 1 2 3 5

FOLKESTONE
Kent
Map **5** TR23

★★★**Clifton** The Leas (Trusthouse Forte) ☎(0303) 41231

Hotel commands fine views of English Channel.

62rm(34 2) (2fb) CTV in all bedrooms Ⓡ sB&B£25 sB&B £31.50 dB&B£38.50 dB&B £49

Lift ☾ *xmas*

Last dinner 9pm

Credit cards 1 2 3 4 5

★★**Chilworth Court** 39–41 Earls Av (Minotels) ☎(0303) 41583

Friendly hotel with well-equipped bedrooms and good quality cooking.

21rm(13 3) (4fb) TV in all bedrooms sB&B£15.95 dB&B £19.80 dB&B£25.30 dB&B £30.25

☾ CTV 20P CFA

English & French Lunch £5 Dinner £7.15&alc Wine £5 Last dinner 9.30pm

S% Credit cards 1 2 3 4 5 **VS**

✕✕**La Tavernetta** Leaside Court ☎(0303) 54955

A well-appointed, lower ground floor restaurant overlooking gardens near the sea front.

Closed Sun & Public Holidays

55 seats *Lunch £4.50&alc Dinner £10 Wine £4.60

Credit cards 1 2 3 5

✕**Emilio's Portofino** 124a Sandgate Rd ☎(0303) 55866

Closed Mon

Good modestly priced Italian cuisine.

Italian 55 seats *Lunch £4.50–£4.90&alc Dinner £8.50alc Wine £4.50 Last dinner 10.30pm

Credit cards 1 2 3 5

✕**Paul's** 2a Bouverie Road West ☎(0303) 59697

Closed Sun, 25 & 26 Dec, & 1 wk early/late summer

Nouvelle Cuisine 44 seats Lunch £9.05alc Dinner £9.05alc Last dinner 9.30pm

S% Credit cards 1 3 5

FORD
Wiltshire
Map **3** ST87

★★**White Hart Inn** ☎Castle Combe (0249) 782213

Quiet 15th century stone inn with beams and log fires.

Annexe: 8 (1fb) 4 CTV in all bedrooms Ⓡ sB&B £22–£28 dB&B £32–£38

→

F

CTV 50P ✽ ⛴ (heated) nc3

English & French V ♧ Bar lunch 95p–£3&alc Dinner £8–£9.50 Wine £3.75 Last dinner 9.30pm

Credit cards 1 3

FORDINGBRIDGE
Hampshire
Map **4** SU11

★★**Ashburn** (Minotel) ☎ (0425) 52060
Reasonably priced but modest hotel with modern bedroom wing.

25rm(9➡) (5fb) TV available in bedrooms Ⓡ sB&B£11.50–£12.50 sB&B➡⋒ £16.50–£18 dB&B£23–£25 dB&B➡⋒ £27.60–£30 B

CTV 70P ✽ ⛴ (heated)

English & Continental V ♧ Lunch £5.75–£6.50 Dinner £6.50–£8 Wine £4 Last dinner 8.30pm

Credit cards 1 3

✕✕**Hour Glass** Burgate ☎ (0425) 52348

Closed Sun, Mon, part Feb, 1 wk May & 1 wk Sep Lunch not served

English & French 35 seats Dinner £9.99–£15.55&alc Wine £4.95 Last dinner 9.45pm 30P

S% Credit cards 1 2 3 5 **VS**

✕**Three Lions Inn** Stuckton ☎ (0425) 52489

Closed Mon, Feb, 1 wk after Etr & 2 wks end July Lunch not served Tue Dinner not served Sun

Continental 32 seats Lunch £8.25alc Dinner £12.50alc Wine £4.50 Last dinner 9pm 20P

VS

FORDWICH
Kent
Map **5** TR15

★★**George & Dragon** ☎ Canterbury (0227) 710661
16th century inn with imaginative above average cooking.

9rm(1➡) Annexe: 4➡ (1fb) CTV in all bedrooms Ⓡ ✱ sB&B£15 sB&B➡ £17.50 dB&B£25 dB&B➡ £29

50P ✽

Mainly Grills V ♧ ☕ ✻ Lunch £2.99–£6.91 Tea 50p Dinner £2.99–£6.91&alc Wine £3.85 Last dinner 10pm

Credit cards 1 2 3 5

FOREST ROW
East Sussex
Map **5** TQ43

★★★**Roebuck** Wych Cross (2m S jct A22/A275) (Embassy) ☎ (034282) 3811 Telex no 957088
An early Georgian country inn with extensive gardens and views over Ashdown Forest.

31➡ CTV in all bedrooms Ⓡ sB➡ £25.50 dB➡ £35 B

120P ✽

English & French V ♧ Lunch fr£7.75 Dinner fr£7.75 Wine £4.30 Last dinner 9.45pm

Credit cards 1 2 3 5

FORFAR
Tayside *Angus*
Map **15** NO45

★★**Royal** Castle St ☎ (0307) 62691
Modernised hotel in the town centre, personally supervised by the owner.

20rm(8➡) TV in 8 bedrooms Ⓡ ✻ sB&B£16.50 sB&B➡ £19 dB&B£26 dB&B➡ £30

CTV 12P 12 Disco Fri/Sat

English & French ♧ ☕ ✻ Lunch £2.45–£3.25 Tea 75p–£1.80 High Tea £2.80–£4.95 Dinner £8alc Wine £4.75 Last dinner 9pm

Credit card 5

FORRES
Grampian *Morayshire*
Map **14** NJ05

★★**Ramnee** ☎ (0309) 72410
Closed Jan
Fine, two-storey stone villa standing back from the main road in well-kept grounds.

20rm(8➡2⋒) Annexe: 2⋒ (4fb) CTV in 10 bedrooms TV in 10 bedrooms Ⓡ ✱ sB&B fr£14.95 sB&B➡⋒ fr£17.25 dB&B fr£26.45 dB&B➡⋒ fr£29.90

CTV 50P 1 ✽

British, French & Italian V ♧ Lunch fr£4.60 Dinner fr£9.20 Wine £3.45 Last dinner 9pm

Credit cards 1 2 3

★★*B* **Royal** ☎ (0309) 72617
Closed Xmas & 1 & 2 Jan
Three-storey building, standing in a quiet area of the town opposite the market and near the station.

20rm(1➡5⋒) (4fb) CTV in all bedrooms Ⓡ ✱ ✻ sB&B£13.50 sB&B➡⋒ £17 dB&B£23 dB&B➡⋒ £29.90

CTV 40P ✽ billiards

V ♧ ☕ ✻ Lunch £3.50 Tea £1.50 High Tea £3.45 Dinner £6.30alc Wine £3.75 Last dinner 8.30pm

Credit cards 1 3

★**Heather** Tyler St ☎ (0309) 72377
Small, pleasant family-run hotel.

6rm(1➡2⋒) Ⓡ sB&B£10–£12 dB&B£20–£24 dB&B➡⋒ £22–£26

CTV 20P

V Lunch £4–£5 High Tea £4–£5 Dinner £8 Wine £3.50

✕✕***Elizabeth Inn*** Mundole ☎ (0309) 72526
Converted and extended cottage on the banks of the River Findhorn, west of Forres.

Closed last wk May, 1st wk Jan, last wk Sep, 1st wk Oct, 2 days Xmas & 2 days New Year. Dinner not served Wed
45 seats Last dinner 8.30pm P

FORSINARD
Highland *Sutherland*
Map **14** NC84

★★***Forsinard*** ☎ Halladale (064 17) 221
RS Dec–Mar

13rm(11➡2⋒) Ⓡ B

CTV 30P ✽

V ♧ ☕ Last dinner 8.15pm

VS

FORT AUGUSTUS
Highland *Inverness-shire*
Map **14** NH30

★★***Inchnacardoch Lodge*** Loch Ness ☎ (0320) 6258 RS Nov–Mar

21rm(3➡6⋒) 1 ✱

CTV 30P ✽ U

♧ ☕ Last dinner 9pm

Credit cards 1 3 5

★★*H* **Lovat Arms** ☎ (0320) 6206
Comfortable, family run hotel with good home cooking and friendly service.

19rm(2➡) Annexe: 6rm (3fb) Ⓡ sB&B£10–£15 sB&B➡ £11.50–£16.50 dB&B£20–£30 dB&B➡ £22.50–£31 B

CTV 50P ✽

V ♧ ☕ Lunch £4.25 Tea 65p Dinner £7.50–£8 Wine £2.20 Last dinner 8pm

VS

★*H* **Caledonian** ☎ (0320) 6256
Closed Oct–Mar

12rm(2⋒) (1fb) sB&B£8.50–£10.50 dB&B£17–£20 dB&B⋒ £20–£23 B

CTV 20P ✽

Scottish & French V ♧ ☕ Bar lunch 50p–£4 Tea fr50p Dinner fr£6.50 Wine £3.75 Last dinner 9.30pm

VS

FORTROSE
Highland *Ross & Cromarty*
Map **14** NH76

★★***Royal*** Union St ☎ (0381) 20236
RS Nov–Feb

11rm ✱ B

CTV 10P

V ♧ ☕ Last dinner 8.30pm

FORT WILLIAM
Highland *Inverness-shire*
Map **14** NN17
See also Banavie

★★★**Alexandra** The Parade ☎ (0397) 2241 Telex no 777210
Victorian building on a corner site just off the main shopping centre and close to the railway station.

92rm(68➡) (6fb) CTV in 65 bedrooms Ⓡ sB&B£17.50–£20.90 sB&B➡ £19.50–

£23.90 dB&B£30.50–£35.30 db&B🛁£34.50–£41.30 B

Lift ☾ CTV 40P *xmas*

Lunch £3.25–£3.90 Tea 75p Dinner £8.50 Wine £3.50 Last dinner 9pm

Credit cards 1 2 3 5 **VS**

☆☆☆**Ladbroke** (on A82) (Ladbroke) ☎(0397) 3117

Modern, low-rise building, standing by the main road on the southern outskirts of town, with splendid hill views over Loch Linnhe.

61🛁 (15fb) CTV in all bedrooms ® ✻ sB🛁 fr£25 dB🛁 fr£38 (room only) B

☾ 61P CFA sauna bath

★★★★

INVERLOCHY CASTLE, FORT WILLIAM

(3m NE A82) ☎(0397) 2177
Closed Nov–Mar

(Rosettes awarded for dinner only.) Still the tops in popularity with the members who can afford it, this hotel offers an example that other fine hotels can only aspire to. It is run with style (and what style!) by the owner, Mrs Greta Hobbs, with the help of her Manager, Mr Leonard. From the moment you arrive, when your car is parked for you, the hospitality is apparent and you know you are going to experience something special. Set in beautiful grounds in view of Ben Nevis, the hotel is an impressive Victorian castle with an even more impressive interior. Fine decorative features include the magnificent painted ceiling in the Great Hall and the splendid staircase. It abounds in fine furniture, Eastern carpets, oil paintings and objets d'art, both in the Great Hall and in the elegantly furnished drawing room. Needless to say the spacious bedrooms are decorated and furnished to an almost equally high standard.
Catering arrangements, under the chef, François Huguet (see p.35), have changed and more choice is now offered. There is a set meal which is thoughtfully composed to present a finely balanced, soigné five course meal. You are advised to choose this meal as representing the best they can offer but there is a further

selection of dishes with the main ones complemented with individual selection of vegetables. Chef Huguet has settled down well and is producing delicious dishes that have earned two rosettes this year. His cooking is influenced by the modern idiom using innovative combinations of ingredients but he does not go 'over the top' as so many promising young chefs do. As befits a hotel with a regular and faithful clientele, the old favourites are not forgotten, however. It would be possible to write a book about the delights of Inverlochy Castle; suffice it to say that a stay here is a memorable experience of grand country house living of the best sort.

14🛁 CTV in all bedrooms ✻ sB&B🛁 £70 dB&B🛁 £98

☾ P2 billiards

International **V** Dinner £21 alc Wine £6.50

S% Credit cards 1 2 3

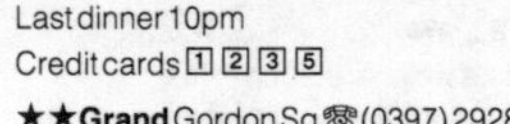

Bar ✻ Lunch fr£6.50 Dinner fr£8.50 Last dinner 10pm

Credit cards 1 2 3 5

★★**Grand** Gordon Sq ☎(0397) 2928

This pre-war, three-storey hotel stands on a corner site in the shopping centre.

33rm(25🛁) (3fb) CTV in 20 bedrooms ® sB&B£11–£18 sB&B🛁£11–£20 dB&B£22–£30 dB&B🛁£22–£33 B

CTV 20P

V Lunch fr£3.95 Tea fr50p Dinner fr£7 Wine £3.95 Last dinner 8.30pm

Credit cards 1 2 3 5 **VS**

★★***Highland*** Union Rd ☎(0397) 2291

An imposing Victorian building with an ornate panelled main hall and stairway.

52rm(28🛁10⋒) CTV in all bedrooms ® B

☾ CTV P ✻ Cabaret nightly in season

Last dinner 9pm

Credit cards 1 2 3 5 **VS**

See advert on page 272

★★**Imperial** Fraser's Sq ☎(0397) 2040

An extended, large Victorian building, near the main shopping area and with views of Loch Linnhe.

40rm(1🛁3⋒) (3fb) CTV in 4 bedrooms TV in 3 bedrooms ® sB&B£12.30–£13 sB&B🛁⋒£16–£17 dB&B£22.70–£25 dB&B🛁⋒£28–£30 B

CTV 12P Cabaret Tue, Thu & Sat

Lunch fr£3.80 High Tea £4.25 Dinner £6.50 Wine £3.50 Last dinner 8.30pm

VS

★★**Milton** ☎(0397) 2331 Telex no 777210 Closed Oct–Apr

61rm(9🛁) (2fb) sB&B£15–£19.40 sB&B🛁⋒£17–£21.40 dB&B£26.50–£31.40 dB&B🛁⋒£30.50–£37.40 B

☾ CTV 200P ✻ Disco wkly Live music and dancing twice wkly

Lunch £2.90–£3.50 Tea 75p Dinner £8.50 Wine £3.50 Last dinner 8.30pm

Credit cards 1 2 3 5 **VS**

★★***Nevis Bank*** Belford Rd ☎(0397) 2595

Roadside hotel near Glen Nevis. →

23rm(6➡)
CTV 20P 🚗
🍵☕ Last dinner 8.30pm

★★**Stag's Head** High St ☎(0397) 4144
Closed Oct–Apr
Converted terraced building located over shops.
46rm(8➡)(6fb) ✶ sB&B£13.50 sB&B➡£15 dB&B£20.40 dB&B➡£27 B
Lift CTV 13P
V 🍵☕ Lunch £4.50 Tea 45p Dinner £8 Last dinner 9pm
Credit cards 1 2 3 5 **VS**

F

FOSSEBRIDGE
Gloucestershire
Map **4** SP01

★★**Fossebridge Inn** ☎(028572) 310
Closed Xmas Day
Stone-built Cotswold inn with a buttery-style restaurant.
8rm(5➡⋒) Annexe: 4➡⋒ Ⓡ ✶
dB&B£20 dB&B➡£20–£30 B
CTV P 🚗 ✽ nc10yrs
🍵✻ Lunch £1.50–£6alc Dinner £6alc Wine £2.70 Last dinner 9.30pm
VS

FOUR MILE BRIDGE
Gwynedd
Map **6** SH27

★★★**Anchorage** ☎Holyhead (0407) 740168 Closed Xmas
Modern, commercial/holiday hotel situated one mile from beaches and shops.
18rm(8➡6⋒) CTV in 16 bedrooms ✶ sB&B£17.50 sB&B➡⋒£19.50 dB&B£27 dB&B➡⋒£29.50 B
CTV 100P 🚗
English & French 🍵✻ Bar lunch £3.50alc Dinner £8alc Wine £4 Last dinner 9.30pm
Credit cards 1 3

FOWEY
Cornwall
Map **2** SX15

★★*H* **Marina** Esplanade ☎(072683) 3315
Georgian hotel in quiet situation with a waterside garden and restaurant.
14rm(8➡)(4fb) CTV in 4 bedrooms sB&B£11–£19.80 sB&B➡£13.20–£24.20 dB&B£22–£30.80 dB&B➡£26.40–£39.60 B
CTV 1P 🚗
English & French V 🍵☕ Dinner £7.70&alc Last dinner 8.30pm
S% Credit cards 1 3 5 **VS**

★★**Old Quay** Fore St ☎(072683) 3302
Closed Xmas & New Year
This hotel stands in an old terrace at the waterside, overlooking the estuary.
13rm(7➡1⋒)(3fb) TV in 10 bedrooms Ⓡ sB&B£10.50–£11.50 sB&B➡⋒£11.50–£12.50 dB&B£19–£21 dB&B➡⋒£21–£25 B
CTV 🚗
English & Continental 🍵☕ Bar lunch £1–£2 Tea 45p Dinner fr£6&alc Wine £4 Last dinner 9pm
Credit cards 1 3

★★**Penlee** The Esplanade ☎(072683) 3220
Friendly, comfortable hotel in an elevated position with unrestricted views of the estuary and the sea.
12rm(8➡)(4fb) 1 CTV in 4 bedrooms Ⓡ sB&B£10–£13 sB&B➡£15.20–£20.50 dB&B£20–£26 dB&B➡£24.40–£35 B
CTV 10P
English & Continental V 🍵☕ Bar lunch £2.50alc Dinner £6.50–£7.50 Last dinner 9pm
Credit cards 1 2 3 5

★★**Riverside** ☎(072683) 2275
Closed Xmas & New Year RS Oct–Mar
Comfortable, well-situated hotel with fine views.

F

14rm(4🛁2🚿) 1🛏 CTV in 3 bedrooms sB&B£12–£16 sB&B🛁🚿£15–£22 dB&B£24–£30 dB&B🛁🚿£30–£44 B

CTV 5P 5

English & French V Bar lunch £1–£3 Dinner £9.50–£12.50 Wine £4 Last dinner 9.30pm

Credit card 1

✕ ***Le Nautique*** Fore St ☎(072683) 3594

Small bistro situated in the centre of the town opposite the harbour.

Closed Oct–mid Apr

65 seats Last dinner 11pm

FOWLMERE
Cambridgeshire
Map **5** TL44

✕✕ **Chequers Inn** ☎(076382) 369

English & French V 30 seats ✱Lunch £12.45alc Dinner £12.45alc Wine £6.35 Last dinner 10pm 50P

Credit cards 1 2 3 4 5

FOWNHOPE
Hereford & Worcester
Map **3** SO53

✕ **Green Man Hotel** ☎(043277) 243

English & French V 73 seats Lunch £4.25alc Dinner £7.15alc Wine £3.95 Last dinner 9.30pm 55P bedrooms available

Credit card 1 **VS**

FOYERS
Highland *Inverness-shire*
Map **14** NH42

★ **Foyers** ☎ Gorthleck (04563) 216

Closed 1–15 Nov

Attractive roadside inn set on the hillside above Loch Ness, 19 miles west of Inverness.

9rm(2🚿) (1fb) ® sB&B£9 dB&B£18 dB&B🚿£19

CTV 25P ✽

V Bar lunch 65p–£2.60alc Tea 50p Dinner £5 Wine £3.90 Last dinner 7.30pm

FRADLEY
Staffordshire
Map **7** SK11

★★ **Fradley Arms** Rykneld St (Best Western) ☎ Burton-on-Trent (0283) 790186

5rm(4🛁1🚿) (2fb) CTV in all bedrooms ® sB&B🛁🚿£19.25–£21.50 dB&B🛁🚿£25.75–£29.75 B

50P ✽

Lunch £4–£5&alc Dinner £5alc Wine £3.80 Last Dinner 9.30pm

Credit cards 1 2 3 5

FRAMFIELD
East Sussex
Map **5** TQ42

✕ ***Coach House*** ☎(082582) 636

Closed Mon & 1st wk May, last 2wks Oct Dinner not served Sun

36 seats Last dinner 9pm 15P

FRAMLINGHAM
Suffolk
Map **5** TM26

★★ **Crown** Market Hill (Trusthouse Forte) ☎(0728) 723521

17rm(4🛁) (2fb) CTV in all bedrooms ® sB&B£30.50 sB&B🛁£33 dB&B£43 dB&B🛁£49.50 B

CTV 15P *xmas*

Last dinner 9.15pm

Credit cards 1 2 3 4 5

✕ ***Market Place*** 18 Market Hill ☎(0728) 723866

Tiny detached cottage with fresh food catering for both the family and the discerning diner.

Closed Sun, Mon & Feb
Dinner not served Tue

English, French & Italian 36 seats Last dinner 9.30pm

FRANT
East Sussex
Map **5** TQ53

✕ **Bassetts** 35 High St ☎(089275) 635

Advance reservations essential.

Closed Sun–Tue, 25 May–Jun Lunch not served

French 24 seats Dinner £8–£9 Wine £3.85 Last dinner 8.45pm P

S% Credit cards 1 2 3

FRECKLETON
Lancashire
Map **7** SD42

✕✕ ***Ledra*** Preston New Rd ☎(0772) 632308

Closed Mon & 24 Dec–31 Jan

Greek & International 40 seats Last dinner 10pm 10P Live music Fri

Credit cards 1 2

FRESHFORD
Avon
Map **3** ST75

❀★★★ ***HBL*** **Homewood Park** Hinton Charterhouse (between A36 & village) ☎ Limpley Stoke (022122) 2643

Closed 25 Dec–16 Jan

Mr and Mrs Ross, the owners of this delightful small country house, have carefully restored it and tastefully decorated it. The drawing room with its log fire is cheerful yet elegant and the restaurant is pleasant and well-appointed, much of the excellent cooking being done by Mr Ross.

8🛁🚿 (3fb) CTV in all bedrooms sB&B🛁🚿£33 dB&B🛁🚿£42–£65
Continental breakfast

20P ✽ (hard) U

French Lunch £8 Tea £1.50 Dinner £13–£16alc Wine £5.75 Last dinner 9.30pm

S% Credit cards 1 2 3 5

FRESHWATER
Isle of Wight
Map **4** SZ38

★★★ ***H*** **Albion** ☎(0983) 753631

Closed Nov–Mar

Comfortable hotel with good lounge and fine sea views.

43rm(37🛁) (21fb) CTV in all bedrooms sB&B£13.50 sB&B🛁£15 dB&B£24–£27 dB&B🛁£30–£31.50

CTV 75P →

V Lunch fr£4.70 Dinner fr£7.75 Wine £4.20 Last dinner 8.15pm
S% Credit cards 1 3 **VS**

★★★**Farringford** Bedbury Ln ☎(0983) 752500
Closed 2 Oct–9 May
Once the home of Alfred Lord Tennyson, set in 33 acres of parkland and gardens.
16 Annexe: 52 (6fb) CTV in 48 bedrooms ® sB&B£20–£25 dB&B£40–£50
CTV 150P 2 (heated) (hard) billiards Disco Wed & Sat
English & French V Lunch £5&alc Tea 55p &alc Dinner £7.50&alc Wine £3.95 Last dinner 9.30pm
Credit cards 1 2 3 5 **VS**

F

FRESSINGFIELD
Suffolk
Map **5** TM27
✕**Fox & Goose** ☎(037 986) 247
Booking essential.
Closed Tue & 21–28 Dec
British & French 28 seats Lunch £11.40–£18.40alc Dinner £11.40–£18.40alc Wine £4.75 Last dinner 8.45pm 30P
VS

FREUCHIE
Fife
Map **11** NO20
★★**Lomond** Parliament Sq (Minotel) ☎Falkland (03375) 329
Modernised and extended former coaching inn.
17rm(9 1)(2fb) TV in all bedrooms ® sB&B fr£12.75 sB&B fr£16 dB&B£23 dB&B fr£26
CTV 50P sauna bath
Scottish & French V *Lunch £5alc Tea 65p High Tea £3.50 Dinner £7 Wine £3.60 Last dinner 9.15pm
Credit cards 1 3 **VS**

FRINTON-ON-SEA
Essex
Map **5** TM21
★★★**Frinton Lodge** 32 The Esplanade (Best Western) ☎(02556) 4391
Spacious and comfortable traditional hotel.
24rm(16 1)(1fb) CTV in all bedrooms ® *sB&B£27 sB&B £29.50–£32 dB&B£45 dB&B £50–£53
Lift CTV 14P 3 Live music and dancing Fri & Sat *xmas*
English & French V Lunch £5.75–£6.95&alc Tea 60p–75p High Tea £4.50alc Dinner £7.95–£9.25&alc Wine £4 Last dinner 9.30pm
Credit cards 1 2 3 5

★★ *H* **Maplin** Esplanade ☎(02556) 3832
Closed Jan
Hospitable, family-run hotel with comfortable rooms and home cooking.
12rm(9 1)(2fb) ® sB&B£19 sB&B £20.50 dB&B £40
CTV 15P 2 (heated) nc10yrs *xmas*
V Lunch £7.50&alc Dinner £10.50&alc Last dinner 9.30pm
S% Credit cards 1 2 3 5 **VS**

★ *H* **Rock** The Esplanade ☎(02556) 5173
Closed Jan
Friendly and efficiently run family hotel.
9rm(1 1)(4fb) ® sB&B£15–£16 dB&B£28–£30 dB&B £30–£32
CTV 9P
V Lunch £6.50&alc Dinner £6.50&alc Wine £4.95
Last dinner 9pm
Credit cards 1 2 3 5 **VS**

FROME
Somerset
Map **3** ST74
☆☆☆**Mendip Lodge** Bath Rd ☎(0373) 63223 Telex no 44832
Edwardian house with attractive public rooms and an adjoining motel bedroom block.
40 (12fb) CTV in all bedrooms ® *sB&B fr£26.50 dB&B fr£37
Continental breakfast
60P CFA *xmas*
English & Continental V *Lunch fr£5.75&alc Tea fr80p Dinner fr£7.55&alc Wine £4.50 Last dinner 9.45pm
S% Credit cards 1 2 3 5

★★ ***George*** 4 Market Pl ☎(0373) 62584
Privately-run town centre hotel catering mainly for the business and touring trade.
16rm(4) TV in all bedrooms ®
18
V Last dinner 10pm
Credit cards 1 2 3 4 5

★★**Portway** Portway ☎(0373) 63508
Closed Xmas day
18rm(11)(2fb) ® sB&B£19 sB&B £21.50 dB&B£27.50 dB&B £31
CTV 30P
Lunch fr£5&alc Dinner fr£7.25&alc Wine £4.50 Last dinner 8.30pm
Credit cards 1 2 3 5 **VS**

✕✕**Halligan's** Vicarage St ☎(0373) 64238
Closed Mon Lunch not served Sat Dinner not served Sun

28 seats Lunch £5.50 Dinner £8–£9alc Wine £4.25 Last dinner 10pm
Credit cards 1 2 3 5

GAIRLOCH
Highland *Ross & Cromarty*
Map **14** NG87
★★★**Gairloch** (Scottish Highland) ☎(0445) 2001 Closed Nov–Mar
Three-storey, red sandstone, Victorian building overlooking Gairloch Bay.
50rm(36 9)(4fb) CTV in 1 bedroom ® sB&B £26 dB&B £42
Lift CTV 50P billiards Disco wkly
V Lunch £2.75–£5 Tea 60p High Tea £2 Dinner £5–£8.50 Wine £4 Last dinner 9pm
Credit cards 1 2 3 5

★**Creag Mhor** Charlestown ☎(0445) 2068
Modern, family run hotel, overlooking the old harbour and quay.
9rm(3 1)(1fb) ® sB&B£12–£13.50 dB&B£21–£24 dB&B £24–£29
CTV 20P billiards
V Bar lunch 90p–£1.20 Tea 75p–£1 Dinner £7–£8 Wine £3.15 Last dinner 7.30pm
VS

GALASHIELS
Borders *Selkirkshire*
Map **12** NT43
★★★**Kingsknowes** Selkirk Rd ☎(0896) 3478
Fine, tastefully decorated mansion house, retaining many country house features, particularly the friendly, informal service.
10rm(7)(1fb) CTV in all bedrooms ® sB&B£22 sB&B £25 dB&B£34 dB&B £38
CTV 50P (hard)
Lunch £9.50alc Dinner £9.50alc Wine £3.20 Last dinner 9pm
Credit cards 1 2 3 5

★**Royal** Channel St ☎(0896) 2918
Commercial hotel situated in the town centre.
21rm(1)(3fb) ® sB&B£11.50 sB&B £15 dB&B£20 dB&B £23
CTV
V Bar lunch fr£1.25 Tea 35p Dinner £3.30 Wine £3.65 Last dinner 8.45pm
Credit cards 1 3

✕**Redgauntlet** 36 Market St ☎(0896) 2098
Cosy little restaurant with iron and stonework features and a friendly staff.
Closed Sun Lunch not served
Scottish, French & Italian V 40 seats Dinner £6alc Wine £3.70 Last dinner 10pm
Credit card 1

GARFORTH
West Yorkshire
Map **8** SE43

☆☆☆**Ladbroke** (& Conferencentre) Garforth Rbt (junc A63/A642 6m E of Leeds) (Ladbroke) ☎ Leeds (0532) 866556 Telex no 556324

Well designed modern hotel in spacious grounds with watermill theme in carvery restaurant.

156 (7fb) CTV in all bedrooms ® *sB fr£32 dB fr£40 (room only) B

300P CFA ✽ Live music and dancing Sat Cabaret Sat

V *Lunch fr£6.50 Dinner fr£8.50 Last dinner 10pm

Credit cards 1 2 3 4 5

GARGRAVE
North Yorkshire
Map **7** SD95

★★**Anchor Inn** ☎ (075678) 666

A stone-built country pub, whose garden leads down to the Leeds-Liverpool Canal.

8rm (4 2) (1fb) CTV in all bedrooms ® sB&B£14–£18 sB&B£16–£20 dB&B£20–£25 dB&B£24–£30 B

100P ✽

English & French *Lunch £4.75&alc Dinner £5.50–£8.50&alc Wine £4.25 Last dinner 9.30pm

Credit cards 1 2 3

GARSTANG
Lancashire
Map **7** SD44

☆☆**Crofters** Cabus (A6) ☎ (09952) 4128

A modern, well-furnished hotel on the A6, close to Garstang.

23rm (3 20) (5fb) CTV in all bedrooms ® sB&B £27.50 dB&B £33.50 B

200P Disco wkly Live music and dancing 3 nights wkly (Jul-Sep)

International V *Lunch fr£4.75 Tea fr£1.25 Dinner fr£6.75 Wine £4.90 Last dinner 10pm

Credit cards 1 2 3 5 VS

GARVE
Highland *Ross & Cromarty*
Map **14** NH36

★★**Garve** ☎ (09974) 205

Closed Nov–Etr

Large stone building set on the main road in the shadow of Ben Wyvis.

34rm (15) (2fb) *sB&B£11–£12.50 sB&B £12.50–£14.50 dB&B£22–£25 dB&B £25–£29 B

CTV 60P 4 ✽

English & French V *Lunch £4.50–£5.50 Tea fr65p Dinner fr£7.50 Wine £4.90 Last dinner 8.30pm

Credit cards 1 3 VS

★**Inchbae Lodge** ☎ Aultguish (09975) 269

Comfortable, family run hotel located 6m W of Garve on A835.

6rm (3) Annexe 6 ® B

25P ✽

International Last dinner 8.30pm

VS

GATEHOUSE OF FLEET
Dumfries & Galloway *Kirkcudbrightshire*
Map **11** NX55

★★★*L* **Murray Arms** (Best Western) ☎ (05574) 207

An historic 17th-century posting house carefully extended to retain its traditional character.

12rm (9 1) (2fb) CTV in all bedrooms ® sB&B£16–£17.50 sB&B £17.50–£19 dB&B fr£32–£35 dB&B £35–£38 B

CTV 20P ✽ (hard) *xmas*

V *Bar lunch £1–£3 Tea £1.50 Dinner £8.75 Wine £3.80 Last dinner 8.45pm

Credit cards 1 2 3 5 **VS**

GATESHEAD
Tyne & Wear
Map **12** NZ26

☆☆☆☆**Five Bridges** High West St (Swallow) ☎ (0632) 771105 Telex no 53534

Seven-storey, glass fronted building opened in 1967

107 (4fb) CTV in all bedrooms ® sB&B£19.50–£30 dB&B£26–£38 B

Lift CTV 100P 100 CFA Live music and dancing Sat

French V Lunch £3.75–£6&alc Tea fr75p High Tea £3.25–£3.75 Dinner £6.95–£7.25&alc Wine £4.95 Last dinner 10pm

Credit cards 1 2 3 5

★★★**Springfield** Durham Rd (Embassy) ☎ (0632) 774121

40 (2fb) CTV in all bedrooms ® sB £31.50 dB £39.50 (room only) B

100P

V Lunch fr£6.70 Dinner fr£6.70 Wine £4.90 Last dinner 9.30pm

Credit cards 1 2 3 4 5

✕✕***Ristorante Italia*** 580A Durham Rd, Low Fell ☎ Low Fell (0632) 879362

Closed Sun

English & Continental 80 seats Last dinner 11pm 50P

Credit cards 1 3 5

GATTONSIDE
Borders *Roxburghshire*
Map **12** NT53

✕✕**Hoebridge Inn** ☎ Melrose (089682) 3082

Converted and extended farmhouse provides the setting for an interesting country restaurant in this Tweedside village.

Closed Mon (Oct–Apr), 2wks Apr & Oct, Xmas Day, Boxing Day & New Year's Day Lunch not served

British, Italian & French 46 seats *Dinner £7.50–£10.50alc Wine £4 Last dinner 10pm 15P

Credit card 3

GATWICK AIRPORT–LONDON
West Sussex
Map **4** TQ24
See plan

☆☆☆☆**Copthorne** Copthorne Rd, Copthorne (on A264 2m E of A264/B2036 Rbt) (Whitbread) ☎ Copthorne (0342) 714971 Telex no 95500 Plan **4**

230rm (185 35) (10fb) CTV in all bedrooms ® sB&B £47 dB&B £64 B

300P CFA ✽ squash sauna bath *xmas*

English & French Lunch £8.10&alc Dinner £12alc Wine £5.50 Last dinner 10.30pm

Credit cards 1 2 3 5

☆☆☆☆**Gatwick Hilton International** ☎ Crawley (0293) 518080 Telex no 877021 Plan **7**

Compact, modern hotel.

333 CTV in all bedrooms sB £43.70–£56.35 dB £52.45–£67.60 (room only)

Lift 40P CFA (heated) sauna bath

English & French Lunch £8&alc Dinner £10&alc Wine £6.50 Last dinner 10.30pm

Credit cards 1 2 3 4 5

☆☆☆☆**Gatwick Penta** Povey Cross Rd, Horley ☎ Horley (02934) 5533 Telex no 87440 Plan **10**

The many amenities offered by this hotel are complemented by its warmth and hospitality.

260 (4fb) 1 CTV in all bedrooms sB £39.90–£46 dB £47.50–£52.50 (room only)

Lift 400P CFA ✽

International V *Lunch £6.95&alc Tea £3.50 Dinner £9.50&alc Wine £5.70 Last dinner 11pm

S% Credit cards 1 2 3 4 5

☆☆☆**Chequers Thistle** Brighton Rd, Horley (Thistle) ☎ Horley (02934) 6992 Telex no 877550 Plan **3**

Originally a Tudor coaching house it has now been extended to form a modern hotel.

78 CTV in all bedrooms ® *sB £33–£36 dB £38–£41 (room only) B

160P CFA

European *Lunch £4.95 Dinner £7.50alc Last dinner 9.30pm

Credit cards 1 2 3 4 5 **VS**

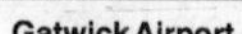

KINGSTON 25m
LONDON 28m
LONDON 28m
LEATHERHEAD
Walton-on-the-Hill
Kingswood
CATERHAM
Woldingham
MAIDSTONE 42m
Oxted
Godstone
REDHILL
GUILDFORD 25m
Betchworth
Dorking
Reigate
Bletchingley
Leigh
Salfords
Blindley Heath
Horley
TUNBRIDGE WELLS 25m
GATWICK AIRPORT (LONDON)
Smallfield
Lingfield
Newdigate
Charlwood
EAST GRINSTEAD
GATWICK AIRPORT and DISTRICT
Copthorne
Crawley Down
Scale
0
3m
CRAWLEY
Turners Hill
EASTBOURNE 50m
HORSHAM
BRIGHTON 28m

Gatwick Airport

1 La Bonne Auberge ✕✕ (*see under South Godstone*)
2 Burford Bridge ★★★★ (*see under Dorking*)
3 Chequers Thistle ☆☆☆
4 Copthorne ☆☆☆☆
5 Forge ✕✕ (*see under Newdigate*)
6 Crest Hotel Gatwick Airport ☆☆☆
6A Felbridge ★★★ (*see under East Grinstead*)
7 Gatwick Hilton International ☆☆☆☆
8 Gatwick Manor ☆☆☆
9 Gatwick Moat House ☆☆☆
10 Gatwick Penta ☆☆☆☆
11 George ★★★
12 Goffs Park ★★★
13 Golden Bengal ✕ (*see under Oxted*)
14 Gravetye Manor ❀★★★ (*see under East Grinstead*)
15 Hoskins ★★ (*see under Oxted*)
16 Ifield Court ★★
16A Pickard Motor ☆☆ (*see under Burgh Heath*)
17 Post House ☆☆☆
18 Punch Bowl Motor ☆☆☆ (*see under Dorking*)
19 Reigate Manor ★★ (*see under Reigate*)
20 Saxon Inn Gatwick ☆☆☆

☆☆☆**Crest** Tushmore Rbt, Langley Dr, Crawley (Crest) ☎Crawley (0293) 29991 Telex no 877311 Plan **6**

Modern, comfortable hotel.

230⇌ CTV in all bedrooms Ⓡ *sB⇌ fr£33 (room only) dB⇌ fr£42 (room only) B

Lift ☾ ⚡300P CFA

International ♁ ☐ *Lunch £4.50–£8.25&alc Tea 55p Dinner £8.25&alc Wine £4.50 Last dinner 10pm

Credit cards 1 2 3 4 5 **VS**

☆☆☆**Gatwick Manor** London Rd, Crawley (Berni) ☎Crawley (0293) 26301 Telex no 87529 Plan **8**

Closed Xmas–New Year

This mock Tudor manor offers all the comforts of a home from home.

30⇌ CTV in all bedrooms Ⓡ ✶ sB&B⇌ £27–£29 dB&B⇌ £38–£42

☾ 250P ✽ ⚑ Disco Sat Live music and dancing Sat Cabaret Sat

Mainly grills Lunch £3.30–£7.50 Dinner £3.30–£7.50 Wine £4 Last dinner 10.30pm

Credit cards 1 2 3 5

☆☆☆**Gatwick Moat House** Longbridge Rbt, Horley (Queens Moat) ☎Horley (02934) 5599 Telex no 877138 Plan **9**

Purpose-built hotel offering comfortable amenities and service.

124⇌⋔ (8fb) CTV in all bedrooms Ⓡ sB&B⇌⋔ £34.50 dB&B⇌⋔ £42 Continental breakfast B

Lift ☾ ## 150 CFA ♿ *xmas*

English & French **V** ♁ ☐ Lunch fr£6.25 Tea 60p Dinner fr£7.25 Wine £4.95 Last dinner 10.30pm

Credit cards 1 2 3 4 5 **VS**

★★★**George** High St, Crawley (Trusthouse Forte) ☎Crawley (0293) 24215 Telex no 87385 Plan **11**

Half-timbered and tile hung 15th-century inn, with extension, featuring a gallows sign outside and a 17th-century stone mantelpiece inside.

76⇌ (3fb) CTV in all bedrooms Ⓡ sB&B⇌ £42 dB&B⇌ £54.50 B

☾ 75P CFA

♁ ☐ Last dinner 9.30pm

Credit cards 1 2 3 4 5

★★★**Goffs Park** 45 Goffs Park Rd, Crawley ☎Crawley (0293) 35447 Telex no 87515 Plan **12**

Popular, commerical hotel.

46rm (18⇌ 21⋔) (2fb) CTV in all bedrooms Ⓡ sB&B £22 sB&B⇌⋔ £25 dB&B £37 dB&B⇌⋔ £41 B

☾ 100P CFA Disco wkly Live music and dancing wkly

English & French **V** ♁ Lunch £5 Dinner £5.75 Wine £4.20 Last dinner 9.30pm

Credit cards 1 2 3 5 **VS**

☆☆☆**Post House** Povey Cross Rd, Horley (Trusthouse Forte) ☎Horley (02934) 71621 Telex no 877351 Plan **17**

Efficient, well-managed modern hotel.

149⇌ (15fb) CTV in all bedrooms Ⓡ sB&B⇌ £44.50 dB&B⇌ £62.50

Lift ☾ 350P ✽ CFA ⛆ (heated) ♿

♁ ☐ Last dinner 10.15pm

Credit cards 1 2 3 4 5

☆☆☆**Saxon Inn Gatwick** Lowfield Heath, Crawley (Saxon Inn) ☎Crawley (0293) 33441 Telex no 87287 Plan **20**

Comfortable airport hotel with above average cooking.

100⇌⋔ CTV in all bedrooms Ⓡ *sB&B⇌⋔ £31.50 dB&B⇌⋔ £39 Continental breakfast

Lift ☾ ## 100P CFA 🚗 Disco Fri *xmas*

International **V** ♁ ☐ *Lunch £5alc Tea £1alc Wine £4.45 Last dinner 10.30pm

Credit cards 1 2 3 4 5 **VS**

★★**Ifield Court** Ifield Av, Crawley ☎(0293) 34807 Plan **16**

Closed 24–26 Dec

Victorian ivy-clad hotel in 4½ acres of grounds.

19rm (13⇌ 6⋔) (7fb) ✶ sB&B⇌⋔ £25–£27.50 dB&B⇌⋔ £39.50–£43.45

☾ CTV 130P 🚗 ✽

V ♁ ☐ Tea fr50p Dinner £10alc Wine £3.85 Last dinner 9.30pm

Credit cards 1 2 3

GAUNTS EARTHCOTT

Avon
Map **3** ST68

✕**Manor House & Junk Shop** ☎Winterbourne (0454) 772225

Reservations essential. Telephone first for instructions on how to locate it as there is no sign. Own alcohol can be brought.

Closed Wed & 4 days Xmas

V Unlicensed 20 seats Lunch £9alc Dinner £9alc Last dinner 10.30pm 8P

S% **VS**

GERRARDS CROSS

Buckinghamshire
Map **4** TQ08

★★★**Bull** (DeVere) ☎(0753) 885995 Telex no 847747

Converted coaching inn dating from 1688 in its own grounds. It is situated on the A40 Oxford road, near the station.

40⇌ 1▣ CTV in all bedrooms *sB&B⇌ £35.70 dB&B⇌ £46.50 B

☾ 133P CFA 🚗 ✽

English & French ♁ ☐ *Lunch £8.70&alc Dinner £8.70&alc Wine £5.50 Last dinner 9.45pm

Credit cards 1 2 3 5

GIFFNOCK

Strathclyde *Renfrewshire*
Map **11** NS55

★★★**MacDonald Thistle** Eastwood Toll Rbt (Thistle) ☎041-638 2225 Telex no 779138

Modern hotel at the Eastwood Toll roundabout (A77), on the southern outskirts of Glasgow.

58rm (50⇌ 8⋔) CTV in all bedrooms Ⓡ *sB⇌⋔ £33–£38 dB⇌⋔ £35–£40 (room only) B

☾ ⚡ CTV 200P CFA

European ☐ *Lunch £5.95&alc Dinner £8.50&alc Last dinner 9.30pm

Credit cards 1 2 3 4 5 **VS**

★★**Stakis Redhurst** Eastwood Mains Rd (Stakis) ☎041-638 6465 Telex no 778704

Modern, L-shaped building in a residential suburb, 5 miles from Glasgow city centre.

16rm(12⇌) CTV in all bedrooms Ⓡ *sB&B fr£23.50 sB&B⇌ fr£32 dB&B⇌ fr£39 B

☾ 50P

Last dinner 10pm

Credit cards 1 2 3 5 **VS**

GIFFORD
Lothian *East Lothian*
Map **12** NT56

★★**Tweeddale Arms** ☎(062081) 240

Country hotel in an attractive village.

10⇌⋒ (1fb) CTV in all bedrooms sB&B£11.50–£12.50 sB&B⇌⋒ £12.50–£16.50 dB&B£22–£24 dB&B⇌⋒ £24–£32 B

✽ *xmas*

English & French **V** Lunch £4.50–£5.50 Tea fr£1.40 High Tea £3.40 Dinner £8 Wine £4.15 Last dinner 8.30pm

Credit cards 2 3 **VS**

★***Goblin Ha'*** ☎(062081) 244

Early-Victorian, painted-stone inn, standing in the centre of an attractive village.

7rm

TV ✽

Last dinner 9pm

GIGHA ISLAND
Strathclyde *Argyllshire*
Map **10** NR64
(Car ferry from Tayinloan (mainland))

★★*HL* **Gigha** ☎(05835) 254

Next to the islands creamery and overlooking the Sound of Gigha. This extended and modernised inn has won an architectural award; equally commendable are the hospitality and home baking.

9rm(3⇌) *sB&B fr£14 sB&B⇌ fr£17.50 dB&B fr£28 dB&B⇌ fr£35

CTV P ✽

V *Lunch £5&alc Tea fr50p&alc Dinner £9&alc Wine £4 Last dinner 8pm

Credit cards 1 3

GILLAN
Cornwall
Map **2** SW72

★**Tregildry** ☎Manaccan (032623) 378
Closed Nov–Etr

Small hotel overlooking Gillans Cove with a private footpath to the beach.

13rm(3⇌1⋒) (3fb) sB&B£11–£12 dB&B£22–£24 sB&B⋒ £27–£29

☾ CTV 24P ✽

English & French **V** Lunch £2.50 Tea £1 High Tea £2 Dinner £7.50&alc Wine £3 Last dinner 9pm

GILLINGHAM
Kent
Map **5** TQ76

★**Park** Nelson Rd ☎Medway (0634) 51546

Popular and comfortable free house.

9rm (1fb) CTV in all bedrooms sB&B£14.25 dB&B£22.95

6P

*Lunch £2.50–£4.95 Tea 50p–£1 Dinner £4.50&alc Wine £3.60 Last dinner 10pm

Credit card 1

GIRVAN
Strathclyde *Ayrshire*
Map **10** NX19

★**Carrick Arms** Dalrymple St ☎(0465) 2261

A roadside inn, simple but pleasant in its character.

9rm(1⇌) (1fb) sB&B£9–£10 sB&B⇌£12.50–£16.50 dB&B£17–£19 dB&B⇌£20–£25 B

CTV 25P ✽

V Lunch £3alc High Tea £3alc Dinner £8alc Wine £2.95 Last dinner 9.30pm

Credit card 2

GISBURN
Lancashire
Map **7** SD84

★★★**Stirk House** ☎(02005) 581 Telex no 635238

A 16th-century manor house with modern extensions, situated in the Ribble Valley.

40rm(37⇌3⋒) Annexe: 12⇌ (2fb) CTV in all bedrooms Ⓡ sB&B⇌⋒ £27 dB&B⇌⋒ £40 B

☾ CTV 100P CFA ✽ (heated) squash sauna bath Disco wkly *xmas*

English, French & Italian Lunch £5.95–£7&alc Dinner £8–£8.70&alc Wine £5.25 Last dinner 9.45pm

Credit cards 1 2 3 4 5 **VS**

GITTISHAM
Devon
Map **3** SY19

★★

✾★★ **COMBE HOUSE, GITTISHAM**

☎Honiton (0404) 2756

(Rosette awarded for dinner only.)
Awarded red stars for the first time last year, our members have been delighted with this hotel. They have enjoyed the historic atmosphere of the public rooms, the country house cooking and the hospitality of the staff – pleasant young girls who are attentive to one's needs and always have a ready smile. Special mention should be made of Mr Jonathan Woollatt who combines all his duties with unfailing friendliness and charm. The house is from the 16th and 17th centuries but the site is originally Saxon. John and Thérèse Boswell converted it from an impressive and private house to an equally impressive hotel with lots of their own furniture and other belongings from their own home in Scotland.
The hall/lounge with its dark panelling and huge fireplace is splendid, but the lighter style of the drawing room is most attractive too. Bedrooms are spacious and individually decorated to good effect, some having murals painted by Mrs Boswell. The bar, walled in green baize and hung with hunting prints,

provides a focal point for guests talking over the day's events. The house is hidden up a valley in 3,000 acres with glorious views, and makes a peaceful retreat or a most agreeable base from which to tour the surrounding historic countryside. Fishing is available on the hotel's stretch of the River Otter.

13rm(8⇌3⋒) CTV in all bedrooms sB&B£21.50 sB&B⇌⋒ £24.50–£34.50 dB&B£43 dB&B⇌⋒ £49–£58 B

50P 3 ✽ *xmas*

French **V** Bar lunch fr£2 Tea £1–£2 Dinner £13.50alc Wine £5.50 Last dinner 9.30pm

S% Credit cards 1 2 3 5

GLAMIS
Tayside *Angus*
Map **15** NO34

✕✕**Strathmore Arms** ☎(030784) 248

Nicely-appointed country restaurant and bar, in a historic village, with the famous Glamis Castle nearby.

Closed Sun

Scottish, English & French **V** 100 seats Lunch £2.50–£5 Dinner £8.70alc Wine

£4.50 Last dinner 9pm 80P
Credit cards 1 2 3 5

GLANTON
Northumberland
Map **12** NU01

★★**Red Lion** ☎Powburn (066578) 216
A stone-built village inn set in the moors.
6rm (1fb) Ⓡ sB&B£9.50–£10.50 dB&B£18–£19
CTV 30P
Bar lunch £1.25–£4 Dinner £3.50–£5 Wine £3 Last dinner 10pm

GLASBURY
Powys
Map **3** SO13

★★*H* **Llwynaubach Lodge** ☎(04974) 473
Good conversion of 18th-century staging post and mill offering comfort, friendly service and home cooking.
6 CTV in all bedrooms Ⓡ sB&B £18 dB&B £35 B
40P ✻ (heated) nc10yr *xmas*
British & Continental V Tea £1–£1.50 Dinner fr£8.25&alc Wine £4.20 Last dinner 9.30pm
Credit cards 1 2 3

GLASGOW
Strathclyde *Lanarkshire*
Map **11** NS56
See plan

★★★★**Albany** Bothwell St (Trusthouse Forte) ☎041-248 2656 Telex no 77440 Central plan **1** *B3*
Large, modern, city-centre hotel with an attractive restaurant.
251 CTV in all bedrooms Ⓡ sB&B £49.50 dB&B £67.50 B
Lift ☾ ## CTV 25P CFA
Last dinner 10.45pm
Credit cards 1 2 3 4 5

☆☆☆☆*BL* **Holiday Inn Glasgow** Argyle St, Anderston (Commonwealth) ☎041-226 5577 Telex no 776355 Central plan **7** *B2*
Centrally located "high rise" hotel close to bus, rail and motorway with good leisure facilities.
296 (88fb) CTV in all bedrooms ✻sB fr£48.88 dB fr£53.48 (room only) B
Lift ☾ ## 200P (heated) squash sauna bath Live music and dancing Mon–Sat nights ♿
English & French V ✻Lunch £9.25–£11.25 Tea 75p Dinner £9.25–£11.25&alc Wine £6.25 Last dinner 11pm
Credit cards 1 2 3 5

★★★★*L* **Stakis Grosvenor** Grosvenor Ter, Gt Weston Rd (Stakis) ☎041-339 8811 Telex no 776247 District plan **23**
Impressively modernised hotel which has retained its traditional character.
96 1 CTV in all bedrooms Ⓡ ✻sB&B fr£42 dB&B fr£50 B
Lift ☾ 200P
International Last dinner 10.30pm
Credit cards 1 2 3 4 5 **VS**

★★★**Bellahouston** 517 Paisley Rd West (Swallow) ☎041-427 3146 Telex no 778795 District plan **15**
Modern hotel on the south side of the city, close to the M8.
122rm (108 14) (1fb) CTV in all bedrooms Ⓡ sB&B £27.50–£36.50 dB&B fr£42 B
Lift ☾ ## CTV 150P CFA *xmas*
V Lunch £4.80–£5.20&alc Dinner £6.80–£7.30&alc Wine £4.50 Last dinner 9.30pm
Credit cards 1 2 3 4 5

☆☆☆**Crest Hotel Glasgow-City** Argyle St, Anderston (Crest) ☎041-248 2355 Telex no 779652 Central plan **5** *B2*
Modern city centre hotel opposite Anderston Bus Station.
123 CTV in all bedrooms Ⓡ ✻sB fr£31 (room only) dB fr£38 (room only) B
Lift ☾ CFA
International V Lunch £5.75–£6.25&alc Tea 60p–70p Dinner £7.95–£8.50&alc Wine £6.25 Last dinner 9.45pm
Credit cards 1 2 3 4 5 **VS**

☆☆☆**Stakis Ingram** Ingram St (Stakis) ☎041-248 4401 Telex no 778704 Central plan **8** *D2*
Modern city centre hotel.
90 CTV in all bedrooms Ⓡ ✻sB&B fr£34 sB&B fr£40 B
Lift ☾ 30P CFA
English & French Last dinner 9.45pm
Credit cards 1 2 3 5 **VS**

☆☆☆**Stakis Pond** Great Western Rd (Stakis) ☎041-334 8161 Telex no 776573 District plan **20**
Modern hotel in the north-west suburbs of the city.
137 CTV in all bedrooms Ⓡ ✻sB&B fr£32 dB&B fr£40 B
Lift ☾ 200P
English & French Last dinner 10pm
Credit cards 1 2 3 5 **VS**

★★★*B* **Tinto Firs Thistle** 470 Kilmarnock Rd (Thistle) ☎041-637 2353 Telex no 778320 District plan **24**
This modern hotel is situated on the A77 in a residential area south of the city.
28rm (24) CTV in all bedrooms Ⓡ ✻sB £33–£40 dB £35–£40 (room only) B
☾ CTV 45P 1 ✻
European ✻Lunch £5.50&alc Dinner £7.95&alc Last dinner 9.30pm
Credit cards 1 2 3 4 5 **VS**

★★*H* **Ewington** Queens Dr, Queens Park ☎041-423 1152 District plan **16**
Friendly, traditional hotel in a terrace overlooking the park.
48rm (4 14) (1fb) ✻sB&B£13–£14 sB&B £16–£17 dB&B£25–£27 dB&B £28–£30 B
Lift ☾ CTV 12P
V ✻Lunch £2.75–£3.50 Tea 65p–£2 High Tea £3.50–£4.75 Dinner £6.25–£6.50 Wine £3.50 Last dinner 8pm

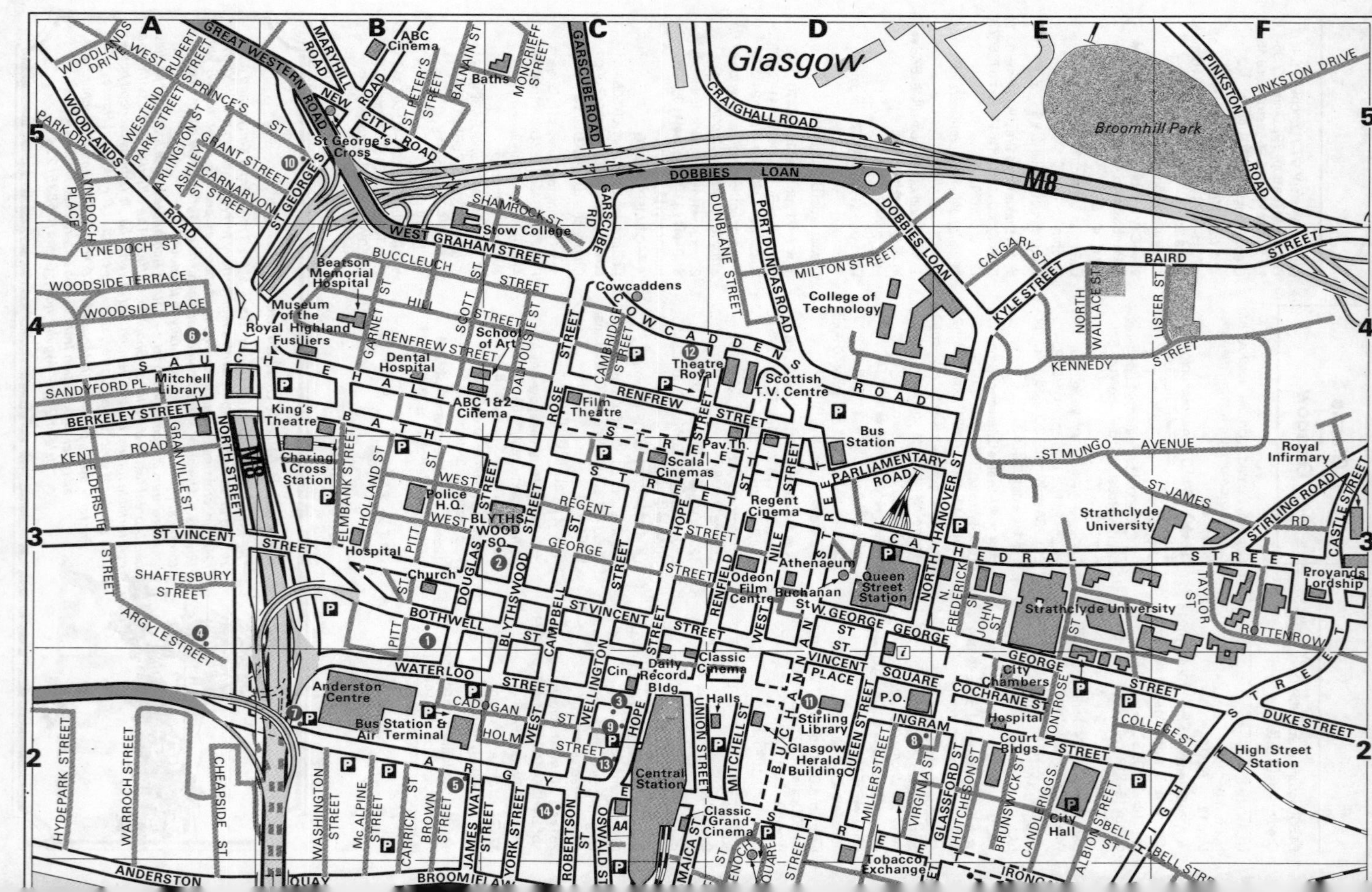

G
Glasgow
A
B
C
D
E
F
1
2
3
4
5
Broomhill Park
PINKSTON ROAD
PINKSTON DRIVE
CRAIGHALL ROAD
GARSCUBE ROAD
GARSCUBE RD
DOBBIES LOAN
M8
PORT DUNDAS ROAD
DUNBLANE STREET
MILTON STREET
College of Technology
KYLE STREET
CALGARY ST
NORTH WALLACE ST
LISTER ST
BAIRD STREET
KENNEDY STREET
ST MUNGO AVENUE
ST JAMES RD
Royal Infirmary
CASTLE STREET
STIRLING ROAD
Provands Lordship
ROTTENROW
TAYLOR ST
CATHEDRAL STREET
Strathclyde University
JOHN ST
N. FREDERICK ST
NORTH HANOVER ST
PARLIAMENTARY ROAD
Bus Station
Queen Street Station
GEORGE SQUARE
GEORGE STREET
City Chambers
MONTROSE ST
COCHRANE ST
Hospital
Court Bldgs
P.O.
INGRAM
COLLEGE ST
HIGH STREET
High Street Station
DUKE STREET
BELL ST
ALBION ST
City Hall
CANDLERIGGS
BRUNSWICK ST
HUTCHESON ST
GLASSFORD ST
VIRGINIA ST
MILLER STREET
Tobacco Exchange
QUEEN STREET
Stirling Library
Glasgow Herald Building
ST ENOCH SQUARE
MITCHELL ST
Classic Grand Cinema
JAMAICA ST
UNION STREET
Halls
Central Station
HOPE STREET
OSWALD ST
ROBERTSON ST
YORK STREET
JAMES WATT STREET
BROWN STREET
CARRICK ST
Mc ALPINE STREET
WASHINGTON STREET
BROOMIELAW
QUAY
CHEAPSIDE ST
WARROCH STREET
HYDEPARK STREET
ANDERSTON
Anderston Centre
Bus Station & Air Terminal
WELLINGTON STREET
Daily Record Bldg.
Cin
Classic Cinema
RENFIELD STREET
WEST NILE STREET
Odeon Film Centre
Athenaeum
Buchanan St
W. GEORGE ST
VINCENT PLACE
WEST GEORGE ST
ST VINCENT STREET
Regent Cinema
BATH STREET
Scala Cinemas
Pav. Th.
SAUCHIEHALL STREET
RENFREW STREET
Scottish T.V. Centre
Theatre Royal
COWCADDENS ROAD
Cowcaddens
CAMBRIDGE STREET
Film Theatre
ROSE STREET
REGENT
CAMPBELL ST
BLYTHSWOOD SQ.
BLYTHSWOOD STREET
WEST BLYTHS WOOD ST
Police H.Q.
DOUGLAS
BOTHWELL
WATERLOO STREET
CADOGAN
HOLM ST
WEST STREET
WEST ST
Church
PITT ST
PITT
HOLLAND ST
ELMBANK STREET
Charing Cross Station
King's Theatre
DALHOUSIE ST
School of Art
ABC 1&2 Cinema
SCOTT ST
HILL STREET
Dental Hospital
GARNET ST
BUCCLEUCH STREET
Beatson Memorial Hospital
Museum of the Royal Highland Fusiliers
WEST GRAHAM STREET
Stow College
SHAMROCK ST
MONCRIEFF STREET
Baths
BALNAIN ST
ST PETER'S STREET
ABC Cinema
NEW CITY ROAD
MARYHILL ROAD
St George's Cross
GREAT WESTERN ROAD
ST GEORGE'S ROAD
PRINCE'S ST
GRANT STREET
CARNARVON STREET
ST. ASHLEY ST
ARLINGTON ST
WEST PRINCE'S STREET
RUPERT STREET
PARK STREET
WESTEND PARK ST
WOODLANDS DRIVE
WOODLANDS ROAD
PARK DR.
LYNEDOCH PLACE
LYNEDOCH ST
WOODSIDE TERRACE
WOODSIDE PLACE
NORTH STREET
Mitchell Library
SANDYFORD PL.
BERKELEY STREET
GRANVILLE ST
KENT ROAD
ELDERSLIE STREET
SHAFTESBURY STREET
ARGYLE STREET

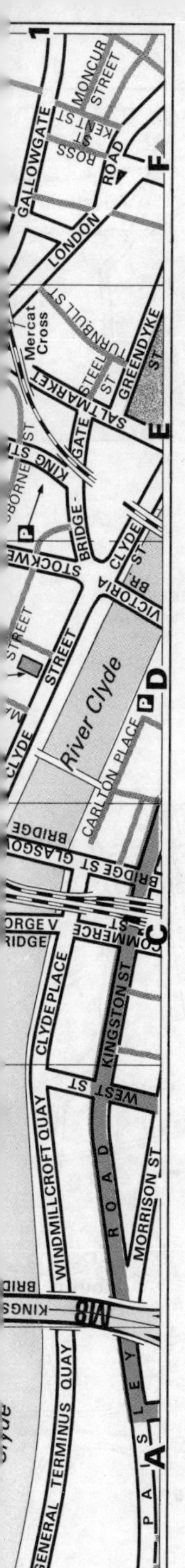
MONCUR STREET
KENT ST
ROSS
GALLOWGATE
LONDON ROAD
TURNBULL ST
Mercat Cross
GREENDYKE ST
SALTMARKET
STEEL ST
KING ST
BRIDGEGATE
CLYDE ST
VICTORIA BR
STOCKWELL STREET
River Clyde
CARLTON PLACE
GLASGOW BRIDGE
BRIDGE ST
COMMERCE ST
KINGSTON ST
CLYDE PLACE
WEST ST
WINDMILLCROFT QUAY
MORRISON ST
PAISLEY ROAD
M8
GENERAL TERMINUS QUAY

Glasgow Central
1 Albany ★★★★
2 Ambassador XXX
3 The Basement at Archie's X
4 Buttery ❀XX
5 Crest Hotel Glasgow City ☆☆☆
6 Fountain XXX
7 Holiday Inn Glasgow ☆☆☆☆
8 Stakis Ingram ☆☆☆
9 Oriental X
10 Pendulum XX
11 Le Provençal XX
12 Trattoria Caruso X
13 Trattoria Lanterna X
14 Trattoria Toscana X

Glasgow

★★**Newlands** 260 Kilmarnock Rd (Scottish & Newcastle) ☎041-632 9171 District plan **18**

Conveniently situated, small hotel, set in the southern suburbs of the city.

17rm(15⇌)(1fb) CTV in all bedrooms Ⓡ *sB&B⇌£17.50 dB&B£32 dB&B⇌£34 B

☾ 🚗

British & French V ♧ ☕ *Lunch £7.25alc Tea £1.95alc Dinner £7.25alc Wine £3.50 Last dinner 11pm

Credit cards 1 2 3 5

★★**Sherbrooke** 11 Sherbrooke Av, Pollokshields ☎041-427 4227 District plan **21**

Traditional red sandstone building located on south side of city with convenient access to motorway.

8rm(5⇌2⋒)(1fb) CTV in all bedrooms Ⓡ B

50P ✽

English & French V ♧ ☕ *Lunch £3.25–£3.75&alc Tea 45–55p High Tea £3–£3.75 Dinner £6.60&alc Wine £4.80 Last dinner 8.15pm

Credit cards 1 2 3 5 **VS**

○**Skean Dhu Glasgow** Renfrew St ☎041-332 3311 Not on plan

320⇌

Due to have opened July 1983

XXX**Ambassador** 19/20 Blythswood Sq ☎041-221 2034 Central plan **2** *C3*

Well appointed basement Italian restaurant.

Closed Sun

International V 100 seats *Lunch £4.80–£6.80&alc Dinner fr£9.50&alc Wine £5.80 Last dinner 10.30pm ♪ Live music and dancing Tue–Sat

Credit cards 1 2 3 4 5

XXX**Fountain** 2 Woodside Cres ☎041-332 6396 Central plan **6** *A4*

Closed Sun Lunch not served Sat

French 55 seats *Lunch £6.75&alc Dinner £9.80alc Wine £5.50 Last dinner 10.30pm ♪ Live music and dancing Tues–Sat

Credit cards 1 2 3 4 5

❀XX**Buttery** 652 Argyle St ☎041-221 8188 Central plan **4** *A3*

Closed Sun Lunch not served Sat

French V 50 seats Lunch £11alc Dinner £14–£15alc Wine £4.50 Last dinner 10pm 25P

S% Credit cards 1 2 3 5

XX**Kensingtons** 164 Darnley St, Pollokshields ☎041-424 3662 District plan **17**

Attractively decorated basement restaurant.

Closed Sun & Mon Lunch not served Sat

International V 30 seats *Lunch £4.95&alc Dinner £10.95&alc Wine £4.95 Last dinner 10.30pm P

Credit cards 1 2 3 5

XX**Pendulum** 17 West Princes St ☎041-332 1709 Central plan **10** *B5*

Italian basement restaurant in West End.

Closed Sun, 1 & 17 Aug, & 1 & 10 Jan Lunch not served Sat Dinner not served Mon

Continental 50 seats Lunch fr£2.80 Wine £4.50 Last Dinner 10.30pm

Credit cards 1 2

❀XX**Poachers** Ruthven Ln ☎041-339 0932 District plan **19**

Bright, ground-floor restaurant located in a lane off the busy Byres Road and popular with business clientele.

45 seats Lunch £7.50alc Dinner £13.50alc Wine £5.25 Last dinner 11pm 10P

Credit cards 1 2 3 5

XX**Le Provençal** 21 Royal Exchange Sq ☎041-221 0798 Central plan **11** *D2*

An attractive bistro and wine bar located below 'Charlie Parkers', a smart lounge bar opposite the Stirling Library.

Closed Sun & local Hols

French 50 seats Lunch £4–£6&alc Dinner £11alc Wine £5 Last dinner 11pm ♪ Live music Fri & Sat (dinner only)

Credit cards 1 2 3 5 **VS**

XX**Shish Mahal** 45 Gibson St ☎041-339 8256 District plan **22**

Popular, well appointed restaurant with tasteful modern decor, situated close to the University.

Indian & Pakistani V Unlicensed No corkage charge 110 seats Lunch £3 Dinner £5alc Last dinner 11.30pm ♪

S% Credit cards 1 2 3 4 5

See advert on page 284

X**Basement at Archie's** 27 Waterloo St ☎041-221 0551 Central plan **3** *C2*

Smart basement cocktail bar and restaurant.

Closed Sun, Public hols, Xmas & New Year Lunch not served Sat

International 43 seats Last dinner 10.30pm ♪

Credit cards 1 2 3 5

X**Oriental** 41 Hope St ☎041-221 1950 Central plan **9** *C2*

Well-appointed modern Chinese restaurant.

Chinese & European 52 seats Lunch £1.95 Dinner £3–£8&alc Last dinner 11.30pm ♪

S% Credit cards 1 2 3 5

X**Trattoria Caruso** 313 Hope St ☎041-331 2607 Central plan **12** *C4*

Italian restaurant with adjoining pizzeria. →

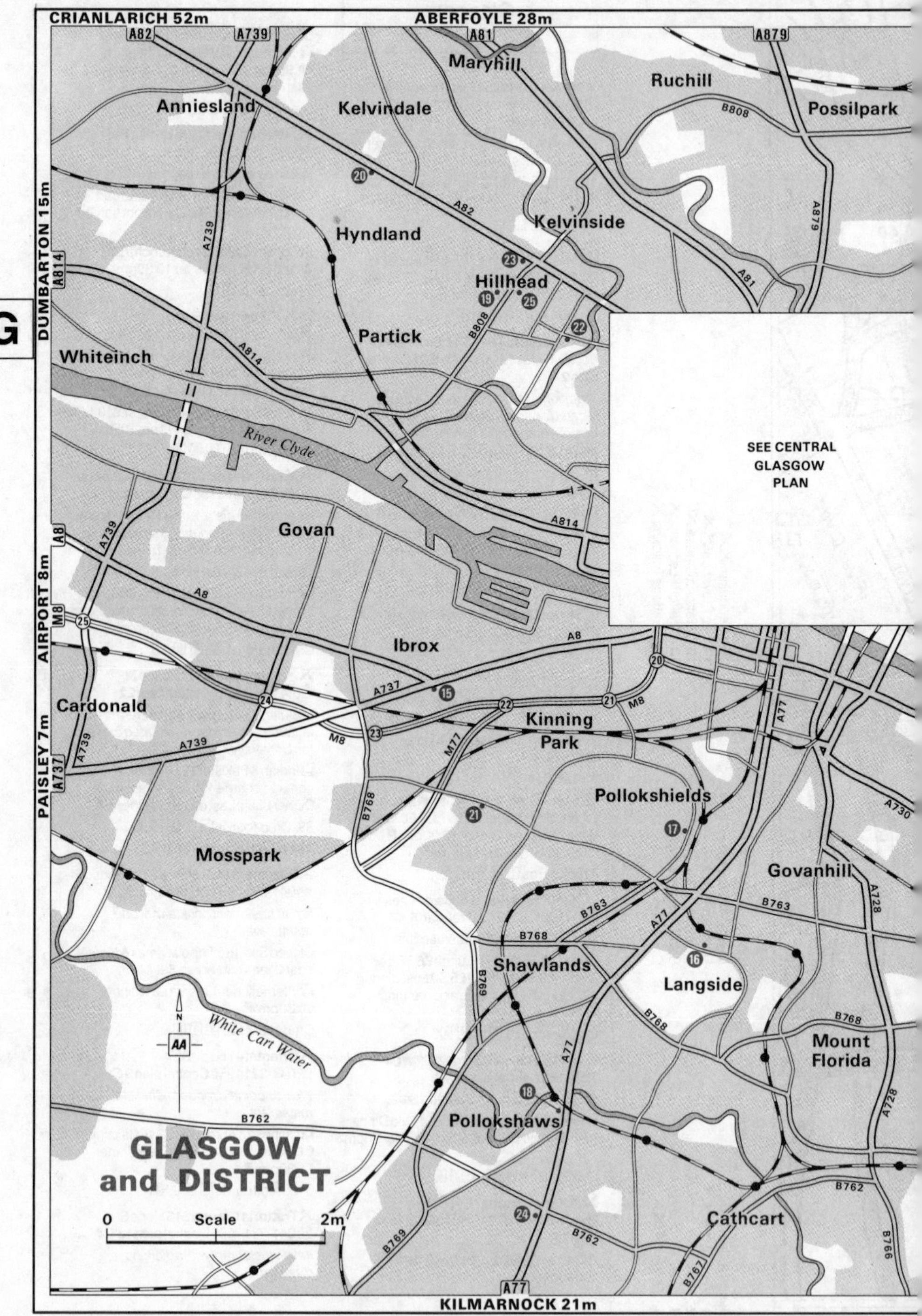

G
CRIANLARICH 52m
ABERFOYLE 28m
DUMBARTON 15m
AIRPORT 8m
PAISLEY 7m
KILMARNOCK 21m
A82
A739
A81
A879
A814
A8
M8
A737
A77
A730
A728
A766
A767
M77
B808
B768
B763
B769
B762
Maryhill
Ruchill
Possilpark
Anniesland
Kelvindale
Hyndland
Kelvinside
Hillhead
Partick
Whiteinch
River Clyde
Govan
Ibrox
Cardonald
Kinning Park
Pollokshields
Mosspark
Govanhill
Shawlands
Langside
Mount Florida
White Cart Water
Pollokshaws
Cathcart
SEE CENTRAL GLASGOW PLAN
N
AA
GLASGOW and DISTRICT
0
Scale
2m

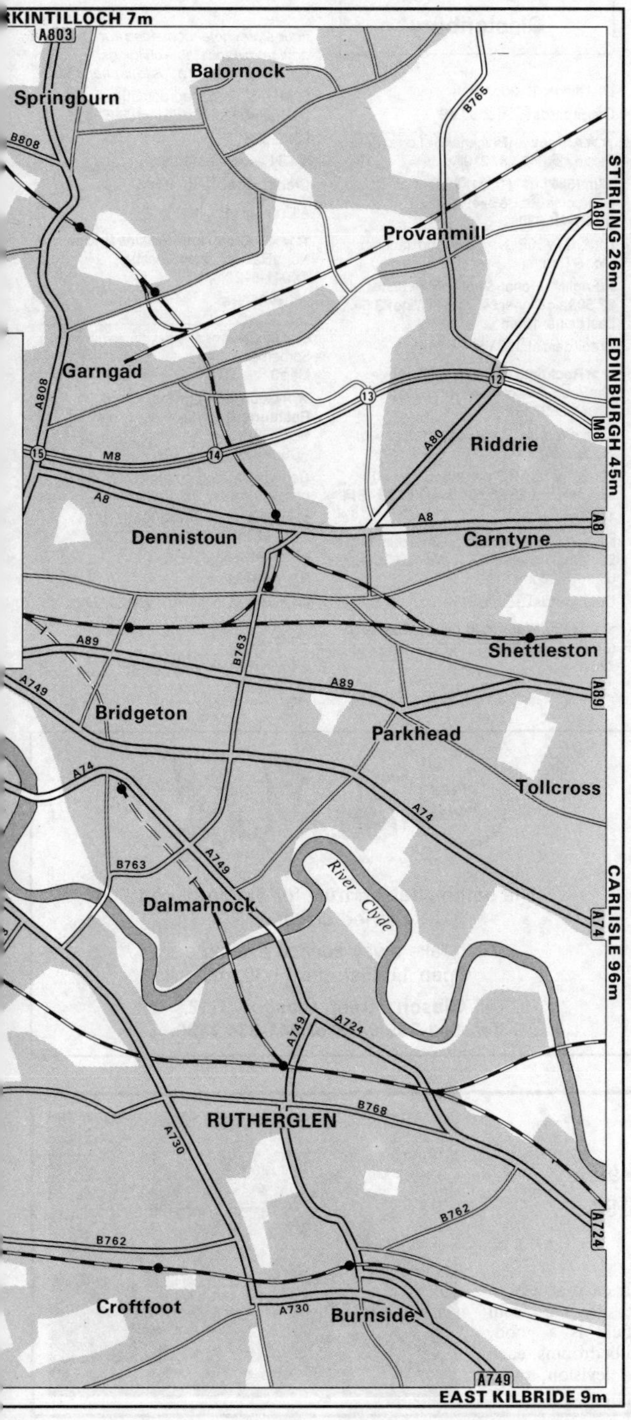

RKINTILLOCH 7m
A803
Balornock
Springburn
B765
B808
STIRLING 26m
A80
Provanmill
EDINBURGH 45m
M8
Garngad
A808
12
13
A80
Riddrie
15
M8
14
A8
A8
A8
Dennistoun
Carntyne
Shettleston
A89
B763
A749
A89
A89
Bridgeton
Parkhead
A74
Tollcross
A74
A749
B763
River Clyde
CARLISLE 96m
Dalmarnock
A74
A749
A724
B768
RUTHERGLEN
A730
B762
A724
B762
Croftfoot
A730
Burnside
A749
EAST KILBRIDE 9m

Glasgow District

15 Bellahouston ★★★
16 Ewington ★★
17 Kensingtons ✕✕
18 Newlands ★★
19 Poachers ❀✕✕
20 Stakis Pond ☆☆☆
21 Sherbrooke ★★
22 Shish Mahal ✕✕
23 Stakis Grosvenor ★★★★
24 Tinto Firs Thistle ★★★
25 Ubiquitous Chip ✕

Closed Sun, last wk Jul & 1st wk Aug

Italian **V** 60 seats Lunch £3.25&alc Dinner £6.50–£8&alc Wine £4.90 Last dinner 11pm P Live music Wed, Fri & Sat

Credit cards 1 2 3 5

✕ ***Trattoria Lanterna*** 35 Hope St ☎041-221 9160 Central plan **13** *C2*

Basement trattoria with authentic cuisine.

Closed Sun

English, French & Italian **V** 65 seats Last dinner 10.20pm P

Credit cards 2 3

✕**Trattoria Toscana** 47 Robertson St ☎041-221 4330 Central plan **14** *C2*

Closed Public hols Lunch not served Sun

Italian 60 seats ✻Lunch fr£2.75 Wine £4.25 Last dinner 11pm

Credit cards 1 2 3

✕ ***Ubiquitous Chip*** Ashton Ln, off Byres Rd ☎041-334 5007 District plan **25**

Unusual restaurant in converted warehouse.

Closed Sun

International 120 seats Last dinner 10.45pm

Credit card 2

At **Bearsden** (6m NW A81)

☆☆**Burnbrae** Milngavie Rd (Stakis) ☎041-942 5951

16rm(13) 100P

GLASGOW AIRPORT
Strathclyde *Renfrewshire*
Map **11** NS46

★★★★**Excelsior** Abbotsinch, Paisley (Trusthouse Forte) ☎041-887 1212 Telex no 777733

Modern, high-rise hotel complex situated at the airport terminal.

316rm(296 9) (9fb) CTV in all bedrooms Ⓡ sB&B £47.50 dB&B £63.50

Lift ☾ ## 35P CFA

Last dinner 10pm

Credit cards 1 2 3 4 5

☆☆☆☆**Stakis Normandy** Inchinan Rd, Renfrew (2m NE A8) (Stakis) ☎041-886 4100 Telex no 778897

Modern hotel complex with golf range.

142 CTV in all bedrooms Ⓡ ✻sB&B fr£35 dB&B fr£42 →

G

Lift ☾ 150P CFA Disco Fri–Sun
⊟ English & French ♧ ▭ Last dinner 10.30pm
Credit cards 1 2 3 5 **VS**

☆☆☆**Dean Park** 91 Glasgow Rd, Renfrew (3m NE A8) ☎041-886 3771 Telex no 779032

Modern, hotel complex with simple, well equipped bedrooms, a striking cocktail bar and attractive function suite.

120🛁 (6fb) CTV in all bedrooms ® sB&B🛁£28.50–£29.50 dB&B🛁£35–£36 ⊞

☾ CTV 250P CFA ✽ Live music and dancing 2 Weds per month *xmas*

⊟ British & Continental ♧ ▭ Lunch £5.50&alc Tea fr£1 Dinner £7.50&alc Wine £4.50 Last dinner 9.45pm
Credit cards 1 2 3 5

★★★**Glynhill** Paisley Rd, Renfrew (2m E A741) ☎041-886 5555 Telex no 779536

Small stone-built hotel, considerably extended, with modern rooms, function suite and bars.

80🛁🚿 (25fb) 2⊟ CTV in all bedrooms ® sB&B🛁🚿£19–£28 dB&B🛁🚿£25.50–£34.50 ⊞

☾ CTV 170P CFA Live music and dancing Wed, Fri, Sat & Sun *xmas*

⊟ International **V** ♧ ▭ Lunch £5.50&alc Tea £1–£2 Dinner £8.50&alc Wine £4.50 Last dinner 10.30pm
Credit cards 1 2 3 5 **VS**

★★**Ardgowan** Blackhall St, Lonend, Paisley ☎041-887 2196

17rm (6🛁11🚿) (1fb) 1⊟ CTV in all bedrooms ® sB&B🛁🚿£20 dB&B🛁🚿£30

Lift ☾ CTV 50P Live music and dancing Mon & Thur

⊟ English, French & Italian **V** ✽Lunch £3.50&alc Dinner £4.50&alc Wine £3.54 Last dinner 10pm
Credit cards 1 3 **VS**

★★**Rockfield** 12 Renfrew Rd, Paisley (2m South East off A741) (Ind Coope) ☎041-889 6182

Converted, two-storey stone house with modern extension.

20rm (8🛁12🚿) CTV in all bedrooms ® sB&B🛁🚿 fr£25.85 dB&B🛁🚿 fr£32.45 ⊞

100P 🚌

⊟ Scottish & European ♧ ▭ Bar lunch £2.50alc Dinner £8.50alc Wine £3.35 Last dinner 8.30pm
Credit cards 1 3 5

☆☆**Stakis Watermill** Lonend, Paisley (3m S) (Stakis) ☎041-889 3201 Telex no 778704

Four-storey hotel, converted from the original mill and stable buildings. A waterfall at the rear adds to its character.

51🛁🚿 CTV in all bedrooms ® ✽sB&B🛁🚿 fr£30 dB&B🛁🚿 fr£38 ⊞

Lift ☾ 50P

♧ ▭ Last dinner 10.30pm
Credit cards 1 2 3 5 **VS**

At **Erskine** (4m NW A8)

☆☆☆☆**Crest Hotel Erskine Bridge** North Barr, Inchinan (Crest) ☎041-812 0123

200🛁 350P

GLASTONBURY
Somerset
Map **3** ST53

★★**George & Pilgrims Hotel & Restaurant** High St (Inter-Hotels) ☎(0458) 31146
RS Sun evening

Centrally located, comfortable, 15th-century hostelry, full of character.

12rm (4🛁1🚿) (4fb) 4⊟ ® sB&B£18 sB&B🛁🚿£19–£22 dB&B£30 dB&B🛁🚿£38–£44 ⊞

CTV 4P 6🏠 *xmas*

⊟ English & Continental **V** ♧ ▭ Lunch fr£3.50 Tea £1.72–£2 Dinner fr£8.50 Last dinner 9pm
Credit cards 1 2 3 4 5 **VS**

✕✕**No 3** Magdalene St ☎(0458) 32129
Closed Mon & 1–14 Feb Lunch not served Tue–Fri Dinner not served Sun (Open Bank Holidays)
V 24 seats Lunch £16 Dinner £13–£16 Wine £4.50 Last dinner 10pm 8P bedrooms available
Credit card 2 5 **VS**

GLENBORRODALE
Highland *Argyllshire*
Map **13** NM66
★★*B* ***Clan Morrison*** ☎(09724) 232
Closed Nov–Mar
Small family run hotel in picturesque lochside position specialising in good food.
6➡Ⓡ
60P CTV ✽
Scottish & French **V** Last dinner 9pm
Credit cards 1 3

★★*BL* **Glenborrodale Castle** (Trusthouse Forte) ☎(09724) 266
Closed Nov–mid Mar
Beautiful red sandstone castle dating from 1900 standing close to Loch Sunart.
23rm(2➡) (5fb) CTV in all bedrooms Ⓡ sB&B£30.50 (incl dinner) dB&B£61 (incl dinner) dB&B➡£67 (incl dinner) B
☾ CTV 40P ✽
Last dinner 9.30pm
Credit cards 1 2 3 4 5

GLENCAPLE
Dumfries & Galloway *Dumfriesshire*
Map **11** NX96
★★**Nith** ☎(038777) 213
Small, family run hotel, set on the side of River Nith.
10rm(2➡2⋔) (1fb) TV in all bedrooms Ⓡ ✽sB&B£13.20 sB&B➡⋔£14.70 dB&B£26.40 dB&B➡⋔£28.90
20P billiards sauna bath Live music and dancing Sat
✽Lunch £3.10alc Tea £1.45alc High Tea £2.90 Dinner £5.75alc Wine £3.30 Last dinner 8.30pm
Credit card 1

GLENCARSE
Tayside *Perthshire*
Map **11** NO12
★★*H* **Newton House** ☎(073886) 250
Former dower house situated on the edge of the village, bordering the main Perth to Dundee road.
7rm sB&B£18–£22 dB&B£24–£26 B
CTV 45P ✽
Scottish & French **V** Lunch £5.50–£7 Tea £1.20–£1.75 High Tea £4.50–£8 Dinner £8.50–£13&alc Wine £4.75 Last dinner 9pm
Credit cards 1 3 5 **VS**

GLENCOE
Highland *Argyllshire*
Map **14** NN15
★★**Glencoe** ☎Ballachulish (08552) 245
Closed Jan–Mar & Nov–Dec
Modernised, stone building at the western end of Glencoe overlooking Loch Leven.
13rm(2➡) (2fb) Ⓡ sB&B£9.50–£12 dB&B£19–£24 dB&B➡£23–£28 B
CTV 40P ✽
Bar lunch £2–£4&alc Tea 70p–£1 Dinner £6.50–£8&alc Wine £3.90 Last dinner 9.15pm
Credit cards 1 2 3 5

★★**Kings House** (12m SE A82) ☎Kingshouse (08556) 259
Closed Nov–Jan
A former inn, modernised and extended, situated admidst the rugged grandeur of Glencoe.
22rm(10➡) (1fb) sB&B£11–£15.50 dB&B£22–£28.50 dB&B➡£25–£35 B
CTV 100P ✽ Live music and dancing Sat
V Bar lunch £3.50alc Tea 60p alc Dinner £6.50–£8.50alc Wine £4.50 Last dinner 8.15pm
Credit cards 1 2

★**Clachaig Inn** ☎Ballachulish (08552) 252
10rm(4➡) (2fb) sB&B£11–£12 dB&B£20–£22 dB&B➡£22–£24 B
TV 40P
✽Dinner £7alc Wine £4.50 Last dinner 7.45pm
Credit card 2

GLENDEVON
Tayside *Perthshire*
Map **11** NN90
✕✕***Tormaukin*** ☎(025982) 252
Closed 3 Jan–Feb
International **V** 74 seats Last dinner 9.45pm bedrooms available

GLENEAGLES
Tayside *Perthshire*
Map **11** NN91
See Auchterarder

GLENFARG
Tayside *Perthshire*
Map **11** NO11
★★**Bein Inn** ☎(05773) 216
Former drovers inn nestling beneath a rock face, offering comfortable and modern accommodation.
9rm(8➡) Annexe: 4➡ (4fb) CTV in all bedrooms Ⓡ ✽sB&B£15.75 sB&B➡£18.75 dB&B£22 dB&B➡£25–£35 B
60P *xmas*
Scottish, English & French **V**
✽Lunch £9alc Tea £1–£1.50 High Tea fr£3.75 Dinner £9alc Wine £4.20 Last dinner 9.30pm
Credit cards 1 3

GLENLIVET
Grampian *Banffshire*
Map **15** NJ12
★★*L* **Minmore House** ☎(08073) 378
10rm(9➡) (3fb) sB&B£12.75 sB&B➡£12.75 dB&B£25.50–£33 dB&B➡£25.50–£33 B
20P 4 ✽ (heated) (hard)
Lunch £3.50–£7&alc Tea 75p&alc High Tea £3.50–£5 Dinner £5.50–£8.50&alc Wine £4.75 Last dinner 9pm
Credit cards 1 3 **VS**
See advert on page 286

G

G

GLENRIDDING
Cumbria
Map **11** NY31

★★★**Ullswater** ☎(08532) 444
47rm(41→6⋒) (7fb) 1⊟ CTV in 4 bedrooms Ⓡ sB&B→⋒£15.50–£27 dB&B→⋒£31–£60 Ɓ
Lift ☾ CTV 120P CFA ✽ *xmas*
⊟English & French ♆ ⊒ Lunch fr£5.50 Tea 60p High Tea fr£4 Dinner £7.50–£8.50&alc Wine £5 Last dinner 8.30pm
Credit cards 1 2 3 5

★★**Glenridding** (Best Western/Minotel) ☎(08532) 228
Hotel occupying an unrivalled position at the head of Ullswater.
43rm(29→8⋒) (5fb) sB&B→⋒£16.50 dB&B→⋒£33 Ɓ
CTV 25P *xmas*
♆ ⊒ Bar lunch £3alc Tea £1–£1.50 Dinner £8–£8.50&alc Wine £4.50 Last dinner 8.30pm
Credit cards 1 2 3 5 **VS**

GLENROTHES
Fife
Map **11** NO20

★★★**Balgeddie House** Leslie Rd ☎(0592) 742511
Large mansion dating from 1936 standing on a hillside in six acres of land.
18rm(17→1⋒) CTV in all bedrooms sB£20.90 sB→£25.30–£26.40 dB→£37.40 (room only) Ɓ
CTV P ✽ U ♿
⊟French ♆ ⊒ Lunch £8–£10alc Tea £1.25alc Dinner £10–£12.50alc Wine £4.95 Last dinner 9pm
S% Credit cards 1 2 3

★★**Greenside** High St, Leslie (2m W A911) ☎(0592) 743453
Extended Victorian house to east of village.
13rm(9→⋒) CTV in 10 bedrooms Ⓡ ✻sB&B£18.17 sB&B→⋒£22.55 dB&B£28.34 dB&B→⋒£33.06 Ɓ
60P
⊟English & French ♆ ✻Lunch £3.20&alc Dinner £6.50&alc Last dinner 8.45pm
Credit cards 1 3

★★***Rothes Arms*** South Park Rd (Scottish & Newcastle) ☎(0592) 753701
Closed 1 Jan
Custom built, commercial hotel, situated in the western residential suburb of this new town.
15rm(7→⋒) CTV in 7 bedrooms Ⓡ
☾ CTV 50P Disco 4 nights wkly Live music and dancing 5 nights wkly
V ♆ ⊒ Last dinner 9pm
Credit cards 1 2 3 4 5

GLENSHEE (Spittal of)
Tayside *Perthshire*
Map **15** NO16

★★*HL* **Dalmunzie House** ☎(025085) 224
Closed 22 Oct–28 Dec
Reputedly the highest hotel in Scotland, its secluded position is convenient for ski slopes. Also six hole private golf course.
19rm(9→) ✻sB&B£15–£18 dB&B£28–£38 dB&B→£34–£44 Ɓ
Lift 20P 4 ✽ (hard)
♆ ⊒ Bar lunch £1 Tea £1.20–£2 Dinner £9.50–£11 Wine £4.05 Last dinner 8.30pm
S% Credit cards 1 5 **VS**

GLOUCESTER
Gloucestershire
Map **3** SO81

★★★**Bowden Hall** Upton St Leonards (3m SE B4073) ☎(0452) 64121
RS Xmas Day & Boxing Day
Imposing hotel in own grounds with popular carvery restaurant.
23rm(22→1⋒) (2fb) CTV in all bedrooms Ⓡ sB&B→⋒£25 dB&B→⋒£38 Ɓ
☾ CTV ✽ sauna bath Live music and dancing Sat Cabaret Sat

V Lunch fr£6.90 Tea 50p Dinner fr£6.90&alc Wine £4.65 Last dinner 10pm
Credit cards 1 2 3 5 **VS**

☆☆☆*B* **Crest** Crest Way, Barnwood (Crest) ☎(0452) 63311 Telex no 437273
RS Xmas
Comfortable modern hotel in quiet and convenient situation for city centre.
100 CTV in all bedrooms Ⓡ *sB fr£36 (room only) dB fr£44 (room only)
178P CFA
International *Lunch £3–£7.50 Tea 55p Dinner £8.50&alc Wine £4.95 Last dinner 9.45pm
Credit cards 1 2 3 4 5 **VS**

★★★*B* **Tara** Upton Hill, Upton St Leonards (3m SE B4073) ☎(0452) 67412
Popular Cotswold stone house, with panoramic views of the Severn Valley.
22rm(9 8) (2fb) CTV in all bedrooms sB&B£23.50 sB&B £35 dB&B£40 dB&B £49.50
100P (heated)
International V Lunch £15alc Tea £2.50alc High Tea £4.50alc Dinner £15alc Wine £5.50 Last dinner 9.45pm
Credit cards 1 2 3 5 **VS**

★★**New Wellington** Bruton Way ☎(0452) 20022
RS Sun
Commercial hotel with good bedrooms and friendly atmosphere.
23rm(4) CTV in all bedrooms Ⓡ *sB&B fr£14.50 sB&B fr£17 dB&B fr£24 dB&B fr£26
Mainly grills *Bar lunch £2.50–£3.50 Tea 75p–£1.50 Dinner £2.50–£3.50 Wine £5.85 Last dinner 9pm
Credit cards 1 3

XX**Peebys** 19 Worcester St ☎(0452) 25636
City centre restaurant with light meals available at lunch time.
Closed Sun Lunch not served Sat
V 40 seats Lunch £3.95&alc Dinner £6.95&alc Wine £4.95 Last dinner 10.30pm
Credit cards 1 3 5

GLYN CEIRIOG
Clwyd
Map **7** SJ23

★★**Plas Owen** ☎(069172) 707
Recently-built hotel set high over the village with views down the Ceiriog Valley.
13rm(12 1) (2fb) Ⓡ sB&B £15.40–£19.80 dB&B £30.80–£35.20
CTV 120P
Lunch £6&alc Tea £2.50 Dinner £6.50&alc Wine £4.90 Last dinner 9pm

★*H* **Glyn Valley** ☎(069172) 210
White-painted, Victorian, village inn, with good picture collection in lounge and bar.
9rm(5) (2fb) 1 Ⓡ sB&B£12 sB&B £13 dB&B£23 dB&B £25
CTV 40P *xmas*
English & French V Lunch £6&alc Tea 90p Dinner £6&alc Wine £3.75 Last dinner 10pm
Credit card 1 **VS**

GOATHLAND
North Yorkshire
Map **8** NZ80

★★**Goathland Hydro** ☎Whitby (0947) 86296
Closed Nov–Mar
32rm(13) (1fb) *sB&B£15 sB&B £17.25 dB&B£30 dB&B £34.50
CTV 25P
V Lunch £4.60 Tea 55p alc Dinner £5.95 Wine £2.50 Last dinner 7.45pm
S%

G

Enjoy the good life..
in Luxury Accommodation
Squash 6 Superb Courts
Golf 18 Hole Course
Skiing 250 Metres Ski Slope
indoor facilities include: Sauna, Solarium, Snooker, Skittles, Pool, Table-tennis. . . .
Special Weekend Break, 2 & 7 Day Holiday Offers
Reductions for children.
FREE Colour Brochure
Gloucester Hotel and Country Club
ROBINSWOOD HILL. GLOUCESTER. TEL: GLOUCESTER (0452) 25653

★**Whitfield House** Darnholm ☎ Whitby (0947) 86215
A converted stone-built 'period' style cottage on the North Yorkshire moors.
12rm (1fb) sB&B£10.20–£11.20 dB&B£18.40–£21.40 B
CTV 10P 2 nc3yrs *xmas*
Lunch £3.95 Tea 50p Dinner £4.25&alc Wine £3.95 Last dinner 7.30pm
VS

GODALMING
Surrey
Map **4** SU94
✕✕**Inn on the Lake** Ockford Rd ☎ (04868) 5575
Well appointed hotel restaurant offering enterprising cuisine.
Dinner not served Sun
English & French 26 seats *Lunch £6.50–£8.50 Dinner £11.50 Wine £4.65 Last dinner 9.45pm 40P bedrooms available
Credit cards 1 2 3 5

G

GOLANT
Cornwall
Map **2** SX15
★★*HL* **Cormorant** ☎ Fowey (072683) 3426
Friendly, well appointed hotel in a beautiful location in this small village, with river views.
10 CTV in all bedrooms ® sB&B £14.50–£17 dB&B £29–£34 B
CTV 25P (heated) *xmas*
V Lunch £3.50 High Tea £2.50 Dinner £8 Wine £3.95 Last dinner 8.30pm
VS

GOLSPIE
Highland *Sutherland*
Map **14** NH89
★★**Golf Links** ☎ (04083) 3408
A converted red stone manse dating from 1870, near the sea front.
10rm (5) ® *sB&B£15 sB&B £17 dB&B£28 dB&B £32 B
CTV 18P

*Bar lunch £1.20alc Tea 60p alc Dinner £8alc Wine £4.25 Last dinner 8pm
Credit cards 1 3 5 **VS**

GOODRICH
Hereford & Worcester
Map **3** SO51
★★**Ye Hostelrie** ☎ Symonds Yat (0600) 890241
Small homely hotel with romantic façade. Popular with the locals.
8rm (2 2) (1fb) ® sB&B£18 sB&B £22 dB&B£29 dB&B £34 B
CTV 30P
Bar lunch £1.20–£2.50 Dinner £8alc Wine £4 Last dinner 9pm

GOODRINGTON
Devon
See **Paignton**

GOODWOOD
West Sussex
See **Waterbeach**

GOOLE
Humberside
Map **8** SE72
★★**Clifton** 1 Clifton Gdns, Boothferry Rd ☎ (0405) 61336
Two-storey, Edwardian building located near the town and the docks.
14rm (6 4) (1fb) CTV in 13 bedrooms sB&B fr£19 sB&B fr£21 dB&B fr£28 dB&B fr£30
CTV 12P 1
English, French & Italian Lunch £5–£6.50&alc Tea 80p Dinner £7.50–£8.50&alc Wine £6 Last dinner 9pm
Credit cards 1 3 5

GOOSNARGH
Lancashire
Map **7** SD53
✕**Ye Horns** ☎ (077 476) 230
Closed Mon
V 100 seats Lunch £5.50–£6 Dinner £8–£8.50 Wine £3.45 Last dinner 9.15pm 50P
Credit cards 2 5

GOREBRIDGE
Lothian *Midlothian*
Map **11** NT36
★*L* **Auld Toll** Newtonloan Toll ☎ (0875) 21253
Former roadhouse, now run as an English inn, it has small but neat bedrooms.
10rm (2 1) (1fb) ® sB&B£11.50 dB&B£20 dB&B £23
CTV 25P
V Lunch £1–£6.50&alc Dinner £1–£6.50&alc Last dinner 10pm
Credit cards 1 2 3 5

GOREY
Jersey, Channel Islands
Map **16**
★★★***Old Court House*** ☎ Jersey (0534) 54444 Telex no 4192032
Closed Nov–Apr
Old courthouse building with a modern frontage and an attractive, beamed restaurant.
27 CTV in all bedrooms
☾ CTV 40P (heated) sauna bath
French Last dinner 10pm
Credit cards 1 2 3 5

★★**Dolphin** Gorey Pier ☎ Jersey (0534) 53370 Telex no 4192085
Small comfortable hotel, with a beamed bar, situated in the town and facing the harbour.
17rm (14) CTV available on request sB&B£13–£15 sB&B £14–£16 dB&B£26–£30 dB&B £28–£32 B
☾ CTV Live music 3 nights wkly *xmas*
English & Continental Lunch £4.20–£4.50&alc Tea 80p–£1.50 Dinner £4–£7.50&alc Wine £3.20 Last dinner 10pm
Credit cards 1 2 3 4

✕***Galley*** ☎ Jersey (0534) 53456
Small restaurant overlooking the harbour, with nautical décor including fishing nets and buoys.

Closed Jan Dinner not served Mon
▣ English & French 80 seats Last dinner 10.15pm ⚠ bedrooms available
Credit cards 3 4

GORLESTON-ON-SEA
Norfolk
See **Yarmouth, Great**

GORRAN HAVEN
Cornwall
Map **2** SX04
★★ ***Llawnroc*** ☎ Mevagissey (0726) 843461
Small, isolated hotel located in the picturesque inlet of Gorran Haven.
10rm(2🛁3⋒) Ⓡ
CTV 60P
▣ Mainly grills ♧ ☐ Last dinner 8.30pm

GOSPORT
Hampshire
Map **4** SZ69
★★ **Anglesey** Crescent Rd, Alverstoke ☎ (07017) 82157
Quiet, Regency-style hotel with comfortable lounge.
19rm(5🛁14⋒)(1fb) 1▭ CTV in all bedrooms Ⓡ sB&B🛁⋒ £18.50–£19.50 dB&B🛁⋒ £25.50–£26.50 B
CTV 3🏠 Live music and dancing twice wkly
▣ English & French V ♧ ☐ Lunch £6–£7&alc Tea £1 alc Dinner £7 alc Wine £3.50 Last dinner 9.30pm
Credit cards 1 3 4 **VS**

GOUDHURST
Kent
Map **5** TQ73
★★ *B* **Star & Eagle** (Whitbread Fremlins, Minotel) ☎ (0580) 211512
RS Xmas
An attractive, 14th-century inn, combining a homely atmosphere and good cooking.
11rm(9🛁) 1▭ CTV in all bedrooms Ⓡ sB&B🛁 £25.50 dB&B🛁 £34 B
30P
V ♧ ☐ Lunch fr £5.50 Dinner fr £5.50&alc Wine £3.80 Last dinner 9.30pm
Credit cards 1 2 3

★ ***Goudhurst*** (1m W of village on A262) ☎ (0580) 211200
RS Xmas day
Small, family-run country free house whose restaurant is furnished with antiques.
6rm Ⓡ B
TV 25P 🚫
♧ Last dinner 9.30pm
Credit cards 1 3 5 **VS**

GOUROCK
Strathclyde *Renfrewshire*
Map **10** NS27
☆☆☆ **Stakis Gantock** Cloch Rd (Stakis) ☎ (0475) 34671 Telex no 778704
Modern building, situated one mile southwest of the town, with views out across the Clyde.
63🛁 CTV in all bedrooms Ⓡ
✱ sB&B🛁 £31 dB&B🛁 £40 B
☾ 80P CFA Live music and dancing Sat *xmas*
♧ ☐ Last dinner 9.30pm
Credit cards 1 2 3 5 **VS**

GRANGE (in-Borrowdale)
Cumbria
Map **11** NY21
See also Borrowdale and Rosthwaite
★★ *L* ***Gates Country House***
☎ Borrowdale (059684) 204 Closed Jan
Comfortable, relaxing hotel with panoramic views of surrounding countryside and fells.
20rm(15🛁) CTV in all bedrooms Ⓡ ✱ B
CTV 30P 1🏠 ✿ 🏠
▣ English & French V ♧ ☐ Last dinner 9pm

GRANGEMOUTH
Central *Stirlingshire*
Map **11** NS98
★★ **Leapark** 130 Bo'ness Rd ☎ (0324) 486733
Large commercial hotel with a popular entertainment programme.
34rm(5🛁)(4fb) CTV in all bedrooms sB&B fr £20.50 sB&B🛁 fr £23 dB&B fr £29 dB&B🛁 fr £33
☾ CTV 120P ✿ Disco twice wkly Cabaret wkly
▣ French ♧ ☐ ✱ Bar lunch £1.20–£2.30 Tea fr £1 High Tea fr £2.30 Dinner fr £5.75&alc Wine £4.50 Last dinner 9.30pm
Credit cards 1 2 3 5

GRANGE-OVER-SANDS
Cumbria
Map **7** SD47
★★★ **Cumbria Grand** ☎ (04484) 2331
Telex no 96215
Large, stone-built hotel with spacious accommodation, set in an elevated position.
95🛁 (4fb) 1▭ CTV in all bedrooms Ⓡ ✱
sB&B🛁 £23–£27 dB&B🛁 £34–£37 B
Lift ☾ CTV 160P 2🏠 CFA ✿ ⚲(hard) billiards Live music and dancing Sat 🏠 *xmas*
▣ English & French V ♧ ☐ Lunch £7–£8&alc Tea 75p Dinner £7.50–£8.50&alc Wine £5.25 Last dinner 9pm
Credit cards 1 2 3

★★ **Grange** Lindale Rd (Best Western) ☎ (04484) 3666
Large, Victorian building with views across Morecambe Bay.
41rm(20🛁10⋒)(4fb) CTV in all bedrooms Ⓡ sB&B £16–£18 sB&B🛁⋒ £20–£22 dB&B £28–£32 dB&B🛁⋒ £36–£40 B
CTV 100P CFA ✿ Live music and dancing Sat 🏠 *xmas*
▣ English & European V ♧ ☐ Lunch £6 Tea 50p High Tea £2.50–£3.50 Dinner £8 Wine £3.90 Last dinner 9pm
Credit cards 1 2 3 5 **VS**

★★ *L* **Graythwaite Manor** Fernhill Rd ☎ (04484) 2001
Large country house in beautiful →

G

grounds with home grown produce used in cooking.

24rm(12⇌) Annexe: 4rm CTV available in bedrooms ★ sB&B£18.50–£25.50 (incl dinner) sB&B⇌£19.50–£28 (incl dinner) dB&B£35–£49 (incl dinner) dB&B⇌£37–£54 (incl dinner) B

CTV 18P 14 ❊ (hard)

English & French V Lunch fr£4 Dinner fr£8 Wine £3.95 Last dinner 8pm

S%

★★ ***Kents Bank*** Kentsford Rd ☎(04484) 2054

Pleasant house in its own grounds, in an elevated position with good views.

8rm(3⇌) B

CTV 28P

Last dinner 8.45pm

Credit cards 1 3

★★ **Netherwood** Lindale Rd ☎(04484) 2552

A large Victorian building, with some oak dècor, standing in its own grounds.

23rm(15⇌2⋒) (6fb) CTV available in bedrooms sB&B£14–£16 sB&B⇌⋒£16–£17 dB&B£28–£32 dB&B⇌⋒£32–£34 B

☾ CTV 60P 12 ❊

V Lunch £3–£4 Tea 45p High Tea £3–£4 Dinner £5–£6.50 Wine £3.60 Last dinner 8.15pm

★ ***Commodore*** Main St ☎(04484) 2381

Pleasant town centre public house with views across Morecambe Bay.

12rm Ⓡ B

CTV 10P 2

V Last dinner 8pm

Credit card 3

★ ***Hardcragg Hall*** ☎(04484) 3353

Small, 400-year-old manor house, with oak panels and beams.

8rm(3⇌) Ⓡ ★ B

CTV 14P ❊

Last dinner 4pm

★*H* **Methven** Kents Bank Rd ☎(04484) 2031 Closed 3 Nov–22 Mar

Small, detached family-run hotel overlooking Morecambe Bay.

14rm(1⇌2⋒) (3fb) TV in 1 bedroom sB&B£9–£11 dB&B£18–£26 dB&B⇌⋒£26–£30 B

CTV 14P ❊ nc3yrs

Lunch £2.75 Tea £1 Dinner £4 Wine £3.30 Last dinner 7pm

S% **VS**

GRANTHAM
Lincolnshire
Map **8** SK93

★★★ **Angel & Royal** High St (Trusthouse Forte) ☎(0476) 5816

Historic town centre inn, originally a hostel for Knights Templar.

32rm(14⇌) CTV in all bedrooms Ⓡ sB&B£30.50 sB&B⇌£33 dB&B£43 dB&B⇌£49.50 B

☾ 53P *xmas*

Last dinner 10pm

Credit cards 1 2 3 4 5

★★★ **George** High St (Best Western) ☎(0476) 3286

Georgian inn, once the home of Isaac Newton.

47rm(41⇌6⋒) (2fb) 1 CTV in all bedrooms Ⓡ sB&B⇌⋒£26.50 dB&B⇌⋒£35 B

☾ 70P 2 Live music and dancing Sat CFA *xmas*

International V Lunch £5.95&alc Tea £1–£2.50 High Tea £1.50–£3.75 Dinner £6.95&alc Wine £5 Last dinner 10pm

Credit cards 1 2 3 5

★★ **Kings** North Pde ☎(0476) 5881

A converted and enlarged former private house standing on the A1174.

14rm(5⇌2⋒) Annexe: 3rm(1⇌2⋒) CTV in all bedrooms Ⓡ sB&B£16 sB&B⇌⋒£22 dB&B£23 dB&B⇌⋒£27.50 B

☾ 50P ✽
V ♈ Lunch £5.30&alc Dinner £6.40&alc Wine £4.25 Last dinner 9.30pm
Credit cards 1 2 3 5

✕✕**Premier** 2–6 North Parade ☎(0476) 77855
Closed Mon Lunch not served Sun Dinner not served Tue
48 seats Wine £4.50 Last dinner 10pm 6P
Credit cards 1 2 3 5

GRANTOWN-ON-SPEY
Highland *Morayshire*
Map **14** NJ02

★★***Ben Mhor*** High St ☎(0479) 2056
Family-run, stone-built hotel, located in the main street.
24rm(20⇌4⋒) TV in all bedrooms
CTV 24P
V ♈ ☐ Last dinner 8.30pm
Credit cards 1 3 5 **VS**

★★**Coppice** Grant Rd ☎(0479) 2688
Detached, two-storey stone building dating from 1890, standing in its own grounds.
25rm (4fb) ✱ sB&B£11.50–£13.50 dB&B£19.50–£23 B
CTV 40P ✽
V ♈ ☐ Bar lunch £1.50–£5 Tea 50p–£1.50 Dinner £6.50 Wine £3.80 Last dinner 7.30pm
VS

★★**Garth** Castle Rd ☎(0479) 2836
Charming, converted, 18th-century house.
14rm(4⇌2⋒) Annexe: 3⇌ sB&B£12–£14 sB&B⇌⋒£15–£17 dB&B£24–£28 dB&B⇌⋒£27–£31 B
✕ CTV 10P 1🏠 ✽ ✽ xmas
English & French V ♈ ☐ Lunch £3–£5 High Tea £3–£6 Dinner £7–£9&alc Wine £4 Last dinner 9pm
Credit cards 3 4 5 **VS**

★★***Rosehall*** The Square ☎(0479) 2721
Distinctive, stone building standing in the square.
14rm(4⇌2⋒) TV available in bedrooms ®
CTV 20P
♈ Last dinner 8pm

★★***Seafield Lodge*** Woodside Av ☎(0479) 2152 Closed Nov
Converted house with extensions, located in a quiet, residential part of the town.
14rm(3⇌6⋒) ® sB&B fr£12.65 dB&B fr£25.30 dB&B⇌⋒ fr£28.75 B
CTV 50P ✽
V ♈ Bar lunch fr£3.20 Tea £1 Dinner fr£9 Wine £5.95 Last dinner 8.15pm
Credit cards 2 3

★**Dunvegan** Heathfield Rd ☎(0479) 2301
Closed 23–27 Dec
Small, family-run hotel in a quiet area opposite playing fields and the golf course.
9rm sB&B£8.75–£10.95 dB&B£17.50–£21.90 B
CTV 9P 1🏠
V ♈ ☐ Bar lunch 65p–£2.50 Tea 60p–£1.25 Dinner £5.80–£7.50 Wine £3.65 Last dinner 7.30pm
VS

★**Spey Valley** Seafield Av ☎(0479) 2942
Attractive, granite-stone hotel with a tidy garden, located in a quiet area.
24rm (6fb) sB&B £10 dB&B £20 B
CTV 24P ✽ *xmas*
♈ ☐ Lunch £3–£6 Tea 75p–£1.50 Dinner £3–£7.75 Wine £3.80 Last dinner 10pm

✕**Craggan Mill** ☎(0479) 2288
Closed 1–22 Feb Lunch not served Oct–Jun
British & Italian V 40 seats Lunch £2.40–£3.60&alc Dinner £6.50–£8.50alc Wine £3.95 Last dinner 10pm 25P Live music Sat

GRASMERE
Cumbria
Map **11** NY30

★★★★**Wordsworth** ☎(09665) 592 Telex no 65329
35rm(34⇌) (1fb) 1 CTV in all bedrooms ✱ sB&B⇌⋒£24–£28 dB&B⇌⋒£48–£70 B
Lift ☾ 55P CFA ✽ (heated) sauna bath *xmas* ♿
English & French V ♈ ☐ Lunch £10–£15alc Tea £3.50 Dinner £11.50–£12&alc Wine £4 Last dinner 9pm
Credit cards 1 2 3 5 **VS**
See advert on page 292

★★★**Gold Rill Country House** ☎(09665) 486
A comfortable hotel with a tranquil atmosphere, situated on the fringe of the village.
21rm(17⇌) (4fb) CTV available in bedrooms ® ✱ sB&B£16–£21 sB&B⇌£18–£23 dB&B£36–£46 dB&B⇌£38–£50 B
CTV 30P ✽ (heated) Live music twice wkly nc5yrs *xmas*
♈ ☐ Bar lunch £1.50–£4 Tea 75p Dinner £10.50 Wine £2.80 Last dinner 8.30pm
Credit cards 1 2 3 5

★★★**Grasmere Red Lion** ☎(09665) 456
Closed mid Nov–mid Mar
A 200-year-old coaching inn, with a modern entrance and interior, opposite the village green.
36rm(28⇌1⋒) (6fb) CTV in all bedrooms ✱sB&B⇌⋒£21–£25 dB&B£33–£39 dB&B⇌⋒£35–£42 B
Lift 40P CFA
English & French V ♈ ☐ Bar lunch 85p–£3.25 Tea 65p Dinner £7&alc Wine £5.10 Last dinner 9pm
S% Credit cards 1 2 3 5 **VS**

❀★★★***HBL* Michael's Nook** ☎(09665) 496 Telex no 65329
(Rosette awarded for dinner only.)
A delightful country house hotel set in secluded gardens overlooking →

Grasmere. Antiques and flowers abound and the drawing room is especially elegant and comfortable. Bedrooms are individually furnished and decorated, and, in the attractive dining room, many local and English specialities are available.
10rm(9⇌1⋒) CTV in all bedrooms ✈
dB&B⇌⋒£75–£112 (incl dinner)
14P 2⌂ ⇉ ✽ xmas ♿
▤ British & French Lunch £14.95 Dinner £19 Wine £4.50
Last dinner 8pm
Credit card ② **VS**

Grasmere

★★★**Prince of Wales** (Mount Charlotte)
☎(09665) 666
A large hotel standing by the lakeside in nine acres of grounds.
81rm(72⇌9⋒) (7fb) CTV in all bedrooms
sB&B⇌⋒£27 dB&B⇌⋒£39.50 ⊟
☾ 90P CFA ✽
▤ English & French **V** ♈ ☐ Lunch £5.75
Dinner £7.25 Wine £5 Last dinner 9pm
Credit cards ① ② ③ ⑤ **VS**

★★★ ***BL* Swan** (Trusthouse Forte)
☎(09665) 551
A 17th-century hotel with later additions, once visited by Sir Walter Scott and William Wordsworth.
41rm(25⇌) (4fb) CTV in all bedrooms ®
sB&B£33 sB&B⇌£39 dB&B£45.50
dB&B⇌£57 ⊟
☾ CTV 40P ⇉ ✽ *xmas*
♈ ☐ Last dinner 8.45pm
Credit cards ① ② ③ ④ ⑤

★★ ***H* Oak Bank** Broadgate ☎(09665) 217
Closed Dec–Jan
14rm(6⇌8⋒) (1fb) sB&B⇌⋒£12–£14
dB&B⇌⋒£24–£28 ⊟
CTV 12P ⇉ ✽ ⌂
▤ English, French & Italian ♈ ☐ Bar lunch £4alc Tea £2alc Dinner £8alc Wine £3.50
Last dinner 8pm
Credit cards ① ③

★★ ***B* Ravenswood** Broadgate
☎(09665) 277
Closed Dec–Jan
Very comfortable hotel, personally supervised by the proprietors and noted for its home cooking.
11rm(1⇌5⋒) (1fb) sB&B£12–£13
sB&B⇌⋒£13–£15 dB&B£24–£26
dB&B⇌⋒£26–£30 ⊟
⚟ CTV 14P ✽ ⌂
▤ English & French **V** ♈ ☐ Bar lunch £1–£3 Tea 70p Dinner £8–£9 Wine £2.95 Last dinner 8pm
VS

★★ **Rothay Bank** ☎(09665) 334
Closed Jan & Feb RS Nov, Dec & Mar
14rm(4⇌⋒) ⊟
CTV 30P ✽
♈ ☐ Last dinner 8pm
Credit cards ① ② ③

★ ***Moss Grove*** ☎(09665) 251
RS Dec–Mar
16rm ✈ ⊟
TV 10P 1⌂ ⇉
♈ Last dinner 7.30pm

❀★ WHITE MOSS HOUSE, GRASMERE

Rydal Water ☎(09665) 295
Closed Nov–mid Mar
This delightful Lakeland stone-built house, with its well tended garden, overlooks Rydal Water and has magnificent views of the surrounding fells. Its very appearance is welcoming and Jean and Arthur Butterworth, most ably assisted by their daughter and son-in-law, Susan and Peter Dixon, ensure that every need is catered for. Indeed, their hospitality and warmth of atmosphere is second to none. This is not a large hotel but the bedrooms and bathrooms have been tastefully designed and furnished to give maximum facilities and comfort. Many thoughtful extras are provided such as hair-dryers, trouser pressers, books and magazines, fresh fruit, flowers and even hot water bottles.
Downstairs, fresh flowers, paintings and polished woodwork abound and an open fire in the very comfortable drawing room gives additional warmth on days when perhaps the Cumbrian weather might not be all that one hopes. Dinner is not really a lavish affair – in many respects it is quite homely – but all will agree that Mrs Butterworth's five course meals, very competently served by Mr Butterworth, are well worthy of our rosette award. Although there is no choice, with the exception of sweets, the standard of cooking is of the highest order. There is an extensive cheese board containing several quite rare English farmhouse cheeses which are served with White Moss oat cakes – a perfect ending to a perfect meal! Mrs Butterworth now gives cookery demonstrations of White Moss dishes in her own home on selected dates, and no doubt would provide details on request.

5⇌ Annexe: 2rm(1⇌1⋒) ✈
dB&B⇌⋒£74 (incl dinner)
10P ⇉ ✽ nc13yrs
Dinner fr£13.95 Wine £4.25 Last dinner 7.30pm
VS

GRASSINGTON
North Yorkshire
Map **7** SE06

★**Grassington House** ☎(0756) 752406
RS Nov–Feb

12rm(1🛁6🚿) Annexe: 6rm (2fb) CTV in 2 bedrooms ® *sB&B fr£12.36 sB&B🛁🚿 fr£13.80 dB&B fr£23 dB&B🛁🚿 fr£26.45

CTV 30P

V ♥ ☕ *Lunch £1.25–£5.70 Tea £1.40–£1.80 High Tea 95p–£2.45 Dinner £3.50–£5.75&alc Wine £3.95 Last dinner 7pm

Credit cards 1 3

GRAVESEND
Kent
Map **5** TQ67

At **Shorne** (4m SE A2)

☆☆☆**Inn on the Lake** ☎Shorne (047482) 3333

78🛁 250P

GRAYS
Essex
Map **5** TQ67

At **North Stifford** (2m N on A13)

☆☆☆***Stifford Moat House*** (Queens Moat) ☎Grays Thurrock (0375) 71451

59🛁🚿 30P

GRAYSHOTT
Hampshire
Map **4** SU83

❀✕**Woods** Headley Rd (1m SW B3002 off A3) ☎Hindhead (042873) 5555

Closed Sun & Mon Lunch not served

French 25 seats Dinner £12alc Wine £3.95 Last dinner mdnt

Credit cards 1 3 5

GREASBY
Merseyside
Map **7** SJ28

✕✕✕***Manor Farm*** Greasby Rd ☎051-677 7034

Comfortable and relaxing 17th-century mansion where lobster is a speciality.

Closed Sun & Public hols Lunch not served Sat

French **V** 120 seats Last dinner 9.30pm 60P

Credit cards 1 2 3 4 5

GREAT
Places incorporating the word 'Great' – eg Great Malvern, Great Yarmouth – are listed under Malvern, Yarmouth, etc

GREENOCK
Strathclyde *Renfrewshire*
Map **10** NS27

★★★**Tontine** 6 Ardgowan Sq (Best Western) ☎(0475) 23316 Telex no 779801

A 19th-century building, with an extension wing, situated in the west end of the town.

32rm(23🛁) CTV in all bedrooms ® sB&B £25 sB&B🛁£28 dB&B £35 dB&B🛁£38 B

☾ 24🚗

British & French **V** ♥ ☕ Lunch £5.25–£5.50&alc Tea £2.30–£2.55 High Tea £3.50–£3.75 Dinner £7.50–£8&alc Wine £5 Last dinner 9pm

Credit cards 1 2 3 5 **VS**

✕***La Taverna*** 6 West Blackhall St ☎(0475) 25391

Lunch not served Sun

English & Italian 46 seats Last dinner 10pm

Credit cards 1 2 5

GRETA BRIDGE
Co Durham
Map **12** NZ01

★★**Morritt Arms** ☎Teesdale (0833) 27232

Old coaching inn retaining Dickensian character.

23rm(14🛁) (2fb) 2 ® sB&B £19.50 sB&B🛁£23 dB&B £27.50 dB&B🛁£36 B

CTV 100P 6🚗 ✽

V ♥ ☕ Lunch £5–£8 Tea 75p–£2.20 Dinner £9–£12 Wine £4.50 Last dinner 9pm

Credit cards 1 3 5 **VS**

GRETNA
Dumfries & Galloway *Dumfriesshire*
Map **11** NY36

★★**Gretna Chase** (¼m S on B721 in England) ☎(04613) 517

Once a marriage house, it has now been modernised while retaining much of its original character.

10rm(1🛁2🚿) (1fb) sB&B £18 sB&B🛁🚿£21 dB&B £30 dB&B🛁🚿£36 B

CTV 40P ✽

English & Continental **V** ♥ Lunch £6.50&alc Dinner £8alc Wine £3.50 Last dinner 9.30pm

Credit cards 1 3 **VS**

★★***Royal Stewart Motel*** ☎(04613) 210

Bungalow-style motel on the outskirts of the town.

13rm(3🛁10🚿) CTV in 3 bedrooms ® B

CTV 20P

Last dinner 9pm **VS**

★★**Solway Lodge** Annan Rd ☎(04613) 266

Two-storey painted-brick building with some bedrooms in modern annexe.

3rm(1🛁) Annexe: 7🛁 (1fb) ® *sB&B🛁£12.50 dB&B🛁£23

CTV 40P Live music and dancing mthly

V ♥ ☕ *Bar lunch 55p–£6 60 Tea 35p Dinner £6.75alc Wine £3.65 Last dinner 9pm

Credit cards 1 2 3 5

GRIMSBY
Humberside
Map **8** TA20

☆☆☆☆**Humber Royal Crest** Littlecoates Rd (Crest) ☎(0472) 50295 Telex no 527776

Modern four-storey brick building on the outskirts of town next to the golf course.

52🛁 CTV in all bedrooms ® *sB🛁 fr£37.50 (room only) dB🛁 fr£44 (room only) B

Lift ☾ 200P CFA ♿

International **V** ♥ *Lunch fr£6.50&alc Dinner fr£8.95&alc Wine £5.25 Last dinner 9.45pm

Credit cards 1 2 3 4 5 **VS**

☆☆☆**Crest** St James's Sq (Crest) ☎(0472) 59771 Telex no 527741

Modern, four-storey hotel near the town centre.

132🛁 CTV in all bedrooms ® *sB🛁 fr£34 (room only) dB🛁 fr£43 (room only) B

Lift ☾ 90P sauna bath CFA

International ♥ *Lunch fr£5.50&alc Tea fr75p Dinner £6.95–£7.75&alc Wine £5.25 Last dinner 9.45pm

Credit cards 1 2 3 4 5 **VS**

✕**Othello** 25 Bethlehem St, Old Market Pl ☎(0472) 56704

Lunch not served Sun

Greek & Continental 80 seats Lunch £11alc Wine £4.20 Last dinner 11pm

Credit cards 1 2 3 5

GRIMSTHORPE
Lincolnshire
Map **8** TF02

✕**Black Horse Inn** ☎Edenham (077832) 247

Closed Sun, Public hols, 10 days Xmas

V 70 seats Lunch £9.95–£12&alc Dinner £12–£15&alc Wine £7.50 Last dinner 9.30pm P bedrooms available

S% Credit cards 1 2 3

GRIMSTON
Norfolk
Map **9** TF72

❀★★★***HBL*** **Congham Hall Country House** Lynn Rd ☎Hillington (0485) 600250

Recently opened as a country house hotel and Midlands winner of the AA Best Newcomer award (see page 26), this Georgian Manor House stands in 44 acres of grounds. It has been most tastefully decorated throughout with very well appointed bedrooms. Good, imaginative meals are served in the very pretty dining room.

10rm(8🛁1🚿) 1 CTV in all bedrooms sB&B £28 sB&B🛁🚿£33 dB&B🛁🚿£42 B

→

CTV 50P 2 🚗 ✽ (heated) (hard) U nc12yrs

V Lunch £7.50alc Dinner £17.50alc Wine £4.50 Last dinner 9.30pm

Credit cards 1 2 3 5

GRINDLEFORD
Derbyshire
Map **8** SK27

★★**Maynard Arms** Main Rd ☎Hope Valley (0433) 30321

Hotel of Victorian origin.

13rm(4 2) (2fb) 2 CTV in all bedrooms Ⓡ ✻sB&B fr£21 sB&B fr£24 dB&B fr£28 dB&B fr£32

80P 5 ✽ *xmas*

English & French V ✻Lunch £4.50–£5.50 Dinner £7–£8.95 &alc Wine £4.50 Last dinner 9.30pm

Credit cards 1 2 3 5

GRIZEDALE
Cumbria
Map **7** SD39

★★**Ormandy** ☎Hawkshead (09666) 532

Closed Jan–Feb

Detached, converted farm house standing in the heart of an 8000 acre forest.

6 Ⓡ sB&B £15.62 dB&B £25

CTV 25P

French Provinçial Dinner £10.50alc Wine £4.40

Last dinner 8.30pm

S% **VS**

GROBY
Leicestershire
Map **4** SK50

★**Brant Inn** Leicester Rd ☎Leicester (0533) 872703

Large, two-storey building with grounds and gardens, situated in a residential area, just off the A50 4m NW of Leicester.

10rm Ⓡ ✻sB&B fr£17 dB&B fr£25.50

200P 2 ✽

✻Lunch fr£3.95&alc Tea fr50p Wine £3.95 Last dinner 10pm

Credit cards 1 3 5

GUERNSEY
Channel Islands (Map 16)
See **Câtel, Fermain Bay, Petit Bôt, St Martin, St Peter Port and St Saviour**

GUILDFORD
Surrey
Map **4** SU94

★★★**Angel** High St (Trusthouse Forte) ☎(0483) 64555

Modernised inn with a friendly staff and informal catering arrangements.

25rm(24 1) (2fb) CTV in all bedrooms Ⓡ sB&B £39 dB&B £54.50

CFA *xmas*

Last dinner 9.30pm

Credit cards 1 2 3 4 5

✕***Rum-Wong*** 16–18 London Rd ☎(0483) 36092

Authentic Thai cuisine is accompanied by friendly service.

Closed Mon & 2–16 Aug, 24–26 Dec, 31 Dec–1 Jan

Thai 60 seats Last dinner 10.45pm Live music and dancing Tue–Sun

Credit cards 1 3

★★★ GREYWALLS, GULLANE

Duncar Rd (Prestige) ☎(0620) 842144 Telex no 727396

Last season our members were becoming a little disenchanted with this hotel but have been quick to report on the improvements made by the new manager, John Robson. He seems to have inculcated new heart among the staff and our members now report an even higher standard of service and particularly welcome the permanent opening of the office hatch: it is an outward sign of the all round improvement in the hospitality that our members have appreciated so much. As we predicted, Julian Waterer has proved a great success and we are pleased to award a rosette for his cooking this year. He follows the modern style and is one of the few to do so in Scotland. His skills manifest themselves in the subtle flavouring and accurate seasoning of his dishes as well as his delicate saucing. He also innovates unusual dishes and the puddings are delicious.

The hotel is owned by the Weaver family and it was once their home. Situated next to the Muirfield Golf Course with the sea beyond and built of mellow stone, it is an architectural gem designed by Sir Edwin Lutyens. The almost equally well known Gertrude Jekyll designed the charming garden and it is worth noting that Mr Walker has tended the gardens for 56 years now. Garden lovers will find it is a privilege to talk to him.

There are four comfortable sitting areas including the original panelled library with its open fire and the airy garden room with television. There is also a cosy little bar where the conversation generally concerns golf. As befits a real home, though, the atmosphere is always warm undoubtedly helped by the Eastern carpets, fine furniture and flowers. A particular decoration in the corridors is the collection of botanical prints of fruit. The hotel provides a good base for golf, touring and for many businessmen who feel it well worth the distance travelling to and from Edinburgh.

19 sB&B £25–£45 dB&B £50–£85

CTV 60P ✽ (hard) nc10yrs

Lunch £5.95&alc Tea £4.95 Dinner £15.95&alc Wine £4.40 Last dinner 9.30pm

Credit cards 1 2 3 5 **VS**

At **Seale** (6m W A31)

☆☆☆**Hog's Back** Hogs Back (on A31) (Embassy) ☎Runfold (02518) 2345

50 130P

GUIST
Norfolk
Map **9** TF92

✕✕***Tollbridge*** ☎Foulsham (036284) 359

Closed Sun, Mon, 1st wk Oct and last 2wks Jan

English & French 40 seats Last dinner 9.30pm 30P

Credit card 3

GULLANE
Lothian *East Lothian*
Map **12** NT48

✕**Colette** 3 Roseberry Pl ☎(0620) 842233

Closed Mon Lunch not served Tue–Fri

French 28 seats ✻Lunch fr£5.95 Dinner £7.50–£15 Wine £5.25 Last dinner 10pm

Credit cards 2 3 5

✕**La Potinière** Main St ☎(0620) 843214

Charming, relaxing little restaurant with superb food and wine list. Must book.

Closed Wed, 1 wk June & Oct Lunch not served Sat Dinner not served Mon, Tue, Thu, Fri & Sun

French 32 seats Lunch £8.50–£9.50 Dinner £12.50 Wine £4.50 10P ⁄

GULWORTHY
Devon
Map **2** SX47
❀✕✕✕**Horn of Plenty** ☎ Tavistock (0822) 832528
Closed Thu Lunch not served Fri
English & French **V** 65 seats ✱Lunch fr£12 Dinner £22&alc Last dinner 9.30pm 20P

GUNNISLAKE
Cornwall
Map **2** SX47
★★**Cornish Inn** (Minotel) ☎ Tavistock (0822) 832475
A small, country inn situated in the glorious Tamar Valley.
9rm(5→) (1fb) Ⓡ B
CTV 24P
Lunch £7alc Dinner £7alc Wine £3.50 Last dinner 9.30pm
Credit cards 1 2 3 5

GWBERT-ON-SEA
Dyfed
Map **2** SN15
★★★*L* **Cliff** (Best Western) ☎ Cardigan (0239) 613241 Telex no 48440
60→⋒ Annexe: 10→ (9fb) 2⊟ CTV in all bedrooms sB&B→⋒ £15–£23 dB&B→⋒ £30–£51 B
☾ CTV 100P CFA ✱ (heated) squash billiards xmas
French **V** Lunch £5–£7.25&alc Tea £1–£3 High Tea £1.50–£3.50 Dinner £7.25–£16&alc Wine £4.75 Last dinner 9.45pm
Credit cards 1 2 3 4 5

GWITHIAN
Cornwall
Map **2** SW54
★★***Glencoe House*** 23 Churchtown Rd ☎ Hayle (0736) 752216
Closed Nov–Feb
Comfortable, small friendly, hotel in a quiet position yet close to the beach.
11rm(10→1⋒) CTV in all bedrooms Ⓡ B
CTV 11P (heated)
English & French **V** Last dinner 9.30pm
Credit cards 1 3

HACKNESS
North Yorkshire
Map **8** SE99
★★★*H* **Hackness Grange Country Hotel** (Best Western) ☎ Scarborough (0723) 69966
13rm(7→6⋒) Annexe: 14rm(12→2⋒) (6fb) CTV in all bedrooms Ⓡ sB&B→⋒ £22–£29 dB&B→⋒ £44–£58 B
⁄ CTV 60P ✱ (heated) (hard) nc3yrs *xmas*
V Lunch £5.80alc Dinner £9.75–£11 Wine £4.25 Last dinner 8.30pm
Credit cards 1 2 3 4 5 **VS**

HADLEY WOOD
Greater London
Map **4** TQ29
★★★★**West Lodge Park** Cockfosters Rd ☎ 01-440 8311
Late-Georgian building with an interesting history, standing in quiet parkland and farmland.
50→ 2⊟ CTV in all bedrooms sB&B→ £38.50 dB&B→ £52 B
Lift ☾ 200P CFA ✱
French Lunch £11alc Dinner £7.50alc Wine £5.20 Last dinner 9.30pm
S% Credit cards 1 2 3 5

HADLOW
Kent
Map **5** TQ65
✕**La Crémaillère** The Square ☎ (0732) 851489
Small restaurant, with separate dining areas, including a conservatory grapevine. →

H

Congham Hall
COUNTRY HOUSE HOTEL
KING'S LYNN NORFOLK PE32 1AH
TELEPHONE HILLINGTON 0485 600250
WINNER – MIDLANDS REGIONAL AWARD – BEST NEWCOMER 1984

Closed Sun, 1 wk Nov & 1 wk Mar Lunch not served Sat

French 33 seats Lunch fr£4 Dinner £10alc Wine £5.25 Last dinner 9.15pm 12P

Credit cards 1 3

HALE BARNS
Greater Manchester
Map **7** SJ78

✕***Borsalino*** 14 The Square ☎061-980 5331

French-style bistro with limited choice from blackboard menu.

Closed Sun, Mon, Xmas & Public hols Lunch not served

French 50 seats Last dinner 10.30pm 100P

Credit cards 1 2 3 5

H

HALIFAX
West Yorkshire
Map **7** SE02

★★★***BL* Holdsworth House** Holdsworth Ln, Holmfield (3m NW off A629 Keighley Rd) ☎(0422) 244270

Closed 25 Dec–1 Jan

Stone-built period house dating from 1633 and standing in its own grounds.

30rm(18 12) (8fb) 2 CTV in all bedrooms ✻sB&B £27.50–£30 dB&B £40

40P CFA billiards

French **V** ✻Lunch fr£6&alc Tea fr60p High Tea fr£2.50 Dinner fr£8&alc Wine £5.20 Last dinner 10pm

Credit cards 1 2 3 4 5

✕**Yorkshireman** 2 Towngate, Hipperholme (2m E on A58) ☎(0422) 206130

Closed Mon Lunch not served Sat Dinner not served Sun

V 46 seats Lunch £4.50–£8&alc Dinner £8.25–£10&alc Wine £3.80 Last dinner 10pm 50P

Credit cards 1 3 5 **VS**

HALSETOWN
Cornwall
Map **2** SW53

✕***Chef's Kitchen*** ☎Penzance (0736) 796218

Terraced stone cottage set in a rural location close to St Ives.

Lunches by appointment only

French 34 seats Last dinner 10pm 10P bedrooms available

Credit cards 1 2

HAMBLE
Hampshire
Map **4** SU40

✕✕***Beth's*** The Quay ☎(042122) 4314

Dinner not served Sun (Oct–Jul)

British & French **V** 45 seats Last dinner 9.30pm

Credit cards 1 3 5 **VS**

HAMILTON
Strathclyde *Lanarkshire*
Map **11** NS75

✕✕**Costa's** 17–21 Campbell St ☎(0698) 283552

Modern Greek-run restaurant offering international cuisine.

Closed Sun. Xmas Day, New Years Day & 1st 3wks Aug

International 60 seats Lunch £3–£12 Dinner £12alc Wine £5.15 Last dinner 10.15pm

Credit cards 1 2 3 5

✕**Il Frate** (Friar Tuck) 4 Barrack St ☎(0698) 284379

An Italian restaurant with a shop-type frontage, and simple but attractive interior décor.

Closed Sun

Continental **V** 90 seats ✻Lunch fr £2.20&alc Dinner £3.80–£7.60&alc Wine £4.10 Last dinner 11pm 12P

Credit cards 1 2 3 5

HAMPOLE
South Yorkshire
Map **8** SE51

✕✕**Hampole Priory** ☎Doncaster (0302) 723740

Closed Sun, Mon & Xmas Lunch not served

English & French 28 seats ✻Dinner £8.95alc Wine £3.80 Last dinner 9.30pm 12P bedrooms available

Credit cards 3 4

HAMPTON LOADE
Shropshire
Map **7** SO78

✕✕**Haywain** (6m SE of Bridgnorth, W off A442) ☎Quatt (0746) 780404

Closed Sun Lunch not served

French **V** 40 seats Dinner £15–£16.50 Wine £3.50 Last dinner 9.30pm 20P

Credit cards 1 2 3 5

HANDFORTH
Cheshire
Map **7** SJ88

★★★★***H* Belfry** Stanley Rd ☎061-437 0511 Telex no 666358

Modern, efficient, family run hotel.

92 CTV in all bedrooms sB £31.75 (room only) dB £42 (room only)

Lift 150P CFA Live music and dancing Tue–Sat

International **V** Lunch fr£7.50&alc Tea fr65p Dinner fr£8.95&alc Wine £4.80 Last dinner 10pm

Credit cards 1 2 3 5 **VS**

HARBERTONFORD
Devon
Map **3** SX75

✕✕***Hungry Horse*** ☎(080423) 441

Beamed, stone-built cottage in the centre of the village close to the river.

Closed Sun, Mon, Feb & 1st 2wks Oct Lunch not served

International 40 seats 8P

Credit card 2

HARDGATE
Strathclyde *Dunbartonshire*
Map **11** NS47

★★**Cameron House** Main St ☎Duntocher (0389) 73535

Small, family-run hotel that caters

especially for functions.
15rm(4⇌11⋒) CTV in all bedrooms sB&B⇌⋒£18 dB&B⇌⋒£30 B
Lift ☾ ## 150P 5⌂ billiards Disco Tue Live music and dancing Sat & Tues *xmas*
V ♔ ☐ Lunch £1.80&alc Tea 50p High Tea £3 Dinner £5.75&alc Wine £3.20 Last dinner 9.30pm

HARLESTON
Norfolk
Map **5** TM28
★★ ***Swan*** The Thoroughfare ☎(0379) 852221
9rm(6⇌3⋒) CTV available in bedrooms ®CTV 50P ⌂
V ♔ Last dinner 9pm
Credit cards 1 3

HARLOSH
Isle of Skye, Highland, *Inverness-shire*
Map **13** NG24
★ ***H* Harlosh** ☎Dunvegan (047022) 367
7rm(1⇌) (2fb) sB&B£7.50–£11 dB&B£15–£22 dB&B⇌£18–£25
TV 20P ## ✽ *xmas*
V Dinner £5.25–£5.75&alc Wine £4.30 Last dinner 9pm
Credit cards 1 3

HARLOW
Essex
Map **5** TL41
☆☆☆ **Green Man** Mulberry Green, Old Harlow (Anchor) ☎(0279) 442521 Telex no 817972 Closed Xmas
Quiet, small hotel, well equipped and managed.
Annexe: 55⇌ (3fb) CTV in all bedrooms ® sB&B⇌£33 dB&B⇌£40 B
☾ ## 75P ✽ Disco Fri
▣ English & French V ♔ ☐ Lunch £7.50–£9.75 Tea £1 Dinner £7.50–£9.75 Wine £4.50 Last dinner 10pm
Credit cards 1 2 3 4 5

☆☆☆ **Saxon Motor Inn** Southern Way (Saxon Inn) ☎(0279) 22441 Telex no 81658
The modern, well-equipped bedrooms, here are complemented by a professional, well-run restaurant.
120⇌ CTV in all bedrooms ® sB&B⇌£31.95 dB&B⇌£43.90 B
☾ CTV 200P CFA Live music and dancing Sat
▣ English & French ♔ ☐ Lunch £5.50&alc Dinner £6.50 Wine £4.50 Last dinner 10.30pm
Credit cards 1 2 3 5 **VS**
See advert on page 298

HARLYN BAY
Cornwall
Map **2** SW87
★ ***L* Polmark** (off B3276) ☎Padstow (0841) 520206 Closed Dec & Jan (except Xmas)
Attractive Cornish stone house in peaceful situation close to the beach.
6rm Annexe: 11rm (3fb) sB&B£10.50–£11.50 dB&B£21–£23
CTV 40P ✽ ⌂ (heated) *xmas*
♔ ☐ Lunch £2.50–£4 Tea 40p–80p Dinner £6–£7&alc Wine £3.20 Last dinner 6pm

HAROME
North Yorkshire
Map **8** SE68
✕ **Star Inn** ☎Helmsley (0439) 70397
Closed Jan Lunch Bar Meals only Dinner not served Sun & Mon
▣ English & French 40 seats ✻ Dinner £9–£11.50 Wine £4.90 Last dinner 9.30pm 30P
Credit cards 1 2 3 5 **VS**

HARPENDEN
Hertfordshire
Map **4** TL11
★★★★ **Harpenden Moat House** 18 Southdown Rd (Queens Moat) ☎(05827) 64111 →

H

This Georgian period house was once known as St Dominic's Convent.

19rm(16⇌3⋒) Annexe: 16⇌ (3fb) 1⊟ CTV in all bedrooms ✱sB&B⇌⋒ £33.50 dB&B⇌⋒ £46.50 Continental breakfast ⊟

☾ 90P

⊟English, French & Italian **V** ☕ ⊟ ✱Lunch £7.20&alc Dinner £9.80&alc Wine £6.90 Last dinner 10pm

Credit cards 1 2 3 5 **VS**

★★★ ***HGlen Eagle*** 1 Luton Rd ☎(05827) 60271 Telex no 925859

Pleasant country-house style hotel with very good facilities.

51rm(47⇌3⋒) 1⊟ CTV in all bedrooms ⊟

Lift ☾ ## 100P CFA ✽ ⌂

⊟French **V** ☕ ⊟ Last dinner 10pm

Credit cards 1 2 3 5

✕✕ **Willow Tree** 6 Church Green ☎(05827) 69358

Closed Xmas

⊟Peking 85 seats Lunch fr£4&alc Dinner fr£4&alc Wine £5 Last dinner 11.15pm 35P⚡

S% Credit cards 1 2 3 4 5

HARRAY
Orkney
Map **16** HY31

★★ ***Merkister*** ☎(085677) 366

RS Oct–Mar

19rm(2⇌⋒)

CTV 30P ## ✽

☕ ⊟ Last dinner 9pm

HARRIS, ISLE OF
Western Isles *Inverness-shire*
Map **13**
See Tarbert

HARROGATE
North Yorkshire
Map **8** SE35

★★★★ **Crown** Crown Pl (Trusthouse Forte) ☎(0423) 67755 Telex no 57652

An 18th-century building near Valley Gardens and the Royal Baths.

120rm(98⇌22⋒) (4fb) CTV in all bedrooms Ⓡ sB&B⇌⋒ £42 dB&B⇌⋒ £55 ⊟

Lift ☾ 50P CFA *xmas*

☕ ⊟ Last dinner 9.30pm

Credit cards 1 2 3 4 5

★★★★ **Hotel Majestic** Ripon Rd (Trusthouse Forte) ☎(0423) 68972 Telex no 57918

Spacious, stylish and comfortable hotel with well-appointed bedrooms.

151rm(150⇌1⋒) (5fb) CTV in all bedrooms Ⓡ sB&B⇌⋒ £44.50 dB&B⇌⋒ £58 ⊟

Lift ☾ 180P CFA ✽ ⊡(heated) ℘(hard) squash ⌂ *xmas*

☕ ⊟ Last dinner 9.15pm

Credit cards 1 2 3 4 5

★★★★ **Old Swan** Swan Rd ☎(0423) 504051 Telex no 57922

140rm(124⇌13⋒) (6fb) CTV in all bedrooms Ⓡ ✱sB&B fr£44 sB&B⇌⋒ fr£44 dB&B fr£66 dB&B⇌⋒ fr£66 ⊟

Lift ☾ 140P CFA ✽ ℘(hard)

⊟English & French **V** ☕ ⊟ Lunch £7.50 Tea fr£3 Dinner fr£7.50&alc Wine £5 Last dinner 10pm

Credit cards 1 2 3 5

★★★ **Cairn** Ripon Rd (Prince of Wales) ☎(0423) 504005 Telex no 57992

A large stone-built, four storey, Victorian hotel situated near the town centre.

140rm(120⇌3⋒) CTV in all bedrooms Ⓡ sB&B⇌⋒ £36 dB&B⇌⋒ £50 ⊟

Lift ☾ 250P CFA ✽ ℘ billiards ⌂ *xmas*

V ☕ ⊟ Lunch £6.25&alc Tea 70p High Tea £2.50 Dinner £6.95&alc Wine £3.95 Last dinner 9.30pm

Credit cards 1 2 3 4 5

★★★**Hospitality Inn** Prospect Pl, West Park (Mount Charlotte) ☎(0423) 64601 Telex no 57530

Six-storey, stone-built Victorian building in the town centre.

71⇌(1fb) CTV in all bedrooms ® ⚒ sB&B⇌£32 dB&B⇌£42.50 B

Lift ☾ 35P CFA

English & French V ♡ ▭ Bar lunch £1.25–£2.75 Dinner £7.75&alc Wine £4.75 Last dinner 10pm

Credit cards 1 2 3 5 VS

★★★**Hotel St George** 1 Ripon Rd (Swallow) ☎(0423) 61431 Telex no 57995

Large hotel with well-proportioned rooms, good restaurant and Lamplight Bar.

82rm(77⇌5⋒) (4fb) CTV in all bedrooms ® *sB&B⇌⋒£35 dB&B⇌⋒£52 B

Lift ☾ CTV 50P CFA ✽ *xmas*

V ♡ ▭ *Lunch £4.75–£5.75 Tea 60palc High Tea £5.75 Dinner £7.60&alc Wine £4.50 Last dinner 9.15pm

Credit cards 1 2 3 5 VS

★★★*B* ***Studley*** Swan Rd ☎(0423) 60425 Telex no 57506

40rm(39⇌1⋒) CTV in all bedrooms ® B

Lift ☾ CTV ⚑ nc8yrs

French V ♡ Last dinner 10.30pm

Credit cards 1 2 3 5

★★**Alphen Lodge** 2 Esplanade ☎(0423) 502882

11rm(6⇌1⋒) 1 CTV in all bedrooms ® *sB&B£15 sB&B⇌⋒£17 dB&B£27 dB&B⇌⋒£32 B

10P *xmas*

V ♡ *Lunch £3.50alc Dinner £6.50 Wine £3.50 Last dinner 8.15pm

Credit cards 1 2 3

★★**Fern** *(formerly Fernlea)* Swan Rd ☎(0423) 523866 Telex no 57583

A pair of stone-built houses with forecourt gardens, near the town centre.

28rm(26⇌) (4fb) TV in all bedrooms ® ⚒ sB&B⇌£25.95–£29.95 dB&B⇌£39.95–£45.95 B

French V Lunch £5alc Tea £1alc Dinner £8.75alc Wine £4.35 Last dinner 9.30pm

Credit cards 1 2 3 5 VS

★★**Green Park** Valley Dr ☎(0423) 504681

A three-storey, stone building on a corner position and overlooking Valley Gardens.

44rm(27⇌17⋒) CTV available in bedrooms ® sB&B⇌⋒£20–£23 dB&B⇌⋒£33–£40 B

Lift ☾ CTV 20P

Cosmopolitan ♡ ▭ Bar lunch £1.15 Tea 60p–£1.75 High Tea £2.50 Dinner £7.65–£10.65 Wine £4.10 Last dinner 8.30pm

Credit cards 1 2 3 5

★★*L* **Hotel Italia** *(formerly Knapping Rise)* 53 King's Rd ☎(0423) 67404

27rm(3⇌2⋒) (1fb) CTV in all bedrooms ® sB&B£17.05–£19.25 sB&B⇌⋒£20.35 dB&B£30.80 dB&B⇌⋒£35.20

CTV 18P *xmas*

English & Italian Bar lunch fr£2.50 Dinner fr£7.20&alc Wine £5 Last dinner 9.30pm

S% Credit cards 2 3 5

★★**Russell** Valley Dr ☎(0423) 509866 Closed 27–30 Dec

Large, converted Victorian house overlooking Valley Gardens.

40rm(8⇌12⋒) (3fb) CTV in all bedrooms sB&B£16.50–£17.25 sB&B⇌⋒£18.95–£21.95 dB&B£29.15–£31.50 dB&B⇌⋒£33.50–£35.95 B

Lift ☾ ⚑ *xmas*

French ♡ Bar lunch 85p–£5 Dinner fr£9.50&alc Wine £5.80 Last dinner 10.30pm

Credit cards 1 2 3 4 5 VS

See advert on page 300

H

★★**Wessex** 22–23 Harlow Moor Dr ☎(0423) 65890

Converted from a pair of stone-built town houses this hotel overlooks Valley Gardens.

14⋒ ®sB&B⋒£14.50 dB&B⋒£29 B̶

CTV ⁋ *xmas*

V ♈ ☕ Lunch £4&alc Tea £1&alc High Tea £3.50&alc Dinner £7 Wine £5 Last dinner 8pm

VS

★**Britannia Lodge** 16 Swan Rd ☎(0423) 58482

Stone-built end of terrace house near the town centre.

11rm(6⇨5⋒) (3fb) CTV in 10 bedrooms ♞ sB&B⇨⋒£13–£17 dB&B⇨⋒£26–£34 B̶

CTV 7P ⩫

🍴French ♈ ☕ Lunch £3.50 Tea £2.50 High Tea £2.50 Dinner £6&alc Wine £4 Last dinner 7.30pm

Credit cards 1 3 **VS**

★*HB* **Gables** 2 West Grove Rd ☎(0423) 55625

9rm(4⇨3⋒) (2fb) CTV in all bedrooms ♞ sB&B£16 sB&B⇨⋒£16 dB&B⇨⋒£30 B̶

6P ⩫

🍴International ♈ ☕ Lunch £3alc Tea £1.50alc High Tea £3alc Dinner £6alc Wine £4 Last dinner 8pm

VS

✕✕**Emilio's** 22 Crescent Rd ☎(0423) 65267

Friendly restaurant specializing in fresh seafood.

Closed Sun

🍴English & Spanish 55 seats Lunch £3.75–£7.20 Dinner £10–£12alc Wine £4 Last dinner 11pm ⁋

Credit cards 1 3 5

❀✕✕**Number Six** 6 Ripon Rd ☎(0423) 502908

Closed Mon, 1st 3wks Aug & Public Hols Lunch not served

🍴French 58 seats Dinner £8.95–£12.50 Wine £4.75 Last dinner 10pm 18P

Credit cards 1 2 5

✕✕**Oliver** 24 King's Rd ☎(0423) 68600

Closed Sun Lunch not served

🍴French V 80 seats ✻Dinner £14.60&alc Wine £5.50 Last dinner 10.30pm ⁋

Credit cards 1 2 3

✕**Burdekin's** 21 Cheltenham Cres ☎(0423) 502610

Closed 1wk Xmas Lunch not served

🍴International V 40 seats Dinner £8.50alc Wine £4.45 Last dinner 9.30pm ⁋

Credit cards 1 2 3

✕***Roman*** 23 Cheltenham Cres ☎(0423) 68568

Closed Sun

🍴French & Italian 50 seats Last dinner 11pm ⁋

Credit cards 1 2 3

HARROW

Greater London,
London plan **5** B5 (page 420)

★★**Cumberland** 1 St John's Rd ☎01-863 4111

Popular hotel with good compact bedrooms.

28rm(8⇨20⋒) Annexe: 52rm(18⇨16⋒) (6fb) CTV in all bedrooms ® ♞ sB&B£21 sB&B⇨⋒£28 dB&B£31 dB&B⇨⋒£37 B̶

☾ CTV 65P

🍴English & French V ♈ ☕ Lunch £4.50–£7.50 Tea 65p Dinner £7.60 Wine £3.70 Last dinner 9.30pm

S% Credit cards 1 2 3 5

✕**Old Etonian** 38 High St ☎01-422 8482

Small French restaurant providing good food.

Closed Sun Lunch not served Sat

🍴French V 75 seats Lunch £15alc Dinner £15alc Wine £4.75 Last dinner 11pm ⁋

Credit cards 1 2 3 4 5 **VS**

HARROW WEALD

Greater London,
London plan **5** B5 (page 420)

★★★**Grim's Dyke Country** Old Redding (Best Western) ☎01-954 4227 Telex no 8954958

Attractive house, once the home of W.S. Gilbert, well-equipped bedrooms in modern annexe.

8⇨⋒ Annexe: 40⋒ (2fb) 1▣ CTV in all bedrooms ® sB&B⇨⋒£36–£39 dB&B⇨⋒£45–£56 B̶

☾ 130P ✽ Cabaret Sun ⌂ *xmas*

🍴English, French & Italian V ♈ ☕ Lunch £9.75 Tea £3.75 Dinner £9.75 Last dinner 10pm

Credit cards 1 2 3 5 **VS**

HARTINGTON

Derbyshire
Map **7** SK16

★**Charles Cotton** ☎(029884) 229

The grounds of this 17th-century inn border the River Dene.

10rm (2fb) ® ✻sB&B£10.45 dB&B £19.25

CTV 50P 1⌂ ⌂

V ♈ ☕ ✻Lunch fr£4.65&alc Tea fr£1.50 High Tea £2.50–£3.50 Dinner fr£5.75&alc Wine £3.50 Last dinner 9.30pm

S%

HARTLAND

Devon
Map **2** SS22

★**Hartland Quay** Hartland Quay ☎(02374) 218

Closed Dec–Feb RS Mar & Nov

Converted from a coastguard cottage beside the demolished harbour, with extensive walks on the cliffs.

16rm(5⇨1⋒) ✻sB&B£10 sB&B⇨⋒ fr£10.50 dB&B£20 dB&B⇨⋒ fr£21 B̶

CTV 100P ⩦

♈ ☕ ✻Dinner £4.50&alc Last dinner 7.45pm

HARTLEPOOL
Cleveland
Map **8** NZ53

★★★**Staincliffe** Seaton Carew ☎(0429) 64301
Converted, three-storey house overlooking the bay at Seaton Carew.
27rm(15⇌1⋒)(1fb) CTV in all bedrooms Ⓡ✻sB&B£20.50 sB&B⇌⋒£25 dB&B£28.50 dB&B⇌⋒£30.50 Ɓ
☾ CTV 58P ✽ ℘ xmas
▣International **V** ✪ ☐ ✻Lunch fr£3&alc Tea fr45p High Tea fr£2.50 Dinner fr£6.25&alc Wine £4.25 Last dinner 9.30pm
Credit cards 1 2 3 5 **VS**

HARTOFT END
North Yorkshire
Map **8** SE79

★★**Blacksmiths Arms** ☎Lastingham (0751) 331
A converted moorland farmhouse dating from the 16th-century, surrounded by attractive scenery.
12rm(8⋒)Ⓡ dB&B£29 dB&B⋒£32 Ɓ
CTV 100P ✽
✪Bar lunch £2–£4.50 Dinner £7.50&alc Last dinner 9.30pm
Credit card 3

HARWICH
Essex
Map **5** TM23

★★**Cliff** Marine Pde, Dovercourt (Minotels) ☎(02555) 3345 (Due to change to (0255) 503345 Telex no 987372
Closed Xmas
Informal seafront hotel with some modern bedroom facilities.
34rm(14⇌4⋒)(5fb) CTV in 33 bedrooms TV in 1 bedroom sB&B£15.18–£16.44 sB&B⇌⋒ fr£16.44 dB&B£30.36–£32.88 dB&B⇌⋒ fr£32.88
☾ CTV 60P 4⌂ Live music Fri
✪ ☐ Lunch £5.06&alc Tea fr65p Dinner fr£6.32&alc Wine £6 Last dinner 9pm
S% Credit cards 1 2 3 5

✕✕**Pier** The Quay ☎(02555) 3363 (Due to change to (0255) 503363
Modern, quay-side restaurant specialising in sea food.
▣English & French **V** 120 seats Lunch £4.50–£9.25&alc Dinner £10alc Wine £4.60 Last dinner 10pm 10P Live music nightly & Sun lunch
S% Credit cards 1 2 3 5

HASLEMERE
Surrey
Map **4** SU93

★★★**Georgian** High St ☎(0428) 51555
Family run 18th century hotel offering comfort and friendly service.
18rm(10⇌1⋒) Annexe: 3⇌(1fb) CTV in all bedrooms Ⓡ sB&B£20.50 sB&B⇌⋒£25.50 dB&B£35 dB&B⇌⋒£40 Ɓ
CTV 30P ✽ squash sauna bath Live music and dancing Sat
▣English & French **V** ✪ ☐ Lunch £6–£8&alc Tea 80p High Tea £2.50–£6 Dinner £8&alc Wine £4.95 Last dinner 9.30pm
Credit cards 1 2 3 5 **VS**

★★★**Lythe Hill** Petworth Rd (1¼m E B2131) (Prestige) ☎(0428) 51251 Telex no 858402 →

H

Most attractive hotel with well equipped modern bedrooms and choice of restaurants and bars.

28➡🚿) Annexe: 6rm (4➡) (8fb) 1 CTV in all bedrooms Ⓡ sB&B➡🚿£30–£33 dB&B➡🚿£43–£47.50 Continental breakfast

☾ 200P CFA ❄ (hard) sauna bath Live music and dancing Sat *xmas*

English & Continental V Lunch £6.75–£7.50&alc Dinner £8.75–£9.50&alc

Credit cards 1 2 3 5 VS

XXX L'Auberge De France (Lythe Hill Hotel) Petworth Rd (1¼m E B2131) ☎(0428) 51251

The service is charming in this 600-year-old, timbered building with a modern addition.

Closed Mon Lunch not served Tue

French 45 seats *Lunch 15alc Dinner £15alc Wine £6.30 Last dinner 10.30pm 200P bedrooms available

Credit cards 1 2 3 5 VS

X Fourteen Petworth Road 14 Petworth Rd ☎(0428) 52625

Small, beamed restaurant with modern décor, and offering an individual but limited choice.

Closed Sun, 2wks Jan, 1wk Aug Lunch not served (except for booked parties)

French 32 seats *Lunch £12alc Dinner £12alc Wine £4.95 Last dinner 10pm 12P

Credit cards 1 2 3 5 VS

❀ **X Morel's** 25 Lower St ☎(0428) 51462

Closed Sun & Public hols

French *Dinner fr£8.50&alc Wine £6.20 Last dinner 10pm

Credit cards 1 2 3 5

HASTINGS & ST LEONARDS
East Sussex
Map **5** TQ80

★★★ **Beauport Park** Battle Rd (3m N off A2100) (Inter-Hotels) ☎(0424) 51222

Busy country house hotel with well kept gardens and lawns.

20rm(17➡) (5fb) CTV in all bedrooms Ⓡ sB&B fr£20 sB&B➡£26–£28 dB&B£30–£40 dB&B➡£38–£40

40P 4 ❄ (heated) (grass) squash billiards sauna bath *xmas*

French V Lunch £6&alc Tea fr£1.30 Dinner fr£7.95&alc Wine £4.50 Last dinner 10pm

Credit cards 1 2 3 5

X *Mitre* 56 High St ☎(0424) 427000

Closed Mon, 2wks Nov & 2wks Feb Lunch not served Tue–Sat Dinner not served Sun

French 26 seats Last dinner 10pm

HATCH BEAUCHAMP
Somerset
Map **3** ST32

★★ ***HBL* Farthing's Country House** ☎(0823) 480664

This elegant Georgian house in an attractive village is comfortable and very well furnished. The bedrooms are decorated to a high standard and very well appointed. George and Claire Cooper, the proprietors, are excellent hosts and dinner in the charming restaurant is of a high standard.

6rm(5➡) CTV in all bedrooms Ⓡ sB&B➡£32–£40 dB&B➡£45–£60

25P ❄

English & French V Lunch £6.50alc Tea £1alc Dinner £11alc Wine £4.50 Last dinner 9.30pm

Credit cards 1 3 VS

HATFIELD
Hertfordshire
Map **4** TL20

★★★ **Comet** 301 St Albans Rd West (junc A1/A414) (Embassy) ☎(07072) 65411
Closed Xmas

The hotel is named after the De Havilland Comet, a model of which stands in the forecourt.

45rm(42➡1⋒)(1fb) CTV in all bedrooms Ⓡ sB£22 (room only) sB➡⋒£32 (room only) dB➡⋒£37 (room only) ⊟

☾ 150P ✽ ♿

V ♧ Lunch fr£6.50 Dinner fr£6.50 Wine £4.50 Last dinner 9.45pm

S% Credit cards 1 2 3 4 5

HATHERSAGE
Derbyshire
Map **8** SK28

★★**George** Main Rd ☎ Hope Valley (0433) 50436

Two-storey, stone-built coaching inn, dating back to the 16th century.

18rm(16➡2⋒)(3fb) CTV in all bedrooms Ⓡ sB&B➡⋒£25 dB&B➡⋒£33 ⊟

CTV 100P ✽

English & Continental V ♧ ☕ ✱ Lunch £6alc Tea 75palc Dinner £7alc Wine £5 Last dinner 10pm

Credit cards 1 2 3 4

★★**Hathersage Inn** Main St (Best Western) ☎ Hope Valley (0433) 50259 Closed Xmas

Stone-built inn on the village main street.

11rm(9➡2⋒) Annexe: 4rm (4fb) CTV in all bedrooms ✱ sB&B£15–£22 sB&B➡⋒£20–£26.50 dB&B£19–£28 dB&B➡⋒£24–£35 ⊟

20P

V ♧ ☕ Lunch £2–£5 Tea fr50p Dinner £6.50–£11.50 Wine £4.60 Last dinner 9.30pm

S% Credit cards 1 2 3 5 **VS**

HAVANT
Hampshire
Map **4** SU70

★★★**Bear** East St (Whitbread Wessex) ☎ (0705) 486501

Town centre converted hotel with parts dating back to the 16th century. With open plan modern restaurant and bar.

35rm(30➡5⋒) CTV in all bedrooms Ⓡ Lift ☾ P *xmas*

Mainly grills ♧ ☕ Last dinner 9.30pm

Credit cards 1 2 3 4 5

HAVERFORDWEST
Dyfed
Map **2** SM91

★★**Hotel Mariners** Mariners Sq ☎ (0437) 3353

A 17th-century inn with stables and old coaching post, situated in the town centre.

29rm(14➡1⋒)(1fb) CTV in all bedrooms Ⓡ ✱ sB&B£17–£18.50 sB&B➡⋒£22.50 dB&B£28 dB&B➡⋒£32 ⊟

☾ 40P

V ♧ ☕ ✱ Lunch fr£4.75 Tea fr75p Dinner fr£6.50&alc Wine £4.50 Last dinner 9.15pm

Credit cards 1 2 3 5

★★**Pembroke House** Spring Gdns ☎ (0437) 3652 Closed Xmas Day

A Georgian terraced building, covered with Virginia creeper.

25rm(15➡5⋒)(1fb) 2 CTV in all bedrooms Ⓡ sB&B£15 sB&B➡⋒£17 dB&B£25 dB&B➡⋒£29 ⊟

☾ CTV 30P sauna bath Disco Fri & Sat

English & French V ♧ ☕ Lunch fr£4.85&alc Tea fr£1.15 High Tea fr£1.15 Dinner fr£6.50&alc Wine £4.75 Last dinner 10pm

Credit cards 1 2 3 4 5

HAWES
North Yorkshire
Map **7** SD88

★★***Fountain*** Market Pl ☎ (09697) 206

Modernised, town centre hotel, family owned and run.

12rm(5➡1⋒) Ⓡ ⊟

CTV 10P

Last dinner 8.45pm

HAWESWATER
Cumbria
Map **12** NY41

★★**Haweswater** ☎ Bampton (09313) 235

→

This hotel offers good views of the lake and surrounding countryside.

16rm Ⓡ ✱ sB&B£12–£13 dB&B£24–£26

CTV 10P 4 *xmas*

✱ Bar lunch £1.50–£2.50&alc Wine £3.50 Last dinner 7.30pm

Credit cards 1 2 3 5

HAWICK
Borders *Roxburghshire*
Map **12** NT51

★★**Kirklands** West Stewart Pl ☎(0450) 72263

Small, well appointed hotel with attractive dining room and thoughtfully equipped bedrooms.

6rm(2 1) CTV in all bedrooms Ⓡ sB&B£17.50–£20.75 sB&B £19.75–£22.75 dB&B£29.50 dB&B £32

20P ✱

British & French V Lunch £3–£4.50 Dinner £8.50–£9&alc Wine £3.50

VS

★★***Teviotdale Lodge Country*** (7m S off A7) (Minotel) ☎Teviotdale (045085) 232

Small, family-run hotel in its own grounds, close to the River Teviot.

8rm(2) 1 CTV in all bedrooms Ⓡ

30P ✱

Last dinner 9pm

Credit cards 1 3

HAWKCHURCH
Devon
Map **3** ST30

★★★**Fairwater Head** (ExecHotel) ☎(02977) 349

Pleasant, extended country house hotel set in its own gardens.

14 (7fb) CTV in all bedrooms Ⓡ sB&B £19.25–£21.50 dB&B £34–£37

CTV 25P ✱ *xmas*

English & French V Lunch £4.50 Dinner £6&alc Wine £4.50 Last dinner 9pm

S% Credit cards 1 3

HAWKHURST
Kent
Map **5** TQ73

★★**Tudor Arms** (Best Western) ☎(05805) 2312 Telex no 945003

A rural yet convivial setting for a hotel, with modern, well-equipped bedrooms and a comfortable lounge.

14rm(6 3) (1fb) CTV in 6 bedrooms sB&B£15 sB&B £17 dB&B£30 dB&B £38

CTV 40P 3 ✱ (hard) *xmas*

English & French Lunch £5–£6.50&alc Tea fr75p Dinner £6.50&alc Wine £5 Last dinner 9.15pm

Credit cards 1 2 3 5 VS

HAWKSHEAD
(nr Ambleside) Cumbria
Map **7** SD39

★★★**Tarn Hows** Hawkshead Hill ☎(09666) 330

Closed Jan

A beautifully situated country-house hotel in 30 acres of garden and parkland.

25rm(5 12) Ⓡ sB&B£10–£16 sB&B £14–£21 dB&B£20–£32 dB&B £28–£42

CTV 30P ✱ (heated) (grass) sauna bath

Bar lunch £1.25–£6.50 Tea fr50p Dinner fr£10.50 Wine £4.50 Last dinner 8.30pm

Credit cards 1 2 3 VS

★***Red Lion*** ☎(09666) 213

A prominent feature of the village is this 15th-century coaching inn.

7rm(12) Annexe: 3rm 1 Ⓡ

CTV 11P nc5yrs

Last dinner 9.30pm

HAWORTH
West Yorkshire
Map **7** SE03

★★**Old White Lion** 6 West Ln ☎(0535) 42313

Stone-built coaching inn standing at the top of the main street.

12rm(4 4) sB&B£16–£17.50 sB&B £16–£17.50 dB&B£25 dB&B £28.50

CTV 10P Live music 3 nights wkly

English & French V Lunch £4.80–£6.50 Tea £3 Dinner £6.75&alc Wine £4.35 Last dinner 5pm

Credit cards 1 2 3 5

HAYDOCK
Merseyside
Map **7** SJ59

☆☆☆☆**Post House** Lodge Ln (adj to M6 junc 23) (Trusthouse Forte) ☎Wigan (0942) 717878 Telex no 677672

Large modern hotel, convenient for the motorway and the racecourse.

98 (36fb) CTV in all bedrooms Ⓡ sB&B £43 dB&B £55.50

☾ 130P CFA

Last dinner 10.15pm

Credit cards 1 2 3 4 5

HAYDON BRIDGE
Northumberland
Map **12** NY86

★**Anchor** John Martin St (Minotels) ☎(043 484) 227

10rm(5) (2fb) Ⓡ sB&B£13–£14 sB&B £15–£16 dB&B£21–£22 dB&B £24–£25

CTV 20P

V Bar lunch £3alc Dinner £6alc Wine £3.50 Last dinner 9pm

VS

✕**General Havelock Inn** Ratcliffe Rd ☎(043484) 376

Closed Mon Dinner not served Sun & Tue

English & French 40 seats Lunch £3.50alc Dinner £9–£11.50 Wine £5.50 Last dinner 9pm 15P

HAYLE
Cornwall
Map **2** SW53

★**Penellen** Rivere Towans, Phillack ☎(0736) 753777

Small, family hotel in its own grounds overlooking the beach, with views of St Ives.

11rm(5⋔)(5fb) ✱sB&B£8.95–£11.95 sB&B⋔£9.95–£12.95 dB&B£16.50–£22 dB&B⋔£18.50–£24 B

CTV 16P (heated)

✱Lunch £4alc Tea 50palc Dinner £4.95–£6.95&alc Wine £3 Last dinner 10.30pm

HAYLING ISLAND
Hampshire
Map **4** SU70

☆☆☆☆**Post House** Northney Rd (Trusthouse Forte) ☎(07016) 5011 Telex 86620

Modern, well-equipped hotel overlooking estuary.

Annexe: 96⇌(4fb) CTV in all bedrooms ®sB&B⇌£40.50 dB&B⇌£53 B

☾ CTV 150P CFA ✱ (heated) *xmas*

Last dinner 10.30pm

Credit cards 1 2 3 4 5

★★*HL* **Newtown House** Manor Rd ☎(07016) 66131
Closed 24 Dec–2 Jan

Well-appointed hotel, personally run with friendly, helpful staff.

22rm(9⇌9⋔) Annexe: 7⇌(5fb) CTV in all bedrooms ✱sB&B£17 sB&B⇌⋔£23 dB&B£30 dB&B⇌⋔£36 B

☾ 45P ✱ (heated) (hard) Live music and dancing Fri

English & Continental V ✱Lunch £4.95–£6.95 Tea 70p High Tea £3.95–£5.95 Dinner £6.50–£7.50&alc Wine £3.95 Last dinner 9pm

Credit cards 1 2 3 5

HAY-ON-WYE
Powys
Map **3** SO24

★**Crown** Broad St ☎(0497) 820435
RS winter

Victorian building in the main street catering mainly for tourists.

14rm(2⇌)(1fb) ✱sB&B£11.50–£12.50 dB&B£20–£21 dB&B⇌£23–£24

CTV 30P 1

V Lunch £4.75–£5.20&alc Dinner £6–£7 Wine £4 Last dinner 8.15pm

S% Credit card 3

★*B* **Old Black Lion** Lion St ☎(0497) 820841

Part 13th-, part 17th-century, two-storey village inn, full of character and charm.

6rm(4⋔) Annexe: 2⋔ (2fb) CTV in all bedrooms ®sB&B£15.50 dB&B⋔£31 B

CTV 20P *xmas*

Welsh & European Lunch £6.45 0alc Tea £3alc Dinner £6.40alc Wine £4.05 Last dinner 9pm

Credit card 1

HAYTOR
Devon
Map **3** SX77

★★*H* **Bel Alp** ☎(03646) 217
Closed Nov–Feb (except Xmas)

Charming, modernised Edwardian country house, quietly situated in grounds with fine views.

11rm(10⇌1⋔) CTV in all bedrooms ® sB&B⇌⋔£19.50–£20.50 dB&B⇌⋔£37–£39 B

Lift 30P ✱ (hard) billiards

English & French V Bar lunch 80p–£3 Tea 70p–£1.50 Dinner £10–£14 Wine £4.50 Last dinner 8.30pm

Credit cards 1 3 5 **VS**

★★**Haytor** ☎(03646) 200

Set in open country in elevated position, this hotel is ideal for touring and walking.

16rm(3⇌2⋔)(1fb) ®sB&B£10.35 dB&B£20.70 dB&B⇌⋔£23 B

CTV 30P ✱ Live music and dancing Sat mthly

V Bar lunch £3.75alc Dinner £6.35 Wine £3.50 Last dinner 8pm

VS

★★**Rock Inn** Haytor Vale ☎(03646) 305
Closed Xmas Day
Busy, family-run, convivial inn, with well appointed bedrooms and good food.
7rm(4→)(1fb) TV available in bedrooms
Ⓡ sB&B£10.30 dB&B£20.55
dB&B→£22.95
10P 🚗 ✽
♔ ✻ Bar lunch £2.75alc Dinner £5.95alc
Wine £3.95 Last dinner 8.45pm
S%

HAYWOOD, GREAT
Staffordshire
Map **7** SJ92
☆☆**Coach & Horses Motel** Pasturefields (on A51) (Minotel) ☎Weston (0889) 270324
42→(1fb) TV in 20 bedrooms Ⓡ
✻sB&B→£15.75 dB&B→£22.50 B
CTV 200P CFA ✽ ⌂
◘ English & French **V** ♔ ✻ Bar lunch £1–£3.10&alc Dinner £5–£7.50 Wine £3.50
Last dinner 9pm
Credit cards 1 2 3 4 5

HEALD GREEN
Greater Manchester
Map **7** SJ88
✕**La Bonne Auberge** ☎061-437 5701
A wide choice of interesting dishes are available in this delightful little French restaurant.
Closed Sun & Public Hols
Dinner not served Mon
◘ French 65 seats Lunch £5.50–£7&alc
Dinner £12alc Wine £4.20
Last dinner 9.30pm P
Credit cards 1 2 5

HEATHROW AIRPORT (London)
Greater London
Map **4** TQ07 **See plan**
☆☆☆☆**Ariel** Bath Rd, Hayes (1½m E junc A4/A437) (Trusthouse Forte)
☎01-759 2552 Telex no 21777 Plan **1** *E4*
Comfortable modern, circular hotel with carvery restaurant.
178→ CTV in all bedrooms Ⓡ
sB&B→£45.50 dB&B→£59.50
Lift ☾ ## 100P CFA
♔ ☕ Last dinner 10.30pm
Credit cards 1 2 3 4 5

☆☆☆☆**Excelsior** Bath Rd, West Drayton (adj M4 Spur at junc with A4) (Trusthouse Forte)
☎01-759 6611 Telex no 24525 Plan **3** *D4*
Large well appointed hotel opposite Heathrow Airport.
662→(11fb) CTV in all bedrooms Ⓡ
sB&B→£52 dB&B→£68
Lift ☾ ## 500P CFA ≈ (heated) sauna bath
♔ ☕ Last dinner 10.45pm
Credit cards 1 2 3 4 5

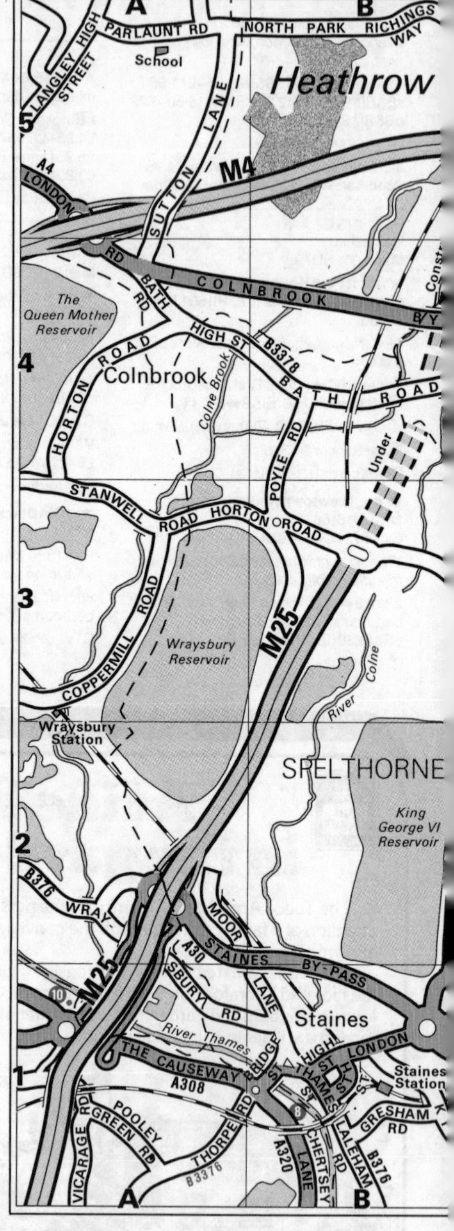

A
B
PARLAUNT RD
NORTH PARK
RICHINGS WAY
School
LANGLEY HIGH STREET
Heathrow
5
M4
SUTTON LANE
A4 LONDON RD
BATH RD
COLNBROOK BY-PASS
The Queen Mother Reservoir
HIGH ST
B3378
4
HORTON ROAD
Colnbrook
Colne Brook
POYLE RD
BATH ROAD
Under
STANWELL ROAD
HORTON ROAD
3
COPPERMILL ROAD
Wraysbury Reservoir
M25
River Colne
Wraysbury Station
SPELTHORNE
King George VI Reservoir
2
B376
WRAYSBURY RD
MOOR LANE
A30
STAINES BY-PASS
Staines
RIVER THAMES
THE CAUSEWAY
A308
BRIDGE ST
HIGH ST
LONDON RD
Staines Station
THAMES ST
1
VICARAGE RD
POOLEY GREEN RD
THORPE RD
B3376
A320
CHERTSEY LANE
LALEHAM RD
B376
GRESHAM RD
A
B

Heathrow Airport
1 Ariel ☆☆☆☆
2 Berkeley Arms ☆☆☆
3 Excelsior ☆☆☆☆
Excelsior Hotel Restaurant (Draitone Manor) ✕✕✕✕
4 Heathrow Penta ☆☆☆☆

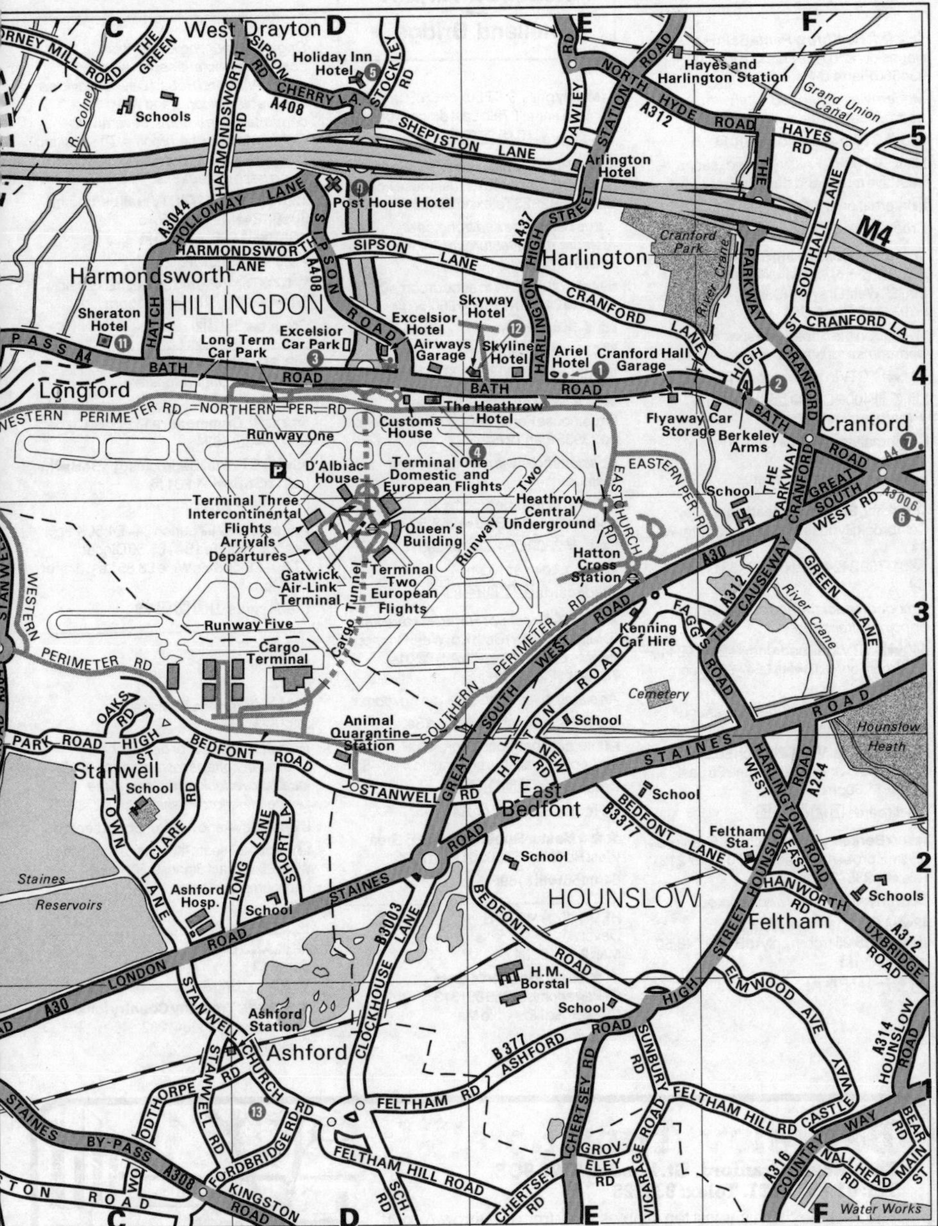
C
D
E
F
West Drayton
Holiday Inn Hotel
Schools
Hayes and Harlington Station
Grand Union Canal
Arlington Hotel
Post House Hotel
M4
Cranford Park
River Crane
Harlington
Harmondsworth
HILLINGDON
Sheraton Hotel
Long Term Car Park
Excelsior Car Park
Excelsior Hotel
Skyway Hotel
Airways Garage
Skyline Hotel
Ariel Hotel
Cranford Hall Garage
Longford
Flyaway Car Storage
Berkeley Arms
Cranford
Customs House
The Heathrow Hotel
Runway One
D'Albiac House
Terminal One Domestic and European Flights
Terminal Three Intercontinental Flights
Arrivals
Departures
Heathrow Central Underground
Queen's Building
Gatwick Air-Link Terminal
Terminal Two European Flights
Hatton Cross Station
Runway Five
Kenning Car Hire
Cargo Terminal
Cargo Tunnel
Cemetery
Hounslow Heath
Animal Quarantine Station
School
Stanwell
East Bedfont
Feltham Sta.
HOUNSLOW
Feltham
Schools
Staines Reservoirs
Ashford Hosp.
H.M. Borstal
Ashford Station
Ashford
Water Works
5
4
3
2
1
H

5 Holiday Inn ☆☆☆☆

6 Hounslow Chinese ✕
(*See under Hounslow*)

7 Master Robert Motel ☆☆☆
(*See under Hounslow*)

8 Pack Horse ★★
(*See under Staines*)

9 Post House ☆☆☆

10 Runnymede ☆☆☆☆
(*See under Egham*)

11 Sheraton-Heathrow ☆☆☆☆

12 Skyway ★★★

13 Terrazza ✕✕
(*See under Ashford*)

☆☆☆☆ ***Heathrow Penta*** Bath Rd, Hounslow ☎01-897 6363 Telex no 934660 Plan **4** *D4*

Modern well-equipped hotel with good bedrooms and restaurant.

670 CTV in all bedrooms Ⓡ

Lift ☾ # 700P CFA (heated) sauna bath Live music and dancing Sat

International **V**

Credit cards 1 2 3 4 5

☆☆☆☆ ***B Holiday Inn*** Stockley Rd, West Drayton (2m N junc M4/A408) (Holiday Inn) ☎West Drayton (08954) 45555 Telex no 934518 Plan **5** *D5*

Well-appointed hotel with spacious bedrooms and popular leisure facilities.

401 CTV in all bedrooms

Lift ☾ # 400P CFA ✽ (heated) (hard) sauna bath

International **V** Last dinner 10.30pm

Credit cards 1 2 3 4 5

☆☆☆☆ ***L* Sheraton-Heathrow** Colnbrook Bypass, West Drayton (2m W A4)

☎01-759 2424 Telex no 934331 Plan **11** *C4*

A modern spacious and comfortably appointed transit hotel.

440 CTV in all bedrooms sB £44–£52 (room only) dB £54–£62 (room only)

Lift ☾ # 350P CFA (heated) sauna bath Live music Mon–Fri

International **V** Lunch £5.25–£7.50&alc Dinner £12alc Wine £6 Last dinner 11.30pm

Credit cards 1 2 3 4 5

☆☆☆ **Berkeley Arms** Bath Rd, Cranford (2½m E on A4) (Embassy) ☎01-897 2121 Telex no 935728 Plan **2** *F4*

Conveniently located airport hotel.

42 CTV in all bedrooms Ⓡ sB £38.25 (room only) dB £48.50 (room only)

Lift ☾ 145P ✽

Mainly grills Lunch £5.50alc Tea 80p alc Dinner £7alc Last dinner 10pm

Credit cards 1 2 3 4 5

☆☆☆ **Post House** Sipson Rd, West Drayton (2m N A408) (Trusthouse Forte) ☎01-759 2323 Telex no 934280 Plan **9** *D5*

Large bedrooms and a choice of restaurants are features of this well appointed hotel.

594 (149fb) CTV in all bedrooms Ⓡ sB&B £47.50 dB&B £60.50

Lift ☾ # 400P CFA

Last dinner 11pm

Credit cards 1 2 3 4 5

★★★ **Skyway** Bath Rd, Hayes (Trusthouse Forte) ☎01-759 6311 Telex no 23935 Plan **12** *E4*

Spacious hotel with well appointed restaurant.

445 CTV in all bedrooms Ⓡ sB&B £45.50 dB&B £58.50

Lift ☾ # 230P CFA (heated)

Last dinner 10pm

Credit cards 1 2 3 4 5

XXXX ***Excelsior Hotel Restaurant*** (Draitone Manor) Bath Rd, West Drayton (adj M4 Spur at junc with A4) ☎01-759 6611 Plan **3** *D4*

An elegant Georgian-style dining room.

Closed Sun Lunch not served Sat

International Open 24hrs 400P bedrooms available Live music Mon–Sat

Credit cards 1 2 3 4 5

At **Hounslow** (3m E on A4)

☆☆☆ **Master Robert Motel** 366 Great West Rd ☎01-570 6261 Plan **7** *F4*

64rm (56 8) 89P

HEDDON'S MOUTH
Devon
Map **2** SS64

★★ ***HBL* Heddon's Gate** ☎Parracombe (059 83) 313
Closed mid Nov–mid Mar

Originally a hunting lodge, this comfortable hotel is set in a wooded valley. Anne and Robert Deville provide a hospitable welcome and very comfortable bedrooms, several with feature Victorian bathrooms. The cooking is original, well prepared and presented using fresh ingredients.

13rm (11 2) 2 CTV in all bedrooms Ⓡ sB&B £13–£20.15 dB&B £26–£40.30

20P ✽ nc7yrs

✽Tea fr45p alc Dinner fr£9.20alc Wine £4.20 Last dinner 8.15pm

Credit cards 1 2

HELENSBURGH
Strathclyde *Dunbartonshire*
Map **10** NS28

☆☆☆ ***BL* Commodore** 112 West Clyde St ☎(0436) 6924

45 CTV in all bedrooms Ⓡ sB&B fr£21 dB&B fr£31

Lift ☾ 150P *xmas*

French **V** Lunch £4–£4.50&alc Tea 50p High Tea £4–£5.50 Dinner £7.50–£8.50&alc Wine £3.85 Last dinner 10.30pm

Credit cards 1 2 3 5 **VS**

HELFORD
Cornwall
Map **2** SW72

❀XX **Riverside** ☎Manaccan (032 623) 443

(Rosette awarded for dinner only.)
Character cottage restaurant idyllically located overlooking the river in the peaceful Helford Passage.

Closed Nov–end Feb Lunch not served

French 30 seats ✽Dinner £17.50alc Wine £5.75 Last dinner 9.30pm 6P bedrooms available

S%

HELLAND BRIDGE
Cornwall
Map **2** SX07

★★★ ***H* Tredethy Country** (off B3266) ☎St Mabyn (020 884) 262
Closed Xmas

Beautiful property, once the much-loved home of the author Prince Chula.

11rm(9➡2⋒)Ⓡ✱sB&B➡⋒£16 dB&B➡⋒£28 B

CTV 30P ✱ ⛆(heated) nc12yrs

English & French ♈ Lunch £6 Tea £1.50 Dinner £7&alc Wine £3.50 Last dinner 8.30pm

VS

HELMSLEY
North Yorkshire
Map **8** SE68

★★★*BL* **Black Swan** Market Pl (Trusthouse Forte) ☎(0439) 70466

Graceful Georgian mansion retaining some older features, this is a comfortable and elegant hotel with good modern facilities and a well tended garden.

38➡(11fb) CTV in all bedrooms Ⓡ sB&B➡£39 dB&B➡£58 B

☾ CTV 36P 2 ✱ *xmas*

Last dinner 9.15pm

Credit cards 1 2 3 4 5

★★★**Feversham Arms** 1 High St (Best Western) ☎(0439) 70766 Closed 24–31 Dec

15➡(4fb) CTV in all bedrooms sB&B➡£28 dB&B➡£36 B

30P ✱ (hard)

English & Continental V Lunch fr£6&alc Dinner fr£10&alc Wine £4 Last dinner 9.30pm

Credit cards 1 3

★★**Crown** Market Sq ☎(0439) 70297

Converted 16th-century inn overlooking the market place.

15rm(1➡9⋒)(2fb) Ⓡ sB&B£15 sB&B➡⋒£17 dB&B£30 dB&B➡⋒£34 B

CTV 15P 3 ✱ *xmas*

V Lunch £3.95–£4.30 Tea 70p–£1.30 High Tea £2–£3.50 Dinner £6.50–£6.90 Wine £3.80 Last dinner 8pm

★★**Feathers** Market Pl ☎(0439) 70275 Closed 24 Dec–3 Jan

Local stone house, partly 14th century and partly 17th century, with Georgian modifications.

18rm(6➡7⋒)(4fb) Ⓡ✱sB&B£13.25 sB&B➡⋒£16 dB&B£26.50 dB&B➡⋒£32 B

CTV 12P

V ✱Lunch fr£4 Tea fr£1.75 Dinner fr£8 Wine £4.95 Last dinner 8.30pm

S% Credit cards 1 2 3 5

HELSTON
Cornwall
Map **2** SW62

★★**Gwealdues** Falmouth Rd ☎(03265) 2808

Small, modern, comfortable hotel located just outside the town centre.

17rm(4➡2⋒)(4fb) CTV in 6 bedrooms Ⓡ ✱sB&B£13.50 sB&B➡⋒£18.50 dB&B£26 dB&B➡⋒£30

CTV 50P ✱ ⛆ nc5yrs

✱Bar lunch £2–£2.75&alc Tea 50p Dinner £4.50–£7.80&alc Wine £3.50 Last dinner 8.15pm

Credit cards 1 3

See advert on page 310

★**Angel** Coinage Hall St ☎(03265) 2701

An inn of character with galleried first floor restaurant.

20rm(3fb) Ⓡ sB&B£14 dB&B£22 B

CTV 12P

V ✱Lunch fr£6&alc Tea fr55p High Tea fr£1.40 Dinner fr£6&alc Last dinner 9.30pm

Credit cards 1 2 3 5 **VS**

See advert on page 310

★*L* **Nansloe Manor Country Hotel** Meneage Rd ☎(03269) 4691

6rm(3➡)(1fb) 1 CTV available in bedrooms Ⓡ✱sB&B fr£11 sB&B➡ fr£13.75 dB&B fr£22 dB&B➡ fr£27.50 →

H

CTV 30P 🚗✽

V✽Dinner fr£6.50&alc Wine £4 Last dinner 9.30pm

Credit cards 1 2 3 5

HEMEL HEMPSTEAD
Hertfordshire
Map **4** TL00

☆☆☆**Hemel Hempstead Moat House** London Rd, Bourne End (Queens Moat) ☎Berkhamsted (04427) 71241

Modern hotel in a pleasant rural situation by a watermill on the River Bulbourne.

Annexe: 40➡ CTV in all bedrooms ® sB&B➡£30.50 dB&B➡£37 ⊟

☾ 80P

⊟International ♈ ☕ Lunch £6.95 Tea 65p Dinner £6.95 Wine £4.95 Last dinner 9.45pm

Credit cards 1 2 3 4 5 **VS**

☆☆☆**Post House** Breakspear Way (Trusthouse Forte) ☎(0442) 51122 Telex no 826902

Attractively decorated and furnished hotel located about 2 miles from the town centre.

Annexe: 107➡ (29fb) CTV in all bedrooms ®sB&B➡£41 dB&B➡£53.50 ⊟

Lift ☾ 140P CFA ✽ *xmas*

♈ ☕ Last dinner 9.45pm

Credit cards 1 2 3 4 5

At **Redbourn** (4m NE on B487)

☆☆☆**Aubrey Park** Hemel Hempstead Rd (Best Western) ☎Redbourn (058285) 2105

57➡ ⋒ 100P

HENLEY-IN-ARDEN
Warwickshire
Map **7** SP16

✕✕✕**Beaudesert** ☎(05642) 2675

Closed Mon & 8–29 Aug Lunch not served Tue–Sat Dinner not served Sun

⊟French 55 seats Lunch fr£6.95 Dinner fr£8.50&alc Wine £4.40 Last dinner 10pm 50P

Credit cards 1 2 3 5

✕✕**Le Filbert Cottage** 64 High St ☎(05642) 2700

Closed Sun, Boxing Day & Public Hols

⊟French 32 seats Lunch £7–£8.50&alc Dinner £16–£18&alc Wine £4.40 Last dinner 10pm ⊁

Credit cards 1 3

✕✕***Othello*** 148 High St ☎(05642) 3089

Closed Sun

⊟Continental 45 seats Last dinner 10.30pm ⊁

Credit cards 1 2 3 5

HENLEY-ON-THAMES
Oxfordshire
Map **4** SU78

★★★**Red Lion** ☎(04912) 2161 (Due to change to (0491) 572161)

Traditional style hotel with some modern comforts.

28rm (19➡) (3fb) 1⊟ CTV in all bedrooms ✝✽sB&B£22.50–£25 sB&B➡£35–£40 dB&B£35–£40 dB&B➡£45–£50 ⊟

☾ 30P 3🏠 🚗 *xmas*

⊟English & French V ♈ ☕ Lunch £4.25–£5.95&alc Tea 75p–£1 High Tea £1.25–£1.50 Dinner fr£7.50&alc Wine £4.70 Last dinner 10pm

Credit cards 2 3

✕✕**Gaylord Tandoori** 60 Bell St ☎(04912) 5157 (Due to change to (0491) 575157)

Well appointed Indian restaurant with imaginative Tandoori cuisine.

⊟Indian 50 seats ✽Lunch £8alc Dinner £8alc Wine £3.45 Last dinner 11pm ⊁

S% Credit cards 1 2 3 5

✕✕**Hamlyn's** Sydney House Hotel, Northfield End ☎(04912) 3412 (Due to change to (0491) 573412)

Closed Mon Dinner not served Sun

⊟English & French 30 seats ✽Lunch fr£2.50alc Dinner £11.50&alc Wine £3.90

H

Last dinner 9.30pm 5P bedrooms available
Credit cards 1 2 3 5 VS

✕ ***Il Rigoletto*** 41 Station Rd ☎ (04912) 2984 (Due to change to (0491) 572984)
Closed Sat, Sun & Mon
Italian 30 seats Last dinner 11pm 8P
Credit cards 1 2 3 5

HEREFORD
Hereford & Worcester
Map **3** SO54

★★★ **Green Dragon** Broad St (Trusthouse Forte) ☎ (0432) 272506
Telex no 35491
Traditional hotel in the centre of Hereford.
88 CTV in all bedrooms ®
sB&B £38.50 dB&B £50 B
Lift ☾ CTV CFA 90 *xmas*
Last dinner 9.30pm
Credit cards 1 2 3 4 5

☆☆☆ **Hereford Moat House** Belmont Rd (Queens Moat) ☎ (0432) 54301
Closed 5 days Xmas
Annexe: 32 CTV in all bedrooms ®
sB&B £26 dB&B £35 B
☾ 150P ✽
English & French V Lunch £5.95&alc Tea 60p Dinner £6.95&alc Wine £4.25 Last dinner 9.45pm
Credit cards 1 2 3 5

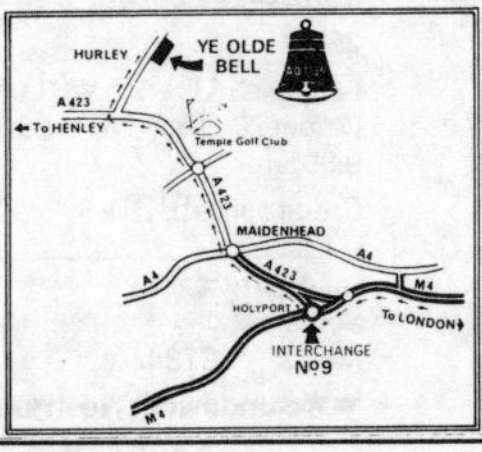

★★ ***Graftonbury*** Grafton Ln ☎ (0432) 56411
20rm(10 5) CTV in 18 bedrooms ® B
Lift CTV 100P ✽ (heated)
Last dinner 9.15pm
Credit cards 1 2 3 5 VS
See advert on page 312

H

★★**Litchfield Lodge** Bodenham Rd ☎(0432) 273258
Closed Xmas
14rm(4➡6⋒) CTV in all bedrooms Ⓡ ★ sB&B£14 sB&B➡⋒£16.50 dB&B£24 dB&B➡⋒£27
CTV 15P ⇌ nc5yrs
♁ ☐ Lunch £6.50&alc Tea 65p Dinner £6.50alc Wine £4 Last dinner 8pm
Credit cards 1 2 3

★★*B* **Merton** Commercial Rd ☎(0432) 265925
Closed 25–31 Dec
Family-run, town centre hotel with a popular, traditional, English menu.
11rm(2➡2⋒) Annexe: 3rm(1fb) CTV in all bedrooms sB&B£17.25 sB&B➡⋒£20.70 dB&B£26.45 dB&B➡⋒£31.20 B
CTV 6P ⇌
V ♁ ☐ Lunch £4.50–£7.50 Tea 50p–£2 High Tea £3–£4.50 Dinner £7&alc Wine £3.25 Last dinner 9pm
Credit cards 1 3

HERSTMONCEUX
East Sussex
Map **5** TQ61
✕✕**Sundial** ☎(0323) 832217
Elegant country restaurant specialising in fish dishes.
Closed Mon, mid Aug–1st wk Sep & Xmas–20 Jan Dinner not served Sun
French **V** 60 seats ✻Lunch fr£8.45&alc Dinner fr£11.50&alc Wine £5.75 Last dinner 9.30pm 20P
Credit cards 3 5

HERTFORD
Hertfordshire
Map **4** TL31
☆☆☆**White Horse Inn** Hertingfordbury (1m W on A414) (Trusthouse Forte) ☎(0992) 56791
Small, attractive inn with modern bedroom block.
30➡ (3fb) CTV in all bedrooms Ⓡ sB&B➡£39 dB&B➡£54.50 B
60P ✽ *xmas*
♁ Last dinner 9.45pm
Credit cards 1 2 3 4 5

★★**Salisbury Arms** Fore St ☎(0992) 53091
RS Xmas
Old inn, with a beamed cocktail bar and a wood-panelled dining room.
32rm(11➡) (1fb) Ⓡ ✻sB&B£16 sB&B➡£18.50 dB&B£24 dB&B➡£29
☾ CTV 35P ⇌
English & Chinese **V** ♁ ✻Lunch fr£3.35&alc Dinner £3.35&alc Wine £3.90 Last dinner 9pm
Credit cards 1 2 3 4 5

✕✕**Marquee** 1 Bircherley Gn ☎(0992) 58999
Closed Xmas Day & Good Fri
International 85 seats Lunch £4.95&alc Dinner £9alc Last dinner 11pm
Credit cards 1 2 3 5

HETHERSETT
Norfolk
Map **5** TG10
★★**Park Farm** ☎Norwich (0603) 810264
6rm(3➡2⋒) Annexe: 14rm(4➡4⋒) (3fb) 1 CTV in 16 bedrooms ★ sB&B£14–£15 sB&B➡⋒£21–£22 dB&B£27–£29 dB&B➡⋒£30–£32 B
CTV 20P ⇌ ✽ (heated) (hard) sauna bath
English & French **V** ♁ ☐ Lunch £4.75&alc Tea 60p–£1 High Tea £3–£5 Dinner £6.50–£7.50&alc Wine £4.20 Last dinner 9pm
S% Credit cards 1 2 3 **VS**

HEVERSHAM
Cumbria
Map **7** SD48
★★★**Blue Bell at Heversham** Prince's Way ☎Milnthorpe (04482) 3159
An attractive 17th-century country inn, once a vicarage, whose history dates back to 1692.
28rm(12➡5⋒) Ⓡ ★ sB&B fr£16.50 sB&B➡⋒ fr£22 dB&B fr£28 dB&B➡⋒ fr£31 B
CTV 100P ⇌
V ♁ ☐ Lunch £5.75 Tea £2.20 Dinner £10 Wine £4.50 Last dinner 9.15pm
S% Credit cards 1 3

HEXHAM
Northumberland
Map **12** NY96
★★**Beaumont** Beaumont St (Minotel) ☎(0434) 602331
Personally-run, commercial and tourist hotel, facing the Abbey grounds.
22rm(2➡14⋒) (3fb) CTV in all bedrooms Ⓡ sB&B£16.50 sB&B➡⋒£17.50–£20 dB&B£25 dB&B➡⋒£25 B
CTV
♁ Lunch £4.50 Dinner £5.50alc Wine £4 Last dinner 10pm
Credit cards 1 2 3 5

★★*HB* **County** Priestpopple ☎(0434) 602030
Warm, comfortable, small hotel with good wholesome food.
10rm(4⋒) (3fb) CTV in all bedrooms Ⓡ ✻sB&B£14–£15 dB&B£22 sB&B⋒£25 B
☾ 2P
V ♁ ☐ ✻Lunch £5 Tea £1.90 High Tea £1.50–£7&alc Dinner £6.50–£12&alc Wine £3.80
Last dinner 9.15pm
Credit cards 1 3 **VS**

★★**Royal** Priestpopple (Exec Hotel) ☎(0434) 602270
An old established inn with the original coaching arch, located in the town centre.
25rm(14➡) (3fb) CTV in all bedrooms Ⓡ sB&B£15 sB&B➡£19.50 dB&B£25.50 dB&B➡£29.50 B
25P
English & French **V** ♁ Lunch £4.50 Dinner £6.50&alc Wine £3.50 Last dinner 9.30pm
Credit cards 1 3 **VS**

HIGHBRIDGE
Somerset
Map **3** ST34
★★**Sundowner** West Huntspill (1m SE

on A38) ☎Burnham-on-Sea (0278) 784766

8rm(2⇌1⋔) (2fb) CTV available in bedrooms sB&B fr£14 sB&B⇌⋔ fr£16 dB&B fr£22 dB&B⇌⋔ fr£26 B

CTV 20P ⊠ ✽

V ♈ Lunch £4.95&alc Dinner £6.25–£8.25&alc Wine £4.25 Last dinner 10pm

Credit cards 1 2 3 5

HIGH EASTER
Essex
Map **5** TL61

✕✕**Punch Bowl** ☎Good Easter (024531) 222

(Classification awarded for dinner only.)

Closed Mon Lunch not served Sat Dinner not served Sun

▤English & French **V** 60 seats Lunch £6.75&alc Dinner £10–£12alc Wine £4.55 Last dinner 10pm 18P

Credit cards 1 2 3 5 **VS**

HIGH LANE
Greater Manchester
Map **7** SJ98

✕✕***Red Lion*** Buxton Rd ☎Disley (06632) 2061

Last dinner 10pm 60P

Credit cards 1 3

HIGH OFFLEY
Staffordshire
Map **7** SJ72

✕✕***Royal Oak*** ☎Woodseaves (078574) 579

Tiny village inn, comfortably modernised, serving imaginative as well as traditional dishes.

Closed last 2wks Aug & Public hols Full lunch by request only
Dinner not served Sun

36 seats Last dinner 9.30pm 12P

Credit cards 1 2 3 5 **VS**

HIGH WYCOMBE
Buckinghamshire
Map **4** SU89

☆☆☆**Crest** Crest Rd, Handy Cross (Crest) ☎(0494) 442100

New hotel with good bedrooms and interesting restaurant.

108⇌ CTV in all bedrooms Ⓡ ✽sB⇌ fr£38 dB⇌ fr£46 (room only) B

Lift ☾ ⚟ 200P CFA ✽

V ♈ ☐ ✽Lunch £4.95–£6.95 Tea 95p–£1.25 Dinner £8.95&alc Last dinner 10.30pm

Credit cards 1 2 3 4 5 **VS**

★★***Falcon*** ☎(0494) 22173

A 14th-century inn of architectural and historical interest, next to the Guildhall in the town centre.

12rm CTV in all bedrooms Ⓡ B

12⌂ Live music and dancing Wed

▤English, French & Italian **V** ♈ ☐ Last dinner 10pm

Credit cards 1 2 3 5

HILLINGDON
Greater London, London plan **5** A4 (page 420)

☆☆☆**Master Brewer Motel** Western Av (A40) ☎Uxbridge (0895) 51199

Modern motel well placed on the A40, each bedroom having a balcony or garden access.

64⇌⋔ CTV in all bedrooms Ⓡ sB&B⇌⋔ £35.50 dB&B⇌⋔ £45.50 B

☾ # CTV 200P CFA ✽

♈ ☐ Lunch £5–£7.95 Dinner £5–£7.95 Wine £4.65 Last dinner 11pm

S% Credit cards 1 2 3 5

HINDHEAD
Surrey
Map **4** SU83

☆☆**Hindhead Motor** Portsmouth Rd (Best Western) ☎(042873) 6666
RS Xmas

16⇌⋔ (3fb) CTV in all bedrooms Ⓡ sB⇌⋔ £23–£25 dB⇌⋔ £32.25–£35.50 B

100P ✽

V ♈ ☐ Lunch £2–£6 Dinner £2–£6 Wine £4.50 Last dinner 10pm

Credit cards 1 2 3 5

HINDON
Wiltshire
Map **3** ST93

★★**Lamb at Hindon** ☎(074789) 225
Closed Xmas

Hotel has modern, well equipped bedrooms and Happy Eater restaurant.

16rm(6⇌) (2fb) 1⊟ Ⓡ ★ sB&B£15–£20 dB&B£28–£30 dB&B⇌£32–£34 B

CTV 12P ⊠ ✽

▤English & Continental **V** ♈ Lunch £5–£6&alc Dinner £7.25–£9&alc Wine £3.60 Last dinner 9pm

Credit card 1

HISTON
Cambridgeshire
Map **5** TL46

○**Post House** (adj A45 3m N of Cambridge)

121⇌

☎Histon (022023) 7000
(Due to have opened July 1983)

HITCHIN
Hertfordshire
Map **4** TL12

★★★**Blakemore** Little Wymondley (2m SE A602) ☎Stevenage (0438) 55821
Telex no 825479

Georgian style house with modern extension in large grounds.

72⇌⋔ (1fb) CTV in all bedrooms ✽sB&B⇌⋔ £30 dB&B⇌⋔ £45 B

Lift ☾ # CTV 300P 1⌂ CFA ✽ ≋ (heated) billiards sauna bath *xmas*

V ♈ ☐ Lunch fr£7.50&alc Tea fr75p Dinner fr£7.50&alc Wine £5.50 Last dinner 10pm

Credit cards 1 2 3 4 5

HOGSTHORPE
Lincolnshire
Map **9** TF57

✕**Belmont** ☎Skegness (0754) 72288

Creeper-clad, Victorian house with pleasant grounds.

Lunch not served Mon & Sat

40 seats ✽Lunch £4.50 Dinner £5.50&alc Wine £3.32 Last dinner 10pm 20P bedrooms available

Credit cards 1 3 **VS**

HOLBETON
Devon
Map **2** SX65

★★★♣***L* Alston Hall** Battisborough Cross ☎(075530) 259

Set in 4½ acres amidst undulating countryside, a beautifully restored country house featuring oak-panelled great hall with minstrel gallery.

9⇌ CTV available in bedrooms ★ ✽sB&B⇌£25.50 dB&B⇌£34.50
Continental breakfast B

⚟ 100P ⊠ ✽ ≋ (heated) ⚲ (hard) ⌂

V ♈ ☐ Lunch £5.95 Tea 60p Dinner £8.25 Wine £4.50 Last dinner 9.30pm

Credit cards 2 5

HOLFORD
Somerset
Map **3** ST14

★★♣***Alfoxton Park*** (Best Western) ☎(027874) 211 Closed 21 Dec–Feb

White, 18th-century house, home of poet William Wordsworth in 1797, set in 50 acres of parkland.

16rm(15⇌) Annexe: 2⇌ 1⊟ CTV in all bedrooms Ⓡ ★

50P ⊠ ✽ ≋ (heated) ⚲ (hard)

▤English & French ♈ ☐ Last dinner 9.30pm

Credit cards 1 2 3 5

See advert on page 314

★★♣**Combe House** ☎(027874) 382
Closed Nov–Feb

Attractive 17th century house in wooded valley, still retaining large water wheel. Bedrooms are well appointed.

16rm(10⇌) sB&B£13.50–£14.75 sB&B⇌£16–£17.75 dB&B£25–£27 dB&B⇌£28–£30 B

CTV 30P ⊠ ✽ ≋ (heated) ⚲ (hard) sauna bath

♈ ☐ Bar lunch £1–£3.75 Tea 60p Dinner £6.50–£7.50 Last dinner 8.15pm

HOLKHAM
Norfolk
Map **9** TF84
See also **Wells-next-the-Sea**

★**Victoria** ☎Fakenham (0328) 710469
A compact building, constructed of local flints, and situated at the entrance to Holkham Hall, it features walled and lawned gardens.

8rm Ⓡ sB&B£12–£14 dB&B£21–£26 B
CTV 50P ✽

English & French Bar lunch 90p–£6 Dinner £5.50&alc Wine £5 Last dinner 8.30pm
VS

HOLLINGBOURNE
Kent
Map **5** TQ85

★★★*L* **Great Danes** Ashford Rd (Rank) ☎Maidstone (0622) 30022 Telex no 96198
Spacious, modern hotel with compact, well-equipped bedrooms.

128 CTV in all bedrooms Ⓡ ✱sB £25–£33 dB £35–£42.50 B
Lift ☾ 450P CFA ✽ (heated) billiards Live music and dancing Sat *xmas*

Lunch £7.50alc Tea 60p alc High Tea 95p alc Dinner £8alc Wine £4.95 Last dinner 10.45pm
Credit cards 1 2 3 4 5 **VS**

HOLLYBUSH
Strathclyde *Ayrshire*
Map **10** NS31

★★★ **Hollybush House** ☎Dalrymple (029256) 214 Telex no 779358
RS Feb & Mar
Early Victorian mansion standing in extensive grounds, with fishing on River Doon.

12rm (6 1) (1fb) ✱sB&B£15–£20 sB&B £20–£25 dB&B£20–£30 dB&B £30–£40 B
☾ CTV 40P 6 ✽

English & French **V** Bar lunch £1.75alc Dinner £10.50&alc Wine £5.60 Last dinner 9.30pm
Credit cards 1 2 3

HOLMES CHAPEL
Cheshire
Map **7** SJ76

✕✕**Yellow Broom** Twemlow Green (1¾m NE A535) ☎(0477) 33289
Closed Mon Lunch not served Tue–Sat Dinner not served Sun

French **V** 40 seats Lunch £3.75–£5.50 Dinner £10.50–£12 Wine £4.50 Last dinner 10.30pm 35P
Credit cards 1 3 **VS**

HOLMROOK
Cumbria
Map **6** SD09

★**Lutwidge Arms** ☎(09404) 230
Victorian fishing inn with grounds bordering on the River Irt.

16rm (8 8) (2fb) CTV in all bedrooms Ⓡ sB&B £13.50 dB&B £26 B
CTV 46P ✽

Bar lunch £2.50alc Dinner £5.50alc Wine £3.10 Last dinner 9pm

HOLYWELL GREEN
West Yorkshire
Map **7** SE01

★★*B* **Rock Inn** ☎Elland (0422) 79721
Converted and extended 17th-century inn overlooking Pennine countryside.

18 CTV in all bedrooms Ⓡ sB&B £18–£27 dB&B £25–£38 B
100P 3 *xmas*

English & French **V** Lunch fr£4.75&alc Tea fr95p Dinner fr£7.50&alc Wine £5.10 Last dinner 9.45pm
Credit cards 1 2 3 4 5 **VS**

HONITON
Devon
Map **3** ST10

★★★ *HL* **Deer Park** Weston (2½m W off A30) ☎(0404) 2064
Old stone manor house, built in 1777, set in its own grounds of 26 acres.

17rm Annexe: 14 (7fb) CTV in all bedrooms sB&B £20–£30 dB&B £35–£55 B
☾ CTV 100P 4 CFA ✽ (heated) (hard) squash billiards sauna bath *xmas*

English & French **V** Lunch fr£5&alc Tea £1.50–£2.50 High Tea £2.50–£4.50 Dinner fr£9.50&alc Wine £4 Last dinner 10.30pm
Credit cards 1 2 3 5 **VS**

★**Angel** High St ☎(0404) 2829 Closed Xmas
Small, 17th-century inn with continental awnings in town centre.

6rm (1) Ⓡ sB&B£13.72 sB&B £15.24 dB&B£22.25 dB&B £25.71 B
CTV 28P nc12yrs

English & French **V** Lunch £3.40–£5.25 Dinner £4.65–£9.50 Wine £3.55 Last dinner 7.30pm

HOOK
Hampshire
Map **4** SU75

☆☆**Raven** Station Rd ☎(025672) 2541
Closed Xmas & New Year
Modernised hotel with comfortable well equipped bedrooms.

29 CTV in all bedrooms Ⓡ ✱sB&B fr£32.20 dB&B fr£43.70 B
☾ 100P CFA Live music and dancing Fri & Sat

English & Italian **V** ✱Lunch £6.50–£7&alc Dinner £8&alc Wine £4.80 Last dinner 10pm
Credit cards 1 2 3 4 5 **VS**

HOPE
Derbyshire
Map **7** SK18

✕✕✕***House of Anton*** Castleton Rd ☎Hope Valley (0433) 20380
Attractive, well-appointed restaurant set in lovely countryside.

English, French & Italian **V** 70 seats Last dinner 9.30pm 30P bedrooms available
Credit cards 1 2 3 5 **VS**

H

HOPE COVE
Devon
Map **3** SX64

★★**Cottage** ☎ Kingsbridge (0548) 561555
Closed 3–31 Jan
Converted and extended house with panoramic views of Hope Cove.
36rm(10➡4⋒) (6fb) sB&B£9.18–£16.08 dB&B£18.36–£32.16 dB&B➡⋒£20.52–£50.96 B
CTV 50P ✽ *xmas*
English & French Lunch £5.38&alc Tea 69p Dinner £9.33&alc Last dinner 8.45pm
S%

★★*HL* **Lantern Lodge** ☎ Kingsbridge (0548) 561280 Closed Jan & Feb
Personally-run hotel in a cliff-top position, overlooking the sea and the village.
16rm(11➡4⋒) (1fb) 3 TV available in bedrooms ® sB&B➡⋒£19 dB&B➡⋒£38 B
CTV 15P ✽ (heated) sauna bath nc8yrs *xmas*
English & French Bar lunch £1.50–£2.75 Dinner fr£10.75 Wine £5.30 Last dinner 9pm
Credit cards 2 3 **VS**

★★**Sun Bay** ☎ Kingsbridge (0548) 561371
Closed Oct–Mar
Modern hotel overlooking Hope Cove Bay.
14rm(11➡1⋒) sB&B fr£10 sB&B➡⋒ fr£10.50 dB&B➡⋒ fr£21 B
CTV 14P ✽

→

♔☕ Tea fr50p Dinner fr£6&alc Wine £3.50 Last dinner 8.15pm

★ ***Greystone*** ☎ Kingsbridge (0548) 561233
Closed Oct–Mar

12rm ⊟

CTV 12P 🚗 ✽ ⌂

♔☕ Last dinner 7.30pm

HORLEY
Surrey
Map **4** TQ24
Hotels are listed under Gatwick Airport

HORNBY
Lancashire
Map **7** SD56

★★ **Castle** Main St ☎ (0468) 21204

Stone-built inn situated in the centre of the village.

11rm (3→1⋒) (2fb) CTV in all bedrooms sB&B£14 sB&B→⋒ £18.50 dB&B£24 dB&B→⋒ £28.50 ⊟

50P ⌂ *xmas*

V ♔☕ ✻ Lunch £5 Tea £1.50&alc Dinner £7–£10&alc Wine £4.50 Last dinner 9.30pm

Credit card 2

HORNCASTLE
Lincolnshire
Map **8** TF26

★ **Bull** Bull Ring ☎ (06582) 3331 Closed Xmas

A 16th-century inn, with a historically decorated banqueting hall, and a cobbled yard.

8rm (1→) (1fb) CTV in 1 bedroom ® sB&B£11.95 sB&B→£16.95 dB&B£19.80 dB&B→£26

☾ CTV 20P Live music and dancing Fri & Sat Cabaret Fri & Sat

V ♔ Lunch 95p–£1.95 Dinner £6.20 Wine £2.65 Last dinner 9.30pm

Credit cards 1 3 5

HORNCHURCH
Greater London
Map **5** TQ58

☆☆☆ **Ladbroke** (& Conference centre) Southend Arterial Rd (Ladbroke) ☎ Ingrebourne (04023) 46789 Telex no 897315

Modern hotel with comfortable bedrooms.

145→ (4fb) CTV in all bedrooms ® ✻sB→ fr£35 (room only) dB→ fr£43 (room only) ⊟

☾ 170P CFA

⊡ French ♔ ✻ Lunch fr£6.50 Dinner fr£8.50 Last dinner 10pm

Credit cards 1 2 3 5

HORNING
Norfolk
Map **9** TG31

★★ **Petersfield House** ☎ (0692) 630741

16rm (13→) (2fb) CTV in all bedrooms sB&B£23 sB&B→£23 dB&B£36.50 dB&B→£36.50 ⊟

100P 🚗 ✽ ♪ *xmas*

⊡ French **V** ♔☕ Lunch £5.50–£10&alc Tea 45p Dinner £7.50–£10&alc Last dinner 9.30pm

Credit cards 1 2 3 5

HORN'S CROSS
Devon
Map **2** SS32

★★ ***BL*** **Foxdown Manor** (Signed from A39 W of village) ☎ (02375) 325

Secluded, personally-run country hotel with many facilities, set in extensive grounds.

7rm (5→1⋒) 2⊞ CTV in all bedrooms ® dB&B→⋒ £38–£46.70 ⊟

30P 🚗 ✽ ⩳ (heated) ⚲ (hard) sauna bath ⌂ *xmas*

⊡ Cosmopolitan **V** ♔☕ Lunch £5.20 Tea 50p High Tea £5 Dinner £10.25&alc Wine £4.75 Last dinner 8.45pm

Credit cards 1 2 3 5

★★**Hoops Inn** ☎(02375) 222
A charming 13th-century thatched inn, personally-run, and having a good restaurant.
6rm Annexe: 8➡⋒ (2fb) 1⊟CTV in 4 bedrooms sB&B£14–£17 sB&B➡⋒£14–£17 dB&B£28–£34 dB&B➡⋒£28–£34 B
CTV 35P ✽ nc5yrs *xmas*
Lunch £5.25&alc Dinner £9&alc Wine £4.15 Last dinner 9.30pm

HORSFORTH
West Yorkshire
Map **8** SE23
✕✕✕**Low Hall** Calverley Ln ☎Leeds (0532) 588221
Closed Sun, Mon, 26–30 Dec & 28 May–4 Jun Lunch not served Sat
▣British & French 80 seats Lunch £6.50&alc Dinner £12 Wine £4.30 Last dinner 10pm 70P
S% Credit cards 1 3 **VS**

HORSHAM
West Sussex
Map **4** TQ13
★★**Ye Olde King's Head** ☎(0403) 53126
Part timbered, two-storey inn situated on Carfax. It was established in 1401, and the cellars date from the 12th century.
24rm(3➡17⋒) Annexe: 5rm(3⋒) (1fb) 1⊟CTV in all bedrooms Ⓡ sB&B fr£21 sB&B➡⋒ fr£29.50 dB&B fr£38.25 dB&B➡⋒ fr£41.25 B
40P 2⌂ CFA
V ♡ ☐ Lunch fr£5.25 Tea fr£1.50 Dinner fr£6.25&alc Wine £3.95 Last dinner 10pm
S% Credit cards 1 2 3

HORSINGTON
Somerset
Map **3** ST72
★★**Horsington House**
☎Templecombe (0963) 70721
Large country house with a friendly atmosphere and catering for both the business and touring clientele.
22rm(16➡4⋒) (3fb) CTV in 12 bedrooms Ⓡ sB&B£19 sB&B➡⋒£21 dB&B➡⋒£33 B
CTV 50P 5⌂✽ ᑭ(hard) Live music and dancing Sat *xmas*
V ♡ ☐ Lunch £5.25&alc Tea fr45p Dinner £7.25&alc Wine £4.90 Last dinner 9.30pm
Credit cards 1 2 3 4 5

HORTON
Northamptonshire
Map **4** SP85
❀✕✕**French Partridge**
☎Northampton (0604) 870033
Dignified country restaurant offering good food and excellent value.
Closed Sun, Mon, 2wks Xmas, 1wk Etr, 3wks end Jul–1st wk Aug Lunch not served
▣French 50 seats Dinner £13 Wine £4.50 Last dinner 9.30pm 50P ⊬
S% **VS**

HORTON-CUM-STUDLEY
Oxfordshire
Map **4** SP51
❀★★★**Studley Priory** ☎Stanton St John (086735) 203 Telex no 23152
Closed 2–19 Jan
Unique, partly 13th century, hotel with Elizabethan panelling and notable restaurant, set in extensive rural grounds.
19rm(15➡4⋒) 2⊟CTV in all bedrooms ✱ sB&B➡⋒£35 dB&B➡⋒£48–£65 B
100P 3⌂✽ ᑭ(grass) *xmas*
▣French **V** Lunch £18alc Dinner £18alc Wine £5.25 Last dinner 9.30pm
Credit cards 1 2 3 4 5

HOUGHTON CONQUEST
Bedfordshire
Map **4** TL04
✕**Knife & Cleaver** ☎Bedford (0234) 740387
Dinner not served Sun
▣English & French 70 seats ✱Lunch £6.80alc Dinner £9.25&alc Wine £3.98 Last dinner 9.30pm
Credit cards 1 3

HOUNSLOW
Greater London, London plan **5** B3 (page 420)
☆☆☆**Master Robert Motel** 366 Great West Rd (A4) ☎01-570 6261 Heathrow plan **7** *F4*
Well appointed comfortable motel with good food and pleasant staff.
64rm(56➡8⋒) CTV in all bedrooms Ⓡ sB&B➡⋒£35.50 dB&B➡⋒£45.50 B
Lift ☾ ⊬ CTV 89P ✽ Live music and dancing Fri
▣English & French ♡ ☐ Lunch £6.75–£9.50&alc Dinner £6.75–£9.50&alc Wine £4.65 Last dinner 11pm
S% Credit cards 1 2 3 5 **VS**

✕**Hounslow Chinese** 261–263 Bath Rd ☎01-570 2161 Heathrow plan **6** *F3*
Comfortable restaurant providing well-flavoured Pekinese dishes.
Closed 25–27 Dec Lunch not served Sun
▣Pekinese 100 seats Lunch fr£6&alc Dinner fr£6&alc Wine £4.70 Last dinner 11.30pm
Credit cards 1 2 3 5

HOVE
East Sussex
See Brighton & Hove

HOVINGHAM
North Yorkshire
Map **8** SE67
★★*L* **Worsley Arms** ☎(065382) 234
14➡ ✱sB&B➡£18–£19.50 dB&B➡£33–£35.50 B
CTV 50P 3⌂✽
▣French & Italian **V** ♡ ☐ ✱Lunch fr£5 Tea 50p–£1.75 Dinner fr£9.75 Wine £5.25 Last dinner 9pm
Credit cards 1 3

HOW CAPLE
Hereford & Worcester
Map **3** SO63
★★**How Caple Grange** ☎(098986) 208
Large hotel in five acres of grounds.
26rm(20➡1⋒) (2fb) CTV in 8 bedrooms Ⓡ sB&B➡⋒£15.52 dB&B£24.15 dB&B➡⋒£26.44 B
CTV 60P ✽ ⩦ sauna bath ⌂
▣English & French ♡ ✱Lunch £3.50–£5 Dinner £6–£11 Wine £4.50 Last dinner 9pm
Credit cards 1 3 **VS**

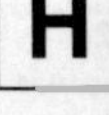

HOWDEN
Humberside
Map **8** SE72
★★**Bowmans** Bridgegate ☎(0430) 30805
A converted merchant's residence and stables, situated in the town centre.
13rm(10➡) (1fb) CTV in all bedrooms sB&B➡£19.50–£23 dB&B➡£30–£33 B
50P
▣English & French **V** ♡ ✱Lunch £7–£12alc Dinner £7–£12alc Wine £4.70 Last dinner 9.30pm
Credit cards 1 2 3 4 5 **VS**

★**Wellington** 31 Bridgegate ☎(0430) 30258
Once a Georgian coaching inn, parts of this hotel date back to the 16th century.
9➡ CTV in all bedrooms sB&B➡£17–£18 dB&B➡£26–£28
100P sauna bath
♡ ☐ Lunch 75p–£5 Tea 50p–£2 High Tea £1–£8 Dinner £1–£8 Wine £4 Last dinner 8pm

HOWGATE
Lothian *Midlothian*
Map **11** NT25
✕✕**Old Howgate Inn** Wester Howgate ☎Penicuik (0968) 74244
Old coaching house reputed to have been used by pilgrims travelling from Edinburgh.
Closed Xmas Day, 1 & 2 Jan
Dinner not served Sun
▣Danish **V** 50 seats ✱Lunch £2.50–£5alc Dinner £2.50–£5alc Wine £4.45 Last dinner 10pm 30P
Credit cards 1 2 3

HOYLAKE
Merseyside
Map **7** SJ28

★★**Stanley** Kings Gap (Whitbread West Pennines) ☎051-632 3311
Large public house with modern bedrooms in the centre of the village.
16rm(2➡)CTV in all bedrooms ® ✗ sB&B£13.95 sB&B➡£15 dB&B£25.20 dB&B➡£27.40 B
☾ CTV 180P
Lunch fr£3.75 Dinner fr£4.75&alc Last dinner 10pm
Credit cards 1 2 3 5

HUDDERSFIELD
West Yorkshire
Map **7** SE11

★★★**George** St George's Sq (Trusthouse Forte) ☎(0484) 25444
Large town centre hotel close to the railway station.
62rm(36➡)CTV in all bedrooms ® sB&B£27 sB&B➡£36.50 dB&B£37.50 dB&B➡£46 B
Lift ☾ 12P CFA
Last dinner 9.45pm
Credit cards 1 2 3 4 5

☆☆☆**Ladbroke** (& Conference centre) Ainley Top (Ladbroke) ☎Elland (0422) 75431 Telex no 517346
Modern building near the M62 motorway.
120➡fi CTV in all bedrooms ® *sB➡fi fr£33.50 (room only) dB➡fi fr£44 (room only) B
Lift ☾ 150P CFA ✲
French *Lunch fr£6.50 Dinner fr£8.50 Last dinner 10pm
Credit cards 1 2 3 5

HUGH TOWN
St Mary's, Isles of Scilly (no map)

★★**Bell Rock** Church St ☎Scillonia (0720) 22575
Closed 27 Nov–16 Jan RS 9 Oct–26 Nov & 17 Jan–8 Apr
Holiday hotel with pleasant service, good food and a swimming pool in the walled garden.
19rm(14➡3fi)(4fb) ® sB&B➡fi £12–£18 dB&B➡fi £24–£26
CTV (heated)
English & French Bar lunch 50p–£1.95 Tea 50p Dinner £7.95 Last dinner 8pm
Credit cards 1 2 3 5

★★**Godolphin** Church St ☎Scillonia (0720) 22316
Closed mid Oct–mid Mar
Large, granite building in St Mary's, near the harbour.
31rm(25➡2fi)(4fb) CTV in all bedrooms ® ✗ sB&B fr£13 sB&B➡fi fr£15 dB&B fr£26 dB&B➡fi fr£30
Bar lunch fr80p Tea fr50p Dinner fr£8.50 Wine £3.90 Last dinner 8pm

★★**Tregarthens** ☎Scillonia (0720) 22540
Closed mid Oct–late Mar
Well-appointed hotel, situated on rising ground near the quay, with views over the harbour and offshore islands.
32rm(24➡)(3fb) CTV in all bedrooms ® ✗ sB&B£15–£25 sB&B➡£18–£28 dB&B£32–£50 dB&B➡£40–£58 B
nc5yrs
International V Bar lunch fr75p&alc Tea fr50p Dinner £8.50–£10 Wine £4 Last dinner 8pm
Credit cards 1 2 3 5

HULL
Humberside
Map **8** TA02

☆☆☆**Crest Hotel Hull–City** Paragon St (Crest) ☎(0482) 26462 Telex no 52431
A town centre, five-storey hotel, situated in a busy shopping street.
125➡ CTV in all bedrooms ® *sB➡ fr£31 (room only) dB➡ fr£41 (room only) B
Lift ☾ CFA
International V *Lunch £5.50 Tea fr70p Dinner £8.35–£8.95 Wine £5.95 Last dinner 9.45pm
Credit cards 1 2 3 4 5 VS

XX**Cerutti's** 10 Nelson St ☎(0482) 28501
Closed Sun, 10 days Xmas & Public Hols
Lunch not served Sat
40 seats *Lunch £12.50alc Dinner £12.50alc Wines £6.25 Last dinner 9.30pm 8P
Credit card 1

At **North Ferriby** (6m W on A63)

☆☆☆**Crest Hotel Hull–Humber Bridge** Ferriby High Rd (Crest) ☎(0482) 645212
102➡100P

At **Willerby** (3¾m NW on A164)

★★★**Willerby Manor** Well Ln ☎(0482) 652616
41rm(27➡14fi) 200P

HUMBIE
Lothian *East Lothian*
Map **12** NT46

★★★ *HBL* **Johnstounburn House** (1m S A6137) ☎(087533) 696 Telex no 727897
A charming house, dating back to 1625 and standing in immaculate gardens, featuring a historic dovecote. The original relaxed atmosphere and traditional character is retained, while the hotel is equipped with all modern facilities.
11rm(9➡2fi)(1fb) CTV in all bedrooms sB&B➡fi £25–£36.50 dB&B➡fi £46–£57 B
☾ 60P ✲ *xmas*
French V Lunch £6.85–£9.50 Tea 75p–£1.50 Dinner £12.50&alc Wine £5.70 Last dinner 9pm
S% Credit cards 1 2 3 5

HUNGERFORD
Berkshire
Map **4** SU36

★★★**Bear** ☎(0488) 82512 Telex no 477575
RS 24–26 Dec
13th century roadside inn, once Charles I's Civil War HQ, it has well equipped (some noisy) bedrooms and good imaginative cooking.
13rm(9➡) Annexe: 15rm(12➡3fi)(3fb) 1 CTV in all bedrooms ® *sB£29.25

(room only) sB➡⋒£32.75 (room only) dB£36 (room only) dB➡⋒£41 (room only) Ƀ

60P ✽

French ♥ Lunch £7.45–£13.45&alc Dinner £8.45–£14.45&alc Wine £4.80 Last dinner 9.30pm

Credit cards [1] [2] [3] [5]

HUNMANBY
North Yorkshire
Map **8** TA07

★★**Wrangham House** Stonegate ☎ Scarborough (0723) 891333
Closed Dec & Jan

9rm (2➡5⋒) (1fb) sB&B£11.50–£13 sB&B➡⋒£12.50–£20 dB&B£23–£26 dB&B➡⋒£25–£28 Ƀ

CTV 20P ✽ nc5yrs

Dinner £7 Wine £3.75 Last dinner 7pm

Credit cards [1] [3]

HUNSTANTON
Norfolk
Map **9** TF64

★★**Le Strange Arms** Sea Front, Old Hunstanton ☎ (04853) 2810

29rm (8➡4⋒) (4fb) Ⓡ sB&B£16–£17.50 sB&B➡⋒£17–£18.50 dB&B£32–£35 dB&B➡⋒£34–£37 Ƀ

☾ CTV 150P 8 ✽ billiards Live music and dancing mthly *xmas*

V ♥ Lunch £6&alc Tea £1 High Tea £2–£4 Dinner £6.50–£8&alc Wine £5 Last dinner 9pm

S%

★**Wash & Tope** Le Strange Ter ☎ (04853) 2250

11rm (2fb) CTV in all bedrooms Ⓡ sB&B£11.50–£13 dB&B£23–£25 Ƀ

CTV 12P 4 Live music and dancing Fri Cabaret Sat *xmas*

English & French V ♥ Lunch fr£4.95 Tea fr60p High Tea fr£1.50 Dinner fr£5.95&alc Wine £4.50

Credit cards [1] [3]

HUNSTRETE
Avon
Map **3** ST66

HUNTINGDON
Cambridgeshire
Map **4** TL27

★★★**Old Bridge** ☎ (0480) 52681 Telex no 32706

22➡ CTV in all bedrooms ✱sB&B➡£29.50–£35 dB&B➡£43–£45 Ƀ

☾ 100P ✽ 18

V ♥ ✱Bar lunch fr£1.95alc Dinner fr£7.35alc Wine £5.80 Last dinner 10.30pm

S% Credit cards [1] [2] [3] [5]

★★**George** George St (Trusthouse Forte) ☎ (0480) 53096

25rm (16➡1⋒) (2fb) CTV in all bedrooms Ⓡ sB&B£33 sB&B➡⋒£35.50 dB&B£45.50 dB&B➡⋒£49.50 Ƀ

71P *xmas*

♥ Last dinner 9.30pm

Credit cards [1] [2] [3] [4] [5]

❀★★★ **HUNSTRETE HOUSE, HUNSTRETE**

Chelwood ☎ Compton Dando (07618) 578 Telex no 449540
Closed 1st wk Jan

(Rosette awarded for dinner only)

Although the cities of Bristol, Bath and Wells are only a 20 minute drive away, this impressive Georgian manor house is very much in the country, standing in 90 acres of garden, pasture land and woodland. This year the pasture at the front of the house has become a small deer park. The essence of this country house hotel is comfort and care. These aspects should be the key word for all hotel keepers but here they are unique. Public rooms and the spacious bedrooms are furnished with a great deal of flair and imagination, reflecting the artistic taste of Mrs Dupays, who is actually a painter. There are comfortable sitting areas, also beautifully decorated and provided with collections of books, antiques and paintings, some by Mrs Dupays. There is also a quaint little bar.

As in the past, inspectors and members have found the cooking to be of a good standard. It is basically country house style cooking but includes some French dishes reflecting the background of their French chef. The menu is changed daily so seasonal dishes and their own garden produce are well in evidence. With its warmth and hospitality, the decor and appointments, as well as the beautiful surroundings you will be delighted with the stay here and although not cheap, it undoubtedly represents value for money.

13➡ Annexe: 7➡2 CTV in all bedrooms sB&B➡⋒£48–£56 dB&B➡⋒£76–£96 Continental breakfast Ƀ

40P ✽ (heated) nc9yrs *xmas*

French V ♥ Buffet lunch £8–£12 Tea fr£2 Dinner £18alc Wine £7 Last dinner 9.30pm

S% Credit cards [2] [3] [4]

H

At **Brampton** (3m W junc A1/A604)

☆☆☆**Brampton** (Kingsmead) ☎(0480) 810434

17🛁 250P

HUNTLY
Grampian *Aberdeenshire*
Map **15** NJ53

★★**Castle** ☎(0466) 2696
Closed Jan & Feb

24rm(7🛁2🚿)(2fb) 1 Ⓡ sB&B£14.50–£16.50 sB&B🛁🚿£16.50–£18.50 dB&B£26–£28 dB&B🛁🚿£28–£31 B

CTV 20P 3 ✽

V ☕ Lunch £3.50–£4 Tea £1–£1.50 High Tea £3.30–£4.60 Dinner £6.50–£7.50 Wine £4.35 Last dinner 10pm

Credit cards 3 5

★★***Gordon Arms*** The Square ☎(0466) 2536
Commercial hotel in town centre.

14rm Ⓡ

CTV 6P ✽

V ☕ Last dinner 8.15pm

Credit cards 1 2 3 5

HURLEY
Berkshire
Map **4** SU88

★★**Ye Olde Bell** ☎Littlewick Green (062882) 4244 Telex no 847035
Remarkable, two-storey, black and white inn, dating back to 1135.

11rm(10🛁1🚿) Annexe: 8🛁 CTV in all bedrooms Ⓡ sB&B🛁🚿£29.50 dB&B🛁🚿£35

100P ✽

International V ☕ Lunch £9&alc Dinner £12&alc Wine £5 Last dinner 9.30pm

Credit cards 1 2 3 5

HURST GREEN
Lancashire
Map **7** SD63

★★*B* **Shireburn Arms** ☎Stonyhurst (025486) 208
A 17th-century coaching inn, family owned and run, and furnished with several fine antiques.

10rm(6🛁1🚿) TV in all bedrooms Ⓡ sB&B fr£16 sB&B🛁🚿£20.50 dB&B fr£26 dB&B🛁🚿 fr£52

CTV 16P ✽

French & Italian Lunch £8alc Dinner £8alc Wine £2.35

Credit card 3

HURSTPIERPOINT
West Sussex
Map **4** TQ21

✕**Barrons** 120 High St ☎(0273) 832183
A small country town restaurant providing simple fare including excellent home made soups.

Closed Sun Lunch not served Mon & Sat

English & French V 32 seats Lunch £6.95–£12.50 Dinner £6.95–£12.50 Wine £4.65 Last dinner 10.30pm

S% Credit cards 1 2 3 4 **VS**

HYTHE
Kent
Map **5** TR13

★★★★**Hotel Imperial** Princes Pde (Best Western) ☎(0303) 67441 Telex no 965082
Imposing sea front hotel with golf course, swimming pool and squash courts.

83rm(81🛁2🚿)(5fb) 2 CTV in all bedrooms Ⓡ ✱ sB&B🛁🚿£30 dB&B🛁🚿£54 B

Lift ☾ 120P 10 CFA ✽ (heated) (hard & grass) squash billiards sauna bath Live music and dancing Sat *xmas*

English & French V ☕ ✱ Lunch £5.95&alc Tea fr60p High Tea fr£3.50 Dinner £9.50&alc Wine £4.90 Last dinner 9pm

Credit cards 1 2 3 5

★★★**Stade Court** West Pde (Best Western) ☎(0303) 68263 Telex no 965082
Comfortable, efficient hotel with sea views, sharing leisure facilities with Hotel Imperial.

32rm(26🛁🚿)(4fb) Ⓡ sB&B£18.50 sB&B🛁🚿£20 dB&B£33.50 dB&B🛁🚿£36 B

Lift CTV 20P 2 CFA *xmas*

English & French V ☕ Lunch £4.50&alc Tea 60p–65p Dinner £7.50–£8&alc Wine £4.40 Last dinner 9pm

Credit cards 1 2 3 5 **VS**

★**Swan** 59 High St ☎(0303) 66236
Closed Xmas Day
Small, family-run inn, with comfortable bedrooms and friendly service.

9rm(2fb) sB&B£14.50 dB&B£26.50

CTV 12P

English & Italian V ☕ Lunch fr£4 Tea fr50p Dinner fr£5.50 Wine £4.80 Last dinner 9pm

Credit cards 1 2 3 5

IGHTHAM
Kent
Map **5** TQ55

✿✕✕**Town House** ☎Borough Green (0732) 884578
Closed Sun, Mon, 24–30 Dec, 3 wks Feb & 2 wks Oct

International 34 seats Lunch £7–£8.50&alc Dinner £14.95alc Wine £4.95 Last dinner 9.45pm 12P

S% Credit cards 1 2 3 5

ILFRACOMBE
Devon
Map **2** SS54

★★**Carlton** Runnacleave Rd ☎(0271) 62446
Closed Dec–Mar (except Xmas)
Detached holiday and touring hotel with popular bar, located in the centre of town.

48rm(11🛁11🚿)(8fb) sB&B£11–£12 sB&B🛁🚿£12–£13 dB&B£22–£24 dB&B🛁🚿£24–£26 B

Lift ☾ CTV 16P Live music and dancing nightly *xmas*

☕ Lunch £2–£3.50 Tea 45p Dinner £7 Wine £3.40 Last dinner 8pm

Credit card 1 **VS**

★★**Cliffe Hydro** Hillsborough Rd ☎(0271) 63606
Closed Dec–Mar
Privately owned and run coaching hotel with fine views of the harbour.
37rm(17⇌5⋒)(7fb) *sB&B£11–£14 sB&B⇌⋒£12–£15 dB&B£24–£28 dB&B⇌⋒£26–£32
Lift CTV 6P ✽ Disco Fri (in season) Live music and dancing 3 nights wkly
Lunch £3.50–£4.50 Tea 50p Dinner £5–£7 Wine £4.15 Last dinner 6.30pm

★★**Harleigh House** Wilder Rd ☎(0271) 63850
RS Oct–May
Centrally located, holiday hotel.
12rm(10⇌) sB&B£7–£12 sB&B⇌£7–£12 dB&B£12–£20 dB&B⇌£12–£20
CTV Live music and dancing *xmas*
Lunch £2–£3 Tea 75p Dinner £3.50–£4.50 Wine £4 Last dinner 8pm

★★ *L* **Imperial** ☎(0271) 62536
Closed Oct–Mar
Large coach and holiday hotel with views over the sea.
100rm(14⇌35⋒) CTV in 10 bedrooms sB&B£12–£14 sB&B⇌⋒£14–£16 dB&B£24–£28 dB&B⇌⋒£28–£32
Lift ☾ CTV 12P Live music and dancing 6 nights wkly
*Lunch £3.75–£4.75 Tea 75p–£1.50 Dinner £5.50–£7 Wine £4.80 Last dinner 8pm

★★**Lee Manor** Lee (3m W on unclass road) ☎(0271) 63920
Closed Oct–mid Apr
Mock-Elizabethan manor, set in 40 acres of wooded grounds.
12rm(4⇌7⋒) CTV in all bedrooms Ⓡ *sB&B£10–£22 sB&B⇌⋒£14–£27 dB&B⇌⋒£20–£44
25P ✽
*Dinner fr£6.50&alc Wine £4.25 Last dinner 9.30pm

★★***St Helier*** Hillsborough Rd ☎(0271) 63862 Closed Nov–Mar RS Apr & Oct
Privately-owned and run holiday touring hotel with its own gardens.
32rm(5⇌) TV available on request
CTV 20P 12 ✽ Disco wkly
English, Austrian, French & Italian
Last dinner 8pm

★★**Tracy House** Belmont Rd ☎(0271) 63933 Closed Nov
Small, privately-owned hotel in a secluded position outside the centre of Ilfracombe.
11rm(4⇌4⋒)(2fb) CTV in 4 bedrooms TV in 2 bedrooms sB&B£12.50–£14 sB&B⇌⋒£15.50–£16.50 dB&B£22–£25 dB&B⇌⋒£28–£31 B
CTV 11P 1 ✽ (heated)
English & Continental Dinner £7.50alc Wine £3.50 Last dinner 8pm
S% **VS**

★**Torrs** Torrs Pk ☎(0271) 62334
Holiday hotel in a quiet situation, personally run by the owners.
14rm(3⇌6⋒)(3fb) Ⓡ sB&B£9–£12.25 sB&B⇌⋒£15.35–£25.35 dB&B£18–£24.50 dB&B⇌⋒£20.70–£27.25 B
CTV 16P *xmas*
Lunch £3.50–£8 Tea 55p–£3 Dinner £3.50–£8 Wine £1.90 Last dinner 7.30pm
Credit cards 1 2 3 5 **VS**

ILKLEY
West Yorkshire
Map **7** SE14

★★★**Cow & Calf** Moor Top ☎(0943) 607335
Large, comfortable stone house overlooking River Wharfe.
17rm(9⇌3⋒) 1 CTV in all bedrooms Ⓡ sB&B£20 sB&B⇌⋒£25 dB&B£27 dB&B⇌⋒£35 B
98P 2 ✽
V Lunch £3alc Tea 75p High Tea £3.25 Dinner £8alc Wine £4.50 Last dinner 9.30pm
Credit cards 1 2 3 4 5

★★★**Craiglands** Cowpasture Rd (Trusthouse Forte) ☎(0943) 607676
Telex no 51137
Converted and extended 19th-century mansion in its own grounds, on the edge of the moor.
46rm(40⇌)(3fb) CTV in all bedrooms Ⓡ sB&B£29.50 sB&B⇌£36.50 dB&B£42 dB&B⇌£52.50 B
Lift ☾ 200P 8 CFA ✽ (hard) billiards *xmas*
Last dinner 9.30pm
Credit cards 1 2 3 4 5

★★**Greystones** 1 Ben Rhydding Rd ☎(0943) 607408
Converted stone built residence in its own secluded grounds and gardens.
10rm(5⇌3⋒)(1fb) Ⓡ sB&B fr£15 sB&B⇌⋒ fr£23 dB&B fr£25 dB&B⇌⋒ fr£30 B
CTV 15P ✽ *xmas*
English & French Lunch fr£5.75 High Tea £2.50–£4 Dinner £7.50–£10 Wine £3.50 Last dinner 9.30pm
Credit cards 1 2 3 5

★★**Lister's Arms** Skipton Rd ☎(0943) 608698
Three-storey, stone-built, coaching inn near the town centre with an attractive rear garden.
17rm(5⇌)(2fb) Ⓡ sB&B£18–£19 sB&B⇌£24–£25 dB&B£24–£25 dB&B⇌£28–£30 B
CTV 150P 3 ✽ Disco 6 nights wkly *xmas*
English & French Lunch £4.50–£4.80 Tea fr75p High Tea fr£4.80 Dinner fr£5.80&alc Wine £3.25 Last dinner 8.45pm

★ *B* **Grove** 66 The Grove ☎(0943) 600298
Closed Dec–mid Jan
Three storey and semi-detached, stone Victorian building, situated close to the town centre.
6rm(2⇌)(2fb) CTV in 2 bedrooms Ⓡ sB&B fr£15 sB&B⇌ fr£20 dB&B fr£20 dB&B⇌ fr£25
CTV 4P nc5yrs →

Lunch £4.50&alc Dinner £6.50&alc Last dinner 7.30pm
Credit cards 1 3

ILKLEY

Church St ☎ (0943) 608484

Though they still do not succumb to the fashion for nouvelle cuisine here, but base their daily set menu on the best of classic traditions, the cooking, under Michael Lawson, achieves the same sort of light delicacy, with honest flavours and careful seasoning. The bar and dining rooms are opulently decorated and furnished, with a profusion of paintings and ornaments, some particularly fine china, and fresh flowers.
Have an aperitif in the bar while you choose your meal from the new à la carte menu. Mr Brian Womersley is in charge of the restaurant and he will advise you well and courteously. Our members have praised the boudin blanc au Roquefort, the old favourite mousseline de sole reputation and the delicious tortellini amongst the first courses. The soups, too are always enjoyable. Among the main courses, the noisettes of lamb, saddle of hare and salmon dishes have been enjoyed, enhanced by their delicate sauces. Puddings are always delicious and universally popular. The wine list is long and comprehensive, reflecting the keen interest of the owners of this restaurant. With its friendly and attentive, yet informal, service it remains one of the finest restaurants in the country under the caring ownership of Colin Long and Malcolm Reid who have dedicated themselves to it for so many years.

Closed Sun & Mon Lunch not served
French 50 seats Dinner £15alc Wine £6.95 Last dinner 9.30pm
Credit cards 1 2 3 5 **VS**

I

✕**Sabera** 9 Wells Rd ☎ (0943) 607104
Closed Xmas Day
English & Indian **V** 44 seats Lunch £2.50&alc Dinner £4.50 alc Wine £3.25 Last dinner mdnt
Credit cards 1 3 **VS**

ILMINSTER
Somerset
Map **3** ST31

★★★**Horton Cross** ☎ (04605) 2144
Modern, purpose-built hotel, with easy access and car park.
23 (7fb) CTV in all bedrooms Ⓡ sB £20.24 (room only) dB £27.83 (room only)
CTV 60P CFA ✽ Live music and dancing Sat mthly *xmas*
English & Continental **V** Lunch £4.45 Tea 35p Dinner £6.50alc Wine £3.50 Last dinner 9.30pm
Credit cards 1 2 3 4 5 **VS**

★★**Shrubbery** ☎ (04605) 2108
Privately-owned hotel catering mainly for touring/business clientele and functions.
12rm (6 2) (3fb) CTV in all bedrooms Ⓡ sB&B £12.50–£16 sB&B £16–£20 dB&B £25–£27.50 dB&B £30–£35
100P ✽ (heated) Live music & dancing wkly
Lunch £6–£6.50 Tea £1.25 Dinner £8.50–£10&alc Wine £4.50 Last dinner 9.30pm
Credit cards 1 2 3 4 5 **VS**

INCHNADAMPH
Highland *Sutherland*
Map **14** NC22

★★***Inchadamph*** ☎ Assynt (05712) 202
Closed Nov–Feb
30rm (7)
TV 30P 4
Last dinner 8pm
Credit cards 1 2 5

INGLESHAM
Wiltshire
Map **4** SU29

✕✕**Inglesham Forge** ☎ Faringdon (0367) 52298
Closed Sun & 25–30 Dec
Lunch not served Mon & Sat
French 35 seats ✱Lunch £18alc Dinner £16alc Wine £4.75 Last dinner 10pm 15P
S% Credit cards 1 2 3 5

INSTOW
Devon
Map **2** SS43

★★★***Commodore*** Marine Pde ☎ (0271) 860347 Closed Xmas
Modern, white stucco building in its own grounds with views of the estuary and the sea.
21rm (20 1) CTV in all bedrooms Ⓡ
150P ✽ Live music and dancing wkly (out of season)
English, French & Spanish
Credit cards 2 3

INVERARAY
Strathclyde *Argyllshire*
Map **10** NN00

★***Fernpoint*** Ferryland ☎ (0499) 2170
Closed Nov–Feb
Built in 1751, the adjoining stables of this historic building have been converted into a Jacobean bar.
6rm (5) CTV in 5 bedrooms Ⓡ
CTV 12P
Last dinner 10pm
Credit cards 1 2 3

INVERGARRY
Highland *Inverness-shire*
Map **14** NH30

★★ *L* **Glengarry Castle** ☎ (08093) 254
Closed 19 Oct–11 Apr
Ruins of Invergarry Castle are to be found in the grounds of this Victorian mansion.
30rm (17) (4fb) Ⓡ sB&B £14–£16 sB&B £18.50–£20.50 dB&B £24–£28 dB&B £29–£33

CTV 45P 2🚗✽ ⛳(hard) 🎣
V 🍵 Lunch fr£4.50 Tea fr£1.50 Dinner £7–£7.50 Wine £3.60 Last dinner 8.15pm
Credit cards 1 5

INVERKEITHING
Fife
Map **11** NT18

★**Queens** Church St ☎(0383) 413075
Stone built inn dating from 1880.
13rm (3fb) Ⓡ sB&B£14 dB&B£22
CTV 40P
British & French 🍵 Lunch £4 High Tea £4–£5.25 Dinner £6.50&alc Wine £3.50 Last dinner 9pm

INVERKIP
Strathclyde *Renfrewshire*
Map **10** NS27

★★***Langhouse*** Langhouse Rd ☎Wemyss Bay (0475) 521211
Converted private house situated on hill overlooking the Firth of Clyde.
8rm (3🛁) Ⓡ
CTV 30P
🍵 Last dinner 9.30pm

INVERMORISTON
Highland *Inverness-shire*
Map **14** NH41

★★**Glenmoriston Arms** Glenmoriston ☎Glenmoriston (0320) 51206 Telex no 75529
Closed Nov–Mar
8rm (6🛁) Ⓡ sB&B£14 dB&B£28 dB&B🛁£32
CTV 24P ✽ 🎣
V 🍵 Bar lunch £3.50alc Dinner £8.50alc Wine £4 Last dinner 8pm
Credit cards 1 2 3

INVERNESS
Highland *Inverness-shire*
Map **14** NH64
See plan

★★★★ ***HBL* Culloden House** (2m E off A96) (Prestige) ☎(0463) 790461 Telex no 75402 Plan **4** *D3*
A charming stately mansion set in 40 acres of parkland, this well appointed hotel offers a high standard of comfort in a house of Georgian elegance. The delightful bedrooms are spacious and have a wide range of facilities.
20🛁 3 CTV in all bedrooms sB&B🛁£49 dB&B🛁£75–£99
☾ 50P 3🚗 ✽ ⛳(hard) sauna bath *xmas*
Scottish & French V 🍵 Lunch £11 Tea £3.50 Dinner £17.50 Wine £5 Last dinner 9.30pm
Credit cards 1 2 3 5 **VS**

☆☆☆**Caledonian** Church St (Allied (Scotland) ☎(0463) 235181 Telex no 76357 Plan **2** *B2*
Large, commercial and coach tour hotel.
120rm (60🛁60) CTV in all bedrooms Ⓡ ✽sB&B🛁 £25 dB&B🛁 £40 ℞
Lift ☾ 40P CFA billiards *xmas*
🍵 Last dinner 9pm
Credit cards 1 2 3 4 5

★★★ ***HBL* Kingsmills** Damfield Rd (Best Western) ☎(0463) 237166 Telex no 75566 Plan **11** *D1*
A tastefully modernised old house with historic associations including Robert Burns and fugitives from the Battle of →

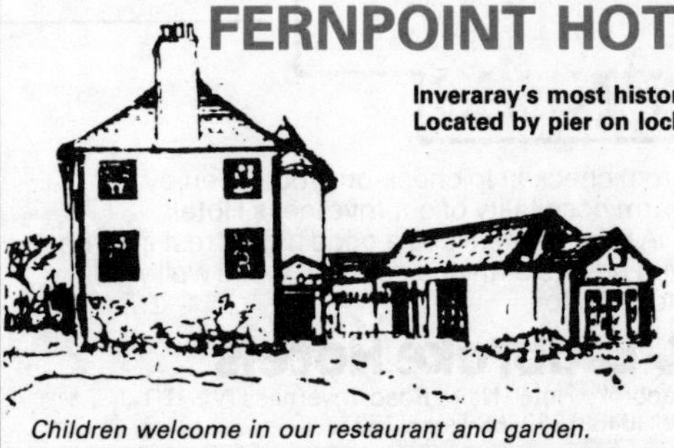

Culloden. Design and décor are beautifully co-ordinated here with some specially made furniture. Modern bedroom wings overlook the well tended garden.

54⇌⋒ (12fb) CTV in all bedrooms ® sB&B⇌⋒ £33.50–£41.50 dB&B⇌⋒ £46–£58 ⛿

☾ CTV 100P ✿ squash

International Lunch £5.50alc Tea 75p–£2 High Tea £4.50alc Dinner £7.75–£9.75&alc Wine £5.50 Last dinner 9.45pm

Credit cards 1 2 3 4 5

Inverness

☆☆☆**Ladbroke** (& Conferencentre) Nairn Rd (junction A9/A96) (Ladbroke) ☎(0463) 239666 Telex no 75377 Plan **12** *D3*

Modern hotel on the eastern edge of the town.

108⇌ (15fb) CTV in bedrooms ® *sB⇌ fr£31.50 (room only) dB⇌ fr£43 (room only) ⛿

Lift ☾ 150P Disco 3 nights wkly

International *Lunch fr£6.50 Dinner fr£8.50 Last dinner 10pm

Credit cards 1 2 3 5

★★★***Station*** 18 Academy St ☎(0463) 231926 Telex no 75275 Plan **17** *C3* Closed 24 Dec–3 Jan

Traditional railway hotel whose features are a pillared foyer and an ornate staircase.

61rm(48⇌6⋒) CTV in all bedrooms ® ⛿ Lift ☾ 10P

European **V** Last dinner 9pm

Credit cards 1 2 3 4 5 **VS**

★★**Beaufort** 11 Culduthel Rd ☎(0463) 222897 Plan **1** *C1*

A stone building with an extension, situated in a residential area near the town centre.

21⋒ CTV in all bedrooms sB&B⋒£20–£21 dB&B⋒£35–£36 B
53P ⛟ ♿ *xmas*
V ✿ ☕ Bar lunch £2.50–£5 Dinner £5–£10&alc Wine £5.25 Last dinner 10pm
Credit cards 1 2 3

★★**Craigmonie** 9 Annfield Rd ☎(0463) 231649 Plan **3** *D1*
Gabled and turreted red sandstone mansion dating from 1832, with a modern extension.
29➡⋒ (5fb) 1⊟ CTV in all bedrooms ® sB&B➡⋒£15.50–£22 dB&B➡⋒£28–£38 B

60P Disco twice wkly Live music and dancing twice wkly *xmas*
V ✿ ☕ Lunch £2.50–£4.75 Tea 75p–85p Dinner £7.50–£8.50&alc Wine £4.50 Last dinner 9.30pm
Credit cards 1 2 3 5
See advert on page 326

★★**Cummings** Church St ☎(0463) 232531 Plan **5** *D3*
Modernised, commercial and tourist hotel.

38rm(4➡1⋒) (2fb) sB&B£15–£17 dB&B£28–£32 dB&B➡⋒£32–£36
Lift ☾ CTV 25P Cabaret 6 nights wkly (Jun–Sep)
✿ Lunch £3.25–£3.75&alc High Tea £3.50–£4.75&alc Dinner £5.50–£6.75&alc Wine £3 Last dinner 8pm
VS

★★**Drumossie** Perth Rd ☎(0463) 236451 Telex no 777967 (att Clan) Plan **7** *D3*
Hotel situated on high ground overlooking town.
81rm(42➡9⋒) Annexe: 20➡ (1fb) 1⊟ →

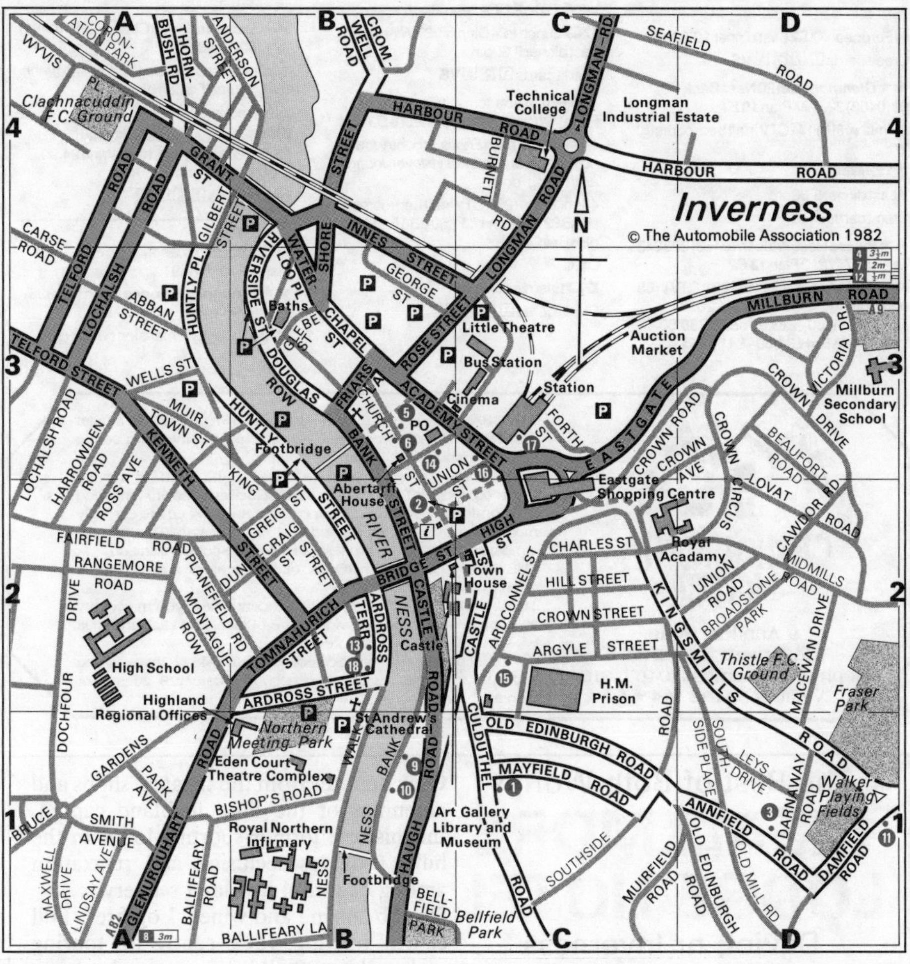
Inverness
© The Automobile Association 1982
A
B
C
D
4
3
2
1
Harbour Road
Longman Road
Longman Industrial Estate
Technical College
Seafield Road
Millburn Road
A9
Eastgate
Eastgate Shopping Centre
Station
Auction Market
Little Theatre
Bus Station
Cinema
Academy Street
Union St
Church St
High St
Bridge St
Castle Street
Castle Road
Ness Bank
River Ness
Castle
Town House
Abertarff House
Baths
Footbridge
Huntly Street
Douglas Row
Friars Bank
Chapel St
Shore Street
Innes Street
George St
Rose Street
Waterloo Pl
Riverside St
Glebe St
Grant St
Gilbert Street
Huntly Pl
Telford Road
Lochalsh Road
Telford Street
Carse Road
Abban Street
Wells St
Muirtown St
Kenneth Street
King St
Greig St
Craig St
Dunbar St
Tomnahurich Street
Ardross Street
Ardross Terr
Fairfield Road
Rangemore Road
Dochfour Drive
Planefield Rd
Montague Row
Harrowden Road
Ross Ave
High School
Highland Regional Offices
Northern Meeting Park
St Andrew's Cathedral
Eden Court Theatre Complex
Bishop's Road
Royal Northern Infirmary
Ballifeary Road
Ballifeary La
Ness Walk
Haugh Road
Bellfield Park
Art Gallery Library and Museum
Culduthel Road
Old Edinburgh Road
Mayfield Road
Southside Road
Ardconnel St
Charles St
Hill Street
Crown Street
Argyle Street
H.M. Prison
Royal Academy
Kingsmills Road
Crown Road
Crown Ave
Crown Circus
Crown Drive
Victoria Dr.
Millburn Secondary School
Beaufort Road
Lovat Road
Cawdor Rd
Midmills Road
Union Road
Broadstone Park
Macewan Drive
Thistle F.C. Ground
Fraser Park
Walker Playing Fields
Annfield Road
Damfield Road
Darnaway Road
Leys Drive
Southside Place
Muirfield Road
Old Mill Rd
Old Edinburgh Road
Clachnacuddin F.C. Ground
Wyvis Pl
Coronation Park
Thornbush Rd
Anderson Street
Cromwell Road
Burnett Rd
Glenurquhart Road
A82
Gardens
Park Ave
Bruce
Smith Avenue
Maxwell Drive
Lindsay Ave
Footbridge
3m
8
3½m
2m
½m

Inverness

1	Beaufort ★★	5	Cummings ★★	10	Glenmoriston ★★	15	Redcliffe ★
2	Caledonian ☆☆☆	6	Dickens ✕✕	11	Kingsmill ★★★	16	Royal ★★
3	Craigmonie ★★	7	Drumossie ★★	12	Ladbroke ☆☆☆	17	Station ★★★
4	Culloden House ★★★★	8	Dunain Park ❀★★	13	Palace ★★	18	Tower ★
		9	Glen Mhor ★★	14	Queensgate ★★		

CTV in 52 bedrooms Ⓡ sB&B£17–£21 sB&B🛁 £19–£22.50 dB&B£30–£36 dB&B🛁 £34–£40 B

☾ CTV 120P CFA ✽ Live music and dancing 3 nights wkly in season xmas

Lunch fr£4.50 Dinner fr£8.50 Wine £4.50 Last dinner 8.30pm

Credit cards 1 2 3 5 VS

★★ ***Glen Mhor*** 10 Ness Bank (Inter Hotels) ☎(0463) 234308 Plan **9** *B1*
Closed 31 Dec–5 Jan

Conversion of Tarradale stone mansion dating from 1870, in a quiet residential area of the town.

26rm(6🛁 8) CTV in all bedrooms Ⓡ B 16P

European Last dinner 10.30pm

Credit cards 1 2 3 5 VS

★★ ***Glenmoriston*** 20 Ness Bank ☎(0463) 223777 Plan **10** *B1*

21rm(2🛁 8) 1 CTV in all bedrooms Ⓡ

☾ # P ✽

V Last dinner 8.30pm

Credit cards 1 3

★★ **Palace** Ness Walk ☎(0463) 223243 Telex no 777210 Plan **13** *B2*

41rm(9🛁) Annexe: 41🛁 (13fb) CTV in 65 bedrooms Ⓡ sB&B£17.50–£20.90 sB&B🛁 £19.50–£23.90 dB&B£30.50–£35.30 dB&B🛁 £34.50–£41.30 B

Lift ☾ CTV 40P *xmas*

Lunch £3.25–£3.75 Tea 75p Dinner £8.90 Wine £3.50 Last dinner 9pm

Credit cards 1 2 3 5 VS

★★ **Queensgate** Queensgate ☎(0463) 237211 Plan **14** *B3*
Closed Xmas & New Year

Modernised, well-appointed tourist hotel of traditional sandstone blocks and set between shops.

60🛁 CTV in 32 bedrooms sB&B🛁 £15–£22.50 dB&B🛁 £25–£35 B

Lift ☾ CTV CFA sauna bath

Lunch fr£4 Dinner fr£7 Wine £3.75 Last dinner 9.30pm

Credit cards 1 2 5 VS

★★ **Royal** Academy St (Trusthouse Forte) ☎(0463) 230665 Plan **16** *C3*

In the image of an English country town hotel, there is an attractive foyer, lounge and dining room.

48rm(21🛁) (2fb) CTV in all bedrooms Ⓡ sB&B£21 sB&B🛁 £31.50 dB&B£34.50 dB&B🛁 £45 B

Lift ☾

Last dinner 9pm

Credit cards 1 2 3 4 5

★ ***Redcliffe*** 1 Gordon Ter ☎(0463) 232767 Plan **15** *C2*
Closed Nov–mid Apr

7rm(2🛁) Ⓡ

CTV 12P ✽

British & French Last dinner 8.30pm

★ **Tower** Ardross Ter ☎(0463) 232765 Plan **18** *B2*

Homely, commercial hotel, dating from 1875 but recently modernised.

10rm ✱ sB&B£13.50–£16.50 dB&B£27.70

CTV

V ✱ High Tea £3.50–£5.50 Last High Tea 8pm

✕✕ **Dickens** 77–79 Church St ☎(0463) 224450 Plan **6** *B3*

Sophisticated Chinese restaurant offering Oriental and French dishes.

Lunch not served Sun

International 64 seats ✱ Lunch fr£2.95&alc Dinner £10alc Wine £4.90 Last dinner 11pm

Credit cards 1 2 3 5

INVERSHIN

Highland *Sutherland*
Map **14** NH59

★★ **Aultnagar Lodge** (2½m N A836) ☎(054 982) 245

Mock Tudor style mansion built in 1910

and standing in 25 acres of tree studded land.

25rm(10➡2⋒)(4fb) sB&B fr£9 sB&B➡⋒ fr£10 dB&B fr£18 dB&B➡⋒ fr£20 B

CTV P ✽ Live music and dancing wkly ⌂ xmas

♡ ⊒ Dinner fr£6.75 Last dinner 8pm

★★ **H Invershin** ☏(054982) 202

Extended drovers inn dating from 1908 and standing in twenty-five acres.

12rm(5➡1⋒) Annexe: 12rm(6⋒)(2fb) CTV in 20 bedrooms TV in 4 bedrooms Ⓡ sB&B£10–£12 sB&B➡⋒£11–£13 dB&B£22–£26 dB&B➡⋒£24–£32

50P ✽ ♪ U ♿

V ⊒ Lunch £3–£6&alc Tea fr£1.25 High Tea £3–£6 Dinner £5–£7.50 Wine £3 Last dinner 9.30pm

Credit cards 1 3 5 **VS**

INVERURIE

Grampian *Aberdeenshire*
Map **15** NJ72

★ **Gordon Arms** The Square ☏(0467) 20314

Small family run hotel of unusual design.

11rm Ⓡ sB&B£12.75 dB&B£19.50

CTV P 🚌

♡ Lunch £3 High Tea £2.50 Dinner £5 Wine £3.90 Last dinner 7.45pm

Credit cards 1 3 5

✕ ***J.G.'s*** Market Pl ☏(0467) 21378

Popular, friendly town centre restaurant.

Closed Sun Dinner not served Mon

50 seats Last dinner 9.30pm 25P

I

IPSWICH
Suffolk
Map **5** TM14

★★★ ***B* Belstead Brook** Belstead Rd ☎(0473) 684241 Telex no 987674
Comfortable, hospitable hotel with country atmosphere.
26→⋒ Annexe: 6→⋒ (8fb) CTV in all bedrooms Ⓡ ✱ sB→⋒ £15–£38.50 (room only) dB→⋒ £28–£51 (room only) Ɓ
☾ 100P CFA ✽ ⌂ *xmas*
English & French V ♈ ☐ Lunch £8.50&alc Dinner £8.50&alc Wine £5.25 Last dinner 9.30pm
Credit cards 1 2 3 5 **VS**

★★★ **Golden Lion** Cornhill ☎(0473) 56645
Listed building in centre of city, thoroughly modernised to offer modern comfortable accommodation.
23rm(20→3⋒) CTV in all bedrooms Ⓡ
☾ 15P
♈ ☐

☆☆☆ **Ipswich Moat House** London Rd (3½m SW A12) (Queens Moat) ☎Copdock (047386) 444 Telex no 987207
47rm(39→) CTV in all bedrooms Ⓡ sB£25.30 sB→£34.10 dB£34.10 dB→£46.20 (room only) Ɓ
☾ 400P ✽ sauna bath Live music and dancing Sat ⌂ *xmas*
English & Continental ♈ ☐ ✻ Lunch £7.95 Tea 70p–£1.65 Dinner £8&alc Wine £5.06 Last dinner 9.20pm
Credit cards 1 2 3 5 **VS**

❀★★★ ***HB* Marlborough** 73 Henley Rd ☎(0473) 57677
Friendly hotel, tastefully modernised, serving good food.
22→ (3fb) CTV in all bedrooms sB&B→£36 dB&B→£46 Ɓ
☾ 60P ✽
English & French V ♈ ☐ Lunch £8.95&alc Tea £1.25–£1.60&alc Dinner £8.95&alc Wine £6.50 Last dinner 9.15pm
Credit cards 1 2 3 5

☆☆☆ **Post House** London Rd (Trusthouse Forte) ☎(0473) 212313 Telex no 987150
Modern holiday complex on the southern outskirts of the town.
118→ (51fb) CTV in all bedrooms Ⓡ sB&B→£40.50 dB&B→£53 Ɓ
☾ 175P CFA ✽ ⩯ (heated) *xmas*
♈ ☐ Last dinner 9.45pm
Credit cards 1 2 3 4 5

★★ **Crown & Anchor (Henekey's)** Westgate St (Trusthouse Forte) ☎(0473) 58506
56rm(24→4⋒) (2fb) CTV in all bedrooms Ⓡ sB&B£26 sB&B→⋒£29.50 dB&B£34.50 dB&B→⋒£41 Ɓ
☾ CTV 30P CFA *xmas*
Mainly grills ♈ ☐ Last dinner 10pm
Credit cards 1 2 3 4 5

★★ **Great White Horse** Tavern St (Trusthouse Forte) ☎(0473) 56558
Historic hotel having links with Dickens and George II.
55rm(10→) (2fb) 1 CTV in all bedrooms Ⓡ sB&B£31 sB&B→£33.50 dB&B£41.50 dB&B→£47.50 Ɓ
☾ CTV *xmas*
♈ ☐ Last dinner 9.15pm
Credit cards 1 2 3 4 5

IRVINE
Strathclyde *Ayrshire*
Map **10** NS33
See also Kilwinning

○ **Skean Dhu Irvine** Roseholme ☎(0294) 74272
128→
Due to have opened September 1983

ISLAY, ISLE OF
Strathclyde *Argyllshire*
Map **10**
See **Bowmore, Port Askaig** and **Port Ellen**

ISLE OF GIGHA
Strathclyde
See **Gigha Island**

ISLE OF MAN
Map **6**
Refer to location atlas (map **6**) for details of places with AA-appointed hotels and restaurants

ISLE OF WHITHORN
Dumfries & Galloway *Wigtownshire*
Map **11** NX43

★ **Queens Arms** ☎Whithorn (09885) 369
Small, family run hotel.
10rm(4→) (1fb) Ⓡ ✱ sB&B£10.50 dB&B£21 dB&B→£23
CTV 10P
♈ Bar lunch £2.10–£4.80 Dinner £7.25–£8.60&alc Wine £3.90 Last dinner 8.30pm
VS

ISLE OF WIGHT
Map **4**
Refer to location atlas (map **4**) for details of places with AA-appointed hotels and restaurants.

ISLE ORNSAY
Isle of Skye, Highland *Inverness-shire*
Map **13** NG61

★★ **Duisdale** ☎(04713) 202
Closed mid Oct–mid Apr
A 19th-century house in 60 acres of sheltered grounds, with moorings for visiting yachts.
24rm(5→) (2fb) Ⓡ ✻ sB&B£14 dB&B£28 dB&B→£34 Ɓ
CTV 30P ✽
♈ ☐ ✻ Lunch £4.30alc Tea £1.50 High Tea £4.75 Dinner £9.75 Wine £3.50 Last dinner 8.30pm
Credit card 1

★★ **Kinloch Lodge** (Minotel) ☎(04713) 214 Telex no 75442
Closed Xmas & New Year
Originally a shooting lodge, Lord & Lady MacDonald welcome guests to enjoy their hospitality and good food.

9rm(5⇌)® sB&B£17.20–£23.90 sB&B⇌£19.20–£23.90 dB&B£34.40–£47.80 dB&B⇌⋔£38.40–£47.80 Ɓ

CTV 30P ✽ ♿

♔☐ Tea 75p High Tea £3 Dinner £11.80 Wine £3.20 Last dinner 8.30pm

S% **VS**

★**Hotel Eilean Iarmain** Camus Croise, Sleat ☎(04713) 266 Telex no 75252

Converted house with turret featured extension. Close to quiet harbour.

7rm Annexe: 4rm 1⇌ sB&B£10–£13.50 dB&B£20–£26

20P

♔☐ Lunch £4–£5.50 Tea 50p–£1 High Tea £3–£4.50 Dinner £8–£10.50 Wine £4 Last dinner 8.30pm

S% **VS**

ISLES OF SCILLY
(No map)
See **Hugh Town, New Grimsby** and **Old Grimsby**

IVINGHOE
Buckinghamshire
Map **4** SP91

✕✕**Kings Head** ☎Cheddington (0296) 668264

Formerly a 17th-century posting house for coaches using the old Roman road.

Dinner not served Sun (Jan & Feb)

International **V** 55 seats ✱Lunch £11.22&alc Dinner £11.22&alc Wine £5.95 Last dinner 9.45pm 12P

S% Credit cards [1] [2] [3] [4] [5]

JEDBURGH
Borders *Roxburghshire*
Map **12** NT62

★★**Jedforest Country House** (3m S of Jedburgh off A68) ☎Camptown (08354) 274

Mansion dating from 1870, standing in 50 acres of tree studded parkland bordering the River Jed.

7rm Annexe: 4⋔ (3fb) TV in 6 bedrooms ® sB&B fr£14.50 sB&B⋔ fr£20 dB&B fr£22.50 dB&B⋔ fr£25.50

CTV 40P ✽

V♔ Bar lunch £1.95–£4.20 Dinner £6.50–£8 Wine £3.75 Last dinner 8.30pm

✕**Carters Rest** ☎(08356) 3414

Friendly, popular restaurant with Tudor decor and open kitchen, situated close to the Abbey.

Closed Sun (Oct–Etr)

Mainly grills 80 seats Lunch fr£4 Dinner £8alc Wine £4 Last dinner 9pm P

S% Credit cards [2] [3]

JERSEY
Channel Islands
Map **16**
Refer to location atlas (map **16**) for details of places with AA-appointed hotels and restaurants.

JEVINGTON
East Sussex
Map **5** TQ50

✕✕**Hungry Monk** ☎Polegate (03212) 2178

Closed 24 & 25 Dec Lunch not served Mon–Sat

English & French **V** 32 seats Lunch £9.40 Dinner £10.25 Wine £4.50 Last dinner 10.30pm 18P

VS

JOHN O'GROATS
Highland *Caithness*
Map **15** ND37

★★**John O'Groats House** ☎(095581) 203

RS Oct–Feb

Said to be the most northerly house on the British mainland, it overlooks the harbour with views across Stroma to the Orkneys.

17rm (1fb) sB&B£8–£12 dB&B£16–£24

CTV 100P ✽ billiards

Scottish & French **V**♔☐✱Lunch £3.25alc Tea 45p–£1.50&alc Dinner £3.75–£7&alc Last dinner 9pm

Credit cards [1] [3] [5]

★**Sea View** ☎(095581) 220

Stone building standing on the roadside overlooking Pentland Firth and the Isles of Stroma and Orkney.

9rm(1⇌1⋔)(1fb)® sB&B£7.50–£8 sB&B⇌⋔£9.50–£10 dB&B£15–£16 dB&B⇌⋔£19–£20

CTV 20P 2

V♔☐ Lunch fr£3.50 Tea fr75p High Tea fr£2.75 Dinner fr£5 Wine £5.25 Last dinner 8pm

JOHNSTONE BRIDGE
Dumfries & Galloway *Dumfriess-shire*
Map **11** NY19

★★**Dinwoodie Lodge** Main Rd ☎(05764) 289

Lodge house on the A74, positioned at the junction for Newton Wamphray.

9rm(2⋔)(3fb) TV in all bedrooms ® sB&B£16–£17 sB&B⋔£21–£22 dB&B£27–£29 dB&B⋔£35–£37 Ɓ

CTV 100P ✽ ♿

V♔☐ Lunch £4–£5&alc High Tea £4.60–£5.50&alc Dinner £5–£6.50&alc Wine £4 Last dinner 9.30pm

Credit cards [1] [2] [3] [5]

JURA, ISLE OF
Strathclyde *Argyllshire*
Map **10**
See Craighouse

KEGWORTH
Leicestershire
Map **8** SK42

★★★**Yew Lodge** 33 Packington Hill ☎(05097) 2518 Telex no 341995

Modernised and extended house near the village centre and close to the M1.

37rm(27⇌9⋔) CTV in all bedrooms ® sB&B£18.50 sB&B⇌⋔ £18.50–£27 dB&B⇌⋔£35–£38 Ɓ

Lift ☾ 70P

V♔☐ Lunch fr£3.30&alc Tea fr65p Dinner fr£4.95&alc Wine £3.90 Last dinner 10pm

Credit cards [1] [2] [3] **VS**

I

KEIGHLEY
West Yorkshire
Map **7** SE04

★★**Beeches** Bradford Rd ☎(0535) 607227
Converted Victorian manor house, ½m from the town centre.
10rm(2➡) Annexe: 14rm(9⋒) (6fb) CTV in 1 bedroom TV in 23 bedrooms Ⓡ ✻sB&B£11.30–£16.50 sB&B➡⋒£12–£19 dB&B£22.60–£26 dB&B➡⋒£23–£28
☾ TV 90P 2🏠✽ Disco
♆▭✻Lunch £5.20–£7.15 Tea fr£1 High Tea £1.75–£3 Dinner £5.20–£7.15 Wine £3.75
Last dinner 8.45pm
Credit cards 1 2 3

KEITH
Grampian *Banffshire*
Map **15** NJ45

★★**Royal** Church Rd ☎(05422) 2528
13rm(3➡) (1fb) sB&B£11–£12 sB&B➡£15–£16 dB&B£18.40–£20 dB&B➡£25.30–£27 Ɓ
CTV 20P 4🏠 *xmas*
V♆▭ Lunch £3.45–£4&alc Tea £1.15–£1.20&alc High Tea £3.50–£4.50&alc Dinner £6.50–£8&alc Wine £3.70 Last dinner 8.30pm
Credit cards 1 3 5

KELSO
Borders *Roxburghshire*
Map **12** NT73

★★★**Cross Keys** 36–37 The Square (Exec Hotel) ☎(0573) 23303
Modernised coaching inn standing in a cobbled square in the town centre.
26rm(9➡4⋒) (4fb) CTV in all bedrooms Ⓡ✻sB&B£16 sB&B➡⋒£19 dB&B£28 dB&B➡⋒£32
Lift ☾ CTV ⚑ billiards Disco Fri/Sat Live music and dancing Fri/Sat
▣Scottish, French & Italian V✻Lunch £4.90 Dinner £8.50&alc Wine £3.70 Last dinner 9pm
Credit cards 1 2 3 4 5

★★★***Ednam House*** Bridge St ☎(0573) 24168 Closed Xmas & New Year
Imposing Georgian mansion in its own gardens on banks of River Tweed.
32rm(19➡4⋒)
CTV 100P 2🏠✽
♆▭ Last dinner 9pm

★★**House O'Hill** ☎(0573) 24594
Closed 1st 2wks Jan
Two-storey house in an elevated position with superb views over the town and the River Tweed.
7rm(1➡) (2fb) CTV in 5 bedrooms ✻sB&B fr£15 dB&B fr£22 dB&B➡⋒£32 Ɓ
CTV 100P ✽ ⚲(hard) ♩ nc3yrs
V♆✻Lunch £4–£4.50 Dinner £8–£10 Wine £3.35 Last dinner 8.30pm

★**Queens Head** Bridge St ☎(0573) 24636
Former coaching inn dating from 1780.
9rm(1➡) (2fb) sB&B£10.30–£13.10 sB&B➡£11.80–£15.20 dB&B£18.90–£20.90 dB&B➡£21.80–£23.60
CTV
▣Scottish & French V♆ Bar lunch £3alc Dinner £6.95–£7.30 Wine £3.85 Last dinner 7.30pm
Credit card 1 **VS**

KENDAL
Cumbria
Map **7** SD59

★★★**County Thistle** Station Rd (Thistle) ☎(0539) 22461
31rm(24➡1⋒) CTV in all bedrooms Ⓡ ✻sB&B➡⋒£24.50–£26.50 dB&B➡⋒£36–£38.50 Ɓ
Lift ☾ ⚡40P
▣European ♆▭ Last dinner 8.45pm
Credit cards 1 2 3 4 5 **VS**

★★★**Woolpack Inn** Stricklandgate (Swallow) ☎(0539) 23852

One-time coaching inn now a modern hotel. The Crown Bar here was once Kendal's wool auction room.

58rm(48→10⋒)(5fb) CTV in all bedrooms Ⓡ sB&B→⋒£39.90 dB&B→⋒£39.90 B

☾ CTV 120P CFA *xmas*

▣English & French **V** ♔ ☐ Lunch fr£5.25&alc Dinner fr£8.25&alc Wine £4.75 Last dinner 9.30pm

Credit cards 1 2 3 4 5

★★**Shenstone Country** (2m S on A6) ☎(0539) 21023

Country-house style building set in three acres of grounds with lawns and beautiful trees.

13rm(2⋒)(2fb) sB&B£14 dB&B£27–£28 dB&B⋒£33

CTV 20P ✽

♔ ☐ Lunch £3.50 Tea 75p Dinner £5.50 Wine £3.50 Last dinner 8pm

S% Credit cards 2 3

❀✕**Castle Dairy** 26 Wildman St ☎(0539) 21170

(Rosette awarded for dinner only.)

Closed Sun, Mon & Tue Lunch not served

48 seats Dinner £12alc Wine £4.50 Last dinner 10pm

S% **VS**

KENILWORTH
Warwickshire
Map **4** SP27

★★★★**De Montfort** The Square (DeVere) ☎(0926) 55944 Telex no 311012

Six-storey building located in the centre of town.

100→ CTV in all bedrooms Ⓡ ✱sB→£31.50 (room only) dB→£42 (room only) B

Lift ☾ 85P CFA Live music and dancing Mon–Sat

▣English & French ♔ ☐ Lunch £5.80&alc Dinner £7&alc Wine £5.50 Last dinner 10pm

Credit cards 1 2 3 4 5 **VS**

★★★**Kenilworth Moat House** Chesford Bridge (Queens Moat) ☎(0926) 58331

Modern, purpose-built hotel, on the outskirts of Kenilworth.

48→ CTV in all bedrooms Ⓡ sB&B→£19–£27 dB&B→£26–£38 B

☾ 200P ✽ ♪ *xmas* ♿

▣English, French & Italian **V** ♔ ☐ Lunch £5.65&alc Tea £1 Dinner £6.65&alc Wine £4.50 Last dinner 9.30pm

Credit cards 1 2 3 4 5 **VS**

★★***Clarendon House*** High St ☎(0926) 54694

Popular, small hotel in Kenilworth old town.

14rm(6→3⋒) 2 B

CTV 20P ✽

▣International Last dinner 9pm

Credit cards 1 2 3 5

❀✕✕**Diments** 121–123 Warwick Rd ☎(0926) 53763

(Rosette awarded for dinner only.)

Closed Sun, Mon & 1st 3wks Aug
Lunch not served Sat

▣French 40 seats Lunch £4.75–£6&alc Dinner £9.95&alc Wine £5.50 Last dinner 10pm 12P

Credit cards 1 2 3 5 **VS**

✕✕**Romano's** 60 Waverley Rd ☎(0926) 57473

Closed Sun & Sep–Jul
Lunch not served Sat

▣English & Italian **V** 26 seats ✱Lunch fr£3.65&alc Dinner £10–£12&alc Wine £3.60 Last dinner 10.30pm 10P

Credit cards 2 3

✕**Restaurant Bosquet** 97a Warwick Rd ☎(0926) 52463

Closed Sun Lunch by reservation only

▣French 26 seats ✱Dinner fr£9.80&alc Wine £5.40 Last dinner 10pm

Credit card 3

✕**Ristorante Portofino** Talisman Sq ☎(0926) 57186

Closed Sun

▣Italian **V** 40 seats Lunch £2.95–£5&alc Dinner £5&alc Wine £4.25 Last dinner 10.30pm

Credit cards 1 2 **VS**

KENMORE
Tayside Perthshire
Map **14** NN74

★★★**Kenmore** Village Sq ☎(08873) 205

Historic, sporting hotel, forming the focal point of the village, and set at the eastern end of Loch Tay.

21→ Annexe: 17→(3fb) 1 CTV in 21 bedrooms ✱sB&B→£17–£19.50 dB&B→£34–£39 B

Lift CTV 100P ✽ ⛳18 ♪ *xmas*

▣Scottish & French ♔ ☐ ✱Lunch fr£5.50 Tea fr£1.50 Dinner fr£9.50 Wine £3.95 Last dinner 9pm

Credit cards 1 2 3

KENNFORD
Devon
Map **3** SX98

☆☆☆**Ladbroke** (on A38) (Ladbroke) ☎Exeter (0392) 832121

Modern hotel complex at foot of Telegraph Hill.

61→⋒(15fb) CTV in all bedrooms Ⓡ ✱sB&B→⋒fr£29 dB&B→⋒fr£37 B

☾ 300P ✽

V ♔ ☐ ✱Lunch fr£6.50 Dinner fr£8.50 Last dinner 9.45pm

Credit cards 1 2 3 5

★★***B*Fairwinds** ☎Exeter (0392) 832911

Closed 16 Dec–7 Jan

Well-appointed tourist and commercial hotel, personally owned and run.

7rm(3→2⋒) CTV in all bedrooms Ⓡ ★ sB&B£15–£17 sB&B→⋒£20–£22 dB&B→⋒£28–£30 B

9P nc12yrs

Lunch £2–£7.15 Tea 40p–60p Dinner £4.65–£7.15 Wine £3.40 Last dinner 8pm

VS

KENTALLEN
Highland *Argyllshire*
Map **14** NN05

❀★★***HBL*** **Ardsheal House** ☎Duror (063174) 227

Closed mid Oct–19 Apr

(Rosette awarded for dinner only.)

Superbly situated overlooking the length of Loch Linnhe this old house dates from 1760. It has been decorated and furnished in country house style and the Taylors provide an informal house party atmosphere with good food and traditional services. (See also p. 30).

12rm(6→2⋒) sB&B£28–£32 sB&B→⋒£32–£38 dB&B£36–£42 dB&B→⋒£42–£56

CTV 14P ✽ (hard) billiards

▣International ♔ ☐ Lunch £2.50–£4 Tea fr65p Dinner fr£13 Wine £4.50 Last dinner 8.30pm

VS

✕✕**Holly Tree** Kentallen Pier ☎Duror (063174) 292

Closed Wed, 13 Nov–15 Dec & Mon & Tue (16 Dec–Etr)

▣International **V** 65 seats Lunch £5.25 Tea 95p alc Dinner £8.50alc Wine £4.25 Last dinner 9.30pm 40P bedrooms available (lunch)

KERNE BRIDGE
Hereford & Worcester
Map **3** SO51

★★**Castle View** ☎Symonds Yat (0600) 890329

8rm(1→1⋒) Ⓡ sB&B£13.50–£14 sB&B→⋒£15.50–£16 dB&B£22–£23 dB&B→⋒£25.50–£26 B

CTV 50P *xmas*

▣English & Italian **V** ♔ ☐ Lunch £5&alc Tea 35p–£1 High Tea £2.50 Dinner £5.50&alc Wine £3.75 Last dinner 10pm

Credit cards 1 2 3 5 **VS**

KESWICK
Cumbria
Map **11** NY22 **See plan**
See map 11 for details of other hotels in the vicinity

K

K

★★★**Derwentwater** Portinscale (Inter-Hotels) ☎(0596) 72538 Telex 64418 Plan **3** *A5*

43rm(33⇌)(4fb) sB&B£22.50–£24.50 sB&B⇌⋒£24.50–£26.50 dB&B£35–£39 dB&B⇌⋒£39–£43 B

Lift ☾ CTV 60P ✽ ♪ billiards *xmas*

⊟English & French **V** ♡ ▭ Lunch £5.25 Tea 75p–£2.25 High Tea £5.25 Dinner £7.75&alc Wine £4.95 Last dinner 9pm

Credit cards 1 2 3 5 **VS**

★★★**Keswick** Station Rd (Trusthouse Forte) ☎(0596) 72020 Telex no 64200

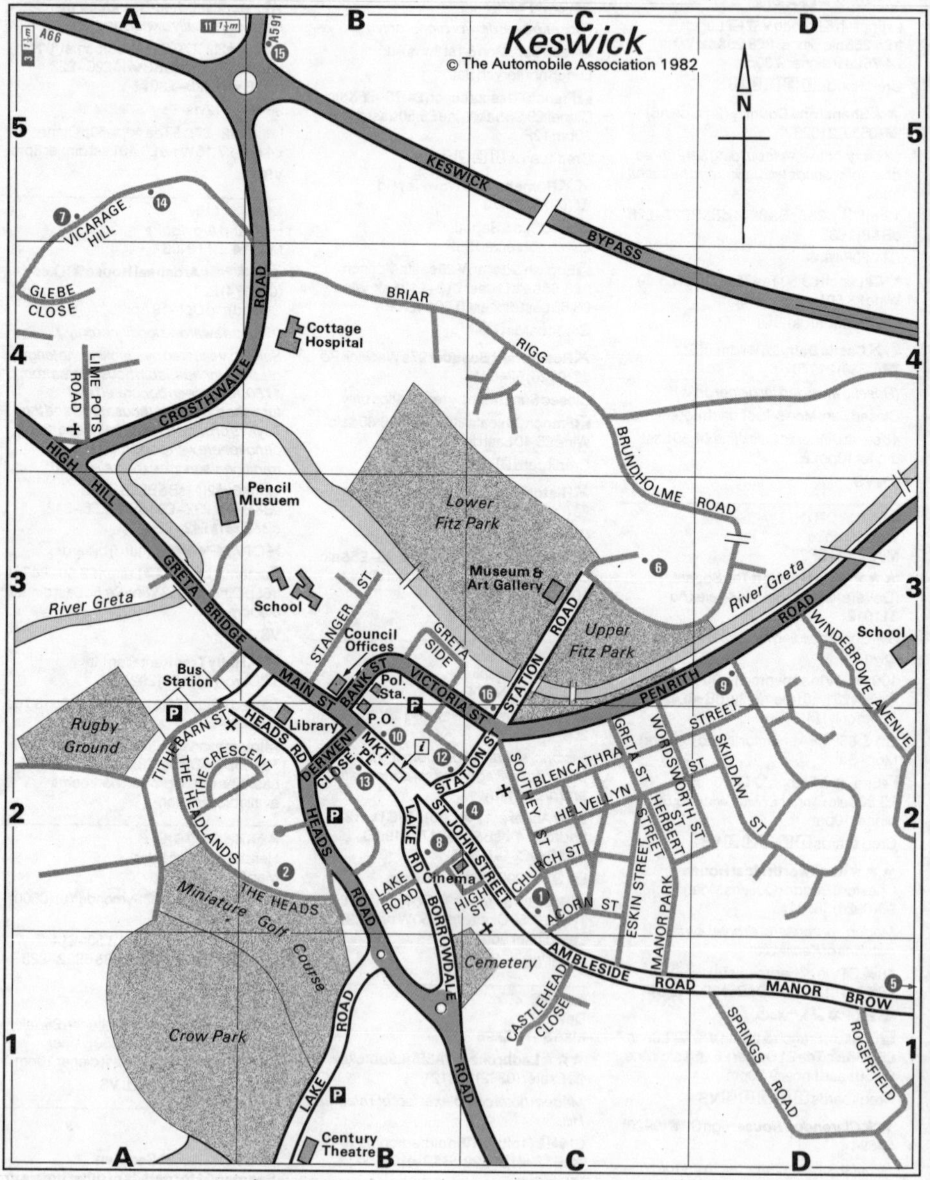

Keswick

© The Automobile Association 1982

Keswick

1 Chaucer House ★
2 Crow Park ★
3 Derwentwater ★★★
5 Grange ★★
6 Keswick ★★★
7 Lairbeck ★
8 Lake ★★
9 Millfield ★★
10 Queen's ★★
11 Red House ★★
12 Royal Oak ★★★
13 Skiddaw ★★
14 Skiddaw Grove ★
15 Underscar ★★
16 Walpole ★★

Plan **6** *C3*
Closed Jan & Feb
Charming, grand old hotel, situated in well tended grounds.
64⇌⋒ (4fb) CTV in all bedrooms ® sB&B⇌⋒ £32.50 dB&B⇌⋒ £50 B
Lift ☾ CTV 50P ✽ ⌂ *xmas*
♉ ☕ Last dinner 9pm
Credit cards 1 2 3 4 5

★★★**Royal Oak** Station St (Trusthouse Forte) ☎(0596) 72965 Plan **12** *B2*
Originating from Elizabethan times and once the centre of a thriving pack-horse trade, this hotel is now a centre for business and social functions.
66rm(26⇌4⋒) (8fb) CTV in all bedrooms ® sB&B£20.50 sB&B⇌⋒ £31 dB&B£33.50 dB&B⇌⋒ £44 B
Lift ☾ 42P CFA *xmas*
♉ ☕ Last dinner 9.15pm
Credit cards 1 2 3 4 5

★★ ***BL*** **Grange** Manor Brow ☎(0596) 72500 Plan **5** *D1*
Charming graceful hotel, with many antiques and set in its own gardens.
12rm(3⇌6⋒) (2fb) 3⊟ CTV in 12 bedrooms ® ✗ sB&B£14 dB&B⇌⋒ £32
⚟ CTV 20P ⛟ ✽ sauna bath nc8yrs *xmas*
V ♉ ☕ ✱ Lunch £3.95 Tea £1.50–£2 High Tea £2.50–£3.50 Dinner £7.50 Wine £3.25 Last dinner 8pm

★★**Lake** Lake Rd ☎(0596) 72069 Plan **8** *B2*
Closed Nov–Mar
20rm(4⇌4⋒) (2fb) ® sB&B fr£12.75 dB&B fr£25.50 dB&B⇌⋒ fr£29.50
CTV 12P 10⌂
♉ Bar lunch £4alc Dinner fr£7.50alc Wine £3 Last dinner 8pm
S%

★★**Millfield** Penrith Rd ☎(0596) 72099 Plan **9** *D3*
Closed Nov–Feb
25rm(6⇌6⋒) (6fb) ® sB&B£14–£16.50 dB&B£15–£33 dB&B⇌⋒ £16–£37 B
Lift CTV 25P ♿
⊟ English & French **V** ♉ Bar lunch 60p–£2.50 Tea 50p–£1 High Tea £4–£5.50 Dinner £7–£8 Last dinner 8.30pm

★★ ***Queen's*** Main St ☎(0596) 73333 Plan **10** *B2*
RS Nov–Feb
Built of local stone and standing in the centre of the town, this hotel is one of the oldest in Keswick.
30rm(18⇌3⋒) CTV in 5 bedrooms B
Lift CTV 25⌂
⊟ English & French **V** ♉ Last dinner 8.30pm
Credit cards 1 2 3 5 **VS**

★★ ♛ **Red House** Skiddaw (on A591) ☎(0596) 72211 Plan **11** *A5*
Closed Dec–Mar
Gabled, red painted, early-Victorian country house set in 10 acres of gardens.
23rm(12⇌) (6fb) sB&B£16.75 sB&B⇌ £17.50 dB&B£32 dB&B⇌ £35
CTV 20P ✽ ≋
V ♉ ☕ Lunch £3–£4 Tea £1 High Tea £4–£5 Dinner £5–£6 Wine £3 Last dinner 8pm
Credit card 2 **VS**

★★**Skiddaw** Main St ☎(0596) 72071 Plan **13** *B2*
Closed 14 Dec–2 Jan
Large town centre hotel with very hospitable atmosphere and service. Bedrooms are well-appointed.
52rm(21⇌1⋒) (5fb) CTV in all bedrooms sB&B fr£13.75 sB&B⇌⋒ fr£16 dB&B fr£27 dB&B⇌⋒ fr£31.50 B
☾ 20P ⛟
♉ ☕ Lunch £4.50–£8 Tea fr45p High Tea £5.50–£8 Dinner £7.75alc Wine £4.25 Last dinner 9pm
S% Credit cards 1 2 3 5

★★ ♛ ***HL*** **Underscar** Applethwaite (1m N off A591) ☎(0596) 72469 Plan **15** *B5*
Closed Dec & Jan
Elegant, comfortable country house hotel in superb setting offering peace, relaxation and excellent food.
12rm(10⇌2⋒) Annexe: 6⋒ (3fb) CTV in all bedrooms ✗ (Main building) sB&B£14–£32 sB&B⇌⋒ £14–£32 dB&B⇌⋒ £28–£60 B
50P ⛟ ✽
V Bar lunch £5alc Tea £1.50alc Dinner £8.50alc Wine £3.90 Last dinner 8.30pm
Credit cards 1 3 **VS**

★★**Walpole** Station St ☎(0596) 72072 Plan **16** *C2*
About 100 years old and one of the finest examples of local slate work.
17rm(6⇌4⋒) (6fb) CTV in all bedrooms ® sB&B£12.95 sB&B⇌⋒ £14.95 dB&B£25.90 dB&B⇌⋒ £29.90
CTV 8P ⛟ *xmas*
⊟ English & French **V** ♉ Lunch £2.25–£2.75&alc Tea 45p–55p Dinner £6.95&alc Wine £4.75 Last dinner 8pm

★**Chaucer House** Ambleside Rd ☎(0596) 72318 Plan **1** *C2*
Closed Nov–Mar
Family-run hotel with views of Skiddaw, Cat Bells, Grisedale and Lake Derwentwater.
32rm(4⇌7⋒) (7fb) ® sB&B£9.50–£10.50 sB&B⇌⋒ £11–£12 dB&B£18.50–£20.50 dB&B⇌⋒ £22–£24 B
CTV 25P ⛟
♉ Dinner £6&alc Wine £3.50 Last dinner 7.30pm
Credit cards 1 2 **VS**

★ ***B*** **Crow Park** The Heads ☎(0596) 72208 Plan **2** *B2*
Closed Nov–Feb
Large, terraced house in an elevated situation close to the shores of Derwentwater.
26rm(9⇌11⋒) (1fb) CTV in 18 bedrooms ® sB&B£10.50 sB&B⇌⋒ £12 dB&B£21 dB&B⇌⋒ £24 B
⚟ CTV 13P
Dinner £3.50–£5.50 Wine £4.30 Last dinner 7.15pm
Credit cards 1 3

★**Lairbeck** Vicarage Hill ☎(0596) 73373 Plan **7** *A5*
12rm(5⇌) (7fb) ✗ ✱ sB&B£11–£12.50 sB&B⇌ £13–£14.50 dB&B£22–£25 dB&B⇌ £26–£29
CTV 25P ✽ ⌂ *xmas*
⊟ English & French ♉ ☕ Lunch £3.75 Tea 55p Dinner £7–£8 Wine £4.14 Last dinner 8pm
VS

★**Skiddaw Grove** Vicarage Hill ☎(0596) 73324 Plan **14** *A5*
11rm(5⇌) (2fb) sB&B£11–£12 dB&B£22–£24 dB&B⇌ £26–£28 B
CTV 10P ⛟ ✽ ≋
Bar lunch £2alc Dinner £6.50alc Wine £4 Last dinner 7.30pm

KETTERING
Northamptonshire
Map **4** SP87

★★**George** Sheep St (Paten) ☎(0536) 518620
Town centre Tudor inn, with mainly commercial clientele.
50rm(21⇌) CTV in all bedrooms ® ✱ sB&B£14.95 sB&B⇌ £27.60 dB&B£24.90 dB&B⇌ £36.80 B
☾ 26P
V ♉ ☕ ✱ Lunch £4.95&alc Tea fr60p Dinner £4.95&alc Wine £3.45 Last dinner 10.30pm
Credit cards 1 2 3 5 **VS**

KETTLEWELL
North Yorkshire
Map **7** SD97

★★**Racehorses** ☎(075676) 233
An 18th-century former coaching inn, situated on the riverside in the centre of the village.
16rm(3⇌2⋒) ✱ sB&B£16.50 dB&B£29 dB&B⇌⋒ £34 B
CTV 20P ⛟ *xmas*
V ✱ Bar lunch £4–£6.75 Dinner £7.50–£10 Wine £3.70 Last dinner 8.30pm
Credit card 1 **VS**

★**Bluebell** Middle Ln ☎(075676) 230
Village inn set close to the riverside in the heart of Wharfedale.
7rm(2⇌) ✱ sB&B£9–£13 dB&B£21–£26 dB&B⇌ £24–£29 B →

CTV 7P *xmas*
V ✿ *Bar lunch 65p–£4.50 Dinner £6.95 Wine £4.95 Last dinner 9pm

KEYNSHAM
Avon
Map **3** ST66
★★**Grange** Bath Rd ☎(02756) 2130
Popular hotel with an informal atmosphere, situated between Bristol and Bath.
11 ⇌ ⋒ Annexe: 20rm (10 ⇌ 10 ⋒) (6fb) CTV in all bedrooms ® ✱ sB&B£19 sB&B ⇌ ⋒ £26 dB&B ⇌ ⋒ £33 ⊟
CTV 36P ✽ Disco mthly
✿ ☐ Lunch £5.50alc Tea 80p alc Dinner £5.50alc Wine £4.50 Last dinner 8.30pm
Credit cards 1 3

KEYSTON
Cambridgeshire
Map **4** TL07
✕✕**Pheasant Inn** ☎Bythorn (08014) 241
▣ English & Continental 45 seats Lunch £8.50alc Dinner £8.50alc Wine £5.80 Last dinner 10pm 50P
S% Credit cards 1 2 3 5

KIDDERMINSTER
Hereford & Worcester
Map **7** SO87
★★★★**Stone Manor** Stone (2m SE on A448) ☎Chaddesley Corbett (056283) 555 Telex no 335661
Converted Georgian house in spacious grounds.
23 ⇌ ⋒ (4fb) 1 ▭ CTV in all bedrooms ® ✱ sB&B ⇌ ⋒ £30.60 dB&B ⇌ ⋒ £44.20
☾ 400P CFA ✽ (hard) Disco Tue & Fri Live music and dancing Sat
▣ French V ✿ ☐ Lunch £5.50&alc Tea 55p Dinner £12alc Wine £5.50 Last dinner 10.15pm
Credit cards 1 2 3 5 **VS**

★★★**Gainsborough House** Bewdley Hill (Best Western) ☎(0562) 754041 Telex 335672
Closed Xmas
Modern hotel with large banqueting facilities.
42 ⇌ 1 ▭ CTV in all bedrooms ® sB&B ⇌ fr£26.75 dB&B ⇌ fr£36.90 ⊟
☾ 130P CFA sauna bath Disco Thu
▣ British & European ✿ ☐ Bar lunch fr£3 Dinner £7 Wine £4 Last dinner 9.30pm
Credit cards 1 2 3 5 **VS**

✕✕**Granary** Heath Ln, Shenstone (3m SE off A450) ☎Chaddesley Corbett (056283) 535
Closed Mon Lunch not served Sat Dinner not served Sun
V 50 seats Lunch £6.95–£7.50 Dinner £9.50–£9.95 Wine £3.95 Last dinner 9pm 40P
Credit cards 1 2 3 5 **VS**
See advert on page 336

✕✕***Westley Court*** Austcliffe Ln, Cookley (3m N off A449) ☎(0562) 850629
Dinner not served Sun
▣ English, French & Italian 75 seats Last dinner 10pm P Live music and dancing Sat Cabaret Sat

KILCHOAN
Highland *Argyllshire*
Map **13** NM46
★★**Kilchoan** ☎(09723) 200
Closed Nov–Etr
Small, family run Highland hotel in an area of outstanding beauty.
6 ⇌ (2fb) TV in all bedrooms ® sB&B ⇌ £13.50 dB&B ⇌ £27
18P ✽
▣ Scottish & French Bar lunch 45p–£3.50 Dinner £5.50–£8.50&alc Wine £3.75 Last dinner 8pm

KILCHRENAN
Strathclyde *Argyllshire*
Map **10** NN02
★★★ *L* **Taychreggan** Lochaweside ☎(08663) 211
Closed 15 Oct–15 Apr

Hotel in superb lochside position with an international atmosphere.

17rm(14⇌)sB&B£16–£20 sB&B⇌⋒£20–£26 dB&B£32–£40 dB&B⇌⋒£40–£52

CTV 40P ✽ ♩

International V ♧ ☕ Lunch £5.50 Tea £1–£1.50 Dinner fr£11 Wine £4.80 Last dinner 9pm

Credit cards 1 2 3 5 VS

KILCREGGAN
Strathclyde *Dunbartonshire*
Map **10** NS28

★★**Kilcreggan** (Minotel) ☎(043684) 2243
Closed 1 Jan
Set high up overlooking gardens and River Clyde.

10rm(5⇌5⋒) (3fb) sB&B⇌⋒£11.50–£14.50 dB&B⇌⋒£23–£29 B

CTV 40P ✽ Live music and dancing Sat

V ♧ ✻ Lunch £5–£6.50 Dinner £6.50–£7.50 Wine £3 Last dinner 8pm

Credit cards 1 3 5

★★★

❀★★★ ARDANAISEIG KILCHRENNAN
☎(08663) 333
Closed mid Oct–Etr

(Rosette awarded for dinner only.)

Dating from 1834, this was until recently a private house which the owners converted to the admirable hotel it has become under the direction of Michael and Frieda Yeo, two experienced hotel keepers. They have created a wonderfully hospitable atmosphere and each of them is only too willing to help in any way they can. The atmosphere is enhanced by the comfortable and tastefully decorated bedrooms as well as the fine public rooms, a well appointed dining room, the library bar and the elegant chintzy drawing room with parquet floor and carpets. There are some nice pieces of furniture and the rooms are cheered by fresh flowers, while coal fires burn in season.

In the dining room, set meals with a small à la carte are provided and the cooking with a slight French influence is enjoyable and well deserving a rosette. At lunch lighter meals are served. There are lots of magazines about and a complementary glass of sherry is sent to your room before dinner. There is also a billiard room, croquet, clay pigeon shooting, boating and fishing on Loch Awe. There is even a selection of wellingtons for those who have forgotten to bring boots suitable for rough walking.

Pride of place, however, must go to the beautiful, informal gardens with rare shrubs and trees that are open to the public. The first owner planted them and, within sight of Cruachan and on the shores of Loch Awe, they provide a magnificent spectacle. For either a retreat or an energetic holiday, Ardanaiseig, now one of the 'Pride of Britain' partners, is a must and very much appreciated by our members.

15⇌ CTV in all bedrooms
sB&B⇌£46.75 (incl dinner)
dB&B⇌£86–£108 (incl dinner)
20P ✽ (hard) ♩ billiards nc8yrs
English & French ♧ ☕ ✻ Lunch £1.20–£8 Tea £1.85 Dinner £14.50 Wine £4.95 Last dinner 9pm
Credit cards 1 2 3 5 VS

KILDRUMMY
Grampian *Aberdeenshire*
Map **15** NJ41

★★★ *HBL* **Kildrummy Castle** (Best Western) ☎(03365) 288
Closed 3 Jan–3 Feb

Dating from 1900, though the ruins of the original 1245 castle can be seen in the beautiful grounds, the hotel is thoughtfully and tastefully decorated. The proprietor and his staff provide warm, friendly country house hospitality.

13rm(9⇌1⋒) (4fb) 1 CTV in all bedrooms ® sB&B£18.50–£24.50 sB&B⇌⋒£19.50–£25.50 dB&B£31–£43 dB&B⇌⋒£33–£45 B

CTV 30P ✽ ♩ billiards *xmas*

V ♧ ☕ Lunch £6.50–£7&alc Tea £1.75–£1.95 Dinner £10.50–£11.50&alc Wine £5.50 Last dinner 9pm

Credit cards 1 2 3 4 VS

KILDWICK
West Yorkshire
Map **7** SE04

★★★ *HB* **Kildwick Hall** ☎Cross Hills (0535) 32244

Elegantly furnished Jacobean manor house overlooking the valley.

12rm(10⇌2⋒) (1fb) 2 CTV in all bedrooms sB&B⇌⋒£30–£40 dB&B⇌⋒£52–£72 B

CTV 60P ✽ *xmas*

English & French V ♧ ☕ Lunch fr£7.95&alc Tea £1.95alc Dinner £10.75–£14.95 Wine £6 Last dinner 10pm

Credit cards 1 2 3 5

KILLEARN
Central *Stirlingshire*
Map **11** NS58

★★**Black Bull** (Ind Coope) ☎(0360) 50215 →

Small, country town inn, dating from 1880 with a garden at the rear.

12rm(5➡)(1fb) 1🛏 Ⓡ sB&B fr£15.68 sB&B➡ fr£19.52 dB&B fr£25.30 dB&B➡ fr£31.35 ℞

CTV 60P ✽

🍴European ♈ ☕ ✻ Lunch £4.25alc Tea 85p High Tea £3.50 Dinner £8alc Wine £3.75 Last dinner 8.30pm

Credit cards 1 2 3 5

KILLIECRANKIE
Tayside *Perthshire*
Map **14** NN96

★★*HL* **Killiecrankie** ☎ Pitlochry (0796) 3220 Closed mid Oct–early Apr

Attractive, white-painted house set amidst woodland and well tended gardens.

12rm(2➡8⋒)(2fb) CTV available in bedrooms sB&B£12–£15 sB&B➡⋒£13.80–£16.80 dB&B£24–£30 dB&B➡⋒£27.60–£33.60

⅟ CTV 30P 2🚗 ✽ ⌂

🍴Scottish & Continental **V** ♈ ☕ Bar lunch 60p–£2.50 Tea 60p Dinner £7.50–£9&alc Wine £3.40 Last dinner 10pm

VS

KILLIN
Central *Perthshire*
Map **11** NN53

★★**Bridge of Lochay** ☎ (05672) 272 Closed Nov–Mar

An 18th-century drovers' inn on the outskirts of the town, close to the River Lochay.

K

17rm(4→3⋔)®sB&B£11 dB&B£22 dB&B→⋔£28 Ɓ
CTV 30P 3🚗🚫🐕✽
V☕🍽 Lunch fr£3.50 Dinner fr£7 Wine £3.90 Last dinner 8.30pm

★★**Killin** (Best Western) ☎(05672) 296
Closed mid Oct–mid Mar
The courthouse that originally stood on this site was replaced by the present hotel which stands on the banks of the River Lochay.
30rm(10→3⋔) (5fb) sB&B£14.75 sB&B→⋔£19.25 dB&B£26.25 dB&B→⋔£29.50 Ɓ
Lift CTV 50P 2🚗✽♪ Live music and dancing wkly
V☕🍽 Lunch £4.75 Tea 60p Dinner £4.50–£7.35 Wine £4.30 Last dinner 8.30pm
S% Credit cards 1 2 3 5 **VS**

★★**Morenish Lodge** ☎(05672) 258
Closed Nov–Mar
Conversion of traditional shooting lodge, overlooking Loch Tay.
12rm(3→) ★ sB&B£14 dB&B£24 dB&B→£27 Ɓ
TV 18P🚫🐕✽ nc4yrs
🍽 Bar lunch £3.50–£5 Tea £1.40 High Tea £4.50–£6 Dinner £7.50 Wine £4.20 Last dinner 8pm
VS

★**Craigard** ☎(05672) 285
closed 15 Oct–14 Jan
A converted stone town house dating from 1867, standing on the main road.
7rm (1fb) ★ sB&B£8–£9 dB&B£16–£18 Ɓ
CTV 10P Disco wkly Live music and dancing wkly
☕🍽 Bar lunch £1.75–£3.50 Tea 40p–60p High Tea £2.45–£4 Dinner £3.50–£6.50&alc Wine £3 Last dinner 8.30pm

★**Falls of Dochart** Main St ☎(05672) 237
Closed 26 Oct–19 Apr
Informal hotel situated in the main street.
9rm(1→) (2fb) ®sB&B£9 dB&B£17 dB&B→£21
CTV 25P 2🚗
🍴Scottish & Continental Lunch £3.75–£5.50&alc High Tea £3.50–£5 Dinner £5.25–£8.50&alc Wine £3.80 Last dinner 8.30pm
VS

KILMARNOCK
Strathclyde *Ayrshire*
Map **10** NS43
☆☆☆**Howard Park** Glasgow Rd (Swallow) ☎(0563) 31211 Telex no 53168
RS 25–26 Dec & 1–2 Jan
Modern, low hotel on outskirts of town.
44→ (6fb) CTV in all bedrooms ®
✽sB&B→£28.50 dB&B→£37.50 Ɓ
Lift ☾ ## 200P
🍴Scottish, English & French V☕🍽
✽Lunch £5.50–£5.65 Tea 45p Dinner £7.15–£7.50&alc Wine £4.75 Last dinner 9.30pm
Credit cards 1 2 3 5

✕✕**Caesar's** 108–112 John Finnie St ☎(0563) 25706
Ultra modern first floor restaurant featuring carvery lunch.
🍴British & Continental **V** 60 seats Lunch £3–£6&alc High Tea £2.50–£5 Dinner £10&alc Wine £5.50 Last dinner 10pm
Credit cards 1 2 3 5 **VS**

KILMARTIN
Strathclyde *Argyllshire*
Map **10** NR89
✕**Cairn** ☎(05465) 254
Closed Nov–Mar Dinner not served Sun
🍴Scottish, French & Italian 50 seats
✽Lunch £3alc Tea 75p alc Dinner £7.50alc Last dinner 9.30pm 10P
Credit cards 2 3 5

KILMORY
Isle of Arran, Strathclyde *Bute*
Map **10** NR92
★★**Lagg** ☎Sliddery (077087) 255
Closed Nov–Feb
17rm(7→) (3fb) ® sB&B£15 sB&B→£16 dB&B£30 dB&B→£32
CTV 40P✽♪⌂
🍴Scottish & French V☕🍽 Lunch £3.50–£6 Tea 80p–£1.50 High Tea £3.50–£5 Dinner £9–£13&alc Wine £5.45 Last dinner 9pm

KILWINNING
Strathclyde *Ayrshire*
Map **10** NS34
See also Irvine
✕***Dalgarven House*** Dalry Rd ☎(0294) 53061
V 80 seats Last dinner 9.30pm 25P bedrooms available
Credit cards 1 2 3

KINBUCK (*near Dunblane*)
Central *Perthshire*
Map **11** NN70
❀★★★***HBL*** **Cromlix House** (4m N of Dunblane, off A9 on the B8033) ☎Dunblane (0786) 822125
Built in 1880, this comfortable hotel is set in a 5,000 acre estate. It is superbly furnished with fine antiques, fresh flowers and has open fires in season. The food is first class with artistically created dishes and a choice of fine wines. The friendly and relaxed hospitality provide a superb country house atmosphere.
10rm(9→1⋔) CTV in 6 bedrooms sB&B→£45 dB&B→£77 Ɓ
40P 1🚗🚫🐕✽🎣♪U⌂
🍴English & French Lunch fr£11 Dinner fr£20 Wine £6.25 Last dinner 9.30pm
S% Credit cards 1 2 3 5 **VS**

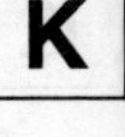
K

KINCLAVEN
Tayside *Perthshire*
Map **11** NO13
★★★***BL*** **Ballathie House**
☎Meikleour (025083) 268 Telex no 727396
RS Nov–Feb
Victorian mansion on the banks of the River Tay, just north of Stanley on an unclassified road. →

21rm(19⇌1⋔) Annexe: 11rm(10⇌) (2fb) CTV in 21 bedrooms TV in 11 bedrooms ® sB&B⇌⋔ £19–£27 dB&B⇌⋔ £36–£50 ⊟

50P CFA ✽ ⚲ ♩ ♿ ⌂

Scottish & French ♆ ☕ Lunch £3–£6 Tea fr£1 Dinner fr£9&alc Wine £5 Last dinner 9.30pm

Credit cards 1 2 5 **VS**

KINCRAIG
Highland *Inverness-shire*
Map **14** NH80

★★ ***H*Ossian** ☎(05404) 242
Closed Nov & 4–31 Jan
Friendly, family-operated hotel with a good reputation for its food.
6rm (1fb) sB&B£14 dB&B£27
CTV 20P ⛟ ✽ Live music and dancing Fri & Sat
International **V** ♆ ☕ Lunch £5–£6 Tea £1.50–£2 High Tea £5–£6 Dinner £8alc Wine £5 Last dinner 9.30pm
Credit card 3

★**Sule** ☎(05404) 344
Converted stone-built house standing in its own grounds overlooking Cairngorm Mountains.
9rm (1fb) ✻sB&B£11–£12.50 dB&B£22–£25
⚟ 30P ⛟ ✽ ♩ billiards nc10yrs
♆ ☕ Bar lunch £1–£2.50 Tea fr50p Dinner £6 Wine £4 Last dinner 7pm

KINGHAM
Oxfordshire
Map **4** SP22

★★**Mill** ☎(060871) 8188
Converted mill and bakehouse with modern extensions on the outskirts of the village.
15rm(13⇌2⋔) Annexe: 4rm(3⇌1⋔) (2fb) CTV in all bedrooms ® sB&B⇌⋔ £15–£16 dB&B⇌⋔ £30–£32 ⊟
60P ✽ ♩ nc5yrs *xmas*
V ♆ ☕ Lunch £5.95&alc High Tea £2.50–£2.90 Dinner £6.95&alc Wine £4.85 Last dinner 9.30pm
Credit cards 1 2 3 4 5 **VS**

★ ***Langston Arms*** Station Rd ☎(060871) 319
Country inn style hotel with extensive views.
8rm(3⇌2⋔) CTV in all bedrooms ® ⊟
60P ⛟ ✽ Live music and dancing Sat
V ♆ ☕ Last dinner 9pm
Credit cards 1 2 3 5

KINGSBRIDGE
Devon
Map **3** SX74

★★ **BUCKLAND-TOUT-SAINTS, KINGSBRIDGE**
(2½m NE on unclass rd) (Best Western) ☎(0548) 3055
Closed 29 Dec–27 Jan

Set among 27 acres of well kept parkland and gardens in the lovely Devon countryside, this elegant Queen Anne house is a delightful hotel in which to spend a holiday. This year, helicopter tours from the grounds are available. The interior retains some of the decorative features of the period and particularly notable are the lovely old pine panelling and rouge Ashburton marble fireplace in the charming dining room, and the unusual Adam fireplace and ornamental ceiling in one of the elegant sitting rooms. This, and another one with television, are comfortable, well decorated and adorned with fresh flowers. The bedrooms, too, are well decorated and provide every comfort.
The hotel is owned and run by the Shepherd family and you have only to ask and your every request will be willingly attended to. With the right sort of guests a house party

atmosphere can be conjured up here, particularly in the snug little panelled bar. It is a cheerful place for an aperitif before sampling the decent food served courteously by cheerful and friendly girls. All in all, this is a sound example of a two Red Star hotel.
13rm(11⇌2⋔) 1⊞ CTV in 5 bedrooms ✻sB&B⇌⋔ £23–£29 dB&B⇌⋔ £41–£49 ⊟
CTV 20P ⛟ ✽
English & French ♆ ☕ ✻Lunch £9alc Tea £1.30 Dinner £10alc Wine £6.35 Last dinner 9pm
Credit cards 1 2 3 4 5 **VS**

★★**Kings Arms** Fore St ☎(0548) 2071
Historical coaching inn located in terraced shopping area of old town.
16rm(7⇌) (2fb) 11⊞ ✻sB&B£12–£13.75 sB&B⇌£13.75–£15.50 dB&B£18–£22 dB&B⇌£21–£25 ⊟
CTV 40P ⛟ *xmas*
♆ ✻Lunch £1–£3 Dinner £6.50alc Wine £4.25 Last dinner 9pm
Credit cards 1 3 **VS**

☆☆**Kingsbridge Motel** The Quay ☎(0548) 2540
Modern tourist and commercial hotel with garden and sun balcony overlooking the quay.

20⇌(3fb) CTV in all bedrooms ® *sB&B⇌£21.50–£23 dB&B⇌£33.50–£36 B

☾ 20P ✽ ♿

English & French *Bar lunch £3.60alc Dinner fr£6.50&alc Wine £5.60 Last dinner 10pm

Credit cards 1 2 3 5 **VS**

★★Rockwood Embankment Rd ☎(0548) 2480

Small villa with new extension overlooking estuary.

6rm(4⇌2fi) TV in all bedrooms ® sB&B⇌fi £13.50 dB&B⇌fi £26

CTV 6P

V Lunch £3.50–£5.50&alc Dinner £5.50&alc Wine £4.50 Last dinner 9pm

Credit cards 1 2 3 5 **VS**

★★*Vineyard* Embankment Rd ☎(0548) 2520 Closed mid Oct–8 Apr

Regency villa in its own grounds overlooking estuary.

11rm(4⇌2fi) B

CTV 18P ✽ Live music Sun lunch

International Last dinner 8.30pm

KINGSKERSWELL
Devon
Map **3** SX86

XXXPitt House ☎(08047) 3374

Two-storey, thatched, cob cottage, dating from the 14th century, in a quiet part of the village.

Closed Sun, Feb & Public Hols Lunch not served

Continental 32 seats Dinner £11alc Wine £4.70 Last dinner 10pm 24P

Credit cards 1 2 3 5

KING'S LYNN
Norfolk
Map **9** TF62

★★★Duke's Head Tuesday Market Pl (Trusthouse Forte) ☎(0553) 4996 Telex no 817349

72⇌(4fb) CTV in all bedrooms ® sB&B⇌£36.50 dB&B⇌£51.50 B

Lift ☾ 50P CFA *xmas*

Last dinner 9.30pm

Credit cards 1 2 3 4 5

★★Mildenhall ☎(0553) 5146

45rm(17⇌) Annexe: 8⇌(2fb) CTV in all bedrooms ® sB&B£16.39 sB&B⇌£18.69 dB&B⇌£26.09 B

☾ CTV 60P Live music and dancing Sat Cabaret Sat

V Lunch £3.75–£4.25 Tea fr£1.50 Dinner £4.25–£4.95 Wine £5.50 Last dinner 9.45pm

Credit cards 1 2 3 5 **VS**

★*Stuart House* Goodwins Rd (Minotel) ☎(0553) 2169

Closed 24 Dec–10 Jan

Converted private residence with a large garden, centrally located in a residential area of King's Lynn.

13rm(5⇌2fi) Annexe: 2⇌ CTV in 10 bedrooms TV in 1 bedroom ® B

CTV 16P ✽

English & European Last dinner 7.45pm

Credit cards 1 3

KINGSTEIGNTON
Devon
Map **3** SX87

XThatchers Crossley Moor Rd ☎Newton Abbot (0626) 65650

Pleasant, white-painted cottage with garden, set in a residential area, off the old Exeter/Newton Abbot Rd.

Closed Tue Dinner not served Sun

35 seats Lunch £2.50–£3 Dinner £10–£12alc Wine £3.35 Last dinner 9.30pm 20P

Credit cards 1 3 **VS**

KINGSWINFORD
West Midlands
Map **7** SO88

★★Summerhill House Swindon Rd (Ansells) ☎(0384) 295254

10rm(3fi) ® sB&B fr£19.25 sB&Bfi fr£22 dB&B fr£25.30 B

CTV 200P

Lunch fr£5.75&alc Dinner fr£6.25&alc Wine £3.90 Last dinner 10pm

Credit cards 1 2 3 **VS**

KINGTON
Hereford & Worcester
Map **3** SO25

★★Burton Mill St ☎(0544) 230323

Personally-run, red brick hotel, popular with local people.

10rm(3⇌2fi)(2fb) ® sB&B£10.70–£11.70 sB&B⇌fi £12.70–£13.70 dB&B£21.40–£23.40 dB&B⇌fi £25.40–£27.40 B

CTV 30P 3 ✽ billiards

English & Continental *Lunch £3.50alc Dinner £6alc Wine £3.50 Last dinner 9.30pm

S% Credit cards 1 3 **VS**

★Swan Church St ☎(0544) 230510 RS Xmas

Small town centre inn.

6rm(1fb) ® sB&B£10 dB&B£20 B

CTV 25P 6

English & French **V** Lunch fr£3&alc Dinner fr£4.50&alc Wine £4.80 Last dinner 10pm

Credit card 1

KINGTON (near Pershore)
Hereford & Worcester
Map **3** SO95

X*Red Hart Inn* ☎Inkberrow (0386) 792221

45 seats Dinner £10alc Last dinner 9.45pm 50P

Credit cards 1 2 3

KINGUSSIE
Highland *Inverness-shire*
Map **14** NH70

★★*Duke of Gordon* Newtonmore Rd ☎(05402) 302

An Edwardian roadside hotel situated in this Highland town.

45rm(40⇌5fi) ® B

Lift CTV 60P billiards Disco wkly Live music and dancing wkly Cabaret wkly →

K

V ♔ ☐ Last dinner 9pm
Credit cards 1 2 3

❀★*H* **Columba House** Manse Rd ☎(05402) 402
RS Nov–Mar
(Rosette awarded for dinner only.)
6rm(2⋒) Annexe: 1➡(1fb) ® sB&B£9.50 sB&B➡⋒£11.50 dB&B£38 dB&B➡⋒£40 B
TV 10P ✽
Scottish & French V ♔ ☐ Bar lunch £1.60–£3.20 Tea 40p–£1.60 Dinner £9.50 Wine £3.20 Last dinner 7.30pm

❀★*H* **Osprey** Ruthven Rd ☎(05402) 510
Closed Nov–26 Dec
(Rosette awarded for dinner only.)
9rm (1fb) sB&B£10–£13 dB&B£20–£26 B
CTV 10P
Scottish, English & French V ♔ ☐ Tea 60p–£1 Dinner £7–£8 Wine £4.50 Last dinner 8pm
Credit cards 1 2 3 5 **VS**

★**Silverfjord** Ruthven Rd ☎(05402) 292
7rm(1➡)(1fb) ® sB&B£9.50–£11 dB&B£17–£20 dB&B➡£19–£22 B
CTV 10P
V ♔ ☐ Bar lunch fr£2.25 Dinner fr£6&alc Wine £3.95 Last dinner 8pm
Credit card 3

KINLOCHBERVIE
Highland *Sutherland*
Map **14** NC25

★★★**Kinlochbervie** ☎(097182) 275
Closed Xmas & New Year RS Nov–Apr
Comfortable and well appointed hotel pleasantly situated overlooking the harbour and Loch Clash.
10➡ CTV in all bedrooms ® sB&B➡ fr£23 dB&B➡ fr£46 B
40P
♔ ☐ Bar lunch £3.50alc Tea fr£1 Dinner £12.50alc Wine £4.85 Last dinner 8.30pm

KINLOCHEWE
Highland *Ross & Cromarty*
Map **14** NH06

★**Kinlochewe** ☎(044584) 253
Closed Dec–Mar
A comfortable little hotel with a friendly atmosphere and ideally situated for fishing and hillwalking.
10rm(1⋒) ✻sB&B£14 dB&B£25–£26 dB&B⋒£29 B
CTV 22P
♔ ☐ ✻Bar lunch fr£2.80 Tea fr£1&alc Dinner £7.75–£11.75&alc Wine £3.35 Last dinner 8pm
Credit cards 1 3

KINLOCH RANNOCH
Tayside *Perthshire*
Map **14** NN65

★★**Dunalastair** (Minotel) ☎(08822) 323
RS Nov–May
23rm(10➡)(4fb) ® sB&B£9.95–£10.95 sB&B➡£12.45–£13.95 dB&B£19.90–£21.90 dB&B➡£24.90–£27.90 B
CTV 40P 8
♔ ☐ Lunch £3.95–£4.95 Tea £1–£1.95 Dinner £6.95–£7.95 Wine £2.95 Last dinner 8.30pm
Credit cards 1 3

★★*Loch Rannoch* ☎(08822) 201
Impressive, late 19th-century hillside hotel with views of Loch Rannoch.
17➡ CTV in all bedrooms ®
40P ✽ (heated) sauna bath Live music and dancing Wed & Sun
European ♔ ☐ Last dinner 9.30pm
Credit cards 1 2 3 5 **VS**

KINROSS
Tayside *Kinross-shire*
Map **11** NO10

★★★**Green** 2 The Muirs (Best Western) ☎(0577) 63467 Telex no 76684
Fully-modernised, former coaching inn standing in six acres of gardens.
48rm(36➡7⋒)(7fb) CTV in all bedrooms sB&B➡⋒£26 dB&B➡⋒£42 B
60P CFA ✽ (heated) squash sauna bath Live music and dancing Fri & Sat *xmas*
French ♔ ☐ Lunch £6.50&alc Tea £3.70 High Tea £5 Dinner £9–£10&alc Wine £3.95 Last dinner 9.30pm
Credit cards 1 2 3 5 **VS**

★★**Bridgend** ☎(0577) 63413
Modest country hotel on the southern outskirts of town.
11rm(3⋒)(2fb) ✻sB&B£10.50 dB&B£19 dB&B⋒£19 B
CTV 50P ✽ Live music and dancing twice wkly *xmas*
V ♔ ☐ ✻Lunch fr£3.25 Tea fr£1 High Tea fr£3.50 Dinner fr£6.50 Wine £3.60 Last dinner 8.30pm

✕✕**Kirklands Hotel** High St ☎(0577) 63313
Two-storey stone inn, in centre of town.
Closed Mon Dinner not served Tue
30 seats Lunch £2.75alc Dinner £10alc Wine £4.32 Last dinner 9.30pm P

✕✕**Windlestrae** ☎(0577) 63217
Large, detached house standing in three acres of gardens.
Closed 3–31 Jan
English & French V 56 seats ✻Lunch £5.95–£6.50 Dinner £11–£12alc 60P bedrooms available
Credit cards 1 2 3 5

KINTBURY
Berkshire
Map **4** SU36

❀✕✕**Dundas Arms** ☎(0488) 58263
A small restaurant, featuring imaginative and skilful professional cooking, and with a cosy cocktail lounge.
Closed Sun, Mon & 1wk Xmas–New Years Eve Lunch not served (except snacks)
English & French 40 seats Dinner £15alc Wine £4.20 Last dinner 9.30pm 70P bedrooms available
Credit cards 1 2 3 5 **VS**

KINVER
Staffordshire
Map **7** SO88

✕✕✕**Berkleys (Piano Room)** High St

☎(0384) 873679
⊟International 35 seats ✻Lunch £4.25alc Dinner £7–£13.50alc Wine £3.80 Last dinner 10pm 10P
Credit cards 1 2 3 5

KIPPFORD
Dumfries & Galloway *Kirkcudbrightshire*
Map **11** NX85
★ ***Anchor*** ☎(055662) 205 RS Oct–Mar
Modernised, stone inn with views over the River Urr.
18rm(1➡)
CTV 18P
V♁ Last dinner 8pm

KIRBY MISPERTON
North Yorkshire
Map **8** SE77
✕✕ ***Bean Sheaf*** ☎(065386) 614
Closed Mon Dinner not served Sun
⊟English & Continental 120 seats ✻Lunch £3.70–£4&alc Dinner £7.50alc Wine £3.50 Last dinner 9.30pm 60P bedrooms available Live music and dancing 2nd & last Fri in mnth

KIRKBY
Merseyside
Map **7** SJ49
★★ ***Golden Eagle*** Cherryfield Dr
☎051-546 4355
Closed Xmas & New Year

Modern, town centre hotel.
70➡⋒ CTV in all bedrooms ® B
Lift ☾ 100P
V♁⊐ Last dinner 9.15pm
Credit cards 1 2 3 4 5

KIRKBY FLEETHAM
North Yorkshire
Map **8** SE29
★★★ ***HB* Kirkby Fleetham Hall**
☎Northallerton (0609) 748226
Restored country mansion offering peace and tranquility, situated 2 miles off the A1.
13➡ 2⊟ CTV in all bedrooms ★ sB&B➡£30 dB&B➡£48–£55 B
50P ✽ *xmas*
⊟English & French Lunch fr£6.95 Dinner £11.95–£12.95 Wine £5 Last dinner 9.15pm
S% Credit cards 2 3 **VS**

KIRKBY LONSDALE
Cumbria
Map **7** SD67
★★★ **Royal** Main St ☎(0468) 71217
One-time coaching inn, now a well furnished hotel, opposite the town square.
22rm(16➡)(1fb) CTV in all bedrooms ®

sB&B£14 sB&B➡£18 dB&B£25 dB&B➡£29 B
CTV 50P 10⌂ ⚲ ♪ billiards *xmas*
V♁⊐✻Lunch £4.50–£6.50 Tea £1.95–£5 High Tea £3.50–£5 Dinner £8–£15&alc Wine £3.50 Last dinner 10.30pm
S% Credit cards 1 2 3 5

★ **Red Dragon Inn** Main St ☎(0468) 71205
RS 15 Nov–Feb
Town centre inn offering modest accommodation.
8rm(1fb) sB&B£9.25–£10.50 dB&B£16–£18.50
CTV 6P 2⌂
♁Bar lunch £2.60–£2.90&alc High Tea £2.60–£2.90&alc Dinner £5&alc Wine £3.80 Last dinner 8.30pm

KIRKBYMOORSIDE
North Yorkshire
Map **8** SE68
★★ ***B* George & Dragon** Market Pl
☎(0751) 31637
Closed Xmas
Welcoming 13th-century inn with modern bedrooms in converted stables at the rear.
17rm(6➡5⋒) Annexe: 6rm(5➡1⋒)(3fb) CTV in 20 bedrooms ★ sB&B➡⋒£9–£18 dB&B£14–£28 dB&B➡⋒£16–£32 B
20P ✽ nc8yrs →

K

International V Lunch £5 Dinner £8–£9alc Wine £4 Last dinner 9.30pm

Credit cards 1 3 **VS**

KIRKBY STEPHEN
Cumbria
Map **12** NY70

★★**King's Arms** Market St ☎(0930) 71378

Modernised, 18th-century inn situated on the main street of this small town.

9rm(1→)(1fb) sB&B£14 sB&B£27 dB&B→£32 B

CTV 3P 9

English & French Lunch £4.95 Dinner £8.75 Wine £4.25 Last dinner 8.45pm

Credit cards 1 3 **VS**

KIRKCALDY
Fife
Map **11** NT29

★★★**Dean Park** Chapel Level ☎(0592) 261635 Closed 1 & 2 Jan

A business hotel located in a large stone mansion with modern bedrooms in the extension. Situated 2 miles from the town centre, off the A910.

K

20rm(13→6)(2fb) CTV in all bedrooms Ⓡ*sB&B→£29 dB&B→£36 B

(100P billiards Live music and dancing Sat *xmas*

V *Lunch £3.65&alc Tea 75p High Tea £1.50–£3.50 Dinner £7.50&alc Last dinner 10pm

Credit cards 1 2 3 5

★★**Station** 4 Bennochy Rd ☎(0592) 262461

Victorian hotel near to town centre opposite railway station.

34rm(6→3) CTV in 9 bedrooms *sB&B£14.50 sB&B→£20 dB&B£25.50 dB&B→£32.50

(25

*Lunch £2.50 Tea 45p Dinner £6 Wine £3.95 Last dinner 10.30pm

Credit cards 1 2 3 4

XXX**Oswald Room** (Dunnikier House Hotel) Dunnikier Park ☎(0592) 268393

Closed Sun

French Lunch fr£7 Dinner fr£7&alc Wine £4.75 Last dinner 9.45pm 100P bedrooms available

Credit cards 1 2 5

KIRKCOLM
Dumfries & Galloway *Wigtownshire*
Map **10** NX06

★★**Knocknassie House** Ervie (3½m W off B738) ☎Ervie (077688) 217

Early 19th-century stone mansion in open countryside.

7rm(1→1)(2fb) CTV in 2 bedrooms TV in 5 bedrooms Ⓡ sB&B£10–£11.50 sB&B→£12.50–£14 dB&B£20–£23 dB&B→£25–£28 B

CTV 30P

V Lunch £3.50–£4 Tea £1.50–£1.75 High Tea £3–£4 Dinner £3–£4&alc Wine £3.70 Last dinner 9pm

VS

★***Corsewall Arms*** Main St ☎(077685) 228

Friendly, family run hotel in small village.

11rm(1→1) B

CTV 20P

Last dinner 7.30pm

KIRKCUDBRIGHT
Dumfries & Galloway *Kirkcudbrightshire*
Map **11** NX65

★★**Royal** St Cuthbert Street ☎(0557) 30551

Tourist/commercial hotel in central location.

18rm(4→2)(2fb) Ⓡ sB&B£10 sB&B→£12 dB&B£20 dB&B→£24 B

CTV 6P 4 Disco wknds Live music and dancing wknds Cabaret wknds *xmas*

Lunch £2–£3.50 Tea 40p–50p High Tea £3–£5 Dinner £6.50–£8 Last dinner 8.30pm

Credit card 1

★★**Selkirk Arms** High St ☎(0557) 30402
18th-century two-storey inn, where Robert Burns wrote the 'Selkirk Grace'.
16rm(2🛁) Annexe: 10rm(2🛁) (5fb) ® sB&B£12.40–£13.65 dB&B£24.80–£27.30 dB&B🛁£28.80–£31.70
CTV 18🏠🚗✽ Live music Tue ♿
V☕ Lunch £4alc Dinner £8 Wine £3.50 Last dinner 8pm
Credit cards 1 3

✕**Ingle** St Mary Street ☎(0557) 30606
Closed Mon & Feb Lunch not served
🍴 Italian 50 seats Last dinner 9.30pm 🚭
Credit cards 1 2 3 5

KIRK LANGLEY
Derbyshire
Map **8** SK23

★★**Meynell Arms** Ashbourne Rd ☎(033124) 515 Closed 27 Dec RS 24–26 Dec
Roadside inn dating back to the 17th century standing on the A52.
9rm(3🛁1🚿)(1fb) 2🛏 CTV in all bedrooms ® ✽sB&B£13.50–£15 sB&B🛁🚿£16 dB&B£21 dB&B🛁🚿fr£24 B
80P✽ Live music Sat & Sun
🍴 English & French V✽ Lunch £5–£7&alc Dinner £6–£10.50&alc Wine £5.15 Last dinner 9.30pm
Credit cards 1 2 3 5 **VS**

KIRKMICHAEL
Tayside *Perthshire*
Map **15** NO06

★★*H* **Log Cabin** (Exec Hotel, Minotel) ☎Strathardle (025 081) 288 Telex no 76277
Attractive, log-built hotel, set 900 feet up amongst heather and pine forest.
13rm(8🛁5🚿) (4fb) CTV available in bedrooms ® sB&B🛁🚿£14–£18 dB&B🛁🚿£28–£36 B
CTV 60P✽🎣U Live music and dancing Sat (in season) 🏠 *xmas* ♿
🍴 Scottish & French V☕☕ Bar lunch fr£2.50alc Tea 60p High Tea fr£3.50 Dinner £9–£10 Wine £3.75 Last dinner 9pm
Credit cards 1 2 3 5

★***Aldchlappie*** ☎Strathardle (025 081) 224 RS Nov–Mar
7rm
CTV 25P 4🏠🚗✽🎣
☕ Last dinner 9pm

★**Strathlene** ☎Strathardle (025081) 347
Small, family-run hotel whose emphasis is on hospitality and good food.
7rm(1🛁) (2fb) ✱ sB&B£9.25–£10.25 sB&B🛁🚿£12.25–£13.25 dB&B£18.50–£20.50 dB&B🛁🚿£20–£22 B
CTV 6P🚗 Live music and dancing Wed & Sat *xmas*
V☕☕ Lunch £4 Tea 75p High Tea £3.25alc Dinner £6.95alc Wine £2.95 Last dinner 8.30pm
Credit cards 1 3 5

KIRKOSWALD
Strathclyde *Ayrshire*
Map **10** NS20

★**Kirkton Jean's** 45 Main St ☎(06556) 220
An attractive family run roadside inn with all accommodation in modern annexe rooms.
Annexe: 9🚿 (1fb) sB&B🚿£12–£16 dB&B🚿£20–£28 B
CTV 40P✽ Live music and dancing Fri & Sat 🏠 *xmas*
🍴 Scottish & Continental V☕☕ Lunch £1.50–£6 Tea £1–£1.50 High Tea £5alc Dinner £10alc Wine £4 Last dinner 10pm

KIRKWALL
Orkney
Map **16** HY41

★★**Ayre** Ayre Rd ☎(0856) 2197
Family run hotel overlooking bay and harbour.
31rm(3🛁) (4fb) ® sB£9.15–£13.80 (room only) dB🛁£17.15–£18.30 (room only) dB£18.30–£24.60 (room only) dB£28.30–£30.60 (room only)
CTV 24P sauna bath Disco wknds Live music and dancing wknds Cabaret wknds
V☕☕ Lunch £2alc Tea 30p–40p alc Dinner £8alc Wine £3.95 Last dinner 9pm
Credit cards 1 3

★★**Kirkwall** Harbour St (Allied Scotland) ☎(0856) 2232 Telex no 76357
Stone building near the pier head, with views across the bay.
40rm(10🛁) (1fb) CTV in all bedrooms ® ✽sB&B£16 sB&B🛁£18 dB&B£30 dB&B🛁£40 B
Lift ☾ CTV 🚭 *xmas* ♿
☕☕ Last dinner 8.30pm
Credit cards 1 2 3 4 5

✕✕***Foveran*** St Ola ☎(0856) 2389
(Classification awarded for dinner only.) Small, modern, purpose built restaurant.
Closed mid Oct–mid Nov Dinner not served Sun & Mon, mid Nov–Apr
45 seats Last dinner 9.30pm 20P bedrooms available
Credit cards 1 2 3 **VS**

K

KIRKWHELPINGTON
Northumberland
Map **12** NY98

★★**Knowesgate** Knowesgate (Inter-Hotels, Minotel) ☎Otterburn (0830) 40261
Modern hotel complex.
14rm(8🛁6🚿) CTV in all bedrooms ® sB&B🛁🚿£16–£20 dB&B🛁🚿£26–£30 B
100P🚗
V☕☕ Bar lunch £1.90–£5.50&alc Tea £1.85 Dinner £7.50&alc Wine £3.50 Last dinner 9pm
Credit cards 1 2 3 5 **VS**

KIRRIEMUIR
Tayside *Angus*
Map **15** NO35

★**Airlie Arms** St Malcolm's Wynd ☎(0575) 72847 →

Homely hotel in the town centre.
6rm
CTV 6P
Lunch £2.50–£5 Tea £1.25 High Tea £2.50–£5 Dinner £4–£5 Last dinner 8pm

KNARESBOROUGH
North Yorkshire
Map **8** SE35

★★★**Dower House** Bond End
Harrogate (0423) 863302
Closed Xmas
16rm(11 3) Annexe: 4rm(3 1) (4fb) CTV in all bedrooms Ⓡ sB&B£21–£33 sB&B £25–£37.95 dB&B£35 dB&B £39.95–£60
60P
V Lunch £5.95–£6.50 Dinner £8.95–£9.55 Wine £4.95 Last dinner 9.30pm
Credit cards 1 3

★★**Mitre** Station Rd Harrogate (0423) 863589
A Georgian-type building set in a picturesque part of the town.
7rm(2 5) CTV in all bedrooms Ⓡ sB&B £21–£25 dB&B £32–£36
CTV *xmas*
English & French **V** Lunch £3.75alc Tea 95palc Dinner £7.50alc Wine £3.80 Last dinner 10pm
Credit card 3 **VS**

KNIGHTWICK
Hereford & Worcester
Map **3** SO75

★**Talbot** (0886) 21235 RS Xmas wk
Old coaching inn with modern extension close to the River Teme.
9rm(3 2) (1fb) sB&B fr£9 sB&B fr£13 dB&B fr£17.50 dB&B fr£20.50
CTV 60P squash sauna bath
V Bar lunch 45p–£4.75&alc Dinner fr£5&alc Wine £3 Last dinner 9pm
VS

KNIPOCH
Strathclyde *Argyllshire*
Map **10** NM82

★★★ ***BL*** **Knipoch** (6m S of Oban)
Kilninver (08526) 251
Modernised and extended Georgian building overlooking sea loch.
21 CTV in all bedrooms sB&B £12.50–£35 dB&B £15–£35 Continental breakfast
40P
Bar lunch £5alc Dinner £15–£18&alc Wine £4 Last dinner 9.30pm
Credit cards 1 2 3 5

KNOCK
Isle of Skye, Highland *Inverness-shire*
Map **13** NG60

★★ ***H*** **Toravaig House** Knock Bay (Inter-Hotels) Isle Ornsay (04713) 231
Closed Nov–Feb
Large, comfortable friendly house in secluded remote location.
10rm(4) Ⓡ sB&B fr£12 dB&B fr£24 dB&B fr£28
CTV 20P
V Lunch fr£4 Tea fr£1.50 Dinner fr£8.50
Credit cards 2 3 5 **VS**

KNOWLE
West Midlands
Map **7** SP17

★★ ***B*** **Greswolde Arms** High St (Ansells)
(05645) 2711
19rm(6) CTV in all bedrooms Ⓡ sB&B fr£21 dB&B fr£27.50 dB&B fr£32
CTV 100P
Mainly grills Lunch fr£5.50&alc Dinner £6alc Wine £3.90
Last dinner 10pm
Credit cards 1 2 3 **VS**

KNOWL HILL
Berkshire
Map **4** SU87

✕✕**Bird in Hand** Littlewick Green (062882) 2781
English & French 70 seats Lunch £6.50&alc Dinner £12.50alc Wine £4.75 Last dinner 10.30pm 100P
S% Credit cards 1 2 3 5

KNOWSLEY
Merseyside
Map **7** SJ49

☆☆☆**Crest Hotel – East Lancs Road**
East Lancs Rd (Crest)
051-546 7531 Telex no 629769
Liverpool plan **5** Closed Xmas wk
Modern motel; situated eight miles from Liverpool.
50 CTV in all bedrooms Ⓡ * sB fr£30 (room only) dB fr£39 (room only)
150P CFA
International **V** * Lunch £4.95–£6.75 Tea 55p Dinner fr£7.50&alc Wine £5.25 Last dinner 9.30pm
Credit cards 1 2 3 4 5 **VS**

KNUTSFORD
Cheshire
Map **7** SJ77

★**Rose & Crown** King St (0565) 52366
Former coaching inn, built in 1647, and restored in 1923, but retaining its original Tudor style.
11rm (2fb) CTV in all bedrooms Ⓡ sB&B£14–£18 dB&B£21–£26
CTV 25P
V Lunch £3–£3.75 High Tea £3–£3.50 Dinner £6.50–£7.50 Wine £3.80 Last dinner 9.15pm
Credit cards 1 3 **VS**

✕✕**La Belle Époque** 60 King St
(0565) 3060
Closed Sun Lunch not served
French 80 seats Dinner £15alc Wine £5.50 Last dinner 10pm bedrooms available
S% Credit cards 1 2 3 4 5

✕✕**David's Place** 10 Princess St
(0565) 3356
Closed Sun & Public Hols
English, French & Italian 70 seats
*Lunch £2–£14&alc Dinner £10–£15 &alc Wine £4.10 Last dinner 9.45pm
Credit cards 1 2 3 5

KYLEAKIN
Isle of Skye, Highland *Inverness-shire*
Map **13** NG72

★★ ***Marine*** Kyle (0599) 4585
RS Nov–Mar
25rm Annexe: 30rm
CTV 10P
Last dinner 7.45pm

KYLE OF LOCHALSH
Highland *Ross & Cromarty*
Map **13** NG72

★★★ ***Lochalsh*** Ferry Rd Kyle (0599) 4202
Situated in a prominent position, with fine views across the Kyle of Lochalsh to Skye.
45rm(29) CTV in all bedrooms Ⓡ
Lift 4P 5
English & French Last dinner 9pm
Credit cards 1 2 3 4 5 **VS**

LACEBY
Humberside
Map **8** TA20

★★**Oaklands Hotel & Country Club**
Grimsby (0472) 72248
53rm(47 3) (2fb) 1 CTV in 39 bedrooms TV in 14 bedrooms Ⓡ sB&B£20 sB&B fr£25 dB&B fr£35
CTV 250P CFA squash sauna bath Disco Sat
International **V** Lunch £5–£7.90 Tea fr£1.80 Dinner fr£7.90&alc Wine £4 Last dinner 9.30pm
Credit cards 1 2 3 4 5

LAGGAN BRIDGE
Highland *Inverness-shire*
Map **14** NN69

★ ***H*** **Monadhliath** (05284) 276
This former manse has been extended and is now a small, family-run hotel.
8rm (3fb) Ⓡ sB&B£9–£11.75 dB&B£18–£21
CTV 40P *xmas*
V Lunch £3.45–£6.25 Tea 55p–£1.20 Dinner £5.45&alc Wine £3.65 Last dinner 9.30pm
Credit cards 1 3

LAIRG
Highland *Sutherland*
Map **14** NC50
★★★**Sutherland Arms** (Scottish Highland) ☎(0549) 2291
Closed mid Oct–mid Apr
Stone-built hotel with views over the River Shin and dam.
24rm(15⇌1⋔) (3fb) Ⓡ ✻ sB&B⇌⋔£26 dB&B⇌⋔£42 B
CTV 30P ✽
V ☕ ✻ Lunch £5.50–£6.75 Dinner £6.50–£8.75&alc Wine £4.60 Last dinner 8.30pm
Credit cards 1 2 3 5 **VS**

LAMLASH
Isle of Arran, Strathclyde *Bute*
Map **10** NS03
✕**Carraig Mhor** ☎(07706) 453
Closed Sun, Mon & Nov
26 seats ✻ Lunch £1.65–£3.30 Dinner £9 Wine £3.55 Last dinner 8.45pm
VS

LAMORNA COVE
Cornwall
Map **2** SW42
★★★*HL* **Lamorna Cove** (Inter-Hotels) ☎Penzance (0736) 731411
Closed Dec & Jan
Comfortable character hotel with well appointed bedrooms, in attractive Lamorna Valley.
19rm(15⇌4⋔) (2fb) 1 CTV in bedrooms sB&B⇌⋔£14–£23 dB&B⇌⋔£28–£46 B
Lift 25P ✽ (heated) sauna bath
V ☕ Lunch fr£5.85 Tea fr£1.25 High Tea fr£4 Dinner £8.50&alc Wine £5.30 Last dinner 9.30pm
Credit cards 1 2 3 5

★★*L* ***Menwinnion Country House***
Lamorna Valley ☎St Buryan (073672) 233
Closed Nov–Jan
Charming, well appointed, tiny country house in secluded gardens offering excellent food.
8rm(2⇌) CTV in all bedrooms B
CTV 12P ✽ nc12yrs
☕ Last dinner 10pm
Credit cards 1 2 3 5

LAMPETER
Dyfed
Map **2** SN54
★★**Black Lion Royal** High St ☎(0570) 422172
Traditional hotel located in the town centre.
17rm(7⇌) (2fb) CTV in all bedrooms Ⓡ sB&B£11.50–£13.50 sB&B⇌£13.50–£15 dB&B fr£20–£22.50 dB&B⇌£22.50–£25 B
CTV 50P ✽
V ☕ Lunch £5 Tea 60–80p Dinner £6&alc Wine £3.95 Last dinner 9.45pm
Credit cards 1 2 3 5 **VS**
See advert on page 346

★★*HB* **Falcondale Country House**
☎(0570) 422910 RS Sun evening
Good quality hotel in extensive grounds.
17rm(2⇌12⋔) (8fb) CTV in all bedrooms Ⓡ sB&B£14.75–£18.50 sB&B⇌⋔£16.75–£21 dB&B£21.50–£27 dB&B⇌⋔£25.75–£32 B
Lift CTV 65P ✽ (hard) *xmas*
English & French ☕ Lunch £5.95&alc Tea £1.50–£1.75 Dinner £5.95&alc Wine £3.95
Last dinner 9.30pm
Credit card 3 **VS**
See advert on page 346

LAMPHEY
Dyfed
Map **2** SN00
★★★ ***Court*** (Best Western) ☎(0646) 672273
Imposing small country house with comfortable bedrooms and small leisure complex. →

14➡ CTV in all bedrooms ✱ ⊟ 100P CFA ✿ ⛵(heated) U ⌂
V ✿ ☐ Last dinner 9.45pm
Credit cards 1 2 3 5 **VS**

LANARK

Strathclyde *Lanarkshire*
Map **11** NS84

★★ ***Cartland Bridge*** ☎ (0555) 4426
Closed New Year's Day
Baronial style mansion in spacious wooded grounds.
15rm ⊟ CTV 300P ✿ ♪ Live music and dancing Sat ⌂
⊟ French **V** ✿ Last dinner 9.30pm
Credit cards 1 2 3 5

LANCASTER

Lancashire
Map **7** SD46

☆☆☆ ***L* Post House** Caton Rd (close to junct. 34, M6) (Trusthouse Forte)
☎ (0524) 65999
120➡ CTV in all bedrooms ® ✱ sB➡ fr£39.50 dB➡ fr£49.50 (room only) ⊟
Lift ☾ ### 166P ⊡(heated) ♪ sauna bath ⌂ *xmas*
⊟ International ✿ ☐ ✱ Lunch fr£7.50&alc Dinner fr£10&alc Wine £5.45 Last dinner 10pm
Credit cards 1 2 3 4 5

★★ **Royal Kings Arms** Market St
☎ (0524) 32451
Solid, Victorian building in the town centre, close to the Castle.
59rm (7➡) (16fb) CTV in 7 bedrooms ®

L

*sB&B£14 sB&B⇌£19 dB&B£26 dB&B⇌£36 B

Lift ☾ CTV 12P *xmas*

V✿☐*Bar lunch £1.40–£1.90 Tea 50p Dinner fr£6 Last dinner 8.15pm

✕✕**Portofino** 23 Castle Hill ☎(0524) 32388

Closed Sun

Italian 40 seats Lunch £3.50–£4.50&alc Dinner £8alc Wine £4.20 Last dinner 10.45pm

Credit cards 1 2 3 5

LANCHESTER
Co Durham
Map **12** NZ14

✕✕***Kings Head Hotel*** ☎(0207) 520054

A large, stone-built, village inn situated on the main through route.

Closed Mon Lunch not served Sat Dinner not served Sun

50 seats Last dinner 9.15pm 120P bedrooms available

Credit cards 1 2 3 5

LANGBANK
Strathclyde *Renfrewshire*
Map **10** NS37

★★★ ***BL*****Gleddoch House**
☎(047554) 711 Telex no 779801
Closed 26–27 Dec & 1–2 Jan

Former family residence of Sir James Lithgow, on a hillside with views towards Dumbarton and the Northern mountains.

19rm(17⇌⋒)(2fb) 1☐ CTV in all bedrooms ® sB&B⇌⋒£44–£51 dB&B⇌⋒£62–£80 B

☾ 100P ✽ ☐(heated) ⚑ ♪ squash U snooker sauna bath

→

▣Scottish & French Lunch fr£9&alc Dinner fr£14&alc Wine £6 Last dinner 9pm

Credit cards [1] [2] [3] [5] **VS**

LANGDALE, GREAT
Cumbria
Map **11** NY30

★★★**Langdales** ☎(09667) 253
Two-storey hotel in the Langdale Valley with attractive gardens bounded by Langdale Beck.

20rm(12🛁4🚿)(3fb) ✻sB&B fr£18 sB&B🛁🚿 fr£21 dB&B fr£36 dB&B🛁🚿 fr£42 B

CTV 50P ✽ *xmas*

V ♧ ▭ Lunch fr£5 Tea fr55p Dinner fr£10 Wine £3.75 Last dinner 8.15pm

LANGHO
Lancashire
Map **7** SD73

✕✕✕**Northcote Manor** Northcote Rd ☎Blackburn (0254) 40555

Lunch not served Sat

▣English & French **V** 75 seats Lunch £3.50 High Tea £2.80 Dinner £6.80&alc Wine £3.95 Last dinner 10pm 40P bedrooms available

Credit cards [1] [2] [3] [5]

L

LANGHOLM
Dumfries & Galloway *Dumfriesshire*
Map **11** NY38

★★**Eskdale** Market Pl (Minotel) ☎(0541) 80357
Built on the site of the former King's Arms Inn which was a famous coaching hostelry.

14rm(3🚿)(2fb) ® ✻sB&B £10.50–£11 sB&B🚿 £12–£12.50 dB&B £21–£22 dB&B🚿 £24–£25 B

CTV 12P

♧ ▭ ✻Lunch £3.50alc Tea 95p alc High Tea £3alc Dinner £6.50alc Wine £3.20 Last dinner 9pm

Credit cards [1] [3] **VS**

★**Crown** High St ☎(0541) 80247
8rm (1fb) sB&B £9.50 dB&B £18 B
CTV 4P

▣English, French, Indian & Italian ♧ Lunch £1–£4.50&alc Dinner £5.50–£6.50&alc Wine £3.50 Last dinner 8.30pm

★**Holmwood House** Holmwood Dr (off B709) ☎(0541) 80211
Neatly-appointed, Victorian house, situated on the edge of a housing estate.

7rm(1🛁1🚿)(1fb) sB&B £12 sB&B🛁🚿 £13.50 dB&B £22 dB&B🛁🚿 £25

CTV 25P ✽

♧Lunch £3.50–£5.50&alc Dinner £6–£7.50&alc Wine £3 Last dinner 8.30pm

LANGLAND BAY
West Glamorgan
Map **2** SS68
See also **Mumbles** and **Swansea**

★★★**Osborne** Rotherslade Rd (Embassy) ☎Swansea (0792) 66274
Popular business hotel overlooking Rotherslade Bay.

42rm(21🛁)(2fb) CTV in all bedrooms ® sB&B £24 sB&B🛁 £33 dB&B £33.75 dB&B🛁 £42 B

Lift ☾ CTV 40P *xmas*

▣Welsh, English & French **V** ♧ ▭ Lunch fr£4.50 Dinner fr£6.75 Wine £4.50 Last dinner 9pm

Credit cards [1] [2] [3] [4] [5]

★★**Brynfield Manor** Brynfield Rd ☎Swansea (0792) 66208
Small country house style hotel with friendly service and commendable food standards.

9rm(6🚿)(1fb) CTV in bedrooms ® sB&B £18–£19.50 sB&B🛁 £21.20–£22 dB&B £32–£34 dB&B🛁 £34–£36 B

CTV 40P ✽ Cabaret Sat & Sun

▣British & French **V** ♧ ▭ Lunch £4.50–£5&alc Tea fr£2.50 Dinner fr£6.50 Wine £5.50 Last dinner 9pm

Credit cards [1] [2]

★★**Langland Court** Langland Court Rd (Best Western) ☎Swansea (0792) 68505

Telex no 497072
Closed 25–31 Dec
Small, family-run hotel in attractive gardens.

13rm(2🛁5🚿) Annexe: 7rm(1🛁)(3fb) CTV in all bedrooms sB&B £16–£18 sB&B🛁🚿 £21–£25 dB&B £30–£35 dB&B🛁🚿 £36–£45 B

☾ CTV 40P 5🚗 ✽ billiards Live music and dancing Sat Cabaret Sat

♧ ▭ ✻Lunch £5–£7&alc Tea 70p–£1.20 High Tea £5 Dinner £6.25–£11 Wine £5 Last dinner 8.30pm

Credit cards [1] [2] [3] **VS**

★**Ael-y-Don** ☎Swansea (0792) 66466
Closed Nov–Feb
A small, family-run hotel with sea views.

18rm(1🛁5🚿)(6fb) ® ✻ sB&B £10.25–£11.25 sB&B🛁🚿 £11.25–£12.25 dB&B £20.50–£22.50 dB&B🛁🚿 £22.50–£24.50 B

CTV 12P 3🚗 ✽ nc5yrs

V ♧ Lunch £4.50–£4.75 Dinner £4.50–£4.75 Wine £3.50 Last dinner 7.30pm

LANGSTONE
Gwent
Map **3** ST38

☆☆**New Inn Motel** (Ansells) ☎Newport (0633) 412426
Conveniently situated just off the M4, north-east of Newport.

36rm(13🛁33🚿)(1fb) CTV in all bedrooms ® ✻ sB&B🛁🚿 fr£23.75 dB&B🛁🚿 fr£31 B

CTV 200P

♧Lunch fr£4.50&alc Dinner fr£4.75&alc Wine £3.90 Last dinner 10pm

Credit cards [1] [2] [3] **VS**

LANGTOFT
Humberside
Map **8** TA06

✕**Old Mill** Mill Ln ☎Driffield (0377) 87284

▣English & Continental **V** 45 seats Lunch £6.50&alc Tea £1.50–£2.50 High Tea £2.85–£4.50 Dinner £6.50&alc Wine £3.50 Last dinner 10pm 30P

Credit cards [1] [3]

LANREATH
Cornwall
Map **2** SX15

★★**Punch Bowl Inn** ☏(0503) 20218
Closed Nov–Mar
Early 17th-century, former coaching inn and smugglers haunt, whose sign was painted by Augustus John.
18rm(11⇌2⋒)(2fb) 3▭ CTV in 16 bedrooms ® sB&B£12.55–£14.15 sB&B⇌£14.75–£16.35 dB&B£25.10–£28.30 dB&B⇌£29.50–£32.70
CTV 50P 4🏠
♆ Bar lunch £2.50alc Dinner £7.20&alc Wine £3.40 Last dinner 9pm
Credit card 1

LARGS
Strathclyde *Ayrshire*
Map **10** NS25

★★**Elderslie** John St, Broomfields ☏(0475) 686460
A 19th-century building on Largs sea front, commanding magnificent views.
25rm(9⇌4⋒)(2fb) ® ✻ sB&B fr£13.20 sB&B⇌⋒ fr£14.80 dB&B fr£26.40 dB&B⇌⋒ fr£29.60
CTV 40P ✿ ⌂
Lunch fr£3.75 Dinner £6.50–£8 Wine £4.50 Last dinner 8.30pm
Credit cards 1 3 **VS**

★★***Queens*** North Esp ☏(0475) 673253
Traditional, seafront hotel, offering modest accommodation at a reasonable price.
14rm ℞
CTV 14P ✿
Last dinner 8.30pm
Credit cards 2 3

★★***St Helens*** 10–16 Greenock Rd ☏(0475) 672328
Detached stone building in own grounds, looking out across the Firth of Clyde.
28rm(4⇌) CTV in 4 bedrooms ℞
CTV 36P 2🏠 ✿ ⌂
♆ ▭ Last dinner 10pm
Credit cards 2 5

★★**Springfield** Greenock Rd ☏(0475) 673119
Popular resort hotel with continental style dining room. Many bedrooms have sea views.
43rm(2⇌12⋒)(5fb) CTV in 6 bedrooms TV in 2 bedrooms sB&B£13.20–£13.85 sB&B⇌⋒£15.20–£15.95 dB&B£23–£24.20 dB&B⇌⋒£27–£28.40
Lift CTV 80P ✿ *xmas*
▣ French **V** ♆ ▭ Lunch £4–£6.50 Tea 50p–£1 High Tea £3.25–£6.50 Dinner £5.50–£6.50&alc Wine £2.95 Last dinner 9pm
Credit cards 1 2 3 5

LARKFIELD
Kent
Map **5** TQ65

☆☆☆**Larkfield** London Rd (Anchor) ☏West Malling (0732) 846858 Telex no 957420
52rm(48⇌4⋒)(3fb) 1▭ CTV in all bedrooms ® ✻ sB&B⇌⋒£33 dB&B⇌⋒£40 ℞
☾ 104P CFA ✿ *xmas* ♿
V ♆ ▭ ✻ Lunch fr£4.95 Tea 75p Dinner fr£4.95 Last dinner 10.15pm
Credit cards 1 2 3 4 5

✕✕✕**Wealden Hall** 773 London Rd ☏West Malling (0732) 840259
Franco Italian cuisine served in attractive wooden beamed surroundings.
Dinner not served Sun
▣ French & Italian 60 seats ✻ Lunch fr£5.75&alc Dinner fr£8.50&alc Wine £4.95 Last dinner 10.30pm
S%

LASTINGHAM
North Yorkshire
Map **8** SE79

★★♣**Lastingham Grange** ☏(07515) 345 →

L

Closed mid Dec–Feb
A 17th-century house of local stone, with extensive gardens, to which a wing was added during the last century.
12➡(2fb) CTV available in bedrooms Ⓡ sB&B➡£25.50 dB&B➡£46 B
30P 2🚗 ✽
V ♔ ☕ Lunch £5.50–£6.25 Tea 45p–£1.50 Dinner £9.50–£10.50 Wine £3.25 Last dinner 8.30pm
Credit cards 2 5 **VS**

LAUDER
Borders *Berwickshire*
Map **12** NT54
★★**Black Bull** Market Pl ☎(05782) 208
13rm(5⋔) Ⓡ sB&B£9.20–£13.15 sB&B⋔£11.50–£14.30 dB&B£18.40–£26.36 dB&B⋔£23–£28.60
CTV 30P
V ♔ ☕ Lunch fr£4.50&alc Tea fr£1.50 High Tea £3–£4.50 Dinner £6–£7.50&alc Last dinner 9pm

★**Eagle** 1 Market Pl ☎(05782) 426
Neatly appointed inn on main village street.
6rm CTV available in bedrooms ✱sB&B fr£8 dB&B fr£16 Continental breakfast
CTV 6P
Mainly grills ♔ ☕ ✱Bar lunch £2.50alc

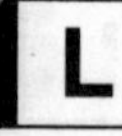
L

High Tea fr£3.75 Dinner £5.50alc Wine £3.50 Last dinner 9pm
Credit card 3

LAUNCESTON
Cornwall
Map **2** SX38
★★**Eagle House** Castle St ☎(0566) 2036
Closed Xmas Day
Georgian mansion close to the castle green and the town centre, with wide, country views.
19rm(2➡3⋔)(4fb) 1▭ TV available in bedrooms ✱sB&B£9 sB&B➡⋔£11 dB&B£17 dB&B➡⋔£19 B
CTV 40P Live music and dancing Sat ♿
V ♔ ☕ ✱Lunch £3.20–£3.60&alc Tea fr25p High Tea fr£1.45 Dinner £3.25–£3.90&alc Wine £2.90 Last dinner 9pm
Credit cards 3 5

★★**White Hart** Broad St ☎(0566) 2013
Former coaching inn of great character but modern facilities.
28rm(13➡2⋔)(2fb) CTV in 15 bedrooms Ⓡ sB&B£12 sB&B➡⋔£14 dB&B£20 dB&B➡⋔£24 B
CTV 18P CFA *xmas*

♔ ☕ Lunch £3–£5.50&alc Tea £1.25 Dinner £5.50–£6&alc Wine £3.65 Last dinner 9.30pm
Credit cards 1 2 3 5 **VS**

LAVENHAM
Suffolk
Map **5** TL94
★★★ *L* **Swan** High St (Trusthouse Forte) ☎(0787) 247477
Four picturesque Tudor houses with authentic beamed ceilings make up this fine hotel.
42➡(2fb) CTV in all bedrooms Ⓡ sB&B➡£39 dB&B➡£57 B
CTV 60P ✽ *xmas*
♔ ☕ Last dinner 9.30pm
Credit cards 1 2 3 4 5

LEAMINGTON SPA (ROYAL)
Warwickshire
Map **4** SP36
★★★**Falstaff** 20 Warwick New Rd ☎(0926) 312044
Neat Victorian house with attractive wood-faced modern extension and a small garden.
50rm(28➡15⋔)(1fb) 3▭ CTV in 39 bedrooms TV in 11 bedrooms Ⓡ sB&B➡⋔£26 dB&B➡⋔£36 B
Lift ☾ 80P sauna bath CFA Disco Fri *xmas*

🍽English, French & Italian ♈ ☐ Lunch £4.95–£6.50&alc Tea fr£2.50 Dinner £5.50–£7&alc Wine £4.25 Last dinner 9.30pm

Credit cards 1 2 3 4 5

★★★**Manor House** Avenue Rd (Anchor) ☎(0926) 23251 Telex no 311653

Large, impressive hotel close to the railway station and the town centre.

53rm(47➡6🚿)(4fb) CTV in all bedrooms Ⓡ ✻sB&B➡🚿£32 dB&B➡🚿£39 Ḃ

Lift ☾ 100P CFA *xmas*

🍽English & French **V** ♈ ☐ Lunch fr£3.75&alc Tea fr55p Dinner fr£6.75&alc Wine £4.50 Last dinner 10pm

Credit cards 1 2 3 5

★★★**Regent** 77 The Parade (Best Western) ☎(0926) 27231

Traditional, town centre hotel.

80rm(69➡3🚿)(7fb) CTV in all bedrooms sB&B➡🚿£26 dB&B➡🚿£37 Ḃ

Lift ☾ CTV 70P 30🏠 CFA Live music and dancing Thu & Fri *xmas*

★★

❀★★🏛MALLORY COURT, LEAMINGTON SPA

Harbury Ln, Bishops Tachbrook (2m S off A452) ☎(0926) 30214 Telex no 317294

Closed 25–30 Dec & 1 Jan

Within its area this hotel stands out for its quality, both in accommodation and food. It was built at the turn of the century by a car manufacturer and was splendidly finished. Set in 10 acres of landscaped gardens it provides a peaceful retreat for the businessman, a staging post for the traveller, but it is also well worth visiting for its own sake! Jeremy Mort and Alan Holland are the two owners who have made such a success of the hotel. It has been beautifully decorated and furnished, and there are two comfortable sitting rooms, both with open fires in season, fresh flowers adding to the attraction of the immaculately kept hotel. Bedrooms are most spacious and provided with everything for your comfort; as well as the usual good quality toiletries, phone, books and bath robes that demonstrate the thought devoted to guests.

Alan Holland supervises the kitchen to good effect and meals are served in two attractive panelled rooms with sparkling table appointments. There

are set menus and the four course dinner is the one that shows the ambition and skill of the cooking. They mainly follow the modern school which is light and well flavoured, and our members tell us how delicious it is. The wine list is also worthy of mention. The owners are to be congratulated on creating so fine a hotel which has many more amenities than its classification might imply.

9rm(7➡) 1🛏 CTV in all bedrooms ✯ sB&B fr£32 dB&B fr£54 dB&B➡ fr£74 Continental breakfast

50P 6🏠🚗❀ ≗ squash

🍽French ♈ ☐ Lunch fr£11.50 Tea fr£4.50 Dinner fr£18 Wine £8.50 Last dinner 9.45pm

S% Credit cards 1 2 3 4

🍽English & French ♈ ☐ Lunch fr£6.25 Tea fr80p Dinner fr£8.50 Wine £5 Last dinner 10.45pm

Credit cards 1 2 3 5

★★**Abbacourt** 40 Kenilworth Rd ☎(0926) 311188

Large, converted house, popular with business people.

19rm(3➡6🚿)(2fb) CTV in 10 bedrooms TV in 12 bedrooms Ⓡ ✻sB&B fr£16.10 sB&B➡🚿 fr£22.42 dB&B fr£36.80 dB&B➡🚿 fr£39.10

30P

🍽International ♈ ☐ ✻Lunch fr£5.50&alc Tea fr£1.50 High Tea fr£3.50 Dinner £10alc Last dinner 9.30pm

Credit cards 1 2 3 5

★★**Angel** 143 Regent St ☎(0926) 23683

RS Sun

17rm(6➡4🚿) CTV in all bedrooms Ⓡ ✯ ✻sB&B £19 sB&B➡£21 dB&B £26 dB&B➡£28 Ḃ

☾ # ⚡ 🅟 50P Live music and dancing Fri & Sat Cabaret Sat

🍽International **V** ♈ ☐ ✻Lunch fr£4.75&alc Tea fr£1.50 Dinner fr£5.75&alc Wine £4 Last dinner 10pm

Credit cards 1 2 3 5

★***Amersham*** 34 Kenilworth Rd ☎(0926) 21637

Small, quiet proprietor run hotel.

14rm CTV available in bedrooms

CTV 14P

🍽English & French ♈ Last dinner 8.30pm

Credit cards 1 3

★***Chesford House*** 12 Clarendon St ☎(0926) 20924

Converted private house, close to the town centre.

10rm(3➡4🚿) CTV in 3 bedrooms TV in 2 bedrooms Ⓡ ✯ Ḃ

10P 1🏠🚗 sauna bath

♈ Last dinner 8pm

Credit card 2 **VS**

See advert on page 352

L

★ *HB* **Lansdowne** 87 Clarendon St ☎(0926) 21313 Telex no 337556
Comfortable hotel on the town centre crossroads.
10rm(2⇌2⋒)(1fb) sB&B£15.85 sB&B⇌⋒£19.50 dB&B£23.95 dB&B⇌⋒£27.50 B
CTV 8P
English, French, Italian & Swiss **V** Lunch £6.95 Tea £3.25 Dinner fr£7.95 Wine £4.95 Last dinner 8.30pm
Credit card 1

★ **Park** 17 Avenue Rd ☎(0926) 28376
Busy hotel set in a quiet area of the town.
16rm(2⇌6⋒)(1fb) sB&B£13.80 sB&B⇌⋒£15.20 dB&B£22.10 dB&B⇌⋒£24.40 B
CTV 14P
V Lunch £1.50–£4 Tea 75p–£1 High Tea £2.50–£3 Dinner £7–£8 Wine £3.75 Last dinner 9pm
VS

LECHLADE
Gloucestershire
Map **4** SU29

✕ **Trout** ☎(0367) 52313
Friendly hospitable Thameside inn where local trout is the speciality.
Lunch not served in restaurant but full menu available in the bar
48 seats ✱Lunch £7.50alc Dinner £7.50alc Wine £3.50 Last dinner 9.30pm 150P
Credit cards 1 2 3 **VS**

L

LECKMELM
Highland *Ross & Cromarty*
Map **14** NH19

★ **Tir-Aluinn** ☎Ullapool (0854) 2074
Closed Oct–19 May
16rm(3⇌) sB&B fr£12.65 sB&B⇌£14 dB&B£25.30 dB&B⇌£28
30P ♿
Bar lunch fr£2 Tea fr£1.50 Dinner fr£5.75 Wine £3.64 Last dinner 8pm

LEDAIG
Strathclyde *Argyllshire*
Map **10** NM93

★★★

★★★ **ISLE OF ERISKA, LEDAIG**
☎(063172) 371 Telex no 727897
Doocot-G (Eriska)
Closed Nov–Mar

A fine example of a British country house, this baronial style granite building set on a peaceful small island provides a wonderful spot for a holiday. There are comfortable sitting rooms with Eastern rugs, antiques, comfortable chairs and lots of fresh flowers. The library bar makes a popular rendezvous to meet other guests – indeed a house party atmosphere generally prevails here – and there are a number of activities available from the hotel such as croquet, sailing, ponies for the children or you could just restfully watch the wildlife and domestic animals in the surrounding fields and on the loch.
The generally spacious bedrooms are comfortable, individually decorated, and provided with complementary toiletries and fresh fruit. Mr and Mrs Buchanan-Smith are the owners who have created a uniquely enjoyable atmosphere. Nothing seems too much trouble for them and this is one aspect that our members comment on most favourably. Another is the food, which is under the care of Mrs Buchanan-

Smith. You can start the day by helping yourself from the sumptuous breakfast laid out on the sideboard, then go out for the day and return to a fine traditional afternoon tea – but leave room for the six course dinner to come! The main course, without choice, is a large joint or turkey carved at your table from a heated trolley. The farm and gardens provide much of the produce and the cooking is of the country house type. Certainly you will not go hungry!
21⇌(1fb) CTV in all bedrooms ® sB&B⇌£59–£65 (incl dinner) dB&B⇌£118–£139 (incl dinner)
P CFA ✽ (hard)
High Tea fr£5.50 Dinner fr£19 Wine £4.20 Last dinner 8.30pm
Credit card 2

LEDBURY
Hereford & Worcester
Map **3** SO73

★★ **Feathers** High St ☎(0531) 2600
A 16th-century, half-timbered, coaching inn for the tourist and businessman alike.

10⋒(1fb) CTV in all bedrooms ® sB&B⋒£18.75–£24 dB&B⋒£37.50 B
☾ 10P 10 squash *xmas*
English & French Lunch £5.95&alc Tea fr£1.50 Dinner fr£5.95&alc Wine £2.75 Last dinner 9.30pm
Credit cards 1 2 5

★★ **Verzons** Trumpet (3m W A438) ☎Trumpet (053183) 381
Comfortable, country hotel with a popular restaurant.

7rm(2→1⋔)(2fb)3⊟CTV in 4 bedrooms TV in 2 bedrooms ® sB&B fr£10.50 dB&B fr£26 dB&B→⋔ fr£26 Ⓑ

40P ✽ U Live music and dancing Sat *xmas*

V ♧ Bar lunch £1.25–£3.45 Dinner £6.50–£10.50alc Wine £3.30 Last dinner 10pm

Credit cards 1 3 **VS**

LEEDS
West Yorkshire
Map **8** SE33
See plan

☆☆☆☆**Ladbroke Dragonara** Neville St (Ladbroke) ☎(0532) 442000 Telex no 557143

Modern, tower-block hotel in the centre of Leeds, next to the railway station.

239rm(207→32⋔) CTV in all bedrooms ® ✻sB→⋔ fr£46 dB→⋔ fr£54.50 (room only) Ⓑ

Lift ☾ # 10P 80 ⌂ CFA Live music and dancing Fri & Sat

⊟ International **V** ♧ ⊒ ✻ Lunch fr£6.50 Dinner fr£8.50 Last dinner 10pm

Credit cards 1 2 3 4 5

★★★★**Queen's** City Sq ☎(0532) 431323 Telex no 55161

Closed 4 days Xmas

Impressive, eight-storey building with a Portland stone façade, adjoining the city station.

195rm(175→) CTV in all bedrooms ® sB&B £20–£30 sB&B→ £28–£38 dB&B→ £40–£60 Ⓑ

Lift ☾ ⚑ CFA sauna bath

⊟ English & French **V** ♧ ⊒ Lunch £3–£7 Tea £1.50–£3 Dinner £6.50–£7&alc Wine £5.75 Last dinner 10pm

S% Credit cards 1 2 3 4 5

★★★**Merrion** Merrion Centre (Kingsmead) ☎(0532) 439191 Telex no 55459

Smart, comfortable modern hotel with stylish bedrooms.

120→(2fb) CTV in all bedrooms ® ✻sB&B→ fr£37 dB&B→ fr£47.50 Ⓑ

Lift ☾ ⚟ 400P CFA Disco Fri & Sat *xmas* ♿

⊟ English & French **V** ♧ ⊒ ✻ Lunch fr£5.95 Tea 75p High Tea £4.50 Dinner £7 Wine £5.25 Last dinner 10.30pm

Credit cards 1 2 3 5 **VS**

★★★**Hotel Metropole** King St (Trusthouse Forte) ☎(0532) 450841 Telex no 557755

110rm(71→3⋔)(3fb) CTV in all bedrooms ® sB&B £31.50 sB&B→⋔ £37.50 dB&B £42 dB&B→⋔ £50 Ⓑ

Lift ☾ 28P CFA

♧ Last dinner 10pm

Credit cards 1 2 3 4 5

☆☆☆**Stakis Windmill** Mill Green View, Seacroft (Stakis) ☎(0532) 732323 Telex no 778704

40→ CTV in all bedrooms ® ✻sB&B→ fr£34 dB&B→ fr£40 Ⓑ

Lift ☾ 200P Disco Fri & Sat ♿

♧ ⊒ Last dinner 10pm

Credit cards 1 2 3 5 **VS**

★**Hartrigg** Shire Oak Rd, Headingley (2½m NW A660) ☎(0532) 751568

Large, Edwardian house with lawns, gardens and mature trees in a quiet position on northern side of town.

28rm (1fb) sB&B £13.80 dB&B £23

CTV 18P 3 ⌂ ⛟

V Lunch £4.60 Tea 65p High Tea £4.60 Dinner £5.20 Wine £3.60 Last dinner 7pm

Credit cards 1 2 3

✕✕✕ ***Gardini's Terrazza*** Minerva House, 16 Greek St ☎(0532) 432880

Closed Sun Lunch not served Sat

⊟ Italian 120 seats Last dinner 11.30pm

⚑ Disco Sat

✕✕ ***New Milano*** 621 Roundhay Rd ☎(0532) 659752

Closed Sun Lunch not served Sat

⊟ Italian 60 seats Last dinner 11pm

Credit cards 1 2 3

L

✕**Rules** 188 Selby Rd ☎(0532) 604564
Closed Mon Dinner not served Sun
French 36 seats Dinner £10alc Wine £5.25 Last dinner 10pm P
Credit cards 1 3

At **Garforth** (6m E junc A63/A642)

☆☆☆**Ladbroke** (& Conference centre) Garforth Roundabout (Ladbroke) ☎(0532) 866556
156 300P

At **Oulton** (6m SE on A639)

☆☆☆**Crest** The Grove (Crest) ☎(0532) 826201
40 200P

LEEK
Staffordshire
Map **7** SJ95

★ ***Red Lion*** Market Sq ☎(0538) 382025
8rm
CTV 50P billiards
V Last dinner 9pm
Credit cards 1 3

LEEMING BAR
North Yorkshire
Map **8** SE28

★**White Rose** ☎Bedale (0677) 22707
Modest, clean roadside hotel.

12rm (2 8) CTV in all bedrooms sB&B£12.50 sB&B £12.50 dB&B£21.50 dB&B £21.50
30P
English & French V Lunch 95p–£3.50 Dinner £5.25–£8&alc Last dinner 10.30pm
Credit cards 1 2 3 VS

LEICESTER
Leicestershire
Map **4** SK50

★★★★**Grand** Granby St (Embassy) ☎(0533) 555599
Impressive, Victorian, city-centre building, standing on the main A6.
93 CTV in all bedrooms Ⓡ sB £33.75 (room only) dB £41.50 (room only)
Lift ☾ 130P 20 CFA Live music and dancing Sat in winter
V Lunch fr£6.70 Dinner fr£6.70 Wine £4.70
Last dinner 9.30pm
Credit cards 1 2 3 4 5

☆☆☆☆**Holiday Inn** St Nicholas Circle (Commonwealth) ☎(0533) 531161
Large, modern, purpose-built hotel close to the city centre.
188 (108fb) CTV in all bedrooms
*sB £37.38 (room only)
dB £44.28 (room only)
Lift ☾ # CFA (heated) sauna bath Live music and dancing Sat
French V Lunch £6.45–£6.95&alc Tea 85p alc Dinner £10alc Wine £4.95 Last dinner 10.15pm
Credit cards 1 2 3 5

★★★**Belmont** De Montfort St (Best Western) ☎(0533) 544773 Telex no 34619
Closed 24 Dec–3 Jan
Large Victorian house close to the A6, ½m south of the city centre.
40rm (33 3) Annexe: 21rm (9) (2fb) CTV in all bedrooms Ⓡ sB&B£24 sB&B fr£34 dB&B£34 dB&B fr£44
Lift ☾ 45P CFA
French Lunch £5–£6.50&alc Tea 75p High Tea £2.50 Dinner £6–£7&alc Wine £4.50 Last dinner 10pm
Credit cards 1 2 3

☆☆☆**Centre** Humberstone Rd ☎(0533) 20471 Telex no 341460
222 CTV in all bedrooms Ⓡ
Lift ☾ # CFA 25 Live music and dancing 4 nights wkly
English & French Last dinner 10.15pm
Credit cards 1 2 3 4 5

☆☆☆**Leicester Forest Moat House** Hinckley Rd, Leicester Forest East (Queens) ☎(0533) 394661
Closed 25–31 Dec
Attractive, modern building on the A47, with a predominantly commercial trade.
30➡⋒ CTV in all bedrooms Ⓡ sB&B➡⋒ £30 dB&B➡⋒ £36 ⊟
☾ 150P ✽
V ♔ ☕ Lunch £6–£9 Tea £1 Dinner £7&alc Wine £4.75 Last dinner 9.45pm
Credit cards ① ② ③ ④ ⑤

★★★**Leicestershire Moat House** Wigston Rd, Oadby (3m SE A6) (Queens Moat) ☎(0533) 719441
RS 25 Dec–2 Jan
29➡ CTV in all bedrooms Ⓡ
*sB&B➡ £16–£28.50 dB&B➡ £24–£36 ⊟
Lift ☾ 200P 6 CFA
French ♔ ☕ *Lunch fr£6.50 Tea fr50p Dinner fr£6.50 Wine £5.25 Last dinner 8.45pm
Credit cards ① ② ③ ⑤

☆☆☆**Post House** Braunstone Lane East (Trusthouse Forte) ☎(0533) 896688
Telex no 341009
Modern, purpose-built complex, located two miles from the city and close to the M1.
179➡ (80fb) CTV in all bedrooms Ⓡ sB&B➡ £39 dB&B➡ £51.50 ⊟
Lift ☾ CTV 102P CFA
♔ ☕ Last dinner 9.45pm
Credit cards ① ② ③ ④ ⑤

★**Rowans** 290 London Rd ☎(0533) 705364
Large Victorian house on the A6, 1m south of the city.
15rm (1fb) TV available in bedrooms sB&B £12–£15 dB&B £17.95–£19.95
CTV 15P
♔ Dinner £5.75–£6.75&alc Wine £3.95 Last dinner 7.30pm
Credit card ① **VS**

✕✕✕**Manor** Glen Parva Manor, The Ford, Little Glen Rd, Glen Parva (3m SW on A426) ☎(0533) 774604
A 16th-century manor house with later additions, approximately three miles from the city centre.
Closed Sun Lunch not served Sat
English and French **V** 80 seats Lunch fr£7 Dinner fr£9.95alc Wine £5.75 Last dinner 10pm 50P
Credit cards ① ② ③

✕✕✕***White House*** Scraptoft Ln ☎(0533) 415951
Lunch not served Sat
Dinner not served Sun
English & Continental 200 seats Last dinner 9.30pm 200P ⅟ Live music and dancing Sat
Credit cards ① ② ③ ⑤

✕✕***Giradot*** Goscote Hotel, Birstall (2m N off A6) ☎(0533) 674191
Closed Sun Lunch not served Sat Dinner not served Mon–Fri
English & French 100 seats Last dinner 10pm 150P
Credit cards ① ②

LEIGH
Greater Manchester
Map **7** SJ69

☆☆☆**Greyhound** Warrington Rd (Embassy) ☎(0942) 671256
Large public house, with a modern motel block at the rear.
56➡⋒ CTV in all bedrooms Ⓡ sB➡⋒ £35.50 (room only) dB➡⋒ £40.50 (room only) ⊟
Lift ☾ ⅟ 242P 8 Disco Sat
♔ ☕ Lunch fr£6.70 Dinner fr£6.70&alc Wine £4.30 Last dinner 9.30pm
S% Credit cards ① ② ③ ⑤

LEIGHTON BUZZARD
Bedfordshire
Map **4** SP92

★★★**Swan** High St ☎(0525) 372148
35➡ (2fb) CTV in all bedrooms Ⓡ sB&B➡ fr£33 dB&B➡ fr£43 ⊟
CTV 10P
V ♔ ☕ Lunch £6–£7.50&alc Tea 75p–£1 Dinner £8.50–£9.50&alc Wine £5.50 Last dinner 9.30pm
Credit cards ① ② ③ ⑤ **VS**

✕**Cross Keys** Market Sq ☎(0525) 373033
1st-floor restaurant run by husband and wife team
Dinner not served Sun & Mon
French & German **V** 48 seats Lunch £5–£6&alc Dinner £5–£6&alc Wine £4.90 Last dinner 10.30pm 4P
Credit cards ① ② ③ ⑤ **VS**

LEINTWARDINE
Hereford & Worcester
Map **7** SO47

✕**Lion** ☎(05473) 203
RS Mon & Sun
English & French **V** 40 seats Lunch £4.75alc Dinner £7.50alc *Wine £3.80 Last dinner 10pm 30P bedrooms available
Credit card ① **VS**

LEOMINSTER
Hereford & Worcester
Map **3** SO45

★★**Royal Oak** South St (Minotel) ☎(0568) 2610
Closed Xmas Day
A bustling, hospitable hotel in the centre of this busy, market town.
17rm (13➡1⋒) (1fb) 1 CTV in 6 bedrooms TV in 11 bedrooms Ⓡ sB&B➡⋒ £17.85 dB&B £26.50–£28.50 dB&B➡⋒ £30–£38 ⊟
CTV 50P
♔ ☕ Lunch £7.75alc Tea 65p alc Dinner £7.75alc Wine £3.70 Last dinner 9pm
Credit cards ① ② ③

★★**Talbot** (Best Western) ☎(0568) 2121
Popular, town-centre hotel, with parts dating from 1470.
31rm (13➡8⋒) (1fb) CTV in 15 bedrooms Ⓡ sB&B fr£16.50 sB&B➡⋒ fr£22 dB&B fr£28.50 dB&B➡⋒ fr£33 ⊟
CTV 60P *xmas*
English & French **V** ♔ ☕ Lunch fr£7.50&alc Tea fr50p Dinner fr£7.50&alc Wine £4.10
Credit cards ① ② ③ **VS**

LERWICK
Shetland
Map **16** HU44

★★★***Kveldsro House*** ☎(0595) 2195
Closed Xmas & New Year
Stone building, in an elevated position overlooking the bay.
14rm (9➡) CTV in all bedrooms Ⓡ ★ 28P nc12yrs
V ♔ ☕ Last dinner 8.30pm

★★★**Lerwick Thistle** Scalloway Rd (Thistle) ☎(0595) 2166 Telex no 75128
Modern hotel on the south side of town, close to the shore, with good views from the dining room.
60rm (56➡4⋒) CTV in all bedrooms Ⓡ *sB➡⋒ £35–£42 (room only) dB➡⋒ £35–£42 (room only) ⊟
☾ ⅟ 60P *xmas*
European ♔ ☕ *Lunch £1.25 Dinner £2.53&alc Last dinner 9pm
Credit cards ① ② ③ ④ ⑤ **VS**

★★**Queens** ☎(0595) 2826
The hotel is a conversion of several stone buildings dating from 1850, and stands off the main road, overlooking the harbour.
34rm (21⋒) (2fb) CTV in 22 bedrooms TV in 12 bedrooms Ⓡ sB&B £20–£24 sB&B⋒ £25–£30 dB&B £25–£30 sB&B⋒ £33–£40 ⊟
CTV
V ♔ ☕ Lunch £1.80–£2.40 Tea 60p–£1 Dinner £8–£10 Wine £4.25 Last dinner 8.30pm

○**Shetland**
64➡ *(due to open March/April 1984)*

L'ETACQ
Jersey, Channel Islands
Map **16**

✕✕✕**Lobster Pot** ☎Jersey (0534) 82888
Attractive, stone-built, cottage restaurant.
Dinner not served Sun →

Continental 100 seats Lunch £4.75–£5.50&alc Dinner £7.50–£8.50&alc Wine £3.50 Last dinner 10.15pm 75P Live music Mon–Sat

Credit cards 1 2 3 4 5

LETCHWORTH
Hertfordshire
Map **4** TL23

★★★**Broadway** The Broadway ☎(04626) 5651

Built in the Georgian style in the mid 1960s, and situated in the centre of Letchworth.

37rm(22➡) (5fb) CTV in all bedrooms Ⓡ ✱sB&B £13.50–£21 sB&B➡£15.50–£27.50 dB&B £19.50–£28.50 dB&B➡£24.50–£35 B

Lift ☾ 60P

Lunch £5.05–£6 Dinner £5.05–£6 Wine £4.10 Last dinner 9.30pm

Credit cards 1 2 3 4 5

LETHAM
Fife
Map **11** NO31

★★★ **BL Fernie Castle** ☎(033781) 209 Telex no 727369

Modernised castle standing in its own grounds with many interesting features relating to its past.

14rm(7➡7⋒) (2fb) 1 CTV in all bedrooms Ⓡ sB&B➡⋒£20 dB&B➡⋒£35 B

CTV 100P ✽ Live music and dancing Sat

Scottish & French V Lunch £5.75–£6.75&alc High Tea £3.50–£4 Dinner £12alc Wine £5 Last dinner 9.30pm

Credit cards 1 2 **VS**

LETTERFINLAY
Highland *Inverness-shire*
Map **14** NN29

★★ *HL* **Letterfinlay Lodge** (off A82) ☎Invergloy (039784) 222

Closed Nov–Feb

A friendly and comfortable family run hotel delightfully situated overlooking Loch Lochy.

15rm(2➡3⋒) (3fb) sB&B £12–£15 sB&B➡⋒£14–£16 dB&B £24–£30 dB&B➡⋒£28–£32

CTV 100P ✽

V Bar lunch 75p–£4 Tea 35p–£2 Dinner £8 Wine £4.50 Last dinner 8.30pm

S% Credit cards 1 2 3 **VS**

LETTERSTON
Dyfed
Map **2** SM92

★★ *B* **Brynawelon** ☎(0348) 840307

Proprietor-run hotel, with comfortable, well-equipped bedrooms.

25rm(23➡2⋒) CTV in all bedrooms Ⓡ ✱sB&B➡⋒£14–£16 sB&B➡⋒£24–£28 B

CTV 120P Disco twice wkly Live music and dancing wkly Cabaret wkly

Bar lunch fr£1.50–£3 Dinner £6.20–£7 Wine £3 Last dinner 9pm

LEVENS (nr Kendal)
Cumbria
Map **7** SD48

★★ **Heaves** (off A6, ½m from junc with A591) ☎Sedgwick (0448) 60396

Closed Xmas

Georgian residence, featuring an Adam style staircase, set in its own grounds.

16rm(5➡1⋒) (3fb) TV in 5 bedrooms Ⓡ sB&B £13–£15 sB&B➡⋒£14.50–£16 dB&B £25–£28 dB&B➡⋒£29–£32 B

Unlicensed CTV 50P ✽

Lunch £4–£5 Tea £1–£1.25 High Tea £3.50–£4.50 Dinner £5.50–£6.50 Last dinner 8pm

Credit cards 1 2 3 5

LEWES
East Sussex
Map **5** TQ41

★★★**Shelleys** High St (Mount Charlotte) ☎(07916) 2361 (Due to change to (0273) 472361)

Gracious Regency-style hotel with elegant antique furnishings.

21rm(8➡13⋒) 1 CTV in all bedrooms sB&B➡⋒£32 dB&B➡⋒£50 B

☾ 24P CFA ✽ *xmas*

English & French V Lunch £6.50–£6.75&alc Dinner £7.50–£7.75&alc Wine £5.75 Last dinner 9.15pm

Credit cards 1 2 3 5 **VS**

★★**White Hart** High St (Best Western) ☎(07916) 4676 (Due to change to (0273) 474676

Famous coaching inn with bedroom annexe. Good food is complemented by friendly service.

19rm(10➡1⋒) Annexe: 14➡ (2fb) 1 CTV in 28 bedrooms sB&B £17.50–£19 sB&B➡£26–£31 dB&B £29–£31 dB&B➡£39–£42 B

☾ CTV 50P

English & French V Lunch £4.45–£5.50&alc Tea fr65p Dinner £6.90&alc Wine £4.10
Last dinner 10.15pm

S% Credit cards 1 2 3 5

✕**Anarkali Tandoori** 13 Fisher St ☎(07916) 71907

Small ground floor restaurant offering good Tandoori cuisine and friendly service.

Closed 25 & 26 Dec

Indian V 30 seats ✱Lunch £6alc Dinner £6alc Wine £3.75 Last dinner mdnt

S% Credit cards 1 2 3 5

✕**La Cucina** 15 Station St ☎(07916) 6707 (Due to change to (0273) 476707)

Closed Sun, Bank Hols & Xmas

Italian & Continental V 50 seats Lunch £4.50alc Dinner £10alc Wine £3.75

Credit cards 1 3

✕**Kenwards** Pipe Passage, 151A High St ☎(07916) 2343 (Due to change to (0273) 472343

Imaginative English cooking served in this converted loft in a 16th-century building.

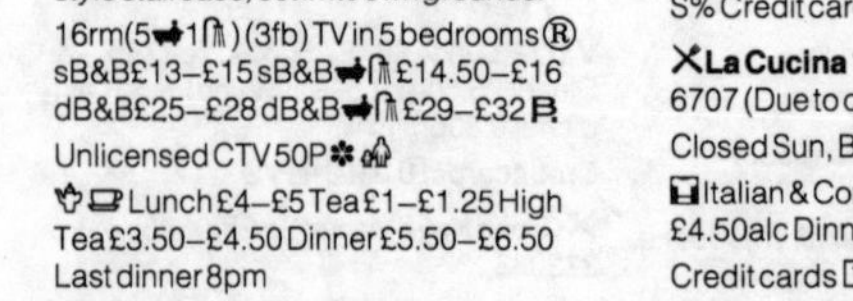

Closed Sun & Mon Lunch not served Sat

V 28 seats ✱Lunch £10alc Dinner fr£6.95&alc Wine £3.75

S% Credit card 2

✕ ***Trumps*** 19–20 Station St ☎ (07916) 3906 (Due to change to (0273) 473906)
Cosy tastefully-furnished restaurant with a variety of speciality dishes.
Closed Sun, Mon & 2wks Xmas Lunch not served
English & French 30 seats Last dinner 10pm
Credit cards 1 2

LEWIS, ISLE OF
Western Isles *Ross & Cromarty*
Map **13**
See **Shawbost** and **Stornoway**

LEYLAND
Lancashire
Map **7** SD52
☆☆☆☆ **Ladbroke** (& Conference centre) (Ladbroke) ☎ (07744) 22922 Telex no 677651
A modern hotel situated at junction 28 of the M6.
93 (9fb) CTV in all bedrooms Ⓡ ✻sB fr£31 dB fr£39 (room only)
CTV 156P CFA ✽ Live music and dancing Fri & Sat
English & Continental V Lunch fr£6.50 Dinner fr£8.50 Last dinner 10pm
Credit cards 1 2 3 4 5

LICHFIELD
Staffordshire
Map **7** SK10
★★★ **George** Bird St (Embassy) ☎ (05432) 23061
40rm (35 5) (2fb) CTV in all bedrooms Ⓡ sB £28 dB £37 (room only)
80P 3 CFA
French V Lunch fr£5.75 Tea 60p Dinner £6.75–£8&alc Wine £4.10 Last dinner 9.30pm
Credit cards 1 2 3 4 5

★★★ **Little Barrow** Beacon St ☎ (05432) 53311
26rm (24) CTV in 24 bedrooms ✻sB&B £24 dB&B £32
CTV 70P

International V Lunch £5.25&alc Tea 40p Dinner £7.50&alc Last dinner 10pm
Credit cards 1 2 3 5

★★ **Angel Croft** Beacon St ☎ (05432) 23147
Closed Xmas RS Sun
Rich brown brick Georgian house, with one acre of grounds, situated close to the Cathedral.
13rm (5) (1fb) 1 ✻sB&B £14–£17 sB&B £16–£21 dB&B £23–£28.50 dB&B £26–£33
CTV 60P ✽
V ✻Lunch £4.75–£8.50 Tea fr65p Dinner £6–£8.75 Wine £4.30 Last dinner 8.45pm
Credit cards 1 3 5 VS

★★ **Swan** Bird St (Embassy) ☎ (05432) 55851
Three-storey Georgian inn, with a mainly commercial trade, situated between the town centre and the Cathedral.
23rm (20 3) Annexe: 8 (3fb) CTV in all bedrooms Ⓡ sB £25.50 (room only) dB £35 (room only)
50P *xmas*
Continental Lunch £3.50–£5 Tea 55p Dinner £6.50–£8.50&alc Wine £4.20 Last dinner 9.30pm
Credit cards 1 2 3 4 5

LIFTON
Devon
Map **2** SX38
★★★ ***Arundell Arms*** (Best Western) ☎ (056 684) 244
Closed Xmas
Early 19th-century building with an old cockpit preserved in the garden.
23rm (16 5) Ⓡ
CTV 80P CFA ✽
English & French Last dinner 9pm
Credit cards 1 2 3 VS

★★ **Lifton Cottage** ☎ (056 684) 439
A small, family-run hotel of character, with an attractive atmosphere.
10rm (4) (3fb) ✻sB&B £9.50 sB&B £11.50–£15 dB&B £19 dB&B £23
CTV 15P ✽
✻Lunch £3.50&alc Tea 50p–£1 Dinner £5&alc Wine £5.75 Last dinner 9pm
Credit cards 1 2 3 5 VS

LIMPLEY STOKE (nr Bath)
Wiltshire
Map **3** ST76
★★★ **Cliffe** (Best Western) ☎ (022 122) 3226
Closed 18 Dec–8 Jan
Converted country residence in wooded grounds with views of the Avon Valley.
12rm (11 1) (3fb) 1 CTV in all bedrooms Ⓡ ✻sB&B £28–£32 dB&B £47–£53
50P ✽ (heated) nc5yrs
V ✻Bar lunch £1.25–£3 Tea £1–£2 Dinner fr£9.25 Wine £5.50 Last dinner 8.30pm
Credit cards 1 2 3 4 5

★★ **Limpley Stoke** ☎ (022 122) 3333
Approached up a steep private road, this country house has good views across the Avon valley.
55rm (43 12) (5fb) 3 CTV in all bedrooms Ⓡ sB&B £18.50–£20 dB&B £28–£32
Lift 60P CFA ✽ *xmas*
V Bar lunch 80p–£3.85 Dinner £6.25–£7.25&alc Last dinner 9pm
Credit cards 1 2 3 5

LIMPSFIELD
Surrey
Map **5** TQ45
✕✕ **Old Lodge** High St ☎ Oxted (08833) 2996
Inventive and creative cooking complemented by impeccable service.
Closed Mon & 1st 3wks Jan Lunch not served Sat Dinner not served Sun
French V 50 seats Lunch £11.50&alc Dinner £11.50&alc Wine £6.25 Last dinner 9.30pm 30P
S% Credit cards 1 2 3 4 5 VS

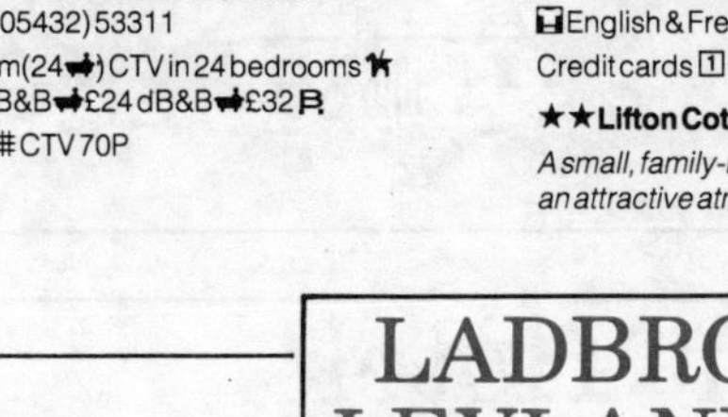

LINCOLN
Lincolnshire
Map **8** SK97
See also **Branston** and **Washingborough**

★★★★**White Hart** Bailgate (Trusthouse Forte) ☎(0522) 26222 Telex no 56304
Early Georgian house with a late Victorian façade, standing in the shadow of Lincoln Cathedral.
68rm(43⇌10⫛)(1fb) CTV in all bedrooms ® sB&B£28.50 sB&B⇌⫛£43 dB&B£44.50 dB&B⇌⫛£58 Ɓ
Lift ☾ CTV 25P 35⌂ CFA *xmas*
♆☕ Last dinner 9.45pm
Credit cards [1] [2] [3] [4] [5]

★★★**Eastgate Post House** Eastgate (Trusthouse Forte) ☎(0522) 20341 Telex no 56316
Large modern hotel near Cathedral.
71⇌(1fb) CTV in all bedrooms ®
sB&B⇌£42 dB&B⇌£54 Ɓ
Lift ☾ 110P CFA ❃ *xmas*
♆☕ Last dinner 9.45pm
Credit cards [1] [2] [3] [4] [5]

★★ *B* **Castle** Westgate ☎(0522) 38801
RS Xmas day
Lovely old building, built as a school in 1852, tastefully modernised and converted.
15⇌⫛ CTV in all bedrooms ® Ɓ
15P
▣ International ♆☕ Last dinner 10pm
Credit cards [1] [2] [4] [5]

★★ *H* **Grand** St Mary's Street ☎(0522) 24211
Modernised, city-centre hotel in the business area, convenient for all the transport terminals.
50rm(43⇌7⫛)(2fb) CTV in all bedrooms ® ✱ sB&B⇌⫛£25 dB&B⇌⫛£36 Ɓ
☾ 40P
▣ International **V** ♆☕ Lunch £5&alc Tea 50p High Tea £3alc Dinner £6&alc Wine £3.55 Last dinner 10pm
Credit cards [1] [2] [3] [5] **VS**

❀✕**White's** The Jews House, 15 The Strait ☎(0522) 24851
Fresh produce, cooked in the modern light style, is served here in one of Britain's oldest houses.
Closed Sun, 1wk Xmas/New Year & 2wks Aug Lunch not served Mon
▣ International **V** 26 seats Last dinner 10pm ⁋ bedrooms available
Credit card [2]

At **Dunholme** (6m NE A46)
☆☆**Four Seasons** Scothern Ln
☎Welton (0673) 60108
Annexe: 12rm(8⇌4⫛)
200P

LINLITHGOW
Lothian *West Lothian*
Map **11** NS97

✕✕✕**Champany** (2m NE off A904)
☎Philpstoun (050683) 4532
Attractive circular restaurant specialising in grills.
Closed 25 Dec–10 Jan
▣ International 48 seats ✱ Lunch £7.40&alc Dinner £12alc Wine £4.80 Last dinner 9.30pm 100P
S% Credit cards [1] [2] [3] [5]

LINWOOD
Strathclyde *Renfrewshire*
Map **10** NS46

★★**Golden Pheasant** Moss Rd (Ind Coope) ☎Johnstone (0505) 21266
Purpose-built hotel standing on the outskirts of this small, commercial and industrial town.
12⇌ CTV in all bedrooms ® sB&B⇌ fr£18.70 dB&B⇌ fr£29.70 Ɓ
100P

Scottish & European ✿ ☕ ✱ Bar lunch 75p–£2.10 Dinner £7alc Wine £3.35 Last dinner 8.30pm

Credit cards 1 2 3 5

LISKEARD
Cornwall
Map **2** SX26

★★ *HL* **Country Castle** Station Rd ☎(0579) 42694

Charming hotel offering friendly service and fine views.

11rm(5→2⋔) (2fb) Ⓡ sB&B£13 sB&B→⋔£15–£18 dB&B£26 dB&B→⋔£36 B

55P ✱

English & French V ✿ ☕ ✱ Bar lunch £1.50–£3.20 Tea fr£1.50 Dinner £7.50&alc Last dinner 8.30pm

Credit card 1 **VS**

★★ ***Lord Eliot*** Castle St ☎(0579) 42717

Small hotel built around the character house of a one-time county landlord.

16rm(1→3⋔) B

CTV 58P Live music and dancing Sat

English & French V ✿ ☕ Last dinner 9pm

★★ **Webbs** The Parade ☎(0579) 43675

Pleasant, Georgian-style hotel within this Charter town.

15rm(10→) (4fb) 1 ⊟ Ⓡ sB&B£14–£18 sB&B→£15–£20 dB&B£27–£32 dB&B→£28–£35

CTV 14P

V ✿ ☕ Lunch £4.60–£5.50&alc Tea 75p–£1 Dinner £5.50–£6.50&alc Wine £4.95 Last dinner 8.30pm

LITTLEBOROUGH
Greater Manchester
Map **7** SD91

★ **Sun** Featherstall Rd ☎(0706) 78957

8rm (1fb) Ⓡ ✱ sB&B£10.50 dB&B£16.50

CTV 6P

✿ ☕ Lunch £2.50–£5.80&alc Tea 50p High Tea £1.50–£2.50 Dinner £1.90–£3.50&alc Wine £3.50 Last dinner 9.30pm

Credit cards 1 2 3

LITTLE HAVEN
Dyfed
Map **2** SM81

★★ **Haven Fort** ☎Broad Haven (043 783) 401
Closed Nov–Mar

Bright, well-maintained hotel, in an elevated postion with sea views.

15rm(8→2⋔) (3fb) Ⓡ ✱ sB&B fr£15.50 sB&B→⋔ fr£15.50 dB&B fr£29 dB&B→⋔ fr£29

CTV 100P nc4yrs

International V ✿ ☕ Bar lunch fr£4.50 Tea fr£1 Dinner fr£6.50&alc Wine £5.50 Last dinner 9pm

★★ ***Little Haven*** Strawberry Hill ☎Broad Haven (043 783) 285

Informal hotel with a lively bar.

9rm(2→) Annexe: 5→ Ⓡ

☾ CTV 20P ✱ nc4yrs

V ✿ ☕ Last dinner 9.30pm

Credit card 1

LITTLE STAUGHTON
Bedford
Map **4** TL16

✕ ***Crown Inn*** ☎Colmworth (023 062) 260

Closed Sat & Sun

French 18 seats Last dinner 9pm 24P

Credit card 2

LITTLE WEIGHTON
Humberside
Map **8** SE93

★★★ **Rowley Manor** ☎Hull (0482) 848248

15rm(11→⋔) 2 ⊟ CTV in all bedrooms sB&B£20.50 sB&B→⋔£28 dB&B£32 dB&B→⋔£40 B

100P 2 ✱ U

English & French V ✿ ☕ Lunch fr£5.50 →

Tea fr60p Dinner fr£7.50&alc Wine £4.95
Last dinner 9pm
S% Credit cards 1 2 3 5 **VS**

LIVERPOOL
Merseyside
Map **7** SJ39 **See plan**
See also **Blundellsands** and **Bootle**

★★★★ **Atlantic Tower Thistle** Chapel St (Thistle) ☎051-227 4444 Telex no 627070 Plan **1** *B5*
226⇌⋒ CTV in all bedrooms Ⓡ sB⇌⋒£40–£44 (room only) dB⇌⋒£50–£60 (room only) Ḅ
Lift ☾ ## CTV 15P 1000 CFA Live music and dancing Fri & Sat
European Lunch £6.95–9.50&alc Dinner fr£7.40&alc Last dinner 9.30pm
Credit cards 1 2 3 4 5 **VS**

☆☆☆☆ ***B* Holiday Inn** Paradise St (Holiday Inn) ☎051-709 0181 Telex no 627270 Plan **8** *C4*
Modern, purpose-built hotel close to the city centre.
273⇌⋒ CTV in all bedrooms sB&B⇌⋒£46 dB&B⇌⋒£63 Ḅ
Lift ☾ ## 500 CFA (heated) sauna bath
French **V** Lunch £5.50&alc Dinner £7&alc Wine £4.95
Last dinner 10.30pm
S% Credit cards 1 2 3 4 5 **VS**

★★★★ **St George's** St John's Precinct, Lime St (Trusthouse Forte) ☎051-709 7090 Telex no 627630 Plan **12** *D4*
155⇌ CTV in all bedrooms Ⓡ sB&B⇌£42 dB&B⇌£58 Ḅ
Lift ☾ CFA
Last dinner 10pm
Credit cards 1 2 3 4 5

☆☆☆ **Crest Hotel Liverpool – City** Lord Nelson St (Crest) ☎051-709 7050 Telex no 627954 Plan **4** *E5*
Tall, modern, city-centre hotel overlooking Lime Street Station.
→

L

Liverpool

1 Atlantic Tower ★★★★
2 Blundellsands ★★★ (*See under Blundellsands*)
3 Bradford ★★
4 Crest Hotel Liverpool – City ☆☆☆
5 Crest Hotel – East Lancs Road ☆☆☆ (*See under Knowsley*)
6 Grange ★★
7 Green Park ★★
8 Holiday Inn ☆☆☆☆
9 Lau's ✕✕
10 Lord Nelson ★★
11 Park ★★★ (*See under Bootle*)
12 St Georges ★★★★
13 Shaftesbury ★★
14 Solna ★

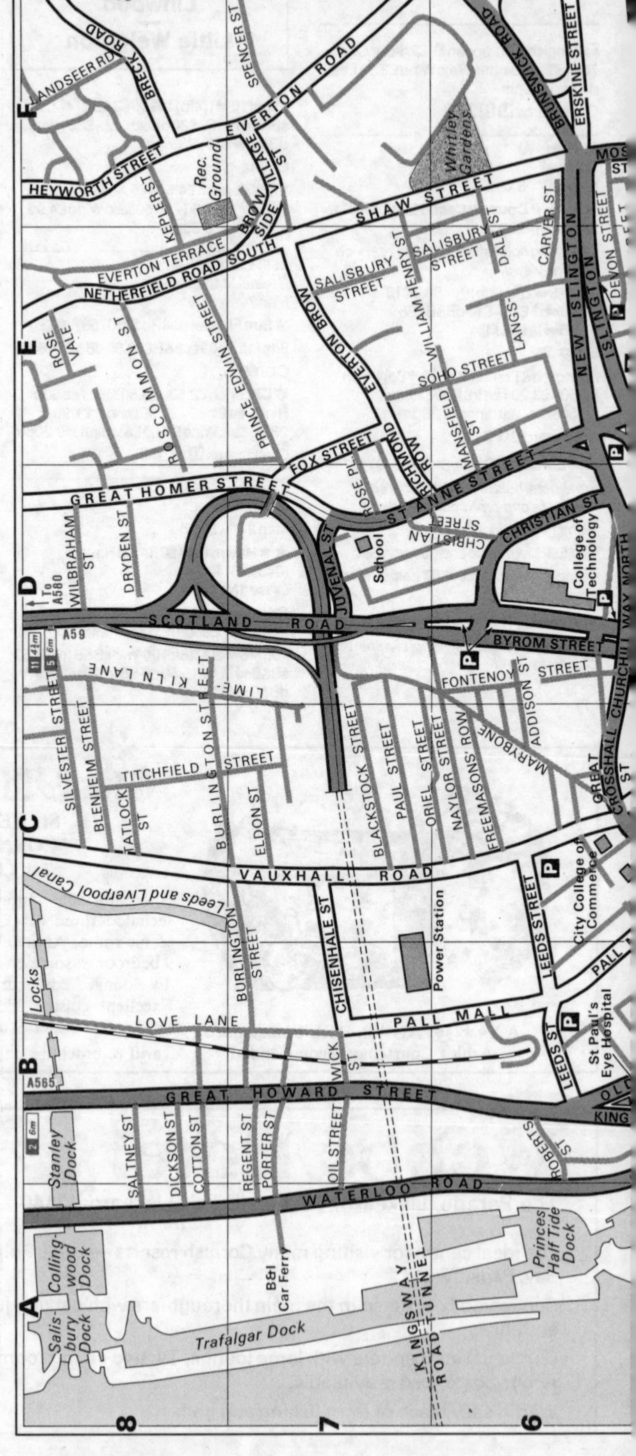

8
7
6
F
E
D
C
B
A
EVERTON ROAD
BRECK ROAD
LANDSEER RD
HEYWORTH STREET
SPENCER ST
EVERTON
Rec. Ground
BROW SIDE
VILLAGE ST
KEPLER ST
EVERTON TERRACE
NETHERFIELD ROAD SOUTH
SHAW STREET
Whitley Gardens
BRUNSWICK ROAD
ERSKINE STREET
SALISBURY STREET
WILLIAM HENRY ST
DALE ST
CARVER ST
NEW ISLINGTON
ISLINGTON
DEVON STREET
ROSE VALE
ROSCOMMON ST
PRINCE EDWIN STREET
EVERTON BROW
SOHO STREET
LANGS
MANSFIELD ST
RICHMOND ROW
FOX STREET
ROSE PL
ST ANNE STREET
GREAT HOMER STREET
CHRISTIAN STREET
CHRISTIAN ST
WILBRAHAM ST
DRYDEN ST
School
College of Technology
To A580
SCOTLAND ROAD
A59
JUVENAL ST
BYROM STREET
KILN LANE
LIME-KILN
FONTENOY STREET
SILVESTER STREET
BLENHEIM STREET
TITCHFIELD STREET
BURLINGTON STREET
TATLOCK ST
ELDON ST
BLACKSTOCK STREET
PAUL STREET
ORIEL STREET
NAYLOR STREET
FREEMASONS' ROW
ADDISON ST
MARYBONE
GREAT CROSSHALL ST
CHURCHILL WAY NORTH
VAUXHALL ROAD
Leeds and Liverpool Canal
City College of Commerce
Power Station
LEEDS STREET
CHISENHALE ST
BURLINGTON STREET
PALL MALL
Locks
LOVE LANE
WICK ST
LEEDS ST
St Paul's Eye Hospital
A565
GREAT HOWARD STREET
Stanley Dock
SALTNEY ST
DICKSON ST
COTTON ST
REGENT ST
PORTER ST
OIL STREET
ROBERTS ST
WATERLOO ROAD
Princes Half Tide Dock
Collingwood Dock
Salisbury Dock
B&I Car Ferry
KINGSWAY ROAD TUNNEL
Trafalgar Dock
P

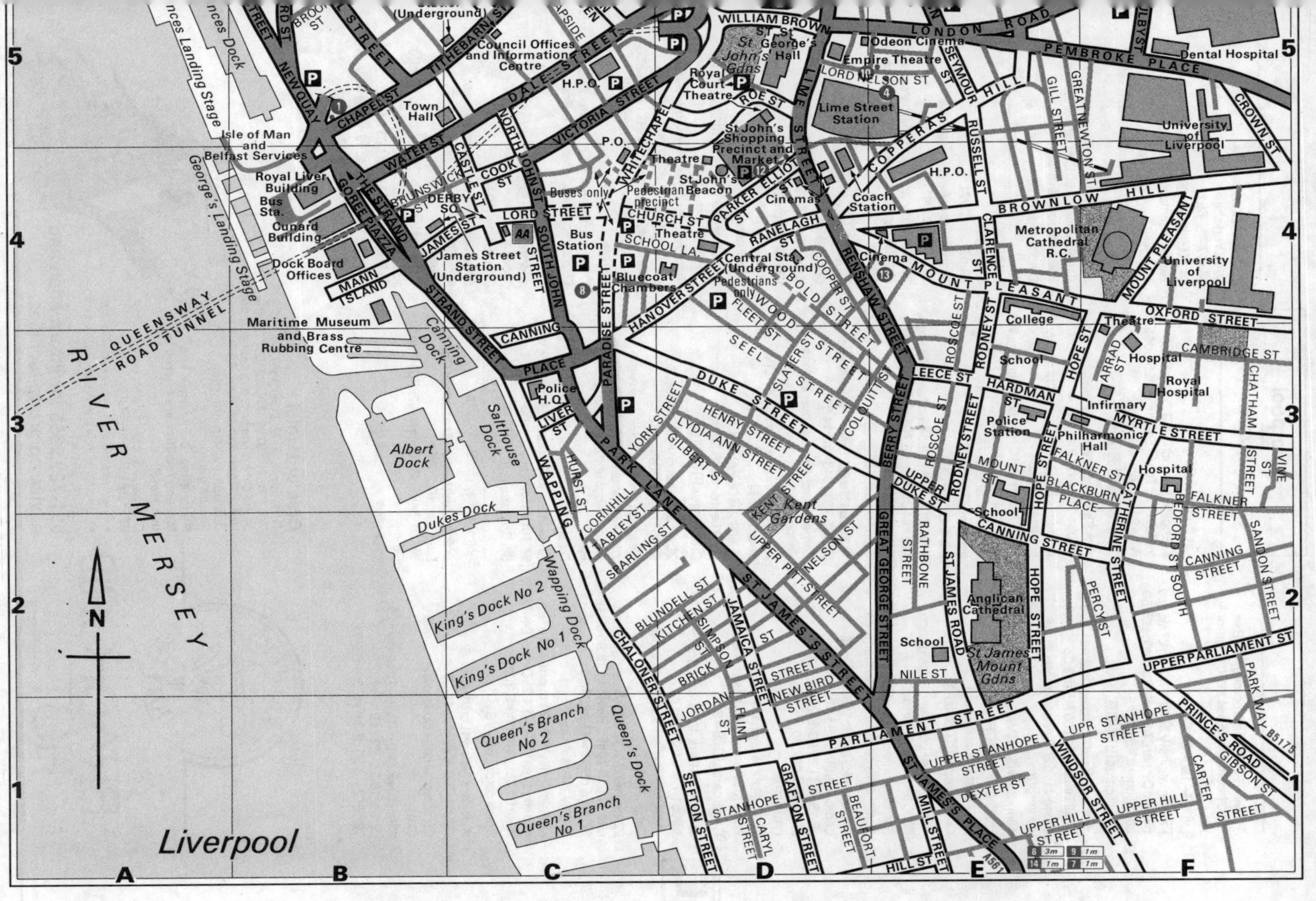

Liverpool
RIVER MERSEY
N
A
B
C
D
E
F
1
2
3
4
5
Dental Hospital
CROWN ST
University of Liverpool
PEMBROKE PLACE
LONDON ROAD
MOUNT PLEASANT
University of Liverpool
OXFORD STREET
CAMBRIDGE ST
CHATHAM STREET
VINE ST
SANDON STREET
UPPER PARLIAMENT ST
PARK WAY
B5175
PRINCE'S ROAD
GIBSON ST
CARTER STREET
Royal Hospital
Hospital
FALKNER STREET
CANNING STREET
BEDFORD ST SOUTH
UPR STANHOPE STREET
UPPER HILL STREET
GREAT NEWTON ST
GILL STREET
BROWNLOW HILL
Metropolitan Cathedral R.C.
Theatre
ARRAD ST
Infirmary
MYRTLE STREET
Philharmonic Hall
FALKNER ST
BLACKBURN PLACE
CATHERINE STREET
PERCY ST
WINDSOR STREET
HOPE ST
College
School
HARDMAN ST
Police Station
HOPE STREET
MOUNT ST
School
CANNING STREET
Anglican Cathedral
St James Mount Gdns
UPPER STANHOPE STREET
DEXTER ST
ST JAMES'S PLACE
A561
SEYMOUR ST
HILL
RUSSELL ST
CLARENCE ST
RODNEY ST
RODNEY STREET
ROSCOE ST
LEECE ST
UPPER DUKE ST
ST JAMES ROAD
School
NILE ST
PARLIAMENT STREET
MILL STREET
HILL ST
Odeon Cinema
Empire Theatre
LORD NELSON ST
Lime Street Station
COPPERAS
H.P.O.
Coach Station
Cinema
RENSHAW STREET
BERRY STREET
RATHBONE STREET
GREAT GEORGE STREET
COLQUITT ST
COOPER ST
BOLD STREET
SLATER ST
WOOD STREET
SEEL ST
FLEET ST
DUKE STREET
HENRY STREET
KENT STREET
Kent Gardens
NELSON ST
UPPER PITT STREET
ST JAMES'S STREET
NEW BIRD STREET
BEAUFORT STREET
GRAFTON STREET
STANHOPE STREET
CARYL STREET
WILLIAM BROWN ST
LIME STREET
St George's Hall
St John's Gdns
ROE ST
Royal Court Theatre
St John's Shopping Precinct and Market
St John's Beacon
Cinemas
RANELAGH ST
Central Sta. (Underground)
Pedestrians only
ELLIOT ST
PARKER ST
CHURCH ST
Theatre
SCHOOL LA.
HANOVER STREET
LYDIA ANN STREET
GILBERT ST
JAMAICA STREET
FLINT ST
SIMPSON ST
BRICK ST
JORDAN
KITCHEN ST
BLUNDELL ST
WHITECHAPEL
Pedestrian precinct
Bluecoat Chambers
YORK STREET
PARK LANE
SPARLING ST
TABLEY ST
CORNHILL
CHALONER STREET
SEFTON STREET
Queen's Dock
P.O.
H.P.O.
VICTORIA STREET
DALE STREET
Buses only
LORD STREET
Bus Station
PARADISE STREET
SOUTH JOHN STREET
CANNING PLACE
Police H.Q.
LIVER ST
HURST ST
WAPPING
Wapping Dock
King's Dock No 2
King's Dock No 1
Queen's Branch No 2
Queen's Branch No 1
Council Offices and Information Centre
NORTH JOHN ST
COOK ST
CASTLE ST
DERBY SQ
JAMES ST
James Street Station (Underground)
STRAND STREET
Salthouse Dock
Dukes Dock
TITHEBARN ST
Town Hall
WATER ST
BRUNSWICK ST
THE STRAND
GOREE PIAZZA
MANN ISLAND
Canning Dock
Albert Dock
(Underground)
CHAPEL ST
NEW QUAY
Royal Liver Building
Bus Sta.
Cunard Building
Dock Board Offices
Maritime Museum and Brass Rubbing Centre
Isle of Man and Belfast Services
George's Landing Stage
QUEENSWAY ROAD TUNNEL

170➡ CTV in all bedrooms Ⓡ *sB➡ fr£33 (room only) dB➡ fr£40 (room only) B

Lift ☾ ⅟ 180P CFA

International V ♧ ☐ *Lunch £7alc Tea 65p alc Dinner £7.50–£8&alc Wine £5.50 Last dinner 9.45pm

Credit cards 1 2 3 4 5 **VS**

★★ ***Bradford*** Tithebarn St ☎051-236 8782 Telex no 627657 Plan **3** *C5*

Stone-built, 200-year old hotel, in the centre of the city.

49rm(23➡⋔) CTV in all bedrooms B

Lift ☾ CTV 15 CFA

♧ ☐ Last dinner 8.15pm

Credit cards 1 2 3 4 5

★★ **Grange** Holmefield Rd, Aigburth ☎051-427 2950 Plan **6** *E1*

Standing in its own grounds, four miles from the city centre in a suburban area.

27rm(17➡2⋔) (1fb) 1 CTV in all bedrooms Ⓡ sB&B£18.40 sB&B➡⋔ £23.90 dB&B£27.70 dB&B➡⋔ £32.30

CTV 25P ✽

English & French V *Dinner £8–£8.50&alc Wine £4.30 Last dinner 9pm

Credit cards 1 3 **VS**

★★ **Green Park** 4/6 Greenbank Dr ☎051-733 3382 Plan **7** *F1*

Detached, red-brick building, close to Sefton Park.

22rm(3➡5⋔) (8fb) CTV in all bedrooms sB&B fr£15.75 sB&B➡⋔ fr£18.95 dB&B fr£20.35 dB&B➡⋔ fr£24.65

☾ CTV 24P ✽ *xmas*

Mainly grills V ♧ ☐ Lunch £4–£6 Tea 45p High Tea £2.25–£4.25 Dinner £4–£6 Wine £3.35 Last dinner 9.30pm

Credit cards 1 3 **VS**

★★ **Lord Nelson** Lord Nelson St ☎051-709 4362 Plan **10** *D8*

Commercial hotel close to Lime Street Station.

58rm(20➡) (3fb) CTV in 46 bedrooms sB&B£16.25–£22 sB&B➡£22–£25 dB&B£24–£30 dB&B➡£30–£36 B

Lift ☾ CTV 16

English & French ♧ ☐ Lunch fr£4.50&alc Tea fr75p Dinner fr£5.50&alc Wine £4 Last dinner 9.30pm

Credit cards 1 2 3 5

★★ **Shaftesbury** Mount Pleasant ☎051-709 4421 Plan **13** *E4*

Modern, city-centre hotel, with a mainly commercial trade..

70rm(25➡) (1fb) CTV in 50 bedrooms sB&B£14.75–£15.75 sB&B➡£17.25–£19.25 dB&B£23.75–£24.25 dB&B➡£24.25–£27 B

Lift ☾ CTV CFA

V ♧ ☐ Lunch fr£4.55&alc Tea fr70p High Tea fr£4 Dinner fr£5.70&alc Wine £5.90 Last dinner 9.30pm

Credit cards 1 2 3 5

★ ***Solna*** Ullet Rd, Sefton Park (Minotel) ☎051-733 1943 Plan **14** *E1*

Large, detached house overlooking Sefton Park.

21rm(1➡) Annexe: 18rm(2➡) CTV in all bedrooms B

☾ 60P 2 Disco Wed

♧ ☐ Last dinner 8.30pm

Credit cards 1 2 3 5

✕✕ **Lau's** Rankin Hall, 44 Ullet Rd ☎051-734 3930 Plan **9** *E1*

Delicious Chinese cuisine served in spacious, ornate Pekinese style surroundings and overlooking Sefton Park.

Closed Sun

Pekinese V 450 seats Lunch £6alc Wine £4.70 Last dinner 11pm 60P

S% Credit cards 1 2 3 5

At **Knowsley** (5m E off A580)

☆☆☆ **Crest Hotel – East Lancs Road** East Lancs Rd (Crest) ☎051-546 7531 Telex no 629769 Plan **5** *D8*

50➡ 150P

LIVERSEDGE

West Yorkshire
Map **7** SE12

✕✕ **Lillibets** Ashfield House, 64 Leeds Rd ☎Heckmondwike (0924) 404911

Lunch by reservation only.

Closed Sun, 10 days after Xmas & 1st 2 wks Aug

40 seats Lunch £5–£7 Dinner £9.50–£10.95 Wine £4.60 Last dinner 9.30pm 25P bedrooms available

Credit cards 1 3

LIZARD

Cornwall
Map **2** SW71

★★ ***L* Housel Bay** Housel Cove ☎(0326) 290417

Hotel of Victorian origin superbly situated in cliffside grounds, with many notable guests.

27rm(13➡3⋔) CTV in 4 bedrooms *sB&B£10–£17 dB&B£20–£34 dB&B➡⋔ £24–£38

☾ ⅟ CTV 30P 5 ✽ nc14yrs

V ♧ ☐ Lunch £6alc Tea £1.45alc Dinner £8.50alc Wine £3.50 Last dinner 8.30pm

Credit card 1

★★ **Lizard** ☎The Lizard (0326) 290456
Closed 20 Oct–Mar

Family-run inn in the centre of the village with busy bars catering for local trade.

10rm(1➡2⋔) (2fb) Ⓡ sB&B£12–£12.50 dB&B£24–£25 dB&B➡⋔ £28–£29

20P

♧ Bar lunch £2.50–£3.50 Dinner £5.50–£6.50&alc Wine £3 Last dinner 8pm

VS

★★ **Polbrean** Sea Front ☎(0326) 290418
Closed Nov–19 Apr

Small hotel near the lighthouse, with unrestricted views of the Lizard and the coastline.

11rm(1➡3⋔) (4fb) TV in all bedrooms Ⓡ sB&B£13.23 sB&B➡⋔ £15.73 dB&B£26.46 dB&B➡⋔ £31.44 B

CTV 25P 3 ✽ Disco 3 nights wkly Live music and dancing wkly

V ♔ ☐ Bar lunch £3alc Tea 60p alc Dinner £5.50&alc Wine £2.90
Last dinner 9.30pm
Credit cards 1 3

LLANARMON DYFFRYN CEIRIOG
Clwyd
Map **7** SJ13

★★★ *H* **Hand** ☎ (069 176) 666
A 16th-century, two-storey hotel in the village, with shooting and fishing facilities.
14rm(9➡) (1fb) CTV in 3 bedrooms ✻sB&B£20 sB&B➡£22 dB&B£32 dB&B➡£35 B
CTV 30P ✽ ⚲(hard) ♩ xmas
International V ♔ ☐ ✻Lunch fr£6.50 Tea fr£1.25 Dinner fr£8.50 Wine £4.95 Last dinner 9pm
Credit cards 1 3 **VS**

★★ *L* **West Arms** ☎ (069 176) 665
Country hotel, over 400 years old, situated in a small picturesque village, 950ft above sea level.
15rm(6➡1⋒) (1fb) sB&B£15 sB&B➡⋒£17.50 dB&B£30 dB&B➡⋒£32 B
CTV 30P ✽ ♩ xmas
♔ ☐ Bar lunch 50p–£4.50 Tea fr65p Dinner £7.50 Last dinner 8.30pm

LLANBEDR
Gwynedd
Map **6** SH52

★★ **Cae Nest Hall** ☎ (034123) 349
Closed 14 Nov–Feb
A 16th-century country house, standing in its own grounds, about one mile from the sea.
9rm(2➡) (3fb) sB&B£10.45–£12.10 dB&B£20.90–£24.20 dB&B➡£23.10–£26.40
CTV 15P ✽
♔ Lunch £4.50alc Dinner £7.50&alc Wine £3.75 Last dinner 9pm
Credit card 3

★★ *H* **Ty Mawr** ☎ (034123) 440
Comfortable, personally run hotel, with good home cooking.
10rm(2➡4⋒) CTV in 6 bedrooms sB&B£12 sB&B➡⋒£16.50 dB&B£24 dB&B➡⋒£27
CTV 20P ✽
V ♔ ☐ Lunch £3–£5 Tea 80p–£1.50 High Tea £1–£2&alc Dinner £5–£8 Wine £4.85 Last dinner 8.45pm

LLANBEDROG
Gwynedd
Map **6** SH33

★★ *B* **Bryn Derwen** ☎ (0758) 740257
Pebble-dashed, Edwardian house in the village set in its own grounds, with views of the sea.
10rm(9➡) (9fb) TV in 9 bedrooms ✶ sB&B£12–£20 sB&B➡£12–£20 dB&B£24–£40 dB&B➡£24–£40 B
CTV 25P ✽ ⌂ xmas
♔ ☐ Lunch £3.50–£5 Tea £2.15–£3 High Tea £3–£5 Dinner £5.75–£9.65 Wine £4.05 Last dinner 8pm
Credit cards 1 3 **VS**

LLANBERIS
Gwynedd
Map **6** SH56

★★ *H* **Gallt-y-Glyn** (Minotel) ☎ (0286) 870370
Part 17th-century, roadside hotel.
10rm (3fb) ✶ sB&B£11.50–£14.50 dB&B£21–£25 B
CTV 15P ✽ ⌂ xmas
V ♔ ☐ Lunch £3.25–£4.50&alc Dinner £6.10&alc Wine £3 Last dinner 8.30pm
Credit cards 1 2 3 5 **VS**

★ **Dol Peris** High St ☎ (0286) 870350
Detached Victorian house in the centre of the village.
10rm (3fb) TV in all bedrooms Ⓡ ✶ sB&B£9–£10.35 dB&B£15–£18.40 B
CTV 12P ⌂ xmas →

L

Mainly grills V Lunch £2.25–£4.50&alc Tea 25p–50p High Tea 95p–£1.50 Dinner £2.75–£4.50&alc Wine £3.50 Last dinner 9.30pm

Credit cards 1 2 5 VS

LLANDDEWI SKYRRID
Gwent
Map **3** SO31

Walnut Tree Inn (3m NE of Abergavenny) Abergavenny (0873) 2797

Closed 25 & 26 Dec Lunch not served

French & Italian 60 seats 36P

LLANDEILO
Dyfed
Map **2** SN62

★★*BL* **Cawdor Arms** (0558) 823500

Closed New Years Day RS Sun eve Jan–Mar

Elegant, bow-fronted Georgian building set in Llandeilo's main road.

17rm(13 4) 2 CTV in all bedrooms sB&B fr£26 dB&B fr£37.50–£45

9P sauna bath *xmas*

English & French V Bar lunch £4.50alc Tea £2.50alc Dinner £11.50 Wine £5 Last dinner 9.30pm

Credit cards 1 2 3 5 VS

★★**King's Head** (0558) 822388

Town hotel with pleasant bedrooms and comfortable lounge bar.

8rm(6) CTV in 6 bedrooms TV in 2 bedrooms sB&B£18 sB&B£20 dB&B£22 dB&B£25

10P

Continental Lunch £4&alc Dinner £4&alc Wine £4 Last dinner 9pm

Credit cards 1 3

LLANDISSILIO (WEST)
Dyfed
Map **2** SN12

★★**Nantyffin Motel** Clynderwen (09912) 329

Friendly hotel with modern bedrooms.

15rm(7) CTV in 7 bedrooms ® sB&B fr£13.80 sB&B fr£15.52 dB&B fr£27.60 dB&B fr£31.04

CTV 150P 7

Welsh, English & French V Lunch £2.50–£5.25 Tea £1.50–£2.50 Dinner £5.25–£6.50 Wine £2.50 Last dinner 9pm

Credit cards 1 2 3 5

LLANDOGO
Gwent
Map **3** · SO50

★★**Old Farmhouse** Dean (0594) 530303

17th century building with modern bedroom block.

8 Annexe: 16 (6fb) CTV in 10 bedrooms ® sB&B£18 sB&B£22 dB&B£25 dB&B£35

CTV 70P Live music and dancing Mon *xmas*

International V Lunch £5.95–£7.95&alc Tea 50p–£1.30 Dinner £7.95&alc Wine £4.50 Last dinner 10pm

S% Credit cards 1 2 3 5

LLANDOVERY
Dyfed
Map **3** SN73

★★ *Llanfair Grange* (0550) 20495

Hospitable country hotel with comfortable bedrooms and mature gardens.

8rm(2) 1 CTV in all bedrooms

45P

English & French
Last dinner 9.30pm

Credit cards 1 3

★ **Picton Court** (0550) 20320

Closed Nov

Small country house in 15 acres of grounds.

10rm(6) (2fb) 1 ® sB&B£11.50–£13 dB&B£22–£24 dB&B£23–£26

CTV 25P

Lunch £7alc Tea 50p–£1.40 Dinner £7alc Wine £3
Last dinner 8.30pm

Credit cards 1 3 VS

LLANDRINDOD WELLS
Powys
Map **3** SO06

★★★**Hotel Metropole** Temple St (Best Western) (0597) 2881 Telex no 35237

Annexe: 135rm(65 34) (1fb) CTV in 18 bedrooms sB&B£16.50 sB&B£21.80–£23.50 dB&B£29.30 dB&B£38–£40

Lift CTV 150P

Lunch fr£5.15 Tea fr75p Dinner fr£7.35 Wine £3.90 Last dinner 8.30pm

Credit cards 1 2 3 5

★★**Hotel Commodore** Spa Rd (0597) 2288

Victorian town centre hotel.

55rm(50 5) (8fb) CTV in 14 bedrooms ® sB&B fr£19.50 dB&B fr£36

Lift CTV 100P 1 CFA (heated) squash sauna bath

V Lunch £4–£5 Tea £1.50–£2.50 Dinner £7–£8 Wine £3.80 Last dinner 8.30pm

Credit cards 1 2 3 VS

LLANDUDNO
Gwynedd
Map **6** SH78 **See plan**

★★★*L* **Empire** Church Walks (0492) 79955 Telex no 617161 Plan **11** *B4*

Closed 18 Dec–3 Jan

Modernised and extended Victorian hotel in a central position close to the Promenade.

56 (7fb) 3 CTV in all bedrooms ® sB&B£19.50–£28 dB&B£28–£44

Lift 40P CFA (heated) sauna bath Live music and dancing Sat

V Lunch fr£6 Tea fr90p Dinner fr£9 Wine £4 Last dinner 9pm

S% Credit cards 1 2 3 4 5

See advert on page 367

★★★**Gogarth Abbey** West Shore (0492) 76211 Plan **14** *A3*

Holiday hotel set on to the Great Orme, facing the West Shore. →

The Old Farmhouse Hotel ★★

Llandogo, Near Monmouth, Gwent
Tel: Dean (0594) 530303/53027

A fully modernised 17th century Monmouthshire homestead. Set off the main road the buildings nestle against the steeply wooded hillside which overlooks the beautiful Wye Valley. A haven for weary travellers, the fully licensed Lounge Bar offers warmth and comfort whilst providing an ideal setting for the special evening out. The hotel bedrooms all have hot and cold and shaver points. Some rooms have private bathroom, radio, intercom and tea and coffer making facilities. Ample parking and the hotel has its own petrol station open 7 days a week. Tofs Restaurant, our well apointed à la carte restaurant, open 7 days a week for the discerning diner. We offer a wide range of international dishes and an excellent wine list to suit every palate. Our friendly and efficient staff will add further enjoyment to your meal.

The Old Farmhouse Hotel is privately owned and we aim for a high standard, both in cuisine and comfort. We look forward to seeing you and hope your visit will be as enjoyable as possible.

L

Llanfair Grange Country House Hotel

LLANDOVERY, DYFED TEL: (0550) 20495

We offer gracious surroundings, excellent cuisine, good wines and personal attention in our compact hotel set in its own grounds with extensive views.

Suite with 4 poster bed available for your special break. Bed and breakfast for £9 per person per day (with evening dinner approximately £18.50 per person per day).

An ideal centre to escape from the busy world. Touring, birdwatching, walking, Pony trekking and fishing by arrangement.

Conference room available.

Resident proprietors:

John & Irene Anderson, Pat & Wally Kilminster

Best Western

The Metropole ★★★

Llandrindod Wells, Powys. LD1 5DY Tel: 0597 2881/2

This spacious hotel was built by the Great Grandmother of the present owners in the Edwardian heyday of the Llandrindod Wells spa. The hotel still retains the same atmosphere of friendly hospitality in keeping with the best traditions of the founder. Ideally situated in mid Wales for the touring visitor or conference organiser. Enjoy free golf (midweek), free fishing with swimming, boating, bowls and tennis.

Llandudno

1 Bedford ★
2 Bodysgallen Hall ★★★
3 Branksome ★
4 Bromwell Court ★★
5 Bron Orme ★
6 Chatsworth House ★★
7 Clarence ★★
8 Clontarf ★
9 Cranleigh ★
10 Dunoon ★★
11 Empire ★★★
12 Esplanade ★★
13 Fairhaven ★
14 Gogarth Abbey ★★★
15 Gwesty Leamore ★
16 Headlands ★★
17 Hilbre Court ★
18 Imperial ★★★
19 Marine ★★★
20 Min-y-Don ★
21 Oak Alyn ★
22 Ormescliffe ★★
23 Osborne ★
24 Plas Fron Deg ★★
25 Ravenhurst ★
26 Richmond ★
27 Risboro ★★
28 Rothesay ★
29 Royal ★★
30 St George's ★★★
31 St Tudno ★★
32 Somerset ★★
33 Sunnymede ★
34 Tan-Lan ★
35 Woodlee ★

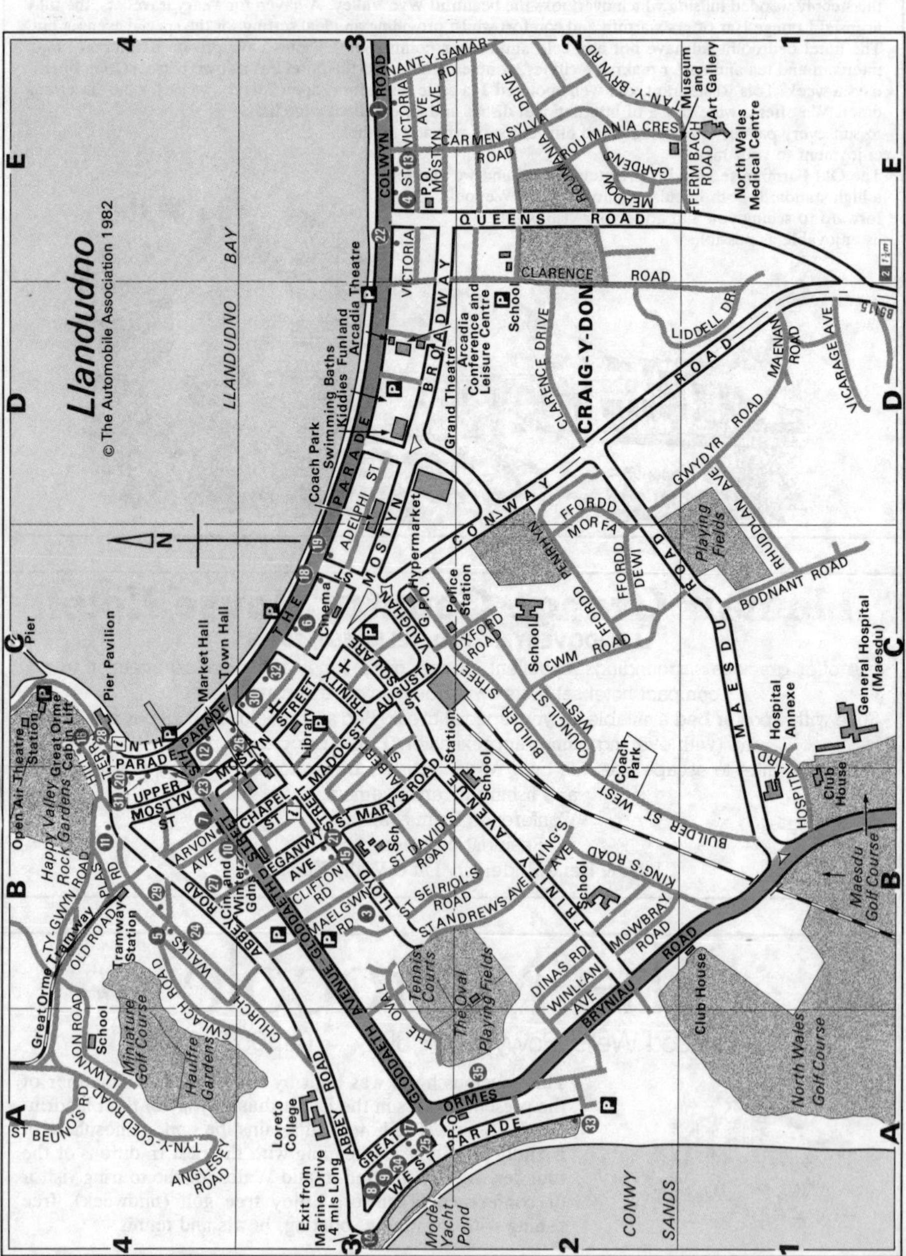
Llandudno
© The Automobile Association 1982
LLANDUDNO BAY
CONWY SANDS
CRAIG-Y-DON
Pier
Pier Pavilion
Market Hall
Town Hall
Happy Valley Rock Gardens
Great Orme Cabin Lift
Open Air Theatre
Tramway Station
Miniature Golf Course
Haulfre Gardens
Loreto College
Exit from Marine Drive 4 mls Long
Model Yacht Pond
The Oval Playing Fields
Tennis Courts
North Wales Golf Course
Maesdu Golf Course
Club House
General Hospital (Maesdu)
Hospital Annexe
Coach Park
Police Station
G.P.O.
Hypermarket
Grand Theatre
Arcadia Conference and Leisure Centre
Arcadia Theatre
Coach Park
Swimming Baths
Kiddies Funland
Cinema
Library
Museum and Art Gallery
North Wales Medical Centre
Playing Fields
School
THE PARADE
MOSTYN ST
GLODDAETH AVENUE
ABBEY ROAD
CHURCH WALKS
TRINITY AVENUE
BRYNIAU ROAD
CONWAY ROAD
MAESDU ROAD
QUEENS ROAD
CLARENCE ROAD
COLWYN ROAD
WEST PARADE

42rm(25⇌⋒)(5fb) CTV in all bedrooms Ⓡ sB&B£15–£18 sB&B⇌⋒£17–£20 dB&B£28–£34 dB&B⇌⋒£32–£38 Ɓ

CTV 50P ✽ (heated) Live music and dancing wkly

V ♆ ☐ Lunch £4–£6 Tea 60p–£1.50 Dinner £6–£8 Wine £2.50 Last dinner 8.15pm

Credit cards 1 2 3 **VS**

★★★ ***Imperial*** Promenade ☎(0492) 77466 Plan **18** *C3*

Impressive, six-storey, Victorian hotel, close to the shops.

145rm(72⇌) 1 CTV available in bedrooms Ⓡ Ɓ

Lift ☾ CTV 50P CFA sauna bath Disco 6 nights wkly Live music and dancing 3 nights wkly

International ♆ ☐ Last dinner 8.15pm

Credit cards 1 2 3 **VS**

★★★ **Marine** Vaughan St (Trusthouse Forte) ☎(0492) 77521 Plan **19** *C3*

Large, Victorian, holiday hotel on a corner position.

79rm(54⇌)(8fb) CTV in all bedrooms Ⓡ sB&B£25.50 sB&B⇌£29.50 dB&B£39 dB&B⇌£44 Ɓ

Lift ☾ 28P CFA *xmas*

♆ ☐ Last dinner 9pm

Credit cards 1 2 3 4 5

★★★ ***L St George's*** Promenade ☎(0492) 77544 Telex no 61520 Plan **30** *C3*

Impressive, Victorian hotel in a central position.

90rm(46⇌44⋒) CTV in all bedrooms Ⓡ Ɓ

Lift ☾ CTV 30P CFA sauna bath

V ♆ ☐ Last dinner 9pm

Credit cards 1 2 3 5

★★ ***B* Bromwell Court** Promenade (Minotel) ☎(0492) 78416 Plan **4** *E3*
Closed Jan

Neat, single-fronted, Victorian, mid-terrace hotel.

12rm(2⇌8⋒)(1fb) CTV in 9 bedrooms Ⓡ sB&B£12.10–£12.50 sB&B⇌⋒£14.50–£15 dB&B£24.20–£25 dB&B⇌⋒£29–£32 Ɓ

CTV nc6 *xmas*

♆ ☐ Lunch £3–£4 Tea £1–£1.50 Dinner £6–£7 Wine £6
Last dinner 7pm

Credit cards 1 3 **VS**

★★★ **BODYSGALLEN HALL, LLANDUDNO**

(off B5115) (Prestige) ☎(0492) 84466 Telex no 8951493 Plan **2** *E1*
Closed 1st wk in Feb

Very much in the grand manner, this historic house has much to offer its guests. It is set in seven acres, with formal gardens including a 17th century 'knot' garden, an 18th century walled rose garden and a useful kitchen plot. The many gabled building dates mainly from Elizabethan times but the tower is 13th century. The interior has been sensitively converted and retains many of the structural features, especially some fine panelling. It has been furnished with suitable antique furniture and the Eastern carpets and oil paintings certainly help to convey an atmosphere of the past. There is a good choice of sitting rooms including the main hall, the drawing room and library as well as the new bar. If you want to retire to your room, you will find it equally well decorated and furnished, and provided with a wide range of facilities such as trouser presses, television, books and biscuits as well as good quality toiletries which, with the comfortable beds and chairs, contribute to your comfort.

The inner man is well looked after, as one would expect. The cooking has been somewhat uneven since the

hotel opened but generally it meets with the approval of our members and our inspectors. Peter Jackson is the young chef and he provides interesting dishes, sometimes traditional, sometimes with a modern influence, yet always with first class materials.

Hospitable service from friendly staff complete the picture but we hope the opening of the conference facilities will not mar the hotels red star qualities.

19⇌ 1 CTV in all bedrooms sB&B⇌£30–£40 dB&B⇌£50–£80 Ɓ

☾ CTV 50P 2 ✽ (hard) nc8yrs *xmas*

♆ ☐ Lunch fr£6.80&alc Tea fr£1 Dinner fr£11.80&alc Wine £5.20
Last dinner 9pm

S% Credit cards 1 2 3 5 **VS**

See advert on page 367

★★ **Chatsworth House** Promenade ☎(0492) 79421 Plan **6** *C3*

Terraced, colour-washed, commercial hotel, situated on the sea front and near to shops.

57rm(37⇌10⋒)(17fb) CTV in all bedrooms Ⓡ sB&B£11–£13.50 sB&B⇌⋒£12.50–£17.50 dB&B£20–£31.90 dB&B⇌⋒£25–£35 Ɓ

Lift 18P Live music and dancing 3 nights wkly (in season) Cabaret 2 nights wkly (in season) *xmas*

♆ ☐ Lunch £3.75 Dinner £6 Wine £3.40 Last dinner 8pm

★★ **Clarence** Gloddaeth St ☎(0492) 76485 Plan **7** *B4*
Closed Oct–Mar

Impressive, Victorian holiday hotel catering mainly for the holiday coach trade.

74rm(4fb) ✻ sB&B£13 dB&B£24 Ɓ

Lift ☾ CTV Live Music & dancing twice wkly

V ♆ ☐ ✻ Lunch £4 Tea 50p–85p Dinner £5–£5.50 Wine £3.90 Last dinner 8pm

Credit cards 1 2 5

★★ **Dunoon** Gloddaeth St ☎(0492) 77078 Plan **10** *B3*
Closed Nov–16 Feb

Victorian hotel in this wide Llandudno street.

59rm(39⇌)(11fb) CTV in all bedrooms Ⓡ sB&B£9–£14 sB&B⇌£11–£16.50 dB&B£18–£26 dB&B⇌£20–£33 Ɓ

Lift CTV 24P

♆ ☐ Lunch £4 Tea 65p Dinner £4.50 Wine £3.50 Last dinner 8pm

★★ **Esplanade** Promenade ☎(0492) 76687 Plan **12** *C4*

Victorian terraced hotel with a verandah.

60rm(40⇌2⋒)(2fb) 5 CTV in 40 bedrooms Ⓡ sB&B£10.50–£14 sB&B⇌⋒£12.50–£16.50 dB&B£21–£24 dB&B⇌⋒£25–£30 Ɓ

Lift ☾ CTV 30P CFA *xmas*

V ♆ ☐ Lunch fr£4.50 Tea fr£1 High Tea fr£3 Dinner fr£6.50 Wine £4.50 Last dinner 7.30pm

Credit cards 1 3

See advert on page 372

★★ **Headlands** Hill Ter ☎(0492) 77485 Plan **16** *C4* Closed Nov–Mar

Built in 1896, this hotel with its tower is set high over Llandudno.

17rm(12⇌3⋒)(5fb) CTV in all bedrooms Ⓡ sB&B£11–£12.50 sB&B⇌⋒£12.50–£15 dB&B⇌⋒£25–£30 Ɓ

CTV 5P

English & French ♆ ☐ Bar lunch 40p–£2.50 Tea fr45p Dinner fr£7 Wine £4.30 Last dinner 8pm

Credit cards 1 3 **VS**

See advert on page 370

L

Llandudno

★★Ormescliffe Promenade ☎(0492) 77191 Plan **22** *E3*
Holiday hotel, located ½m from the shopping area.
64rm(22→13⋒)(15fb) CTV in 35 bedrooms ® sB&B£11.95–£13.95 sB&B→⋒£13.95–£15.95 dB&B£23.90–£27.90 dB&B→⋒£27.90–£31.90 B
Lift CTV 15P CFA xmas
Lunch fr£4.70 Tea fr60p Dinner fr£6.25 Wine £4.50 Last dinner 8pm
Credit cards [1] [3] [5] **VS**

★★Plas Fron Deg 48 Church Walks ☎(0492) 77267 Plan **24** *B4*
Pleasant hotel in an elevated position, with extensive front lawn with shrubs and flowers.
9rm(4⋒) B
CTV
Last dinner 9.30pm
Credit cards [1] [2] [3] [5]

★★Risboro Clement Av (Exec Hotel) ☎(0492) 76343 Plan **27** *B4*
70rm(52→18⋒) CTV in all bedrooms ® sB&B→⋒£13–£15 dB&B→⋒£26–£30 B
Lift 16P (heated) sauna bath Disco twice wkly Live music and dancing 4 nights wkly Cabaret 3 nights wkly *xmas*
✱Lunch £4.50 Tea £1 Dinner £6.50 Last dinner 7.45pm
Credit cards [1] [3]

★★Royal Church Walks ☎(0492) 76476 Plan **29** *B4* Closed Dec–early Feb
Pebble-dashed, detached building located under Great Orme in a residential area.
41rm(8→3⋒)(5fb) ® sB&B£7.50–

Headlands Hotel

AA★★

Llandudno Tel: 0492 77485

Situated on the Great Orme with superb sea and mountain views this 18 bedroomed hotel offers excellent food, comfort and a convivial atmosphere. Ideal for the businessman attending conferences or the holidaymaker, each guest receives individual attention from the proprietors. 12 rooms en suite with colour TV. All rooms tea/coffee making facilities. Central heating, 5 car spaces, Cocktail Bar, TV Lounge, Sun Terrace. Terms from: £11.50 Bed & Breakfast, from £16.00 Dinner, Bed & Breakfast. Light Luncheons available.
Resident Proprietors: C A Lonsdale FHCIMA, Mrs W A Lonsdale BA
Open Easter to October.

L

THE Ormescliffe ★★

LLANDUDNO

On sea front overlooking bay. An hotel of high reputation.
65 bedrooms many with private bath or shower, colour TV & tea/coffee making facilities.
Dancing in season. Fully licensed. Table tennis, snooker, pool table and darts.
Free parking facilities at rear of Hotel.
Children welcome. Cots, high-chairs provided. Kiddies play-room.
Washing facilities. Special baby teas. Listening service every night.
Special terms for children under 12. Children under 5 free.
Fire Certificate.
We are here to make your stay a happy one.
Under the personal supervision of Mr & Mrs Brian Butterworth.
Ring or write for Brochure and Tariff — Telephone 77191

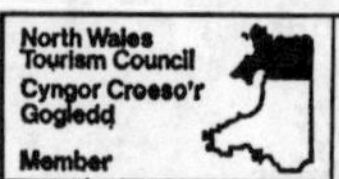
North Wales Tourism Council
Cyngor Croeso'r Gogledd
Member

Plas Fron Deg

HOTEL & RESTAURANT

Church Walks, Llandudno, Gwynedd LL30 2HL Tel: (0492) 77267

The hotel is situated in a sheltered position at the foot of the Great Orme, yet commands superb views of Llandudno and of the hills beyond the sparkling Conwy estuary. The dining room overlooks the garden as does the lounge, with its elegant furniture. The attractively-styled bedrooms have been furnished for your complete relaxation, with wonderful views from the window, hot and cold water, heating, radio and shaver points. Some bedrooms are fitted with private shower and WC. The unusual bar lounge, a most pleasant rendevous, is always well-stocked with a fine range of wines, spirits and beers.
Our aim at Plas Fron Deg is a combination of the services of a large hotel with added assurances of personal attention from the resident proprietors of a small hotel.
The efforts of the Proprietors have been recognised by winning the Sunday Times 'Taste of Wales Restaurant of the Year Award' for 1982.

LLANDUDNO HOTELS AND RESTAURANTS ASSOCIATION LHRA

£10.50 dB&B£15–£21.90 dB&B⇥£18–£24.90 ⊟

Lift CTV 30P ✽ ♿ Live music & dancing twice wkly

V ♡ ⊒ Bar lunch 50p–£1.50 Tea 50p Dinner £4.95–£5.95 Wine £3.50 Last dinner 7.30pm

S%

★★ ***HBL*** **St Tudno** North Pde ☎ (0492) 76309 Plan **31** *B4* Closed Jan

A warm and relaxed atmosphere pervades this high quality hotel personally run by Martin and Janette Bland. The public areas are delightful and attractive and the new dining room is fresh and bright. The 6 course menu is excellent value. The bedrooms are comfortable and extremely well equipped.

21rm(18⇥3⋒)(2fb) CTV in all bedrooms ® sB&B⇥⋒£16.50–£26.50 dB&B⇥⋒£25–£45 ⊟

Lift ⅄ 5P 2⌂ ⌗

⊟ British & French V ♡ ⊒ Lunch £5.50 Tea 75p Dinner £7.95 Wine £3.80 Last dinner 8.30pm

Credit cards ① ③

★★ **Somerset** Central Prom ☎ (0492) 76540 Plan **32** *C3* Closed Dec–Feb

36rm(28⇥8⋒)(9fb) CTV in all bedrooms sB&B⇥⋒£10.50–£12.50 dB&B⇥⋒£21–£25 ⊟

Lift 20P 3⌂

♡ ⊒ ✽ Lunch £2.50–£3.45 Tea 40p Dinner £3.45–£5.50 Wine £3.45 Last dinner 7.30pm

See advert on page 372

★ **Bedford** Promenade ☎ (0492) 76647 Plan **1** *E3*

Detached Victorian building, ¾m from the →

main shopping area, catering mainly for holidaymakers.

30rm(2➡3⋒)(8fb) sB&B£7.50–£8.50 sB&B➡⋒£8.50–£9.50 dB&B£15–£18 dB&B➡⋒£17–£20

CTV 30P *xmas*

French & Italian **V** Lunch fr£4.50 Tea fr£2 Dinner £6.50–£7.50 Wine £3.90 Last dinner 7.30pm

★ ***Branksome*** Lloyd St ☎(0492) 75989 Plan **3** *B3*
Closed Nov–Feb

Holiday hotel situated in a quiet residential area, ½m from the beach and ¼m from the shops.

50rm(3➡4⋒) Annexe: 5rm

CTV 12P

Last dinner 7.30pm

★ **Bron Orme** Church Walks ☎(0492) 76735 Plan **5** *B4*
Closed Oct–Mar

Located at the foot of Great Orme, only a short distance from the beach and the town centre.

11rm(4fb) sB&B£8–£8.50 dB&B£15–£16

CTV nc4yrs

Continental **V** Lunch fr£3.75 Dinner fr£4.75 Wine £3.80 Last dinner 7.30pm

L

★ **Clontarf** West Shore ☎(0492) 77621 Plan **8** *A3*
Closed Nov–Feb

Detached hotel situated in residential area, close to the West Shore.

10rm(1➡3⋒)(1fb) sB&B£11.50 dB&B£20.50 dB&B➡⋒£23.50

CTV 10P nc7yrs

Lunch fr£4 Tea fr40p Dinner fr£7.90 Wine £4.50 Last dinner 7.30pm

★ **Cranleigh** Great Ormes Rd, West Shore ☎(0492) 77688 Plan **9** *A3*
Closed Oct–19 Apr

Detached hotel in residential area, near West Shore.

13rm(3⋒)(5fb) Ⓡ sB&B£9–£11 sB&B⋒£10.50–£12.50 dB&B£18–£22 dB&B⋒£21–£25

CTV 13P nc2yrs

Lunch fr£4.50 Dinner fr£6.50 Wine £3.30 Last dinner 7.30pm

Credit card 1

★ *B* **Fairhaven** Promenade, Craigydon Pde ☎(0492) 76123 Plan **13** *E3*
Closed Nov–Mar

Neat, single-fronted, mid-terrace, Victorian building.

11rm(5➡3⋒)(1fb) CTV in all bedrooms Ⓡ sB&B£10.75–£11.75 sB&B➡⋒£12.50–£13.50 dB&B£21.50–£23.50 dB&B➡⋒£25–£27

CTV 6P nc6yrs

Lunch £2.50–£3.50 Dinner £3–£5 Wine £3 Last dinner 7pm

VS

★ **Gwesty Leamore** 40 Lloyd St ☎(0492) 75552 Plan **15** *B3*
Closed Dec

Holiday hotel in a corner position, close to the shops and ½m from the beach.

12rm(3⋒)(5fb) CTV in 2 bedrooms Ⓡ sB&B£8–£9 sB&B⋒£10–£11 dB&B£16–£18 dB&B⋒£20–£22

CTV 4P

Bar lunch fr£2.50alc Tea fr£1.20alc Dinner £5alc Wine £4 Last dinner 7.30pm

VS

★ **Hilbre Court** Great Ormes Rd, West Shore ☎(0492) 76632 Plan **17** *A3*
Closed Nov–Feb

Edwardian house in residential area, near West Shore.

10rm(3➡)(1fb) CTV in 3 bedrooms TV in 7 bedrooms sB&B£10.30–£11.50 dB&B£20.60–£23.20 dB&B➡£23–£26.40

CTV 5P nc3yrs

V ✱ Bar lunch £2–£5 Dinner £7.85&alc Wine £4.20 Last dinner 7pm

Credit cards 1 3 **VS**

★*H***Min-y-Don** North Pde ☎(0492) 76511 Plan **20** *B4*
Closed Nov–Feb
Family run holiday hotel on the sea front, near the shops.
20rm(2⇌1⋔)(10fb)Ⓡ✠sB&B£9–£9.25 dB&B£18–£18.50 dB&B⇌⋔£20.73–£21.96 𝐁
CTV 6P *xmas*
V⚘☕ Bar lunch £2–£2.50 Tea £1–£1.50 High Tea £1.95–£2.25 Dinner £4–£4.70 Wine £3.75 Last dinner 7.30pm
VS

★**Oak Alyn** Deganwy Av ☎(0492) 76497 Plan **21** *B3*
RS Jan–Mar
Three-storey Victorian house in a central position.
15rm(2⇌2⋔)(1fb) CTV in 5 bedrooms TV in 4 bedrooms Ⓡ sB&B£5.50–£6.50 sB&B⇌⋔£8–£9 dB&B£11–£13 dB&B⇌⋔£16–£18 Continental breakfast 𝐁
CTV 15P *xmas*
⚘Lunch £1–£2.50 Dinner £3.50 Wine £3.50 Last dinner 7.30pm
Credit cards [1] [3]

★**Osborne** North Pde ☎(0492) 77087 Plan **23** *B4*
Closed Nov–Etr
Double-fronted, Victorian holiday hotel facing North Parade, adjacent to the shops.
29rm(11⇌)(6fb) sB&B£8–£8.50 sB&B⇌£9 dB&B£16–£20 dB&B⇌£20 𝐁
CTV 12 billiards *xmas*
V⚘☕ Lunch fr£2.80 Tea fr60p Dinner £3.75 Wine £4.50 Last dinner 8pm
Credit cards [1] [2] [3] **VS**

★**Ravenhurst** West Pde ☎(0492) 75525 Plan **25** *A3*
Closed Nov–Jan
This hotel faces the West Shore, and has good views of the Snowdonia Range.
22rm(8⇌1⋔) Annexe: 1⇌(5fb) CTV available in bedrooms Ⓡ sB&B£10.50–£12.50 sB&B⇌£11.50–£13.50 dB&B£21–£24 dB&B⇌£23–£27 𝐁
CTV 14P
V⚘☕ Lunch £3&alc Tea 60p–£1.50&alc Dinner £4.50–£7.50&alc Wine £3.95 Last dinner 7.30pm
Credit card [3] **VS**

★**Richmond** St Georges Pl ☎(0492) 76347 Plan **26** *C3*
Closed Nov–Mar
Large, terraced hotel with a verandah.
26rm(13⇌1⋔)(8fb)Ⓡ✠sB&B£8.50–£9 sB&B⇌⋔£9.85–£10.35 dB&B£17–£18 dB&B⇌⋔£19.70–£20.70 𝐁
Lift CTV ⊅
☕ Bar lunch 95p–£3.50 Tea 35p Dinner £5.25 Wine £3.50 Last dinner 7.30pm
VS

★**Rothesay** 83 Church Walks ☎(0492) 76844 Plan **28** *C4*
Closed Oct–Apr
Victorian terraced hotel just off North Parade.
22rm(1⋔)(3fb) sB&B£9–£9.50 dB&B£18–£19
CTV ⊅ Live music and dancing twice wkly
⚘☕ Tea 40p Dinner £3.75–£4.50 Wine £3 Last dinner 7pm

★*L***Sunnymede** West Pde ☎(0492) 77130 Plan **33** *A2*
Closed Dec–Feb
Comfortable hotel with olde worlde lounge bar.
18rm(7⇌4⋔)(6fb) CTV in 2 bedrooms Ⓡ sB&B£8–£12 sB&B⇌⋔£10–£14 dB&B£16–£24 dB&B⇌⋔£20–£48 𝐁
CTV 18P
V⚘☕ Lunch £3.15&alc Tea 70p High Tea £2 Dinner £3–£5.50&alc Wine £4 Last dinner 6.30pm
VS

★**Tan-Lan** Great Ormes Rd, West Shore ☎(0492) 75981 Plan **34** *A3*
Closed Nov–Feb
Located in a residential area with a small garden at the front.
18⇌(7fb) CTV in all bedrooms Ⓡ sB&B⇌£14.70–£15.50 dB&B⇌£29–£32.50 𝐁
CTV 10P ♣ ⌂
▣ Welsh, English & French V⚘☕ Bar lunch 70p–£2&alc Tea 50p–60p Dinner £4–£5 Wine £4.20 Last dinner 7pm
VS

★**Woodlee** Great Ormes Rd, West Shore ☎(0492) 77702 Plan **35** *A2*
Closed Nov–mid Mar
Family run holiday hotel with home cooking dominating the menu.
21rm Ⓡ ✱sB&Bfr£10 dB&Bfr£20 𝐁
CTV ⊅
⚘☕ ✱Lunch fr£1&alc Tea fr30p Dinner fr£5&alc Wine £3 Last dinner 7.30pm
Credit card [3]

LLANELLI
Dyfed
Map **2** SN50

★★★**Stradey Park** Furnace (Trusthouse Forte) ☎(05542) 58171
Telex no 48521
Conveniently positioned company owned hotel with purpose built accommodation designed for business clients.
77⇌(3fb) CTV in all bedrooms Ⓡ sB&B⇌£31.50 dB&B⇌£44 𝐁
Lift ☾ 120P CFA
⚘☕ Last dinner 9.30pm
Credit cards [1] [2] [3] [4] [5]

L

★★**Diplomat** Ael-y-Bryn ☎(05542) 56156
A good quality hotel with comfortable restaurants.
12rm CTV in all bedrooms Ⓡ sB&B£19.50–£22 dB&B£26.50–£28.50
Lift 200P ♣ Ⓒ Live music and dancing Sat Cabaret Sat *xmas*
▣ English & French V⚘☕ Lunch fr£4.95&alc Tea fr£1.75 High Tea fr£2.95 Dinner fr£5.50&alc Wine £4.50 Last dinner 9.45pm
Credit cards [1] [2] [3] [5]
See advert on page 374

LLANFAIR PWLLGWYNGYLL
Gwynedd
Map **6** SH57
★★**Carreg Bran Country** Church Ln
☎Llanfairpwll (0248) 714224
Regency-style country house set below Britannia Bridge.
9➡ (4fb) CTV in all bedrooms ®
*sB&B➡£21.79–£25.05
dB&B➡£37.55–£43.64 B
80P ✽ *xmas*
V ✽Lunch £4.50&alc Tea £1.15–£2.20 Dinner £5.95&alc Wine £5.60 Last dinner 9.30pm
Credit cards 1 2 3 5

LLANFYLLIN
Powys
Map **6** SJ11
★★ *BL* **Bodfach Hall** ☎(069184) 272
Closed Nov–Feb
A 17th-century, oak-panelled, country house situated in 15 acres of grounds.
9rm(6➡1⋒) (1fb) CTV in all bedrooms ®
sB&B➡⋒ fr£15 dB&B➡⋒ fr£30 B
20P ✽
Lunch fr£4.50 Tea fr£1.20 Dinner fr£6.75 Wine £4.90 Last dinner 9pm
Credit card 5 **VS**

★★**Cain Valley** ☎(069184) 366
A 15th-century country inn with a Jacobean stairway and an oak-panelled lounge bar set in the centre of the village.
13rm(6➡5⋒) (2fb) TV in all bedrooms
sB&B➡⋒ £16.50 dB&B➡⋒ £25 B
CTV 18P *xmas*
French & German Lunch £4–£5.50&alc Dinner £5.65&alc Wine £3.60 Last dinner 9.15pm

L

LLANGADOG
Dyfed
Map **3** SN72

★★ **H *Plas Glansevin*** (Inter-Hotels)
☎ (05503) 238 Closed Xmas
Comfortable country hotel with an elegant restaurant.
8rm (3 2) CTV in all bedrooms ®
50P ✽ (heated)
 Last dinner 9pm
Credit cards 1 2 3 4 5 **VS**

LLANGAMMARCH WELLS
Powys
Map **3** SN94

★★★ **Lake** ☎ (05912) 202
Closed Jan
Three-storey, red brick and half-timbered hotel set in its own grounds.
29rm (13 2) (4fb) 1 CTV in all bedrooms ® *sB&B£17 sB&B £20.50 dB&B£30 dB&B £33.50
40P 3 ✽ (hard) billiards *xmas*
V *Lunch £4.95–£5.50 Tea 50p–£1.50 Dinner £8.50–£9.50 Wine £2.70 Last dinner 8.45pm
S% Credit card 1

LLANGOLLEN
Clwyd
Map **7** SJ24

★★★ **Bryn Howel** (2¾m E A539)
☎ (0978) 860331 Closed Xmas Day
Mock Tudor house with modern extensions with fine views up the Dee Valley and good salmon and trout fishing facilities.
34rm (30 29) (1fb) CTV in 30 bedrooms ® sB&B£15 sB&B £22–£24 dB&B£20 dB&B £33–£36
CTV ✽
International V Lunch *£5–£5.50 Tea 75p–£2.25 High Tea £2–£3 Dinner fr£7&alc Wine £4 Last dinner 9.30pm
S% Credit cards 1 2 3

★★★ **Hand** (Mount Charlotte, Best Western) ☎ (0978) 860303 Telex no 61160
Three-storey coaching inn overlooking the river.
59rm (50 9) (6fb) CTV in all bedrooms sB&B £25 dB&B £38
☾ 50P CFA ✽ Live music and dancing nightly (May–Oct)
V Lunch £4.50–£4.75&alc Dinner £7.50–£7.75&alc Wine £5 Last dinner 10pm
Credit cards 1 2 3 5 **VS**

★★★ **Royal** Bridge St (Trusthouse Forte) ☎ (0978) 860202
Three-storey stone hotel, situated in the centre of the town on the bank of the River Dee.
33 (4fb) CTV in all bedrooms ®
sB&B £33 dB&B £49.50
23P 2 *xmas*
 Last dinner 9pm
Credit cards 1 2 3 4 5

★★ **L Ty'n-y-Wern** (1m E on A5)
☎ (0978) 860252 Closed 3 Jan–Feb
An 18th-century farmhouse set in seven acres of lawns and grazing land overlooking the River Dee and the Vale of Llangollen.
10rm (2) (3fb) TV in all bedrooms ® sB&B fr£14 dB&B fr£30 dB&B fr£32
TV 80P ✽
 Bar lunch £2.50–£6.50 Dinner £7–£10 Wine £5.25 Last dinner 9pm
Credit card 3

LLANGORSE
Powys
Map **3** SO12

★ **Red Lion** ☎ (087484) 238
Small character inn positioned close to The Brecon Beacons and Black Mountains.
10rm (5) ® sB&B fr£12.50 dB&B fr£20.50 dB&B fr£23.50
CTV 30P 2 ✽ *xmas* →

L

Welsh, English & French V Bar lunch £3.50–£5 Tea £1.50–£2.15 Dinner fr£7&alc Wine £4.25 Last dinner 9.15pm

LLANGURIG
Powys
Map **6** SN98

★*L* **Glan Severn Arms** Pant Mawr ☎(05515) 240
RS 1wk Xmas

Small country-style inn, situated beside the road, with panoramic views from the rear of the building.

7rm(5) CTV in all bedrooms sB&B£15 dB&B£22 dB&B£25 B
40P

Lunch fr£7.50 Tea fr£1 Dinner fr£8.75 Wine £4.50 Last dinner 8.15pm

LLANGYNOG
Powys
Map **6** SJ02

★*H* **New Inn** ☎Pennant (069174) 229

Comfortable family run inn set in mountain hamlet.

8rm(2)(2fb) sB&B£10–£11 dB&B£20–£22 dB&B£22–£24 B
CTV 70P

V Lunch £3.75–£4&alc Tea 75p–£1&alc High Tea £2–£3&alc Dinner £4.50–£5&alc Wine £3.95 Last dinner 10pm

LLANIDLOES
Powys
Map **6** SN98

★ **Red Lion** Longbridge St ☎(05512) 2270

Town centre inn

6rm(2fb) Ⓡ *sB&B£8 dB&B£16–£17
CTV 8P

*Bar lunch £4.95&alc Wine £3.95 Last dinner 9.30pm

LLANRHAEADR
Clwyd
Map **6** SJ06

★★★ ***Bryn Morfydd*** ☎Llanynys (074578) 280

Country mansion, ½m from the main road and set amongst green fields and trees.

17 Annexe: 8 TV in all bedrooms B

CTV 100P CFA (heated) (hard)

Welsh, English & French Last dinner 9.30pm

LLANRWST
Gwynedd
Map **6** SH76

★★★ *L* **Gwesty Plas Maenan** Maenan (3m N) ☎Dolgarrog (049269) 232

Quiet, secluded hotel in an elevated position, overlooking the vale of Conwy and the river.

15(3fb) CTV in all bedrooms Ⓡ
*sB&B£18.15–£21.75 dB&B£28.60–£33.50 B
110P Live music wkly *xmas*

V Lunch £3.65–£6.80&alc Tea 50p–£3.65 High Tea £3.65–£6.80 Dinner £6.50–£7&alc Wine £4.75 Last dinner 10pm

S% Credit cards 1 2 3 5 VS

★★ **Eagles** ☎(0492) 640454

Impressive stone hotel on the banks of the River Conwy.

12rm(10 2)(4fb) CTV in 6 bedrooms TV in 4 bedrooms Ⓡ sB&B£13.50–£15.50 dB&B£23–£26 B

CTV 50P 3 billiards Disco Sat

Bar lunch £1.50–£6 Tea £1.20–£1.50 High Tea £2.50–£3.50 Dinner fr£7 Wine £3.50 Last dinner 9pm

Credit cards 1 2 3

★★ **Maenan Abbey** Maenan ☎Dolgarrog (049269) 247

19th-century stone building with a galleried hall and the staircase as a feature. On the site of an old monastery, alongside A470.

12rm(9 3) Annexe: 3(2fb) CTV in 1 bedroom TV in 1 bedroom Ⓡ

sB&B£13.80–£16.10 dB&B£21.85–£25.30 B

CTV 60P sauna bath *xmas*

Welsh, English, French & Italian V *Lunch £3.95–£5.95&alc Tea £1.75–£2.25 High Tea £2.95–£3.95 Dinner £6.95–£8 Wine £3.95 Last dinner 9.45pm

Credit cards 1 2 3 5

★★ **Meadowsweet** Station Rd ☎(0492) 640732

Victorian hotel alongside the A470 on the outskirts of town. Overlooking meadows.

10(1fb) TV in all bedrooms sB&B£16–£19 dB&B£24–£33 B
10P *xmas*

French Lunch £6 Tea 75p High Tea £2.50 Dinner £9.50–£11.50&alc Wine £4.95 Last dinner 9.30pm

Credit cards 1 2 3 VS

LLANSANTFFRAID-YM-MECHAIN
Powys
Map **7** SJ22

★ **Lion** ☎(069181) 207

6rm(2)(1fb) CTV in 1 bedroom Ⓡ
*sB&B£9.50 sB&B£11–£11.50 dB&B£19 dB&B£22–£23 B
CTV 40P

English & Continental *Bar lunch £4.50alc Tea 60p–£1 Dinner £8alc Wine £3.85 Last dinner 10pm

Credit card 1

LLANSTEPHAN
Dyfed
Map **2** SN31

★★ ***Mansion House*** Pant-yr-Atho ☎(026783) 515

Family run hotel with fine views.

10 B
CTV 50P

Last dinner 9pm

LLANTWIT MAJOR
South Glamorgan
Map **3** SS96

★★ **West House** West St ☎(04465) 2406

Small, character country house style of hotel, offering commendable grill menu.

20rm(14⇌)(1fb) CTV in 15 bedrooms TV in 5 bedrooms Ⓡ sB&B fr£15 sB&B⇌ fr£20 dB&B fr£21 dB&B⇌ fr£28 Ꞵ

50P Live music and dancing Fri & Sat *xmas*

Mainly grills Lunch fr£5.50&alc Tea fr£2 Dinner £8–£9alc

Credit cards 1 3

✕✕✕ **Colhugh Villa** Flanders Rd ☎(04465) 2022

Situated in an elevated position in the centre of the village.

Closed Mon Lunch not served Tue–Sat Dinner not served Sun

English & French 60 seats Lunch fr£6 Dinner fr£7&alc Wine £4.80 Last dinner 9.30pm 35P

Credit cards 1 2 3 5

LLANWNDA
Gwynedd
Map **6** SH45

☆☆☆ ***B*Stables** (Inter-Hotels) ☎(0286) 830711

Modern bedrooms with excellent facilities plus good food in attractive restaurant are features of this rural hotel.

Annexe: 12⇌(2fb) CTV in all bedrooms Ⓡ sB&B⇌ £21.50–£23.50 dB&B⇌ £32.50–£35 Ꞵ

☾ 60P ✽ *xmas*

International **V** Lunch £5.75–£6.50&alc Tea £2.75 High Tea fr£5 Dinner £7.50–£9&alc Wine £4.50 Last dinner 9.45pm

Credit cards 1 2 3 **VS**

LLANWRTYD WELLS
Powys
Map **3** SN84

★ **Neuadd Arms** ☎(05913) 236

Small country inn in centre of village.

18rm(1fb) ✻sB&B£10–£11 dB&B£20–£22 Ꞵ

CTV 10P

International **V** Lunch £4.25 Tea £1.50 Dinner £5–£5.50&alc Wine £3.50 Last dinner 8.30pm

Credit card 3 **VS**

LLYSWEN
Powys
Map **3** SO13

★ **Griffin Inn** ☎(087485) 241

Small, personally run inn with comfortable bedrooms.

6rm(4⇌2⋂) Ⓡ sB&B⇌⋂ £12.50–£14 dB&B⇌⋂ £20–£24 Ꞵ

15P 2 nc10yrs

V Bar lunch £3alc Dinner £8 Last dinner 9pm

Credit cards 1 3 5

LOCHAILORT
Highland *Inverness-shire*
Map **13** NM78

★ **Lochailort Inn** ☎(06877) 208

7rm (1fb) Ⓡ sB&B£9.50–£12 dB&B£19–£24

CTV 20P *xmas*

V Lunch £3.50alc Tea 50p alc High Tea £3.50alc Dinner £6.50alc Wine £4.10 Last dinner 9.30pm

LOCHAWE
Strathclyde *Argyllshire*
Map **10** NN12

★★ ***L*Carraig-Thura** ☎Dalmally (08382) 210

Closed Dec–Feb RS Mar

Turreted grey-stone hotel in picturesque setting with friendly service and good home cooking.

20rm(11⇌5⋂)(3fb) Ⓡ sB&B£14 sB&B⇌⋂ £17–£21 dB&B£22–£26 dB&B⇌⋂ £28–£40 Ꞵ

CTV 40P ✽ *xmas*

V Bar lunch £2.50–£5 Tea £1.50–£2 Dinner £8–£10 Wine £3 Last dinner 8pm

Credit cards 1 3 **VS**

L

LOCHBOISDALE
Isle of South Uist, Western Isles *Inverness-shire*
Map **13** NF71
★★ ***Lochboisdale*** ☎(08784) 332
Traditional tourist/fishing hotel close to pier.
20rm(8⇌)
CTV 30P ⚑ ⌡
⚘ ⊟ Last dinner 8.30pm
Credit card ③

LOCHCARRON
Highland *Ross & Cromarty*
Map **14** NG93
★**Lochcarron** ☎(05202) 226
Closed Xmas & New Year
Stone-built building on edge of village close to the loch shore.
7rm(4⇌) Ⓡ sB&B£12–£13 dB&B£24–£26 dB&B⇌£28–£32
CTV 20P ⛟
⚘ ⊟ Lunch £3.50alc Tea £1alc Dinner £5alc Wine £3.25 Last dinner 8.30pm
Credit cards ① ③ **VS**

LOCHEARNHEAD
Central *Perthshire*
Map **11** NN52
★★ ***Clachan Cottage*** Lochside ☎(05673) 247
Two modernised, converted and extended cottages form this hotel which overlooks Loch Earn and the Perthshire hills.
30rm(9⇌⋒) Ⓡ B
CTV 70P ✽ billiards Disco wkly Live music and dancing 3 nights wkly
⚘ ⊟ Last dinner 8.30pm
Credit cards ① ② ③

★ *L* **Craigroyston House** Lochside ☎(05673) 229
Closed Nov–Mar
14rm(1⇌3⋒) Ⓡ sB&B£10–£17 sB&B⇌⋒£15–£17 dB&B£15–£25 dB&B⇌⋒£21–£25
CTV 14P ⛟

⊟ International **V** ⚘ ⊟ Lunch £3alc Tea 75palc High Tea £3.85alc Dinner £6alc Wine £3.50 Last dinner 9.30pm
Credit cards ① ③ **VS**

LOCHGILPHEAD
Strathclyde *Argyllshire*
Map **10** NR88
★★**Stag** Argyll St ☎(0546) 2496
A painted hotel, with a small turret, situated on a corner site, halfway up the main street.
28rm (2fb) sB&B£10 dB&B£20
CTV 10P
V ⚘ ⊟ Bar lunch fr£2.90 Tea 50p High Tea £3.50 Dinner £6.50alc Wine £3.60 Last dinner 8.30pm
Credit card ③

LOCHINVER
Highland *Sutherland*
Map **14** NC02
★★★**Culag** (Best Western) ☎(05714) 209
Closed Nov–Apr
Spacious traditional hotel beside the pier.
42rm(19⇌) (1fb) Ⓡ sB&B£17.50 sB&B⇌£20 dB&B£35 dB&B⇌£40 B
Lift ☾ CTV 50P ✽ ⌡ ⌂ ♿
⊟ Scottish & French ⚘ ⊟ Lunch £4.50 Tea £1.50 High Tea £3.50 Dinner £9 Wine £3.50 Last dinner 9pm
Credit cards ① ② ③ **VS**

LOCHMADDY
Isle of North Uist, Western Isles *Inverness-shire*
Map **13** NF96
★★**Lochmaddy** ☎(08763) 331
15rm(1⇌1⋒) Ⓡ sB&B£12–£14.50 dB&B£23–£27 dB&B⇌⋒£25–£29
CTV 30P ⛟ ⌡ Live music and dancing Wed & Sat
⊟ Scottish & Continental **V** ⚘ ⊟ Bar lunch £1.50–£4 Tea 50p–£2 Dinner £6–£8.50 Wine £3.75 Last dinner 8.30pm

LOCHWINNOCH
Strathclyde *Renfrewshire*
Map **10** NS36
✕ ***Gable End*** 45 High St ☎(0505) 842775
Family-run restaurant in the town centre, near Castle Semple.
Closed Mon
⊟ Continental 50 seats Last dinner 9pm 30P
Credit cards ① ② ③ ⑤

LOCKERBIE
Dumfries & Galloway *Dumfriesshire*
Map **11** NY18
★★**Dryfesdale** ☎(05762) 2427
An 18th-century, former manse, standing in its own seven-acre grounds.
11rm(4⇌1⋒) (2fb) TV in all bedrooms sB&B£15–£16 sB&B⇌⋒£17.50–£19.50 dB&B£20.50–£22.50 sB&B⇌⋒£26–£28 B
CTV 70P ⛟ ✽ U ♿
⊟ British & French **V** ⚘ ⊟ Lunch £4.80–£6.20&alc Tea 80p alc Dinner £7.50–£9.80&alc Last dinner 9pm
Credit cards ① ② ③ ⑤ **VS**

★★**Somerton House** Carlisle Rd ☎(05762) 2583
RS 25 Dec & 1 Jan
A robust Victorian house standing in its own grounds.
6rm(3⇌) (1fb) sB&B£11.50–£12.50 sB&B⇌£12.50–£13.50 dB&B£23–£24 dB&B⇌£25–£26.50
CTV 90P 1⌂ ⛟ ✽
⊟ Mainly grills ⚘ ⊟ ✱ Bar lunch £2.50–£5 Tea 50p–£1 High Tea £2–£3 Dinner £6.50–£7.50 Last dinner 7.45pm

★**Blue Bell** High St ☎(05762) 2309
18th-century town centre inn.
6rm (1fb) Ⓡ ✱ sB&B£9.50 dB&B£16.50
CTV 10P Live music and dancing 3 nights wkly
⊟ Mainly grills ⚘ Bar lunch £1.60–£5 Dinner £6.95 Last dinner 9pm

★**Townhead** Townhead St ☎ (05762) 2298

Small, three-storey hotel with a modern extension standing on the main road at the north end of the town.

9rm (2fb) Ⓡ sB&B£8.50–£9.50 dB&B£17–£19

CTV 25P

Lunch £2–£4.50&alc Tea 50p–£1.50&alc Dinner £2.50–£7 Wine £3.50 Last dinner 9.30pm

LOFTUS
Cleveland
Map **8** NZ71

★★★**Grinkle Park** ☎ Guisborough (0287) 40515

20rm (10) CTV in all bedrooms Ⓡ *sB&B£12.75–£16.80 sB&B£19.15–£28.90 dB&B£24.20–£31.85 dB&B£26.80–£37.90

CTV 80P *xmas*

International V *Lunch £4.95 Dinner £8.50&alc Wine £4.02 Last dinner 9pm

S% Credit cards 1 3

LOGIERAIT
Tayside *Perthshire*
Map **14** NN95

★**Logierait** ☎ Ballinluig (079682) 423

Friendly, personally supervised historic inn.

7rm (2fb) sB&B£10 dB&B£18

CTV 30P 2 Live music and dancing wknds Cabaret wknds *xmas*

V Lunch £4 Tea fr 75p Dinner £7.50 Wine £4.50 Last dinner 10pm

DISPLAY OF HOTEL PRICES

All hotels, motels, inns, and guesthouses in Britain, with four bedrooms or more (including self-catering accommodation) and offering accommodation to guests, are required to display notices showing minimum and maximum overnight charges. The notice must be displayed in a prominent position in the reception area, or at the entrance.

The prices shown must include any service charge, and may include Value Added Tax, and it must be made clear whether or not these items are included. If VAT is not included then it must be shown separately. If meals are provided with the accommodation, this must be made clear too. If prices are not standard for all rooms, then only the lowest and highest prices need be given.

Alphabetical List of London Hotels and Restaurants

L

L

L

LONDON
Greater London Plans **1–5**, pages **411–421** (Small scale maps 4–5 at back of book)

A map of the London postal area appears on pages 422–423.

Places within the London postal area are listed below in postal district order commencing East, then North, South and West, with a brief indication of the area covered. Detailed plans **1–4** show the locations of AA-appointed hotels and restaurants within the Central London postal districts which are indicated by a number, followed by a grid reference e.g. *A5* to help you find the location. Plan **5** shows the districts covered within the outer area keyed by a grid reference, e.g. *A1*. **Other places within the county of London are listed under their respective place names and are also keyed to this plan or the main map section.**

If more detailed information is required the *AA Motorists Map of London*, on sale at AA offices, is in two parts: the 'West End and the City' shows one-way systems, banned turns, car parks, stations, hotels, places of interest, etc: 'Outer London gives primary routes, car parks at suburban stations, etc. A theatre map of the West End is included.

For London Airports see under Gatwick & Heathrow.

E1 Stepney *and east of the Tower of London*
London plan **5** E4

★★★★**Tower Thistle** St Katharine's Way (Thistle) ☎01-481 2575 Telex no 885934 Plan 4: **7** *C3*
834⇌⋔ CTV in all bedrooms ★
✱sB⇌⋔£48–£58 (room only) £55–£68 (room only) Ɓ
Lift ☾ ##90P90 ⌂ CFA ♿
☐European ✿ ☐ ✱Lunch £6–£8.95&alc Dinner £6–£11.95&alc Last dinner 9.30pm
Credit cards ① ② ③ ④ ⑤ **VS**

✕***Blooms*** 90 Whitechapel High St ☎01-247 6001
Closed Sat Dinner not served Fri
☐Kosher Unlicensed 150 seats 80P

E14 Poplar
London plan **5** E4

✕**Good Friends** 139 Salmon Ln ☎01-987 5541
Closed Xmas Day, Boxing Day & New Years Day
☐Cantonese **V** Unlicensed No corkage charge 80 seats ✱Lunch fr£4.50&alc Dinner fr£5.50&alc
Credit cards ① ② ③ ⑤

EC1 City of London; *Barbican Clerkenwell, Farringdon*
London plan **5** D4

❀✕**Bubb's** 329 Central Markets ☎01-236 2435 Plan 3: **7** *E6*
Good food, pleasantly served in French market-style restaurant
Closed Sat, Sun Public Hols & Aug
☐French 80 seats ✱Lunch £15alc Dinner £17alc Wine £4.50 Last dinner 9.30pm ♪
S%

EC2 City of London; *Bank of England, Liverpool Street Station*

✕✕✕**Baron of Beef** Gutter Ln
☎01-606 6961 Plan 4: **1** *A4*
Spacious, panelled basement restaurant specialising in English cuisine.
Closed Sat & Sun
80 seats ✱Lunch £9&alc Dinner £9&alc Wine £6.50 Last dinner 9.30pm ♪ Live music Thu
S% Credit cards ① ② ③ ⑤

❀❀✕✕✕**Le Poulbot London EC2**
45 Cheapside ☎01-236 4379 Plan 4: **5** *B4*
(Rosettes awarded for lunch only)
Those who want to know how that hackneyed dish, tournedos chasseur, should be done could do worse than try it here! Christopher Oakley, the English chef and protegé of the Roux brothers, continues to produce food of delicious flavour and demonstrates a sure touch with his well composed dishes. Favourites from the old à la carte menu still appear on the set menu now in use, and dishes that have pleased everyone include mousseline de saumon beurre de ciboulettes, marmite du pêcheur, terrine de laperau gèlée de romarin, and a ragout de coquilles au champagne among the first courses. More importantly, main courses include a ragout de homard aux fonds d'artichauts, noisettes de chevreuil au genièvre, and assiette de gibier a l'estragon. Not everyone likes the selection of vegetables around the edge of the plate but they are invariably well cooked and complement the main item. There is a selection of fine French cheeses from Philippe Oliver and a more limited selection of puddings that do not impress quite so much as the other dishes. Nevertheless, with a wine from the very good list, you can be assured of a delicious meal here. All this is especially commendable in a City restaurant where the normal clientele does not always give first priority to the food. Here it would be foolish not to do so because the cooking is very polished and the three course meal and coffee represents excellent value for money. The restaurant is plushly furnished with some high backed booths and, although they are always very busy, Jean Cottard, the manager, looks after you with unfailing charm and efficiency.
Closed Sat, Sun & Public Hols
Dinner not served
☐French 50 seats Lunch £16.50 Wine £9 ♪
S% Credit cards ① ② ③ ④ ⑤

L

EC3 City of London; *Monument, Tower of London*

✕✕✕ ***Viceroy*** Colonial House, Mark Ln ☎01-626 2271 Plan 4: **8** *C3*

Closed Sat, Sun & Public hols

Dinner not served

French 60 seats

Credit cards 1 2 3 5

✕✕ ***Shares*** 12–13 Lime St ☎01-623 1843 Plan 4: **6** *C3*

A modern, tastefully furnished, lunch-time restaurant with a small bar.

Closed Sat, Sun & Public hols

Dinner not served

International 78 seats

Credit cards 1 2 3 5

EC4 City of London; *Blackfriars, Cannon Street and Fleet Street*

✕❀ **Le Gamin** 32 Old Bailey ☎01-236 7931 Plan 4: **3** *A4*

French restaurant with authentic atmosphere and cuisine.

Closed Sat, Sun & Public Hols

Dinner not served

French 100 seats Lunch £15.75

S% Credit cards 1 2 3 4 5

✕ ***Ginnan*** 5 Cathedral Pl ☎01-236 4120 Plan 4: **4** *A4*

Simple modern Japanese restaurant with small party room.

Closed Sat, Sun, 1–3 Jan & Public Hols

Japanese 80 seats Last dinner 10pm

Credit cards 1 2 3 5

N1 Islington
London plan **5** D4

❀✕✕✕ **Carriers** 2 Camden Passage ☎01-226 5353

Owned by Robert Carrier, this modern-style restaurant occupies three floors of a double-fronted building in Camden Passage.

Closed Sun & Public Hols

French & International 78 seats ✻Lunch £15–£22 Dinner £25–£27 Wine £5.90 Last dinner 11.30pm

Credit cards 1 2 3 5

✕✕ **Frederick's** Camden Passage ☎01-359 2888

Closed Sun

French **V** 150 seats ✻Lunch £12.25alc Dinner £12.25alc Wine £3.95 Last dinner 11.30pm

Credit cards 1 2 3 4 5

✕ **M'sieur Frog** 31A Essex Rd ☎01-226 3495

Closed 3 wks Aug, 1 wk Xmas

Dinner not served Sun

French 63 seats ✻Dinner £14alc Wine £4.25 S%

✕ **Portofino** 39 Camden Passage ☎01-226 0884

Simple, Italian restaurant, where the walls are decorated with hanging bottles.

Closed Sun, Xmas, Etr & Public Hols

French & Italian 65 seats ✻Lunch £15alc Dinner £15alc Wine £3.95 Last dinner 11.30pm Live music Thu–Sat

S% Credit cards 1 2 3 5

N6 Highgate
London plan **5** D5

✕✕ **San Carlo** 2 High St ☎01-340 5823

Good modern Italian restaurant with patio.

Closed Mon & Public hols

Italian **V** 100 seats ✻Lunch £15alc Dinner £15alc Wine £4.75 Last dinner mdnt 30P

S% Credit cards 1 2 3 4 5

NW1 Regents Park; *Baker Street, Euston and King's Cross Stations*
London plan **5** D4

☆☆☆☆ **White House** Albany St, Regents Park (Rank) ☎01-387 1200 Telex no 24111 Plan 3: **44** *A6*

590 CTV in all bedrooms ✻sB £39.50–£55 dB fr£55–£60 (room only)

Lift CFA

English, French & Continental **V** Lunch £11–£15 Dinner £12–£15 Wine £6 Last dinner 11.30pm

Credit cards 1 2 3 4 5

☆☆☆ ***Harewood*** Harewood Row (Inter-Hotel) ☎01-262 2707 Telex no 291855

Modern hotel with comfortable bedrooms and grill restaurant.

93rm (79 14) CTV in all bedrooms ®

Lift 10P

Mainly grills Last dinner 10pm

Credit cards 1 2 3 4 5 **VS**

★★★ **Kennedy** Cardington St (Forum) ☎01-387 4400 Telex no 28250

Closed 23 Dec–27 Dec

320 (35fb) CTV in all bedrooms sB&B £37 dB&B £47 Continental breakfast

Lift # 11

English & International **V** Lunch £6.45&alc Tea £1alc High Tea £6.50alc Dinner £8.50alc Wine £5.60 Last dinner 10.30pm

Credit cards 1 2 3 4 5

✕✕ ***Viceroy of India*** 3–5 Glentworth St ☎01-486 3401

Indian **V** 125 seats Last dinner 11.30pm

Credit cards 1 2 3 4 5

✕ ***Froops*** 17 Princess Rd, Regents Pk ☎01-722 9663

Closed Sun Lunch not served

Swedish **V** 45 seats Last dinner 11.30pm

Credit cards 1 2 3 5

NW3 Hampstead *and Swiss Cottage*
London plan **5** D4

☆☆☆☆ **Clive** (& Conference centre) Primrose Hill Rd (Ladbroke) ☎01-586 2233 Telex no 22759

Closed Xmas

Modern commercial and conference hotel with well equipped bedrooms.

83 CTV in all bedrooms ® ✻sB fr£36.60 dB fr£45 (room only)

Lift 16P 2 CFA

English & Continental **V** ✻Lunch fr£6 Dinner fr£8.50 Last dinner 10pm

Credit cards 1 2 3 5

☆☆☆☆ ***BL Holiday Inn*** King Henry's Rd, Swiss Cottage (Commonwealth) ☎01-722 7711 Telex no 267396

291 CTV in all bedrooms

Lift # 75P 60 (heated) sauna bath Live music and dancing Tue–Sat

International **V** Last dinner 10.30pm

Credit cards 1 2 3 4 5

★★★ **Charles Bernard** 5 Frognal ☎01-794 0101 Telex no 23560

Informal modern hotel with pleasant bedrooms.

57 CTV in all bedrooms ® sB&B £32.20 dB&B £41.40

Lift CTV 25P

Dinner £6–£9 Last dinner 9.30pm

S% Credit cards 1 2 3 5 **VS**

☆☆☆ **Post House** Haverstock Hill (Trusthouse Forte) ☎01-794 8121 Telex no 262494

Popular modern hotel with well equipped bedrooms.

140 (50fb) CTV in all bedrooms ® sB&B £43.50 dB&B £56

Lift 70P

Last dinner 10pm

Credit cards 1 2 3 4 5

✕✕ **Keats** 3 Downshire Hill ☎01-435 3544

Intimate French restaurant with good wine list. Special gastronomic evenings.

Closed Sun & 2 wks Aug Lunch not served

French 45 seats Dinner £17&alc Wine £8–£9 Last dinner 11.30pm

Credit cards 1 2 3 5

✕ **Lee Ho Fook** New College Parade, Finchley Rd ☎01-734 9578

Cantonese **V** 150 seats Lunch £3.50alc Dinner £6.50&alc Wine £4.30 Last dinner 11.30pm

S% Credit cards 1 2 3 5

NW4 Hendon
London plan **5** C5

☆☆☆☆**Hendon Hall** Ashley Ln (Kingsmead) ☎01-203 3341 Telex no 8956088

52rm(48→ 4⋒) CTV in all bedrooms ® sB&B→⋒ £37–£39 dB&B→ £42.50 B

☾ 100P CFA Live music and dancing Sat *xmas*

English & French **V** Lunch £7&alc Tea 90p High Tea £2 Dinner £7.35&alc Wine £5.25
Last dinner 10.15pm
Credit cards 1 2 3 5

NW6 Kilburn
London plan **5** C4

✕**Capability Brown** 351 West End Ln ☎01-794 3234

Quiet sophisticated, French restaurant on two levels, connected by a spiral staircase.

French 45 seats Lunch fr£8&alc Dinner £9alc Wine £4.50 Last dinner 11.30pm
Credit cards 1 2 3 5

✕**Peter's Bistro** 65 Fairfax Rd ☎01-624 5804

Lunch not served Sat Dinner not served Sun

French **V** 55 seats Lunch £6.50&alc Dinner £10alc Wine £4.25 Last dinner 11.30pm Live music nightly
S% Credit cards 1 2 3 4 5

✕**Vijay** 49 Willesden Ln ☎01-328 1087

South Indian **V** 100 seats Lunch £4–£6 Dinner £4–£6alc Wine £4.50 Last dinner 11pm
Credit cards 1 2 5

NW7 Mill Hill
London plan **5** C5

☆☆☆**TraveLodge** M1 Scratchwood Service Area (Access from Motorway only) (Trusthouse Forte) ☎01-906 0611 Telex no 8814796

The restaurant facilities (mainly grills) are located in the adjacent service area.

100→ (12fb) CTV in all bedrooms ® sB&B→ £28 dB&B→ £40 B
120P CFA
Credit cards 1 2 3 4 5

✕✕**Good Earth** 143–145 Broadway, Mill Hill ☎01-959 7011
Closed 24–26 Dec

Chinese **V** 90 seats Lunch £7.85–£12.95&alc Dinner £7.85–£12.95&alc Wine £4.30 Last dinner 11.15pm 10P
S% Credit cards 1 2 3 5

NW8 St John's Wood
London plan **5** D4

☆☆☆☆**Ladbroke Westmoreland** (& Conference centre) 18 Lodge Rd (Ladbroke) ☎01-722 7722 Telex no 23101

Pleasant, modern hotel with well-equipped bedrooms.

350→⋒ (4fb) CTV in all bedrooms ® *sB→⋒ fr£50 dB→⋒ fr£62 (room only) B

Lift ☾ ## 44P 26 CFA

V Last dinner 11.30pm
Credit cards 1 2 3 4 5

✕✕**Lords Rendezvous** 24 Finchley Rd ☎01-722 4750

Modern, elegant Chinese restaurant with good food.

Closed Xmas & Boxing Day & Public hols

Chinese **V** 120 seats *Lunch £12.65–£18.40&alc Dinner £12.65–£18.40&alc Wine £5.75 Last dinner 11.15pm
S% Credit cards 1 2 3 5 **VS**

✕✕**Oslo Court** Prince Albert Rd ☎01-722 8795

A traditional, comfortable restaurant overlooking Regent's Park.

Closed Sun & Mon

French **V** 45 seats Lunch £10alc Dinner fr£10alc Wine £4.50 Last dinner 11pm
Credit cards 1 2 3 5

NW10 Harlesden, Willesden
London plan **5** C4

✕**Kuo Yuan** 217 High Rd, Willesden ☎01-459 5801

Lunch not served

Pekinese 150 seats *Dinner £5&alc Wine £3.80 Last dinner 11pm
S%

NW11 Golders Green
London plan **5** C5

✕✕**Luigi's** 1–4 Belmont Parade, Finchley Rd ☎01-455 0210

Closed Mon

Italian **V** 96 seats *Lunch £3.50–£4.50&alc Dinner £10alc Wine £4.50 Last dinner 10.30pm
Credit cards 1 2 3 5

✕***Hong*** 30 Temple Fortune Pde, Finchley Rd ☎01-455 9444

Modern nicely appointed Chinese restaurant offering cuisine from several regions.

Closed Mon

Cantonese

SE1 Southwark *and Waterloo*

✕**RSJ's** 13A Coin St ☎01-928 4554 Plan 3: **30** *E3*

Closed Sun Lunch not served Sat

French 40 seats *Lunch £8alc Dinner £10alc Wine £4.75 Last dinner 11pm

✕**South of the Border** Joan St ☎01-928 6374 Plan 3: **35** *E3*

Closed Sun & 1–23 Aug Lunch not served Sat

Cosmopolitan **V** 85 seats Lunch £9alc Dinner £9alc Wine £4.50 Last dinner 11.30pm
S% Credit cards 1 2 3 5 **VS**

SE10 Greenwich
London plan **5** E3

✕**Le Papillion** 57 Greenwich Church St ☎01-858 2668

Lunch not served Sat Dinner not served Sun

French 40 seats Lunch £5.80–£8.75&alc Dinner £13.50alc Wine £4.95 Last dinner 10.30pm
Credit cards 1 2 3 5

L

SE11 Kennington
London plan **5** D3

★★ ***London Park*** Brook Dr, Elephant & Castle 01-735 9191 Telex 919161

388rm(251) CTV in all bedrooms Ⓡ

Lift 16P CFA

Last dinner 8.45pm

Credit cards 1 2 3 5

SE13 Lewisham
London plan **5** E2

✕ **Curry Centre** 37 Lee High Rd 01-852 6544

Indian **V** 60 seats ✱Lunch £5alc Dinner £7.50&alc Wine £5.25 Last dinner 11.30pm

S% Credit cards 1 2 3 5 **VS**

SE19 Upper Norwood
London plan **5** D2

★★ **Aucklands** 153 Auckland Rd, Upper Norwood 01-771 5161 RS Sun

Small friendly, country house style hotel with well-equipped bedrooms.

35rm(13 22) (2fb) CTV in all bedrooms Ⓡ sB&B £27–£30 dB&B £37–£40

CTV 35P

English & French **V** Lunch £4.50–£5.50 Dinner £6.95&alc Wine £5 Last dinner 9.45pm

Credit cards 1 2 3 5

SW1 Westminster; *St James's Park, Victoria Station, Knightsbridge, (Lower) Regent St*

★★★★★ **Hyatt Carlton Tower**
2 Cadogan Pl 01-235 5411 Telex no 21944 Plan 2: **61A** *D3*

(Rosette awarded for Chelsea Room Restaurant)

This modern eighteen storey hotel has several fine suites and two restaurants, the Rib Room and the Chelsea Room.

228 CTV in all bedrooms sB fr£70 dB fr£102 (room only)

Lift # 40 CFA

American & French **V** ✱Lunch £12.50&alc Tea £5.50&alc Dinner £20alc Wine £6.50 Last dinner 11pm

Credit cards 1 2 3 4 5

★★★★★***B*** **Hyde Park** Knightsbridge (Trusthouse Forte) 01-235 2000 Telex no 262057 Plan 2: **62** *D4*

Traditional, elegant and very English in style, this hotel is small enough to permit personal and friendly service. Except for those on the top floor, the bedrooms are, arguably, the best of any London hotel.

179 CTV in all bedrooms sB&B £98.50 dB&B £116

Lift CFA

Last dinner 10pm

Credit cards 1 2 3 4 5

★★★★★***B*** **Sheraton Park Tower**
101 Knightsbridge 01-235 8050
Plan 2: **109** *D4*

★★★★★

★★★★★ BERKELEY HOTEL, LONDON SW1

Wilton Pl, Knightsbridge 01-235 6000 Telex no 919252 Plan 2: **13** *D4*

Probably the last example of a traditional luxury hotel to be built in London – or perhaps anywhere for that matter – the Berkeley provides the highest standards of modern comfort combined with the elegance of the past. This is helped by the retention of furniture and other items from the old building. It is also helped by the dignified service from the friendly, efficient staff under the direction of Mr Sebastini. There are no shops or bar and their absence helps to create something of the atmosphere of a town house with its gracious sitting rooms, one of which is used as a cocktail lounge for the restaurant.
The design of the restaurant is essentially modern and provides a stimulating background to the delicious classical menus provided by Chef Auduc. The old Perroquet has been revamped under the name Berkeley Buttery and Perroquet. At luncheon there is still the same type of buffet; but at dinner the food has a Venetian influence and features many fish dishes. Unfortunately, we have not been able to sample this before we go to press but it sounds an interesting venture. For the same reason we are unable to say whether they are to continue with music and dancing.
The comfortable bedrooms which are air conditioned and individually decorated, provide every comfort. Room service is amongst the best in London and with the swimming pool and sauna, as well as the usual 5 star amenities, our members think this is one of the very nicest London hotels.

150 CTV in all bedrooms ✱sB&B £80 dB&B £99–£115 (room only)

Lift # 50 (heated) sauna bath

French & Italian ✱Lunch fr£10&alc Tea £4.25 Dinner fr£10&alc Wine £7.10 Last dinner 10.45pm

Credit cards 1 3

★★★★ GORING, LONDON SW1

Beeston Pl, Grosvenor Gdns 01-834 8211 Telex no 919166 Plan 3: **12** *A2*

THE GORING

Not a luxury hotel, but this is one of the last hotels in London under family ownership and direction; it is a rarity, a hotel of character, and provides old fashioned services. They are friendly but discreet, dignified without being stuffy, yet always efficient. It is an oasis of calm in this busy part of London. The bedrooms here are a bit variable, but mostly they are of good size, comfortable and well equipped, including direct dial phones and hair dryers. The two pleasant sitting rooms which overlook the garden, one with a bar counter in one section, are comfortably furnished and retain some of the contemporary structural features. So does the elegant dining room with its plaster decorated ceiling and frieze. It has good table appointments and comfortable elbow chairs, while the cooking, from both the set meals and à la carte is carefully done and enjoyable. After a short absence, we are pleased to award Red Stars again and congratulate Mr George Goring on quickly restoring the old standards.

100 CTV in all bedrooms sB £61 (room only) dB £84 (room only)

Lift 10P 4

English & French **V** Lunch fr£10&alc Tea fr£3.75 Dinner fr£12&alc Wine £6.50 Last dinner 10.30pm

S% Credit cards 1 2 3 5

Circular-shaped hotel with large, well-appointed bedrooms and friendly service.

293⇌⋒ CTV in all bedrooms ★ sB⇌⋒ £98.55–£110.05 dB⇌⋒ £114.30–£125.80 (room only) B

Lift ☾ ## 80 CFA *xmas*

English & French V ♀ ☕ ✱ Lunch £4.95&alc Tea £3.25–£4.75 Dinner £14.50&alc Wine £7.50 Last dinner 11pm

Credit cards 1 2 3 4 5

★★★★ **Cavendish** Jermyn St (Trusthouse Forte) ☎01-930 2111 Telex no 263187 Plan 1: **8** *A2*

Comfortable modern hotel with efficient friendly service.

253⇌ CTV in all bedrooms sB&B⇌ £68.50 dB&B⇌ £92.50 B

Lift ☾ 10P 80 CFA

♀ ☕ Last dinner 11pm

Credit cards 1 2 3 4 5

★★★★ **Duke's** St James's Pl (Prestige) ☎01-491 4840 Telex no 28283 Plan 1: **16** *A1*

Gracious building with brick and stone façade situated in a quiet courtyard off St James's Park.

56⇌⋒ (4fb) CTV in all bedrooms ★ sB⇌⋒ £65 dB⇌⋒ fr£89 (room only)

Lift ☾

V ♀ ☕ ✱ Lunch £16–£20alc Tea £2alc Dinner £16–£20alc Wine £6.90 Last dinner 10pm

Credit cards 1 2 3 4 5

☆☆☆☆ *L* **Holiday Inn Chelsea** 17–25 Sloane St (Holiday Inn) ☎01-235 4377 Telex no 919111 Plan 2: **60** *D3*

Modern hotel with good leisure facilities and helpful staff.

206⇌ (24fb) CTV in all bedrooms ★ ✱ sB⇌ fr£67.85 dB⇌ fr£78.20 (room only) B

Lift ☾ ## 6P CFA (heated) Cabaret nightly

International V ♀ ☕ ✱ Lunch fr£8.50&alc Tea £3.50alc Dinner £12alc Wine £6.35 Last dinner 10.30pm

S% Credit cards 1 2 3 4 5

☆☆☆☆ **Royal Westminster Thistle** 49 Buckingham Palace Rd (Thistle) ☎01-834 1821 Telex no 916821 Plan 3: **29** *A1*

Modern, well appointed hotel with interesting bedrooms and friendly willing staff.

135⇌⋒ (6fb) CTV in all bedrooms ★ ✱ sB⇌⋒ £45–£50 (room only) dB⇌⋒ £55–£60 (room only) B

Lift ☾ CFA

European ☕ ✱ Lunch £7.95&alc Dinner £10&alc Last dinner 10.30pm

Credit cards 1 2 3 4 5 **VS**

★★★★ ***H* Stafford** 16–18 St James's Place (Prestige) ☎01-493 0111 Telex no 28602 Plan 1: **50A** *A1*

Small comfortable, secluded hotel with elegant restaurant and lounges.

★

★ EBURY COURT, LONDON SW1

26 Ebury St ☎01-730 8147 Plan 2: **40** *E3*

A great favourite with so many of our members, this charming little hotel is unique in London. It was opened before the War by Diana and Romer Topham and over the years has been enlarged by the acquisition of neighbouring houses. These extensions have given it a quaint, rambling air that is quite appealing. Bedrooms vary in style, but they are prettily furnished with some decent pieces of furniture and are very comfortable. There are two cosy little sitting rooms, one with television, which are comfortable and homely. Good honest food is served in the basement dining room, and good afternoon teas, and light refreshments are available throughout the day. This is not one of the smart, stylish Red Star hotels but, more importantly, it is one of honest character where the good natured

staff are obliging and make you feel at home. It represents particularly good value for money in this part of London.

39rm (11⇌) 4 CTV available in bedrooms ✱ sB&B £24.50 dB&B £36.50 dB&B⇌ £45.50 B

Lift ☾ CTV nc5yrs

English & French V ☕ Lunch £7.75alc Dinner £8.75alc Wine £4.20 Last dinner 9pm

Credit cards 1 3

60⇌ CTV in all bedrooms ★

Lift ☾ 2P 2

English & French ♀ ☕ Last dinner 9.30pm

Credit cards 2 4 5

★★★ ***B* Lowndes Thistle** 19 Lowndes St (Thistle) ☎01-235 6020 Telex no 919065 Plan 2: **80** *D3*

A modern and somewhat exclusive hotel in Belgravia with elegant Adam style sitting area and particularly attractive bedrooms.

80⇌⋒ CTV in all bedrooms ★ ✱ sB⇌⋒ £62–£69 (room only) dB⇌⋒ £73–£83 (room only) B

Lift ☾

European ☕ ✱ Lunch £9.50&alc Dinner £10.30&alc

Credit cards 1 2 3 4 5 **VS**

L

★★★ *L* **Royal Horseguards Thistle** Whitehall Court (Thistle) ☎01-839 3400 Telex no 917096 Plan 1: **44** *D1*

Modern very comfortable hotel with attractive restaurant.

284 CTV in all bedrooms

*sB £45–£50 (room only) dB £51–£59 (room only)

Lift ☾ TV CFA

European *Lunch £8.95&alc Dinner £8.95&alc Last dinner 9.45pm

Credit cards 1 2 3 4 5 **VS**

★★★ ***Rubens*** Buckingham Palace Rd ☎01-834 6600 Telex no 916577 Plan 3: **30A** *A2*

Modernised hotel with nicely-appointed rooms.

173rm(148 25) CTV in all bedrooms

Lift ☾

Last dinner 9.30pm

Credit cards 1 2 3 4 5

★★★ **Stakis St Ermins** Caxton St (Stakis) ☎01-222 7888 Telex no 917731 Plan 3: **32** *B2*

244 (16fb) CTV in all bedrooms *sB&B £43 dB&B £56

Continental breakfast

Lift ☾ 22P

English, French & International **V** *Lunch £8.75&alc Tea £1.25 High Tea £2.25 Dinner £8.75&alc Wine £5.75 Last dinner 10pm

Credit cards 1 2 3 4 5

XXXX ***Hunting Lodge*** 16 (Lower) Regent St ☎01-930 4222 Plan 1: **23** *B2*

Cheerful, friendly restaurant with hunting theme and charcoal grill.

Closed Sun Lunch not served Sat

100 seats Last dinner 11.30pm

Credit cards 1 2 3 4 5

XXX ***Kundan*** 3 Horseferry Rd ☎01-834 3434 Plan 3: **16** *C1*

Comfortable, elegant basement restaurant offering skillful speciality cooking.

Closed Sun & Public hols

Indian & Pakistani 135 seats Last dinner 11.30pm

Credit cards 1 2 3 4 5

XXX **Lafayette** 32 King St, St James's ☎01-930 1131 Plan 1: **28** *A1*

Closed Sat & Sun

French 100 seats Lunch £11&alc Dinner £11&alc Wine £5.25 Last dinner 11.30pm

S% Credit cards 1 2 3 4 5 **VS**

XX ***L'Amico*** 44 Horseferry Rd ☎01-222 4680 Plan 3: **1** *C1*

Closed Sat & Sun

Italian 70 seats Last dinner 11pm

Credit cards 1 2 3 5

London SW1 — London SW3

XX **Le Caprice** Arlington House, Arlington St ☎01-629 2239 Plan 1: **7B** *A1*

Modern, French restaurant, with large plants, and prints around the walls.

Closed Xmas–New Year

Lunch not served Sat

French **V** 70 seats Lunch £11alc Dinner £11alc Wine £4.50 Last dinner mdnt Live music nightly

Credit cards 1 2 3 5

XX **Dolphin Square** Rodney House, Dolphin Sq ☎01-828 3207

French restaurant/brasserie overlooking indoor swimming pool.

Closed Xmas Day Dinner not served Sun

French 120 seats *Lunch £7.50–£13.50&alc Tea 50p–£2 Dinner £11–£13.50&alc Wine £4.80 Last dinner 11.30pm Live music nightly Live music & dancing Sat

S% Credit cards 1 2 3 5

XX **Gavvers** 61 Lower Sloane St ☎01-730 5983 Plan 2: **49B** *E2*

The short, fixed-price menu here, offers superb value for money in very comfortable surroundings.

Closed Sun Lunch not served

French 60 seats *Dinner £15.75 Wine £4.80 Last dinner 11pm

S%

❀XX **Ken Lo's Memories of China** 67 Ebury St ☎01-730 7734 Plan 3: **15A** *A1*

Closed Sun & Public hols

Chinese **V** 90 seats Lunch £11–£15&alc Dinner £15–£22&alc Wine £5.50 Last dinner 11pm

S% Credit cards 1 2 3 5

❀XX **Mijanou** 143 Ebury St ☎01-730 4099 Plan 2: **88B** *E2*

Restaurant offers French specialities with attractive ambience.

Closed Sat, Sun, 3wks Aug & 2wks Xmas & New Year

French 30 seats Lunch £8.95&alc Dinner £15alc Wine £4.95 Last dinner 10pm

Credit cards 1 2 5

XX ***Os Arcos*** 44 High St ☎01-828 1486 Plan 3: **24** *A1*

Small, intimate basement Portuguese restaurant.

Closed Sun Lunch not served Sat

Portuguese 40 seats Last dinner 11.15pm Live music Thu–Sat

Credit cards 1 2 3 5

❀XX **Pomegranates** 94 Grosvenor Rd ☎01-828 6560

Cuisine from at least 14 countries features in this basement restaurant.

Closed Sun & Public hols

Lunch not served Sat

Cosmopolitan **V** 50 seats *Lunch fr£11&alc Dinner £17alc Wine £7 Last dinner 11.15pm

S% Credit cards 1 2 3 5

❀XX **Salloos** 62–64 Kinnerton St ☎01-235 4444 Plan 2: **106A** *D3*

Comfortable well run family restaurant, with take away service as well.

Closed Sun & Public hols

Pakistani **V** 70 seats Last dinner 11.30pm

Credit cards 1 2 3 4 5

XX **Tate Gallery** Millbank Embankment ☎01-834 6754 Plan 3: **36** *C1*

Closed Sun, Good Fri, May Day, 24–26 Dec & New Years Day Dinner not served

V 120 seats *Lunch £12alc Wine £4.50 Last lunch 3pm

X **Ciboure** 21 Eccleston St ☎01-730 2505 Plan 2: **26A** *E3*

Closed Sun Lunch not served Sat

French 35 seats *Lunch £10.50 Dinner fr£15alc Wine £5.10 Last dinner 11.30pm

S% Credit cards 1 2 3 4 5

X **Eatons** 49 Elizabeth St ☎01-730 0074 Plan 2: **39** *E2*

Closed Sat, Sun & Public hols

Continental 40 seats Lunch £11.50alc Dinner £11.50alc Wine £5.80 Last dinner 11.15pm

S% Credit cards 1 2 3 5

X **Tapas** 30 Winchester St ☎01-828 3366

Atmospheric basement restaurant with large international selection of hors d'oeuvres.

Closed Sun & Public hols Lunch not served

Cosmopolitan **V** 40 seats *Dinner £5.40–£12.15&alc Wine £5.50 Last dinner 11.30pm

S% Credit cards 1 2 3 5

X **Tent** 15 Eccleston St ☎01-730 6922 Plan 2: **119** *E2*

Small bistro-style restaurant with good cooking.

Closed Sat

International 46 seats *Lunch £9.03 Dinner £9.03 Wine £4.35 Last dinner 11.15pm

S% Credit cards 1 2 3

SW3 Chelsea

★★★ *L* **Basil Street** Basil St, Knightsbridge ☎01-581 3311 Telex no 28379 Plan 2: **12** *D3*

Antique furniture and plenty of flowers help create a country house atmosphere here.

92rm(66) CTV in 60 bedrooms sB&B £30–£33 sB&B £49.50–£53 dB&B £52.50–£54 dB&B £68.75–£74

❀★★★★THE CAPITAL, LONDON SW3

Basil St, Knightsbridge ☎01-589 5171 Telex no 919042 Plan 2: **18** *D3*

To reverse the common description of restaurant with rooms, this hotel, in fashionable Knightsbridge, might fairly be called rooms with a restaurant! There is no conventional lounge but the lack is compensated for by the excellent bedrooms, some newly refurbished. They are very well furnished and decorated as well as being well equipped and provided with many thoughtful touches such as bath robes and fresh fruit. They have mini bars, but that is not to say that room service is neglected, on the contrary, it deserves special mention. The bar and restaurant have established themselves over the years and both are very successful; perhaps too much so because the bar is very busy during the early evening. Excellent food, provided by chef Brian Turner, is most enjoyable and thoroughly deserves our rosette. Dieter Schultz, the maitre d'hotel looks after the restaurant with unfailing charm, courtesy and industry. The good and reasonably priced wine list complements the food in a most worthwhile fashion. Mr David Levin is to be congratulated on creating this hotel where traditional standards of service by warm and friendly staff have earned the plaudits of our members.

60➡ CTV in all bedrooms
sB&B➡£77.36 dB&B➡£95.22
Continental breakfast

Lift ☾ # 12

French **V** Lunch £12.50&alc Dinner £19alc Wine £7.94 Last dinner 10.30pm

S% Credit cards 1 2 3 4 5

Lift ☾ CTV CFA *xmas*

International **V** Lunch £8–£9 Tea £2.95–£3.25&alc Dinner £9alc Wine £4.40 Last dinner 9.45pm

Credit cards 1 2 3 5

❀XXXXWaltons 121 Walton St ☎01-584 0204 Plan 2: **124** *C2*

Modern, comfortable elegant restaurant offering international cuisine.

International 65 seats Lunch £9.20&alc Dinner £16.10&alc Wine £6 Last dinner 11.30pm

S% Credit cards 1 2 3 4 5

XXXParkes 4 Beauchamp Pl ☎01-589 1390 Plan 2: **97** *C3*

Modern, intimate, basement restaurant offering an individual and imaginative five-course menu.

Closed Sun, 4 days Xmas & 4 days Etr Lunch not served Sat

60 seats Last dinner 11pm

Credit cards 1 2 3 4 5

XXBewick's 87–89 Walton St ☎01-584 6711 Plan 2: **14** *C2*

Closed Etr & 1 wk Xmas Lunch not served Sat & Sun

French 65 seats ✱Lunch £6.95–£8.50&alc Dinner £16alc Wine £6.50 Last dinner 11.30pm

Credit cards 1 2 3 4 5

❀❀XXTante Claire, London SW3

68 Royal Hospital Rd ☎01-352 6045 Plan 2: **118** *D1*

A long, narrow room nicely furnished with comfortable banquettes and attractively decorated with Klimt prints, this has become a restaurant of renown under its excellent chef/patron, Pierre Koffman. His cooking is unique in its daring even compared with the other great chefs in this country. Sometimes it is too daring: for those accustomed to the more subtle use of chocolate with game in Italy, Mr Koffman's use of it can be a bit overpowering! But that pales beside the skill he brings to the composition of the rest of his dishes: the touch of ginger with sweetbreads, fruit vinegars with certain dishes and his delicate spicing all demonstrate his gastronomic flair with dishes that are perfect in conception and execution.

At lunch, the set meal represents superb value for money while the à la carte menu features well loved dishes like andouillette de la mer au vinaigre au cassis, caneton rôtie au épices and the unusual pied de cochon farcie aux morilles. He understands fish and his changing daily offering according to the vagaries of the market never fail to please with their perfect cooking and delicate saucing. His puddings are excellent: charlotte au citron et son coulis de fraises and fondant au chocolat, sauce orange have been commended as have all his mouth watering sorbets and various ice preparations such as mousse or biscuit glacé. A fine selection of French cheeses in the peak of condition also deserves mention. It will not be difficult to choose an appropriate wine from the list of some 170 wines with vintages reaching back to 1948.

This is certainly a restaurant to be reckoned with. With the friendly service provided by a brigade of attentive staff, you are assured of a memorable meal.

Closed Sat, Sun, 10 days Etr, 3 wks Aug 10 days Xmas & New Year & Public Hols

French **V** 32 seats ✱Lunch £11.50&alc Dinner £20alc Wine £6.40 Last dinner 11pm

Credit cards 2 5

XXBrasserie St Quentin 243 Brompton Rd ☎01-589 8005 Plan 2: **16** *C3*

Stylish brasserie serving adventurous tempting food.

Closed 1 wk Xmas

French **V** 83 seats Lunch £8.50&alc Tea £2.50alc Dinner £14alc Wine £5.60 Last dinner mdnt

Credit cards 1 2 3 5 **VS**

XXChelsea Rendezvous 4 Sydney St ☎01-352 9519 Plan 2: **23** *C2*

Busy, basement restaurant with extensive menu.

Closed 24–26 Dec & Public hols

Chinese **V** 100 seats ✱Lunch £10alc Dinner £10alc Wine £5 Last dinner 11.30pm

S% Credit cards 1 2 3 4 5 **VS**

❀XXDaphne's 112 Draycott Av ☎01-589 4257 Plan 2: **34** *C2*

Warm cosy restaurant with fine French and English cooking.

Closed Sun Lunch not served

English & French 90 seats Dinner £15alc Wine £5.80 Last dinner mdnt

Credit cards 1 2 3 5

❀XXEnglish Garden 10 Lincoln St ☎01-584 7272 Plan 2: **42B** *D2*

Closed Xmas Day & Good Friday **V** 70 seats ✱Lunch £5&alc Dinner £8.50&alc Wine £6 Last dinner 11.30pm

S% Credit cards 1 2 3 5

❀**XX English House** 3 Milner St ☎01-584 3002 Plan 2: **43** *D2*
Intimate English restaurant with garden atmosphere serving well prepared traditional dishes.
Closed 24 Dec–26 Dec
V 35 seats ✱Lunch £6.50&alc Dinner £10.50&alc Wine £6 Last dinner 11.30pm Ᵽ
Credit cards [1] [2] [3] [5]

XX Le Français 259 Fulham Rd ☎01-352 4748 Plan 2: **45** *B1*
Small, intimate restaurant with simple décor, noted for its regional specialities.
Closed Sun
■French 65 seats Lunch £8.50–£14 Wine £7.90 Last dinner 10.45pm Ᵽ
Credit cards [2] [3]

XX Ménage à Trois 15 Beauchamp Pl ☎01-589 4252 Plan 2: **88A** *D3*
Closed 4 days Xmas & Aug Bank Hol
■International **V** 70 seats Lunch £12alc Dinner £12alc Wine £5.25 Last dinner 12.15am Ᵽ Live music lunch & dinner daily
Credit cards [1] [2] [3] [4] [5]

XX San Frediano 62 Fulham Rd ☎01-584 8375 Plan 2: **107** *C2*
Closed Sun
■Italian **V** 85 seats ✱Lunch £12alc Dinner £12alc Wine £4 Last dinner 11.15pm Ᵽ
S% Credit cards [1] [2] [3] [5]

XX Tandoori 153 Fulham Rd ☎01-589 7749 Plan 2: **116** *C2*
Good quality Tandori dishes and curries served in this intimate basement restaurant.
Closed Xmas Lunch not served Mon–Sat
■Indian 70 seats Lunch £7alc Dinner £8alc Last dinner 12.30am Ᵽ
S% Credit cards [1] [2] [3] [5]

X Al Ben Accolto 48 Fulham Rd ☎01-589 0876 Plan 2: **2** *C2*
Closed Sun
■Italian 45 seats Lunch £10alc Dinner £10alc Wine £4.10 Ᵽ
Credit cards [1] [2] [5]

❀**X Dans** 119 Sydney St ☎01-352 2718 Plan 2: **33A** *C1*
Small restaurant with light modern decor and plants. Delicious soufflé aux fruits frais.
Closed Sat & Sun
■French 50 seats Last dinner 11.30pm Ᵽ
Credit cards [2] [3]

X *Don Luigi's* 33c Kings Rd, Chelsea ☎01-730 3023 Plan 2: **36** *D2*
Comfortable Italian restaurant with authentic cuisine.
■Italian 60 seats Last dinner 11.30pm Ᵽ
Credit cards [1] [2] [3] [4] [5] **VS**

X Luba's Bistro 6 Yeoman's Row ☎01-589 2950 Plan 2: **81** *C3*
Candle-lit restaurant with very simple décor.
Closed Sun, 1 wk Xmas & 1 wk Etr
■Russian & Continental **V** Unlicensed No corkage charge 50 seats ✱Lunch £3–£8&alc Dinner £5–£10&alc Last dinner 11.45pm Ᵽ
Credit cards [1] [2] [3]

❀**X Ma Cuisine** 113 Walton St ☎01-584 7585 Plan 2: **82** *C2*
Closed Sat, Sun, 15 Jul–15 Aug & Public hols
■French **V** 32 seats Lunch £12alc Dinner £14alc Wine £6.75 Last dinner 11pm Ᵽ
Credit cards [2] [5]

X Poissonerie Restaurant 82 Sloane Ave ☎01-589 2457 Plan 2: **100** *C2*
Closed Sun, 23 Dec–3 Jan, Etr & Public hols
■French 80 seats Dinner £16alc Wine £6.50 Last dinner 11.30pm Ᵽ
S% Credit cards [1] [2] [3] [5]

X Le Suquet 104 Draycott Av ☎01-581 1785 Plan 2: **115** *C2*
Closed Mon, 2wks Xmas Lunch not served Tue
■French 48 seats Lunch £24alc Dinner £24alc Wine £6 Last dinner 11.30pm Ᵽ
S% Credit card [2]

SW5 Earl's Court

☆☆☆☆**London International** 147 Cromwell Rd, Kensington (Swallow) ☎01-370 4200 Telex no 27260 Plan 2: **78** *A2*
Large, friendly hotel with well-equipped bedrooms.
413➡⋒ (40fb) CTV in all bedrooms sB&B➡⋒ fr£34.50 dB&B➡⋒ fr£48.50 Continental breakfast ℞
Lift ☾ Ᵽ CFA
✿▭ Lunch £3.95&alc Tea 85p Dinner £5.25&alc Wine £5 Last dinner mdnt
Credit cards [1] [2] [3] [5] **VS**

★★★**Barkston** Barkston Gdns (Trusthouse Forte) ☎01-373 7851 Telex no 8953154 Plan 2: **11** *A2*
Quiet, friendly and comfortable family hotel.
74rm(69➡5⋒) (8fb) CTV in all bedrooms Ⓡ sB&B➡⋒ £39 dB&B➡⋒ £51 Continental breakfast ℞
Lift ☾ Ᵽ CFA
✿Last dinner 9.30pm
Credit cards [1] [2] [3] [4] [5]

★★★***Elizabetta*** Cromwell Rd ☎01-370 4282 Telex no 918978 Plan 2: **42** *A2*
Modern, quiet comfortable hotel with compact well-equipped bedrooms.
84➡⋒ CTV in all bedrooms ★
Lift ☾ ## CTV 20⌂
■International **V** ✿▭ Last dinner 10pm
Credit cards [1] [2] [3] [5]

☆☆☆***Hogarth*** Hogarth Rd (Inter-Hotel) ☎01-370 6831 Telex no 8951994 Plan 2: **58A** *A2*
Closed 24–28 Dec
Bedrooms are modern and well-appointed but lunch facilities are limited.
86rm(66➡20⋒) CTV in all bedrooms Ⓡ ★℞
Lift ☾ 26⌂
■Mainly grills ✿ Last dinner 8.30pm
Credit cards [1] [2] [5]

X L'Artiste Affamé 243 Old Brompton Rd ☎01-373 1659 Plan 2: **7** *A1*
French bistro-style restaurant.
Closed Sun & Public hols
■French 60 seats Lunch £9–£10&alc Dinner £9–£10&alc Wine £5.20 Last dinner 11.30pm Ᵽ
Credit cards [1] [2] [3] [5]

X Tiger Lee 251 Old Brompton Rd ☎01-370 2323 Plan 2: **121** *A1*
Small Chinese restaurant specialising in fish dishes.
Lunch not served
■Cantonese **V** 64 seats Dinner £16.50alc Wine £6.90 Last dinner 11pm Ᵽ⚡
S% Credit cards [2] [3] [5]

SW7 South Kensington

☆☆☆☆**Forum Hotel London** Cromwell Rd (Forum) ☎01-370 5757 Telex no 919663 Plan 2: **44A** *A2*
Very large, busy modern hotel with self service breakfast.
914➡ (99fb) CTV in all bedrooms Ⓡ ✱sB&B➡£38 dB&B➡£47 Continental breakfast ℞
Lift ☾ Live music and dancing 6 nights wkly ♿ *xmas*
✿▭✱Lunch fr£5.50 Tea fr£1.30 Dinner fr£5.50 Wine £5.30 Last dinner 1am
Credit cards [1] [2] [3] [4] [5] **VS**

★★★★**Gloucester** 4–18 Harrington Gdns (Rank) ☎01-373 6030 Telex no 917505 Plan 2: **52** *A2*
Modern, friendly hotel with choice of restaurant.
550➡⋒ (2fb) CTV in all bedrooms Ⓡ sB➡⋒ fr£59 dB➡⋒ fr£69 (room only) ℞
Lift ☾ ##⚡130⌂ CFA sauna bath *xmas*
■International **V** ✿▭✱Lunch £8.95–£10.45 Tea £1.75 High Tea £2.50alc Dinner £14alc
Credit cards [1] [2] [3] [4] [5]

☆☆☆**Embassy House** 31–33 Queen's Gate (Embassy) ☎01-584 7222 Telex no 8813387 Plan 2: **42A** *B3*

Hotel has modern well-appointed bedrooms and limited facilities for lunch.

70⇌(17fb) CTV in all bedrooms ®
✻sB&B⇌£36 dB&B⇌£47 ⛿

Lift ☾ ⚐

V ♔ ⊒ Lunch fr£7.50 Dinner fr£7.50 Wine £4.50 Last dinner 9.45pm

Credit cards 1 2 3 5

★★★ ***Onslow Court*** 109–113 Queen's Gate ☎01-589 6300 Telex no 262180 Plan 2: **96** *B2*

Comfortable hotel with good size bedrooms and efficient services, offering good value for money.

146rm(112⇌) CTV in all bedrooms ⛿

Lift ☾ ⚐

▣ Mainly grills ♔ ⊒ Last dinner 8.30pm

Credit cards 1 2 3 5

★★★ ***Rembrandt*** Thurloe Pl ☎01-589 8100 Telex no 295828 Plan 2: **102A** *C3*

Modern bedrooms are well equipped and restaurant is partially self service.

190rm(138⇌14⋒) CTV in 99 bedrooms TV in 91 bedrooms ✱ ⛿

Lift ☾ #

▣ International **V** ♔ ⊒ Last dinner 9.30pm

Credit cards 1 2 3 4 5

❀✕✕ **Shezan** 16–22 Cheval Pl ☎01-589 7918 Plan 2: **110** *C3*

Well-appointed Indian restaurant with a high standard of service and food.

Closed Sun & Public hols

▣ Indian & Pakistani 104 seats ✻Lunch £18alc Dinner £18alc Wine £6.80 Last dinner 11.30pm ⚐

S% Credit cards 1 2 3 4 5

✕ ***Chanterelle*** 119 Old Brompton Rd ☎01-373 5522 Plan 2: **22** *B2*

Small restaurant with pleasant décor, divided into bays by natural wood partitions.

Closed last 3wks Aug, Xmas

▣ English & French 47 seats Last dinner mdnt ⚐

Credit cards 1 2 3 5

✕ **Gondolière** 3 Gloucester Rd ☎01-584 8062 Plan 2: **54** *A3*

Highly coloured Trattoria with bright murals and paintings.

Closed Sun Lunch not served Sat

▣ Italian 36 seats Lunch £4.95&alc Dinner £8.30&alc Wine £4.85 Last dinner 11pm ⚐

Credit cards 1 3

✕ **Montpeliano** 13 Montpelier St ☎01-589 0032 Plan 2: **91A** *C3*

Popular, fashionable Italian restaurant featuring authentic cuisine and efficient, friendly service.

Closed Sun

▣ Italian 75 seats ✻Lunch £10alc Dinner £10alc Wine £4.50 Last dinner 11.30pm ⚐

SW8 Battersea
London plan **5** D3
(see also SW11)

❀✕✕ **Alonso's** 32 Queenstown Rd ☎01-720 5986

Lively restaurant serving imaginative, consistently sound French cuisine.

Closed Sun & Public hols Lunch not served Sat

▣ French 80 seats ✻Lunch £7.75 Dinner £11.75 Wine £4.25 Last dinner 11.30pm ⚐

Credit cards 2 3 5

❀❀✕✕ **Chez Nico London SW8** 129 Queenstown Rd ☎01-720 6960

Our members were delighted with our two rosette award, given for the first time last year to this restaurant, and we are pleased that Nico Ladenis, the chef/patron, has continued to warrant our faith in him. Not in the most salubrious part of London, his charming little restaurant is a Mecca for the discerning diner. One has to knock to gain admittance to the two cosy little rooms, prettily decorated – no doubt influenced by Mrs Ladenis, who will greet you and helpfully take your order. The atmosphere here has something of the traditionally French family restaurant.

Mr Ladenis is helped by his skilled sous-chef, Jean Villa. Their style is influenced by the modern school but without so many of the gimmicks associated with the less skilled of its practitioners which can mar the finished result. The fillet of superb beef with a fumet from cêpes is a good example where the flavour of the beef marries well with the gutsy sauce flavoured delicately with the fungi. Other dishes to please have been the delice de turbot en feuilleté à la crème de sauternes and the mousse de canard au jus de truffes et Porto among the starters; while among the main ones, fresh fish of the day is usually notable as are a supreme de canard grillé aux herbes, sauce vin rouge and a blanc de poulet à la vapeur farcies de petits legumes et de poivres verts, sauces a la crème de girolles. Puddings are equally delicious from the light parfait au kirsch, sauce framboise to the richly solid marquise au chocolat. A first and main course is priced together according to the main dish chosen and puddings etc. are priced separately. For this standard of cooking, the prices are not unreasonable.

Closed Sun, 4days Etr, last 2wks Jul & 1st wk Aug & 10days Xmas

Lunch not served Sat

▣ French 31 seats Lunch fr£10.50 Dinner £20alc Wine £8.50 Last dinner 10.45pm

Credit cards 1 3 **VS**

L

❀✕✕**L'Arlequin** 123 Queenstown Rd ☎01-622 0555

Modern restaurant offering excellent French cuisine and ambience. (See p 34.)

Closed Sat, Sun & Mon, 3wks Aug & Public Hols Lunch not served Sat

▣French 32 seats ✱Lunch £9.50–£10.50&alc Wine £6 Last dinner 10.45pm ⁋

S% Credit cards [1] [3]

SW10 West Brompton

London plan **5** C3

✕✕**Martin's** 88 Ifield Rd ☎01-352 5641 Plan 2: **87** *A1*

A fashionable and comfortable restaurant featuring a fixed price menu.

Closed Sun Lunch not served

▣French 36 seats ✱Dinner fr£13.50 Wine £7.50 Last dinner 11.30pm ⁋

S% Credit cards [1] [3]

✕✕**Nikita's** 65 Ifield Rd ☎01-352 6326 Plan 2: **94** *A1*

Dinner not served Sun

▣Russian 45 seats Dinner £10alc Wine £4.75 Last dinner 11.30pm ⁋⁄

S% Credit cards [1] [2] [5]

✕✕**Santa Croce** 112 Cheyne Walk ☎01-352 7534

Closed Sun & Public Hols

▣Italian **V** 120 seats Lunch £10–£12alc Dinner £10–£12alc Wine £4.15 Last dinner 11.15pm ⁋

S% Credit cards [1] [2] [3] [4] [5]

✕✕**September** 457 Fulham Rd ☎01-352 0206

Fashionable, popular, modern restaurant featuring enterprising and reliable cooking.

Lunch not served

▣English & French **V** 44 seats ✱Dinner £18alc Wine £5 Last dinner 11.30pm ⁋

✕**Bagatelle** 5 Langton St ☎01-351 4185

Closed Sun

▣French 55 seats ✱Lunch fr£9&alc Dinner £12.50alc Wine £4.80 Last dinner 11pm ⁋

Credit cards [1] [2] [3] [5]

✕**La Croisette** 168 Ifield Rd ☎01-373 3694 Plan 2: **32** *A1*

Popular small French restaurant specialising in shell fish. Good main basement ambience.

Closed Mon & 2wks Xmas Lunch not served Tue

▣French 42 seats Lunch £11 Dinner £11 Wine £6 Last dinner 11.30pm ⁋

S% Credit card [2]

✕***La Fringale*** 4 Hollywood Rd ☎01-351 1011 Plan 2: **46** *A1*

Closed Sun & Public hols Lunch not served

▣French & Italian **V** 50 seats Last dinner 11.45pm

Credit cards [1] [2] [3] [5]

✕**Golden Duck** 6 Hollywood Rd ☎01-352 3500 Plan 2: **53** *A1*

▣Pekinese & Szechwan **V** ✱Dinner £9–£12 Wine £4.95 Last dinner mdnt ⁋

S% Credit cards [1] [2] [3] [5]

✕**Hungry Horse** 196 Fulham Rd ☎01-352 7757 Plan 2: **61** *B1*

Closed Good Fri & Xmas Day Lunch not served Sat

54 seats Lunch £5.90–£7.35&alc Dinner £11alc Wine £4.20 Last dinner mdnt ⁋

Credit cards [1] [3] [5]

SW11 Battersea

London plan **5** D3

(see also SW8)

✕***Ormes*** 245 Lavender Hill ☎01-228 9824

Lunch not served Mon–Sat Dinner not served Sun

▣French 50 seats Last dinner 11.30pm ⁋

Credit cards [1] [2] [3]

✕**Pollyanna's** 2 Battersea Rise ☎01-228 0316

Fashionable bistro-style decor is complemented by skilful and reliable cooking.

Lunch not served Mon–Sat

▣English & French **V** 36 seats ✱Lunch fr£5.95 Dinner £13alc Wine £4.25 Last dinner mdnt ⁋

SW13 Barnes

London plan **5** C3

✕**Barnaby's** 39B High Street, Barnes ☎01-878 4750

Small high street restaurant offering French specialities.

Closed Sun, Etr, Xmas & Public hols Lunch not served Mon & Sat

▣French 25 seats Lunch £9.50alc Dinner £9.50alc Wine £4.95 Last dinner 10.15pm ⁋

S% Credit cards [1] [2] [3] [5] **VS**

SW14 East Sheen

London plan **5** C3

✕**Crowthers** 481 Upper Richmond Rd West, East Sheen ☎01-876 6372

Small family-run, tastefully decorated restaurant offering a fixed price menu.

Lunch not served Sat Dinner not served Sun

▣English & French 28 seats ✱Dinner £10.75 Wine £4.85 Last dinner 11pm

Credit cards [1] [2]

✕**Janine's** 505 Upper Richmond Rd West, East Sheen ☎01-876 5075

Small, intimate, candlelit Anglo-French restaurant.

Closed Mon Dinner not served Sun

▣English & French 30 seats ✱Lunch fr£5.95&alc Dinner fr£5.95&alc Wine £3.80 Last dinner 10.30pm ⁋

S% Credit cards [1] [3]

SW15 Putney

London plan **5** C3

✕**Cassis** 30 Putney High St ☎01-788 8668

Closed Sun Lunch not served Sat

▣French 50 seats Lunch £11–£15&alc Dinner £11–£15&alc Wine £4.50 Last dinner 10.50pm ⁋

✕**Wild Thyme** 96 Felsham Rd ☎01-789 3323

Closed Sun Lunch not served

▣International **V** 30 seats ✱Dinner £9alc Wine £4 Last dinner 11pm ⁋

Credit cards [1] [3] [5]

SW16 Norbury

London plan **5** D2

✕**Malean** 1585 London Rd, Norbury ☎01-764 2336

Small family-run Chinese restaurant.

Lunch not served Sun

▣Pekinese & Szechwan Unlicensed ✱Lunch fr£2.20&alc Dinner fr£4.50&alc Wine £4.20 Last dinner mdnt ⁋

Credit cards [2] [3]

SW19 Wimbledon

London plan **5** C2

✕**Les Amoureux** 156 Merton Hall Rd ☎01-543 0567

Closed Sun & Aug Lunch not served

▣French **V** 50 seats Dinner £8.55&alc Wine £4.50 Last dinner 10pm ⁋

S% Credit cards [1] [2]

W1 West End; *Piccadilly Circus, Soho, St Marylebone and Mayfair*

★★★★★**Churchill** Portman Sq ☎01-486 5800 Telex no 264831 Plan 2: **26** *D6*

This modern hotel has become well established on the London scene over the years. It has luxurious décor with a Regency flavour.

489⇌⋒ CTV in all bedrooms ✱sB&B⇌⋒ fr£98.33 dB&B⇌⋒ fr£114.65

Lift ☾ ⌗60 ⛍ CFA ⛟

▣French & International ✿ ☕ ✱Lunch £10alc Tea £4.50 High Tea fr£6alc Dinner £14&alc Wine £7.20 Last dinner 1am

Credit cards [1] [2] [3] [4] [5] **VS**

See advert on page 395

❀❀❀★★★★★**THE DORCHESTER**

See page 394

★★★★★

★★★★★CLARIDGE'S, LONDON W1

Brook St ☎01-629 8860 Telex no 21872 Plan 2: **27** *E6*

So long as the capable and kindly Mr Lund Hansen remains general manager of this historic hotel, we are sure that the traditional standards will be maintained to the great satisfaction of its distinguished clients. The interior lends itself to this atmosphere with its splendid, lofty public areas which are all sumptuously furnished and decorated. From the moment you walk into the marble hall you are aware of the discreet luxury. In the main sitting rooms – there is no bar – you are attended to by staff in knee breeches and live music is played at luncheon and during the evenings. The bedrooms and luxurious suites are appropriately furnished to equally high standards while new guests always express their pleasure at the spacious, old fashioned, yet efficient bathrooms.

The Causerie, with its Smörgasbord has always been a popular rendezvous for less formal eating, while the restaurant maintains its

classical menus. Mr Kruder is the maitre d'hotel and Chef Souprand is in charge of the kitchen; between them they look after you well and provide enjoyable food – not perhaps for the 'foodies' – but for those who appreciate exceptionally fine raw materials decently cooked.

205⇌⋒ CTV in all bedrooms ★ sB&B⇌⋒£80 dB&B⇌⋒£105 (room only) ⊟

Lift ☾ ⊁ ⇌

▣French **V** ✿ ✻Lunch £15alc Dinner £18alc Wine £7.10 Last dinner 11pm

Credit cards 1 3

✿✿★★★★★THE CONNAUGHT, LONDON W1

Carlos Pl ☎01-499 7070 Plan 2: **30** *E5*

Our members claim that this is probably the best luxury hotel in London; certainly it is the most friendly and enjoyable to stay at. Mr Zago inspires his staff, many with years of service in the hotel, but we are equally sure that the staff have their own pride in working at a hotel with such a reputation. From the moment you are welcomed by the linkmen and reception until your departure you will be delighted. You will also revel in the very English atmosphere here with its splendid staircase and handsome mahogany panelling in the bar and restaurant. There are two elegant and comfortable sitting rooms, one of which is a favourite for afternoon tea. Bedrooms vary in size but are appropriately furnished and decorated, with the usual amenities. Everything contributes to the feeling of the Mayfair house which this hotel once was.

The food is probably even better than in the distant past. It is served in the popular panelled restaurant under Mr Chevalier, and in the Grill Room, with its Georgian decor, under Mr

Bovo. The latter provides an à la carte menu while the former provides a table d'hote priced according to the main course chosen plus specialities and a further list of extra dishes. The kitchens are controlled by Chef Michel Bourdin and he succeeds admirably in providing something for everybody in traditional international hotel style as opposed to a pure restaurant. The dishes in heavy type on the menu are the ones to go for. All our members and our inspectors enjoy this hotel as much as any.

90⇌ CTV in all bedrooms ★

Lift ☾ ⊁ ⇌

▣English & French ⊒ Last dinner 10.30pm

S% Credit card 1

★★★★★*L* Grosvenor House Park Ln (Trusthouse Forte) ☎01-499 6363 Telex no 24871 Plan 2: **57** *E5*

This large, traditional hotel overlooking Hyde Park has excellent public areas and amenities which include a shopping arcade and swimming pool. The accommodation is of various styles and standards and there is limited car parking.

478⇌ CTV in all bedrooms sB&B⇌£95 dB&B⇌£112

Lift ☾ 20P 100⌂ CFA ⛆ (heated) sauna bath

✿ ⊒ Last dinner 10.30pm

Credit cards 1 2 3 4 5

★★★★★*L* Hilton International 22 Park Ln (Inter-Continental) ☎01-493 8000 Telex no 24873 Plan 2: **58** *E4*

Constantly alive and interesting, this thirty-storey hotel includes five restaurants, three bars and a disco as well as live music and dancing in the Roof Top Restaurant. The bedrooms are of various styles and standards.

503⇌⋒ (51fb) CTV in all bedrooms sB⇌⋒£84.70–£104.70 dB⇌⋒£107.40–£133.40

Lift ☾ ## 300⌂ CFA ⇌ Disco Mon–Sat Live music and dancing Mon–Sat

▣English, American, Chinese & International **V** ✿ ⊒ Lunch £12–£16.75&alc Tea £4.50&alc High Tea £7.50alc Dinner £17.50&alc Wine £6 ⱠLast dinner 12.30am

Credit cards 1 2 3 4 5

★★★★★*BL* Inn on the Park Hamilton Pl, Park Lane (Prestige) ☎01-499 0888 Telex no 22771 Plan 2: **64** *E4*

Possibly the best modern hotel in London, it has splendid suites, excellent bathrooms and two restaurants.

228⇌⋒ CTV in all bedrooms sB⇌⋒£104.15 dB⇌⋒£116.15 (room only) ⊟

Lift ☾ ## ⊬ 80⌂ CFA ⇌ *xmas*

▣International **V** ✿ ⊒ Lunch £12.85–£15.85&alc Tea fr£5.50 Dinner fr£20&alc Wine £8.50 Last dinner mdnt

Credit cards 1 2 3 4 5

★★★★★*Inter-Continental* 1 Hamilton Pl, Hyde Park Corner (Inter-Continental) ☎01-409 3131 Telex no 25853 Plan 2: **65** *E4*

This modern hotel overlooking Hyde Park Corner has large, well-appointed bedrooms, mostly small bathrooms and efficient service.

492⇌ CTV in all bedrooms ★

Lift ☾ ## ⊬ 100⌂ CFA ⇌ sauna bath Disco Mon–Sat Live music and dancing Sat, Live music Sun lunch

▣International ✿ ⊒ Last dinner 11.45pm

Credit cards 1 2 3 4 5

L

★★★★★**May Fair** Berkeley St (Inter-Continental) ☎01-629 7777 Telex no 262526 Plan 3: **20** *A4*

Long established hotel, with friendly service.

390 CTV in all bedrooms sB£75.90–£92 dB£95.45–£109.25 (room only)

Lift ☾ Live music and dancing 6 nights wkly

English, French & Polynesian V ∗Lunch £5.95–£12.50&alc Tea £3.25 Dinner £11.50–£22.50&alc Wine £7.95 Last dinner 11.30pm

Credit cards 1 2 3 4 5 VS

★★★★★ *L* **Ritz** Piccadilly ☎01-493 8181 Telex no 267200 Plan 3: **28** *A3*

Fine food, magnificent lounges, the ornate Louis XVI restaurant, and the many luxurious bedrooms all combine to make this an opulent, elegant and traditional hotel.

139 CTV in all bedrooms ∗sB£85.60 dB£112.55

Lift ☾ Live music and dancing Fri & Sat

International V ∗Lunch £16&alc Tea £6.50 Dinner £19.50&alc Wine £9.25 Last dinner 11pm

Credit cards 1 2 3 4 5

★★★★**Britannia** Grosvenor Sq (Inter-Continental) ☎01-629 9400 Telex no 23941 Plan 2: **15** *E5*

Smart, comfortable hotel with good, intimate restaurant and popular coffee shop.

440 (11fb) CTV in all bedrooms sB£63.25–£65.55 dB£74.75–£77.05 (room only)

Lift ☾ CFA Live music and dancing nightly *xmas*

English, French & Japanese V Lunch £10.50–£11.75&alc Tea £1.50alc High Tea £7alc Dinner £15alc Wine £5.50 Last dinner 12.30am

Credit cards 1 2 3 4 5

★★★★ *L* **Brown's** Dover St, Albemarle St (Trusthouse Forte) ☎01-493 6020 Telex no 28686 Plan 3: **6** *A4*

Gracious building, founded in the early 19th century by a butler of Lord Byron's family.

130 (26fb) CTV in all bedrooms sB&B£79.50 dB&B£107.50

Lift ☾ CFA *xmas*

Last dinner 9.30pm

Credit cards 1 2 3 4 5

★★★★**Cumberland** Marble Arch (Trusthouse Forte) ☎01-262 1234 Telex no 22215 Plan 2: **33** *D6*

A commercial and tourist hotel with limited room service, but good coffee shop facilities.

910 (29fb) CTV in all bedrooms sB&B£58 dB&B£79.50

Lift ☾ CFA

Last dinner 10.30pm

Credit cards 1 2 3 4 5

★★★★**London Marriot** *(formerly Europa Hotel)* Grosvenor Sq ☎01-493 1232 Telex no 268101 Plan 2: **44** *E6*

Modern tastefully furnished hotel with good restaurant.

276 (10fb) CTV in all bedrooms sB£63.25 dB£77.05 (room only)

Lift ☾ CFA Live music and dancing nightly *xmas*

English & French V Lunch £9.75&alc Tea £1.50alc High Tea £7alc Dinner £15alc Wine £5.50 Last dinner 12.30am

Credit cards 1 2 3 4 5

☆☆☆☆ *BL* **Holiday Inn** 134 George St (Commonwealth) ☎01-723 1277 Telex no 27983 Plan 2: **59** *C6*

Well appointed hotel with attractive garden style coffee shop.

241 (135fb) CTV in all bedrooms ∗sB£69 dB£87.40 (room only)

Lift ☾ # 50 CFA (heated) sauna bath *xmas*

French & Cosmopolitan ∗Lunch £3.50–£12&alc Tea £1.50 Dinner £9.50–£15&alc Wine £6.25 Last dinner mdnt

Credit cards 1 2 3 4 5

★★★★★THE DORCHESTER, LONDON W1

Park Ln ☎01-629 8888 Telex no 887704 Plan 2: **37** *E5*

(Rosette awarded only to Terrace Room.)

Chef Mosimann goes from strength to strength and our members have reported a further improvement in the Terrace Room, an opinion shared by our inspectors. We are delighted to award three rosettes here for the first time – this is now the only luxury hotel to be awarded them! There is an à la carte menu and a set four course dinner as well as the, now famous, 'Menu Surprise' of six courses. The cooking is in the light, modern style and is absolutely superb, rivalling that of the great chefs of France. Recommended dishes among the first courses have been feuilleté de ris de veau aux ecrivisses, consommé d'homard and crab tarlet flavoured with bacon and dill. Fish dishes are lightly cooked and beautifully sauced, turbot aux tomates à la moutarde de meaux being a good example while rosettes de boeuf aux echalottes, canard d'Aylesbury Nossi Be and medaillons d'agneau aux fleurs de thym have been pronounced excellent. Desserts show the same artistic skill, notably a feuilleté de poire Dorchester. There is also the Grill Room where sound English fare is provided.

Mr Udo Schlentrich, the general manager, after what must have been the traumatic experience of the alterations, has succeeded admirably in imbuing his staff with the right attitude and they seem in great heart, showing their pride in working in a hotel of international renown. Needless to say, the bedrooms,

The Dorchester

suites and public rooms all reflect the comfort and luxury that one expects. The Promenade is a popular rendezvous throughout the day as is the smart, luxurious bar where Mike McKenzie entertains at the piano; piano music in the afternoon and evening is also provided in The Promenade. An unusual and welcome addition is the library where guests can relax since, besides books there are games and a selection of music cassettes. The efficient room service deserves special mention. With all the improvements, coupled with the smiling, courteous service, the Dorchester has become a very special hotel reconciling the virtues of a traditional one with modern demands.

280 CTV in all bedrooms ∗sB£75–£85 dB£95–£105 (room only)

Lift ☾ 6P 50 CFA Live music and dancing 6 nights wkly

International ∗Lunch fr£14.20&alc Tea fr£5.20 Dinner fr£14.20&alc Wine £9.50 Last dinner 11.30pm

Credit cards 1 2 3 4 5

★★★★ **THE ATHENAEUM, LONDON W1**

Piccadilly (Rank) ☏01-499 3464 Telex no 261589 Plan 2: **8** *E4*

Mr Ron Jones, the general manager of this modern hotel, is dedicated to achieving the highest standards. The bedrooms are a reasonable size for a new hotel, comfortably furnished, adorned with attractive soft furnishing, and are well equipped. The public areas include a panelled club-like bar which has become a popular rendezvous, and the fresh, pale green lounge is a comfortable room in which to relax over a drink or afternoon tea. The restaurant is attractive and provides an à la carte menu, as well as a very good value set price luncheon which includes wine; theatre dinners are provided during the early evening. Good raw materials and sound cooking makes for enjoyable eating here. There are many 5 star features, including excellent room service. Cheerful and friendly service complete your enjoyment of your stay so it is no

wonder that our members express their enthusiasm for this hotel.

112 CTV in all bedrooms sB £93.25–£102.25 dB £119.50–£130.50 (room only)

Lift ☾ # CFA Live music 6 nights wkly *xmas*

International **V** *Lunch £13.50–£15.50&alc Tea £1–£3.75 Dinner £10.50–£15.50&alc Wine £7.50 Last dinner 10.30pm

S% Credit cards 1 2 3 4 5

★★★★ ***L Park Lane*** Piccadilly ☏01-499 6321 Telex no 21533 Plan 2: **99** *E4*

The Palm Court lounge is very well appointed offering the elegance and atmosphere of the twenties.

284 CTV in all bedrooms

Lift ☾ 180 CFA

International Last dinner 10.30pm

Credit cards 1 2 3 5

★★★★ **Piccadilly** Piccadilly (Forum) ☏01-734 8000 Telex no 25795 Plan 1: **37** *A2*

Hotel has limited facilities and services, and carvery restaurant.

290 (17fb) CTV in all bedrooms sB fr£53 dB fr£68 (room only)

Lift ☾ CFA

V Lunch £8.90 Tea £1.50 High Tea £3.50 Dinner £8.90 Wine £5.65 Last dinner 10pm

Credit cards 1 2 3 4 5 **VS**

★★★★ **Portman Inter-Continental** 22 Portman Sq (Inter-Continental) ☏01-486 5844 Telex no 261526 Plan 2: **101** *A6*

Well-appointed, modern hotel with efficient and friendly service.

276 CTV in all bedrooms *sB £83.95 dB £95.45 (room only)

Lift ☾ # 400 CFA →

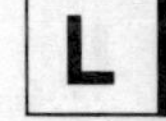

French V ✿ ☐ *Lunch £5.85–£9.95&alc Dinner fr£6.50&alc Wine £7.90 Last dinner 11pm

Credit cards 1 2 3 4 5

☆☆☆☆**Regent Crest** Carburton St (Crest) ☎01-388 2300 Telex no 22453 Plan 3: **27** *A6*

Purpose-built hotel with modern, well-equipped bedrooms.

322 CTV in all bedrooms Ⓡ *sB fr£40 (room only) dB fr£49 (room only)

Lift ☾ CFA

International V ✿ ☐ *Lunch £7alc Tea fr65p Dinner £12.50alc Wine £6.35 Last dinner 10.30pm

Credit cards 1 2 3 4 5 **VS**

★★★★**St George's** Langham Pl (Trusthouse Forte) ☎01-580 0111 Telex no 27274 Plan 3: **33** *A5*

Modern hotel whose top floor restaurant gives panoramic views across London.

85 CTV in all bedrooms Ⓡ sB&B £60 dB&B £82 B

Lift ☾ ## 2P

✿ ☐ Last dinner 10pm

Credit cards 1 2 3 4 5

★★★★**Selfridge Thistle** Orchard St (Thistle) ☎01-408 2080 Telex no 22361 Plan 2: **108** *E6*

A modern hotel with small bedrooms and bathrooms, but comfortable and attractive public lounge and restaurant.

298 CTV in all bedrooms *sB £68–£72 (room only) dB £74–£80 (room only) B

Lift ☾ ## 7 CFA

European ✿ ☐ *Lunch £9.50–£12.50&alc High Tea £4.75–£6 Dinner £9.80–£12.75&alc Last dinner 10pm

Credit cards 1 2 3 4 5 **VS**

★★★★**Westbury** New Bond St (Trusthouse Forte) ☎01-629 7755 Telex no 24378 Plan 3: **41** *A4*

Comfortable, commercial and tourist hotel with attractive wood-panelled lounges.

256 CTV in all bedrooms sB&B £78 dB&B £97.50 B

Lift ☾ CFA

✿ ☐ Last dinner 10.30pm

Credit cards 1 2 3 4 5

★★★ *B* **Berners** Berners St ☎01-636 1629 Telex no 25759 Plan 1: **5A** *A5*

Modern, very elegant hotel.

236 CTV in all bedrooms sB £49.50–£54.50 dB £63.80–£70.20 (room only) B

Lift ☾ CFA ♿

✿ ☐ Lunch £8.75&alc Dinner £8.75&alc Wine £5.50 Last dinner 10pm

Credit cards 1 2 3 5

★★★ *HB* **Chesterfield** 35 Charles St (Forum) ☎01-491 2622 Telex no 269394 Plan 2: **24** *E5*

Closed Xmas

Traditional and tastefully appointed hotel retaining a warm and friendly atmosphere.

85 CTV in all bedrooms *sB £53 dB £73 (room only) B

Lift ☾

French ✿ ☐ Lunch £9.75&alc Dinner £9.75&alc Wine £6.50 Last dinner 10.30pm

Credit cards 1 2 3 4 5

★★★**Clifton-Ford** Welbeck St (Forum) ☎01-486 6600 Telex no 22569 Plan 2: **28** *E6*

A commercial and tourist hotel providing reasonable comfort.

227 CTV in all bedrooms sB&B £47 dB&B £59 Continental breakfast B

Lift ☾ CTV 20 CFA *xmas*

International V ✿ ☐ Lunch £12alc Tea £1.35 Dinner £9.50&alc Wine £5.75 Last dinner 10.15pm

Credit cards 1 2 3 4 5 **VS**

★★★**Mount Royal** Bryanston St, Marble Arch (Forum) ☎01-629 8040 Telex no 23355 Plan 2: **92** *D6*

Commercial hotel with good coffee shop facilities.

700 (30fb) CTV in all bedrooms Ⓡ sB&B £41 dB&B £50.50 Continental breakfast B

Lift ☾ CFA Cabaret Sun (summer)

English, Asian & French ✿ ☐ Lunch £5.75&alc Dinner £5.75&alc Wine £5.75 Last dinner 10.30pm

Credit cards 1 2 3 4 5 **VS**

☆☆☆**Rathbone** Rathbone St (Comfort) ☎01-636 2001 Telex no 28728 Plan 1: **41** *B5*

Modern hotel whose restaurant décor depicts the 1926 general strike.

64rm (56 8) CTV in all bedrooms Ⓡ *sB&B fr£30 dB&B fr£40.50 Continental breakfast

Lift ☾

Mainly grills *Lunch fr£5.75&alc Dinner fr£5.75&alc Wine £3.95 Last dinner 10pm

Credit cards 1 2 3 4 5 **VS**

★★★ ***Stratford Court*** 350 Oxford St ☎01-629 7474 Telex no 22270 Plan 2: **114** *E6*

Small, friendly, central hotel.

139 CTV in all bedrooms B

Lift ☾

Mainly grills ✿ ☐ Last dinner 10.30pm

Credit cards 1 2 3 4 5

★★★ ***Washington*** Curzon St ☎01-499 7030 Telex no 24540 Plan 3: **40** *A3*

A commercial and tourist hotel with a military theme evident in the décor and furnishings in the restaurant and bar.

160 CTV in all bedrooms B

Lift ☾ CFA

✿ ☐ Last dinner 9.30pm

Credit cards 1 2 3 4 5 **VS**

★★ *H* **Bryanston Court** 56 Great Cumberland Pl ☎01-262 3141 Telex no 262076 Plan 2: **17** *D6*

Comfortable, hospitable hotel with many tasteful features.

56rm(6➡50⚐) CTV in all bedrooms ★ sB&B➡⚐ £30 dB&B➡⚐ £40 Continental breakfast ⊟
Lift ☾ 🚗

⊟English & French ☕ 🍽 Lunch £6–£8 Dinner £8–£10 Wine £5

Credit cards 1 2 3 4 5

★★ *Green Park* Half Moon St ☎01-629 7522 Telex no 28856 Plan 3: **11A** *A3*

Modest hotel with well appointed lounge and bar.

175rm(89➡) TV available in bedrooms ★ ⊟
Lift ☾ CTV sauna bath
☕ 🍽 Last dinner 9.30pm
Credit cards 1 2 3 4 5

★★ Regent Palace Glasshouse St, Piccadilly (Trusthouse Forte) ☎01-734 7000 Telex no 23740 Plan 1: **42** *B3*

Well-situated hotel with good accommodation and friendly service.

1002rm (51fb) CTV in all bedrooms Ⓡ ★ sB&B £25.50 dB&B £42.50 ⊟
Lift ☾ CTV 🚫 CFA *xmas*
☕ 🍽 Last dinner 9pm
Credit cards 1 2 3 4 5

★★ *Royal Angus* 39 Coventry St ☎01-930 4033 Telex no 24616 Plan 1: **43** *B3*

Corner site hotel with well-equipped comfortable bedrooms.

92rm(90➡2⚐) CTV in all bedrooms ★ ⊟
Lift ☾ 🚫
⊟Mainly grills ☕ 🍽 Last dinner 9.45pm
Credit cards 1 2 3 4 5

XXXXX *Café Royal (Grill Room)* 68 Regent St ☎01-437 9090 Plan 1: **7** *B3*
Lunch not served alternate Sat
⊟French 56 seats Wine £7.50 🚫

XXXXX 'Ninety Park Lane' 90 Park Lane ☎01-499 6363 ext 4206 Plan 2: **57** *E5*

Luxurious and elegant surroundings, combine here with professional service.

Closed Sun Lunch not served Sat →

❀❀❀ XXXX Le Gavroche 43 Upper Brook St ☎01-730 2820 Plan 2: **49A** *E5*
Closed 23 Dec–2 Jan

It is an odd facet of human nature that when someone reaches a certain eminence in their chosen field, there always seems to be a section of the populace which delights in denigrating them. Of course, no restaurant is perfect, and it is easy to pick holes if one is determined to do so. Yet Albert Roux has set standards in Britain that have not been equalled. Our reports do not lead us to believe that there has been any falling off in their high standards; indeed, our members and inspectors continue to be delighted. As one of our inspectors said, 'Having completed my inspection of multiple rosetted establishments, I have no doubt that Le Gavroche stands out amongst them'.

Albert Roux dedicates himself to producing food that is innovative and which stands comparison with that from the great chefs in France. Influenced by, but not an imitative slave to, the modern school his cooking is an example of true gastronomic art, producing rich but beautifully balanced dishes that defy description. The various mousses are light and flavoursome, composite dishes well arranged sauces enhance their dishes and the puddings are all delectable; nor must one forget the effort put into the selection of French cheeses all served here in prime condition. To match the food there is a long and extensive wine list with old vintages reaching back to 1918.

Your order will be helpfully taken either in the bar or downstairs at your table, perhaps while you enjoy an aperitif; some of the dishes which are artistically presented will be displayed to help you choose. Then, at your table, in the well decorated and comfortable room with immaculate table appointments you are set for a memorable meal. There is a five course Menu Exceptionelle (for a minimum of two people), the à la carte and, at luncheon, a good value set meal of three courses. Highly praised dishes have included soupe aux moules, terrine de sole au beurre de champagne and cervelas de saumon Curnonski among the first courses, while among the fish and main courses were escalope de saumon à l'oseille (said to be as good as that of the frères Troisgros), carré d'agneau en crepinette au Porto and all their game dishes. Perfect sorbets are mouthwatering and puddings such as the sable aux fraises and marquise au chocolat were described as perfect. Good coffee with excellent petits fours are usually served in the anteroom and make a fitting conclusion to your meal. Only supreme artistry can produce dishes of such flavour and delicacy. As you would expect, the service is up to the same high standard and you will be attended to by an immaculately clad French brigade who are knowledgeable and attentive to a fault. Such an experience is not cheap, but for those who appreciate the finest of food it is very worthwhile. This is among the three best restaurants in Britain, and can do nothing but good for the reputation of British catering. Its example has inspired many others to excellent effect.

⊟French 70 seats Lunch £22&alc Dinner £38alc Wine £11 Last dinner 11pm 🚫
S% Credit cards 1 2 3 4 5

L

French 75 seats *Lunch £13.50–£16&alc Dinner £22.50alc Wine £8.50 Last dinner 11.30pm bedrooms available Live music nightly
Credit cards 1 2 3 4 5

XXXX Hilton Hotel (Trader Vic's) Park Ln ☎01-493 7586 Plan 2: **58** *E4*
Lively Polynesian restaurant below Hilton Hotel.
Lunch not served Sat
International 150 seats *Lunch fr£9.50&alc Dinner £12.50–£15.50&alc Wine £6.50 Last dinner 11.30pm
Credit cards 1 2 3 4 5

XXXX *Tiberio* 22 Queen St ☎01-629 3561 Plan 2: **120** *E5*
Elegant, modern Italian restaurant in a white, vaulted cellar. There is an impressive entrance with tropical plants and fountains.
Closed Sun Lunch not served Sat
Italian 90 seats Last dinner 1am Live music and dancing Mon–Sat
Credit cards 1 2 3 4 5

XXX Braganza 56–57 Frith St ☎01-437 5412 Plan 1: **5** *B4*
Spacious, panelled restaurant specialising in fish dishes.
Closed Sun & Public hols
French 145 seats *Lunch £14alc Dinner £14alc Wine £4.95 Last dinner 11.15pm
S% Credit cards 1 2 3 4 5

XXX Chesa (Swiss Centre) 10 Wardour St ☎01-734 1291 Plan 1: **11** *C3*
Closed Xmas Day
Swiss 60 seats *Lunch £9.50–£10.50&alc Dinner £9.50–£10.50&alc Wine £7.20 Last dinner mdnt
S% Credit cards 1 2 3 4 5

XXX Greenhouse 27A Hays Mews ☎01-499 3331 Plan 2: **55A** *E5*
Closed Sun & Xmas–New Year
Lunch not served Sat
English & French 80 seats Lunch £11.50alc Dinner £11.50alc Wine £5.05 Last dinner 11pm
Credit cards 1 2 3 4 5

XXX Masako 6–8 St Christopher Pl ☎01-935 1579 Plan 2: **88** *E6*
Authentic Japanese décor with armour, bamboo walls and waitresses in national costume.
Closed Sun & Public Hols
Japanese 100 seats *Lunch £6.90–£8.20 Dinner £15.10–£19.60 Wine £4.80 Last dinner 10pm Live music Fri & Sat
Credit cards 1 2 3 5

XXX *Snooty Fox* 52 Hertford St ☎01-499 1150 Plan 2: **112** *E5*
Elegant Mayfair restaurant with modern paintings on green baize walls.
Closed Sun Lunch not served Sat

French 50 seats Last dinner mdnt
Credit cards 1 2 3 5

XXX Tandoori of Mayfair 37a Curzon St ☎01-629 0600 Plan 2: **117** *E5*
Skillful Tandoori cooking and well cooked curries are found in this attractively decorated basement restaurant.
Closed Xmas
Indian **V** 140 seats Lunch £8.50alc Dinner £10alc Wine £4.80 Last dinner mdnt
Credit cards 1 2 3 4 5

XXX Terrazza 19 Romilly St ☎01-437 8991 Plan 1: **53** *B4*
Soho restaurant on two floors, with cool, modern décor, tiled floor and murals.
Closed Xmas Day
Italian **V** 149 seats *Lunch £6.10–£9.60&alc Dinner £6–£12alc Wine £4.50 Last dinner 11.30pm
S% Credit cards 1 2 3 4 5 **VS**

XXX *Verrey's* 233 Regent St ☎01-734 4495 Plan 3: **39A** *A5*
A basement restaurant in three parts whose walls are made up of elegant light and dark wood panels.
Closed sun Lunch not served Sat
English & French 140 seats Last dinner 11.30pm Live music Tue–Sat
Credit cards 1 2 3 5 **VS**

XXX White Tower 1 Percy St ☎01-636 8141 Plan 1: **59** *B5*
Busy Greek restaurant with many faithful regulars.
Closed Sat & Sun, 1wk Xmas, 3wks Aug
Greek 80 seats *Lunch £15alc Dinner £15alc Wine £5 Last dinner 10.30pm
Credit cards 1 2 3 4 5 **VS**

XX Au Jardin des Gourmets 5 Greek St ☎01-437 1816 Plan 1: **2** *B4*
Well established restaurant with good food and a very good wine list.
Closed Sun Lunch not served Sat
French **V** 90 seats Lunch £9.50–£10.50&alc Dinner £9.50–£10.50&alc Wine £4.50 Last dinner 11pm
S% Credit cards 1 2 3 4 5 **VS**

XX La Cucaracha 12 Greek St ☎01-734 2253 Plan 1: **14** *C4*
A maze of small white-arched rooms that were once the cellars of an 18th-century monastery.
Closed Sun & Public hols Lunch not served Sat
Mexican **V** 85 seats Lunch £10–£12alc Dinner £10–£12alc Wine £6.20 Last dinner 11.30pm Live music nightly
S% Credit cards 1 2 3 4 5

XX *Gallery Rendezvous* 53 Beak St ☎01-734 0445 Plan 1: **17** *A3*
Chinese paintings are permanently exhibited in the restaurant.
Closed Public hols
Pekinese 150 seats Last dinner 11pm P
Credit cards 1 2 3 5

XX Gay Hussar 2 Greek St ☎01-437 0973 Plan 1: **18** *B4*
Small, comfortable restaurant with authentic Hungarian cooking.
Closed Sun & Public hols
Hungarian 35 seats Lunch £9–£10&alc Dinner £16alc Wine £5 Last dinner 11pm

XX *Gaylord, 16 Albermarle St* ☎01-629 9802 Plan 3: **9** *A4*
Indian 120 seats Last dinner 11.30pm
Credit cards 1 2 3 5 **VS**

XX Gaylord, Mortimer St ☎01-636 0808 Plan 3: **10** *A5*
Well established restaurant with modern decor, serving well cooked curries and Tandoori specialities.
Indian **V** 96 seats Lunch £6.55alc Dinner £6.55alc Wine £5.35 Last dinner 11.30pm
Credit cards 1 2 3 5 **VS**

XX *Geetanjli of Mayfair* 23 Brook St ☎01-493 1779 Plan 3: **11** *A4*
Closed 24 & 25 Dec
Northern Indian 120 seats Last dinner 11.10pm
Credit cards 1 2 3 4 5

XX Içi Paris 2A Duke St ☎01-935 1864 Plan 2: **63** *E6*
An elegant basement restaurant with Louis XV furnishings.
Closed Sun, last wk Jul & 1st 2wks Aug
Lunch not served Sat
French 32 seats Lunch £15alc Dinner £15alc Wine £6 Last dinner 10.30pm Live music nightly
S% Credit cards 1 2 3 5

XX Lal Qila Tottenham Court Rd ☎01-387 4570 Plan 3: **17** *A6*
Good, modern Indian restaurant.
Closed Xmas Day & Boxing Day
Indian 70 seats *Lunch £30 Dinner £30 Wine £4 Last dinner 11.30pm
Credit cards 1 2 3 5

XX Langan's Brasserie Stratton St ☎01-493 6437 Plan 3: **18** *A3*
Closed Sun & Public hols
Lunch not served Sat
French 200 seats Lunch £13alc Dinner £13alc Wine £4.95 Last dinner 11.45pm Live music nightly
S% Credit cards 1 2 3 5

XX *La Loggia* 39 Upper Berkeley St ☎01-723 0554 Plan 2: **74** *D6*

L

An elegant restaurant with northern Italian décor.
Closed Sun
70 seats Live music nightly
Credit cards 1 2 3 4 5

XXMikado 110 George St
☎01-935 8320 Plan 2: **89** *D6*
Closed Sun, 10 days Aug/Sep & Public hols Lunch not served Sat
Japanese 70 seats ✻Lunch £5.50–£9.50&alc Dinner £15–£20&alc Wine £5 Last dinner 10.15pm
Credit cards 2 3 5

XX*Mr Kai of Mayfair* 65 South Audley St
☎01-493 8988 Plan 2: **91** *E5*
Closed Public hols
Pekinese & Chinese 104 seats Last dinner 11.15pm
Credit cards 1 2 3 4 5

❀**XX*Odin's*** 27 Devonshire St
☎01-935 7296
First-class food and interesting surroundings are features of this restaurant.
Closed Sun & Public hols Lunch not served Sat
English & French 60 seats Last dinner 11.15pm
Credit cards 1 2 3 4 5

XXVendôme 20 Dover St ☎01-629 5417 Plan 3: **39** *A4*
Three-storey Victorian style seafood restaurant.
Closed Sat & Public hols
French 81 seats ✻Lunch £14alc Dinner £14alc Wine £4.95 Last dinner 10.45pm
S% Credit cards 1 2 3 4 5

XXWheeler's 19 Old Compton St
☎01-437 2706 Plan 1: **58** *C4*
Long established fish restaurant with intimate rooms.
Closed Sun & Public hols
French 123 seats ✻Lunch £14alc Dinner £14alc Wine £4.95 Last dinner 11pm
S% Credit cards 1 2 3 4 5

London W1

XArirang 31–32 Poland St
☎01-437 6633 Plan 1: **1** *A4*
Closed Sun, Xmas Day & New Years Day
Korean **V** 80 seats Lunch £10alc Dinner £12alc Last dinner 11pm
S% Credit cards 1 2 3 4 5

XAunties 126 Cleveland St
☎01-387 3226 Plan 3: **2** *A6*
English restaurant specialising in home-made pies.
Closed Sat, Sun, 1wk Xmas–New Year, & Public Hols
V 30 seats ✻Lunch £8.50–£10.50 Dinner £8.50–£10.50 Wine £4.50 Last dinner 10pm
S% Credit cards 1 2 3 5

XChez Zorba 11 Charlotte St
☎01-631 0895 Plan 1: **12A** *B5*
Greek & French **V** 120 seats Lunch £5alc Dinner £5alc Wine £3.95 Last dinner 3am
S% Credit cards 1 2 3 5

❀**XChuen Cheng Ku** 17–23 Wardour St
☎01-734 3281 Plan 1: **13** *B3*
Large, busy restaurant with excellent variety of unusual dishes.
Chinese **V** 400 seats ✻Lunch £3.75alc Dinner £4.80 Wine £4.50 Last dinner 11.45pm
Credit cards 1 2 3 5

XD'Artagnan 19 Blandford St ☎01-935 1023
Small, intimate, friendly French restaurant.
Closed Sun Lunch not served Sat
French 31 seats ✻Lunch fr£10.50&alc Dinner fr£10.50&alc Wine £5.90 Last dinner 10.30pm
S% Credit cards 1 2 3 5

XDragon Gate 7 Gerrard St ☎01-734 5154 Plan 1: **14A** *C3*
First Szechwan restaurant in London serving specialities from south west China.
Closed 25 & 26 Dec
Szechwan 55 seats ✻Lunch £7.50alc Dinner £7.50alc Wine £4.75 Last dinner 11.30pm
S%

XKerzenstuberl 9 St Christopher's Pl
☎01-486 3196 Plan 2: **68** *E6*
Popular Austrian restaurant with live music and staff in traditional dress.
Closed Sun, 7 Aug–7 Sep & Public hols Lunch not served Sat
Austrian **V** 50 seats ✻Lunch £10.50alc Dinner £12.50alc Wine £5.95 Last dinner 11pm Live music and dancing Mon–Sat
Credit cards 1 2 3 5 **VS**

XLee Ho Fook 15 Gerrard St
☎01-734 9578 Plan 1: **29** *B3*
Authentic chinatown atmosphere in this intimate restaurant.
Cantonese **V** 120 seats Lunch fr£3.50alc Dinner fr£6.50alc
S% Credit cards 1 2 3 5 **VS**
See advert on page 400

XLittle Akropolis 10 Charlotte St
☎01-636 8198 Plan 1: **30** *B5*
Small, intimate, candlelit, Greek restaurant.
Closed Sun & 3wks Jul Lunch not served Sat
30 seats Lunch £8.50alc Dinner £8.50alc Wine £5.50 Last dinner 10.30pm
Credit cards 1 2 3 5

XMayflower 66–70 Shaftesbury Ave
☎01-734 9207 Plan 1: **32** *B3*
Small ground floor and basement restaurant with small alcoves and good food.
Closed Xmas Day
Chinese **V** 100 seats ✻Lunch £6.50–£7.50&alc Dinner £6.50–£7.50&alc Wine £6 Last dinner 3am
S% Credit cards 1 2 3 5

X*Orient* 43 Grafton Way ☎01-387 6363 Plan 3: **23** *A6*
A basement Indian restaurant featuring a belly dancer as cabaret. →

L

Indian V 84 seats Last dinner 11pm
Cabaret 5 nights wkly
Credit cards 1 2 3 5

X **Pavillion** 165 Oxford St ☎01-437 8774 Plan 1: **36** *A4*
Small 1st-floor Italian restaurant with a friendly atmosphere.
Closed Sun & Public hols Lunch not served Sat
Italian V 40 seats Last dinner 11pm
Live music nightly
Credit cards 1 2 3 5

X **Raj of India** 60–62 Old Compton St ☎01-734 4379 Plan 1: **39A** *B4*
Modern Indian restaurant in heart of Soho. Window between restaurant and kitchen shows chefs at work.
Indian 50 seats *Lunch £5.95–£8.55&alc Dinner £5.95–£8.55&alc Wine £4.75 Last dinner mdnt
S% Credit cards 1 2 3 5

X **Saga** 43 South Molton St ☎01-408 2236 Plan 2: **106** *E6*
Closed Sun & Public hols
Japanese 77 seats Last dinner 10.30pm
Credit cards 1 2 3 4 5

X **Soho Rendezvous** 21 Romilly St ☎01-437 1486 Plan 1: **49** *B4*
Comfortable, friendly restaurant offering well-prepared Peking cuisine with most attentive service.
Closed Sun & Public hols
Pekinese 100 seats Last dinner 11pm
Credit cards 1 2 3 5

W2 Bayswater, Paddington

☆☆☆☆ **London Embassy** 150 Bayswater Rd (Embassy) ☎01-229 1212 Telex no 27727 Plan 2: **76** *A5*
A busy, commercial and tourist hotel with helpful staff, providing some lounge and room service.
193 (5fb) CTV in all bedrooms sB&B £46 dB&B £56 Continental breakfast B
Lift ☾ 10P 36 CFA *xmas*
V *Lunch fr£7 Dinner fr£8.15&alc Wine £4.70 Last dinner 10.15pm
Credit cards 1 2 3 4 5

★★★★ *L* **Royal Lancaster** Lancaster Ter (Rank) ☎01-262 6737 Plan 2: **105** *B5*
435 (10fb) CTV in all bedrooms
*sB £55–£60 dB £67.50–£72.50 (room only) B
Lift ☾ 100P CFA
English, French & Italian *Lunch £8–£10.50&alc Tea £2.75alc Dinner £8–£13.95&alc Wine £5.60 Last dinner 10.45pm
Credit cards 1 2 3 4 5

☆☆☆ **Central Park** Queensborough Ter ☎01-229 2424 Telex no 27342 Plan 2: **21** *A5*
Busy modern commercial hotel.
291rm(127 164) (10fb) CTV in all bedrooms sB&B £26–£29 dB&B £38–£42 Continental breakfast B
Lift ☾ 20 sauna bath
Mainly grills V Lunch £6.50alc Tea £1.50alc Dinner £7.50alc Wine £5 Last dinner 10pm
Credit cards 1 2 3 5 **VS**

★★★ **Coburg** 129 Bayswater Rd (Best Western) ☎01-229 3654 Telex no 268235 Plan 2: **29** *A5*
RS Xmas & New Year
125rm(70 10) CTV in 70 bedrooms TV in 55 bedrooms ® sB&B £19.50 sB&B £33 dB&B £32 dB&B £48 B
Lift ☾ CFA
V Lunch £6.50 Tea fr75p High Tea fr£4.50 Dinner £7.50 Wine £4.50 Last dinner 9.30pm
Credit cards 1 2 3 4 5

☆☆☆**Hospitality Inn** 104/105 Bayswater Rd (Mount Charlotte) ☎01-262 4461 Telex no 22667 Plan 2: **102** *A5*

Modern hotel with buffet style breakfast and lunch.

175⇌ (13fb) CTV in all bedrooms ® sB⇌£31.50 dB⇌£41.50 (room only) B

Lift ☾ 80P CFA

International V Lunch £5.95–£6.25&alc Dinner £8.50alc Wine £5 Last dinner 10.15pm

Credit cards 1 2 3 5 **VS**

★★★**Park Court** 75 Lancaster Gate (Mount Charlotte) ☎01-402 4272 Telex no 23922 Plan 2: **98** *A5*

Hotel with informal restaurant and well-equipped bedrooms.

442⇌ (9fb) CTV in all bedrooms ® sB⇌£31.50–£32.50 dB⇌£41.50–£42.50 (room only) B

Lift ☾ CFA *xmas*

European V Lunch fr£5&alc Dinner fr£5&alc Wine £5 Last dinner 11pm

Credit cards 1 2 3 5

★★★**White's** Lancaster Gate (Mount Charlotte) ☎01-262 2711 Telex no 23922 Plan 2: **125** *B5*

Small friendly hotel overlooking Hyde Park.

61⇌ (2fb) CTV in all bedrooms ® sB⇌£37 dB⇌£47 (room only) B

Lift ☾ 40P Live music and dancing 6 nights wkly

European V Lunch £7.50–£7.75&alc Dinner £9.50–£9.75&alc Wine £5 Last dinner 10.15pm

Credit cards 1 2 3 5

✕✕**Bali** 101 Edgware Rd ☎01-723 3303 Plan 2: **10** *C6*

Indonesian & Malaysian 80 seats Lunch £4–£5alc Dinner £9&alc Wine £4.75 Last dinner 11pm

Credit cards 1 2 3 4 5

✕✕***Trat-West*** 143 Edgware Rd ☎01-723 8203 Plan 2: **122** *C6*

Italian 70 seats Last dinner 11.30pm

Credit cards 1 2 3 4 5

✕**Chez Franco** 3 Hereford Rd ☎01-229 5079

Small, pleasant, ground-floor restaurant with photographs of famous actors and actresses on the walls.

Closed Sun, 1st 3wks Aug & Public hols Lunch not served Sat

French & Italian 45 seats Lunch £3.50–£6&alc Dinner £3.90–£6&alc Wine £3.90 Last dinner 11pm

Credit card 2 **VS**

✕***Ganges*** 101 Praed St ☎01-262 3835 Plan 2: **48** *B6*

Closed Sun & 2wks Xmas

Indian V 28 seats Last dinner 11pm

Credit cards 1 2 3 5

✕**Kalamaras** 76–78 Inverness Mews ☎01-727 9122 Plan 2: **66** *A5*

Closed Sun & Public hols

Greek V 86 seats Dinner £10alc Wine £5.05 Last dinner mdnt Live music nightly

Credit cards 1 2 3 5

✕**Le Mange Tout** 34 Sussex Pl ☎01-723 1199 Plan 2: **85** *C6*

Cosy little restaurant serving reasonably priced French cuisine.

Closed Public Hols Lunch not served Sat & Sun

French V 35 seats ✱Lunch fr£8.95&alc Dinner fr£9.50&alc Wine £4.95 Last dinner 10.30pm

S% Credit cards 1 2 3 4 5

✕***Romantica Taverna*** 12 Moscow Rd ☎01-727 7112 Plan 2: **102B** *A5*

Closed 23 Dec–1 Jan

French & Greek 80 seats Last dinner 1am

Credit cards 1 2 3 4 5

W5 Ealing

London plan **5** B4

See also W13 Ealing (Northfields)

☆☆☆**Carnarvon** Ealing Common ☎01-992 5399 Telex no 935114

Modern purpose-built hotel, sited on the North Circular.

145⇌⋒ CTV in all bedrooms ® sB&B⇌⋒ fr£39.50 dB&B⇌⋒ fr£49.50 Continental breakfast B

Lift ☾ 150P CFA

Lunch £9.50alc Dinner £9.50alc Wine £6 Last dinner 9.30pm

Credit cards 1 2 3 5

W6 Hammersmith

London plan **5** C3

☆☆☆☆**Cunard International** 1 Shortlands, Hammersmith ☎01-741 1555 Telex no 934539

Closed Xmas

Modern hotel with well-equipped bedrooms, traditional restaurant, carvery and 24 hour coffee shop.

640⇌⋒ CTV in all bedrooms ® ✱sB⇌⋒ fr£42.55 dB⇌⋒ fr£51.75 (room only) B

Lift ☾ ## 130 CFA squash

English & French ✱Lunch £7.95&alc Dinner £7.95&alc Wine £5.25 Last dinner 10.30pm

Credit cards 1 2 3 4 5 **VS**

✕**Anarkali** 303 King St ☎01-748 1760

Indian ✱Lunch £6.50alc Dinner £7.70alc Wine £6 Last dinner 11.30pm

S% Credit cards 1 2 3 5

✕***Aziz*** 116 King St ☎01-748 1826

Closed Sun & Xmas

Indian 60 seats Last dinner 11.45pm

Credit cards 2 3 5

W8 Kensington

London plan **5** C3

★★★★★**Royal Garden** Kensington High St (Rank) ☎01-937 8000 Telex no 263151 Plan 2: **104** *C1*

A large, modern hotel with live music and dancing in the romantic Roof-Top restaurant. The bedrooms are large and spacious.

427⇌⋒ (36fb) CTV in all bedrooms ✱sB⇌⋒ £63.50–£83 dB⇌⋒ £79–£98.50 (room only) B

Lift ☾ 160 CFA Live music and dancing 6 nights wkly

English, French & International V Lunch ✱£10.50&alc Tea £3.50&alc Dinner £13.50&alc Wine £6.50 Last dinner 11pm

Credit cards 1 2 3 4 5

★★★★**Kensington Close** Wright's Ln (Trusthouse Forte) ☎01-937 8170 Telex no 23914

Large busy hotel with many modern facilities.

530⇌ (11fb) CTV in all bedrooms sB&B⇌£43.50 dB&B⇌£57 B

Lift ☾ 100 CFA (heated) squash sauna bath *xmas*

Last dinner 10pm

Credit cards 1 2 3 4 5

★★★★**Kensington Palace Thistle** DeVere Gdns (Thistle) ☎01-937 8121 Telex no 262422 Plan 2: **67** *A3*

316⇌⋒ (14fb) CTV in all bedrooms ✱sB⇌⋒ 44.75–£49.75 (room only) dB⇌⋒ £55–£61.75 (room only) B

Lift ☾ 150 CFA *xmas*

European ✱Lunch £9&alc Dinner £9&alc Last dinner 10pm

Credit cards 1 2 3 4 5 **VS**

See advert on page 402

☆☆☆☆***London Tara*** Scarsdale Pl, off Wright's Ln (Best Western) ☎01-937 7211 Telex no 918835

Modern hotel with comfortable bedrooms, choice of restaurants and night spot.

843⇌ CTV in all bedrooms B

Lift ☾ 60P 65 CFA Disco 6 nights wkly Live music and dancing 6 nights wkly

International Last dinner 1am

Credit cards 1 2 3 4 5

★★**Hotel Lexham** 32–38 Lexham Gdns (Minotel) ☎01-373 6471 Plan 2: **75** *A2*

Quiet, traditional family-type hotel.

64rm (11⇌5⋒) (10fb) sB&B£15–£16 sB&B⇌⋒ £18–£19 dB&B£23–£25 dB&B⇌⋒ £30 B

Unlicensed Lift ☾ CTV  →

International V ♆ ☕ Lunch £3alc Tea 75palc Dinner £4.95 Last dinner 8pm
Credit cards 1 3

✕✕✕ *Trattoo* 2 Abingdon Rd, Kensington ☎01-937 4448
Italian 100 seats Last dinner 11.30pm ⊘
Credit cards 1 2 3 4 5

✕✕ La Grenouille 21 Abingdon Rd ☎01-937 5832
This Kensington restaurant has striking, modern décor.
Closed Sun & Mon, 1 wk Xmas, last wk Aug & 1st wk Sep.
French V 39 seats ✻ Lunch £8.50&alc Dinner £12alc Wine £4.50 Last dinner 11.30pm ⊘
Credit cards 1 2 3 5

✕✕ *Sailing Junk* 59 Marloes Rd ☎01-937 2589
A large mural dominates this basement Chinese restaurant.
Closed 24–26 Dec Lunch not served
Chinese 48 seats Last dinner 11.30pm ⊘
Credit cards 1 2 3 5

✕ Ark 35 Kensington High St ☎01-937 4294 Plan 2: **5** *A3*
Lunch not served Sun
French 90 seats Lunch £8alc Dinner £8alc Wine £3.95 Last dinner 11.25pm ⊘
Credit cards 1 3 5

✕ *Il Barbino* 32 Kensington Church St ☎01-937 8752
Closed Sun & Public hols Lunch not served Sat
Italian 45 seats Last dinner 11.45pm ⊘
Credit cards 1 2 3 4 5

✕ C.J. Kane's 5 Campden Hill Rd ☎01-938 1830
Closed Sun
American & Mexican V 75 seats Lunch £5.45–£10.15 Tea £1.85–£2.65 Dinner £5.45–£10.15 Wine £4.50 Last dinner 11.30pm ⊘
Credit cards 1 2 3 5

London W8 — London W11

✕ *Holland Street* 33c Holland St ☎01-937 3224
Closed Sat, Sun, Public hols, Xmas & Etr
20 seats Last dinner 10pm ⊘
Credit cards 1 2 3 5

✕ Siam 12 St Albans Grove ☎01-937 8765 Plan 2: **111** *A3*
Small restaurant decorated in traditional style, featuring traditional Thai dance shows nightly.
Lunch not served Mon & Sat
Thai V 85 seats Lunch £4.50–£6&alc Dinner £8.50–£9.50&alc Wine £4.90 Last dinner 11.15pm ⊘ ⊁
Credit cards 1 2 3 4 5 VS

✕ *Twin Brothers* 51 Church St ☎01-937 4152
Closed Sun Lunch not served
32 seats Last dinner 11pm

W9 Maida Vale
London plan **5** B3

✕ Didier 5 Warwick Pl ☎01-286 7484
Small friendly restaurant.
Closed Sat, Sun & Public hols
French 35 seats Lunch £6.95&alc Dinner £12alc Wine £4.50 Last dinner 10.30pm ⊘
Credit cards 1 2 VS

W11 Holland Park, Notting Hill
London map Plan **5** C3

☆☆☆☆ Hilton International Kensington Holland Park Av ☎01-603 3355 Telex no 919763
Modern hotel with comfortable bedrooms and a Japanese restaurant.
606 ⇄ ⋒ CTV in all bedrooms Ⓡ
sB&B ⇄ ⋒ £45.95–£61.95
dB&B ⇄ ⋒ £62.90–£83.90
Lift ☾ ## ⊁ 20P 110 ⌂ CFA nc18yrs *xmas*
English, French & Japanese V ♆ ☕ Lunch £8.50&alc Tea fr£4 Dinner fr£10&alc Wine £7 Last dinner 11.30pm
Credit cards 1 2 3 4 5

❀✕✕✕ Leith's 92 Kensington Park Rd ☎01-229 4481
Closed 24–27 Dec & 1 day Aug Bank hol
Lunch not served
International V 95 seats ✻ Dinner £22alc Wine £7.90 Last dinner mdnt ⊘
S% Credit cards 1 2 3 5

❀✕✕ Chez Moi 1 Addison Av ☎01-603 8267
Popular, small French restaurant, with an intimate, friendly atmosphere and good food.
Closed Sun, 2 wks Xmas & 2 wks Aug
Lunch not served Sat
French 50 seats Lunch £18.20alc Dinner £18.20alc Wine £5.25 Last dinner 11.30pm ⊘
Credit cards 1 2 3 5

✕✕ La Pomme d'Amour 128 Holland Park Av ☎01-229 8532
Closed Sun & Public hols Lunch not served Sat
French 70 seats Lunch £9.50&alc Dinner £14alc Wine £5 Last dinner 11pm ⊘
S% Credit cards 1 2 3 5 VS

✕ La Jardinière 148 Holland Park Av ☎01-221 6090
Small, pleasantly decorated restaurant with warm ground floor atmosphere and cool basement area. Friendly service.
Closed Mon & Public hols Lunch not served Tue–Sat
French 75 seats Lunch £7.75&alc Dinner £11alc Wine £4.80 Last dinner mdnt ⊘
S% Credit cards 1 2 3 5 VS

✕ Monsieur Thompsons 29 Kensington Park Rd ☎01-727 9957
Closed Sun
French ✻ Lunch £13alc Dinner £13alc Wine £5.75 Last dinner 10.30pm

✕ Rama Sita 6 Clarendon Rd ☎01-727 9359

L

Closed Sun & 15–31 Aug

French & Indian V 42 seats Lunch £4.50–£6.50&alc Dinner £7.50–£15 Wine £4.35 Last dinner 11pm

S% Credit cards 1 2 3 5

✕ ***Singapore Mandarin*** 120–122 Holland Park Av ☎01-727 6341

Closed 24–26 Dec

Singapore Chinese V 90 seats Last dinner 11.45pm Live music Fri & Sat

Credit cards 2 3 5

W12 Shepherds Bush

London plan **5** C3

✕ ***Shireen*** 270 Uxbridge Rd ☎01-749 5927

Closed Sun

Indian V 36 seats Last dinner 11.30pm

Credit cards 1 2 3 5 **VS**

W13 Ealing (Northfields)

London plan **5** B4

(See also W5)

✕ **Maxims Chinese** 153–155 Northfield Av ☎01-567 1719

Closed 25–28 Dec Lunch not served Sun

Pekinese V 100 seats Lunch £4.95–£13.80&alc Dinner £4.95–£13.80&alc Wine £4.90 Last dinner mdnt

S% Credit cards 1 2 5 **VS**

W14 West Kensington

London plan **5** C3

☆☆☆ **Royal Kensington** 380 Kensington High St (Comfort) ☎01-603 3333 Telex no 22229

Modern hotel with simple restaurant operation.

409⇌ CTV in all bedrooms ® *sB&B⇌ fr£30 dB&B⇌ fr£40.50 Continental breakfast

Lift ☾ 50 CFA

V ☕ *Lunch fr£5.75&alc Dinner fr£5.75&alc Wine £3.95 Last dinner 11pm

Credit cards 1 2 3 4 5 **VS**

London W11 — London WC1

✕ ***Bamboo House*** 7 Rockley Rd, Shepherds Bush ☎01-740 0333

A colourfully decorated Chinese restaurant.

Pekinese V 100 seats Last dinner 11.30pm 10P

Credit cards 1 2 3 5

WC1 Bloomsbury, Holborn

★★★★ **Hotel Russell** Russell Sq (Trusthouse Forte) ☎01-837 6470 Telex no 24615 Plan 3: **31** *C6*

Large hotel facing Russell Square with compact modern bedrooms.

318⇌ CTV in all bedrooms sB&B⇌ £50 dB&B⇌ £66.50 B

Lift ☾ CFA *xmas*

☕ Last dinner 10pm

Credit cards 1 2 3 4 5

☆☆☆ **Bloomsbury Crest** Coram St, Russell Sq (Crest) ☎01-837 1200 Telex no 22113

Modern hotel with carvery restaurant.

250⇌ CTV in all bedrooms ® *sB⇌ fr£37 (room only) dB⇌ fr£44 (room only) B

Lift ☾ CFA

International V ☕ *Lunch £6.25–£8.75&alc Tea £1.85 High Tea £3 Dinner £6.25–£8.75&alc Wine £5.25 Last dinner 11pm

Credit cards 1 2 3 4 5 **VS**

★★★ **Kingsley** Bloomsbury Way (Mount Charlotte) ☎01-242 5881 Telex no 21157 Plan 1: **27** *D5*

An old-fashioned hotel, operating a partly self-service carvery restaurant.

169rm (98⇌5⋒) CTV in all bedrooms ® sB&B£29 sB&B⇌⋒ £31 dB&B⇌⋒ £42 Continental breakfast B

Lift CTV

V ☕ Lunch £8.50 Dinner £8.50 Wine £5 Last dinner 9pm

Credit cards 1 2 3 5

☆☆☆ **London Ryan** Gwynne Pl, Kings Cross Rd (Mount Charlotte) ☎01-278 2480 Telex no 27728

Modern hotel, with well equipped bedrooms.

213⇌ (19fb) CTV in all bedrooms sB&B⇌ £32 dB&B⇌ £42.80 Continental breakfast B

Lift ☾ 50P

V ☕ Bar lunch £5–£6.75 Dinner £6.75–£7.75&alc Wine £5 Last dinner 9.45pm

Credit cards 1 2 3 4 5 **VS**

☆☆☆ **Royal Scot Thistle** 100 Kings Cross Rd (Thistle) ☎01-278 2434 Telex no 27657

A modern hotel providing bedrooms with many facilities, formal restaurant and coffee shop.

349⇌⋒ CTV in all bedrooms ® *sB&B⇌⋒ £35 dB&B⇌⋒ £38 Continental breakfast B

Lift ☾ # 35P CFA sauna bath

European *Lunch £8.25&alc Dinner £8.25&alc Last dinner 9.30pm

Credit cards 1 2 3 4 5 **VS**

★★ ***Bedford Corner*** 11–13 Bayley St ☎01-580 7766 Plan 3: **4** *B6*

Closed 25 Dec–3 Jan

Small, modernised, Victorian hotel with friendly staff.

85rm (49⇌⋒) CTV in all bedrooms ® B

Lift ☾

Mainly grills ☕ Last dinner 9.30pm

Credit cards 1 2 3 4 5 **VS**

★★ **Cora** Upper Woburn Pl ☎01-387 5111 Telex no 23175 (Cora G)

Well-run hotel, close to Euston main line railway station.

144rm (50⇌2⋒) (8fb) CTV in all bedrooms *sB&B£14–£20 sB&B⇌⋒ £20.50–£31 dB&B£28–£35 dB&B⇌⋒ £35–£42 B

Lift ☾ CTV CFA

English & Continental ☕ *Lunch £4.80–£6.50&alc Tea 75palc Dinner £4.80–£6.50&alc Wine £5.30 Last dinner 9.30pm

Credit cards 1 2 3 5

L

★★*Grand* 126 Southampton Row
☎01-405 2006 Telex no 25757 Plan 3: **13** *C6*

Traditional hotel offering good value for money.

92rm(53➡) CTV in all bedrooms ® B

Lift ☾ CTV 🐕

🍷☕ Last dinner 8.45pm

Credit cards 1 2 3 5

✕✕**Kites Chinese** 50 Woburn Pl
☎01-580 1188 Plan 3: **15B** *C6*

A modern, well-run restaurant with friendly and attractive Manderin waitresses.

Closed Public Hols

Chinese **V** 120 seats ✱Lunch £7.50alc Dinner £9alc Wine £4.70 Last dinner 11.30pm Live music Mon–Fri 🐕

S% Credit cards 1 2 3 5 **VS**

✕**Les Halles** 57 Theobalds Rd
☎01-242 6761 Plan 3: **18A** *D6*

A simple French brasserie with interesting food and wine.

Closed Sat, Sun, Xmas & Public Holidays

French **V** 80 seats Lunch £8.50&alc Dinner £8.50&alc Wine £4.15 Last dinner 11pm bedrooms available

Credit cards 1 2 3 5 **VS**

WC2 Covent Garden; *Leicester Square, Strand and Kingsway*

★★★★*L* **Waldorf** Aldwych (Trusthouse Forte) ☎01-836 2400 Telex no 24574 Plan 1: **57** *E4*

Gracious, elegant hotel with good range of accommodation.

310➡ (12fb) CTV in all bedrooms sB&B➡£60 dB&B➡£82 B

Lift ☾ 🐕 CFA *xmas*

🍷Last dinner 10pm

Credit cards 1 2 3 4 5

★★★**Drury Lane Moat House** 10 Drury Ln (Queens Moat) ☎01-836 6666 Telex no 8811395 Plan 1: **15** *D5*

Hotel with comfortable bedrooms and Maudies Restaurant.

128➡⋒ (6fb) CTV in all bedrooms ✱ sB➡⋒ fr£50.50 dB➡⋒ fr£69.50 (room only) B

Lift ☾ ## 8P 8🚗

French 🍷Lunch £8.25–£9.95&alc Dinner £10.25–£12.50&alc Wine £5.50 Last dinner 10pm

Credit cards 1 2 3 5

★★★**Royal Trafalgar Thistle**
Whitcomb St (Thistle) ☎01-930 4477 Plan 1: **44A** *C2*

Comfortable hotel with well-equipped compact accommodation.

107➡⋒ CTV in all bedrooms ✱
✱sB➡⋒ £41.50–£47.50 (room only)
dB➡⋒ £47.50–£52.50 (room only) B

Lift ☾ 🐕

European ☕ ✱Lunch £7.75&alc Dinner £7.57&alc Last dinner 10pm

Credit cards 1 2 3 4 5

London WC1 – London WC2

★★★**Strand Palace** Strand (Trusthouse Forte) ☎01-836 8080 Telex no 24208 Plan 1: **52** *E3*

Modernised, compact Regency styled hotel.

761➡ (16fb) CTV in all bedrooms ® ✱ sB&B➡£44.50 dB&B➡£57 B

Lift ☾ 🐕 *xmas*

🍷☕ Last dinner 10.30pm

Credit cards 1 2 3 4 5

✕✕✕✕✕**Savoy Hotel Grill**
Embankment Gdns, Strand ☎01-836 4343 Plan 1: **46** *E3*

Closed Sat, Sun & Aug

French **V** 120 seats ✱Lunch £20alc Dinner £17.50–£25.50&alc Wine £8.05 Last dinner 11.15pm 🐕 Live music nightly

S% Credit cards 1 2 3 5

❀✕✕✕✕**Inigo Jones** 14 Garrick St
☎01-836 6456 Plan 1: **24** *D3*

On the first floor of old building in Covent Garden, the restaurant's unusual ecclesiastical décor includes elegant Gothic arches, illuminated stained glass windows and wood carvings of prelates.

Closed Sun & Public hols Lunch not served Sat

French 85 seats Last dinner 11.45pm 🐕

Credit cards 1 2 3 5

✕✕✕✕**Simpsons** 100 The Strand
☎01-836 9112 Plan 1: **48** *E3*

Closed Sun, Xmas Day, New Years Day & Public hols

350 seats Lunch £12alc Dinner £9–£11.50&alc Wine £7.25 Last dinner 10pm 🐕

S% Credit cards 1 3 4 5

❀✕✕✕**Boulestin** 25 Southampton St
☎01-836 7061 Plan 1: **4** *D3*

Elegant, Edwardian-style restaurant featuring imaginative and classic cooking and excellent fresh vegetables.

Closed Sun, Public hols, 1wk Xmas & last 3wks Aug Lunch not served Sat

★★★★★**SAVOY HOTEL, LONDON, WC2**

Strand ☎01-836 4343 Telex no 24234
Plan 1: **46** *E3*

It is rare for a hotel steeped in tradition to carry the hallmark of one man since the days of Charles Ritz and a few others; but unquestionably this now applies at the Savoy. That man is Willy Bauer who has recently completed his second year as general manager here. Unceasing in his endeavours to improve standards, the effect and success can be gauged immediately one approaches the entrance. The instant and courteous attention is the same whether one arrives in a Rolls or a 2CV and the spring in the steps of the staff show that pride has returned. Formality, discretion, politeness, efficiency – these aspects of service have always been evident at this great hotel but there is new warmth and hospitality as well, typified by regular greetings in the corridors, lounge, lifts by all members of staff. The splendour remains despite certain physical refurbishing and the vast majority of the bedrooms are spacious, tastefully decorated and well appointed. The legendary deep baths and lovely 'thunderstorm' showers are much appreciated as are the bath sheets and luxurious, soft beds. Many rooms and suites overlook the Thames and these have air conditioning as well. Very few hotels can match the comfort of the public areas; besides a small, quiet lounge in which one can relax, there is the large Thames Foyer where not only are drinks served but also one of the best afternoon teas in London is available. A pianist plays and the music adds to the atmosphere. There is also the American Bar which is a popular rendezvous and provides excellent cocktails. The restaurant, The River Room, provides good value table d'hote meals for lunch and dinner as well as an à la carte. A new chef, Mr Edelmann has taken over and, although the style has changed a little, first impressions are very favourable. The Grill Room remains as popular as ever and it is with regret we report the departure of its excellent maitre d'hotel, Mr Aldo Fiorintini. We wish his successor well.

201➡⋒ CTV in all bedrooms ✱
✱sB➡⋒ £80 (room only)
dB➡⋒ £100 (room only) B

Lift ☾ 58🚗 CFA Live music and dancing Mon–Sat

French 🍷☕ ✱Lunch £15.50&alc Tea £5.80 Dinner £18.50–£19.50&alc Wine £8.05 Last dinner 10.30pm

Credit cards 1 2 3 5

French 67 seats Last dinner 11.15pm
Credit cards 1 2 3 4 5

✕✕✕ ***La Bussola*** 42 St Martin's Ln ☎01-240 1148 Plan 1: **6** *D3*
Closed Sun Lunch not served Sat
International 160 seats Last dinner 11.45pm
Credit cards 1 2 3 5

✕✕✕ **Grange** 39 King St ☎01-240 2939 Plan 1: **20** *D3*
Sophisticated, popular restaurant offering excellent value for money.
Closed Sun & 4wks Aug/Sep Lunch not served Sat
English & French 65 seats Lunch £12–£17 Dinner £12–£17 Wine £6 Last dinner 11.30pm
S% Credit card 2

✕✕✕ **P S Hispaniola** Victoria Embankment, River Thames ☎01-839 3011 Plan 1: **21** *D1*
The restaurant is located on board a paddle steamer.
Lunch not served Sat
Continental 250 seats Lunch £9.50&alc Dinner £12.50alc Wine £3.75 Last dinner 11.15pm
Credit cards 3 4 5

✕✕✕ **Ivy** 1–5 West St ☎01-836 4751 Plan 1: **26** *C4*
Quiet but popular restaurant with attractive decor.
Closed Sun & Public hols Lunch not served Sat
French 105 seats ✻Lunch £9.50&alc Dinner £9.50&alc Wine £5 Last dinner 11pm
S% Credit cards 1 2 3 4 5

✕✕✕ **Neal Street** 26 Neal St ☎01-836 8368 Plan 1: **33** *D4*
Modern restaurant with tasteful basement cocktail bar serving very original English and French cuisine.
Closed Sat, Sun, Xmas & Public hols
International 65 seats Lunch £22alc Dinner £22alc Wine £7.50 Last dinner 11pm
Credit cards 1 2 3 4 5

✕✕✕ **L'Opera** 32 Great Queen St ☎01-405 9020 Plan 1: **35** *D5*
Splendid, plush Edwardian restaurant in gilt and crimson occupying two floors in the centre of theatreland.
Closed Sun Lunch not served Sat
French 100 seats Lunch £11&alc Dinner £11&alc Wine £5.25 Last dinner mdnt
S% Credit cards 1 2 3 4 5 **VS**

✕✕✕ **Rules** 35 Maiden Ln, Strand ☎01-836 5314 Plan 1: **45** *D3*
Well established traditional restaurant with professional, efficient service.
Closed Sun, 1st 3wks Aug, Xmas & New Year & all Public Holidays Lunch not served Sat
150 seats Lunch £10alc Dinner £10alc Wine £5.40 Last dinner 11.15pm
Credit cards 1 2 3 5

✕✕ **Chez Solange** 35 Cranbourn St ☎01-836 0542 Plan 1: **12** *C3*
Good quality home cuisine in this elegant West End restaurant.
French **V** 84 seats Lunch £10&alc Dinner £15alc Wine £5.25 Last dinner 12.15am Live music nightly
S% Credit cards 1 2 3 4 5 **VS**

❀✕✕ **Interlude de Tabaillau** 7–8 Bow St ☎01-379 6473 Plan 1: **25** *D4*
Informal atmosphere, honest French cooking and good value for money.
Closed Sun, 3wks Aug/Sep, 1wk Xmas & 10days Etr Lunch not served Sat
French 40 seats ✻Lunch fr£16.50 Dinner fr£21
Credit cards 1 2 3 5

❀✕✕ **Poons 41 King St** ☎01-240 1743 Plan 1: **38** *D3*
Comprehensive selection of Cantonese cuisine prepared before your eyes in this friendly restaurant.
Closed Sun & 4days Xmas
Cantonese **V** 120 seats Lunch £7.50alc Dinner £10.50alc Wine £6.90 Last dinner 11.30pm
Credit cards 2 3 5

✕✕ ***Terrazza-Est*** 125 Chancery Ln ☎01-242 2601 Plan 3: **38** *E5*
Closed Sat & Sun
Italian 140 seats Last dinner 11.30pm
Credit cards 1 2 3 4 5 **VS**

✕✕ **Thomas de Quincey's** 36 Tavistock St ☎01-240 3972 Plan 1: **54** *E3*
Attractive hospitable restaurant serving original unusual dishes.
Closed Sun, 3wks Aug & Public hols Lunch not served Sat
French 50 seats Lunch £25alc Dinner £25alc Wine £6.40 Last dinner 11pm
S% Credit cards 1 2 3 4 5 **VS**

✕ ***Azami*** 13–15 West St ☎01-240 0634 Plan 1: **3** *C4*
Traditional and authentic Japanese cuisine featuring a Sushi and Tempura counter and basement Cattleya lounge.
Closed Mon
Japanese 54 seats Last dinner 10.30pm
Credit cards 1 2 3 5

✕ **Le Café des Amis du Vin** 11–14 Hanover Pl ☎01-379 3444 Plan 1: **6A** *D4*
Traditional French street cafe with imaginative menu.
Closed Sun
French **V** 130 seats Lunch £7.50–£10&alc Dinner £7.50–£10&alc Wine £4.50 Last dinner 11.45
S% Credit cards 1 2 3 5

✕ **Cellier de Medici** 8 Mays Court ☎01-836 9180 Plan 1: **9** *D3*
Small, intimate, informal Italian restaurant.
Closed Sun Lunch not served Sat
Continental 50 seats Lunch £8alc Dinner £8alc Wine £4.20 Last dinner 11.15pm
S% Credit cards 1 2 3 5

✕ **Il Passetto** 230 Shaftesbury Av ☎01-836 9391 Plan 1: **23A** *D5*
Modern Italian restaurant with good home made food.
Closed Sun
Italian 42 seats ✻Lunch £8alc Dinner £8alc Wine £4.25 Last dinner 11pm
Credit cards 1 2 3 5

✕ **Joy King Lau** 3 Leicester St ☎01-437 1133 Plan 1: **26A** *C3*
Good quality, authentic Cantonese cuisine served in this popular five-storey restaurant.
Cantonese **V** 200 seats Lunch £5–£8&alc Tea £5–£8&alc Dinner £5–£8&alc Wine £4.40 Last dinner 11.30pm
S% Credit cards 2 4 5

✕ **Last Days of The Raj** 22 Drury Ln ☎01-836 1628 Plan 1: **28A** *D5*
Bright, popular co-operative featuring authentic, honest and skilful Indian cuisine.
Indian 44 seats ✻Lunch £8alc Dinner £8alc Wine £4.10 Last dinner 11.30pm
S% Credit cards 1 3

✕ **Manzi's** 1–2 Leicester St ☎01-734 0224 Plan 1: **31** *C3*
An Edwardian atmosphere in London's oldest seafood restaurant.
Closed Xmas Day & Boxing Day Lunch not served Sun, 1 Jan & Good Friday
Seafood 125 seats ✻Lunch £7–£10alc Dinner £7–£10alc Wine £4.20 Last dinner 11.40pm bedrooms available
Credit cards 1 2 3 5

✕ ***New Rasa Sayang*** 3 Leicester Pl ☎01-437 4556 Plan 1: **34** *C3*
Interesting Indonesian restaurant with the interior covered with traditional wall murals.
Indonesian **V** 52 seats Last dinner 11.15pm
Credit cards 2 5

❀✕ **Poon's 4 Leicester St** ☎01-437 1528 Plan 1: **39** *C3*
Small, bustling restaurant specialising in wind dried food. →

Closed Sun, 25 & 26 Dec
Cantonese V 100 seats ✻Lunch £3.80–£5&alc Dinner £3.80–£5&alc Wine £3.80
Last dinner 11.30pm

✕Sheekey's 29–31 St Martin's Court
☎01-240 2565 Plan 1: **47** *C3*

One of the oldest fish restaurants in London specialising in oysters.

Closed Sun & Public hols
100 seats ✻Lunch £13alc Dinner £13alc
Wine £4.95 Last dinner 11pm
S% Credit cards 1 2 3 5

London restaurants open Sundays in 1984

❀❀❀✕✕✕✕	Le Gavroche (W1)	❀✕✕✕✕	Waltons (SW3)
✕✕✕✕	Hilton Hotel (Trader Vic's) (W1)		

✕✕✕	Chesa (*Swiss Centre*) (W1)	✕✕✕	Tandoori of Mayfair (W1)
✕✕✕	PS Hispaniola (WC2)	✕✕✕	Terrazza (W1)
❀✕✕✕	Leith's (dinner only) (W11)		

✕✕	Bali (W2)	✕✕	Kites Chinese (WC1)
✕✕	Bewick's (dinner only) (SW3)	✕✕	Lal Qila (W1)
✕✕	Brasserie St Quentin (SW3)	✕✕	Lords Rendezvous (NW8)
✕✕	Le Caprice (SW1)	✕✕	Luigi's (NW11)
✕✕	Chelsea Rendezvous (SW3)	✕✕	Ménage à Trois (SW3)
✕✕	Dolphin Square (lunch only) (SW1)	✕✕	Nikita's (lunch only) (SW10)
❀✕✕	English Garden (SW3)	✕✕	San Carlo (N6)
❀✕✕	English House (SW3)	✕✕	September (SW10)
✕✕	Gaylord (Mortimer St) (W1)	✕✕	Tandoori (SW3)
✕✕	Good Earth (NW7)	✕✕	Vendôme (W1)

✕	Anarkali (W6)	✕	Lee Ho Fook (15 Gerrard St) (W1)
✕	Ark (dinner only) (W8)	✕	Malean (dinner only) (SW16)
❀✕	Capability Brown (NW6)	✕	Le Mange Tout (W2)
✕	Chez Zorba (W1)	✕	Manzil's (dinner only) (WC2)
❀✕	Chuen Cheng Ku (W1)	✕	Maxim's Chinese (dinner only) (W13)
✕	La Croisette (SW10)		
✕	Crowthers (lunch only) (SW14)	✕	Mayflower (W1)
✕	Curry Centre (SE13)	✕	M'sieur Frog (N1)
✕	Dragon Gate (W1)	✕	Le Papillion (lunch only) (SE10)
✕	Good Friends (E14)	✕	Peter's Bistro (lunch only) (NW6)
✕	Hungry Horse (SW10)	✕	Pollyanna's (SW11)
✕	Janine's (lunch only) (SW14)	✕	Raj of India (SW1)
✕	La Jardinière (W11)	✕	Siam (W8)
✕	Joy King Lau (WC2)	✕	Le Suquet (SW3)
✕	Kuo Yuan (NW10)	✕	Tent (SW1)
✕	Last Days of the Raj (WC2)	✕	Vijay (NW6)
✕	Lee Ho Fook (New College Pde) (NW3)		

London hotels & restaurants open for meals after 11pm

★★★★★	Churchill (W1)	01.00	★★★★★	Inn on the Park (W1)	Midnight
❀❀❀★★★★★	Dorchester (W1)	23.30	★★★★★	May Fair (W1)	23.30
★★★★★	Hilton International (W1)	00.30			

★★★★	Britannia (W1)	00.30	☆☆☆☆	Ladbroke Westmoreland (NW8)	23.30
★★★★	Europa (W1)	00.30			
☆☆☆☆	Forum Hotel London (SW7)	01.00	☆☆☆☆	London International (SW5)	Midnight
☆☆☆☆	Hilton International Kensington (W11)	23.30			
☆☆☆☆	Holiday Inn (W1)	Midnight	☆☆☆☆	White House (NW1)	23.30

Rating	Restaurant	Time
✕✕✕✕✕	Ninety Park Lane (W1)	23.30
✕✕✕✕✕	Savoy Hotel Grill (WC2)	23.15
✕✕✕✕	Hilton Hotel (Trader Vic's) (W1)	23.30
❀✕✕✕✕	Inigo Jones (WC2)	23.45
❀✕✕✕✕	Waltons (SW3)	23.30
❀✕✕✕	Boulestin (WC2)	23.15
✕✕✕	Braganza (W1)	23.15
❀✕✕✕	Carriers (N1)	23.30
✕✕✕	Chesa (*Swiss Centre*) (W1)	Midnight
✕✕✕	Grange (WC2)	23.30
✕✕✕	PS Hispaniola (WC2)	23.15
✕✕✕	Lafayette (SW1)	23.30
❀✕✕✕	Leith's (W11)	Midnight
✕✕✕	L'Opera (WC2)	Midnight
✕✕✕	Rules (WC2)	23.15
✕✕✕	Tandoori of Mayfair (W1)	Midnight
✕✕✕	Terrazza (W1)	23.30
✕✕✕	Verrey's (W1)	23.30
❀✕✕	Alonso's (SW8)	23.30
✕✕	Bewick's (SW3)	23.30
✕✕	Brasserie St Quentin (SW3)	Midnight
✕✕	Le Caprice (SW1)	Midnight
✕✕	Chelsea Rendezvous (SW3)	23.30
❀✕✕	Chez Moi (W11)	23.30
✕✕	Chez Solange (WC2)	00.15
✕✕	La Cucaracha (W1)	23.30
❀✕✕	Daphne's (SW3)	Midnight
✕✕	Dolphin Square (SW1)	23.30
❀✕✕	English Garden (SW3)	23.30
❀✕✕	English House (SW3)	23.30
✕✕	Frederick's (N1)	23.30
✕✕	Gaylord (Mortimer St) (W1)	23.30
✕✕	Good Earth (NW7)	23.15
✕✕	La Grenouille (W8)	23.30
❀✕✕	Keats (NW3)	23.30
✕✕	Kites Chinese (WC1)	23.30
✕✕	Lal Qila (W1)	23.30
✕✕	Langan's Brasserie (W1)	23.45
✕✕	Lords Rendezvous (NW8)	23.15
✕✕	Martin's (SW10)	23.30
✕✕	Ménage à Trois (SW3)	00.15
✕✕	Nikita's (SW10)	23.30
❀✕✕	Pomegranates (SW1)	23.15
❀✕✕	Poon's (King St) (WC2)	23.30
❀✕✕	Salloos (SW1)	23.30
✕✕	San Carlo (N6)	Midnight
✕✕	San Frediano (SW3)	23.15
✕✕	Santa Croce (SW10)	23.15
✕✕	September (SW10)	23.30
❀✕✕	Shezan (SW7)	23.30
✕✕	Tandoori (SW3)	00.30
✕	Anarkali (W6)	23.30
✕	Ark (W8)	23.25
✕	L'Artiste Affamé (SW5)	23.30
✕	Le Café des Amis du Vin (WC2)	23.45
❀✕	Capability Brown (NW6)	23.30
✕	Cellier de Medici (WC2)	23.15
✕	Chez Zorba (W1)	03.00
✕	Chuen Cheng Ku (W1)	23.45
✕	Le Croisette (SW10)	23.30
✕	Curry Centre (SE13)	23.30
❀✕	Dan's (SW3)	23.30
✕	Dragon Gate (W1)	23.30
✕	Eatons (SW1)	23.15
✕	Gibourne (SW1)	23.30
✕	Hungry Horse (SW10)	Midnight
✕	La Jardinière (W11)	Midnight
✕	Joy King Lau (WC2)	23.30
✕	Kalamaras (W2)	Midnight
✕	C J Kane's (W8)	23.30
✕	Last Days of the Raj (WC2)	23.30
✕	Lee Ho Fook (New College Pde) (NW3)	23.30
✕	Luba's Bistro (SW3)	23.45
✕	Malean (SW16)	Midnight
✕	Manzi's (WC2)	23.40
✕	Maxim's Chinese (W13)	Midnight
✕	Mayflower (W1)	03.00
✕	Montpeliano (SW7)	23.30
✕	Le Papillion (SE10)	23.30
✕	Peter's Bistro (NW6)	23.30
✕	Poissonerie (SW3)	23.30
✕	Pollyanna's (SW11)	Midnight
❀✕	Poon's (Leicester St) (WC2)	23.30
✕	Portofino (N1)	23.30
✕	Raj of India (W1)	Midnight
✕	Siam (W8)	23.15
✕	South of the Border (SE1)	23.30
✕	Le Suquet (SW3)	23.30
✕	Tapas (SW1)	23.30
✕	Tent (SW1)	23.15

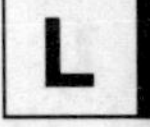

London restaurants with specialised food

Cuisine	Rating	Restaurant	Rating	Restaurant
Chinese	✕✕✕	Fu Tong (**C**) (W8)	✕	Bamboo House (**P**) (W14)
C–Cantonese	✕✕	Chelsea Rendezvous (**P**) (SW3)	❀✕	Chuen Cheng Ku (**C**) (W1)
	✕✕	Gallery Rendezvous (**P**) (W1)	✕	Golden Duck (**P**) (SW10)
P–Pekinese	❀✕✕	Ken Lo's Memories of China (**C**) (SW1)	✕	Joy King Lau (**C**) (WC2)
			✕	Lee Ho Fook (**C**) (W1)
	✕✕	Kites Chinese (**P** & **C**) (WC1)	✕	Maxim's Chinese (**P**) (W13)
	✕✕	Lords Rendezvous (**P**) (NW8)	❀✕	Poon's (Leicester St) (**C**) (WC2)
	✕✕	Mr Chow (**P**) (SW1)	✕	Singapore Mandarin (**P**) (W11)
	✕✕	Mr Kai of Mayfair (**P**) (W1)	✕	Soho Rendezvous (**P**) (W1)
	❀✕✕	Poon's (King St) (**C**) (WC2)	✕	Tiger Lee (**C**) (SW5)
	✕✕	Sailing Junk (**C**) (W8)		
English	✕✕✕✕	Hunting Lodge (SW1)	❀✕✕	English House (SW3)
	✕✕✕✕	Simpson's (WC2)	✕✕	Tate Gallery (SW1)
	✕✕✕	Baron of Beef (EC2)	✕	Aunties (W1)
	✕✕✕	Neal Street (WC2)	✕	Holland Street (W8)
	✕✕✕	Rules (WC2)		
Fish Dishes	✕✕✕	Braganza (W1)	✕	La Croisette (SW10)
	✕✕	Fisherman's Wharf (W1)	✕	Poissonnerie (SW3)
	✕✕	Wheeler's (W1)	✕	Sheekeys (WC2)
French	✕✕✕✕✕	Café Royal *(Grill Room)* (W1)	✕✕	Shares (EC3)
	✕✕✕✕✕	Ninety Park Lane (W1)	❀❀✕✕	Tante Claire (SW3)
	❀❀❀✕✕✕✕	Le Gavroche (W1)	✕✕	Thomas de Quincey's (WC2)
	❀✕✕✕✕	Inigo Jones (WC2)	✕	Les Amoureux (SW19)
	❀✕✕✕	Boulestin (WC2)	✕	Ark (W8)
	✕✕✕	Braganza (W1)	✕	Didier (W9)
	❀✕✕✕	Carriers (N1)	✕	Bagetelle (SW10)
	✕✕✕	Lafayette (SW1)	❀✕	Bubb's (EC1)
	✕✕✕	Neal Street (WC2)	❀✕	Capability Brown (NW6)
	✕✕✕	L'Opera (WC2)	✕	Le Café des Amis du Vin (WC2)
	❀❀✕✕✕	Le Poulbot (EC2)		
	✕✕✕	Snooty Fox (W1)	✕	Cassis (SW15)
	❀✕✕	L'Arlequin (SW8)	✕	Cellier de Medici (WC2)
	✕✕	Le Caprice (SW1)	✕	Chez Franco (W2)
	✕✕	Au Jardin des Gourmets (W1)	✕	Dan's (SW3)
	✕✕	Brasserie St Quentin (SW3)	✕	La Croisette (SW10)
	✕✕	Le Caprice (SW1)	✕	La Fringale (SW10)
	❀✕✕	Chez Moi (W11)	❀✕	Le Gamin (EC4)
	❀❀✕✕	Chez Nico (SW8)	✕	Les Halles (WC1)
	✕✕	Chez Solange (WC2)	✕	Hungry Horse (SW10)
	❀✕✕	Daphne's (SW3)	✕	La Jardinière (W11)
	✕✕	La Grenouille (W8)	❀✕	Ma Cuisine (SW3)
	✕✕	Le Français (SW3)	✕	Le Mange Tout (W2)
	✕✕	Frederick's (N1)	✕	M'sieur Frog (N1)
	✕✕	Gavvers (SW1)	✕	Peter's Bistro (NW6)
	✕✕	Ici Paris (W1)	✕	Poissonnerie (SW3)
	❀✕✕	Interlude de Tabaillau (WC2)	✕	South of the Border (SE1)
	❀✕✕	Keats (NW3)	✕	Le Suquet (SW3)
	✕✕	La Pomme D'Amour (W11)	✕	Wild Thyme (SW15)
Greek	❀✕✕✕	White Tower (W1)	✕	Little Akropolis (W1)
	✕	Chez Zorba (W1)	✕	Romantica Tavern (W2)
Hungarian	✕✕	Gay Hussar (W1)		

Cuisine		Restaurant		Restaurant
Indian & Pakistani	XXX	Kundan (SW1)	X	Aziz (W6)
	XX	Gaylord (Abermarle St) (W1)	X	Curry Centre (SE13)
	XX	Gaylord (Mortimer St) (W1)	X	Ganges (W2)
	XX	Geetanjli of Mayfair (W1)	X	Orient (W1)
	❀XX	Salloos (SW1)	X	Rama Sita (W11)
	❀XX	Shezan (SW7)	X	Shireen (W12)
	XX	Tandoori (SW3)	X	Vijay (NW6)
	XX	Viceroy of India (NW1)		
Indonesian	XX	Bali (W2)	X	New Rasa Sayang (WC2)
Italian	XXXX	Tiberio (W1)	XX	Santa Croce (SW10)
	XXX	La Bussola (WC2)	XX	Terrazza-Est (WC2)
	XXX	Terrazza (W1)	X	Al ben Accolto (SW3)
	XXX	Trattoo (W8)	X	Anarkali (W6)
	XX	L'Amico (SW1)	X	Il Barbino (W8)
	XX	La Loggia (W1)	X	La Capannina (W1)
	XX	San Carlo (N6)	X	Don Luigi's (SW3)
	XX	San Ferdiano (SW3)	X	Portofino (N1)
Japanese	XXX	Masako (W1)	X	Ginnan (EC4)
	XX	Mikado (W1)	X	Saga (W1)
	X	Azami (WC2)		
Jewish	X	Blooms (E1)		
Mexican	XX	La Cucaracha (W1)		
Original Dishes	❀XXXX	Walton's (SW3)	❀XX	Daphne's (SW3)
	❀XXX	Carriers (N1)	❀XX	Mijanou (SW1)
	❀XXX	Leith's (W11)	❀XX	Odin's (W1)
	❀XXX	Parkes (SW3)	X	Froops (NW1)
	❀XXX	White Tower (W1)		
Polish & Russian	XX	Nikita's (SW10)	X	Luba's Bistro (SW3)
Polynesia	XXXX	Hilton Hotel *(Trader Vic's)* (W1)		
Portuguese	XX	Os Arcos (SW11)		
Siamese (Thai)	X	Siam (W8)		
Spanish	XXX	PS Hispaniola (WC2)		
Swiss	XXX	Chesa *(Swiss Centre)* (W1)		

DISPLAY OF HOTEL PRICES

All hotels, motels, inns, and guesthouses in Britain, with four bedrooms or more (including self-catering accommodation) and offering accommodation to guests, are required to display notices showing minimum and maximum overnight charges. The notice must be displayed in a prominent position in the reception area, or at the entrance.

The prices shown must include any service charge, and may include Value Added Tax, and it must be made clear whether or not these items are included. If VAT is not included then it must be shown separately. If meals are provided with the accommodation, this must be made clear too. If prices are not standard for all rooms, then only the lowest and highest prices need be given.

London Plans - Key map

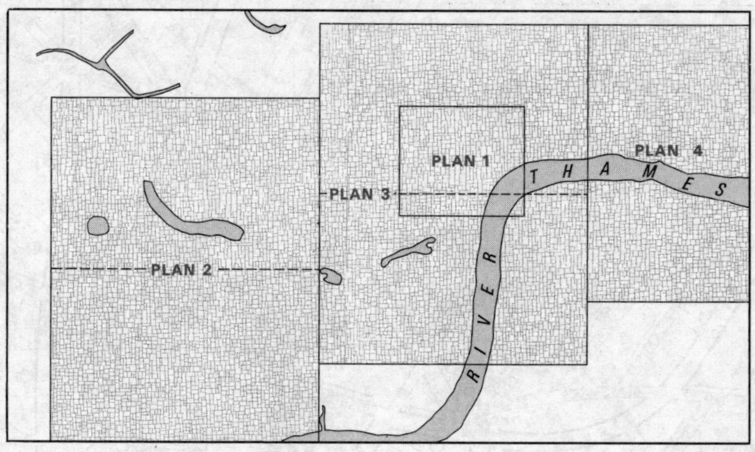
PLAN 1
PLAN 2
PLAN 3
PLAN 4
RIVER THAMES

London
Plan 1

L

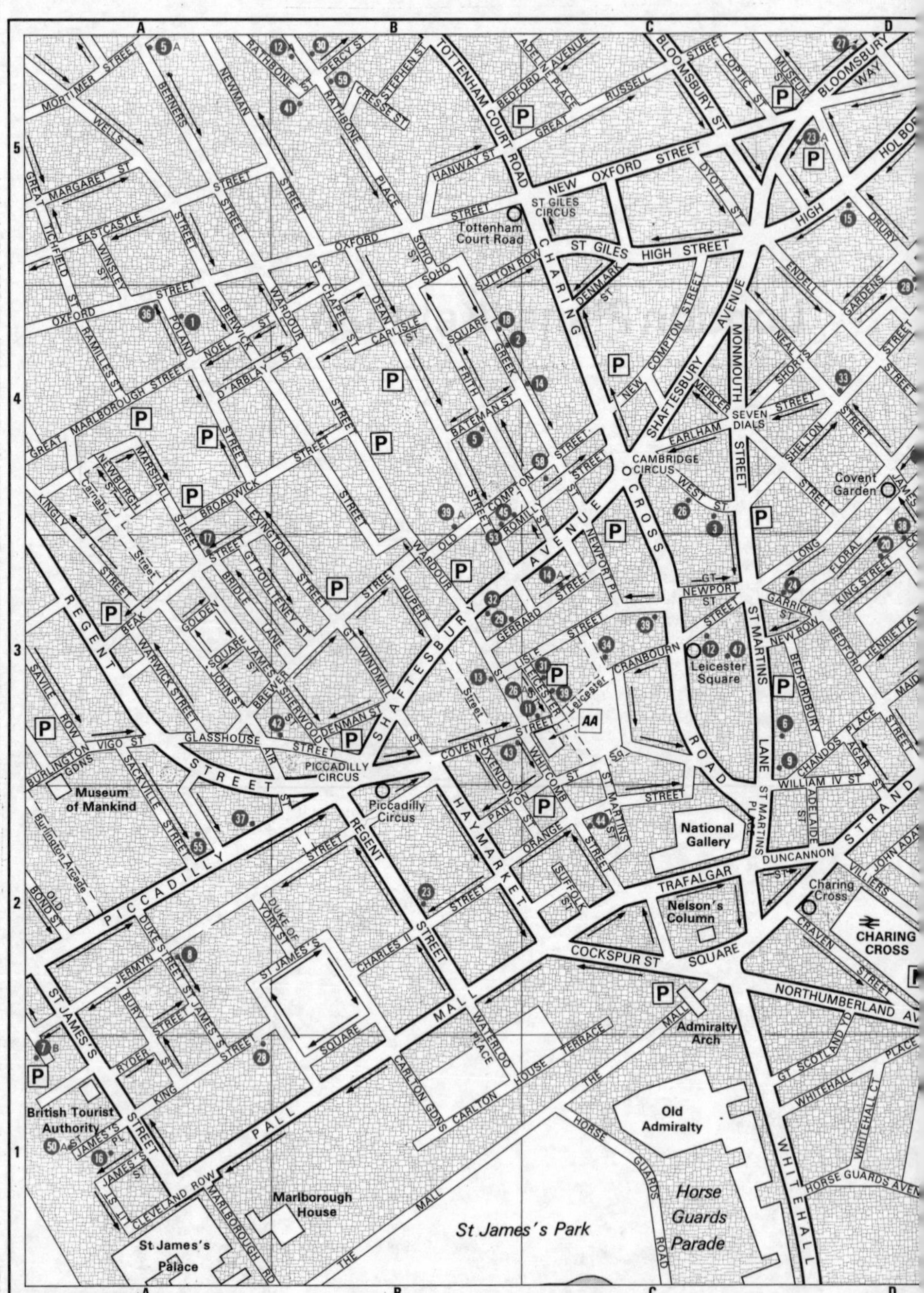

A
B
C
D
5
4
3
2
1
MORTIMER STREET
WELLS
BERNERS
NEWMAN
RATHBONE
PERCY ST
STEPHEN ST
CRESSE ST
RATHBONE PLACE
TOTTENHAM COURT ROAD
BEDFORD AVENUE
ADELINE PLACE
GREAT RUSSELL
BLOOMSBURY ST
COPTIC ST
MUSEUM ST
BLOOMSBURY WAY
HOLBORN
GREAT MARGARET ST
HANWAY ST
NEW OXFORD STREET
DYOTT ST
HIGH
DRURY
EASTCASTLE STREET
OXFORD STREET
ST GILES CIRCUS
Tottenham Court Road
ST GILES HIGH STREET
TICHFIELD ST
WINSLEY ST
SOHO ST
SOHO SQUARE
SUTTON ROW
CHARING CROSS ROAD
DENMARK ST
ENDELL
EARLHAM
GARDENS
POLAND
BERWICK
WARDOUR
GT CHAPEL ST
DEAN
CARLISLE ST
GREEK
FRITH
NEW COMPTON STREET
SHAFTESBURY AVENUE
MONMOUTH
NEAL ST
SHORTS
RAMILLIES ST
NOEL ST
D'ARBLAY ST
GREAT MARLBOROUGH STREET
BATEMAN ST
MERCER
SEVEN DIALS
EARLHAM STREET
SHELTON
KINGLY
NEWBURGH ST
MARSHALL STREET
BROADWICK
LEXINGTON
OLD COMPTON
ROMILLY ST
CAMBRIDGE CIRCUS
WEST ST
Covent Garden
JAMES
Carnaby Street
GT POULTENEY ST
BRIDLE LANE
NEWPORT PL
GT NEWPORT ST
LONG
FLORAL
KING STREET
GARRICK ST
REGENT
BEAK
GOLDEN SQUARE
JAMES ST
WARDOUR
RUPERT
GERRARD STREET
GT WINDMILL
LISLE ST
LEICESTER
Leicester Square
CRANBOURN
ST MARTINS LANE
NEW ROW
BEDFORDBURY
BEDFORD
HENRIETTA
SAVILE ROW
WARWICK STREET
JOHN ST
BREWER
SHERWOOD ST
DENMAN ST
AA
CHANDOS PLACE
AGAR
BURLINGTON GDNS
VIGO ST
GLASSHOUSE STREET
AIR
PICCADILLY CIRCUS
COVENTRY STREET
WHITCOMB
WILLIAM IV ST
ADELAIDE ST
STRAND
Museum of Mankind
SACKVILLE STREET
Piccadilly Circus
HAYMARKET
OXENDON
PANTON ST
ST MARTINS ST
National Gallery
ST MARTINS PLACE
Burlington Arcade
PICCADILLY
ORANGE
DUNCANNON
JOHN ADAM
VILLIERS
SUFFOLK ST
TRAFALGAR
Nelson's Column
Charing Cross
CHARING CROSS
CRAVEN STREET
OLD BOND ST
DUKE OF YORK ST
CHARLES II
COCKSPUR ST
SQUARE
NORTHUMBERLAND AV
JERMYN
DUKE STREET ST JAMES'S
ST JAMES'S SQUARE
BURY
ST JAMES'S
MALL
WATERLOO PLACE
Admiralty Arch
GT SCOTLAND YD
WHITEHALL PLACE
RYDER ST
KING STREET
CARLTON GDNS
CARLTON HOUSE TERRACE
THE MALL
WHITEHALL CT
British Tourist Authority
PALL
HORSE GUARDS ROAD
Old Admiralty
JAMES'S PL
CLEVELAND ROW
MARLBOROUGH RD
Marlborough House
Horse Guards Parade
HORSE GUARDS AVE
WHITEHALL
St James's Park
St James's Palace

London Plan
Plan 1

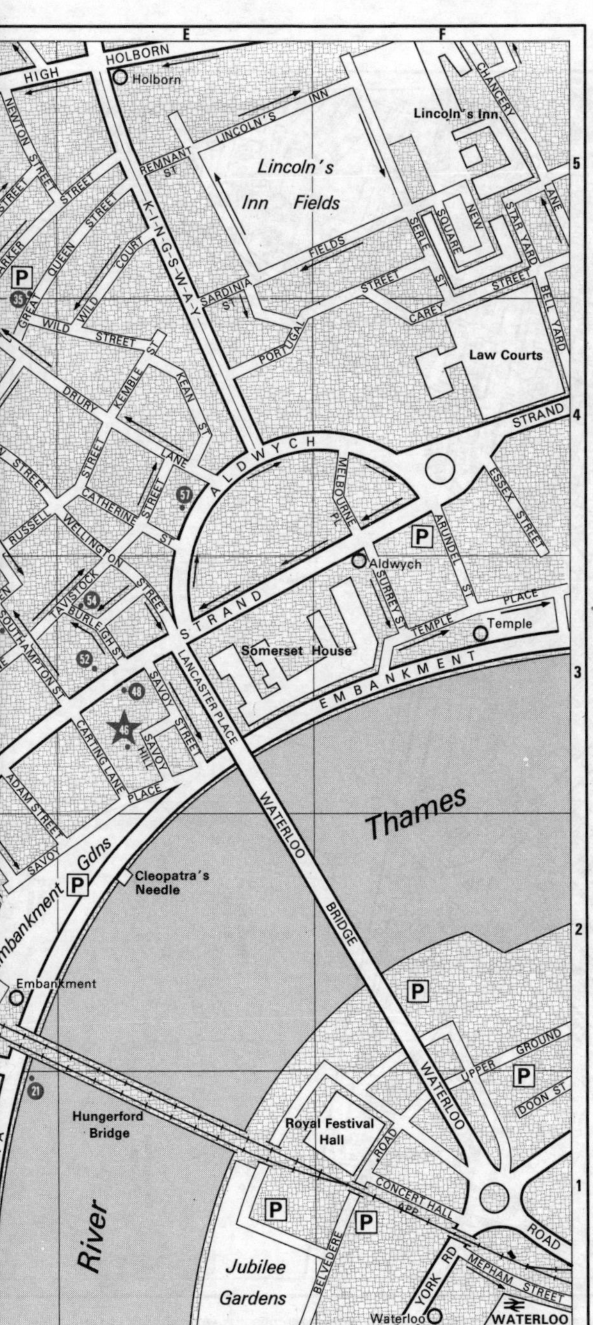

E
F
HOLBORN
HIGH
Holborn
NEWTON STREET
STREET
STREET
QUEEN
PARKER
GREAT
WILD
WILD
COURT
KINGSWAY
REMNANT ST
LINCOLN'S
INN
Lincoln's Inn
CHANCERY
Lincoln's
Inn Fields
FIELDS
SERLE
SQUARE
NEW
STAR YARD
LANE
SARDINIA ST
STREET
ST
CAREY
STREET
BELL YARD
PORTUGAL
Law Courts
STREET
DRURY
KEMBLE
ST
KEAN
ST
LANE
STREET
CATHERINE
STREET
RUSSELL
WELLINGTON
ST
STREET
ALDWYCH
MELBOURNE PL
STRAND
ESSEX
STREET
ARUNDEL
ST
Aldwych
SURREY ST
STRAND
PLACE
TEMPLE
Temple
TAVISTOCK
BURLEIGH ST
SOUTHAMPTON ST
Somerset House
EMBANKMENT
SAVOY
STREET
LANCASTER PLACE
CARTING LANE
SAVOY HILL
PLACE
ADAM STREET
SAVOY
Thames
WATERLOO
BRIDGE
Embankment Gdns
Cleopatra's Needle
Embankment
UPPER
GROUND
DOON ST
WATERLOO
Hungerford Bridge
Royal Festival Hall
ROAD
CONCERT HALL APP
ROAD
River
Jubilee
Gardens
BELVEDERE
YORK RD
MEPHAM STREET
Waterloo
WATERLOO
5
4
3
2
1

London Plan 1

1	Arirang (W1) ✕	A4
2	Au Jardin des Gourmets ✕✕	B4
3	Azami ✕	C4
4	Boulestin ❀✕✕✕	D3
5	Braganza ✕✕✕	B4
5A	Berners ★★★	A5
6	La Bussola ✕✕✕	D3
6A	Le Café des Amis du Vin ✕	D4
7	Café Royal (Grill Room) ✕✕✕✕✕	B3
7B	Le Caprice ✕✕	A1
8	Cavendish ★★★★	A2
9	Cellier de Medici ✕	D3
11	Chesa *(Swiss Centre)* ✕✕✕	C3
12	Chez Solange ✕✕	C3
12A	Chez Zorba ✕	B5
13	Chuen Cheng Ku ❀✕	B3
14	La Cucaracha ✕✕	C4
14A	Dragon Gate ✕	C3
15	Drury Lane Moat House ★★★	D5
16	Duke's ★★★★	A1
17	Gallery Rendezvous ✕✕	A3
18	Gay Hussar ❀✕✕	B4
20	Grange ✕✕✕	D3
21	PS Hispaniola ✕✕✕	D1
23	Hunting Lodge ✕✕✕✕	B2
23A	Il Passetto ✕	D5
24	Inigo Jones ❀✕✕✕✕	D3
25	Interlude de Tabaillau ❀✕✕	D4
26	Ivy ✕✕✕	C4
26A	Joy King Lau ✕	C3
27	Kingsley ★★★	D5
28	Lafayette ✕✕✕	A1
28A	Last Days of the Raj ✕	D5
29	Lee Ho Fook ✕	B3
30	Little Akropolis ✕	B5
31	Manzi's ✕	C3
32	Mayflower ✕	B3
33	Neal Street ✕✕✕	D4
34	New Rasa Sayang ✕	C3
35	L'Opera ✕✕✕	D5
36	Pavillion ✕	A4
37	Piccadilly ★★★★	A2
38	Poon's (King St) ❀✕✕	D3
39	Poon's (Leicester St) ❀✕	C3
39A	Raj of India ✕	B4
41	Rathbone ☆☆☆	B5
42	Regent Palace ★★	B3
43	Royal Angus ★★	B3
44	Royal Horseguards Thistle ★★★	D1
44A	Royal Trafalgar Thistle ★★★	C2
45	Rules ✕✕✕	D3
46	Savoy ★★★★★	E3
	Savoy Hotel Grill ✕✕✕✕✕	
47	Sheekey's ✕	C3
48	Simpson's ✕✕✕✕	E3
49	Soho Rendezvous ✕	B4
50A	Stafford ★★★★	A1
52	Strand Palace ★★★	E3
53	Terrazza ✕✕✕	B4
54	Thomas de Quincey's ✕✕	E3
57	Waldorf ★★★★	E4
58	Wheeler's ✕✕	C4
59	White Tower ✕✕✕	B5

To help you find details of establishments shown on this map first consult the Alphabetical List of London Hotels and Restaurants on pages 380–382.

London
Plan 2

London Plan 2

2	Al Ben Accolto ✕	C2
5	Ark ✕	A3
7	L'Artiste Affamé ✕	A1
8	Athenaeum ★★★★	E4
10	Bali ✕✕	C6
11	Barkston ★★★	A2
12	Basil Street ★★★	D3
13	Berkeley ★★★★★	D4
14	Bewick's ✕✕	C2
15	Britannia ★★★★	E5
16	Brasserie St Quentin ✕✕	C3
17	Bryanston Court ★★	D6
18	Capital ✿ ★★★★	D3
21	Central Park ☆☆☆	A5
22	Chanterelle ✕	B2
23	Chelsea Rendezvous ✕✕	C2
24	Chesterfield ★★★	E5
26	Churchill ★★★★★	D6
26A	Ciboure ✕	E3
27	Claridge's ★★★★★	E6
28	Clifton-Ford ★★★	E6
29	Coburg ★★★	A5
30	Connaught ✿✿ ★★★★★	E5
32	La Croisette ✕	A1
33	Cumberland ★★★★	D6
33A	Dan's ✕	C1
34	Daphne's ✿ ✕✕	C2
36	Don Luigi's ✕	D2
37	Dorchester ✿✿ ★★★★★	E5
39	Eatons ✕	E2
40	Ebury Court ★	E3
42	Elizabetta ★★★	A2
42A	Embassy ☆☆☆	B3
42B	English Garden ✕✕	D2
43	English House ✿ ✕✕	D2
44	Europa ★★★★	E6
44A	Forum Hotel London ☆☆☆☆	A2
45	Le Français ✕✕	B1
46	La Fringale ✕	A1
48	Ganges ✕	B6
49A	Le Gavroche ✿✿✿ ✕✕✕✕	E5
49B	Gavvers ✕✕	E2
52	Gloucester ★★★★	A2
53	Golden Duck ✕	A1
54	Gondolière ✕	A3
55A	Greenhouse ✕✕✕	E5
57	Grosvenor House ★★★★★ Ninety Park Lane ✕✕✕✕✕	E5
58	Hilton International ★★★★★ Hilton Hotel (Trader Vic's) ✕✕✕✕	E4
58A	Hogarth ☆☆☆	A2
59	Holiday Inn (W1) ☆☆☆☆	C6
60	Holiday Inn Chelsea ☆☆☆☆	D3
61	Hungry Horse ✕	B1
61A	Hyatt Carlton Tower ✿ ★★★★	D3
62	Hyde Park ★★★★★	D4
63	Içi Paris ✕✕	E6
64	Inn on the Park Hotel ★★★★★	E4
65	Inter-Continental ★★★★★	E4
66	Kalamaras ✕	A5
67	Kensington Palace Thistle ★★★★	A3
68	Kerzenstuberl ✕	E6
74	La Loggia ✕✕	D6
75	Hotel Lexham ★★	A2
76	London Embassy ☆☆☆☆	A5
78	London International ☆☆☆☆	A2
80	Lowndes Thistle ★★★	D3

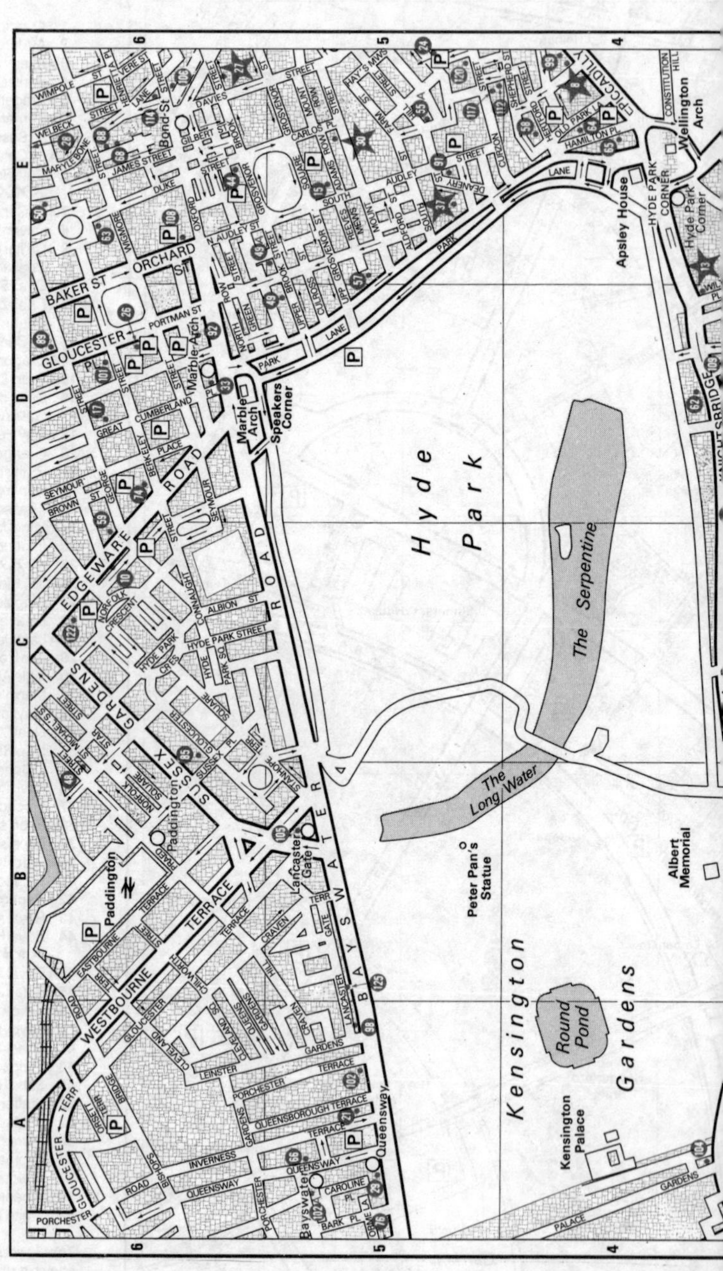

Hyde Park
The Serpentine
The Long Water
Kensington Gardens
Round Pond
Kensington Palace
Peter Pan's Statue
Albert Memorial
Apsley House
Hyde Park Corner
Wellington Arch
Marble Arch
Speakers Corner
Paddington
Lancaster Gate
Queensway
Bayswater
Bond St
Piccadilly
Park Lane
Bayswater Road
Edgeware Road
Westbourne Terrace
Sussex Gardens
Oxford Street
Baker St
Gloucester Pl
Orchard St
Portman St
Seymour St
Great Cumberland Place
Knightsbridge

To help you find details of establishments shown on this map first consult the Alphabetical List of London Hotels and Restaurants on pages 380–382.

London Plan
Plan 2

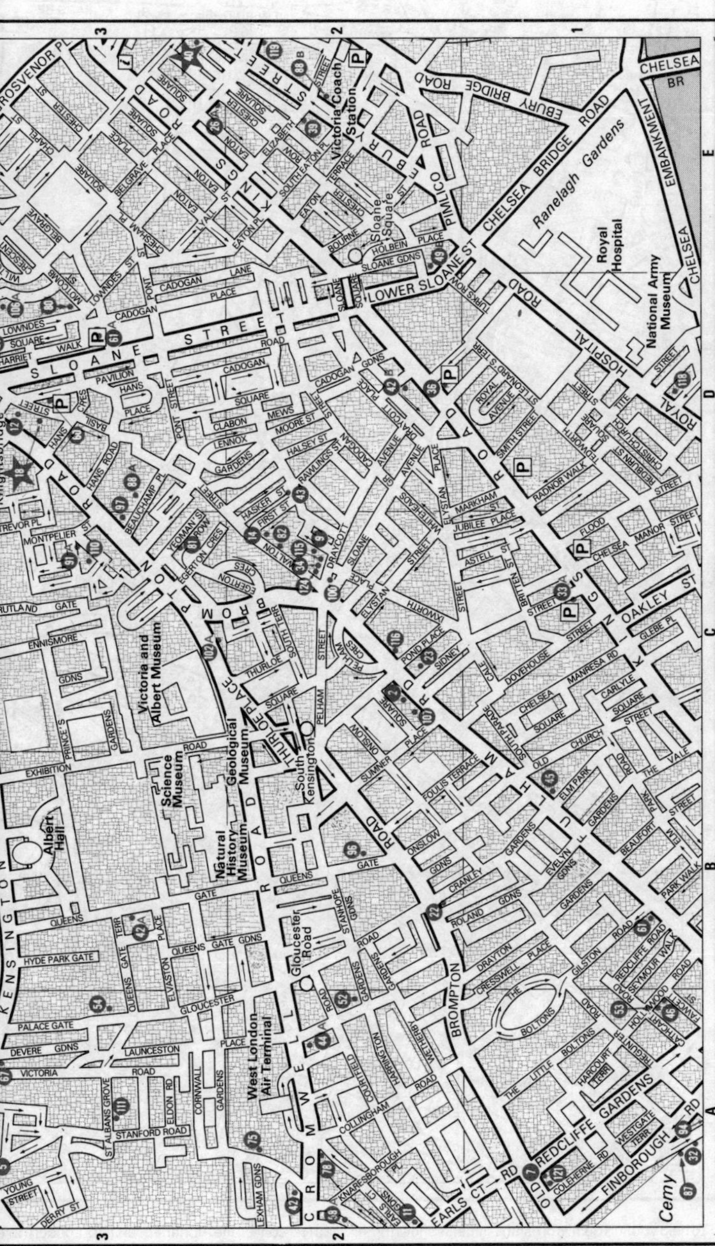

Victoria Coach Station
Sloane Square
Ranelagh Gardens
Royal Hospital
National Army Museum
Victoria and Albert Museum
Science Museum
Geological Museum
Natural History Museum
Albert Hall
South Kensington
Gloucester Road
West London Air Terminal
Knightsbridge
EBURY BRIDGE ROAD
CHELSEA BRIDGE ROAD
CHELSEA EMBANKMENT
LOWER SLOANE ST
SLOANE STREET
ROYAL HOSPITAL ROAD
KING'S ROAD
FULHAM ROAD
BROMPTON ROAD
CROMWELL ROAD
OLD BROMPTON ROAD
KENSINGTON GORE
EXHIBITION ROAD
QUEENS GATE
GLOUCESTER ROAD
REDCLIFFE GARDENS
FINBOROUGH RD
EARLS CT. RD
OAKLEY ST
Cemy

81	Luba's Bistro ✕	C3
82	Ma Cuisine ❀ ✕	C2
85	Le Mange Tout ✕	C6
87	Martins ✕✕	A1
88	Masako ✕✕✕	E6
88A	Ménage à Trois ✕✕	D3
88B	Mijanou ❀ ✕✕	E2
89	Mikado ✕✕	D6
91	Mr Kai of Mayfair ✕✕	E5
91A	Montpeliano ✕	C3
92	Mount Royal ★★★	D6
94	Nikita's ✕✕	A1
96	Onslow Court ★★★	B2
97	Parkes ❀ ✕✕✕	C3
98	Park Court ★★★	A5
99	Park Lane ★★★★	E4
100	Poissonnerie ✕	C2
101	Portman Inter-Continental ★★★★	A6
102	Hospitality Inn ☆☆☆	A5
102A	Rembrandt ★★★	C3
102B	Romantica Taverna ✕	A5
104	Royal Garden ★★★★★	A4
105	Royal Lancaster ★★★★	B5
106	Saga ✕	E6
106A	Salloos ❀ ✕✕	D3
107	San Frediano ✕✕	C2
108	Selfridge Thistle ★★★★	E6
109	Sheraton Park Tower ★★★★★	D4
110	Shezan ❀ ✕✕	C3
111	Siam ✕	A3
112	Snooty Fox ✕✕✕	E5
114	Stratford Court ★★★	E6
115	Le Suquet ✕	C2
116	Tandoori ✕✕	C2
117	Tandoori of Mayfair ✕✕✕	E5
118	Tante Claire ❀❀ ✕✕	D1
119	Tent ✕	E2
120	Tiberio ✕✕✕✕	E5
121	Tiger Lee ✕	A1
122	Trat-West ❀ ✕✕	C6
124	Waltons ❀ ✕✕✕✕	C2
125	White's ★★★	B5

London
—
Plan 3

London Plan 3

No.	Establishment	Grid
1	L'Amico ✕✕	C1
2	Aunties ✕	A6
4	Bedford Corner ★★	B6
6	Brown's ❀★★★★	A4
7	Bubb's ❀✕	E6
9	Gaylord (Abemarle St) ✕✕	A4
10	Gaylord (Mortimer St) ✕✕	A5
11	Geentanjli of Mayfair ✕✕	A4
11A	Green Park ★★	A3
12	Goring ★★★★	A2
13	Grand ★★	C6
15A	Ken Lo's Memories of China ❀✕✕	A1
15B	Kites Chinese ✕✕	C6
16	Kundan ✕✕✕	C1
17	Lal Qila ✕✕	A6
18	Langan's Brasserie ✕✕	A3
18A	Les Halles ✕	D6
20	May Fair ★★★★★	A4
23	Orient ✕	A6
24	Os Arcos ✕✕	A1
27	Regent Crest ☆☆☆☆	A6
28	Ritz ★★★★★	A3
29	Royal Westminster ☆☆☆☆	A1
30	RSJ's ✕	E3
30A	Rubens ★★★	A2
31	Hotel Russell ★★★★	C6
32	St Ermins ★★★	B2
33	St George's ★★★★	A5
35	South of the Border ✕	E3
36	Tate Gallery ✕✕	C1
38	Terazza-Est ✕✕	E5
39	Vendôme ✕✕	A4
39A	Verrey's ✕✕✕	A5
40	Washington ★★★	A3
41	Westbury ★★★★	A4
44	White House ☆☆☆☆	A6

6
5
4
A
B
C
D
E
BLACKFRIARS BR
Thames
River
WATERLOO BRIDGE
Cleopatra's Needle
FARRINGDON ROAD
Farringdon
FARRINGDON
NEW BRIDGE ST
Blackfriars
HOLBORN VIADUCT
Holborn Viad
CLERKENWELL ROAD
ROSEBERY AVE
Gray's Inn
GRAY'S INN ROAD
THEOBALD'S ROAD
Chancery Lane
HOLBORN
HIGH HOLBORN
Lincoln's Inn
Law Courts
FLEET STREET
Temple Church
The Temple
Temple
Aldwych
ALDWYCH
Somerset House
EMBANKMENT
KINGSWAY
Holborn
STRAND
SOUTHAMPTON ROW
Russell Sq
RUSSELL SQUARE
British Museum
BLOOMSBURY
NEW OXFORD ST
GREAT RUSSELL ST
Covent Garden
MONMOUTH ST
SHAFTESBURY AVENUE
ST MARTINS LA
Leicester Square
CHARING CROSS ROAD
National Gallery
Charing Cross
TRAFALGAR SQ
Nelson's Column
Tottenham Court Road
ST GILES
GOWER STREET
TOTTENHAM COURT ROAD
Goodge St
HAYMARKET
Piccadilly Circus
REGENT STREET
PICCADILLY
Museum of Mankind
Oxford Circus
OXFORD CIRCUS
REGENT ST
PORTLAND PL
EUSTON RD

To help you find details of establishments shown on this map first consult the Alphabetical List of London Hotel and Restaurants on pages 380–382.

London Plan
—
Plan 3

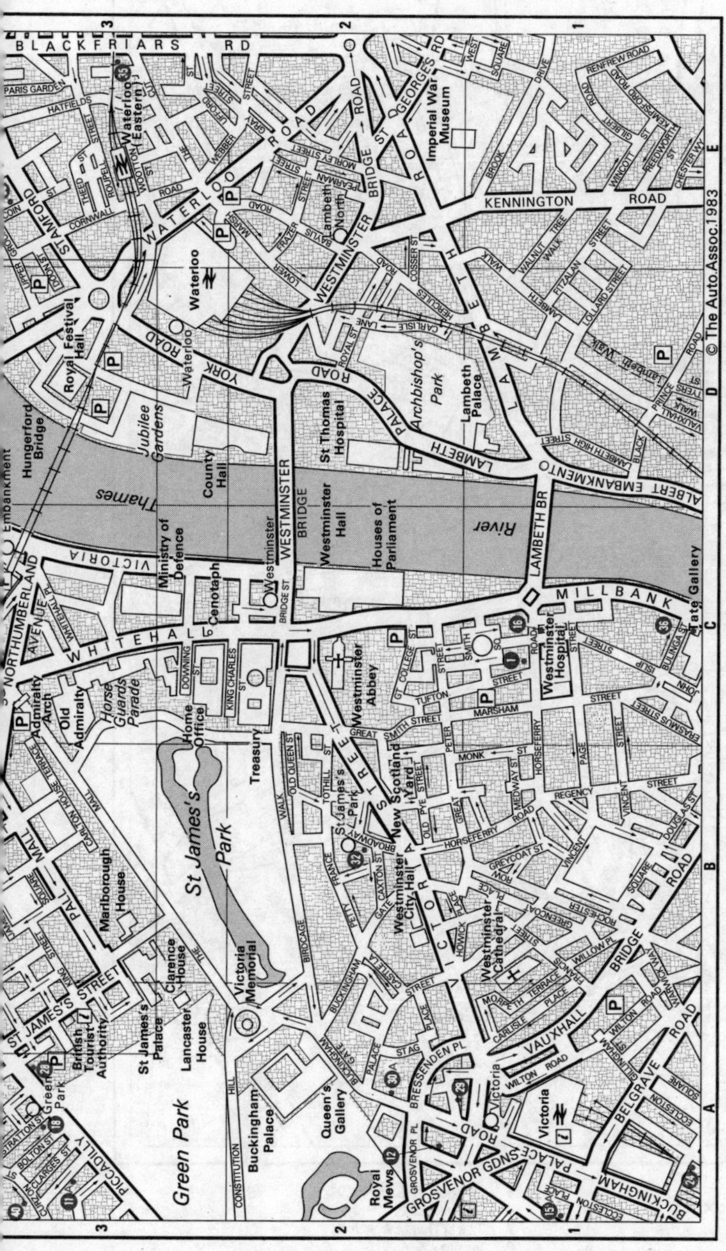

BLACKFRIARS RD
WATERLOO ROAD
Waterloo (Eastern)
Waterloo
Royal Festival Hall
Jubilee Gardens
Hungerford Bridge
Embankment
County Hall
River Thames
WESTMINSTER BRIDGE
Westminster Hall
Houses of Parliament
St Thomas Hospital
Lambeth Palace
Archbishop's Park
LAMBETH PALACE ROAD
LAMBETH BR
ALBERT EMBANKMENT
KENNINGTON ROAD
Imperial War Museum
Lambeth North
ST GEORGES RD
MILLBANK
Tate Gallery
Westminster Hospital
WHITEHALL
Ministry of Defence
Cenotaph
Westminster
NORTHUMBERLAND AVENUE
VICTORIA EMBANKMENT
Admiralty Arch
Old Admiralty
Horse Guards Parade
Home Office
Treasury
Westminster Abbey
New Scotland Yard
St James's Park
Westminster City Hall
Westminster Cathedral
VICTORIA STREET
VAUXHALL BRIDGE ROAD
BELGRAVE ROAD
Victoria
BUCKINGHAM PALACE ROAD
GROSVENOR GDNS
Royal Mews
Queen's Gallery
Buckingham Palace
Victoria Memorial
Green Park
CONSTITUTION HILL
Lancaster House
St James's Palace
Clarence House
Marlborough House
British Tourist Authority
ST JAMES'S STREET
PICCADILLY
PALL MALL
THE MALL
© The Auto. Assoc. 1983

L

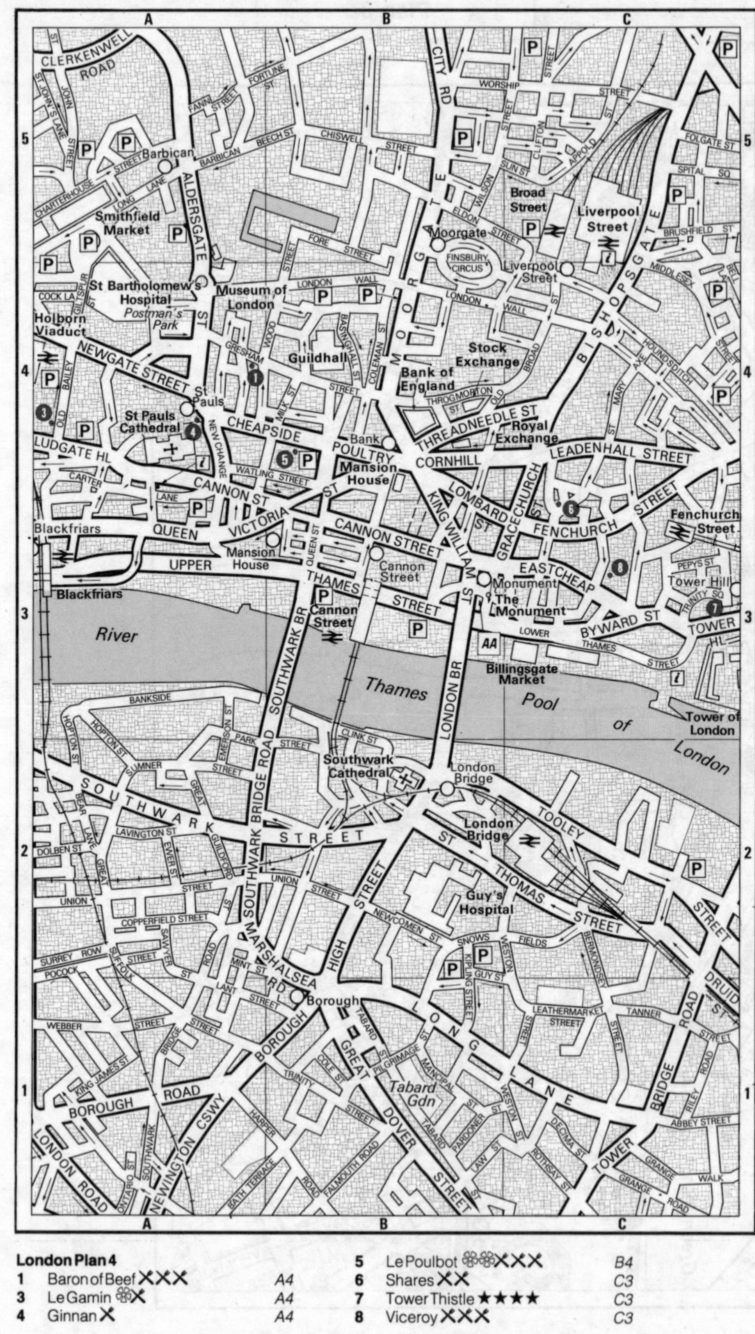

A
B
C
5
4
3
2
1
CLERKENWELL ROAD
ST JOHN'S LANE
ST JOHN STREET
CHARTERHOUSE STREET
LONG LANE
Barbican
BARBICAN
BEECH ST
CHISWELL STREET
FORTUNE ST
FANN ST
ALDERSGATE
Smithfield Market
St Bartholomew's Hospital
Postman's Park
Museum of London
COCK LA
GILTSPUR ST
Holborn Viaduct
NEWGATE STREET
OLD BAILEY
St Pauls
St Pauls Cathedral
NEW CHANGE
LUDGATE HL
CARTER LANE
CHEAPSIDE
WATLING STREET
CANNON ST
QUEEN VICTORIA ST
Blackfriars
UPPER THAMES STREET
Mansion House
QUEEN ST
GRESHAM
WOOD ST
MILK ST
Guildhall
BASINGHALL ST
COLEMAN ST
LONDON WALL
FORE STREET
MOORGATE
CITY RD
Moorgate
FINSBURY CIRCUS
ELDON ST
WILSON ST
SUN ST
CLIFTON ST
APPOLD ST
WORSHIP STREET
Broad Street
Liverpool Street
Liverpool Street
FOLGATE ST
SPITAL SQ
BRUSHFIELD ST
MIDDLESEX ST
BISHOPSGATE
HOUNDSDITCH
ST MARY AXE
BELL LANE
Stock Exchange
OLD BROAD ST
Bank of England
THROGMORTON ST
THREADNEEDLE ST
Royal Exchange
Bank
POULTRY
Mansion House
CORNHILL
LEADENHALL STREET
LOMBARD ST
GRACECHURCH ST
FENCHURCH STREET
Fenchurch Street
KING WILLIAM ST
CANNON STREET
Cannon Street
EASTCHEAP
PEPYS ST
Tower Hill
TRINITY SQ
Monument
The Monument
BYWARD ST
TOWER HL
LOWER THAMES STREET
Cannon Street
Blackfriars
River Thames
Pool of London
Billingsgate Market
Tower of London
SOUTHWARK BR
LONDON BR
BANKSIDE
HOPTON ST
EMERSON ST
PARK STREET
SUMNER ST
GREAT
CLINK ST
Southwark Cathedral
London Bridge
London Bridge
TOOLEY STREET
SOUTHWARK STREET
SOUTHWARK BRIDGE ROAD
BEAR LANE
GREAT
LAVINGTON ST
DOLBEN ST
EMERSON ST
GUILDFORD ST
UNION STREET
UNION
COPPERFIELD STREET
SAWYER ST
SURREY ROW
POCOCK
SUFFOLK ST
MARSHALSEA RD
MINT ST
LANT STREET
ST THOMAS STREET
Guy's Hospital
NEWCOMEN ST
SNOWS FIELDS
WESTON ST
KIPLING STREET
GUY ST
BERMONDSEY STREET
HIGH STREET
Borough
BOROUGH HIGH STREET
TABARD ST
LONG LANE
LEATHERMARKET STREET
TANNER
WEBBER
KING JAMES ST
BOROUGH ROAD
BRIDGE ST
TRINITY
COLE ST
GREAT DOVER STREET
PILGRIMAGE ST
MANCIPLE ST
Tabard Gdn
PARDONER ST
LAW ST
ROTHSAY ST
DECIMA ST
TOWER BRIDGE ROAD
RILEY ROAD
ABBEY STREET
GRANGE WALK
GRANGE ROAD
DRUID ST
LONDON ROAD
SOUTHWARK
ONTARIO ST
NEWINGTON CSWY
HARPER
BATH TERRACE
FALMOUTH ROAD

L

London Plan 4

1	Baron of Beef XXX	A4	5	Le Poulbot ✿✿XXX	B4
3	Le Gamin ✿X	A4	6	Shares XX	C3
4	Ginnan X	A4	7	Tower Thistle ★★★★	C3
			8	Viceroy XXX	C3

To help you find details of establishments shown on this map first consult the Alphabetical List of London Hotels and Restaurants on pages 380–382.

London — Plan 5

L

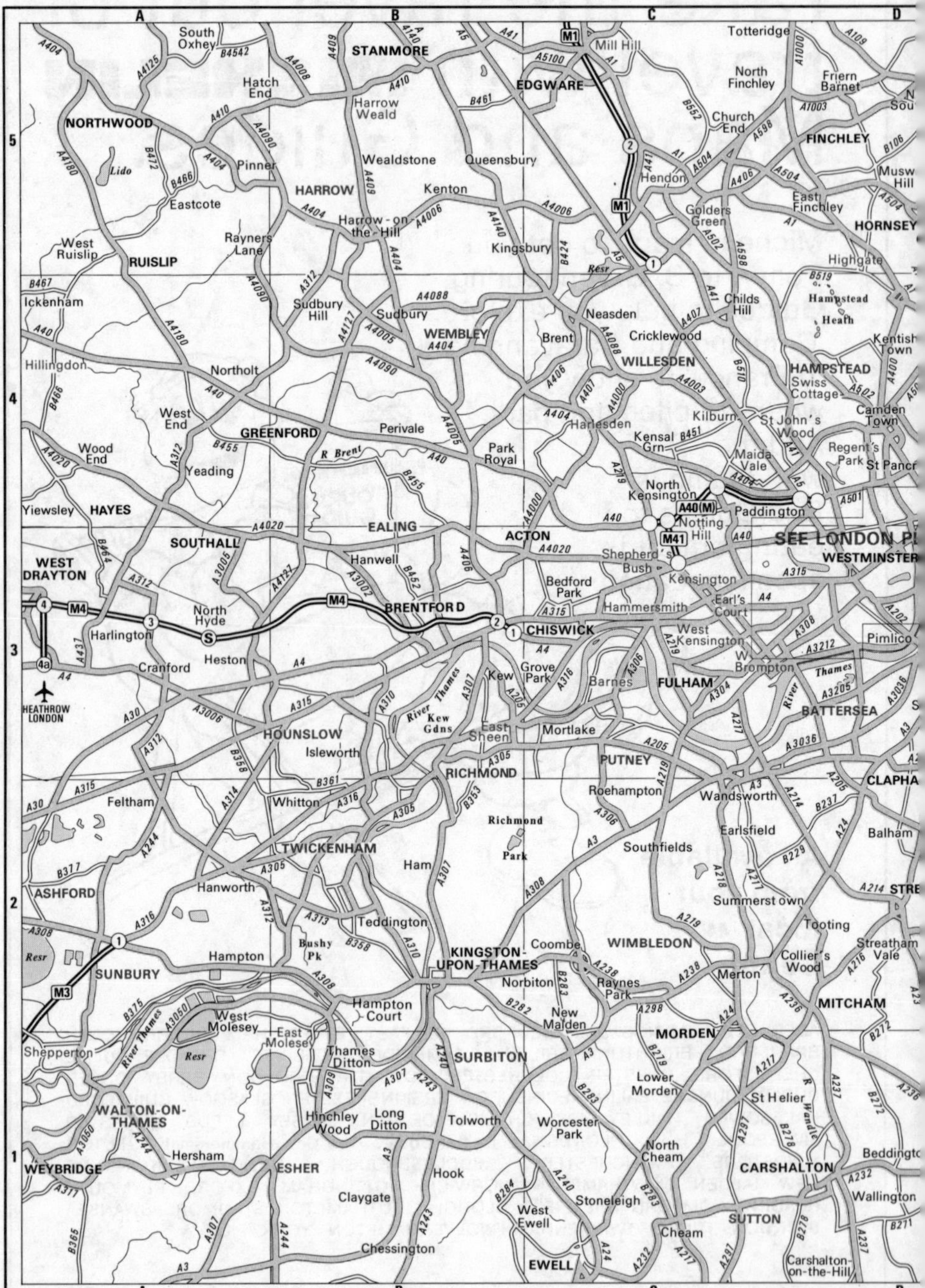

London
Plan 5

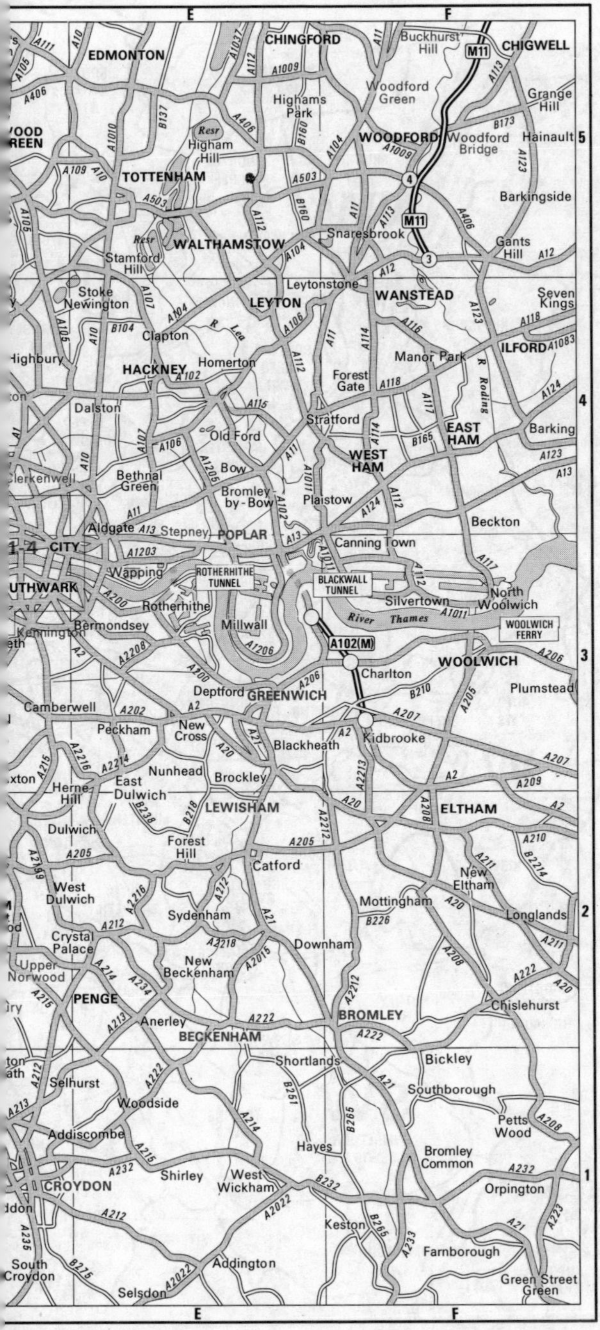

The placenames shown in **red** are locations of AA Hotels and Restaurants outside the Central London plan area (*Plans 1–4*). Some of these fall within the London Postal District area and can therefore be found in the gazetteer under London, in postal district order (*see London Postal District map on following page*). Others outside the London Postal District area can therefore be found under their respective placenames in the main gazetteer.

L

London Postal Districts and ways in and out of London

L

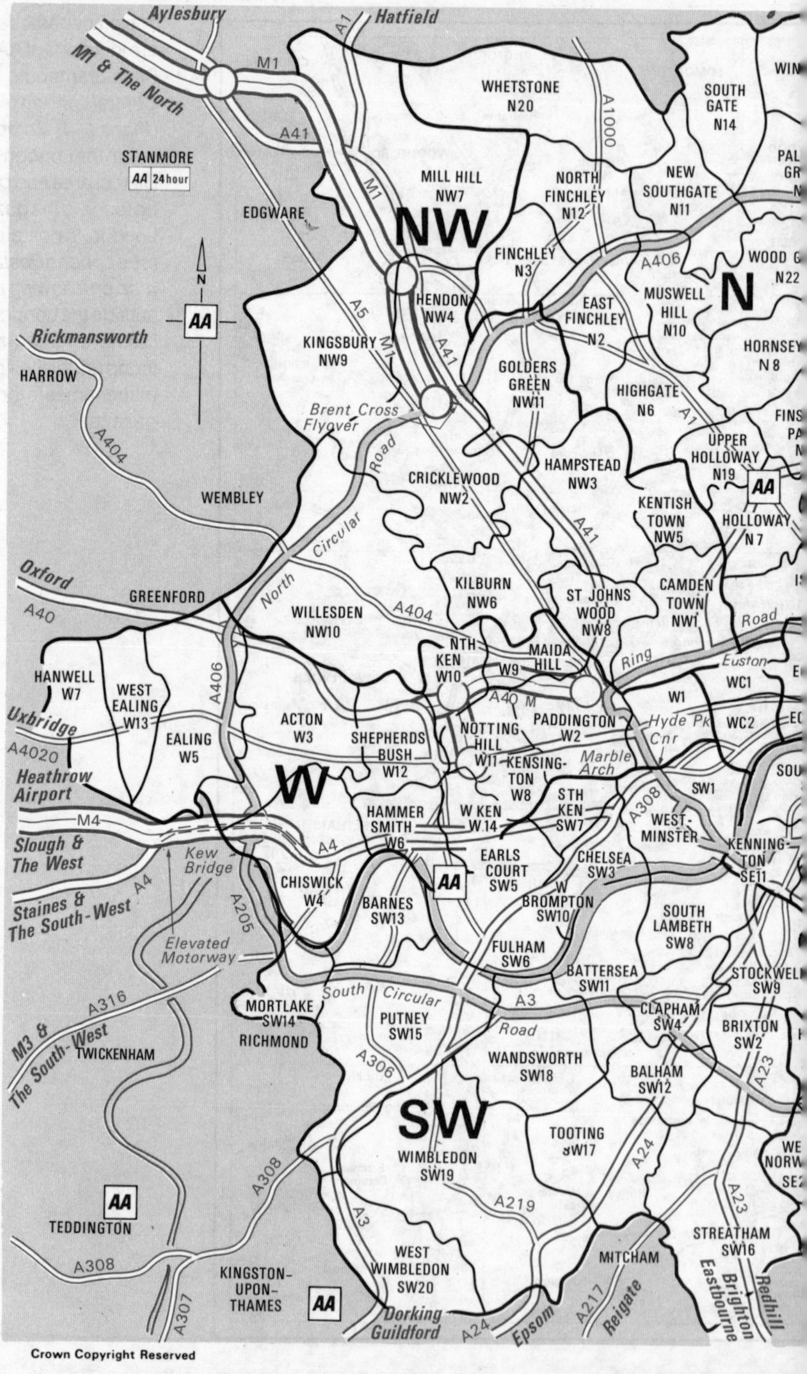

Crown Copyright Reserved

London Postal Area Boundary
London Postal District Boundaries
Main Roads into and out of London
Signposted North and South Circular
Roads & Ring Road
Other Main Roads
Service Centre AA
Scale of Miles
0 1 2 3 4
Cambridge
A10
LOWER EDMONTON N9
CHINGFORD E4
UPPER EDMONTON N18
Epping
Bishops Stortford
A104
M11
TOTTENHAM N17
WOODFORD E18
A406
Chelmsford
Southend
SOUTH TOTTENHAM N15
A503
WALTHAMSTOW E17
A12
GANTS HILL
A114
Romford
STOKE NEWINGTON N16
LEYTON E10
LEYTONSTONE E11
ILFORD
CLAPTON E5
E
FOREST GATE E7
MANOR PARK E12
HOMERTON E9
HACKNEY E8
A11
BARKING
A117
BETHNAL GREEN E2
BOW E3
STRATFORD E15
Tilbury
A13
PLAISTOW E13
EAST HAM E6
R THAMES
EC3
Road
STEPNEY E1
POPLAR E14
NORTH WOOLWICH E16
THAMESMEAD SE28
Ring
Free Ferry
ROTHERHITHE SE16
ABBEY WOOD SE2
DEPTFORD SE8
CHARLTON SE7
Rd
A205
A102 M
Erith
A206
GREEN WICH SE10
WOOLWICH SE18
A202
NEW CROSS SE14
A2
SE
PECKHAM SE15
BLACKHEATH SE3
WELLING
BROCKLEY SE4
A21
EAST DULWICH SE22
LEWISHAM SE13
A207
A20
South
ELTHAM SE9
FOREST HILL SE23
SE21
A205
LEE SE12
Rochester
Motorway
Dover
CATFORD SE6
SYDENHAM SE26
SIDCUP
ANERLEY SE20
E19
SOUTH NORWOOD SE25
BROMLEY
Sevenoaks
BECKENHAM
Sevenoaks
Hastings
A224
Maidstone
Folkestone

L

LONDON AIRPORTS
See under Gatwick, Heathrow

LONG EATON
Derbyshire
Map **8** SK43
See also Sandiacre

☆☆☆**Novotel Nottingham Derby**
Bostock Lane (S of M1 junc 25) ☎(06076) 60106 (Due to change to (0602) 720106 Telex no 377585
Large modern motor hotel close to Junction 25 on the M1.
112 CTV in all bedrooms
*sB £28.40 dB £33 (room only)
Lift 160P CFA (heated)
English & French Dinner £10–£14alc Last dinner mdnt
Credit cards 1 2 3 5

★★**Europa** 20 Derby Rd ☎(06076) 68481 (Due to change to (0602) 728481)
Three-storey Victorian building standing by the A6005 close to town centre.
18rm(5) CTV in 12 bedrooms *sB&B fr£12 sB&B fr£16 dB&B fr£20 dB&B fr£24
CTV 15P
*Tea fr50p Dinner fr£4.95 Wine £4.60 Last dinner 8.30pm
Credit cards 1 2 3 5

LONGFRAMLINGTON
Northumberland
Map **12** NU10

✕✕**Angler's Arms** Weldon Bridge (2m S off B6344) ☎(066570) 655
English & Portuguese 50 seats Lunch £2.50–£5&alc Tea £2–£3 High Tea fr£3 Dinner £5–£10alc
Credit cards 2 3

LONGHORSLEY
Northumberland
Map **12** NZ19

★★★★*BL* **Linden Hall** (Prestige)
☎Morpeth (0670) 56611 Telex no 538224
Luxurious, Georgian country house in 300 acres of parkland offering every comfort and charming friendly service.
45 2 CTV in all bedrooms Ⓡ
sB&B £35.65 dB&B £46.75–£52.50
Lift CTV 180P CFA
billiards sauna bath *xmas*
V Lunch £3–£11.50 Tea £2.25 Dinner £11.75alc Wine £4.95 Last dinner 9.30pm
S% Credit cards 1 2 3 4 5 **VS**

LONG MELFORD
Suffolk
Map **5** TL84

★★★**Bull** (Trusthouse Forte)
☎Sudbury (0787) 78494
Historical, timbered inn offering traditional hospitality.
27 (4fb) CTV in all bedrooms Ⓡ sB&B fr£39 dB&B £58
40P 4 *xmas*
Last dinner 10pm
Credit cards 1 2 3 4 5

★**Crown Inn** Hall St ☎Sudbury (0787) 77666
Situated in the main street of the village, the hotel has 15th-century walled gardens.
18rm(2) (1fb) Annexe: 3 CTV in 5 bedrooms Ⓡ sB&B £18 sB&B £22 dB&B £30 dB&B £36
10P *xmas*
V Lunch £5.50&alc Tea £1.25 Dinner £6.50&alc Wine £4.75 Last dinner 9.30pm
Credit cards 1 2 3 5 **VS**

LONGNOR
Staffordshire
Map **7** SK06

★***Crewe & Harpur*** ☎(029883) 205
Closed Xmas
An old, stone-built, coaching inn in this small Peak District village.
6rm
CTV 35P Live music and dancing Sat & Sun Cabaret Sat & Sun
V Last dinner 9.30pm

✕✕***Ye Old Cheshire Cheese*** High St ☎(029883) 218
Closed Mon Dinner not served Sun
English & Continental 70 seats Last dinner 9.30pm 60P bedrooms available
Credit cards 1 2 3 4 5

LONGRIDGE
Lancashire
Map **7** SD63

★★***Blackmoss Country House*** (2m NE off Chipping road) ☎(077478) 3148
11rm(2) Ⓡ
CTV 60P (heated) sauna bath
V Last dinner 10pm
Credit cards 1 2 5

✕**Corporation Arms** Lower Rd ☎(077478) 2644
Closed Xmas Day
V 50 seats Lunch £6alc Dinner £6alc Wine £4.50 Last dinner 9.30pm 80P
S% Credit cards 1 2

LONGTOWN
Cumbria
Map **11** NY36

★★***Graham Arms*** English St ☎(0228) 791213
Town centre hotel conveniently situated for fishing holidays.
15rm(2) CTV available in bedrooms Ⓡ
CTV 10P 4
V Last dinner 8.45pm

★*H* **March Bank Country House** Scotsdyke (3m N A7 Gaiashiels rd) ☎(0228) 791325
Friendly, family-run hotel providing good home cooking and standing well back from the road.
7rm (1 1) (1fb) sB&B £13–£14 dB&B £26–£28 dB&B £30–£32
CTV 25P
V Lunch £3.50–£5.50&alc Tea £1.80 High Tea £3.50–£5.50&alc Dinner £10 Wine £3.75 Last dinner 7.30pm
S%

LOOE
Cornwall
Map **2** SX25

★★★*L* **Hannafore Point** Marine Dr, Hannafore (Exec Hotel/Best Western) ☎(05036) 3273
Closed Nov–15 Mar
Modern, well-appointed hotel, in superb situation with some of the best views of the coast.
39rm(37➡2⋒) (2fb) CTV in all bedrooms Ⓡ*sB&B➡⋒£19–£25 dB&B➡⋒£30–£45 B
33P 7⌂ ⩫(heated) xmas
English, French & Italian V Lunch £3–£5&alc Tea £1 High Tea £1.50&alc Dinner £8–£9&alc Wine £4 Last dinner 9.30pm
Credit cards 1 2 3 5

★★**Fieldhead** Portvan Rd, Hannafore ☎(05036) 2689 Closed 8 Nov–Feb
Family-run hotel overlooking Looe harbour and the coastline.
16rm(5➡) (5fb) CTV in all bedrooms Ⓡ sB&B£13–£20 dB&B£27–£37 dB&B➡£36–£42 B
☾ 12P 12⌂ ✽ ⩫(heated) nc5yrs
V Lunch £1.50alc Tea 55p High Tea £1.50alc Dinner £8alc Wine £4.20 Last dinner 8pm
Credit cards 1 2 3 5

★★*L* **Klymiarven** Barbican Hill ☎(05036) 2333
Closed Jan & Feb RS Dec
Georgian manor house set in wooded gardens with unique views of the harbour.
15rm(6➡2⋒) (2fb) CTV in all bedrooms Ⓡ*sB&B£15.50–£22.50 sB&B➡⋒£17.50–£26.50 dB&B£31–£45 dB&B➡⋒£35–£58
15P ✽ ⩫(heated)
English & French V *Bar lunch 65p–£3 Tea 60p–£1.25 Dinner £7 Wine £4.25 Last dinner 7.30pm

★★**Rock Towers** Hannafore Rd, Hannafore ☎(05036) 2140
Closed early Nov–mid Jan
Personally run hotel overlooking sea and having private foreshore.
27rm(8➡1⋒) (2fb) CTV in 9 bedrooms Ⓡ sB&B£10.80–£11.50 dB&B£21.60 dB&B➡⋒£31,44–£35.72 B
Lift CTV 14P 8⌂ xmas
English & French V *Lunch £4.50–£6&alc Dinner £6.25&alc Wine £4.30 Last dinner 9.30pm

★**Portbyhan** West Looe Quay ☎(05036) 2071
Small friendly holiday hotel situated by West Looe harbour.
43rm(12⋒) (8fb) sB&B£8.50–£11.50 sB&B⋒£9–£12 dB&B£17–£23 dB&B⋒£18–£24 B
Lift CTV billiards sauna bath xmas
V Lunch £3–£5 Tea 65p–£1 High Tea £1.50–£2.50 Dinner £4–£7 Wine £3 Last dinner 7.45pm

✕✕**Trelaske County Hotel** Polperro Rd, Trelaske (2m W on A387) ☎(05036) 2159
Lunch not served Mon–Sat
V 60 seats Lunch £5.45 Tea £1.50 Dinner £7.95&alc Wine £3.75 Last dinner 9.30pm
40P bedrooms available
Credit card 3

LOSSIEMOUTH
Grampian *Morayshire*
Map **15** NJ27

★★**Stotfield** ☎(034381) 2011
Closed mid Oct–mid Apr
50rm(14➡1⋒) (2fb) Ⓡ sB&B£13 sB&B➡⋒£17 dB&B£22.50 dB&B➡⋒£30 B
☾ CTV 12P 4⌂ billiards Live music and dancing 3 nights wkly
Scottish Lunch £2.75–£3.50 Dinner £4.95–£5.50 Wine £5.95 Last dinner 8pm
VS

L

LOSTWITHIEL
Cornwall
Map **2** SX15

★★**Carotel Motel** Hillside Gdns
☎Bodmin (0208) 872223
Small, comfortable motel conveniently situated on the A390 in the ancient town of Lostwithiel.
32rm(25⇛7⋒) (3fb) CTV in all bedrooms ®✻sB&B⇛⋒£20 dB&B⇛⋒£29 B
60P✿ Live music and dancing Sat *xmas*
♉☐✻Lunch £3.50–£6 Dinner £6&alc Wine £3
Credit cards 1 2 3 5 **VS**

★★**Royal Oak Inn** ☎Bodmin (0208) 872552
An inn dating from the 13th century supposedly once used by smugglers as an ale house.
6rm(2⋒) (2fb) CTV in all bedrooms ® sB&B£10.50–£11.50 sB&B⋒£14–£16 dB&B£18.80–£19.50 dB&B⋒£22–£24
20P
♉Lunch fr£2.25&alc Dinner fr£2.25&alc Wine £3.30 Last dinner 10pm
Credit cards 1 3

LOUGHBOROUGH
Leicestershire
Map **8** SK51

★★★**King's Head** High St (Embassy)
☎(0509) 214893
Town centre inn with a large modern extension, standing on the A6.
82rm(63⇛6⋒) (4fb) CTV in all bedrooms ®✶sB£22 sB⇛⋒£31 dB£31 dB⇛⋒£36 (room only) B
Lift ☾ CTV 80P CFA
V♉Lunch fr£6.50 Dinner fr£6.50 Wine £4.50 Last dinner 9.15pm
Credit cards 1 2 3 4 5

★★**Cedars** Cedar Rd ☎(0509) 214459
Closed 26, 27 & 28 Dec
A 200-year-old former manor house just off the A6, 1 mile south of the town centre.
37rm(26⇛11⋒) (3fb) CTV in all bedrooms ®✻sB&B⇛⋒£11.50–£19 dB&B⇛⋒£20–£30 B
50P✿ (heated)
V♉☐✻Lunch £4.25–£5.90 Tea 90p–£1.95 Dinner £5.35–£9.90 Wine £3.75 Last dinner 9pm
VS

★★**Great Central** Great Central Rd (Minotel) ☎(0509) 263405
Large Victorian hotel close to the old Great Central railway line.
16rm(4⇛8⋒) (1fb) CTV in all bedrooms ® sB&B£12.50–£16 sB&B⇛⋒£13.50–£20 dB&B£17–£21 dB&B⇛⋒£20–£25 B
20P3
English & Italian **V**♉Lunch fr£2 Dinner £4.50–£6.25 Wine £4.95 Last dinner 9pm
Credit cards 1 2 3

✕✕***Harlequin*** 11 Swan St ☎(0509) 215235
Ground and first floor restaurant in the town centre.
Closed Sun & 5–19 Jul
Lunch not served Sat
Italian 70 seats Last dinner 11pm
Credit cards 2 3 5

LOUTH
Lincolnshire
Map **8** TF38

★★**Priory** Eastgate ☎(0507) 602930
Magnificent, Gothic-style building set in its own impressive gardens, approximately ¼ mile from the town centre.
12rms(6⇛2⋒) (2fb) ®✶sB&B£14.38–£16.68 sB&B⇛⋒£18.40–£20.70 dB&B£26.45–£28.75 dB&B⇛⋒£28.75–£32.20
CTV 24P✿ (grass)
V Dinner fr£6.50&alc Wine £3.75 Last dinner 9pm
Credit cards 1 3

LOWER BEEDING
West Sussex
Map **4** TQ22

✕✕Cisswood House ☎(040376) 216
Excellent cuisine is offered in this very elegant country restaurant.
Closed Sun, Mon, 3 wks Etr & Public hols Lunch not served Sat
English & Continental 100 seats Lunch £8.50–£14alc Dinner £8.50–£14alc Wine £4.25 Last dinner 10pm 34P bedrooms available
Credit cards 1 2 3 5

LOWER SLAUGHTER
Gloucestershire
Map **4** SP12

★★★ *BL* **Manor** ☎Bourton-on-the-Water (0451) 20456
Interesting 17th-century house with lovely garden. Service is friendly and good; bedrooms are particularly comfortable.
11🛁 (3fb) 2⊠ CTV in all bedrooms ✻sB&B🛁£42 dB&B🛁£54 B
50P ✣ (heated) (grass) ¥ nc8yrs
English & French V Lunch £6.50–£7.50&alc Tea £2 Dinner £14alc Wine £4.50 Last dinner 9.30pm
Credit cards 1 2 3 5 **VS**

LOWESTOFT
Suffolk
Map **5** TM59

★★★**Victoria** Kirkley Cliff ☎(0502) 4433
Modernised Victorian hotel situated on the cliff top at the southern end of the town.
50rm(26🛁5🚿) (5fb) CTV in 49 bedrooms ® sB&B£27 sB&B🛁🚿£29.50 dB&B£39.50 dB&B🛁🚿£44 B
Lift ☾ CTV 70P ✣ (heated)
V Bar lunch £1.95–£5 Dinner £7.75&alc Last dinner 9pm
Credit cards 1 2 3 4 5

☆☆ ***Oulton Motel*** Bridge Rd, Oulton Broad (2m W A1114) (Minotel) ☎(0502) 2157
Motel situated above the Oulton Broad shopping centre and offering friendly and efficient service.
24🛁🚿 CTV in 7 bedrooms ® B
☾ CTV 30P
English & Continental Last dinner 10.30pm
Credit cards 1 2 3 5

LOWESWATER
Cumbria
Map **11** NY12

★***Grange*** ☎Lamplugh (094686) 211
RS Jan–Feb
Comfortable, 17th-century country hotel situated in its own grounds at the head of Loweswater.
8rm(1🛁3🚿) Annexe: 9rm(3🛁2🚿) ® B
CTV 20P 2 ✣
V Last dinner 8pm

LOWICK GREEN
Cumbria
Map **7** SD28

★**Farmers Arms** ☎Barrow-in-Furness (0229) 86376
A 14th-century inn, well furnished throughout and with good restaurant facilities.
12rm(1🛁) ® ✻sB&B£11.50 dB&B£23 dB&B🛁£24.50 B
CTV 100P ✣
Mainly grills ✻Lunch £3–£4.10 Dinner £7.50alc Wine £3.70 Last dinner 9.30pm
Credit cards 1 2 3

LOW ROW
North Yorkshire
Map **7** SD99

★***Punch Bowl*** ☎Richmond (0748) 86233
Closed Nov–Dec
Stone-built 17th-century inn facing south with views over Upper Swaledale.
16rm(4🛁)
CTV 22P ✣
English & French Last dinner 8.30pm
Credit cards 2 5 **VS**

LUDLOW
Shropshire
Map **7** SO57

★★★ *HB* **Feathers** Bull Ring ☎(0584) 5261 Telex no 35637
A beautifully restored hotel dating from 1603, containing some lovely panelled lounges with elaborate ceilings and fireplaces.
35🛁🚿 (3fb) 5⊠ CTV in all bedrooms ® sB&B🛁🚿£29–£33 dB&B🛁🚿£46–£52 B
☾ 40P CFA *xmas*
V Lunch £3.95–£5.95&alc Tea £2 Dinner £8.95–£11.95&alc Wine £4.35 Last dinner 9pm
Credit cards 1 2 3 4 5 **VS**
See advert on page 428

★★**Angel** Broad St ☎(0584) 2581
This hotel was frequented by Lord Nelson.
16rm(4🛁) (3fb) ✻sB&B£16 sB&B🛁£24 dB&B£27.50 dB&B🛁£35 B
CTV 25P 8
Lunch £6alc Dinner £6.50alc Last dinner 9pm

★★**Overton Grange** (1½m S of Ludlow off B4361) ☎(0584) 3500
17rm(4🛁2🚿) (2fb) CTV in all bedrooms ® ✻sB&B£14.50–£15.75 sB&B🛁🚿£19.50–£21 dB&B£28.50–£32 dB&B🛁🚿£37.50–£40 B
80P 2 ✣ *xmas*
English & French V ✻Lunch £6.75–£7.25&alc Tea 35p–45p High Tea £2–£2.75 Dinner £6.75–£7.50 Wine £4.85 Last dinner 9.30pm
Credit cards 1 2 3 5 **VS**

★**Cliff** Dinham ☎(0584) 2063
12rm (2fb) ® sB&B fr£10 dB&B fr£20
CTV 20P ✣
V Lunch £3.50–£6&alc Tea £1–£1.50 Dinner £3.50–£6 Wine £3 Last dinner 9.45pm
Credit cards 2 3

✕**Eagle House** Corve St ☎(0584) 2325
English & Spanish V 150 seats Lunch £2–£3.65&alc Tea 70p–£1.75&alc High Tea £1.50–£5&alc Dinner £5.75– →

L

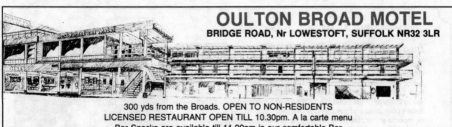

£8.45&alc Wine £3.30 Last dinner 10pm 24P

✕Penny Anthony 5 Church St ☎(0584) 3282

Closed Sun & 30 Apr–10 May

French **V** 50 seats Lunch £4.50–£9.50&alc Dinner £4.50–£9.50&alc Wine £3.70 Last dinner 10pm

Credit cards 2 5 **VS**

LUDWELL
Wiltshire
Map **3** SY92

★Grove House (Minotel) ☎Donhead (074 788) 365 Closed Dec

Hospitable small hotel with pleasant garden.

12rm(1 6) (1fb) CTV in 3 bedrooms ® sB&B£16–£17 dB&B£25–£26 dB&B £29–£30.50

CTV 12P ✽ nc5yrs

Lunch fr£5.50 Dinner £6.20–£6.75 Wine £3.95 Last dinner 7.30pm

Credit cards 1 3 **VS**

LULWORTH
Dorset
Map **3** SY88

★★Lulworth Cove ☎West Lulworth (092 941) 333

This hotel has an attractive terrace and gardens at the side, and some of the rooms overlook Lulworth Cove.

17rm(3 8) (2fb) TV in all bedrooms ® sB&B£10–£12 sB&B £15–£17 dB&B£23–£27 dB&B £23–£27

TV 10P Live music and dancing twice wkly *xmas*

V Lunch fr£3.33&alc Tea fr£1.30 High Tea 75p–£4 Dinner fr£5.25&alc Wine £3.75 Last dinner 10.15pm

Credit cards 1 2 3 4 5

★Bishop's Cottage ☎West Lulworth (092 941) 261 Closed Nov–Etr

Three adjoining stone cottages have been converted to form this hotel which nestles into the hillside on the edge of Lulworth Cove.

11rm(1) Annexe: 3rm(2) (3fb) ® sB&B£8.50–£9.50 dB&B£17–£19 dB&B £18–£20

CTV 6P ✽ (heated)

V Lunch £2.50–£7 Tea 45p–£1.50 High Tea £1.50–£3 Dinner £5–£10 Last dinner 8.30pm

S% Credit cards 1 3

LUMBY
North Yorkshire
Map **8** SE43

★★★Selby Fork (Southern junc A1/A63) (Anchor) ☎South Milford (0977) 682711 Telex no 557074

109rm(59 50) (16fb) CTV in all bedrooms ® ✻sB&B £33 dB&B £39

200P 40 CFA ✽ (heated) (hard) sauna bath Disco Sat *xmas*

✻Lunch £5.95–£6.50&alc Tea 45p Dinner £5.95–£7.50&alc Wine £4.50 Last dinner 10pm

Credit cards 1 2 3 5

LUNAN BAY
Tayside *Angus*
Map **15** NO65

★★Lunan Bay ☎Inverkeilor (02413) 265

Closed 1–3 Jan

11rm(9 2) (1fb) CTV in all bedrooms ® sB&B £25 dB&B £34

CTV 150P ✽

V Lunch £11.50alc High Tea £3.50–£4.25 Dinner £11.50alc Wine £5.80 Last dinner 9pm

Credit cards 1 2 3 5

LUSS
Strathclyde *Dunbartonshire*
Map **10** NS39

★★Colquhoun Arms ☎(043 686) 282 Telex no 727289

Village hotel by Loch Lomond.

23rm(1 4) (2fb) sB&B£12.50–£15 dB&B£22–£26 dB&B £27.50–£29

CTV 50P 3 ✽ *xmas*

L

▣Scottish & French V♕☕ Lunch £2.50–£4.50 Tea 60p–75p High Tea £3.50–£3.90 Dinner £5.50–£7.50&alc Wine £3.85 Last dinner 9.45pm

Credit cards 1 2 3 4 5

★★**Inverbeg Inn** Inverbeg (3m N on A82) (Inter-Hotel/ExecHotel) ☎(043 686) 678 Telex no 777205

Attractive roadside inn with modern shutters.

14rm(7➡) (1fb) CTV in 3 bedrooms sB&B£21.50 sB&B➡£27 dB&B£34 dB&B➡£40 Ƀ

☾ CTV 80P ✿ ♪ *xmas*

▣British & French V♕☕ Lunch 80p–£10 Tea £1 High Tea £3–£6 Dinner £6.50–£7.50&alc Wine £4.50 Last dinner 11.45pm

Credit cards 1 2 3 4 5 **VS**

LUSTLEIGH
Devon
Map **3** SX78

✕**Moorwood Cottage** ☎(06477) 341

Thatched cottage set in four acres of grounds.

Closed Mon & Xmas Day (Open Bank Holiday Mondays)

▣European V 28 seats Lunch £4alc Dinner £8.50alc Wine £4.25 Last dinner 9.15pm 12P

LUTON
Bedfordshire
Map **4** TL02

☆☆☆☆**Chiltern** Waller Av, Dunstable Rd (Crest) ☎(0582) 55911 Telex no 825048

Comfortable modern hotel with friendly restaurant.

99➡ CTV in all bedrooms ® *sB➡ fr£37 (room only) dB➡ fr£44 (room only) Ƀ

Lift ☾ ⊬ 190P CFA

▣International V♕☕ *Lunch £7.25&alc Tea 75p Dinner fr£8.75&alc Wine £4.55 Last dinner 10.15pm

Credit cards 1 2 3 4 5 **VS**

☆☆☆☆**Strathmore Thistle** Arndale Centre (Thistle) ☎(0582) 34199 Telex no 825763

Modern, comfortable hotel with well appointed restaurant, pleasant coffee shop and friendly service.

151➡⋒ CTV in all bedrooms ® ♜ *sB➡⋒ £39–£42 (room only) dB➡⋒ £46–£48 (room only) Ƀ

Lift ☾ # ⊬ 750⛟ CFA

▣European ☕ *Lunch £8.75&alc Dinner £8.75&alc Last dinner 10pm

Credit cards 1 2 3 4 5 **VS**

☆☆☆**Crest Hotel – Luton** Dunstable Rd (Crest) ☎(0582) 55955 Telex no 826283 Closed Xmas wk

Modern hotel with well-equipped bedrooms.

139➡ CTV in all bedrooms ® *sB➡ fr£33 (room only) dB➡ fr£39 (room only) Ƀ

Lift ☾ ⊬ 120P CFA

▣Mainly grills V♕ *Lunch £4.95–£6.95 Tea 55p Dinner £7.50–£8.50&alc Wine £6.45 Last dinner 9.45pm

Credit cards 1 2 3 4 5 **VS**

★★**Red Lion (Henekey)** Castle St (Trusthouse Forte) ☎(0582) 413881

Comfortable, welcoming hotel with steakhouse grill.

47rm(11➡1⋒) (5fb) CTV in all bedrooms ® sB&B£26 sB&B➡⋒ £29.50 dB&B£36.50 dB&B➡⋒ £39 Ƀ

☾ 16P *xmas*

▣Mainly grills ♕☕ Last dinner 10.30pm

Credit cards 1 2 3 4 5

LUTTERWORTH
Leicestershire
Map **4** SP58

★★**Moorbarns** Watling St (2m W on A5) ☎(04555) 2237

Closed 26 Dec–5 Jan

There is modern accommodation in the annexe of this large hotel on the A5. →

L

Annexe: 11rm(6➡5⋔) CTV in all bedrooms Ⓡ ✱sB&B➡⋔£23 dB&B➡⋔£34–£38

40P ✽ (heated) Live music and dancing Sat nc14yrs

International Lunch fr£5.50&alc Tea fr£1.75 Dinner £6.50–£7.50 Wine £4.95 Last dinner 9.45pm

Credit cards 1 2 5

LYDDINGTON
Leicestershire
Map **4** SP89

★★*L* **Marquess of Exeter Inn** Main Rd ☎Uppingham (0572) 822477

This charming 17th-century rural village inn has an annexe with modern bedrooms.

Annexe: 9rm(5➡4⋔) (1fb) CTV in all bedrooms Ⓡ sB&B➡⋔£25 dB&B➡⋔£35

CTV 50P Live music and dancing mthly

V Lunch £4.50–£9.50&alc Tea £1.50–£2.50 Dinner £1.50–£7.50&alc Wine £4.50 Last dinner 9.30pm

Credit cards 1 2 3 5

LYDFORD
Devon
Map **2** SX58

★*H* **Lydford House** ☎(082 282) 347 Closed Xmas & Boxing Day

Standing in 1½ acres of grounds with views of Dartmoor.

11rm(4➡1⋔) (4fb) sB&B£11.25 sB&B➡⋔£12.75 dB&B£22.50 dB&B➡⋔£25.50 Ḃ

CTV 30P ✽ U nc5yrs

Bar lunch £3.50alc Dinner £6&alc Wine £3.40 Last dinner 8.30pm

S% Credit cards 1 2 5 **VS**

★**Manor Inn** Lydford Gorge (Minotel) ☎(082 282) 208
Closed Dec–Mar

Small holiday and touring hotel serving good food, close to the Gorge.

7rm(2➡2⋔) ✱sB&B£12.50–£14 sB&B➡⋔£14.50–£16 dB&B£25–£27 dB&B➡⋔£27–£29 Ḃ

CTV 20P ✽ nc10yrs

English & Continental V ✱Bar lunch £1–£3 Dinner £5–£6.50&alc Wine £3 Last dinner 9.30pm

Credit cards 1 3 5 **VS**

LYME REGIS
Dorset
Map **3** SY39
See also Uplyme

★★★**Alexandra** Pound St ☎(02974) 2010 Closed Dec & Jan

An 18th-century former residence of the Dowager Countess Poulett, with unrivalled views across the lawns to Lyme Bay.

26rm(11➡8⋔) (6fb) CTV in all bedrooms Ⓡ sB&B£12.50–£20 sB&B➡⋔£15.50–£21 dB&B£25–£44 dB&B➡⋔£31–£52 Ḃ

CTV 17P 1 ✽

V Lunch £4.25–£4.95&alc Tea 90p–£1 Dinner £6.95–£7.25&alc Wine £3.50 Last dinner 8.30pm

Credit cards 1 2 3 5 **VS**

★★★**High Cliff** Sidmouth Rd ☎(02974) 2300 Closed mid Dec–Mar

11rm(3➡3⋔) (1fb) TV available on request ✱sB&B£16.50–£25 sB&B➡⋔£20–£25 dB&B£25–£34 dB&B➡⋔£35–£44 Ḃ

CTV 25P 4 ✽ billiards

✱Tea 50p–60p High Tea fr£1 Dinner fr£6.90 Wine £3.75 Last dinner 8.30pm

Credit card 5

★★★*H* **Mariners** Silver St ☎(02974) 2753 Telex no 04606 (ICCG) Closed Nov–Feb

17th century coaching inn with pleasant atmosphere.

16rm(8➡4⋔) (2fb) CTV in 14 bedrooms sB&B£19 dB&B£38 dB&B➡⋔£38 Ḃ

CTV 22P

Lyme Regis

International Bar lunch 85p–£3 Tea 90p alc Dinner £10.50alc Wine £4.50 Last dinner 8.15pm

Credit cards 1 2 3 4 5

★★**Bay** Marine Pde (02974) 2059 Closed Dec–Feb

Gabled hotel with pleasant, attentive service and a sun terrace overlooking Lyme Bay and the Cobb.

25rm(5 2)(4fb) Ⓡ sB&B£13–£15 dB&B£26–£28 dB&B £30–£32 B

CTV 25

French V Bar lunch £1.50–£5 Dinner £7.50–£8.50 Wine £3.75 Last dinner 6pm

★★**Buena Vista** Pound St (Inter-Hotels) (02974) 2494 Closed 17 Dec–14 Feb RS Nov–Mar

Two-storey Regency house in its own grounds, overlooking the bay.

20rm(8)(2fb) TV in 9 bedrooms sB&B£16.20–£20.50 sB&B £17.80–£22 dB&B£30–£34.50 dB&B £32.40–£47.50 B

CTV 17P 2

Lunch fr£3.75 Tea fr55p Dinner £6.50–£8 Wine £3.80 Last dinner 8pm

Credit cards 1 2 3 5 **VS**

★★**Royal Lion** Broad St (02974) 2768

Fine panelling and oak beams still exist in this 16th-century coaching inn.

23rm(8 7)(4fb) 1 CTV in 15 bedrooms sB&B fr£14.60 sB&B fr£16.60 dB&B fr£29.20 dB&B fr£31.20

CTV 30P 2

V Bar lunch £1.50–£3 Dinner fr£8 Wine £3.50 Last dinner 9pm

Credit cards 1 3 **VS**

★★**St Michaels** Pound St (02974) 2503 Closed Oct–Etr

A basically Georgian hotel with modern additions.

15rm(5)(2fb) sB&B£17.25–£19 (incl dinner) dB&B£34.50–£38 (incl dinner) dB&B £36.50–£40 (incl dinner) B

CTV 10P

V Lunch fr£5 Dinner fr£6.50 Last dinner 8pm

Credit cards 1 2 5

★★**Three Cups** Broad St (Minotel) (02974) 2732

Situated on Lyme's main street, the rear gardens of this hotel have spectacular views across the Cobb.

21rm(6)(4fb) CTV in 8 bedrooms TV in 2 bedrooms Ⓡ sB&B£15.95 sB&B £17.95 dB&B£31.90 dB&B £35.90 B

CTV 22P

English & French Lunch £3.25&alc Dinner £8.50&alc Wine £4.45 Last dinner 9pm

Credit cards 1 2 3 5

★**Dorset** Silver St (02974) 2482

13rm(4)(3fb) sB&B£9–£12.50 sB&B £10.25–£13.75 dB&B£18–£25 dB&B £20.50–£27.50 B

CTV 14P

Bar lunch £2alc Dinner £4.95 Wine £3.89 Last dinner 7.30pm

Credit card 3

★**Stile House** Pound St (02974) 2052 Closed Nov–Jan

Comfortable Georgian hotel with personal attention from owners.

16rm (3fb) Ⓡ * sB&B£12.50–£14 dB&B£24.50–£28

CTV 16P

* Lunch £3.50 Tea 60p Dinner £7 Wine £4.80 Last dinner 7pm

Credit card 1

★**Tudor House** Church St (02974) 2472 Closed mid Oct–mid Mar

Historic Elizabethan hotel with comfortable accommodation. Bar contains old water well.

17rm(4)(9fb) sB&B£9–£13.50 sB&B £9.50–£14 dB&B£18–£27 dB&B £19–£28

→

CTV 12P

Tea 50p Dinner £5.50–£7.50 Last dinner 7.30pm

S% **VS**

XX Toni Ristorante Italiano 14–15 Monmouth Rd (02974) 2079

Closed Sun & Mon, & Oct–Etr Lunch not served

Italian 30 seats *Dinner £9alc Wine £4.25 Last dinner 9pm

Credit cards 2 3 5

LYMINGTON
Hampshire
Map **4** SZ39

★★★ *HL* Passford House Mount Pleasant (2m NW on Sway rd) (0590) 682398

Comfortable country house in large grounds with many modern facilities.

51 1 CTV in all bedrooms ® *sB&B £27 dB&B £42–£54

CTV 80P 2 CFA (heated) (hard) sauna bath *xmas*

English & French V *Lunch fr£6&alc Tea 75p &alc Dinner £9&alc Wine £5 Last dinner 8.30pm

Credit card 2

★★ *B* Stanwell House (0590) 77123

An attractive hotel with tastefully furnished bedrooms.

21rm (14 2) (2fb) CTV in all bedrooms sB&B £16–£18 sB&B £24–£26 dB&B £32–£34 dB&B £36–£39

English & French Lunch £5.45–£6 Dinner £8–£9 Wine £4.50 Last dinner 9.30pm

S% Credit cards 1 2 3 5

X Fagin's 135 High St (0590) 73074

Simple bistro style restaurant with interesting home-made cuisine.

Closed Wed & Tue in winter Lunch not served

French 42 seats Dinner £8.75alc Wine £3.70 Last dinner 10.30pm

Credit cards 1 3

X Limpets 9 Gosport St (0590) 75595

Bistro style restaurant with pine decor.

Closed Sun & Mon in winter, Nov, 25 & 26 Dec Lunch not served

Continental 45 seats Dinner £10alc Wine £4.60 Last dinner 10.30pm

Credit cards 1 2

LYMM
Cheshire
Map **7** SJ68

★★ Lymm Whitbarrow Rd (Greenall Whitley) (092575) 2233 Telex no 629462

24rm (7 17) Annexe: 26 CTV in all bedrooms ® sB&B £30.80–£31.80 dB&B £41.80–£42.80

120P CFA

English & French V Lunch £5.50–£8.75&alc Tea 60p Dinner £7–£8.75&alc Wine £5.15 Last dinner 10pm

S% Credit cards 1 2 3 5

LYMPSHAM
Avon
Map **3** ST35

★★ *HL* Batch Farm Country Edingworth (093472) 371 Closed Nov–Etr RS Oct

Small family run hotel, also a working farm.

10rm (2) (4fb) *sB&B £13.22–£13.70 dB&B £21.85–£23.85 dB&B £23.30–£27.30

CTV 40P billiards nc4yrs

*Bar lunch £1.50–£3 Dinner £4.50–£6.50&alc Wine £3.90 Last dinner 8pm

Credit cards 1 3

LYNDHURST
Hampshire
Map **4** SU30

★★★ Crown High St (Anchor) (042 128) 2722 Telex no 858875

L

Gothic style hotel with mullioned windows. Services are traditional with some modern facilities.

42➡⋒(3fb) 1⊟CTV in all bedrooms Ⓡ ✗
✻sB&B➡⋒£28.50 dB&B➡⋒£38 Ꞵ
Lift ☾ CTV 50P 8🚗 CFA *xmas*
⊟English & French V☆☐✻Lunch £6.50&alc Tea fr50p Dinner £6.50&alc Wine £4.50 Last dinner 9.30pm
Credit cards ① ② ③ ④ ⑤

★★★**Lyndhurst Park** High St (Forest Dale) ☎(042 128) 2823 Telex no 477802
Large hotel with a modern extension and attractive garden.
64rm(59➡) 4⊟CTV in all bedrooms Ⓡ sB&B➡⋒ fr£25 dB&B➡⋒ fr£34
Lift ☾ 150P CFA ✽ ≋(heated) ⚲(hard) Live music and dancing Sat ⌂ *xmas*
V☆Lunch £2.75–£6.25 Dinner £6.95–£9.25 Wine £4.35 Last dinner 10pm
Credit cards ① ② ③ ⑤ **VS**

★★★ ♛ ***L* Parkhill House** ☎(042 128) 2944 Closed 1 wk Jan
Elegant, finely furnished Georgian mansion in extensive grounds.
16rm(14➡2⋒) Annexe: 6➡(3fb) CTV in all bedrooms Ⓡ ✻sB&B➡⋒£20–£30 dB&B➡⋒£40–£50 Ꞵ
40P 3🚗 ✽ ≋(heated) ♩ *xmas*
☆✻Lunch £5.7&alc Dinner £9.25&alc Wine £5.25 Last dinner 9pm
Credit cards ① ② ③ ④ ⑤ **VS**

★★**Evergreens** Romsey Rd ☎(042 128) 2175
Small holiday hotel with attractive garden. Vegetable garden supplies kitchen.
18rm(1➡7⋒)(2fb) CTV available in bedrooms Ⓡ ✻sB&B£14 dB&B£28 dB&B➡⋒£32 Ꞵ
CTV 32P ✽ ≋(heated) *xmas*
V☆☐✻Lunch £5.50alc Tea 65p&alc High Tea £5.50alc Dinner £6.50&alc Wine £4.50 Last dinner 9.30pm

★★***Pikes Hill Forest Lodge*** Pikes Hill, Romsey Rd ☎(042 128) 3677
20rm(11➡4⋒) CTV in all bedrooms Ⓡ Ꞵ
CTV 45P ✽ ≋(heated)
⊟French V☆☐ Last dinner 9.30pm
Credit cards ① ③ ⑤ **VS**

★***H* Forest Point** Romsey Rd (A337) ☎(042 128) 2420
Closed Jan & Feb
Small, homely, family-run hotel sited on the edge of the town close to the New Forest.
10rm(1➡1⋒)(2fb) sB&B£10–£15 sB&B➡⋒£11.50–£16.50 dB&B£20–£30 dB&B➡⋒£23–£33 Continental breakfast Ꞵ
CTV 20P 3🚗 ✽ U *xmas* ♿
V☆☐Lunch £5.50–£8.50 Tea 50p–£1.50 High Tea £2–£5.50 Dinner £6–£18 Wine £4.75 Last dinner 9.30pm
Credit cards ① ② ③

LYNMOUTH
Devon
Map **3** SS74
See also Lynton

★★★**Tors** ☎Lynton (05985) 3236
Closed mid Nov–early Mar
Comfortable hotel in five acres of grounds, set on a hill above Lynmouth. There are fine views over the bay.
39rm(32➡) CTV available in bedrooms ✻sB&B£14–£15 sB&B➡£18.50–£19.50 dB&B£28–£30 dB&B➡£37–£42 Ꞵ
Lift CTV 28P CFA ✽ ≋(heated) ⌂
⊟English & French ☆☐✻Lunch £4.50&alc Tea 60p Dinner £7.50&alc Wine £4.25 Last dinner 9pm
Credit cards ① ② ③ ⑤

★★**Bath** Sea Front ☎Lynton (05985) 2238 Closed Dec–Feb RS Mar & Nov
Traditional, family-run hotel situated in the centre of the village.
24rm(12➡1⋒)(4fb) CTV available in bedrooms Ⓡ sB&B£9–£15 sB&B➡⋒£16–£17 dB&B£18–£30 dB&B➡⋒£32–£34 Ꞵ
CTV 13P 4🚗 ⌂
⊟English & French V☆☐Lunch £3.50&alc Tea 50p Dinner £7 Wine £4.20 Last dinner 8.30pm
S% Credit cards ① ② ③ ⑤ **VS**

★★ ♛ **Beacon** Countisbury Hill ☎Lynton (05985) 3268 Closed Dec & Jan
This small holiday hotel has magnificent views over Lynmouth.
7rm(2➡3⋒) TV in all bedrooms ✗ ✻sB&B£13.25 sB&B➡⋒£13.75 dB&B£23.50–£24.50 dB&B➡⋒£26.50–£28.50 Ꞵ
10P 🚗 ✽ nc12yrs
⊟English & Continental V☆☐✻Lunch £4.95&alc Dinner £6.75–£8&alc Wine £4.25 Last dinner 8pm

★**Rising Sun** The Harbour ☎Lynton (05985) 3223
Closed 13 Dec–12 Feb
Stone-built inn, set into the hill beside the harbour.
17rm(1⋒)(2fb) CTV in 9 bedrooms Ⓡ sB&B£11–£15 dB&B£22–£30 Ꞵ
CTV ⚑ ✽ ♩
Lunch £2–£7.50&alc Dinner £3.50–£10&alc Wine £3.95 Last dinner 9.30pm
S% Credit cards ① ③

★***Shelley's Cottage*** ☎Lynton (05985) 3219 Closed 6 Nov–6 Mar
The origin of this hotel's name is that Shelley wrote part of 'Queen Mab' here in 1812.
15rm Ꞵ
CTV ⚑ nc4yrs
V☆☐Last dinner 7pm
VS

LYNTON
Devon
Map **3** SS74
See also Lynmouth

★★★**Lynton Cottage** ☎(05985) 2342
Closed Nov–Feb
Touring hotel in a secluded position with fine views.
22rm(9➡5⋒)(4fb) sB&B£12.25–£13.55 sB&B➡⋒£14.75–£16 dB&B£24.50–£27.12 dB&B➡⋒£29.50–£32 Ꞵ
☾ CTV 26P ✽ ⌂
V☆☐✻Lunch £3.95&alc Tea £1.20 →

L

Dinner £6.95&alc Wine £3.75 Last dinner 8.30pm

Credit cards 1 3

★★*B* **Crown** Sinai Hill (Inter-Hotels) ☎(05985) 2253

A well-appointed inn, centrally situated and convenient for touring the Exmoor countryside and coastline.

16rm(15⇌1⋔)(6fb) 5⊟ CTV in 10 bedrooms ® sB&B⇌⋔£14.75–£16.25 dB&B⇌⋔£27.50–£30.50 B

CTV 20P

English & French V Bar lunch 50p–£1.75 Dinner £6.25–£6.75 Wine £3.25 Last dinner 8.15pm

Credit cards 1 3 5 **VS**

★★*HB* **Rockvale** ☎(05985) 2279 Closed Nov–Mar

Former Bristol merchant's holiday home, the hotel has been modernised and offers comfortable accommodation.

10rm(6⇌1⋔)(1fb) 1⊟ CTV in all bedrooms ® sB&B£10–£12 sB&B⇌⋔£11.50–£13 dB&B£20–£24 dB&B⇌⋔£23–£26 B

CTV 12P ✽

English & Continental Bar lunch £1.50–£3 Dinner £6.50 Wine £4 Last dinner 8pm

★★**Sandrock** Longmead ☎(05985) 3307 Closed Dec & Jan

Comfortable touring holiday hotel, close to the town centre.

10rm(4⇌1⋔)(3fb) ® sB&B£8–£10 sB&B⇌⋔£9–£11.50 dB&B£16–£20 dB&B⇌⋔£18–£23 B

CTV 9P

Bar lunch fr£1 Tea fr95p Dinner fr£6 Wine £3 Last dinner 8pm

Credit card 1 **VS**

Lynton

★*B* **Chough's Nest** North Walk ☎(05985) 3315 Closed mid Oct–19 Apr

Comfortable holiday hotel, situated high above the bay.

11rm(7⇌2⋔)(2fb) 2⊟ sB&B£9–£10 sB&B⇌⋔£10–£11 dB&B£18–£20 dB&B⇌⋔£20–£22 B

CTV ✽ nc2yrs

V Dinner £5–£6 Wine £4 Last dinner 8.30pm

VS

★*HL* **Combe Park** Hillsford Bridge ☎(05985) 2356 Closed mid Oct–Etr

Former hunting lodge set in six acres of woodland.

9rm(6⇌2⋔) ® * sB&B£13–£14 sB&B⇌⋔£13–£14 dB&B£26–£28 dB&B⇌⋔£26–£28

CTV 12P ✽ nc12yrs

Dinner £8.50 Wine £4.75 Last dinner 7.30pm

★**Conway** Castle Hill ☎(05985) 2291 Closed 7 Oct–6 Apr

Small, privately-run, holiday hotel situated in the town.

9rm(2⇌1⋔)(2fb) TV in 1 bedroom ® sB&B£8–£8.25 dB&B£16–£16.50 dB&B⇌⋔£18.50–£19 B

CTV

Bar lunch 75p Dinner £4.50 Wine £3.20 Last dinner 7.30pm

Credit cards 1 3

★**Neubia House** Lydiate Ln ☎(05985) 2309

Closed Dec & Jan (except Xmas)

Small, friendly, well-appointed hotel in a quiet situation.

13rm(10⇌3⋔)(3fb) sB&B⇌⋔£11.55–£12.60 dB&B⇌⋔£23.10–£25.20 B

CTV 14P *xmas*

French Bar lunch £1.50–£3.50&alc Dinner £7&alc Wine £3.20 Last dinner 7.30pm

VS

★*B* **Seawood** North Walk ☎(05985) 2272

Closed Nov–Feb

The high, secluded position of this hotel ensures fine views over the bay.

12rm(8⋔)(2fb) 5⊟ sB&B£8.50–£10.50 sB&B⋔£10.50–£13 dB&B£17–£21 dB&B⋔£21–£26 B

CTV 10P ✽

English, French & Italian Lunch £5.50 Tea 50p Dinner £6.50 Wine £4.25 Last dinner 7.30pm **VS**

LYONSHALL
Hereford & Worcester
Map **3** SO35

✕**Penrhos Court** ☎Kington (0544) 230720

Closed Jan Lunch not served

60 seats *Dinner £5–£13.50&alc Wine £4.50 Last dinner 9.30pm 30P

Credit cards 1 3

LYTHAM ST ANNES
Lancashire
Map **7** SD32

★★★★**Clifton Arms** West Beach, Lytham (Whitbread West Pennines) ☎(0253) 739898 Telex no 677463

49rm(43 4) (4fb) 1 CTV in all bedrooms ® sB&B£24 sB&B £28.60 dB&B£44 dB&B £38.50

Lift ☾ CTV 100P CFA *xmas*

V Lunch fr£5.50&alc Tea fr£1.65 Dinner fr£8.25&alc Wine £4.29 Last dinner 9.45pm

S% Credit cards 1 2 3 5

★★★*B* **Grand Crest** South Prom, St Annes (Crest) ☎(0253) 721288

Grand Edwardian building now modernised throughout, situated on the sea front.

40rm(38 2) CTV in all bedrooms ® *sB fr£29 (room only) dB fr£39 (room only)

Lift ☾ 150P CFA Live music and dancing Sat in winter Cabaret Sat in summer *xmas*

International **V** *Lunch £5.50&alc Tea 70p–£2.50 Dinner £8.25&alc

Credit cards 1 2 3 4 5 **VS**

★★**Chadwick** South Prom, St Annes ☎(0253) 720061

Large, family hotel in a seafront location.

70rm(62 8) (30fb) 2 CTV in all bedrooms sB&B £14.50–£16 dB&B £24–£26

☾ CTV 45P 1 CFA Live music and dancing wkly *xmas*

Lunch £3.80 Tea £1.50 Dinner £5.60 Wine £3.50 Last dinner 8pm

Credit cards 1 2 3 5 **VS**

★★**Fernlea** 15 South Prom, St Annes ☎(0253) 726726 Telex no 677150

93 (40fb) CTV in all bedrooms sB&B £17 dB&B £34

Lift ☾ CTV 60P CFA (heated) squash sauna bath *xmas*

Lunch £5.50 Tea £2 Dinner £6.50 Wine £3.50 Last dinner 8pm

Credit cards 1 2 3 5

★★**Hotel Glendower** North Prom, St Annes ☎(0253) 723241

Large, stone building overlooking the sea front.

68rm(65) (6fb) CTV in 6 bedrooms *sB&B £12–£14.50 dB&B £24–£29

☾ CTV 50P (heated) *xmas*

*Lunch fr£4 Tea fr50p Dinner fr£6 Wine £3.75 Last dinner 8pm

Credit cards 1 3 **VS**

★★**St Ives** 7 South Prom, St Annes ☎(0253) 720011

74rm(68) (44fb) CTV in all bedrooms sB&B fr£16.65 sB&B fr£17.65 dB&B fr£28.50 dB&B fr£29.50

☾ CTV 80P CFA (heated) sauna bath Disco wkly Live music and dancing 4 nights wkly Cabaret wkly *xmas*

English & French **V** Lunch fr£4.50 Tea 40p Dinner £5.85 Wine £4.20 Last dinner 10pm

Credit cards 1 2 3

★★**Savoy** 314 Clifton Drive North, St Annes ☎(0253) 728441

Modern, family-owned hotel with good furnishings throughout.

17rm(14) (3fb) 1 CTV in all bedrooms ® sB&B £11.50–£14.95 dB&B £23–£29.90

Lift CTV 6P Live music and dancing & Cabaret twice wkly in season *xmas*

V *Lunch £2.50–£4.95 Tea £1–£1.50 High Tea £2.50–£3.50 Dinner £4.95–£6.95&alc Wine £3.20 Last dinner 10.30pm

Credit cards 1 2 5

★**Carlton** 61 South Prom, St Annes ☎(0253) 721036 Closed Dec–Feb

Pleasant, family-run hotel overlooking the Promenade gardens.

22rm(3 3) (7fb) ® *sB&B£11.50 dB&B£23 dB&B £24–£25

CTV 12P

*Bar lunch £2alc Dinner £5 Wine £3.50 Last dinner 7.30pm

★**Lindum** 63–67 South Prom, St Annes ☎(0253) 721534

Conveniently situated sea-front hotel.

80rm(58 20) (29fb) CTV in all bedrooms ® sB&B£12.50–£13.50 sB&B £13–£14 dB&B£22–£25 dB&B £24–£26

Lift ☾ CTV 21P CFA sauna bath *xmas*

V Bar lunch 65p–£1.40 Tea 35p–50p Dinner £5.75–£6 Wine £3.30 Last dinner 7.30pm

S% Credit cards 1 2 3 **VS**

See advert on page 436

MACCLESFIELD
Cheshire
Map **7** SJ97
See also Bollington

✕**Da Topo Gigio** 15 Church St ☎(0625) 22231

Friendly, informal restaurant with an emphasis on colourful and tasty Italian dishes.

Closed Sun, Mon & Aug

English, French & Italian **V** 66 seats *Lunch £4.25–£8&alc Dinner £10alc Wine £3.95 Last dinner 10.30pm

Credit card 1

✕**Oliver's Bistro** 101 Chestergate ☎(0625) 32003

Lunch not served

French **V** 64 seats *Dinner £6.50 →

£8.50 Wine £4.25 Last dinner 10.15pm

S% Credit cards 1 3

MACDUFF
Grampian *Banffshire*
Map **15** NJ76

★★**Deveron House** 27 Union Rd (Inter-Hotels) ☎(0261) 32309

A compact and well modernised hotel situated by the harbour.

17rm(13⇛) (4fb) CTV in all bedrooms ® sB&B£17.50–£20 sB&B⇛£19.50–£22.50 dB&B£30–£33 dB&B⇛£35–£40 B

CTV 8P Disco Sat Live music and dancing Sat *xmas*

V Lunch £5–£6 High Tea £1.60–£3 Dinner £7.50–£8.50&alc Wine £4.50 Last dinner 9.30pm

Credit cards 1 2 3 5 **VS**

★★**Fife Arms** Shore St (Minotels) ☎(0261) 32408

Situated in the town centre overlooking the harbour.

13rm(3⇛3⋔) (2fb) ® sB&B£10–£12 sB&B⇛⋔£12.50–£16 dB&B£18–£22 dB&B⇛⋔£22–£26 B

CTV 12P 6 Disco twice wkly Live music and dancing wkly *xmas*

V ✻ Bar lunch £1.50–£3 Tea fr40p High Tea fr£2.95 Dinner £5.95–£7&alc Wine £4 Last dinner 10.30pm

Credit cards 1 3 **VS**

M

MACHYNLLETH
Powys
Map **6** SH70

★★**Wynnstay** Maengwyn St (Trusthouse Forte) ☎(0654) 2003

Former coaching inn situated in the centre of this market town.

31rm(10⇛1⋔) (2fb) CTV in all bedrooms ® sB&B£30.50 sB&B⇛⋔£33 dB&B£40.50 dB&B⇛⋔£46.50 B

42P

Last dinner 8.30pm

Credit cards 1 2 3 4 5

MADINGLEY
Cambridgeshire
Map **5** TL36

✕✕**Three Horseshoes** High St ☎(0954) 210221

Dinner not served Xmas Day

English & French **V** 38 seats Lunch £9.50alc Dinner £10.50alc Wine £5.50 Last dinner 9.30pm P

Credit cards 1 2 3 5

MAIDENCOMBE
Devon
See under Torquay

MAIDENHEAD
Berkshire
Map **4** SU88

☆☆☆☆**Crest** Manor Ln (Crest) ☎(0628) 23444 Telex no 847502

Attractively decorated and furnished hotel.

190⇛ CTV in all bedrooms ® ✻ sB⇛ fr£38 dB⇛ fr£46 (room only) B

Lift ☾ 300P CFA Cabaret Sat

International **V** ✻ Lunch £4.75–£7.80&alc Tea fr75p Dinner £6.50–£9.25&alc Last dinner 9.45pm

Credit cards 1 2 3 4 5 **VS**

★★★**Fredrick's** Shoppenhangers Rd ☎(0628) 35934

Well run, comfortable hotel and restaurant, featuring imaginative and evocative cooking.

10rm(3⇛6⋔) Annexe: 21⇛⋔ (1fb) CTV in all bedrooms sB&B⇛⋔£42.50 dB&B⇛⋔£50.50–£59.50

☾ 90P *xmas*

French **V** Lunch £14.50–£19.50&alc Dinner £19.50–£24.50&alc Wine £7.50 Last dinner 9.45pm

Credit cards 1 2 3 5

★★**Bear** High St (Anchor) ☎(0628) 25183 Telex no 858875

Centrally situated hotel with well equipped bedrooms.

12rm CTV in all bedrooms ® sB&B£28–£30 dB&B£38–£40 B

English & French **V** Lunch £6.40–£7.20&alc Tea £1.30–£2.50 Dinner £6.40–£7.20&alc Wine £4.80 Last dinner 9.30pm

Credit cards 1 2 3 4 5

✕✕***Franco's La Riva*** Raymead Rd ☎(0628) 33522

Closed Sun

Italian 45 seats 18P

Credit cards 1 2 3 5

✕***Chef Peking*** 74 King St ☎(0628) 32851

Popular Chinese restaurant with authentic cuisine.

Chinese 75 seats Last dinner 11pm

✕**Chez Michel et Valerie** Bridge Av ☎(0628) 22450

Closed Sun, Mon, 24 Dec–4 Jan & 1st 3wks Aug Lunch not served Sat

French 38 seats ✻ Lunch fr£7.90&alc Dinner fr£7.90&alc Last dinner 10.15pm

Credit cards 1 2 3 5

✕***Maidenhead Chinese*** 45–47 Queen St ☎(0628) 24545

Pekinese restaurant with attentive and friendly service.

Closed Sun & Xmas

Pekinese 80 seats Last dinner 11pm

Credit cards 2 5

MAIDSTONE
Kent
Map **5** TQ75

★★**Royal Star** High St (Embassy) ☎(0622) 55721 Closed Xmas

Commercial hotel with comfortable bedrooms and limited personal services.

33rm(8⇛6⋔) (2fb) CTV in all bedrooms ® sB&B£24.75 sB&B⇛⋔£33.75 dB&B£35 dB&B⇛⋔£40.50 B

☾ 20P 70

Mainly grills **V** Lunch fr£5 Dinner fr£5 Wine £4.80 Last dinner 10pm

Credit cards 1 2 3

✕✕**Running Horse** Sandling ☎(0622) 52975

Tudor-style roadhouse with a small restaurant.

Closed Sun

▣English & Continental 68 seats Lunch £9.50alc Dinner £9.50alc Wine £6.50 Last dinner 10pm 70P

S% Credit cards 1 2 3 5

At **Larkfield** (5m NW on A20)

☆☆☆**Larkfield** London Rd (Anchor) ☎West Malling (0732) 846858

52rm(48➡4⋔) 104P

MALDON
Essex
Map **5** TL80

★★**Blue Boar** Silver St (Trusthouse Forte) ☎(0621) 52681

An ancient inn, with pleasant well-equipped bedrooms and small public areas.

21➡ Annexe: 5➡ (3fb) CTV in all bedrooms ® sB&B➡£33 dB&B➡£49.50 ₿

43P *xmas*

♈▭ Last dinner 9.30pm

Credit cards 1 2 3 4 5

✕**Francine's** 1A High St ☎(0621) 56605

A very small restaurant with restricted surroundings, offering imaginative and skilful French cooking.

Closed Sun, Mon & 2wks Aug & 24–30 Dec Lunch not served

▣French 26 seats Dinner £8.50alc Wine £4.40 Last dinner 9.30pm 8P

Credit cards 1 3

MALHAM
North Yorkshire
Map **7** SD96

★**Buck Inn** (Minotels) ☎Airton (07293) 317

Imposing stone built inn in the centre of the village.

10rm(1➡) (4fb) TV in 1 bedroom ® sB&B£9–£14 dB&B£18–£28 dB&B➡£12–£31

CTV 50P *xmas*

V Bar lunch £1.50–£2.15 Dinner £4.50–£5.50&alc Wine £4 Last dinner 9pm

VS

MALLAIG
Highland *Inverness-shire*
Map **13** NM69

★★**Marine** ☎(0687) 2217

Close to the harbour and the railway station.

21rm(6➡) (2fb) ® sB&B£9.50–£12 sB&B➡£12–£14 dB&B£19–£23 dB&B➡£23–£27 ₿

⁄CTV 10P 🚌 Cabaret Thu

♈▭ Lunch £3alc Tea 50p–£1 Dinner £5.50–£7.50&alc Wine £3.70 Last dinner 8pm

Credit card 2 **VS**

★★**West Highland** ☎(0687) 2210

Closed Nov–Mar

Large stone building overlooking the fishing port and the islands of Rhum, Eigg and Skye.

26rm(10➡) (6fb) ® sB&B£13.50–£17 dB&B£23–£30 dB&B➡£26–£33 ₿

CTV 30P ✽

V♈▭ Lunch £4–£5 Tea fr60p Dinner fr£8 Wine £2.90 Last dinner 8.30pm

Credit cards 1 2 3 5 **VS**

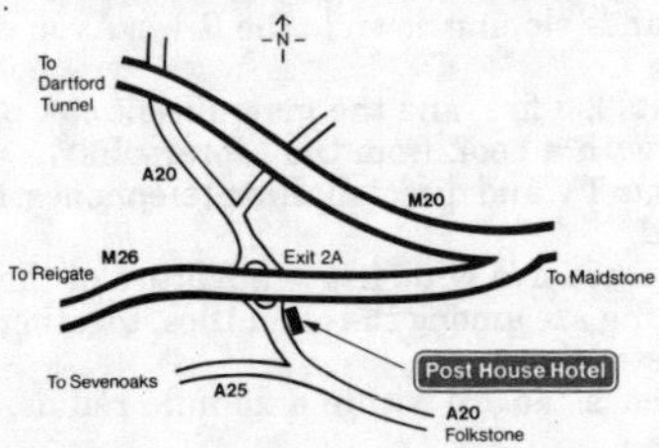

MALLWYD
Gwynedd
Map **6** SH81

★**Brigand's Inn** ☎Dinas Mawddwy (06504) 208

Closed Nov

15th-century coaching inn with good atmosphere. A popular fishing hotel.

13rm(3➡) (1fb) ® sB&B£9.95–£12.50 dB&B£19.90–£25 dB&B➡£23–£29 ₿

CTV 40P 2🏠 ✽ ♪ *xmas*

♈▭ Lunch £4.50alc Tea £1.25 Dinner £5.95–£7.50&alc Wine £3.60 Last dinner 9pm

Credit cards 1 3

MALMESBURY
Wiltshire
Map **3** ST98

★★★ ***H*** **Old Bell** Abbey Row ☎(06662) 2344 Closed 24–31 Dec RS Public Hols

Comfortable relaxing hotel with well appointed restaurant and attentive staff.

19rm(10⇌2⫛) CTV in all bedrooms sB&B£19–£20 sB&B⇌⫛£30–£32 dB&B£32–£34 dB&B⇌⫛£37–£44 B

25P 2⌂ ⍉ ✽

English & Continental ♈ ☐ Lunch £6.50–£7 Tea 70p Dinner £9–£9.50 Wine £4.30 Last dinner 9.30pm

Credit cards 1 2 3 5 **VS**

★★★ ***HL*** **Whatley Manor** Easton Grey ☎(06662) 2888

Finely restored country manor house with large comfortable rooms and charming courteous staff.

12⇌ Annexe: 3⇌ (2fb) CTV in all bedrooms ✠ sB&B⇌ fr£35 dB&B⇌ fr£42 B

☾ 60P ⍉ ✽ ≈ (heated) ♪ U nc7yrs *xmas* ♿

English & French ♈ ☐ Lunch £6–£7 Tea fr£1.50 Dinner £11.50–£14.50 Wine £4.60 Last dinner 9.30pm

Credit cards 1 2 3 5

★ **Kings Arms** 29 High St ☎(06662) 3383

Friendly modest hotel offering value for money.

6rm (2fb) CTV in all bedrooms Ⓡ sB&B£10–£11 dB&B£18–£20

20P ⍉

♈ ✻ Lunch £6.50alc Dinner £6.50alc Wine £4.20 Last dinner 9pm

S%

MALTON
North Yorkshire
Map **8** SE77

★★ ***Green Man*** Market Pl ☎(0653) 2662 Closed Xmas

25rm(15⇌⫛) B

CTV 3P 2⌂

♈ Last dinner 8.45pm

Credit card 2

★★ **Talbot** Yorkersgate (Trusthouse Forte) ☎(0653) 4031

24rm(7⇌) CTV in all bedrooms Ⓡ sB&B£30.50 sB&B⇌£35.50 dB&B£40.50 dB&B⇌£49.50 B

CTV 20P 10⌂ ✽ *xmas*

♈ ☐ Last dinner 9pm

Credit cards 1 2 3 4 5

★ **Wentworth Arms** Town St, Old Malton ☎(0653) 2618 Closed Xmas

Former 17th-century coaching inn.

7rm ✠ sB&B fr£10.50 dB&B fr£21

30P ⍉ nc6yrs

♈ ☐ Lunch £4.50alc Tea £1.50alc High Tea £5.50alc Dinner £6.50alc Wine £2.80 Last dinner 8.45pm

Credit card 3

MALVERN, GREAT
Hereford & Worcester
Map **3** SO74

★★★ **Abbey** Abbey Rd (DeVere) ☎(06845) 3325 Telex no 335008

Imposing, creeper-clad, Gothic-style mansion with a modern wing, catering mainly for a commercial clientele.

110rm(82⇌) CTV in all bedrooms Ⓡ ✻sB&B£21 sB&B⇌£30.45 dB&B£38.85 dB&B⇌£45.15 B

Lift ☾ 140P CFA ✽

♈ ☐ ✻ Lunch £5.25&alc Dinner £6.30&alc Wine £5.50 Last dinner 8.30pm

S% Credit cards 1 2 3 4 5 **VS**

★★★ **Foley Arms** (Best Western) ☎(06845) 3397 Telex no 437269

Family-run hotel, situated in the centre of Malvern.

26rm(18⇌3⫛) (1fb) CTV in all bedrooms Ⓡ sB&B£26.50 sB&B⇌⫛£28.75 dB&B£36.50 dB&B⇌⫛£42 B

☾ ⍁ 45P 4⌂ CFA ⍉ ✽

M

V ⚘ ☕ Lunch £3.95–£5.15&alc Tea 70p Dinner £5.50–£6alc Wine £3.65 Last dinner 9.15pm
Credit cards 1 2 3 4 5

★★Beauchamp Graham Rd (Minotels) ☎(06845) 63411
Small hotel in Malvern centre.
14rm(3🛁) CTV in all bedrooms ® sB&B£12.50–£13.50 sB&B🛁£16.50–£17.50 dB&B£24–£26 dB&B🛁£28–£30 B
6P
V ⚘ Lunch £4.50–£6 Dinner £5.50–£8.50 Wine £4 Last dinner 8.30pm
Credit cards 1 3 **VS**

★★Broomhill West Malvern Rd, West Malvern (2m W B4232) ☎(06845) 64367
Closed Nov–Feb
Three-storey Victorian house with magnificent views.
10rm(3🛁2🚿)(2fb) ✱sB&B£11.80 dB&B£21 dB&B🛁🚿£25 B
⊬ CTV 10P 🚗 ✽ nc5yrs
⚘ ✱Bar lunch £1.50–£2.50 Dinner £6.25 Wine £3.52 Last dinner 7.30pm
VS

★★*H* Cotford Graham Rd ☎(06845) 2427
RS Dec (B&B only)
Comfortable, family-run hotel situated in a quiet road leading to the town centre.
14rm(4🛁2🚿)(4fb) TV available in bedrooms ® ★ sB&B£14 sB&B🛁🚿£16–£18 dB&B£24–£25 dB&B🛁🚿£28–£30 B
CTV 14P 🚗 ✽
⚘ ☕ Lunch £5–£6&alc Tea 75p High Tea £2–£3 Dinner £6–£6.50&alc Wine £4.50 Last dinner 8pm
VS

★★Montrose 23 Graham Rd ☎(06845) 2335
A family-run hotel in a quiet road near the town centre.
14rm(1🛁6🚿)(1fb) ® sB&B£12.50–£15 sB&B🛁🚿£13.50–£20 dB&B fr£21 dB&B🛁🚿 fr£25 B
CTV 16P 🚗 ✽ *xmas*
V ⚘ Lunch fr£3 Dinner fr£5.50 Wine £3.95 Last dinner 8pm
Credit cards 1 3

★★*Thornbury* Avenue Rd ☎(06845) 2278
Family-run hotel in a quiet suburb of Malvern.
15rm(5🚿) Annexe: 5rm B
CTV 14P 🚗 ✽
V ⚘ ☕ Last dinner 7.45pm
Credit cards 1 2

❀★★Walmer Lodge 49 Abbey Rd ☎(06845) 4139 Closed Public hols
(Rosette awarded for dinner only.)
Small, quiet, family-run hotel.
9rm(4🛁3🚿) ★
CTV 8P 🚗 ✽ nc12yrs
English & French Last dinner 9pm

MALVERN WELLS
Hereford & Worcester
Map **3** SO74

★★★ *L* Cottage in the Wood Holywell Rd ☎(06845) 3487 Telex no 261507
Impressive, comfortable, country hotel nestling in the Malvern hillside.
9🛁 Annexe: 8🛁(1fb) 1 CTV in all bedrooms ® ★ dB&B🛁£40–£52 Continental breakfast B
30P 🚗 ✽ *xmas*
V ⚘ ☕ Lunch £6.95&alc Tea 75p–£2.50 Dinner £11.50&alc Wine £4.95 Last dinner 9.15pm
Credit cards 1 3 **VS**

★★Essington Holywell Rd ☎(06845) 61177
10rm(3🛁1🚿)(2fb) CTV in all bedrooms sB&B fr£14 sB&B🛁🚿 fr£16 dB&B fr£28 dB&B🛁🚿 fr£32 B
30P ✽ *xmas*
⚘ Bar lunch fr£4.50 Dinner fr£8 Wine £5 Last dinner 8.15pm
Credit cards 1 3

M

Manchester

1 Armenian ✕
2 Armenian Taverna ✕
3 Casa España ✕✕
4 Gaylord ✕✕
5 Grand ★★★★
6 Isola Bella ❀✕✕
7 Kai's Chinese ✕
8 Kwok Man ✕✕
9 Market ✕
10 Hotel Piccadilly ★★★★
11 Portland Thistle ★★★★
12 Post House ☆☆☆
13 La Première ✕✕
14 Rajdoot ✕✕
15 Sam's Chop House ✕
16 Simpsons ★★
17 Steak & Kebab ✕
18 Terrazza ✕✕✕
19 Truffles ✕✕
20 Willow Bank ★★★
21 Woo Sang ✕✕
22 Yang Sing ❀✕

★★ **Holdfast Cottage** Welland (on A4104 midway between Welland & Little Malvern) ☎ Hanley Swan (0684) 310288

9rm(4→2⋒) ✻sB&B fr£15 sB&B→⋒ fr£17 dB&B fr£28 dB&B→⋒ fr£32 ⊟

CTV 16P ✿ *xmas*

V ♈ ☐ Tea fr75p High Tea fr£2.50 Dinner fr£8.50 Wine £5.95 Last dinner 8.45pm

VS

❀✕✕ **Croque-en-Bouche** 221 Wells Rd ☎ (06845) 65612

Closed Sun, Mon & Tue Lunch not served

French 22 seats Dinner fr£14.50 Wine £4.50 Last dinner 9.15pm

S% Credit cards 1 3

MALVERN (WYNDS POINT)

Hereford & Worcester

Map **3** SO74

★★ ***Malvern Hills*** (Minotel) ☎ Colwall (0684) 40237

Situated high in the Malvern Hills, with lovely views of Worcestershire and Herefordshire.

16rm(10→) CTV in 10 bedrooms ® ⊟

CTV 30P ✿

English & French V ♈ ☐ Last dinner 9.30pm

Credit cards 1 5

See advert on page 442

MAN, ISLE OF

Map **6**

Refer to location atlas (Map **6**) for details of places with AA-appointed hotels and restaurants.

MANCHESTER

Greater Manchester

Map **7** SJ89

See plan. See also Salford

★★★★ **Grand** Aytoun St (Trusthouse Forte) ☎ 061-236 9559 Telex no 667580

Plan **5** *E4*

→

M

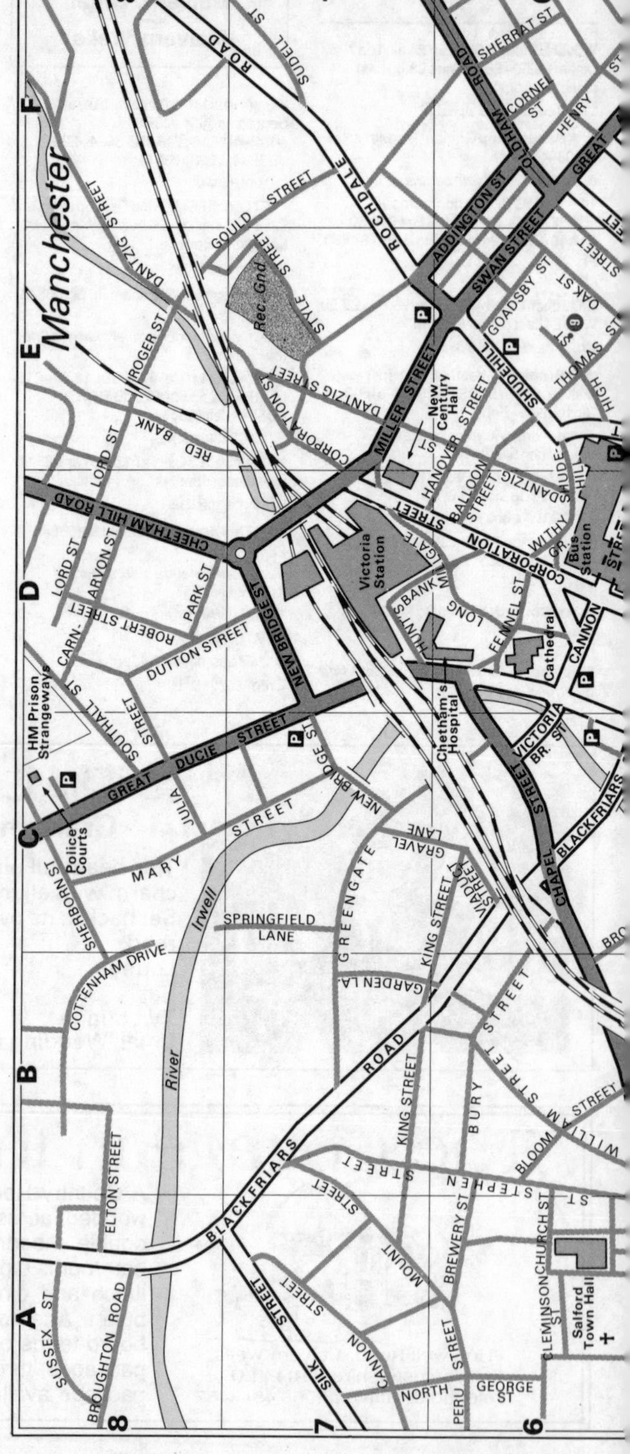

Manchester
Victoria Station
Cathedral
New Century Hall
Chetham's Hospital
HM Prison Strangeways
Police Courts
Rec. Gnd.
Bus Station
Salford Town Hall
River Irwell
CHEETHAM HILL ROAD
GREAT DUCIE STREET
NEW BRIDGE ST
CORPORATION STREET
MILLER STREET
ROCHDALE ROAD
SWAN STREET
ADDINGTON ST
OLDHAM ROAD
SHUDEHILL
DANTZIC STREET
BLACKFRIARS ROAD
CHAPEL STREET
VICTORIA BR. ST
DUTTON STREET
ROBERT STREET
MARY STREET
GREENGATE
KING STREET
BURY STREET
SPRINGFIELD LANE
COTTENHAM DRIVE
SHERBORN ST
ELTON STREET
BROUGHTON ROAD
SUSSEX ST
SILK STREET
CANNON STREET
NORTH GEORGE ST
CLEMINSON ST
CHURCH ST
STEPHEN STREET
BLOOM STREET
WILLIAM STREET

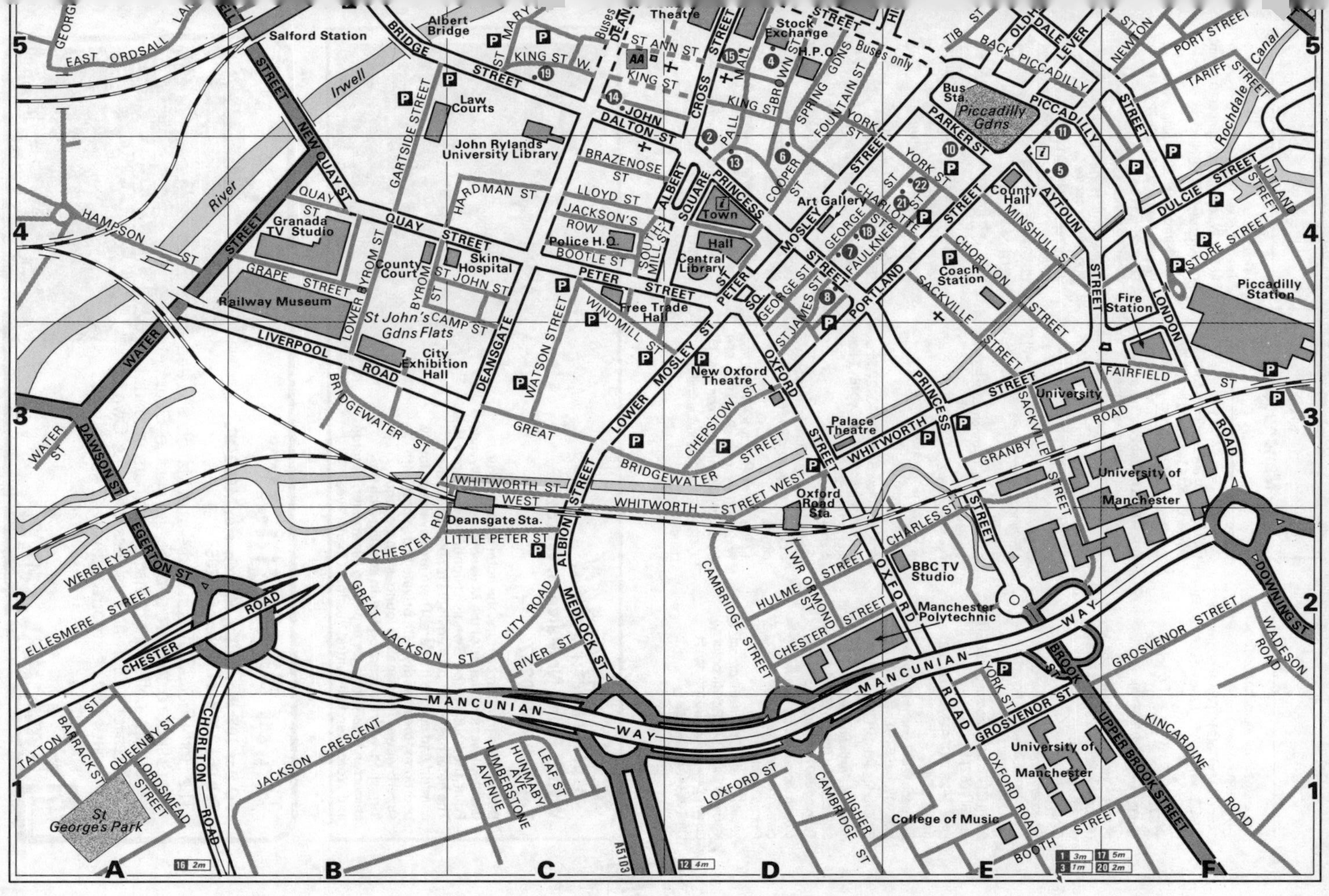
Salford Station
Albert Bridge
Theatre
Stock Exchange
H.P.O.
Buses only
Irwell
River
Law Courts
John Rylands University Library
Granada TV Studio
Railway Museum
County Court
Skin Hospital
Police H.Q.
Town Hall
Central Library
Art Gallery
County Hall
Coach Station
Fire Station
Piccadilly Station
Piccadilly Gdns
Bus Sta.
Rochdale Canal
Free Trade Hall
New Oxford Theatre
Palace Theatre
St John's Gdns Flats
City Exhibition Hall
Deansgate Sta.
Oxford Road Sta.
University
University of Manchester
BBC TV Studio
Manchester Polytechnic
College of Music
St George's Park
NEW QUAY ST
QUAY STREET
DEANSGATE
LIVERPOOL ROAD
WATER STREET
DAWSON ST
EGERTON ST
CHESTER ROAD
CHORLTON ROAD
MANCUNIAN WAY
PETER STREET
LOWER MOSLEY STREET
OXFORD STREET
OXFORD ROAD
PORTLAND STREET
PRINCESS STREET
WHITWORTH STREET
WHITWORTH STREET WEST
ALBION STREET
MEDLOCK ST
CAMBRIDGE STREET
UPPER BROOK STREET
DOWNING ST
LONDON ROAD
PICCADILLY
AYTOUN STREET
MOSLEY STREET
CROSS STREET
JOHN DALTON ST
GROSVENOR ST
A5103

Large six-storey, Victorian building in the city centre.

146rm(131→15⋒) CTV in all bedrooms ®sB&B→⋒£47.50 dB&B→⋒£61.50 B

Lift ☾ CFA

♆☐ Last dinner 10pm

Credit cards 1 2 3 4 5

★★★★**Hotel Piccadilly** Piccadilly (Embassy) ☎061-236 8414 Telex no 668765 Plan **10** *E4*
Closed 25–28 Dec

Fourteen-floor sky-scraper block (1965) in city centre, having panoramic views from the restaurant.

250⋒ CTV in all bedrooms ®sB&B⋒£49 dB&B⋒£62 B

Lift ☾ ⅟250P CFA Live music and dancing Sat

▣French ♆☐ Lunch fr£8.90 Dinner fr£8.90 Wine £5.20 Last dinner 10.30pm

S% Credit cards 1 2 3 4 5

★★★★**Portland Thistle** 3–5 Portland St, Piccadilly (Thistle) ☎061-228 3400 Telex no 669157 Plan **11** *E5*

Modern hotel behind a restored 19th-century warehouse façade, facing Piccadilly Gardens.

221→⋒ (13fb) CTV in all bedrooms ® *sB→⋒£36.50–£42.50 (room only) dB→⋒£44–£47.50 (room only) B

Lift ☾ ## ⅟34P CFA

▣European ☐ *Lunch £3–£10&alc Dinner £6–£11&alc Last dinner 9.30pm

Credit cards 1 2 3 4 5 **VS**

☆☆☆**Post House** Palatine Rd, Northenden (Trusthouse Forte) ☎061-998 7090 Telex no 669248 Plan **12** *D1*

A building of modern structure, 7m south of the city centre at the junction of the B5167/A5103. It is close to motorways M56 and M63 and convenient for the airport.

201→ CTV in all bedrooms ®sB&B→£43 dB&B→£55 B

Lift ☾ 243P CFA

♆☐ Last dinner 10.30pm

Credit cards 1 2 3 4 5

★★★**Willow Bank** 340–342 Wilmslow Rd, Fallowfield ☎061-224 0461 Telex no 668222 Plan **20** *E1*
RS Public Hols

Large, Victorian house with modern extensions, situated 2 miles from city centre.

123rm(112→6⋒) (2fb) CTV in 120 rooms ★sB£20 (room only) sB→⋒£24–£26 (room only) dB→⋒£38 (room only) B

☾ CTV 100P 40 Live music and dancing Sat

▣International ♆☐ Lunch £3.50&alc Tea fr£1.50alc High Tea fr£2 Dinner £6&alc Wine £3.50 Last dinner 10.15pm

Credit cards 1 2 3 5

★★**Simpsons** 122 Withington Rd, Whalley Range ☎061-226 2235 Telex no 667822 Plan **16** *A1*
Closed 24 Dec–2 Jan

Family-run hotel in the suburbs, 2 miles from the city centre.

40rm(7→2⋒) (4fb) CTV in 17 bedrooms *sB&B£17.25 sB&B→⋒£23 dB&B£23 dB&B→⋒£27.60 B

☾ CTV 42P

▣English, French, Indian & Italian ♆☐ *Lunch £2.30–£3.50&alc Tea 87p–£1.73 Dinner £6.90&alc Wine £4.20 Last dinner 11.30pm

Credit cards 1 2 3 5 **VS**

XXX**Terrazza** 14 Nicholas St ☎061-236 4033 Plan **18** *D4*

Closed Sun Lunch not served Sat

▣Italian 110 seats *Lunch £7.10alc Dinner £14.05alc Wine £4.35 Last dinner 11.30pm

S% Credit cards 1 2 3 4 5

XX***Casa España*** 100 Wilmslow Rd, Rusholme ☎061-224 6826 Plan **3** *E1*

Colourful Spanish restaurant with cheerful service.

Closed Sun & Public hols

M

Spanish 56 seats Last dinner 10.30pm
Credit card 2

✕✕**Gaylord** Amethyst House, Marriot's Court, Spring Gdns ☎061-832 6037 Plan **4** *D5*
Indian **V** 90 seats ✱Lunch fr£4.35&alc Dinner £10&alc Wine £6 Last dinner 11.30pm
Credit cards 1 2 3 5

✕✕**Isola Bella** Booth St ☎061-236 6417 Plan **6** *D4*
Popular Italian restaurant featuring delicious selections of hors d'oeuvres, salads and sweets.
Closed Public Hols
Italian 70 seats Lunch £13alc Dinner £13alc Wine £5.80 Last dinner 10.45pm
S% Credit cards 2 3 5

✕✕**Kwok Man** 28–32 Princess St ☎061-228 2620 Plan **8** *D4*
Cantonese **V** 180 seats Lunch £2.50 Dinner £6alc Wine £5.20 Last dinner 4am 25P Cabaret Wed evening
Credit cards 1 2 3 5

✕✕**La Première** Clarence St ☎061-236 6657 Plan **13** *D4*
Intimate and romantic French basement restaurant.
Closed Sun & Public Hols Lunch not served Sat
French 40 seats Lunch £3.75–£6.95&alc Dinner £6.50–£8.25&alc Wine £4.60 Last dinner mdnt Live music Fri & Sat evening
Credit cards 1 2 3 5

✕✕**Rajdoot** St James House, South King's St ☎061-834 2176 Plan **14** *C5*
Closed Sun & Xmas Lunch not served Public Hols
Indian **V** 85 seats Lunch £4–£8&alc Dinner £5–£9&alc Wine £4.80 Last dinner 11.30pm
S% Credit cards 1 2 3 5

✕✕***Truffles*** 63 Bridge St ☎061-832 9393 Plan **19** *C5*
Closed Sun & Mon Lunch not served Sat
French **V** 40 seats Last dinner 11pm
Credit cards 1 2 3 5 **VS**

✕✕**Woo Sang** 19 George St ☎061-236 3697 Plan **21** *E4*
Busy Cantonese restaurant with extensive menu above Chinese supermarket.
Cantonese **V** 200 seats Lunch £2&alc Dinner £9alc Wine £6 Last dinner 11.45pm
Credit cards 1 2 3 5

✕***Armenian*** (Granada Hotel) 404 Wilmslow Rd, Withington ☎061-434 3480 Plan **1** *E1*
Closed 25 Dec Lunch not served Sat & Sun
Armenian 50 seats Last dinner 11.30pm 12P bedrooms available
Credit cards 2 5

✕***Armenian Taverna*** 3–5 Princess St ☎061-834 9025 Plan **2** *D4*
Lunch not served Sat & Sun
Armenian 60 seats Last dinner 11.30pm
Credit cards 2 5

✕***Kai's Chinese*** 16 Nicholas St ☎061-236 2041 Plan **7** *D4*
Cantonese 90 seats Last dinner 5am

✕**Market** 30 Edge St ☎061-834 3743 Plan **9** *E6*
Closed Sun, Mon, 1wk Xmas, 2wks Spring & Aug Lunch not served
Cosmopolitan **V** 28 seats ✱Dinner £6.50alc Wine £3.50 Last dinner 10.30pm

✕**Sam's Chop House** Black Pool Fold, Chapel Walks ☎061-834 1526 Plan **15** *D5*
Dinner not served
100 seats Lunch fr£5.50&alc Wine £4.35 Last lunch 3pm
Credit cards 1 2 3 5

✕***Steak & Kebab*** 846 Wilmslow Rd, Didsbury ☎061-445 2552 Plan **17** *E1*
A simple, cottage-style restaurant, adjoining a public house in the southern suburbs.
Closed 25 & 26 Dec & 1 Jan Lunch not served Sat
International 110 seats Last dinner 11.30pm 20P

✕**Yang Sing** 17 George St ☎061-236 2200 Plan **22** *E4*
Small, crowded restaurant featuring Cantonese cooking at its very best.
Cantonese **V** 70 seats ✱Lunch fr£2&alc Dinner £10alc Wine £4.25 Last dinner 11.30pm
S% Credit cards 1 2

MANCHESTER AIRPORT
Greater Manchester
Map **7** SJ78

☆☆☆☆**Excelsior** Ringway Rd, Wythenshawe (Trusthouse Forte) ☎061-437 5811 Telex no 668721
Large, modern hotel near the airport.
304 (3fb) CTV in all bedrooms Ⓡ sB&B £49.50 dB&B £63.50
Lift ☾ 350P CFA ✽ (heated)
Last dinner 10.15pm
Credit cards 1 2 3 4 5

★★★**Valley Lodge** Altrincham Rd ☎Wilmslow (0625) 529201 Telex no 666401
Tyrolean style hotel.
87rm(74 13) CTV in all bedrooms Ⓡ sB&B £30.50 dB&B £37.50 Continental breakfast
Lift ☾ 300P CFA Disco Wed–Sat
International Lunch fr£6 Dinner fr£7 Wine £4.85 Last dinner 10.30pm
Credit cards 1 2 3 5
See advert on page 444

MANORBIER
Dyfed
Map **2** SS09

★★***Castle Mead*** ☎(083 482) 358
Closed Oct–Mar
Small, peaceful, friendly, comfortable, country-house style hotel with attractive garden.
8rm(6) Annexe: 3 Ⓡ
CTV 20P ✽
Last dinner 8pm

MANSFIELD
Nottinghamshire
Map **8** SK56

★★**Midland** Midland Pl (Home Brewery) ☎(0623) 24668

27rm(16⇌4⋒) CTV in all bedrooms Ⓡ ✵sB&B£16.56 sB&B⇌⋒£18.86 dB&B£28.52 dB&B⇌⋒£31.05

CTV 20P

V ♧ ⊒ Last dinner 9pm

Credit cards 1 3

MARAZION
Cornwall
Map **2** SW53

★ ***Cutty Sark*** The Square ☎ Penzance (0736) 710334

A comfortable inn with convivial atmosphere in the heart of the village.

12rm(2⇌) CTV in 10 bedrooms B

CTV 32P

Mainly grills ♧ ⊒ Last dinner 9.30pm

Credit card 3 **VS**

MARGATE
Kent
Map **5** TR37

★★**Walpole Bay** Fifth Av, Cliftonville (1m E) ☎ Thanet (0843) 21703

Closed 4 Oct–14 May (except Xmas)

Friendly, old fashioned hotel with good accommodation.

46rm(18⇌) (9fb) TV in 5 bedrooms sB&B£14–£19 sB&B⇌£20–£25 dB&B£25–£30 dB&B⇌£30–£38 B

Lift ☾ CTV 2 *xmas*

V ♧ ⊒ Lunch £5–£5.50 Tea 70p Dinner £6–£7.50 Wine £3.70 Last dinner 7.45pm

Credit cards 1 3 5 **VS**

MARKET DRAYTON
Shropshire
Map **7** SJ63

★★**Corbet Arms** High St ☎ (0630) 2037

Ancient inn with a Georgian façade and a pillared entrance.

9⇌ (2fb) TV in all bedrooms Ⓡ sB&B⇌£18.50 dB&B⇌£28 B

CTV 45P 2

Mainly grills **V** ♧ ⊒ Lunch £4 Tea £1.10 Dinner £7&alc Wine £3.65 Last dinner 9pm

Credit cards 1 2 3 5

★★**Tern Hill** (on A53) ☎ Tern Hill (063 083) 310

10rm(6⇌) CTV in all bedrooms Ⓡ sB&B⇌£13–£15 dB&B⇌£29–£30

150P 8 ✽

V ♧ Lunch fr£4.50&alc Dinner fr£6.50&alc Wine £3.80 Last dinner 9pm

Credit cards 1 2 3 5

MARKET HARBOROUGH
Leicestershire
Map **4** SP78

★★★**Three Swans** High St ☎ (0858) 66644

Historic inn dating from the 15th century, on the A6 near the town centre.

18rm(11⇌7⋒) (1fb) 2 CTV in all bedrooms Ⓡ sB&B⇌⋒£25 dB&B⇌⋒£32 B

50P 10

English & French ♧ ⊒ Lunch £5.50–£6&alc Tea £1.50 High Tea £3.50 Dinner £10alc Wine £4.85 Last dinner 9.45pm

Credit cards 1 2 3 4 5

★★**Angel** High St ☎ (0858) 63123

Closed Xmas

Old coaching inn standing in the High Street, close to the town centre.

18rm (4fb) TV in 10 bedrooms Ⓡ ✵sB&B£12 dB&B£24 B

CTV 40P 4

V ♧ ⊒ ✵Lunch £5.80alc Tea fr55p Dinner £8–£9 Wine £3.95 Last dinner 9.15pm

S% Credit cards 1 2 3 5

★★**Grove Motel** Northampton Rd ☎ (0858) 64082

30rm(25⇌1⋒) (2fb) CTV in all bedrooms Ⓡ sB&B⇌⋒£22.14 dB&B⇌⋒£29.10 B

CTV 65P ✽ CFA billiards

M

V ✿ ✱ Lunch 60p–£6&alc Dinner £4–£10&alc Last dinner 9.15pm

Credit cards 1 3 VS

MARKET RASEN
Lincolnshire
Map **8** TF18

★★*H* **Limes** Gainsborough Rd (Exec Hotel) ☎ (0673) 842357
RS 25 Dec–2 Jan

13rm (11 ⇌ 2 ⋒) (3fb) CTV in all bedrooms ® sB&B ⇌ ⋒ £25–£28 dB&B ⇌ ⋒ £30–£32 B

30P ✽ ⚲ (grass) squash Cabaret Fri

English & French V ✿ ☐ Lunch £5.50–£6&alc Tea £2.50–£3.50 High Tea £3.50–£4.50 Dinner £6.25–£6.75&alc Wine £4.50 Last dinner 9.30pm

Credit cards 1 3

MARKET WEIGHTON
Humberside
Map **8** SE84

★★ ***Londesborough Arms*** 44 High St ☎ (0696) 72219

10rm ★

CTV 50P

✿ ☐ Last dinner 9.30pm

Credit cards 1 2 3 4 5

MARKINGTON
North Yorkshire
Map **8** SE26

★★★ *BL* **Hob Green** ☎ Harrogate (0423) 770031 Telex no 57780

11 ⇌ 1 CTV in all bedrooms ® sB&B ⇌ £30–£35 dB&B ⇌ £42.50–£47.50 B

50P ✽ *xmas*

English & French V Dinner £9.75–£12.50 Wine £4.95 Last dinner 10pm

Credit cards 1 2 3 5

MARKS TEY
Essex
Map **5** TL92

☆☆☆ **Marks Tey** London Rd (Paten) ☎ Colchester (0206) 210001 Telex no 987176

Friendly, modern hotel with good bedrooms.

106 ⇌ CTV in all bedrooms ® ✱ sB&B ⇌ fr£27.60 dB&B ⇌ fr£36.80 B

☾ CTV 160P CFA *xmas*

English & French V ✿ ☐ ✱ Lunch £5.45–£6.65&alc Tea fr60p Dinner £5.45–£6.65&alc Wine £3.45 Last dinner 10pm

Credit cards 1 2 3 5

MARKYATE
Hertfordshire
Map **4** TL01

☆☆☆ **Hertfordshire Moat House** London Rd (Queens Moat) ☎ Luton (0582) 840840

Modern, convenient hotel.

97 ⇌ (6fb) CTV in all bedrooms ® sB&B ⇌ £23–£33 dB&B ⇌ £26–£36 B

☾ # 200P CFA ✽ Disco Thu Live music and dancing Sat *xmas* ♿

English & French V ✿ ☐ Lunch £5.75–£12&alc Tea 65p–£1.95 Dinner £6.95–£12&alc Wine £4.75 Last dinner 10pm

Credit cards 1 2 3 5 VS

MARLBOROUGH
Wilsthire
Map **4** SU16

★★ **Castle & Ball** High St (Trusthouse Forte) ☎ (0672) 52002

A 17th-century inn with a tile-hung Georgian façade. The interior has been completely modernised yet retains its charm and character.

30rm (6 ⇌) (2fb) CTV in all bedrooms ® sB&B £33 sB&B ⇌ £35.50 dB&B £43 dB&B ⇌ £49.50 B

CTV 50P *xmas*

✿ ☐ Last dinner 9.30pm

Credit cards 1 2 3 4 5

MARLOW
Buckinghamshire
Map **4** SU88

★★★★ *BL* **Compleat Angler** Marlow Br →

M

(Trusthouse Forte) ☎(06284) 4444 Telex no 848644

A gem of a place in luxuriant fragrant gardens with uninterrupted river views. The house has fine period furniture and tapestries.

42➡ CTV in all bedrooms sB&B➡£61 dB&B➡£81

☾ 100P 4🏠 CFA ✽ 🎾(hard)

Last dinner 10pm

Credit cards 1 2 3 4 5

✕✕Cavaliers (Restaurant Français) 24 West St ☎(06284) 2544

Closed Public Hols Lunch not served Mon

French 50 seats Lunch £8.75&alc Dinner £12alc Wine £5.50 Last dinner 10pm 6P Live music Thu, Fri & Sat evenings & Sun lunch

S% Credit cards 1 2 3 5

MARSH GIBBON
Buckinghamshire
Map **4** SP62

✕Greyhound Inn ☎Stratton Audley (08697) 365

Closed Mon Dinner not served Sun & Tue

English & French **V** 30 seats ✱Lunch £5.75–£11.25 Dinner £5.75–£11.25 Wine £4 Last dinner 9.30pm 100P

Credit cards 1 2 3 5

MARSTON TRUSSELL
Northamptonshire
Map **4** SP68

★★***Sun Inn*** ☎Market Harborough (0858) 65531 Closed Sun

Modern accommodation is provided in the extension of this traditional, rural, village inn.

10rm(9➡) Ⓡ ⊞

CTV 50P 4🏠

English & French **V** Last dinner 9.45pm

Credit cards 2 3 5

MARTINHOE
Devon
Map **3** SS64

★ ***HBL* Old Rectory** ☎Parracombe (05983) 368 Closed Nov–Feb

This quiet, charming, Georgian house stands in its own grounds within the Exmoor National Park. It is a comfortable, well-appointed and tastefully decorated hotel offering friendly, personal service provided by Terry Pring and well prepared meals from the kitchen of Elizabeth Pring.

11rm(6➡1⋒) (2fb) CTV in 4 bedrooms sB&B£8–£10 sB&B➡⋒£12–£14 dB&B£16–£20 dB&B➡⋒£22–£32 ⊞

14P ✽ nc6yrs ♿

V Lunch £3.75–£4.75 Dinner £8.50–£9.50 Wine £4.25 Last dinner 7.30pm

Credit cards 1 2 3 4 5 **VS**

MARTOCK
Somerset
Map **3** ST41

★**White Hart** ☎(0935) 822246

Friendly inn situated in the town centre opposite the Corn Exchange.

8rm (3fb) CTV in 2 bedrooms TV in 6 bedrooms Ⓡ sB&B fr£12.50 dB&B fr£25

CTV 20P snooker

Lunch £2alc Dinner £7.50alc Wine £5.25 Last dinner 9.30pm

VS

MARYPORT
Cumbria
Map **11** NY03

★★**Waverley** Curzon St ☎(0900) 812115

Situated on the edge of the town, this hotel is within easy reach of the sea, lakes and fells.

20rm(1➡) (1fb) CTV in 4 bedrooms Ⓡ sB&B fr£10 sB&B➡ fr£15 dB&B fr£19 dB&B➡ fr£23 ⊞

☾ CTV 10P

V Lunch fr£3.80 Tea fr£1.20 High Tea fr£1.60 Dinner fr£6.80 Wine £3.10 Last dinner 8.30pm

Credit cards 1 3 **VS**

M

MARYTAVY
Devon
Map **2** SX57

★**H Moorland Hall** ☏(082281) 466
Family run hotel, Victorian built featuring a 'Victorian Christmas'.
10rm(1→2⋒) ® *sB&B fr£10.50 sB&B→⋒ fr£15.50 dB&B fr£19 dB&B→⋒ fr£24 B
CTV 15P ✽ billiards *xmas*
*Tea fr£1.40 Dinner fr£6.50 Wine £4.50 Last dinner 8.30pm
Credit cards 1 3

MASHAM
North Yorkshire
Map **8** SE28

★★**H Jervaulx Hall** ☏Bedale (0677) 60235 Closed 20 Dec–Feb
Early 19th-century country house adjoining Jervaulx Abbey, with its own lawns and gardens.
8→ (2fb) ® dB&B→£38
CTV 20P ✽ ♿
Tea £2 Dinner £9.50&alc Wine £3.80 Last dinner 8pm
Credit cards 1 3 **VS**

★★***Kings Head*** Market Pl ☏Ripon (0765) 89295
An 18th-century, stone-built hotel situated in the Market Place.
14rm ® B
CTV
V Last dinner 9pm

MATLOCK
Derbyshire
Map **8** SK36

★★★**New Bath** New Bath Rd (2m S A6) (Trusthouse Forte) ☏(0629) 3275
Large, much extended, Georgian-style building in an elevated position above the A6.
56→ (16fb) CTV in all bedrooms ® sB&B→£35.50 dB&B→£51.50 B
250P CFA ✽ & (heated) (hard) sauna bath *xmas*
Last dinner 9.30pm
Credit cards 1 2 3 4 5

★★★***B* Riber Hall** Riber ☏(0629) 2795
Elizabethan manor house 3 miles from Matlock, next to Riber Castle.
Annexe: 11→⋒ 11 CTV in all bedrooms ® *sB&B→£30–£34.50 dB&B→£40–£46 Continental breakfast B
45P 1 ✽ nc10yrs
English & French **V** *Lunch £6.35 Tea £1.75 Dinner £15alc Wine £5.50 Last dinner 9.30pm
Credit cards 1 2 3 5

★**Greyhound** Market Pl Cromford (2½m S on A5012 at junc with A6) ☏Wirksworth (062982) 2551

Large 3-storey Georgian inn in centre of old town.
6rm
CTV 80P
Last dinner 8.30pm

★**High Tor** Artist's Corner, Dale Rd ☏(0629) 2031
The former home of Admiral Collingwood, standing on the A6.
17rm (2fb) 4 *sB&B£12–£20 dB&B£18–£30
CTV 20P ✽ sauna bath
V *Lunch £3.95&alc Tea 75p Dinner £5&alc Wine £3.95 Last dinner 9pm

MAUCHLINE
Strathclyde *Ayrshire*
Map **11** NS42

✕***La Candela*** 5 Kilmarnock Rd ☏(0290) 51015
Small village restaurant with dark wood frontage and a red canopy.
Lunch not served Sun
European 40 seats Last dinner 10pm 15P

MAWGAN PORTH
Cornwall
Map **2** SW86

★★**H Tredragon** (Minotels) ☏St Mawgan (06374) 213 Closed Nov–Etr (except Xmas)
Comfortable, family holiday hotel, with fine views over the beach and direct access to it.
30rm(13→11⋒) (11fb) sB&B£11–£13 dB&B£22–£26 dB&B→⋒£26–£30
CTV 30P ✽ (heated) sauna bath Live music and dancing Tue *xmas*
British & Continental Bar lunch 65p–£2.50 Tea 50p High Tea £4.75 Dinner fr£6 Wine £3.50 Last dinner 8pm
Credit card 1 **VS**

MAWNAN SMITH
Cornwall
Map **2** SW72

★★★**Meudon** ☏Falmouth (0326) 250541 Telex no 45478
Closed mid Nov–mid Feb
Manor house hotel overlooking sub-tropical gardens leading to the beach.
36rm(30→⋒) (1fb) CTV in 30 bedrooms ® sB&B£11–£18 sB&B→⋒£22–£36 dB&B→⋒£44–£68 B
50P CFA ✽
Lunch £5–£6 Tea 50p–£1 High Tea £2–£5 Dinner £8.50–£12.50&alc Wine £4 Last dinner 9pm
Credit cards 1 2 3 5 **VS**

★★★**Trelawne** ☏Falmouth (0326) 250226
Closed 5 Nov–17 Mar
Small, family-run, holiday hotel situated on the coast with two acres of grounds and gardens.
16rm(10→2⋒) (1fb) ® *sB&B£15–£18 sB&B→⋒£17–£20 dB&B£30–£36 dB&B→⋒£34–£40
CTV 20P ✽ (heated)
*Lunch £2.90–£3.85 Tea 55p Dinner £6.90–£8.50 Wine £3.90 Last dinner 8.30pm
Credit cards 1 2 3 5 **VS**

✕**Dionysus** ☏Falmouth (0326) 250714
Small, modern restaurant situated in the heart of the village.
Lunch not served
English & Greek 34 seats Dinner £6.50alc Wine £4 Last dinner 10.30pm 20P
Credit cards 1 2 3 4 5 **VS**

MAYPOOL (*near Churston*)
Devon
Map **3** SX85

✕**Firwood Country Hotel** ☏Churston (0803) 842442
A converted row of cottages in a quiet position with a garden and fine views.
V 32 seats Lunch £3.50alc Dinner £6.25alc Wine £3.20 Last dinner 10.30pm P bedrooms available
Credit cards 1 3 **VS**

MEALSGATE
Cumbria
Map **11** NY24

★★***Pink House*** ☏Low Ireby (09657) 229
Closed Nov RS Sun
Detached rural hotel in ½ acre of gardens.
8rm
CTV 15P ✽
Last dinner 8pm

MEASHAM
Leicestershire
Map **8** SK31

☆☆**Measham Inn** Tamworth Rd ☏(0530) 70095 Telex no 34610
RS Public Hols
32→ (9fb) CTV in all bedrooms ® *sB&B→£17–£23.50 dB&B→£22.50–£29 B
70P CFA
Mainly grills *Lunch £5.50alc Tea 45p alc Dinner £5.50alc Wine £4.50 Last dinner 9.30pm
Credit cards 1 2 3 5 **VS**

MEIGLE
Tayside *Perthshire*
Map **11** NO24

★★**H Kings of Kinloch** ☏(08284) 273
Closed Jan
An 18th-century mansion set in its own grounds, off the A94 1½m west of Meigle.
7rm(1→) (3fb) TV available in bedrooms *sB&B£14.50–£16.50 sB&B→£16.50 dB&B£25–£27 dB&B→£27 →

M

45P2 ✽

Cosmopolitan V ✻Lunch £5.30–£10 Tea fr60p High Tea £3–£7 Dinner fr£8.50&alc Wine £5.30 Last dinner 9pm

Credit card 1

MELBOURN
Cambridgeshire
Map **5** TL34

✕**Pink Geranium** Royston (0763) 60215

Pink-washe thatched cottage.

Closed S Mon., last 2wks Aug & Xmas Lunch no served Sat

Engl & French 45 seats Lunch fr£5.75 Dinner £8.50–£10alc Wine £3.75 Last dinner 9.30pm 25P

MELKSHAM
Wiltshire
Map **3** ST96

★★★*B* **Beechfield House** Beanacre (1m N A350) (0225) 703700

Ornate but comfortable Victorian style hotel, personally run.

8 1 CTV in all bedrooms sB&B £29.50 dB&B £38.50–£60

45P ✽ (heated) (grass) *xmas*

English & French Lunch £6.75–£7.50&alc Tea £1.25–£1.50 Dinner £13alc Wine £4.95 Last dinner 9pm

Credit cards 1 2 3 5

★★**Kings Arms** Market Pl (0225) 703217

Friendly, clean, comfortable town centre hotel.

13rm(5)(1fb) CTV in all bedrooms sB&B £15.50 sB&B £20 dB&B £20 dB&B £25

CTV 50P *xmas*

V Lunch fr£5&alc Tea fr50p High Tea fr£1.50 Dinner fr£5.50&alc Wine £4 Last dinner 9.30pm

Credit cards 1 3 **VS**

✕✕**Mr Bumbles** Conigre Farm Hotel, Semington Rd (0225) 702229

Dinner not served Sun

V 40 seats Lunch £4.95 Dinner £7.95&alc Wine £4.95 Last dinner 10.30pm 25P bedrooms available

Credit cards 1 2 3 5 **VS**

MELLING
Lancashire
Map **7** SD57

★★***Melling Hall*** Hornby (0468) 21298

A converted 17th-century manor house, set in open country on the edge of the village.

13rm(3 1) CTV in 2 bedrooms TV in 1 bedroom Ⓡ

CTV 3 ✽

French Last dinner 9pm

Credit cards 1 3 **VS**

MELROSE
Borders *Roxburghshire*
Map **12** NT53

★★*L* **Burt's** The Square (089682) 2285

Dating from 1722, this converted town house is of architectural interest.

23rm(5 4)(2fb) Ⓡ sB&B £13–£14.50 sB&B £15–£16 dB&B £26–£29 dB&B £29–£31

CTV 36P ✽

English & Continental V Lunch £4.50–£5.50 Dinner £8.25–£9.25&alc Wine £4.50 Last dinner 9.30pm

Credit cards 1 2 3 4 5 **VS**

★★**George & Abbotsford** (089682) 2308

Three-storey, stone, coaching inn standing on the main road in the centre of this Border town.

21rm(13 1)(1fb) CTV available on request Ⓡ sB&B £14 sB&B £16 dB&B £25 dB&B £28

CTV 100P ✽

V ✻Lunch £8.50&alc Tea £1.50 High Tea £4 Dinner £8.50 Last dinner 9.30pm

Credit cards 1 2 3 4 5

M

★ ***Bon-Accord*** The Square ☎(089682) 2645
Small family run country town hotel.
8rm Ⓡ
CTV Live music and dancing Sat & Sun
♔ Last dinner 8pm

MELTHAM
West Yorkshire
Map **7** SE01
★★★**Durker Roods** ☎Huddersfield (0484) 851413
Converted Victorian building, originally a mill owner's mansion.
32rm(26⇌6⋒)(3fb) CTV in all bedrooms Ⓡ sB&B⇌⋒£24–£30.50 dB&B⇌⋒£31.50–£37 B
☾ 80P ✽
V ♔ Lunch £4–£6&alc Dinner £7&alc Wine £4.50 Last dinner 9.30pm
Credit cards 1 2 3 5

MELTON MOWBRAY
Leicestershire
Map **8** SK71
★★★*HB* ***George*** High St (Inter-Hotels) ☎(0664) 62112
Old world inn situated in the centre of the town.
19rm(17⇌2⋒) 4▭ CTV in all bedrooms Ⓡ B
CTV 15P
▭ English & French **V** ♔ Last dinner 10pm
Credit cards 1 2 3 5
★★★**Harboro'** Burton St (Anchor) ☎(0664) 60121 Telex no 858875
Commercial hotel, which was a former coaching inn, situated on the A606.
27rm(23⇌4⋒)(1fb) CTV in all bedrooms Ⓡ ✽sB&B⇌⋒£18.50–£30 dB&B⇌⋒£29.50–£39 B
☾ CTV 40P ⌂ *xmas*
V ♔ ▭ ✽Lunch £1.80–£11.95 Tea 45p–£2.95 Dinner £6.95–£11.95 Wine £4.50 Last dinner 10pm
Credit cards 1 2 3 4 5 **VS**
★★**Kings Head** Nottingham St (Home Brewery) ☎(0664) 62110
Victorian-style building in the town centre offering modern accommodation.
15rm(4⇌8⋒)(1fb) CTV in all bedrooms Ⓡ ✽ ✽sB&B£14.74 sB&B⇌⋒£15.81 dB&B£26.18 dB&B⇌⋒£28.84
CTV 50P 15⌂
V ♔ ▭ Last dinner 9pm
S% Credit cards 1 3

MEMBURY
Devon
Map **3** SY29
★★**Lea Hill Farm** ☎Stockland (040488) 388
Converted 14th-century farmhouse situated in very remote countryside. Attractive dining room featuring polished flagstones and exposed timbers.
5⇌ Annexe: 3 CTV in 2 bedrooms ✽sB⇌ fr£12.50 dB⇌ fr£25 (room only) B
⁄ CTV 50P ⌿ ✽
▭ English & French **V** ▭ ✽Lunch 75p–£2.50 Tea 50p Dinner fr£5.85&alc Wine £4.25 Last dinner 9.15pm
Credit card 1

MENAI BRIDGE
Gwynedd
Map **6** SH57
★★**Gazelle** Glyn Garth (2m NE A545) ☎(0248) 713364
Holiday, touring hotel, situated at the edge of the Menai Straits.
10rm Annexe: 3rm(1⇌)(1fb) TV in 6 bedrooms Ⓡ ✽ ✽sB&B£14 dB&B£23 dB&B⇌£28 B
CTV 30P ✽
♔ ▭ Lunch £4.75 Tea 75p Dinner £9alc Wine £4 Last dinner 9.30pm
Credit cards 1 3

MENDHAM
Suffolk
Map **5** TM28
★ ***Sir Alfred Munnings*** Studio Corner ☎Harleston (0379) 852358
14rm(6⋒) CTV in 2 bedrooms B
CTV 40P 2⌂ ⌓ (heated) Live music and dancing Sun
V ♔ ▭ Last dinner 10pm
Credit cards 1 2 **VS**

MERE
Wiltshire
Map **3** ST83
★★**Old Ship** Castle St (Inter-Hotels) ☎(0747) 860258
Modernised former coaching inn, featuring an oak-beamed dining room.
14rm(6⇌) Annexe: 11rm(9⇌2⋒)(3fb) 1▭ CTV in 17 bedrooms TV in 8 bedrooms Ⓡ sB&B£17.90 sB&B⇌⋒£19.90 dB&B£29.90 dB&B⇌⋒£33.40–£36.50 B
40P 3⌂ *xmas*
▭ English & French ♔ ▭ Lunch £1.85–£4.50&alc Tea 70p Dinner £6–£7&alc Wine £3.95 Last dinner 9.15pm
Credit cards 1 2 3 5 **VS**
★**Talbot** ☎(0747) 860427
Formerly the 'George Inn' where Charles II dined in 1651.
7rm(2⇌)(1fb) CTV in 3 bedrooms sB&B £12 sB&B⇌£15 dB&B£24 dB&B⇌£28 B
CTV 25P
♔ Lunch £4.80&alc Dinner £6.50&alc Last dinner 9pm
Credit cards 1 3

MERE BROW
Lancashire
Map **7** SD41
✕**Crab & Lobster** (Legh Arms) ☎Hesketh Bank (077473) 2734
The restaurant is housed in an old cottage, which was converted in 1962, and has been recently extended.
Closed Sun, Mon & Xmas–mid Jan Lunch not served
50 seats ✽Dinner £11 alc Wine £4.30 Last dinner 9pm P
S% **VS**

MERIDEN
West Midlands
Map **4** SP28
★★★**Manor** (DeVere) ☎(0676) 22735

→

M

Telex no 311011

Originally a Georgian house, located in the heart of England.

32⇌ CTV in all bedrooms *sB⇌£28 (room only) dB⇌£40.50 (room only) B

☾ CTV 270P CFA ✿ ≘ (heated) Live music and dancing Sat Cabaret Sat ♿

English & Continental ✿ ☐ Lunch £5.50&alc Dinner £12.60alc Wine £5.50 Last dinner 10pm

S% Credit cards 1 2 3 4 5 VS

MERTHYR TYDFIL
Mid Glamorgan
Map **3** SO00

★★**Castle** Castle St ☎(0685) 2327

Modern, commercial hotel situated in the town centre.

47⇌ (4fb) CTV in all bedrooms ® sB&B⇌ £23 dB&B⇌ £29 B

Lift ☾ CTV *xmas*

✿ Lunch £6.50 Tea 55p Dinner £8.35alc Wine £3.60 Last dinner 9.45pm

Credit cards 1 2 3 5 VS

MESSING
Essex
Map **5** TL81

✕ ***Old Crown Inn*** ☎ Tiptree (0621) 815575

Closed Mon Dinner not served Sun

French **V** 55 seats Last dinner 9.30pm 30P

Credit cards 3 5

MEVAGISSEY
Cornwall
Map **2** SX04

★★**Spa** Polkirt Hill ☎(0726) 842244

10rm(4⇌) (1fb) ® sB&B£11.50–£13 sB&B⇌£13.50–£15 dB&B£23–£26 dB&B⇌£27–£30 B

CTV 14P 2 ✿ (hard) nc5yrs

English & Continental ✿ ☐ Bar lunch £1.80–£4.50 Tea 50p–£2 Dinner £6.50 Wine £3.35 Last dinner 8pm

Credit cards 1 2 3 5 VS

★★**Tremarne** Polkirt Hill (Minotel) ☎(0726) 842213

Closed Nov–Mar

Meriden — Middlesbrough

Small friendly hotel in an elevated position with views of the coastline.

14rm(4⇌5) (3fb) CTV in all bedrooms ® sB&B£11–£14 sB&B⇌ £14 dB&B£18–£24 dB&B⇌ £22–£30 B

CTV 14P ≘ (heated) nc5yrs

English, French, Indian & Italian ✿ ☐ Bar lunch £1.50 Tea 70p Dinner £7 Wine £4.25 Last dinner 8pm

Credit cards 1 3

★★**Trevalsa Court** Polstreath ☎(0726) 842468

Closed Feb

Country house of character in a peaceful situation overlooking the sea.

10rm(3⇌2) ® sB&B£12–£13 sB&B⇌ £14–£15 dB&B£24–£26 dB&B⇌ £28–£30 B

CTV 45P ✿

English, French & Italian **V** ✿ Bar lunch £1.50–£4.50 Dinner £6.50&alc Wine £3.95 Last dinner 9.30pm

Credit cards 1 2 3 5

MICKLETON
Gloucestershire
Map **4** SP14

★★★**Three Ways** (Inter-Hotel) ☎(038 677) 231

Large, country-house hotel, that is a good touring centre for the Cotswolds.

39rm(37⇌) (2fb) CTV in 28 bedrooms sB&B£15 sB&B⇌£19.40–£23 dB&B£25 dB&B⇌£32.20–£37.50 B

☾ CTV 70P CFA ✿ *xmas* ♿

British & Continental **V** ✿ ☐ Lunch £6–£7.15&alc Tea £1.50–£2.50 High Tea £3.50 Dinner £7–£8.50&alc Wine £4.80 Last dinner 10pm

Credit cards 1 2 3

MIDDLEHAM
North Yorkshire
Map **7** SE18

★**Millers House** Market Pl ☎ Wensleydale (0969) 22630

An 18th-century former merchant's house, in the corner of the Market Place.

6rm(5⇌) TV in all bedrooms ® sB&B£15 dB&B⇌£30 B

10P *xmas*

English & Continental ✿ * Bar lunch £1.50–£1.90 Dinner £8alc Wine £3.50 Last dinner 9pm

Credit card 5

MIDDLESBROUGH
Cleveland
Map **8** NZ42

☆☆☆☆**Ladbroke Dragonara** (& Conferencentre) Fry St (Ladbroke) ☎(0642) 248133 Telex 58266

Multi-storey modern hotel near the town centre.

140rm(126⇌14) CTV in all bedrooms ® *sB⇌ fr£32 (room only) dB⇌ fr£42 (room only) B

Lift ☾ 30 CFA Live music and dancing Fri & Sat (in season)

V ✿ * Lunch fr£6.50 Dinner fr£8.50 Last dinner 10.30pm

Credit cards 1 2 3 5

☆☆☆**Blue Bell Motor Inn** Acklam (Swallow) ☎(0642) 593939 Telex no 53168

A two-storey hotel with a modern wing, standing by a busy roundabout.

60⇌ CTV in all bedrooms ® sB&B⇌£19.50–£28.50 dB&B⇌£28–£37.50 B

Lift ☾ CTV 200P CFA

Mainly grills **V** ✿ ☐ * Lunch £3–£4.50&alc Tea 50p–£1.50 Dinner £7&alc Wine £5 Last dinner 10pm

Credit cards 1 2 3 5

★★★***Marton*** Stokesley Rd, Marton (3m S A172) ☎(0642) 317141

A modern functionally built three storey hotel at the junction of the A172 and A174. Spacious public areas and conference banqueting facilities. Bright and cheerful bedrooms, warm and comfortable facilities.

54⇌ CTV in all bedrooms ® B

CTV 320P CFA billiards Live music and dancing Sat Cabaret Sat

V ✿ ☐ Last dinner 9.15pm

Credit cards 2 3

CASTLE HOTEL

☆☆☆**Marton Way** Marton Rd ☎(0642) 817651
Modern, comfortable hotel surrounding a courtyard car park.
Annexe: 53→ (4fb) CTV in all bedrooms Ⓡ *sB&B→£15–£22.50 dB&B→£21.50–£29.50 B
☾ 250P CFA
V ♧ ☐ *Lunch £3.95–£6.30&alc Dinner £3.95–£6.30&alc Last dinner 9.45pm
Credit cards 1 2 3 5

MIDDLETON-IN-TEESDALE
Co Durham
Map **12** NY92
★★ *B* **Teesdale** Market Pl ☎Teesdale (0833) 40264
14rm(7→) (1fb) sB&B fr£10.95 sB&B→ fr£12.95 dB&B fr£21.90 dB&B→ fr£25.90 B
CTV 20P
English, French, German & Italian ♧ ☐ Bar lunch 70p–£3.50 Dinner fr£7 Wine £4.50 Last dinner 8.30pm
Credit card 3

MIDDLETON-ON-SEA (nr Bognor Regis)
West Sussex
Map **4** SU90
★ ***Manor Farm*** Elmer Sands ☎(024 369) 3154
Closed Dec–Feb
Coastal hotel in thatched manor farm house.
6rm(1→4⋒) CTV in all bedrooms Ⓡ ★
35P nc10yrs
V Last dinner 9.30pm
Credit card 3

MIDDLETON STONEY
Oxfordshire
Map **4** SP52
★★ **Jersey Arms Inn** ☎(086 989) 234
Closed Xmas
6→ Annexe: 3→ (1fb) CTV in all bedrooms ★ sB&B→£20 dB&B→£30 B
CTV 100P 1
♧ Lunch £8alc Dinner £8alc Wine £5.50 Last dinner 9.30pm
Credit cards 1 2 3

MIDDLE WALLOP
Hampshire
Map **4** SU23
★★ *L* **Fifehead Manor** ☎Andover (0264) 781565
Closed 2wks Xmas & New Year
Small manor house hotel, providing comfortable rooms in the main building as well as further rooms in a modern annexe.
7rm(6→) Annexe: 5⋒ TV in all bedrooms sB&B→⋒£27 dB&B→⋒£42 Continental breakfast B
50P 2 ✽
International **V** ♧ ☐ Lunch £11alc Tea £2.50alc Dinner £11alc Wine £4.10 Last dinner 9.30pm
Credit cards 1 2 3 5 **VS**

✕ **Old Drapery Stores** ☎Andover (0264) 781301
Good continental cuisine is offered at this Dutch-owned restaurant.
Closed Sun, Boxing Day & New Years Day
Lunch not served Sat
English & Continental **V** 44 seats *Lunch £4.95 Dinner £7.36–£9.56&alc Wine £4.35 Last dinner 10pm 12P bedrooms available
S% Credit cards 2 3

MIDHURST
West Sussex
Map **4** SU82
★★★ ***Spread Eagle*** South St (Best Western) ☎(073 081) 2211 Telex no 86853
Historic (1430's) hotel with comfortable old bar and restaurant.
23→ Annexe: 4rm(2→) 2 CTV in all bedrooms B
☾ CTV 100P CFA
♧ ☐ Last dinner 9.30pm
Credit cards 1 2 3 5

MILDENHALL
Suffolk
Map **5** TL77

★★ **Bell** High St (Best Western) ☎(0638) 712134
Parts of this former coaching inn date from 1600.
18rm(12→1⋒) (3fb) CTV in all bedrooms Ⓡ sB&B£19 sB&B→⋒£21 dB&B£30 dB&B→⋒£32 B
20P *xmas*
V ♧ ☐ Lunch £5.40 Tea 60p High Tea 80p Dinner £8alc Wine £3.60 Last dinner 9pm
Credit cards 1 2 3 5

MILFORD HAVEN
Dyfed
Map **2** SM90
★★ **Lord Nelson** Hamilton Ter (Wessex Taverns) ☎(06462) 5341
Comfortable, modern hotel.
24rm(22→3⋒) CTV in all bedrooms Ⓡ ★ sB&B→⋒£25 dB&B→⋒£35 B
☾ 30P 8 *xmas*
English & French **V** ♧ ☐ Lunch £1.50–£2.20
Credit cards 1 2 3 5

☆☆ **Sir Benfro** Herbrandston (3m W on unclass rd) ☎(06462) 4242
Small friendly hotel.
12→ TV in all bedrooms Ⓡ sB&B→£15–£17.50 dB&B→£21–£25 B
TV 70P ✽ Live music and dancing wknds
English & French **V** ♧ ☐ *Lunch £3.50–£5.50 Tea 75p–£1.50 High Tea £1.50–£2.50 Dinner £4.50–£5.95&alc Wine £3.75 Last dinner 9.15pm
VS

MILFORD-ON-SEA
Hampshire
Map **4** SZ29
✕ **Mill House** 1 High St ☎(059 069) 2611
Small personally run village restaurant with baked prawns a delicious speciality.
Closed Mon, 18 Oct–5 Nov
Dinner not served Sun
English & French 50 seats Lunch £3.80–£4.15&alc Dinner £8alc Wine £3.60 Last dinner 9.30pm
Credit cards 1 2 3 5 **VS**

M

MILNATHORT
Tayside *Kinross-shire*
Map **11** NO10

★**Thistle** New Rd ☎ Kinross (0577) 63222
6rm (1fb) ® sB&B£9 dB&B£18
CTV 40P Disco twice wkly Live music and dancing twice wkly
V ♈ Bar lunch £1.20–£2.20 High Tea £3.20 Dinner £6.50alc Wine £3.80 Last dinner 8pm

MILNGAVIE
Strathclyde *Dunbartonshire*
Map **11** NS57

★★★**Black Bull Thistle** Main St (Thistle) ☎ 041-956 2291 Telex no 778323
Former coaching inn dating from 1740 with a modern extension.
27rm (24➡3⋒) CTV in all bedrooms ® ✱sB➡⋒ £30–£35 (room only) dB➡⋒ £32–£38 (room only) Ᵽ
☾ CTV 70P Live music and dancing Sat
⊡ European ☕ ✱Lunch £4&alc Dinner £8.50&alc Last dinner 8.30pm
Credit cards 1 2 3 4 5 **VS**

✕✕**Gavin's Mill** ☎ 041-956 1439
Closed Sun
⊡ French & Italian 60 seats Lunch £3.50–£4&alc Dinner £7&alc Wine £4.20 Last dinner 10.30pm 120P
Credit cards 1 2 3 4 5 **VS**

MILTON
Dyfed
Map **2** SN00

★★**Milton Manor** ☎ Carew (06467) 398
Georgian manor house in 2½ acres of secluded grounds, personally run.
26rm (14➡7⋒) (9fb) CTV in 7 bedrooms ® sB&B£12.15–£13.25 sB&B➡⋒ £13.25–£15.75 dB&B£24.30–£26.50 dB&B➡⋒ £26.50–£31.50 Ᵽ
CTV 40P ✽ ⌂
⊡ International V ♈ ☕ Lunch fr£2.25 Tea 50p–£2 High Tea £2–£3 Dinner £6&alc Wine £3.70 Last dinner 9.30pm
VS

MILTON ABBAS
Dorset
Map **3** ST80

★★♛**Milton Manor** ☎ (0258) 880254
Closed Nov–Mar
Tudor-style manor house hotel in its own grounds amidst the Dorset countryside.
12rm (4➡3⋒) (3fb) ✱ sB&B£15–£17 dB&B£26 dB&B➡⋒ £30
CTV 20P ✽ nc12yrs
Bar lunch £2.50–£3.50 Dinner £6 Wine £4.20 Last dinner 7.30pm

MILTON COMMON
Oxfordshire
Map **4** SP60

★★**Belfry** Brimpton Grange (Inter-Hotels) ☎ Great Milton (08446) 381 Telex no 837968
Closed 25–27 Dec
Big, half-timbered, country house in large grounds, with an adjoining banqueting hall.
43rm (27➡9⋒) 1⊟ CTV in all bedrooms ® sB&B£23 sB&B➡⋒ £28 dB&B£28 dB&B➡⋒ £35–£39 Continental breakfast Ᵽ
☾ 200P CFA ✽ ≋ billiards ⌂
⊡ International ♈ ☕ Lunch fr£7&alc Tea 65p Dinner £8.50–£10.50&alc Wine £5.75 Last dinner 9.30pm
Credit cards 1 2 3 5

MILTON KEYNES
Buckinghamshire
Map **4** SP83

★★**Cock** Watling St, Stony Stratford ☎ (0908) 562109
Small country town hotel with a warm friendly atmosphere and good food.
18rm (3➡3⋒) Annexe: 2rm (2fb) CTV in all bedrooms ✱sB&B£16.50–£22 dB&B£22.50–£32 dB&B➡⋒ £30–£39 Ᵽ
CTV 100P 3⌂
⊡ International ♈ ✱Lunch £8alc Dinner £8alc Wine £4.65 Last dinner 9.45pm
Credit cards 1 2 3 5 **VS**

★★**Woughton House** Woughton on the Green ☎ (0908) 661919
Closed 25–27 Dec
Country house style hotel with informal atmosphere.
10rm (8➡2⋒) CTV in all bedrooms sB&B➡⋒ £20–£31 dB&B➡⋒ £30–£43 Ᵽ
☾ 60P ✽ Live music and dancing Fri, Sat & Sun
V ♈ ☕ Lunch £4.50–£10&alc Tea 60p Dinner £5–£10&alc Wine £3.45 Last dinner 10pm
Credit cards 1 2 3

MILTON ON STOUR
Dorset
Map **3** ST82

★★★♛**Milton Lodge** ☎ Gillingham (07476) 2262
Georgian house situated in 5½ acres of grounds.
10rm (9➡1⋒) (4fb) CTV available in bedrooms sB&B➡⋒ £14–£24 dB&B➡⋒ £26–£43 Ᵽ
CTV 50P ✽ ≋ (heated) ♪ U ⌂ *xmas*
⊡ English & French V ♈ ☕ Lunch £3.50–£6 Tea 50p–£1 High Tea £1.50–£3.50 Dinner £8.50–£10.50 Wine £5 Last dinner 9.30pm
Credit cards 1 2

MINCHINHAMPTON
Gloucestershire
Map **3** SO80
See **Amberley**

MINEHEAD
Somerset
Map **3** SS94

★★★**Beach** The Avenue (Trusthouse Forte) ☎ (0643) 2193
Built in 1874 of local brick and now fully modernised, the hotel is close to the Esplanade and the beach.
35rm (33➡2⋒) (6fb) CTV in all bedrooms ® sB&B➡⋒ £34.50 dB&B➡⋒ £47 Ᵽ
40P ≋ (heated) ⌂
♈ ☕ Last dinner 8.45pm
Credit cards 1 2 3 4 5

Minehead

★★★*H* **Benares** Northfield Rd ☎(0643) 2340 Closed last 2 wks Oct & 2 wks Xmas
Friendly holiday and business hotel, with good restaurant and fine garden.
21rm(16→1⋒)(1fb) CTV in all bedrooms ®sB&B£24.15 sB&B→⋒£28.35 dB&B£42 dB&B→⋒£47.30 ⊟
CTV 20P 1⌂✽
⊟English & French V ♁ ☐ Lunch £4.75–£5 Dinner £6.50–£6.75&alc Wine £3.10 Last dinner 8.15pm
Credit cards 1 2 3 5

★★★*HL* **Northfield** Northfield Rd ☎(0643) 5155 Telex no 42513
Friendly holiday hotel with attractive garden.
27rm(21→3⋒)(2fb) CTV in all bedrooms ®sB&B£22.50–£27 sB&B→⋒£24.50–£29 dB&B£42–£51 dB&B→⋒£46–£57 ⊟
Lift 24P 3⌂ ✽ nc5yrs *xmas*
V ♁ ☐ Lunch £5.75–£7.75 Tea £1 Dinner £8.50–£10.50 Wine £3.25 Last dinner 8.15pm
Credit cards 1 2 3 5 VS

★★**Beaconwood** Church Rd, North Hill ☎(0643) 2032
Closed 2wks Nov RS rest of Nov
Peaceful, family-run hotel outside the town centre.
16rm(3→2⋒)(5fb) sB&B£11.50–£12 sB&B→⋒£13–£13.50 dB&B£23–£24 dB&B→⋒£26–£27 ⊟
CTV 30P ✽ ⌒(heated) *xmas*
V Lunch £3.50–£4.50&alc Dinner £5.50–£6&alc Wine £4 Last dinner 8pm
Credit cards 1 3 VS

★★**Merton** Western Ln, The Parks ☎(0643) 2375
Closed Nov–Mar
Small, holiday and business hotel, that is comfortable and personally run.
12rm(3→3⋒)(2fb) sB&B£9.45–£11.55 dB&B£18.90–£23.10 dB&B→⋒£21.80–£26 ⊟
CTV 14P ✽
V ♁ ☐ Lunch £2.50–£3.50 Tea fr 75p Dinner fr £7 Wine £3.50 Last dinner 8pm

★★*HL* **Hotel Remuera** Northfield Rd ☎(0643) 2611
Closed Nov RS Dec–Feb
Small country-house style hotel which is personally-run.
8rm(3→) Annexe: 2rm(1→)(3fb) CTV available in bedrooms ®sB&B£15.75–£17.50 sB&B→£17.50–£19.50 dB&B£25.50–£28.50 dB&B→£28.25–£32.50 ⊟
CTV 9P ✽ nc12yrs
♁ ☐ Lunch fr £4.25 Tea fr £2.50 Dinner fr £6&alc Wine £4.90 Last dinner 10pm
VS

★★*L* **Winsor** The Avenue ☎(0643) 2171
Closed Nov–Apr
Large, seasonal, holiday hotel run by the owners.
38rm(10→)(4fb) CTV in 10 bedrooms ® sB&B£11 dB&B£22 dB&B→£24
CTV 26P
♁ Bar lunch £2 Dinner £5.75 Wine £2.90 Last dinner 8pm
Credit cards 1 2 3

★★*H* **Woodcombe Lodge** Bratton Ln ☎(0643) 2789
Quietly situated on the edge of town with spacious garden.
10rm(2→4⋒)(1fb) CTV in all bedrooms ®sB&B→⋒£17–£18 dB&B→⋒£34–£36 ⊟
16P ✽ nc9yrs *xmas*
⊟English & Continental ♁ ☐ Lunch £8alc Tea 40p–50p Dinner £6.50–£7&alc Wine £3.95 Last dinner 9.30pm
Credit cards 1 3 5
See advert on page 454

★★**York** The Avenue ☎(0643) 5151
Business and holiday hotel situated in the centre of Minehead. →

M

20rm(5⇒4⋒)Ⓡ✶sB&B£10–£12 dB&B£20–£24 dB&B⇒⋒£24–£28 B

CTV 16P nc10yrs

♆☐ Bar lunch £2.50alc Tea 75palc Dinner £6.50alc Wine £4.10 Last dinner 9.30pm

Credit cards 1 2 3 4 5

★ *H* **Kingsway** Ponsford Rd ☎(0643) 2313

Closed Oct–19 Apr

Comfortable, privately-owned and run holiday hotel.

10rm (2fb) sB&B£12 dB&B£24 B

CTV 10P ⇎ nc5yrs

Lunch £5 Dinner £7 Wine £2.85 Last dinner 7pm

Credit cards 1 3

★ *H* **Mentone** The Parks ☎(0643) 5229

Closed Nov–Feb

Small, privately-owned hotel situated in Minehead, forming an ideal centre for touring the surrounding countryside and coastline.

8rm(4⇒2⋒) (2fb) CTV in all bedrooms Ⓡ sB&B£9–£10 sB&B⇒⋒£15 dB&B£18–£20 dB&B⇒⋒£20–£24 B

5P 4⌂ ⇎ nc10yrs

☐ English & French ♆ Lunch £3.25 Dinner £5.50 Wine £3.28 Last dinner 8pm

Credit cards 1 2 3

M

MINSTEAD
Hampshire
Map **4** SU21

✕ **Honeysuckle Cottage**
☎ Southampton (0703) 813122

Closed Sun–Tue

V 48 seats ✱ Dinner £13alc Wine £5.50 Last dinner 9pm 20P

Credit card 1

MINSTER LOVELL
Oxfordshire
Map **4** SP31

★★ **Old Swan** ☎ Witney (0993) 75614

Quiet, comfortable hotel with formal restaurant.

5rm(4⇒) 1⊟ ✶ ✱ sB&B⇒£29.70 dB&B⇒£40.15 B

CTV 50P ⇎ ✽ nc6yrs *xmas*

♆☐ ✱ Lunch £5 Tea 75p Dinner fr£10alc Wine £4.65 Last dinner 9.30pm

Credit cards 1 2 3 5 **VS**

MOCHRUM
Dumfries & Galloway *Wigtownshire*
Map **10** NX34

★ **Greenmantle** ☎ Port William (09887) 357

Converted from a 17th-century manse, this hotel stands in its own grounds in the centre of this small, country village.

7rm(6⋒) (2fb) ✶ sB&B£8.50–£12.50 sB&B⋒£9.50–£13.50 dB&B£19–£27 dB&B⋒£19–£27 B

CTV 20P ⇎ ✽

☐ International ♆☐ Lunch £4.50–£5 Tea £1–£1.20 High Tea £2.50–£3 Dinner £6–£7.50&alc Wine £3.20 Last dinner 9.30pm

S%

MODBURY
Devon
Map **3** SX65

★ **Modbury Inn** Brownston St ☎(0548) 830275

6rm(1⇒) (2fb) CTV in all bedrooms Ⓡ ✶ sB&B£11.50 dB&B£23 dB&B⇒£27.60

CTV 12P 2⌂ ⇎ ✽ nc4yrs

☐ Mainly grills **V** ♆☐ Lunch fr£1 Dinner fr£2.50 Wine £3.25 Last dinner 9.30pm

VS

✕ **Modbury Pippin** 35 Church St ☎(0548) 830765

Terraced cottage in the main street with a plate-glass frontage and a canopied entrance.

Closed Sun & Jan

☐ Cosmopolitan **V** 26 seats Lunch £2.50alc Tea £1alc Dinner £4.95&alc Wine £3.60 Last dinner 9.30pm ⸙ bedrooms available

Credit cards 1 3 **VS**

MOELFRE
Gwynedd
Map **6** SH58

✕✕ **Old Ship's Bell** ☎(024 888) 693

Closed Mon Lunch not served Oct–May

☐ English & French 60 seats Lunch £2.95–£4.50 Dinner £7.50–£12&alc Wine £3.75 Last dinner 9.30pm ⸙

Credit cards 1 3

MOFFAT
Dumfries & Galloway *Dumfriesshire*
Map **11** NT00

☆☆☆ **Ladbroke** Ladyknowe (Ladbroke) ☎(0683) 20464

A modern, two-storey building at the foot of the main square.

51⇒ (4fb) CTV in all bedrooms Ⓡ ✱ sB⇒ fr£25 (room only) dB⇒ fr£37 (room only) B

☾ 70P

✱ Lunch fr£6.50 Dinner fr£8.50 Last dinner 9.30pm

Credit cards 1 2 3 5

★★ **Annandale** High St ☎(0683) 20013

Closed Dec–Feb RS Mar

A modernised and extended coaching inn dating from 1780.

19rm Annexe: 5⇒ (4fb) TV in 5 bedrooms Ⓡ sB&B£12–£13 sB&B⇒£16–£17 dB&B£24–£26 dB&B⇒£28–£30

CTV 50P

V ♆ Bar lunch £3.95–£5 Dinner £6–£6.25 Wine £3.75 Last dinner 8.15pm

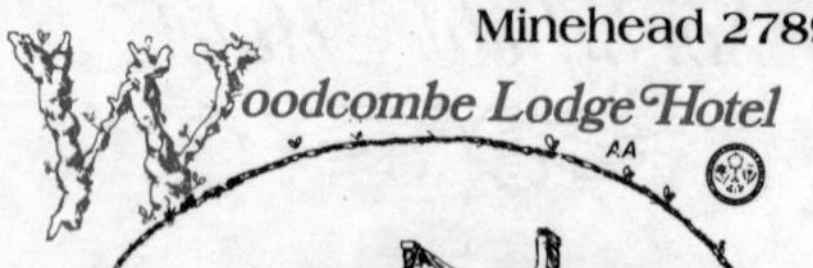

Credit cards 1 2 3 5

★★ ***Balmoral*** High St ☎(0683) 20288

Two-storey hotel with characteristic shutters.

18rm(2⇒) B

CTV 12P

☐ Scottish, Belgian & French ♆☐ Last dinner 9pm

Credit cards 1 2 3 5

✿★★ *HB* **Beechwood Country House** ☎(0683) 20210

Closed Jan

(Rosette awarded for dinner only.)

Small, intimate, nicely decorated hotel.

8rm(4➡2⋒)Ⓡ✱sB&B£13–£16 sB&B➡⋒£15–£18 dB&B£26–£32 dB&B➡⋒£30–£36 Ᵽ

CTV 20P ✽

Lunch £6.60alc Tea 75p alc Dinner £10alc Wine £4 Last dinner 9pm

Credit cards 1 2 3 4 5

★★Moffat House High St ☎(0683) 20039

Fine 18th-century Adam mansion with wide country views at rear. Nicely decorated rooms and attentive service.

15rm(4➡7⋒)(3fb)Ⓡ sB&B£16 sB&B➡⋒£18 dB&B£29 dB&B➡⋒£33 Ᵽ

CTV 30P 6 ✽ ♿

International V Lunch £5.75 High Tea £3.90–£4.90 Dinner £8.50 Wine £5.50 Last dinner 8.45pm

Credit cards 2 3 5 **VS**

See advert on page 456

MOLD
Clwyd
Map **7** SJ26

★★*Bryn Awel* Denbigh Rd ☎(0352) 3285 Closed 25 Dec–9 Jan

Business and tourist hotel situated on the edge of the town.

7rm(3➡⋒) Annexe: 12rm(2➡) CTV in all bedrooms Ⓡ✱

60P 5

English & French V Last dinner 10.15pm

Credit cards 1 3 5

MONIAIVE
Dumfries & Galloway *Dumfriesshire*
Map **11** NX79

★★Woodlea ☎(08482) 209

RS Nov–Mar (advance bookings advised)

A family hotel with many recreational facilities, set in five acres of grounds.

15rm(5➡)(3fb)Ⓡ sB&B£9.80–£13 dB&B£19.60–£26 dB&B➡£13.80–£34 Ᵽ

CTV 40P ✽ (heated) (grass) sauna bath nc1mth

International V Lunch £3.45–£3.50 Tea £1.40–£1.50 Dinner £6.20–£6.50&alc Wine £3.80 Last dinner 8.30pm

★*Craigdarroch Arms* ☎(08482) 205

9rm

CTV 8P

Last dinner 9pm

MONK FRYSTON
North Yorkshire
Map **8** SE52

★★★Monk Fryston Hall ☎South Milford (0977) 682369

A medieval country mansion, standing in its own grounds and ornamental gardens, popular with businessmen.

24➡ CTV in all bedrooms Ⓡ sB&B➡£29–£32 dB&B➡£38–£40 Ᵽ

☾ 60P 2 ✽ *xmas* ♿

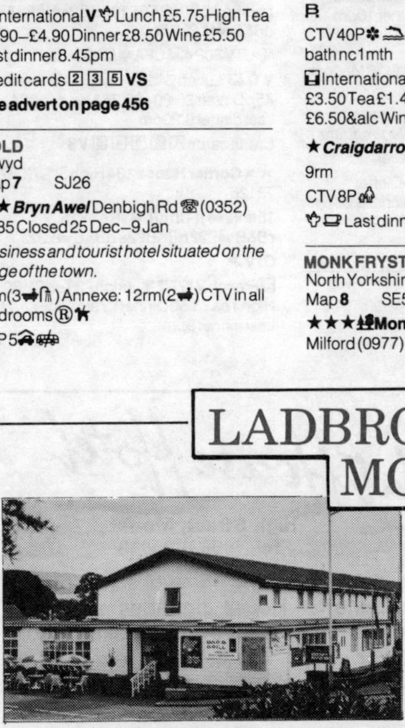

Lunch £5.75–£6&alc Dinner £8.75–£9&alc Wine £6.25 Last dinner 9.30pm

Credit cards 1 2 3

MONKLEIGH
Devon
Map **2** SS42

★★*Beaconside* ☎Bideford (02372) 77205 Closed mid Nov–Feb

Comfortable, small, secluded hotel with good food and atmosphere.

9➡⋒ CTV in all bedrooms Ⓡ✱Ᵽ

CTV 15P ✽ (grass) nc10yrs

French Last dinner 8pm

MONMOUTH
Gwent
Map **3** SO51

★★★King's Head Agincourt Sq (Inter-Hotels) ☎(0600) 2177

Comfortable, traditional hotel with Charles I associations.

25rm(19➡6⋒) Annexe: 3➡(2fb) 1 CTV in all bedrooms sB➡⋒ fr£29 (room only) dB➡⋒ fr£39.50 (room only) Ᵽ

☾ 20P CFA *xmas* →

Monmouth — Montrose

🍴Welsh, English & French V☕Lunch fr7&alc Dinner fr£9.50&alc Wine £4.50 Last dinner 9pm

Credit cards 1 2 3 5 VS

★★ ***Beaufort Arms*** Agincourt Sq (Trusthouse Forte) ☎(0600) 2411

Early 18th-century coaching inn with a Georgian façade adjoining the old Shire hall.

26rm(3⇌) CTV in all bedrooms ® ⊟

CTV 28P

☕Last dinner 9pm

Credit cards 1 2 3 4 5

★ ***Talocher Farmhouse*** Wonastow Rd ☎Dingestow (060083) 236

Small, character, rural hotel.

9rm(1⇌⋒) ⊟

⅟CTV 20P 2⌂ ✿ ⛰ sauna bath

☕☐ Last dinner 11pm

★ **White Swan** Priory St ☎(0600) 2045

Closed 24–26 Dec & New Year

Listed, former coaching inn situated conveniently in the town centre.

19rm(4⇌) sB&B£12.50–£13.50 sB&B⇌£17 dB&B£23 dB&B⇌£26.50 ⊟

CTV 7P 10⌂

🍴English & French ☕Lunch £3.20 Dinner £6.50alc Wine £4 Last dinner 9.30pm

Credit cards 1 2 3 VS

MONTACUTE
Somerset
Map **3** ST41

★★ **Kings Arms Inn** Bishopston ☎Martock (0935) 822513

Closed Xmas Day

Most attractive inn with fine rooms and interesting food.

10⇌⋒ CTV in all bedrooms ® ★ sB&B⇌⋒£22.50–£25 dB&B⇌£35–£38 ⊟

20P ✿

🍴International V☕☐ Buffet lunch £1.25–£3.95 Tea fr£1.25 Dinner £5.50–£12&alc Wine £5.25 Last dinner 10pm

Credit cards 1 2 3 5

✕✕ **Milk House** The Borough ☎Martock (0935) 823823

Old stone house with lattice windows, attractively situated in the village square.

Closed Sun & Mon Lunch not served

🍴English & French 50 seats Dinner £11.50alc Wine £3.85 Last dinner 9.30pm

Credit cards 1 3

MONTROSE
Tayside *Angus*
Map **15** NO75

★★★ **Links** Mid Links (Minotel) ☎(0674) 72288

Businessman's hotel with its own popular disco.

22rm(18⇌) (4fb) CTV in 16 bedrooms TV in 2 bedrooms ® ✱sB&B19 sB&B⇌£23 dB&B£27 dB&B⇌£33 ⊟

☾ CTV 50P Disco nightly

☕☐✱Lunch £4.50–£5.50 Tea 80p–£1.50 High Tea £3.50–£4.50 Dinner £6.50–£8.50 Wine £4 Last dinner 10.45pm

Credit cards 1 2 3 5

★★★ **Park** John St ☎(0674) 73415

Telex no 76367

59rm(40⇌12⋒) (4fb) CTV in all bedrooms ® sB&B£19 sB&B⇌⋒£27 dB&B⇌⋒£37 ⊟

☾ CTV 80P 4⌂ CFA ✿ ∪ *xmas*

V☕☐ Lunch £4.25–£4.65&alc Tea 40p–45p Dinner £5.20–£5.75&alc Wine £4 Last dinner 9.30pm

Credit cards 1 2 3 4 5 VS

★★ **Corner House** 134 High St ☎(0674) 73126

15rm(2⇌) (1fb) ® ✱sB&B£15 sB&B⇌£22 dB&B£28 dB&B⇌£32

CTV

🍴French V☕☐✱Lunch £3 Tea £1.30 High Tea £3.50 Dinner £7alc Wine £4.75 Last dinner 9pm

M

MONYMUSK
Grampian *Aberdeenshire*
Map **15** NJ61

★★**Grant Arms** ☎(04677) 226
RS Nov–Mar (Dining Room closed)
Friendly inn dating from 18th century.
10rm(1) Annexe: 5rm(3 2) (2fb) Ⓡ *sB&B£15.62 sB&B £17.60 dB&B£31.90 dB&B £35.20
CTV 12P Live music Fri & Sat
*Lunch £3.50–£5 Tea 40p–£1.20 High Tea £2.60–£5.50 Dinner £8 Wine £3.84 Last dinner 9pm
S% Credit card 5

MORAR
Highland *Inverness-shire*
Map **13** NM69

★★**Morar** ☎Mallaig (0687) 2346
Closed Nov–Mar
Family run hotel above white sands of Morar.
28rm(10) (3fb) Ⓡ sB&B£13–£17.50 sB&B £16–£20.50 dB&B£23–£30 dB&B £29–£36 B
CTV 50P
Scottish & French **V** Lunch £3–£5 Tea 50–75p High Tea £3–£6 Dinner £4–£8 Wine £3.95 Last dinner 8.30pm
VS

MORECAMBE
Lancashire
Map **7** SD46

★★★**Elms** Bare ☎(0524) 411501
39rm(29 3) (3fb) CTV in 20 bedrooms *sB&B£16 sB&B £18.50 dB&B£32 dB&B £34.50 B
Lift ☾ CTV 80P CFA 11 Live music and dancing Tue & Sat *xmas*
V *Lunch £3.25–£4&alc Tea 40p High Tea £4.50–£6 Dinner fr£6.50 Wine £3.40 Last dinner 9pm
Credit cards 1 2 3 **VS**

★★★**Midland** Marine Rd ☎(0524) 417180
Large building, occupying a prominent position overlooking Morecambe Bay.
46rm(31 12) (3fb) CTV in all bedrooms Ⓡ *sB&B £29.50–£31 B
Lift ☾ 80P *xmas*
English & French **V** *Lunch £4.50&alc Tea £1 Dinner £6.95&alc Wine £4.10 Last dinner 9.30pm
Credit cards 1 2 5

★★**Clarendon** Promenade, West End ☎(0524) 410180 Closed Xmas & New Year
Tall, sea-front hotel overlooking the bay.
31rm(25 2) (4fb) CTV in 29 bedrooms Ⓡ sB&B fr£13 sB&B fr£18.50 dB&B fr£23 dB&B fr£26 B
Lift ☾ CTV billiards sauna bath
Lunch £2.75–£3.75 Dinner £3.50–£7&alc Wine £2.85 Last dinner 9pm
S% Credit cards 1 3 5 **VS**

★★**Strathmore** Marine Rd East ☎(0524) 411314
Friendly traditional hotel with resident proprietors.
55rm(29 11) CTV in all bedrooms Ⓡ *sB&B£14.50–£15.50 sB&B £20–£25 dB&B£28–£30 dB&B £35–£37 B
Lift ☾ 30P 12 *xmas*
English & French **V** Lunch £4–£6.50 Tea 50p High Tea £3 Dinner £4.50–£6.50&alc Wine £4 Last dinner 10.45pm
Credit cards 1 2 3 5

★**Rimington** 70–72 Thornton Rd ☎(0524) 415668
A stone-built corner sited house, situated in a side road off the promenade.
6 (1fb) CTV in all bedrooms Ⓡ *sB&B fr£13.50 dB&B fr£21
English & French **V** *Bar lunch fr£1.25 Dinner £5.50&alc Wine £4.75 Last dinner 9pm

MORETONHAMPSTEAD
Devon
Map **3** SX78

★★**White Hart** The Square ☎(06474) 406 (Due to change to (0647) 40406)
Built in 1637, this traditional inn has been modernised but retains its original character.
17rm(12 2) (3fb) CTV in all bedrooms Ⓡ sB&B£14.50 sB&B £18 dB&B£25 dB&B £29 B
8P billiards nc 10yrs *xmas*
English & French Bar lunch £1–£3 Tea 50p Dinner £6–£7 Wine £4.25 Last dinner 8.30pm
Credit cards 1 2 3 5

MORETON-IN-MARSH
Gloucestershire
Map **4** SP23

★★★*B***Manor House** High St (Best Western) ☎(0608) 50501 Telex no 837151
Elegant, traditional hotel with a good restaurant.
37rm(29 3) (1fb) 4 CTV in all bedrooms sB&B£18.50–£19.50 sB&B £27.50–£29.50 dB&B£32.50–£35 dB&B £42.50–£45
Lift ☾ ## CTV 40P 10 (heated) sauna bath nc 9yrs *xmas*
British & French **V** Lunch fr£5.75 Tea fr75p High Tea fr£1.50 Dinner fr£9.50 Wine £4.50 Last dinner 9pm
Credit cards 1 2 3 5 **VS**

★★***Redesdale Arms*** High St ☎(0608) 50308
Comfortable well run hotel with good restaurant.
8rm(3) Annexe: 6rm(2) CTV in all bedrooms Ⓡ B
40P
English & French
Credit cards 1 2 3 5
See advert on page 458

★★**White Hart Royal** High St (Trusthouse Forte) ☎(0608) 50731
A company-owned hotel with a cobbled hallway and a character lounge bar.
21rm(6) Annexe: 6rm CTV in all bedrooms Ⓡ sB&B£33 sB&B £35.50 dB&B£45.50 dB&B £49.50 B
CTV 10P *xmas*
Last dinner 9.30pm
Credit cards 1 2 3 4 5

M

❀XXX**Lambs** High St ☎(0608) 50251
A well-appointed country town restaurant with a high standard of cooking and service. Informal light meals are provided at lunch time.
Dinner not served Sun
⊟English & French 70 seats ✱Lunch 95p–£4.75 Dinner £9.50&alc Wine £4.25 Last dinner 10.30pm ⚡⊬
Credit cards 1 3

MORFA NEFYN
Gwynedd
Map **6** SH24
★★***Woodlands Hall*** Edern ☎Nefyn (0758) 720425
Georgian, country house hotel set in its own grounds, 1m from Morfa Nefyn and the beach, with large function facility.
13rm(5⇌2⋒) Ⓡ ⊟
⊬CTV 100P ✽ Live music and dancing wkly Cabaret mthly
V ♡ ⊐ Last dinner 9pm
Credit card 3

★**Bryn Noddfa** ☎Nefyn (0758) 720843
Family run holiday hotel in quiet situation.
9rm(1⇌5⋒) (2fb) sB&B£8.50 sB&B⇌⋒£9 dB&B£17 dB&B⇌⋒£18
CTV 16P
⊟English, French & Indian V ♡ ⊐ Lunch £4alc Tea £1alc High Tea £3.50alc Dinner £4.50alc Wine £4 Last dinner 9.30pm
Credit card 1

MORLEY
Derbyshire
Map **8** SK34
★★★**Breadsall Priory** (on unclass rd linking B6179 [Little Eaton] & A608) ☎Derby (0332) 832235
Large, Elizabethan manor house in extensive grounds which include a golf course.
17rm(14⇌3⋒) Annexe: 6⇌ (3fb) 1⊟ CTV in all bedrooms Ⓡ sB&B⇌⋒£26.50 dB&B⇌⋒£40 ⊟
150P ✽ ⚑18 squash billiards
⊟Continental V ♡ ⊐ Lunch £5.25–£5.75&alc Dinner £8.25&alc Wine £4.50 Last dinner 9.45pm
Credit cards 1 2 3 5

MORPETH
Northumberland
Map **12** NZ18
★★**Queen's Head** Bridge St (Scottish & Newcastle) ☎(0670) 512083
Closed Xmas Day
Tastefully modernised old coaching inn which retains old world comfort and atmosphere.
23rm(10⇌) CTV in all bedrooms Ⓡ ✱ ✱sB&B fr£16 sB&B⇌fr£18.50 dB&B fr£26.50 dB&B⇌fr£29
☾ 7P 14⌂
V ♡ ⊐ ✱Lunch £1.70–£3 Tea £1.50 High Tea £2.25–£4.10 Dinner £6.50–£10&alc Last dinner 9.45pm
Credit cards 1 2 3 5

MORTEHOE
Devon
Map **2** SS44
★**Glenhaven** Chapel Hill ☎Woolacombe (0271) 870376
Small, holiday hotel with a friendly atmosphere, in a peaceful location.
12rm(1⇌4⋒) (4fb) 3⊟ sB&B£7.50–£9.50 sB&B⇌⋒£8.50–£10.50 dB&B£15–£19 dB&B⇌⋒£17–£21 ⊟
CTV 7P ✽ ⌂ *xmas*
♡ ⊐ Bar lunch 45p–95p Tea fr30p Dinner fr£5.50 Wine £3 Last dinner 7.30pm

MOTHERWELL
Strathclyde *Lanarkshire*
Map **11** NS75
See also **Wishaw** (Strathclyde)
★★★**Garrion** Merry St ☎(0698) 64561
Large, commercial hotel in the town centre.
51rm(29⇌8⋒) CTV in all bedrooms Ⓡ sB&B£20 sB&B⇌⋒£25 dB&B£29 dB&B⇌⋒£34 ⊟

M

Lift ☾ 100P CFA sauna bath Disco wkly
Scottish, English & French V Lunch £3.45&alc Tea 60p High Tea £2–£2.75 Dinner £5.95&alc Wine £3.75 Last dinner 9.30pm
Credit cards 1 2 3 5

MOTTRAM ST ANDREW
Cheshire
Map **7** SJ87
★★★*B* **Mottram Hall** (Greenall Whitley) ☎Prestbury (0625) 828135 Telex no 668181
Georgian mansion built in 1721, standing in formal gardens surrounded by 120 acres of parkland.
72rm(68➡4⋔) 6 CTV in all bedrooms ®sB&B➡⋔£36.50–£37.50 dB&B➡⋔£49–£50 B
☾ CFA 200P ✽ (grass) billiards
French V Lunch fr£6.50&alc Tea fr60p Dinner fr£8&alc Wine £5.25 Last dinner 10pm
Credit cards 1 2 3 5

MOULTON
North Yorkshire
Map **8** NZ20
✕✕**Black Bull Inn** ☎Barton (032 577) 289
Closed Sun & 24–31 Dec Lunch not served Sat
English & French 90 seats ✱Lunch £8–£9alc Dinner £9–£11alc Wine £4.50 50P

MOUNT HAWKE
Cornwall
Map **2** SW74
★*HL* **Tregarthen Country Cottage**
Banns Rd ☎Porthtowan (0209) 890399
Comfortable, privately owned small cottage hotel, with well appointed bedrooms and good garden.
6rm(3➡1⋔) ✱sB&B fr£9 sB&B➡⋔ fr£10 dB&B fr£18 dB&B➡⋔ fr£20 B
CTV 12P ✽
✱Bar lunch 50p–£3.50 Tea fr40p Dinner fr£4 Wine £3.50 Last dinner 7.30pm
S% Credit card 1

MOUSEHOLE
Cornwall
Map **2** SW42
★★**Carn Du** Raginnis Hill ☎Penzance (0736) 731233
Small, comfortable, personally-run hotel above the village with views over Mount's Bay.
6rm(1➡1⋔) ® sB&B£10–£14 sB&B➡⋔£12–£16 dB&B£20–£28 dB&B➡⋔£24–£32.50 B
CTV 20P ✽ *xmas*
V Bar lunch £1.75–£2.50 Tea 50p Dinner £7 Wine £3.85 Last dinner 8.30pm
Credit cards 1 2 3 5

★★*H* **Lobster Pot** ☎Penzance (0736) 731251
Closed end Nov–early Mar
Well-appointed character hotel and restaurant overhanging the small village harbour.
14rm(11➡2⋔) Annexe: 4➡ (3fb) ✱sB&B£9.90–£16.22 sB&B➡⋔£11.55–£23.60 dB&B£19.80–£32.44 dB&B➡⋔£23.10–£47.20
CTV
English & French Lunch £3.50 Tea £1.30 Dinner £7.25 Wine £5 Last dinner 9.45pm
S% **VS**

★**Old Coastguard** ☎Penzance (0736) 731222
RS Jan & Feb
Small hotel at the entrance to the village, with a rear garden enjoying commanding views.
14rm(3➡1⋔) (4fb) 1 TV available in bedrooms ® sB&B£10.95–£12.95 dB&B£20.70–£24.10 dB&B➡⋔£26.20–£29.30 B
CTV 5P ✽ Live music and dancing 2 nights wkly *xmas*
V Bar lunch £1–£3.75&alc Tea 75p Dinner £5.50&alc Wine £4.30 Last dinner 9.30pm
S% Credit cards 1 2 3

MUCH BIRCH
Hereford & Worcester
Map **3** SO53
★★★*B* **Pilgrim House** ☎Golden Valley (0981) 540742
Fully modernised hotel in quiet surroundings.
15➡⋔ CTV in all bedrooms ® ✱sB&B➡⋔£24.50 dB&B➡⋔£35 B
100P ✽
French & Italian ✱Lunch £4.50–£10 Dinner £5.50–£10&alc Wine £2.50 Last dinner 9.30pm
Credit cards 1 2 3 4 5

MUDEFORD
Dorset
see **Christchurch**

MUIRHEAD
Strathclyde *Lanarkshire*
Map **11** NS66
★★***Crow Wood House*** (Scottish & Newcastle) ☎041-779 3861
Large, white painted inn situated on the busy A80.
18➡ CTV in all bedrooms ® B
☾ CTV 200P
Englsh & French V Last dinner 9.15pm
Credit cards 1 2 3 5

✕✕***La Campágnola*** 112 Cumbernauld Rd ☎041-779 3405
Smart little Italian restaurant with good atmosphere.
Closed Sun
International 60 seats Last dinner 11pm 20P
Credit cards 1 2 3 5

MUIR OF ORD
Highland *Ross & Cromarty*
Map **14** NH55
★★*B* ***Ord Arms*** ☎(0463) 870286
Closed New Year
Attractive, sandstone building set back from the main road on the northern outskirts of town.
15rm(4➡3⋔) CTV in all bedrooms ® B
200P ✽ Live music and dancing Fri
V Last dinner 8.30pm
Credit card 1

★★*L* **Ord House** ☎(0463) 870492
RS Nov–Mar
A 17th-century listed building retaining a traditional country house character.
14rm(8➡) (1fb) ® sB&B£11.75–£16.50 sB&B➡£12.75–£17.50 dB&B£23.50–£33 dB&B➡£25.50–£35 B
☾ CTV 20P ✽
Scottish, English & French V Bar lunch £1–£5 Tea £1.20–£2 Dinner £8–£10 Wine £4 Last dinner 8.30pm **VS**

MULL, ISLE OF
See **Salen** and **Tobermory**

MULLION
Cornwall
Map **2** SW61
★★★**Polurrian** ☎(0326) 240421
Closed 27 Oct–19 Apr
Family holiday hotel superbly situated in 12 acres of terraced grounds overlooking Polurrian Cove with its fine surfing sands.
43rm(39➡) (16fb) 4 CTV in all bedrooms ✱sB&B£13.50–£25.50 sB&B➡£15.50–£27.50 dB&B£27–£51 dB&B➡£31–£55 B
☾ CTV 60P 3 CFA ✽ (heated) (hard) squash Disco twice wkly Live music and dancing wkly
English & French V ✱Lunch £1–£6.50&alc Tea 70p–£1.20 High Tea £1.50–£3.50 Dinner £8.50&alc Wine £3.90 Last dinner 9.30pm
Credit cards 1 3 **VS**
See advert on page 462

MUMBLES (nr Swansea)
West Glamorgan
Map **2** SS68
See also **Langland Bay** and **Swansea**
★**St Annes** Western Ln ☎Swansea (0792) 69147 Closed Xmas
Small, quiet, modern hotel overlooking Swansea Bay.
25rm(12➡2⋔) (1fb) CTV in all bedrooms ® sB&B£12.65 sB&B➡⋔£16.10 dB&B£18.98 dB&B➡⋔£20.13
CTV 40P →

M

Bar lunch fr£1 Tea fr£1.25 Dinner £4.60–£5.46 Wine £4 Last dinner 6.30pm

XX **Norton House** Norton Rd
Swansea (0792) 404891
A well-appointed Georgian house offering comfortable surroundings.
Closed Sun, Xmas Day & New Years Day Lunch not served
French 70 seats Dinner fr£7.50&alc Wine £5 Last dinner 9.30pm 60P bedrooms available
Credit cards 1 3

MUNDESLEY-ON-SEA
Norfolk
Map **9** TG33
★★★ **Continental** (Mount Charlotte)
(0263) 720271
Closed Sep–Apr
44rm(26 1)(13fb) sB&B£18.50–£19 sB&B £20–£21 dB&B£28–£30 dB&B £30–£32 B
Lift CTV 100P CFA (heated) (hard) Live music and dancing wkly
V Lunch £4.25 Dinner £6.75&alc Wine £5 Last dinner 9pm
Credit cards 1 2 3 5

★★ **Manor** (0263) 720309
Closed 3–15 Jan
26rm(8 10)(2fb) CTV available in bedrooms sB&B£15–£17

sB&B £17.50–£20 dB&B£24 dB&B £26.50 B
CTV 40P (heated) Live music and dancing Sat *xmas*
Lunch £3.90&alc Tea 45p&alc Dinner £4.90&alc Wine £3.35

MUSSELBURGH
Lothian *Midlothian*
Map **11** NT37
☆☆ **Drummore** North Berwick Rd
031-665 2302 Telex no 8811232
Motor hotel with compact chalets and character restaurant.
Annexe: 47 CTV in all bedrooms ® *sB&B £16.50 dB&B £30 B
150P CFA *xmas*
Scottish & French *Bar lunch £1.30–£2.50 Tea 60p High Tea £3.50 Dinner £5.50&alc Wine £3.75 Last dinner 9.30pm
Credit cards 1 2 3 5 VS

★ **Pittencrieff** 59–60 Linkfield Rd
031-665 2104
RS Xmas & New Year
A tourist/commercial hotel on the east side of town, overlooking the race course.
17rm (4fb) sB&B£12.50–£14.50 dB&B£21–£25

CTV 30P
V Lunch £5alc Tea 80p alc High Tea £3.75alc Dinner £6.50alc Wine £3.50 Last dinner 8.30pm
Credit cards 1 3 VS

NAIRN
Highland *Nairnshire*
Map **14** NH85
★★★★ **Golf View** Seabank Rd
(0667) 52301 Telex no 777967
Traditional hotel catering for tourists and a business clientele, in a residential area with views across the Moray Firth.
55rm(45 10) CTV in all bedrooms sB&B £26–£30 dB&B £42–£50 B
Lift CTV 30P CFA (heated) (hard) sauna bath Live music, dancing & cabaret wkly *xmas*
Lunch fr£5.25 Tea fr£1.95 Dinner fr£9.75 Wine £4.95 Last dinner 9pm
Credit cards 1 2 3 5 VS

★★★★ **Newton** (0667) 53144
Telex no 777967 (att Clan)
Closed Nov–Mar
Imposing combination of Georgian and Scottish Baronial architecture with fine views over Moray Firth to the Ross-shire Hills.
34 Annexe: 14 CTV in all bedrooms ® sB&B £26–£30 dB&B £42–£50 B
Lift CTV 50P (hard) sauna bath

M

Lunch fr£5.25 Tea fr£1.95 Dinner fr£10.50 Wine £4.95 Last dinner 9pm
Credit cards 1 2 3 5

★★★**Royal Marine** Marine Rd ☎(0667) 53381 Telex no 75460
Large stone building convenient for beach and recreational area.
43rm(29⇌6⋒)(4fb) CTV in 4 bedrooms sB&B⇌⋒£19 dB&B⇌⋒£28–£33 B
Lift CTV 25P 2 ✽ Live music and dancing twice wkly Cabaret wkly *xmas*
Scottish, French & Italian **V** ✽Lunch £3.50–£4 Tea £1.25–£1.50 High Tea £3.50–£4 Dinner £8–£8.50 Last dinner 8.30pm
Credit cards 1 2 3 5

★★★**Windsor** Albert St ☎(0667) 53108
60rm(18⇌23⋒)(4fb) CTV in all bedrooms Ⓡ sB&B£16.45–£17.50 sB&B⇌⋒£19–£22 dB&B£30.05–£33 dB&B⇌⋒£35–£40 B
Lift ☾ ## CTV 50P CFA ✽ Live music and dancing & Cabaret Sat *xmas*
English & Continental Lunch £3.50–£5.50&alc Tea £1.75 High Tea £5–£7 Dinner £8.50–£9.50&alc Wine £3.50 Last dinner 6.15pm
Credit card 1 2 3 4 5

★★***Alton Burn*** Alton Burn Rd ☎(0667) 52051 Closed Nov–Mar
24rm(5⇌) Annexe: 10rm B
CTV 60P ✽ (heated) (hard)
Last dinner 8.30pm
Credit card 3

❀★★***HBL*****Clifton** ☎(0667) 53119 Closed Nov–Feb
(Rosette awarded for dinner only.)
All who appreciate good food and wine are welcome at this ivy-covered Victorian Hotel, owned for many years by Mr MacIntyre and his wife. The Victorian interior has been splendidly renovated and there are plenty of flowers, paintings and objets d'art. Each bedroom is individually designed and decorated. Dinner is almost a theatrical production of great taste.
17rm(10⇌) 2
CTV 20P ✽
French Last dinner 9.30pm
Credit card 2

★***Ross House*** Seabank Rd ☎(0667) 53731 Closed end Oct–mid Apr
Modestly appointed but comfortable and homely family and holiday hotel situated in a residential area.
17rm
CTV 17P ✽
Last dinner 8pm

★**Washington** 8 Viewfield St ☎(0667) 53351
Traditional, family hotel in a detached mansion, set in a residential area.
20rm(7⋒)(7fb) Ⓡ sB&B£10–£11 sB&B⋒£11.50–£12.50 dB&B£20–£22 dB&B⋒£23–£25 B
CTV 20P ✽
Bar lunch £1–£2.50 Tea £1 High Tea £3.25 Dinner £4.50–£5.50 Wine £3 Last dinner 7pm

NANT-DDU (near Merthyr Tydfil)
Powys
Map **3** SO01

★★**Nant Ddu Lodge** Cwm Taf ☎Merthyr Tydfil (0685) 79111
A former hunting lodge of Lord Tredegar, situated in spectacular scenery of the Brecon Beacons.
9rm(3⇌5⋒) CTV in all bedrooms
60P ✽
Last dinner 9pm

NANTWICH
Cheshire
Map **7** SJ65

★★**Alvaston Hall** Middlewich Rd (Best Western) ☎(0270) 624341 Telex no 36690
Large 19th-century building with a modern extension in an attractive rural setting.
40rm(25⇌15⋒) Annexe: 27rm(20⇌7⋒) (3fb) CTV in all bedrooms Ⓡ sB&B⇌⋒£24.15–£31.05 dB&B⇌⋒£31.05–£36.80 B
☾ 300P CFA ✽ (heated) (hard) squash sauna bath Disco Sat *xmas*
Lunch £6–£6.90&alc Tea £1–£1.90 Dinner £7.40–£8.50&alc Wine £4.60 Last dinner 10pm
Credit cards 1 2 3 5 **VS**

★★**Lamb** Hospital St ☎(0270) 625286
A 200-year-old coaching inn in the centre of town.
16rm(6⇌2⋒)(1fb) ✽sB&B£13.50 sB&B⇌⋒£18 dB&B£22 dB&B⇌⋒£27
CTV 15P 10
V ✽Lunch fr£3.50 High Tea £3.50 Dinner £8.50 Wine £6.50 Last dinner 9.30pm →

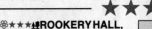

❀★★★ **ROOKERY HALL, NANTWICH**
Worleston (2m N B5074) (Prestige) ☎(0270) 626866

Mr Norton writes a regular column about the many problems which hotel keepers have to face, and it is therefore of particular credit to Mr and Mrs Norton and their staff that they have been able to maintain the impeccable standards that are now so much part of this hotel. Known as The English Château, this mansion is reputed to be Georgian in origin and was rebuilt early in the 19th century. It stands amidst 28 acres of gardens and wooded parkland, close to the River Weaver and with views over the verdant Cheshire Plain. It is a Grade 2 listed building and has been lovingly restored by the Nortons. It has individually decorated and furnished bedrooms, elegant and comfortable public rooms with some fine pieces of antique as well as reproduction furniture and a beautiful mahogany panelled dining room which reminds one of the opulence and style of days long gone. This past year has seen the addition of two new rooms, one with sitting area, in the converted Palladian stable block.
We award a single Rosette where the cuisine is considered to be of a higher standard than is expected within the classification; but this does not show the amount of dedication and skill which enables this high standard to be reached and much credit in this respect must go to Mrs Norton whose domain is well and truly the kitchen. She is currently one of only 23 Master Chef members of the British Chapter of the Master Chefs Institute and her skills are clearly evident in the mainly French provincial style of cooking. Additionally, Mrs Norton now runs a cookery enjoyment course in the hotel and husbands are tactfully invited to make a present of the course to their wives as a pleasurable and lasting gift. A visit to Rookery Hall will certainly be memorable: for its food, its wines (they are a hobby of Mr Norton and an extensive list is available) and most importantly, the hospitality and service provided by the Nortons and their friendly staff.
10⇌ Annexe: 2⇌ 1 CTV in all bedrooms sB&B⇌£39.95–£49.95 dB&B⇌£66.35–£105.60 B
Lift 50P ✽ (hard) nc 10yrs *xmas*
French **V** Lunch £6.25–£9.25&alc (Lunch not served Mon & Sat) Dinner £17.95–£18.95 Wine £6.45 Last dinner 8.30pm (8.45 Sat)
Credit cards 1 2 3 4 5 **VS**

N

Credit cards 1 3

✕✕**Churche's Mansion** Hospital St ☎(0270) 625933

Remarkable, 16th-century, half-timbered mansion, with beamed and panelled dining room.

Closed 25–28 Dec & 1 Jan Dinner not served Sun

60 seats Lunch £4.95–£5.95 Dinner £9.95–£10.95 Last dinner 8.30pm 30P

VS

NARBERTH
Dyfed
Map **2** SN11

★★**Plas-Hyfryd** Morfield Rd (Minotel) ☎(0834) 860653

A family-run hotel in an 18th-century mansion, which was formerly the rectory.

12rm(9→3⋒)(3fb)Ⓡ sB&B→⋒£15 dB&B→⋒£24.50 B

CTV 30P ✽ ⛆(heated) ⌂

Lunch £4.50&alc Dinner £5.50&alc Wine £3.20 Last dinner 9.30pm

Credit cards 1 3 **VS**

NARBOROUGH
Leicestershire
Map **4** SP59

★★**Charnwood** 48 Leicester Rd (Off A46 2m S of M1, junc 21) ☎Leicester (0533) 862218

Closed 26 Dec–2 Jan

Converted Victorian house in a Leicester suburb, conveniently near the M1.

23rm(8→2⋒) CTV in all bedrooms Ⓡ ★ sB&B£15.50–£16.50 sB&B→£18.50–£19.50 dB&B£24.50–£25.50 dB&B→£27.50–£28.50 B

40P ✽

English & French Lunch fr£3.25&alc Tea fr55p Dinner £5.95–£7.95&alc Wine £3.95 Last dinner 9.30pm

VS

NEASHAM
Co Durham
Map **8** NZ31

★★**Newbus Arms** Newbus Grange ☎Darlington (0325) 721071

9→⋒ 100P

V Lunch £4.75–£9.25&alc Dinner £9.25&alc Wine £4.95 Last dinner 10.15pm

Credit cards 1 2 3 5

NEATH
West Glamorgan
Map **3** SS79

★★**Castle** The Parade ☎(0639) 3581

Commercial hotel in the town centre.

30rm(5→18⋒)(1fb) CTV in all bedrooms Ⓡ ★ sB&B fr£22 sB&B→⋒ fr£24 dB&B fr£33 dB&B→⋒ fr£37.50 B

☾ 20P

Mainly grills Lunch £5&alc Dinner £5&alc Wine £4.75 Last dinner 10pm

Credit cards 1 2 3 5 **VS**

★★**Cimla Court Motel** Cimla Rd ☎(0639) 3771 RS Xmas

Privately-owned commercial hotel on the outskirts of the town.

25rm(19→6⋒)(1fb) CTV in all bedrooms Ⓡ *sB&B→⋒£18.08 dB&B→⋒£27.83

☾ 100P Live music and dancing Sat ⌂ ♿

Welsh, English, French & Italian **V** *Lunch £5–£6&alc Tea fr£1.75 High Tea fr£3 Dinner fr£5.50–£6&alc Wine £3.75 Last dinner 9.30pm

S% Credit cards 1 2 3 5 **VS**

NEEDHAM MARKET
Suffolk
Map **5** TM05

★★*B* **Limes** ☎(0449) 720305

Originally built in 1485 as a Boule House, a Georgian front was added to this hotel in 1751.

11→(3fb) CTV in all bedrooms Ⓡ sB&B→£26 dB&B→£38 B

CTV 60P

English & French Lunch £5.95&alc Tea 40p High Tea £1.50 Dinner £6.50&alc Wine £4 Last dinner 9.30pm

Credit cards 2 5

NEFYN
Gwynedd
Map **6** SH34

★★**Nanhoron Arms** St Davids Rd ☎(0758) 720203

20rm(3→)(6fb) CTV & TV available in bedrooms Ⓡ sB&B£11 sB&B→£12.50 dB&B£22 dB&B→£23.50 B

CTV 123P 4 ✽ billiards Live music and dancing & Cabaret three nights ⌂ *xmas*

V Lunch £3.50 Tea £2 High Tea £3.50 Dinner £4 Wine £4.30 Last dinner 9.30pm

★**Caeau Capel** Rhodfar Mor ☎(0758) 720240

Closed late Sep–Mar RS Etr–Spring Bank Hol

Detached holiday hotel set in its own grounds in a quiet cul-de-sac.

23rm(4→)(7fb) *sB&B£9.20–£10.93 sB&B→£11.50–£13.22 dB&B£18.40–£21.86 dB&B→£23–£26.44 B

CTV 40P ✽ (grass) ⌂

*Bar lunch 35p–£3 Tea fr50p Dinner £4.03–£6.33 Wine £3.42 Last dinner 7.30pm

Credit cards 1 3

NELSON
Lancashire
Map **7** SD83

★★***Great Marsden*** Barkerhouse Rd ☎(0282) 64749

Victorian building in its own grounds on the outskirts of town.

14rm(1→1⋒) TV in all bedrooms Ⓡ ★ Lift CTV 110P ✽ Disco Sat

Last dinner 9pm

NESSCLIFF
Shropshire
Map **7** SJ31

✕***Old Three Pigeons*** ☎(074 381) 279

Closed Mon Dinner not served Sun

Continental 60 seats Last dinner 9pm 100P

NETHYBRIDGE
Highland *Inverness-shire*
Map **14** NJ02
★★★*H* **Nethybridge** (Best Western)
☎(047 982) 203 Telex no 75261
Closed Nov
Large, traditional Highland hotel offering friendly service, comfortable lounges and spacious bedrooms.
63rm(61⇌1⋔) (3fb) CTV in 15 bedrooms sB&B⇌⋔£17 dB&B⇌⋔£34 B
Lift ☾ CTV 50P CFA ✽ U Disco, Live music and dancing, Cabaret Fri & Sat
V ♥ ☐ Lunch £4 Tea 75p Dinner £7.50–£8.50 Wine £2.75 Last dinner 9pm
Credit cards 1 2 3 5

NEW ABBEY
Dumfries & Galloway *Kirkcudbrightshire*
Map **11** NX96
★ ***Abbey Arms*** 1 The Square ☎(038 785) 215
Small, two-storey granite inn dating from 1840 standing in this border village.
6rm Ⓡ
CTV 6P
♥ ☐ Last dinner 7pm

NEWARK-ON-TRENT
Nottinghamshire
Map **8** SK75
★★ ***Midland*** Muskham Rd ☎(0636) 73788
10rm(1⇌1⋔)
CTV 15P
♥ ☐ Last dinner 8.30pm

★★ **Ram** (Home Brewery) ☎(0636) 702255
21rm(1⇌) Ⓡ ✱ sB&B£13.54 dB&B£27.20 dB&B⇌£30.11 B
CTV 9P 5
V ♥ ☐ Last dinner 8.45pm
Credit cards 1 3 **VS**

★★ **Robin Hood** Lombard St (Anchor) ☎(0636) 703858 Telex no 858875
Closed Xmas Day
20⇌ (4fb) CTV in all bedrooms Ⓡ ✱ sB&B⇌£28.50 dB&B⇌£39 B
☾ 50P 2 CFA
V ♥ ☐ ✱ Lunch £6.15–£6.95&alc Tea 45p–£1.75 Dinner £6.15–£6.95&alc Wine £4.50 Last dinner 9.45pm
Credit cards 1 2 3 4 5 **VS**

XX ***Queens Head*** Market Pl ☎(0636) 702327
Closed Mon
65 seats Last dinner 9.45pm
Credit cards 1 2 3 4 5

NEWBRIDGE
Cornwall
Map **2** SW43
XX **Enzo** ☎ Penzance (0736) 3777
Warm, friendly Cornish stone cottage restaurant specializing in Italian evenings.
Closed Sun (in winter) & 2–3 wks Xmas
English & Italian **V** 32 seats Dinner £9alc Wine £4.20 Last dinner 10.30pm 40P
Credit cards 1 2 5 **VS**

NEWBRIDGE-ON-WYE
Powys
Map **3** SO05
★ ***New Inn*** ☎(059 789) 211
A 16th-century village inn with a modern restaurant.
10rm(1⇌)
CTV 100P
Welsh & French ♥ ☐
Last dinner 8.30pm
Credit card 1 **VS**

NEW BRIGHTON
Merseyside
See **Wallasey**

NEWBURGH
Grampian *Aberdeenshire*
Map **15** NJ92
❀★★★*BL* **Udny Arms** Main St ☎(03586) 444 →

N

(Rosette awarded for dinner only.)
Small Victorian hotel overlooking estuary.
26⇌⋔ CTV in all bedrooms
sB&B⇌⋔£26 dB&B⇌⋔£39.50 B
☾ 57P CFA
V ✿ ☕ Lunch £3.25–£7.25&alc Tea £1 Dinner £12.50&alc Wine £4.05 Last dinner 9.30pm
Credit cards 1 2 3

NEWBURY
Berkshire
Map **4** SU46
See also **Elcot**
See advert on page 463

★★★**Chequers** Oxford St (Trusthouse Forte) ☎(0635) 43666 Telex no 849205
Well appointed coaching inn with delightful restaurant.
58rm(35⇌5⋔) Annexe: 11⇌ (2fb) CTV in all bedrooms ® sB&B£33 sB&B⇌⋔£39 dB&B£43 dB&B⇌⋔£54.50 B
☾ 60P CFA *xmas*
✿ ☕ Last dinner 9.30pm
Credit cards 1 2 3 4 5

✕**La Riviera** 26 The Broadway ☎(0635) 47499
Small Greek-style taverna offering a varied choice of specialized dishes.
Closed Sun, 25 & 26 Dec, Etr, 1st 3wks Apr & Public hols
Continental & Greek 40 seats ✱Lunch £7–£9alc Dinner £7–£12alc Wine £4.50 Last dinner 10.15pm
Credit cards 1 2 3 5

N

✕***Sapient Pig*** 29 Oxford Rd ☎(0635) 47425
Closed Sun Lunch not served Sat Dinner not served Mon
French 60 seats Last dinner 9.50pm
Credit cards 1 3

NEWBY BRIDGE
Cumbria
Map **7** SD38

★★★**Swan** (ExecHotel, Inter-Hotels) ☎(0448) 31681
Closed 1–11 Jan
36⇌ (12fb) CTV in all bedrooms ® ✱
sB&B⇌£23.65–£32 dB&B⇌£42–£48 B
CTV 100P ✿ *xmas*
English & French V ✿ ☕ Bar lunch £1.25–£3.85 Tea £1.25–£2 Dinner £9.50–£9.75&alc Wine £4.80 Last dinner 9pm
Credit cards 1 2 3 5

NEWCASTLE EMLYN
Dyfed
Map **2** SN34

★★**Emlyn Arms** (Inter-Hotels) ☎(0239) 710317
Originally a coaching inn, hotel has new wing of comfortable bedrooms.
18rm(9⇌⋔) Annexe: 20⇌⋔ (2fb) CTV in all bedrooms ® sB&B£13–£14 sB&B⇌⋔£15–£22 dB&B£24–£26 dB&B⇌⋔£26–£32 B
CTV 200P Disco & Live music and dancing wkly *xmas*
V ✿ ☕ Lunch £5.45–£5.95&alc Dinner £6.45–£6.95&alc Wine £4.50 Last dinner 9pm
Credit cards 1 2 3 5

NEWCASTLETON
Borders *Roxburghshire*
Map **12** NY48

✕**Copshaw Kitchen** ☎Liddesdale (054121) 250
Charming, well-furnished little country restaurant.
Closed Tue Dinner not served Mon
V 35 seats Tea £1.20 High Tea £1.50–£3.25 Dinner £6.50alc Wine £4.25 Last dinner 9pm 12P bedrooms available

NEWCASTLE-UNDER-LYME
Staffordshire
Map **7** SJ84

★★★**Clayton Lodge** Newcastle Rd, Clayton (A519) (Embassy) ☎Stoke-on-Trent (0782) 613093
51rm(40⇌) CTV in all bedrooms ® sB&B£21.50 sB&B⇌£33.75 dB&B£33.75 dB&B⇌£38.25 (room only) B
☾ 400P CFA ✿
✿ ☕ Lunch £7.25 Dinner £7.25 Wine £4.50 Last dinner 10pm
Credit cards 1 2 3 4 5

☆☆☆**Crest** Liverpool Rd (Crest) ☎Stoke-on-Trent (0782) 612431 Telex no 36681
RS Xmas wk
47⇌ Annexe: 28⇌ CTV in all bedrooms ® ✱sB⇌ fr£32 dB⇌ fr£38 (room only) B
☾ 150P CFA
International V ✿ ✱Lunch fr£5.25&alc Dinner fr£7.95&alc Wine £5.25 Last dinner 9.45pm
Credit cards 1 2 3 4 5 VS

☆☆☆**Post House** Clayton Rd (Trusthouse Forte) ☎Stoke-on-Trent (0782) 625151 Telex no 36531
126⇌ (46fb) CTV in all bedrooms ® sB&B⇌£38.50 dB&B⇌£52 B
☾ 128P ✿
✿ ☕ Last dinner 10.15pm
Credit cards 1 2 3 4 5

★ *H***Deansfield** 98 Lancaster Rd ☎(0782) 619040
9⋔) (2fb) CTV in all bedrooms sB&B⋔£11–£15 dB&B⋔£18–£24 B
CTV 12P ✿ billiards Disco nightly *xmas*
English & French V ✿ ☕ Lunch £2alc Tea 90palc High Tea £1.50alc Dinner £6alc Wine £3 Last dinner 10.30pm
Credit cards 1 2 3 5

NEWCASTLE UPON TYNE
Tyne & Wear
Map **12** NZ26
See plan on pages 466/467

★★★★ *B***Gosforth Park Thistle** High Gosforth Park, Gosforth (Thistle) ☎(0632) 364111 Telex no 53655
Plan **5** *D8*
Large modern hotel set in 167 acres of woodland overlooking Newcastle racecourse.
178⇌ CTV in all bedrooms
✱sB⇌£43.50–£46 dB⇌£52.50–£60 (room only) B

Lift ☾ #⚡300P CFA ✽ ⊡(heated) squash sauna bath ♿ *xmas* ♿

▣European ♣ ☕ ✱ Lunch £6.95&alc Dinner £12&alc Last dinner 9.30pm

Credit cards 1 2 3 4 5 **VS**

★★★**County Thistle** Neville St (Thistle) ☎(0632) 322471 Telex no 537873 Plan **2** *C4*

A traditional town centre hotel offering comfortable accommodation, situated opposite the main railway station.

115🛁⛆ (1fb) CTV in all bedrooms ® ✱sB🛁⛆ £30.50–£34 dB🛁⛆ £35–£40 (room only) ₿

Lift ☾ ⚡50🚗 CFA

▣European ♣ ☕ ✱ Lunch £6.75&alc Dinner £6.75&alc Last dinner 9.30pm

Credit cards 1 2 3 4 5 **VS**

★★★**Imperial** Jesmond Rd (Swallow) ☎(0632) 815511 Telex no 537972 Plan **6** *F8*

130🛁⛆ CTV in all bedrooms ® sB&B🛁⛆ £20.35–£33 dB&B🛁⛆ £30.80–£41.80 ₿

Lift ☾ 120P CFA ⊡(heated) sauna bath Disco Sat

♣ ☕ ✱ Lunch £4.70 Dinner £7.15&alc Wine £4.50 Last dinner 10pm

Credit cards 1 2 3 5

☆☆☆**Newcastle Crest** New Bridge St (Crest) ☎(0632) 326191 Telex no 53467 Plan **3** *E5*
Closed Xmas wk

180🛁 CTV in all bedrooms ® ✱sB🛁 fr£34 dB🛁 fr£41 (room only) ₿

Lift ☾ ⚡250P sauna bath CFA

▣International **V** ♣ ☕ ✱ Lunch £3.95–£5.95&alc Tea fr£2 Dinner £8.25–£10&alc Wine £6.25 Last dinner 10pm

Credit cards 1 2 3 4 5 **VS**

★★★**Northumbria** 63 Osborne Rd, Jesmond (Mount Charlotte) ☎(0632) 814961 Telex no 53636 Plan **9** *E8*

71rm(23🛁32⛆) (3fb) CTV in all bedrooms ® sB&B£27 sB&B🛁⛆ £30 dB&B£33 dB&B🛁⛆ £35 ₿

Lift ☾ 30P 3🚗 sauna bath

▣English & French **V** ♣ ☕ Lunch £4.50–£5&alc Dinner £7–£7.50&alc Wine £4.75 Last dinner 9.45pm

Credit cards 1 2 3 5 **VS**

Newcastle upon Tyne

★★★**Royal Turks Head Thistle** Grey St (Thistle) ☎(0632) 326111 Plan **12** *D5*

Traditional city centre hotel with spacious lounges and sweeping staircase.

91rm(74🛁⛆) (3fb) CTV in all bedrooms ® ✱sB🛁⛆ £25–£28.50 dB🛁⛆ £30–£32.50 (room only) ₿

Lift ☾ ⚑ CFA

▣European ☕ ✱ Lunch £4 Dinner £6&alc Last dinner 9pm

Credit cards 1 2 3 4 5 **VS**

☆☆☆**Swallow** Newgate Arcade (Swallow) ☎(0632) 325025 Telex no 538230 Plan **13** *C5*

Modern, purpose-built hotel with a roof-top restaurant, situated in the city centre precinct.

92🛁⛆ (4fb) CTV in all bedrooms ® sB&B🛁⛆ £35 dB&B🛁⛆ £48 ₿

Lift ☾ 150P CFA Disco Sat

▣International **V** ♣ ☕ Lunch £3&alc Tea £1.25 High Tea £3–£5 Dinner £6–£9&alc Wine £4.75 Last dinner 9.30pm

S% Credit cards 1 2 3 4 5 **VS**

★★**Avon** 64 Osborne Rd, Jesmond (Mount Charlotte) ☎(0632) 814961 Telex no 53636 Plan **1** *E8*

A mainly commercial hotel, converted from a terraced private residence.

91rm(37🛁4⛆) (9fb) CTV in all bedrooms ® sB&B£27 sB&B🛁⛆ £32 dB&B£37 dB&B🛁⛆ £40 ₿

Lift ☾ 52P 3🚗

▣English & French **V** ♣ ☕ Lunch £4.50–£5&alc Dinner £7–£7.50&alc Wine £4.75 Last dinner 9.45pm

Credit cards 1 2 3 5 **VS**

★**Osborne** Osborne Rd, Jesmond ☎(0632) 814778 Plan **10** *E8*

Comfortable, hospitable hotel in residential area.

25rm(1🛁9⛆) (1fb) CTV in all bedrooms ® ✱sB&B£18 sB&B🛁⛆ £24–£26 dB&B£30 dB&B🛁⛆ £36 ₿

5P 🚗

♣ ☕ ✱ Lunch £4 Dinner £5 Last dinner 8pm

S% Credit cards 1 3

✕✕✕**Michelangelo** 25 King St, Quayside ☎(0632) 614415 Plan **8** *E4*

Closed Sun & Bank hols Lunch not served Sat

▣French & Italian 80 seats Lunch fr£4.95 Dinner £12alc Last dinner 11pm

S% Credit cards 1 2 3 5 **VS**

✕✕**Fishermans Lodge** Jesmond Dene, Jesmond ☎(0632) 813281 Plan **4** *F8*

Converted Victorian house now provides comfortable restaurant with two dining rooms and two lounges.

Closed Sun, Public Hols & 25 Dec–2 Jan Lunch not served Sat

V 65 seats Lunch £7.50–£8&alc Dinner £16alc Wine £6.50 Last dinner 11pm 45P

Credit cards 1 2 3 5

✕✕**Mandarin** 14–16 Stowell St ☎(0632) 617881 Plan **7** *C5*

Comfortable town centre restaurant serving traditional Cantonese dishes.

▣Cantonese 150 seats ✱ Lunch £2&alc High Tea £2&alc Dinner £6–£7&alc Wine £4 Last dinner 11.45pm 20P

S% Credit cards 1 2 3

✕✕***Three Mile Inn*** Great North Rd, Gosforth (3m N A1) ☎(0632) 856817 Plan **14** *D8*

▣English & French 72 seats Last dinner 10.30pm 200P

Credit cards 1 3 5

✕**Ristorante Roma** 22 Collingwood St ☎(0632) 320612 Plan **11** *C4*

An intimate city centre restaurant close to the railway station.

Lunch not served Sun

▣English & Italian **V** 85 seats Lunch £2.95–£5.95&alc Dinner £8&alc Wine £3.85 Last dinner 11.30pm ⚑ Disco nightly Live music Tue–Sat

Credit cards 1 3 **VS**

N

Newcastle upon Tyne

1 Avon ★★
2 County Thistle ★★★
3 Crest ☆☆☆
4 Fishermans Lodge ✕✕
5 Gosforth Park Thistle ★★★★
5A Holiday Inn ☆☆☆☆ *(Listed under Seaton Burn)*
6 Imperial ★★★
7 Mandarin ✕✕
8 Michelangelo ✕✕✕
9 Northumbria ★★★
10 Osborne ★
11 Ristorante Roma ✕
12 Royal Turks Head Thistle ★★★
13 Swallow ☆☆☆
14 Three Mile Inn ✕✕

At **Seaton Burn** (6m N junc A1/A108)

☆☆☆☆*B* **Holiday Inn** Great North Rd (Commonwealth) ☎(0632) 365432

150⇨ 230P

At **Wallsend** (5m E at junc A1/A1058)

☆☆☆**Newcastle Moat House** Coast Rd (Queens Moat) ☎(0632) 628989

172⇨ 500P

NEWCASTLE UPON TYNE AIRPORT
Tyne & Wear
Map **12** NZ17

☆☆☆**Stakis Airport** Woolsington (Stakis)
☎Ponteland (0661) 24911 Telex no 537121

A modern, purpose-built hotel within the airport complex.

100⇨ CTV in all bedrooms ® ✻ sB&B⇨ fr£34 dB&B⇨ fr£40 Ⓑ

Lift ☾ 100P CFA

English & French Last dinner 9.45pm

Credit cards 1 2 3 5 **VS**

N

NEWDIGATE
Surrey
Map **4** TQ14

✕✕**Forge** Parkgate Rd ☎(030 677) 582
Gatwick plan **5**

Restaurant serving varied à la carte menu, with seasonal specialities.

Closed Mon & 1st 3wks Aug Lunch not served Sat Dinner not served Sun

French 36 seats Lunch £7.50&alc Dinner £13alc Wine £6.60 Last dinner 10pm 20P

Credit cards 1 2 3 5

NEWENT
Gloucestershire
Map **3** SO72

✕**Soutters** Culver St ☎(0531) 820896

Small, personally run bistro with relaxed atmosphere. Must book.

Closed Sun & Mon Lunch not served

French **V** 18 seats Dinner £11alc Wine £3.95 Last dinner 9.30pm

Credit cards 2 5 **VS**

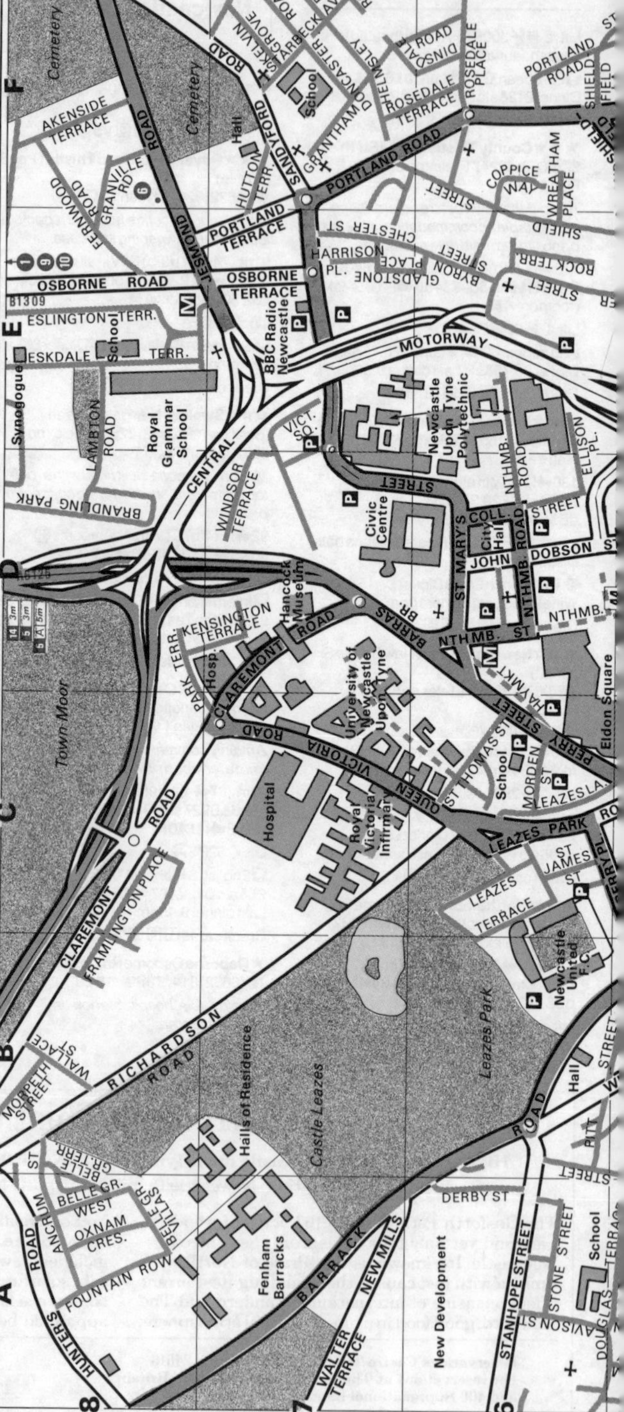

Cemetery
AKENSIDE TERRACE
GRANVILLE RD
FERNWOOD ROAD
JESMOND ROAD
Hall
HUTTON TERR.
SANDYFORD
School
GRANTHAM
PORTLAND ROAD
ROSEDALE TERRACE
ROSEDALE PLACE
PORTLAND TERRACE
COPPICE WAY
WREATHAM PLACE
CHESTER ST
HARRISON PL.
OSBORNE ROAD
OSBORNE TERRACE
B1309
ESLINGTON TERR.
ESKDALE TERR.
School
BBC Radio Newcastle
MOTORWAY
Synagogue
LAMBTON ROAD
Royal Grammar School
CENTRAL
VICT. SQ.
Newcastle Upon Tyne Polytechnic
WINDSOR TERRACE
BRANDLING PARK
Civic Centre
City Hall
JOHN DOBSON ST
A6125
Hancock Museum
KENSINGTON TERRACE
CLAREMONT ROAD
BARRAS BR.
University of Newcastle Upon Tyne
Town Moor
Hosp.
VICTORIA ROAD
QUEEN VICTORIA
Hospital
Royal Victoria Infirmary
Eldon Square
PERCY STREET
LEAZES PARK RD
ST JAMES ST
LEAZES TERRACE
Newcastle United F.C.
FRAMLINGTON PLACE
CLAREMONT
RICHARDSON ROAD
WALLACE ST
MORPETH STREET
Halls of Residence
Castle Leazes
Leazes Park
BELLE GR. WEST
OXNAM CRES.
FOUNTAIN ROW
HUNTER'S ROAD
Fenham Barracks
BARRACK ROAD
NEW MILLS
WALTER TERRACE
New Development
DERBY ST
STANHOPE STREET
STONE STREET
School

Newcastle Upon Tyne
River Tyne
High Level Bridge
King Edward Bridge
Redheugh Bridge
Tyne Bridge
Swing Bridge
Newcastle Central Station
Cathedral
Moot Hall
The Keep
Guildhall
Custom House
Manors Station
Gas Works
Rec. Gnd
Town Hall
Central Shopping Precinct
Shopping Precinct
Newgate Shopping Centre
County Court
Telephone Exchange
Theatre Royal
Tyne Tees T.V.
Coach Station
Hospital
College
Clinic
Baths
Cinema
Library
School
QUAYSIDE
SCOTSWOOD ROAD
WESTGATE ROAD
NEVILLE STREET
REDHEUGH BRIDGE ROAD
ASKEW ROAD
HIGH STREET
OAKWELL GATE
BENSHAM ROAD
GEORGE STREET
WESTMORLAND ROAD
MELBOURNE STREET
NEW BRIDGE ST
CITY ROAD
FORTH BANKS
THE CLOSE
BLENHEIM STREET
RYE HILL
PRINCE CONSORT ROAD
HIGH WEST ST
WEST CENTRAL ROUTE
PARK LANE
SOUTH SHORE ROAD
HAWKS ROAD
A
B
C
D
E
F
1
2
3
4
5

NEW GALLOWAY
Dumfries & Galloway *Kirkcudbrightshire*
Map **11** NX67

★ ***Crosskeys*** ☎ (06442) 218
RS Nov & Feb
Modest, old fashioned inn.
8rm
CTV 8P 2🚗 ⊘
✿ ☕ Last dinner 8pm
Credit cards ① ③

NEWGATE STREET
Hertfordshire
Map **4** TL30

★★★ ***L* Ponsbourne** ☎ Potters Bar (0707) 875221 Telex no 299912
26rm(20➡ 6⋒) Annexe: 6➡ (1fb) CTV in all bedrooms sB&B➡⋒ £22.40–£29.70 dB&B➡⋒ £39.60 B
☾ 200P 2🚗 ⊘ ❀ ≋ ⛳ 🎾(hard) ⌂ *xmas*
🍴French V ✿ Lunch £8.80–£11&alc Tea £1 Dinner £12&alc Wine £5.50 Last dinner 9.30pm
S% Credit cards ① ② ③ ⑤ **VS**

NEW GRIMSBY
Tresco Isles of Scilly (No map)

★**New Inn** ☎ Scillionia (0720) 22844
Closed Nov
Tresco's only inn, it is near sandy beach.
12rm(10➡) (2fb) Ⓡ ✱ sB&B£19.05–£30.35 (incl dinner) dB&B➡£38.10–£60.70 (incl dinner)
CTV ≋ (heated) ⌂
🍴English & Continental V ✿ Bar lunch £3.50alc Dinner £8.50&alc Wine £3.75 Last dinner 8.30pm
Credit cards ① ③ **VS**

NEWHAVEN East Sussex
See **Seaford**

NEWMARKET
Suffolk
Map **5** TL66

★★★**Newmarket Moat House** Moulton Rd (Queens Moat) ☎ (0638) 667171
Modern hotel close by Newmarket Heath yet adjoining town centre.
49➡ CTV in all bedrooms Ⓡ sB&B➡£30 dB&B➡£40 B
Lift ☾ 60P 5🚗 CFA ❀
🍴English & French V ✿ ☕ Lunch fr£7.75 Dinner fr£7.75 Wine £5 Last dinner 9.45pm
Credit cards ① ② ③ ⑤ **VS**

★★**Bedford Lodge** Bury Rd (Best Western) ☎ (0638) 663175
A quiet but centrally-situated hotel.
14rm(5➡ 4⋒) (1fb) CTV in all bedrooms Ⓡ sB&B£18–£31 sB&B➡⋒ £24.50–£31 dB&B£33–£44.50 dB&B➡⋒ £36.50–£44.50 B
☾ CTV 100P ❀ ⌂ *xmas*
🍴International V ✿ ☕ Lunch £6.25&alc Tea £1.50 High Tea £4.50 Dinner £6.25&alc Wine £4.20 Last dinner 10.30pm
S% Credit cards ① ② ③ ⑤ **VS**

★★**Rosery Country House** 15 Church St, Exning (2m NW B1103)
☎ Exning (063877) 312
11rm(7➡ 1⋒) 1⊟ CTV in all bedrooms Ⓡ ✱ sB&B£17 sB&B➡⋒ £26.50 dB&B➡⋒ £35.50
20P ⊘ ❀
✱Lunch £5.75alc Dinner £10.50alc Wine £5.20
Credit cards ① ② ③ ⑤ **VS**

★★**Rutland Arms** High St (Paten)
☎ (0638) 664251
The main building is a Georgian coaching house built round a cobbled courtyard.
49rm(41➡) CTV in all bedrooms Ⓡ ✱sB&B£14.95 sB&B➡£27.60 dB&B£24.90 dB&B➡£36.80 B
☾ CTV 26P 8🚗 CFA
V ✿ ☕ ✱Lunch £4.95&alc Tea fr60p Dinner £4.95&alc Wine £3.45 Last dinner 9pm
Credit cards ① ② ③ ⑤

N

★★**White Hart** High St (Trusthouse Forte) ☎(0638) 663051

Three-storey gabled building standing on the site of a 17th-century inn.

21rm(10⇌) CTV in all bedrooms ® sB&B£30.50 sB&B⇌£33.50 dB&B£42 dB&B⇌£48 B

25P

☆☐ Last dinner 9.30pm

Credit cards 1 2 3 4 5

NEW MILTON
Hampshire
Map **4** SZ29

❀❀★★★★**CHEWTON GLEN, NEW MILTON**

Christchurch Rd (Prestige)
☎Highcliffe (04252) 5341 Telex no 41456

This 18th century mansion, converted to a wonderful hotel by the owner, Martin Skan, is situated a little way out of town in its own grounds near the New Forest. When you arrive you are immediately aware that here is a hotel of international standards, one that cannot help but give a very favourable impression to overseas guests. One is made welcome and shown all the service and courtesy in keeping with a fine English country house. The gardens boast a helipad, swimming pool, croquet lawn and putting green, while there is a billiard room to one side. On a fine day it is a pleasure to have refreshments or a light luncheon on the terrace. Both the stylish public rooms and the bedrooms are impeccably furnished and decorated with many a thoughtful touch to provide everything for your comfort.
Then there is the Marryat Room, the sumptuously comfortable and well-appointed restaurant where Pierre Cheviallard, the chef, provides such excellent food. He is a worthy successor to Christian Delteil and we are delighted to restore our two rosette award this year. A set meal is provided at a moderate price at lunchtime while the one at dinner demonstrates his real skill and flair.

Among the first courses our inspectors have enjoyed were mussels with thyme, pigeon paté and quails' breast in perfect puff pastry with delicious Madeira sauce. Breast of duck flavoured with pepper with its liver mousseline and another delicate sauce, veal in a leek and cream sauce as well as all fish dishes sampled have been specially recommended amongst the main ones. Vegetables are well done as is the mouthwatering selection of puddings. This hotel really is one of the 'great' hotels.

50⇌(6fb) CTV in all bedrooms sB&B⇌£45–£70 dB&B⇌£72–£90 Continental breakfast B

☾ 100P CFA ❀ (heated) billiards nc7yrs *xmas*

French ☆☐ Lunch £9.50&alc Tea £1.75 Dinner £18.50&alc Wine £5.50 Last dinner 9.30pm

S% Credit cards 1 2 3 4 5

NEWPORT
Gwent
Map **3** ST38

★★★★ ***BL* Celtic Manor** The Coldra ☎(0633) 413000

17⇌(16fb) 2 CTV in all bedrooms ✻sB&B⇌£42.50 dB&B⇌£57.44 B

☾ CTV 150P ❀ Live music and dancing 4 nights wkly *xmas*
(continued below)

French V ☆☐ ✻Lunch £6alc Tea £2.50alc Dinner £10alc Wine £5.95 Last dinner 10.30pm

Credit cards 1 2 3 5

See p 25 and advert on page 470

☆☆☆**Ladbroke** (& Conference centre) The Coldra (Ladbroke) ☎(0633) 412777 Telex 497205

Modern, well equipped hotel with comfortable bedrooms.

125⇌(44fb) CTV in all bedrooms ®

✻sB⇌£31 dB⇌£41 (room only) B

☾ CTV 300P ❀ Live music and dancing Sat Cabaret mthly

English & French ☆☐ ✻Lunch fr£6.50 Dinner fr£8.50 Last dinner 10pm

Credit cards 1 2 3 4 5

See advert on page 470

★★**Priory** High St, Caerleon (3m NE B4236) ☎(0633) 421241

22⇌ CTV in all bedrooms ® sB&B⇌ fr£28.60 dB&B⇌ fr£35.75 B

100P ❀

Dinner fr£7&alc Wine £3.90 Last dinner 10pm

Credit cards 1 2 3 **VS**

★★**Queens** 19 Bridge St (Anchor) ☎(0633) 62992 Telex no 858875

A traditional hotel located in the town centre.

43rm(29⇌23) (2fb) CTV in all bedrooms ® sB&B fr£20.50 sB&B⇌ fr£29 dB&B fr£31 dB&B⇌ fr£36 B

☾ CTV Live music and dancing Fri

V ☆ ✻Lunch fr£6.35&alc Dinner fr£6.35&alc Wine £4.50 Last dinner 10pm

Credit cards 1 2 3 5

★★**Westgate** Commercial St ☎(0633) 66244 Telex no 498173

Traditional hotel situated in the town centre.

72rm(30⇌) (5fb) CTV in all bedrooms ® sB&B£11.25–£27.50 sB&B⇌£15–£32.50 dB&B£22.50–£32.50 dB&B⇌£30–£38.50 B

Lift ☾ CTV 30P CFA *xmas*

English & French ☆☐ Lunch £1.95–£4.95&alc Tea £1.50–£3.50 High Tea £1.50–£3.50 Dinner £5.95–£6.55&alc Wine £4.10 Last dinner 10pm

Credit cards 1 2 3 4 **VS**

At **Castleton** (6m W A48)

☆☆☆**Ladbroke Wentloog Castle** (Ladbroke) ☎(0633) 680591

55⇌ 75P

At **Langstone** (4m E A48)

☆☆**New Inn Motel** (Ansells) ☎(0633) 412426

36rm(3⇌33) 200P

NEWPORT
Gloucestershire
Map **3** ST69

☆☆***Newport Towers Motel*** (on A38) ☎Dursley (0453) 810575

Modern, privately-owned hotel on the A38, close to the M5.

60⇌ ® B

CTV 250P 3 ❀

☆☐ Last dinner 10pm

Credit cards 1 2 3

NEWPORT
Isle of Wight
Map **4** SZ48

★**Wheatsheaf** St Thomas' Sq ☎(0983) 523835

Attractive hotel with cobbled stone bar and old dining room.

11rm(7) (2fb) CTV available in bedrooms ✻sB&B fr£13 sB&B fr£15 dB&B fr£20 dB&B fr£22 B

CTV Live music and dancing 3 nights wkly *xmas*

English & French **V** ☆☐ ✻Lunch fr£5.95 Tea fr50p Dinner fr£6.95&alc Wine →

N

£4.50 Last dinner 9.30pm
Credit card 3

NEWPORT
Shropshire
Map **7** SJ71
★★**Royal Victoria** St Mary's St (Wolverhampton & Dudley) ☎(0952) 810831
21rm(13⇌3⋒)(1fb) CTV in all bedrooms Ⓡ*sB&B£14.25 sB&B⇌£16.75 dB&B£22 dB&B⇌£26 B
☾ CTV 100P
English & French ✿ ⊒ *Lunch fr£4.50&alc Dinner fr£5.75&alc Wine £3.75 Last dinner 9.30pm
Credit cards 1 3 **VS**

NEWPORT PAGNELL
Buckinghamshire
Map **4** SP84
✕✕**Glovers** 18–20 St John St ☎(0908) 616398
Closed Sun, Mon, 25 Dec–5 Jan & Public Hols Lunch not served Sat
English & French 38 seats *Lunch £11.75–£12.75 Dinner £11.75–£12.75 Wine £4 7P
Credit cards 1 2 3 5

NEWPORT PAGNELL SERVICE AREA
(M1 Motorway) Buckinghamshire
Map **4** SP84
☆☆☆**TraveLodge** M1 Motorway Service Area (Trusthouse Forte) ☎(0908) 610878 Telex no 826186
Catering facilities are provided in the adjacent service area.
100⇌ CTV in all bedrooms Ⓡ sB&B⇌£26 dB&B⇌£37 Continental breakfast B 120P
Mainly grills
Credit cards 1 2 3 4 5

NEWQUAY
Cornwall
Map **2** SW86
See plan on pages 472 & 473

★★★ ***Atlantic*** Dane Rd ☎(06373) 2244
Plan **1** *B3*
Closed Oct–mid May except Etr wk
Spacious family hotel, situated in 10 acres of grounds on the headland.
80rm(64⇌) TV available in bedrooms
Lift ☾ CTV 100P CFA 6🚗❀
⊡ & ⛵ (heated) squash billiards sauna bath Disco 3 nights wkly in season Live music and dancing twice wkly in season
🏠♿
V♈☐ Last dinner 8.45pm
Credit cards 1 2 3 5 **VS**

★★★ **Barrowfield** Hillgrove Rd
☎(06373) 2560 Plan **2** *D2*
Modern, family hotel, under personal supervision, close to the beach.
61rm(59⇌2⋒) (11fb) CTV in all bedrooms ® sB&B⇌⋒ £10.50–£12.50 dB&B⇌⋒ £21–£25 ₿
Lift ☾ CTV 38P 14🚗 CFA ⊡ & ⛵ (heated) sauna bath Disco 4 nights wkly Live music and dancing 2 nights wkly Cabaret 2 nights wkly 🏠 *xmas*
▣ English & French V♈☐ Lunch £4.65 Tea £1.25 Dinner £7.45&alc Wine £3.60
Last dinner 8.30pm
Credit card 3
See advert on page 474

★★★ ***HL*** **Hotel Bristol** Narrowcliff
☎(06373) 5181 Plan **5** *D2*
In an ideal position, directly overlooking Tolcarne beach, this hotel has been under the same ownership since 1927. →

Newquay
1 Atlantic ★★★
2 Barrowfield ★★★
3 Beachcroft ★★
4 Bewdley ★★
5 Hotel Bristol ★★★
6 Cedars ★★
7 Corisande Manor ★★
8 Cross Mount ★★
9 Edgcumbe ★★★
10 Glendorgal ★★★
11 Great Western ★★
12 Kilbirnie ★★★
13 Hotel Kontiki ★★
15 Minto House ★★
16 Hotel Mordros ★★★
17 Pine Lodge ★★
18 Porth Veor Manor ★★
19 Hotel Riviera ★★★
20 St Rumons ★★★
21 Sandy Lodge ★★
22 Trebarwith ★★★
23 Trevone ★
24 Water's Edge ★★
25 Whipsiddery ★★
26 Windsor ★★★

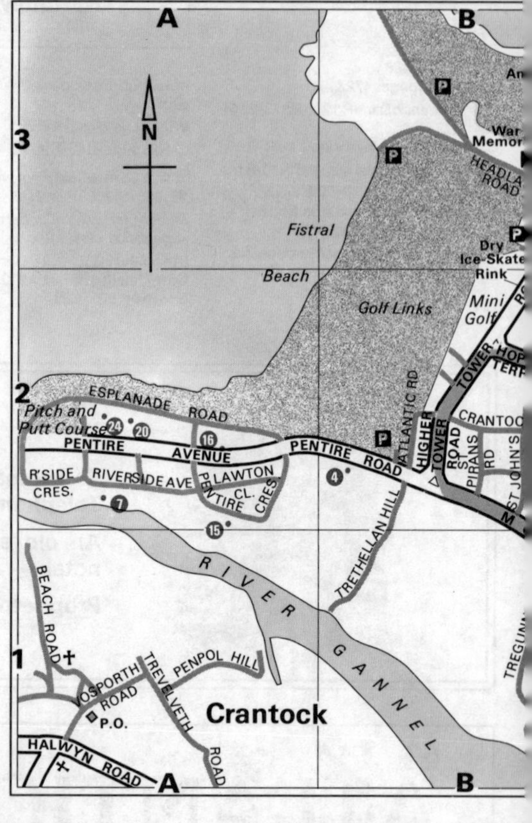

A
B
3
2
1
N
Fistral
Beach
Golf Links
Dry
Ice-Skate
Rink
Pitch and
Putt Course
ESPLANADE ROAD
PENTIRE AVENUE
PENTIRE ROAD
R'SIDE CRES.
RIVERSIDE AVE
LAWTON CL.
PENTIRE CRES
ATLANTIC RD
HIGHER TOWER ROAD
ST PIRANS RD
TRETHELLAN HILL
RIVER GANNEL
BEACH ROAD
VOSPORTH ROAD
TREVELVETH ROAD
PENPOL HILL
P.O.
Crantock
HALWYN ROAD

100rm(66→) CTV in 66 bedrooms sB&B£17–£20 sB&B→⋔£21–£25 dB&B£32–£38 dB&B→⋔£38–£48 B
Lift ☾ CTV 100P 5[garage symbol] CFA[pool symbol](heated) billiards sauna bath *xmas*
V[restaurant symbol] Lunch £5.75–£7.50 Tea £2 Dinner £7.75–£10.50 Wine £4 Last dinner 8.30pm
Credit cards 1 2 3 5 **VS**

N

★★★ ***HL*** **Edgcumbe** Narrowcliff
☎(06373) 2061 Plan **9** *E3*
Closed Dec–Feb
Family holiday hotel with traditional services and good facilities.
89rm(62→27⋔)(39fb) CTV in 58 bedrooms ® sB&B→⋔£13.50–£24.50 dB&B→⋔£27–£49 B
Lift ☾ CTV 70P[parking symbol][pool symbol]&[pool symbol](heated) billiards sauna bath Disco wkly Live music and dancing 3 nights wkly Cabaret twice wkly[symbol]
V[restaurant symbol] Lunch fr£5.50&alc Tea 45p–£3&alc Dinner fr£8&alc Wine £4.25 Last dinner 8.30pm
VS

★★★ *L* ***Glendorgal*** Lusty Glaze Rd
☎(06373) 4937 Plan **10** *E3*
Friendly, personally-run, secluded hotel in 15 acres of grounds and headland.
30rm(27→) 1[symbol] CTV in all bedrooms ®
70P[symbol][pool symbol][tennis symbol](hard)[symbol] sauna bath[symbol]
[symbol]English & Continental[restaurant symbol] Last dinner 8.30pm
Credit card 5
See advert on page 474

★★★ **Kilbirnie** Narrowcliff
☎(06373) 5155 Plan **12** *E3*
Closed 4 days Xmas
Family holiday-hotel ¾m from town centre. Comfortably appointed with fine coastal views.
73rm(53→)(6fb) CTV in 53 bedrooms sB&B£11.75–£17.50 sB&B→£14.75 dB&B£23.50–£35 dB&B→£29.50–£41 B

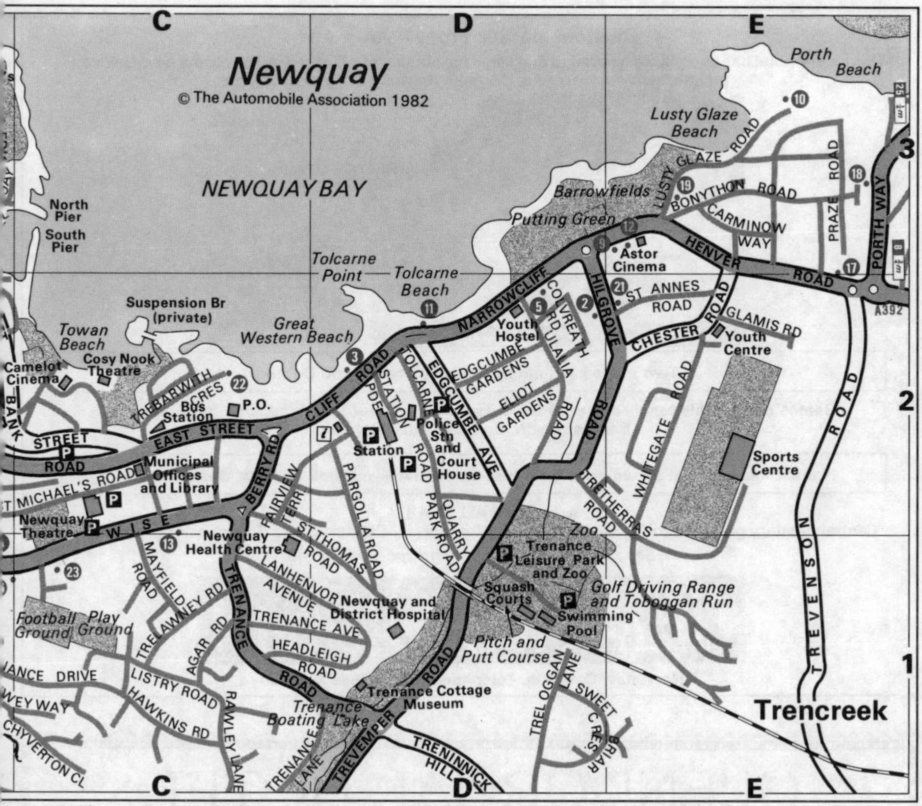

Newquay

© The Automobile Association 1982

N

☾ 60P (heated) billiards sauna bath Disco wkly in season Live music and dancing 4 nights wkly in season

Lunch fr£4.50 Dinner fr£8 Wine £3.65 Last dinner 8.30pm

Credit cards 1 3 **VS**

★★★**Hotel Mordros** Pentire Av ☎(06373) 6700 Plan **16** *A2*

Closed mid Oct–Etr

Modern, purpose-built hotel, close to Fistral Beach.

30 (4fb) sB&B £8.55–£15.52 dB&B £17.10–£31.04

CTV 30P CFA (heated) Disco 5 nights wkly Cabaret 3 nights wkly

English & Continental Bar lunch £1.50–£4 Tea 80p Dinner £6–£8 Wine £3.50 Last dinner 8.30pm

★★★ **Hotel Riviera** Lusty Glaze Rd (Best Western) ☎(06373) 4251

Plan **19** *E3*

Closed Xmas

Situated in cliff-top gardens overlooking the sea, close to the town centre and the beaches.

50rm(23 8) (9fb) CTV in all bedrooms sB&B£18.50–£25 sB&B £19.50–£26 dB&B£37–£50 dB&B £39–£52 →

N

Lift ☾ CFA 60P ✽ ⛴ (heated) squash billiards sauna bath Disco 6 nights wkly (summer) (Sat in winter) ♎

▣ Continental V ♧ ☐ Lunch fr£2.50 Tea 45p–£1.25 High Tea £2–£4 Dinner fr£6&alc Wine £5.50 Last dinner 10pm

Credit cards 1 3

★★★ St Rumons Esplanade Rd, Fistral Bay ☎ (06373) 2978 Plan **20** *A2*
Closed Nov–Mar

Modern family hotel overlooking Fistral Bay.

75rm(53⇌) (37fb) CTV in 53 bedrooms ® sB&B£15.52–£17.82 dB&B£31.04–£35.64 dB&B⇌£34.50–£39.10

Lift ☾ ✗ CTV 55P ▭ & ⛴ (heated) sauna bath Disco twice wkly Live music and dancing 3–4 nights wkly ♎

▣ English & Continental V ♧ ☐ ✽ Lunch £5.18&alc Tea 50p alc Dinner £6.33&alc Wine £4 Last dinner 8.30pm

Credit cards 2 3

★★★ *L* Trebarwith Island Estate ☎ (06373) 2288 Plan **22** *C2*
Closed mid Nov–Mar

Family owned and run hotel, with a garden having its own steps to the beach.

46rm(29⇌ 4⋔) (4fb) 5 ⊟ CTV in all bedrooms ✱ sB&B£11–£24 sB&B⇌⋔ £13–£26 dB&B£22–£48 dB&B⇌⋔ £26–£52 ℞

☾ 40P ⇌ ✽ ▭ (heated) billiards sauna bath Live music and dancing 3 nights wkly Cabaret wkly ♎

V ♧ ☐ Bar lunch 60p–£2 Tea fr£1 Dinner £7–£8.50&alc Wine £3.50 Last dinner 8.30pm

Credit cards 1 3 VS

★★★ *L* Windsor Mount Wise ☎ ((06373) 5188 Plan **26** *B1*
Closed Nov–Etr →

Large, well-appointed family hotel close to the town centre and the beaches.
46rm(31⇌2⋒)(12fb) CTV available in bedrooms Ⓡ ★ sB&B£10–£20 sB&B⇌⋒£12–£23 dB&B£20–£40 dB&B⇌⋒£24–£46
CTV 40P ✽ & ⋍(heated) squash sauna bath Disco wkly Live music and dancing 4 nights wkly Cabaret wkly
Bar lunch 70p–£2.75 Tea 35p Dinner £7.50 Wine £3.60 Last dinner 8.30pm
Credit cards 1 3

★★**Beachcroft** Cliff Rd ☎(06373) 3022
Plan **3** *D2*
Closed early Oct–end Apr
Large, family hotel in its own gardens, close to the town centre and beach.
69rm(19⇌12⋒)
Lift CTV 65P ✽ ⋍(heated) (hard) sauna bath Live music and dancing 4 nights wkly
V Last dinner 8pm
VS

★★**Bewdley** Pentire Rd ☎(06373) 2883
Plan **4** *B2*
Closed Nov–Feb
On the outskirts of town overlooking Fistral Beach and the Gannel Estuary.
30rm(4⇌12⋒)(6fb) sB&B£8.50–£12.50 sB&B⇌⋒£9.50–£13 dB&B£17–£25 dB&B⇌⋒£19–£26 B
☾ CTV 40P ✽ ⋍(heated) Disco wkly Live music and dancing twice wkly Cabaret wkly *xmas*
V Lunch £3 Tea £3 High Tea £3 Dinner £5.50 Last dinner 7.30pm
Credit cards 1 3 **VS**

★★**Cedars** Mount Wise ☎(06373) 4225
Plan **6** *B1*

N

Closed Oct–mid Apr
Small, friendly, family-run hotel close to the town centre and beaches.
35rm(12➡7⋒) CTV available in bedrooms Ⓡ
CTV 40P ⛆ (heated) sauna bath
V ♆ ☕ Last dinner 8pm
VS

★★**Corisande Manor** Riverside Ave, Pentire ☎(06373) 2042 Plan **7** *A2*
Closed 30 Oct–6 May
Character, country-house style hotel with a pleasant, rural view of the Gannel estuary.
9rm(3⋒) Annexe: 4➡(3fb) sB&B£7–£12 dB&B£14–£24 dB&B⋒£16–£26 B
CTV 32P ✤ nc3yrs
English, French & Italian ♆ ☕ Bar lunch £1–£3.50 Tea 37p–56p Dinner £5.25–£5.75 Wine £3.95 Last dinner 8pm

★★*HL* **Cross Mount** Church St, St Columb Minor ☎(06373) 2669 Plan **8** *E3*
Closed Nov & Xmas
Attractive, cottage style hotel, personally run by owners and with interesting home cooking.
12rm(4➡2⋒)(3fb) Ⓡ sB&B£8.50–£12.50 sB&B➡⋒£9.50–£13.50 dB&B£17–£25 dB&B➡⋒£19–£27 B
CTV 11P
♆ ☕ Lunch £3.50–£5 Tea 90p–£1.20 High Tea 90p–£3 Dinner £4.25–£8&alc Wine £2.86 Last dinner 9.45pm
Credit cards 1 3 **VS**

★★***Great Western*** Cliff Rd ☎(06373) 2010 Plan **11** *D2*
RS Nov–Mar
Close to the beaches, this hotel is situated in the centre of town and has good views.
50rm(25➡25⋒) TV in all bedrooms Ⓡ
Lift CTV 30P 20 CFA ✤ Live music and dancing nightly in season
British, French & Italian V ♆ ☕ Last dinner 8pm
Credit cards 1 2 3 5

★★**Hotel Kontiki** Mount Wise (cars use Brecken Ter) ☎(06373) 71137 Plan **13** *C2*
Large, family hotel, close to the town centre and beaches.
58rm(48➡5⋒) Annexe: 12rm(8➡)(26fb) CTV in 32 bedrooms Ⓡ sB&B£9–£14.50 sB&B➡⋒£10.50–£18.50 dB&B£18–£29 dB&B➡⋒£21–£37 B
☾ CTV 52P 20 (heated) sauna bath wkly Live music and dancing nightly xmas
English, Italian & French V ♆ ☕ Lunch £2–£3.24 Tea 35p–£1 High Tea £1–£1.50 Dinner £3.50–£7.50 Last dinner 9.30pm
Credit cards 1 2 3 5
See advert on page 478

★★**Minto House** 38 Pentire Cres, Pentire
☎(06373) 3227 Plan **15** *A2*
Closed Nov–19 Apr
Family hotel situated on the banks of the Gannel Estuary.
29rm(11➡12⋒) Annexe: 2rm (6fb) CTV in all bedrooms Ⓡ sB&B£10.25–£15 sB&B➡⋒£11–£16 dB&B£20.50–£30 dB&B➡⋒£22–£32 B
16P ✤ sauna bath Disco wkly in season Live music and dancing twice wkly in season Cabaret wkly in season
English & Continental ♆ ☕ Bar lunch 55p–£5 Tea 50p–£2.50 Dinner £7–£8.50 Wine £3.20 Last dinner 8pm
Credit cards 1 2 3 5
See advert on page 478

★★**Pine Lodge** Henver Rd
☎(06373) 2549 Plan **17** *E3*
Closed Xmas
Small, friendly, family-run hotel close to the town centre and beaches.
10rm(2➡1⋒) Annexe: 5rm(1➡4⋒) CTV in all bedrooms Ⓡ sB&B£11.50–£15.50 sB&B➡⋒£13.50–£17.50 dB&B£23–£32 dB&B➡⋒£27–£34
CTV 20P ⛆ (heated)
♆ ☕ Bar lunch £1.20–£3 Tea 80p Dinner £5.25&alc Wine £3.65 Last dinner 8pm
Credit card 3 **VS**

N

Newquay

★★Porth Veor Manor House Porthway ☎(06373) 3274 Plan **18** *E3*
Closed Nov–6 Jan
In a peaceful situation, this hotel is personally run by the owners.
14rm(12➡2⋒) (5fb) CTV in all bedrooms Ⓡ✱B
CTV 50P ✿ ⌂
English & French ♆ ☕ Lunch £3.75–£5.50&alc Tea fr45p High Tea £1–£2.50 Dinner £5–£6.50&alc Wine £3.45 Last dinner 9pm
Credit cards 1 3 **VS**

★★Sandy Lodge Hillgrove Rd ☎(06373) 2851 Plan **21** *E2*
Closed 14 Oct–22 Apr
Small, family hotel situated close to Barrowfield and Tolcarne beach.
46rm(8➡13⋒) (14fb) ✱ sB&B£9–£12 dB&B£18–£23 dB&B➡⋒£22–£26.45 B
CTV 50P ⊡ & ≈ (heated) sauna bath Disco, Live music and dancing, Cabaret 2 nights ⌂
V ♆ ☕ Lunch £2.85–£3.50&alc Tea 55p–75p&alc Dinner £4.85–£6.50&alc Wine £3.85 Last dinner 8pm

★★Water's Edge Esplanade Rd, Fistral Bay ☎(06373) 2048 Plan **24** *A2*
Closed Nov–Mar
Small, family-owned hotel near Fistral Beach.
20rm(12➡4⋒) (5fb) Ⓡ ✱ sB&B£11.50–£17.83 dB&B£23–£35.66 dB&B➡⋒£25.30–£39.10 B
CTV 18P 1⌂ ✱ ⌂
English & French ♆ ☕ ✱ Bar lunch £1–£1.85 Tea 50p–£1.25 Dinner £7.95 Wine £3.95 Last dinner 8.15pm
VS

Newquay — New Quay

★★ *HL* **Whipsiderry** Trevelgue Rd, Porth ☎(06373) 4777 Plan **25** *E3*
Closed Oct–mid Apr
18rm(2⇌16⋒)(6fb)Ⓡ sB&B£6.75–£9.95 sB&B⇌⋒£9.21–£12.41 dB&B£13.50–£19.90 dB&B⇌⋒£18.42–£39.80 Ᵽ
CTV 25P ✽ ⊡(heated) Disco twice wkly Cabaret twice wkly
English & Continental V ✿ ⊒ Bar lunch 75p–£2 Tea 30p–75p Dinner £4.75–£7.50 Wine £3.70 Last dinner 8pm

★ **Trevone** Mount Wise ☎(06373) 3039 Plan **23** *C1*
Closed 13 Oct–21 Apr
Small, family hotel situated close to town centre and beaches.
35rm(11⋒)(5fb) ★ ✽sB&B£6.32–£9.20 sB&B⋒£7.47–£10.35 dB&B£12.64–£18.40 dB&B⇌⋒£14.94–£20.70
CTV 20P Disco Mon & Fri Cabaret Tue–Thu & Sun
English & Continental ✿ ✽Tea fr40p Dinner fr£4 Wine £3.75 Last dinner 7.30pm
VS
See advert on page 480

NEWQUAY
Dyfed
Map **2** SN35

★ **New Quay** ☎(0545) 560282
A convivial hotel on the sea front with modest bedrooms.
11rm Ⓡ ✽sB&B£8.50–£12 dB&B£16–£23 Ᵽ
CTV ⊁
✿ ✽Bar lunch £1.75–£6 Dinner fr£4&alc Wine £3.50 Last dinner 9.30pm
Credit cards 1 3

NEWTON ABBOT
Devon
Map **3** SX87

★★★**Globe** Courtenay St ☎(0626) 4106
Principal town centre hotel.
18rm(6⇌5⋔)(2fb) CTV in all bedrooms Ⓡ sB&B£17.50 sB&B⇌⋔£22.50 dB&B£26 dB&B⇌⋔£32 B
1⌂⇌ Live music and dancing twice wkly *xmas*
▣English, American & French V♁ Lunch £4.50&alc Dinner £6.95–£8.95&alc Wine £4.35 Last dinner 10pm
Credit cards 1 2 3 5

★★***Queens*** Queen St (Inter-Hotels) ☎(0626) 65216
Commercial, corner-sited, town hotel, with good service and attentive staff.
26rm(15⇌1⋔) CTV in 24 bedrooms TV in 2 bedrooms Ⓡ B
9P *xmas*
▣English & French ♁☐ Last dinner 9.45pm
Credit cards 1 2 3 5 **VS**

✕**Old Rydon Inn** Rydon Rd, Kingsteignton (1½m E A380) ☎(0626) 4626
Closed Sun & Mon
▣European 45 seats ✱Dinner £10.50alc Wine £4.25 Last dinner 9.30pm 30P
Credit cards 1 2 3 5

NEWTON FERRERS
Devon
Map **2** SX54

★★⌂*H* **Court House** ☎Plymouth (0752) 872324
Creeper-clad manor set in spacious, terraced lawns and gardens.
10rm(8⇌) sB&B£13–£18 sB&B⇌£14–£19 dB&B£26–£36 dB&B⇌£28–£38 B
CTV 25P ⇌✽ ≈(heated) nc8yrs
▣English & Continental V♁☐ Lunch £3–£5 Tea £1–£2 Dinner £8.50–£10&alc Wine £4.50 Last dinner 8.30pm
Credit card 3 **VS**
See advert on page 515

★★**River Yealm** Yealm Rd ☎Plymouth (0752) 872419
Gabled building in its own grounds with river frontage and jetty.
23rm(6⇌)(1fb) Ⓡ sB&B£15–£16 sB&B⇌£16–£17 dB&B£30–£32 dB&B⇌£32–£34 B
CTV 60P 1⌂✽ ♪
V♁☐ Bar lunch fr£2&alc Tea fr40p&alc Dinner fr£7.50&alc Wine £3.60 Last dinner 8.30pm

NEWTONMORE
Highland *Inverness-shire*
Map **14** NN79

★★***Glen*** Main St ☎(05403) 203
Converted, small, stone house with a modern extension to the side and at the front.
10rm(5⇌⋔)
CTV 25P
Last dinner 9pm

★★**Highlander** ☎(05403) 341
Closed 8–30 Nov
33⋔ (5fb) Ⓡ sB&B⋔£13.35–£15.35 dB&B⋔£22.70–£26.70
CTV 100P ✽ snooker Disco Sat (Dec–Apr) Live music and dancing & Cabaret Mon–Thu (Mar–Oct) *xmas*
V♁☐ Lunch £8&alc Tea 50p alc High Tea £2.25alc Dinner £8&alc Wine £3.25 Last dinner 8.30pm
Credit cards 1 2 3 5

★★**Mains** Main St ☎(05403) 206
Closed Nov
Grey, stone-built hotel in a prominent position at the crossroads of the A86 & the A9.
26rm(7⇌9⋔)(3fb) Ⓡ sB&B£9.50–£12.50 sB&B⇌⋔£10.50–£13.50 dB&B£18–£24 dB&B⇌⋔£20–£26 B
⚟CTV 100P billiards Disco & Cabaret wkly ⌂

Bar lunch £1.10–£4.95 Tea 45p–65p High Tea £2.50–£2.75 Dinner £6–£8.50 Wine £3.40 Last dinner 8.30pm

Credit cards 1 2 3 5

★ *H* **Ard-Na-Coille** Kingussie Rd (05403) 214
Closed Nov–Dec

10rm (1 3) (2fb) sB&B £10–£13 dB&B £18–£26 dB&B £20–£28
CTV 15P 2

English & French Tea fr 60p Dinner £7.50 Wine £4.25 Last dinner 8pm

NEWTON POPPLEFORD
Devon
Map **3** SY08

✕ **Bridge End House** Harpford (½m E A3052) Colaton Raleigh (0395) 68411
Detached, white-painted cottage, built around the 17th century, set by the main road.
Closed Mon, 25–27 Dec & 2–7 Oct
Lunch not served Sat Dinner not served Sun

English & French 42 seats *Lunch £3.57–£8.25 Dinner £4.20–£15&alc Wine £3.80 Last dinner 10pm 20P bedrooms available

Credit cards 1 3

NEWTON SOLNEY
Derbyshire
Map **8** SK22

★★★ **Newton Park** (Embassy) Burton-on-Trent (0283) 703568
Closed Xmas & New Year RS Public hols
Large, Georgian-style building on the B5008, about 3 miles from Burton-on-Trent.

27 (1fb) CTV in all bedrooms Ⓡ sB&B £31 dB&B £37
200P

English & French V Lunch £6.20 Tea fr 60p Dinner £7.90 Wine £4.50 Last dinner 9pm

Credit cards 1 2 3 4 5

NEWTON STEWART
Dumfries & Galloway *Wigtownshire*
Map **10** NX46

★★★ **Bruce** Queen St (0671) 2294
Modern, family-run hotel in the village centre.

16 (2fb) CTV in all bedrooms Ⓡ sB&B £19–£22 dB&B £32–£36
16P 4

French Lunch £2.50–£3 Tea 50p–£1 Dinner £8–£9&alc Wine £4.75 Last dinner 8.30pm

Credit cards 1 2 3 5

★★★ *BL* **Kirroughtree** Minnigaff (0671) 2141
Closed 23 Dec–Feb
An 18th-century mansion set in an elevated position in parkland, 2 miles outside the town. Free golf for residents.

22rm (21 1) Annexe: 2 (4fb) 4 CTV in all bedrooms Ⓡ sB&B £18–£23 dB&B £36–£46
60P nc 10yrs

British & French V Lunch £5.75&alc Tea 90p Dinner £12.50alc Wine £4.90 Last dinner 9.30pm

See advert on page 482

★★ **Creebridge House** (0671) 2121
A very pleasant country house style hotel set in secluded grounds on the town outskirts.

20rm (11 1) (1fb) CTV in 9 bedrooms TV in 6 bedrooms Ⓡ sB&B £14–£15.50 sB&B £17–£18.50 dB&B £28–£31 dB&B £34–£37
40P xmas

European V Lunch £5–£6 Tea fr 60p Dinner £9–£10 Wine £4.20 Last dinner 9.30pm

Credit cards 1 3

★★ **Crown** 101 Queen St (0671) 2727
Closed Xmas Day
A border-town coaching inn maintaining its traditional Galloway appearance and hospitality.

9rm (4 1) (1fb) CTV available in bedrooms Ⓡ sB&B £10.50 sB&B £18 dB&B £21 dB&B £25
CTV 25P sauna bath

V Lunch fr £3.45&alc Tea fr £1.20 High Tea fr £3.75 Dinner fr £8 Wine £5.20 Last dinner 8.30pm

Credit cards 1 2 3 5

★★ **Galloway Arms** Victoria St (0671) 2282
Old building set between shops in the centre of this market town.

23rm (14 2) (3fb) CTV in all bedrooms Ⓡ sB&B £16–£18 sB&B £18 dB&B £32–£35 dB&B £35
8P 15 *xmas*

Mainly grills V Bar lunch £1.75–£3.50 Tea £1.85–£2 High Tea £3.50–£6&alc Dinner £9.50–£10&alc Wine £4.50 Last dinner 10pm

Credit cards 1 2 3 5 **VS**

NEWTOWN
Powys
Map **6** SO19

★★★ **Bear** Broad St (0686) 26964
Telex 35205
Coaching inn dating from Tudor times, situated in the town centre, with a modern extension at the rear.

37rm (28 5) (13fb) CTV in all bedrooms Ⓡ sB&B £22.50–£24 dB&B £31.40–£33.40
CTV 60P

English, Welsh & French V Lunch £5.50&alc Tea 50p Dinner £6.50&alc Wine £3.95 Last dinner 9.30pm

Credit cards 1 2 3 5

NEWTOWN LINFORD
Leicestershire
Map **4** SK50

★★ **Johnscliffe** 73 Main St (Exec Hotel) Markfield (0530) 242228
RS 21 Dec–4 Jan

7rm (2 3) (1fb) 2 CTV in 5 bedrooms Ⓡ sB&B £15 sB&B £18.50 dB&B £25–£35
CTV 25P

English & French V Lunch £3–£6 Tea 50p–£1.50 Dinner £6.50–£7.50&alc Wine £4.95 Last dinner 9.45pm

S% Credit cards 1 3 5

N

NORMAN CROSS
Cambridgeshire
Map **4** TL19

☆☆☆**Crest** Great North Rd (Crest)
☎Peterborough (0733) 240209
Telex no 32576 RS Sun & Bank hols

97rm(77→20⋔) CTV in all bedrooms Ⓡ
*sB→⋔ fr£30 dB→⋔ fr£39 (room only) Ɓ

☾ ⚡200P CFA ♿

🅴International **V** ✿ ☕ *Lunch £2.25–£6 Tea fr50p High Tea fr£1 Dinner £6.25–£7.95 Wine £4.25 Last dinner 9.45pm

Credit cards ① ② ③ ④ ⑤ **VS**

NORTHALLERTON
North Yorkshire
Map **8** SE39

★★★**Solberge Hall** Newby Wiske (3¼m S off A167) (Best Western)
☎(0609) 779191

15rm(14→1⋔) 2▭ CTV in all bedrooms Ⓡ sB&B→⋔ £25 dB&B→⋔ £35–£45 Ɓ

CTV 60P ✽ billiards

🅴French ✿ ☕ *Lunch £2.45–£6 Tea £1.95 Dinner £8.50alc Wine £4.50 Last dinner 9.30pm

Credit cards ① ③ ⑤

★★**Golden Lion** Market Pl (Trusthouse Forte) ☎(0609) 2404

Sympathetically modernised inn with Georgian façade offering comfortable old world atmosphere and stylish dining room.

29rm(10→) (1fb) CTV in all bedrooms Ⓡ sB&B£33 sB&B→£35.50 dB&B£45.50 dB&B→£49.50 Ɓ

CTV 60P *xmas*

✿ ☕ Last dinner 9.30pm

Credit cards ① ② ③ ④ ⑤

NORTHAMPTON
Northamptonshire
Map **4** SP76

★★★**Grand** Gold St ☎(0604) 34416

54rm(36→) (2fb) CTV in all bedrooms Ⓡ *sB&B£20 sB&B→£26.75 dB&B£30.35 dB&B→£36 Ɓ

Lift ☾ 60P CFA

V ✿ ☕ *Lunch £5.90–£7.40&alc Tea 50p–£2.50 High Tea £5.90–£7.40&alc Dinner £5.90–£7.40&alc Wine £3.90 Last dinner 10pm

Credit cards ① ③ ⑤

★★★**Saxon Inn** Silver St, Town Centre (Saxon Inn) ☎(0604) 22441 Telex no 311142

133→⋔ (4fb) CTV in all bedrooms Ⓡ sB&B→⋔ fr£34.95 dB&B→⋔ fr£45.90 Ɓ

Lift ☾ 250P CFA Live music and dancing wkly ♿

🅴International **V** ✿ ☕ *Lunch £5.95&alc Dinner £6.95&alc Wine £4.60 Last dinner 10.30pm

Credit cards ① ② ③ ④ ⑤ **VS**

★★★**Westone Moat House** Ashley Way, Weston Favell (3m E off A45) (Queens Moat) ☎(0604) 406262
Closed 27–31 Dec

29→ Annexe: 34→ (4fb) CTV in all bedrooms Ⓡ sB&B→£31 dB&B→£41 Ɓ

Lift ☾ CTV 100P 1🚗 CFA ✽ sauna bath Live music and dancing mthly

🅴English & French **V** ✿ ☕ *Lunch £5.50&alc Tea 70p Dinner £6.25&alc Wine £4.75 Last dinner 9.45pm

Credit cards ① ② ③ ④ ⑤ **VS**

✕**Napoleon's Bistro** 9–11 Welford Rd
☎(0604) 713899

Closed Sun 25–31 Dec & Public hols
Lunch not served Mon & Sat

🅴French **V** 44 seats *Lunch £5.35–£6.95 Dinner £8.95–£9.95 Wine £4.50 Last dinner 10pm

Credit cards ① ③ ⑤

✕***Vineyard*** 7 Derngate ☎(0604) 33978
Closed Sun, 24 Dec–3 Jan & Bank hols
Lunch not served Sat Dinner not served Mon

🅴English & European 35 seats Lunch £5.25&alc Dinner £9.80alc Wine £4.70 Last dinner 10.30pm ⚡

Credit cards ① ③ ⑤

N

NORTH BALLACHULISH
Highland *Inverness-shire*
Map **14** NN06

★**Loch Leven** ☎Onich (08553) 236
10rm (1fb) Ⓡ sB&B£10 dB&B£20 B
CTV 100P ✽ Live music and dancing wkly
Bar lunch £1.50–£4&alc Tea £1–£2 Dinner £4–£6&alc Wine £3.60 Last dinner 8.30pm
See advert on page 484

NORTH BERWICK
Lothian *East Lothian*
Map **12** NT58

★★★*L* **Marine** Cromwell Rd (Trusthouse Forte) ☎(0620) 2406 Telex no 727363
Built in the grand resort style, this hotel has excellent views across the Firth of Forth.
85rm (75 10) (9fb) CTV in all bedrooms Ⓡ sB&B £33.50 dB&B £52.50 B
Lift ☾ CTV 200P CFA ✽ (heated) (hard) squash billiards sauna bath *xmas*
Last dinner 9.30pm

Credit cards 1 2 3 4 5

★★**Blenheim House** Westgate ☎(0620) 2385
Centrally-situated hotel, very close to the beach, with fine views across West Bay.
11rm (5 1) (2fb) sB&B£12–£14 sB&B £14–£16 dB&B£24–£28 dB&B £28–£32 B
CTV 30P ✽
V Lunch £4–£4.50 Dinner fr £8&alc Wine £5.10 Last dinner 9pm

★★**Nether Abbey** Dirleton Ave ☎(0620) 2802
Closed Nov–Feb →

N

16rm(4➡6⋒)(4fb)Ⓡ★sB&B£12.50 sB&B➡⋒£15.50 dB&B£25 dB&B➡⋒£28

CTV 60P✽

V♔Bar lunch £1.50–£2.50&alc Dinner £7.50–£8 Wine £4.50 Last dinner 8pm

Credit cards 1 3 **VS**

★★**Point Garry** West Bay Rd ☎(0620) 2380

Closed Nov–Feb

Family run hotel with pleasant garden.

15rm(2➡6⋒)(4fb) sB&B£13.75 sB&B➡⋒£15.40 dB&B£25 dB&B➡⋒£28

CTV 10P billiards

V♔ Lunch £3.50 Tea 50p Dinner £5.50&alc Wine £4.35 Last dinner 9pm

VS

✕**Al Vagabondo** 35 High St ☎(0620) 3434

Closed Mon (in winter) Lunch not served Sun

Continental 50 seats ✱Lunch £3–£4.85&alc Dinner fr£8&alc Wine £4.60 Last dinner 10.45pm

Credit cards 1 2 3 5

NORTH FERRIBY
Humberside
Map **8** SE92

☆☆☆**Crest Hotel Hull–Humber Bridge** Ferriby High Rd (Crest) ☎Hull (0482) 645212 Telex no 52558

A multi-storey, modern hotel with views of the Humber Bridge.

102➡CTV in all bedroomsⓇ✱sB➡ fr£35 dB➡fr£45 (room only)

☾100P Live music and dancing Sun CFA

International V♔✱Lunch £6–£8.50&alc Tea fr50p Dinner £8.50&alc Wine £5.25 Last dinner 9.45pm

Credit cards 1 2 3 4 5 **VS**

NORTH HUISH
Devon
Map **3** SX75

★★**Brookdale Country House** Hillgrove Rd ☎Gara Bridge (054 882) 402

Closed Jan

Secluded hotel in wooded grounds.

8rm(2➡2⋒)(1fb) 1 CTV in all bedroomsⓇsB&B£14–£17 sB&B➡⋒£17 dB&B£26–£29 dB&B➡⋒£29

30P✽ *xmas*

♔ Lunch £5–£8 Tea 90p–£1.40 Dinner £6–£9.50&alc Wine £3.95 Last dinner 9pm

Credit cards 1 2 3 5

NORTHIAM
East Sussex
Map **5** TQ82

★★**Hayes Arms** Village Green ☎(07974) 3142

Comfortable, Tudor timbered house with Georgian extension, run by Canadian couple.

7➡1 CTV in all bedroomsⓇ★ sB&B➡£22–£35 dB&B➡£32–£45

CTV 40P✽ nc12yrs

English & Continental ♔ Bar lunch £8–£14&alc Tea 75p alc High Tea £1.75 Dinner £8–£14&alc Wine £4.25 Last dinner 9.30pm

Credit cards 1 2 3 5

NORTHLEACH
Gloucestershire
Map **4** SP11

★**Wheatsheaf** ☎(04516) 244

A small, friendly hotel with a cosy bar.

8rm(2fb) sB&B£12 dB&B£19

CTV 15P✽

♔Bar lunch 45p–£1.90 Dinner £4–£7.50 Wine £2.90 Last dinner 8.30pm

✕**Country Friends** Market Pl ☎(04516) 421

An enchanting small restaurant serving carefully prepared and interesting dishes.

Closed Sun Lunch not served Tue–Sat Dinner not served Mon

English & French V 20 seats ✱Lunch £5.60–£6.60&alc Dinner fr£7.80&alc Wine £4.40 Last dinner 9.30pm bedrooms available

Credit cards 2 5

NORTHOPHALL
Clwyd
Map **7** SJ26

★★★**Chequers** (Inter-Hotels) ☎Deeside (0244) 816181 Telex no 617112

Well equipped hotel in its own grounds offering some Welsh cuisine.

30rm(28➡2⋒)(3fb) CTV in all bedrooms ⓇsB&B➡⋒£22.50–£25 dB&B➡⋒£40–£45

200P 2✽

V♔Lunch £4–£6&alc Tea 45p Dinner £8–£9&alc Wine £3.95 Last dinner 9.45pm

Credit cards 1 2 3 5 **VS**

NORTH PETHERTON
Somerset
Map **3** ST23

★★ *B* **Walnut Tree Inn** (Exec Hotel) ☎(0278) 662255

6rm(6➡⋒) Annexe: 5➡⋒)(1fb) CTV in all bedroomsⓇ★sB&B➡⋒ fr£22 dB&B➡⋒ fr£32

70P

Mainly grills V♔Lunch £4.80alc Dinner £8.20alc Wine £3.20 Last dinner 10pm

Credit cards 1 2 3 5 **VS**

NORTHREPPS
Norfolk
Map **9** TG23

✕✕***Northrepps Cottage*** ☎Overstrand (026 378) 202

Closed Mon Dinner not served Sun

English & Continental 336 seats Last dinner 9pm 100P

NORTH STIFFORD
Essex
Map **5** ST68

☆☆☆**Stifford Moat House** (Queens Moat) ☎Grays Thurrock (0375) 71451

RS Dec

Quiet hotel with modern, well-equipped bedrooms and friendly, well-run restaurant.

64🛁 CTV in all bedrooms Ⓡ sB&B🛁 fr£36.50 dB&B🛁 fr£41 Ⓑ

☾ 80P CFA ✿ 🎾(hard) Live music and dancing Sat

▣English & French ♕ ☕ Lunch £5–£7&alc Tea £1–£2.50 Dinner £7–£10.50&alc Wine £4.75 Last dinner 9.30pm

Credit cards 1 2 3 4 5

NORTH STOKE
Oxfordshire
Map **4** SU68

★★★ ***HL*** **Springs** ☎ Wallingford (0491) 36687 Telex no 849794

Hospitable, attractive, elegant hotel whose restaurant overlooks lake. Guitar-shaped swimming pool and tennis court.

23🛁 (7fb) 1▣ CTV in all bedrooms sB&B🛁 fr£36 dB&B🛁 fr£62 Continental breakfast Ⓑ

100P 🚫 ✿ ≋(heated) 🎾(hard) sauna bath *xmas*

▣English & French **V** ♕ ☕ Lunch £7.50&alc Tea £1–£2.50 Dinner £10.75&alc Wine £7 Last dinner 10pm

S% Credit cards 1 2 3 4 5 **VS**

NORTH TAWTON
Devon
Map **3** SS60

★ **Kayden Arms** High St (Minotel) ☎ (083 782) 242

Small, privately-run hotel in the village centre.

7rm(2🛁 1🚿)(1fb) CTV in 5 bedrooms ✻sB&B£9–£11 sB&B🛁🚿 £10–£12 dB&B£16–£21 dB&B🛁🚿 £18–£25 Ⓑ

CTV ⚑ Live music and dancing Wed *xmas*

♕ ☕ ✻Lunch £3alc Tea fr50p Dinner £6alc Wine £3.25 Last dinner 10pm

Credit cards 1 3

NORTH UIST, ISLE OF
Western Isles *Inverness-shire*
Map **13**
See **Lochmaddy**

NORTHWICH
Cheshire
Map **7** SJ67

★★★ **Hartford Hall** Hartford (2m SW off bypass A556) ☎ (0606) 75711
RS Xmas & New Year

Gabled, 16th-century country house in its own grounds.

21🛁🚿 (2fb) CTV in all bedrooms Ⓡ ✗ sB&B🛁🚿 £28 dB&B🛁🚿 £38 Ⓑ

☾ CTV 50P 🚫 ✿

V ♕ ✻Lunch £7alc Dinner £8.25alc Wine £3.95 Last dinner 10pm

Credit cards 1 2 3 5
See advert on page 486

★★ **Woodpecker** London Rd (Greenall Whitley) ☎ (0606) 45524 Telex no 629462
RS 24–28 Dec

35rm(28🛁 2🚿)(2fb) CTV in all bedrooms Ⓡ ✗ sB&B🛁🚿 £29.70–£30.70 dB&B🛁🚿 £39.60–£40.60 Ⓑ

☾ 80P ✿

V ♕ ☕ Lunch £6.50&alc Tea 50p High Tea £3 Dinner fr£6.50&alc Wine £4.50 Last dinner 10pm

S% Credit cards 1 2 3 5

NORWICH
Norfolk
Map **5** TG20

★★★ **Lansdowne** 116 Thorpe Rd (Embassy) ☎ (0603) 20302

44rm(21🛁 3🚿)(1fb) CTV in all bedrooms Ⓡ sB fr£22 sB🛁🚿 fr£30 dB fr£32 dB🛁🚿 fr£37 Ⓑ

Lift ☾ 70P CFA

▣English & French **V** ♕ ☕ Lunch fr£5.40 Dinner fr£6.75&alc Wine £4.50 Last dinner 9.15pm

Credit cards 1 2 3 4 5
See advert on page 486

★★★**Maids Head** Tombland (Queens Moat) ☎(0603) 28821 Telex no 975080
Part of the hotel is more than 700 years old, showing the original fireplace and king-pin pillars.
82rm(60⇌18⋒)(5fb) 1⊟ CTV in all bedrooms sB&B£26 sB&B⇌⋒£32.25 dB&B⇌⋒£46.50 Ɓ
Lift ☾ ⚡80P CFA 20⌂ *xmas*
V♆☕ Lunch £3.41–£6.82 Tea £1.36–£1.68 Dinner fr£7&alc Wine £5.40 Last dinner 10.30pm
Credit cards 1 2 3 5 **VS**

☆☆☆**Hotel Nelson** Prince of Wales Rd (Best Western) ☎(0603) 28612 Telex no 975203
The hotel stands on the banks of the River Wensum close to the city centre.
94⇌⋒ CTV in all bedrooms Ⓡ ★ sB&B⇌⋒£36 dB&B⇌⋒£43.50 Ɓ
Lift ☾ ⚡96P 32⌂ sauna bath *xmas*
V♆ Lunch fr£7 Dinner fr£7 Wine £4 Last dinner 9.45pm
Credit cards 1 2 3 5

☆☆☆**Hotel Norwich** 121–131 Boundary Rd (Best Western) ☎(0603) 410431 Telex no 975337
102⇌⋒ (16fb) CTV in all bedrooms Ⓡ ★ sB&B⇌⋒£34 dB&B⇌⋒£42 Ɓ
☾ ⚡225P CFA *xmas*
⊟ English & French V♆☕ Lunch fr£7 Dinner fr£7 Wine £4 Last dinner 10pm
Credit cards 1 2 3 5

☆☆☆**Post House** Ipswich Rd (Trusthouse Forte) ☎(0603) 56431 Telex no 975106
120⇌ (58fb) CTV in all bedrooms Ⓡ sB&B⇌£38.50 dB&B⇌£52 Ɓ
☾ 200P CFA ✽ ⇌ (heated) *xmas*
♆☕ Last dinner 9.45pm
Credit cards 1 2 3 4 5

★★★***Sprowston Hall*** Wroxham Rd, Sprowston (2m NE A1151) (Inter-Hotel) ☎(0603) 410871
Imposing building reached up a long driveway, offering a pleasant, relaxing break.
30⇌⋒ Annexe: 7⇌⋒ CTV in 30 bedrooms
☾ 60P CFA ✽ ⚑
♆☕

★★**Castle** Castle Meadow (DeVere) ☎(0603) 611511 Telex no 975582
79rm(26⇌) CTV in all bedrooms Ⓡ ✻sB&B fr£16.80 sB&B⇌£29 dB&B fr£28.50 dB&B⇌ fr£35.70 Ɓ
Lift ☾ ⚐ CFA
⊟ English & French ♆☕✻ Lunch fr£5.25&alc Dinner fr£5.25&alc Wine £5.50 Last dinner 9pm
Credit cards 1 2 3 4 5 **VS**

★★**Oaklands** 89 Yarmouth Rd ☎(0603) 34471
Closed 24 & 25 Dec
42rm(22⇌3⋒) (3fb) CTV in all bedrooms sB&B£16.50 sB&B⇌⋒£19.50 dB&B£26.50 dB&B⇌⋒£29.50 Ɓ
90P ✽
⊟ English & French V♆☕ Lunch £4.25–£4.95&alc Tea 40p Dinner £5.25–£6.25&alc Wine £3.65 Last dinner 10pm
Credit cards 1 3

✕✕**Marco's** 17 Potter Gate ☎(0603) 24044
Closed Sat & Sun, 2wks Etr, 2wks Aug
⊟ Italian **V** 35 seats Lunch £8–£10&alc Dinner £10–£15&alc Wine £6 ⚐
Credit cards 1 2 3 5

NOTTINGHAM
Nottinghamshire
Map **8** SK54
See plan on pages 488–489

★★★★**Albany** St James's Street (Trusthouse Forte) ☎(0602) 470131 Telex no 37211 Plan **1** *C4*
160⇌ CTV in all bedrooms Ⓡ sB&B⇌£45.50 dB&B⇌£61.50 Ɓ
Lift ☾ ⌗ CFA

N

Last dinner 10.30pm

Credit cards 1 2 3 4 5

★★★★**Stakis Victoria** Milton St (Stakis) ☎(0602) 419561 Telex no 37401 Plan **14** *D5*

167 CTV in all bedrooms ® *sB&B fr£33 dB&B fr£39

Lift 8P Disco Fri & Sat *xmas*

English & French Last dinner 10pm

Credit cards 1 2 3 5 **VS**

★★★*L* **Bestwood Lodge** Bestwood Country Park, Arnold (3m N off A60) (Exec Hotel) ☎(0602) 203011 Plan **2** *C8*

A former hunting lodge, built in 1865, situated in 70 acres of parkland and woods.

35rm(11 19) (3fb) 1 CTV in all bedrooms ® sB&B £21 dB&B £28

150P Disco wkly

International **V** Lunch £6alc Tea 65palc High Tea £2.95alc Dinner £7alc Wine £4.45 Last dinner 10.30pm

Credit cards 1 2 3 5 **VS**

★★★**George** George St (Best Western) ☎(0602) 475641 Telex no 378150 Plan **5** *D4*

75rm(44 1) 1 CTV in all bedrooms ® *sB&B fr£17 sB&B £26 dB&B fr£21 dB&B £30

Lift CFA

*Lunch £1–£6 Tea 75p–£2 Dinner £6.50–£8 Wine £5 Last dinner 9.30pm

Credit cards 1 2 3 4 5

★★★*L* ***North Lodge*** 2 North Rd, The Park ☎(0602) 475215 Plan **8** *A3*

10rm(5 5) CTV in all bedrooms ®

30P sauna bath

International **V** Last dinner 10pm

Credit cards 1 2 3 5

★★★**Savoy** Mansfield Rd ☎(0602) 602621 Telex no 377429 Plan **11** *C8*

Closed Xmas Day

125 CTV in all bedrooms ® *sB fr£28.50 dB fr£37 (room only)

Lift 250P 50

English & Continental **V** *Lunch £2.55–£4.50 Tea fr45p Dinner £3.85–£6.25 Wine £3.30 Last dinner 11pm

Credit cards 1 3 4

★★★**Strathdon Thistle** Derby Rd (Thistle) ☎(0602) 418501 Telex no 377185 Plan **12** *B5*

64rm(20 44) CTV in all bedrooms ® *sB £31–£34 dB £36.50–£39.50 (room only)

Lift CFA

European *Lunch £5.60&alc Dinner £8&alc Last dinner 9.30pm

Credit cards 1 2 3 4 5 **VS**

★★***Edwalton Hall*** Edwalton (3½m S A606) ☎(0602) 231116 Plan **3** *E1*

12rm(2) ®

CTV 60P 2 Cabaret Sun

International **V** Last dinner 10pm

Credit card 2

★★**Flying Horse** Poultry (Berni) ☎(0602) 52831 Plan **4** *C4*

56rm(27) CTV in all bedrooms ® *sB&B £16 sB&B £20 dB&B £28 dB&B £32

14

Mainly grills *Lunch £2.32–£5 Dinner £3.60–£9 Wine £3.96 Last dinner 10.30pm

Credit cards 1 2 3 5

★★**Nottingham Knight** Loughborough Rd, Ruddington (junc A60/A614) (Home Brewery) ☎(0602) 211171 Plan **9** *E1*

9rm(6) (1fb) CTV in all bedrooms ® sB&B £16.56 sB&B £18.97 dB&B £23.80 dB&B £27.60

Lift 200P

Mainly grills **V** Last dinner 10.15pm

Credit cards 1 3

✕✕***Rhinegold*** King John Chambers, Fletcher Gate ☎(0602) 51294 Plan **10** *D4*

Closed Sun

English, French & Spanish 46 seats Last dinner 10.30pm

Credit cards 1 2

✕✕**Trattoria Conti** 14–16 Wheeler Gate ☎(0602) 474056 Plan **13** *C4*

Closed Sun, Last 2wks Jul 1st 3wks Aug & Public hols

English, French & Italian 72 seats *Lunch £3.75–£10&alc Dinner £10–£12alc Wine £4.25 Last dinner 11.15pm

Credit cards 1 2 3 5

✕**La Grenouille** 32 Lenton Boulevard ☎(0602) 411088 Plan **6** *A5*

Closed 24 Dec–2 Jan & Public hols Lunch not served

French **V** 38 seats Dinner £7–£15 Wine £5.50 Last dinner 9.30pm 10P

✕**Moulin Rouge** Trinity Sq ☎(0602) 472845 Plan **7** *C5*

Closed 26 Dec

International **V** 34 seats *Lunch £1.95–£3 Dinner £4.75–£5 Wine £3.70 Last dinner 11pm

Credit cards 1 2 3 5 **VS**

NUNEATON

Warwickshire

Map **4** SP39

★★**Chase** Higham Ln (Ansells) ☎(0203) 341013

Modernised hotel, popular with business clientele.

28 CTV in all bedrooms ® sB&B fr£29.25 dB&B fr£35.25

CTV 350P

Lunch fr£5.75&alc Dinner fr£5.75&alc Wine £3.90 Last dinner 10pm

Credit cards 1 2 3 **VS**

★★***Griff House*** Coventry Rd ☎Coventry (0203) 382984

The former home of George Eliot, the hotel has a modern bedroom extension.

23rm(13 3) 1 CTV in all bedrooms ® →

N

Nottingham

1 Albany ★★★★
2 Bestwood Lodge ★★★
3 Edwalton Hall ★★
4 Flying Horse ★★
5 George ★★★
6 La Grenouille X
7 Moulin Rouge X
8 North Lodge ★★★
9 Nottingham Knight ★★
10 Rhinegold XX
11 Savoy ★★★
12 Strathdon Thistle ★★★
13 Trattoria Conti XX
14 Stakis Victoria ★★★★

☾ CTV 200P ♪ Disco Thur Live music and dancing Sun

Last dinner 10pm

Credit cards 1 2 3

See advert on page 490

☆☆**Longshoot Motel** Watling St (Charrington)

☎(0203) 329711 Telex no 311100

Modern hotel, situated by a busy road junction.

Annexe: 47 CTV in all bedrooms ®

*sB&B £15.50–£26.50

dB&B £23–£33.50 B

☾ 47P

*Lunch fr£5.50 Dinner fr£5.50 Wine £3.80 Last dinner 10.30pm

Credit cards 1 2 3

NUNNINGTON
North Yorkshire
Map **8** SE67

XX**Ryedale Lodge** ☎(04395) 246

Lunch not served

French **V** 30 seats Dinner £10.95 Wine £4.95 Last dinner 9pm 25P bedrooms available

Credit cards 1 3 **VS**

OAKFORD
Devon
Map **3** SS92

X**Higher Western** (2m W on A361)

☎Anstey Mills (03984) 210

Closed Mon & 2wks Feb Dinner not served Sun

English & French 26 seats Lunch £5alc Tea £1.30 Dinner £8.60&alc Wine £4.25 Last dinner 9.30pm bedrooms available

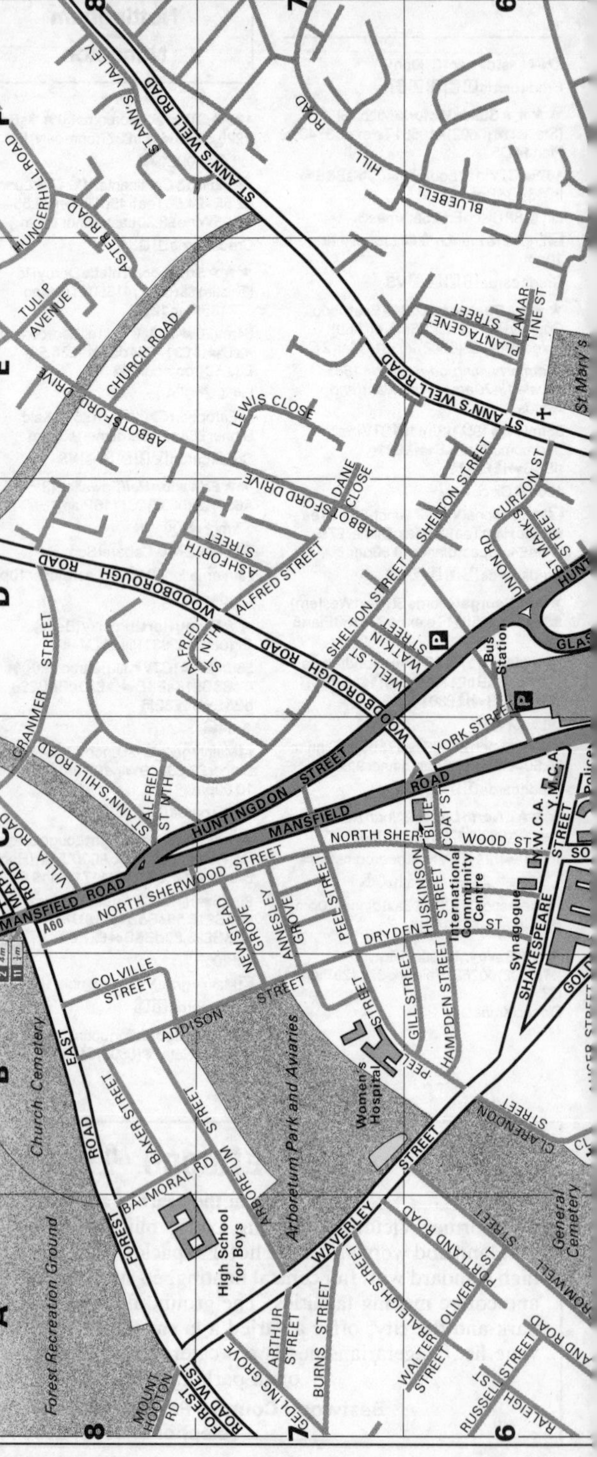

ST ANN'S WELL ROAD
ST ANN'S VALLEY
HUNGERHILL ROAD
HILL ROAD
BLUEBELL HILL
TULIP AVENUE
CHURCH ROAD
ABBOTSFORD DRIVE
LEWIS CLOSE
DANE CLOSE
PLANTAGENET STREET
LAMARTINE ST
St Mary's
SHELTON STREET
CURZON ST
UNION RD
ST MARK'S STREET
ASHFORTH STREET
ALFRED STREET
WOODBOROUGH ROAD
CRANMER STREET
ST ANN'S HILL ROAD
ALFRED ST NTH
WATKIN STREET
WELL ST
Bus Station
YORK STREET
HUNTINGDON STREET
MANSFIELD ROAD
NORTH SHERWOOD STREET
NORTH SHER
BLUE COAT ST
WOOD ST
Y.W.C.A.
Y.M.C.A.
International Community Centre
Synagogue
SHAKESPEARE STREET
HUSKINSON STREET
DRYDEN ST
NEWSTEAD GROVE
ANNESLEY GROVE
PEEL STREET
VILLA ROAD
A60
COLVILLE STREET
ADDISON STREET
EAST ROAD
BAKER STREET
ARBORETUM STREET
Church Cemetery
Arboretum Park and Aviaries
Women's Hospital
GILL STREET
HAMPDEN STREET
CLARENDON STREET
BALMORAL RD
FOREST ROAD
High School for Boys
WAVERLEY STREET
Forest Recreation Ground
MOUNT HOOTON RD
FOREST ROAD WEST
GEDLING GROVE
ARTHUR STREET
BURNS STREET
RALEIGH STREET
WALTER STREET
OLIVER ST
PORTLAND ROAD
RUSSELL STREET
General Cemetery
ROMWELL STREET

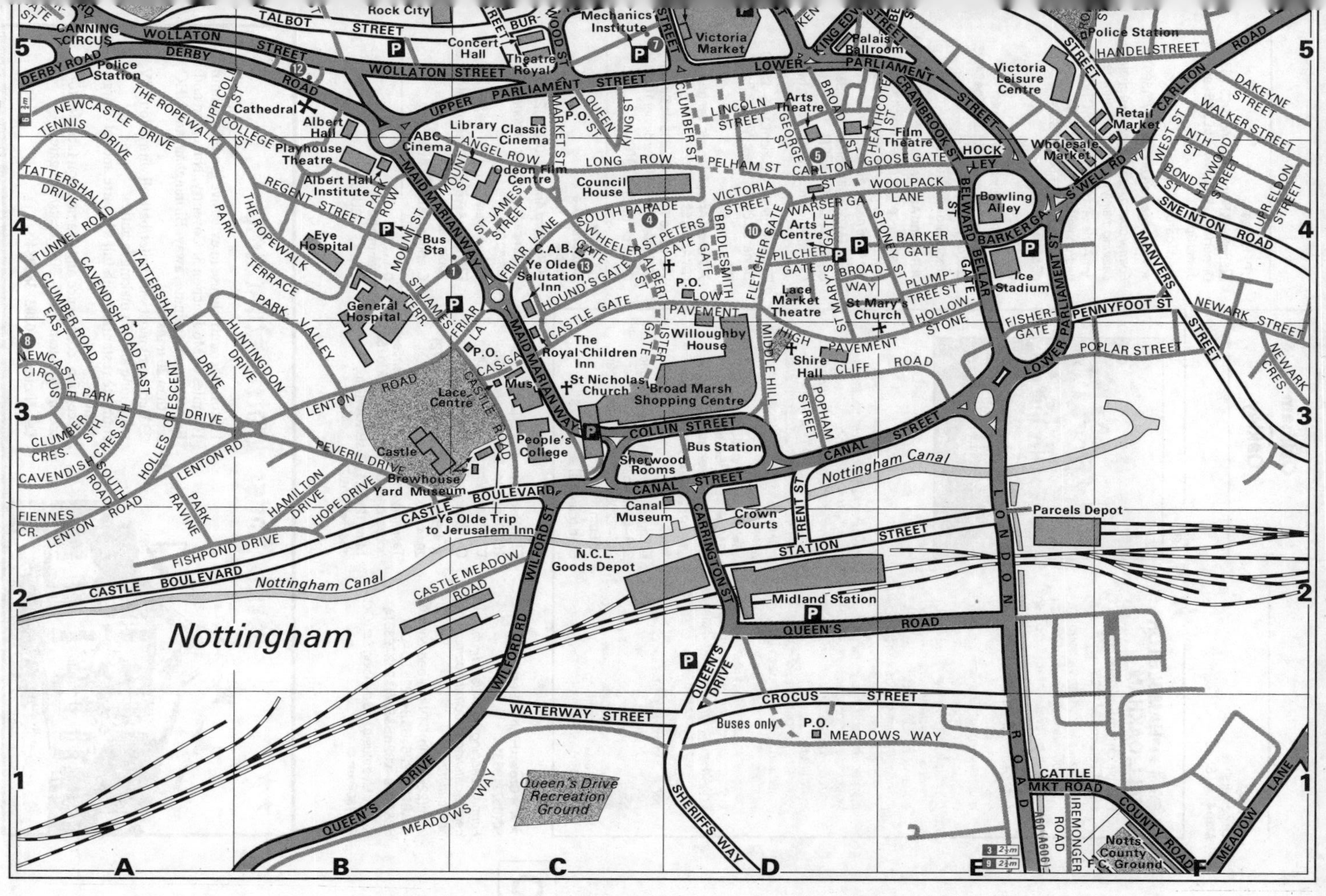
Nottingham
LONDON ROAD
MAID MARIAN WAY
UPPER PARLIAMENT STREET
LOWER PARLIAMENT STREET
WOLLATON STREET
DERBY ROAD
CANNING CIRCUS
CANAL STREET
COLLIN STREET
CARRINGTON ST
STATION STREET
TRENT ST
QUEEN'S ROAD
QUEEN'S DRIVE
WILFORD ST
WILFORD RD
CASTLE BOULEVARD
CASTLE MEADOW ROAD
WATERWAY STREET
CROCUS STREET
MEADOWS WAY
SHERIFFS WAY
CATTLE MKT ROAD
IREMONGER ROAD
COUNTY ROAD
MEADOW LANE
A60 (A606)
MANVERS STREET
SNEINTON ROAD
CARLTON ROAD
PENNYFOOT ST
POPLAR STREET
NEWARK STREET
HANDEL STREET
Nottingham Canal
Midland Station
Parcels Depot
Crown Courts
Bus Station
Canal Museum
N.C.L. Goods Depot
Broad Marsh Shopping Centre
Council House
Castle
Brewhouse Yard Museum
Ye Olde Trip to Jerusalem Inn
Lace Centre
People's College
Sherwood Rooms
General Hospital
Eye Hospital
Cathedral
Albert Hall
Playhouse Theatre
Albert Hall Institute
ABC Cinema
Library
Classic Cinema
Odeon Film Centre
Concert Hall
Theatre Royal
Mechanics Institute
Victoria Market
Palais Ballroom
Victoria Leisure Centre
Police Station
Retail Market
Wholesale Market
Bowling Alley
Ice Stadium
Arts Theatre
Film Theatre
Arts Centre
Lace Market Theatre
St Mary's Church
Shire Hall
St Nicholas Church
The Royal Children Inn
Willoughby House
Ye Olde Salutation Inn
Queen's Drive Recreation Ground
Notts County F.C. Ground
Rock City
Buses only

OAKHAM
Leicestershire
Map **4** SK80

★★★

❀★★★ **HAMBLETON HALL, OAKHAM**

Hambleton (3m E off A606) ☎ (0572) 56991 Telex no 341995

Tim and Stefa Hart are the couple who have converted this lovely old house near Rutland Water into the popular hotel it has become. They employed Nina Campbell to decorate the interior and she has used her skill to charming effect. The drawing room is quite lovely with its attractive views over the water and there is also a small bar. The bedrooms have been equally well done and the fresh looking soft furnishings add their own air of distinction. They are comfortable and thoughtfully equipped with practically everything you could possibly need when away from home.
In the sparklingly appointed restaurant, Chef Nicholas Gill, who won the 1983 Mouton Cadet competition, provides excellent food in the modern manner and shows considerable promise with his dishes on the set four course menu. They are light and delicate and often enhanced with superb sauces. Mr Hart is enthusiastic about wine and has compiled a long list with some interesting examples from which you can choose something to complement your meal. The Harts,

together with their new manager, have inspired their friendly staff to offer the best of hospitality: nothing seems too much trouble for them and they are most solicitous of your needs. Such an attitude cannot fail to make your stay one you will remember.

15➡⋔ 1 CTV in all bedrooms sB&B➡⋔ £45 dB&B➡⋔ £65 Continental breakfast

Lift 32P 1 ✽ (hard) nc9yrs *xmas*

English & French **V** ✻Lunch £13–£15&alc Tea fr£1.50 Dinner £15–£20&alc Wine £7 Last dinner 9.15pm

Credit cards 1 2 3 5 **VS**

★★★**Crown** High St (Best Western) ☎ (0572) 3631

Former coaching inn, situated in the town centre, catering for both the commercial and tourist trade.

25rm(22➡)(2fb) CTV in all bedrooms Ⓡ sB&B£22–£25 sB&B➡£26.50–£30 dB&B£29–£32 dB&B➡⋔£32–£38

☾ CTV Live music and dancing Sat (Oct–Feb) 30P *xmas*

English & French **V** Lunch £4.40–£5.40 Tea 60p–£3.25 Dinner £5.95–£7.50&alc Wine £4 Last dinner 10pm

Credit cards 1 2 3 5

★★**Boultons** 4 Catmos St ☎ (0572) 2844

Tastefully and extensively modernised house, parts of which date back to 1604.

14rm(12➡2⋔) Ⓡ sB&B➡⋔ fr£18 dB&B➡⋔ fr£23

CTV 16P ✽

English & French Lunch fr£3.75&alc Dinner fr£5.25&alc Wine fr£3.95 Last dinner 9pm

Credit cards 1 3

★★**George** Market Pl ☎ (0572) 56971

Former coaching inn in the town centre, catering mainly for commercial trade.

3rm Annexe: 16rm(8➡)(1fb) CTV in all bedrooms Ⓡ ✻sB&B£14.95 sB&B➡£17–£23.50 dB&B£24 dB&B➡£29.50

CTV 10P

English & French **V** ✻Lunch £6.85&alc Dinner £6.85&alc Wine £4.25 Last dinner 10pm

Credit cards 1 2 3 5 **VS**

★**Rutland Angler** Mill St ☎ (0572) 55839

This 18th-century house which was a former nursing home, is situated just off the A606 near the town centre.

9rm(1➡) TV in all bedrooms Ⓡ sB&B£15 dB&B£24 dB&B➡£26

CTV 18P Live music and dancing twice wkly

Mainly grills **V** Lunch £1.95–£3.70 Dinner £2.80–£4.45alc Wine £3.98

VS

✕✕**Noel Arms** Bridge St, Langham (2m NW A606) ☎ (0572) 2931

V 40 seats ✻Lunch £8.50&alc Dinner £8.50&alc Wine £6 Last dinner 10pm 30P

Credit cards 1 2 3 5

OAKLEY
Bedfordshire
Map **4** TL05

✕***Bedford Arms*** ☎ (02302) 2280

A 17th-century inn, with a stone-built dining room.

Closed Xmas

English & French 50 seats Last dinner 10pm 75P

Credit cards 1 2 3 5

OAKLEY
Hampshire
Map **4** SU55

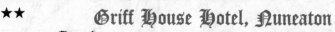

★★**Beach Arms** (on B3400)
☎Basingstoke (0256) 780210

Main hotel building has old beams and there are separate modern compact chalets.

5rm(1🛁1🚿) Annexe: 12rm(12🛁) CTV in all bedrooms ® sB&B£25 sB&B🛁🚿£31 dB&B£29 dB&B🛁🚿£38 B̶

CTV 60P ✽ ♿

V ♧ Lunch £6.50&alc Dinner £6.50&alc Wine £3.50 Last dinner 10pm

S% Credit cards 1 2 3 5

OBAN

Strathclyde *Argyllshire*
Map **10** NM83

★★★*L* **Alexandra** Corran Esp (Scottish Highland) ☎(0631) 62381 Telex no 778215 Plan **1** *A5*
Closed mid Oct–mid Apr

Stone building with gables, tower and a Regency-style porch leading to front, also having views of Oban Bay.

56rm(40🛁1🚿) (1fb) ® sB&B🛁🚿£26 dB&B🛁🚿£42 B̶

Lift ☾ CTV 35P ✽ Live music and dancing twice wkly

International **V** Bar lunch £3alc Dinner fr £8.50 Wine £4.60 Last dinner 8.30pm

Credit cards 1 2 3 5 **VS**

★★★**Caledonian** Station Sq ☎(0631) 63133 Telex no 777210 Plan **2** *B2*
Closed 16 Nov

Set in the town centre close to the railway and bus stations, this five-storey Victorian building overlooks the bay and harbour.

72rm(36🛁) (8fb) ® sB&B£17–£19.40 sB&B🛁£19–£23.40 dB&B£29–£34.30 dB&B🛁£33–£40.30 B̶

Lift ☾ CTV 3P Live music and dancing twice wkly

♧ Lunch £3.25–£3.75 Tea 75p Dinner £8.90 Wine £3.50 Last dinner 9pm

Credit cards 1 2 3 5 **VS**

★★★**Great Western** The Esplanade (Scottish Highland) ☎(0631) 63101 Telex no 778215 Plan **4** *B4*
Closed Nov–Mar RS Apr, May & Oct

Large hotel in commanding seafront location with superb views of the bay from the ornate lounge and cocktail bar.

74rm(64🛁2🚿) (2fb) ® sB&B🛁£26 dB&B🛁🚿£42

Lift ☾ CTV 25P Live music and dancing twice wkly Cabaret 4 nights wkly

V ♧ Lunch £1.20–£3.75 Tea fr 60p Dinner £6.50–£8.75 Wine £4.40 Last dinner 8.30pm

Credit cards 1 2 3 5

★★★***Regent*** Esplanade ☎(0631) 62341 Plan **9** *B3*

Previously the Regent and Marine Hotel, this is a large, privately-owned hotel on the Esplanade.

75rm(27🛁9🚿) ® B̶

Lift ☾ CTV 11P

♧ Last dinner 8.30pm

Credit cards 1 2 3 4 5

See advert on page 492

★★**Columba** North Pier ☎(0631) 62183 Plan **3** *B3*
Closed Nov–Mar

Large, traditional-style hotel at Oban's North Pier.

54rm(3🛁11🚿) (3fb) sB&B£12–£13.50 sB&B🛁🚿£14–£15.50 dB&B£24–£27 dB&B🛁🚿£28–£31

Lift ☾ CTV 9P Live music and dancing 3 nights wkly Cabaret wkly

♧ Lunch £4 Tea 30p Dinner £6 Wine £4.50 Last dinner 8pm

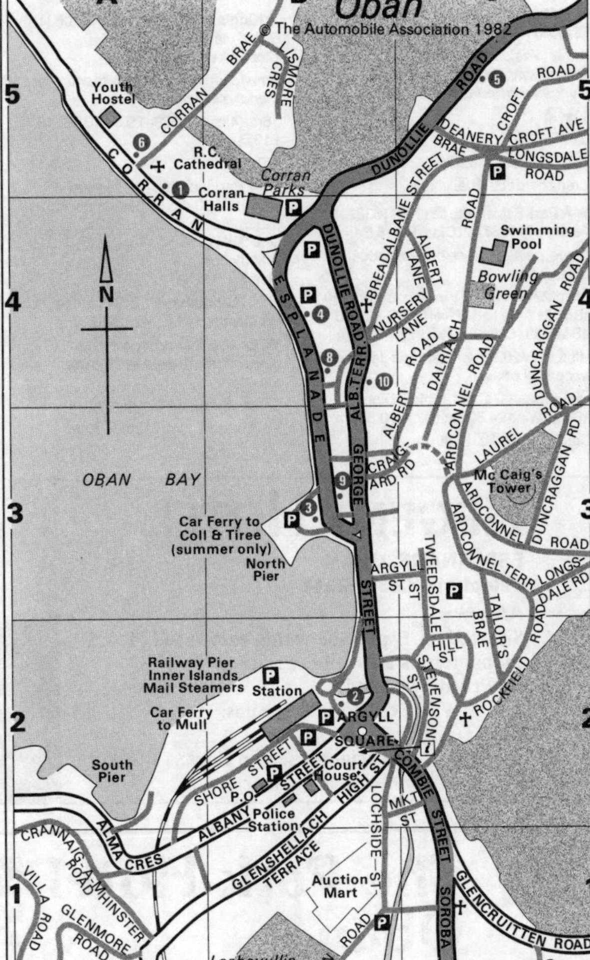
Oban
© The Automobile Association 1982
A
B
C
5
4
3
2
1
N
Youth Hostel
R.C. Cathedral
Corran Halls
Corran Parks
CORRAN ESPLANADE
CORRAN BRAE
LISMORE CRES
DUNOLLIE ROAD
DEANERY BRAE
CROFT ROAD
CROFT AVE
LONGSDALE ROAD
BREADALBANE STREET
ALBERT LANE
NURSERY LANE
ALBERT ROAD
DALRIACH ROAD
ARDCONNEL ROAD
DUNCRAGGAN ROAD
Swimming Pool
Bowling Green
ESPLANADE
ALB. TERR
GEORGE STREET
CRAIGARD RD
LAUREL ROAD
Mc Caig's Tower
ARDCONNEL TERR
LONGSDALE RD
OBAN BAY
Car Ferry to Coll & Tiree (summer only)
North Pier
ARGYLL ST
TWEEDSDALE ST
TAILOR'S BRAE
ROCKFIELD ROAD
HILL ST
STEVENSON ST
Railway Pier Inner Islands Mail Steamers
Station
Car Ferry to Mull
ARGYLL SQUARE
South Pier
SHORE STREET
STREET
Court House
P.O.
ALBANY
Police Station
HIGH ST
GLENSHELLACH TERRACE
COMBIE STREET
MKT ST
LOCHSIDE ST
ALMA CRES
CRANNAIG-A-MHINSTER ROAD
VILLA ROAD
GLENMORE ROAD
Auction Mart
LOCHAVULLIN ROAD
SOROBA ROAD
GLENCRUITTEN ROAD
Lochavullin Playing Fields
SINCLAIR DRIVE
QUARRY ROAD

Oban

1 Alexandra ★★★
2 Caledonian ★★★
3 Columba ★★
4 Great Western ★★★
5 King's Knoll ★
6 Lancaster ★★
7 Manor House ★★
8 Park ★★
9 Regent ★★★
10 Rowan Tree ★★

O

★★*L* **Lancaster** Corran Esp ☎(0631) 62587 Plan **6** *A5*
Seafront hotel popular with tourist and business trade alike.
28rm(3➡2⋔)(3fb) CTV available on request Ⓡ ✱sB&B fr£12 sB&B➡⋔ fr£14 dB&B fr£24 dB&B➡⋔ fr£28
CTV 24P (heated) sauna bath
V ✱Lunch £3.50–£4.65&alc Tea fr50p High Tea fr£3.50 Dinner £5.75–£6.90 Wine £4.40 Last dinner 8pm

★★***Manor House*** Gallanach Rd ☎(0631) 62087 Plan **7** *A2*
Attractive stone built small hotel on south side of Oban Bay with comfortable lounges and bedrooms.
11➡⋔
CTV P ✽
Last dinner 8.30pm
Credit cards 1 3 5

★★**Park** Esplanade ☎(0631) 63621 Telex no 777967 (att Clan) Plan **8** *B4*
Large, painted, stone hotel overlooking Oban Bay.
81rm(22➡17⋔) CTV in 40 bedrooms Ⓡ sB&B£17–£21 sB&B➡⋔£19–£22.50 dB&B£30–£36 dB&B➡⋔£34–£40 B
Lift ☾ CTV 20P Live music and dancing twice wkly *xmas*
European Lunch fr£4.50 Dinner fr£8.50 Wine £4.50 Last dinner 8.30pm
Credit cards 1 2 3 5

★★***Rowan Tree*** George St ☎(0631) 62954 Plan **10** *B4* Closed Nov–Mar
Modern hotel with open plan lounges.
24rm(16➡) TV available on request
☾ CTV 20P Live music and dancing 3 nights wkly Cabaret wkly
Last dinner 8.30pm
Credit cards 2 3

★**King's Knoll** Dunollie Rd ☎(0631) 62536 Plan **5** *C5*
Closed mid Oct–Mar
Small comfortable hotel with snug bar and friendly service.
18rm(4fb) sB&B£9–£9.50 dB&B£18–£19 B
CTV 12P ✽
Bar lunch 50p–£2 Tea 50p–£1 Dinner £4.50–£5.50 Last dinner 8pm

OLDBURY
W Midlands
Map **7** SO98
✽✕✕**Jonathans'** 16 Wolverhampton Rd, Quinton ☎021-429 3757
Victorian dishes are served in an authentically re-created intimate atmosphere.
Closed Sun Lunch not served Sat
V 100 seats Lunch £12alc Dinner £13.90&alc Wine £4.90 Last dinner 10pm 8P
Credit cards 1 2 3 5 **VS**

OLD GRIMSBY
Tresco Isles of Scilly (No map)
✽★★★*H* **Island** ☎Scillonia (0720) 22883
Closed mid Oct–mid Mar
Attractive hotel of stone and timber, set in attractive gardens overlooking the sea.
36rm(29➡⋔) CTV in 20 bedrooms
sB&B£34–£38 (incl dinner)
sB&B➡⋔£48–£52 (incl dinner)
dB&B£36.50–£38.50 (incl dinner)
dB&B➡⋔£38.50–£63 (incl dinner)
CTV ✽ (heated)
English & Continental Lunch £8.50alc Tea fr70p Dinner £15.50 Wine £5.60 Last dinner 8.15pm

OLDHAM
Great Manchester
Map **7** SD90
★★★**Bower** Hollinwood Av, Chadderton (2¼m SW A6104) (Greenall Whitley)
☎061-682 7254 Telex no 666883
50rm(28➡22⋔) CTV in all bedrooms Ⓡ B
☾ 120P CFA ✽ Live music and dancing Sat

O

V ♔ ☐ Lunch fr£5.50 Tea fr50p Dinner fr£6 Wine £5 Last dinner 9.30pm
S% Credit cards 1 2 3 5 **VS**

✕✕ ***Inzievar Hotel*** 5 Alexandra Rd
☎061-624 3830
Closed Sun Lunch not served Sat Dinner not served Mon
100 seats Last dinner 9pm 20P ⚡
Credit cards 1 2 3 4 5

OLD RAYNE
Grampian *Aberdeenshire*
Map **15** NJ62
★**Lodge** ☎(04645) 205
Traditional granite building with modern extensions including attractive wooden chalet annexe accommodation. It is located just off the A96.
2rm Annexe: 4 CTV in 4 bedrooms Ⓡ sB&B£11.50
CTV 70P billiards
♔ ☐ Lunch £4 Tea 75p High Tea £3 Dinner £7 Wine £3.25 Last dinner 8pm

OLD SODBURY
Avon
Map **3** ST78
★★**Cross Hands** ☎Chipping Sodbury (0454) 313000
Mellow Cotswold stone building in a rural setting alongside the main A46 Bath/Stroud road.
15rm(2 2) (2fb) CTV in all bedrooms Ⓡ ✻ sB&B£15 sB&B £22 dB&B£26.50 dB&B £33.50
Continental breakfast B
100P ✽
Mainly grills V ♔ Lunch £4.85–£10 Dinner £4.85–£10 Last dinner 10.30pm
Credit cards 1 2 3 5

OLLERTON
Nottinghamshire
Map **8** SK66
★**Hop Pole** ☎Mansfield (0623) 822573
Ivy-covered coaching inn.
12rm(1) Ⓡ sB&B£7.50–£19.50 sB&B £21 dB&B£24–£28 dB&B £28–£30
CTV 30P ✽ sauna bath
♔ ☐ Lunch £5–£7 Dinner £5–£7 Wine £3.80 Last dinner 10pm
Credit cards 1 3

OMBERSLEY
Hereford & Worcester
Map **3** SO86
✕✕**Crown & Sandys Arms** ☎Worcester (0905) 620252
Closed Sun, Mon & 25 Dec–3 Jan
48 seats Lunch £2.25–£9.45 Dinner £9.45–£10.45 Wine £3.95 Last dinner 10pm 100P
Credit card 1 **VS**

ONICH
Highland *Inverness-shire*
Map **14** NN06
★★***Allt-Nan-Ros*** ☎(08553) 210
Closed Nov–Mar
Roadside hotel standing in its own grounds with pleasant views across loch.
20rm B
CTV 30P ✽
♔ ☐ Last dinner 8pm
Credit card 3

★★***L* Creag Dhu** (Inter-Hotels)
☎(08553) 238 Closed 29 Oct–15 Apr
Hospitable, inviting hotel in superb loch-side and mountain setting, facing south with panoramic views.
20rm(5 3) (1fb) sB&B£14.50–£16.50 sB&B £17–£19 dB&B£29–£33 dB&B £34–£38 B
CTV 25P ✽ Cabaret wkly
♔ ☐ ✻ Bar lunch £2.80alc Tea 80p–£1.20 Dinner £8&alc Wine £3.85
Last dinner 8.30pm
Credit cards 1 2 3 5 **VS**

See advert under Fort William

★★**Onich** ☎(08553) 214
Building dating from 1880 standing on the loch side in its own grounds.
22rm(6 1) (4fb) Ⓡ sB&B fr£11 sB&B fr£13.50 dB&B fr£20 dB&B fr£25 B
CTV 50P ✽
V ♔ ☐ Bar lunch £1.50–£5 Tea fr65p High Tea fr£3.50 Dinner fr£7.75 Wine £4.25 Last dinner 8.30pm
Credit cards 1 2 3

ORFORD (near Woodbridge)
Suffolk
Map **5** TM44
★★**Crown & Castle** (Trusthouse Forte)
☎(03945) 205
An 18th-century posting house associated with smugglers.
10rm(1) Annexe: 10 (9fb) CTV in all bedrooms Ⓡ sB&B£30.50 sB&B £35.50 dB&B£43 dB&B £49.50 B
20P ✽ *xmas* ♿
♔ ☐ Last dinner 9pm
Credit cards 1 2 3 4 5

✕✕**Kings Head Inn** ☎(03945) 271
Remarkable, two-storey, medieval inn, in the shadow of St Bartholomew's Church.
Closed 3–30 Jan RS Sun & Mon
International V 36 seats ✻ Lunch £5alc Dinner £9alc Last dinner 9pm 100P bedrooms available
Credit card 5

✕**Butley Oysterage** Market Hill
☎(03945) 277
Closed Jan
50 seats Lunch £2.50–£6&alc Dinner £2.50–£6&alc Wine £3.56 Last dinner 8.30pm

ORKNEY
Map **16**
See **Harray, Kirkwall, St Margaret's Hope** and **Stromness**

ORTON
Cumbria
Map **12** NY60
✕**Gilded Apple** ☎(05874) 345
Closed Mon & Tue–Thu Nov–Mar
Lunch not served Tue–Sat
English, French, Greek & Italian 35 seats Lunch £4.35–£4.95 Dinner £6.55–£9.90&alc Wine £4.75 Last dinner 10pm 4P bedrooms available
VS

OSWESTRY
Shropshire
Map **7** SJ22
★★★**Wynnstay** Church St (Trusthouse Forte) ☎(0691) 655261
31rm(16 2) CTV in all bedrooms Ⓡ sB&B£30.50 sB&B £33 dB&B£40.50 dB&B £46.50 B
70P ✽
♔ Last dinner 9.30pm
Credit cards 1 2 3 4 5

★★***L* Sweeney Hall** Morda (1m S on A483) ☎(0691) 652450
10rm(6) Ⓡ sB&B£14–£17 dB&B£21–£24 dB&B £27–£36.30
CTV 80P ✽
V ♔ Lunch fr£6&alc Tea fr60p Dinner fr£7.70&alc Wine £4.70 Last dinner 9.30pm

OTHERY
Somerset
Map **3** ST33
★**Townsend House** Glastonbury Rd
☎Burrowbridge (082 369) 382
Closed 23 Dec–21 Jan
Small, friendly, country hotel, personally-run by the owners, with a separate restaurant of character.
7rm (1fb) sB&B£10–£11 dB&B£19–£20 B
CTV 18P
English & Continental ♔ ☐ Lunch £3.80alc Tea 50p alc Dinner £4.90–£6.50&alc Last dinner 8.30pm
Credit card 3

OTTERBURN
Northumberland
Map **12** NY89
★★★**Percy Arms** (Swallow) ☎(0830) 20261 Telex no 53168
33rm(16) (2fb) 1 CTV in 3 bedrooms Ⓡ ✻ sB&B£16–£22 sB&B £19.50–£24 dB&B£30–£38 dB&B £39–£40 B
⚡ CTV 40P 8 ✽ U Live music and dancing Sat *xmas* →

O

V♈☕✱Lunch fr£4.80 Tea fr£2 High Tea fr£4 Dinner fr£8.50 Last dinner 8pm

Credit cards 1 2 3 5 **VS**

★★🏰**Otterburn Tower** ☎(0830) 20620

13rm(2➡) (2fb) 1🛏 CTV in 5 bedrooms ® sB&B£15 dB&B£25 dB&B➡£28–£35 Ꞵ

CTV 70P 2🚗✽ ♪ Disco Sat *xmas*

🍽Portuguese V♈☕ Lunch £5.50–£20&alc Tea fr£2 High Tea fr£3 Dinner fr£7&alc Wine £4.50 Last dinner 10pm

Credit cards 1 2 3 5

OTTERY ST MARY
Devon
Map **3** SY19

★★★*H***Salston** (Best Western) ☎(040481) 2310 Telex 42551

Country house of historical and architectural interest, standing in 6 acres of grounds.

33rm(25➡⋒) (15fb) 1🛏 CTV in all bedrooms ® sB&B£19–£22 sB&B➡⋒£26–£30 dB&B£27–£30 dB&B➡⋒£30–£44 Ꞵ

100P CFA✽ 🏊(heated) ♪ squash sauna bath Disco Sat 🎪 *xmas*

🍽English & French ♈☕ Lunch £6alc Tea 55p alc Dinner £7.50–£9.10&alc Wine £5 Last dinner 8.30pm

Credit cards 1 2 3 5

★***Kings Arms*** Gold St ☎(040481) 2486

Small hotel in the town centre with simple but sound appointments.

6rm ®

CTV 10P billiards

♈Last dinner 9.30pm

Credit cards 1 3

✕✕***Lodge*** 17 Silver St ☎(040481) 2356

Village centre restaurant run by proprietor.

Closed Mon, 1wk Nov, 2wks Jan/Feb & 1wk Jun Dinner not served Sun

🍽English & Continental 20 seats Last dinner 9.30pm bedrooms available

OULTON
West Yorkshire
Map **8** SE32

☆☆☆**Crest** The Grove (Crest) ☎Leeds (0532) 826201 Telex no 557646

40➡ CTV in all bedrooms ® ✱sB➡fr£34 dB➡fr£44 (room only) Ꞵ

☾ ⚡200P Disco Mon Live music and dancing Wed ♿

🍽International V♈✱Lunch £7.50–£8&alc Tea 45p Dinner £8–£8.95&alc Wine £5.25 Last dinner 10pm

Credit cards 1 2 3 4 5 **VS**

OUNDLE
Northamptonshire
Map **4** TL08

★★**Talbot** New St (Anchor) ☎(0832) 73621 Telex no 32364

Period stone and slate building with the original coaching entrance.

42rm(39➡) (2fb) CTV in all bedrooms ® ✱sB&B£23 sB&B➡£31 dB&B➡£41 Ꞵ

☾ 60P CFA 🎪 *xmas*

V♈☕✱Lunch £5.50alc Tea 30p–60p Dinner £7.50–£10.50alc Wine £4.50 Last dinner 9.45pm

Credit cards 1 2 3 4 5

OVERSCAIG
Highland *Sutherland*
Map **14** NC42

★***Overscaig*** ☎Merkland (054983) 203

RS Oct–mid Apr

10rm(4➡⋒) ®

CTV 20P✽ ♪

♈☕ Last dinner 8pm

OXFORD
Oxfordshire
Map **4** SP50

See plan on pages 496–497

★★★★**Randolph** Beaumont St (Trusthouse Forte) ☎(0865) 247481 Telex no 83446 Plan **13** *C3*

Large, mid-Victorian building in Gothic style with pointed gables and lancet and dormer windows.

109➡ (8fb) CTV in all bedrooms ® sB&B➡£45.50 dB&B➡£61.50 Ꞵ

Lift ☾ 60🚗 CFA *xmas*

♈☕ Last dinner 10.15pm

Credit cards 1 2 3 4 5

★★★**Ladbroke Linton Lodge** Linton Rd, Park Town (Ladbroke) ☎(0865) 53461 Telex no 837093 Plan **6** *C5*

Hotel offers a blend of modern and more traditional accommodation.

72rm(65➡1⋒) CTV in all bedrooms ® ✱sB➡⋒fr£35 dB➡⋒fr£47 (room only) Ꞵ

Lift ☾ 40P CFA✽

V☕✱Dinner fr£8.50 Last dinner 9.30pm

Credit cards 1 2 3 5

☆☆☆**Oxford Moat House** Godstow Rd, Wolvercote Roundabout (Queens Moat) ☎(0865) 59933 Telex no 837926 Plan **10** *B5*

Large modern hotel with well equipped bedrooms.

155➡ CTV in all bedrooms ® sB&B➡fr£33 dB&B➡fr£42 Ꞵ

☾ CTV 300P 8🚗✽ Live music and dancing Tue, Thu & Sun *xmas*

V♈☕ Lunch £4–£6&alc Tea fr60p Dinner £5–£8&alc Wine £4.50 Last dinner 9.45pm

Credit cards 1 2 3 4 5 **VS**

☆☆☆**TraveLodge** Peartree Roundabout (junc A34/A43) (Trusthouse Forte) ☎(0865) 54301 Telex no 83202 Plan **16** *B5*

Modern hotel with a grill and carvery restaurant.

102➡ (42fb) CTV in all bedrooms ® sB➡£28 dB➡£40 Continental breakfast Ꞵ

☾ 102P CFA✽ 🏊(heated)

♈

Credit cards 1 2 3 4 5

★★**Cotswold Lodge** 66A Banbury Rd ☎(0865) 512121 Plan **1** *C5*

Closed Xmas Day evening–30 Dec

A hotel with many modern bedrooms, where the Greek proprietors give the food a Mediterranean flavour.

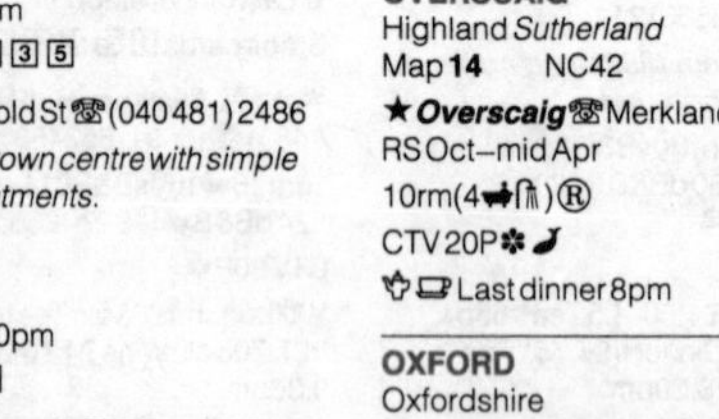

52⇌ CTV in all bedrooms ★ sB&B⇌£31.50–£35 dB&B⇌£41.50–£45 B

☾ 60P Live music and dancing Sat

English & French V ♔ Lunch £7.50–£9&alc Dinner £8–£9.50&alc Wine £3.85 Last dinner 10.30pm

Credit cards 1 2 3 5

See advert on page 498

★★**Eastgate** The High, Merton St (Anchor) ☎(0865) 248244 Telex no 83302 Plan **3** *E2*

Late 19th century building with overhanging, leaded bay windows.

34rm(28⇌6⋒) (4fb) CTV in all bedrooms ® sB&B£28 sB&B⇌⋒£36 dB&B⇌⋒£44 B

Lift ☾ CTV 25P CFA *xmas*

V ♔ ☕ *Lunch £3.85–£12&alc Tea 50p–£3 Dinner £6.50–£12 Wine £4.50 Last dinner 9.15pm

S% Credit cards 1 2 3 5

★★***Isis*** 47–53 Iffley Rd ☎(0865) 248894 Plan **5** *F1*

Traditional, but modest hotel.

36rm(5⇌) B

CTV 14P 8🚗

♔ ☕ Last dinner 8.30pm

Credit cards 1 3 **VS**

See advert on page 498

★★**Royal Oxford** Park End St (Embassy)

☎(0865) 248432 Plan **15** *B2*

Traditional hotel with modern bedroom facilities.

25rm(12⇌) (2fb) CTV in all bedrooms ® sB fr£22 sB⇌ fr£30 dB fr£32 dB⇌ fr£37 (room only) B

☾ 15P *xmas*

V ♔ Bar lunch 70p–£3 Dinner fr£6.75 Wine £4.30 Last dinner 9.30pm

Credit cards 1 2 3 5

See advert on page 498

★**River** 17 Botley Rd ☎(0865) 243475 Plan **14** *A2*

Closed Xmas & New Year

Small, family run hotel.

17rm(6⇌4⋒) (4fb) CTV in all bedrooms sB&B£15–£20 sB&B⇌⋒£20–£25 dB&B£25–£30 dB&B⇌⋒£30–£35

CTV 20P

♔ Tea fr50p Dinner £3.50–£5.50 Wine £5 Last dinner 8pm

❀❀✕✕**Les Quat' Saisons** 272 Banbury Rd, Summertown ☎(0865) 53540 Plan **11** *C5*

Raymond Blanc, the young chef/patron of this unpretentious little restaurant on the outskirts of Oxford continues to earn the enthusiastic appreciation of members and inspectors alike. His refined cooking is classically based, influenced by the modern school but thankfully free of those gimmicky aberrations that mar the results of lesser cooks who seemingly are only trying to be different! He has a profound knowledge of gastronomy which he is able to use to good effect in the clever composition of his dishes which are always superb examples of his art as well as being beautifully presented. There is a basic à la carte menu with some old favourites and a section of seasonal items as well as some daily dishes where advantage can be taken of the market. At lunch there is a set meal which is a real bargain for cooking of this quality. Among the first courses to be so much appreciated have been crème de faisane, moules de saffran, salade de coquilles St. Jacques aux blanc des pireaux et artichauts and the trio petits bonheur. Main courses such as sarcelle rôtie aux petits legumes d'hiver et fumet St. Emilion, medaillons de chevreuil au cassis and medaillon de veau truffé et son rognon au vinaigre de Xeres have been much enjoyed. Bouquetieres de legumes are near perfect as are the puddings; delectable mousses, various ways with ices and mouth-watering sorbets as well as the lightest of pastry never fail to please. Service is by a pleasant brigade of young staff under the able supervision of Mr Alain Desenclos, the restaurant manager. Mr Blanc has enlarged his horizons: besides his bakery and charcuterie offshoots, he plans to move to new premises at the Manor House, Great Milton. The present restaurant will continue but in bistro style.

Closed Sun, Mon, Last 2wks July & 23 Dec–6 Jan

French V 48 seats Lunch £9.50–£14.50&alc Dinner £20alc Wine £6.50 Last dinner 10.15pm

S% Credit cards 1 2 3 4

❀✕✕✕**Restaurant Elizabeth** 84 St Aldates ☎(0865) 242230 Plan **4** *C1*

The consistently good cuisine is complemented by an extensive wine list and formal, yet friendly service.

Closed Mon, Last 2wks Aug & last 2wks Dec

French 40 seats *Lunch £10&alc Dinner £14.40alc Wine £6 Last dinner 11pm

S% Credit cards 1 2 3 5 **VS**

✕✕**Paddyfield** 39/40 Hyther Bridge St ☎(0865) 248835 Plan **12** *B3*

Chinese 80 seats *Lunch fr£2.20&alc Dinner £8alc Wine £4.75 Last dinner mdnt

S% Credit cards 1 3

✕***Clements*** 37 St Clements ☎(0865) 241431 Plan **2** *F2*

Popular informal restaurant serving imaginative dishes.

Closed 23 Dec–2 Jan

Lunch not served Mon

English & French 35 seats Last dinner 10.30pm

Credit cards 1 3

O

✕***Lotus House*** 197 Banbury Rd, Parktown, Summertown ☎(0865) 54239 Plan **7** *C5*

Closed Xmas

Cantonese & Pekinese **V** 70 seats Last dinner 11.45pm 4P

Credit cards 2 3 5

✕**Michel's Bistro** 146 London Rd, Headington ☎(0865) 62587 Plan **8** *F2*

Sound, French bistro offering a short, seasonal menu.

French **V** 50 seats ✱Lunch fr£5.95&alc Dinner fr£8.95&alc Wine £4.80 Last dinner 11pm

Credit cards 1 2 3 5

✕**Opium Den** 79 George St ☎(0865) 248680 Plan **9** *B3*

Busy city centre restaurant specialising in sizzling Cantonese dishes.

Chinese 125 seats Lunch fr£1.50&alc Dinner fr£4&alc Wine £5 Last dinner 11.45pm

Credit cards 1 2 3 5 **VS**

❀✕**Wren's** 29 Castle St ☎(0865) 242944 Plan **17** *C2*

Closed Sun Lunch not served Sat

French 40 seats Last dinner 10.30pm

Credit cards 1 2 3 4 5

OXTED
Surrey
Map **5** TQ35

★★**Hoskins** Station Rd West ☎(08833) 2338 Gatwick plan **15**

Modern circular hotel with well equipped bedrooms.

10 CTV in all bedrooms sB&B £25 dB&B £30

CTV 30P

Mainly grills Lunch £3.50–£7 Dinner £3.50–£7 Wine £4.15 Last dinner 9.30pm

Credit cards 1 2 3 5

✕***Golden Bengal*** 51 Station Rd East ☎(08833) 7373 Gatwick plan **13**

Indian 46 seats Last dinner mdnt

✕**Wine and Tandoori** 111–113 Station Rd East ☎(08833) 7459

Skilful and authentic Indian cuisine featuring Tandoori specialities and traditional curries.

Indian 60 seats ✱Lunch £10alc Dinner £10alc Wine £3.60 Last dinner mdnt

PADSTOW
Cornwall
Map **2** SW97

★★★**Metropole** Station Rd (Trusthouse Forte) ☎(0841) 532486

Closed 4 Nov–2 Mar

Large, detached, traditional hotel in an elevated position overlooking the river estuary.

44 (4fb) CTV in all bedrooms Ⓡ sB&B £33.50 dB&B £55.50

Lift CTV 40P (heated) →

O

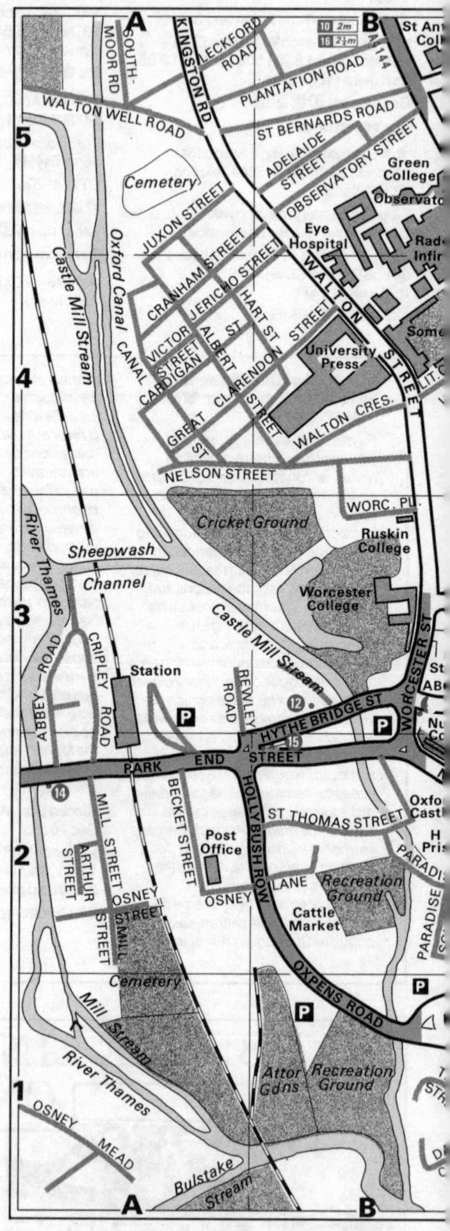
A
B
SOUTH-MOOR RD
KINGSTON RD
LECKFORD ROAD
PLANTATION ROAD
WALTON WELL ROAD
ST BERNARDS ROAD
ADELAIDE STREET
OBSERVATORY STREET
Green College
Cemetery
JUXON STREET
Eye Hospital
Oxford Canal
Castle Mill Stream
CANAL
CRANHAM STREET
JERICHO STREET
HART ST
WALTON STREET
VICTOR STREET
CARDIGAN
ALBERT ST
CLARENDON STREET
University Press
GREAT ST
WALTON CRES.
NELSON STREET
WORC. PL.
Cricket Ground
Ruskin College
River Thames
Sheepwash Channel
Worcester College
Castle Mill Stream
ABBEY ROAD
CRIPLEY ROAD
Station
REWLEY ROAD
HYTHE BRIDGE ST
WORCESTER ST
PARK END STREET
MILL STREET
BECKET STREET
HOLLY BUSH ROW
ST THOMAS STREET
ARTHUR STREET
Post Office
OSNEY LANE
OSNEY STREET
Recreation Ground
Cattle Market
PARADISE
Cemetery
OXPENS ROAD
Mill Stream
River Thames
Attor Gdns
Recreation Ground
OSNEY MEAD
Bulstake Stream
1
2
3
4
5

Oxford
1 Cotswold Lodge ★★
2 Clements ✕
3 Eastgate ★★
4 Restaurant Elizabeth ❀✕✕✕

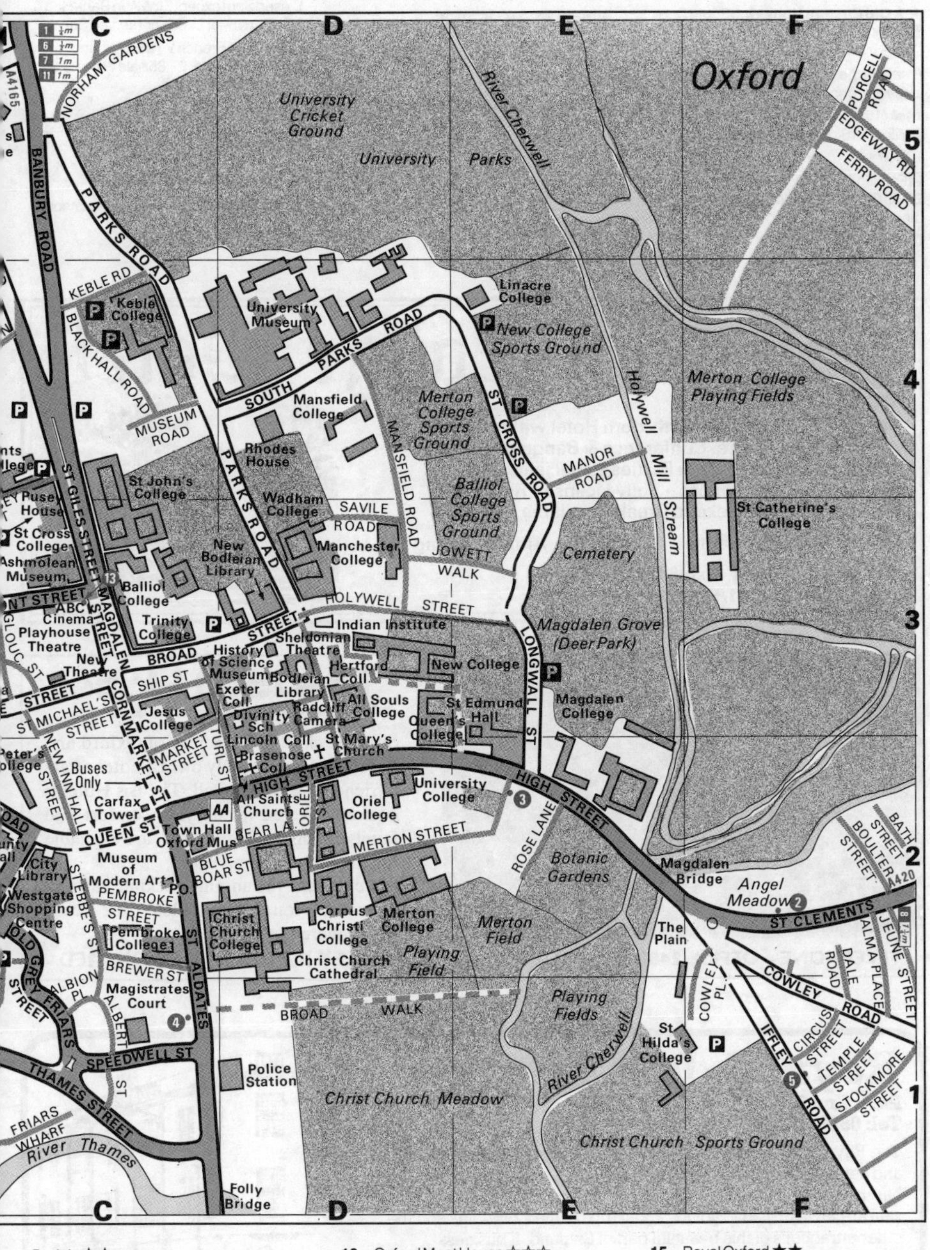

Oxford
C
D
E
F
5
4
3
2
1
NORHAM GARDENS
A4165
BANBURY ROAD
PARKS ROAD
University Cricket Ground
University Parks
River Cherwell
PURCELL ROAD
EDGEWAY RD
FERRY ROAD
KEBLE RD
Keble College
BLACK HALL ROAD
University Museum
SOUTH PARKS ROAD
Linacre College
New College Sports Ground
Merton College Playing Fields
Holywell Mill Stream
MUSEUM ROAD
Mansfield College
Merton College Sports Ground
ST CROSS ROAD
MANOR ROAD
St Catherine's College
Rhodes House
St John's College
Wadham College
SAVILE ROAD
MANSFIELD ROAD
Balliol College Sports Ground
Cemetery
Pusey House
St Cross College
Ashmolean Museum
ST GILES STREET
New Bodleian Library
Manchester College
JOWETT WALK
Balliol College
HOLYWELL STREET
Trinity College
Indian Institute
LONGWALL ST
Magdalen Grove (Deer Park)
ABC Cinema
Playhouse Theatre
MAGDALEN STREET
BROAD STREET
History of Science Museum
Sheldonian Theatre
Hertford Coll.
New College
New Theatre
SHIP ST
Bodleian Library
Exeter Coll.
Radcliff Camera
All Souls College
St Edmund Hall
Magdalen College
ST MICHAEL'S STREET
Jesus College
Divinity Sch
Lincoln Coll.
Queen's College
St Mary's Church
CORNMARKET ST
MARKET STREET
TURL ST
Brasenose Coll
HIGH STREET
University College
NEW INN HALL STREET
Buses Only
Carfax Tower
All Saints Church
Oriel College
ROSE LANE
BATH STREET
BOULTER STREET
QUEEN ST
Town Hall
Oxford Mus
BEAR LA.
MERTON STREET
Botanic Gardens
Magdalen Bridge
City Library
Museum of Modern Art
BLUE BOAR ST
Angel Meadow
A420
ST CLEMENTS
Westgate Shopping Centre
ST EBBE'S ST
PEMBROKE STREET
P.O.
Christ Church College
Corpus Christi College
Merton College
Merton Field
The Plain
JEUNE STREET
ALMA PLACE
DALE ROAD
Pembroke College
ST ALDATES
Playing Field
COWLEY ROAD
COWLEY PL.
BREWER ST
Christ Church Cathedral
Playing Fields
OLD GREY FRIARS STREET
ALBION PL
Magistrates Court
ALBERT ST
BROAD WALK
River Cherwell
St Hilda's College
CIRCUS STREET
TEMPLE STREET
IFFLEY ROAD
STOCKMORE STREET
SPEEDWELL ST
Police Station
THAMES STREET
Christ Church Meadow
Christ Church Sports Ground
FRIARS WHARF
River Thames
Folly Bridge

P

5 Isis ★★
6 Ladbroke Linton Lodge ★★★
7 Lotus House ✕
8 Michel's Bistro ✕
9 Opium Den ✕
10 Oxford Moat House ☆☆☆
11 Les Quat' Saisons ❀❀✕✕
12 Paddyfield ✕✕
13 Randoph ★★★★
14 River ★
15 Royal Oxford ★★
16 TraveLodge ☆☆☆
17 Wren's ❀✕

Last dinner 8.45pm
S% Credit cards 1 2 3 4 5

★★Old Custom House Inn South Quay ☎(0841) 532359
Closed Nov–19 Apr
Pleasant, personally run inn by harbours edge and once the old custom house.
14➡(1fb) CTV in all bedrooms Ⓡ sB&B➡£16–£17 dB&B➡£28–£30 ℞
CTV
English & French Bar lunch £1.50–£3.50 Dinner £5–£7 Wine £3.52 Last dinner 9pm
Credit cards 1 3 **VS**

★Dinas ☎(0841) 532326
Closed Nov–Mar
The hotel overlooks Padstow and the river estuary.
26rm(3➡) (1fb) Ⓡ sB&B£8.05 sB&B➡£8.05 dB&B£16.10 dB&B➡£18.40 ℞
CTV 50P ✽ Disco wkly
V Bar lunch £1–£2.50 Tea £1 Dinner £4 Wine £4.50 Last dinner 8pm

✕Seafood ☎(0841) 532485
Informal nautical restaurant with friendly service.
Closed Sun (except Etr & Aug Bank Hol) & 2 Oct–mid Mar Lunch not served Sat
English & French **V** 70 seats Lunch £7.85&alc Dinner £7.85&alc Wine £3.95 Last dinner 9.45pm
Credit cards 1 2 3 5

PAIGNTON
Devon
Map **3** SX86

★★★Palace Esplanade Rd (Trusthouse Forte) ☎(0803) 555121

P

Impressive, sea-front hotel with views of the sea and the beach. The staff are attentive and pleasant.

54⇌(11fb) CTV in all bedrooms ® sB&B⇌£34.50 dB&B⇌£56.50 ⊟

Lift ☾ 60P CFA ✽ ⛵(heated) 𝓟(hard) ⌂ *xmas*

♆ ▭ Last dinner 8.45pm

Credit cards 1 2 3 4 5

★★★ *H* **Redcliffe** Marine Dr ☎(0803) 526397

Unusual, mid-Victorian building with a central tower, pinnacles and battlements, overlooking the sea.

63rm(56⇌7⋒)(8fb) sB&B⇌⋒£17–£24 dB&B⇌⋒£34–£48 ⊟

Lift ☾ CTV 100P CFA ✽ ⛵(heated) 𝓟(hard) Live music and dancing 6 nights wkly ⌂ *xmas*

▣ English & French V ♆ ▭ Lunch £2.75–£5.25 Tea 60–70p Dinner £6.75–£7.25 Wine £4.50 Last dinner 8.30pm

Credit card 2 **VS**

★★ ***Alta Vista*** Alta Vista Rd, Goodrington (from A379 follow signs Roundham St Anne's) ☎(0803) 551496

Closed Nov–Mar

Hotel overlooks Goodrington Sands.

28rm(15⇌) CTV in all bedrooms ® ✭ ⊟

CTV 30P ✽ Disco 3 nights in season ⌂

♆ ▭ Last dinner 7.30pm

Credit cards 1 3

★★ ***Hunters Lodge*** Roundham Rd, Goodrington ☎(0803) 557034

Closed Nov–Apr

Hotel's hillside position gives panoramic sea views.

32rm

CTV 30P 4🚗 ✽

V ♆ ▭ Last dinner 7.30pm

Paignton — Painswick

★★**St Ann's** Alta Vista Rd, Goodrington ☎(0803) 557360
Closed Dec–Feb
Hotel overlooks Goodrington Sands.
28rm(23⇌5⋔) Annexe: 2rm 4▣ CTV in all bedrooms Ⓡ sB&B⇌⋔ £10.93–£17.25 dB&B⇌⋔ £21–£35 ₿
CTV 30P ≋(heated) sauna bath Disco twice wkly Cabaret wkly ⌂
▣English & French V ✪ Bar lunch £1–£2.50 Dinner £4.50–£7 Wine £3 Last dinner 8pm
Credit card [1]

★★**Seaford** Stafford Rd (off Sands Rd) ☎(0803) 557341
Detached gabled villa with newly extended frontage.
24rm(12⇌9⋔) (8fb) CTV in all bedrooms Ⓡ sB&B £9–£12 dB&B⇌⋔ £18–£24 ₿
Lift 14P Live music and dancing wkly *xmas*
▣English & French V ✪ ▭ Lunch fr£3 Dinner fr£4 Last dinner 9.30pm
VS

★**Danethorpe** 23 St Andrew's Rd ☎(0803) 551251
Detached hotel with new wing.
13rm (3fb) Ⓡ ∗ sB&B £7 dB&B £14
CTV 10P 1⌂ *xmas*
V ✪ ▭ Lunch £2.50–£3 Tea £1 High Tea £2.50 Dinner £4–£4.25 Wine £3.75 Last dinner 7pm

★***Oldway Links*** Southfield Rd ☎(0803) 559332
Large hilltop villa with good views.
19rm sB&B £11
CTV 20P ✽ ⌂
Last dinner 7.15pm
Credit card [3]

☆**Torbay Holiday Motel** Totnes Rd ☎(0803) 558226
Hotel complex with a pleasant restaurant, catering for the tourist and commercial clientele.
16⋔ CTV in all bedrooms Ⓡ sB&B⋔ £14.95 dB&B⋔ £23.92 ₿
CTV 150P ✽ ▭(heated) Live music and dancing 3 nights wkly ⌂
▣English & French V Lunch £3alc Dinner £5alc Wine £3 Last dinner 9.30pm
Credit cards [1] [3]

✕**Luigis** 59 Torquay Rd ☎(0803) 556185
▣English & Italian V 40 seats Lunch £3.15–£5&alc Dinner fr£8.25&alc Wine £4.75 Last dinner 11pm ⁋
Credit card [3] **VS**

PAINSWICK
Gloucestershire
Map **3** SO80

★★★***HBL* Painswick** Kemps Ln ☎(0452) 812160 Telex no 43605
Painswick Hotel, once a Georgian vicarage, is a delightful hotel with the aura of a country house, yet situated in the pretty village of Painswick in the Cotswolds. The well appointed public rooms are comfortable and there is a gallery room for those guests requiring more privacy for their relaxation. The bedrooms have been refurbished to a high standard. Traditional caring service and hospitality are provided by the proprietors, Mr and Mrs Hill, and excellent meals are produced by chef Kevin Hooper.
16rm(14⇌) (2fb) CTV in all bedrooms sB&B £26 sB&B⇌ £30 dB&B £36 dB&B⇌⋔ £44–£50 ₿
25P ✽ ⌂ *xmas*
▣English & French V ✪ ▭ Lunch £6.50–£11.50 Dinner £7.75–£11.50&alc Wine £5 Last dinner 9.30pm
Credit cards [1] [2] [3] [5] **VS**

✕✕***Country Elephant*** ☎(0452) 813564
A well-appointed, popular, small restaurant with a warm, informal atmosphere.
Closed Mon, 1 wk Etr, 1 wk Xmas & 3 wks Oct–Nov Lunch not served Tue–Sat Dinner not served Sun
36 seats Last dinner 10.30pm ⁋
Credit cards [2] [3] [5]

P

PAISLEY
Strathclyde *Renfrewshire*
Map **11** NS46
Hotels and restaurants are listed under Glasgow Airport

PANDY
Gwent
Map **3** SO32
★★ ***Park*** ☎Crucorney (087 382) 630
Very comfortable country house style of hotel with friendly service.
7rm TV in 1 bedroom
CTV 30P
English & Continental Last dinner 11.30pm
Credit cards 1 2 3 **VS**

PANGBOURNE
Berkshire
Map **4** SU67
★★★ **Copper Inn** (Best Western)
☎(07357) 2244
RS 4 days Xmas
A 19th-century posting house situated near the River Thames.
21 (2fb) 1 CTV in all bedrooms ® sB&B£37.50 dB&B£48.75
29P
English & French **V** *Lunch £6.75&alc Tea 85p Dinner £11alc Wine £5.05 Last dinner 9.30pm
Credit cards 1 2 3 5

PARBOLD
Lancashire
Map **7** SD41
★★ **Lindley** Lancaster Ln (Whitbread West Pennines) ☎(02576) 2804
RS Xmas Day & New Years Day
This well-equipped hotel is located in a quiet suburb.
13rm (6 7) (1fb) CTV in all bedrooms ® *sB&B £22 dB&B £26
75P
English & French *Lunch £7.50alc Dinner £7.50alc Wine £4.45 Last dinner 10pm
Credit cards 1 3

✗ **Prescotts Farm** Lees Ln, Dalton (1m S on unclass rd off A5209) ☎(02576) 4137
Closed Sun & Mon Lunch not served Sat & Tue
V 50 seats Lunch £2.75alc Dinner £10.34alc Wine £3.85 Last dinner 10pm
45P
Credit cards 1 2 5

PARKGATE
Cheshire
Map **7** SJ27
★★ **Parkgate** Boathouse Ln
☎051-336 5101
A large house with modern extensions. Close to the Dee Estuary.
30rm (6 24) (2fb) 1 CTV in all bedrooms ® sB&B £22.50–£27 dB&B £35.50–£43
125P *xmas*
French Lunch £4.95–£10&alc Tea 65p–95p Dinner £6.25–£9&alc Wine £5.25 Last dinner 10.30pm
Credit cards 1 2 3 5 **VS**

★★ ***B*** **Ship** The Parade (Anchor)
☎051-336 3931
Attractive, stone fronted inn with modern bedrooms, overlooking the Dee Estuary.
26 CTV in all bedrooms ® *sB&B fr£29 dB&B fr£38.50
80P
English & French *Lunch fr£4.60&alc Dinner fr£6&alc Wine £4.50 Last dinner 9pm
Credit cards 1 2 3 4 5

✗✗ **Boat House** The Parade
☎051-336 4187
Dinner not served Sun
English & French **V** 60 seats Lunch £3.50–£4.75&alc Dinner £10alc Wine £4.50 Last dinner 10pm 80P
S% Credit cards 1 2 3 5

PATHHEAD
Lothian *Midlothian*
Map **11** NT36

★★ **Stair Arms** (Scottish & Newcastle)
☎Ford (0875) 320277
A small, former coaching inn.
6rm CTV in all bedrooms ® sB&B£16.50 dB&B£26.50
60P
V Lunch £4–£6.50 Dinner £8–£10 Wine £4.30 Last dinner 9pm
Credit cards 1 2 3 5

PATTERDALE
Cumbria
Map **11** NY31
★★ **Patterdale** ☎Glenridding (08532) 231
Closed Dec–Feb
This hotel lies at the foot of the Kirkstone Pass facing Ullswater.
55rm (12 12) Annexe: 6rms (2fb) ® *sB&B fr£12.60 sB&B fr£14.50 dB&B fr£25.20 dB&B fr£29
CTV 50P
V *Tea fr£1.20 Dinner fr£7 Wine £4.70 Last dinner 8pm
Credit card 2

PEASMARSH
East Sussex
Map **5** TQ82
★★ **Flackley Ash** (Best Western)
☎(079 721) 381
Peaceful, Georgian manor house with modern bedrooms and traditional hospitality.
17 (7fb) 2 CTV in all bedrooms ® sB&B £26.50 dB&B £43
CTV 50P
English & French **V** Lunch £8alc Tea 60p Dinner £6.50&alc Wine £3.95 Last dinner 9.30pm
Credit cards 1 2 3 5

PEAT INN
Fife
Map **12** NO40
✗✗ **Peat Inn** ☎(033 484) 206
(Rosette awarded for dinner only.)
A small roadside inn near St Andrews. →

P

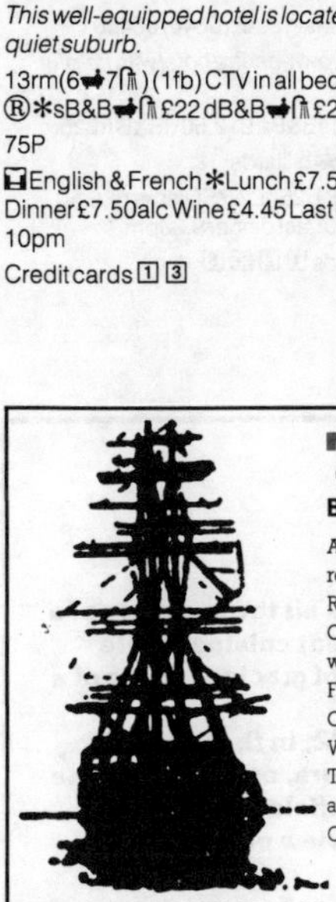

Closed Sun, Mon, 1st wk Jan, 1 wk Apr & 1 wk Oct

🍴French 42 seats Lunch £7 Dinner £13.50alc Wine £6 Last dinner 9.30pm 30P 🚭

S% Credit cards 2 3

PEEBLES
Borders *Peeblesshire*
Map **11** NT24

★★★**Park** Innerleithen Rd (Swallow) ☎(0721) 20451 Telex no 53168

Traditional Scottish building with a modern extension, overlooking the River Tweed and the Border hills.

26rm(21➡2⋒) 1📺 CTV in all bedrooms Ⓡ sB&B£21.50–£26.50 sB&B➡⋒£23–£28 dB&B£33.50–£41.30 dB&B➡⋒£35–£42.80 B

☾ 60P ✽ *xmas* ♿

V ♉ ☕ Lunch £3.75–£6&alc Tea 55p–£1.40 High Tea fr£4.50 Dinner fr£8.25 Wine £5.25 Last dinner 9pm

Credit cards 1 2 3 5

★★★**Peebles Hydro** ☎(0721) 20602 Telex no 72568

Overlooking the Tweed Valley, this large conference and family hotel stands in its own grounds above the town.

135rm(127➡8⋒) (26fb) CTV in all bedrooms Ⓡ ✶ sB&B➡⋒£28.50–£30.50 dB&B➡⋒£38–£49 B

Lift ☾ CFA ✽ (heated) 🎾(hard) squash U billiards sauna bath Live music and dancing twice wkly ⌂ *xmas*

V ♉ ☕ Lunch £5.75–£7.75 Tea 75p Dinner £8.50–£12 Wine £5.35 Last dinner 9pm

Credit cards 1 2 3

★★★**Tontine** High St (Trusthouse Forte) ☎(0721) 20892

Traditional hotel with attractive Adam dining room.

37rm(36➡1⋒) (3fb) CTV in all bedrooms Ⓡ sB&B➡⋒£33 dB&B➡⋒£49.50 B

☾ CTV 30P 6🚗 *xmas* CFA

♉ ☕ Last dinner 9.30pm

Credit cards 1 2 3 4 5

★★🏛*HL* **Cringletie House** ☎Eddleston (07213) 233 Closed Jan & Feb

A superior country house hotel located off A703, 2 miles north of Peebles.

16rm(8➡1⋒) sB&B£17.50 sB&B➡⋒£19.50 dB&B➡⋒£41 B

Lift CTV 40P 🐕 ✽ 🎾(hard)

🍴International ♉ ☕ Lunch £3.75–£7.50 Tea £2.50 Dinner £12 Last dinner 8.30pm

★★**Dilkusha** Chambers Ter ☎(0721) 20590

Closed New Year's Day

Quiet hotel with panelled dining room and cocktail bar.

6rm(4➡2⋒) (2fb) CTV in all bedrooms Ⓡ sB&B➡⋒£16–£20 dB&B➡⋒£25–£32 16P 3🚗 ✽

🍴Scottish & French V ♉ Lunch fr£4.40&alc High Tea £2.80–£6.50 Dinner £6.60–£7.50&alc Wine £4.20 Last dinner 9.30pm

Credit cards 2 3 VS

★★🏛**Venlaw Castle** Edinburgh Rd ☎(0721) 20384 Closed Nov–Mar

Baronial-style mansion, on a wooded hillside. Attractive cocktail bar.

12rm(1➡4⋒) (2fb) Ⓡ sB&B£13.50–£14.50 dB&B£25–£26 dB&B➡⋒£27–£29 B

CTV 20P 2🚗 ✽

♉ Bar lunch 70p–£4 Dinner £7.50–£9 Wine £4.50 Last dinner 8pm

Credit cards 1 2 4 5 VS

★**Riverside** Neidpath Rd ☎(0721) 20776

Converted, three-storey manse dating from 1865 with terraced gardens leading to the River Tweed.

8rm (2fb) ✱ sB&B£9–£9.50 dB&B£18–£19 B

CTV 40P 1🚗 ✽

V ♉ Lunch £2.50–£3 High Tea £3–£3.50 Dinner £4–£5 Wine £3.80 Last dinner 8pm

PEEL
Isle of Man
Map **6** SC28

✕**Lively Lobster** The Harbour ☎(062 484) 2789

Closed Oct–Mar

40 seats ✱Lunch £9alc Dinner £9alc Wine £4 Last dinner 9.30pm 🚭

PELYNT
Cornwall
Map **2** SX25

★★**Jubilee Inn** ☎Lanreath (0503) 20312

A charming inn that has been completely modernised.

10rm(6➡1⋒) (2fb) 1📺 CTV in 4 bedrooms sB&B£12.90 sB&B➡⋒£12.90 dB&B fr£25.80 dB&B➡⋒ fr£25.80 B

CTV 60P 5🚗 🐕 ✽ ⌂ *xmas*

V ♉ ☕ Lunch 60p–£3.80 Tea 50p–75p High Tea £1.50–£2 Dinner fr£5.50 Last dinner 10pm

Credit cards 1 3

PEMBROKE
Dyfed
Map **2** SM90

See also **Lamphey**

★★ ***Coach House Inn*** 116 Main St (Exec Hotel) ☎(0646) 684602

Proprietor-run hotel with comfortable, purpose-built bedrooms and a convivial bar.

Annexe: 14rm(13➡1⋒) CTV in all bedrooms Ⓡ ✶ B

CTV 10P ✽ ⌂

🍴English & French V ♉ Last dinner 10pm

Credit cards 1 2 3 VS

★★**Lion** Main St ☎(0646) 684501

A friendly town-centre hotel with helpful staff.

11rm (1fb) sB&B fr£12.50 dB&B fr£25

CTV 12P 🐕 billiards

Bar lunch £1.25–£2.75 Dinner fr£6.50 Wine £4.20 Last dinner 9.30pm

Credit cards 1 2 3 5

★★**B *Old King's Arms*** Main St ☎(0646) 683611
Closed Xmas wk & New Year
A traditional hotel with a popular restaurant.
21➡ CTV in all bedrooms Ⓡ
22P ✽
☐ English & French ✿ Last dinner 10pm
Credit cards ① ③

PEMBROKE DOCK
Dyfed
Map **2** SM90

☆☆☆**Cleddau Bridge** The Avenue ☎(0646) 685961
Modern well appointed hotel with commanding views.
24➡⋒ (3fb) CTV in all bedrooms Ⓡ
sB&B➡⋒ £27.50 dB&B➡⋒ £37.50 ₿
☾ CTV 200P ✽ Live music and dancing Fri & Sat, Cabaret Fri & Sat ♘ *xmas*
☐ English & French **V** ✿ ☕ ✻ Lunch £7.25&alc Tea fr55p High Tea fr£2 Dinner £7.25&alc Wine £4 Last dinner 9.30pm
Credit cards ① ② ③ ⑤

PENARTH
South Glamorgan
Map **3** ST17

★**Glendale** 8–10 Plymouth Rd ☎(0222) 706701
A small, well-kept friendly hotel
19rm (11➡2⋒) (4fb) CTV in all bedrooms Ⓡ sB&B £13.50 sB&B➡⋒ £17.50 dB&B £22 dB&B➡⋒ £30 ₿
CTV
☐ Italian **V** ✿ Lunch fr£3 Tea fr75p High Tea fr£3.50 Dinner fr£5.75&alc Wine £2 Last dinner 10pm
S% Credit cards ① ③ **VS**

Penarth — Pencraig

★**Walton House** 37 Victoria Rd ☎(0222) 707782
RS Xmas Day
Pleasant small hotel near town centre.
13rm(4⇌1⋒)(1fb) CTV in all bedrooms sB&B£12 sB&B⇌⋒£14 dB&B£22 dB&B⇌⋒£25
TV
English, French & Italian **V** Lunch £4.25 Tea 50p High Tea £3.50 Dinner £5.50 Wine £4.50 Last dinner 8pm
Credit cards 1 3 **VS**

✕✕✕**Caprice** The Esplanade
☎(0222) 702424
A comfortable, first-floor restaurant overlooking the Bristol Channel.
Closed Sun
English & Continental **V** 80 seats Lunch £7.25 Dinner £10.75&alc Wine £4.25 Last dinner 11pm
S% Credit cards 1 2 3 5 **VS**

PENCRAIG
Hereford & Worcester
Map **3** SO52

★★**Pencraig Court** ☎Llangarron (098984) 306 Closed Nov–Mar
Peaceful, small, country hotel set in gardens and woodland.
11rm(5⇌)(1fb) 1 CTV available in bedrooms sB&B£13–£15 sB&B⇌£15–£17 dB&B£23–£27 dB&B⇌£27–£31
CTV 25P
English & French **V** Bar lunch fr£2 Tea fr60p Dinner fr£6.50 Wine £3.50 Last dinner 8pm
Credit cards 1 2 3 **VS**

P

PENDOGGETT
Cornwall
Map **2** SX07

★★ ***H Cornish Arms*** ☎ Port Isaac (020888) 263 Closed Xmas

Delightful, small hotel in a 17th-century former ale house, with beamed ceilings.

7rm(4➡) ⊟

50P ⊘ ✽ nc14yrs

Last dinner 9.30pm

Credit cards 1 2 3 5

PENNAL
Gwynedd
Map **6** SH60

★★★ ***B* Talgarth Hall** Plas Talgarth Estate ☎ (065475) 631

10➡ CTV in all bedrooms Ⓡ sB&B➡£25 dB&B➡£40

P ⊘ ✽ ⊡ & ⛆(heated) ⚲(hard) squash sauna bath Live music and dancing wkly ⌂ *xmas*

⊟ English, Welsh & French **V** ⚘ ⊑ Lunch £3.50alc Tea 60p–£1.20 Dinner £10alc Wine £3.96 Last dinner 9.30pm

Credit cards 1 2 3 4 5 **VS**

★★ ***L* Llugwy Hall Country House** (1m E on A483) ☎ (065 475) 228

Gracious, Elizabethan country house in wooded surroundings alongside the River Dovey.

11➡ (3fb) CTV in all bedrooms Ⓡ sB&B➡£19.50 dB&B➡£26 ⊟

40P ✽ ⌂ *xmas*

V ⚘ ⊑ Lunch fr£1.25 Tea fr60p High Tea fr£3.75 Dinner £6.50–£8.50&alc Wine £3.95 Last dinner 9pm

Credit cards 1 2 3 4 5 **VS**

★ **Riverside** ☎ (065 475) 285

Roadside village inn catering for local and tourist clientele.

7rm (1fb) sB&B£12.50–£14 dB&B£25–£28

CTV 50P 6⌂ ✽

⚘ ⊑ Bar lunch £1.75–£3.50 Tea 80p–£1.50 Dinner £5.50–£7.50 Wine £3 Last dinner 8.30pm

PENN STREET
Buckinghamshire
Map **4** SU99

✕✕ **Hit or Miss** ☎ High Wycombe (0494) 713109

Old coaching inn providing tasty well-cooked food.

Closed Mon & last wk Jul–1st wk Aug Dinner not served Sun

⊟ International 40 seats Lunch £6.50&alc Dinner £12.50alc Wine £4.50 Last dinner 9.30pm 110P

Credit cards 1 5

PENPILLICK
Cornwall
Map **2** SX05

★★ **Penpillick House** ☎ Par (072 681) 2742

Small Georgian house with views of St Austell Bay and Luxulyan Valley.

10rm(3➡) Annexe: 2rm (2fb) CTV in all bedrooms sB&B£12.50–£14 sB&B➡£12.50–£14 dB&B£25–£28 dB&B➡£25–£28 ⊟

CTV 20P ⊘ ✽ ⛆(heated) ⚲ sauna bath Live music and dancing wkly *xmas*

⊟ English & French **V** ⚘ ⊑ Lunch £2–£5.50 Tea 50p–£1.50 High Tea £1.50 Dinner £4.50–£6.50&alc Wine £3.50 Last dinner 9pm

Credit cards 1 2 3 5

PENRHYNDEUDRAETH
Gwynedd
Map **6** SH63

★ **Brynllydan** Llanfrothen ☎ (0766) 770442

Converted farmhouse at the end of a long lane, 1 mile from the village.

10rm(5➡) (1fb) TV in 5 bedrooms Ⓡ ✻sB&B fr£9.78 sB&B➡ fr£11.50 dB&B fr£17.25 dB&B➡ fr£20.75 ⊟

☾ ⚟ CTV 50P ⊘ ✽ ⌂

⊟ French ⚘ ⊑ ✻Dinner £4.50&alc Wine £3.60 Last dinner 10pm

PENRITH
Cumbria
Map **12** NY53

See also **Edenhall**

★★ **Clifton Hill** Clifton (2¾m S A6) ☎ (0768) 62717

Large Edwardian house with several later additions.

56rm(54➡2⋔) CTV in all bedrooms sB&B➡⋔ fr£14.95 dB&B➡⋔ fr£21

CTV 200P 30⌂ ✽ *xmas*

V ⚘ ⊑ ✻Lunch fr£3.75 Tea fr£1.75 High Tea fr£2.85 Dinner fr£6.90 Wine £3.15 Last dinner 8.30pm

★★ **Crown** Eamont Bridge (1m S A6) ☎ (0768) 62566

Old world country inn with a comfortable, modern dining room.

14rm (1fb) ✦ sB&B fr£13.50 dB&B fr£26 ⊟

CTV 100P ✽ ⚓

V ⚘ Lunch £5.25–£7.50&alc High Tea £3.50–£5.20 Dinner £7.50–£9.60&alc Wine £4.50 Last dinner 9pm

Credit cards 1 2 5

★★ ***H George*** Devonshire St ☎ (0768) 62696 Closed Xmas

Former coaching inn, offering courteous and personal service, situated in the town centre.

31rm(11➡19⋔) Ⓡ sB&B fr£16.50 sB&B➡⋔ fr£17 dB&B fr£28 dB&B➡⋔ fr£29 ⊟

☾ CTV 40P

⚘ ⊑ Lunch fr£3.75 Tea 60p Dinner fr£6.25 Wine £4.30 Last dinner 8.30pm

★★ ***Strickland*** Corney Sq ☎ (0768) 62262 Closed 25, 26 & 31 Dec

Late Victorian hotel, was former schoolhouse.

17rm(3➡3⋔) TV in 2 bedrooms Ⓡ ✦

11P

⚘ ⊑ Last dinner 10pm

★ **Abbotsford** Wordsworth St ☎ (0768) 63940

The hotel is situated beneath the wooded Penrith Beacon.

11rm(9➡2⋔) (3fb) 1⊟ Ⓡ ✻sB&B➡⋔ £13–£14 dB&B➡⋔ £24–£26 ⊟

CTV 12P 4⌂ ✽ *xmas*

⊟ English & Italian **V** ⚘ ✻Lunch fr£3.50&alc High Tea fr£3.50 Dinner fr£6.75&alc Last dinner 9.30pm

Credit cards 1 2 3 5

★ **Glen Cottage** Corney Sq ☎ (0768) 62221

Closed Xmas & New Year's Day

White, stucco-faced cottage of charm and character, built in 1756.

7rm(2➡) (2fb) CTV in all bedrooms sB&B£11.50 sB&B➡£14.50–£15.50 dB&B£20–£21 dB&B➡£23–£24 ⊟

3⌂ ⊘

⚘ Lunch fr£2.75 Dinner fr£3.75 Wine £3.25 Last dinner 9.15pm

Credit cards 1 2 3 4 5

★ ***Station*** Castlegate ☎ (0768) 62072

Pleasant rather old fashioned hotel with friendly hospitality.

20rm TV in 2 bedrooms Ⓡ ⊟

CTV 10P

⚘ ⊑ Last dinner 8pm

PENSHURST
Kent
Map **5** TQ54

★★ **Leicester Arms** ☎ (0892) 870551

Closed Xmas

Picturesque 17th-century inn with modern well equipped bedrooms and friendly management.

7➡ CTV in all bedrooms Ⓡ sB&B➡ fr£21.50 dB&B➡ fr£33.50 ⊟

40P

⊟ English, French & Italian **V** ⚘ ✻Bar lunch fr£4 Dinner fr£5.50&alc Wine £3.80 Last dinner 9.30pm

Credit cards 1 2 3

PENZANCE
Cornwall
Map **2** SW43

★★★ ***HL* Higher Faugen** Newlyn (off B3315) ☎ (0736) 2076

Closed Nov–Feb

Holiday hotel in secluded surroundings, set in 10 acres of grounds.

12rm(8➡4⋔) (2fb) 1⊟ CTV in all bedrooms Ⓡ ✦ sB&B➡⋔ £16.10–£22 →

P

db&B→⋒£32.20–£44 B
☾ 15P3 ⌂ ✽ (heated) (hard) billiards
International Bar lunch 65p–£2.50 Tea fr50p Dinner fr£9.20 Wine £3.60 Last dinner 8.30pm
Credit cards 1 2 5 VS

★★★**Mount Prospect** Britons Hill ☎(0736) 3117
Well appointed hotel in quiet location.
26rm(23→3⋒) (2fb) CTV in all bedrooms Ⓡ sB&B→⋒£28.75 dB&B→⋒£46 B
☾ CTV 16P ✽ (heated) Live music and dancing wkly, Cabaret wkly *xmas*

Continental V Lunch £4.60&alc Tea 50p Dinner £9.20&alc Wine £5.25 Last dinner 9pm
Credit cards 1 2 3 5 VS

★★★***Queen's*** The Promenade ☎(0736) 2371
Large, traditional hotel on the sea front with exceptional views over Mount's Bay.
71rm(47→3⋒) CTV in all bedrooms Ⓡ B
Lift ☾ CTV 60P
English & French V Last dinner 9pm

Credit cards 1 2 3 5

★★**Sea & Horses** 6 Alexandra Ter ☎(0736) 61961
Small, comfortable, well-run hotel in a quiet garden terrace on the sea front.
11rm(1→) (6fb) Ⓡ sB&B£9–£10.50 sB&B→£9–£10.50 dB&B£18–£21 dB&B→£18–£21 B
CTV 11P2
V Bar lunch 95p–£1.60 Dinner £5.35–£5.60 Wine £4 Last dinner 8pm
VS

★**Minalto** Alexandra Rd ☎(0736) 2923
Small, family hotel in a quiet location close

P

Penzance

to the beach and the town centre.

10rm (3fb) sB&B£10.35 dB&B£20.70 B

CTV 10P *xmas*

V ♈ ☕ Lunch £3.45&alc Tea fr46p Dinner £5.75–£6.90&alc Last dinner 8pm

★**Smuggler's** Fore St, Newlyn Harbour ☎(0736) 4207

A 250-year-old Cornish building situated in a commanding position overlooking Newlyn Harbour.

16rm (2⇌4⋒) (3fb) CTV in all bedrooms Ⓡ sB&B£14 sB&B⇌⋒£18 dB&B£24 dB&B⇌⋒£28

☾ CTV 6P 2🚗 ⇌ *xmas*

V ♈ ☕ Lunch £1–£3&alc Tea £1 alc Wine £4.85 Last dinner 9.30pm

Credit card 2

★***H*** **Southern Comfort** Alexandra Ter ☎(0736) 66333

RS Nov–Feb

12rm (3⋒) ★ sB&B fr£8.50 sB&B⋒ fr£11.50 dB&B fr£17 dB&B⋒ fr£20 B

CTV 11P ⇌

♈ ☕ Bar lunch 50p–£3 Tea fr50p Dinner fr£4&alc Wine £2.65 Last dinner 7.30pm

★**Yacht Inn** The Promenade ☎(0736) 2787 Closed Nov & Feb

Small inn located on the Promenade, close to the town centre.

8rm (2fb) Ⓡ sB&B£8.90–£10 dB&B£17.80–£20

CTV 8P ⇌ nc5yrs

V ♈ Lunch £3–£5 Tea £1–£1.50 Dinner £5–£7.50 Wine £3 Last dinner 7.30pm

✕✕**Le Tarot** 19 Quay St ☎(0736) 3118

A cellar restaurant with a marble floor and alcove interior, situated close to the Old Harbour.

Closed Tue Nov–May Lunch not served Mon–Sat

→

P

⊟French 80 seats Lunch £5.50 Dinner £5.50&alc Last dinner 10pm ♬ Live music Sat

Credit cards 1 2 3 5

PERRANPORTH
Cornwall
Map **2** SW75

★★**Promenade** ☎(087 257) 3118
Closed end Sep–Apr
Family, holiday hotel near to and overlooking the beach.
35rm(15→)(5fb) 🛏 ✻sB&B£13.50–£19 dB&B£27–£38 dB&B→£31.50–£61
☾ CTV 27P
♧

★*H***Beach Dunes** Ramoth Way, Reen Sands ☎(087257) 2263
RS Nov
6rm(2→1⋔) Annexe: 3→ CTV in all bedrooms Ⓡ ✻sB&B fr£14 sB&B→⋔ fr£17 dB&B fr£28 dB&B→⋔ fr£31 B
10P ✻ (heated) squash *xmas*
♧Bar lunch 50p–£2.50 Dinner £6.50 Wine £3.40 Last dinner 7.30pm
Credit cards 1 3

PERSHORE
Hereford & Worcester
Map **3** SO94

★★**Angel Inn** ☎(0386) 552046
Closed Xmas
Old coaching inn, whose gardens at the back reach down to the River Avon.
18rm(6→3⋔)(1fb) Ⓡ sB&B£19.80 sB&B→⋔£22 dB&B£29.70 dB&B→⋔£35.20 B
CTV 50P ✻ ♪
V♧⊟ Lunch £2–£10&alc Dinner fr£7&alc Wine £4.50 Last dinner 10pm
Credit cards 1 2 3 5 **VS**

★★**Manor House** Bridge St ☎(0386) 552713
Closed Xmas Day
8rm (2fb) sB&B£11.50 dB&B£23
CTV 60P
V♧Lunch £3.50–£12&alc Dinner £3.50–£12&alc Wine £3.75 Last dinner 9.30pm
Credit cards 1 2 3 5 **VS**

★***Star*** Bridge St ☎(03865) 552704
Closed Xmas Day
Town-centre inn with a small garden, bordering the banks of the River Avon.
8rm Ⓡ
CTV 50P ♪
♧⊟ Last dinner 9.30pm
Credit cards 1 3

✕***Zhivago's*** 22 Bridge St ☎(0386) 553828
Closed Sun
⊟English, French & Italian 48 seats Last dinner 10pm ♬
Credit cards 1 2 3 5

PERTH
Tayside *Perthshire*
Map **11** NO12
See plan

★★★**Isle of Skye** Queen's Bridge, Dundee Rd ☎(0738) 24471
Plan **4** *D2*
Recently refurbished traditional hotel standing on the north bank of the river.
44→⋔ CTV in all bedrooms Ⓡ sB&B→⋔£24 sB&B→⋔£40 B
☾ 80P CFA Live music and dancing wkly Cabaret wkly *xmas*
⊟Scottish & French ♧⊟ Lunch fr£4.50 Tea fr£1.50 High Tea £3.25–£5.25 Dinner fr£8.50&alc Wine £4 Last dinner 9.45pm
Credit cards 1 2 3 5

★★★**Royal George** Tay St (Trusthouse Forte) ☎(0738) 24455 Plan **8** *C3*
Three-storey stone building overlooking the River Tay.
43→(2fb) CTV in all bedrooms Ⓡ sB&B→£33 dB&B→£52.50 B
☾ 20P 12⌂ *xmas*
♧⊟ Last dinner 10pm
Credit cards 1 2 3 4 5

P

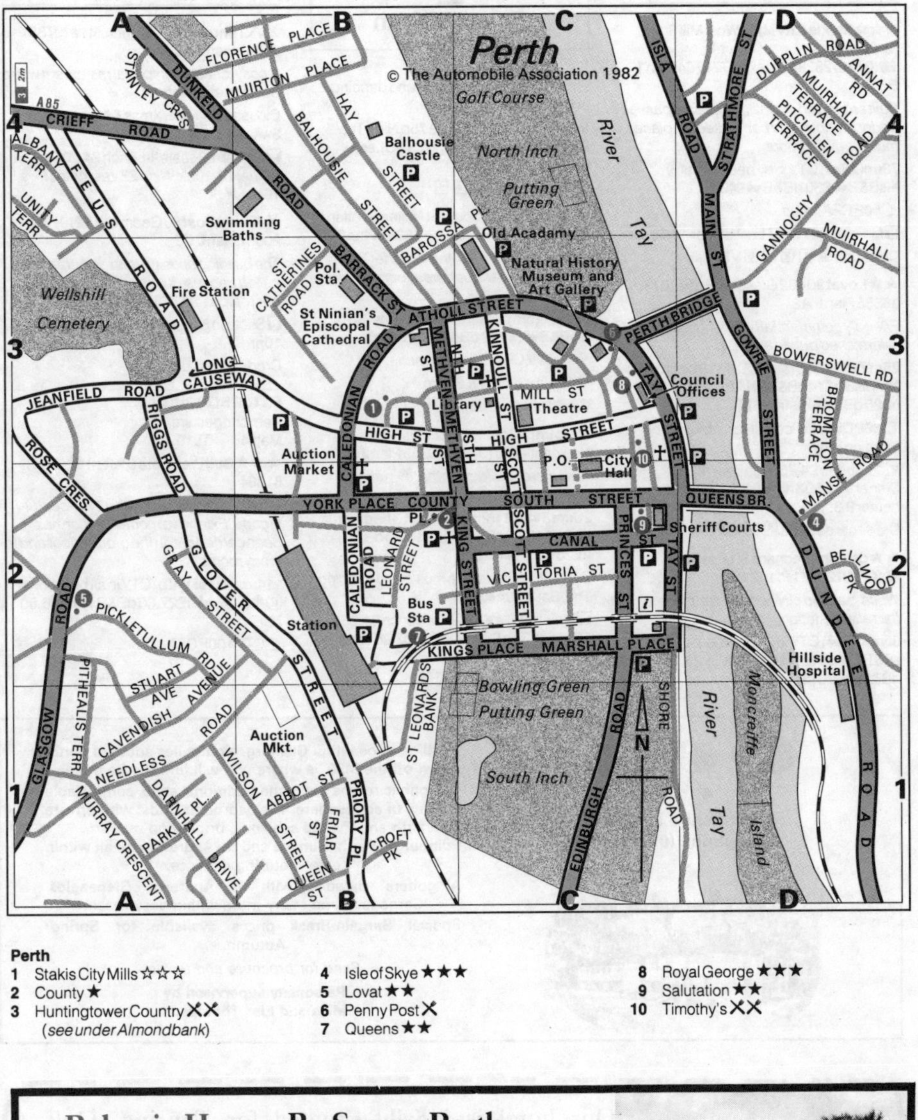

Perth

© The Automobile Association 1982

Perth

1 Stakis City Mills ☆☆☆
2 County ★
3 Huntingtower Country ✕✕ (*see under Almondbank*)
4 Isle of Skye ★★★
5 Lovat ★★
6 Penny Post ✕
7 Queens ★★
8 Royal George ★★★
9 Salutation ★★
10 Timothy's ✕✕

P

☆☆☆**Stakis City Mills** West Mill St (Stakis)
☎(0738) 28281 Telex no 778704 Plan **1** *B3*

Built around an old mill, the stream passes under the hotel and can be seen in places through glass floors.

78rm(76➡) CTV in all bedrooms ®
✻sB&B➡£30 dB&B➡£40 ₿

☾ 50P CFA *xmas*

▣Mainly grills ♆ ▭ Last dinner 10.30pm

Credit cards 1 2 3 5 **VS**

★★**Lovat** 90–92 Glasgow Rd ☎(0738) 36555 Plan **5** *A2*

Friendly commercial hotel with recently refurbished public areas.

25rm(11➡2⋔) (5fb) CTV in 19 bedrooms ✶sB&B fr£14 sB&B➡⋔ fr£22 dB&B fr£20 dB&B➡⋔ fr£30 ₿

☾ 60P Disco twice wkly Live music and dancing wkly

V♆ Lunch fr£4.75 High Tea fr£2.50 Dinner fr£4.50&alc Wine £4.50 Last dinner 9.30pm

Credit cards 1 2 3 5 **VS**

★★**Queens** Leonard St (Travco)
☎(0738) 25471 Plan **7** *B2*

White-painted city centre hotel close to the railway station.

55rm(28➡) CTV in 28 bedrooms ®
sB&B£14 sB&B➡£17 dB&B£23 dB&B➡£26 ₿

Lift ☾ CTV 20P Live music and dancing twice wkly ⌂

V♆ ▭ Lunch £3.75 Tea 75p High Tea £3.75 Dinner £5.25 Wine £3.95 Last dinner 8.30pm

Credit cards 1 2 4 5

★★**Salutation** South St (Allied Scotland)
☎(0738) 22166 Telex no 76357 Plan **9** *C2*

Established in 1699, this was the temporary headquarters of Bonnie Prince Charlie.

67➡⋔ (5fb) CTV in all bedrooms ®
✻sB&B➡⋔£23 dB&B➡⋔£46 ₿

☾ # CTV CFA billiards *xmas*

♆ ▭ Last dinner 8.30pm

Credit cards 1 2 3 4 5

★**County** County Pl (Scottish & Newcastle) ☎(0738) 23355 Plan **2** *B2*

Two-storey building in the town centre, close to the Motorail terminal.

20rm(3➡8⋔) (2fb) 2▤ TV in 3 bedrooms sB&B£12.50 sB&B➡⋔£12.50 dB&B fr£23 dB&B➡⋔£25

CTV 10P billiards Live music and dancing Thu, Sat & Sun ⌂ *xmas*

▣Mainly grills **V**♆ ▭ Bar lunch £1.25 Tea 55p High Tea £2.45 Dinner £2.45 Wine £2.26 Last dinner 11pm

Credit cards 1 2 3 4 5

✕✕**Timothy's** 24 St John St ☎(0738) 26641 Plan **10** *C3*

A cosy, cheerful, informal restaurant with a bustling atmosphere.

Closed Sun, Mon, Xmas & New Year & 3wks summer

▣Danish 60 seats ✻Lunch £4.20alc Dinner £6.10alc Wine £3 Last dinner 10pm ⚑

✕***Penny Post*** 80 George St ☎(0738) 20867 Plan **6** *C3*

The building housing this restaurant is so called because it was one of Perth's first post offices in 1773.

▣Scottish & French 45 seats Last dinner 10pm

Credit cards 1 2 3 5

PETERBOROUGH
Cambridgeshire
Map **4** TL19

★★★**Bull** Westgate (Paten) ☎(0733) 61364

Former coaching inn with a 17th-century façade. Extensive modernisation has been carried out on the ground floor and in many rooms.

114rm(107➡) (4fb) CTV in all bedrooms ®✻sB&B➡ fr£27.60 dB&B➡ fr£36.80 ₿

☾ CTV 100P CFA

P

English & French V ♧ ☕ *Lunch £2.80–£5.35&alc Tea fr60p Dinner £2.80–£5.65&alc Wine £3.45 Last dinner 10.30pm
Credit cards 1 2 3 5

☆☆☆**Saxon Inn Motor** (Saxon Inn) ☎(0733) 260000 Telex no 32708
98 (4fb) CTV in all bedrooms Ⓡ sB&B £33.50 dB&B £47.50 B
Lift ☾ 200P CFA Live music and dancing Sat
English & French V ♧ ☕ Lunch £6.25 Tea fr60p Dinner £7.25 Wine £4.95 Last dinner 10pm
Credit cards 1 2 3 5 **VS**

At **Norman Cross** (6m SW junc A1/A15)
☆☆☆**Crest** Great North Rd (Crest) ☎(0733) 240209
97rm(77 20) 200P

PETERHEAD
Grampian *Aberdeenshire*
Map **15** NK14
☆☆☆*B* **Waterside Inn** Fraserburgh Rd ☎(0779) 71121 Telex no 739413
80 Annexe: 40 (40fb) CTV in all bedrooms Ⓡ sB&B £21–£35 dB&B £24–£40 B
☾ 250P CFA ✽ Billiards sauna bath Disco Sat

British & French V ♧ ☕ Lunch £3–£5 Tea £1 High Tea £3–£5 Dinner £5–£10&alc Wine £3.95 Last dinner 10.30pm
Credit cards 1 2 3 5

PETERLEE
Co Durham
Map **12** NZ44
★★★**Norseman** Bede Way ☎(0783) 862161
Comfortable modern hotel with reasonably priced feature restaurant.
26 CTV in all bedrooms Ⓡ *sB&B £22.50 dB&B £32.50
Lift ☾ 50P billiards
V ♧ *Lunch £1.95–£2.75 Dinner £4.50–£12 Wine £4.30 Last dinner 9.30pm
S% Credit cards 1 2 3 5 **VS**

PETIT BÔT
Guernsey, Channel Islands
Map **16**
★**Manor** ☎Guernsey (0481) 37788
Closed Nov–Mar
Large hotel situated in wooded valley with spacious public rooms and modest bedrooms.
62rm(20) sB&B £10–£12 sB&B £11–£13 dB&B £20–£24 dB&B £22–£26 B

Lift CTV 28P ✽
♧ ☕ Lunch £2.50–£3.50 Tea 25p–£1 High Tea 50p–£2 Dinner £3.50–£4.50 Last dinner 8pm
Credit card 1

PETT BOTTOM
Kent
Map **5** TR15
✕**Duck Inn** ☎Canterbury (0227) 830354
Nestling in a hollow, this country inn has a cosy dining room and wood fires.
Closed Mon, Tue, Xmas, 2wks Mar & 2wks Oct
English & French 36 seats Lunch fr£11.25 Dinner fr£11.25 Wine £6.90 Last dinner 9.15pm 25P
Credit cards 2 5

PETTY FRANCE
Avon
Map **3** ST78
★★★**Petty France** ☎Didmarton (045 423) 361 Telex no 43232
Closed 27 Dec–5 Jan
Georgian hotel with large gardens and country house atmosphere.
8rm(7 1) Annexe: 8rm(7 1) (1fb) 1 CTV in 16 bedrooms Ⓡ sB&B fr£25.50 dB&B £38–£44 Continental breakfast B
30P ✽ *xmas* →

P

▣English & French ♆Lunch £10alc Dinner £10alc Wine £5.05 Last dinner 9.45pm
S% Credit cards 1 2 3 5 **VS**

PEVENSEY
East Sussex
Map **5** TQ60
★★**Priory Court** Pevensey Castle ☎Eastbourne (0323) 761494 Telex no. 878172
A partly 18th-century hotel situated opposite Pevensey castle.
8rm(4➡)(2fb) CTV available in bedrooms ♜✱sB&B£22 sB&B➡£27 dB&B£34 dB&B➡£40
☾ CTV 60P ✽ *xmas*
V♆☕✱Bar lunch £3.50alc Tea £1alc Dinner £8.50&alc Wine £3.90
Credit cards 1 2 3 5

PEWSEY
Wiltshire
Map **4** SU15
✕**Close** ☎(06726) 3226
Closed Mon & 31 Dec & 1 Jan Dinner not served Sun
▣International 36 seats Lunch £7alc Tea 90p–£1.80 Dinner £9.40–£9.90 Wine £3.70 Last dinner 9.30pm 20P
Credit cards 1 2 3 5

PICKERING
North Yorkshire
Map **8** SE78
★★**Forest & Vale** 2 Hungate, Malton Rd ☎(0751) 72722
Comfortable country hotel with well kept garden. Large restaurant serving mainly English food.
17rm(7➡6⋒) Annexe: 6rm(5➡1⋒)(1fb) CTV available in bedrooms Ⓡ sB&B£15–£17 sB&B➡⋒£15–£17 dB&B£30–£34 dB&B➡⋒£30–£34B
CTV 70P ✽
▣English & French V♆☕✱Lunch £5.50&alc Tea £1–£2 High Tea £2.50–£5 Dinner £8.50&alc Wine £4.35 Last dinner 9pm
Credit cards 1 2 3 5 **VS**

✕**Blacksmiths Arms** Aislaby (2m NW on A170) ☎(0751) 72182
A congenial atmosphere pervades this 18th century stone inn where French and British dishes can be enjoyed.
Closed Tue
V 60 seats Lunch £4.85alc Dinner £7.90alc Wine £3.70 Last dinner 9.30pm 20P
Credit cards 1 3

PIDDLETRENTHIDE
Dorset
Map **3** SY79
★★**Old Bakehouse** ☎(03004) 305
Rendered, colourwashed cottage in the village main street, overlooking an outdoor pool and gardens.
3➡ Annexe: 6➡ CTV in 4 bedrooms TV in 5 bedrooms Ⓡ sB&B➡£16–£18 dB&B➡£25–£29B
25P ⛟ ✽ ⛱(heated) sauna bath nc12yrs
▣English & French Dinner £6.50&alc Wine £4 Last dinner 9pm
Credit cards 1 3 **VS**

PILLATON
Cornwall
Map **2** SX36
★★***Weary Friar*** ☎St Dominick (0579) 50238
A 12th-century inn with oak beams and period furniture.
12➡ CTV in all bedrooms
CTV 50P ⛟ nc5yrs
V♆☕ Last dinner 9.40pm
Credit cards 1 2 3 5 **VS**

PITLOCHRY
Tayside *Perthshire*
Map **14** NN95
See plan

P

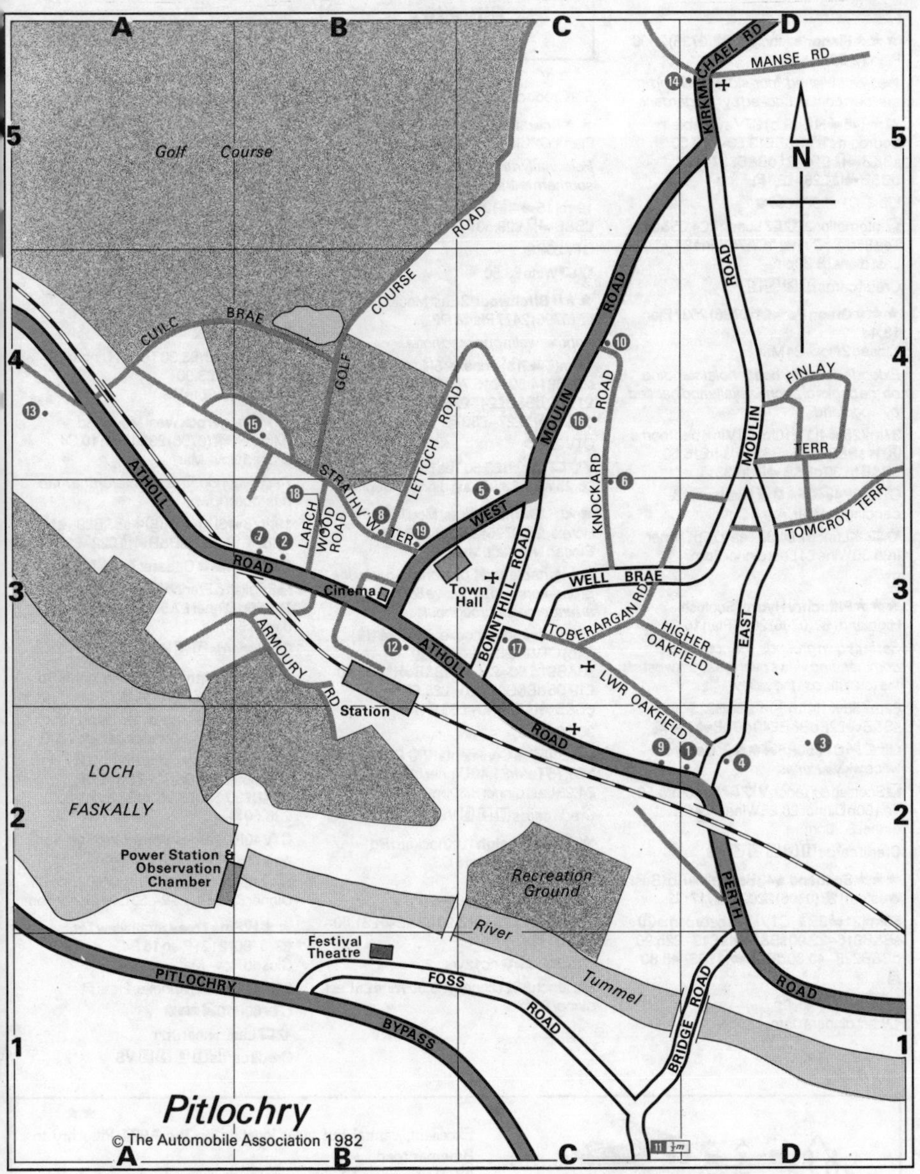
A
B
C
D
5
4
3
2
1
Golf Course
CUILC BRAE
GOLF COURSE ROAD
KIRKMICHAEL RD
MANSE RD
N
MOULIN ROAD
EAST MOULIN ROAD
FINLAY TERR
TOMCROY TERR
KNOCKARD ROAD
LETTOCH ROAD
STRATHV W. TER
LARCH WOOD ROAD
WEST
ATHOLL ROAD
BONNTHILL ROAD
WELL BRAE
TOBERARGAN RD
HIGHER OAKFIELD
LWR OAKFIELD
Cinema
Town Hall
ARMOURY RD
Station
LOCH FASKALLY
Power Station & Observation Chamber
Recreation Ground
River Tummel
Festival Theatre
FOSS ROAD
PITLOCHRY BYPASS
BRIDGE ROAD
PERTH ROAD
Pitlochry
© The Automobile Association 1982

P

★★★ *L* **Atholl Palace** (Trusthouse Forte) ☎ (0796) 2400 Telex no 76406 Plan **3** *D2*

Large imposing hotel with superb views and very good leisure facilities.

92⇌ (4fb) CTV in all bedrooms ® sB&B⇌£33.50 dB&B⇌£54.50 B

Lift ☾ CTV 150P CFA ✽ ≋ (heated) ⚲ (hard) sauna bath *xmas*

♆ ▭ Last dinner 9pm

Credit cards 1 2 3 4 5

Pitlochry

1 Acarsaid ★★
2 Airdanier ★
3 Atholl Palace ★★★
4 Birchwood ★★
5 Burnside ★★
6 Castlebeigh ★★
7 Claymore ★★
8 Craigard ★★
9 Craig Urrard ★
10 Craigvrack ★★
11 Dunfallandy House ★
12 Fisher's ★★★
13 Green Park ★★★
14 Moulin Inn ★★
15 Pinetrees ★★
16 Pitlochry Hydro ★★★
17 Scotland's ★★★
18 Tigh-na-Cloich ★
19 Wellwood ★★

Pitlochry

★★★**Fisher's** Atholl Rd ☎(0796) 2000 Plan **12** *B3*
Well-established, four-storey building in the town centre, backed by fine gardens.
77rm(46→5⋒)(9fb) CTV available in bedrooms ✗ sB&B£13.50–£18.50 sB&B→⋒£14–21 dB&B£27–£37 dB&B→⋒£28–£39 ℞
Lift ☾ CTV 55P 10⌂ ✽
▣International ♡ ☐ Lunch fr£4.25&alc Tea 85p alc Dinner fr£7.75 Wine £4 Last dinner 8.30pm
Credit cards 1 2 3 5

★★★**Green Park** ☎(0796) 2537 Plan **13** *A4*
Closed 2 Nov–24 Mar
Extended country house hotel standing on the banks of Loch Faskally and backed by woodland.
37rm(25→4⋒)(10fb) CTV in 8 bedrooms Ⓡ ✗ sB&B fr£15 sB&B→⋒ fr£16.50 dB&B fr£30 dB&B→⋒ fr£33 ℞
CTV 50P 4⌂ CFA ✽ ♪ Live music & dancing Sat Mar, Apr & Oct
♡ ☐ ✱ Lunch fr£4.30 Tea fr75p Dinner fr£8.30 Wine £4 Last dinner 8pm
S%

★★★**Pitlochry Hydro** (Scottish Highland) ☎(0796) 2666 Plan **16** *C4*
Set in its own grounds, the hotel offers commanding views over the south west of the town across the valley.
62rm(58→)(4fb) Ⓡ ✱ sB&B£25 sB&B→£28 dB&B£40 dB&B→£44 ℞
Lift ☾ ⚟ CTV 60P 5⌂ ✽ ⚑ ⚲ Cabaret twice wkly ⌂ *xmas*
▣Scottish & French **V** ♡ ☐ Lunch £5.50 Tea 60p Dinner £8.25 Wine £4.45 Last dinner 8.30pm
Credit cards 1 2 3 4 5 **VS**

P

★★★**Scotland's** 40 Bonnethill Rd (Best Western) ☎(0796) 2292 Plan **17** *C3*
50rm(21→25⋒) CTV in 10 bedrooms Ⓡ sB&B£16–22.90 sB&B→⋒£19–£25.90 dB&B£28–40.80 dB&B→⋒£33–45.80 ℞
Lift ☾ CTV 50P CFA
♡ Last dinner 10pm

S% Credit cards 1 2 3 5 **VS**

★★**Acarsaid** 8 Atholl Rd ☎(0796) 2389 Plan **1** *D2* Closed end Oct–19 Apr
Personally run, modern hotel, at the southern entrance to the town.
19rm(15→4⋒) Ⓡ ✗ sB&B→⋒£14.75 dB&B→⋒£29.50 ℞
CTV 20P ✽
♡ ☐ Wine £3.50

★★*B* **Birchwood** 2 East Moulin Rd ☎(0796) 2477 Plan **4** *D2*
Popular well appointed hotel.
11rm(6→2⋒) Annexe: 5⋒ (4fb) Ⓡ sB&B£14.50–£15.75 sB&B→⋒£15.75–£17.50 dB&B£24–£26.50 dB&B→⋒£27–£30 ℞
CTV 25P ✽
V ♡ ☐ Lunch £3.50 Tea £1.75 Dinner £6.25 Wine £3.90 Last dinner 7.30pm

★★*HL* **Burnside** West Moulin Rd (Inter-Hotels) ☎(0796) 2203 Plan **5** *C3*
Closed Nov–late Mar
Comfortable hotel, personally-run by the proprietors with attractive floral arrangements throughout.
17rm(12→5⋒) Annexe: 6rm(1→1⋒) (8fb) CTV in all bedrooms Ⓡ sB&B£15.60–£16.42 sB&B→⋒£18.20–£19.08 dB&B£27.20–£28.62 dB&B→⋒£32.40–£33.97 ℞
30P ✽ ⌂
▣Scottish & Continental **V** ♡ ☐ Lunch fr£3.75 Tea fr£1.40 Dinner fr£7.75 Wine £4.25 Last dinner 8.30pm
Credit cards 2 3 5 **VS**

★★**Castlebeigh** 10 Knockard Rd ☎(0796) 2925 Plan **6** *C3*
Closed Nov–Mar
19→ CTV in all bedrooms Ⓡ sB&B→£10.90–£12.90 dB&B→£21.80–£25.80 ℞
CTV 36P ⛌ ✽ nc12yrs
Bar lunch fr£2 Dinner fr£8.50 Wine £5 Last dinner 8pm

★★**Claymore** 162 Atholl Rd ☎(0796) 2888 Plan **7** *B3*
Closed Nov–mid Apr
8rm(2→) Annexe: 4rm(1⋒)(1fb) Ⓡ sB&B fr£13 dB&B fr£26 dB&B→⋒ fr£30 ℞
CTV 25P ⛌ ✽ nc5yrs
Bar lunch £4alc Dinner fr£8 Wine £3.85 Last dinner 8.30pm

★★*L* **Craigard** Strathview Ter ☎(0796) 2592 Plan **8** *B3* Closed Nov–Mar
10rm(3→3⋒) Annexe: 8rm(4→⋒)(1fb) CTV in all bedrooms Ⓡ sB&B£13–£15.50 sB&B→⋒£14.25–£16.75 dB&B£24–£28.50 dB&B→⋒£27–£31.50 ℞
⚟ 10P ⛌ ✽ ♿
V ♡ ☐ Lunch £3.30 Tea £1 Dinner £7–£9.50 Wine £3.90 Last dinner 8pm **VS**

★★**Craigvrack** West Moulin Rd (Minotel) ☎(0796) 2399 Plan **10** *C4*
Closed Nov–Mar
Recently modernised hotel on the road east out of town.
19rm(6→3⋒)(4fb) Ⓡ ✱ sB&B£9–£11.50 dB&B£18–£23 dB&B→⋒£22–£27.60 ℞
CTV 22P ⛌ ✽ Cabaret Tue & Thu
▣English & French ♡ ☐ ✱ Lunch £5–£6 Tea 55p Dinner £7.50 Wine £3.25 Last dinner 8pm
Credit cards 1 3 **VS**

★★**Moulin Inn** 11–13 Kirkmichael Rd ☎(0796) 2196 Plan **14** *D5*
Charming little hotel on the hillside above the town. Its history dates back to 1700.
18rm(13→) Annexe: 5rm (1fb) CTV in 18 bedrooms Ⓡ sB&B£16.50–£18 dB&B£30.50–£33.50 dB&B→£33.50–£36.50 ℞
CTV 40P Live music and dancing 4 nights wkly in summer, wkly in winter
▣Continental **V** ♡ ☐ Bar lunch 75p–£3 Dinner £8.25 Wine £4.50 Last dinner 9pm

★★♣**Pine Trees** Strathview Ter ☎(0796) 2121 Plan **15** *B4*
Closed Nov–Mar
22rm(13→4⋒) Annexe: 2rms ℞
CTV 60P 10⌂ ⛌ ✽
♡ ☐ Last dinner 9pm
Credit cards 1 2 3 5 **VS**

★★ ***Wellwood*** West Moulin Rd ☎(0796) 2879 Plan **19** *B3* Closed Nov–Mar
Privately owned hotel standing in its own grounds. Close to the town centre.
14rm CTV available in bedrooms
CTV 20P 1⌂ ✽ nc8yrs
▣International ♈ ▭ Last dinner 8pm

★**Airdaniar** 160 Atholl Rd ☎(0796) 2266 Plan **2** *B3* Closed Nov–Mar
10rm(1➡3⋔)(2fb) Ⓡ sB&B£14.75–£15.75 dB&B£23.50–£25.50 dB&B➡⋔£27.50–£29.50 B̶
CTV 14P ✽ ♪
♈ ▭ Bar lunch £2.40alc Tea £1.35alc Dinner £6.75 Wine £3.30 Last dinner 8pm
VS

★***Craig Urrard*** 10 Atholl Rd ☎(0796) 2346 Plan **9** C2
12rm(3⋔) Annexe: 2rm B̶
CTV 16P ▦ ✽
V ♈ Last dinner 7.30pm

★**Dunfallandy House** Logierait Rd (2m S unclass road) ☎(0796) 2648 Plan **11** *C1*
Converted 18th century house overlooking River Tummel.
8rm (2fb) Ⓡ sB&B£12 dB&B£20 B̶
CTV 30P 3⌂ ▦ ✽ Disco wkly Live music and dancing twice wkly Cabaret wkly
V Lunch £1.50–£3&alc Wine £3 Last dinner 9pm
Credit cards 1 2 3 5

★**Tigh-na-Cloich** Larchwood Rd ☎(0796) 2216 Plan **18** *B3* Closed Nov–Mar
14rm(2➡3⋔)(1fb) CTV in 4 bedrooms Ⓡ sB&B£11–£12.50 dB&B£22–£25 dB&B➡⋔£25–£28 B̶
CTV 10P 2⌂ ✽
♈ ▭ Bar lunch £4alc Tea 50p–80p Dinner £5–£6alc Wine £3.90 Last dinner 7.45pm

PLOCKTON
Highland *Ross & Cromarty*
Map **14** NG83

★***HL* Haven** ☎(059984) 223 Closed Nov–Mar
Comfortable and attractive family-run hotel in one of Scotland's most beautiful villages.
13rm(2➡) CTV in all bedrooms Ⓡ ✱sB&B fr£11 sB&B➡ fr£13 dB&B fr£19 dB&B➡ fr£23
CTV 8P ▦
♈ ▭ ✱Lunch fr£2.50 Tea fr70p Dinner fr£6.75 Wine £3.60 Last dinner 7.45pm

PLYMOUTH
Devon
Map **2** SX45
See plan
See also **Down Thomas**

☆☆☆☆*L* **Holiday Inn** Armada Way (Commonwealth) ☎(0752) 662866 Telex no 45637 Plan **9** *C3*
Purpose-built modern hotel with well-appointed, spacious rooms adjacent to the Hoe.
218➡ (122fb) CTV in all bedrooms sB&B➡£35 dB&B➡£44.50 B̶
Lift ☾ ## 130P CFA ▭(heated) sauna bath
▣International **V** ♈ ▭ Lunch fr£8.25&alc Tea fr70p Dinner fr£9&alc Wine £6.50 Last dinner 11pm
Credit cards 1 2 3 4 5

★★★*L* **Astor** Elliott St, The Hoe (Inter-Hotels) ☎(0752) 25511 Plan **1** *C2* Closed Xmas
Dating from the 1800s, this hotel has been modernised with well appointed rooms, catering for the commercial/tourist clientele.
58rm(54➡4⋔)(3fb) CTV in all bedrooms ✱sB&B➡⋔£27.50–£29.50 dB&B➡⋔£39.50–£42.50 Continental breakfast B̶
Lift ☾ CFA
V ♈ Lunch £4.50–£4.75&alc Dinner £6.50–£7.50&alc Wine £4.05 Last dinner 9.30pm
Credit cards 1 2 3 5 **VS**
See advert on page 518

★★★**Duke of Cornwall** Millbay Rd (Best Western) ☎(0752) 266256 Telex no 45424 Plan **4** *B3* Closed 24–27 Dec
A splendid example of Victorian Gothic architecture, the hotel is built in heavy grey stone with turrets, gables and wrought-iron balconies.
67rm(50➡17⋔)(10fb) CTV in all bedrooms Ⓡ sB&B➡⋔ fr£24 dB&B➡⋔ fr£36 B̶
Lift ☾ 60P Disco Tue–Sat Live music and dancing Sat
▣English & French ♈ ▭ ✱Lunch £4.75&alc Tea fr50p Dinner £6.75&alc Wine £4 Last dinner 9.45pm
Credit cards 1 2 3 5

☆☆☆**Mayflower Post House** Cliff Rd, The Hoe (Trusthouse Forte) ☎(0752) 662828 Telex no 45442 Plan **11** *B2*
A modern hotel in a fine position with views of The Hoe.
104➡ (79fb) CTV in all bedrooms Ⓡ sB&B➡£42 dB&B➡£55 B̶
Lift ☾ 149P CFA ✽ ⩯(heated) *xmas*
♈ ▭ Last dinner 10.30pm
Credit cards 1 2 3 4 5

☆☆☆**Novotel Plymouth** Marsh Mills Roundabout, 254 Plymouth Rd ☎(0752) 21422 Telex no 45711 Plan **14** *F4*
100➡ CTV in all bedrooms ✱sB&B➡£31.90 dB&B➡£41 B̶
Lift ☾ 140P CFA ✽ ⩯(heated) ♿
▣French **V** ♈ ▭ ✱Lunch £5–£7&alc Tea £1–£1.50 Dinner £5–£8&alc Wine £5 Last dinner 12mdnt
Credit cards 1 2 3 5 **VS**

★★★**Strathmore** Elliott St, The Hoe (Exec Hotel) ☎(0752) 662101 Plan **15** *C2*
A three-storey tourist and commercial hotel within walking distance of The Hoe and the town centre.
63rm(36➡14⋔)(5fb) CTV in 63 bedrooms Ⓡ sB&B£18 sB&B➡⋔£23 dB&B£28 dB&B➡⋔£34 B̶
Lift ☾ CTV 7P CFA Disco 3 nights wkly Live music and dancing wkly Cabaret twice wkly *xmas* →

Plymouth

1 Astor ★★★
2 Chez Nous ❀✕
3 Drake ★
4 Duke of Cornwall ★★★
5 Elfordleigh ★★
6 Green Lanterns ✕✕
7 Grosvenor ★★
8 Highlands ★★
9 Holidy Inn ☆☆☆☆
10 Khyber ✕✕
11 Mayflower Post House ☆☆☆
12 Merchantman ★
13 Merlin ★
14 Novotel Plymouth ☆☆☆
15 Strathmore ★★★

English & French **V** Lunch £4&alc Tea 60p Dinner £6.25&alc Wine £4.25 Last dinner 10pm

Credit cards 1 2 3 5

See advert on page 518

★★**Elfordleigh** Plympton (3m E off A38) ☎(0752) 336428 Plan **5** *F4*
RS Xmas

Hotel has extensive grounds, swimming pool and golf course.

18rm(2🛁7🚿)(2fb) sB&B£19.55 sB&B🛁🚿£22 dB&B£26.45 dB&B🛁🚿£32 B

CTV 50P ✽ (heated) (hard) squash billiards sauna bath

Bar lunch £3 Tea 40p Dinner £7 Last dinner 8pm **VS**

★★**Grosvenor** 9 Elliott St, The Hoe ☎(0752) 260411 Plan **7** *C3*

Georgian-style terraced house with comfortable rooms and good food, in the centre of the city.

14rm(9🛁5🚿)(1fb)Ⓡ
sB&B🛁🚿£18.17–£21.33
dB&B🛁🚿£30.70 B

P

2

French **V** Lunch £3.50–£3.80&alc Dinner £6.50–£6.80&alc Wine £4.90 Last dinner 9.45pm

Credit cards 1 3 **VS**

See advert on page 519

★★**Highlands** Dean Cross Rd, Plymstock (3m SE off A379) ☎(0752) 43643 Plan **8** *F4*

Family-run hotel with good food and pleasant staff. 3 miles from Plymouth.

9rm(4🛁2🚿)(1fb) CTV in 1 bedroom TV in all other bedrooms Ⓡ sB&B£16 sB&B🛁🚿£18.50 dB&B£22 dB&B🛁🚿£25

24P

V Lunch £5.30&alc Dinner £5.30&alc Wine £4.80 Last dinner 9pm **VS**

★**Drake** 1 Windsor Villas, Lockyer St, The Hoe ☎(0752) 29730 Plan **3** *C3*
Closed Xmas & New Year

Soundly-appointed hotel offering personal service by the resident owner, situated within walking distance of The Hoe. →

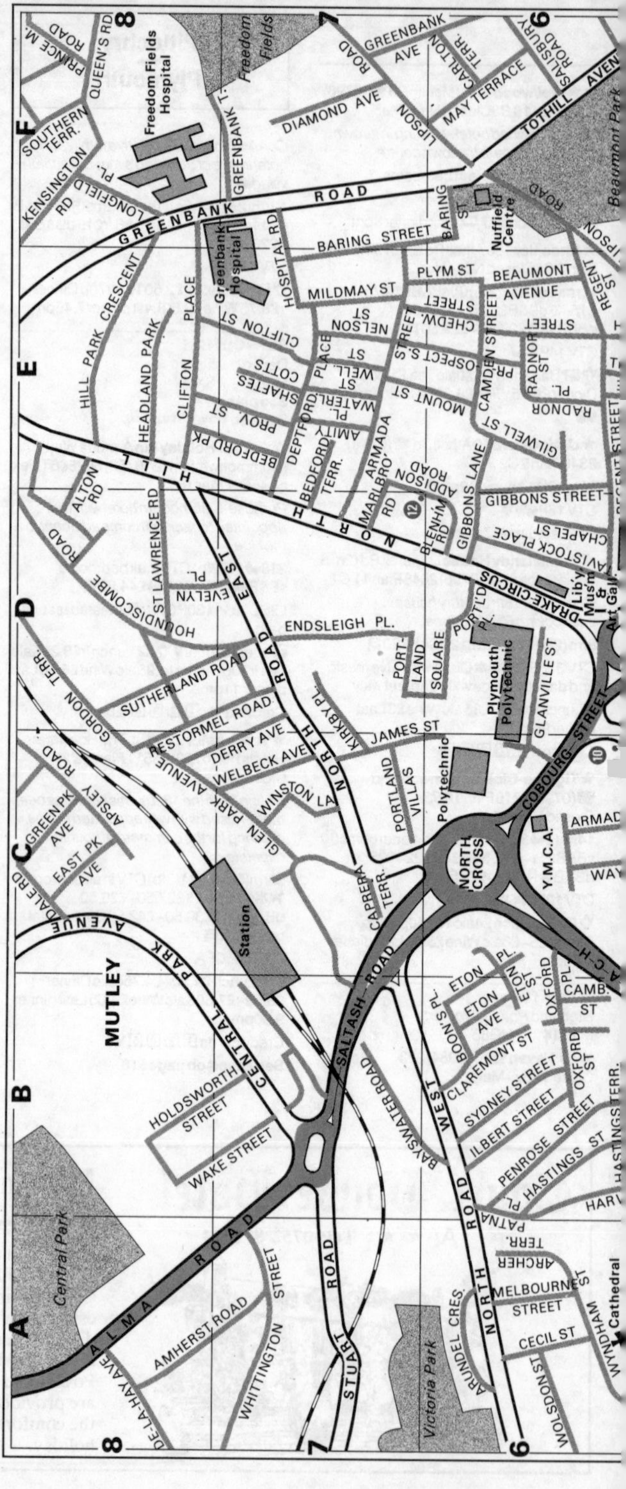

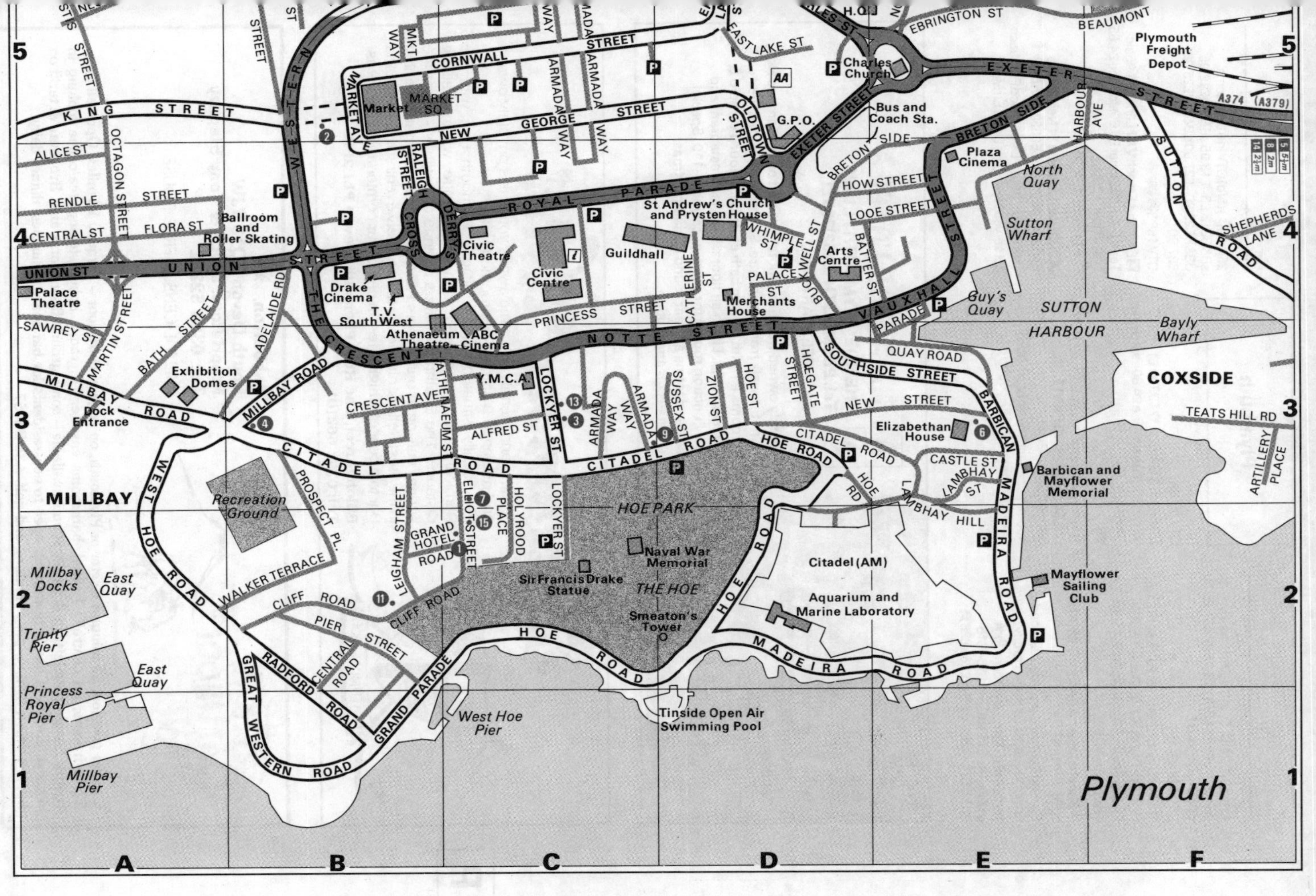

Plymouth
Plymouth Freight Depot
A374
(A379)
5 5½m
8 2m
14 2¼m
COXSIDE
SUTTON HARBOUR
Bayly Wharf
Sutton Wharf
North Quay
Guy's Quay
TEATS HILL RD
ARTILLERY PLACE
SUTTON ROAD
SHEPHERDS LANE
HARBOUR AVE
BEAUMONT
EXETER STREET
BRETON SIDE
EBRINGTON ST
Plaza Cinema
Bus and Coach Sta.
Charles Church
G.P.O.
AA
EAST LAKE ST
OLDTOWN STREET
HOW STREET
LOOE STREET
BATTER ST.
Arts Centre
BUCKWELL ST
WHIMPLE ST
PALACE ST
Merchants House
VAUXHALL STREET
PARADE
QUAY ROAD
SOUTHSIDE STREET
BARBICAN
Barbican and Mayflower Memorial
NEW STREET
Elizabethan House
CASTLE ST
LAMBHAY ST
LAMBHAY HILL
MADEIRA ROAD
Mayflower Sailing Club
Citadel (AM)
Aquarium and Marine Laboratory
CITADEL ROAD
HOE RD
HOE ROAD
HOEGATE STREET
HOE ST
ZION ST
SUSSEX ST
ARMADA WAY
St Andrew's Church and Prysten House
ROYAL PARADE
CATHERINE ST
NOTTE STREET
Guildhall
PRINCESS STREET
Civic Centre
Civic Theatre
HOE PARK
THE HOE
Naval War Memorial
Smeaton's Tower
Tinside Open Air Swimming Pool
Sir Francis Drake Statue
LOCKYER ST
HOLYROOD PLACE
ELLIOT STREET
GRAND HOTEL ROAD
ATHENAEUM ST
Athenaeum Theatre
ABC Cinema
Y.M.C.A.
ALFRED ST
CRESCENT AVE
LEIGHAM STREET
CLIFF ROAD
West Hoe Pier
GRAND PARADE
PIER STREET
CENTRAL ROAD
RADFORD ROAD
GREAT WESTERN ROAD
WALKER TERRACE
PROSPECT PL.
Recreation Ground
WEST HOE ROAD
CORNWALL STREET
ARMADA WAY
NEW GEORGE STREET
MARKET SQ.
Market
MARKET AVE
MKT WAY
RALEIGH STREET
DERRY'S CROSS
Drake Cinema
T.V. South West
THE CRESCENT
MILLBAY ROAD
ADELAIDE RD
Exhibition Domes
BATH STREET
Ballroom and Roller Skating
UNION STREET
WESTERN APPROACH
KING STREET
OCTAGON STREET
FLORA ST
CENTRAL ST
RENDLE STREET
ALICE ST
UNION ST
Palace Theatre
SAWREY ST
MARTIN STREET
Dock Entrance
MILLBAY
Millbay Docks
East Quay
Trinity Pier
Princess Royal Pier
Millbay Pier
A
B
C
D
E
F
1
2
3
4
5

16rm(3⫛)(4fb) TV in 3 bedrooms sB&B£14.95 sB&B⫛£16.95 dB&B£25.30 dB&B⫛£27.30 B

CTV 12P

Lunch £3.80–£5.20 Tea £1–£1.50 High Tea £1.50–£2.50 Dinner £5.20–£9.50 Wine £4.20 Last dinner 9.15pm

Credit cards 1 3

★**Merchantman** Addison Rd ☎(0752) 669870 Plan **12** *D7*

Formed from two converted terraced houses situated ½m from the city centre.

14rm(4⫛) CTV in 1 bedroom ® sB&B£14–£16 sB&B⫛£16–£18 dB&B£24–£26 dB&B⫛£26–£28 B

CTV 5P

English & German Tea £1–£2 Dinner £5–£9&alc Wine £4.80 Last dinner 10pm

VS

★**Merlin** 2 Windsor Villas, Lockyer St, The Hoe ☎(0752) 28133 Plan **13** *C3*

Closed 25 Dec–2 Jan

A commercial and tourist hotel within walking distance of The Hoe and city centre.

25rm(9⫛)(5fb) CTV in 9 bedrooms sB&B£12.95–£13.95 sB&B⫛£12.95 dB&B£25.90–£27.90 dB&B⫛£25.90–£27.90

CTV 16P 3

English & French **V** Lunch £4.95alc Tea £1–£1.50 Dinner £6.60alc Wine £4.65 Last dinner 9.30pm

Credit cards 1 2 3 5

XX**Green Lanterns** 31 New St, The Barbican ☎(0752) 660852 Plan **6** *E3*

Closed Sun, 25–27 Dec & Good Fri, Lunch not served New Years Day & Etr Mon

35 seats Lunch £3.–£4 Dinner £8.50–£15&alc Wine £4.25 Last dinner 10.45pm

Credit cards 1 2 3 5

XX**Khyber** 44 Mayflower St ☎(0752) 266036 Plan **10** *C6*

Closed 25 & 26 Dec

North Indian **V** 56 seats Lunch £4.10–£4.75&alc Dinner fr£6.95&alc Wine £4.95 Last dinner 11pm

Credit cards 1 2 3 5

X**Chez Nous** 13 Frankfort Gate ☎(0752) 266793 Plan **2** *B5*

Small simple restaurant providing excellent French cuisine.

Closed Sun & Mon, 1st 10 days Feb & Sept & Public Hols

French 28 seats *Lunch fr£12&alc Dinner fr£12&alc Wine £5.80 Last dinner 10.30pm

Credit cards 1 2 3 5

POCKLINGTON
Humberside
Map **8** SE84

★★**Feathers** Market Sq (Scottish & Newcastle) ☎(07592) 3155

Traditional, three-storey coaching inn in the village.

6rm(3 1) Annexe: 6 (1fb) 1 CTV available in bedrooms Ⓡ

sB&B £16 dB&B £28

CTV 50P 6 *xmas*

V Lunch £3.95&alc Tea 50p–£1.50 High Tea £3.50 Dinner £5.75&alc Wine £3.95 Last dinner 9pm

Credit cards 1 2 3 4 5 **VS**

POLKERRIS
Cornwall
Map **2** SX05

X**Rashleigh Inn** (Rashleigh Room) ☎Par (072 681) 3991 →

P

Well-appointed dining room of the 'Inn on the Beach'.

Dinner not served Sun Lunch not served (buffet only)

French **V** 24 seats ✻ Dinner £10.72alc Wine £3.10 Last dinner 8.45pm 25P

Credit cards [1] [3] **VS**

POLMONT
Central *Stirlingshire*
Map **11** NS97

★★★**Inchyra Grange** Grange Rd (Inter-Hotels) ☎(0324) 711911 Telex no 777693

Converted mansion with modern bedroom wing.

30⇌ CTV in all bedrooms ® ✻sB&B⇌ £27.50 dB&B⇌ £38.50 B

☾ 200P ✿ Live music and dancing Sat Cabaret Sat

French **V** ✻ Lunch fr£5.50&alc Dinner fr£7.20&alc Wine £4.45 Last dinner 9.30pm

Credit cards [1] [2] [3] [5] **VS**

POLPERRO
Cornwall
Map **2** SX25

★**Claremont** ☎(0503) 72241
Closed Nov–mid Apr

Small, personal hotel in an elevated position, overlooking the picturesque village of Polperro.

11rm(4fl) sB&B fr£11 dB&B fr£22 dB&Bfl fr£25

Unlicensed CTV 16P

Lunch fr£4 Dinner fr£6.50 Last dinner 7.30pm

✕**Kitchen** Fish Na Bridge ☎(0503) 72780

An intimate, cottage style restaurant, personally run and offering good food.

Closed Mon (except Public hols) also Sun, Tue, Wed & Thu Nov–Mar Lunch served by arrangement only

English & French **V** 22 seats Lunch £4.95 Dinner £6.95 Wine £4.45 Last dinner 9.30pm

Credit cards [1] [2] [3] [5] **VS**

✕**Polmary** The Coombs ☎(0503) 72828

A small, friendly bistro style restaurant in a slate and granite building with a sun terrace.

Closed wk days Nov–19 Apr

40 seats Lunch £2.95–£3.25 Tea £1–£1.50 High Tea £1–£2.25 Dinner £6&alc Wine £2.80 Last dinner 9.30pm 5P bedrooms available

Credit cards [1] [3] [5] **VS**

PONTARGOTHI
Dyfed
Map **2** SN52

★★*H* **Cothi Bridge** (Minotel) ☎Nantgaredig (026 788) 251

A comfortable, small hotel with a convivial bar, overlooking the River Cothi.

16rm(3⇌4fl)(1fb) sB&B£16 sB&B⇌fl £19 dB&B£28 dB&B⇌fl £30 B

CTV 30P ✿ xmas

French **V** Lunch fr£3.80&alc Dinner fr£6.75&alc Wine £4 Last dinner 9.30pm

Credit cards [1] [2] [3] [5]

PONTERWYD
Dyfed
Map **6** SN78

★★**Dyffryn Castell** ☎(097 085) 237

Historic coaching house set on the A44 in the heart of the countryside.

7rm(1⇌)(2fb) ® sB&B£11.95 sB&B⇌ £12.95 dB&B£19.90 dB&B⇌ £21.90 B

CTV 50P

V Bar lunch £1.25–£5.75 Dinner £7.50alc Wine £3.45 Last dinner 9pm

VS

POOLE
Dorset
Map **4** SZ09

For additional hotels see **Bournemouth**

★★★★*H* **Hospitality Inn** The Quay (Mount Charlotte) ☎(0202) 671200 Telex no 418374

Modern hotel with comfortable rooms and attentive staff.

68rm(65⇌3fl) CTV in all bedrooms ® sB&B⇌fl £36.50 dB&B⇌fl £42 B

Lift ☾ 120P CFA Live music and dancing 5 nights wkly *xmas*

English & French **V** Lunch £4.50–£4.75&alc Dinner £7–£7.50&alc Wine £4.75 Last dinner 10pm

Credit cards [1] [2] [3] [5] **VS**

★★★**Dolphin** High St ☎(0202) 673612

Located in the new shopping complex, within walking distance of the quay and the harbour.

71rm(49⇌13fl) CTV in all bedrooms ® sB&B£18.50–£19.50 sB&B⇌fl £26–£28 dB&B£29–£31 dB&B⇌fl £34–£36 B

Lift ☾ 30P Disco nightly

English & French **V** Lunch £3.75–£6.85&alc High Tea £2.50–£3.75 Dinner £3.75–£6.85&alc Wine £3.85 Last dinner 10pm

S% Credit cards [1] [2] [3] [5]

★★★***Harbour Heights*** 73 Haven Rd, Sandbanks ☎(0202) 707272

A large modern hotel with fine harbour views.

35rm(19⇌14fl) CTV in all bedrooms ® B

Lift ☾ 80P Live music and dancing 4 nights wkly

English & French Last dinner 9.30pm

Credit cards [1] [2] [3] [5]

★★★***Mansion House*** Thames St ☎(0202) 685666 Telex no 41495
Closed Public hols RS Sun

19⇌ 1 CTV in all bedrooms B

CTV 40P nc7yrs

V

Last dinner 10pm

Credit cards [1] [2] [3] [5] **VS**

★★★**Sandbanks** Banks Rd, Sandbanks ☎(0202) 707377 Closed Nov–Mar

Family holiday hotel on the Sandbanks peninsula, with sea views to one side, and Poole harbour on the other.

120rm(82➡11⋒)(40fb) CTV in 30 bedrooms Ⓡ ★ sB&B£17–£25.50 sB&B➡⋒£18.50–£27 dB&B£34–£51 dB&B➡⋒£38–£54

Lift ☾ ⚡CTV 200P CFA ⊡(heated) ⛳ sauna bath Disco twice wkly Live music and dancing wkly ⌂

🍽International V ✿ ☕ Lunch fr£5.50 Tea fr50p Dinner fr£6.50 Wine £3 Last dinner 8.30pm

★★ ***H*** **Sea Witch** 47 Haven Rd, Canford Cliffs ☎(0202) 707697 Westbourne & Branksome plan **73** *A1*

Attractive friendly hotel with pleasant accommodation and good food.

10➡ CTV in all bedrooms Ⓡ
*sB&B➡£23.20–£27.50 dB&B➡£33.50–£40 B

30P

🍽English & French V ✿ ☕ Lunch £4.45–£4.95&alc Tea £1 Dinner £12–£15&alc Wine £4.80 Last dinner 9.45pm

Credit cards 1 2 3 4 5

✕✕ **Warehouse** The Quay ☎(0202) 677238

Converted quayside warehouse with views across the docks to Brownsea Island and Sandbanks.

Closed Sun Lunch not served Sat

🍽French 80 seats Lunch £3.25–£20&alc Dinner £3.25–£20&alc Wine £4.10 Last dinner 10pm ⚡

S% Credit cards 1 2 3 5 **VS**

✕ **Gulliver's** 292 Sandbanks Rd, Lilliput ☎(0202) 708810

Lunch not served Mon–Sat Dinner not served Sun

🍽English, French & Oriental V 32 seats Lunch £4.50 Dinner £6.50–£8.50 Wine £3.90 Last dinner 10pm 20P

Credit cards 1 3

✕ **Hidden House** 54–56 Commercial Rd, Lower Parkstone ☎(0202) 743645

Closed Mon, Lunch not served Sat, Dinner not served Sun

🍽French 60 seats *Lunch £4.95–£8.75&alc Dinner fr£8.75&alc Wine £4.25 Last dinner 10.30pm P

Credit card 5

✕ **Isabel's** 32 Station Rd, Lower Parkstone ☎(0202) 747885

Closed Sun, 25 & 26 Dec Lunch not served

🍽English & French V 56 seats *Dinner £8alc Wine £4.80 Last dinner 10.30pm ⚡

S% Credit cards 2 3 5 **VS**

POOLEWE

Highland *Ross & Cromarty*
Map **14** NG88

★★ **Pool House** ☎(044 586) 272

14rm(3➡) Ⓡ sB&B£11–£14 dB&B£22–£28 dB&B➡£27–£33 B

CTV 30P

✿ ☕ *Lunch £3.50alc Tea fr50p Dinner £7–£8 Wine £3.55 Last dinner 8.15pm

Credit card 3

POOLEY BRIDGE

Cumbria
Map **12** NY42

★★★

❀❀★★★ **SHARROW BAY HOTEL, POOLEY BRIDGE**

Sharrow Bay (1¾m S unclass road)
☎(08536) 301
Closed 5 Dec–5 Mar

Sharrow Bay country house hotel has been described by one inspector as elegant, luxurious and a haven of peace. It is all of these things and many others as well. Situated at the edge of Ullswater, with spectacular views over the lake towards the fells and beyond, it has been the pride and joy of the owners, Brian Sack and Francis Coulson, for 35 years, during which time their continued search for perfection never appears to have waned.

The bedrooms, including those in the lodge annexe and the cottage, both in the grounds, Thwaite Cottage about 4 miles away and delightful Bank House a mile away, are extremely comfortable. All are individually furnished and decorated to a very high standard with many thoughtful touches including plants, books, games, magazines, sewing kits, trouser presses and a complimentary glass of sherry on arrival. At Bank House, an old barn has been tastefully converted into a banqueting hall, complete with minstrel's gallery, stained glass windows, original beams and an ornate stone fireplace brought from Warwick Castle, as well as many other original and authentic items of furniture. Guests staying at Bank House can also enjoy breakfast in the baronial elegance of this room, although dinner is served at Sharrow Bay. The lounge and dining room in the main hotel show the same comfort and attractive soft furnishings as the bedrooms; porcelain, fresh flowers and paintings abound and the

picture window in the drawing room gives magnificent views of the lake.

Meals at Sharrow are truly memorable and Francis Coulson's culinary art is known and praised far from the shores of Ullswater. Five course luncheons and six course dinners have included many mouth watering and delectable dishes. Examples such as biscuit de poisson, beignets de fromage, selle de chevreuil Saint Hubert, filet de boeuf en croute have all been highly praised, not forgetting the famous old English syllabub. The fine wine list complements the delicious food, and regular visitors to the hotel will notice a change in both the wine list and menu covers, demonstrating yet again that the search for perfection never ends.

12rm(7➡) Annexe: 18rm(13➡2⋒) CTV in all bedrooms Ⓡ ★ sB&B£48–£49 (incl dinner) sB&B➡⋒£54–£60 (incl dinner) dB&B£80–£98 (incl dinner) dB&B➡⋒£106–£140 (incl dinner)

⚡20P 3🚗 ⚡ ✽ nc13yrs ♿

🍽English & French V ✿ ☕ Lunch fr£15.50 Tea fr£3.50 Dinner fr£20.50 Wine £4.85 Last dinner 8.45

S%

POOL-IN-WHARFEDALE

West Yorkshire
Map **8** SE24

❀✕✕✕ **Pool Court** Pool Bank
☎Arthington (0532) 842288

An elegant, friendly, comfortable Georgian house, providing cuisine of a high standard.

Closed Sun & Mon, 2wks Xmas & 1st 2wks Aug Lunch not served

🍽International 65 seats Dinner fr£10&alc Wine £5.95 Last dinner 9.15pm 65P bedrooms available

Credit cards 2 3 5

PORLOCK

Somerset
Map **3** SS84

★★ **Castle** ☎(0643) 862504

Centrally-located touring and commercial inn with busy bars and a first-floor lounge.

10rm(4➡2⋒) Ⓡ ★ sB&B£12–£13 dB&B£22–£24 dB&B➡⋒£27–£30 B

CTV 8P *xmas*

✿ Bar lunch £1–£5 Dinner £9.50alc Wine £4.50 Last dinner 9.30pm

Credit cards 1 3

★★ ***Oaks*** Doverhay ☎(0643) 862265
Closed 10 Nov–10 Feb
Charming, small, tourist hotel with fine views and standing in its own grounds.
12rm(1➡5⋒) CTV in all bedrooms ✱ ⊟
14P ⇎ ✽ nc8yrs
☐ Last dinner 8.30pm
Credit cards 1 3

★ ***Ship Inn*** High St ☎(0643) 862507
RS Nov–Mar
Attractive, well-appointed, 13th-century inn, with friendly atmosphere and good food.
11rm(5➡1⋒) Ⓡ ⊟
CTV 20P 2⌂ ✽ U
V ♡ Last dinner 8pm

PORLOCK WEIR
Somerset
Map **3** SS84

★★ ***H Cottage*** ☎Porlock (0643) 862749
Comfortable, privately owned and run holiday hotel with pleasant gardens and sea views.
6rm(4➡) TV in 6 bedrooms ⊟
3P
♡ ☐ Last dinner 8.30pm
Credit cards 1 2 3

★★ **Anchor Hotel & Ship Inn** ☎Porlock (0643) 862753
Closed Jan
A complex of converted stables and the former post office, offering differing styles of accommodation.
24rm(14➡) Annexe: 1➡(4fb) 1⊟ CTV in all bedrooms Ⓡ sB&B£16.50 sB&B➡⋒£18–£19.50 dB&B£33 dB&B➡£36–£39 ⊟
20P ✽ *xmas*
♡ Lunch £4–£5&alc Dinner £8.25–£9.25&alc Wine £3.95 Last dinner 9pm
S% Credit cards 1 2 3 4 5

PORT APPIN
Strathclyde *Argyllshire*
Map **14** NM94

★★

❀★★ **AIRDS, PORT APPIN**
☎Appin (063 173) 236
Closed mid Nov–Mar
(Rosette awarded for dinner only)
Overlooking Loch Linnhe, this unassuming and homely little hotel, once an old ferry inn dating from 1700, offers a peaceful retreat made welcoming by good hearted hospitality. The owners, Mr and Mrs Allan, together with their friendly young staff, are most kind and make sure that you enjoy your stay. Mrs Allan looks after the kitchen and provides excellent country house fare including Scottish dishes from local produce. There is also a long wine list that provides something for everyone.
The bedrooms are compact and modern but enlivened by pretty, co-ordinated soft furnishings, and thoughtful extras include bath salts and reading matter. There are two comfortable lounges (one with television) overlooking the loch, one small bar, and another larger one, where you can meet the locals over a game of darts. This is one of those hotels where sheer honest-to-goodness Scottish hospitality is always evident yet at reasonable cost. It makes an ideal base to tour this part of Scotland or to take advantage of the local amenities.

13rm(6➡3⋒)(1fb) sB&B£18 dB&B£36 dB&B➡⋒£40
30P ⇎ ✽
♡ ☐ Lunch fr£3 Tea fr75p Dinner fr£12 Wine £5 Last dinner 7.30pm
VS

PORT ASKAIG
Isle of Islay, Strathclyde *Argyllshire*
Map **10** NR46

★★ ***Port Askaig*** ☎(049 684) 245
A picturesque Highland inn beside small harbour and pier, overlooking the sound towards Jura.
9rm(2➡2⋒) Ⓡ ⊟
CTV 14P 6⌂ ⇎ ✽ nc6yrs
♡ ☐ Last dinner 8.30pm

PORT DINORWIC
Gwynedd
Map **6** SH56

✕ **Sea Horse** 20 Snowdon St ☎(0248) 670546
A small, Victorian, terrace house on a road leading to the Menai Straits.
Closed Sun, 2wks Oct, 1wk Feb Lunch not served
☐ French **V** 50 seats Dinner £9alc Wine £3.75 Last dinner 9.30pm
Credit cards 1 3

PORTELET BAY
Jersey, Channel Islands
Map **16**
★★★★**Portelet** ☎Jersey (0534) 41204 Telex no 4192039
Closed Oct–mid Apr
86 (10fb) CTV in all bedrooms sB&B£20.50–£29.50 dB&B£41–£59
☾ 120P (heated) (hard) Live music and dancing nightly Cabaret wkly mid May–Sep
English & Continental V Lunch £6&alc Tea 85p–£1.90 Dinner £8&alc Wine £3.20 Last dinner 8.45pm
Credit cards 1 2 3 4 5

PORT ELLEN
Isle of Islay Strathclyde *Argyllshire*
Map **10** NR34
★ *H* **Dower House** Kildalton (3m E A846) ☎Kildalton (049 683) 225
Small, friendly, family run hotel with good home cooking. Located beside a small bay to the east of Port Ellen.
6rm (5 1) (1fb) Ⓡ sB&B£12–£16 dB&B£22–£28
☾ CTV 12P Live music and dancing mthly
V Lunch £4–£6&alc Tea £1–£1.70&alc High Tea £4.60–£7&alc Dinner £5–£7.80&alc Wine £4.50 Last dinner 9pm

PORT GAVERNE
Cornwall
Map **2** SX08
★★ ***Headlands*** ☎Port Isaac (020 888) 260 Closed Nov–Feb
Family hotel in a commanding position overlooking the coast.
14rm (6)
CTV 40P
English & French
Last dinner 8.30pm
See advert on page 525

★★ *L* **Port Gaverne** ☎Port Isaac (020 888) 244 Closed 21 Jan–24 Feb
Well-appointed, friendly hotel nestled in a valley and next to the beach.
18rm (11) Annexe: 2 sB&B£15.50–£17.50 dB&B£31–£35 dB&B£35–£43
☾ CTV 20P 2 xmas
International V Lunch £2.55–£4.60 Dinner £7.95&alc Wine £3.65 Last dinner 9.30pm
S% Credit card 1 2 3 5 **VS**
See advert on page 524

PORTHCAWL
Mid Glamorgan
Map **3** SS87
★★**Atlantic** West Drive ☎(065 671) 5011
Popular, businessman's hotel in a seafront location, close to beaches and the golf course.
15 Annexe: 1rm (2fb) 1 CTV in all bedrooms Ⓡ *sB&B£25 dB&B£35
Lift ☾ 20P *xmas*
British & Continental V *Bar lunch £3.50alc Tea £1.20alc Dinner £6.75&alc Wine £4.50 Last dinner 9.30pm
Credit cards 1 2 3 4 5

★★**Fairways** Sea Front ☎(065 671) 2085
Traditional hotel with friendly service.
27rm (5 9) (2fb) CTV available in bedrooms sB&B£15–£16.50 sB&B£16.50–£19.50 dB&B£22.50–£27.50 dB&B£30–£33
Lift ☾ CTV 30P 2 *xmas*
International V Lunch £3.95&alc Tea 90p–£1.25 Dinner £5.95–£6.95&alc Wine £4.25 Last dinner 9.15pm
Credit cards 1 3

★★ *B* **Maid of Sker** West Rd, Nottage ☎(065 671) 2172
Closed Xmas night RS Sun eve
Small, modern hotel located conveniently for the M4 in village of Nottage.
10 CTV in all bedrooms Ⓡ *sB&B£25 dB&B£35
100P →

V🍷☕ Bar lunch £2.25–£4.15 Tea fr65p Dinner £5.50–£6.15&alc Wine £4.85 Last dinner 9.30pm

Credit cards 1 2 3 5

★**B Brentwood** 37/41 Mary St ☎(065671) 2725

Small personally run friendly hotel, with comfortable modern bedrooms.

24rm(19🛁) CTV in all bedrooms ® sB&B fr£13 sB&B🛁 fr£17 dB&B fr£26 dB&B🛁 fr£28

CTV 15P *xmas*

▣ English & Continental Lunch fr£4.95&alc Dinner fr£5.25&alc Wine £4.25 Last dinner 11pm

Credit cards 1 3

★**Rose & Crown** Nottage (2m N B4283) ☎(065671) 4850

RS Sun eve

Small comfortable inn with charming bars.

7🛁 CTV in all bedrooms ® ✱ sB&B🛁 £18 dB&B🛁 £27

CTV 20P

V🍷☕ Bar lunch 90p–£2 Tea 90p Dinner £7alc Wine £3.60 Last dinner 10pm

S% Credit cards 1 3 5

★**Seaways** 26–28 Mary St ☎(065671) 3510

12rm(2🛁4⫛)(1fb) CTV in 8 bedrooms ® ✱ sB&B£12.50 sB&B🛁⫛ £17 dB&B£20 dB&B🛁⫛ £28 B

CTV 🅿 🚗 nc5yrs

Bar lunch £1.60alc Dinner £4.50&alc Wine £3.50 Last dinner 9.30pm

Credit cards 1 2 3 5 **VS**

PORTHLEVEN
Cornwall
Map **2** SW62

★**Torre Vean Manor House** ☎Helston (03265) 62412

Closed Nov–Feb

Small, personally-run, 150-year-old hotel in the heart of this small fishing village.

7rm (2fb) sB&B£9.95 dB&B£19.90–£21.90

CTV 10P 🚗 ✽

▣ English & French 🍷 Bar lunch £2.50–£3.95&alc Dinner £5.95&alc Wine £4.25 Last dinner 9pm

PORTHMADOG
Gwynedd
Map **6** SH53

★★**Royal Sportsman** High St (Trusthouse Forte) ☎(0766) 2015

Centrally situated, two-storey, stone-fronted hotel.

21rm(5🛁)(6fb) CTV in all bedrooms ® sB&B£25.50 sB&B🛁 £33 dB&B£40.50 dB&B🛁 £46.50 B

28P

🍷☕ Last dinner 8.45pm

Credit cards 1 2 3 4 5

★★**Tyddyn Llwyn** Black Rock Rd ☎(0766) 2205

Modern hotel in rural setting.

12rm (2fb) ® ✱ *sB&B fr£14.50 dB&B fr£29 B

CTV 50P ✽ nc2yrs

▣ Welsh, English & French V🍷 *Bar lunch £1.35–£5 Dinner fr£4.50&alc Wine £4.20 Last dinner 9.30pm

Credit cards 1 3

See advert on page 526

PORT ISAAC
Cornwall
Map **2** SW98
See also **Port Gaverne** and **Trelights**

★★**Castle Rock** ☎(020888) 300

Closed Nov–Mar RS Apr

Set in an elevated position with commanding sea views, this hotel is close to the beach and the town centre.

17rm(4🛁2⫛) CTV in 5 bedrooms TV in 1 bedroom sB&B£8.60–£10.60 dB&B£17.20–£21 dB&B🛁⫛ £24–£30 B

CTV 20P 🚗 ✽

🍷☕ Bar lunch £1–£2.50 Tea 45p Dinner £6.90 Last dinner 8.15pm

Credit cards 1 5

P

PORTLAND
Dorset
Map **3** SY67
☆☆☆**Portland Heights** Yeates Corner (Best Western) ☎(0305) 821361 Telex no 418493
Modern style hotel with good amenities overlooking Chesil Beach.
33rm(31 2) CTV in all bedrooms ®
sB&B £27.60–£29
dB&B £37.60–£39
☾ 100P CFA (heated) sauna bath
 Lunch £6.50alc Tea 75p–£2.50 Dinner £8.50alc Wine £4.30 Last dinner 9.45pm
Credit cards 1 2 3 5 VS

★★***Pennsylvania Castle*** Pennsylvania Rd ☎(0305) 820561
An 18th-century mock castle standing in grounds overlooking the sea.
13rm(6 6) 1 CTV in all bedrooms ®

Lift ☾ 100P
 French V Last dinner 10pm
Credit cards 1 2 3 5

PORTLOE
Cornwall
Map **2** SW93
★★***HB* Lugger** (Inter-Hotels) ☎Truro (0872) 501322
Closed early Nov–mid Mar
A charming old inn on harbour edge with small, delightful bedrooms and a large rear annexe of modern bedrooms.
21rm(15 6) (1fb) ®
sB&B £18–£22 dB&B £36–£44

CTV 20P sauna bath nc12yrs →

P

English & Continental Bar lunch £3.50alc Dinner £9 Wine £3.95 Last dinner 9pm

Credit cards 1 2 3 5 VS

PORTMAHOMACK
Highland *Ross & Cromarty*
Map **14** NH98

★★**Caledonian** ☎(086287) 345

A friendly, family run commercial/tourist hotel situated close to the shore overlooking the Dornoch Firth.

16 (3fb) TV in 16 bedrooms Ⓡ sB&B £12–£18 dB&B £22–£28

CTV 25P Disco wkly Live music and dancing twice wkly *xmas*

Scottish, English & French V Lunch £9alc Tea 50p–£1.20 Dinner fr£7&alc Wine £4.20 Last dinner 9pm

Credit cards 1 2 3

PORTPATRICK
Dumfries & Galloway *Wigtownshire*
Map **10** NX05

★★

★★ KNOCKINAAM LODGE, PORT PATRICK

(2m S on unclass road) ☎(077 681) 471

Closed early Jan–mid Mar

Approached down a long drive, this charming little hotel is situated at the edge of a small cove with lawns running down to the sea, one of which is laid out for croquet. It is situated about as far south as you can go on Scotland's west coast, and was built as a holiday home in 1869. Many of the original structural features are retained inside including a nice oak panelled bar and several fireplaces. There are two sitting rooms, one with television, and the morning room together with the dining room have views over the sea. There are lots of fresh flowers which combine with the summery décor in the public rooms and the attractively furnished bedrooms to create a very fresh atmosphere. There are also many decent pieces of furniture in the house.

The dining room is candle lit during the evening and, with its good appointments, makes a fitting background to the excellent food that earns our rosette. The style is mostly country house cooking with fashionably modern touches. A four course dinner with coffee is served

but there is also a small à la carte menu.

Mr and Mrs Pilkington are the owners who have created this delightful hotel and have clearly inspired their staff by example to give the friendly and hospitable service that our members comment on so favourably. With traditional services and its delightful setting it is ideal for a restful holiday or as a base for touring this relatively unappreciated part of Scotland.

11rm(7 1) sB&B £22.50 dB&B £32.20 dB&B fr£51

CTV 50P *xmas*

British & French V Bar lunch fr£3.50 Tea £1 Dinner £13.50&alc Wine £5.95 Last dinner 9pm

Credit cards 2 3

★★★**Fernhill** ☎(077 681) 220

Closed Nov–Feb

11rm(7) Annexe: 4rm(1 3) (3fb) TV in 15 bedrooms Ⓡ sB&B £15.50–£16.50 sB&B £24–£25 dB&B £29–£31 dB&B £31–£36

CTV 40P

French V Lunch £4.95 Tea fr80p Dinner fr£8.50&alc Wine £2.50 Last dinner 9.30pm

Credit cards 1 3

★★**Braefield House** Braefield Rd ☎(077 681) 255

Closed Nov–Mar

Small hotel standing in its own grounds and overlooking the village harbour and North Channel.

7rm(3) (1fb) sB&B £11.50–£13 dB&B £22–£25 dB&B £24–£27

CTV 18P

V Bar lunch £2.75–£3.50 Dinner £7.50alc Wine £3.75 Last dinner 8pm

★★**Portpatrick** (Mount Charlotte) ☎(077 681) 333

Closed Oct–Apr

Large cliff top resort hotel with good amenities for families with children.

60rm(26 1) sB&B £18.50–£19 sB&B £20–£21 dB&B £28–£30 dB&B £30–£32

Lift CTV 100P CFA (heated) (grass) billiards Live music and dancing twice wkly

V Lunch £4.75–£5 Dinner £6.50–£7&alc Wine £5 Last dinner 9pm

Credit cards 1 2 3 5

★**Mount Stewart** South Cres ☎(077 681) 291

Closed Feb & Nov

Two-storey stone house set on a hillside overlooking the harbour.

8rm(1) (5fb) Ⓡ sB&B £12.50–£14 dB&B £25–£28 dB&B £29–£32

CTV 20P

Bar lunch £3.50–£6.50 Tea £1.25–£1.75 High Tea £3.50–£5.50 Dinner £7.50–£10.50 Wine £4.05 Last dinner 9pm

P

PORTREE
Isle of Skye, Highland *Inverness-shire*
Map **13** NG44

★★★**Coolin Hills** ☎(0478) 2003
Converted shooting lodge with fine views over Portree Bay.
18rm(11➡2⋔) Annexe: 10rm(4➡) (5fb) Ⓡ sB&B£13.50–£18 sB&B➡⋔£16–£20 dB&B£26–£30 dB&B➡⋔£32–£36
CTV 100P ✽ billiards ♿
V ♆ ☕ Lunch fr£3.50 Tea fr50p Dinner fr£7 Wine £4.10 Last dinner 8pm
Credit card 1

★★**Rosedale** ☎(0478) 2531
Closed early Oct–mid May
18rm(9➡7⋔) Annexe: 3➡ (2fb) Ⓡ sB&B£13–£14.50 sB&B➡⋔£15.50–£17 dB&B£25–£26 dB&B➡⋔£30–£33
CTV 15P
♆ ☕ Bar lunch £1–£3 Dinner £8–£8.50 Wine £4 Last dinner 8pm
VS

★★**Royal** ☎(0478) 2525
A well-appointed hotel in a central location overlooking the harbour.
28rm(17➡⋔) (2fb) sB&B£12–£17 dB&B£23–£30 dB&B➡⋔£27–£36
☾ CTV 20P 8🏠
♆ ☕ ✽ Lunch £4–£4.50&alc Tea £1.20&alc High Tea £4.50–£5.50&alc Dinner £6.50–£8&alc Wine £3.50 Last dinner 8.30pm

★**Isles** Somerled Sq ☎(0478) 2129
Closed Nov–Apr
A well appointed, small, family run hotel in central location near shops.
10rm (1fb) sB&B£10.75–£11.50 dB&B£21.50–£23 B
CTV
V Lunch £4.15alc Dinner £8alc Wine £4.75 Last dinner 8.30pm

★**King's Haven** Bosville Ter ☎(0478) 2290 Closed Nov–Mar
Comfortable, small hotel with friendly hospitality, an attractive dining room with log burning stove and good food.
7rm(1➡4⋔) Ⓡ
CTV 🚗 ✽
V ♆ ☕ Last dinner 9pm
Credit cards 1 3

PORTSCATHO
Cornwall
Map **2** SW83

★★★**Rosevine** Porthcurnick Beach ☎(087 258) 206
Closed Nov–23 Dec & 3 Jan–Mar
Comfortably appointed country hotel in secluded setting with good views over the sea.
16rm(10➡1⋔) (1fb) CTV & TV available in bedrooms ✽ sB&B£15–£17 sB&B➡⋔£16.50–£18.50 dB&B£30–£34 dB&B➡⋔£33–£37
☾ CTV 40P 🚗 ✽ *xmas*
English & French **V** ♆ ☕ Lunch fr£2 Tea fr50p Dinner £9&alc Wine £3.80 Last dinner 8.45pm
Credit cards 1 3 5 **VS**

★★*HL* **Gerrans Bay** Gerrans ☎(087 258) 338 Closed mid Oct–19 Apr
Small hotel located in the heart of the Roseland Peninsula with rural and coastal views.
15rm(11➡) (2fb) Ⓡ sB&B£13.50–£14.50 sB&B➡£14.50–£15.50 dB&B£26–£28 dB&B➡£28–£30
CTV 16P 🚗
♆ ☕ Lunch £2.75–£3.25&alc Tea 60p Dinner £6.50&alc Wine £4 Last dinner 8.30pm
Credit cards 1 2 3 **VS**

★★**Roseland House** Rosevine ☎(087 258) 644
Closed Dec & Jan
Small, comfortable, friendly hotel in a commanding position with unrestricted views.
20rm(7➡) Annexe: 5rm (3fb) 1 🛏 sB&B£14–£20 (incl dinner) sB&B➡£14–£20 (incl dinner) dB&B£24–£40 (incl dinner) dB&B➡⋔£28–£40 (incl dinner) B
CTV 25P 3🏠 🚗 ✽

V ♆ ☕ Bar lunch £1alc Tea £1alc Dinner £7alc Wine £3 Last dinner 7.30pm
VS

PORTSMOUTH AND SOUTHSEA
Hampshire
Map **4** SZ69

☆☆☆☆*BL* **Holiday Inn** North Harbour (Commonwealth) ☎(0705) 383151 Telex no 86611
Very comfortable hotel with excellent leisure facilities.
170➡⋔ (76fb) CTV in all bedrooms sB&B➡⋔£50–£52 dB&B➡£65–£70 B
Lift # 200P CFA (heated) squash sauna bath Disco 4 nights wkly Live music and dancing twice wkly *xmas* ♿
French **V** ♆ ☕ Lunch £10.50–£12.50 Dinner £8.50–£9.50&alc Wine £6.25 Last dinner 11pm
Credit cards 1 2 3 4 5

☆☆☆**Crest** Pembroke Rd, Southsea (Crest) ☎(0705) 827651 Telex no 86397
RS Xmas
Modern hotel, well decorated and furnished.
170➡ CTV in all bedrooms Ⓡ ✽ sB➡ fr£35 dB➡ fr£42 (room only) B
Lift ☾ 125P CFA Live music and dancing Wed, Fri & Sat ♿
International **V** ♆ ☕ ✽ Lunch fr£4 Dinner fr£8.25&alc Wine £5.25 Last dinner 9.45pm
Credit cards 1 2 3 4 5 **VS**

★★★**Pendragon** Clarence Pde, Southsea (Trusthouse Forte) ☎(0705) 823201 Telex no 86376
Overlooking Southsea Common, this is a traditional hotel with many modern facilities.
58rm(37➡) CTV in all bedrooms Ⓡ sB&B£30 sB&B➡£33.50 dB&B£42 dB&B➡£49 B
Lift ☾ CFA 8🏠 *xmas*
♆ ☕ Last dinner 9pm
Credit cards 1 2 3 4 5

★★★**Royal Beach** South Pde, Southsea (Mount Charlotte) ☎(0705) 731281 Telex no 86719 →

P

111➡CTV in all bedrooms sB&B➡£28.50 dB&B➡£37 B

Lift ☾ CTV 40P CFA

▣English & French V♧☐ Lunch £5.50–£6&alc Dinner £6.50–£7&alc Wine £4.50 Last dinner 9.45pm

Credit cards 1 2 3 5 **VS**

★★**Berkeley** South Pde, Southsea ☎(0705) 735059
Closed mid Oct–mid Apr

Family run sea front hotel in Regency style building.

44rm(20➡)(3fb) CTV available in bedrooms ® sB&B£16–£22 sB&B➡£18–£25 dB&B£30–£40 dB&B➡£34–£46

Lift CTV 3P 6🚗

V♧☐ Lunch £6.50–£7.50 Tea 60p–£1.20 Dinner £8–£10 Wine £3.20 Last dinner 8pm

Credit cards 1 3

★★**Keppels Head** The Hard (Anchor) ☎(0705) 821954 Telex no 858875

Victorian hotel with modern well equipped bedrooms.

25rm(17➡8⋒)(6fb) CTV in all bedrooms ®✱sB&B➡⋒£35 dB&B➡⋒£46 B

Lift ☾ 20P *xmas*

V♧☐ Lunch £7.50–£10.50&alc Tea 75p Dinner £7.50–£10.50&alc Wine £4.95 Last dinner 10pm

Credit cards 1 2 3 4 5

★★**Ocean** St Helens Pde, Southsea ☎(0705) 734233
Closed 24–31 Dec

Large, seafront hotel with a family atmosphere.

50rm(7➡)(4fb) CTV in all bedrooms ® sB&B£18.75 sB&B➡£20.75 dB&B£31.95 dB&B➡£33.95

Lift CTV 20P 🚗 squash billiards sauna bath

▣Mainly grills V♧ Bar lunch £1.40–£3.50 Dinner £6&alc Wine £3.75 Last dinner 10pm

Credit card 3 **VS**

PORTSONACHAN

Strathclyde *Argyllshire*
Map **10** NN01

★★***Portsonachan*** (Minotel) ☎Killchrenan (08663) 224

On the banks of picturesque Loch Awe, the hotel is popular for fishing providing simple but comfortable accommodation.

19rm(3➡) ® B

CTV 20P 🚗✽ ⸙

V♧☐ Last dinner 9pm

Credit cards 1 3

PORT TALBOT

West Glamorgan
Map **3** SS79

★★★**Aberafon** Aberafon Seafront ☎(0639) 884949 Telex no 48222

Comfortable modern hotel overlooking beach.

72➡⋒ (6fb) CTV in all bedrooms ® ✱sB&B➡⋒£25.50 dB&B➡⋒£31 B

Lift ☾ ## 150P CFA ✽ Disco Thu & Sun Live music and dancing Fri & Sat Cabaret Sat *xmas*

▣French & Italian V♧☐✱ Lunch £1.75–£2.50&alc Tea fr£1 Dinner fr£6.55&alc Wine £4.95 Last dinner 11pm

Credit cards 1 2 3 5

★★★**Ladbroke Twelve Knights** Margam Rd, Margam (2m SE A48) (Ladbroke) ☎(0639) 882381

Small business hotel with good bedrooms.

11⋒ (1fb) CTV in all bedrooms ® sB&B⋒£15–£30 dB&B⋒£22–£42 B

200P *xmas*

▣International V♧☐ Lunch £5.45alc Dinner £5.95alc Wine £3.75 Last dinner 10.30pm

Credit cards 1 2 3 5

PORT WILLIAM

Dumfries & Galloway *Wigtownshire*
Map **10** NX34

P

★★★BL **Corsemalzie House** (ExecHotel) ☎Mochrum (098 886) 254
Country house hotel in extensive grounds.
15rm(10→5⋒) (1fb) CTV in all bedrooms ® sB&B→⋒£19–£23 dB&B→⋒£34–£39 B
30P 2 ✽ xmas
Scottish & French V Lunch £6 Tea 90p–£1.75 Dinner £8.75&alc Wine £4.10 Last dinner 9.15pm
Credit cards 1 2 3 VS

★★**Monrieth Arms** ☎(09887) 232
Traditional homely, family run hotel.
13rm(1→) sB&B£11.30 dB&B£22.60 dB&B→£24.10
CTV 6P 3
Lunch fr£4 Tea fr£1.25 Dinner fr£6 Wine £4 Last dinner 8pm

POTARCH

Grampian *Aberdeenshire*
Map **15** NO69

★***Potarch*** ☎Kincardine O'Neil (033984) 339
Closed Jan RS Nov–Dec
7rm(3→) ®
CTV 30P 2 ✽
Last dinner 8.30pm

POUNDISFORD

Somerset
Map **3** ST22

✕✕***Well House*** ☎Blagdon Hill (082342) 566
Closed Mon Lunch not served wk dys in winter Dinner not served Sun
English & Continental 40 seats Last dinner 9.15pm 20P
Credit cards 1 5

POWFOOT

Dumfries & Galloway *Dumfriesshire*
Map **11** NY16

★★**Powfoot Golf** Links Av ☎Cummertrees (04617) 254
20rm(7→) (1fb) ® sB&B fr£11.50 sB&B→fr£17 dB&B fr£23 dB&B→fr£29 B
CTV 40P xmas
Bar lunch £2.50alc Tea 90p High Tea £5 Dinner £6.50–£8 Wine £4.20 Last dinner 9pm
Credit cards 1 2 3 VS

PRAA SANDS

Cornwall
Map **2** SW52

★★**Prah Sands** ☎Germoe (073676) 2438
Closed Oct–19 Apr
Family hotel positioned at the water's edge.
22rm(9→) (6fb) sB&B£12.50–£15.50 sB&B→£14–£17 dB&B£24–£30 dB&B→£27–£33 B
CTV 30P (hard)
Lunch £3.80–£4.20 Tea 50p–90p Dinner £6.50–£7 Wine £3.90 Last dinner 8pm
Credit card 1 VS

PRESTBURY

Cheshire
Map **7** SJ97

✕✕✕**Bridge** ☎(0625) 829326
Formal but friendly restaurant, with a spacious lounge bar and situated between the River Bollin and the church.
Closed Sun
English & French 90 seats Lunch £4.50–£5.10&alc Dinner £7.50–£8.20&alc Wine £5.95 Last dinner 9.45pm 30P bedrooms available Live music Tue–Sat
Credit cards 1 2 3 5

✕✕✕**Legh Arms** ☎(0625) 829130
Smart, attractive restaurant with adjoining bars, dating from the 15th century and situated in the village centre.
English & French V 150 seats Lunch £5.25–£6.50&alc Dinner £9.50–£10.50&alc Wine £5 Last dinner 10pm 40P
S% Credit cards 1 2 3 5

✕✕***White House*** ☎(0625) 829376
Closed Mon Dinner not served Sun
English & French 75 seats Last dinner 10.15pm 25P Disco Wed, Fri & Sat
Credit cards 1 2 3 5

PRESTEIGNE

Powys
Map **3** SO36

★★L **Radnorshire Arms** High St (Trusthouse Forte) ☎(0544) 267406
Attractive, half-timbered coaching house with an annexe providing more modern accommodation.
6→ Annexe: 10→ (2fb) CTV in all bedrooms ® sB&B→£35.50 dB&B→£49.50 B
CTV 20P 6 ✽ xmas
Last dinner 8.15pm
Credit cards 1 2 3 4 5

PRESTON

Lancashire
Map **7** SD52
See also Bartle and Barton

★★★**Broughton Park House** Garstang Rd, Broughton (3m N on A6) ☎(0772) 864087
Elegant Edwardian country house with most bedrooms in modern extension. Also extensive leisure complex.
65rm(59→6⋒) (5fb) 1 CTV in all bedrooms ® ✱ sB&B→⋒£30 dB&B→⋒£40 B
☾ # 220P ✽ (heated) sauna bath
V Lunch £4.50&alc Tea fr45p High Tea £2 Dinner £6.50&alc Last dinner 10pm
Credit cards 1 2 3 4 5

☆☆☆**Crest** The Ringway (Crest) ☎(0772) 59411 Telex no 677147
RS Xmas
132→ CTV in all bedrooms ® ✱ sB→ fr£33 dB→ fr£42 (room only) B
Lift ☾ 30P CFA
International V ✱ Lunch fr£4 Tea 55p Dinner fr£8.50&alc Wine £4.95 Last dinner 9.45pm
Credit cards 1 2 3 4 5 VS

P

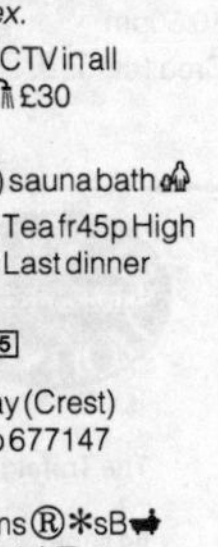

☆☆☆**Tickled Trout** Preston New Rd, Samlesbury (Junc 31 M6/A59) ☎Samlesbury (077 477) 671 Telex no 677625
Large, modern hotel on the banks of the River Ribble at the junction of the M6 and the A59.
66➡ CTV in all bedrooms Ⓡ
*sB&B➡£19–£31 dB&B➡£28.50–£40 ₿
☾ 160P 12🏠 CFA ♪ Disco twice wkly
▣International ♔ ☕ Lunch fr£6&alc Tea £2–£3 High Tea £2–£3 Dinner £7–£9alc Last dinner 10.15pm
Credit cards 1 2 3 5
See advert on page 529

☆☆☆**Trafalgar** Preston New Rd, Samlesbury (junc A59/A677) ☎Samlesbury (077 477) 351 Telex no 677362
Modern hotel and conference centre, situated at the junction of the A59 and the A677, 1 mile from junction 31 of the M6.
54➡⋒ CTV in all bedrooms Ⓡ
sB➡⋒ £33.30 dB➡⋒ £47.60 (room only) ₿
Lift ☾ ## 300P CFA ▭ (heated) squash *xmas*
▣French **V** ♔ ☕ Lunch £6alc Tea 50palc Dinner £8alc Wine £4.70 Last dinner 10.30pm
Credit cards 1 2 3 4 5

✕**French Bistro** Miller Arcade, Church St ☎(0772) 53882
Lunch not served Sun
▣French **V** 34 seats Lunch fr£2.50&alc Dinner £5–£6.50&alc Wine £3.75 Last dinner 12.15am ₽
Credit cards 1 2 3 5 **VS**

At **Leyland** (6m S junc 28/M6)
☆☆☆☆**Ladbroke** (& Conference centre), Leyland Way (Ladbroke) ☎Leyland (07744) 22922
93➡⋒ 156P

PRESTWICK

Strathclyde *Ayrshire*
Map **10** NS32

☆☆**Carlton Motor** ☎(0292) 76811
Modern, low-rise hotel in its own grounds, standing on the main road.
34➡ (2fb) CTV in all bedrooms Ⓡ
sB&B➡£21 dB&B➡£36 ₿
☾ ## CTV 150P ✽ Live music and dancing twice wkly *xmas*
▣European **V** ♔ ☕ Lunch £3.75 Tea £1.25 High Tea £3.75–£6 Dinner £7.25&alc Wine £3.75 Last dinner 9.30pm
Credit cards 1 2 3 4 5

★★**Links** Links Rd ☎(0292) 77792
Traditional, seaside hotel overlooking Prestwick Championship golf course.
13rm(5➡) (1fb) CTV in all bedrooms Ⓡ
CTV 100P ##
♔ Wine £3.50 Last dinner 8.30pm
S%

★★**Parkstone** Esplanade ☎(0292) 77286
Detached building situated on the Esplanade, looking out to the Isle of Arran.
30rm(3➡11⋒) (2fb) CTV in 27 bedrooms Ⓡ ✱ sB&B fr£15.85 sB&B➡⋒ fr£17.85 dB&B fr£26.65 dB&B➡⋒ fr£29.65
CTV 60P
V ♔ ☕ Lunch fr£4.85 Tea fr£1.75 High Tea fr£3.40 Dinner fr£6.95 Wine £3.95 Last dinner 8.30pm
Credit card 2

★★**Queen's** Esplanade ☎(0292) 70501
28rm(8➡4⋒) (2fb) sB&B £14.50–£15.50 sB&B➡⋒ £16–£17 dB&B £29–£31 dB&B➡⋒ £32–£34 ₿
☾ CTV 10P Live music and dancing Sat Cabaret Sat 🏠 *xmas*
▣French & Italian **V** ♔ ☕ Lunch £4.50–£6 Tea £1.50–£2.75 High Tea £3–£6.50 Dinner £7.50–£15 Wine £3.30 Last dinner 7pm
Credit cards 1 2 3 5

★★**St Nicholas** 41 Ayr Rd ☎(0292) 79568
13rm(4⋔)(4fb)Ⓡ★sB&B fr£13 dB&B fr£24 dB&B⋔ fr£26
CTV 50P billiards
V Bar lunch £1.90–£2.50 High Tea £2.60–£4.80 Dinner £6.50–£8 Wine £3 Last dinner 9pm
S% Credit cards 1 3 5

★**Auchencoyle** 13 Links Rd ☎(0292) 78316
6rm(3⋔)(3fb)Ⓡ sB&B£8.75–£9 sB&B⋔£10.25–£10.50 dB&B£17.50–£18 dB&B⋔£20.50–£21
CTV 20P
Lunch £2.25–£3.50&alc Tea £1–£1.50&alc High Tea £1.50–£6.50&alc Dinner £4.50–£7.50&alc Wine £4 Last dinner 8.45pm

★***Golden Eagle*** 132 Main St ☎(0292) 77566
6rm TV available in bedrooms
CTV 75P 2 Disco twice wkly Live music Sun Cabaret mthly
Mainly grills V Last dinner 7.30pm

★**North Beach** Links Rd ☎(0292) 79069
Closed 30 Dec–2 Jan
Small hotel standing near the beach opposite the golf course.
9rm(1fb)Ⓡ sB&B£9.50–£10 dB&B£18 B
CTV 14P Disco twice wkly Live music and dancing twice wkly
Lunch £2.30–£3.30&alc Tea 50p–75p High Tea £2.50–£6&alc Dinner £5.50–£6&alc Wine £3.20 Last dinner 7.30pm
VS

PRINCETHORPE
Warwickshire
Map **4** SP37

★★**Woodhouse** ☎Marton (0926) 632303
Closed 25 & 26 Dec
Converted country house in a quiet setting, offering a variety of sporting facilities.
8rm(4⇌1⋔) Annexe: 14rm TV in all bedrooms Ⓡ*sB&B£16.50 sB&B⇌⋔£24.50 dB&B£29 dB&B⇌⋔£37 B
100P✽ (heated) (hard) Disco Sat
French & Swiss V *Lunch £5.95–£8.25&alc Tea fr50p High Tea fr£2.50 Dinner £5.95–£8.25&alc Wine £4.95 Last dinner 10.30pm
Credit cards 1 2 5

PRIORS HARDWICK
Warwickshire
Map **4** SP45

✕✕**Butchers Arms** ☎Byfield (0327) 60504
Lunch not served Sat Dinner not served Sun
100 seats Lunch £5.50&alc Dinner £15alc Wine £4.05 Last dinner 9.30pm 100P
S%

PUDDINGTON
Cheshire
Map **7** SJ37

✕✕✕***Craxton Wood*** Parkgate Rd, Ledsham (on A540 junc A550)
☎051-339 4717
Charming country house with elegant, attractive restaurant.
Closed Sun, Public hols & last 2 wks Aug
French 85 seats Last dinner 10pm 60P bedrooms available
Credit cards 1 2 3 5

PUDSEY
West Yorkshire
Map **8** SE23

✕**Tiberio** 68 Galloway Ln ☎Bradford (0274) 665895
Closed Mon & 1st wk Jan Lunch not served Sat
Continental 50 seats *Lunch £3.55–£9.15&alc Dinner £5–£11&alc Wine £4.75 Last dinner 11pm 30P
Credit cards 1 2 3

PULBOROUGH
West Sussex
Map **4** TQ01

★**Chequers** Church Pl (Minotel) ☎(07982) 2486
Friendly family country hotel overlooking Arun valley.
9rm(6⇌1⋔)(1fb) sB&B£13.75 sB&B⇌⋔£14.75 dB&B£25 dB&B⇌⋔£26.50 B
CTV 10P ✽ *xmas*
Lunch £4.50 Tea 50p–£2.50 High Tea £1.50–£3.50 Dinner £7.50 Wine £3.95 Last dinner 8.30pm
Credit cards 1 2 3 5 **VS**

✕**Stane Street Hollow** Codmore Hill ☎(07982) 2819
Small, intimate restaurant, with good food.
Closed Sun, Mon, Xmas–New Year 3 wks May & 2 wks end Oct Lunch not served Tue & Sat
French & Swiss 38 seats Lunch £4.90–£5.20&alc Dinner £11.50alc Wine £5.65 Last dinner 9.15pm 16P

PUTSBOROUGH
Devon
Map **2** SS44

★★★*H* **Putsborough Sands** ☎Croyde (0271) 890555
Closed Oct–Etr
Purpose-built, comfortable, holiday hotel, family owned and run in a fine coastal situation.
61rm(30⇌2⋔)(16fb)★sB&B£12–£20 sB&B⇌⋔£15–£23 dB&B£24–£40 dB&B⇌⋔£30–£46 B
CTV 40P (heated) squash sauna bath Disco twice wkly Live music and dancing twice wkly
International Bar lunch £3.10 Tea 50p Dinner £8.75 Wine £3.95 Last dinner 8.30pm
Credit cards 1 3 **VS**

QUEENSFERRY (SOUTH)
Lothian *West Lothian*
Map **11** NT17

☆☆☆**Forth Bridges Moat House** Forth Road Bridge (Queens Moat)
☎031-331 1199 Telex no 727430
Situated close to the southern approach to the Forth Road Bridge, the hotel has splendid views over the Firth of Forth.
108⇌⋔(4fb) CTV in all bedrooms Ⓡ *sB⇌⋔£35.35 dB⇌⋔£46.20 B
200P ✽ billiards
English & French *Lunch £6.50&alc Dinner £7.25&alc Wine £4.40 Last dinner 9.45pm
Credit cards 1 2 3 4 5 **VS**

✕✕**Hawes Inn** ☎031-331 1990
Historic inn overlooking the Firth of Forth where Robert Louis Stevenson is said to have started 'Kidnapped'.
Lunch not served Sat Dinner not served Sun in winter
60 seats *Lunch fr£4.95 Dinner £10alc Wine £4.20 Last dinner 9.30pm 60P bedrooms available
S% Credit cards 1 2 3 5 **VS**

RADLETT
Hertfordshire
Map **4** TL10

★★**Red Lion (Henekey's)** Watling St (Trusthouse Forte) ☎(09276) 5341
The majority of the bedrooms here are of a good standard and there is a limited lounge but good bars.
17rm(7⇌1⋔)(1fb) CTV in all bedrooms Ⓡ sB&B£26 sB&B⇌⋔£29.50 dB&B£36.50 dB&B⇌⋔£41 B
21P
Mainly grills Last dinner 10pm
Credit cards 1 2 3 4 5

RAINHILL
Merseyside
Map **7** SJ49
See also St Helens

★**Rockland** View Rd (Minotel)
☎051-426 4603
Large Georgian house with a modern extension set in its own pleasant gardens.
10rm(2⇌) Annexe: 3⋔ TV in 8 bedrooms Ⓡ sB&B£14.50 sB&B⇌⋔£17.50 dB&B£25 dB&B⇌⋔£28 B
CTV 30P ✽
Lunch £3.50–£4 Tea 40p Dinner £6&alc Wine £3.50 Last dinner 8.15pm

R

RAMPSIDE (nr Barrow-in-Furness)
Cumbria
Map **7** SD26

★★Clarke's Arms (Whitbread West Pennines) ☎Barrow-in-Furness (0229) 20303
Closed 25 & 26 Dec
Small, country hotel set in its own grounds overlooking Morecambe Bay.
10⋒ (4fb) CTV in all bedrooms ® ✽sB&B⋒£21.50 dB&B⋒£27.50 B
50P 🚗
English & French **V** ✽Lunch £7alc Dinner £7.25&alc Wine £4.45 Last dinner 9.45pm
Credit cards 1 3

RAMSBOTTOM
Greater Manchester
Map **7** SD71

★★Old Mill Springwood ☎(070682) 2991
The waterwheel is intact in this black and white building which has modern style bedrooms.
17➡ 1 CTV in all bedrooms ® sB&B➡£25.30 dB&B➡£36.80
☾ CTV 100P ✽ Live music and dancing Sat Cabaret Thu
French **V** ✽Lunch £4&alc Dinner £6.50–£8.50&alc Wine £4.15 Last dinner 9.45pm
Credit cards 1 2 3 5

RAMSBURY
Wiltshire
Map **4** SU27

✕✕Bell The Square ☎Marlborough (0672) 20230
Closed Mon, Dinner not served Sun
French 54 seats Lunch £6.50–£10.50 Dinner £10.50 Wine £3.95 Last dinner 9.30pm 40P
Credit cards 1 2 3 5 **VS**

RAMSGATE
Kent
Map **5** TR36

★★San Clu Victoria Pde ☎Thanet (0843) 52345
Old fashioned family run hotel with reasonable accommodation.
51rm(20➡) CTV in 3 bedrooms TV in 18 bedrooms sB&B£15–£21 sB&B➡£18–£21 dB&B£24–£36 dB&B➡£30–£36 Continental breakfast B
Lift ☾ CTV 15P 1 CFA Live music and dancing wkly in summer *xmas*
English & French **V** Lunch £3–£5.95&alc Tea £1–£1.50 High Tea £5.50–£7.50 Dinner £6.50–£7.50&alc Wine £4 Last dinner 9pm
Credit cards 1 2 3

★★*H* Savoy Grange Rd ☎Thanet (0843) 52637
Closed Feb
Friendly hotel with modern bedrooms and skilful good cooking.
13rm(1➡2⋒) Annexe: 12rm(2➡11⋒) (4fb) CTV in 20 bedrooms ® sB&B£11.50–£12.50 sB&B➡⋒£17–£18 dB&B£19–£20 dB&B➡⋒£23–£26
☾ CTV 20P
English & French **V** Lunch £4–£4.75&alc Tea fr75p Dinner £7alc Wine £3.50 Last dinner 10pm
Credit cards 1 2 3 4 5

RANGEWORTHY
Avon
Map **3** ST68

★Rangeworthy Court Wooton Rd ☎(045 422) 347
Closed 24 Dec–4 Jan
This ancient Cotswold manor, which is a listed building, is beautifully furnished with antiques.
14rm(1➡7⋒) (2fb) 1 sB&B£17.75 sB&B➡⋒£20 dB&B£26.50 dB&B➡⋒£30 B
CTV 50P 🚗 ✽
English & Continental Lunch £3–£7 Tea 60p Dinner £6–£9.95 Wine £4.25 Last dinner 8.30pm
VS

RANTON
Staffordshire
Map **7** SJ82

✕✕✕Yew Tree ☎Seighford (078 575) 278
Extended, comfortable furnished farmhouse with choice of classical and some unusual dishes.
Closed Mon Dinner not served Sun
French **V** 90 seats ✽Lunch £3.60–£5.60&alc Dinner £10alc Wine £4.60 Last dinner 9pm 25P
Credit cards 1 2 3 5

RATHO
Lothian *Midlothian*
Map **11** NT17

✕Bridge Inn ☎031-333 1320
Compact, friendly restaurant alongside Union Canal.
Dinner not served Sun
Scottish, English & French **V** 60 seats ✽Lunch £2.50–£5&alc Dinner £9alc Wine £5.50 Last dinner 10pm 40P
Credit cards 1 2 5 **VS**

RAVENGLASS
Cumbria
Map **6** SD09

★Pennington Arms ☎(06577) 222
A country inn in a quiet village on an estuary of the Rivers Esk, Mite and Irt.
16rm(3➡) Annexe: 20rm (11fb) sB&B£10.90–£12.90 sB&B➡⋒£12.40–£14.40 dB&B£21.80–£25.80 dB&B➡⋒£24.80–£28.80 B
CTV 50P 1 ♿
V Lunch £3.50–£4&alc Tea £1.75–£2 High Tea £2.75–£6 Dinner £4.50–£8&alc Wine £3.50 Last dinner 10pm
VS

RAVENSCAR (near Scarborough)
North Yorkshire
Map **8** NZ90

★★*H* Raven Hall ☎Scarborough (0723) 870353 Closed early Dec–early Apr
A cliff-side mansion overlooking the sea, on the site of a Roman signal station.
57rm(37➡2⋒) (13fb) CTV available in bedrooms ® sB&B£12.50–£25 sB&B➡⋒£17.50–£35 dB&B£25–£50 dB&B➡⋒£35–£70 B
☾ CTV 200P 2 ✽ (hard) billiards Disco wkly Live music and dancing 3 nights wkly
V Lunch £4.50–£6&alc Tea 75p–£2&alc High Tea £1.50–£4&alc Dinner £3.50–£9&alc Wine £2.50 Last dinner 8.45pm
Credit cards 1 2 3 **VS**

RAVENSTONEDALE
Cumbria
Map **12** NY70

★★Black Swan ☎Newbiggin-on-Lune (05873) 204
Family-run, stone-built inn situated in the centre of a peaceful village.
6rm(2➡) sB&B£12.50–£14.50 sB&B➡£15.50–£17.50 dB&B£24–£26 dB&B➡£27–£29 B
CTV 15P 2 🚗 (hard) *xmas*
English & French Bar lunch £1.50–£6 Tea £1.50–£2 Dinner £7.50–£8 Last dinner 8.30pm
Credit card 3

READ
Lancashire
Map **7** SD73

✕✕Belvedere Hotel ☎Padiham (0282) 72170
Large country house featuring friendly Italian restaurant.
Closed Mon Lunch not served Sat & Sun
Italian 100 seats Dinner £7.95alc Wine £5.50 Last dinner 9.30pm 40P
Credit cards 1 3

READING
Berkshire
Map **4** SU77

☆☆☆Post House Basingstoke Rd (Trusthouse Forte) ☎(0734) 875485 Telex no 849160
Modern well managed hotel with good amenities for families with children.
143➡ (57fb) CTV in all bedrooms ® sB&B➡£46.50 dB&B➡£58.50 B
☾ 240P CFA ✽ (heated)
Last dinner 10.30pm
Credit cards 1 2 3 4 5

★★**Ship** Duke St (Anchor) ☎(0734) 583455 Telex no 858875
Closed Xmas
Friendly well run hotel with popular carving room.
32rm(20🛁2🚿)(2fb) CTV in all bedrooms Ⓡ*sB&B £22.50 sB&B🛁🚿 £33 dB&B🛁🚿 £38 B
☾ CTV 20P 6🏠 CFA
V ♆ *Lunch £5.35–£7.30&alc Dinner £5.35–£7.30&alc Wine £4.75 Last dinner 9.15pm
Credit cards 1 2 3 4 5

○**Ramada** Oxford Rd ☎(0734) 586222
200🛁
(Due to open Sep 1983)

REDBOURN
Hertfordshire
Map **4** TL11
☆☆☆**Aubrey Park** Hemel Hempstead Rd (Best Western) ☎(058285) 2105 Telex no 825562
Busy hotel in quiet setting with modern bedrooms and two restaurants.
57🛁🚿(2fb) CTV in all bedrooms Ⓡ sB🛁🚿 £21–£33 dB🛁🚿 £30–£41 (room only) B
☾ ## 100P ✽ (heated) (hard) ♿ *xmas*
English & French V ♆ Lunch £4.75–£5.50&alc Tea 70p Dinner £6.50–£8.50&alc Wine £4.50 Last dinner 10pm
Credit cards 1 2 3 4 5

REDBROOK
Clwyd
Map **7** SJ54
★★***Redbrook Hunting Lodge***
Wrexham Rd ☎Redbrook Maelor (094873) 204
On a prominent corner site in a rural position on the A495/A525, 1m from Whitchurch, the hotel has pleasant gardens.
11rm(5🛁1🚿) B
CTV 100P ✽ Live music and dancing Sat
English, French & Italian V ♆ Last dinner 9.30pm

Credit cards 1 2 3

REDCAR
Cleveland
Map **8** SZ62
☆☆☆**Royal York** Coatham Rd ☎(0642) 486221
51🛁(2fb) CTV in all bedrooms sB&B🛁 £21.50 dB&B🛁 £29.50 B
Lift ☾ CTV 300P CFA billiards Disco Sat *xmas*
English, French, German & Italian ♆ Lunch fr£3.50&alc Tea fr£1.25 Dinner £5.45&alc Wine £3.95 Last dinner 10pm
Credit cards 1 2 3

★★***Clarendon*** High St (Scottish & Newcastle) ☎(0642) 484301
11rm CTV 10P Live music and dancing twice wkly
Last dinner 9.45pm
Credit cards 1 3

REDRUTH
Cornwall
Map **2** SW74
★★★**Penventon** ☎(0209) 214141
60rm(29🛁8🚿)(3fb) 1 CTV in all bedrooms Ⓡ sB&B £8.50 sB&B🛁🚿 £10.50 dB&B £20–£34 dB&B🛁🚿 £24–£38 B
☾ 200P ✽ (heated) sauna bath Disco Tue–Sun *xmas*
English, French & Italian V ♆ Lunch fr£5&alc Tea fr85p High Tea fr£1.85 Dinner fr£7&alc Wine £3.95 Last dinner 9.30pm
Credit cards 1 2 3 VS

☆☆***Crossroads Motel*** Scorrier (2m E off A30) ☎St Day (0209) 820551
Modern, friendly hotel, with good restaurant and character bars.
30rm(25🛁5🚿) CTV in all bedrooms Ⓡ B
80P ♿
♆ Last dinner 10pm
Credit cards 1 2 3 5

RED WHARF BAY
Gwynedd
Map **6** SH58
★*L* ***Min-y-Don*** ☎Tynygongl (0248) 852596
Holiday hotel set on the edge of Red Wharf Bay, with good views.
18rm(3🛁🚿) B
CTV 200P ✽
♆ Last dinner 9pm
Credit cards 1 2 3

REIGATE
Surrey
Map **4** TQ25
★★**Reigate Manor** Reigate Hill (Best Western) ☎(07372) 40125
Gatwick plan **19**
Georgian manor house with some well equipped bedrooms and imaginative good cooking.
15🚿 Annexe: 12🛁(1fb) CTV in all bedrooms Ⓡ sB🛁🚿 £27.25–£29.25 dB🛁🚿 £35.90–£37.90 (room only) B
100P Live music and dancing Sat
V ♆ Lunch £8.50alc Dinner £12alc Wine £5 Last dinner 10pm
S% Credit cards 1 2 3 5

RENFREW
Strathclyde *Renfrewshire*
Map **11** NS56
For hotels and restaurants see Glasgow Airport.

RETFORD (EAST)
Nottinghamshire
Map **8** SK78
★★★*BL* **West Retford** North Rd ☎(0777) 706333 Telex no 56143
Annexe: 31🛁(15fb) CTV in all bedrooms Ⓡ sB🛁 £31.50 dB🛁 £38 (room only) B
☾ CTV 100P CFA ✽ Disco Sat Live music and dancing Fri (twice mthly)
French V ♆ Lunch £6.35–£6.60&alc Tea 75p Dinner £8.65&alc Wine £5.75 Last dinner 10.30pm
S% Credit cards 1 2 3 5 VS
See advert on page 534

★★**Elms** London Rd ☎(0777) 702977
Closed Xmas RS Public hols
10rm(1⇌)(1fb) CTV in all bedrooms ® *sB&B£17.25 sB&B⇌£20.70 dB&B£32.20 dB&B⇌£39.10
100P ✽ Disco twice wkly
V ♔ ☕ *Lunch £5–£5.50 Tea £1.50–£2.50 High Tea £3–£4.50 Dinner £8–£10 Last dinner 8.30pm
Credit cards 1 3

RHAYADER
Powys
Map **6** SN96

★★**Elan Valley** Elan Valley (2½m SW B4518) ☎(0597) 810448
Closed Xmas
Detached hotel in rural surroundings between the town and the Elan Lakes.
12rm(3⇌3⋔)(1fb) sB&B£14 sB&B⇌⋔£15 dB&B£24 dB&B⇌⋔£26 ⊟
CTV 50P 6 ✽
V ♔ ☕ Lunch £5.50 Tea 50p–£1.50 Dinner £6 Wine £4 Last dinner 8pm
Credit card 2 **VS**

★**Elan** West St ☎(0597) 810373
A 16th-century cottage-style hotel near the centre of the town.
15rm(1⇌)(2fb) sB&B£8.50–£11 dB&B£16.50–£20 dB&B⇌£18.25–£22.50
CTV 12P

English & French ♔ ☕ Lunch £3.95–£4.75 Tea 50p–£1.50&alc Dinner £6–£8 Wine £3.50 Last dinner 7.30pm
S%

★***Lion Royal*** ☎(0597) 810202
Closed 2wks Xmas
Town-centre tourist hotel.
21rm(2⇌3⋔) ® ⊟
CTV 20P
♔ Last dinner 8pm

RHOS
Dyfed
Map **2** SN33

★★***Lamb*** ☎ Velindre (0559) 370576
A pleasant, small hotel on the A484 between Carmarthen and Cardigan.
7⇌⋔ CTV in all bedrooms ® ★ ⊟
100P Live music and dancing Fri & Sat
♔ Last dinner 10pm
Credit cards 1 2 3

RHOSNEIGR
Gwynedd
Map **6** SH37

★***Maelog Lake*** ☎(0407) 810204
Prominent, detached hotel on the outskirts of Rhosneigr, 1m from the beach.
13rm
CTV 60P Cabaret wkly
♔ ☕ Last dinner 4pm

RHOSSILI
West Glamorgan
Map **2** SS48

★★**Worms Head** ☎ Gower (0792) 390512
Closed 24 & 25 Dec
Bright cliff-top hotel with magnificent views of the sea and the bay.
21rm(2⇌3⋔)(2fb) ® ★ sB&B£11.50 dB&B£23 dB&B⇌⋔£25 ⊟
CTV 20P
V ♔ Lunch £3.50alc Dinner £5.50alc Wine £4.50 Last dinner 8pm

RHU
Strathclyde *Dunbartonshire*
Map **10** NS28

★★★L ***Rosslea Hall*** ☎(0436) 820684
The tower and façade date from 1849, but modern bedrooms combine to provide a mixture of the past and present.
16rm(11⇌5⋔) CTV in all bedrooms ® sB&B⇌⋔£27 dB&B⇌⋔£40 ⊟
30P 1 ✽ *xmas*
V ♔ ☕ Lunch £10alc Tea £2–£2.50&alc Dinner £9.50&alc Wine £4.50 Last dinner 9pm
Credit cards 1 2 3 5 **VS**

R

★ *L* **Ardencaple** (Ind Coope) ☎(0436) 820200

Attractive inn with interior theme linked to Clyde steamers.

10rm(4⇌) (2fb) 1⊟ CTV in all bedrooms ®sB&B fr£16.75 sB&B⇌ fr£20.63 dB&B fr£26.40 dB&B⇌ fr£32.45 ⓑ

CTV 100P Disco twice wkly

⊟European ☕ ☐ ✻Lunch £5.50alc Tea 50p High Tea £3alc Dinner £7alc Wine £3.75 Last dinner 9pm

Credit cards 1 3 5

RHYDWYN
Gwynedd
Map **6** SH38

✕**Lobster Pot** Church Bay ☎Llanfaethlu (040 788) 241

Closed Mon–Thu in winter Lunch not served

64 seats Dinner £10alc Wine £4.20 Last dinner 9.45pm P

S% Credit cards 1 2 5

RHYL
Clwyd
Map **6** SJ08

★★★ ***Westminster*** East Pde ☎(0745) 2241 Telex no 629462

Four-storey hotel set on the Promenade close to the High St.

56rm (28⇌⋒) CTV in all bedrooms ® ⓑ

Lift ☾ 12P

☕ ☐ Last dinner 9pm

Credit cards 1 2 3 5

RICHMOND
North Yorkshire
Map **7** NZ10

★★**Frenchgate** 59–61 Frenchgate ☎(0748) 2087 Closed Xmas wk

Stone-built, Georgian, gentleman's town house, enclosing a 16th-century cottage. →

R

12rm(3⇌3⋔)CTV in 5 bedrooms TV in 7 bedrooms Ⓡ sB&B£17.50 sB&B⇌⋔£19.75–£21.75 dB&B£31.50 dB&B⇌⋔£33.50 B
6P nc7yrs
English & French Lunch £7alc Dinner £7.50&alc Wine £3.85 Last dinner 8.30pm
Credit cards 1 3

★★**King's Head** Market Sq (Swallow) ☎(0748) 2311
25rm(17⇌)(2fb) CTV in all bedrooms Ⓡ sB&B£13–£16.65 sB&B⇌£19–£20.95 dB&B£22.75–£30.95 dB&B⇌£29.70–£35.90 B
CTV 25P
V Lunch £5.25 Tea 45p–£1.20 High Tea £3.70–£5 Dinner £7.50alc Wine £4.50 Last dinner 9.15pm
Credit cards 1 2 3 5

RICHMOND UPON THAMES
Greater London, London plan **5** B3 (page 420)

★★★**Petersham** Nightingale Ln, Richmond Hill ☎01-940 7471 Telex no 928556
Closed Xmas
Victorian hotel overlooking the Thames.
52⇌ CTV in all bedrooms ★ *sB&B⇌ fr£34.50 dB&B⇌ fr£44 Continental breakfast B
Lift ☾ CTV 50P
*Lunch fr£8.50&alc Tea fr60p Dinner fr£8.50&alc Wine £5.50 Last dinner 9.15pm
Credit cards 1 2

★★★**Richmond Gate** 158 Richmond Hill ☎01-940 0061 Telex no 928556
A comfortably appointed commercial hotel with attractive and well equipped lounges.
50⇌ 2 CTV in all bedrooms ★ sB&B⇌£40 dB&B⇌£50 B
☾ 40P 2 ✽
V Lunch £6alc Dinner £9.50–£11 Wine £5.50 Last dinner 9.30pm
Credit cards 1 2

★★★**Richmond Hill** 146–150 Richmond Hill (Best Western) ☎01-940 2247 Telex no 21844
Comfortable informal hotel with attractive restaurant offering good food.
128rm(120⇌)(6fb) CTV in all bedrooms Ⓡ sB&B⇌£32.50 dB&B⇌£42
Lift ☾ 150P CFA squash Live music and dancing Sat *xmas*
English & French V Lunch £6.50 Dinner £7.25 Wine £5.50 Last dinner 9pm
Credit cards 1 2 3 4 5

✕✕***Evergreen*** 102–104 Kew Rd ☎01-940 9044
Attractive restaurant featuring authentic Chinese dishes and specialities like crab with ginger and onion.
Closed Xmas
Chinese 150 seats Last dinner 11pm P
Credit cards 1 2 3 5

✕✕***Kew Rendezvous*** 110 Kew Rd ☎01-948 4343
Simple, smart restaurant with Pekinese menu.
Closed Public hols
Pekinese 200 seats Last dinner 11pm P
Credit cards 1 2 3 5

✕✕**Lichfields** Lichfield Ter, Sheen Rd ☎01-940 5236
Well appointed friendly restaurant offering skilful traditional French cooking.
Closed Sun, Mon, 1wk Xmas, 1wk Whit & 2wks Sep Lunch not served Sat
French 38 seats Lunch £11.50–£15 Dinner £27alc Wine £5.50 Last dinner 10.45pm
Credit cards 1 2

✕**Red Lion Chinese** 18 Red Lion St ☎01-940 2371
Small modern Pekinese restaurant with attractive decor.
Closed 24 & 25 Dec
Pekinese 88 seats *Lunch £5–£8&alc Dinner £5–£8&alc Wine £4 Last dinner 11pm
Credit cards 1 2 3 5 VS

✕***Richmond Rendezvous*** 1 Paradise Rd ☎01-940 6869
Pekinese 150 seats Last dinner 11pm
Credit cards 1 2 3 5

✕***Valcheras*** The Quadrant ☎01-940 0648
Closed Xmas, Public hols, last wk Jul & 1st wk Aug Dinner not served Sun
Continental 75 seats Last dinner 10.30pm
Credit cards 3 5

RIPLEY
Surrey
Map **4** TQ05

✕✕✕**Clock House** ☎Guildford (0483) 224777
Dinner not served Sun
French 85 seats *Lunch £5.50–£6.50&alc Dinner £8.50–£12&alc Wine £4.45 Last dinner 10.30pm
Credit cards 1 2 3 5

RIPON
North Yorkshre
Map **8** SE37

★★★**Ripon Spa** Park St (Best Western) ☎(0765) 2172 Telex no 57780
An Edwardian building in a garden setting, five minutes walk from the city centre.
41rm(35⇌6⋔)(5fb) CTV in all bedrooms Ⓡ sB&B⇌⋔£24–£25.50 dB&B⇌⋔£35–£48 B
Lift ☾ CTV 100P CFA ✽ Live music and dancing mthly *xmas*
V Lunch £6–£7&alc Tea £2.50 Dinner £8.50–£9.50&alc Wine £4.50 Last dinner 9pm
Credit cards 1 2 3 5 VS

★★***Unicorn*** Market Sq (Galleon) ☎(0765) 2202
28rm(14⇌⋔) Ⓡ ★ B
☾ CTV P
Last dinner 6.30pm
Credit cards 1 3 VS

✕**New Hornblower** Duck Hill ☎(0765) 4841
Closed Feb Lunch not served Dinner not served Mon
French 18 seats Dinner £7–£12 Wine £4.50 Last dinner 10pm
Credit cards 1 3

RIPPONDEN
West Yorkshire
Map **7** SE01

✕✕***Over the Bridge*** Millfold ☎(042 289) 3722
Smart, comfortable little restaurant in attractive setting, offering delectable 4 course menu.
Closed Sun Lunch not served Dinner not served Public hols
English & French 45 seats Last dinner 9.30pm 50P
Credit card 2

RISHWORTH
West Yorkshire
Map **7** SE01

★★***Royal*** Oldham Rd ☎Halifax (0422) 822382
An 18th-century, stone-built coaching inn.
9rm(2⇌7⋔) 1 CTV in all bedrooms ★ 80P ✽
English & French Last dinner 9.15pm
Credit cards 1 3 5 VS

ROBESTON WATHEN
Dyfed
Map **2** SN01

✕✕**Robeston House** ☎Narberth (0834) 860392
Lunch by reservation only.
English & Continental V 50 seats Lunch £7.50alc Tea £1alc Dinner £11alc Wine £3.75 Last dinner 9.15pm 50P bedrooms available
Credit card 1

ROBIN HOOD'S BAY
North Yorkshire
Map **8** NZ90

★★**Grosvenor** Station Rd ☎Whitby (0947) 880320
14rm(2fb) ★ sB&B£10–£12.75 dB&B£20–£25 B
CTV 10P *xmas*

V ✿ ☕ Bar lunch £1–£5 Tea £1–£3 Dinner £7.25&alc Wine £5.20 Last dinner 8.30pm

Credit cards 1 3 **VS**

★★**Victoria** ☎ Whitby (0947) 880205

Two-storey, late-Victorian villa in its own grounds on the cliff top overlooking the village and the bay.

16rm(1⋒)(3fb)® sB&B£11.75 sB&B⋒£11.75 dB&B£23.50 dB&B⋒£23.50 B

CTV 30P 4 Live music and dancing monthly

V ✿ Bar lunch 60p–£2.75 Dinner £6.25 Wine £4.70 Last dinner 8.30pm

ROCHDALE
Greater Manchester
Map **7** SD91

★★**Midway** Manchester Rd, Castleton ☎(0706) 32881

Closed Xmas Day & New Year's Day

29rm(2⇌19⋒)(1fb) 1 CTV in all bedrooms ® sB&B£20 sB&B⇌⋒£25 dB&B⇌⋒£35

☾ CTV 200P

English, French & Italian V ✿ ☕ Lunch fr£5.25 Tea fr40p Dinner fr£6.95 Wine £3.85 Last dinner 10.30pm

Credit cards 1 2 3 5 **VS**

✕✕✕**Moorcock** Huddersfield Rd, Milnrow (3m SE on A640) ☎ Saddleworth (04577) 2659

Closed Mon Lunch not served Sat Dinner not served Sun

International **V** 75 seats Lunch £5.75–£6.50&alc Wine £5.70 Last dinner 9.30pm 50P

Credit cards 1 2 3 5

ROCHESTER
Kent
Map **5** TQ76

☆☆☆**Crest** Maidstone Rd (On A229 1m N of M2 jct 3) (Crest) ☎ Medway (0634) 687111 Telex no 965933

Ideally located for Rochester Airport, a modern professional hotel with good size well-appointed bedrooms.

106⇌⋒(10fb) CTV in all bedrooms ® ✱sB&B⇌⋒£34 dB&B⇌⋒£42 (room only) B

Lift ☾ ## 180P ♿

International V ✿ ☕ ✱Lunch £6.95alc Tea 60p Dinner £10–£12alc Wine £6.45 Last dinner 10pm

Credit cards 1 2 3 4 5 **VS**

ROCHESTER
Northumberland
Map **12** NY89

★**Redesdale Arms** ☎ Otterburn (0830) 20668

11rm(1fb) 2 ® ✱sB&B£9.50–£11.50 dB&B£19–£26 B

CTV 28P

Continental **V** ✱Bar lunch 65p–£4.25&alc Dinner £2.20–£6.50&alc Wine £3.95 Last dinner 8pm

Credit cards 1 2 **VS**

ROCHFORD
Essex
Map **5** TQ89

✕✕**Renoufs** 1 South St ☎ Southend-on-Sea (0702) 544393

Well-managed restaurant with attentive service.

Closed Sun, Mon, 1–24 Jan & 15–28 Jun Lunch not served Sat

French **V** 65 seats Lunch £7&alc Dinner £7&alc Wine £4.75 Last dinner 9.45pm

Credit cards 1 2 3 5

ROCK (near St Minver)
Cornwall
Map **2** SW97

★★**St Enodoc** ☎ Trebetherick (020 886) 2311

Comfortable hotel in an elevated position, with unrestricted views of the Camel estuary.

14rm(6⇌2⋒)(3fb) CTV available in bedrooms sB&B£15–£20 sB&B⇌⋒£16–£21 dB&B£30–£40 dB&B⇌⋒£32–£42 B

17P ✽ *xmas*

English & French V ✿ ☕ Bar lunch £1.70 Tea 75p Dinner £6.75–£7.25&alc Wine £4.90 Last dinner 9.30pm

S% Credit cards 1 3 **VS**

ROCKCLIFFE
Dumfries & Galloway *Kirkcudbrightshire*
Map **11** NX85

★★★ *L* **Baron's Craig** ☎ (055 663) 225

Closed mid Oct–Mar

27rm(20⇌)(2fb) CTV in all bedrooms sB&B£21.20–£23.73 sB&B⇌£29–£33.60 dB&B£39.90–£45 dB&B⇌£50–£60 B

50P 4 ✽

✿ ☕ Bar lunch fr£2.60 Tea 80p–£2.10 Dinner fr£10.50 Wine £4.60 Last dinner 9pm

ROMALDKIRK
Co Durham
Map **12** NY92

★★*B* **Rose & Crown** (Best Western) ☎ Teesdale (0833) 50213 Closed Xmas Day

Charming old village inn with wide ranging inexpensive bar meals.

10rm(3⇌2⋒) 1 Annexe: 5rm(4⇌1⋒)(1fb) CTV in all bedrooms ® sB&B£11.50–£17 sB&B⇌⋒£11.50–£20 dB&B£23–£32 dB&B⇌⋒£23–£34 B

60P

V ✿ ☕ Lunch £2.25–£5.50 Tea £1.50 High Tea £3.50 Dinner fr£8.50&alc Wine £4.75

Last dinner 10pm

Credit cards 1 2 3 5

ROMILEY
Greater Manchester
Map **7** SJ99

✕**Waterside** 166 Stockport Rd ☎061-430 4302

Stone and brick built cottage, about 200 years old, beside the Peak Forest Canal.

Closed Mon Dinner not served Sun

English & French **V** 36 seats Lunch £4.95–£5.50 Dinner £7.95–£8.95&alc Wine £4.95 Last dinner 9.45pm 20P

Credit card 1

R

ROMSEY
Hampshire
Map **4** SU32

★★★**White Horse** Market Pl (Trusthouse Forte) ☎(0794) 512431
Comfortable lounges and helpful staff make this hotel popular with business people and tourists alike.
33⇌ Annexe: 7rm (7fb) CTV in all bedrooms Ⓡ sB&B⇌£39 dB&B⇌£54.50 Ᵽ
60P CFA
✿ ☐ Last dinner 9.30pm
Credit cards 1 2 3 4 5

★***Dolphin*** Cornmarket ☎(0794) 512171
Modest, proprietor-run hotel.
7rm(2⇌) 1 ▭ CTV in 4 bedrooms Ⓡ
CTV 20P
V ✿ ☐ Last dinner 10pm
Credit cards 1 2 3 5

✕✕**Old Manor House** 21 Palmerston St ☎(0794) 517353
Closed Mon, Xmas & Etr Sun Dinner not served Sun
▣ French 55 seats ✻ Lunch fr£5.95&alc Dinner £10.10alc Wine £4.95 Last dinner 10.30pm 15P
S% Credit cards 1 2 3 5

At **Ampfield** (4m E A31)
☆☆☆**Potters Heron** (Whitbread Wessex) ☎Chandlers Ford (04215) 66611
42⇌ 120P

ROSEBANK
Strathclyde *Lanarkshire*
Map **11** NS84

★★★***Popinjay*** (Best Western) ☎Crossford (055 586) 441
Tudor style hotel with grounds extending to River Clyde.
37rm(27⇌7⋒) 1 ▭ CTV in all bedrooms Ⓡ Ᵽ
☾ 100P ✽ ♩ ⌂
V ✿ ☐ Last dinner 10pm
Credit cards 1 2 3 4 5

ROSEDALE ABBEY
North Yorkshire
Map **8** SE79

★**White Horse Farm** (Minotel, Exec Hotel) ☎Lastingham (07515) 239
Closed 25 Dec
Converted 17th-century farmhouse overlooking unspoilt Rosedale.
15rm(8⇌7⋒) (3fb) CTV in all bedrooms Ⓡ sB&B⇌⋒£16–£24 dB&B£29–£35 dB&B⇌⋒£35 Ᵽ
50P ⚘ ✽ *xmas*
▣ English & Continental ✿ Bar lunch £3.80–£7 Tea £2 Dinner £8&alc Wine £4.50 Last dinner 9pm
Credit card 5 **VS**

ROSEHALL
Highland *Sutherland*
Map **14** NC40

★★**Achness** ☎(054 984) 239
Closed Oct–Feb
5rm Annexe: 7⇌ TV in 6 bedrooms Ⓡ sB&B£10 sB&B⇌£12 dB&B£20 dB&B⇌£24
CTV 50P ⚘ ✽ ♩ Live music and dancing wkly
✿ ☐ ✻ Bar lunch £2–£4 Tea 50p Dinner fr£7.50 Wine £3 Last dinner 8pm
S%

ROSEMARKIE
Highland *Ross & Cromarty*
Map **14** NH75

★★***HL*** **Marine** ☎Fortrose (0381) 20253
Closed Oct–Mar RS early Apr
A long established golfing and family hotel noted for its hospitality and comfortable lounges.
50rm(9⇌4⋒) (4fb) sB&B£9–£11.55 sB&B⇌⋒£10.50–£13.15 dB&B£18–£23.10 dB&B⇌⋒£21–£26.25 Ᵽ
CTV 50P 10⌂ ⚘ ✽ ♿
V ✿ ☐ Lunch fr£4.50 Tea fr£1 Dinner fr£6.50 Wine £3.60 Last dinner 8.30pm
VS

R

ROSLIN
Lothian *Midlothian*
Map **11** NT26

✕**Ye Olde Original Rosslyne Inn** Main St ☎031-440 2384
A period theme and pieces of Victoriana enhance the atmosphere at this restaurant.
Lunch not served Sat & Sun
▣Mainly grills **V** 60 seats ✱Lunch £2–£5 Dinner £6–£12&alc Wine £3.50 Last dinner 9pm 24P bedrooms available
Credit card 3

ROSSINGTON
South Yorkshire
Map **8** SK69

★★**Mount Pleasant** (Minotel) (on A638 Great North Rd 1½m E of village) ☎Doncaster (0302) 868696 Closed Xmas Day
Converted 18th-century estate house with 80 acres of woodland and farmland.
21rm(3⇛5⋒) Annexe: 8rm(2⇛) 1⊟(1fb) CTV in 11 bedrooms TV in 6 bedrooms Ⓡ ✱sB&B£12.50 sB&B⇛⋒£16.50 dB&B£22–£30 dB&B⇛⋒£25–£40
CTV 100P 5⌂ ✱ ♿
V ♡ ▭ Lunch £2.95–£7 Tea £1.60–£2.50 High Tea £3.50–£6 Dinner £4.95–£8 Last dinner 9.30pm

ROSS-ON-WYE
Hereford & Worcester
Map **3** SO62
See also Kerne Bridge and Pencraig

★★★*H* ***Chase*** Gloucester Rd ☎(0989) 63161
Georgian style hotel set in gardens, close to Ross town centre.
38rm(34⇛4⋒) 4⊟ CTV in all bedrooms Ⓑ
☾ 200P CFA ✱ ⌂
▣English & French **V** ♡ ▭ Last dinner 9.45pm
Credit cards 1 2 3 5

★★★*H* **Pengethley** (4m N on A49 Hereford rd) (Best Western) ☎Harewood End (098987) 211
Fully-modernised, Georgian house, set in peaceful surroundings.
13rm(11⇛2⋒) Annexe: 7⇛(4fb) CTV in all bedrooms sB&B⇛⋒£30–£47 dB&B⇛⋒£50–£74 Ⓑ
CTV 70P 2⌂ ✱ ≋(heated) ♪ Live music and dancing Thu *xmas*
V ♡ ▭ Lunch fr£7.25 Tea fr70p Dinner fr£12.27&alc Wine £6.75 Last dinner 9.30pm
Credit cards 1 2 3 5 **VS**

★★★*H* **Royal** Palace Pound (Trusthouse Forte) ☎(0989) 65105
Comfortable hotel with extensive views of Wye valley.
31⇛(6fb) CTV in all bedrooms Ⓡ sB&B⇛£39 dB&B⇛£52.50 Ⓑ
20P ✱ *xmas*
♡ ▭ Last dinner 9.15pm
Credit cards 1 2 3 4 5

★★★**Wye** Weston under Penyard (2m E A40) ☎(0989) 63541
Modernised country hotel specialising in conferences and banquets.
43rm(36⇛⋒) CTV in all bedrooms sB&B fr£21 sB&B⇛⋒ fr£26 dB&B fr£32 dB&B⇛⋒ fr£36 Ⓑ
☾ CTV 150P 10⌂ CFA ✱ squash ⌂ *xmas*
▣English & Continental **V** ♡ ▭ Bar lunch fr£1 Tea fr£2 High Tea fr£3 Dinner fr£8 Wine £4.50 Last dinner 9.15pm
Credit cards 1 2 3 5

★★♔**Chasedale** Walford Rd ☎(0989) 62423
Quiet family-run hotel on the edge of Ross-on-Wye.
12rm(6⇛)(3fb) CTV in 6 bedrooms sB&B£15.50–£16.50 sB&B⇛£18.50–£19.75 dB&B£25–£26.50 dB&B⇛£31–£33 Ⓑ
CTV 16P ✱ *xmas*
▣English & French **V** ♡ ▭ Lunch £4.50–£5 Tea 45–50p Dinner £6.50&alc Wine £4.50 Last dinner 9pm
Credit cards 1 3

★★**Hunsdon Manor** Weston-under-Penyard (2m E A40) ☎(0989) 62748
A 15th-century manor house with later additions, standing in 2½ acres of lawns and gardens.
12rm(2⇛4⋒)(2fb) CTV in 5 bedrooms Ⓡ sB&B£13 sB&B⇛⋒£18 dB&B£22 dB&B⇛⋒£27 Ⓑ
CTV 40P ✱ *xmas*
▣English & Continental **V** ♡ ▭ Lunch £4.50–£5.50 Tea 30–50p Dinner £6&alc Wine £3.50
Last dinner 9.30pm
Credit cards 1 2 3 5

★★**King's Head** 8 High St ☎(0989) 63174
13rm(16⇛) CTV in all bedrooms Ⓡ sB&B£14 sB&B⇛£19 dB&B£25 dB&B⇛£29 Ⓑ
CTV 20P *xmas*
♡ ▭ Bar lunch £3–£5 Tea £1–£2 Dinner £6.50–£9.50alc Wine £4.20 Last dinner 9.30pm

★★♔**Walford House** Walford Rd (2m S B4228) ☎(0989) 63829
9rm(7⇛2⋒)(2fb) 1⊟ CTV in 9 bedrooms Ⓡ sB&B⇛⋒£17–£19 dB&B⇛⋒£32–£38 Ⓑ
80P ✱ *xmas*
▣French **V** ♡ ▭ Lunch £5.50–£6.50&alc Tea fr50p Dinner £7.50–£8.50&alc Wine £5.10 Last dinner 9.30pm
Credit cards 1 3 5

★**Brookfield House** Over Ross ☎(0989) 62188 Closed Nov & Jan
Small, comfortable, family-run hotel, close to the town centre.
7rm(1⇛2⋒) TV available in bedrooms Ⓡ sB&B£12–£14 dB&B£20–£24 dB&B⇛⋒£24–£28 Ⓑ
CTV 15P 3⌂ ✱
♡Lunch fr£4.50 Dinner fr£6 Wine £3.50 Last dinner 7pm
Credit cards 1 3
See advert on page 540

★**Orles Barn** Wilton ☎(0989) 62155
Small, family-run hotel in well kept gardens, close to the junction of the A40 and the A49. →

R

8rm(2⇌)(2fb) CTV in 4 bedrooms ® sB&B£12–£15 sB&B⇌£15–£18 dB&B£24–£28 dB&B⇌£30–£36 Ᵽ

CTV 15P ✽ (unheated)

English, French & Spanish V Lunch fr£5–£6.50&alc Tea 65p–85p High Tea £1.25–£2 Dinner £5.95–£6.95&alc Wine £4.30 Last dinner 9.30pm

Credit cards 1 2 3

★**Rosswyn** 17 High St ☎(0989) 62733

19rm(3⇌1⋒)(1fb) 3 CTV in 1 bedroom ® sB&B£10–£12 sB&B⇌⋒£16 dB&B£24–£28 dB&B⇌⋒£32 Ᵽ

CTV 3P ✽ Live music and dancing fortnightly Sat *xmas*

English & French V Bar lunch 60p–£3&alc Dinner £8–£9&alc Wine £4.50 Last dinner 10pm

VS

★**Wilton Court** Wilton ☎(0989) 62569

Sandstone hotel, originally a 16th century courthouse, on the banks of the River Wye.

8rm(2⇌4⋒)(2fb) CTV in all bedrooms ® sB&B£14.50 sB&B⇌⋒£15.50 dB&B£27 dB&B⇌⋒£29 Ᵽ

25P ✽

English & French Bar lunch £3.50alc Dinner £5.95&alc Wine £4.25 Last dinner 9.30pm

Credit cards 1 3

ROSTHWAITE
Cumbria
Map **11** NY21
See also **Borrowdale** and **Grange-in-Borrowdale**

★★★**Scafell** ☎Borrowdale (059684) 208

Closed Jan, RS end Oct–end Mar (wknds only)

R

21rm(14⇌)(1fb)CTV available in bedrooms ® sB&B£14.75–£16.75 sB&B⇌£15.95–£17.95 dB&B£29.50–£33.50 dB&B⇌£31.90–£35.90 B
50P ✽
V ♧ Bar lunch £2.75–£5 Tea £1–£1.25 Dinner £9.25 Wine £3 Last dinner 9.30pm

ROSUDGEON
Cornwall
Map **2** SW52

★★ *H* **Rosudgeon** ☎ Penzance (0736) 710476 Closed Jan RS Dec & Feb
Comfortable, quiet and very conveniently situated hotel with pleasant garden and good home cooking.
11rm(5⋒)(1fb) TV in 1 bedroom CTV in 1 bedroom ® sB&B£14.60 sB&B⋒£16.10 dB&B£29.20 dB&B⋒£32.20 B
CTV 20P nc6 *xmas*
♧ Tea 90p–£1.50 Dinner £6–£7 Wine £2.80 Last dinner 8pm
Credit cards 1 3 **VS**

ROTHBURY
Northumberland
Map **12** NU00

★★ ***Coquet Vale*** Station Rd ☎ (0669) 20305
Large, detached grey-stone building in an elevated position overlooking the valley.
9rm ® B
CTV 28P ✽ billiards
English & French ♧ Last dinner 9.30pm

★ ***Queens Head*** Town Foot ☎ (0669) 20470 RS Oct–Apr
Public house with good-sized bedrooms, in the village centre, one minute's walk from the river.
8rm B
CTV 10P 2
English & French V ♧ Last dinner 8.30pm

ROTHERHAM
South Yorkshire
Map **8** SK49

☆☆☆☆ *L* **Carlton Park** Moorgate Rd ☎ (0709) 64902 Telex no 547810
A modern, luxury hotel offering comprehensive facilities, particularly for the business executive.
62⇌ CTV in all bedrooms ® ✱ sB⇌ £36.75 dB⇌£43.50 (room only) B
Lift ☾ 92P CFA ✽ sauna bath Disco 3 nights wkly Live music and dancing 5 nights wkly
English & French V ♧ ✱ Lunch £4alc Dinner £6.50&alc Wine £4.80 Last dinner 9.45pm
Credit cards 1 2 3 4 5 **VS**

★★ **Brentwood** Moorgate Rd ☎ (0709) 2772 Telex no 547291
A stone-built Victorian residence in its own grounds, with a modern extension.
15rm(2⇌7⋒) Annexe: 20rm(16⇌1⋒) (1fb) 1 CTV in 21 bedrooms ® ✱ sB&B£17 sB&B⇌⋒£23 dB&B£25 dB&B⇌⋒£30 B
CTV 50P ✽ *xmas*
♧ ✱ Lunch £2.90–£5.75&alc Dinner £7.50–£7.95&alc Wine £3.70 Last dinner 9pm
Credit cards 1 2 3 5

★ **Elton** Main St, Bramley (3m E A631) ☎ (0709) 545681
A two-storey stone building, which was originally a farmhouse.
15rm(2⇌3⋒) CTV in 8 bedrooms ® ✱ sB&B£13.75 sB&B⇌⋒£18.75–£20.75 dB&B£23.75 dB&B⇌⋒£26.75–£28.75
☾ 26P
English & French ♧ ✱ Lunch £4.25–£5.50&alc Tea 70p Dinner £8&alc Wine £4.95 Last dinner 10pm
Credit card 1 2 3

ROTHES
Grampian *Morayshire*
Map **15** NJ24

★★★ *L* **Rothes Glen** ☎ (03403) 254 Closed mid Nov–Feb
Charming, castle-like building by the designer of "Balmoral" standing in 40 acres of its own grounds at the head of Glen of Rothes.
19rm(14⇌)(1fb) sB&B£24.50 sB&B⇌£27 dB&B£44.45 dB&B⇌£49.50
CTV 40P ✽
V ♧ Lunch £6.50&alc Dinner £13.50&alc Wine £2.75 Last dinner 8.30pm
S% Credit cards 2 3 5

★ ***Station*** 51 New St ☎ (03403) 240
10rm ®
CTV 6P 3
V ♧ Last dinner 9pm

ROTHESAY
Isle of Bute Strathclyde *Bute*
Map **10** NS06

★ *H* **Ardmory House** Ardmory Rd, Ardbeg ☎ (0700) 2346
A converted private house, built in 1833, standing on a hillside with panoramic views.
6rm(4⇌2⋒)(2fb) TV in all bedrooms ✱ sB&B⇌⋒ fr£12.50 dB&B⇌⋒ fr£25 B
CTV 28P ✽
V ✱ Lunch fr£3.50 Dinner fr£5.95&alc Wine £3.05 Last dinner 9.30pm
Credit cards 1 2 3

★ **St Ebba** 37 Mountstuart Rd, Craigmore ☎ (0700) 2683 Closed Nov–Mar
16rm(8⋒)(3fb) TV in 8 bedrooms sB&B£11.50–£14 sB&B⋒£13–£15 dB&B£23–£25 dB&B⋒£26–£29 B
CTV 6P
♧ Bar lunch £1.50–£3 Tea 75p–£1.25 Dinner £6–£7 Wine £3.35 Last dinner 7.30pm
VS

ROTHLEY
Leicestershire
Map **8** SK51

★★★ *L* **Rothley Court** Westfield Ln (Best Western) ☎ Leicester (0533) 374141 Telex no 341789
Closed 25 & 26 Dec RS Pub hols
13rm(11⇌2⋒) Annexe: 20rm(17⇌) CTV in all bedrooms ® ✱ sB&B£25.30 sB&B⇌⋒£36.22 dB&B£35.42 dB&B⇌⋒£41.97 B
☾ 100P CFA ✽
French V ♧ ✱ Lunch £8.53&alc Tea 58p Dinner £11.37&alc Wine £6.02 Last dinner 9.30pm
S% Credit cards 1 2 3 5 **VS**

R

XX Red Lion Inn ☎ Leicester (0533) 302488
The restaurant is in a single-storey building to the rear of this large inn at the junction of the A6 and the B5328.
Lunch not served Sat Dinner not served Sun
English & French **V** 65 seats Lunch £5–£10 Dinner £6–£12 Wine £2.95 Last dinner 10pm 100P
Credit cards 1 2 3 5 **VS**

ROTTINGDEAN
East Sussex
Map **5** TQ30
see also Brighton and Hove
★★*B* **White Horse** Marine Dr ☎ Brighton (0273) 31955
The hotels tastefully decorated rooms look out over English Channel; restaurant specialises in local sea food.
18 (2fb) 2 CTV in all bedrooms Ⓡ sB&B £21.45 dB&B £32.45
Lift ☾ 70P *xmas*
English & Continental **V** Lunch £5.50&alc Dinner fr£5.50&alc Wine £4.45 Last dinner 10pm
S% Credit cards 1 2 3 5

ROUSDON
Devon
Map **3** SY29
★★*B* ***Orchard Country*** ☎ Lyme Regis (02974) 2972 Closed Nov–Feb
Peaceful secluded country hotel.
15rm (7 2)
CTV 16P nc8yrs
V Last dinner 8.30pm
Credit cards 1 5

ROWARDENNAN
Central *Stirlingshire*
Map **10** NS39
★★**Rowardennan** ☎ Balmaha (036 087) 273 Closed Nov, RS Dec–Mar
Personally run historic inn near Loch Lomond.
9rm (1) *sB&B £12 sB&B £15 dB&B £20 dB&B £24
CTV 50P

V *****Bar lunch £1.40–£4.95 Tea fr50p High Tea fr£3.50 Dinner £7 Wine £4 Last dinner 9pm
VS

ROWEN
Gwynedd
Map **6** SH77
★*BL* **Tir-y-Coed** ☎ Tynygroes (049 267) 219 Closed Nov–Feb
Detached, Edwardian house situated in a small, peaceful village.
7rm (5 1) Annexe: 1 CTV in 7 bedrooms Ⓡ sB&B £12.50–£15.25 dB&B £23–£28.50
CTV 10P nc3yrs
Bar lunch £1–£4 Dinner £6.50 Wine £4.50 Last dinner 7.15pm

ROWSLEY
Derbyshire
Map **8** SK26
★★★*L* **Peacock** (Embassy) ☎ Darley Dale (0629) 733518
Former Dower house, built in 1652, on the A6, 2m from South Bakewell.
14rm (10 4) Annexe: 6rm (1) CTV in all bedrooms Ⓡ sB £22 sB £31.50 dB £35 dB £47.25
☾ 30P 5 *xmas*
V Lunch fr£7.90 Tea fr90p Dinner fr£11.25 Wine £4.80 Last dinner 9pm
Credit cards 1 2 3 4 5

ROY BRIDGE
Highland *Inverness-shire*
Map **14** NN28
★★**Glenspean Lodge** ☎ Spean Bridge (039781) 224
15rm (1) (2fb) sB&B £10–£12 dB&B £20–£24 dB&B £20–£24
CTV 30P 2 *xmas*
V Lunch £5.25 Tea 60p High Tea £2.75 Dinner £7–£8&alc Wine £2.20 Last dinner 9.30pm

RUABON
Clwyd
Map **7** SJ34
★★**Wynnstay Arms** High St ☎ (0978) 822187
Stone-built tourist hotel, located in the centre of the town.
9rm (1fb) CTV in all bedrooms Ⓡ sB&B £16 dB&B £26
☾ 80P 1
English & French Lunch fr£4.50&alc Dinner £5.50–£7.50&alc Wine £2.40 Last dinner 9.45pm
Credit cards 1 3

RUAN HIGH LANES
Cornwall
Map **2** SW93
★★**Hundred House** ☎ Truro (0872) 501336 Closed Nov–Feb, RS Xmas
Small, family-run hotel, set in three acres of gardens and grounds.
10rm (3 5) sB&B £18–£20 sB&B £18–£20 dB&B £30–£36 dB&B £35–£40
CTV 20P *xmas*
Bar lunch 80p–£1.50 Tea 30p–£1.25 Dinner £6.50&alc Wine £3.35 Last dinner 9pm
Credit cards 1 2 3 5 **VS**

★★**Pendower** Gerrans Bay ☎ Truro (0872) 501257 Closed 29 Sep–27 Apr
Situated on headland in secluded grounds with commanding unrestricted views.
20rm (4) (1fb) sB&B £12.50–£13.50 dB&B £25–£27 dB&B £27–£29
CTV 20P 10
Lunch £3.80 Dinner £6 Wine £3.45 Last dinner 7.45pm
S% **VS**

★★*L* **Polsue Manor** ☎ Truro (0872) 501270
Closed early Oct–mid Apr
Charming 18th-century manor in secluded setting and with a relaxed atmosphere.
13rm (9) (4fb) Ⓡ sB&B £13.50–£14.50 sB&B £14.50–£15.50 dB&B £27–£29

dB&B⇌£29–£31 B
☾ CTV 20P ✽
V ♧ Dinner £6.50&alc Wine £3.60 Last dinner 8.30pm
S%

★**Pendower Beach House** ☎ Truro (0872) 501241 Closed Nov–Feb
Character hotel with relaxed atmosphere set in 8 acres close to the sea.
15rm (1⋔) sB&B£10–£14 sB&B⋔£15–£17 dB&B£20–£28 dB&B⋔£30–£34 B
CTV 50P ✽ (hard)
V ♧ Lunch £4–£5.50&alc Tea 65p Dinner £7–£9&alc Wine £4.50 Last dinner 7pm
Credit cards 1 2 3 4 5 **VS**

RUGBY
Warwickshire
Map **4** SP57

★★★**Clifton Court** Lilbourne Rd, Clifton upon Dunsmore ☎ (0788) 65033 RS xmas wk
14rm (10⇌4⋔) CTV in all bedrooms Ⓡ ✱sB⇌⋔ fr31.50 dB⇌⋔ fr£37.50 (room only) B
120P ✽ nc3
English, French & Italian ♧ ✱Lunch £5.45–£6.05&alc Tea fr£1 Dinner fr£6.85–£7.45&alc Wine £5 Last dinner 9.30pm
Credit cards 1 3

★★★**Three Horse Shoes** Sheep St (Porter) ☎ (0788) 4585
Popular and busy, modernised hotel.
32rm (19⇌13⋔) (2fb) CTV in all bedrooms Ⓡ sB&B⇌⋔£21.50–£37.50 dB&B⇌⋔£28–£47 Continental breakfast B
☾ CFA *xmas*
English & French V ♧ Lunch fr£6.50&alc Dinner fr£7.25&alc Wine £5.25
Last dinner 10.30pm
Credit cards 1 2 3 5 **VS**

★★**Dun Cow** The Square, Dunchurch (3m S A426) ☎ (0788) 810233 Telex no 312242

A 16th-century inn, beside the main road.
17rm (1⇌9⋔) (2fb) 1 CTV in all bedrooms Ⓡ ✱sB&B£14–£22 sB&B⇌⋔£19–£29 dB&B£22–£40 dB&B⇌⋔£30–£40 B
☾ 120P 6 *xmas*
V ♧ ✱Lunch £5.95–£9.50&alc Tea 80p–£1.30 High Tea £2.95 Dinner £6.50–£9.50&alc Wine £4.60
Last dinner 10pm
Credit cards 1 2 3 5

✕***Andalucia*** 10 Henry St ☎ (0788) 76404
Dinner not served Sun
Spanish **V** 120 seats
Last dinner 10.30pm
Credit cards 1 2 3 4 5

At **Crick** (6m E A428)
☆☆☆☆**Post House** (Trusthouse Forte) ☎ Crick (0788) 822101
96⇌ 150P

RUGELEY
Staffordshire
Map **7** SK01

★★**Cedar Tree** Main Rd, Brereton ☎ (08894) 4241 Closed Sun evening
A three-storey, white-painted, 18th century building located between Lichfield and Rugeley.
25rm (6⇌8⋔) (1fb) CTV in 1 bedroom Ⓡ sB&B£14 sB&B⇌⋔£15 dB&B£26 dB&B⇌⋔£28 B
CTV 150P squash Disco wkly Live music and dancing twice wkly Cabaret wkly
Continental ♧ Lunch £5–£9 Tea 30p–45p Dinner £6–£10 Wine £4.20 Last dinner 9.30pm
S% Credit cards 1 2 3 5

★★**Eaton Lodge** Wolseley Rd (Wolverhampton & Dudley) ☎ (08894) 3454
12rm (1⇌) (1fb) CTV in all bedrooms Ⓡ ✱sB&B£13.75 sB&B⇌£15.25 dB&B£20 dB&B⇌£24 B
250P ✽

♧ ✱Lunch fr£2.95–£3.95&alc Dinner fr£3.95&alc Wine £3.75
Last dinner 9.15pm
Credit cards 1 3 **VS**

RUNCORN
Cheshire
Map **7** SJ58

☆☆☆**Crest** Wood Ln, Beechwood (Crest) ☎ (0928) 714000 Telex no 627426 RS Public hols
141⇌ CTV in all bedrooms Ⓡ ✱sB⇌ fr£33.50 dB⇌ fr£42 (room only) B
Lift ☾ 250P CFA ✽ Disco Sat Live music and dancing Sat
International **V** ♧ ✱Lunch £3.95–£6.45 Tea 50p Dinner £8.25–£9.75&alc Wine £5.25 Last dinner 9.45pm
Credit cards 1 2 3 4 5 **VS**

RUSHDEN
Northampton
Map **4** SP96

★**Westward** Shirley Rd ☎ (0933) 312376 Closed 24 Dec–1 Jan
16rm (1⋔) Annexe: 10rm (3fb) CTV in 4 →

R

bedrooms TV in 22 bedrooms ® ✗
sB&B £14.50–£18.50 sB&B⋔ £22.50
dB&B £25 dB&B⋔ £30

CTV 16P ▭ (heated)

V ♧ Lunch £3.50–£4.50&alc Tea 50p&alc Dinner £4.50–£6.50&alc Wine £4.80 Last dinner 8pm

RUSHLAKE GREEN
East Sussex
Map **5** TQ61

★★★

★★★ PRIORY COUNTRY HOUSE, RUSHLAKE GREEN

☎ (0435) 830553
Closed 25 Dec–12 Jan

Standing in a tranquil rural area not far from the towns of Hastings and Battle, this small but fine 15th century stone and tile hung manor house is situated in its own extensive grounds and parkland close to the charming village of Rushlake Green. Once an Augustinian priory, the house has been lovingly converted by its owners, Jane and Peter Dunn, with great attention to detail. The interior is comfortable and homely and has a foyer lounge with a fine inglenook fireplace and there is a further comfortable lounge with deep armchairs and flowers. In the absence of a formal bar, the pre-dinner aperitif and crudités are served in these rooms by pleasant staff. The traditional-style beamed bedrooms have lovely soft furnishings and contain several thoughtful touches such as books, magazines, a sewing kit, a tin of biscuits, fresh fruit and toiletries and, naturally are comfortable.
Imaginative meals are served in the two small, beamed dining rooms where tables are set with Laura Ashley tablecloths. The young cook is producing well prepared and presented dishes of interest such as hot crab and vegetable timballe with spinach sauce, flavoursome sea bass served in a light cream and

ginger sauce as well as mouth watering sweets including well made and presented sorbets. It is a fixed price menu of country house style cooking and these enjoyable meals are prepared with a great deal of skill from fresh ingredients.
As well as the structural and decorative features of the hotel with its pleasing architecture, another attractive aspect of it must be the easy, gentle atmosphere and unique manner of service. Apart from the owners, young staff serve with cheerfulness and nothing seems too much trouble for them but yet, they never intrude.

6→ Annexe: 6→ CTV in all bedrooms
sB&B→ £31.05 dB&B→ £44.86–£67.86

P ✽ ♪ nc9yrs

English & French ♧ ☕ Lunch £9.15alc Tea £1.25alc Dinner £14.40alc Wine £5.95 Last dinner 9pm

RUSHYFORD
Co Durham
Map **8** NZ22
★★★ **Eden Arms** (Swallow) ☎ Bishop Auckland (0388) 720541 Telex no 53168

51→ (4fb) 1 ▭ CTV in all bedrooms ®
sB&B→ £26 dB&B→ £33 B

☾ CTV 20P 6 ⌂ CFA billiards Disco Sat (Sep–May)

V ♧ ☕ Lunch £4.30&alc Tea £1.60 High Tea £2.30 Dinner fr£6.25&alc Wine £4.75 Last dinner 9.15pm

S% Credit cards 1 2 3 4 5 **VS**

RUTHERGLEN
Strathclyde *Lanarkshire*
Map **11** NS66
★★ **Stakis Burnside** East Kilbride Rd, Burnside, Cambuslang (Stakis) ☎ 041-634 1276 Telex no 778704

Commercial hotel with a painted, timber exterior, situated on the outskirts of the town.

16rm(13→) CTV in all bedrooms ®
✱ sB&B→ £28 dB&B→ £36 B

☾ 100P

♧ ☕ Last dinner 9.30pm

Credit cards 1 2 3 5 **VS**

RUTHIN
Clwyd
Map **6** SJ15
★★★ **Ruthin Castle** (Best Western) ☎ (08242) 2664 Telex no 61169

Impressive, 15th-century stone castle situated in its own, well-kept grounds.

58rm(55→3⋔) (4fb) sB&B→⋔ £22.50
dB&B→⋔ £42–£47 B

Lift ☾ CTV 200P CFA ✽ ♪ *xmas*

English & Continental **V** ♧ ☕ Lunch £5&alc Tea £1.55&alc Dinner £7.75&alc Wine £4.20 Last dinner 9pm

Credit cards 1 2 3 5

RYDE
Isle of Wight
Map **4** SZ59
★★ **Yelf's** Union St (Trusthouse Forte) ☎ (0983) 64062

Informal hotel with warm friendly atmosphere.

21→ CTV in all bedrooms ® sB&B→ £35
dB&B→ £50 B

🍵☕ Last dinner 8.45pm
Credit cards 1 2 3 4 5

RYE
East Sussex
Map **5** TQ92

★★**George** High St (Trusthouse Forte) ☎(0797) 222114
Historic coaching inn with many original features, well appointed bedrooms and country kitchen style restaurant.
20rm(12➡)(1fb) CTV in all bedrooms ® sB&B➡£35.50 dB&B➡£52.50 B
CTV 9P 8🚗 *xmas*
🍵 Last dinner 9pm
Credit cards 1 2 3 4 5

★★**Hope Anchor** Watchbell St ☎(0797) 222216
Warm comfortable 17th century hotel of great character.
15rm(6➡)(1fb) CTV in 1 bedroom ® ★ sB&B£11–£14.30 dB&B£23–£30.25 dB&B➡£26–£35 B
CTV 20P 1🚗🐕 *xmas*
English & French 🍵☕ Lunch £5–£7.50&alc Tea 50p Dinner £7.50–£8&alc Wine £2.90 Last dinner 9.30pm
S% Credit cards 1 2 3 4 5

★★**Saltings** Hilders Cliff, High St ☎(0797) 223838
Family run hotel with nautical dècor.
15rm(1➡5⋒)(3fb) CTV available in bedrooms ® sB&B£15 sB&B➡⋒£18.50 dB&B£26 dB&B➡⋒£31 B
☾ CTV 35P Live music and dancing Sat in season *xmas*
English & Continental **V** 🍵☕ Lunch £5.05&alc Tea £1.50alc Dinner £7.05&alc Wine £4.75 Last dinner 9.30pm
Credit cards 1 2 3 5

✕**Flushing Inn** Market St ☎(0797) 223292
Closed Tue, 26 Dec–2nd wk Jan Dinner not served Mon
36 seats Lunch £6.60–£7.60&alc Dinner £8.80–£11.50&alc Wine £6 Last dinner 9.15pm 🚭
Credit cards 1 2 3 5

✕**Monastery** 6 High St ☎(0797) 223272
Lunch reservations necessary weekdays.
Closed Mon (Nov–mid Apr) & Tue Dinner not served Sun (Nov–mid Apr)
50 seats Lunch £7.50–£7.75&alc Dinner fr£9.35alc Wine £3.95 Last dinner 9.30pm
🚭 bedrooms available
Live music Fri & Sat, plus Sun lunch
S% **VS**

SAFFRON WALDEN
Essex
Map **5** TL53

★★*H* **Saffron** 10–18 High St ☎(0799) 22676
RS Sat & Sun
A 16th-century hotel combining old world charm with modern comfort, and featuring an inner, terraced patio.
18rm(4➡2⋒)(1fb) CTV in all bedrooms sB&B£14.50 sB&B➡⋒£25 dB&B£20 dB&B➡⋒£34 continental breakfast B
CTV 12P Disco Fri
English & French Lunch £5.50–£8.50&alc Dinner £5.50–£8.50&alc Wine £4.50 Last dinner 9.30pm
Credit cards 1 3 **VS**

ST AGNES
Cornwall
Map **2** SW75

★★**Rose in Vale** Mithian ☎(087 255) 2202 Closed Nov–Mar
14rm(6➡2⋒)(3fb) ®
sB&B£10.50–£12.50 sB&B➡⋒£12–£14 dB&B£21–£25 dB&B➡⋒£24–£28
CTV 25P 🐕 ✽ ≈(heated) nc5yrs
V ✻ Bar lunch fr£1.20 Dinner fr£5.50 Last dinner 8pm
VS

★★***Rosemundy House*** ☎(087 255) 2101 Closed Nov–Mar
Country-house style hotel in four acres of private, wooded gardens.
44rm(18➡12⋒) CTV in 2 bedrooms ★
CTV 70P ✽ ≈(heated) nc5yrs
🍵☕ Last dinner 5pm
Credit card 3
See advert on page 546

★**Lamorna House** Chapel Porth Rd, Goonvrea ☎(087 255) 2670
Closed Nov–Mar
Small hotel in a quiet location.
10rm(2fb) ® ★ sB&B£8.50–£11 dB&B£17–£22
CTV 12P 🐕
🍵☕ Bar lunch 50p–£2.60 Tea £1.05 Dinner £6.25 Wine £5.25 Last dinner 7.30pm

★**Sunholme** Goonvrea Rd ☎(087255) 2318 Closed Nov–Feb
Small, family hotel in a rural location.
11rm(1⋒)(3fb) sB&B£7.50–£10.50 dB&B£15–£21 dB&B⋒£19–£25 B
CTV 20P ✽
🍵☕ Bar lunch £1.25–£3 Tea 35p–£1.10 Dinner fr£5.50&alc Wine £3.75

ST ALBANS
Hertfordshire
Map **4** TL10

☆☆☆**Noke Thistle** Watford Rd (2¾m S at junc A405/A412) (Thistle) ☎(0727) 54252 Telex no 893834
Convenient, comfortable hotel.
57➡(1fb) CTV in all bedrooms ® ✻sB&B➡£35–£38 dB&B➡£42–£45 (room only) B
☾ 200P CFA ✽
European ☕ ✻ Lunch £7&alc Dinner £8&alc Last dinner 9.30pm
Credit cards 1 2 3 4 5 **VS**

★★★**St Michael's Manor** Fishpool St ☎(0727) 64444
Gracious 16th century manor house in beautiful setting with many modern facilities added.
22rm(15➡4⋒) 1 CTV in all bedrooms sB&B£25.75 sB&B➡⋒£33.50 dB&B£39.50 dB&B➡⋒£46 B
☾ 70P 🐕 ✽
English & French **V** Lunch →

fr£7.50&alc Dinner fr£10.50&alc Wine £4.70 Last dinner 9.30pm

Credit cards 1 2 3 VS

★★★**Sopwell House** Cottonmill Ln ☎(0727) 64477

An 18th-century mansion, surrounded by three acres of gardens, and reputed to have once had royal connections.

20⇌ (1fb) CTV in all bedrooms sB&B⇌ fr£32.74 dB&B⇌ fr£41.35

☾ 100P CFA ✿

French Lunch fr£6.90&alc Dinner fr£9&alc Wine £5.06 Last dinner 10pm

Credit cards 1 2 3 5

St Albans

XX ***Aspelia*** 17 Heritage Cl ☎(0727) 66067

Closed Sun & Public hols

Modern restaurant serving interesting Greek food.

Greek V 80 seats Last dinner 11pm

Credit cards 1 2 3 4 5

X ***Jade Garden*** 16–20 Spencer St ☎(0727) 56077

Closed 25–27 Dec & 13 Feb

Town centre restaurant serving good Cantonese cuisine.

Cantonese 70 seats Last dinner 11.30pm

Credit cards 1 2 3 5

❀X **La Province** 13 George St ☎(0727) 52142

Closed Sun, Mon, 25 Dec–2 Jan & 1 wk Etr & last 2 wks Aug

Small French restaurant offering reasonably priced sound cooking.

French 38 seats Lunch £5–£7&alc Dinner £12alc Wine £4.80 Last dinner 10pm

Credit cards 1 2 3 5

ST ANDREWS
Fife
Map **12** NO51

★★★★**Rusacks Marine** Pilmour Links ☎(0334) 74321
Closed 1st 2wks Jan
50rm(49⇌1⋒) (12fb) CTV in all bedrooms sB&B⇌⋒£20–£36 dB&B⇌⋒£40–£72 B
Lift ☾ 30P Live music and dancing wkly *xmas*
French & International V Lunch £5.50&alc Tea £2.75 High Tea £4.50–£7.50 Dinner £9.75&alc Wine £6.50 Last dinner 9.30pm
Credit cards 1 2 3 4 5

★★★*HL* **Rufflets** ☎(0334) 72594
Closed mid Jan–mid Feb
Large, country house hotel with its own grounds and gardens.
18rm(16⇌2⋒) Annexe: 3⇌ (2fb) CTV in all bedrooms ® sB&B⇌⋒£25 dB&B⇌⋒£42 B
100P 6 *xmas*
Scottish & French Lunch £5–£6.50&alc Tea £2.50–£3.50 Dinner £9–£9.50&alc Wine £5.50 Last dinner 9pm
Credit cards 1 2 3 5 **VS**

★★★***St Andrews Golf*** 40 The Scores (Inter-Hotels) ☎(0334) 72611 Telex no 777205
Situated on the sea front with views over sandy beaches and rock pools.
22rm(20⇌2⋒) CTV in all bedrooms ® B
Lift ☾ CFA sauna bath Live music and dancing Sat
Last dinner 9.30pm
Credit cards 1 2 3 5 **VS**

★★★***Scores*** (Best Western) ☎(0334) 72451
30⇌ CTV in all bedrooms B
Lift ☾ CTV
Scottish & Continental V Last dinner 9pm
Credit cards 1 2 3 5 **VS**

★**Ardgowan** 2 Playfair Ter ☎(0334) 72970 RS Oct–Apr
16rm(1⇌) (2fb) TV in all bedrooms ®
*sB&B£9.50 dB&B£19 dB&B⇌£19
CTV
French Bar lunch £1.15–£1.80&alc High Tea £3.25 Wine £3.80 Last high tea 9.15pm

★**Russell** 26 The Scores ☎(0334) 73447
Closed 24 Dec–7 Jan RS Nov–Apr
Small, family-run hotel with views of the sea.
8rm (3fb) CTV in all bedrooms ® sB&B fr£14 dB&B fr£28
Bar lunch £2 Dinner £8.50 Wine £4.50 Last dinner 9.30pm
Credit cards 1 3

✕✕**Grange Inn** Grange ☎(0334) 72670
Closed Mon; 25, 26 Dec, 1 & 2 Jan
Scottish & French V 36 seats Lunch £5.50–£5.95&alc Dinner £10.50alc Wine £4.75 Last dinner 9.30pm 40P bedrooms available
VS

ST ANNES
Lancashire
See **Lytham St Annes**

ST ASAPH
Clwyd
Map **6** SJ07

★★★***Oriel House*** Upper Denbigh Rd ☎(0745) 582716
Modernised hotel set in picturesque area alongside private stretch of river.
19rm(12⇌7⋒) Annexe: 1⇌1 CTV in 12 bedrooms TV in 8 bedrooms ®
150P
English & French V Last dinner 9.30pm
Credit cards 1 3
See advert on page 548

★★**Plas Elwy** The Roe ☎(0745) 582263
Small, converted old mansion house →

situated off main (A55) Chester to Colwyn Bay road.
7⋒ CTV in 7 bedrooms ⓡ ★ sB&B⋒ £15–£16 dB&B⋒ £23–£25 B
20P ✽ (heated)
International V Lunch £3.50–£4&alc Dinner £5–£7&alc Wine £5 Last dinner 10.30pm
Credit cards 1 2 3 5

ST AUBIN
Jersey, Channel Islands
Map **16**

★★★ **La Haule Manor** ☎ Jersey (0534) 41426 Telex no 4192225
Closed Oct–Apr
An 18th-century manor house standing in its own ground facing sea with attractive lounges.
20rm(14⇌) (2fb) ✽sB&B£14–£20 sB&B⇌£20–£26 dB&B£22–£34 dB&B⇌£28–£40
CTV 40P ✽
V ✽Lunch £4&alc Tea 40p Dinner £6 Wine £2.80 Last dinner 8.30pm
Credit cards 2 3 4 5

✕✕ **Old Court House Inn** St Aubin's Harbour ☎ Jersey (0534) 41156
17th Century harbourside restaurant (featured in 'Bergerac'), offering seafood specialities.
Closed 25 & 26 Dec
English & French V 56 seats ✽Lunch £6&alc (Sun only) Dinner £12alc Wine £3 Last dinner 11pm bedrooms available Live music (5 nights wkly)
S%

ST AUSTELL
Cornwall
Map **2** SX05

★★★**Porth Avallen** Sea Rd. Carlyon Bay (Exec Hotel) ☎Par (072681) 2802 RS Xmas & New Year

Comfortable hotel in secluded position.

25rm(16⇌1⋒)(4fb) 2⊟ CTV in 20 bedrooms ✈ sB&B £17.50–£20.50 sB&B⇌⋒ £22.50–£27 dB&B £29–£32.75 dB&B⇌⋒ £34.25–£38 B

CTV 50P ⊕ ✽ ⌂

⊡ English & French ♡ ⊑ Lunch £4–£7&alc Tea 65p–£2&alc High Tea £2.50–£3.50&alc Dinner £7.50–£10.50&alc Wine £3.10 Last dinner 8.30pm

Credit cards 1 2 3 5 **VS**

★★**Clifden** 36–39 Aylmer Sq ☎(0726) 3691 Closed Xmas

15rm(1⇌) CTV in all bedrooms Ⓡ sB&B fr£15 sB&B⇌ fr£19 dB&B fr£24 dB&B⇌ fr£27

CTV

V ♡ ⊑ Lunch £2.50–£3.50&alc Tea fr40p High Tea fr75p Dinner £3.75–£6&alc Wine £3.25 Last dinner 9pm

S% Credit cards 1 3 **VS**

★★**Cliff Head** Sea Rd, Carlyon Bay ☎Par (072681) 2125 RS Oct–Mar

Large, family hotel in its own grounds and gardens overlooking Carlyon Bay.

50rm(12⇌)(2fb) sB&B fr£13.23 sB&B⇌ fr£15.53 dB&B £23 dB&B⇌ £28.74 B

⊁ CTV 60P ✽ ⊡ (heated) nc6

Bar lunch 65p–£2.50 Dinner £6.05 Wine £4.95 Last dinner 8pm

Credit cards 1 3

★★**Pier House** Harbour Front, Charlestown ☎(0726) 5272 Closed Xmas–mid Feb

Small harbour-side character hotel in unspoilt village.

12rm(4⇌)(3fb) sB&B £10 sB&B⇌ £13 dB&B £18–£20 dB&B⇌ £21–£24

CTV 12⌂

⊡ English & French **V** ♡ Dinner £4&alc Wine £3.95 Last dinner 10.30pm **VS**

★★**White Hart** Church St ☎(0726) 2100 Closed Xmas

Well appointed, busy inn, centrally located.

20rm(4⇌) CTV in all bedrooms Ⓡ sB&B fr17.25 sB&B⇌ fr£21.20 fr dB&B £26.40 dB&B⇌ fr£30 B

⊁ ⊕

V ♡ ⊑ Lunch fr£3 Tea £1.20 Dinner fr£7.30 Last dinner 8.30pm

S% Credit cards 1 2 3 **VS**

✕✕**Boscundle Manor** Tregrehan (2m E off A390) ☎Par (072681) 3557

A beautiful 18th-century county house offering good food, fine wines and personal service.

Closed Sun, 23 Dec–mid Feb Lunch not served

⊡ International **V** 20 seats ✽ Dinner £11alc Wine £4.75 Last dinner 9pm 12P bedrooms available

S% Credit cards 1 2 3 **VS**

ST BEES
Cumbria
Map **11** NX91

★★**Queens** Main St ☎Egremont (0946) 822287
Closed 24 Dec–2 Jan

9rm(1⇌3⋒)(1fb) ✈ sB&B £11.50–£13 sB&B⇌ £13.50–£15 dB&B £18.50–£21.50 dB&B⇌ £22.50–£25

CTV 8P

⊡ Mainly grills **V** ♡ Lunch £3.50alc Dinner £4.75alc Wine £3.95 Last dinner 9pm

Credit card 1

ST BOSWELLS
Borders, *Roxburghshire*

★★★**Dryburgh Abbey**
See Dryburgh for Gazetteer entry
See advert on page 550

ST BRELADE
Jersey, Channel Islands
Map **16**

★★★★**Atlantic** La Moye (Best Western) ☎Jersey (0534) 44101 Telex no 4192405
Closed 1 Jan–3 Mar

Modern, purpose-built hotel standing in its own grounds, with views across lawns and trees to the sea.

46⇌⋒ CTV in all bedrooms ✈ ✽ sB&B⇌⋒ fr£26 dB&B⇌⋒ £42–£73

Lift ☾ 50P CFA ⊕ ✽ ⊡ (heated) ⚲ (hard)

⊡ Continental ♡ ⊑ Lunch £5.25–£5.75&alc Tea fr70p Dinner fr£8.25&alc Wine £3 Last dinner 9.15pm

Credit cards 1 2 3 4 5

❀★★★★**Hotel l'Horizon** St Brelade's Bay (Prestige) ☎Jersey (0534) 43101 Telex no 4192281

(Rosette awarded for the Star Grill.)

Hotel with comfortable bedrooms and lounges, overlooking the beach.

104⇌⋒(5fb) CTV in all bedrooms ✈ ✽ sB&B⇌⋒ £22–£26.60 dB&B⇌⋒ £51.25–£70.50 B

Lift ☾ 110P CFA ⊕ ⊡ (heated) sauna bath Live music and dancing nightly ♿

⊡ English, French, Italian **V** ♡ ⊑ ✽ Lunch £8alc Tea £1.75alc Dinner £10&alc Wine £3.50 Last dinner 9.45pm

S% Credit cards 1 2 3 5

See advert on page 550

★★★★**BL La Place** Route du Coin, La Haule ☎Jersey (0534) 44261 Telex no 4191462 RS Nov–Mar (except Xmas)

41⇌ CTV in all bedrooms

☾ 30P CFA ⊡ (heated) sauna bath Live music twice wkly *xmas*

⊡ French ♡ ⊑ Lunch £13.50alc Tea £1.50alc Dinner £13.50alc Wine £3.75 Last dinner 9.30pm
Credit cards 1 2 3 5

❀★★★**Château Valeuse** Rue de Valeuse, St Brelade's Bay ☎Jersey (0534) 43476
Closed Nov–Feb

Small, comfortable, hotel in elevated position with fine view across lawns to the sea.

26rm(18⇌5⋒) ✈ ✽ sB&B £12–£15 sB&B⇌⋒ £15–£18 dB&B £24–£30 dB&B⇌⋒ £30–£36

☾ CTV 50P ⊕ ✽ ⊡ (heated) nc5yrs

⊡ French **V** ♡ ⊑ ✽ Lunch fr£4.50&alc Tea fr50p Dinner fr£6&alc Wine £2.75 Last dinner 9.15pm
Credit cards 1 3

S

S

✕**Herbie's Inn** St Brelade's Bay ☎Jersey (0534) 41081

Closed Mon & Xmas–1 Mar Dinner not served Sun

English & Continental 85 seats Last dinner 10.30pm 30P Live music nightly

Credit cards 3 5

ST BURYAN
Cornwall
Map **2** SW42

★ *H* **Treverven Country House** ☎(073672) 280

7rm(2→1) (2fb) ® sB&B£11.25–£16.50 dB&B£24–£32 dB&B→£26–£36

CTV 40P Live music and dancing Fri & Sat *xmas*

V *Lunch £3.50–£4.95&alc Tea fr60p High Tea fr£2 Dinner £3.50–£4.95&alc Wine £4.50 Last dinner 11pm

Credit cards 1 2 3

ST CLEMENT'S BAY
Jersey, Channel Islands
Map **16**

★★★ *L* ***Ambassadeur*** Le Greve d'Azette ☎Jersey (0534) 24455 Telex no 4192296
Closed 2 Jan–14 Feb

Comfortable, modern family hotel overlooking the sea.

41rm(39→2) CTV in all bedrooms

Lift 40P9 (heated) Cabaret wkly

International **V** Last dinner 8.30pm

Credit cards 1 2 3 4 5 **VS**

✕✕✕**Shakespeare Hotel** Samares Coast Rd ☎Jersey (0534) 51915

Lunch not served Mon–Sat

English & French **V** 120 seats Lunch £5.50&alc Dinner £6.50–£10&alc Wine £3.05 Last dinner 10pm 50P bedrooms available Disco Sat

Credit cards 1 2 3 5 **VS**

ST COLUMB MAJOR
Cornwall
Map **2** SW96

★★ *H* **Old Rectory Hotel & Country Club** Bridge Hill ☎(0637) 880656
Closed Jan

Delightful, 14th-century, character building with a moat in its own attractive grounds.

12rm(2fb) 1 sB&B£12.50 dB&B£25

CTV 40P (heated) (hard)

French **V** Lunch fr£3&alc Dinner fr£6.50&alc Wine £4.95 Last dinner 10.30pm

Credit cards 2 3 5 **VS**

ST COMBS
Grampian *Aberdeenshire*
Map **15** NK06

★★**Tufted Duck** ☎Inverallochy (03465) 2481

Modern hotel overlooking bay.

18rm(11→7) (1fb) CTV in all bedrooms ® sB&B→£19–£25 dB&B→£35–£40

50P sauna bath

French Lunch £5.50&alc Tea 75p Dinner £8.95&alc Wine £4.75 Last dinner 9pm

Credit cards 1 2 3 5 **VS**

See advert on page 552

ST DAVID'S
Dyfed
Map **2** SM72

★★★ *B* **Warpool Court** (Inter-Hotels) ☎(0437) 720300 Closed Jan

Country house hotel standing in seven acres of Italian gardens, with views of St Bride's Bay.

25rm(17→8) CTV in all bedrooms ® *sB&B→£22.40–£25.85 dB&B→£35.10–£43.70

40P (heated) billiards Live music and dancing Sat (winter) Cabaret Fri (winter) *xmas*

English & French **V** *Lunch £1.35–£6.95 Tea £1.20 High Tea £2–£5 Dinner £9.95&alc Wine £3.75 Last dinner 9.30pm

S% Credit cards 1 2 3 **VS**

★★**Grove** High St ☎(0437) 720341
Closed 25–31 Dec

Small, informal, Regency-style hotel.

10rm(7→2) (1fb) 1 CTV in all bedrooms ® sB&B→£14.50–£19 dB&B→£25.50–£33

65P

Bar lunch £1–£2.95 Tea £1.25 Dinner £6.95 Wine £3.90 Last dinner 8.30pm

Credit cards 1 3

See advert on page 552

★★**Old Cross** Cross Sq ☎(0437) 720387
Closed Nov–Feb

An 18th-century house, recently extended, facing the market cross in the square.

17→ (4fb) ® sB&B→£12.70–£18 dB&B→£34–£45

CTV 20P

V *Bar lunch £1–£2.40 Tea fr£1.50 Dinner fr£6.50&alc Wine £3.10 Last dinner 8.30pm

VS

★★**St Non's** ☎(0437) 720239
RS Nov–Feb

A comfortable hotel situated close to the cathedral and the Bishop's Palace.

20→ (5fb) CTV available in bedrooms ® sB&B→£13–£16 dB&B→£26–£32

CTV 40P Live music and dancing Sat *xmas*

International Lunch £2.60–£3.85 Tea 50p High Tea £4 Dinner fr£8.50&alc Wine £4.65 Last dinner 9.30pm

Credit cards 1 2 3 5 **VS**

ST FILLANS
Tayside *Perthshire*
Map **11** NN62

★★★**Four Seasons** ☎(076485) 333
Closed Nov–Mar

A bright and airy hotel with a continental atmosphere. →

S

12rm(11⇌1⋔)(6fb) TV in 12 bedrooms ®sB&B⇌⋔£24.50–£29.50 dB&B⇌⋔£41–£51 ₿
50P 3⌂ ❀
🍽British, French & Italian V ♡ ☕ Lunch £6.50&alc Tea £1–£2 Dinner £9 Wine £4.90 Last dinner 9.45pm
S% Credit cards 1 2

★★*Drummond Arms* (Inter-Hotels) ☎(076485) 212
Closed 17 Oct–10 May
Four-storey, roadside hotel in an attractive position overlooking the wooded shore of Loch Earn.
36rm(14⇌) ₿
CTV 50P ❀ ⌂
🍽English & French ♡ ☕
Last dinner 8.15pm
Credit cards 1 2 3 4 5

ST HELENS
Isle of Wight
Map **4** SZ68
❀ ✕**Hay Loft** Upper Green
☎Bembridge (098387) 2014
Small, simple bistro with lively atmosphere.
Closed Sun & end Sep Spring Bank hol
Lunch not served
🍽Cosmopolitan 40 seats Dinner £7alc Wine £3.70 Last dinner 9.15pm
VS

ST HELENS
Merseyside
Map **7** SJ59
See also Rainhill
★★★**Fleece** Church St (Greenall Whitley) ☎(0744) 26546 Telex no 629811
This modernised hotel dates back to 1792 when it was a coaching inn.
73rm(71⇌2⋔)(4fb) CTV in all bedrooms ®sB&B⇌⋔£29.50–£30.50 dB&B⇌⋔£39–£40 ₿
Lift ☾ 70P CFA
♡ Bar lunch 90p–£3 Dinner £6–£6.50&alc Wine £5 Last dinner 9.15pm
Credit cards 1 2 3 5

At **Haydock** (5m E junc M6/A580)
☆☆☆☆**Post House** Lodge Lane (Trusthouse Forte) ☎Wigan (0942) 717878
98⇌ 130P

ST HELIER
Jersey, Channel Islands
Map **16**
❀ ★★★★*L* **Grand** The Esplanade
☎Jersey (0534) 22301 Telex no 4192104
(Rosette awarded for Victoria's.)
Large, recently-modernised hotel with an excellent swimming pool and a health and beauty centre.
118⇌ CTV in all bedrooms
✻sB&B⇌£21–£31 dB&B⇌£42–£62 ₿
Lift ☾ 30P CFA ▭(heated) billiards sauna bath Live music and dancing Fri & Sat in season *xmas*
🍽English & Continental ♡ ☕ ✻ Tea £1 Dinner £6.50&alc Wine £3 Last dinner 9pm
Credit cards 1 2 3 5

★★★★**Hotel La Plage** Havre des Pas
☎Jersey (0534) 23474 Telex no 4192328
Closed Nov–Feb
97⇌(3fb) CTV in all bedrooms
✻sB&B⇌£20.50–£25.50 dB&B⇌£39–£63
Lift ☾ 80P 20⌂ CFA Live music and dancing 6 nights wkly
🍽English & French ♡ ☕ Lunch £5.50&alc Tea fr65p Dinner £7.15&alc Wine £2.75 Last dinner 9pm
Credit cards 1 2 3 4 5

★★★**Apollo** St Saviour's Rd ☎Jersey (0534) 25441 Telex no 4192086
Comfortable, modern town centre hotel.
53⇌⋔(4fb) CTV in all bedrooms
sB&B⇌⋔£21–£25 dB&B⇌⋔£35–£45 ₿
Lift ☾ CTV 45P Disco Wed & Sat Cabaret Wed *xmas*

French ☕ ☕ Lunch fr£4&alc Dinner fr£6.50&alc Last dinner 8.30pm

Credit cards 1 2 3

See advert on page 554

★★★ **Beaufort** Green St ☎ Jersey (0534) 32471 Telex no 4192160

54🛁🚿 (1fb) CTV in all bedrooms ★ sB&B🛁🚿 £22–£26 dB&B🛁🚿 £36–£42 B

Lift ☾ CTV 30P disco wkly Live music and dancing wkly cabaret wkly *xmas*

French ☕ ☕ Lunch £4.50–£5&alc Dinner £6.50–£7.50&alc Last dinner 9pm

Credit cards 1 2 3 4 5

★★★ **Ommaroo** Havre des Pas ☎ Jersey (0534) 23493 Telex no 4192225

84rm(51🛁23🚿) (8fb) CTV in 73 bedrooms ✱sB&B£14–£20 sB&B🛁🚿 £20–£26 dB&B🛁🚿 £28–£40

Lift ☾ CTV 80P CFA ✿ Disco wkly Cabaret wkly in season ♨ *xmas*

English & French V ☕ ☕ ✱Lunch fr£4&alc Tea 40p Dinner £6&alc Wine £2.80 Last dinner 8.30pm

Credit cards 2 3 4 5

★★★ *BL* **Pomme D'or** The Weighbridge ☎ Jersey (0534) 78644 Telex no 4192309

Recently-modernised hotel, with comfortable bedrooms and extensive bars in a central location.

151🛁🚿 (3fb) CTV in all bedrooms ® ✱sB&B🛁🚿 £19–£25 dB&B🛁🚿 £30–£46 B

Lift ☾ *xmas*

English & French V ☕ ☕ ✱Lunch £4.50–£5&alc Tea 50palc Dinner £6–£6.50&alc Wine £2.55 Last dinner 9pm

Credit cards 1 2 3 5

S

★★ *L* **Hotel Savoy** Rouge Bouillon
☎ Jersey (0534) 30012
Closed Dec–Feb
65rm(35⇌4⋒)(2fb) CTV in all bedrooms ✱ *sB&B£9–£13.50 sB&B⇌⋒£11.25–£15.75 dB&B£18–£27 dB&B⇌⋒£22.50–£31
Lift ☾ 50P (heated) Live music and dancing wkly Cabaret wkly
English, French & Italian ✱Lunch £3.50&alc Tea 40p Dinner £5&alc Wine £2.60 Last dinner 8.30pm
Credit cards 1 3 **VS**

★★ **Mountview** St John's Rd Minotel)
☎ Jersey (0534) 78887 Telex no 4192341
Closed mid Dec–mid Mar
An attractive holiday hotel providing pleasant service.
36rm(11⇌20⋒)(2fb) CTV in all bedrooms sB&B£16–£20.50 sB&B⇌⋒£18–£22.50 dB&B£26–£35 dB&B⇌⋒£30–£39
Lift ☾ 12P
Lunch £3.50–£4.50 Tea 45p–55p High Tea £2–£3.50 Dinner £4.50–£6&alc Wine £3 Last dinner 8pm
Credit card 1 3

★★ **Royal Yacht** The Weighbridge
☎ Jersey (0534) 20511 Telex no 4192085
45rm(18⇌27⋒)(9fb) CTV in all bedrooms sB&B⇌⋒£15.50–£18 dB&B⇌⋒£31–£36
Lift ☾ # CTV *xmas*
English & French ✱Lunch £2.25–£5.50&alc Tea 80p Dinner £6.75&alc Wine £3.50 Last dinner 8.30pm
Credit cards 1 3

✕✕ **La Capannina** 67 Halkett Pl
☎ Jersey (0534) 34602
Closed Sun & Public hols
French & Italian 80 seats Lunch

S

£7.50alc Dinner £7.50alc Wine £3.95 Last dinner 10pm

S% Credit cards 1 2 3 5

✕✕**Mauro's** 37 La Motte St ☎ Jersey (0534) 20147

Closed Sun, Public hols & 20 Dec–2 Feb

French & Italian 48 seats Last dinner 10pm

Credit card 3

ST IVES
Cambridgeshire
Map **4** TL37

★★★**Slepe Hall** Ramsey Rd ☎ (0480) 63122 Closed Xmas

14rm(9) (2fb) 3 CTV in all bedrooms sB&B£25 sB&B£33 dB&B£35 dB&B£42

120P 1

International V Lunch £9.85alc Tea 75palc Dinner £10alc Wine £5.50 Last dinner 10pm

Credit cards 1 2 3 5

★★**Golden Lion** Market Hill ☎ (0480) 63159 Closed Xmas night & Boxing day

Modernised, 16th-century inn situated in the town centre, popular with business and tourist clientele alike.

21rm(17) (3fb) CTV in 17 bedrooms Ⓡ *sB&B£12 sB&B£19 dB&B£31

CTV

*Lunch £3.50 Dinner £3.50–£7.50 Wine £3 Last dinner 10.30pm

Credit cards 1 3

☆☆**St Ives Motel** London Rd ☎ (0480) 63857 Closed 25–27 Dec

16 (2fb) CTV in all bedrooms Ⓡ sB fr£24.75 dB fr£36

TV 80P

Lunch £9.50alc Tea 60palc Dinner £9.50alc Wine £4.60 Last dinner 9.30pm

Credit cards 1 2 3 5

ST IVES
Cornwall
Map **2** SW54
See plan

★★★**Carbis Bay** Carbis Bay ☎ Penzance (0736) 795311 Plan **2** *B2*

Closed Nov–Mar

Large, detached property close to its own beach with beautiful views across St Ives Bay.

28rm(18) (7fb) CTV in all bedrooms Ⓡ sB&B£15–£20 sB&B£17–£22 dB&B£30–£40 dB&B£34–£44

CTV 200P 6 (heated) Live music and dancing 4 nights wkly (in season) *xmas*

English & French Lunch £3.50 Tea 40p–60p Dinner £7.50&alc Wine £4.50 Last dinner 9.30pm

Credit cards 1 2 3 5 **VS**

★★★**Chy-an-Drea** The Terrace (Inter-Hotels) ☎ Penzance (0736) 795076 Plan **5** *B4*

Closed Nov–Mar

Hotel situated in a commanding position overlooking Porthminster Beach and St Ives Bay.

35rm(20 9) (3fb) CTV in 30 bedrooms Ⓡ sB&B£16–£19 sB&B£17–£21 dB&B£30–£38 dB&B£34–£42

CTV 5P 20 nc4yrs

Lunch £3alc Dinner fr£7 Last dinner 8.30pm

Credit cards 1 2 3 5

★★★*H* **Garrack** Higher Ayr (Exec Hotel) ☎ Penzance (0736) 796199 Plan **9** *A5*

Closed Dec–Mar

Secluded hotel with a country house atmosphere, set in its own grounds giving panoramic views of St Ives Bay.

19rm(11 2) Annexe: 2rm (3fb) CTV in 6 bedrooms sB&B£13.25–£16.50 dB&B£26.50–£33 dB&B£36–£43.50

CTV 30P (heated) Sauna bath →

S

English & French Lunch £7alc Tea £2alc Dinner £7.50alc Wine £4.20 Last dinner 8.30pm

Credit cards 1 2 3 4 5 **VS**

★★★**Porthminster** The Terrace ☎Penzance (0736) 795221 Plan **15** *B4*
Closed mid Dec–mid Jan

Traditional hotel in a commanding position overlooking St Ives Bay.

50rm(25→25⋒)(7fb) CTV in all bedrooms ® sB&B→⋒£18–£20.50 dB&B→⋒£36–£41 ℞

Lift ☾ CTV 32P 10 ✽ (heated) sauna bath Disco wkly

St Ives

V Lunch £7alc Tea fr50p Dinner £7&alc Wine £3.60
Last dinner 8.30pm

Credit cards 1 2 3 4 5

★★★***Tregenna Castle*** Tregenna Park, St Ives Rd ☎Penzance (0736) 795254 Telex no 45128 Plan **18** *B3*

An imposing, granite-built house in superb grounds with good sporting facilities.

79rm(66→2⋒) CTV in all bedrooms ® ℞

Lift ☾ 50P 20 CFA ✽ (heated) 18 (hard & grass) squash Live music and dancing wkly

English & French V Last dinner 9pm

Credit cards 1 2 3 4 5 **VS**

★★*HL* **Boskerris** Boskerris Rd, Carbis Bay ☎Penzance (0736) 795295 Plan **1** *A2*
Closed early Oct–19 Apr

Well appointed hotel with country house atmosphere.

20rm(15→)(3fb) sB&B£11–£12.50 dB&B£22–£25 dB&B→£25–£27 ℞

CTV 20P ✽ (heated) →

S

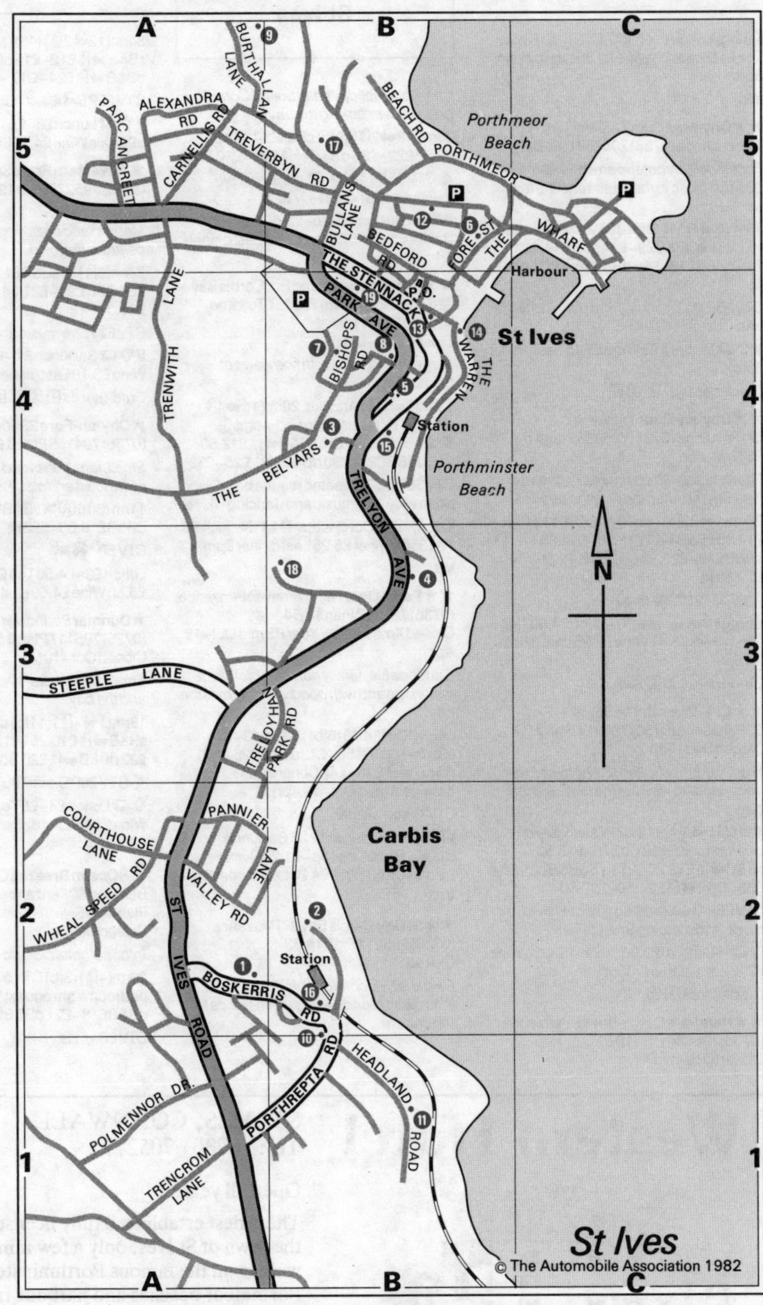
A
B
C
5
4
3
2
1
BURTHALLA LANE
ALEXANDRA RD
PARC AN CREET
CARNELLIS RD
TREVERBYN RD
BEACH RD
Porthmeor Beach
PORTHMEOR
BULLANS LANE
BEDFORD RD
FORE ST
THE WHARF
Harbour
THE STENNACK
P.O.
PARK AVE
BISHOPS RD
TRENWITH LANE
St Ives
THE WARREN
Station
THE BELYARS
TRELYON AVE
Porthminster Beach
N
STEEPLE LANE
TRELOYHAN PARK RD
COURTHOUSE LANE
PANNIER LANE
Carbis Bay
WHEAL SPEED RD
VALLEY RD
ST IVES ROAD
BOSKERRIS RD
HEADLAND ROAD
PORTHREPTA RD
POLMENNOR DR.
TRENCROM LANE
St Ives
© The Automobile Association 1982

St Ives

1 Boskerris ★★
2 Carbis Bay ★★★
3 Chy-an-Albany ★★
4 Chy-an-Dour ★★
5 Chy-an-Drea ★★★
6 Chy-an-Fore ★
7 Chy-Morvah ★★
8 Dunmar ★
9 Garrack ★★★
10 Hendra's ★★
11 Karenza ★★
12 Ocean Breezes ★
13 Outrigger ✕
14 Pedn-Olva ★★
15 Porthminster ★★★
16 St Uny ★★
17 Trecarrell ★
18 Tregenna Castle ★★★
19 Western ★★

S

English & French V Lunch £3.50 Tea £1 Dinner £8 Wine £3.80 Last dinner 8pm

VS

★★**Chy-an-Albany** Albany Ter Penzance (0736) 796759 Plan **3** *B4*

Family holiday hotel in an elevated position close to the beach and the town centre.

36rm(5 5) (10fb) Ⓡ TV available on request sB&B£9–£14 sB&B £11–£16 dB&B£18–£28 dB&B £22–£32

CTV 35P Live music and dancing twice wkly

V Dinner fr£5 Wine £2.75 Last dinner 8pm

Credit cards 1 2 3 5

★★**Chy-an-Dour** Trelyon Av Penzance (0736) 796436 Plan **4** *B3*
RS Nov–Feb

Family hotel with commanding views of St Ives Bay, situated close to the beach.

29rm(1 20) (4fb) Ⓡ sB&B£11.50–£14.95 sB&B £11.50–£14.95 dB&B£23–£29.90 dB&B £23–£29.50

Lift ☾ CTV 22P

English & Belgian Lunch £4.60 Tea 50p Dinner £6.44 Wine £3.95 Last dinner 8.15pm

Credit cards 1 2 3

★★**Chy-Morvah** The Belyars Penzance (0736) 796314 Plan **7** *B4*
Closed Dec–Feb

From its high situation, the hotel enjoys commanding views of the town and the bay.

40rm(11 4) (12fb) TV available in bedrooms *sB&B£10.75–£16.50 sB&B £12.25–£18.75 dB&B£21.50–£33 dB&B £24.50–£37.50

CTV 25P (heated) Disco wkly Live music and dancing 6 nights wkly

*Lunch fr£2.50 Dinner fr£4.50 Wine £2.95 Last dinner 8.30pm

Credit cards 1 3

★★**Hendra's** Carbis Bay Penzance (0736) 795030 Plan **10** *B1*
Closed Oct–mid May

34rm(12 2) (4fb) sB&B£10–£12 sB&B £12–£15 dB&B£20–£24 dB&B £24–£30

CTV 25P 5 nc5yrs *xmas*

V Lunch £3–£5 Tea fr50p Dinner fr£8&alc Wine £4.20 Last dinner 8pm

★★**Western** Royal Sq Penzance (0736) 795277 Plan **19** *B4* Closed Xmas RS Oct–Apr

Modernised coaching inn, located in the centre of the town.

23rm(2) sB&B£11.49–£13.92 dB&B£23.98–£27.84 dB&B £26.20–£30.06

CTV 8 Live music and dancing wkly

V Bar lunch £1–£3.50 Dinner £5.50 Wine £3.18 Last dinner 8pm

Credit cards 1 2 3 5

★**Chy-an-Fore** 28 Fore St Penzance (0736) 794155 Plan **6** *B5*

Small, family terraced hotel set in the heart of the town and close to the beach.

11rm (3fb) Ⓡ sB&B£8.25–£11 dB&B£16.50–£22

CTV 5P 1

Lunch £3–£4.50 Tea £1.30 Dinner £4.50–£5.50 Wine £4.60 Last dinner 7pm

★**Dunmar** Pednolver Ter Penzance (0736) 796117 Plan **8** *B4*
Closed Oct–19 Mar

Small, family hotel overlooking the town and the bay.

18rm(1 4) (11fb) sB&B£8.80–£11 sB&B £10.25–£13.25 dB&B£17.60–£22 dB&B £20.50–£26.50

☾ CTV 20P Disco Thu

Lunch £4–£5 Tea £2 Dinner £5–£7 Wine £3.05 Last dinner 7pm

VS

★*H* **Ocean Breezes** Clodgy View, Barnoon Penzance (0736) 795587 Plan **12** *B5*
Closed Nov

Informal hotel close to the old town.

20rm(4) (3fb) CTV available in bedrooms on request sB&B£9–£10.50 dB&B£18–£21 dB&B £20–£23

CTV 8P *xmas*

Character holiday hotel built of Cornish granite, overlooking the bay.

38rm(13 2) (9fb) sB&B£11–£13 dB&B£22–£26 dB&B £26–£30.14

☾ CTV 16P 14 (heated) Live music and dancing wkly

V Bar lunch 60p–£2.50 Tea 50p Dinner £5.50–£7 Wine £2.95 Last dinner 8pm

★★**Karenza** Headland Rd, Carbis Bay Penzance (0736) 795294 Telex no 337363 Plan **11** *B1*
Closed Nov–Mar

Large, family hotel with fine views of Carbis Bay.

12rm(5 3) Annexe: 20rm(14 4) (10fb) CTV available in bedrooms Ⓡ *sB&B£11.50–£15 sB&B £12.50–£16 dB&B£23–£30 dB&B £25–£32

CTV 30P (heated) sauna bath Disco twice wkly Live music and dancing wkly

English & Continental *Lunch £3 Tea 35p Dinner £5.25 Last dinner 8pm

VS

★★**Pedn-Olva** The Warren Penzance (0736) 796222 Plan **14** *B4*
Closed Xmas & New Year RS mid Oct–19 Apr

Comfortable, family holiday hotel by the waterside and with good views across the bay.

34rm(13 14) (6fb) sB&B£13–£20 sB&B £14.50–£22 dB&B£26–£40 dB&B £28–£42 Continental breakfast (mid Oct–19 Apr)

CTV Disco wkly

English & French Bar lunch £1.30–£2.50 Tea 45p–£1.20 Dinner £6.50–£7.50 Wine £4.20 Last dinner 8pm

VS

★★**St Uny** Carbis Bay Penzance (0736) 795011 Plan **16** *B2*
Closed Oct–Mar

Castle-style, comfortable, family hotel, set in its own grounds and gardens close to the beach.

S

Bar lunch £1.10–£2.50 Tea 80p Wine £3.75 Last dinner 7pm
Credit cards [1] [2] [3] [5] **VS**

★**Trecarrell** Carthew Ter ☎Penzance (0736) 795707 Plan **17** *B5* Closed Nov & Dec RS Jan & Feb
Personally-managed, small hotel in a quiet position above the town.
14rm(1 7) (3fb)
CTV 14P Live music and dancing wkly Cabaret wkly
International Lunch £4.50 Tea 60p High Tea £3 Dinner £5.25&alc Wine £4
Last dinner 7.45pm
Credit cards [1] [2] [3] [5]

✕***Outrigger*** Street-an-Pol ☎Penzance (0736) 795936 Plan **13** *B4*
Intimate, friendly bistro, serving interesting local seafood.
Closed Mon Lunch not served
French 32 seats Last dinner 10.15pm
Credit cards [1] [3] [5] **VS**

ST KEYNE
Cornwall
Map **2** SX26
★★ *L* **Old Rectory** ☎Liskeard (0579) 42617 Closed Nov–mid Mar
Small, stone-built Victorian house, in relaxing grounds with friendly service.
9rm(1 2) (3fb) sB&B £11.50–£14 dB&B £23–£28 dB&B £27.30–£32.30
CTV 20P
Dinner £7.50–£8 Wine £4.09 Last dinner 7.30pm
Credit cards [1] [3] **VS**

ST LAWRENCE
Jersey, Channel Islands
Map **16**
★★★ *HB* **Little Grove** Rue de Haut ☎Jersey (0534) 25321
Attractive, granite-built house in pleasant grounds and with good restaurant and attentive staff.
13rm(10 3) CTV in all bedrooms sB&B £20–22 dB&B £40–£44

25P (heated)
French Lunch fr£6.05&alc Tea fr£1&alc Dinner fr£7.15&alc Wine £3 Last dinner 10pm
Credit cards [1] [2] [3]

ST LAWRENCE
Isle of Wight
Map **4** SZ57
★★ *H* **Rocklands** ☎Ventnor (0983) 852964
Closed Nov–May RS Oct
Mr and Mrs Exposite run a very friendly family hotel with many facilities for children.
16rm(9 2) Annexe: 4rm (10fb) 1 CTV in all bedrooms sB&B £15.95–£18.45 sB&B £16.95–£19.45 dB&B £32.90–£36.90 dB&B £34.90–£38.90
CTV 18P (heated) billiards sauna bath
V Lunch fr£3.45 Tea fr50p Dinner £9–£11alc Last dinner 8.30pm

ST LEONARDS-ON-SEA
E. Sussex
Map **5** TQ80
See Hastings & St Leonards

ST MARGARET'S HOPE
Orkney
Map **16** ND49
✕**Creel** Front St ☎(085 683) 311
Closed Mon & Tue Lunch not served
44 seats Dinner £7.50–£8alc Wine £4.80 Last dinner 10.30pm P
S% **VS**

ST MARTIN
Guernsey, Channel Islands
Map **16**
★★★**Hotel Bella Luce** La Fosse ☎Guernsey (0481) 38764
31rm(24 4) (10fb) CTV in all bedrooms sB&B £13.50–£22 dB&B £20–£41
65P (heated) sauna bath

International **V** Lunch £3.85&alc Tea 50p–£1.50&alc High Tea £1.50–£3&alc Dinner £5–£6.95&alc Wine £2.95 Last dinner 10pm

★★★**Green Acres** Les Hubits ☎Guernsey (0481) 35711
Rural hotel with good modern furniture.
48rm(44 4) (3fb) CTV in all bedrooms sB&B £8.50–£21 dB&B £17–£34
75P (heated) *xmas*
English & French Lunch £3.75 Tea 40p–£1.85 High Tea £1.50–£3 Dinner £5 Wine £2.70 Last dinner 8.30pm

★★★ *H* **Ronnie Ronalde's St Martin's Hotel** Les Merriennes (Best Western) ☎Guernsey (0481) 35644
Spacious holiday hotel standing in its own grounds, offering good amenities.
57rm(53 4) (23fb) CTV in all bedrooms sB&B £20–£26 dB&B £40–£52
Lift 200P 3 CFA (heated) (hard) Live music and dancing 6 nights wkly *xmas*
English & French **V** Lunch £4–£7&alc Tea 50p–£1&alc Dinner £6.25–£7&alc Wine £2.50 Last dinner 9pm
Credit cards [1] [2] [3] [5]

★★★**St Margaret's Lodge** Forest Rd ☎Guernsey (0481) 35757
Holiday hotel with an attractive bar and restaurant and within reach of the airport.
43 CTV in all bedrooms sB&B £13.50–£22.50 dB&B £27–£45
Lift CTV 200P CFA (heated) Live music and dancing twice wkly *xmas*
English & French **V** Lunch £3.50–£4.50&alc Tea 45p&alc High Tea £1.25 Dinner £7alc Wine £2.85 Last dinner 9.45pm
S% Credit cards [1] [2] [3] [5]

ST MARYCHURCH
Devon
Map **3** SX96
See **Torquay**

S

ST MAWES
Cornwall
Map **2** SW83

★★★

★★★**TRESANTON, ST MAWES**
☎(0326) 270544
Closed Nov–Mar

In the words of one of our inspectors, this is 'quite simply the most charming and delightful hotel I have ever stayed in'. Generous praise indeed, but it is a view widely shared by many of our members who report on this hotel. From the busy beach road, you enter another world where the two houses which make up this hotel are set among pretty terrace gardens with views of the bay and the Roseland peninsula; they offer every comfort and a unique atmosphere. The original building contains the reception, a small television room and a bar with a piano – this room is one where the owner, Mrs Farquharson Oliver, can be met in the evening offering her own special brand of hospitality. At the house higher up the hill are most of the bedrooms, individually decorated in soft pastel shades and very well appointed; television or radio can be arranged on request. There is a small sitting area as well as the delightful drawing room which offers every comfort. The whole hotel is adorned by antiques, pictures and objets d'art – some of them very fine indeed – as

well as fresh flowers. The dining room offers fairly simple fare, featuring local fish which is well cooked and of excellent quality. Afternoon tea, too, deserves special mention. The word 'quality' together with the considerate and friendly service from all the staff, epitomises the virtues of this splendid hotel.

21rm(6➡) CTV available in bedrooms ✱sB&B£46.50 (incl dinner) sB&B➡£46.50 (incl dinner) dB&B£118 (incl dinner) dB&B➡£118.00 (incl dinner)

CTV 40P 🚫 ✽ nc10yrs

British & French **V** ✱Lunch £15alc Dinner £15 Wine £6 Last dinner 8.45pm

S% Credit cards 2 3

★★★**Idle Rocks** (Inter-Hotels)
☎(0326) 270771 Closed late Oct–late Mar

Family owned hotel situated on the harbour-side with pleasant views from the public rooms.

15rm(13➡2⋒) Annexe: 8➡ (5fb) Ⓡ sB&B➡⋒£18–£22 dB&B➡⋒£36–£44 Ɓ

CTV 🚫 nc6yrs

English & Continental Bar lunch £3.50alc Tea £1.50 Dinner £9 Wine £3.95 Last dinner 9.30pm

Credit cards 1 2 3 5 **VS**

★★**Green Lantern** Marine Pd ☎(0326) 270502 Closed Dec–Jan

The hotel is in a central position on the sea front with views of the harbour.

11rm(2➡4⋒) CTV in 6 bedrooms ✱ sB&B£10.50 sB&B➡⋒£10.50 dB&B£21 dB&B➡⋒£21

CTV 🚫 nc12yrs

English & Continental Lunch £5.50 Dinner £7.50&alc Wine £4.50 Last dinner 9.30pm

Credit cards 1 2 3 5

★★**Rising Sun** ☎(0326) 270233
Closed 15 Nov–Feb

Small, character inn at the harbour's edge.

13rm(7➡) Ⓡ sB&B£17.50–£20 sB&B➡£17.50–£20 dB&B£35–£40 dB&B➡£40–£43

CTV 6P 🚫 nc10yrs

Bar lunch 75p–£5 Dinner £7.50 Wine £3.30
Last dinner 8.45pm

Credit cards 1 2 5

★★**Ship & Castle** Harbourside
☎(0326) 270401 Closed Nov–Mar

Pleasant, family holiday hotel on the waterfront.

47rm (46➡) (2fb) CTV in 3 bedrooms Ⓡ ✱sB&B£14–£19 sB&B➡£14–£19 dB&B£20–£38 dB&B➡£20–£38

Lift CTV 10P Live music and dancing 3 nights wkly

English & French **V** Lunch £3–£5 Dinner £4.95 Last dinner 9pm

Credit cards 1 3 **VS**

★**St Mawes** The Seafront ☎(0326) 270266 Closed Dec & Jan

Comfortable, small village hotel on seafront.

7rm(2➡) Ⓡ sB&B£13.20–£15.40 dB&B£22–£25.50 dB&B➡£30.80–£35

CTV 🚫 nc3yrs

V Lunch £6–£8&alc Dinner £7.25–£8.80&alc Wine £3.95 Last dinner 8pm

S% Credit cards 1 2 3 **VS**

ST MAWGAN
Cornwall
Map **2** SW86

★**Dalswinton Country House**
☎(06374) 385 Closed Xmas
Small hotel in a secluded position with pleasant rural views.

S

10rm(3➡2⋒)(3fb)Ⓡ sB&B£9.20–£12.08 sB&B➡⋒£12.65–£15.53 dB&B£18.40–£24.15 dB&B➡⋒£21.85–£27.60 Ᵽ

CTV 15P ✽ (heated)

Bar lunch £2.25alc Dinner £5.75&alc Wine £3.50 Last dinner 7.30pm

Credit card 1 **VS**

★ ***Pen-y-Morfa Country*** ☎(06374) 363

Small modern hotel in the heart of the village.

11rm CTV available in 6 bedrooms Ᵽ

40P (heated) sauna bath

Credit cards 2 5

ST MELLION
Cornwall
Map **2** SX36

☆☆☆*L* **St Mellion** ☎St Dominick (0579) 50101 Closed Xmas

Modern hotel in a rural location, just off the A388 Callington road.

24➡⋒(24fb) CTV in all bedrooms Ⓡ sB&B➡⋒£29.75–£35 dB&B➡⋒£51.20–£60 Ᵽ

☾ CTV 500P CFA (heated) squash billiards sauna bath

V ✻ Lunch £2 Tea 40p High Tea £2 Dinner £8.50&alc Wine £5.60 Last dinner 9.30pm

Credit cards 1 2 3 5

ST MELLONS
South Glamorgan
Map **3** ST28

★★ **St Mellons Hotel & County Club** ☎Castleton (0633) 680355 RS 25 Dec eve

A comfortable hotel, well situated between Cardiff and Newport, where the new annexe rooms are particularly well-appointed and there is a leisure complex on site. →

S

S

13 Annexe: 14 (10fb) CTV in 25 bedrooms TV in 2 bedrooms ® sB&B £23–£31 dB&B £33–£48

CTV 200P CFA (heated) (hard) squash billiards sauna bath

English & French V Lunch fr£5.50&alc Dinner fr£7&alc Wine £4.90 Last dinner 10pm

Credit cards 1 2 3 4 5 VS

ST PETER
Jersey, Channel Islands
Map **16**

★★★★ ***Mermaid*** Airport Rd Jersey (0534) 41255 Telex no 4192249

68 CTV in all bedrooms

150P CFA (heated) Live music and dancing 3 nights wkly (in season)

English, French & Italian V Last dinner 9pm

Credit cards 1 2 3 4

XXX ***Governor's Grill*** (Mermaid Hotel) Airport Rd Jersey (0534) 41255

Closed Mon

English, French & Italian 52 seats Last dinner 10pm 50P bedrooms available Live music 3 nights wkly Live music and dancing wkly

Credit cards 1 2 3 4

ST PETER PORT
Guernsey, Channel Islands
Map **16**

★★★★ **Duke of Richmond** Cambridge Park Guernsey (0481) 26221 Telex no 4191462

Purpose-built commercial and holiday hotel, with good amenities.

75rm(70 5) (11fb) CTV in all bedrooms ® sB&B £20–£27.50 dB&B £37–£50

Lift CFA (heated) Live music and dancing 3 nights wkly *xmas*

English & French V Lunch £3.50–£4.50&alc Tea 55p–£1 High Tea £2.85–£4&alc Dinner £7–£7.50&alc Wine £3.25 Last dinner 9.30pm

Credit cards 1 2 3 5

★★★★ ***Old Government House*** Ann's Pl Guernsey (0481) 24921 Telex no 4191144

Long-established, well-appointed, traditional hotel, with sea views.

73 1 CTV in all bedrooms

Lift CTV 30P CFA (heated) Disco Mon–Sat Live music and dancing Mon–Sat

English & French V Last dinner 9.15pm

Credit cards 1 2 3 4 5 VS

★★★ **La Frégate** Les Côtils Guernsey (0481) 24624

Small, comfortable hotel with a good restaurant overlooking the town and sea.

13 ® sB £20–£25 dB £40–£50 (room only)

24P nc14yrs

French V Lunch £6.50–£6.90 Dinner £9–£9.40&alc Wine £3.50 Last dinner 9.30pm

Credit cards 1 2 3 5

★★★ ***Royal*** Glategny Esp Guernsey (0481) 23921 Telex no 4191221

Traditional, large hotel, on the seafront, overlooking the harbour and the neighbouring islands.

79rm(70) CTV in all bedrooms

Lift 120P CFA (heated) Live music and dancing 3 nights wkly

English & French V Last dinner 9pm

Credit cards 1 2 3 5

★★ *L* **Duncholille** Guelles Rd Guernsey (0481) 22912

Closed Nov–mid Mar (except Xmas)

24rm(7 13) (5fb) ® sB&B £10.50–£16 sB&B £11.75–£17.25 dB&B £21–£32 dB&B £23.50–£35.50

CTV 10P (heated) *xmas* →

S

English, French & Italian Tea 40p Dinner £4.50 Wine £2.75 Last dinner 8pm VS

★★**Grange Lodge** Grange Rd
☎Guernsey (0481) 25161
Closed Dec & Jan
Late Georgian house set in own grounds.
33rm (21) CTV in all bedrooms sB&B£11–£12.50 sB&B£12–£13.50 dB&B£22–£25 dB&B£24–£27
CTV 50P ✽
English & French **V** ✻Bar lunch fr40p&alc Tea 45p High Tea 70p Dinner fr£3.50 Wine £1.80 Last dinner 7.15pm
Credit cards 1 3

★★**Hotel de Havelet** Havelet
☎Guernsey (0481) 22199
Attractive old Guernsey residence with modern 'Wellington Boot' restaurant and a bar in the annexe.
33rm (30 1) CTV in all bedrooms sB&B £15.50–£17.50 dB&B£25–£29 dB&B £29–£33
30P ✽
English, Austrian & French Lunch £4alc Dinner £4.25–£6&alc Last dinner 9pm
Credit cards 1 2 3 4 5

★★**Moore's** Pollet ☎Guernsey (0481) 24452
Tourist and commercial hotel close to the shopping centre in town.
34rm (20) Annexe: 6rm (3) CTV in all bedrooms sB&B£11.50–£16 sB&B £12.60–£18.20 dB&B£19.25–£29.70 dB&B £22.80–£34.10
Lift ☾ *xmas*
English & French Lunch £3–£4.50 Dinner £4–£5 Wine £2.50 Last dinner 8.45pm
Credit cards 1 2 3
See advert on page 563

○**St Pierre Park** Rohais ☎Guernsey (0481) 28282 Telex no 4191662
Attractive, new hotel on the edge of town with well appointed public rooms and bedrooms.
132 CTV in all bedrooms Ⓡ ✻sB&B£29.15–£33 dB&B£53–£60
Lift ☾ 200P ✽ (heated) (hard) sauna bath Live music and dancing wkly in season *xmas*
English & French Lunch fr£6.50&alc Tea £1.40–£1.60 Dinner fr£7.50&alc Wine £3.35 Last dinner 10.30pm
Credit cards 1 2 3 5

✕✕✕**Le Nautique** Pier Steps
☎Guernsey (0481) 21714
Attractive popular converted harbour warehouse, with food (especially local fish) of high standard.
Closed Sun & 3wks Jan
French 66 seats Lunch £9alc Dinner £9alc Wine £3.30 Last dinner 10pm

S% Credit cards 1 2 3 5 VS

✕**Nino's Ristorante Italiano** Lefevre St
☎Guernsey (0481) 23052
Popular restaurant serving pasta and fish. Grill and pizza restaurant below.
Closed Sun
English, French & Italian **V** 70 seats ✻Lunch £3–£3.50&alc Dinner £5–£6.25&alc Wine £3 Last dinner 10.30pm
Credit cards 1 2 3 5

ST SAVIOUR
Guernsey, Channel Islands
Map **16**

★★★*L* **L'Atlantique** Perelle Bay
☎Guernsey (0481) 64056
Attractive, modern style stone-built hotel with well appointed public rooms.
21 (1fb) CTV in all bedrooms Ⓡ sB&B£12–£26 dB&B£24–£42
70P ✽ (heated) nc4yrs *xmas*
Continental **V** Lunch £2.90–£4.10&alc Dinner £6.75&alc Wine £2.90 Last dinner 9.30pm
S% Credit cards 1 2 3 4 5 VS

ST SAVIOUR
Jersey, Channel Islands
Map **16**

❀★★★★**LONGUEVILLE MANOR, ST SAVIOUR, JERSEY**
(off St Helier/Grouville rd, A3)
☎Jersey (0534) 25501 Telex no 4192306
Longueville Manor is a lovely creeper clad, Norman style house situated in 15 acres of well tended grounds and gardens. It offers peaceful seclusion, yet is only a short drive from St Helier town centre. The hotel has been owned by the Lewis family for some 30 years and recently changes have been made to the management structure here. Mr & Mrs Lewis are in semi-retirement, and the day-to-day running of the hotel is now left to their daughter and son-in-law, Mr and Mrs Dufty. A further member of the family, Malcolm Lewis, son of Mr and Mrs Lewis, joined the management team in 1981. Improvements continue to be made, and, rather than increasing the number of rooms, they are being reduced so as to provide more spacious accommodation and greater comfort for guests. There are pleasant public sitting rooms and a delightful newly decorated bar from which French windows open into the garden. The bedrooms are also very well decorated and comfortable, so you are sure of a comfortable stay.

The dining room is well appointed and now serves food in the modern style, demonstrating real skill and thoroughly deserving our rosette award. This hotel with its friendly staff and warm atmosphere, together with the good food, makes it a hotel not to be missed when visiting the Channel Islands.
35 1 CTV in all bedrooms sB&B £31–£38 dB&B £56–£70
Lift ☾ 30P ✽ (heated) nc7yrs
Lunch fr£8.80 Dinner fr£13&alc Wine £5 Last dinner 9.30pm
Credit cards 1 2 3 4 5 VS

ST WENN
Cornwall
Map **2** SW96

★**Wenn Manor** ☎Roche (0726) 890240
Old manor house which is full of character and situated in an isolated position.
9rm (6 1) (2fb) Ⓡ sB&B£10–£12 sB&B £10.50–£12.50 dB&B £20–£25
CTV 20P 1 ✽ (heated) *xmas*
Bar lunch £1.50 Tea fr80p High Tea fr£3 Dinner fr£5.50 Wine £3 Last dinner 8pm
Credit cards 1 3

SALCOMBE
Devon
Map **3** SX73

★★★★*HL* **Marine** Cliff Rd (Prestige)
☎(054 884) 2254 Telex no 45185
Closed Nov–Feb
This hotel is in a superb position at the edge of the estuary, and has private landing stages.
51 (8fb) CTV in all bedrooms ✻sB&B £26.75–£40.50 dB&B £53.50–£71
Lift ☾ 60P CFA ✽ (heated) (grass) sauna bath Live music Sat
English & French ✻Lunch £2.50–£5.50&alc Tea £1.50&alc–£3.50&alc

Dinner £9.95–£14.95&alc Wine £5 Last dinner 9pm

Credit cards 1 2 3 5 **VS**

★★★*H* **Bolt Head** (Best Western) ☎(054 884) 2780 Closed Nov–5 Apr

Swiss chalet-style hotel, standing 140 feet above sea level, overlooking the sea and the estuary.

29rm(26⇌2⋒) CTV in all bedrooms Ⓡ sB&B⇌⋒ £21.30–£25.20 dB&B⇌⋒ £42.60–£50.40 B

45P ✽ (heated)

English & French V ♀ Bar lunch £1.65–£2 Tea 70p Dinner £8.95&alc Wine £4.90 Last dinner 9.30pm

Credit cards 1 2 3 5 **VS**

★★★ **St Elmo** Sandhills Rd, North Sands ☎(054 884) 2233 Closed Nov–Etr

An Edwardian house situated on the hillside overlooking the estuary and North Sands Bay.

25rm(22⇌4⋒) CTV in all bedrooms Ⓡ *sB&B£17.25–£19.55 sB&B⇌⋒ £18.98–£20.70 dB&B£34.50–£39.10 dB&B⇌⋒ £37.96–£41.40 B

CTV 40P

English & French V ♀ *Bar lunch £1.25–£4.75 Tea 75p–£2 Dinner £8.80–£10.50 Wine £4.60 Last dinner 8.30pm

Credit cards 1 3

★★★*H* **Salcombe** Fore St (Inter-Hotels) ☎(054 884) 2991 Closed Nov–Feb

Hotel is located at waters edge, with good views.

51rm(27⇌2⋒) (6fb) CTV available in bedrooms *sB&B£19.50–£32 (incl dinner) dB&B£37–£62 (incl dinner) dB&B⇌⋒ £42–£69 (incl dinner) B

☾ CTV 45P ✽ (heated)

V ♀ *Lunch £1–£4.25 Tea 60p–£1.25 Dinner £10.25–£10.50 Wine £4 Last dinner 9pm

S% Credit cards 1 2 3 5

See advert on page 566

❀★★★*HBL* **Tides Reach** South Sands ☎(054 884) 3466 Closed Dec–Feb

(Rosette awarded for dinner only.)

Set in a quiet, tree-fringed cove with sandy beach, this is a pleasant and extremely comfortable hotel. The public rooms are bright and fresh looking over the gardens and sea and there are excellent leisure facilities including a large indoor pool. Bedrooms are attractively furnished and well appointed. Good food is served in the attractive dining room.

40rm(36⇌4⋒) (2fb) CTV in all bedrooms Ⓡ sB&B⇌⋒ £25–£39 (incl dinner) dB&B⇌⋒ £50–£78 (incl dinner) B

Lift ☾ 100P ✽ (heated) squash sauna bath nc8yrs

English & Continental V ♀ Bar lunch £2.50–£7 Tea 75p Dinner £10.50–£11&alc Wine £5.20 Last dinner 10pm

Credit cards 1 2 3 5

See advert on page 566

★★*H* **Castle Point** Sandhills Rd ☎(054 884) 2167 Closed mid Oct–19 Apr

Private grounds of this hotel give access to the estuary and the ruins of Salcombe Castle.

20rm(6⇌4⋒) (1fb) sB&B£12–£19 dB&B£18–£32 dB&B⇌⋒ £30–£42 B

CTV 40P 3 ✽ nc6yrs

French V ♀ Bar lunch £1.50alc Tea 85palc Dinner £8–£8.50 Wine £4.10 Last dinner 8pm

Credit cards 1 3 4

★★ **Grafton Towers** Moult Rd, South Sands (ExecHotel) ☎(054 884) 2882 Closed 4 Oct–Mar

Edwardian hotel overlooking bay.

14rm(6⇌3⋒) (1fb) CTV in 9 bedrooms TV in 2 bedrooms Ⓡ *sB&B£9–£12 sB&B⇌⋒ £11–£16 dB&B£18–£24 dB&B⇌⋒ £22–£32 B

14P ✽ →

S

🍴English & Continental ♈ ☕ ✱Lunch £2–£3 Tea 50p Dinner £7–£8 Wine £3.95 Last dinner 8pm

Credit cards 1 3

★★ *H* **Soar Mill Cove** Soar Mill Cove, Malborough (3m W of town off A381 at Malborough) ☎ Galmpton (0548) 561566 Closed Oct–Mar

14rm(13➡1⋒) (3fb) CTV in all bedrooms ® sB&B➡⋒ £24–£30 dB&B➡⋒ £48–£60 B

50P ✱ (heated) Live music twice wkly nc3yrs ♿

🍴European ♈ ☕ Lunch £5–£10 Tea £1–£3 High Tea £3–£5 Dinner £15.50&alc Wine £4.50 Last dinner 10pm

Credit cards 1 3

★★ *H* **South Sands** ☎ (054 884) 2791 Closed Jan

Tourist and commercial hotel situated on South Sands with direct access to the beach.

20rm(13➡7⋒) (3fb) CTV in all bedrooms ® sB&B➡⋒ £16–£25 dB&B➡⋒ £30–£40 B

15P 17 *xmas*

🍴International ♈ ☕ Lunch £6.50alc Tea 50p Dinner £8.25&alc Wine £3.50 Last dinner 9.30pm

S% Credit cards 1 2 3 5

★ **Knowle** Onslow Rd ☎ (054 884) 2846 Closed Nov–Mar

Salcombe

Hotel overlooks estuary.

11rm(1➡5⋒) Annexe: 6rm(1➡1⋒) (3fb) TV available in bedrooms ® sB&B £11.50–£15.50 sB&B➡⋒ £11.50–£15.50 dB&B £23–£31 dB&B➡⋒ £23–£31 B

CTV 40P ✱

🍴English & Continental V ♈ ☕ Lunch fr£4.30 Tea fr75p High Tea fr£1.50 Dinner fr£6.60 Wine £4.14 Last dinner 7.45pm

Credit cards 1 3 VS

★ **Melbury** Devon Rd ☎ (054 884) 2883 Closed 22 Sep–11 May (except Etr)

Gabled villa with new extension.

14rm(4➡5⋒) (2fb) ® ✱ sB&B £9.60–£12.60 sB&B➡⋒ £11–£14 dB&B £19.20–£25.20 dB&B➡⋒ £22–£28

CTV 18P ✱ nc5yrs

♈ Bar lunch £1alc Dinner £6 Wine £2.45 Last dinner 7.30pm

★ **Sunny Cliff** Cliff Rd ☎ (054 884) 2207 Closed Nov–Mar

Comfortable hotel on the clifftop with fine estuary views.

15rm(2➡) Annexe: 3rm (4fb) sB&B £12.50–£16 dB&B £25–£32 dB&B➡ £26–£36 B

CTV 14P 1 ✱ (heated)

🍴English & French ♈ ☕ Bar lunch 65p–£2.35 Tea 50p High Tea £1–£2.25 Dinner £6.50 Wine £4.75 Last dinner 8pm

VS

★ *H* **Wells** Herbert Rd ☎ (054 884) 3484

Comfortable hotel in a quiet residential area, within walking distance of the town and the beach.

12rm(4➡6⋒) (2fb) ✱ ✱ sB&B £10–£12 sB&B➡⋒ £11–£13 dB&B➡⋒ £22–£26 B

CTV 20P ✱ nc4yrs

V ♈ ☕ Lunch £1.50–£3&alc Tea 50p&alc High Tea £2.50–£3&alc Dinner £6.95&alc Wine £4.50 Last dinner 8pm

Credit cards 1 2 3 4 5 VS

✕✕ **Galley** Fore St ☎ (054 884) 2828

Cottage style restaurant overlooking the harbour.

Closed Mon out of season Lunch not served Mon–Sat Dinner not served Sun

🍴English & French V 60 seats Lunch £4.95 Dinner £7.50&alc Wine £4 Last dinner 10.30pm

Credit cards 1 2 3 4 5

S

SALEN
Island of Mull, Strathclyde *Argyllshire*
Map **10** NM54

✕**Puffer Aground** Main Rd ☎Aros (06803) 389
Old roadside cottages have been converted to make this restaurant which has an adjoining craft shop.
Closed Sun, Mon (Etr–Spring Bank hol) & mid Oct–19 Apr
V 40 seats Dinner £5.25&alc Last dinner 9pm 15P

SALFORD
Greater Manchester
Map **7** SJ89
See also Manchester

★★**Racecourse** Littleton Rd (Greenall Whitley) ☎061-792 1420 Telex no 629462
20rm(5⇌) (1fb) Ⓡ sB&B£19.50–£20.50 sB&B⇌£21–£22.50 dB&B£28–£30 dB&B⇌£33–£35 B
CTV 100P
V Lunch fr£4.50 Tea fr35p Dinner fr£5.50 Wine £3.80 Last dinner 7.30pm
Credit cards 1 2 3 5

★**Beaucliffe** 254 Eccles Old Rd, Pendleton ☎061-789 5092
21rm(1⇌16⋒) (1fb) sB&B£17 sB&B⇌⋒£19 dB&B£27 dB&B⇌⋒£29 B
CTV 40P 1 billiards nc6yrs
V Lunch £2.50–£4 Dinner fr£6.25&alc Wine £2.95 Last dinner 8pm
Credit cards 1 2 3

SALISBURY
Wiltshire
Map **4** SU12

★★★**Rose & Crown** Harnham Rd, Harnham (Queens) ☎(0722) 27908
A thirteenth-century building with new wing, comfortable bedrooms and good food.
27⇌⋒ 1 CTV in all bedrooms Ⓡ sB&B⇌⋒£35–£44 dB&B⇌⋒£47.50–£54.50 B
☾ 43P CFA xmas

V Lunch £5.95–£14.50&alc Tea £1.10–£2.25 Dinner £7.95–£14.50&alc Wine £5.50 Last dinner 9.30pm
Credit cards 1 2 3 4 5

★★★**White Hart** St John St (Trusthouse Forte) ☎(0722) 27476
72rm(56⇌) (2fb) CTV in all bedrooms Ⓡ sB&B£30.50 sB&B⇌£35.50 dB£45.50 dB⇌£52.50 B
☾ 85P *xmas*
Last dinner 9.45pm
Credit cards 1 2 3 4 5

★★**Cathedral** Milford St ☎(0722) 20144
Terraced hotel in the centre of the town amidst shops and many other attractions.
32rm(9⇌1⋒) (3fb) CTV in 20 bedrooms sB&B£14.50–£19.50 sB&B⇌£18.50–£23.50 dB&B£23.50–£26.50 dB&B⇌£26.50–£29.50 B
Lift CTV
Mainly grills **V** Lunch £3.50–£5.75 Tea 60p Dinner £4–£10&alc Wine £4.15 Last dinner 9pm
Credit card 3 **VS**

★★***King's Arms*** St John Street (Wessex Taverns) ☎(0722) 27629
A 16th-century, half-timbered and gabled inn near the cathedral.
11rm(5⇌) Annexe: 6⇌ 1 CTV in 8 bedrooms TV in 1 bedroom Ⓡ B
CTV
Credit cards 1 2 3 4 5

★★*H* **Old Bell Inn** 2 St Anne Street ☎(0722) 27958
RS Sun
14th-century inn near Cathedral with good food and very comfortable bedrooms.
7rm(6⋒) 2 Ⓡ dB&B⋒£29–£36
CTV 6P nc10yrs
V Lunch £4.50 Dinner £10alc Wine £4 Last dinner 10pm
Credit cards 1 2 3 5 **VS**

★★**Red Lion** Milford St (Best Western) ☎(0722) 23334
Former coaching inn dating from 1320, containing many items of historic interest.
55rm(40⇌) (5fb) 2 CTV in 40 bedrooms Ⓡ sB&B£20–£22 sB&B⇌£25–£28 dB&B£30–£32.50 dB&B⇌£40–£45 B
☾ 12P 12 CFA *xmas*
Lunch £4–£8 Tea 75p–£1.25 Dinner £7.50–£8 Wine £4 Last dinner 8.45pm
Credit cards 1 2 3 5

✕✕**Old Dutch Mill** 58A Fisherton St ☎(0722) 23447
Lunch by reservation only.
French **V** 24 seats ✻Lunch £10–£12.50alc Dinner £10–£12.50alc Wine £4.50 Last dinner 11pm 200P
S% Credit cards 1 3 5

✕**Cranes** 90 Crane St ☎(0722) 3471
Closed Sun & Public hols (except Xmas Day) Dinner not served Mon (Nov–19 Apr)
English & French 34 seats Lunch £3.50–£10alc Dinner £7.50–£15 Wine £4.50 Last dinner 9.30pm
S% Credit cards 1 2 3 5 **VS**

✕**Provençal** Market Pl ☎(0722) 28923
French 34 seats ✻Lunch £6&alc Dinner £9.75&alc Last dinner 10pm
Credit cards 1 2 3 5

SALTASH
Cornwall
Map **2** SX45

★**Holland Inn** (07555) 3635
Busy inn with separate chalet bedrooms.
Annexe: 30⇌ CTV in all bedrooms Ⓡ sB&B⇌£20 dB&B⇌£34 B
30P
V Lunch £3–£8.50 Dinner £9.50alc Wine £4.75 Last dinner 9.30pm
Credit cards 1 3

SAMPFORD PEVERELL
Devon
Map **3** ST01

S

★**Green Headland** ☎Tiverton (0884) 820255
Closed Dec RS Oct–Nov & Jan–Apr
Comfortable, small, privately-run hotel, popular with tourists and businessmen.
6rm (3fb) sB&B£10–£11 dB&B£19–£21
CTV 100P ✽
Lunch £3.50–£5 Tea 40p–£1 High Tea £2–£3.50 Dinner £4.50–£7 Wine £3.50 Last dinner 8.30pm
Credit card 1

SANDBACH
Cheshire
Map **7** SJ76
★★★**Chimney House** Congleton Rd (Whitbread West Pennines) ☎(09367) 4141 Telex no 66971
RS Public hols
Large country house in Tudor style.
20 (1fb) CTV in all bedrooms
*sB&B£25 dB&B£30 B
☾ 50P ✽
English & French **V** *Lunch fr£4.50&alc Tea 75p Dinner £10alc Wine £4 Last dinner 10pm
Credit cards 1 3

☆☆☆**Saxon Cross** Holmes Chapel Rd (M6 junc 17) ☎(09367) 3281 Telex no 367169 RS 24–27 Dec
52 (11fb) CTV in all bedrooms Ⓡ sB&B£18–£27 dB&B£26.50–£32 B
☾ 200P ✽ CFA ♿
V Lunch £4.50&alc Dinner £7.50&alc Last dinner 9.30pm
Credit cards 1 2 3 4 5 **VS**

★★**Old Hall** Newcastle Rd ☎(09367) 61221
RS Xmas
12rm (7 5) (1fb) CTV in all bedrooms *sB&B£15–£20 sB&B£20–£30 B
60P ✽
English & French **V**
*Lunch £4.95–£5.95&alc Tea 50p Dinner fr£6.95&alc Wine £4.25 Last dinner 9.30pm
Credit cards 1 2 3 5

SANDBANKS
Dorset
See **Poole**

SANDERSTEAD
Greater London
Map **4** TQ36
★★★★**Selsdon Park** (Best Western) ☎01-657 8811
Large mansion in 200 acre grounds. Popular with conferences and has excellent leisure facilities.
160 (4fb) CTV in all bedrooms sB&B£41–£49 dB&B£55–£67 B
Lift ☾ 200P 20 ✽ CFA (heated) 18 billiards sauna bath Live music and dancing Sat *xmas*

Sampford Peverell — Saundersfoot

International Lunch £9.25–£9.75&alc Dinner £10.25–£11.75&alc Wine £5.75 Last dinner 9pm
Credit cards 1 2 3 5 **VS**

SANDIACRE
Derbyshire
Map **8** SK43
See also Long Eaton
☆☆☆**Post House** Bostocks Ln (N of M1 junc 25) (Trusthouse Forte) ☎(0602) 397800
106 (11fb) CTV in all bedrooms Ⓡ sB&B£42 dB&B£54 B
☾ 180P CFA
Last dinner 10pm
Credit cards 1 2 3 4 5

SANDOWN
Isle of Wight
Map **4** SZ58
★★★**Broadway Park** Melville St ☎(0983) 402007
Closed 30 Sep–27 Apr RS 28 Apr–26 May & 9–29 Sep
Country house in landscaped gardens with good recreation facilities.
53rm (34 1) (5fb) Ⓡ sB&B£15–£17.50 sB&B£15.50–£20.50 dB&B£30–£35 dB&B£30–£40 B
Lift ☾ CTV 100P ✽ (heated) (grass) Disco twice wkly Live music and dancing 3 nights wkly *xmas*
English & French Lunch £3.50 Tea fr40p Dinner £6–£7.50 Wine £3.20 Last dinner 8.30pm
Credit cards 1 3

★★★**Melville Hall** Melville St ☎(0983) 403794
Closed Oct–Apr RS Apr–26 May & 9–30 Sep
Large house in quiet area with attractive gardens.
38rm (18 1) (3fb) *sB&B£15.25–£20.50 dB&B£27.25–£36.25 dB&B£32–£45.50
☾ CTV 30P ✽ (heated) Live music and dancing Mon, Tue, Thu & Fri nc3yrs
English & French Lunch £4.50–£5.50 Tea 60p–£2 Dinner £6.50–£8 Wine £4.50 Last dinner 8.30pm
Credit cards 1 3 **VS**

★**Rose Bank** 6 High St ☎(0983) 403854
Closed Xmas wk
Small friendly family run hotel overlooking the sea.
9rm (2fb) sB&B£10.35–£11.50 dB&B£20.70–£23
CTV nc6yrs
*Lunch fr£4 Tea fr75p Dinner fr£6 Wine £3.25 Last dinner 7pm

SANDYHILLS
Dumfries & Galloway *Kirkcudbrightshire*
Map **11** NX85

✕**Granary** Barend (B794) ☎Southwick (038 778) 663
Closed Jan–19 Apr (Lunch & Dinner served Sat only Nov–23 Dec)
50 seats *Lunch 90p–£2 Dinner £4–£9 Wine £4.25 Last dinner 9pm P bedrooms available **VS**

SANQUHAR
Dumfries & Galloway *Dumfriesshire*
Map **11** NS70
★★**Mennockfoot Lodge** ☎(06592) 382
Converted from former farm buildings, this hotel stands in its own grounds.
4rm (2) Annexe: 8rm (2) (2fb) sB&B£13 sB&B£14 sB&B£15 dB&B£22 dB&B£24 B
CTV 25P ✽ ♿
V Lunch £5alc Tea £1.80alc High Tea £6alc Dinner £7.70alc Last dinner 8.30pm

★**Nithsdale** High St (Minotel) ☎(06592) 506
Converted 18th-century stone building standing in the High St.
6rm (2fb) sB&B£9.75 dB&B£19.50
CTV Disco wkly
Lunch fr£3.50&alc Dinner fr£5.50&alc Wine £3.75 Last dinner 7.30pm
Credit cards 1 2 3 **VS**

SARK
Channel Islands
Map **16**
✕✕**Aval du Creux** Harbour Hill ☎(048 183) 2036
(Rosette awarded for dinner only.)
Small and very friendly hotel and restaurant.
Closed Oct–Apr
Austrian & French **V** 50 seats Lunch £5.50&alc Dinner £8&alc Wine £2.80 Last dinner 8.30pm bedrooms available
Credit card 3

SAUNDERSFOOT
Dyfed
Map **2** SN10
★★★**St Brides** St Brides Hill (Inter-Hotels) ☎(0834) 812304 Telex no 48350
Comfortable cliff top hotel with good sea views.
49rm (31 18) (6fb) CTV in all bedrooms Ⓡ sB&B£28.50 dB&B£47 B
☾ 70P CFA ✽ (heated) sauna bath Live music and dancing wkly *xmas*
English & French **V** Bar lunch £2–£5 Tea 75p–£3.25 Dinner fr£7.95&alc Wine £5
Last dinner 9.30pm
Credit cards 1 2 3 5

★★**Glen Beach** Swallow Tree Woods ☎(0834) 813430
Small, personally run, family hotel. →

S

12rm(1⇌9⋒) CTV available in bedrooms ® sB&B⇌⋒£14–£17.25 dB&B⇌⋒£28–£34.50 Ƀ

CTV 60P ⊞ ✽ Disco Mon (Jul & Aug) Live music and dancing Thu (Jul & Aug) *xmas*

V ♈ ☐ Lunch £4.95 Tea £1.30 Dinner £6.50&alc Wine £4.80 Last dinner 9.30pm

Credit cards 1 3

SAUNTON
Devon
Map **2** SS43

★★★★ ***H*** **Saunton Sands** (Brend) ☎ Croyde (0271) 890212

Purpose-built coastal hotel with good facilities.

90⇌ CTV in all bedrooms ✻ sB&B⇌£19–£25.50 dB&B⇌£33–£50 Continental breakfast Ƀ

Lift ☾ CTV 200P 8⌂ CFA ✽ ⊡ (heated) ℘ (hard) squash billiards sauna bath ⌂ *xmas*

⊟ English & French ♈ ☐ ✻ Lunch £5.75 Tea 55p Dinner £8.45&alc Wine £4.60 Last dinner 9.30pm

Credit cards 1 2 3 5

SAVERNAKE
Wiltshire
Map **4** SU26

★★ **Savernake Forest** (Best Western) ☎ Marlborough (0672) 810206 Closed Jan

10rm(9⇌) (2fb) ® sB&B£20–£25 sB&B⇌⋒£20–£25 dB&B£32–£42 dB&B⇌⋒£32–£42 Ƀ

CTV 50P ⊞ ✽ ♩

⊟ English & French ♈ ☐ Bar lunch £4alc Tea £1.50alc Dinner £9.50&alc Wine £3.90 Last dinner 9pm

Credit cards 1 2 3 5

SCALASAIG
Isle of Colonsay, Strathclyde *Argyllshire*
Map **10** NR39

★ ***H*** **Colonsay** ☎ (09512) 316

Comfortable island hotel which is a listed building, set amidst island scenery.

11rm(2⋒) (2fb) TV available on request sB&B£8–£19 sB&B⇌⋒£8–£19 dB&B£15–£35 dB&B⇌⋒£15–£35 Ƀ

TV 32P ⊞ ✽ ⚑18 ♩

⊟ French ♈ ☐ Bar lunch £1.50alc Tea fr90p High Tea fr£5.50 Dinner fr£9 Wine £3.50
Last dinner 7.30pm

Credit cards 1 2 3 5 **VS**

SCARBOROUGH
North Yorkshire
Map **8** TA08
See plan

★★★★ **Crown** Esplanade ☎ (0723) 73491 (due to change to 373491) Telex no 52580 Plan **3** *C3*

Regency period hotel overlooking the bay from South Cliffs.

81⇌ (9fb) CTV in all bedrooms ★ ✻ sB&B⇌£21.50–£24 dB&B⇌£41–£43 Continental breakfast Ƀ

Lift ☾ 6P CFA 6⌂ billiards *xmas*

⊟ French V ♈ ☐ ✻ Bar lunch £2.75 Tea 70p–£2.50 Dinner £10alc Wine £6.15 Last dinner 9pm

Credit cards 1 2 3 5

★★★★ **Holbeck Hall** Seacliffe Rd ☎ (0723) 74374 (due to change to 374374) Plan **6** *D1*

A former Victorian residence in 3 acres of gardens and grounds, offering panoramic views over Scarborough.

31⇌ (4fb) CTV in all bedrooms ★ sB&B⇌£22.50–£28.50 dB&B⇌£45–£57

☾ 50P 3⌂ ✽ ⚑ ⌂ *xmas*

⊟ French V ♈ ☐ ✻ Lunch fr£5.25&alc Tea fr£1.95 Dinner fr£9.75&alc Wine £5.95 Last dinner 9.30pm

Credit cards 2 3 5 **VS**

★★★★ ***B*** **Royal** St Nicholas St ☎ (0723) 64333 (due to change to 364333) Telex no 52472 (Toscar) Plan **10** *C3*

Elegant, Regency building by town centre with very comfortable, modern bedrooms. →

S

THE SAUNTON SANDS

Enjoy 4 star luxury overlooking 5 miles of unspoilt golden beaches

The Saunton Sands is a friendly, family owned and managed hotel in a glorious position overlooking Barnstaple Bay and the nearby championship golf course. There's a first class restaurant with a choice of 130 fine wines, and every comfort and entertainment facility you could wish for – including **heated indoor pool, sauna, solarium, squash, tennis, billiards room, putting, ballroom, nursery, hairdresssing salon etc.** Open throughout the year with luxury self contained apartment suites also available. Exceptional value in low season. Free colour brochure on request.

X. Brend, Saunton Sands Hotel, Nr. Braunton EX33 1LQ **Tel (0271) 890212**

NORTH DEVON

CROWN HOTEL

SCARBOROUGH

The premier hotel on the Yorkshire coast

Write or telephone for colour brochure and full details.

CROWN HOTEL, ESPLANADE, SCARBOROUGH
Telephone (0723) 73491

AA ★★★★

S

HOLBECK HALL HOTEL

★★★★AA **BTA Commendation**

A superb old country house hotel, overlooking the South Bay with panoramic views of Scarborough. All rooms with private bathroom, colour TV and telephone. Public Bar. Private car parking for over fifty cars. Helicopter landing space available within the grounds. The nearest hotel to the South Cliff Golf Club (¼ mile). Children welcome. Pets by arrangement only.

Brochure on request from
Holbeck Hall Hotel,
Sea Cliff Road, Scarborough,
or telephone (0723) 74374 with your enquiry.

Scarborough

© The Automobile Association

Scarborough

1 Brookland ★★
2 Carlton ★★
3 Crown ★★★★
4 Dorchester ★
5 Esplanade ★★
6 Holbeck Hall ★★★★
7 Lanterna Ristorante ✕✕
8 Mayfair ★★
9 Norbreck ★★
10 Royal ★★★★
11 St Nicholas ★★★
12 Southlands ★★
13 Wrea Head Country ★★[country house symbol]

135rm(30[shower])(19fb) CTV in all bedrooms Ⓡ[symbol]✱sB&B[shower]£17–£24 dB&B[shower]£34–£42[symbol]

Lift ☾ CTV CFA billiards sauna bath Disco wkly Live music and dancing wkly Cabaret wkly in season [symbol] *xmas*

[symbol][symbol] Lunch £3.50–£5.50 Tea fr40p Dinner £7.50&alc Wine £5 Last dinner 10.30pm

Credit cards 1 2 3 5 **VS**

★★★**St Nicholas** St Nicholas Cliff ☎(0723) 64101 (due to change to 364101) Telex no 52351 Plan **11** *C3*

Large, terraced Victorian houses have been converted into a hotel which is situated near to the beach and town centre.

166rm(100[bath]5[shower])(22fb) 2[symbol] CTV in 150 bedrooms [symbol]✱sB&B£19–£20 sB&B[bath][shower]£23–£24 dB&B£32–£34 dB&B[bath][shower]£42–£44[symbol]

Lift ☾ CTV 2P 38[garage] CFA [symbol] *xmas*

English & Continental V ♀ Lunch £4.50–£5.50&alc Tea 60p–£1 Dinner £8.50–£9.50&alc Wine £4.95 Last dinner 9pm

Credit cards 1 2 3 **VS**

★★**Brookland** Esplanade Gdns, South Cliff ☎(0723) 76576 (due to change to 376576) Plan **1** *C1*

52rm(33🛁) (5fb) CTV in all bedrooms Ⓡ sB&B£12–£15.47 sB&B🛁£13–£17.19 dB&B£24–£28.64 dB&B🛁£26–£32 B

Lift ☾ CFA

♀ Bar lunch £1–£5 Tea 70p High Tea £1.20 Dinner £7 Wine £5.50 Last dinner 7.30pm

Credit cards 1 3 **VS**

★★**Carlton** Belmont Rd ☎(0723) 60938 (due to change to 360938) Plan **2** *C2*
Closed Nov–Mar (expect Xmas)

40rm(3🛁) (10fb) sB&B£14.50–£15.50 sB&B🛁£18 dB&B£28–£30 dB&B🛁£36 B

Lift ☾ CTV ✽ Disco twice wkly *xmas*

V ♀ Lunch fr£3.50&alc Tea 50p High Tea £2.75–£3.75 Dinner fr£3.75&alc Wine £5.60 Last dinner 9.30pm

★★**Esplanade** Belmont Rd (Travco) ☎(0723) 60382 (due to change to 360382) Plan **5** *C2*
Closed Dec–Feb

Large seaside hotel overlooking South Cliffs and the sea.

78rm(50🛁12🚿) (5fb) CTV in 62 bedrooms Ⓡ sB&B£13–£16 sB&B🛁🚿£15–£19 dB&B£26–£31 dB&B🛁🚿£30–£34 B

Lift ☾ CTV 25P CFA ✽ Live music and dancing wkly Cabaret wkly *xmas*

V ♀ Lunch fr£4 Tea fr75p Dinner fr£6 Wine £3.95 Last dinner 8.30pm

Credit cards 1 2 3 5

★★**Mayfair** 42 The Esplanade ☎(0723) 60053 (due to change to 360053)
Plan **8** *D1*
Closed Dec–Feb

Regency style with bright cheerful bedrooms and comfortable lounges.

19rm(11🛁) (4fb) CTV in 11 bedrooms TV in 8 bedrooms Ⓡ sB&B£11.50–£13.50 sB&B🛁£13.50–£16 dB&B£23–£27 dB&B🛁£27–£32 B

Lift ☾

V ♀ ✻ Dinner £4.50–£5 Wine £4 Last dinner 7.15pm

Credit cards 1 3

★★**Norbreck** Castle Rd, North Bay (Travco) ☎(0723) 66607 (due to change to 366607) Plan **9** *C4*

55rm(41🛁) (5fb) CTV in 41 bedrooms Ⓡ ✻sB&B£10.50–£16 sB&B🛁£11.50–£19 dB&B£21–£27 dB&B🛁£23–£30 B

Lift ☾ CTV 14P CFA Live music and dancing wkly *xmas*

♀ Lunch £4.50 Tea 55 High Tea £1.75 Dinner £6&alc Wine £3.95 Last dinner 8.30pm

Credit cards 1 2 3 5 **VS**

★★***Southlands*** 15 West St, South Cliff (Galleon) ☎(0723) 61461 (due to change to 361461) Plan **12** *C2*

61rm(25🛁🚿) CTV in 25 bedrooms Ⓡ B

Lift ☾ CTV P CFA Disco wkly Cabaret wkly

♀ Last dinner 10.30pm

Credit cards 1 3 **VS**

See advert on page 574

★★ *L* **Wrea Head Country** Scalby (3m NW off A171) ☎(0723) 78211 (due to change to 378211) Plan **13** *A2*

Converted, Victorian, country residence standing in 14 acres of landscaped gardens.

20rm(13🛁7🚿) (2fb) CTV in all bedrooms Ⓡ ✻sB&B🛁🚿£14–£18 dB&B🛁🚿£28–£36 B

40P 2 ✽ *xmas*

V ♀ ✻ Lunch £5 Tea £1.75 Dinner £8.50–£10.50 Wine £5.95 Last dinner 9pm

Credit card 2

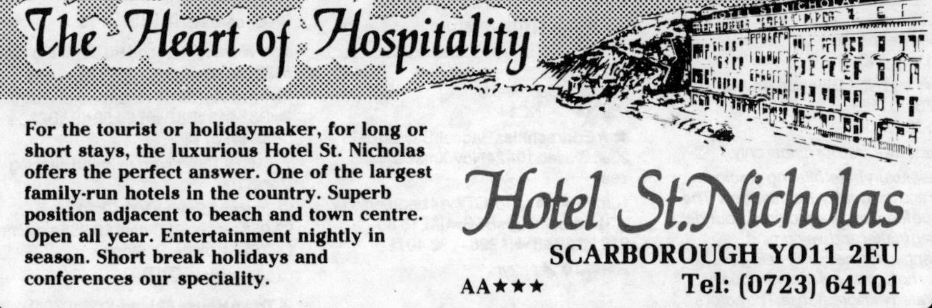

★*H* **Dorchester** Filey Rd ☎(0723) 61668 (due to change to 361668) Plan **4** *C1*
Closed mid Sep–May

45rm(12⇌) (2fb) *sB&B£10.50 sB&B⇌£10.50 dB&B£21 dB&B⇌£21

Lift CTV 30P ♿

Lunch £4 Tea £1.50 Dinner £7 Last dinner 7.15pm

S%

✕✕**Lanterna Ristorante** 33 Queen St ☎(0723) 63616 (due to change to 363616) Plan **7** *C4*

Closed Sun & Mon Lunch not served

Italian 36 seats Dinner £8.75alc Wine £5 Last dinner 9.30pm

Credit card 3 **VS**

SCILLY, ISLES OF
No map
See **Hugh Town, New Grimsby** and **Old Grimsby**

SCOLE
Norfolk
Map **5** TM17

★★**Scole Inn** (Best Western) ☎(037978) 481

8rm(2⇌⋔) Annexe: 12⇌⋔ (2fb) 1 CTV in all bedrooms Ⓡ sB&B£17.50 sB&B⇌⋔£21.50 dB&B£25 dB&B⇌⋔£32 B

CTV 60P *xmas*

V Lunch fr£6.50 Dinner fr£6.50&alc Wine £4 Last dinner 10pm

S% Credit cards 1 2 3 5 **VS**

SCONE
Tayside *Perthshire*
Map **11** NO12

❀★★★*HBL* **Balcraig House** ☎(0738) 51123
Closed 2–20 Jan

(Rosette awarded for dinner only.)

A small, luxury hotel offering gracious living and top quality in all respects. The antique furniture, fine pictures, abundant reading matter and welcoming atmosphere immediately help guests relax. The bedrooms are individually decorated with great style. The hotel's own farm provides much of the produce for the enterprising and splendid meals. Awarded AA Best Newcomer in Scotland (see page 24).

10⇌ 1 CTV in 4 bedrooms sB&B⇌£32–£36 dB&B⇌£50–£60 B

20P (hard) U *xmas*

Tea £2.75&alc Dinner £13&alc Wine £4.50 Last dinner 10.45pm

S% Credit cards 1 2 3 5

★★★ ***Murrayshall House*** Montague ☎(0738) 51171 Telex no 76197

9rm(1⇌4⋔) CTV in all bedrooms

50P ⛳18

British & French **V** Last dinner 10.30pm

Credit cards 2 3 5

SCOTCH CORNER (near Richmond)
North Yorkshire
Map **8** NZ20

★★★**Scotch Corner** Great North Rd (Scottish Highland) ☎Richmond (0748) 2943

Established hotel in its own grounds and gardens, situated at the junction of the A1 and the A66.

45rm(37⇌) (5fb) CTV in all bedrooms Ⓡ *sB&B⇌£26 dB&B⇌£42

Lift ☾ CTV 250P 10 CFA

English & French **V** Lunch £5.80alc Tea fr60p High Tea fr£3.75 Dinner £7.50&alc Wine £2.50 Last dinner 10pm

Credit cards 1 2 3 5 **VS**

SCOURIE
Highland *Sutherland*
Map **14** NC14

★★**Eddrachilles** Badcall Bay ☎(0971) 2080 Closed 10–24 Nov, Xmas & New Year

10rm(3⇌7⋔) (1fb) CTV in 4 bedrooms TV in 3 bedrooms Ⓡ sB&B⇌⋔£15.60–£19.20 dB&B⇌⋔£26–£32.40 B

20P nc2yrs

Continental Bar lunch £3 Dinner £5.10–£5.40&alc Wine £3.60 Last dinner 8.30pm

★★**Scourie** ☎(0971) 2396
Closed mid Oct–mid Mar

A shingle-clad building and part of a 17th-century tower house, make up this hotel.

22rm(10⇌1⋔) sB&B£11.50–£13 sB&B⇌⋔£15–£16.80 dB&B£23–£26 dB&B⇌⋔£26.50–£29.80

TV 30P

*Lunch £4.50–£5.50 Tea 55p Dinner £6.50–£7 Wine £3.30 Last dinner 8.30pm

Credit card 3

SCRATCHWOOD
(M1 Motorway Service Area) **Access only from Motorway** Greater London
Map **4** TQ19

☆☆☆**TraveLodge** See **London** under **NW7**

SCUNTHORPE
Humberside
Map **8** SE81

★★**Royal** Doncaster Rd (Anchor) ☎(0724) 868181

Villa-style building with a pillared entrance, near the town centre.

33rm(31⇌2⋔) (1fb) CTV in all bedrooms Ⓡ *sB&B⇌⋔£31 dB&B⇌⋔£39 B

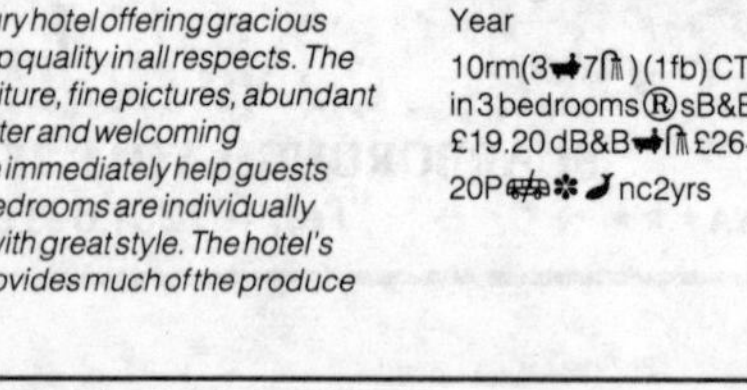

☾ 40P CFA

V Lunch fr£3.75 Tea fr35p Dinner fr£5.35 Wine £4.50
Last dinner 10pm

Credit cards 1 2 3 4 5 **VS**

★★**Wortley** Rowland Rd ☎(0724) 842223

28rm(22⇌) 2 CTV in all bedrooms Ⓡ *sB&B£18 sB&B⇌£29.50 dB&B£22 dB&B⇌£37 B

☾ # CTV 150P Live music and dancing Mon & Thu

English & French **V** *Lunch £3.95&alc Tea £1 Dinner £3.95&alc Wine £4.75 Last dinner 9.30pm

Credit cards 1 2 3 5

✕**Town House** 62 Mary St ☎(0724) 863692

Closed Sun Lunch not served Sat
Continental V 40 seats Lunch £2.50–£3.50&alc Dinner £4.80–£5.50&alc Wine £3.50 Last dinner 10pm
Credit cards 1 2 3 5

SEAFORD
East Sussex
Map **5** TV49

☆☆**Ladbroke** (on A259) (Ladbroke) ☎(0323) 891055 Telex no 877796
A chalet-type motel with parking outside each chalet.
70 (4fb) CTV in all bedrooms ® *sB fr£25 dB fr£33 (room only) B
(70P
V Last dinner 9pm
Credit cards 1 2 3 5

★**Clearview** 36/38 Claremont Rd ☎(0323) 890138
Well-run, friendly hotel.
12rm(7 3) (5fb) CTV in 10 bedrooms TV in 2 bedrooms ® sB&B£12.50–£15 sB&B £18.50–£22 dB&B£20–£22 dB&B £24–£26
CTV Cabaret Sun
Mainly grills Bar lunch £1.30–£4 Dinner £5.50–£7.50 Wine £3.50 Last dinner 9pm

SEAHOUSES
Northumberland
Map **12** NU23

★★*L* **Dunes** Sea Front ☎(0665) 720378
Closed mid Oct–May
Natural stone building on the seafront, overlooking the beach and Farne Islands.
29rm(6) (2fb) *sB&B£13.50 sB&B £15.50 dB&B£27 dB&B £31 B
CTV 30P 8
V *Dinner £7.25–£9.75 Wine £3 Last dinner 7.45pm

★★**Olde Ship** ☎(0665) 720200
Closed mid Oct–Mar
9rm(2 3) (1fb) CTV in all bedrooms ® sB&B£11–£12 sB&B £12.50–£13.50 dB&B£22–£24 dB&B £25–£27
CTV 10P 2
V Lunch fr£3 Tea fr75p Dinner fr£6.50 Wine £2 Last dinner 7.50pm

★**Beach House** Sea Front ☎(0665) 720337 Closed Dec–mid Mar
14rm(7 7) (2fb) 1 CTV in 5 bedrooms TV in 9 bedrooms ® sB&B £13–£15.50 dB&B £26–£31 B
CTV 16P
Dinner £6.50–£7 Wine £3.50 Last dinner 7.30pm
VS

★**St Aidans** ☎(0665) 720355
Closed Dec–Jan
Seafront hotel with a cosy bar and a comfortable restaurant.
8rm(1 3) (3fb) CTV in all bedrooms ® sB&B£12–£16 sB&B £13–£17 dB&B£24–£32 dB&B £26–£34 B
(10P
English & French V Bar lunch £2.50–£5.50&alc Dinner £6–£7&alc Wine £3 Last dinner 8pm
Credit cards 1 3 5 VS

★**White Swan** North Sunderland (1½m SE) (Minotel) ☎(0665) 720211
A modest country inn with neat, bright bedrooms 1m from the village and the sea.
19rm(4) (4fb) ® sB&B fr£11.50 dB&B fr£23 dB&B fr£27 B
CTV 40P
V Lunch £3.50–£4.50 Dinner £6–£8&alc Wine £3.50 Last dinner 10pm
Credit cards 1 3

SEALE
Surrey
Map **4** SU84

☆☆☆**Hog's Back** Hog's Back (on A31) (Embassy) ☎Runfold (02518) 2345
Converted private residence in its own gardens and grounds with lovely views.
50 (6fb) CTV in all bedrooms ® sB&B £35 dB&B £41 (room only) B
(130P
V Lunch fr£7.50&alc Dinner fr£8.50&alc Wine £4.50 Last dinner 9.30pm
Credit cards 1 2 3 4 5

SEASCALE
Cumbria
Map **6** NY00

★★**Wansfell** Drigg Rd ☎(0940) 28301
This hotel offers distant views of the Isle of Man.
14rm (2fb) *sB&B£11.50–£12 dB&B£18–£19 B
CTV 50P
V *Lunch £3.50–£5.50&alc Tea fr£1.50&alc High Tea £2.50–£5 Dinner £3.50–£8&alc Wine £4.05 Last dinner 9.30pm

SEATON
Devon
Map **3** SY29

★★**Bay** East Walk ☎(0297) 20073
A large holiday hotel situated on the promenade with good sea views.
33rm(11 4) (2fb) CTV in all bedrooms ® sB&B£12.65 sB&B £13.80 dB&B£25.30 sB&B £27.60
100P Live music and dancing twice wkly *xmas*
English, French & Italian V Lunch £3.45–£9.75&alc Tea 50p Dinner £3.45–£5.50&alc Wine £2.75 Last dinner 9pm

SEATON BURN
Tyne & Wear
Map **12** NZ27

☆☆☆☆*B* **Holiday Inn** Great North Rd (Commonwealth) ☎Newcastle-upon-Tyne (0632) 365432 Telex no 53271
Newcastle-upon-Tyne Plan **5A**
150 (72fb) CTV in all bedrooms *sB fr£36.50 dB fr£44.50 (room only) B
(# 230P CFA (heated) sauna bath Live music and dancing 4 nights wkly *xmas*
English & French V
Credit cards 1 2 3 4 5

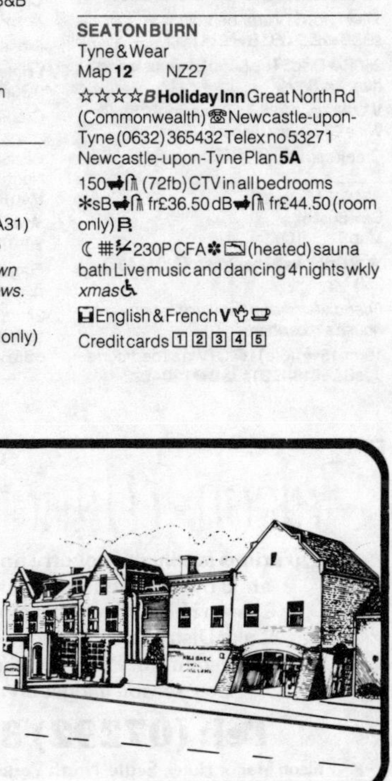

S

SEAVIEW
Isle of Wight
Map **4** SZ69

★★**Seaview** High St ☎(098371) 2278
Friendly, family run hotel in attractive situation.
14rm(7🛁🚿)(1fb) CTV in 2 bedrooms Ⓡ sB&B£13.50 sB&B🛁🚿£17 dB&B£25 dB&B🛁🚿£30.50 B
CTV 12P 🚗 *xmas*
English & French **V** Lunch £4.95&alc Tea 40p Dinner £5.95–£6.95&alc Wine £4.50 Last dinner 9.30pm
Credit cards 1 3 **VS**

SEAVINGTON ST MARY
Somerset
Map **3** ST41

✕✕**Pheasant** ☎South Petherton (0460) 40502
Lunch not served
English, French & Italian **V** 52 seats Dinner £6.75&alc Wine £3.95 Last dinner 9.30pm 60P bedrooms available
Credit cards 1 2 3 5 **VS**

SEDGEFIELD
Co Durham
Map **8** NZ32

★★★**Hardwick Hall** ☎(0740) 20253 Telex no 537681
Comfortable hotel within country park with attractive bars and splendid fireplaces.
17🛁(1fb) CTV in all bedrooms sB&B🛁£27 dB&B🛁£34 B
250P ✽ Disco Tue & Thu Live music and dancing Sat
V ✻Lunch fr£5.75 Dinner fr£7.75&alc Wine £3.50 Last dinner 9.45pm
Credit cards 1 2 3 5

SEDLESCOMBE
East Sussex
Map **5** TQ71

★★**Brickwall** The Green ☎(042487) 253
Friendly family run hotel with country house atmosphere.
19rm(15🛁)(3fb) 1 CTV in all bedrooms Ⓡ sB&B£18–£20 sB&B🛁£20–£22 dB&B£30–£32 dB&B🛁£34–£36 B
CTV 20P 5🚗 ✽ (heated) *xmas*
✻Lunch £4.75–£5.75 Dinner £7–£7.75 Wine £4.50 Last dinner 8.30pm
Credit cards 1 2 5

✕✕**Holmes House** ☎(042487) 450
Chef Patron provides very good food in this converted 17th century cottage filled with paintings and antiques.
Closed Mon Lunch not served Sat Dinner not served Sun
International 40 seats Lunch £6.50&alc Dinner £7.50&alc Wine £4.50 Last dinner 9pm
S% Credit cards 1 2 5

✕***Tithe Barn*** Lower Green ☎(042487) 393
Small, intimate, family-run restaurant with welcoming, open log fires.
Closed Mon Dinner not served Sun
English & French **V** 40 seats Last dinner 10pm 25P
Credit cards 1 2 3 5

SEIGHFORD
Staffordshire
Map **7** SJ82

✕***Hollybush Inn*** ☎(078575) 280
Country inn with old beams, traditional hospitality and wholesome food.
Dinner not served Sun
International 50 seats Last dinner 9.30pm 100P
Credit cards 1 3

SELBY
North Yorkshire
Map **8** SE63

★★**Londesborough Arms** Market Pl ☎(0757) 707355
Former coaching inn standing in the town centre beside the Abbey.
34rm(12🛁2🚿) CTV in all bedrooms Ⓡ sB&B£19 sB&B🛁£24 dB&B£26 dB&B🛁£35 B
☾ 24P 6🚗 billiards Disco nightly
Lunch £4.85–£5.75&alc Dinner £5.95–£6.50&alc Wine £3.85 Last dinner 9.30pm
Credit cards 1 2 3 5

SELKIRK
Borders *Selkirkshire*
Map **12** NT42

★***Heatherlie Hill*** Heatherlie Park ☎(0750) 21200
Detached Victorian house just off town centre, a small family run hotel.
6rm B
CTV 15P 🚗 ✽
V Last dinner 8.30pm
Credit cards 1 2 3 4 5 **VS**

SELMESTON
East Sussex
Map **5** TQ50

✕**Corins** Church Farm ☎Ripe (032183) 343
Home-cooked food served in 17th-century farmhouse surroundings.
Closed Mon Lunch not served Tue–Sat Dinner not served Sun
English, French & Italian 24 seats Lunch £5.50 Dinner £10.50 Wine £4.25 Last dinner 11pm 24P
S% Credit cards 1 2 3 5 **VS**

SENNEN
Cornwall
Map **2** SW32

★★*L* **Tregiffian** ☎(073687) 408
Closed Nov–Feb
A converted Cornish granite farmhouse set amidst moorland with a view of Sennen Cove.
8rm(3🛁1🚿)(1fb) Ⓡ ✻sB&B£11 dB&B£22 dB&B🛁🚿£26 B
CTV 20P 🚗 ✽
International **V** ✻Bar lunch 75p–£2.50 Tea fr 30p Dinner fr£6.60&alc Wine £4 Last dinner 8.30pm
Credit cards 1 3 5 **VS**

SETTLE
North Yorkshire
Map **7** SD86

S

★★★**Falcon Manor** Skipton Rd ☎(07292)3814
16rm(13→2⋒)(1fb) CTV in all bedrooms Ⓡ sB&B→⋒£20–£23 sB&B→⋒£30–£35 ⊟
80P ✽ ⌒(grass) ⌂ *xmas*
⊟English & Continental V ♡ ⊐ Lunch £1–£3.95 Tea 65p–£3 High Tea £2.50–£5.50 Dinner £7.90–£11 Wine £3.50 Last dinner 9.30pm
Credit cards 1 3 5

★★**Royal Oak** Market Pl ☎(07292) 2561
6rm(2⋒) Ⓡ sB&B£17.75 sB&B⋒£20.50 dB&B£28.50 dB&B⋒£32.50
CTV 15P
♡✱Lunch £5 Dinner £7alc Wine £3.50 Last dinner 10pm

SHAFTESBURY
Dorset
Map **3** ST82

★★★**Grosvenor** The Commons (Trusthouse Forte) ☎(0747) 2282
Modernised, former coaching inn whose central archway leads to an inner courtyard.
48rm(40→2⋒)(4fb) CTV in all bedrooms Ⓡ sB&B→⋒£33 dB&B£40.50 dB&B→⋒£49 ⊟
☾ ⊘ *xmas*
♡⊐ Last dinner 9pm
Credit cards 1 2 3 4 5

★★★**Royal Chase** Royal Chase Roundabout (Best Western) ☎(0747) 3355
A former monastery, the hotel also has Georgian and some Victorian parts. It offers modern comforts without losing its original character.
18rm(10→4⋒)(4fb) 1⊟ CTV in all bedrooms Ⓡ sB&B£21.25 sB&B→⋒£26–£28 dB&B£36.75 dB&B→⋒£42–£47.50 ⊟
CTV 200P ✽ ⌂ *xmas*
V ♡ ⊐ Lunch £8alc Tea 65p High Tea £1.75 Dinner £8alc ✱Wine £4.80 Last dinner 9.30pm
S% Credit cards 1 2 3 5 **VS**

SHANKLIN
Isle of Wight
Map **4** SZ58
(Shanklin telephone numbers due to change during the currency of this guide.)

★★★***Cliff Tops*** Park Rd ☎(098386) 3262 Telex no 86725
Hotel has good Channel views and large well-kept gardens.
102rm(87→3⋒) Annexe: 8rm CTV in all bedrooms ⊟
Lift ☾ 40P CFA ✽ ⌒(heated) sauna bath
Live music and dancing 5 nights wkly (May–Sep) ⌂
⊟English & French ♡ ⊐
Last dinner 8.45pm
Credit cards 1 2 3 5
See advert on page 578

★★★***Shanklin*** Eastmount Rd ☎(098386) 2286 Closed Nov–Mar
Modern luxury hotel with extensive sea and country views.
67rm(46→) Annexe: 20rm CTV in 15 bedrooms ⊟ ♿
Lift ☾ CTV 100P Disco 6 nights wkly Live music and dancing 6 nights wkly
V ♡ ⊐ Last dinner 8.30pm

★★**Luccombe Hall** Luccombe Rd (Exec Hotel) ☎(098386) 2719 Closed Dec & Jan RS Feb, Mar & Nov
Well-appointed, comfortable hotel with good leisure facilities.
32rm(23→3⋒)(12fb) CTV in 20 bedrooms TV in 12 bedrooms sB&B£13–£18 sB&B→⋒£16.25–£22.50 dB&B£22–£31 dB&B→⋒£26–£36 ⊟ ♿
CTV 25P ⌂ ✽ ⌒(heated) ⌒(grass)
⊟English & Continental Lunch £4–£4.50 Dinner £8.50–£9.50 Wine £3.50 Last dinner 9.30pm
VS
See advert on page 578

S

S

★★**Melbourne Ardenlea** Queen's Rd ☎(098386) 2283 Closed mid Oct–Mar

Family run hotel, set in well tended gardens.

47rm(16⇌2⋒)(6fb) sB&B£10–£12 sB&B⇌⋒£12–£14 dB&B£20–£24 dB&B⇌⋒£24–£28 B

CTV 12P ✽ Live music and dancing twice wkly

English & French Lunch fr£4.60 Dinner fr£5.75 Wine £4 Last dinner 5.30pm

VS

SHAP
Cumbria
Map **12** NY51

★★**Shap Wells** (situated 3m SW of Shap Village off A6) ☎(09316) 628 Closed Jan–14 Feb

73rm(39⇌) sB&B£10.75–£12.50 sB&B⇌⋒ £13.30–£15.50 dB&B£21.50–£25 dB&B⇌⋒£26.60–£31 B

CTV 200P ✽ (hard) billiards

English & French

Credit cards 1 2 3 5

SHAPWICK
Somerset
Map **3** ST43

★★**Shapwick House** Monks Dr (Best Western) ☎Ashcott (0458) 210321

Spacious, modernised country hotel in a peaceful location, yet with easy access to the A39.

12rm(6⇌6⋒)(2fb) Ⓡ ✻sB&B⇌⋒ fr£21 dB&B⇌⋒ fr£32 B

CTV 100P 2 ✽

✻Lunch fr£6.60 Tea fr60p Dinner fr£8.80 Wine £3.50 Last dinner 9pm

Credit cards 1 2 3 5

SHARDLOW
Derbyshire
Map **8** SK43

✕✕***Lady in Grey*** Wilne Ln ☎Derby (0332) 792331

Large Victorian house near the River Trent and just off the A6.

Closed Public hols Dinner not served Sun

English & French 72 seats Last dinner 9.30pm 50P bedrooms available

Credit cards 1 2 3 5

SHAWBOST
Isle of Lewis, Western Isles *Ross & Cromarty*
Map **13** NB24

✕**Raebhat House** ☎(085171) 205 Closed Sun

Unlicensed No corkage charge 40 seats Lunch £3.50–£4&alc Tea 50p High Tea £2.50–£3.50 Dinner £8&alc Last dinner 9.30pm 30P bedrooms available Live music Fri

SHEDFIELD
Hampshire
Map **4** SU51

☆☆☆**Meon Valley** Sandy Ln ☎Wickham (0329) 833455 Telex no 86272 Closed Xmas Day

Country hotel with many outdoor facilities.

54rm⇌⋒ (5fb) CTV in all bedrooms Ⓡ sB&B⇌⋒£31 dB&B⇌⋒£39 B

☾ CFA 250P ✽ (heated) 18 (hard) squash billiards sauna bath

English & French V Lunch £4.50–£5.95 Tea fr40p High Tea fr£1.75 Dinner £7.50&alc Wine £4.50 Last dinner 9.45pm

Credit cards 1 2 3 5

SHEFFIELD
South Yorkshire
Map **8** SK38

★★★★**Grosvenor House** Charter Sq (Trusthouse Forte) ☎(0742) 20041 Telex no 54312

Modern, fourteen-storey hotel in the town centre.

121rm(103⇌) CTV in all bedrooms Ⓡ sB&B⇌£43 dB&B⇌£57 B

Lift ☾ 82 CFA →

♆☐ Last dinner 9.45pm
Credit cards 1 2 3 4 5

★★★★**Hallam Tower Post House** Manchester Rd, Broomhill (Trusthouse Forte) ☎(0742) 686031 Telex no 547293
Twelve-storey, modern tower block hotel, overlooking the city.
135➡ (2fb) CTV in all bedrooms ® sB&B➡£42 dB&B➡£54 Ḃ
Lift ☾ 120P CFA ✽
♆☐ Last dinner 9.30pm
Credit cards 1 2 3 4 5

★★★**Hotel St George** Kenwood Rd (Swallow) ☎(0742) 583811 Telex no 547030
76➡⋒ CTV in all bedrooms ® ✱sB&B➡⋒£22–£32 dB&B➡⋒£32–£42 Ḃ
Lift ☾ ## 120P CFA ✽ ♪ ♿ *xmas*
▣ English & French ♆☐ ✱Lunch £4.95&alc Tea 55p Dinner £6.75&alc Wine £4.75 Last dinner 9.30pm
Credit cards 1 2 3 5

★★★**Mosborough Hall** High St, Mosborough (7m SE A616) ☎(0742) 484353 RS Sat, Sun & Mon
A period manor house with Elizabethan elements, in a village setting
13rm(8➡5⋒) (2fb) 5▭ CTV in all bedrooms ★ sB&B➡⋒£19–£30 dB&B➡⋒£34–£38 Ḃ
☾ 100P ✽ Live music and dancing Sat ⌂
V ♆☐ Lunch £4.75–£5.75&alc Tea 65p Dinner £7.75–£8.25&alc Wine £5 Last dinner 9.30pm
Credit cards 1 2 3 **VS**

★★★**Royal Victoria** Victoria Station Rd ☎(0742) 78822 RS Xmas & Etr
Large four-storey Victorian hotel near the former railway station in the town centre.
63rm(32➡6⋒) (2fb) CTV in 32 bedrooms TV in 31 bedrooms ® sB&B£24.75 sB&B➡⋒£36.85 dB&B£38.50 dB&B➡⋒£46.20 Ḃ
Lift ☾ 200P CFA
♆☐ ✱Lunch £5.35 Tea 65p Dinner £7 Wine £4.15 Last dinner 9.15pm
Credit cards 1 2 3 5 **VS**

S

★★**Roslyn Court** 178–180 Psalter Ln, Brincliffe ☎(0742) 666188 RS wknds
Three-storey building in a residential area.
31rm (2fb) CTV in 2 bedrooms ® ✱sB&B£15–£19.50 dB&B£24–£30 Ḃ
☾ CTV 40P
V ♆☐ ✱Bar lunch 60p–£1.50 Tea fr60p Dinner fr£4.60 Wine £4 Last dinner 8.45pm
Credit cards 1 2 5

★★**Rutland** 452 Glossop Rd, Broomhill (Inter-Hotels) ☎(0742) 665215 Telex no 547500
The hotel is made up from seven stone houses joined by walkways to the public areas.
78rm(53➡3⋒) Annexe: 17rm(16➡1⋒) (11fb) CTV in all bedrooms ✱sB&B£15–£19 sB&B➡⋒£20–£27.50 dB&B➡⋒£28–£36 Ḃ
Lift ☾ CTV 80P CFA
V ♆☐ ✱Lunch £3.80–£4.25&alc Dinner £5.75&alc Wine £4.50 Last dinner 9.30pm
Credit cards 1 2 3 5

★★**St Andrew's** 46–48 Kenwood Rd (Swallow) ☎(0742) 550309 Telex no 547030
RS Xmas
41rm(9➡21⋒) (2fb) CTV in 24 bedrooms ® ✱sB&B£16 sB&B➡⋒£20–£26 dB&B£26 dB&B➡⋒£29–£38 Ḃ
☾ CTV 100P ✽
V ♆☐ ✱Lunch £4.50&alc Tea 60p Dinner £5.85&alc Wine £4.75 Last dinner 8.45pm
Credit cards 1 2 3 5

✕✕**Dore** Church Ln ☎(0742) 365948
Closed Mon Dinner not served Sun
▣ English & French 65 seats Lunch fr£4.50&alc Dinner £6.50&alc Last dinner 10pm 15P Live music and dancing Fri
Credit cards 1 2 3 5 **VS**

✕*La Bella Roma* 216–218 London Rd ☎(0742) 53872
Closed Sun Lunch not served Sat
▣ French & Italian 60 seats Last dinner 11.30pm ₽̸
Credit cards 1 3

SHEPPERTON
Surrey London plan **5** 1A (page 422)

☆☆☆**Shepperton Moat House** Felix Ln (Queens Moat) ☎Walton-on-Thames (09322) 41404 Telex no 928170
Closed 25–30 Dec
Busy commercial hotel with a smart bar and restaurant.
180➡⋒ CTV in all bedrooms ✱sB&B➡⋒£31–£34.25 dB&B➡⋒£38.50–£43.25 Ḃ
Lift ☾ CTV 225P CFA ✽ ♪ sauna bath Live music and dancing Sat (in winter)
▣ English & French V ♆ ✱Lunch £7.80&alc Dinner £8.50&alc Wine £5.25 Last dinner 10pm
S% Credit cards 1 2 3 5

SHEPTON MALLET
Somerset
Map **3** ST64

★★**Shrubbery** Commercial Rd ☎(0749) 2555
Owner-managed, small tourist hotel, with a cellar restaurant, in the centre of the town.
7rm(3➡1⋒) (2fb) ★ sB&B£15 sB&B➡⋒£17.50 dB&B£25 dB&B➡⋒£29 Ḃ
CTV 20P ⛟ ✽
V ♆☐ Bar lunch £1–£3 Tea fr75p Dinner £8alc Wine £3.95 Last dinner 9pm
Credit cards 1 2 3 5

✕✕**Bowlish House** Coombe Ln, Bowlish (on the Wells road A371) ☎(0749) 2022
Relaxed informal Georgian country house restaurant with superb wine list.
Lunch not served
▣ International 26 seats Dinner £9.50–£12 Wine £3 Last dinner 10.30pm 22P bedrooms available ⚟
VS

✕✕**Thatched Cottage** Frome Rd ☎(0749) 2058
Closed Mon Lunch not served Sat Dinner not served Sun
36 seats ✱Lunch £5.95 Dinner £11.50alc Wine £4.95 Last dinner 9.45pm 40P
Credit cards 1 2 3 5

✕**Blostin's** 29 Waterloo Rd ☎(0749) 3648
Closed Sun Lunch not served
▣ English & French 28 seats ✱Dinner £6.95–£7.95&alc Wine £4.65 Last dinner 9pm ₽̸
Credit cards 1 3 5

SHERBORNE
Dorset
Map **3** ST61

☆☆☆**Post House** Horsecastles Ln (Trusthouse Forte) ☎(0935) 813191 Telex no 46522
60➡ (36fb) CTV in all bedrooms ® sB&B➡£37.50 dB&B➡£50 Ḃ
☾ 100P CFA ✽ ⌂ *xmas*
♆☐ Last dinner 9.45pm
Credit cards 1 2 3 4 5

★★**Eastbury** Long St ☎(0935) 813387
Georgian town house with pleasant lawns and gardens in a quiet position, near the shops and Abbey.
15rm(5➡) (3fb) sB&B£14–£15 dB&B➡£16–£17 dB&B£25–£27 dB&B➡£29–£31 Ḃ
TV 15P 4⛟ ✽ ⌂
▣ English & Continental ♆☐ Lunch £4 Tea 50p–60p High Tea 50p–£3alc Dinner £6 Wine £3.80 Last dinner 8.30pm

★★**Saffron House** The Avenue ☎(0935) 812734
Closed Xmas–New Year
Detached stone house in a quiet residential area, only a short walking distance from town.
6rm(5➡1⋒) sB&B➡⋒£16.20 dB&B➡⋒£32.40
CTV 30P ✽
▣ English & Continental Lunch £5.50–£6 Tea 60p High Tea £4–£5.50 Dinner £7.30–£8.50 Wine £3.50 Last dinner 8pm
VS

✕✕**Grange** Oborne (1½m NE off A30) ☎(0935) 813463

Closed Mon Lunch not served Tue–Sat Dinner not served Sun
English, French & Italian **V** 50 seats Lunch £5.75 Dinner £7.50–£11alc Wine £4.75 Last dinner 10.30pm 25P bedrooms available
Credit cards 1 3

SHERBURN IN ELMET
North Yorkshire
Map **8** SE43
✕ ***Bon Viveur*** 19 Low St ☎ South Milford (0977) 682146
Closed Sun, Mon, 2wks Jan & all Aug Lunch not served
French 40 seats Last dinner 9.30pm 20P

SHERINGHAM
Norfolk
Map **9** TG14
★★ **Beaumaris** South St ☎ (0263) 822370
Closed Nov–Mar
28rm(11→2⋒) (5fb) TV available on request Ⓡ *sB&B£12.50–£15 sB&B→⋒£13.50–£16 dB&B£24–£30 dB&B→⋒£26–£32 B
CTV 25P
Lunch £4–£5.50 Tea 75p Dinner £6.50–£8.50 Wine £4.50 Last dinner 8.15pm
Credit card 3

★★ **Southlands** South St ☎ (0263) 822679
Closed Oct–mid Apr
21rm(9→) (1fb) CTV in all bedrooms Ⓡ sB&B fr£15 sB&B→ fr£17 dB&B fr£30 dB&B→ fr£34
20P
Bar lunch fr£1.50 Tea fr£1 Dinner fr£8.50 Wine £3.10 Last dinner 8pm

★ **Two Lifeboats** Promenade ☎ (0263) 822401
Closed Xmas night
Established in 1720, this hotel was once used by smugglers.
8rm Ⓡ sB&B£13 dB&B£26 B
CTV

V Bar lunch £2.25 High Tea fr£1.75 Dinner fr£5.50&alc Wine £3 Last dinner 9pm

SHETLAND
Map **16**
See Brae, Lerwick, Virkie and Whiteness

SHIELDAIG
Highland *Ross & Cromarty*
Map **14** NG85
★*B* **Tigh an Eilean** ☎ (05205) 251
Closed Nov–Etr
A small, family-run hotel, beautifully situated on the shores of Loch Torridon.
13rm (1fb) Ⓡ sB&B£12.50–£14 dB&B£22–£26
20P nc6yrs
Bar lunch £1.25alc Dinner £6.50 Wine £3.35 Last dinner 8pm

SHIFNAL
Shropshire
Map **7** SJ70
★★★*H* ***Park House*** Park St ☎ Telford (0952) 460128
RS 24–30 Dec
24rm(14→10⋒) 1 CTV in all bedrooms B
☾ 80P Disco Wed & Thu Live music and dancing Fri
English & French Last dinner 9.45pm
Credit cards 1 2 3 5 **VS**

SHINFIELD
Berkshire
Map **4** SU76
✕✕ **Milton Sandford** Church Rd Ln ☎ Reading (0734) 883783
Closed Sun Lunch not served
38 seats Dinner £16 Wine £4.90 Last dinner 9.30pm 25P
S% Credit cards 1 2 3 5

SHIPDHAM
Norfolk
Map **5** TF90

★★*BL* **Shipdham Place** Church Cl ☎ Dereham (0362) 820303
Closed Xmas & Feb RS Jan & Mar
5→ *sB&B→£27.50–£30 dB&B→£32.50–£35
CTV 20P
English & French Tea £1–£1.75 Dinner £14.75–£16.50 Wine £5.50 Last dinner 8.30pm

SHIPHAM
Somerset
Map **3** ST45
★★*H* **Daneswood House** Luck Hill ☎ Winscombe (093 484) 3145
10rm(1→2⋒) CTV in all bedrooms sB&B£19 sB&B→⋒£21.50 dB&B£27.50 dB&B→⋒£30 B
CTV 30P 3 *xmas*
Continental Lunch £4.95–£7.95&alc Tea 75p–£1.50&alc Dinner £7.95–£9.95&alc Wine £5.50 Last dinner 9pm
Credit cards 1 2 3 5

★ **Penscot Farmhouse** The Square (Minotel) ☎ Winscombe (093 484) 2659
Attractive, personally-run, cottage hotel, with a separate restaurant serving good food.
18rm(6→6⋒) (2fb) 1 Ⓡ sB&B£11–£13.50 sB&B→⋒£13.50–£15.50 dB&B£22–£27 dB&B⋒£27–£31 B
CTV 40P *xmas*
V Lunch 75p–£3.50 Tea 30p–£1 Dinner £3.50–£8.50&alc Wine £3.50 Last dinner 9.30pm
Credit cards 1 3 5 **VS**
See advert on page 582

SHIPLEY
Shropshire
Map **7** SO89
✕✕ **Thornescroft** Bridgnorth Rd ☎ Pattingham (0902) 700253
Georgian farmhouse with a matching extension.
Closed Sun, Mon, Tue following Bank hols, Xmas & New Year →

S

⊟English & Continental 50 seats Lunch £3.25–£5.25&alc Dinner £8.25–£8.75&alc Wine £5 Last dinner 9pm P

Credit cards 1 2 5

SHIPSTON-ON-STOUR
Warwickshire
Map **4** SP24

✕✕**Old Mill** ☎(0608) 61880

Dinner not served Sun

45 seats Lunch £6.25 Dinner £9.50&alc Wine £4.80 Last dinner 9.30pm 15P bedrooms available

Credit cards 1 2 3 5

SHIPTON-UNDER-WYCHWOOD
Oxfordshire
Map **4** SP21

★★***Shaven Crown*** ☎(0993) 830330

Traditional cosy hotel with galleried lounge and formal restaurant.

8rm(2➡) CTV in all bedrooms Ⓡ ✶ 30P ✽

V ♈ ☕ Last dinner 9.30pm

Credit cards 1 2 3 5

✕**Lamb Inn** High St ☎(0993) 830465

Lunch not served Mon–Sat Dinner not served Sun

20 seats ✻Lunch fr£6 Dinner fr£8.50 Wine £5 Last dinner 9.30pm 20P bedrooms available

Credit cards 1 2 3 5

SHORNE
Kent
Map **5** TQ67

☆☆☆**Inn on the Lake** Watling St (A2) ☎(047 482) 3333

Hotel has spacious modern bedrooms, some overlooking lake.

78➡⋔ (2fb) CTV in all bedrooms Ⓡ ✶ sB&B➡⋔ £27–£35 dB&B➡⋔ £33–£47

☾ 250P CFA ✽ ♩ Live music and dancing Sat

⊟English & French ♈ Lunch £7–£9&alc Dinner £8&alc Wine £5 Last dinner 9.45pm

Credit cards 1 2 3 5

SHREWSBURY
Shropshire
Map **7** SJ41

★★★**Ainsworth's Radbrook Hall** Radbrook Rd ☎(0743) 4861

This was originally the house of the Head of the Clan McPherson.

43rm(35➡8⋔) Annexe: 5⋔ CTV in all bedrooms Ⓡ sB&B➡⋔ fr£25 dB&B➡⋔ fr£36 ⊟

☾ CTV 250P CFA ✽ squash sauna bath Disco Sat Live music and dancing Sat *xmas*

V ♈ ☕ Lunch fr£5&alc Tea fr50p Dinner fr£6&alc Wine £4.75 Last dinner 9.30pm

Credit cards 1 2 4 5 **VS**

See advert on page 584

★★★**Lion** Wyle Cop (Trusthouse Forte) ☎(0743) 53107 Telex no 35648

60➡ (5fb) CTV in all bedrooms Ⓡ sB&B➡ £35.50 dB&B➡ £52.50 ⊟

Lift ☾ 32P 40⌂ CFA *xmas*

♈ Last dinner 9.45pm

Credit cards 1 2 3 4 5

★★★**Lord Hill** Abbey Foregate (Greenall Whitley) ☎(0743) 52601

Closed 26 Dec RS Xmas & New Year

23rm(7➡14⋔) Annexe: 24➡ (2fb) CTV in all bedrooms Ⓡ sB&B➡⋔ £25–£26 dB&B➡⋔ £36–£37 ⊟

☾ 200P CFA

V ♈ ☕ Lunch £5.28&alc Tea 50p Dinner £6.16 Wine £5.22 Last dinner 9.15pm

Credit cards 1 2 3 5

★★★**Prince Rupert** Butcher Row ☎(0743) 52461 Telex no 35100

Dating back to the 15th century, the hotel is named after James I's grandson. It is privately owned and managed and caters for conferences and meetings.

64rm(52➡10⋔) (4fb) CTV in all bedrooms ✻sB&B£24 sB&B➡⋔ £28 dB&B£34 dB&B➡⋔ £38 ⊟

Lift ☾ ⋕ CTV 50P CFA billiards ♿ →

RELAX IN A COUNTRY HOUSE GARDEN.

Set in 300 acres of beautiful Shropshire countryside, and just 14 miles from Shrewsbury, Hawkstone Park Hotel is the perfect holiday centre, and the home of Sandy Lyle. Convenient for trips to the historical towns of Shrewsbury, Chester and Ludlow, other local interests include the famous Hodnet Hall gardens, just a country stroll away.

Enjoy all the comforts of a relaxed country house atmosphere. **All rooms with bath and colour TV.** Our elegant restaurant serves traditional cuisine and flambé specialities, all accompanied by wines at moderate cost. Or why not sample Real Ale in the Hawkstone Park Arms.

And of course there's plenty to do at Hawkstone Park! Leisure facilities include **two splendid 18-hole golf courses,** tennis, croquet, outdoor swimming pool, sauna, solarium and trimnasium.

Excellent inclusive terms with up to 75% reduction for children.

SUPER VALUE BARGAIN BREAKS AND SPECIALITY WEEKENDS, AVAILABLE SUMMER AND WINTER

Brochure and details from:
Hawkstone Park Hotel,
Weston-under-Redcastle, Shrewsbury,
Shropshire, SY4 5UY.
Tel: Lee Brockhurst **(093924) 611**

Best Western

HAWKSTONE PARK HOTEL ★★★

NEW CONFERENCE
FACILITIES
OPENING
AUTUMN
'83

THE HOME OF SANDY LYLE

S

S

🍴International V ♔ ☕ ✱Lunch fr£6&alc Tea fr75p Dinner fr£8&alc Wine £4 Last dinner 10.15pm

Credit cards ① ② ③ ⑤

★★ ***Beauchamp*** The Mount (Scottish & Newcastle) ☎(0743) 3230

25rm(9🛁6🚿) CTV in all bedrooms Ⓡ ✱ B

CTV 80P ✽ Disco wknds

♔ ☕ Last dinner 9 & 9.30pm wknds

Credit cards ① ② ③ ⑤

★★ **Britannia** Welsh Bridge (Greenall Whitley) ☎(0743) 61246 Telex no 629462 RS Xmas & New Year

28rm(12🛁🚿) (3fb) CTV in 13 bedrooms Ⓡ sB&B£20.35–£21.35 sB&B🛁£24.75–£25.75 dB&B£28.60–£29.60 dB&B🛁£35.20–£36.20 B

☾ 40P 8🚗

🍴English & French V ♔ ☕ Lunch £4.75–£8.50&alc Tea 55p Dinner £7–£9&alc Wine £4.50 Last dinner 9.45pm

S% Credit cards ① ② ③ ⑤

✕✕ ***Albright Hussey*** Albright Hussey (3m N off A528) ☎Bowmore Heath (0939) 290523

The battle of Shrewsbury (1406) was fought on the site of this restaurant.

Closed Mon Dinner not served Sun

🍴English & French 60 seats Last dinner 10pm 200P

Credit cards ① ② ③ ⑤

See advert on page 582

✕ **Penny Farthing** Abbey Foregate ☎(0743) 56119

A small restaurant with beams and a cottage atmosphere, next to the Abbey.

Lunch not served Sat Dinner not served Tue

🍴English & French 55 seats Lunch £2.50alc Tea £1.75alc Dinner £15alc Wine £5.60 Last dinner 10pm

Credit cards ① ② ⑤ **VS**

SIDCOT

Avon
Map **3** ST45

★★ **Sidcot** ☎Winscombe (093 484) 2271

Small, personally-run, holiday hotel set in four acres of grounds with access to A38.

9🛁 (3fb) CTV in 6 bedrooms TV in 1 bedroom Ⓡ sB&B🛁🚿£18–£20 dB&B🛁🚿£28–£30 B

65P ✽ sauna bath

🍴English & French V ♔ ☕ Lunch £5–£6&alc Tea £1.20–£2.50 High Tea £2–£4 Dinner £6–£6.50&alc Wine £4 Last dinner 9.30pm

Credit cards ① ② ③ ⑤

SIDMOUTH

Devon
Map **3** SY18

★★★★ ***HL*** **Victoria** Esplanade (Brend) ☎(03955) 2651

Large hotel in its own grounds, set in an elevated position overlooking the sea.

63🛁 CTV in all bedrooms ✱sB&B🛁£27.60–£31.63 dB&B🛁£41.40–£50.60 B

Lift ☾ CTV 75P CFA 4🚗 ✽ & (heated) (hard) billiards sauna bath *xmas*

🍴English & French ♔ ☕ ✱Lunch £7.19 Tea 69p Dinner £9.78&alc Wine £4.95 Last dinner 9pm

Credit cards ① ② ③ ⑤

★★★ **Bedford** Esplanade ☎(03955) 3047

Closed 22 Oct–Mar

Large, traditional hotel on a corner of the promenade. There are fine sea views.

40rm(21🛁5🚿) (10fb) CTV in all bedrooms Ⓡ ✱sB&B£11.50–£15.50 sB&B🛁🚿£15–£17.50 dB&B£27–£35 dB&B🛁🚿£35–£43 B

Lift ☾ CTV

♔ ☕ Lunch £3.50 Dinner £6.50 Wine £3.50 Last dinner 8.30pm

S% Credit card ③

S

Sidmouth

★★★**Belmont** Sea Front ☎(03955) 2555
Closed Jan
Set in own grounds, hotel has imposing façade with some balconies.
50🛁 CTV in all bedrooms ® sB&B🛁£22–£24 dB&B🛁£44–£48 [B]
Lift ☾ 26P ✽ nc2yrs
🍷☕ Lunch £6.50–£7&alc Tea fr£1.75 Dinner £7.50–£8 Wine £5 Last dinner 8.30pm
S% Credit cards 1 2 3

★★★**Fortfield** Station Rd ☎(03955) 2403
Victorian-style hotel overlooking the sea.
56rm(27🛁1🚿)(10fb) CTV in 2 bedrooms ® sB&B£18.50–£21.50 sB&B🛁🚿£23–£25 dB&B£34–£37 dB&B🛁🚿£39–£50 [B]
Lift ☾ CTV 60P CFA ✽ sauna bath 🏠 *xmas*
V🍷☕ Bar lunch £4alc Tea 50p Dinner £6.50&alc Wine £3.50 Last dinner 8.30pm
Credit cards 1 3 5 VS

★★★*H* **Riviera** The Esplanade ☎(03955) 5201 Telex no 42551 (Exonia)
Attractive hotel in a fine position on the sea front, with its own sun patio.
34rm(20🛁3🚿)(6fb) CTV in all bedrooms sB&B£16.50–£24 sB&B🛁🚿£19–£26.50 dB&B£33–£48 dB&B🛁🚿£38–£53 [B]
Lift ☾ CTV 7P 9🏠🅿 *xmas*
🍽 English & French V🍷☕ Lunch £7.50&alc Tea 80p Dinner £9&alc Wine £4.50 Last dinner 9pm
Credit cards 2 5 VS

★★★**Salcombe Hill House** Beatland Rd ☎(03955) 4697
Closed Dec–Feb
Standing in own grounds, hotel is short distance from sea front.
33rm(22🛁3🚿)(5fb) CTV in all bedrooms ® sB&B£16–£23 sB&B🛁🚿£17–£24 dB&B£32–£46 dB&B🛁🚿£34–£48 [B]
Lift ☾ CTV 35P 5🏠🅿 ✽ [pool] (heated) [golf] (grass) nc3yrs
V🍷☕ Lunch £4.50–£5.50 Tea £1 Dinner £6–£7 Wine £3.80 Last dinner 8pm
S% Credit cards 1 3

★★★*H* **Westcliff** Manor Rd ☎(03955) 3252
RS Nov–mid Mar
Comfortable hotel with spacious grounds, close to the beach.
38rm(29🛁1🚿)(15fb) CTV available on request sB&B£12.65–£24.40 sB&B🛁🚿£14.65–£26.40 dB&B£25.30–£48.80 dB&B🛁🚿£29.30–£52.80 [B]
Lift CTV 50P 🅿 ✽ [pool] (heated) Disco Thu Live music and dancing Sat
🍽 English, French & Italian 🍷☕ Lunch £5.25alc Tea 70p Dinner £8.80 Wine £3.80 Last dinner 8.30pm
Credit cards 1 2 3

★★**Abbeydale** Manor Rd ☎(03955) 2060
Closed Dec–Feb
Comfortable, friendly holiday hotel.
17rm(13🛁2🚿)(3fb) CTV in all bedrooms ® ★ ✽ sB&B£12.75–£15 sB&B🛁🚿£14–£16.50 dB&B£25.50–£30 dB&B🛁🚿£28–£33
24P 🅿 ✽ nc4yrs
🍽 English & French 🍷☕ ✽ Bar lunch £1 Tea 50p Dinner £6 Wine £3.50 Last dinner 8.30pm
VS

★★ [country house] ***Brownlands*** Sid Rd ☎(03955) 3053 Closed Nov–Mar
Standing in 5 acres of grounds with panoramic view towards the sea within one mile from the town.
17rm(4🛁5🚿) [B]
[no smoking] CTV 30P 4🏠 ✽ ⛺
V🍷 Last dinner 8pm

★★***Byes Links*** Sid Rd ☎(03955) 3129
Closed Nov–Mar
→

S

Situated in quiet district within walking distance of the shops and beach.
18rm(9→7⋒)®Ƀ
CTV 40P ✽ Live music and dancing 3 nights wkly
V♔☕ Last dinner 8.15pm

★★*H***Littlecourt** Seafield Rd ☎(03955) 5279
Closed Nov–Mar
Regency house with its own garden, in a quiet position only a short distance from the shops and the sea.
21rm(12→3⋒)(3fb) CTV available on request ®*sB&B£15.95–£17.45 (incl dinner) sB&B→⋒£16.95–£21.50 (incl dinner) dB&B£31.90–£34.90 (incl dinner) dB&B→⋒£41–£46 (incl dinner) Ƀ
CTV 14P ✽ (heated)
V♔☕*Bar lunch 70p–£3 Tea £1 Dinner £5.45 Wine £3.80 Last dinner 8pm

★★**Royal Glen** Glen Rd ☎(03955) 3221
This hotel was once a Royal residence.
37rm(18→9⋒)(5fb) CTV in 14 bedrooms TV in 17 bedrooms *sB&B£10.55–£17.15 sB&B→⋒£13.18–£20.40 dB&B£21.10–£28.40 dB&B→⋒£24.20–£40.80 Ƀ
CTV 16P 8🚘 nc8yrs
♔☕*Lunch £4.25–£4.50&alc Tea 50p–£1 Dinner £4.50&alc Wine £3.60 Last dinner 7.30pm
Credit cards 2 3

★★**Royal York & Faulkner** Esplanade ☎(03955) 3043
Regency-style, building personally-run on the sea front, close to shopping facilities.
71rm(18→2⋒)(8fb) CTV in all bedrooms ®sB&B£12.50–£14.50 sB&B→⋒£14–£16.50 dB&B£25–£29 dB&B→⋒£28–£33 Ƀ
Lift CTV 5P

S

V ♀ ☕ Lunch fr£4.50 Tea fr75p Dinner fr£6 Wine £3 Last dinner 8pm

S% Credit card 3 **VS**

★★**Woodlands** Station Rd ☎(03955) 3120

A converted period house on the approach road to the sea front, offering a quiet atmosphere.

30rm(15⇌) ® sB&B£12–£16.50 sB&B⇌£13–£18.25 dB&B£24–£33 dB&B⇌£26–£36.50 B

CTV 25P ⇌ ✽ nc3yrs *xmas*

♀ ☕ ✱Lunch £3–£4 Dinner £4–£4.50 Wine £2.90 Last dinner 8pm

★**Applegarth** Church St, Sidford (2m N B3175) ☎(03955) 3174

Closed mid Oct–Nov & 27–30 Dec

Cottage hotel on the edge of the town with very pleasant gardens.

6rm ® sB&B£12–£13 dB&B£24–£26 B

CTV 15P ⇌ ✽ nc10yrs

English & French V ♀ Lunch £4alc Dinner £5&alc Wine £3 Last dinner 9pm

Credit cards 2 3 **VS**

SILLOTH
Cumbria
Map **11** NY15

★★★**Skinburness** ☎(0965) 31468

One of Cumbria's oldest hotels, it has fine views of the Solway Firth and the Scottish mountains.

23rm(8⇌) (2fb) CTV in all bedrooms ® ★ sB&B£13.50 sB&B⇌£15.50 dB&B£17 dB&B⇌£20 B

CTV 70P ✽ Disco Sat Live music and dancing Sat *xmas*

Mainly grills ♀ ✱Lunch £3.55alc Dinner £5.10alc Wine £3.50 Last dinner 9pm

Credit card 1

★★**Golf** Criffel St ☎(0965) 31438

23rm(13⇌1⇌) (8fb) CTV in all bedrooms ® sB&B£16–£18 sB&B⇌£18–£20 dB&B£25–£29 dB&B⇌£28–£34 B

CTV

V ♀ ☕ Lunch £3.75&alc Tea fr£1.60&alc High Tea £2–£4.80 Dinner £6.50&alc Wine £4.20 Last dinner 9.30pm

Credit cards 1 2 5

★★**Queens** Park Ter, Criffel St ☎(0965) 31373

Situated on the sea front with excellent views.

22rm(11⇌) (4fb) CTV in all bedrooms ® ✱sB&B£13 sB&B⇌£16 dB&B£24 dB&B⇌£28 B

CTV 5

V ♀ ✱Lunch £4.50 High Tea £2 Dinner £6.50–£7.50&alc Wine £3.50 Last dinner 9.30pm

Credit card 1

SILVERDALE
Lancashire
Map **7** SD47

★**Silverdale** Shore Rd ☎(0524) 701206

RS Oct–Mar

9rm(1⇌1⇌) (1fb) sB&B£12 sB&B⇌£13.50 dB&B£22 dB&B⇌£25

CTV 30P squash Disco wkly

♀ Bar lunch £1.70 Dinner £4.20&alc Wine £2.70 Last dinner 9pm

Credit cards 1 2 3

SIMONSBATH
Somerset
Map **3** SS73

★★

★★**SIMONSBATH HOUSE, SIMONSBATH**

☎Exford (064 383) 259

RS Nov–Feb

This hotel makes an ideal, and most atmospheric base from which to tour Exmoor. The house was built in 1654 for the warden of Exmoor and was the first house to be built on the moor itself. Mr and Mrs Brown, both experienced in hotel management, bought the house five years ago and converted it to the pleasant and welcoming hotel it has become. The bedrooms are modern, comfortable and thoughtfully equipped, but it is the public rooms with fresh flowers which retain the atmosphere; the cosy oak panelled bar with bookshelves becomes the centre to talk over the day's events while the main sitting room is also most attractive and comfortable. Both have roaring log fires in season and it is a delight to come in and enjoy a traditional cream tea on a cold day. Mr Brown looks after the front of the house ably and with unfailing warmth, while Mrs Brown works hard to produce fine meals from fresh local produce. Much of the cooking is traditional, adventurously so sometimes, and is most enjoyable. It

is served in a well appointed room with an attractive blue colour scheme. The Browns are to be congratulated on achieving such a warm and welcoming atmosphere that our members appreciate so much. This year they have devised a number of literary tours to increase guests' further enjoyment of North Devon and Somerset.

9rm(6⇌) 1 CTV in 6 bedrooms TV in 3 bedrooms ★ ✱sB&B£23 sB&B⇌£34.25 dB&B£41.50 dB&B⇌£54

25P 2 ⇌ ✽ squash nc10yrs *xmas*

V ♀ ☕ Lunch £8.50 Dinner £12.50 Wine £3.95 Last dinner 9pm

Credit cards 1 2 3 **VS**

SITTINGBOURNE
Kent
Map **5** TQ96

★★***Coniston*** London Rd ☎(0795) 23927

Friendly hotel with modern well equipped bedrooms.

50rm(32⇌4⇌) CTV in all bedrooms

☾ CTV 100P ✽

V ♀ Last dinner 10.30pm

Credit cards 1 2 3 5

SIXMILE BOTTOM
Cambridgeshire
Map **5** TL55

★★★ ***B*** **Swynford Paddocks** ☎(063 870) 234

12⇌ CTV in all bedrooms ® sB&B⇌£33–£37 dB&B⇌£51–£68 B

30P ⇌ ✽ (hard) *xmas*

English & French V ♀ Lunch £10alc Dinner £12alc Wine £5.50 Last dinner 9pm

S% Credit cards 1 2 3 5

SKEABOST BRIDGE
Isle of Skye, Highland *Inverness-shire*
Map **13** NG44

★★★ *L* **Skeabost House** ☎(047 032) 202

Closed mid Oct–19 Apr

Fine, family-run Scottish mansion at the head of a loch.

21rm(13⇌) (3fb) ® sB&B£15 sB&B⇌£20 dB&B£28 dB&B⇌£40

☾ CTV 40P 2 ⇌ ✽ billiards

V ♀ ☕ Bar lunch £3.50–£4.80 Tea 40p–45p High Tea £1.50–£1.75 Dinner £9 Wine £5.50 Last dinner 8pm

SKEGNESS
Lincolnshire
Map **9** TF56

★★**County** North Pde ☎(0754) 2461

Large, four-storey sea front hotel to the north of the town centre.

42rm(10⇌) CTV in 10 bedrooms ✱sB&B£16 sB&B⇌£21 dB&B£28 dB&B⇌£32 B

→

Lift ☾ CTV 40P 6 sauna bath xmas
V Lunch £5.50&alc Tea 60p Dinner £5.50&alc Wine £3.60 Last dinner 9.30pm
Credit cards 1 2 3 5

★★**Links** Drummond Rd ☎(0754) 3605
A large gabled building, ¼ mile from the town centre and close to the sea front.
21rm(2 4)(2fb) sB&B£10.50–£12.50 sB&B £12–£14 dB&B£21–£25 dB&B £24–£28 B
CTV 40P Live music and dancing Fri & Sat *xmas*
Lunch £3–£4.50 Dinner £5.50–£6.50&alc Wine £3.50 Last dinner 9pm
Credit cards 1 3

SKELMORLIE
Strathclyde *Ayrshire*
Map **10** NS16
★★★ *BL* **Manor Park** ☎Wemyss Bay (0475) 520832
Closed 3 Jan–mid Feb
Imposing mansion set in its own magnificent grounds, 2m south of Skelmorlie.
18rm(5 12)(4fb) CTV available in bedrooms ® sB&B fr£24.50 dB&B fr£45 B
150P *xmas*
Scottish & Continental Lunch £11alc Tea fr£2 Dinner £8.50&alc Wine £4.50 Last dinner 9pm
VS

SKINFLATS
Central *Stirlingshire*
Map **11** NS98
✕ ***Dutch Inn*** Main Rd ☎Grangemouth (03244) 3015
Closed Sun
Mainly grills 80 seats Last dinner 8pm 150P
VS

SKIPTON
North Yorkshire
Map **7** SD95
★**Midland** Broughton Rd ☎(0756) 2781
10rm(2fb) ® sB&B£11.50 dB&B£22
CTV 30P
V Lunch fr£3.95 High Tea £2.80–£4.50 Dinner £4.95–£6.50 Wine £3.90 Last dinner 9pm
Credit cards 2 3

✕ ***Le Caveau*** 86 High St ☎(0756) 4274
Closed Thu Lunch not served
French 26 seats Last dinner 10pm
Credit card 3

SKYE, ISLE OF
Highland *Inverness-shire*
Map **13**
Refer to location atlas (Map **13**) for details of places with AA appointed hotels and restaurants.

SLEAFORD
Lincolnshire
Map **8** TF04
★**Carre Arms** ☎(0529) 303156
Predominantly commercial public house hotel next to the railway and close to the town centre.
14rm *sB&B£10 dB&B£18
CTV 20P 10
*Lunch £3–£4.50&alc Tea fr£1.50&alc High Tea fr£2.50&alc Dinner fr£3.50&alc Wine £3.25 Last dinner 8.30pm
Credit cards 1 2 5

★**Lion** Northgate ☎(0529) 302127
Small coaching inn with the original entrance and courtyard.
10rm *sB&B£11 dB&B£18 B
CTV

SLIGACHAN
Isle of Skye, Highland, *Inverness-shire*
Map **13** NG42

S

★★★**Sligachan** ☎(047852) 204
Closed Oct–9 May
This stone building replaces the original 18th-century coaching inn which stood nearby.
23rm(9➡) sB&B£17.50 sB&B➡£19 dB&B£34 dsB&B➡£38
CTV 24P 6🏠 ✽ nc8yrs
V♈☕ Bar lunch £3.50alc Tea £1.80 Dinner £8 Wine £4.30 Last dinner 8.30pm

SLOUGH
Berkshire
Map **4** SU97
☆☆☆☆ ***B*** **Holiday Inn** Ditton Rd, Langley (Commonwealth) ☎(0753) 44244 Telex no 848646
Modern hotel with extensive leisure facilities.
239➡⋒ (104fb) CTV in all bedrooms ✻sB&B➡⋒£33–£49.10 dB&B➡⋒£44.60–£64.85 Ƀ
Lift ☾ ## 250P CFA ✽ ⊡(heated) 🎾(hard) sauna bath Live music and dancing Fri & Sat ⌂ *xmas* ♿
▣ International V♈☕ Lunch £9.25–£11&alc Tea fr£3 Dinner fr£8.65&alc Wine £6.75 Last dinner 10.30pm
Credit cards ① ② ③ ④ ⑤

SMALLWAYS
North Yorkshire
Map **12** NZ11
★ ***A66 Motel*** ☎ Teesdale (0833) 27334
Closed Xmas and New Year
A single-storey extension to an inn, with a motel unit.
6rm(1➡) CTV in all bedrooms
20P ✽
V♈ Last dinner 11pm
Credit cards ① **VS**

SNAINTON
North Yorkshire
Map **8** SE98
★★**Coachman Inn** ☎ Scarborough (0723) 85231
An 18th-century, stone-built coaching inn close to the North Yorkshire moors.
10rm(5➡3⋒) Annexe: 2⋒ (5fb) TV in 2 bedrooms Ⓡ ✻sB&B£16.50–£18 sB&B➡⋒£16.50–£18 dB&B£30–£33 dB&B➡⋒£30–£33 Ƀ
CTV 80P ✽
V♈ ✻Bar lunch £2.50–£7 Dinner £7.75 Wine £4.75 Last dinner 9pm
Credit cards ① ② ③ ⑤

SOLIHULL
West Midlands
Map **7** SP17
★★★**George** High St (Embassy) ☎021-704 1241
RS Xmas & New Year
An old coaching inn with modern extensions overlooking a medieval bowling green.
47rm(41➡) (1fb) CTV in all bedrooms Ⓡ sB&B fr£24 sB&B➡ fr£33.75 dB&B fr£31.50 dB&B➡ fr£37 Ƀ
☾ 200P
▣ English & French V♈☕ Lunch fr£6.50 Dinner fr£7 Wine £4.50 Last dinner 9.15pm
Credit cards ① ② ③ ⑤

★★★**St Johns** 651 Warwick Rd (Inter-Hotels) ☎021-705 6777 Telex no 339352
Popular hotel with extensive conference facilities.
218rm(198➡2⋒) (10fb) CTV in all bedrooms Ⓡ sB&B£19.50–£21 sB&B➡⋒£22–£30.50 dB&B£26–£28 dB&B➡⋒£28–£40
Lift ☾ 350P CFA
V♈☕ Lunch £5.50&alc Tea £1.25 High Tea £2.50 Dinner £8&alc Wine £5 Last dinner 9.45pm
Credit cards ① ② ③ ④ ⑤

★★**Flemings** 141 Warwick Rd, Olton ☎021-706 0371 Birmingham district plan **23**
Closed Xmas wk
75rm(5➡70⋒) (4fb) CTV in all bedrooms Ⓡ sB&B➡⋒£19.75 dB&B➡⋒£29 Ƀ
☾ CTV 91P ✽ billiards ⌂

▣ International V♈☕ Lunch £4.50&alc Tea 45palc Dinner £6.75&alc Wine £4 Last dinner 9.30pm
Credit cards ① ③

SONNING
Berkshire
Map **4** SU77
★★★ ***H*** **White Hart** ☎ Reading (0734) 692277 Telex no 847938
The hotel dates back to pre-Elizabethan times, and the annexe is converted from a row of 13th-century cottages, set in lovely gardens leading down to the Thames.
12➡ Annexe: 13➡ (7fb) CTV in all bedrooms Ⓡ sB&B➡£35–£38 dB&B➡£44–£48 Ƀ
☾ 40P ✽ *xmas*
▣ English & French V♈☕ ✻Lunch £8&alc Tea £1.50 High Tea £6–£8 Dinner £8–£14&alc Wine £5.25 Last dinner 9.45pm
Credit cards ① ② ③ ⑤

SOUTHAM
Warwickshire
Map **4** SP46
★★**Craven Arms** ☎(092681) 2452
Old coaching inn with a courtyard and a post box which was used for recording coach journeys.
10rm(1➡) (2fb) CTV in all bedrooms sB&B£16.95 sB&B➡£20.55 dB&B£28.95 dB&B➡£30.90
CTV 100P *xmas*
▣ English & French V♈☕ Lunch £3.45–£5.95&alc Tea £1–£1.25 High Tea £2.55–£3.25 Dinner £5.25–£7.25&alc Wine £3.95 Last dinner 10pm
Credit cards ① ② ③ ⑤

SOUTHAMPTON
Hampshire
Map **4** SU41
See plan
★★★★**Polygon** Cumberland Pl (Trusthouse Forte) ☎(0703) 26401 Telex no 47175 Plan **6** *B3*
Town centre hotel with spacious public areas. →

119⇀(7fb) CTV in all bedrooms Ⓡ sB&B⇀£45.50 dB&B⇀£59 B̶
Lift ☾ 120P CFA 16 *xmas*
Last dinner 9.45pm
Credit cards [1] [2] [3] [4] [5]

★★★**Dolphin** High St (Trusthouse Forte) ☎(0703) 26178 Telex no 477735 Plan **3** *C1*
Traditional hotel with spacious public rooms and modest bedrooms.
72⇀(2fb) CTV in all bedrooms Ⓡ sB&B⇀£35.50 dB&B⇀£49.50 B̶
Lift ☾ 70P CFA *xmas*
Last dinner 9.45pm
Credit cards [1] [2] [3] [4] [5]

☆☆☆**Post House** Herbert Walker Av (Trusthouse Forte) ☎(0703) 28081 Telex no 477368 Plan **7** *B1*
Modern comfortable hotel with some most attractive bedrooms.
132⇀(10fb) CTV in all bedrooms Ⓡ sB&B⇀£42 dB&B⇀£54 B̶
Lift ☾ 250P CFA ✽ (heated)
Last dinner 10pm
Credit cards [1] [2] [3] [4] [5]

★★★**Southampton Moat House** 119 Highfield Ln (Queens Moat) ☎(0703) 559555 Plan **8** *C5*
Modern hotel with well appointed bedrooms.
74rm(62⇀6⋂)(9fb) CTV in 68 bedrooms Ⓡ sB&B£16 sB&B⇀⋂£30.50 dB&B⇀⋂£39.75 B̶
Lift ☾ 120P CFA
English & French **V** Lunch £5.85&alc Tea 50p High Tea £3.50 Dinner £7.15&alc Wine £4.25 Last dinner 9.45pm
Credit cards [1] [2] [3] [5] **VS**

★★★**Southampton Park** Cumberland Pl (Forest Dale) ☎(0703) 23467 Telex no 47439 Plan **9** *B3*
Closed 25 & 26 Dec
Comfortable hotel with canopied log fire a focal point.
77⇀ CTV in all bedrooms Ⓡ sB&B⇀ fr£29.50 dB&B⇀ fr£36.50 B̶
Lift ☾ CFA

V Lunch £3.75–£6.45 Dinner £7.25–£8.25 Wine £4.35 Last dinner 11pm
Credit cards [1] [2] [3] [5] **VS**

★★**Albany** Winn Rd, The Avenue ☎(0703) 554553 Plan **1** *B5*
RS Xmas
Small friendly hotel in quiet area.
38rm(10⇀14⋂) Annexe: 2rm(1⇀1⋂)(6fb) TV in 26 bedrooms Ⓡ sB&B£16.50–£17 sB&B⇀⋂£23–£25 dB&B⇀⋂£32–£34 B̶
Lift ☾ CTV 50P ✽
English & French **V** Lunch £5.65&alc Tea 35p Dinner £5.65&alc Wine £4.20 Last dinner 9.15pm
S% Credit cards [1] [3]

★★***Star*** High St (Inter-Hotels) ☎(0703) 26199 Telex no 477777 Plan **10** *B2*
Closed Xmas
Family run hotel with good home made food.
34rm(16⇀) CTV in all bedrooms Ⓡ B̶
Lift ☾ CTV 20P 4
French Last dinner 9.15pm
Credit cards [1] [3] [5]
See advert on page 594

✕✕**Olivers** Ordnance Rd ☎(0703) 24789 Plan **5** *C4*
Charming wood panelled restaurant, with candlelit tables offering homemade French cuisine.
Closed Sun & 24 Dec–3 Jan Lunch not served Sat
French **V** 70 seats Lunch £6.25 Dinner £8.95 Wine £4.75 Last dinner 10pm 25P
Credit cards [1] [2] [3] [5] **VS**

✕**Golden Palace** Above Bar St ☎(0703) 26636 Plan **4** *B2*
Modern Chinese restaurant with excellent Cantonese cuisine.
Chinese **V** 140 seats ✱Lunch £1.80–£3.50&alc High Tea £2.50–£4&alc Dinner £2.50&alc Wine £3.90 Last dinner mdnt
Credit cards [1] [2] [3] [5]

SOUTHBOROUGH
Kent
Map **5** TQ54

★★**Hand & Sceptre** 21 London Rd ☎Tunbridge Wells (0892) 37055
Friendly hotel with well equipped compact bedrooms.
23⇀ CTV in all bedrooms Ⓡ sB&B⇀£15.25–£18.25 dB&B⇀£26.50–£29.75 B̶
40P CFA
English & French **V** ✱Bar lunch £1.50–£2 Tea 50p Dinner £6.75&alc Wine £4.25 Last dinner 8.45pm
Credit cards [1] [2] [5]

SOUTH BRENT
Devon
Map **3** SX66

★**Glazebrook House** ☎(03647) 3322
Closed 25 & 26 Dec
Detached two-storey house about one hundred years old set in 20 acres of grounds.
12rm(8⇀) TV in 2 bedrooms Ⓡ sB&B£15 sB&B⇀£15 dB&B£25 dB&B⇀£25 B̶
CTV 60P ✽ (heated) billiards
English & French **V** High Tea fr£1.20 Dinner fr£4&alc Wine £4.20 Last dinner 10pm
Credit cards [1] [2] [3] [5] **VS**

SOUTHEND-ON-SEA
Essex
Map **5** TQ88

☆☆☆***Airport Moat House*** Aviation Way (Queens Moat) ☎(0702) 546344
Modern single storey motel with well equipped bedrooms.
Annexe: 65⇀⋂ CTV in all bedrooms Ⓡ B̶
☾ 300P CFA Disco 5 nights wkly Live music and dancing twice wkly
English & French Last dinner 9.50pm
Credit cards [1] [2] [3] [5]

★★**Roslin** Thorpe Esp, Thorpe Bay (2m E B1016) (Exec Hotel) ☎(0702) 586375 Telex no 99450 (Chacom)
Friendly, family-run hotel with some bedrooms facing the sea. →

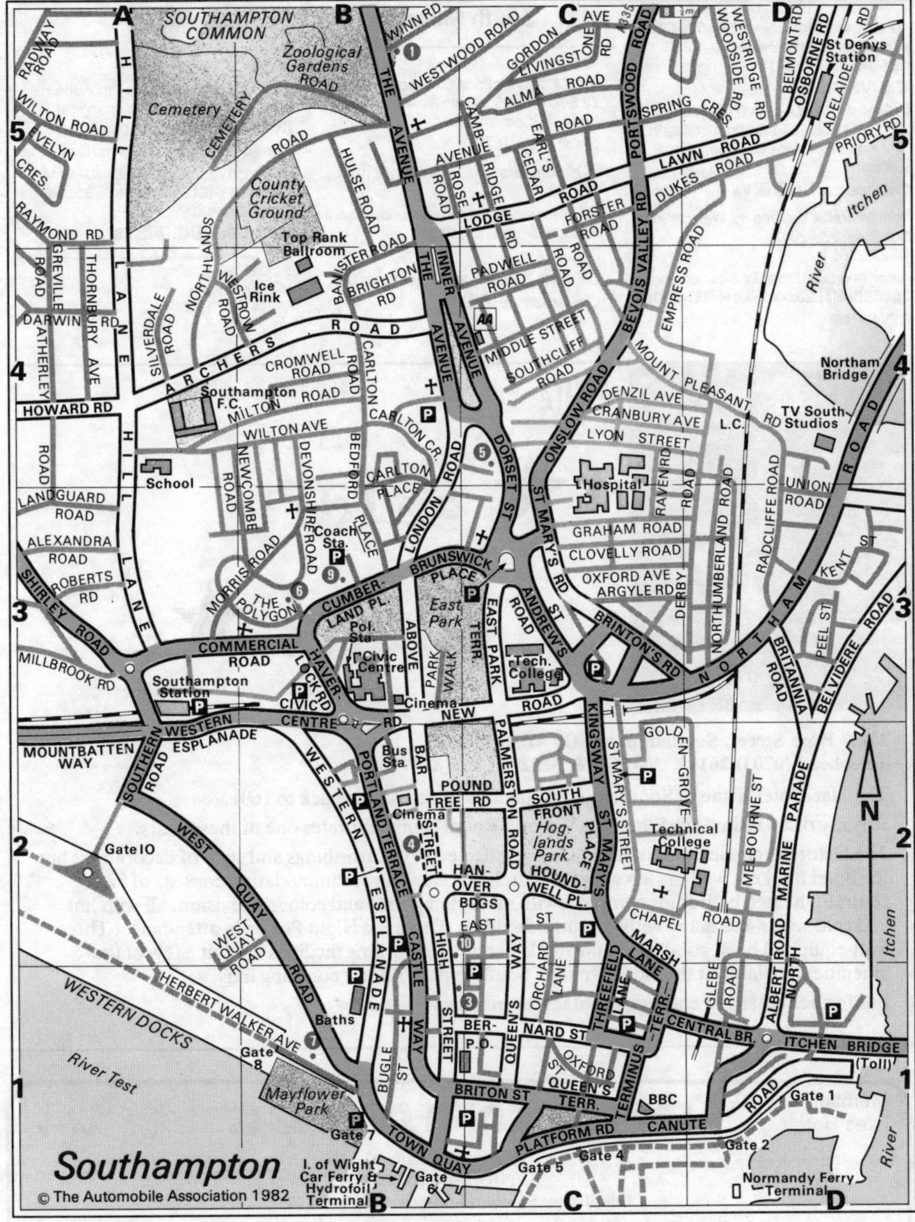
Southampton
© The Automobile Association 1982
A
B
C
D
1
2
3
4
5
SOUTHAMPTON COMMON
Zoological Gardens
Cemetery
County Cricket Ground
Top Rank Ballroom
Ice Rink
Southampton F.C.
School
Coach Sta.
THE POLYGON
Pol. Sta.
Civic Centre
Cinema
Southampton Station
East Park
Tech. College
Hospital
AA
St Denys Station
River Itchen
Northam Bridge
TV South Studios
L.C.
Bus Sta.
Hoglands Park
Technical College
Baths
Mayflower Park
P.O.
BBC
WESTERN DOCKS
River Test
Gate 10
Gate 8
Gate 7
Gate 6
Gate 5
Gate 4
Gate 2
Gate 1
I. of Wight Car Ferry & Hydrofoil Terminal
Normandy Ferry Terminal
ITCHEN BRIDGE (Toll)
N
THE AVENUE
WINN RD
WESTWOOD ROAD
GORDON AVE
LIVINGSTONE RD
ALMA ROAD
CAMBRIDGE RD
EARL'S ROAD
CEDAR RD
PORTSWOOD ROAD
WESTRIDGE RD
WOODSIDE RD
BELMONT RD
OSBORNE RD
ADELAIDE RD
SPRING CRES
LAWN ROAD
DUKES ROAD
PRIORY RD
AVENUE ROAD
ROSE ROAD
LODGE ROAD
FORSTER ROAD
BEVOIS VALLEY RD
EMPRESS ROAD
PADWELL ROAD
MIDDLE STREET
SOUTHCLIFF ROAD
MOUNT PLEASANT RD
HULSE ROAD
BANISTER ROAD
BRIGHTON RD
THE INNER AVENUE
RADWAY ROAD
WILTON ROAD
EVELYN CRES.
RAYMOND RD
GREVILLE ROAD
THORNBURY AVE
DARWIN RD
ATHERLEY ROAD
HILL LANE
HOWARD RD
LANDGUARD ROAD
ALEXANDRA ROAD
ROBERTS RD
SHIRLEY ROAD
MILLBROOK RD
CEMETERY ROAD
NORTHLANDS ROAD
WESTROW ROAD
SILVERDALE ROAD
ARCHERS ROAD
CROMWELL ROAD
MILTON ROAD
WILTON AVE
CARLTON ROAD
CARLTON CR.
CARLTON PLACE
NEWCOMBE ROAD
DEVONSHIRE ROAD
BEDFORD PLACE
MORRIS ROAD
LONDON ROAD
DORSET ST
ONSLOW ROAD
ST MARY'S RD
DENZIL AVE
CRANBURY AVE
LYON STREET
RAVEN RD
DERBY ROAD
NORTHUMBERLAND ROAD
GRAHAM ROAD
CLOVELLY ROAD
OXFORD AVE
ARGYLE RD
BRINTON'S RD
RADCLIFFE ROAD
UNION ROAD
KENT ST
PEEL ST
NORTHAM ROAD
BRITANNIA ROAD
BELVIDERE ROAD
BRUNSWICK PLACE
CUMBERLAND PL.
COMMERCIAL ROAD
HAVELOCK RD
ABOVE BAR
PARK WALK
EAST PARK TERR.
ST ANDREW'S RD
CIVIC CENTRE RD
NEW ROAD
KINGSWAY
MOUNTBATTEN WAY
WESTERN ESPLANADE
SOUTHERN ROAD
PORTLAND TERRACE
POUND TREE RD
PALMERSTON ROAD
SOUTH FRONT
HOUNDWELL PL.
GOLDEN GROVE
ST MARY'S STREET
MELBOURNE ST
MARINE PARADE
WEST QUAY ROAD
HERBERT WALKER AVE
HANOVER BDGS
EAST ST
HIGH STREET
CASTLE WAY
QUEEN'S WAY
ORCHARD LANE
THREEFIELD LANE
MARSH LANE
CHAPEL ROAD
GLEBE ROAD
ALBERT ROAD NORTH
CENTRAL BR.
BERNARD ST
BUGLE ST
OXFORD ST
QUEEN'S TERR.
TERMINUS TERR.
BRITON ST
TOWN QUAY
PLATFORM RD
CANUTE ROAD

Southampton

1 Albany ★★
3 Dolphin ★★★
4 Golden Palace ✽ ✕
5 Olivers ✕✕
6 Polygon ★★★★
7 Post House ☆☆☆
8 Southampton Moat House ★★★
9 Southampton Park ★★★
10 Star ★★

S

40rm(25➡15⋒) Annexe: 5➡ (5fb) CTV in all bedrooms ✻sB&B➡⋒£20–£26 dB&B➡⋒£28–£34 B̶

☾ CTV 24P 🏠 *xmas*

English & Continental ✻Lunch £1.80–£4.50&alc Tea fr60p High Tea fr£3 Dinner fr£6&alc Wine £3.80 Last dinner 9.30pm

Credit cards 1 2 3 5 **VS**

★**Balmoral** 34 Valkyrie Rd, Westcliff-on-Sea ☎(0702) 42947
RS 25 & 26 Dec

19rm(14➡5⋒) (2fb) CTV in all bedrooms Ⓡ sB&B➡⋒£20.50 dB&B➡⋒£33.50 B̶
CTV 18P

V ✻Lunch £5.50&alc High Tea £2.50 Dinner £5.50&alc Wine £3.30 Last dinner 7.30pm

Credit cards 1 3 **VS**

✕✕***Schulers*** 161 Eastern Esp ☎(0702) 610172

Sophisticated sea-front restaurant, also featuring a menu Gourmand.

Closed Mon

French 75 seats Last dinner 10pm 12P

Credit cards 1 2 3 5

SOUTH GODSTONE
Surrey
Map **5** TQ34

✕✕**La Bonne Auberge** Tilburstow Hill ☎(034 285) 2318 (due to change to (0342) 892318) Gatwick plan **1**

Closed Mon Dinner not served Sun

French 75 seats Lunch £7.80–£11 Dinner £11–£12&alc Wine £5.35 Last dinner 10pm 60P

Credit cards 1 2 3 5 **VS**

SOUTH MIMMS
Hertfordshire
Map **4** TL20

S

☆☆☆**Crest** Bignells Corner (junc A1/A6) (Crest) ☎Potters Bar (0707) 43311 Telex no 299162
RS Xmas
Modern, commercial hotel.
120⇌ CTV in all bedrooms ® sB⇌ fr£36 dB⇌ fr£45 (room only) B
☾ CTV 150P CFA
International V Lunch £5.25–£7.50&alc Tea fr75p Dinner £7.50–£8.50&alc Wine £5.25 Last dinner 10pm
Credit cards 1 2 3 4 5 VS

SOUTH MOLTON
Devon
Map **3** SS72
✕ ***Stumbles*** 134 East St ☎(07695) 3683
Closed Sun
French V 36 seats Last dinner 10pm 20P 5 bedrooms available
Credit cards 1 2 3 5

SOUTH NORMANTON
Derbyshire
Map **8** SK45
☆☆☆☆**Swallow** Carter Ln East (junc 28 M1 Motorway) (Swallow) ☎Ripley (0773) 812000 Telex no 377264
Large, modern hotel, conveniently situated next to the M1.
123⇌ CTV in all bedrooms ® sB&B⇌ £26.40–£39.60 dB&B⇌ £32.45–£48.40 B
☾ CTV 120P CFA sauna bath
International V Dinner £6.25–£7.75&alc Wine £4.75 Last dinner 10pm
Credit cards 1 2 3 4 5

SOUTH PETHERTON
Somerset
Map **3** ST41
✕✕**Oaklands** Palmer St ☎(0460) 40272
Closed Mon Lunch not served Tue–Sat Dinner not served Sun
French 48 seats *Lunch £6.75 Dinner £9.30&alc Wine £4.20 Last dinner 9.30pm 14P bedrooms available
S% Credit cards 1 2 3 5

SOUTHPORT
Merseyside
Map **7** SD31
★★★★**Prince of Wales** Lord St (Prince of Wales) ☎(0704) 36688 Telex no 67415
98rm (81⇌ 17) (6fb) CTV in all bedrooms ® sB&B⇌ fr£38 dB&B⇌ fr£52.80 B
Lift ☾ 95P CFA Disco 4 nights wkly *xmas*
French V Lunch £5.50–£10 Tea fr£3 Dinner fr£7 Wine £5.50 Last dinner 10pm
Credit cards 1 2 3 4 5 VS

★★★***Royal Clifton*** Promenade (Prince of Wales) ☎(0704) 33771 Telex no 67415
115rm (74⇌) CTV in all bedrooms ®
Lift ☾ CTV 150P CFA billiards Live music and dancing 4 nights wkly
English & Continental
Credit cards 2 3 4 5

★★**Bold** Lord St ☎(0704) 32578
Former coaching house at the northern end of this fashionable street.
26rm (12⇌) (3fb) CTV in all bedrooms ® sB&B£18 sB&B⇌ £22 dB&B£30 dB&B⇌ £35
☾ 14P *xmas*
V Lunch fr£4.50&alc Dinner fr£6.50&alc Wine £4.40 Last dinner 10pm
Credit cards 1 2 3

★★***Carlton*** 86–88 Lord St ☎(0704) 35111
25rm (9⇌ 4) CTV in all bedrooms ® B
Lift ☾ 18P
English & Continental V Last dinner 10pm
Credit cards 1 2

★★**Lockerbie House** 11 Trafalgar Rd, Birkdale ☎(0704) 65298
Detached house in a residential area close to Birkdale Station and the famous golf course.
14rm (4⇌ 6) (2fb) TV in all bedrooms ® *sB&B£13–£16 sB&B⇌ £15–£18 dB&B£25–£27 dB&B⇌ £27–£29
CTV 12P nc5yrs
Dinner £5–£6&alc Wine £4 Last dinner 7.30pm

★★**Scarisbrick** Lord St ☎(0704) 38321
53rm (19⇌) CTV in all bedrooms ® sB&B£17.50 sB&B⇌ £23 dB&B£24 dB&B⇌ £32 B
Lift ☾ CTV Live music and dancing twice wkly *xmas*
English & French V Lunch £2.95–£4.15 Dinner £7.50–£8.50 Wine £4 Last dinner 9.15pm
Credit cards 1 2 3 4 5

★**Metropole** Portland St ☎(0704) 36836
27rm (8⇌ 7) (1fb) CTV in 10 bedrooms sB&B£12–£15 sB&B⇌ £14–£17 dB&B£24–£26 dB&B⇌ £27–£30 B
CTV 12P *xmas*
V Lunch £3–£3.50 Tea 70p Dinner £4.75–£5.25 Wine £3 Last dinner 8.30pm
Credit cards 1 2 3 VS

✕✕**Squires** 78–80 King St ☎(0704) 30046
Closed Sun, 26 Dec & Good Fri Lunch not served
International 40 seats Dinner £8.75&alc Wine £4.95 Last dinner 10.30pm
Credit cards 1 2 3 5

✕**Le Coq Hardi** 1 Royal Ter, West St ☎(0704) 38855
Closed Sun & last wk Jul–1st wk Aug Lunch not served
French 25 seats Dinner £10.50alc Wine £4.70 Last dinner 10pm
Credit card 2

SOUTHSEA
Hampshire
Map **4** SZ69
See **Portsmouth and Southsea**

SOUTH SHIELDS
Tyne & Wear
Map **12** NZ36
★★★**Sea** Sea Rd ☎(0632) 566227
27rm (24⇌ 3) (2fb) CTV in all bedrooms ® sB&B⇌ £25.50 dB&B⇌ £33.50 B
☾ 40P 10
English & French Lunch £2–£4.95&alc Tea 50p–£2 Dinner £5.50–£5.95&alc Wine £4.20 Last dinner 9.30pm
Credit cards 1 2 3 5 VS

★★**New Crown** Mowbray Rd (Scottish & Newcastle) ☎(0632) 553472
11rm (3⇌) (1fb) CTV in all bedrooms ® *sB&B£13.50 sB&B⇌ £15.50 dB&B£20 dB&B⇌ £22
30P Live music and dancing twice wkly
V *Lunch fr£4.40&alc Tea fr£1 Dinner fr£4.40&alc Last dinner 9pm
Credit cards 1 2 3 5

SOUTH UIST, ISLE OF
Western Isles *Inverness-shire*
Map **13**
See **Lochboisdale**

SOUTHWELL
Nottinghamshire
Map **8** SK75
★★★**Saracens Head** Market Pl (Anchor) ☎(0636) 812701 Telex no 858875
Charles I surrendered to the Scots here in 1647.
23⇌ (1fb) CTV in all bedrooms ® sB&B⇌ fr£34 dB&B⇌ fr£44 B
☾ CTV 80P 2 CFA
Continental V Lunch fr£5&alc Dinner fr£8.50&alc Wine £5.75 Last dinner 9.45pm
S% Credit cards 1 2 3 4 5

SOUTHWOLD
Suffolk
Map **5** TM57
★★★**Swan** Market Pl ☎(0502) 722186 Telex no 97223
An 18th-century former coaching inn with the original Georgian fireplace and doorframes; as well as many fine paintings, engravings and maps.
35rm (10⇌) Annexe: 18⇌ CTV in 33 bedrooms *sB&B£15.75–£19.45 sB&B⇌ £18.40–£22.10 dB&B£31.50–£38.90 dB&B⇌ £35.25–£42.70 B
Lift ☾ CTV 60P
V *Lunch £6.15 Tea £1.15 Dinner £7.25&alc Wine £4.20 Last dinner 8.30pm
Credit cards 1 2 3 5 VS

S

★★**Crown** High St ☎(0502) 722275 Telex no 97223 (Adnams)
Dates from the early Georgian period when it was a coaching inn.
21rm(12➡5⋒)(1fb) CTV in all bedrooms *sB&B£15.50–£16.65 sB&B➡⋒£18–£19 dB&B£29.85–£32.05 dB&B➡⋒£32.35–£34.55 Ⓑ
13P9🏠
🍴English & French V 🍷 ☕ *Lunch £3.55–£5.80&alc Tea fr85p Dinner fr£6.85&alc Wine £4.65 Last dinner 8.30pm
Credit cards 1 2 5 **VS**

★★**Pier Avenue** Pier Av ☎(0502) 722632
13rm(4➡3⋒)(1fb) CTV in all bedrooms Ⓡ sB&B£12–£15.50 sB&B➡⋒£13.50–£17 dB&B£24–£31 dB&B➡⋒£27–£34 Ⓑ
CTV 10P
🍷Lunch £4.20–£7.20&alc Dinner £6.50–£9&alc Wine £4.50 Last dinner 9pm

★★**Randolph** Wangford Rd, Reydon ☎(0502) 723603
Closed Nov–19 Apr
This hotel is situated in the village, only 1m from Southwold Beach.
12rm(2➡)(3fb) TV in all bedrooms sB&B£10–£14 sB&B➡£12–£16 dB&B£20–£24 dB&B➡£24–£28
15P2🏠
Dinner £6–£6.50 Wine £3.80 Last dinner 8pm

✕✕**Dutch Barn** Ferry Rd ☎(0502) 723172
Closed Mon & Jan Lunch not served Nov–May
🍴English & French V 45 seats Lunch £4.95–£6.95&alc Dinner £4.95–£6.95&alc Wine £4.95 Last dinner 10pm 30P Live music Sat
Credit cards 1 2 3 **VS**

SOUTH WOODHAM FERRERS
Essex
Map **5** TQ89
☆☆**Oakland** Merchant St ☎Chelmsford (0245) 322811
RS Xmas
Commercial traditional style hotel with comfortable bedrooms.
28➡⋒(4fb) CTV available in bedrooms Ⓡ *sB&B➡⋒£20 dB&B➡⋒£28 Ⓑ
☾ CTV 20P Disco wknds Live music and dancing wknds Cabaret wknds
V 🍷 Lunch £7–£14&alc Dinner £7–£14&alc Wine £3 Last dinner 9.30pm
Credit cards 1 2 3 5

✕✕**Ruchita Tandoori** Unit 1B Town Sq ☎Chelmsford (0245) 320821
🍴Indian 50 seats Last dinner mdnt

SOUTH ZEAL
Devon
Map **3** SX69
★★**Oxenham Arms** ☎Sticklepath (083 784) 244
Closed Xmas Day evening
A 12th-century inn of great character located in the village centre.
8rm(6➡)(2fb) CTV in 6 bedrooms Ⓡ *sB&B£14 sB&B➡£18 dB&B£24 dB&B➡£30 Ⓑ
CTV 8P ✽ *xmas*
V 🍷 ☕ Lunch £3.75–£6.50&alc Tea 45p alc Dinner £7.50–£9.50&alc Wine £3.80 Last dinner 9pm
Credit cards 1 2 3 5 **VS**

SPALDING
Lincolnshire
Map **8** TF22
★★**Dembleby** Broad St ☎(0775) 67060
Situated close to the town centre, the hotel features a large walled garden, part of which stands on the site of an old abbey.
8rm(3⋒) CTV in 6 bedrooms *sB&B fr£13.80 sB&B⋒ fr£17.60 dB&B fr£25.07 dB&B⋒ fr£27.60
15P ✽
🍷Wine £3.90 Last dinner 9.30pm
Credit cards 1 3

★★***Red Lion*** Market Pl ☎(0775) 2869
Former coaching inn.
27rm(4➡1⋒) Annexe: 6rm TV in 8 bedrooms Ⓑ
CTV 30P ♿
🍴English, French & Italian V 🍷 ☕ Last dinner 9.30pm
Credit cards 1 3

★★**White Hart** Market Pl (Trusthouse Forte) ☎(0775) 5668
28rm(4➡) CTV in all bedrooms Ⓡ sB&B£30.50 sB&B➡£33 dB&B£43 dB&B➡£46.50 Ⓑ
35P
🍷 ☕ Last dinner 10pm
Credit cards 1 2 3 4 5

SPEAN BRIDGE
Highland *Inverness-shire*
Map **14** NN28
See also **Letterfinlay** and **Roy Bridge**
★★**Spean Bridge** (Minotel) ☎(039 781) 250
Closed Dec–Jan
Originally a coaching inn, log fires still provide a welcome.
8rm(2➡) Annexe: 16rm(14➡)(4fb) Ⓡ sB&B£11.50–£13.50 sB&B➡£12.50–£14.50 dB&B£23–£27 dB&B➡£25–£29 Ⓑ
CTV 60P 1🏠 ♪ Live music and dancing mthly Cabaret mthly
🍷 ☕ Bar lunch £2.50–£4&alc Tea fr50p Dinner £8–£10&alc Wine £4.75 Last dinner 9.30pm
Credit cards 1 3 4 5

SPELDHURST
Kent
Map **5** TQ54
✕✕**George & Dragon Inn** ☎Langton (089 286) 3125
Lunch not served Sat Dinner not served Sun
🍴International V 50 seats Lunch £7–£9&alc Dinner £17.50alc Wine £5.50 Last dinner 10pm 70P
Credit cards 1 2 3 5

SPEY BAY
Grampian *Morayshire*
Map **15** NJ36
★★**Spey Bay** (Minotel) ☎Fochabers (0343) 820424
Closed 1 Jan

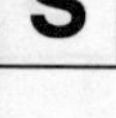

A friendly, seafront hotel next to the golf course.
9rm(5➡4⋔)(2fb)ⓡ✻sB&B➡⋔£17.50 dB&B➡⋔£27.50 Ⓑ
CTV 50P Live music and dancing Sat
V ♔ ☕ ✻ Bar lunch £1.25&alc Tea £1.25 High Tea £1.70–£4.50&alc Dinner fr£7&alc Wine £3.74 Last dinner 7.15pm
Credit cards ⑤ **VS**

STABLEFORD
Staffordshire
Map **7** SJ83
✕✕**Cock Inn** ☎Newcastle (Staffs) (0782) 680210
This 18th-century inn with its original stone fireplace is said to be haunted.
▣French **V** 100 seats ✻Lunch £1.95–£4.65&alc Dinner £8.95alc Wine £5.85 Last dinner 10pm 120P Disco Wed, Thu, Fri & Sat
Credit cards ① ② ③ ⑤

STADDLE BRIDGE
North Yorkshire
Map **8** SE49
✕✕***McCoys (Tontine Inn)*** ☎East Harlsey (060982) 207
Closed Sun, Xmas & Public hols
▣International 60 seats Last dinner 11pm 80P bedrooms available
Credit card ③

STAFFORD
Staffordshire
Map **7** SJ92
See also **Haywood, Great**
☆☆☆**Tillington Hall** Eccleshall Rd (Greenall Whitley) ☎(0785) 535331 Telex no 36566
93rm(90➡3⋔)(1fb) CTV in all bedrooms ⓡsB&B➡⋔£32.50–£33.50 dB&B➡⋔£42–£43 Ⓑ
Lift ☾ 200P 1🚗 CFA Live music and dancing Fri & Sat ⌂
▣English & French **V** ♔ ☕ Lunch £5.50&alc Tea 55p Dinner £6.50&alc Wine £4.30 Last dinner 10pm
S% Credit cards ① ② ③ ⑤

★★**Swan** Greengate St (Berni) ☎(0785) 58142
Closed 23 Dec–3 Jan
31rm(29➡2⋔)(5fb) 1▤ CTV in all bedrooms ⓡ★✻sB&B➡⋔£21 dB&B➡⋔£37 Ⓑ
☾ 60P CFA
▣Mainly grills ♔ Last dinner 10.15pm
Credit cards ① ② ③ ⑤

★**Garth** Wolverhampton Rd, Moss Pit (Wolverhampton & Dudley) ☎(0785) 56124
32rm(24➡)(2fb) CTV in all bedrooms ⓡ sB&B£13.50–£17.50 sB&B➡£21 dB&B£22–£24.50 dB&B➡£28 Ⓑ
☾ 100P ✽
♔ ☕ Lunch fr£3.75&alc Dinner £5.75alc Wine £3.75 Last dinner 9.45pm
Credit cards ① ③ **VS**

★**Romaline** 73 Wolverhampton Rd ☎(0785) 54100
Closed 25 & 26 Dec
14rm(2⋔)(3fb) sB&B£12.25–£13.50 dB&B£16.50–£22 dB&B⋔£22.50–£24.75
14P
V ♔ ☕ ✻Lunch £3alc Tea £1.50alc Dinner £6.40alc Wine £4 Last dinner 9.45pm
Credit cards ① ② ⑤ **VS**

★**Vine** Salter St (Wolverhampton & Dudley) ☎(0785) 51071
23rm ⓡ✻sB&B£14 dB&B£19.50 Ⓑ
CTV 10P
♔ ☕ Lunch £3.25alc Dinner fr£3.95&alc Wine £3.75 Last dinner 9.15pm
Credit cards ① ③ **VS**

STAINES
Surrey
Map **4** TQ07
★★*L* **Pack Horse** Thames St (Anchor) ☎(0784) 54221 Heathrow plan **8** *D1*
Closed 24–29 Dec
Large Victorian building with a riverside patio, boat moorings and wide windowed dining room overlooking the Thames.
17rm(13➡) CTV in all bedrooms ⓡ sB&B fr£22.50 sB&B➡fr£34.50 dB&B fr£34 dB&B➡fr£41 Ⓑ
☾ 45P
▣English & French **V** ♔ ✻Lunch fr£5.50&alc Tea fr65p Dinner £8alc Wine £5 Last dinner 10pm
Credit cards ① ② ③ ④ ⑤ **VS**

STALISFIELD GREEN
Kent
Map **5** TQ95
✕**Plough Inn** ☎Eastling (079589) 256
Lunch not served Mon–Sat Dinner not served Sun
30 seats ✻Lunch fr£5 Dinner £7.50alc Wine £4.75 Last dinner 9.30pm 45P
VS

STAMFORD
Lincolnshire
Map **4** TF00
★★★**George** St Martins ☎(0780) 55171 Telex no 32578
A large, tastefully modernised, historic coaching inn.
48rm(39➡) 1▤ CTV in all bedrooms sB&B£25 sB&B➡£33 dB&B£40 dB&B➡£47 Ⓑ
☾ ⚟ 75P 5🚗 CFA ✽ ⌂ *xmas*
▣English, French & Italian **V** ♔ ☕ Lunch £16alc Wine £5.45 Last dinner 10.30pm
Credit cards ① ② ③ ⑤

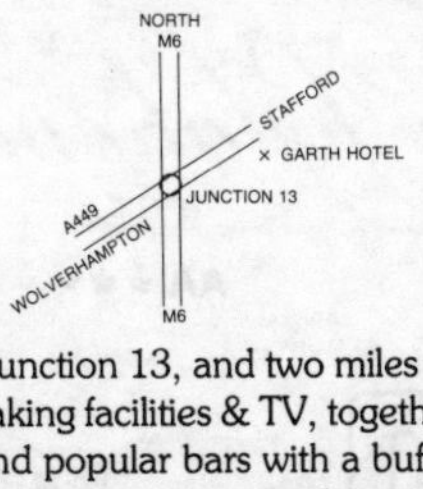

★★**Crown** ☎(0780) 63136
Closed Xmas Day
An old two-storey, stone-built hotel in the town centre, catering for a predominantly commercial clientele.
18rm(6➡3⋔)(1fb) 1▤ CTV in all bedrooms Ⓑ
CTV 40P
▣English & French ♔ ☕ Lunch £5.95alc Tea 50p alc Dinner £6.90alc Wine £4.50 Last dinner 9.30pm
Credit cards ① ② ③ ④ ⑤

★★**Lady Anne's** 37–38 High St, St Martins ☎(0780) 53175
An 18th-century stone-built house in 3½ acres of ground on the B1081. →

S

25rm(13➡6⋔)(5fb)1🛏CTV in all bedrooms Ⓡ ✱sB&B£11.50–£20 sB&B➡⋔£11.50–£26 dB&B£23.50 dB&B➡⋔£23.50–£36 🅱

CTV 150P ✽ ⌂

V ♔ ☕ Lunch £1.85–£5.50 Tea 70p–£1.50 High Tea £2–£2.50 Dinner £6.50–£7.50 Wine £5.95 Last dinner 10pm

Credit cards 1 2 3 5 **VS**

★**St Martin's Garden House** St Martin's ☎(0780) 63359

Closed early Jan

10rm CTV in all bedrooms ✶ ✱sB&B fr£15 dB&B fr£25 🅱

6P ✽

♔ ☕ ✱Dinner fr£7 Wine £4.50 Last dinner 9.30pm

Credit cards 1 3

STANDISH
Gt Manchester
Map **7** SD51

☆☆☆**Cassinellis Almond Brook Motor Inn** Almond Brook Rd ☎(0257) 425588 Telex no 677662

43➡⋔ Annexe: 20➡⋔ (15fb) CTV in all bedrooms Ⓡ ✶ sB&B➡⋔£15–£26 dB&B➡⋔£20–£35 🅱

☾ ### 300P CFA Disco Thu, Fri & Sun Live music and dancing Sat Cabaret Sat *xmas*

🍴English & Italian V ♔ Lunch fr£3.50 Dinner fr£6.50&alc Wine £4 Last dinner 9.30pm

Credit cards 1 2 3 5

STANHOPE BRETBY
Derbyshire
Map **8** SK22

✕✕***Stanhope Arms*** Ashby Road East (on A50) ☎Burton-on-Trent (0283) 217954

🍴English & French 120 seats Last dinner 10pm 150P bedrooms available

STANSTED
Essex
Map **5** TL52

✕✕***Bury Lodge Hotel*** Bury Lodge Ln ☎Bishop's Stortford (0279) 813345

Good specialist French cooking.

Closed Sun, Mon & last wk Dec

🍴French 39 seats Last dinner 10.30pm P

Credit cards 1 2 3 5

STAPLETON
North Yorkshire
Map **8** NZ21

✕***Bridge Inn*** ☎Darlington (0325) 50106

Village public house features Victorian style restaurant offering delicious food and good wine list.

Closed Mon Lunch not served Tue–Sat Dinner not served Sun

🍴Cosmopolitan 30 seats Wine £4.30 Last dinner 9.30pm 100P

STAVERTON
Devon
Map **3** SX76

★**Sea Trout Inn** ☎(080426) 274

A comfortable village inn in a peaceful situation offering attentive service from the resident owners.

6rm Ⓡ sB&B£13.50 dB&B£27

CTV 70P

V ♔ ✱Bar lunch 80p–£4.25 Dinner £8alc Wine £3.50 Last dinner 10pm

Credit cards 1 3 5

STEPPINGLEY
Bedfordshire
Map **4** TL03

✕**French Horn** ☎Flitwick (0525) 712051

Beamed 16th century pub, offering sound, mainly French food.

Closed Mon Dinner not served Sun

🍴English & Continental V 65 seats ✱Lunch £8–£10alc Dinner £8–£10alc Wine £4 Last dinner 9.45pm 60P

Credit cards 1 2 3 5 **VS**

STEVENAGE
Hertfordshire
Map **4** TL22

☆☆☆**Grampian** The Forum ☎(0438) 350661 Telex no 825697

Modern, purpose-built hotel.

100➡ CTV in all bedrooms Ⓡ sB&B➡£30–£31 dB&B➡£37–£38 🅱

Lift ☾ CFA ⚑ *xmas*

🍴English & French V ♔ ☕ Lunch £2.15–£2.55&alc Tea 60p Dinner £6.70–£7.25&alc Wine £4.80 Last dinner 9.30pm

Credit cards 1 2 3 5

☆☆☆**Roebuck Inn** London Rd, Broadwater (Trusthouse Forte) ☎(0438) 65444 Telex no 825505

Charming 15th century inn with modern bedrooms.

54➡ (12fb) CTV in all bedrooms Ⓡ sB&B➡£35.50 dB&B➡£49.50 🅱

☾ 80P CFA ✽

♔ Last dinner 9.45pm

Credit cards 1 2 3 4 5

☆☆☆**Stevenage Moat House** High St, Old Town (Queens Moat) ☎(0438) 359111

Historically interesting old world hotel with modern, well-equipped bedrooms.

61rm(60➡1⋔)(5fb) CTV in all bedrooms Ⓡ sB&B➡⋔£30.75 dB&B➡⋔£38.50 🅱

☾ 100P ✽ ⌂

🍴International V ♔ ☕ Lunch £6.95&alc Tea 60p Dinner £6.95 Wine £4.95 Last dinner 9.45pm

Credit cards 1 2 3 4 5

TELEPHONE NUMBERS

In some areas telephone numbers are likely to be changed by British Telecom during the currency of this publication. If any difficulty is experienced when making a reservation it is advisable to check with the operator.

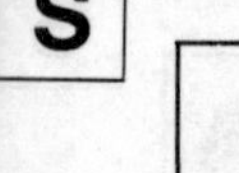
S

STEWARTON
Strathclyde *Ayrshire*
Map **10** NS44

★★★

❀★★★♜**CHAPELTOUN HOUSE, STEWARTON**
☎(0560) 82696
Closed Xmas, 1st wk Jan & last 3wks Jul

Although open fires burn in season in the public rooms, these are not the warmest features of this hotel; that quality is most apparent in the hospitality provided here by the owners, Alan and Elizabeth Russell and their team of cheerful, friendly girls. In 1976 they converted this turn of the century baronial residence set in 20 acres of grounds into a most welcoming hotel and restaurant. There are six spacious bedrooms appropriately furnished in Victorian and Edwardian style but with modern comforts. They are well equipped and besides the usual thoughtful touches, fresh fruit, sweets and sherry are provided. On the ground floor is a splendid oak panelled hall with comfortable seating and, overlooking the garden, the attractive sitting room with its contemporary plaster decorative features; there is also a large cocktail bar.
The restaurant consists of two rooms with chairs upholstered in tapestry and pleasing table appointments. Here, chef Ian McGregor utilises his skills to provide delicious cooking of

Continental as well as Scottish dishes, which well deserves our rosette. At lunch there is a modest set meal together with an à la carte menu; at dinner a set meal of four courses and coffee is served. There is abundant choice, particularly of the puddings laid out on a buffet for self help. The hotel makes a good out of town resting stage for Glasgow (30 minutes away) or as a base from which to tour the Ayrshire coast.

6rm(4⇨2⋔) CTV in all bedrooms ♜ sB&B⇨⋔ £35 dB&B⇨⋔ £60
50P ✽ nc12yrs
International V ♈ Lunch £7&alc Dinner £15.50alc Wine £6 Last dinner 9.30pm
Credit cards 1 2 VS

STICKLEPATH
Devon
Map **2** SX69

★★♜**Skaigh House** Belstone (1m W on Belstone rd unclass) ☎(083784) 243
Closed Oct–Mar
8rm(2⇨) ♜ ✽sB&B£15 dB&B£30–£36 dB&B⇨£38
CTV 16P ✽
✽Lunch £2.50–£3.50 Tea 80p Dinner £8–£10 Wine £3.50 Last dinner 8pm

STINCHCOMBE
Gloucestershire
Map **3** ST79

★★♜*B* **Stinchcombe Manor Country House** ☎Dursley (0453) 2538
A 19th-century manor house, recently extended and modernised, providing comfortable accommodation and a good restaurant.
16rm(9⇨7⋔) (4fb) 4 CTV in all bedrooms ® sB&B⇨⋔ fr£25 dB&B⇨⋔ fr£35 B

80P ✽ (heated) (hard) xmas
International V ♈ Lunch £7 Tea £1.20–£2 High Tea £4 Dinner fr£10.50 Wine £5.50 Last dinner 9.30pm
Credit cards 1 2 3 5

STIRLING
Central *Stirlingshire*
Map **11** NS79

★★★**Golden Lion** King St ☎(0786) 5351 Telex no 777546
75rm(30⇨7⋔) (5fb) CTV in all bedrooms ® sB&B£16.50–£17.50 sB&B⇨⋔ £23.50–£25 dB&B£29–£30.50 dB&B⇨⋔ £36–£38 B
Lift ☾ 40P CFA Live music and dancing 3 nights wkly in season *xmas*
British & French V ♈ Lunch £3.50–£5&alc Tea 95p–£1.50 High Tea £3–£4 Dinner £6.50–£7.50&alc Wine £4.25 Last dinner 10pm
Credit cards 1 2 3 5

★★***King Robert*** Glasgow Rd ☎(0786) 811666
Modern building on the outskirts of town, close to the Bannockburn monument and battlefield.
21⇨ CTV in all bedrooms ® B
☾ CTV 100P CFA ✽ Disco wkly Live music and dancing twice wkly Cabaret wkly
V ♈ Last dinner 9pm
Credit cards 1 2 3 4 5

★★**Stakis Station** 56 Murray Pl (Stakis) ☎(0786) 2017 Telex no 778704
Adjoining buildings, including a former coaching inn, have been converted to this town-centre hotel, close to the railway station.
25rm(10⇨15⋔) CTV in all bedrooms ® ✽sB&B⇨⋔ fr£21 dB&B⇨⋔ fr£29 B
☾
Mainly grills ♈ Last dinner 9.30pm
Credit cards 1 2 3 5 VS

★★**Terraces** 4 Melville Ter (Minotel) ☎(0786) 2268
14rm(8⇨3⋔) (1fb) CTV in all bedrooms ® ✽sB&B£11.95–£15.50 sB&B⇨⋔ £11.95–£19.95 dB&B£23.90–£25.50 dB&B⇨⋔ £23.90–£29.50 B →

S

☾25P

V♔☐ Lunch £2.95&alc Tea £1.15–£1.75 High Tea £2.75–£3.50 Dinner £5.95&alc Wine £3.95 Last dinner 9pm

Credit cards 1 2 3 VS

★**Kings Gate** 5 King St ☎(0786) 3944

A 19th-century hotel in the shopping area.

15rm(5⇌) (2fb) Ⓡ sB&B £13 sB&B⇌⋒ £16 dB&B £22 dB&B⇌⋒ £24.50

CTV 5P

V♔☐ Lunch £3.80–£5.80 Tea £1–£1.50 High Tea £3.60–£5.20 Dinner £6.50–£9&alc Wine £5.50 Last dinner 8.30pm

Credit cards 1 2 3

✕✕**Heritage** 16 Allan Park ☎(0786) 3660

An 18th-century, painted, stone building of architectural interest situated at the foot of Castle Rock.

Closed Xmas & New Year

▣International V 50 seats Lunch £5.50&alc Dinner £10–£11&alc Wine £3.80 Last dinner 10pm 12P bedrooms available

Credit cards 1 3 5 VS

✕✕**Hollybank** Glasgow Rd ☎(0786) 812311

▣International 33 seats Lunch £6.60&alc High Tea £3.60–£6.50 Dinner £12.75&alc Wine £5.50 Last dinner 10pm 50P bedrooms available

Credit cards 1 2 3 5

STOCKBRIDGE
Hampshire
Map 4 SU33

★★**Grosvenor** High St (Whitbread Wessex) ☎Andover (0264) 810606

Popular fishing inn with spacious bedrooms and cosy public rooms.

14rm(1⇌) CTV in 13 bedrooms ✶ sB&B fr£18 dB&B fr£30 dB&B⇌ fr£33 ℞

CTV 30P

▣English & French ♔ Lunch fr£5&alc Dinner fr£7&alc Wine £4.75 Last dinner 9.30pm

Credit cards 1 2 3 5

STOCKPORT
Gt Manchester
Map 7 SJ88

★★★**Alma Lodge** 149 Buxton Rd (Embassy) ☎061-483 4431

A converted Victorian house with a modern extension, standing on the A6 1½m south-east of the town.

72rm(55⇌) CTV in all bedrooms Ⓡ sB £22 sB⇌ £32 dB⇌ £34.50 dB⇌ £40.50 (room only) ℞

☾ CTV 150P ⛟ CFA Live music and dancing wkly

V♔☐ Lunch fr£6.70&alc Dinner fr£6.70&alc Wine £4.50 Last dinner 9.30pm

Credit cards 1 2 3 4 5

★★★**Belgrade** Dialston Ln ☎061-483 3851 Telex no 667217

160⇌⋒ (8fb) CTV in all bedrooms Ⓡ ✶ sB&B⇌⋒ £26.50 dB&B⇌⋒ £32

Lift ☾ 300P CFA

▣English & French ♔☐ Lunch £3.75–£5&alc Tea £1–£1.50 Dinner £8.50&alc Wine £3.75 Last dinner 10.30pm

Credit cards 1 2 3 5 VS

★★**Wycliffe Villa** 74 Edgeley Rd, Edgeley ☎061-477 5395

Closed Xmas RS Aug

12rm(3⇌8⋒) CTV in all bedrooms Ⓡ ✶ sB&B⇌⋒ £23 dB&B⇌⋒ £32

CTV 20P ⛟ nc5yrs

▣English & Italian Lunch fr£3&alc Dinner £7alc Wine £4.95 Last dinner 9.30pm

Credit cards 1 2 3 5 VS

★**Acton Court** Buxton Rd ☎061-483 6172

26rm(4⇌) (2fb) CTV in 22 bedrooms Ⓡ sB&B £12.88–£14.03 sB&B⇌⋒ £20.70 dB&B fr£28.06 dB&B⇌⋒ fr£34.50 ℞

CTV 250P Disco Tue

▣Italian V♔☐ Lunch fr£2.25 Tea fr£2 Dinner fr£4.50 Wine £4.50 Last dinner 10pm

Credit cards 1 2 3 5

At **Bramhall** (3½m south A5102)

☆☆☆**Bramhall Moat House** Bramhall Ln South (Queens Moat) ☎061-439 8116

40⇌⋒ 132P

STOCKTON-ON-TEES
Cleveland
Map 8 NZ41

☆☆☆☆**Swallow** 10 John Walker Sq (Swallow) ☎(0642) 619721 Telex no 587895

Modern, multi-storey hotel in the town centre.

126⇌ (61fb) CTV in all bedrooms Ⓡ sB&B⇌ £33 dB&B⇌ £45 ℞

Lift ☾ ⌗ CFA

▣French V♔☐ Lunch fr£7.25&alc Tea 55p High Tea £4.50 Dinner £8.45&alc Wine £4.75 Last dinner 10.30pm

Credit cards 1 2 3

★★★**Billingham Arms Thistle** Town Sq, Billingham (3m NE A19) (Thistle) ☎(0642) 553661 Telex no 587746

Modern brick building close to the shopping area.

64rm(43⇌12⋒) CTV in all bedrooms Ⓡ ✻sB⇌⋒ £27–£35 dB⇌⋒ £36.50–£40 (room only) ℞

☾ ⚞ CTV 100P 2🚗 CFA ♿

▣English & Continental ☐ ✻Lunch fr£4.90&alc Dinner fr£8&alc Last dinner 10pm

Credit cards 1 2 3 4 5 VS

☆☆☆**Golden Eagle Thistle** Trenchard Av, Thornaby-on-Tees (1m E A174) (Thistle) ☎(0642) 766511

Large, modern hotel in a residential and shopping area.

54⇌⋒ CTV in all bedrooms Ⓡ ✻sB⇌⋒ £27–£29 dB⇌⋒ £35–£40 (room only) ℞

Lift ☾ ⌗ 80P CFA Live music & dancing Thur, Fri & Sat

S

English & Continental ✱Lunch £5.50&alc Dinner £7.50&alc Last dinner 9.15pm

Credit cards 1 2 3 4 5 **VS**

☆☆☆**Post House** Low Ln, Thornaby-on-Tees (Trusthouse Forte) ☎(0642) 591213 Telex no 58426

Situated on the A1044 close to the interchange with the A174 towards Yarm.

140 (22fb) CTV in all bedrooms ® sB&B £36.50 dB&B £49

250P CFA

Last dinner 10.15pm

Credit cards 1 2 3 4 5

★★*B* **Parkmore** 636 Yarm Rd, Eaglescliffe (3m S A19) (Best Western) ☎(0642) 786815

40rm(26 13) (2fb) CTV in all bedrooms ® sB&B £18–£20 sB&B £20–£22.50 dB&B £27.50–£29.50

CTV 50P (grass)

English & French **V** Lunch fr£4.80 High Tea fr£4 Dinner fr£7.50&alc Wine £5.70 Last dinner 8.45pm

Credit cards 1 2 3 **VS**

★**Stonyroyd** 187 Oxbridge Ln ☎(0642) 607734

14rm (3fb) sB&B £12.75 dB&B £18.25

CTV 12P

V Lunch £3 Tea £1.75 High Tea £3 Dinner £4.25 Wine £2 Last dinner 7pm

VS

STOKE FLEMING

Devon

Map **3** SX84

★★**Stoke Lodge** Cinders Ln ☎(080427) 523

Closed 2nd Jan–1 Feb

14rm(2 8) (8fb) CTV available on request ® sB&B £10–£13 sB&B £18–£24 dB&B £20–£28

CTV 40P (heated) *xmas*

V Lunch £3.95–£4.95&alc Tea 40p–£1.25&alc High Tea £1.50–£2.50&alc Dinner £4.95–£5.95&alc Wine £3.99 Last dinner 9.30pm

STOKE GABRIEL

Devon

Map **3** SX85

★★*H* ***Gabriel Court*** ☎(080428) 206

A feature of the hotel is its long-established, walled garden (c 1480) with yew arches, box hedges and magnolia trees.

25rm(15 5)

CTV 15P 8 (heated) (grass)

V Last dinner 8.30pm

Credit cards 1 3 5

STOKEINTEIGNHEAD

Devon

Map **3** SX97

✕✕ ***Harvest Barn*** Stoke Rd ☎Shaldon (062687) 3670

(Classification awarded for dinner only.)

This attractive, white-painted cottage restaurant is situated on the edge of the village in the heart of the countryside.

Closed Mon Lunch not served Tue–Sat Dinner not served Sun

English & French 38 seats Last dinner 9.30pm 18P

Credit cards 1 3

STOKE-ON-TRENT

Staffordshire

Map **7** SJ84

See also Newcastle-under-Lyme

★★★★**North Stafford** Station Rd (Trusthouse Forte) ☎(0782) 48501 Telex no 36287

Traditional hotel opposite the station, with imposing rooms, formal service and displays of pottery.

70rm(42) (1fb) CTV in all bedrooms ® sB&B £41 dB&B £55

Lift 120P CFA

Last dinner 9.45pm

Credit cards 1 2 3 4 5

★★★**Haydon House** 5–9 Haydon St, Basford ☎(0782) 629311 Telex no 36413

19rm(6 8) CTV in all bedrooms sB&B fr£18.50 sB&B fr£25.50 dB&B fr£36.50

40P nc3yrs

Lunch £5–£7&alc Tea £1.05–£1.25 Dinner £7.45–£8.45&alc Wine £4.95 Last dinner 10pm

Credit cards 1 2 3 5 **VS**

★★★**Stakis Grand** 66 Trinity St, Hanley (Stakis) ☎(0782) 22361 Telex no 778704

This Victorian hotel in the city centre is popular with businessmen.

93 CTV in all bedrooms ® ✱sB&B fr£29 dB&B fr£38

Lift 50P CFA Disco Sat

English & French Last dinner 10pm

Credit cards 1 2 3 5 **VS**

★★**George** Swan Sq. Burslem (Embassy) ☎(0782) 84021 Closed Xmas

Traditional, commercial hotel in a central position in the city.

36rm(5) CTV in all bedrooms ® sB&B £20.25 sB&B £26.50 dB&B £30.50 dB&B £35.50

Lift CTV 12P

V Lunch fr£2.25 Dinner fr£5.75 Wine £4.55

Last dinner 9.30pm

S% Credit cards 1 2 3 4 5

✕✕ ***Poachers Cottage*** Stone Rd, Trentham (3m S A34) ☎(0782) 657115

An extended cottage serving traditional meals, situated on the A34 on the edge of the city.

Dinner not served Sun & Mon

120 seats Last dinner 9.30pm 60P

STOKE PRIOR

Hereford & Worcester

Map **3** SO55

✕ ***Wheelbarrow Castle*** ☎Leominster (0568) 2219

Lunch not served

English, French & Italian 24 seats Last dinner 9.30pm 20P bedrooms available

STOKESLEY

North Yorkshire

Map **8** NZ50

✕ ***Golden Lion*** High St ☎(0642) 710265

Dinner not served Sun

French 60 seats Last dinner 9.15pm 10P bedrooms available

STONE

Staffordshire

Map **7** SJ93

★★★**Brooms** (Exec Hotel) ☎(0785) 815531

Closed Xmas

16rm(12) (1fb) CTV in all bedrooms ✱sB&B £15–£18 sB&B £15–£24.50 dB&B £25 dB&B £25–£35

40P

English & French **V** ✱Lunch £6–£8.50&alc Tea 55p Dinner £6–£8.50&alc Wine £4.90 Last dinner 9.30pm

Credit cards 1 2 3 5 **VS**

★★★*B* **Crown** High St ☎(0785) 813535

13 Annexe: 16 CTV in all bedrooms ® ✱sB&B £21 dB&B £32–£35

200P 2

V Lunch £3.75–£4 Dinner £5.50–£8.50 Wine £3.95 →

S

Last dinner 9.30pm
Credit cards 1 2 3

✕**La Casserole** 6 Oulton Rd ☎(0785) 814232
Tucked into a quiet residential area this restaurant serves simple French dishes.
Closed Sun Lunch not served Mon–Sat
French **V** 45 seats Dinner £9.50 Wine £4 Last dinner 11pm

STON EASTON
Somerset
Map **3** ST65

★★★

❀★★★**STON EASTON PARK, STON EASTON**
(Prestige) ☎Chewton Mendip (076121) 631 Telex no 444738
Closed Jan
(Rosette awarded for dinner only)
This hotel is everything you would expect from an estate started in 1739, the golden age of the English country house. The lovely grounds were designed by the famous Humphry Repton, and they contain a croquet lawn, an ice house and even a castle folly as well as a stream which runs to one side of the house. The stone mansion, now coloured with lichen, was designed in the Palladian style and the interior contains fine architectural and decorative features. It has been beautifully restored after near dereliction, and Jean Monro has made a quite exceptional success of it, particularly with regard to the décor and furniture. The main drawing room is elegantly done but just as charming is another smaller, more restful room with a soft colour scheme and its wood panelling ragged, stippled and dragged in the revived modern fashion. There is also a library, impressive with its mahogany shelving and there is a fine Regency table in the Yellow Dining Room, used for private parties. Open fires burn in season. The whole abounds with Eastern rugs, antiques, objets d'art and pictures. Plenty of fresh flowers contribute their charm to the overall effect as well.
The dining room is in a quite different, much lighter style but with refined

table appointments and comfortable chairs. The cooking is in the charge of a promising young chef and he cooks in the modern style. Excellent raw materials are used to good effect which ensures that his efforts earn our rosette. Service is by friendly and cheerful young girls. Bedrooms are also well and appropriately furnished with attractive, usually matching soft furnishings. They are well equipped with television, direct dial telephones and good toiletries. All in all this is a beautiful hotel in which to experience country house living at his best – a rare experience indeed.
16⇌ 6 CTV in all bedrooms
sB&B⇌£45–£55 dB&B⇌£65–£105
80P 6 ✽ billiards nc9yrs *xmas*
English & French **V** Lunch £10.50–£11.50 Tea £2.25 Dinner £16.50alc Wine £6 Last dinner 9.30pm
Credit cards 1 2 3 5

STONE CROSS
East Sussex
Map **5** TQ60

★★★**Glyndley Manor** Hailsham Rd (2m NW off B2104) (Exec Hotel)
☎Hailsham (0323) 843737 Telex no 877440
Charming, family run country house with well appointed lounge.
21rm(18⇌3⋒) (6fb) CTV in all bedrooms
sB&B⇌⋒£25.30–£27.50

dB&B⇌⋒£50.60–£55
100P ✽ (heated) (hard) *xmas*
English & Continental **V** Lunch £5.75&alc Tea 80p–£2 Dinner £7.50&alc Wine £5 Last dinner 9.30pm
S% Credit cards 1 2 3 4 5

STONEHAVEN
Grampian *Kincardineshire*
Map **15** NO88

☆☆☆**Commodore** Cowie Park
☎(0569) 62936 Telex no 739111
Friendly, modern commercial hotel.
40⇌ CTV in all bedrooms Ⓡ sB&B⇌£22 dB&B⇌£32
CTV 200P Disco Sat Live music & dancing Sat *xmas*
International **V** ✽Lunch £3.95 Dinner £7.95&alc Wine £5.75 Last dinner 10pm
Credit cards 1 2 3 5 **VS**

★★**County** Arduthie Rd ☎(0569) 64386
Closed 1 Jan
14rm(10⇌2⋒) (4fb) CTV in all bedrooms Ⓡ sB&B£15 sB&B⇌£17 dB&B£26 dB&B⇌£30
CTV 80P squash sauna bath *xmas*
✽Lunch £2.35–£3.20 Tea 80p–£2 High Tea £3–£6.50 Dinner £7.50–£10 Wine £4 Last dinner 9.30pm

★★**St Leonard's** Bath St ☎(0569) 62044
Closed 1–2 Jan
14rm(10⇌1⋒) (1fb) CTV in all bedrooms Ⓡ sB&B£22.50–£27.50 sB&B⇌£22.50–£27.50 dB&B£30–£35 dB&B⇌£30–£37.50
CTV 40P ✽
French **V** Lunch £5–£6&alc Dinner £7.75–£8.50&alc Wine £6 Last dinner 9pm
Credit card 3

STORNOWAY
Isle of Lewis, Western Isles *Ross & Cromarty*
Map **13** NB43

★★★***Caberfeidh*** ☎(0851) 2604
A purpose built hotel on northern edge of town.
36⇌ CTV in 6 bedrooms
Lift CTV 100P CFA Live music and dancing Thu & Fri
International **V** Last dinner 9pm
Credit cards 1 2 3 5 **VS**

★★★**Seaforth** James St ☎(0851) 2740
A city style but friendly hotel.
72rm(70⇌) (5fb) CTV in 6 bedrooms
sB&B⇌£22.50–£25.50 dB&B⇌£32.50–£35.50
Lift CTV 50P CFA Disco twice wkly Live music and dancing wkly Cabaret wkly
Lunch £4 Tea 90p Dinner £8–£10&alc Wine £4.25 Last dinner 9pm
Credit cards 1 2 3 **VS**

★★**Royal** Cromwell St (Scottish & Newcastle) ☎(0851) 2109
Homely, traditional, commercial hotel close to harbour and town centre.
19rm (1fb) Ⓡ sB&B£12.75 dB&B£25.50
CTV billiards
Lunch £1.50–£3.50 Tea 85p Dinner £4.50alc Wine £3 Last dinner 9pm
Credit cards 1 3

STORRINGTON
West Sussex
Map **4** TQ01

❀✕✕✕**Manleys** Manleys Hill
☎(09066) 2331
Very fine French cuisine is served in this beautifully furnished restaurant with its beams and log fire.
Closed Mon, 1st wk Jan, last wk Aug & 1st 2wks Sep Dinner not served Sun
French 36 seats Last dinner 9.15pm
18P

S

STOURBRIDGE
West Midlands
Map **7** SO88

★★**Bell** Market St (Wolverhampton & Dudley) ☎(03843) 5641 (due to change to (0384) 396783)
Small hotel close to the shopping centre, popular with businessmen.
21rm(1➡) CTV in all bedrooms Ⓡ sB&B£11.50–£13.25 sB&B➡⋒£13–£14.75 dB&B£18–£20 dB&B➡⋒£20–£22 B
CTV 100P
♧Lunch fr£3.50&alc Dinner fr£4.75&alc Wine £3.75 Last dinner 8.45pm
Credit cards 1 3 **VS**

★★**Talbot** High St (Wolverhampton & Dudley) ☎(03843) 4350 (due to change to (0384) 394350)
Busy hotel in the main street, popular with local business people.
21rm(6➡2⋒) (2fb) 2⊟ CTV in all bedrooms Ⓡ ✱sB&B£13.75–£15.50 sB&B➡⋒£15.50–£17.25 dB&B£21–£23 dB&B➡⋒£23–£25 B
CTV 35P
♧Lunch £3.50 Dinner fr£4.50&alc Wine £3.75 Last dinner 9.15pm
Credit cards 1 3 **VS**

✕**Gallery** 121 Bridgnorth Rd, Wollaston ☎(03843) 2788 (due to change to (0384) 392788)
A friendly restaurant, located over a butchers shop.
Closed Mon Lunch not served Tue–Sat Dinner not served Sun
40 seats ✱Lunch £6alc Dinner £12alc Wine £3.90 Last dinner 9.30pm
S% Credit card 1

STOURPORT-ON-SEVERN
Hereford & Worcester
Map **7** SO87

★★★**Mount Olympus** 35 Hartlebury Rd ☎(02993) 77333 Telex no 335494
Modernised hotel with sports and conference facilities.
42rm(37➡5⋒) 1⊟ CTV in all bedrooms Ⓡ ✱sB&B➡⋒£27.50 dB&B➡⋒£36 B
600P CFA ✽ (heated) (hard) squash Disco Thu *xmas*
International **V** ♧ ✱Lunch £4.50–£6.95&alc Tea £2 High Tea £2.50 Dinner £6.95–£8.95&alc Wine £4.95 Last dinner 10pm
Credit cards 1 2 3 5

★★**Swan** High St (Ansells) ☎(02993) 2050
35rm(8➡27⋒) CTV in all bedrooms Ⓡ sB&B➡⋒ fr£24.25 dB&B➡⋒ fr£31.50 B
CTV 80P Lunch fr£4.35&alc Dinner fr£5.25&alc Wine £3.90 Last dinner 10pm
Credit cards 1 2 3 **VS**

STOW-ON-THE-WOLD
Gloucestershire
Map **4** SP12

★★**Fosse Manor** ☎(0451) 30354
Closed Xmas
Modernised Cotswold manor house, situated 1m south of the historic market town.
17rm(4➡6⋒) Annexe 6rm(2➡) (4fb) 1⊟ CTV in 2 bedrooms Ⓡ ✱sB&B£8.96–£16.31 sB&B➡⋒£11.25–£18 dB&B£18–£31.50 dB&B➡⋒£22.50–£38.25 B
CTV 40P ✽
English & Continental **V** ♧ ✱Lunch fr£7.50&alc Dinner fr£7.75&alc Wine £3.90 Last dinner 9.30pm
Credit cards 1 2 3 5

★★ *H* **Old Stocks** The Square ☎(0451) 30666 Closed 25–30 Dec
Hospitable small hotel with well appointed bedrooms.
19rm(6➡2⋒) (6fb) CTV available in bedrooms Ⓡ sB&B➡⋒£15–£17 dB&B➡⋒£27.50–£30 B
CTV 3P 4 ✽
♧ Lunch £4.15–£6.75 Tea 50p Dinner £4.15–£6.75 Wine £4.15 Last dinner 9.30pm
Credit cards 1 3 5 **VS**

★★**Royalist** Digbeth St ☎(0451) 30670
The hotel is the oldest building in this historic town and has comfortable bedrooms.
8rm(5➡) Annexe: 4rm(1➡3⋒) (2fb) 1⊟ CTV in all bedrooms Ⓡ sB&B£14–£15 dB&B£28–£30 dB&B➡⋒£30–£32.50 B
10P nc5yrs
V ♧ Bar lunch 60p–£4.25 Tea £1–£1.50 Dinner £8.60alc Wine £5.25 Last dinner 9pm
Credit cards 1 2 3 5 **VS**

★★**Stow Lodge** The Square ☎(0451) 30485
Closed 1 Jan–4 Feb & 21–31 Dec
Comfortable, privately-owned hotel in its own grounds, set back from the Market Square.
22➡⋒ (2fb) CTV in all bedrooms Ⓡ ✱dB&B➡⋒£33.50–£36.50 B
30P ✽ nc5yrs
♧✱Bar lunch £5alc Dinner £6&alc Wine £4 Last dinner 9pm
Credit cards 2 5
See advert on page 604

★★**Talbot** The Square ☎(0451) 30631 Telex no 43434
17rm(3➡) (1fb) Ⓡ sB&B fr£13.50 sB&B➡⋒ fr£19 dB&B fr£23.50 dB&B➡⋒ fr£28.50 B
CTV *xmas*
V ♧ Lunch fr£5.95&alc Tea 50p Dinner £6.50&alc Wine £5.25 Last dinner 9.30pm
Credit cards 1 2 3 4 5

★★ *B* **Unicorn Crest** Sheep St (Crest) ☎(0451) 30257
Former 16th-century coaching inn with recently refurbished bedrooms.
20➡ CTV in all bedrooms Ⓡ ✱sB➡£28.50 dB➡£38 (room only) B
50P
International **V** ♧ Lunch £5.75 Dinner £8.50&alc Wine £5.75 Last dinner 9.30pm
Credit cards 1 2 3 5 **VS**

★**King's Arms** Market Sq ☎(0451) 30364 →

S

A 16th-century inn located in the Market Square.
8rm (2fb) 1 TV in all bedrooms ® sB&B£10.50–£12 dB&B£21–£24 B
CTV 9P
V ✿ ✱ Lunch 50p–£5&alc Dinner £6.50–£9&alc Wine £3.25 Last dinner 9pm
Credit cards 1 2 3 5 VS

✿ ✕ **Rafter's** Park St ☎ (0451) 30200
An attractive country town restaurant offering seasonal menus in a relaxed atmosphere.
Closed Sun & Public hols
English & French 45 seats Lunch £9.95&alc Dinner £9.95&alc Wine £5.25 Last dinner 10pm
S% Credit cards 1 2 3 5 VS

STRACHUR
Strathclyde *Argyllshire*
Map **10** NN00
★★★ **Creggans Inn** ☎ (036986) 279 Telex no 727396 (attn Creggans)
A 17th-century inn, extensively and tastefully modernised, with compact bedrooms.
22rm (15⇌ 2⋔) TV available in bedrooms ✱sB&B£22–£24 sB&B⇌⋔£25.50–£31 dB&B£32–£35 dB&B⇌⋔£40–£48 B
CTV 80P ✽ billiards *xmas*
Scottish & French V ✿ ✱ Lunch £5.50alc Tea £1.50alc Dinner £12alc Wine £5.65 Last dinner 9.30pm
Credit cards 1 2 3

STRANRAER
Dumfries & Galloway *Wigtownshire*
Map **10** NX06
★★★*L* ***North West Castle*** (Exec Hotel) ☎ (0776) 4413 Telex no 777088
Tasteful combination of old and new buildings with good leisure facilities.
79⇌ Annexe: 4rm (4⇌) CTV in all bedrooms ® B
Lift ☾ 100P CFA (heated) billiards sauna bath Live music and dancing Sat
English & French V ✿ Last dinner 9.30pm

★ ***Bucks Head*** 44 Hanover St ☎ (0776) 2064
14rm B
CTV 12P Disco twice wkly Live music and dancing wkly
✿ Last dinner 7.30pm
Credit cards 1 3

★ ***Enyhallow*** Castle Kennedy (3½m E A75) ☎ Dunragit (05814) 256
Converted, two-storey, 19th-century building with a modern extension.
7rm (5⋔) ®
CTV 20P ✽
Scottish & French V Last dinner 9.30pm
Credit cards 1 2 3 4 5

✕✕ **Bay House** Cairnryan Rd ☎ (0776) 3786
V 55 seats Lunch £2.95–£4.20 Dinner £8.75alc Wine £3.70 Last dinner 9.30pm
30P Live music Sat
Credit cards 1 2 3 5

STRATFORD-UPON-AVON
Warwickshire
Map **4** SP25
See plan
★★★★*L* **Hilton** Bridgefoot ☎ (0789) 67511 Telex no 311127 Plan **10** *C2*
A modern hotel, close to the theatre and the town centre.
249⇌ CTV in all bedrooms sB⇌£38.85–£51.75 dB⇌£54.85–£72.10 (room only) B
Lift ☾ CTV 350P CFA ✽ Live music and dancing Mon–Sat *xmas*
International V ✿ Lunch fr£6.95 Tea fr85p High Tea fr£6 Dinner fr£7.10 Last dinner 10.30pm
Credit cards 1 2 3 5

★★★★ **Shakespeare** Chapel St (Trusthouse Forte) ☎ (0789) 294771 Telex no 311181 Plan **13** *B2*

S

Famous black and white timbered 16th-century building whose bedrooms are named after Shakespearian characters.

66→(3fb) CTV in all bedrooms ® sB&B→£45.50 dB&B→£65.50 ℞

Lift ☾ 35P CFA *xmas*

♔☐ Last dinner 9.30pm

Credit cards 1 2 3 4 5

★★★★*H* ***Welcome*** Warwick Rd ☎(0789) 295252 Telex no 31347 Plan **15** *C3*

Comfortable, Jacobean-style mansion house standing in 150 acres of parkland.

84→⋔ CTV in all bedrooms ℞

☾ 100P 5🚗 CFA ✽ ⛳ billiards ♿

English & French **V** ♔☐ Last dinner 9.15pm

Credit cards 1 2 3 4 5

★★★**Alveston Manor** Clopton Bridge (Trusthouse Forte) ☎(0789) 204581 Telex no 31324 Plan **1** *C1*

Popular tourist hotel, said to have Shakespearian connections.

112→(3fb) CTV in all bedrooms ® sB&B→£39 dB&B→£55.50 ℞

☾ 200P CFA ✽ *xmas*

♔ Last dinner 9.15pm

Credit cards 1 2 3 4 5

★★★**Arden** Waterside ☎(0789) 294949 Telex no 291855 Plan **2** *B2*

The building dates from the Regency period and is situated opposite the Royal Shakespeare Theatre.

63rm(40→14⋔)(6fb) CTV in 20 bedrooms TV in 43 bedrooms ® *sB&B£17 sB&B→£24.25 dB&B→£38.75 ℞

☾ CTV 40P CFA ✽ ⌂

English & International **V** ♔ *Lunch £5.50alc Dinner £6.75&alc Wine £4.80 Last dinner 9.30pm

Credit cards 1 2 3 4 5

★★★*B* **Falcon** Chapel St (Queens Moat) ☎(0789) 205777 Telex no 312522 Plan **6** *B2*

A modernised hotel in the town centre. Origins date from the 15th century.

73→⋔ 1⊟ CTV in all bedrooms ® sB&B→⋔£25–£35 dB&B→⋔£45–£48 ℞

Lift ☾ 100P 24🚗 CFA *xmas*

English & French **V** ♔☐ Lunch £5.50–£6.50&alc Tea £3.50 Dinner £7–£8&alc Wine £1.40 Last dinner 9pm

Credit cards 1 2 3 4 5 **VS**

★★★**Grosvenor House** Warwick Rd (Best Western) ☎(0789) 69213 Telex no 311699 Plan **8** *C3*

Closed 24–28 Dec

A busy, family-run hotel, popular with tourists and business people.

57rm(23→30⋔)(13fb) 2⊟ CTV in all bedrooms ✶ *sB&B£17.50 sB&B→⋔£22–£25 dB&B£27.50 dB&B→⋔£33.50–36 ℞

☾ ⚟ CTV 50P CFA ✽

V ♔☐ *Lunch £4–£5&alc Tea 50p–£1 Dinner £7&alc Wine £3.70 Last dinner 8.45pm

Credit cards 1 2 3 5 **VS**

★★★**Swan's Nest** Bridgefoot (Trusthouse Forte) ☎(0789) 66761 Telex no 31419 Plan **14** *C1*

A brick-built hotel whose grounds border the River Avon.

70rm(44→8⋔)(2fb) CTV in all bedrooms ® sB&B£33 sB&B→⋔£35.50 dB&B£45.50 dB&B→⋔£52.50 ℞

☾ 100P ✽ CFA *xmas* ♿

♔☐ Last dinner 9.15pm

Credit cards 1 2 3 4 5

★★★**White Swan** Rother St (Trusthouse Forte) ☎(0789) 297022 Plan **16** *A3*

Traditional 15th century inn in the town centre.

55rm(22→2⋔)(4fb) CTV in all bedrooms ® sB&B£30.50 sB&B→⋔£33 dB&B£43 dB&B→⋔£49.50 ℞ →

S

☾ ⁄P CFA *xmas*
⚘Last dinner 8.30pm
Credit cards 1 2 3 4 5

★★**Haytor** Avenue Rd ☎(0789) 297799 Plan **9** *C4*
Closed 29 Dec–2 Jan
Friendly quiet hotel with secluded walled garden.
18rm(10⇌6⋒) (2fb) 3⊞ ⁄★ sB&B£20 sB&B⇌⋒£22–£24 dB&B£35–£37 dB&B⇌⋒£37–£40
CTV 20P ✽ billiards *xmas*
⚘ Tea £1–£1.25 Dinner £5.50–£7.50 Wine £6 Last dinner 7.30pm

✕✕**Christophi's** 21–23 Sheep St ☎(0789) 293546 Plan **5** *B2*
Closed Sun Lunch not served
International **V** 140 seats ✻Dinner £9.50alc Wine £4.95 Last dinner mdnt ⁄P bedrooms available Live music and dancing nightly Cabaret Fri & Sat
S% Credit cards 1 2 3 5

✕✕**Marlowe's** 18 High St ☎(0789) 204999 Plan **12** *B2*
English & French 150 seats ✻Lunch £2.50–£7&alc Dinner £2.50–£7&alc Last dinner 11pm ⁄P
Credit cards 1 2 3 **VS**

✕**Buccaneer** 11 Warwick Rd ☎(0789) 292550 Plan **3** *C3*
Closed last 2 wks Feb & 1st 2 wks Mar Lunch not served
International **V** 30 seats Dinner £5–£6&alc Wine £3.85 Last dinner 11.30pm 6P bedrooms available
Credit cards 1 2 3 4 5

✕**Giovanni** Ely St ☎(0789) 297999 Plan **7** *B2*
Closed Sun & Public hols
English, French & Italian **V** 70 seats Last dinner 11.30pm ⁄
Credit cards 1 3

✕**Marianne Français** 3 Greenhill St ☎(0789) 293563 Plan **11** *A3*
French **V** 50 seats ✻Lunch £10–£15alc Dinner £10–£15alc Wine £5.85 Last dinner 11pm ⁄P

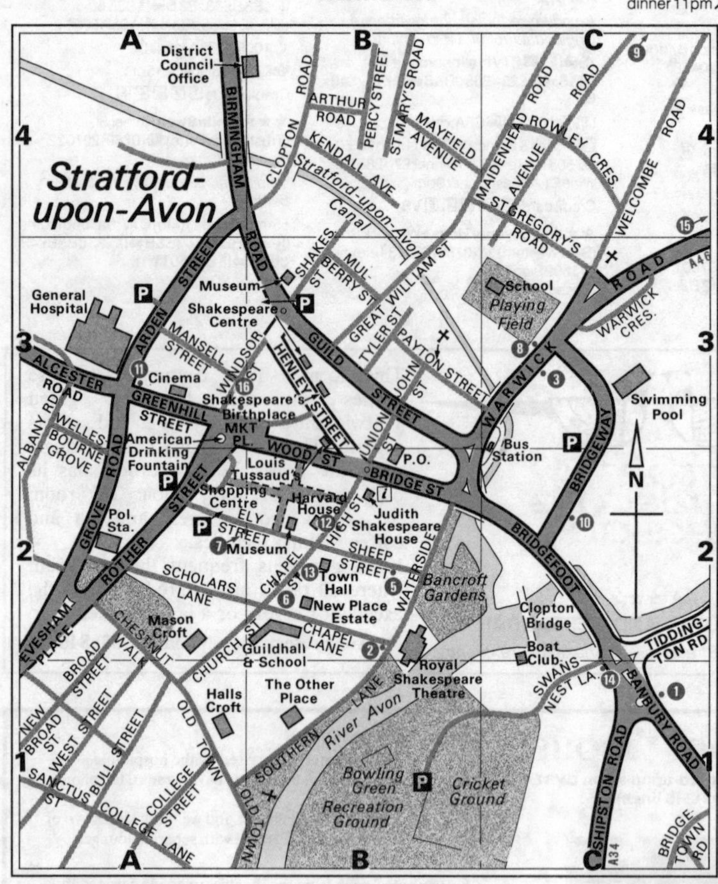
Stratford-upon-Avon
District Council Office
General Hospital
Museum
Shakespeare Centre
Cinema
Shakespeare's Birthplace
American Drinking Fountain
Louis Tussaud's
Shopping Centre
Harvard House
Judith Shakespeare House
Museum
Town Hall
New Place Estate
Mason Croft
Guildhall & School
Halls Croft
The Other Place
Royal Shakespeare Theatre
Bancroft Gardens
Clopton Bridge
Boat Club
School Playing Field
Swimming Pool
Bus Station
P.O.
Bowling Green
Recreation Ground
Cricket Ground
River Avon
Stratford-upon-Avon Canal
BIRMINGHAM ROAD
CLOPTON ROAD
ARTHUR ROAD
PERCY STREET
ST MARY'S ROAD
MAYFIELD AVENUE
KENDALL AVE
MAIDENHEAD ROAD
ROWLEY CRES.
WELCOMBE ROAD
ST GREGORY'S ROAD
WARWICK ROAD
WARWICK CRES.
ARDEN STREET
MANSELL STREET
WINDSOR ST
HENLEY STREET
GUILD STREET
GREAT WILLIAM ST
TYLER ST
PAYTON STREET
JOHN ST
UNION ST
ALCESTER ROAD
GREENHILL STREET
WELLESBOURNE GROVE
ALBANY ROAD
GROVE ROAD
ROTHER STREET
WOOD ST
BRIDGE ST
ELY STREET
SHEEP STREET
HIGH ST
WATERSIDE
CHAPEL ST
CHAPEL LANE
SCHOLARS LANE
CHESTNUT WALK
EVESHAM PLACE
CHURCH ST
BROAD STREET
NEW BROAD ST
WEST STREET
BULL STREET
SANCTUS ST
COLLEGE STREET
COLLEGE LANE
OLD TOWN
SOUTHERN LANE
BRIDGEFOOT
BRIDGEWAY
TIDDINGTON RD
SWANS NEST LA.
BANBURY ROAD
SHIPSTON ROAD
BRIDGETOWN RD
A46
A34
MKT PL.
Pol. Sta.
N

Stratford-upon-Avon

1 Alveston Manor ★★★
2 Arden ★★★
3 Buccaneer ✕
4 Charlecote Pheasant ☆☆☆ *(Listed under Charlecote)*
5 Christophi's ✕✕
6 Falcon ★★★
7 Giovanni ✕
8 Grosvenor House ★★★
9 Haytor ★★
10 Hilton ★★★★
11 Marianne Francais ✕
12 Marlowe's ✕✕
13 Shakespeare ★★★★
14 Swan's Nest ★★★
15 Welcome ★★★★
16 White Swan ★★★

S% Credit cards 2 5

At **Charlecote** (5m E off B4086)

☆☆☆**Charlecote Pheasant Country Hotel** ☎(0789) 840649 Annexe: 15rm(4⇌11⋒)

130P

STRATHAVEN
Strathclyde *Lanarkshire*
Map **11** NS74

★**Strathaven** Hamilton Rd ☎(0357) 21778

7rm (1fb) CTV in 7 bedrooms Ⓡ ✱ sB&B£13.50 dB&B£27 ⛿

100P ✽ ⌂ *xmas*

French V ♆ ☕ Lunch £3–£5.50 Tea £1.50 High Tea £4 Dinner £6.50–£9.50&alc Wine £5.50 Last dinner 9pm

Credit cards 1 2 3 5

STRATHBLANE
Central *Stirlingshire*
Map **11** NS57

★★★ ***B Country Club*** Milngavie Rd (Inter-Hotel) ☎Blanefield (0360) 70491
Closed New Year's Day

Converted country mansion with popular restaurant.

10rm(7⇌3⋒) CTV in all bedrooms Ⓡ ✱ ⛿

100P ✽ ♩ ⌂

Scottish & French V ♆ ☕ Last dinner 10pm

Credit cards 1 2 3 5

See advert on page 608

★★*B* **Kirkhouse Inn** ☎Blanefield (0360) 70621

Hotel with good standards throughout, situated in a lovely village. →

S

17rm(11⇌)CTV in all bedrooms sB&B£19 sB&B⇌⋒£21 dB&B£24 dB&B⇌⋒£28 B
☾⚡CTV 300P ✽ ♪ U ⌂ *xmas*
French V ✿ Lunch £4.50&alc Tea 75p Dinner £7.50&alc Wine £3.50 Last dinner 9.30pm
Credit cards 1 2 3 5 **VS**

STRATHCARRON
Highland *Ross & Cromarty*
Map **14** NG94
✕**Carron** Cam Allt ☎Lochcarron (05202) 488
Closed Sun Lunch not served 15 Oct–30 Mar Dinner not served Sun–Tue & Thu 15 Oct–30 Mar
V 43 seats Lunch £3.50alc Tea £1.10alc High Tea £3.50alc Dinner £10.50alc Wine £3.80 Last dinner 9.15pm 25P
Credit cards 1 3

STRATHDON
Grampian *Aberdeenshire*
Map **15** NJ31
★**Colquhonnie** ☎(09752) 210
Small Highland hotel in spectacular scenery.
9rm (4fb) ® sB&B£8 dB&B£16 B
CTV 20P 4⌂ ♪ billiards
V ✿ Lunch fr£3.50 Tea 75p High Tea £3 Dinner fr£7 Last dinner 7.30pm
VS

STRATHMIGLO
Fife
Map **11** NO21
✕✕**Strathmiglo Inn** ☎(03376) 252
Closed Thu, Xmas, New Year & last 2 wks Jul Dinner not served Sun
26 seats Lunch fr£6&alc Dinner £12alc Last dinner 9pm 8P
S% Credit cards 1 2 3

STRATHPEFFER
Highland *Ross & Cromarty*
Map **14** NH45
★**Brunstane Lodge** ☎(09972) 261
RS Nov–Apr
7rm(1⇌1⋒) (2fb) sB&B£9–£10 dB&B£18–£20 dB&B⇌⋒£20–£22
CTV 10P ✽
Bar lunch £1–£1.50 Dinner £6.50–£7.50 Wine £3.50 Last dinner 8pm
VS

★**Dunraven Lodge** Golf Course Rd ☎(09972) 210
14rm (2⇌2⋒) ® ★ sB&B£9–£12 dB&B£14–£20 dB&B⇌⋒£16–£22 B
CTV 16P ✽ nc12yrs
V ✿ Lunch £2–£3 Tea 50p–75p Dinner £7.50–£8.50 Wine £4.20 Last dinner 8pm
Credit cards 1 3 **VS**

❀★*HL* **Holly Lodge** ☎(09972) 254
Closed Dec–Feb
(Rosette awarded for dinner only.)
Delightful little family hotel with a reputation for its hospitality and comfortable lounges.
7rm(2⇌3⋒) ® sB&B£14–£16 sB&B⇌⋒£15–£18 dB&B£30–£36 dB&B⇌⋒£30–£36
CTV 12P 1⌂ ✽
Dinner £8.50–£10 Wine £3.75 Last dinner 8pm

STRATHTUMMEL
Tayside *Perthshire*
Map **14** NN86
★★*B* **Port-an-Eilean** ☎Tummel Bridge (08824) 233 Closed mid Oct–mid Apr
Comfortable hotel in a splendid location by the loch side, personally supervised by the proprietors.
12rm(6⇌) (1fb) sB&B£14 sB&B⇌£16.50 dB&B£28 dB&B⇌£31
20P 2⌂ ✽ ♪
Cosmopolitan ✿ Tea 60p–£1.50 Dinner £7.50 Wine £3.70 Last dinner 9pm

STRATHYRE
Central *Perthshire*
Map **11** NN51
★**The Inn** Main St ☎(08774) 224
Attractively modernised roadside Inn.

S

6rm(4➡1⋒)B
CTV 120P🚗✽
🍴Mainly grills ♧☕ Last dinner 9pm

STRATTON
Cornwall
Map **2** SS20
★**Stamford Hill House** ☎Bude (0288) 2709 Closed Oct–19 Apr
Small, family hotel in an elevated position with good rural views.
18rm(7➡1⋒)(11fb)✯sB&B£6.50–£10.50 sB&B➡⋒£9.50–£12.50 dB&B£13–£21 dB&B➡⋒£19–£25 B
CTV 20P✽♩⌂
♧☕Lunch £2.50–£4.50&alc Tea £1–£1.50 Dinner £4–£5&alc Wine £3.20 Last dinner 8.30pm

STREATLEY
Berkshire
Map **4** SU58
★★★ *L* **Swan** ☎Goring (0491) 873737
26➡⋒ CTV in all bedrooms Ⓡ sB➡⋒£33–£40.25 dB➡⋒£56–£62 (room only) B
☾ 120P✽♩ *xmas*
🍴French V♧☕✻Lunch £6.50–£8&alc Tea fr95p High Tea fr£1.75 Dinner £8.50–£14 Wine £6 Last dinner 5pm
Credit cards 1 2 3 5 **VS**

STREET
Somerset
Map **3** ST43
☆☆☆**Wessex** ☎(0458) 43383
Useful modern hotel near town centre.
50➡ CTV in 25 bedrooms TV in 25 bedrooms Ⓡ sB&B➡£23.80 dB&B➡£33.80 B
Lift ☾ 30P 30⌂ CFA Live music and dancing Sat
V♧☕Lunch fr£1.90 Tea fr£2.50 Dinner fr£5.50 Wine £3.95 Last dinner 9.45pm
Credit cards 1 2 3 5 **VS**
See advert on page 610

STREETLY
West Midlands
Map **7** SP09
☆☆**Parson & Clerk Motel** Chester Rd (junct A452/B4138) (Ansells) ☎021-353 1747
This hotel has a separate, modern bedroom block set away from the main building.
30⋒ Ⓡ ✯ sB&B⋒ fr£23.25 dB&B⋒ fr£28.75 B
CTV 200P🚗
Lunch fr£5.75&alc Dinner fr£5.75&alc Wine £3.90 Last dinner 10pm
Credit cards 1 2 3 **VS**

STRETE
Devon
Map **3** SX84
✕**Laughing Monk** ☎Stoke Fleming (080 427) 639
Stone-built former school house with a front patio in the centre of the village.
Closed Mon & Tues (Oct–Mar) Lunch not served Mon–Sat Dinner not served Sun
V 70 seats Lunch £4.95 Dinner £8–£9.25alc Wine £4.50 Last dinner 10pm 20P Disco Fri
S% Credit cards 1 2 3 5 **VS**

STROMNESS
Orkney
Map **16** HY21
★★**Stromness** Victoria St ☎(0856) 850298
40rm(15➡21⋒)(3fb) TV available in bedrooms Ⓡ sB&B£8.50–£14.95 sB&B➡⋒£10.80–£17.25 dB&B£17–£25.30 dB&B➡⋒£20–£28.75 B
Lift CTV 5P✽ billiards
♧☕Lunch £2–£2.70 Tea 30p–£1 High Tea £2–£3.50 Dinner £3.20–£6.50&alc Wine £3.70 Last dinner 8.30pm

STRONTIAN
Highland *Argyllshire*
Map **14** NM86
★★**Kilcamb Lodge** ☎(0967) 2257
Situated on the outskirts of the village with grounds stretching down to Loch Sunart.
11rm(3⋒)(1fb) Ⓡ sB&B£11.90 dB&B£23 dB&B⋒£23.80
CTV 50P🚗✽♩
♧Lunch £2–£6 Dinner £8–£9&alc Wine £2 Last dinner 9pm
★★ ***Loch Sunart*** ☎(0967) 2471
Closed Nov–Mar
This hotel in a small village on Loch Sunart, overlooks the bay and the loch.
11rm(5➡) Ⓡ B
CTV 30P🚗♩
V♧Last dinner 7pm

STROUD
Gloucestershire
Map **3** SO80
See also Amberley and Painswick
★★★**Bear of Rodborough** Rodborough Common (½m SW) (Anchor) ☎Amberley (045 387) 3522 Telex no 858875
Character hotel set in Cotswold countryside, with extensive grounds adjoining National Trust land.
30rm(27➡3⋒) Annexe: 18➡(4fb) 1🛏 CTV in all bedrooms Ⓡ sB&B➡⋒ fr£35 dB&B➡⋒ fr£42 B
☾ 120P CFA✽ Live music and dancing Sat Cabaret Sat *xmas*
🍴English & French ♧Lunch £4.95–£12&alc Tea 50p High Tea £1.30 Dinner £8–£12&alc Wine £4.50 Last dinner 9.15pm
Credit cards 1 2 3 5 **VS**
★★♜ *H* **Burleigh Court** Brimscombe (2½m SE off A419) ☎Brimscombe (0453) 883804
Closed 24–30 Dec
Hospitable country house hotel with comfortable bedrooms.
11rm(6➡3⋒)(1fb) CTV available in bedrooms Ⓡ sB&B£22.50 sB&B➡⋒£22.50 dB&B£33 dB&B➡⋒£33 B
CTV 40P 2⌂🚗✽⩯(heated)⌂
🍴English & Continental V♧☕Lunch £4.50–£12&alc Tea £1–£1.50&alc High Tea £1.50–£3&alc Dinner £8.95–£12.50&alc Wine £3.95 Last dinner 8.30pm
Credit cards 1 2 3 **VS**

S

★★London 30–31 London Rd ☎(04536) 79992
Town centre hotel with attractive restaurant.
10rm(2⇌6⋔) CTV in all bedrooms ✱ sB&B fr£15 sB&B⇌⋔ fr£18 dB&B fr£26 dB&B⇌⋔ fr£30 ⊟
12P nc6yrs
V Dinner fr£6.50&alc Wine £3.90 Last dinner 9.30pm
Credit cards 1 2 5

★*Alpine Lodge* Stratford Rd ☎(04536) 4949
A privately-owned hotel with popular bars.
10rm(8⇌) CTV in all bedrooms ®
30P
Mainly grills **V** ♁ ☐ Last dinner 9.30pm
VS

★Imperial (Berni) ☎(04536) 4077
Closed Xmas
Town centre hotel with popular grill restaurants and bars.
20rm ✱ ✻sB&B fr£13 dB&B fr£26 ⊟
CTV 6P
Mainly grills ♁ ✻Lunch £2.95–£7.78 Dinner £2.95–£7.78 Wine £3.90 Last dinner 10pm
Credit cards 1 2 3 5

STRUY
Highland *Inverness-shire*
Map **14** NH43

★★Cnoc Erchless Castle Estate ☎(046376) 264 RS Oct–May
Small, family run country hotel within the grounds of The Erchless Castle Estate.
9rm(2⇌2⋔) (2fb) ® ✻sB&B£11 sB&B⇌⋔ £13 dB&B£18 dB&B⇌⋔ £22
CTV 40P
✻Lunch £3.15alc Dinner fr£7 Wine £3.90 Last dinner 9pm

STUDLAND
Dorset
Map **4** SZ08

★★★Knoll House Ferry Rd ☎(092944) 251 Closed mid Oct–Mar
A rambling building amid pine trees with lawns and gardens extending down to the beach.
104rm(83⇌) Annexe: 7rm CTV available in bedrooms sB&B£21–£30 sB&B⇌£25–£34 dB&B£42–£60 dB&B⇌£46–£68
☾ CTV 100P ✻ (heated) (hard)
V ♁ ☐ Lunch £7 Tea 65p–£1.45 Dinner £7 Wine £3.95 Last dinner 8.30pm

★★*Manor House* ☎(092944) 288
Closed late Oct–Mar
Gothic-style manor house with secluded gardens and grounds overlooking the sea and cliffs.
19rm(10⇌5⋔) 3 CTV in 3 bedrooms
CTV 30P ✻ nc5yrs
♁ ☐ Last dinner 8pm

STURMINSTER NEWTON
Dorset
Map **3** ST71

✿✕✕**Plumber Manor** (2m SW on Hazelbury Bryan road) ☎(0258) 72507
(Rosette awarded for dinner only.)
A 17th-century grey stone manor house in 15 acres of parkland.
Closed Mon, Feb, 1st 2wks Nov & Sun (mid Nov–Jan & Mar) Lunch not served
English & French 60 seats Dinner £12.60–£13.50 Wine £4.50 Last dinner 9.30pm 20P bedrooms available

SUDBURY
Suffolk
Map **5** TL84

★★★Mill Walnut Tree Ln ☎(0787) 75544 Telex no 919161
46⇌ CTV in all bedrooms ® sB&B⇌£27.50 dB&B⇌£38 ⊟
☾ CTV 80P 6 CFA *xmas*

S

♔☐ Lunch £7.50&alc Tea £2 High Tea £3 Dinner £8.50&alc Wine £4.75 Last dinner 9.30pm

S% Credit cards 1 2 3 5

★★**Four Swans** North St ☎(0787) 78103

Originally a coaching inn, this 18th-century building has been substantially modernised and a bedroom block built alongside.

5rm Annexe: 12➡ CTV in 14 bedrooms Ⓡ ✱sB&B£11.20 sB&B➡£14.65 dB&B£18.95 dB&B➡£22.40 Continental breakfast

CTV 20P *xmas* ♿

♔✱Lunch fr£1.50&alc Dinner £8alc Wine £4.10 Last dinner 9.30pm

Credit cards 1 2 3 4 5

SULGRAVE

Northamptonshire
Map **4** SP54

✕**Thatched House Hotel** ☎(029 576) 232

A 17th-century Cotswold stone restaurant in a quiet country village.

▣English & French **V** 56 seats ✱Lunch £3.75–£7.75 Tea 75p–£2.45 Dinner £5–£9.95 Wine £4 Last dinner 9.30pm 10P bedrooms available

Credit cards 1 2 3 5

SUNBURY-ON-THAMES

Surrey
London plan **5** A2 (page 422)

✕**Castle** 21 Thames St ☎(09327) 83647

Converted, 17th-century small inn, close to the River Thames.

Closed Sun & Boxing day–30 Dec

▣French 80 seats Lunch £11alc Dinner £11alc Wine £6.50 Last dinner 10pm 30P Live music Fri

Credit cards 1 2 3 5 **VS**

SUNDERLAND

Tyne & Wear
Map **12** NZ35

★★★**Seaburn** Queen's Pde, Seaburn (Swallow) ☎(0783) 292041 Telex no 53168

82rm(79➡3⋂)(4fb) CTV in all bedrooms Ⓡ sB&B➡⋂£17.50–£31 dB&B➡⋂£25.75–£40 B

Lift ☾ CTV 120P 3🚗 CFA Live music and dancing Sat

V♔☐ Lunch £6–£6.75&alc Tea £2.25 High Tea £3–£4.50 Dinner £6.50&alc Wine £4.75 Last dinner 9.30pm

Credit cards 1 2 3 5 **VS**

★**Gelt House** St Bede's Ter ☎(0783) 672990 Closed Xmas

15rm(3➡3⋂) Annexe 8rm(2➡6⋂)(3fb) CTV in 16 bedrooms Ⓡ ★✱sB&B fr£12 sB&B➡⋂ fr£18.40 dB&B fr£22.50 dB&B➡⋂ fr£24.50

CTV 14P 🚗 sauna bath

▣English & Continental **V**♔✱Lunch fr£4.95 Tea fr£2.50 Dinner fr£5.75 Wine £4 Last dinner 7.30pm

SURBITON

Gt London
London Plan **5** B1 (page 422)

❀✕✕**Chez Max** 85 Maple Rd ☎01-399 2365

Restaurant offering very individualistic French cuisine.

Closed Sun & Mon Lunch not served Sat

▣French 30 seats Lunch £16alc Dinner £16alc Wine £6.10 Last dinner 10.30pm

Credit cards 1 2 3 5

SUTTON

Gt London
Plan **5** C1 (page 422)

❀✕**Partners 23** 23 Stonecot Hill ☎01-644 7743

(Rosette awarded for dinner only.)

Small, well-run restaurant serving good fresh food.

Closed Sun, Mon, 25–30 Dec & 2wks Aug Lunch not served Sat

▣French 26 seats Lunch £7–£9 Dinner £11.50 Wine £4.20 →

S

Last dinner 9.30pm ₽̸
Credit cards 1 3 VS

SUTTON BENGER
Wiltshire
Map **3** ST97

★★★**Bell House** ☎Seagry (0249) 720401
Comfortable village hotel with good bedrooms and attractive restaurant.
14➡ (2fb) CTV in all bedrooms ® sB&B➡£23–£28 dB&B➡£46–£50 B̶
50P ✽
V ♧ ☐ Lunch £8alc Tea 50p–£1 Dinner £7–£10 Wine £6 Last dinner 11pm
Credit cards 1 2 3 5

SUTTON COLDFIELD
West Midlands
Map **7** SP19

★★★★**Penns Hall** Penns Ln (Embassy) ☎021-351 3111 Telex no 335789
Considerably extended mansion, with grounds and a lake.
116➡⋒ CTV in all bedrooms ® sB➡£38 dB➡£46 B̶
Lift ☾ 600P CFA ✽ ♪ Live music and dancing Sat (Sep–May)
▣International ♧ Lunch £6.75&alc Dinner £8.50&alc Wine £4.70 Last dinner 10pm
Credit cards 1 2 3 4 5

★★★**Moor Hall** Moor Hall Dr, Four Oaks (Best Western) ☎021-308 3751
57rm(52➡⋒) (3fb) CTV in all bedrooms ® ✻sB&B£27.50–£28.50 sB&B➡⋒£32.50–£34 dB&B➡⋒£37.50–£41 B̶
☾ 200P CFA ✽ ⌂
▣English & French V ♧ ☐ Lunch fr£6&alc Tea fr£1.50 Dinner fr£7.75&alc Wine £4.75 Last dinner 10.30pm
Credit cards 1 2 3 5 VS

★★**Sutton Court** 66 Lichfield Rd ☎021-355 2135
RS 26 Dec–1 Jan
Turreted house on busy cross roads leading into the town centre.
11rm (2➡8⋒) CTV in all bedrooms ® sB&B➡⋒£20.87 dB&B➡⋒£29.72
⚡30P
▣English & French V ♧ ☐ Lunch £2.95–£7.50&alc Tea £2 Dinner £7.50–£10&alc Wine £4.75 Last dinner 9.30pm
S% Credit cards 1 2 3 5 VS

✕✕**Le Bon Viveur** 65 Birmingham Rd ☎021-355 5836
Closed Sun, Mon, & Aug Lunch not served Sat
▣French 48 seats ✻Lunch £4.20–£5.35&alc Dinner £9.50alc Wine £4.45 Last dinner 10.30pm 10P
Credit cards 1 2 3 5 VS

✕✕**La Gondola** Lichfield Rd, Mere Green ☎021-308 6782
Lunch not served Sat Dinner not served Sun
▣Italian 80 seats ✻Lunch £4.45&alc Dinner £8.50&alc Wine £4.95 Last dinner 10.30pm 40P Live music Fri & Sat
Credit cards 1 2 3

SUTTON-ON-SEA
Lincolnshire
Map **9** TF58

★★**Bacchus** High St (Home Brewery) ☎(0521) 41204
A predominantly holiday hotel with large grounds, close to the seafront.
22rm(6➡) CTV available in bedrooms ® ★ ✻sB&B£12.90–£14.35 dB&B£25.80–£27.45 dB&B➡£28.59–£31.62 B̶
CTV 40P 6⌂ ✽ *xmas*
V ♧ Last dinner 9pm
S% Credit cards 1 3

★★**Grange & Links** Sea Ln, Sandilands ☎(0521) 41334
16rm(11➡3⋒) (1fb) 1⊞ CTV in all bedrooms ® ✻sB&B£13.80 sB&B➡⋒£20.70 dB&B➡⋒£31.05 B̶
CTV 60P ⇌ ✽ ⚲(hard) Disco Sat Live music and dancing Sat *xmas*
▣English & French V ♧ ✻Lunch £6.50alc Dinner £8alc Wine £3.50 Last dinner 8.30pm
Credit cards 2 3

SUTTON UPON DERWENT
Humberside
Map **8** SE74

★★**Old Rectory** ☎Elvington (090 485) 548
Charming, relaxing, well-converted country vicarage with its own pleasant gardens.
6rm(2⋒) CTV in all bedrooms ® ✻sB&B fr£12.50 sB&B⋒ fr£15.50 dB&B fr£25 dB&B⋒ fr£31 Continental breakfast
40P ✽
✻Lunch fr£5.50 Tea fr£1.75 High Tea fr£3.75 Dinner fr£6.90&alc Last dinner 8.30pm

SWALLOWFIELD
Berkshire
Map **4** SU76

✕✕**Mill House** Basingstoke Rd ☎Reading (0734) 883124
Closed Sun, Mon, 3–9 Jan & 14–27 Aug Lunch not served Sat
▣English & French 75 seats ✻Lunch £9.50–£14 Dinner £11.50–£16 Wine £5.25 Last dinner 9.15pm 50P
Credit cards 1 2 3 5

SWANAGE
Dorset
Map **4** SZ07

★★★***Corrie*** De Moulham Rd ☎(0929) 423104
Long, low pebble-dashed building with enclosed veranda and sun balcony overlooking the sea.
53➡ CTV available in bedrooms
Lift ☾ CTV 36P 9⌂ ⇌ ▭(heated) sauna bath Disco 3 nights wkly Live music and dancing 4 nights wkly ⌂
♧ ☐ Last dinner 7.45pm

★★★**Grosvenor** ☎(0929) 422292
Closed Nov–Mar
Set in private grounds with its own beach, this hotel enjoys panoramic views across Swanage Bay.

95rm(56⇌1⋒) Annexe: 10rm(7⇌) (30fb) CTV in 20 bedrooms ® ✱ sB&B£18–£25.50 sB&B⇌⋒£19.50–£27 dB&B£36–£51 dB&B⇌⋒£39–£54 ⛿

Lift ☾ ✂ CTV 200P CFA ❀ ▭ ⛵ (heated) ⛳ ℘ (hard) ♩ sauna bath Disco twice wkly Live music and dancing wkly ⌂

⊟ International **V** ♧ ▭ Lunch fr£5.50 Tea fr50p Dinner fr£6.50 Wine £3 Last dinner 8.30pm

VS

★★★ ***H*****Pine's** Burlington Rd ☎ (0929) 425211 Telex no 418297 (PH)

Bedrooms and good food, modern cliff top hotel with attentive staff, well

Swanage

appointed.

51rm(46⇌3⋒) (15fb) CTV in all bedrooms sB&B£17.25–£21.85 sB&B⇌⋒£17.25–£21.85 dB&B⇌⋒£34.50–£43.70 ⛿

Lift ☾ 60P ⛟ CFA ❀ Live music and dancing twice wkly (in season) ♿ *xmas*

⊟ English & Continental **V** ♧ ▭ Lunch £5.18–£5.75 Tea 63p–70p High Tea £1.15–£2.88 Dinner £7.75–£8.35 Wine £4.30 Last dinner 9pm

VS

★★ **Cliff Top** 8 Burlington Rd ☎ (0929) 422091 Closed Nov–Apr

Purbeck stone building with fine views across the bay.

16rm(11⇌3⋒) (4fb) sB&B£9.50 sB&B⇌⋒£10.50 dB&B£19 dB&B⇌⋒£21 ⛿

CTV 10P 3⌂ ⛟ ⌂

⊟ English & Austrian ♧ ▭ Bar lunch £1–£2 Dinner £7.50 Wine £2.95 Last dinner 7.30pm

★★ **Grand** Burlington Rd ☎ (0929) 423353 Closed Nov–Feb except xmas RS 24–28 Dec

In an elevated position with fine views. →

60rm(9⇌)(10fb)Ⓡ*sB&B£13–£15 sB&B⇌£15–£16.50 dB&B£24–£26 dB&B⇌£28–£30 B
Lift ☾ CTV 10P ✽ *xmas*
Bar lunch 50p–£4 Tea 50p–£1.50 Dinner £6 Wine £3.75 Last dinner 7.50pm
Credit cards 1 2 3

★**Malverns** Park Rd ☎(0929) 422575
Red-brick, terraced building at the top of the hill, away from the town centre and the beach.
19rm(1⇌3⋒)(8fb) TV available on request sB&B£8.75–£11.50 sB&B⋒£10.75–£14 dB&B£17.50–£23 dB&B⋒£19.50–£25.50 B
CTV 12P nc3yrs
V Bar lunch 50p–£3&alc Tea £42p–£2.50 Dinner £3.75–£5.50&alc Wine £3.50 Last dinner 7.30pm
Credit cards 1 2 3 5 **VS**

★*H* **Sefton** Gilbert Rd ☎(0929) 423469
Closed Dec–Mar
15rm(5⋒)(1fb)Ⓡ sB&B£10–£15 sB&B⋒£12–£17 sB&B£20–£30 dB&B⋒£24–£34 B
CTV 9P 1 ✽ nc8yrs
International **V** Bar lunch £1–£5 Tea 50p–£1 Dinner £9–£10 Wine £3.85 Last dinner 7.30pm
Credit card 1 **VS**

★***Suncliffe*** Burlington Rd ☎(0929) 423299
Closed Oct–Mar
Detached, brick gabled hotel in a quiet residential area.
14rm(1⇌5⋒)
CTV 14P 3 ✽
Last dinner 7.30pm

★**York** Cauldon Av ☎(0929) 422704
Closed mid Oct–19 Apr
Detached colour-washed hotel with a mansard roof, in a quiet location within walking distance of the sea front and facing tennis courts.
22rm(4⇌)(3fb) sB&B£10–£11.50 sB&B⇌£13.75–£15.25 dB&B£20–£23 dB&B⇌£23.75–£26.75
CTV 20P 4
V Tea 40p High Tea £2.50 Dinner £5 Last dinner 8pm

✕✕***Cobblers*** 4 Institute Rd ☎(0929) 423001
Lunch not served Dinner not served Mon & Tue in winter
42 seats Last dinner 11pm
Credit cards 1 3

✕***La Trattoria*** 12 High St ☎(0929) 423784
Closed 17 Oct–20 Nov & Sun, Mon, Tue from Nov–mid Mar
Italian **V** 40 seats Last dinner 11pm
Credit cards 1 2 3 5

SWANSEA
West Glamorgan
Map **3** SS69

☆☆☆☆**Dragon** Kingsway Circle (Trusthouse Forte) ☎(0792) 51074 Telex no 48309
A purpose-built, city-centre hotel.
118⇌ CTV in all bedrooms Ⓡ sB&B⇌£43 dB&B⇌£59 B
Lift ☾ CTV 40P CFA *xmas*
Last dinner 9.30pm
Credit cards 1 2 3 4 5

☆☆☆**Fforest Motel** Pontardulais Rd, Fforestfach (on A483 ¼m S of M4 junct 47) ☎(0792) 588711
Comfortable modern motel conveniently located close to M4.
18⇌ CTV in all bedrooms Ⓡ
☾ 180P Live music and dancing Sat
Mainly grills Last dinner 10.30pm
Credit cards 1 2 3 4 5

★★**Llwyn Helyg** Ffynone Rd, Ffynone ☎(0792) 465735
11rm(8⇌3⋒)(3fb) TV in all bedrooms *sB&B⇌⋒£17 dB&B⇌⋒£27
☾ CTV 15P
French **V** *Lunch £4&alc Dinner £6&alc Wine £4.10 Last dinner 9.30pm
Credit cards 1 3 **VS**

★*HB* **Windsor Lodge** Mount Pleasant ☎(0792) 42158 Closed 25 Dec
Comfortable small hotel, close to the city centre.
18rm(11⇌3⋒) CTV in all bedrooms Ⓡ sB&B£18.50 sB&B⇌⋒£25 dB&B£26 dB&B⇌⋒£32 B
20P sauna bath
V Lunch £4–£10 Tea £1–£3.50 Dinner £8–£12 Wine £4.20 Last dinner 9pm
Credit cards 1 2 3 **VS**

✕✕**Drangway** 66 Wind St ☎(0792) 461397
Popular city restaurant offering imaginative menus.
Closed Sun
English & French **V** 34 seats *Lunch £5.30–£11.25 Dinner £9.30–£11.30&alc Wine £4.95 Last dinner 10.15pm
Credit cards 1 2 3 5

✕✕***Oyster Perches*** Uplands Cres ☎(0792) 473173
Closed Mon Dinner not served Sun
54 seats Last dinner 10pm
Credit cards 1 2 3 4 5

✕**Riverside** 20 Castle St ☎(0792) 55210
Cantonese 40 seats *Lunch £6–£9alc Dinner £6–£9alc Wine £4 Last dinner mdnt

SWAY
Hampshire
Map **4** SZ29

★★★**White Rose** Station Rd (Exec Hotel) ☎Lymington (0590) 682754
Small, friendly family run hotel.
13rm(9⇌)(3fb) CTV in 11 bedrooms Ⓡ *sB&B£14–£16 sB&B⇌£18–£21.50 dB&B£28–£31 dB&B⇌£31–£35 B
Lift 50P ✽ *xmas*
English & French **V** *Lunch £5&alc Dinner £6&alc Wine £4 Last dinner 8.45pm
Credit cards 1 3 **VS**

SWINDON
Wiltshire
Map **4** SU18

S

★★★★*H* **Blunsdon House** Blunsdon (3m N off A419) (Best Western) ☎(0793) 721701 Telex no 444423
Friendly, family run hotel, with well appointed restaurant and separate carvery.
72rm(70⇌2⋒) (16fb) 5⊟ CTV in all bedrooms ® ✱sB&B⇌⋒ fr£33 dB&B⇌⋒ fr£40 ⊟
Lift ☾ 250P CFA ✽ ⌂ *xmas*
⊟English & French V ✿ ⊐ ✱Lunch £6.50&alc Dinner £6.95–£8&alc Wine £4.50 Last dinner 10pm
Credit cards 1 2 3 4 5 VS

☆☆☆**Crest** Oxford Rd, Stratton St Margaret (3m NE A420) (Crest) ☎(0793) 822921 Telex no 444456
A modern, pale brick building in a rural setting.
98⇌ CTV in all bedrooms ® ✱sB⇌ fr£34 dB⇌ fr£44 (room only) ⊟
☾ 150P ⌂ ♿
⊟English & International V ✿ ✱Lunch £5.50–£9.50 Tea 60p Dinner £8.95–£12.50&alc Wine £5.25 Last dinner 9.45pm
Credit cards 1 2 3 4 5 VS

★★★**Goddard Arms** High St, Old Town (Anchor) ☎(0793) 692313 Telex no 444764
Grey-tiled, creeper-clad inn in one of the old parts of town, with a modern motel in the grounds.
19⇌ Annexe: 47⇌ CTV in all bedrooms ® sB&B⇌⋒ £36–£38 dB&B⇌⋒ £42–£44 ⊟
☾ # CTV 100P CFA ♿
✿ ✱Lunch £6.50–£10 Tea 75p High Tea £4.50 Dinner £6.50–£10 Wine £4.80 Last dinner 9.45pm
Credit cards 1 2 3 4 5

☆☆☆**Post House** Marlborough Rd (Trusthouse Forte) ☎(0793) 24601 Telex no 444464
103⇌ (50fb) CTV in all bedrooms ® sB&B⇌ £42 dB&B⇌ £54 ⊟
☾ 200P CFA ✽ ⌒ (heated)
✿ ⊐ Last dinner 10pm
Credit cards 1 2 3 4 5

★★★**Wiltshire** Fleming Way (Kingsmead) ☎(0793) 28282 Telex 444250
Modern, purpose-built hotel situated close to the main shopping area.
85⇌⋒ (2fb) CTV in all bedrooms ® sB&B⇌ £37 dB&B⇌ £47 ⊟
Lift ☾ # CFA Live music and dancing Wed, Sat & Sun ⌂ *xmas* ♿
⊟English & French V ✿ ⊐ Lunch £4.95–£6.75&alc Tea 90p–£1.20 Dinner £6.75–£7.50&alc Wine £5.25 Last dinner 10.30pm
Credit cards 1 2 3 4 5

SYMONDS YAT (WEST) (nr Ross-on-Wye)
Hereford & Worcester
Map **3** SO51
★★**Wye Rapids** ☎(0600) 890366
Secluded and relaxing hotel standing high above the Wye Rapids.
16rm(4⇌2⋒) ✱sB&B£15 sB&B⇌⋒ £18 dB&B£22 dB&B⇌⋒ £27 ⊟
CTV 20P 10⌂ ✽ *xmas*
⊟English & French V ✿ ⊐ ✱Bar lunch 75p–£2.75 Tea 50p–£2 Dinner £7.50&alc Wine £3.65
Last dinner 8.15pm
Credit cards 1 3 5

TADDINGTON
Derbyshire
Map **7** SK17
✕✕**Waterloo** ☎(029885) 230
A roadside inn on the A6, 5m east of Buxton.
⊟English & French 150 seats Lunch £5.15–£10 Dinner £5.50–£12 Wine £4.50 Last dinner 8.30pm 70P
Credit cards 1 2 3

TAIN
Highland *Ross & Cromarty*
Map **14** NH68
★★★**Royal** High St ☎(0862) 2013
25rm(15⇌7⋒) CTV in all bedrooms ® ✱sB&B£14.50–£16 sB&B⇌⋒ £19–£21 dB&B£25–£32 dB&B⇌⋒ £25–£32
☾ 8P 6⌂
⊟Scottish & French V ✿ ⊐ ✱Lunch £10alc Dinner £10alc Wine £3 Last dinner 9.30pm
Credit cards 1 2 3 5 VS

★★**Mansfield** Scotsburn Rd ☎(0862) 2052
Imposing mansion with some recently built modern rooms. Located on the western fringe of town.
21rm(15⇌⋒) (2fb) CTV in all bedrooms ® ✱sB&B£14–£15 sB&B⇌⋒ £18–£19.50 dB&B£24 dB&B⇌⋒ £32–£34
☾ CTV 50P ✽
✿ ⊐ ✱Bar lunch £2–£5 Tea 60p–70p Dinner £5.50–£6 Wine £5.50 Last dinner 9pm

TALLADALE
Highland *Ross & Cromarty*
Map **14** NG97
★*H* **Loch Maree** ☎Lochmaree (044589) 200
Closed Nov–Apr RS Oct
A traditional Highland fishing hotel with a reputation for hospitality and good home cooking.
15rm ✱sB&B£18–£20 dB&B£35–£41
12P 4⌂
V ✿ ⊐ ✱Lunch £4–£4.50 Tea 33p–75p Dinner £7–£7.50 Wine £3.35 Last dinner 8pm
S%

TALLAND BAY
Cornwall
Map **2** SX25
★★★*L* **Talland Bay** (Inter-Hotels) ☎Polperro (0503) 72667
Closed 15 Dec–1 Feb
Well-appointed hotel in a secluded position with good views and access to beach.
18rm(16⇌) Annexe: 2⇌ 1⊟ CTV in all bedrooms sB&B£15.15–£24.20 sB&B⇌ £17.15–£31.90 dB&B£30.30–£41.80 dB&B⇌ £34.30–£63.80 ⊟
20P ✽ ⌒ (heated) ⌂ →

T

English & French V Lunch £4.35–£4.85&alc Tea £1.50–£1.85 High Tea £2.85–£3.25 Dinner £7.75–£8.55&alc Last dinner 9pm

Credit cards 1 2 3 5

TALSARNAU
Gwynedd
Map **6** SH63

★★ **Maes y Neuadd** (2m SE on unclass rd off B4573) Harlech (0766) 780200

The original wing of this country house was built in the 14th century, and Cromwell is said to have visited here.

12rm(10 1) CTV in all bedrooms sB&B £16.50–£27 dB&B £33–£44

50P nc7yrs *xmas*

English & French Bar lunch £3.25alc Tea £1alc Dinner £9.25alc Wine £4.50 Last dinner 9pm

Credit cards 1 2 3 **VS**

TAL-Y-BONT
Gwynedd
Map **6** SH76

☆☆ **Lodge** (Inter-Hotels) Dolgarrog (049 269) 534 Closed Xmas Day–2 Jan

(Rosette awarded for dinner only) Single-storey accommodation is available behind the main hotel facilities, in this quiet Conwy valley village.

10 CTV in all bedrooms Ⓡ sB&B £17.50–£21.50 dB&B £27.50–£32.50

30P

British & French V Lunch £4.75–£7.50&alc Tea £1–£1.50&alc Dinner £6–£8.95&alc Wine £3.50 Last dinner 9.30pm

S% Credit cards 1 2 3 5 **VS**

TAL-Y-LLYN
Gwynedd
Map **6** SH70

★★ **Tynycornel** Abergynolwyn (065 477) 282 Closed Xmas & Jan RS Dec

Delightful lakeside hotel where most rooms have beautiful views.

4rm(2) Annexe: 12rm(11 3) Ⓡ sB&B £16–£22 sB&B £18–£22

dB&B £36–£44 dB&B £36–£44

60P 3 sauna bath

English & Continental Bar lunch 70p–£1.90 Tea 55p–£1.20 Dinner £7.50–£8&alc Wine £4 Last dinner 9.30pm

Credit cards 1 3 **VS**

★ *HB* **Minffordd** Corris (065 473) 665 Closed Jan RS Nov–Dec & Feb–Mar

Small, welcoming 350-year-old coaching inn at the foot of Cader Idris.

7rm(3 2) (1fb) Ⓡ sB&B £13–£19 sB&B £15–£21 dB&B £22–£34 dB&B £26–£38

12P nc3yrs

Dinner £9 Wine £3.95 Last dinner 8.30pm

TAMWORTH
Staffordshire
Map **4** SK20

★★ **Castle** Ladybank (0827) 57181

24 (2fb) TV in 17 bedrooms Ⓡ sB&B £24.50 dB&B £32.50

CTV CFA Disco 6 nights wkly *xmas*

V Bar lunch 60p–£2.95 Tea 50p Dinner £4.95–£8.95&alc Wine £5.25 Last dinner 10pm

Credit cards 1 2 3 5

✕✕ **Kealeys** 36 Market St (0827) 55444

Closed Sun & Mon

English & French V 36 seats Lunch £1.95–£3.50 Dinner £8.95–£9.50&alc Wine £3.50 Last dinner 10pm

Credit cards 1 2 3 5

TANGMERE
West Sussex
Map **4** SU90

✕ ***Old Timbers*** Arundel Rd Chichester (0243) 773294

Wholesome, spicy, simple fare is offered at this 18th century timbered cottage restaurant.

Closed Sun, Tue, 1wk Apr & 2wks Oct

English & French 80 seats Last dinner 10pm (winter) & 10.30pm (summer) 50P

Credit card 3

TARBERT Harris, Isle of,
Western Isles *Inverness-shire*
Map **13** NB10

★★ **Harris** Harris (0859) 2154

Closed mid Oct–mid Mar

26rm(12 2) (2fb) sB&B £12.15 sB&B £15.15 dB&B £23 dB&B £28

CTV 25P

V Lunch £4.50–£6 Tea £1–£1.50 Dinner £6–£6.80 Last dinner 8pm

VS

TARBERT Loch Fyne
Strathclyde *Argyllshire*
Map **10** NR86

★★★ ***Stonefield Castle*** (08802) 207

Closed Oct–Mar

Stone castle in 100 acres of wooded grounds surrounded by hills and overlooking Loch Fyne.

34rm(28 4) Ⓡ

Lift CTV 50P (heated) (hard) sauna bath

V Last dinner 9pm

Credit cards 1 2 3 4 5

★★ **Bruce** Harbour St (08802) 577

A modern town-centre hotel.

11rm(2 9) (1fb) TV available Ⓡ sB&B fr£13.50 dB&B fr£25

CTV 5P Live music and dancing Sat

Bar lunch £3alc Tea 75p alc High Tea £3.50alc Dinner £7.50alc Wine £4.75 Last dinner 9.30pm

Credit cards 1 2 3 5 **VS**

★ **West Loch** (08802) 283

Closed Nov

(Rosette awarded for dinner only.)

White-painted coaching inn providing simple accommodation and excellent food.

6rm (2fb) sB&B £16.50 dB&B £24

CTV 20P

T

🍽 International V ☕ Lunch £5alc Tea £1.25alc High Tea £2.75alc Dinner £10.50 Wine £4 Last dinner 8.30pm

TARPORLEY
Cheshire
Map **7** SJ56

★★**Swan** 50 High St ☎(08293) 2411
RS Xmas Day

Formerly Georgian coaching house. A friendly, unpretentious hotel.

9rm (1fb) TV in all bedrooms Ⓡ sB&B£18 dB&B£30
CTV 50P
V ☕ Lunch £6&alc Dinner £7&alc Wine £4.20 Last dinner 9.15pm
Credit cards [1] [2] [3] [5]

★★**B Willington Hall** (3m NW off unclass rd linking A51 and A54) ☎Kelsall (0829) 52321
Closed Xmas Day RS Mon
5🛁 CTV in all bedrooms Ⓡ sB&B🛁£23 dB&B🛁£36
60P ✱ (hard)
Lunch £8.50alc Dinner £8.50 Wine £3.80 Last dinner 9.30pm
Credit cards [1] [2] [3] [5] VS

TAUNTON
Somerset
Map **3** ST22

★★★★**H Castle** Castle Green (Prestige) ☎(0823) 72671 Telex no 46488

Impressive, stone turreted castle, parts of which are medieval.

40🛁 (1fb) 5 CTV in all bedrooms sB🛁£40–£49.50 dB🛁🚿£65–£77 (room only) B
Lift ☾ 35P 10 CFA *xmas*
☕ Lunch £6.20–£7.90&alc Tea 70p Dinner £12.90&alc Last dinner 9pm
Credit cards [1] [2] [3] [4] [5]

★★★**County** East St (Trusthouse Forte) ☎(0823) 87651 Telex no 46484

Former coaching inn with modern facilities.

72rm (60🛁) (2fb) CTV in all bedrooms Ⓡ sB&B£29.50 sB&B🛁£35.50 dB&B£42 dB&B🛁£50 B
Lift ☾ CTV 100P 8 CFA
☕ Last dinner 9.30pm
Credit cards [1] [2] [3] [4] [5]

★★**Corner House** Park St ☎(0823) 84683

Privately owned and run holiday hotel in a central situation.

22rm (5🛁) (4fb) CTV in all bedrooms Ⓡ sB&B£17.25 sB&B🛁£21.25 dB&B£29.90 dB&B🛁£33.90
CTV 32P 2
🍽 English & French V Lunch £5alc Dinner £8alc Wine £4.50 Last dinner 9.45pm
Credit cards [1] [2] [3] [5]

★★**Creech Castle** Bathpool (on A38) ☎(0823) 73512 Closed Xmas

Touring and business hotel with a busy bar, close to the M5.

19rm (2🛁18🚿) Annexe: 9rm (1🛁7🚿) (1fb) TV in all bedrooms Ⓡ sB&B£15.84 sB&B🛁🚿£19.91 dB&B🛁🚿£29.70 B
200P Disco Mon–Sat
🍽 English & Continental V ☕ Lunch £2–£3.50 Tea fr30p High Tea £1 Dinner £4.90alc Wine £4.50 Last dinner 9.45pm
S% Credit cards [1] [2] [3] [5]

★★**Falcon** Henlade (3m E A358) (Exec Hotel) ☎(0823) 442502
Closed 24 Dec–15 Jan

Small, informal hotel with comfortable, well appointed bedrooms with easy access to the motorway.

9rm (6🛁2🚿) CTV in all bedrooms Ⓡ sB&B🛁£22.50 dB&B🛁£35 B
CTV 25P ✱ nc5yrs
☕ Bar lunch £3.50alc Tea £1alc Dinner £7.25alc Wine £3.30 Last dinner 9pm
Credit cards [1] [3]

★★**Heatherton Grange** Wellington Rd, Bradford-on-Tone (3m SW off A38) ☎Bradford-on-Tone (042346) 777

A privately owned and run 18th-century former coaching inn with a friendly and lively atmosphere.

18rm (1🛁3🚿) (3fb) CTV in all bedrooms Ⓡ ✱ sB&B£16.68 sB&B🛁🚿£16.68 dB&B£26.45 dB&B🛁🚿£27.60 B
CTV 160P *xmas*
🍽 Mainly grills V ☕ ✱ Lunch £4.95–£6.25&alc Tea fr£1 Dinner £6.25–£7.25&alc Wine £3.60 Last dinner 10pm
Credit cards [1] [2] [3] [4] [5]

★★**St Quintin** Bridgwater Rd, Bathpool ☎(0823) 73016

Small, comfortable holiday hotel, family owned, with friendly atmosphere.

6rm Annexe: 4rm (2fb) TV in all bedrooms Ⓡ sB&B£16.75–£18.50 dB&B£29.50–£33.50 B
CTV 30P ✱
V ☕ Lunch £2.50–£4.50&alc Tea 60p–£1&alc Dinner £3.50–£6.50&alc
Credit cards [1] [2] [3] [5] VS

See advert on page 618

✕✕**Quorum** 148 East Reach ☎(0823) 88876

Lunch by reservation only.

Closed Sun & Public hols
V 50 seats Lunch £5.95&alc Dinner £10alc Wine £4.30 Last dinner 10.30pm
Credit cards [1] [2] [3] [5] VS

TAVISTOCK
Devon
Map **2** SX47

★★★**Bedford** Plymouth Rd (Trusthouse Forte) ☎(0822) 3221

Family hotel, parts of which date from the 15th century, offering modern amenities.

32rm (30🛁2🚿) CTV in all bedrooms Ⓡ sB&B🛁🚿£35.50 dB&B🛁🚿£52.50 B
12 ✱ *xmas*
☕ Last dinner 9pm
Credit cards [1] [2] [3] [4] [5]

✕**Graham's** 67 West St ☎(0822) 66520
Closed Sun & 2wks Jan
V 24 seats Dinner £7.50alc Wine £4.50 Last dinner 9.15pm

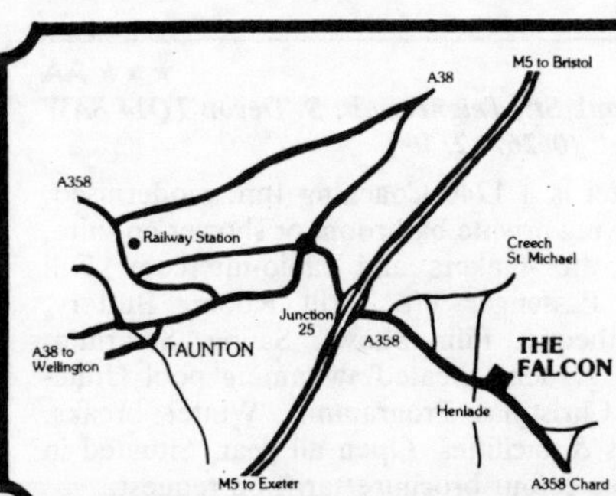

A38
M5 to Bristol
A358
Railway Station
Creech St. Michael
Junction 25
A358
A38 to Wellington
TAUNTON
THE FALCON
Henlade
M5 to Exeter
A358 Chard

TAYNUILT
Strathclyde *Argyllshire*
Map **10** NN03

★ ***Netherlorn*** Bridge of Awe ☎ (08662) 243
A modern, family-run hotel.
26rm(15🛁) Ⓡ
CTV 40P ✽
V ☕ Last dinner 8pm
Credit card 1

★ **Polfearn** ☎ (08662) 251
Closed Oct–Apr
Family-run, small, granite hotel with gardens and a grazing field at the front.
14rm(1🚿)(2fb) CTV in all bedrooms Ⓡ sB&B£9–£11 dB&B£18–£22
CTV 20P ✽ nc5yrs
V ☕ Bar lunch £3alc Tea £80p alc High Tea £3 Dinner £5.50 Wine £3.50 Last dinner 9.30pm
VS

TEBAY (WEST SERVICE AREA)
(M6 Motorway) Cumbria
Map **12** NY60

☆☆ **Tebay Mountain Lodge** ☎ Orton (05874) 351
Closed Nov–Feb
There are good views of the Cumbrian mountains, from this hotel which lies between the Lake District and the Yorkshire Dales.
30🛁🚿(10fb) CTV in all bedrooms Ⓡ sB&B🛁🚿£23–£25.50 dB🛁🚿£33–£37
Continental breakfast
☾ 40P
English & French V ☕ Lunch £1.50–£3&alc Tea £1.50&alc High Tea £1.50–£2.50 Dinner £4–£5.75&alc Wine £3.95 Last dinner 9.30pm
Credit cards 1 2 3 5 **VS**

TEDBURN ST MARY
Devon
Map **3** SX89

★★ **King's Arms Inn** ☎ (06476) 224
Closed Xmas
Pleasant village-centre inn with a congenial atmosphere and a popular bar. It is conveniently located for the A30.
7rm(1🛁)(1fb) CTV in 5 bedrooms Ⓡ sB&B£10.50 dB&B£17.50 dB&B🛁£21.50
CTV 50P 2 ✽
V ☕ Lunch £4.35 Dinner £6.60alc Wine £4.20 Last dinner 9.15pm

TEES-SIDE AIRPORT
Co Durham
Map **8** NZ31

★★★ **St George** Middleton St George (Mount Charlotte) ☎ Darlington (0325) 332631
Modern hotel within airport complex.
58🛁(1fb) CTV in all bedrooms Ⓡ sB&B🛁£28.50 dB&B🛁£37
☾ 100P CFA squash sauna bath Live music and dancing twice wkly
☕ Lunch £4.95–£5&alc Dinner £8–£8.25&alc Wine £4.50 Last dinner 9.45pm
Credit cards 1 2 3 5

TEIGNMOUTH
Devon
Map **3** SX97

★★★ **London** Bank St ☎ (06267) 2776
Well modernised coaching inn with lovely setting. Rooftop swimming pool.
26rm(20🛁6🚿)(9fb) CTV in all bedrooms Ⓡ sB&B🛁🚿£15–£22 dB&B🛁🚿£24–£36
Lift ☾ CTV 10P CFA (heated) sauna bath Disco twice wkly Live music and dancing twice wkly *xmas*
English & French V ☕ Lunch £4–£5&alc Tea 70p–£1&alc High Tea £2.50–£4&alc Dinner £7–£8&alc Wine £3.50 Last dinner 10.30pm
Credit cards 1 3 **VS**

★★ **Glendaragh** Barn Park Rd ☎ (06267) 2881 Closed Nov–Jan
19th century manor house, close to sea front.

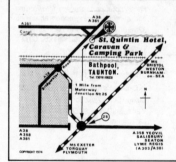

T

10rm(8⇌)(2fb)CTV in all bedrooms ® sB&B£14.38–£16.10 dB&B⇌£21.85–£23 B
10P 2🚗 ⇎ ✽
Wine £3.50 Last dinner 8pm
Credit cards 1 3 VS

★★ H **Venn Farm Country House** Higher Exeter Rd (Best Western) ☎(06267) 2196
Peaceful countryside surrounds this Devon farmhouse.
10rm(8⇌2⋔)(2fb) CTV in all bedrooms ® ✱ sB&B£19–£22 sB&B⇌⋔£20–£25 dB&B£32–£38 dB&B⇌⋔£36–£40 B
50P ⇎ ✽
V ♔ ✱ Lunch fr£6&alc Dinner fr£8&alc Wine £5 Last dinner 8.45pm
Credit cards 1 2 3 5

★**Bay** Sea Front ☎(06267) 4123
Closed Nov–mid Apr
20rm(5⇌5⋔)(4fb) CTV in all bedrooms sB&B£10–£13 sB&B⇌⋔£13–£14 dB&B£20–£26 dB&B⇌⋔£26–£28 B
15P
V ♔ ☐ Lunch £3 Tea £1.50 Dinner £4–£5 Wine £2.50 Last dinner 7.30pm
Credit cards 1 2 3 5 VS

★***Belvedere*** Barnpark Rd ☎(06267) 4561
Four-storey, detached building, dating from 1850, set in a quiet position.
15rm(1⇌1⋔) ® B
CTV 10P 1🚗 ⇎
Last dinner 7.30pm
Credit card 1 VS

★**Glenside** Ringmoor Rd, Shaldon (1m S off A379) (Minotel) ☎Shaldon (062687) 2448
10rm(2⇌4⋔)(4fb) CTV in all bedrooms ® sB&B£8–£10 sB&B⇌⋔£10–£12 dB&B£16–£20 dB&B⇌⋔£19–£23 B
10P ⇎
▣ English & French V Dinner £5.50&alc Wine £4.50 Last dinner 6pm
Credit cards 1 3 4

✕✕**Minadab** 60 Dawlish Rd ☎(06267) 2044
Thatched cottage of the early 1800s, on the main Dawlish/Teignmouth road.
Closed Sun
▣ French & Italian 30 seats ✱ Dinner £7.75–£10&alc Wine £4.15 Last dinner 10pm 7P bedroom available ⍻
Credit cards 1 2 3 5 VS

TELFORD
Shropshire
Map **7** SJ60

★★★ B **Buckatree Hall** Ercall Ln, Wellington ☎(0952) 51821
Large, gabled house standing in attractive and well-tended grounds at the foot of the Wrekin.
25⇌ CTV in all bedrooms ® sB&B⇌ fr£29.50 dB&B⇌ fr£36 B
☾ 110P ✽ *xmas*
▣ English & French ♔ ☐ Lunch fr£6.50 Dinner fr£6.50 Last dinner 10pm
Credit cards 1 2 3 5 VS

☆☆☆ B **Telford Hotel Golf & Country Club** Great Hay, Sutton Hill ☎(0952) 585642 Telex no 35481
58rm(56⇌)(2fb) CTV in all bedrooms ® sB&B⇌£29.50–£33 dB&B⇌£37.50–£43.50 B
☾ 150P ⊡(heated) ⚑ squash billiards sauna bath
▣ International V Lunch £6.45&alc Dinner £7.15&alc Wine £5.45 Last dinner 9.45pm
Credit cards 1 2 3 5

★★**Charlton Arms** Wellington (Greenall Whitley) ☎(0952) 51351 Telex no 629462
Closed 25 Dec–1 Jan RS Public Hols
27rm(22⇌1⋔)(1fb) CTV in all bedrooms ® sB&B£22–£23 sB&B⇌£26.95–£27.95 dB&B£30.80–£31.80 dB&B⇌£39.60–£40.60 B
☾ 130P
♔ ☐ Lunch fr£5&alc Dinner fr£6.50&alc Wine £5.25 Last dinner 9.30pm
Credit cards 1 2 3 5

★★**Falcon** Holyhead Rd, Wellington ☎(0952) 55011 Closed Xmas
14rm(3⋔)(1fb) ✱ sB&B fr£14 sB&B⇌⋔ fr£16 dB&B fr£18.50 dB&B⇌⋔ fr£21
CTV 35P nc3yrs
V ✱ Bar lunch £1.40–£3.85 Dinner £6.50alc Wine £3.60 Last dinner 9pm

★**White House** Wellington Rd, Donnington (off A518) ☎(0952) 604276
10rm(4fb) CTV available in bedrooms sB&B£14.50 dB&B£19.50
CTV 100P ⇎ ✽
▣ English & French ♔ Lunch £4.75–£6 Dinner £8alc Wine £3.75 Last dinner 9pm
Credit card 1 VS

TEMPLE SOWERBY
Cumbria
Map **12** NY62

★★ BL **Temple Sowerby House** ☎Kirkby Thore (0930) 61578
Closed Jan & Feb
8rm(6⋔)(1fb) 2▭ sB&B£16 sB&B⇌£18–£20 dB&B£32 dB&B⇌£36–£40 B
CTV 12P ⇎ ✽ nc5yrs
♔ Dinner £11–£12 Wine £3.50 Last dinner 8pm
Credit cards 1 3
See advert on page 620

TENBURY WELLS
Hereford & Worcester
Map **7** SO56

★**Royal Oak** ☎(0584) 810417
Timber framed building dating from the 16th century, situated in the centre of the town.
6rm(1fb) ® ✱ sB&B£10 dB&B£20
CTV 100P
♔ ✱ Lunch 60p–£5 Dinner £6.20 Wine £3.90 Last dinner 9.45pm

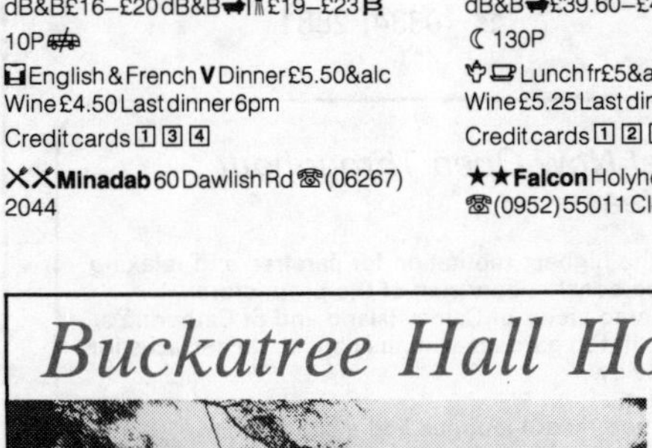

TENBY
Dyfed
Map **2** SN10

★★★ ***Imperial*** The Paragon (Best Western) ☎(0834) 3737
Closed Jan & Feb
Traditional seaside hotel with historic perimeter walls.
48rm(38⇌8⋔) CTV in all bedrooms B →

T

Lift ☾ 16P 16⛟ CFA ⛳(hard) ♪ Live music and dancing wkly Live music Thu ⌂

🍴English & French **V** ⛭ ☕ Last dinner 9.30pm

Credit cards 1 2 3 4 5

★★***H*** **Atlantic** Esplanade ☎(0834) 2881

Comfortable seaside hotel with friendly service and good food.

33rm(24⇌5⋔) CTV in all bedrooms Ⓡ B

CTV 28P CFA ⛟ ✽ ♪

🍴French ⛭ ☕ Last dinner 9.15pm

Credit cards 1 2 3 5 **VS**

★★**Fourcroft** The Croft ☎(0834) 2516

Closed Nov–19 Apr

Well-equipped hotel with a relaxed atmosphere, overlooking the harbour.

38rm(34⇌4⋔) (10fb) CTV in all bedrooms Ⓡ sB&B⇌⋔ £14–£16.50 dB&B⇌⋔ £25–£30

Lift CTV ✽ ⌂

🍴Welsh & International **V** ⛭ ☕ Bar lunch 75p–£3.50 Tea 50p–60p Dinner £7–£8.50 Last dinner 8.30pm

Credit cards 1 3

★★**Royal Lion** ☎(0834) 2127

Closed Nov–Mar

36rm(14⇌1⋔) (10fb) CTV in 6 bedrooms TV in 30 bedrooms Ⓡ sB&B£12–£18 sB&B⇌⋔ £14–£20 dB&B£24–£40 dB&B⇌⋔ £26–£42 B

Lift CTV 4P ⌂

V ⛭ Lunch £2–£4&alc Dinner £7&alc

Credit cards 1 3

★**Buckingham** Esplanade (Minotel) ☎(0834) 2622 Closed Dec–Feb

Friendly holiday hotel overlooking the beach and Caldey Island.

23rm(11⇌1⋔) (1fb) CTV in 8 bedrooms Ⓡ sB&B£11–£13 sB&B⇌⋔ £13–£15 dB&B£22–£26 dB&B⇌⋔ £26–£34 B

CTV **P** ⛟

🍴British & Continental ⛭ ☕ Bar lunch 95p–£2 Tea 90p Dinner fr£6.75 Wine £3.85 Last dinner 8pm

Credit cards 1 2 3 5

★**Croft** ☎(0834) 2576

Closed Nov–Mar

Traditional, informal, holiday hotel overlooking the harbour.

20rm(10⇌) (3fb) Ⓡ sB&B£10–£10.50 dB&B£20–£21 dB&B⇌ £23–£24

CTV 5P

⛭ ☕ Tea fr50p High Tea fr£1.50 Dinner fr£6 Last dinner 7.30pm

Credit cards 1 2 3 **VS**

★**Harbour Heights** 11, The Croft ☎(0834) 2132

Closed Nov–Etr

Small comfortable hotel overlooking Carmarthen Bay and Tenby Harbour, offering commendable food standards.

10rm(7⇌) CTV in all bedrooms Ⓡ ★ *sB&B fr£11.50 sB&B⇌ fr£14 dB&B fr£23 dB&B⇌ fr£28 B

⛭ ☕ *Lunch fr£4 Dinner fr£5 Last dinner 8pm

Credit cards 1 2 3

TENTERDEN

Kent

Map **5** TQ83

★★**White Lion** High St ☎(05806) 2921

Comfortable hotel with modern bedrooms and popular bar and restaurant.

12rm(8⇌) 3⛶ CTV in 2 bedrooms sB&B£17.25–£19.25 sB&B⇌ £24.75–£26 dB&B£26.50–£28 dB&B⇌ £32.25–£34 B

CTV 45P *xmas*

🍴English, French & Italian **V** ⛭ Lunch £5.25–£6.50&alc Dinner £6.95–£7.50&alc Last dinner 9.30pm

Credit cards 1 2 3 5

TETBURY

Gloucestershire

Map **3** ST89

See also **Westonbirt**

★★★***H*** **Close** 8 Long St (Prestige) ☎(0666) 52272 Telex no 43232 (ref CLH)

Closed 27 Dec–5 Jan →

A 16th-century wool merchant's house with a walled garden, offering comfortable bedrooms and good service.

11rm(10⇌1⋒)(2fb) 1⊟ CTV in all bedrooms Ⓡ ✱ sB&B⇌⋒ £26–£36 dB&B⇌⋒ £44–£65 Continental breakfast Ⓑ

15P *xmas*

French ✿ ☐ Last dinner 9.45pm

Credit cards 1 2 3 5 **VS**

★★★**Snooty Fox** Market Pl ☎(0666) 52436

Traditional, market-square hotel with good bedroom facilities and attentive service.

12rm(11⇌1⋒)(2fb) 2⊟ CTV in all bedrooms Ⓡ ✱ sB&B⇌⋒ £22.50 dB&B⇌⋒ £39.50 Ⓑ

xmas

English & French ✿ ✱ Lunch fr£6 Dinner £12alc Wine £4.45 Last dinner 9.45pm

Credit cards 1 2 3 5

✕**Hubbits** 7 New Church St ☎(0666) 53306

Small, personally-run, restaurant.

Closed Mon, 1st wk Jan & last wk Dec Lunch not served Tue–Fri Dinner not served Sun

V 28 seats Lunch £4.95–£5.50 Dinner £7.95–£10.75 Wine £4.25 Last dinner 9.30pm

Credit cards 1 2 3 **VS**

TETFORD

Lincolnshire
Map **8** TF37

★ ***White Hart*** ☎(065 883) 255

6rm TV in 1 bedrooms Ⓡ ✱ Ⓑ

CTV 60P 3 ✿

French **V** Last dinner 9pm

Credit cards 1 2 3

TEWKESBURY

Gloucestershire
Map **3** SO83

★★★**Bell** Church St ☎(0684) 293293

Comfortable, traditional hotel dating from Elizabethan times with well appointed bedrooms and attractive new restaurant.

25⇌(2fb) 2⊟ CTV in all bedrooms Ⓡ sB&B⇌ £21–£33 dB&B⇌ £25–£44 Ⓑ

☾ CTV 70P 20 CFA *xmas*

Mainly grills **V** ✿ ☐ Lunch £4–£6.25&alc Tea £2–£3 High Tea £4 Dinner £7.25–£7.95&alc Wine £4 Last dinner 6pm

Credit cards 1 2 3 4 5 **VS**

★★★**Royal Hop Pole Crest** Church St (Crest) ☎(0684) 293236

Attractive hotel with comfortable bedrooms and courtyard garden.

29rm(25⇌4⋒) CTV in all bedrooms Ⓡ ✱ sB⇌⋒ fr£31 dB⇌⋒ fr£42 (room only) Ⓑ

☾ 40P CFA

International **V** ✿ ☐ ✱ Lunch £5.75&alc Dinner £8.25&alc Last dinner 9.30pm

Credit cards 1 2 3 4 5 **VS**

☆☆☆***B*** **Tewkesbury Park Golf & Country Club** Lincoln Green Ln (Inter-Hotels) ☎(0684) 295405 Telex no 43563

Modern comfortable hotel with extensive leisure facilities.

52⇌⋒ (4fb) CTV in all bedrooms Ⓡ sB&B⇌⋒ £28–£29.50 dB&B⇌⋒ £38–£40 Ⓑ

☾ CTV 200P CFA ✿ (heated) 18 squash billiards sauna bath Disco wkly Live music and dancing wkly *xmas*

✿ Lunch £5.95–£6.45 Dinner £7.10–£7.70&alc Wine £4.10

Credit cards 1 2 3 5 **VS**

★***B*** **Tudor House** High St ☎(0684) 297755

Historic Tudor building with fine staircase and especially comfortable bedrooms.

8rm(3⇌1⋒)(1fb) 1⊟ CTV in all bedrooms Ⓡ sB&B£20 sB&B£24 dB&B£32 dB&B⇌⋒ £36 Ⓑ

✿ ☐ Lunch £5.95 Tea 60p–95p Dinner £5.95&alc Wine £3.55 Last dinner 9.15pm

Credit cards 1 3 5

T

THAKEHAM (nr Storrington)
West Sussex
Map **4** TQ11

★★★ **BL Little Thakeham** Merrywood Ln ☎ Storrington (09066) 4416
Closed Xmas
Tastefully decorated Edwardian manor house featuring English cuisine set in spacious orchard and gardens.
8rm(7⇌1⋒) CTV in all bedrooms ★
sB&B⇌⋒ fr£51.40 dB&B⇌⋒ fr£67.50
30P ✽ ≋(heated) 𝒫(grass)
V Lunch £15alc Dinner £15alc Wine £5.50
Last dinner 9.30pm
Credit cards 1 2 3 5

★★ ***Abingworth Hall*** ☎ West Chiltington (07983) 2257
A delightful country hotel, standing in its own grounds on the Sussex Downs, by the side of a natural lake.
26rm(12⇌1⋒) ® B
CTV 50P 2🚗 ✽ ≋(heated) 𝒫(hard) ⤴ U billiards ♿
English, American & Continental **V**
Last dinner 9pm
Credit cards 1 2 3

THAME
Oxfordshire
Map **4** SP70

★★★ ***H Spread Eagle*** Cornmarket (Best Western) ☎ (084 421) 3661
A very special hotel with warm hospitality and modern bedrooms.
29rm(16⇌⋒) ★ B
☾ CTV 80P Disco wkly Live music and dancing mthly
French Last dinner 9.30pm
Credit cards 1 3

THETFORD
Norfolk
Map **5** TL88

★★★ ***HBL* Bell** King St (Trusthouse Forte) ☎ (0842) 4455
Originally a 15th-century coaching house, this elegantly restored hotel has always occupied a central place in the town's life. The friendly welcome by the staff and the comfortable bedrooms with their many thoughtful touches make this an extremely pleasant hotel of much historic interest.
42⇌ CTV in all bedrooms ® sB&B⇌£45 dB&B⇌£65 B
☾ 65P *xmas*
Last dinner 9.15pm
Credit cards 1 2 3 4 5

★★ **Historical Thomas Paine** White Hart St ☎ (0842) 5631
Partly Georgian hotel, reputed to be the birthplace of Thomas Paine, a famous son of Thetford.
14rm(7⇌7⋒) CTV in all bedrooms ®
✽sB&B fr£21.95 sB&B⇌⋒ fr£23.95

dB&B⇌⋒ fr£33.95 B
33P *xmas*
✽Lunch fr£4.95&alc Dinner fr£7.50&alc Wine £4.10 Last dinner 9.30pm
Credit cards 1 2 3 5

THIRLSPOT
Cumbria
Map **11** NY31

★★ ***Kings Head*** ☎ Keswick (0596) 72393
RS Nov–Mar
13rm(5⇌2⋒) ®
CTV 60P
Last dinner 8.30pm

THIRSK
North Yorkshire
Map **8** SE48

★★ **Golden Fleece** Market Pl (Trusthouse Forte) ☎ (0845) 23108
Three-storey coaching inn in the market square.
22rm(6⇌) CTV in all bedrooms ®
sB&B£33 sB&B⇌£35 dB&B£43 dB&B⇌£49.50 B
50P 2🚗 *xmas*
Last dinner 9pm
Credit cards 1 2 3 4 5 **VS**

★★ **Three Tuns** Market Pl ☎ (0845) 23124
A three-storey coaching inn situated in the market square.
12rm(7⇌) (3fb) CTV in all bedrooms ®
sB&B£22.50–£25 sB&B⇌⋒ £24.50–£27.50 dB&B£30–£33 dB&B⇌⋒ £32–£35 B
☾ 20P 2🚗 *xmas*
English & Continental **V** Lunch £5.25–£5.75 Dinner £7.50alc Wine £4.75
Last dinner 9.30pm
Credit cards 1 2 3 5

THORNBURY
Avon
Map **3** ST69

★★★

✿★★★ **THORNBURY CASTLE, THORNBURY**
(Prestige) ☎ (0454) 412647 Telex no 449986
Closed Xmas

In the early 16th century this manor was converted to a castle but since then part had fallen to picturesque ruin. It was bought by Kenneth Bell – only the fifth owner – and converted to a notable restaurant some years ago. The planting of a flourishing vineyard reflects his great interest in wine and also adds to the medieval atmosphere of the castle and grounds with its walled garden. Last year he added to the amenities by converting some of the rooms to bedrooms and it has now become a very well run hotel. The rooms have been most attractively decorated with locally made furniture and lovely soft furnishings. They are well equipped and thoughtful touches include flowers, fruit, books and hair dryers. They are very relaxing. The other public areas are suitably baronial and appropriately decorated, having antique furniture. There is a cosy little sitting room with open fire in season.
The panelled restaurant is also striking with improved table appointments, and it provides a fitting setting for Mr Bell's food.

Traditional in approach, eclectic in choice, and cooked with skill, it is hearty and enjoyable with something to appeal to everyone. With wine from the long and interesting list to complement your choice from the à la carte menu you will be very pleased. Friendly staff offer cheerful hospitality and that, too, contributes to the feeling of well being that Mr Bell is so insistent upon.
10⇌ CTV in all bedrooms ★
sB&B⇌£40–£48 dB&B⇌£55–£110
Continental breakfast
36P ✽ nc12yrs
Continental Lunch fr£15.50 Dinner £18.50alc Wine £6 Last dinner 9.30pm
S% Credit cards 1 2 3 4 5
See advert on page 624

THORNE
South Yorkshire
Map **8** SE61

★★ **Belmont** Horsefair Green ☎ (0405) 812320 Closed 24 Dec–3 Jan
Conversion of a detached house, near the town centre and the M18 Motorway.
26rm(8⇌) (2fb) sB&B£14 sB&B⇌£19.50 dB&B£25 dB&B⇌£28
CTV 30P ♿ →

V Lunch £5.50&alc Tea 75p Dinner £5.50&alc Wine £4 Last dinner 8pm
VS

THORNHILL
Dumfries & Galloway *Dumfriesshire*
Map **11** NX89

★★**Buccleuch & Queensberry** (0848) 30215
Red sandstone country-town hotel dating from 1858 with main road location.
11rm(3 1) (2fb) Ⓡ sB&B£9–£13 sB&B £11–£15 dB&B£18–£23 dB&B £20–£26 B
CTV 25P 4
V Bar lunch £2.60alc Tea 50p–£1.85 High Tea £4alc Dinner £7.75alc Wine £4
Last dinner 8pm
S% Credit cards 1 3 **VS**

★★**Trigony House** Closeburn (2m S off A76) Closeburn (08484) 211
Nicely appointed hotel in secluded grounds.
6rm(1 2) Annexe: 3rm Ⓡ sB&B£13–£17.50 sB&B £20.50–£24 dB&B£24 dB&B £27.50–£33 B
CTV 30P 2
Lunch £4.50–£7 Dinner £6–£6.50&alc Wine £4.20 Last dinner 8.45pm
VS

THORNTHWAITE
Cumbria
Map **11** NY22

★★**Swan** Braithwaite (059682) 256
Closed Nov–19 Apr
A 17th-century coaching inn amid fine mountain scenery overlooking Lake Bassenthwaite with Skiddaw in the background.
15rm(3 3) *sB&B£10.35–£12.05 sB&B £12.20–£16.10 dB&B£20.70–£24.10 dB&B £24.20–£32.20 B
CTV 60P 3
English & Continental Lunch £5alc Tea £1 Dinner £8–£9.25&alc Wine £3.50 Last dinner 8.30pm
S%

★★**Thwaite Howe** Braithwaite (059682) 281 Closed 3 Nov–24 Mar
Victorian villas on the edge of a forest built for the owners of the local lead mines.
8 (2fb) sB&B £12–£13 dB&B £24–£26 B
CTV 25P nc5yrs
V Lunch £4–£5 Tea £1.20 High Tea £2.50 Dinner £6.50–£7.50 Wine £4 Last dinner 6pm

★★***Woodend Country House***
Braithwaite (059682) 206
Closed Jan RS Feb
7rm(2) CTV in all bedrooms
20P nc8yrs
English & French Last dinner 7.45pm

THORNTON
West Yorkshire
Map **7** SE03

XX**Cottage** 869 Thornton Rd
Bradford (0274) 832752
Closed Sun Lunch not served Sat
French 80 seats Lunch £8–£9alc Dinner £8–£9alc Wine £6.05 Last dinner 10.15pm 80P
Credit cards 1 2 3 **VS**

THORNTON CLEVELEYS
Lancashire
Map **7** SD34

★★**Regal** Victoria Rd Cleveleys (0253) 852244
40rm(8 3) (4fb) CTV in all bedrooms Ⓡ sB&B£14.50 sB&B £16.55 dB&B£29 dB&B £33.10 B
Lift CTV 15P Disco 4 nights wkly
Lunch £2.25–£3.50 High Tea £1.50–£5 Dinner £5.50–£8 Wine £4 Last dinner 8.15pm
Credit cards 1 2 3 5

X**River House** Skippool Creek, Thornton-le-Fylde (2m E A585)
Cleveleys (0253) 883497
Closed Mon

45 seats *Lunch £6&alc Dinner £6.50&alc Wine £5 Last dinner 9.30pm 20P bedrooms available
Credit cards 2 4 5

THORNTON DALE
North Yorkshire
Map **8** SE88

★**New Inn** Pickering (0751) 74226
A 17th-century inn at the village centre, close to the North Yorkshire Moors.
8rm (1fb) Ⓡ *sB&B fr£12 dB&B fr£18
CTV 8P 1
V *Lunch £3.50 Dinner £5.50–£7 Wine £2.95 Last dinner 8pm

THORNTON HOUGH
Merseyside
Map **7** SJ38

★★★**Thornton Hall** 051-336 3938
36 CTV in all bedrooms Ⓡ sB&B £27.83 dB&B £40.48 B
150P CFA
English, French, Italian & Hungarian **V** *Lunch £4.14–£7.27&alc Tea 57p–£1.27 Dinner fr£7.27&alc Wine £5.06 Last dinner 9.30pm
Credit cards 1 2 3 4 5

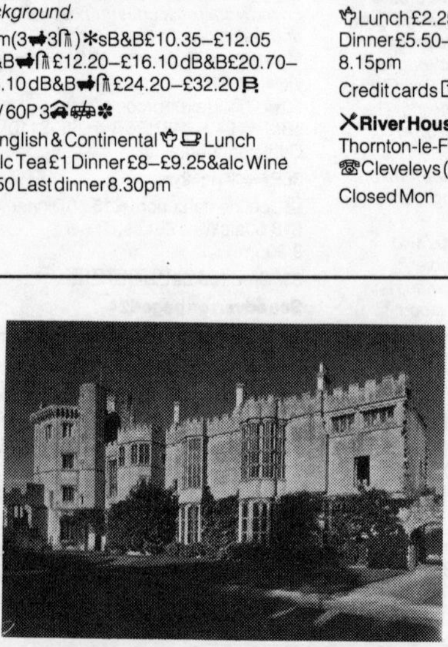

THORNTON WATLASS
North Yorkshire
Map **8** SE28

★***Buck Inn*** Bedale (0677) 22461
Village inn overlooking the cricket ground on the green.
7rm B
CTV 40P 7 nc7yrs
Last dinner 9.30pm
Credit cards 1 3 **VS**

THORPE (DOVEDALE)
Derbyshire
Map **7** SK15

★★★**Izaak Walton** (1m W on Ilam rd)
Thorpe Cloud (033529) 261
A much extended 18th-century farmhouse enjoying excellent views of Dovedale.
27 2 CTV in all bedrooms
sB&B £28–£30 dB&B £40–£42

☾ 100P ✽ xmas
V Lunch £4.50–£6.50&alc Tea 80p High Tea £2 Dinner £8.50&alc Wine £5 Last dinner 9.15pm
Credit cards 1 2 3 4 5 VS

★★★ *B* **Peveril of the Peak** (Trusthouse Forte) ☎ Thorpe Cloud (033 529) 333
Much extended and modernised old house with splendid views.
41➡ (7fb) CTV in all bedrooms ® sB&B➡ £36 dB&B➡ £50 B
100P CFA ✽ *xmas*
Last dinner 9.30pm
Credit cards 1 2 3 4 5

THORPE BAY
Essex
See **Southend-on-Sea**

THORPE-LE-SOKEN
Essex
Map **5** TM12
✕ **Lobiollies** High St ☎ Clacton-on-Sea (0255) 861616
Imaginative and skilful cooking of fresh food is efficiently served, in this unpretentious restaurant.
Closed Mon Dinner not served Sun Lunch not served Tue–Sat
French **V** 52 seats Lunch £6.50 Dinner £9–£11&alc Wine £4.50 Last dinner 9.45pm 12P
Credit cards 1 3

THORVERTON
Devon
Map **3** SS90
★ **Berribridge House** ☎ Exeter (0392) 860259
Small cottage hotel, run by the owners, with a warm, friendly atmosphere and an attractive restaurant.
6rm (2⋒) sB&B £12–£15 sB&B⋒ £14–£17 dB&B £24–£30 dB&B⋒ £28–£34 B
CTV 6P 1 ✽
V Lunch £5&alc Dinner £7.50&alc Wine £4.50 Last dinner 9pm

THRAPSTON
Northamptonshire
Map **4** SP97
★★ **Bridge** Bridge St ☎ (08012) 2128
15rm (7➡) (1fb) CTV in 5 bedrooms TV in 1 bedroom ✱ sB&B fr£10.25 sB&B➡ fr£17 dB&B fr£25 dB&B➡ fr£30 B
CTV 70P squash billiards sauna bath *xmas*
V Bar lunch £1.20–£5 Tea £1 Dinner £2.20–£6.85 Wine £3.85 Last dinner 9.30pm
Credit cards 1 2 3 5 **VS**

THREE COCKS
Powys
Map **3** SO13
❀ ★★ *H* **Three Cocks** ☎ Glasbury (04974) 215 Closed Jan–mid Feb
(Rosette awarded for dinner only.)
Warm friendly 15th-century roadside inn. 1m from Glasbury.
7rm sB&B £13.50–£14.85 dB&B £27–£29.70 B
CTV 50P ✽
French Dinner fr£11.50&alc Wine £4.75 Last dinner 9.30pm
Credit cards 1 2 3 4

THREE LEGGED CROSS
Dorset
Map **4** SU00
✕✕ **Capercaizie** Ringwood Rd ☎ Bournemouth (0202) 822374
Closed Mon & mid 2wks Jan Dinner not served Sun
French & International 100 seats Lunch £5alc Dinner £10alc Wine £3.85 Last dinner 9.30pm 50P
Credit cards 1 2 3 5 **VS**

THRESHFIELD
North Yorkshire
Map **7** SD96
★★★ ***Wilson Arms*** (Best Western) ☎ (0756) 752666 Telex no 517357 →

T

Large hotel in its own grounds on the edge of the village.

28 CTV in 1 bedroom

Lift ☾ CTV 50P 6

English & French Last dinner 8.30pm

Credit cards 1 2 3 5

THURLESTONE
Devon
Map **3** SX64

★★★*HL* **Thurlestone** (Best Western) ☎(054 857) 382

Spacious hotel, built, owned and managed by the Grose family for 90 years, which has fine country and sea views.

74rm(60)(20fb) CTV in all bedrooms sB&B£19.50–£30 sB&B£22–£36 dB&B£29–£55 dB&B£36–£70

Lift ☾ 100P 15 CFA ✽ & (heated) 18 (hard) squash billiards sauna bath *xmas*

Lunch £3.25–£3.75&alc Tea 75p–80p High Tea £2.75–£2.95 Dinner £8.50–£9&alc Wine £4.95 Last dinner 9pm

Credit cards 1 2 3 5

See advert on page 625

★★*H* **Furzey Close** ☎(054 857) 333
Closed Nov–Feb

Well-appointed, family-run hotel with a relaxing atmosphere and a fine garden.

10rm(5 2)(2fb) CTV in all bedrooms Ⓡ sB&B£11.50–£16.50 dB&B£24–£38 dB&B£24–£38

12P ✽

V Bar lunch £1.75 Tea 75p–£1 Dinner £8 Wine £3.75 Last dinner 8pm

THURSO
Highland *Caithness*
Map **15** ND16

★★**Pentland** Princes St ☎(0847) 63202

56rm(11)(3fb) sB&B£11 sB&B£13–£20 dB&B£22 dB&B£30

☾ CTV

Scottish & French V Lunch £1.75alc Tea 75palc High Tea £3.40alc Dinner £3.75alc Wine £3.70 Last dinner 8.30pm

★ ***St Clair*** Sinclair St ☎(0847) 63730

27rm(2 4) CTV in 6 bedrooms

☾ CTV 6

V Last dinner 9pm

TINTAGEL
Cornwall
Map **2** SX08

★★*H* **Atlantic View** Treknow ☎Camelford (0840) 770221
Closed Nov–Mar (except Xmas)

Small, comfortable, family hotel in a prominent position with good sea views.

10rm(8 2)(3fb) 2 sB&B£13.50–£15.50 sB&B£13.50–£15.50 dB&B£27–£31 dB&B£27–£31

CTV 16P ✽ (heated) nc3yrs *xmas*

English & French Bar lunch £1–£2.50 Tea £1.28–£2.28 Dinner £7.50–£9.50 Wine £3.50 Last dinner 8.15pm

Credit cards 1 2 3 5 **VS**

★★**Bossiney House** ☎Camelford (0840) 770240
Closed 8 Oct–Mar

Modern holiday hotel in its own grounds, with sea views.

20rm(11 6)(1fb) sB&B£12.50–£14.25 sB&B£14–£15.75 dB&B£25–£28 dB&B£28–£31.50

CTV 30P ✽

English & Continental ✽ Bar lunch £2–£3 Tea 45p–£1.25alc Dinner £6.25 Wine £4.30 Last dinner 8pm

VS

TINTERN
Gwent
Map **3** SO50

★★**Beaufort** (Embassy) ☎(02918) 202

Small hotel overlooking Tintern Abbey.

26rm(15 11)(1fb) CTV in all bedrooms Ⓡ sB&B£30.50 dB&B£41

CTV 100P ✽ *xmas*

English, Welsh & French V Bar lunch 95p–£6.75 Dinner £6.95&alc Wine £3.90 Last dinner 9pm

Credit cards 1 2 3 4 5

★★ ***Royal George*** (Trusthouse Forte) ☎(02918) 205

Traditional hotel a few minutes' walk from the river.

19rm(15) CTV in all bedrooms Ⓡ

CTV 30P ✽

Last dinner 9.30pm

Credit cards 1 2 3 4 5

★ ***Wye Valley*** ☎(02918) 441

Pleasant, proprietor-run hotel with a relaxed atmosphere, close to the river.

8rm(4) Ⓡ

CTV 20P

English & French Last dinner 9.30pm

Credit cards 1 3 **VS**

TITCHWELL
Norfolk
Map **9** TF74

★★*H* **Manor** (Best Western) ☎Brancaster (048 521) 221
Closed 24–30 Dec

Comfortable and friendly family hotel facing the bird watching area of the salt marshes.

7rm(4 1)(2fb) Annexe: 3 Ⓡ ✽sB&B£16.25–£18.95 sB&B£17.75–£20.45 dB&B£27.50–£32.90 dB&B£30.50–£35.90

CTV 30P ✽ Live music and dancing twice mthly

V ✽Lunch £4.75alc Tea £1alc High Tea £2alc Dinner £7.50alc Wine £4.25 Last dinner 9pm

Credit cards 1 2 3 5 **VS**

TIVERTON
Devon
Map **3** SS91

☆☆☆**Tiverton Motel** Blundells Rd ☎(0884) 256120

Modern, privately-owned and run, purpose-built hotel, ideal for tourists and business people.

T

29➡(15fb) CTV in all bedrooms Ⓡ sB&B➡⋒£15–£25 dB&B➡⋒£25–£38 ₿

☾ 150P CFA ❀ Disco twice wkly Live music and dancing wkly *xmas*

▣English & French **V** ♧ ▭ Lunch £4.50–£7 Tea fr50p Dinner £6.75&alc Wine £4.25 Last dinner 9.45pm

Credit cards 1 2 3 5 **VS**

★★**Hartnoll Country House** Bolham (1½m N on A396) ☎(0884) 252777

Georgian house in its own grounds, with busy bars and varied styles of bedrooms.

12rm(8➡) CTV in all bedrooms Ⓡ ✻sB&B fr£11 sB&B➡fr£15 dB&B fr£19 dB&B➡fr£25 ₿

CTV 80P 2⌂ ❀ ♩

♧ ▭ ✻Bar lunch fr£1.95 Wine £3.65 Last dinner 9pm

Credit cards 3 5

✕✕***Henderson's*** 18 Newport St ☎(0884) 254256

Closed Sun

▣English, French & Italian **V** 45 seats Last dinner 10pm

Credit cards 1 3

TOBERMORY
Isle of Mull, Strathclyde *Argyllshire*
Map **13** NM55

★**Mishnish** Main St ☎(0688) 2009

Small, traditional, Highland hotel overlooking the picturesque Tobermory Bay.

14rm(6➡1⋒) ✻sB&B£10–£15 dB&B£20–£30 dB&B➡⋒£22–£32 ₿

CTV 5P ♩ Live music nightly in season

♧ ▭ ✻Lunch fr£4&alc Tea fr50p Dinner fr£7&alc Last dinner 9pm

TODWICK
South Yorkshire
Map **8** SK48

✕✕***Red Lion*** ☎Worksop (0909) 771654

▣English & French **V** 90 seats Last dinner 10pm

Credit cards 1 3 **VS**

TOMINTOUL
Grampian *Banffshire*
Map **15** NJ11

★★***Gordon Arms*** The Square ☎(08074) 206

Situated in the village square with views of the surrounding hills.

29rm(5➡1⋒)

CTV 20P ♩

♧ ▭ Last dinner 8pm

★★***Richmond Arms*** ☎(08074) 209

RS Nov & Dec

Traditional hotel in Highland village square.

26rm(8➡) Ⓡ ₿

CTV 15P 2⌂ ❀ ♩ ∪ ⌂

V ♧ ▭ Last dinner 8pm

VS

TONBRIDGE
Kent
Map **5** TQ54

★★**Rose & Crown** High St (Trusthouse Forte) ☎(0732) 357966

Early 18th-century building of blue and red chequered brick; the interior has panelling and oak beams.

52➡(1fb) CTV in all bedrooms Ⓡ sB&B➡£35.50 dB&B➡£52.50 ₿

☾ 62P CFA *xmas*

♧ ▭ Last dinner 10pm

Credit cards 1 2 3 4 5

TONGUE
Highland *Sutherland*
Map **14** NC55

★★**Ben Loyal** ☎(08005) 216

RS Nov–Mar

13rm(2➡3⋒) Annexe: 6rm sB&B£12–£14 dB&B£24–£28 dB&B➡£32

⇎.

♧ ▭ Dinner £7alc Wine £3.55 Last dinner 7.45pm

Credit cards 1 3

★★***Tongue*** ☎(08005) 206 Telex no 778215

Closed Oct–Apr

A comfortable and friendly family run traditional hotel offering special facilities for fishing.

21rm(12➡) Ⓡ ₿

☾ CTV 30P ❀ ♩

V ♧ ▭ Last dinner 8.30pm

Credit cards 1 2 3 4 5

TORBAY
Devon
See under **Brixham, Churston Ferrers, Paignton** and **Torquay**

TORCROSS
Devon
Map **3** SX84

★**Grey Homes** ☎Kingsbridge (0548) 580220

Closed Nov–Mar

Modestly-appointed, family-run hotel occupying a superb position looking down on the beach.

7rm sB&B£12–£14 dB&B£24–£28 ₿

CTV 15P 3⌂ ⇎ ❀ ℘(grass)

♧ ▭ Bar lunch 80p Tea 95p Dinner £6.50 Wine £3.50 Last dinner 7.30pm

TORMARTON
Avon
Map **3** ST77

★★**Compass Inn** (Inter-Hotel, Minotel) ☎Badminton (045 421) 242

Old, family-run inn offering modern facilities.

11rm(6➡1⋒)(3fb) CTV in 7 bedrooms TV in 4 bedrooms Ⓡ sB&B£20.95 sB&B➡⋒£26.95 dB&B£29.95 dB&B➡⋒£37.95 ₿

160P ❀

▣English ♧ Bar lunch £4.50–£6 Dinner £4.50–£6&alc Wine £4.75 Last dinner 9.30pm

Credit cards 1 2 3 5

TORQUAY
Devon
Map **3** SX96
See Central and District plans

★★★★★ **Imperial** Park Hill Rd (Trusthouse Forte) ☎(0803) 24301 Telex no 42849 Central plan **18** *F1*
An impressive hotel with ornate lounge areas and a refurbished restaurant; the bedrooms are being refurbished to a high standard.
164 (8fb) CTV in all bedrooms sB&B £47 dB&B £81 B
Lift ☾ CTV 200P 60 CFA ✽ & (heated) (hard) squash sauna bath Live music and dancing Mon–Sat *xmas*
Last dinner 9.30pm
Credit cards 1 2 3 4 5

★★★★ **Grand** Sea Front ☎(0803) 25234 Telex no 42891 Central plan **13** *B1*
Large, family hotel with large public rooms and overlooking the sea.
120 CTV in all bedrooms sB&B £21–£33 dB&B £42–£62 B
Lift ☾ 35 CFA ✽ (heated) (hard) sauna bath Disco Tue Live music and dancing Sat *xmas*
English & Continental **V** Lunch £5.50–£7.50&alc Tea 70p–80p High Tea £2.50–£3.50&alc Dinner £8.50–£9.50&alc Wine £4.95 Last dinner 9.30pm
Credit cards 1 2 3 5 **VS**

★★★★ **Palace** Babbacombe Rd ☎(0803) 22271 Telex no 42606 District plan **53**
Standing in some 20 acres, this hotel offers a relaxing atmosphere and extensive sporting facilities.
138rm(112) (10fb) CTV in all bedrooms sB&B £29.50–£32.50 dB&B £57–£65 B
Lift ☾ CTV 100P CFA 40 ✽ & (heated) (hard) squash billiards sauna bath Live music and dancing 6 nights wkly *xmas*
English & French **V** Lunch fr£5 Tea fr£1.50 High Tea fr£3 Dinner fr£10&alc Wine £4.75 Last dinner 9.15pm
Credit cards 1 2 3 5 **VS**

★★★ **Belgrave** Sea Front ☎(0803) 28566 Central plan **3** *C2*
Sea front hotel next to Abbey gardens.
54rm(50 4) (12fb) CTV in all bedrooms ® sB&B £17–£23 dB&B £34–£46 B
Lift ☾ 80P CFA 6 ✽ (heated) Live music and dancing Mon–Fri (Jun–Sep) Cabaret Mon–Fri (Jun–Sep) *xmas*
English & French Bar lunch £2–£4 Tea 35p Dinner fr£6&alc Wine £4.60 Last dinner 8.30pm
Credit cards 1 2 3 5 **VS**
See advert on page 630

★★★ **Corbyn Head** Sea Front, Livermead ☎(0803) 213611 District plan **42**
Large, modernised hotel with an attractive exterior.
52rm(44 3) (13fb) CTV in 12 bedrooms TV available in bedrooms ® sB&B £18.70–£27.50 sB&B £18.70–£27.50 dB&B £40.50–£57.50 dB&B £40.50–£57.50 B
☾ CTV 60P 5 CFA ✽ (heated) billiards Live music and dancing Sat Cabaret Sat *xmas*
Credit cards 1 2 3 5

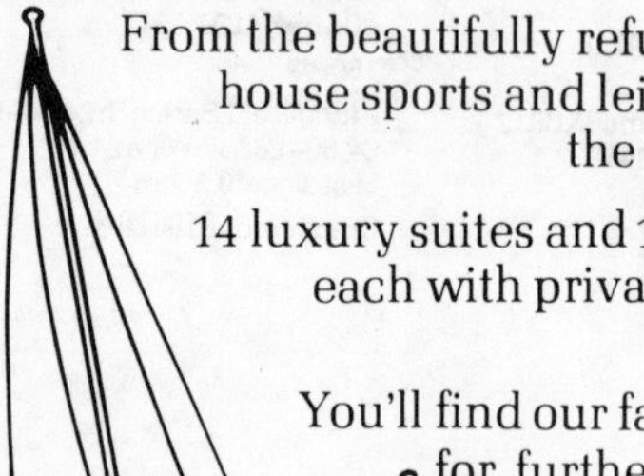

★★★ *H* **Devonshire** Park Hill Rd ☎(0803) 24850 Telex no 42712 Plan **10** *F1*
Large, detached hotel with pleasant garden, set in a quiet position.
54rm(29 4) Annexe: 12rm(10 2) (9fb) CTV in 35 bedrooms ® sB&B £10–£15 sB&B £13–£18 dB&B £20–£30 dB&B £26–£36 B
☾ CTV 50P 3 CFA ✽ (heated) (hard) Live music and dancing twice wkly Cabaret wkly (May–Oct) *xmas*
English, French, German & Italian **V** Lunch £4.15–£5.50 Tea 60p–£1.25→

T

High Tea £1.25–£1.95 Dinner £5.80–£7 Wine £3.95

Credit cards 1 2 3 5 VS

★★★ ***Gleneagles*** Asheldon Rd, Wellswood ☎ (0803) 23637 District plan **46**

Closed Nov–Mar

Modern hotel in quiet residential area, 1m from the town centre.

42rm(39 3) CTV available in bedrooms

CTV 27P (heated) Live music and dancing twice wkly

English & French V Last dinner 8pm

VS

★★★ ***HBL*** **Homers** Warren Rd ☎ (0803) 213456 Central plan **15** *D2*

Closed 20 Nov–8 Mar

A small, bright, well-appointed hotel with good views over the bay. The proprietors, Helen and Andre Bisonette are very hospitable and make guests most comfortable. Bedrooms have good facilities, and the peaceful lounges are tastefully furnished. Dinner is of a good standard with a comprehensive wine list.

17rm(9 4) (2fb) CTV in all bedrooms sB&B£19.50 sB&B £19.50 dB&B£39 dB&B £39

5P nc7yrs *xmas*

English & French Lunch £5.95 Tea 65p–£1.50 Dinner £12.95 Wine £4.95 Last dinner 8.30pm

Credit cards 1 2 3 5 **VS**

★★★ ***HL*** **Kistor** Belgrave Rd (Inter-Hotels) ☎ (0803) 23219 Central plan **19** *C2*

Commercial and tourist hotel close to the beach, affording personal attention.

52rm(51 1) (14fb) CTV in all bedrooms sB&B £14–£25 dB&B £28–£44

Lift CTV 40P CFA (heated) sauna bath Disco wkly Live music and dancing twice wkly *xmas*

English & Continental V Lunch £4 Tea 32p–£1.50 High Tea £1.50–£3.50 Dinner £5.50–£7.50 Wine £4 Last dinner 8.30pm

S% Credit cards 1 2 3 **VS**

See advert on page 634

★★★ **Lincombe Hall** Meadfoot Rd (Travco) ☎ (0803) 213361 Central plan **21** *F2*

Large, detached Victorian-style building, ¼m from the beach and the town centre.

44rm(31) (6fb) 1 CTV in 20 bedrooms Ⓡ sB&B£15 sB&B £18 dB&B£27 dB&B £30

CTV CFA (heated) (hard) Disco wkly Live music and dancing wkly *xmas*

Lunch £4.50 Tea £1 Dinner £6.50 Wine £3.75

Last dinner 8.30pm

Credit cards 1 2 4 5

★★★ ***HL*** **Livermead Cliff** Torbay Rd (Best Western) ☎ (0803) 22881 Telex no 42918 Central & District plan **22**

Castellated, three-storey, red stone building whose grounds are enclosed by a sea wall. (Sports facilities at nearby sister hotel 'Livermead House' available to guests.)

64rm(53 7) (18fb) CTV in 45 bedrooms TV in 19 bedrooms Ⓡ sB&B£16–£19.50 sB&B £20.50–£25 dB&B£32–£40 dB&B £40–£49

Lift CTV 60P CFA 12 (heated) *xmas*

English & Continental V Lunch £5–£5.75&alc Tea 70p Dinner £7–£7.75&alc Wine £4.75 Last dinner 8.30pm

S% Credit cards 1 3 **VS**

★★★ ***HL*** **Livermead House** Torbay Rd (Best Western) ☎ (0803) 24361 Telex no 42918 Central & District plan **23**

Attractive hotel standing in its own grounds. →

THE DEVONSHIRE HOTEL

AA★★★

Park Hill Road, Torquay, South Devon, TQ1 2DY
Tel: (STD 0803) 24850 Telex: 42712

Privately owned and situated in quiet garden setting of great charm – 'away from it all' – yet close to the harbour, beaches walk, entertainment and shopping centre. The ideal all seasons holiday hotel. Outdoor swimming pool (heated May-October). Spacious restaurant. Dancing in high season, excellent cuisine and extensive wine list. Large free car park. Own hard tennis court and games room, 69 well-equipped bedrooms (including 12 in a new annex within the hotel grounds), majority with bathroom en suite, all with radio and intercom, some on ground floor. Licensed lounge bar, colour TV lounge. Central heating throughout. Friendly service, midweek bookings accepted. Colour brochure and tariff on request.

homers
hotel
torquay
AA
***
H.B.L.
Merit
Awards
TO
PLEASE PLEASES
US

A Renaissance of Graciousness

An oasis of COMFORT and LUXURY for the individual visitor who expects ELEGANCE, REFINEMENT and SERVICE when choosing an Hotel. Our breathtaking panoramic seaviews complete the enchantment. All rooms have Colour TV, dialling phone, radio and Mini Bar.

A Gourmet's Delight

Good food is a way of life at Homers. Superb cuisine, friendly efficient service supported by a most extensive wine list, make any meal a special occasion when you stay with us.

Your Hosts, Helen & Andre Bissonnette welcome your inquiries for their 3 or 5 night GOURMET BREAKS, Weekly Holidays, Christmas programme and our Executives Welcome scheme.

Homers Hotel, Warren Road, Torquay. TQ2 5TN.
Reservations or Inquiries on Torquay (0803) 213456.

T

T

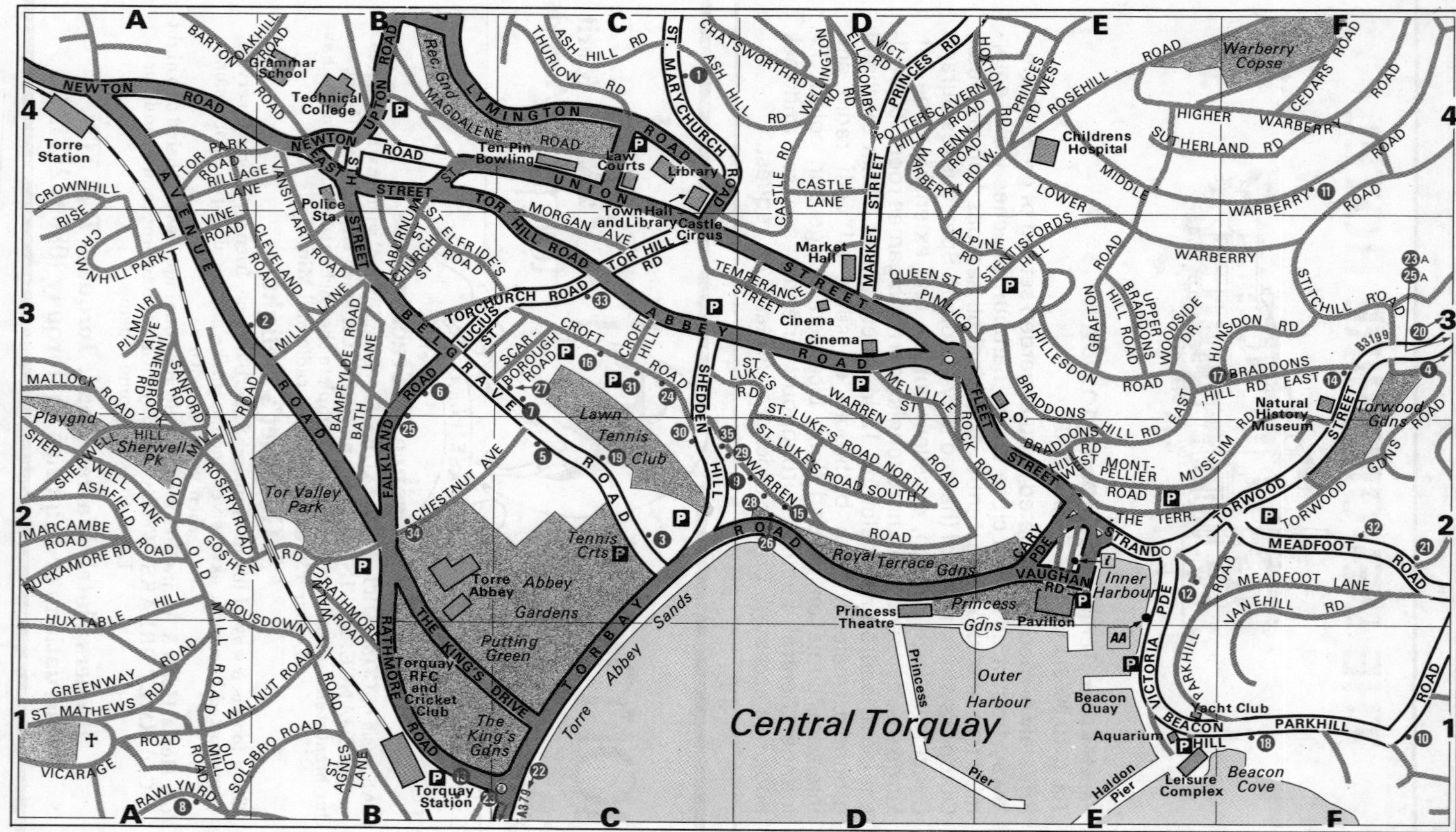
Central Torquay
Outer Harbour
Inner Harbour
Princess Pier
Beacon Quay
Beacon Cove
Haldon Pier
Leisure Complex
Aquarium
Yacht Club
Princess Theatre
Princess Gdns
Pavilion
Royal Terrace Gdns
Torre Abbey Sands
Torre Abbey Gardens
Torre Abbey
Putting Green
The King's Gdns
Torquay Station
Torquay RFC and Cricket Club
Tor Valley Park
Torre Station
Sherwell Pk
Playgnd
Lawn Tennis Club
Tennis Crts
Market Hall
Cinema
Town Hall and Library
Law Courts
Library
Childrens Hospital
Warberry Copse
Natural History Museum
Torwood Gdns
Police Sta.
Technical College
Grammar School
Ten Pin Bowling
Rec. Gnd

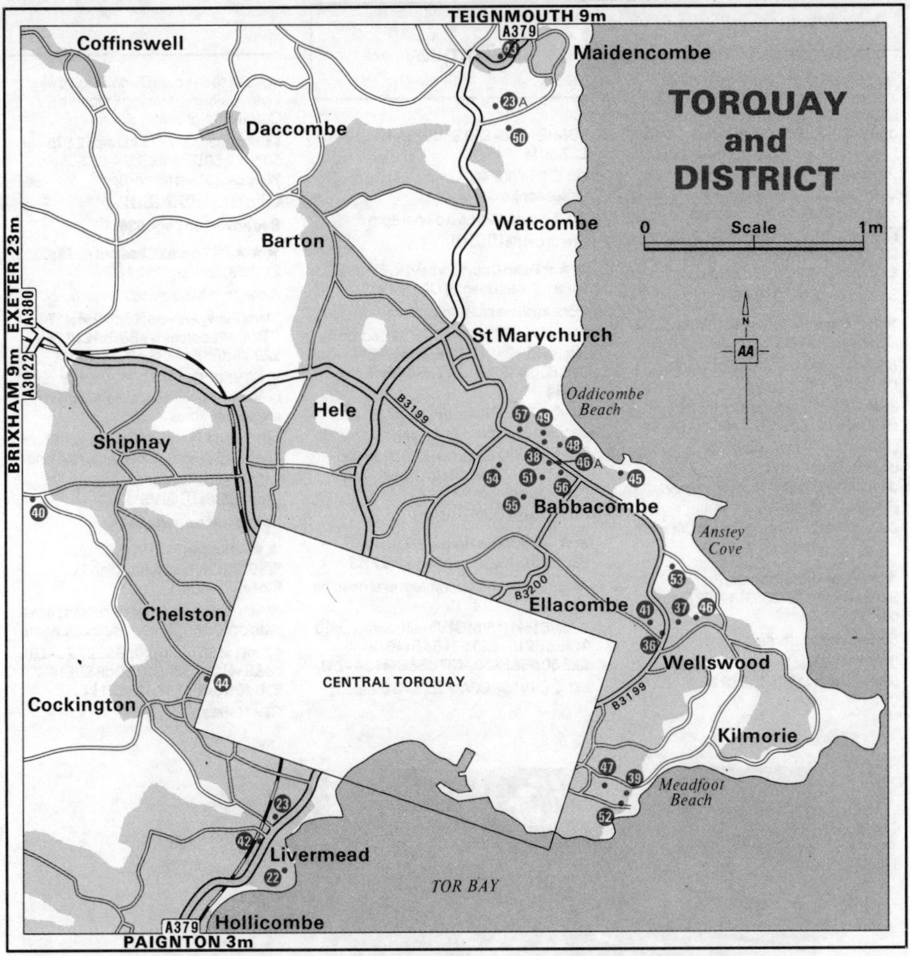

TORQUAY and DISTRICT

TEIGNMOUTH 9m A379 Maidencombe Coffinswell Daccombe Watcombe Barton EXETER 23m A380 BRIXHAM 9m A3022 St Marychurch Hele B3199 Oddicombe Beach Shiphay Babbacombe Anstey Cove Ellacombe B3200 Chelston Wellswood CENTRAL TORQUAY Cockington B3199 Kilmorie Meadfoot Beach Livermead TOR BAY A379 Hollicombe PAIGNTON 3m

Scale 0 1m

Torquay District
36 Ansteys Lea ★★
37 Ardmore ★★
38 Ashley Rise ★
39 Hotel Balmoral ★★
40 Brigantine Manor ★★
41 Coppice ★★
42 Corbyn Head ★★★
43 Dartmoor Maiden ★★
44 Fairmount House ★
45 Glen ★★
46 Gleneagles ★★★
46A Green Mantle ✕
22 Livermead Cliff ★★★
23 Livermead House ★★★
23A Maidencombe House ★★
47 Meadfoot Bay ★★
48 Morningside ★★
49 Norcliffe ★★
50 Orestone House ★★
51 Oswald's ★★★
52° Overmead ★★
53 Palace ★★★★
54 Penrhyn ★
55 Sunray ★★
56 Viscount ★★
57 Woodland Park ★

T

Torquay Central
1 Albaston ★★
2 Bancourt ★★
3 Belgrave ★★★
4 Burlington ★★
5 Bute Court ★★
6 Carlton ★
7 Cavendish ★★
8 Chelston Towers ★★★
9 Conway Court ★★★
10 Devonshire ★★★
11 Fonthill ★★
12 Café Garbo ✕
13 Grand ★★★★
14 Gresham Court ★★★
15 Homers ★★★
16 Howden Court ★★★
17 Hunsdon Lea ★★★
18 Imperial ★★★★★
19 Kistor ★★★
20 Lansdowne ★★
21 Lincombe Hall ★★★
22 Livermead Cliff ★★★
23 Livermead House ★★★
23A Lisburne ✕
24 Nepaul ★★★
25 Nethway ★★
25A Café Old Vienna ✕
26 Palm Court ★★★
27 Rainbow House ★★★
28 Rock Walk ★★
29 Hotel Roseland ★★★
30 Shedden Hall ★★
31 Shelley Court ★
32 Sydore ★★
33 Templestowe ★★
34 Toorak ★★★
35 Vernon Court ★★

Torquay

76rm(60➡6⋒) Annexe: 2➡⋒ (8fb) CTV in 40 bedrooms TV in 25 bedrooms ® sB&B£16–£19.50 sB&B➡⋒£20–£24 dB&B£30–£38 dB&B➡⋒£38–£47 Ⓑ

Lift ☾ CTV 120P 5🚗✽ ≋ (heated) 𝒫(hard) ♪ squash billiards sauna bath Live music and dancing twice wkly (in summer, Xmas & Etr) ⌂ *xmas* ♿

▣English & Continental **V** ♡ ☐ Lunch £5–£5.75&alc Tea fr70p Dinner £7–£7.75&alc Wine £4.75 Last dinner 8.30pm

S% Credit cards 1 3 **VS**

★★★**Nepaul** Croft Rd ☎(0803) 22745 Central plan **24** *C3*

Soundly-appointed hotel in a good position with fine views.

39➡ (4fb) CTV in all bedrooms ® sB&B➡£14–£22 dB&B➡£28–£44 Ⓑ

Lift ☾ CTV 18P CFA 6🚗 ✽ ⊡ (heated) billiards Disco wkly Live music and dancing twice wkly Cabaret wkly ⌂ *xmas*

▣French **V** ♡ Lunch £4.25&alc Dinner £6.95 Wine £3.90 Last dinner 8.30pm

Credit cards 1 3

★★★**Oswald's** Palermo Rd, Babbacombe ☎(0803) 39292 District plan **51**

Set in residential area of Babbacombe near sea front.

55rm(19➡4⋒) ® sB&B£9.35–£13.75 dB&B£14.50–£18.95 dB&B➡⋒£18.70–£27.50 Ⓑ

Lift ☾ CTV 30P ✽ Live music and dancing (in season) *xmas*

♡ ☐ Wine £4.25 Last dinner 8pm

Credit cards 1 2 3

★★★**Palm Court** Torbay Rd ☎(0803) 24881 Central plan **26** *D2*

Hotel in prime sea front position.

72rm(37➡3⋒) (7fb) CTV in all bedrooms ® sB&B£12–£14.50 sB&B➡⋒£14–£16.50 dB&B£24–£29 dB&B➡⋒£24–£33 Ⓑ

Lift ☾ CTV 15P billiards Live music and dancing 3 nights wkly (in season) ⌂ *xmas*

▣French **V** ♡ ☐ Lunch £4.50 Tea 40p High Tea £1.25 Dinner £7.75&alc Wine £3.45 Last dinner 7.30pm

Credit cards 1 2 3 5 **VS**

★★★**Rainbow House** Belgrave Rd ☎(0803) 213232 Central plan **27** *C3*

Modern, soundly appointed hotel near the sea front.

92rm(81➡) (15fb) CTV in all bedrooms ® ★ sB&B£15–£20.50 sB&B➡£19–£22.50 dB&B£30–£37 dB&B➡£34–£41

Lift ☾ CTV 90P CFA ✽ ⊡ & ≋ (heated) squash sauna bath Disco 3 nights wkly Live music and dancing 6 nights wkly Cabaret 3 nights wkly ⌂ *xmas*

▣International **V** ♡ ☐ Lunch £4.75 Tea 50p–£2.50 Dinner £6.50–£7.50&alc Wine £4.25 Last dinner 9pm

Credit cards 1 2 3 5

See advert on page 636

★★★ *HL* **Toorak** Chestnut Av ☎(0803) 211866 Central plan **34** *B2*

A comfortable, personally-run hotel.

31rm(29➡) Annexe: 10rm(9➡) (17fb) CTV in all bedrooms sB&B➡£16.75–£29.75 dB&B➡£33.50–£59.50 Ⓑ

☾ CTV 50P CFA ✽ ≋ (heated) 𝒫(hard) billiards Live music and dancing Sat (in season) ⌂ *xmas*

▣English & French **V** ♡ ☐ Lunch £5.25 Tea £1.25 Dinner £8.50&alc Last dinner 8.30pm

Credit cards 1 3 **VS**

See advert on page 636

★★**Albaston** 27 St Mary Church Rd ☎(0803) 26758 Central plan **1** *C4*

Closed Dec

Small, family-run hotel, occupying a main road position, ½m from the town centre.

12rm(1➡5⋒) (4fb) ® sB&B£7.20–£9 sB&B➡⋒£8.55–£10.50 dB&B£14.40–£18 dB&B➡⋒£17.10–£21 Ⓑ

CTV 12P ⌂ →

KISTOR HOTEL

Belgrave Road Torquay TQ2 5HF Devon

Mr. and Mrs. Jonathan Hassell personally run this progressive family hotel, OPEN THROUGHOUT THE YEAR and situated 150 yards from the sea front centre, in its own large garden. Thoroughly modernised, the hotel offers: rooms with private bath and colour television and radio; dances most Fridays and Saturdays throughout the year, also Mondays during the season. Indoor heated swimming pool, spa bath, sauna and exercise area, for the free use of resident guests. Cocktail Bar; Lift; Car Park. AA★★★. Bookings from any day on Full Board; Dinner, Bed and Breakfast; or Bed and Breakfast basis. Special out-of-season terms. Ideal for residential conferences.

Write for Brochure T1 or telephone 0803 23219.

T

T

Torquay

English & French V Lunch £2.50–£3.75&alc Tea 50p–75p High Tea £1.50–£2 Dinner £3.75–£5.75&alc Last dinner 10pm

Credit cards 1 3 VS

★★**Ansteys Lea** Wellswood ☎(0803) 24843 District plan **36**

Closed Nov–Feb (except Xmas) RS Mar & Oct

Villa-style hotel with a pleasant garden, 1m from the town.

27rm(5→4⋒)(8fb) CTV in 9 bedrooms *sB&B£9.50–£12.50 sB&B→⋒£11–£14 dB&B£19–£25 dB&B→⋒£23–£28 B

CTV 20P ✽ (heated) *xmas*

*Dinner £5 Wine £3.85 Last dinner 7.15pm

★★*H***Ardmore** Asheldon Rd, Wellswood ☎(0803) 24792 District plan **37**

RS Nov–Mar

The hotel stands in its own grounds just off the Babbacombe road.

30rm(9→) sB&B£8–£10.50 sB&B→£9–£11.50 dB&B£16–£21 dB&B→£18–£23 B

CTV 30P ✽ (heated)

Bar lunch £1–£2 Tea 50p–£1 Dinner £5–£5.50 Wine £6 Last dinner 8pm

★★*L***Hotel Balmoral** Meadfoot Sea Rd ☎(0803) 23381 District plan **39**

Closed Nov

A comfortable, family-run hotel in a quiet position, with views over Meadfoot Beach.

23rm(7⋒)(6fb) sB&B£9–£10.50 dB&B£18–£21 dB&B⋒£21–£24 B

CTV 18P ✽ Disco wkly Cabaret wkly *xmas*

English & French V Lunch £4.25 Tea £1.50 Dinner £6.50&alc Wine £3.95 Last dinner 9.30pm

Credit cards 1 3 VS

★★**Bancourt** Avenue Rd ☎(0803) 25077 Central plan **2** *A3*

Modern hotel complex a short distance from the shops and sea front.

40rm(20→)(9fb) CTV in all bedrooms Ⓡ sB&B£9.35–£15.40 sB&B→£10.60–£16.65 dB&B£18.70–£30.80 dB&B→£21.20–£33.30 B

☾ 35P ✽ (heated) *xmas*

English & Continental V Bar lunch £2.75–£3 Tea 45p Dinner £5.60 Wine £4.50 Last dinner 8pm

S% VS

★★**Bowden Close** Teignmouth Rd, Maidencombe ☎(0803) 38029 Not on plan

Closed Dec–Feb.

Hotel stands in own grounds with panoramic sea views.

21rm(1→7⋒)(5fb) 1 Ⓡ sB&B£8.80–£10.10 sB&B→⋒£10.10–£11.40 dB&B£16–£18.60 dB&B→⋒£18.70–£21.20 B

CTV 50P 2 ✽ *xmas*

Bar lunch £2–£3 Tea 70p–£1 Dinner £5 Wine £3 Last dinner 8pm

Credit card 3 VS

★★**Brigantine Motor** 56 Marldon Rd, Shiphay ☎(0803) 63162 District plan **40**

Closed Xmas wknd

An extended private house, now a family-run tourist/commercial hotel, situated in a residential position.

14rm(5→2⋒)(3fb) CTV in all bedrooms Ⓡ sB&B fr£13.50 sB&B→⋒ fr£16.25 dB&B fr£17.30 dB&B→⋒ fr£20.05 B

☾ CTV 40P 1 ✽

Lunch 60p–£5 Tea £1.20 Dinner £4.25&alc Last dinner 10pm

Credit cards 1 3 VS

★★**Burlington** 462–466 Babbacombe Rd (Minotel) ☎(0803) 24374 Central plan **4** *F3*

Closed Nov–Mar except Xmas

A tourist hotel situated on a main road about ¼m from the beach and the town centre.

46rm(1→10⋒)(10fb) sB&B£7.50–£10.50 sB&B→⋒£9–£12.25 dB&B£15–£21 dB&B→⋒£18–£24.50 B

☾ CTV 30P ✽ Live music and dancing twice wkly *xmas*

Bar lunch £2.25–£3.50 Tea £1–£1.75 Dinner £5–£6 Wine £4.50 Last dinner 8pm

Credit cards 1 3

★★**Bute Court** Belgrave Rd ☎(0803) 23771 Central plan **5** *C2*

Closed Nov–Mar

White-painted, Victorian building whose spacious and modernised rooms have good sea views.

47rm(30→2⋒)(12fb) CTV in all bedrooms sB&B£10–£15 sB&B→⋒£11.50–£17 dB&B£20–£30 dB&B→⋒£23–£34 B

Lift ☾ CTV 35P 5 ✽ (heated) billiards Disco wkly Live music and dancing twice wkly Cabaret wkly *xmas*

English & French V Lunch £3.45–£5 Tea 50p–£1 High Tea £3–£4 Dinner £4.50–£6.50 Last dinner 8pm

Credit cards 1 2 3 5 VS

★★**Cavendish** Belgrave Rd ☎(0803) 23682 Central plan **7** *C3*

Closed Nov–Mar (except for Conferences)

Imposing villa with extension near shops and sea front.

59rm(8→5⋒)(10fb) Ⓡ sB&B£14.50–£16.80 sB&B→⋒£16.60–£19.15 dB&B£28–£32.50 dB&B→⋒£32–£37.20 B

☾ CTV 24P (heated) sauna bath Live music and dancing twice wkly Cabaret wkly nc5yrs

English & Continental Lunch £4.90&alc Tea £1.25 Dinner £6.25&alc Wine £3.75 Last dinner 8pm

Credit cards 1 2 3 5

★★**Chelston Tower** Rawlyn Rd ☎(0803) 607351 Central plan **8** *A1*

Closed Dec–27 Jan except 31 Dec–2 Jan

Built about 120 years ago, this hotel stands on high ground.

22rm(7→2⋒)(11fb) sB&B£12.50–£13.50 sB&B→⋒£14.50–£15.50 dB&B£25–£27 dB&B→⋒£29–£31 B →

T

CTV 40P ✽ ⛆ (heated)
♆ ☕ Dinner £5.50–£6 Wine £3.50 Last dinner 8pm
VS

★★**Conway Court** Warren Rd ☎ (0803) 25363 Central plan **9** *D2*
Closed mid Nov–mid Mar
Converted split level mansion with good sea views.
40rm (14→ 17⋒) (4fb) 4▣ ® ✻ sB&B £12–£16 sB&B→⋒ £13.35–£17.35 dB&B £23–£31 dB&B→⋒ £25.70–£33.70 ⊟
CTV ⚑ ✽ *xmas*
V ♆ ☕ ✻ Lunch £2.60–£5.65 Tea fr65p High Tea fr40p Dinner £5.75&alc Wine £4.15 Last dinner 8pm

★★**Coppice** Barrington Rd ☎ (0803) 27786 District plan **41**
Closed Nov–4 Apr
Just outside the town centre, yet within easy reach of all the amenities.
29rm (23→ 3⋒) (5fb) sB&B £6–£9 sB&B→⋒ £7–£10 dB&B £12–£18 dB&B→⋒ £14–£20
CTV 30P ✽ ⛆ (heated) Cabaret wkly ⌂ *xmas*
V ♆ ☕ Lunch £1.50–£4 High Tea £1.50–£2 Dinner £3–£5&alc Wine £3.70 Last dinner 7.30pm

★★**Dartmoor Maiden** Maidencombe ☎ (0803) 38760 District plan **43**
Closed last 2wks Jan
Small, detached, inn-style hotel near Maidencombe beach, 2½m from the town centre.
6rm (2→) (1fb) ✈ sB&B £7–£8 sB&B→ £9.50–£10.50 dB&B £14 dB&B→ £19–£21 ⊟
CTV 16P ⛟ ✽ nc7yrs
▤ English & French ♆ Lunch £1–£10 Dinner £1–£10&alc Wine £3.95 Last dinner 9pm
Credit cards ② ③ ⑤

★★**Fonthill** Lower Warberry Rd ☎ (0803) 23894 Central plan **11** *F4*
Closed mid Oct–mid Apr
Modern hotel with many balconied rooms overlooking pool.
32rm (30→) (9fb) CTV in 15 bedrooms ® sB&B→ £9.96–£12.78 dB&B→ £19.92–£25.56
CTV 26P ✽ ⛆ (heated) disco Wed
♆ ☕ Bar lunch £1–£2.50 Tea fr50p Dinner £4.80 Wine £4.40 Last dinner 8pm
VS

★★***Glen*** Babbacombe Beach ☎ (0803) 38340 District plan **45**
Closed mid Oct–Mar
Hotel stands high on cliff side overlooking beach.
18rm ⊟
CTV 15P ⛟ ✽
♆ ☕ Last dinner 8pm

★★**Gresham Court** Babbacombe Rd ☎ (0803) 23007 Central plan **14** *F3*
Closed Dec–mid Apr
34rm (7→ 6⋒) (5fb) ® ✈ sB&B £8.50–£10.75 dB&B £16–£20.25 dB&B→ £18–£22.50 ⊟
Lift CTV 4P Live music and dancing twice wkly nc3yrs
Lunch fr£2.85 Dinner fr£3.50 Wine £2.40 Last dinner 8pm
Credit card ③ **VS**

★★**Howden Court** Croft Rd ☎ (0803) 24844 Central plan **16** *C3*
Closed Oct–Apr
Large villa in its own grounds.
32rm (12→ 20⋒) (9fb) sB&B→⋒ £10–£12 dB&B→⋒ £18–£20
CTV 20P billiards
♆ Lunch £3.75 Dinner £5 Wine £3.90 Last dinner 8pm

★★**Hunsdon Lea** Hunsdon Rd ☎ (0803) 26538 Central plan **17** *F3*
Closed Nov–Mar (except Xmas & New Year)
Quiet hotel within short walking distance of town centre.
18rm (8→ 1⋒) (5fb) CTV in 9 bedrooms sB&B £11.50–£15 sB&B→⋒ £13.50–£17 dB&B £23–£30 dB&B→⋒ £27–£34 ⊟
⚟ CTV 12P ✽ ⛆ (heated) Live music and dancing twice wkly *xmas*
♆ ☕ Lunch £2.50–£4&alc Tea 60p–£1 High Tea £1.75–£2.25alc Dinner £3.50–£5.50&alc Wine £3.90 Last dinner 8.30pm
VS

★★***Lansdowne*** Babbacombe Rd ☎ (0803) 22822 Central plan **20** *F3*
Closed Nov–Mar
Hotel with a modern exterior in a quiet position, ¼m from the town centre.
31rm (22→ 2⋒) ⊟
CTV 30P ✽ ⛆ (heated) Disco Thu Live music and dancing Tue ⌂
▤ English & French ♆ ☕ Last dinner 8pm
VS

★★**Maidencombe House** Teignmouth Rd ☎ (0803) 36611 District plan **23A**
28rm (15→ 1⋒) (7fb) CTV in 12 bedrooms ® ✈ sB&B £12–£14 sB&B→⋒ £14–£16 dB&B £16–£20 dB&B→⋒ £24–£26 ⊟
☾ CTV 40P ✽ ⛆ (heated) Live music and dancing twice wkly ⌂
▤ English & French V ♆ ☕ Lunch £4 Tea 50p High Tea £2 Dinner fr£6 Wine £3.10 Last dinner 8.30pm
Credit card ①

★★**Meadfoot Bay** Meadfoot Sea Rd ☎ (0803) 24722 District plan **47**
Closed Oct–Mar
Double-fronted villa standing in its own grounds in the Meadfoot Bay area.
26rm (9→ 2⋒) (5fb) CTV in 11 bedrooms TV in 15 bedrooms ® sB&B £9–£15.50 dB&B £16–£29 dB&B→⋒ £21–£34 ⊟
CTV 20P ✽ nc3yrs *xmas*
Wine £3.95
Credit card ① **VS**

★★**Morningside** Sea Front, Babbacombe Downs ☎ (0803) 37025 District plan **48**
Closed Oct–mid Apr
On Babbacombe Downs with panoramic views towards Lyme Bay.

T

18rm(1⋔)(2fb) CTV available on request ® ✱ sB&B£12–£14 dB&B£24–£30 dB&B⋔£24–£30

CTV 14P 🚗 nc5yrs

V ♆ ☕ Bar lunch £2–£4 Tea 40p–60p Dinner £5–£6.50 Wine £3 Last dinner 7pm

★★**Nethway** Falkland Rd ☎(0803) 27630 Central plan **25** *B2*
Closed Nov–Mar (except Xmas)

Hotel is in elevated position near Abbey gardens.

26rm(12➡12⋔)(6fb) sB&B£10–£15 sB&B➡⋔£11.50–£16.50 dB&B➡⋔£22–£32 ℞

☾ CTV 26P ✽ ⛲(heated) ▶ Live music and dancing 3 nights wkly Cabaret wkly *xmas* ♿

♆ Bar lunch 50p–£1.50 Tea fr50p Dinner fr£5 Wine £3.50 Last dinner 8pm

Credit card 3 **VS**

★★**Norcliffe** Sea Front, Babbacombe ☎(0803) 38456 District plan **49**
Closed Nov–mid Apr

Imposing villa on Babbacombe sea front, offering fine views, and near to the shops.

22rm(8➡1⋔)(4fb) CTV in 6 bedrooms ® sB&B£9.50–£15 dB&B£19–£30 dB&B➡⋔£23–£34 ℞

CTV 17P 🚗 🏠

English & French V ♆ ☕ Bar lunch £1–£3 Tea £1.25–£2 Dinner £5–£7 Wine £2.95 Last dinner 7.45pm

Credit cards 1 3

★★*HB* **Orestone House** Rockhouse Ln, Maidencombe (Exec Hotel) ☎(0803) 38099 District plan **50**
Closed 27 Nov–4 Mar (except Xmas) →

MAGNIFICENT SEA VIEWS ....
Norcliffe Hotel

T

Set on a hillside in a quiet valley this hotel has good sea views.

15rm(5➡6⋒)(7fb) CTV in all bedrooms ®sB&B£15–£17 sB&B➡⋒£17–£20 dB&B£30–£34 dB&B➡⋒£34–£40 ₿

CTV 28P ⛟ ✽ ≋ (heated) ⌂ *xmas*

V ♧ ☐ ✻ Lunch £4.25 Tea 55p–£1 Dinner £6.50&alc Wine £3.30 Last dinner 8.30pm

Credit cards 1 2 5 **VS**

★★ ***Overmead*** Daddyhole Rd ☎(0803) 27633 District plan **52**
Closed Dec–Mar
Stone-built, split-level hotel with a modern wing extension set in a quiet position.

60rm(16➡⋒) ✈ ₿

Lift ☾ CTV 7P 13⌂ ≋ (heated) billiards

♧ ☐ Last dinner 7pm

Credit cards 1 3 **VS**

★★ **Rock Walk** Warren Rd ☎(0803) 28775 Central plan **28** *D2*
Closed end Nov–mid Mar
Simply-appointed, holiday hotel overlooking Torbay.

31rm(7➡12⋒)(9fb) CTV available on request sB&B£8.95–£11.75 sB&B➡⋒£10.30–£13.10 dB&B£17.90–£23.50 dB&B➡⋒£20.60–£26.20 ₿

☾ CTV 10P Live music and dancing wkly ⌂ *xmas*

V ♧ ☐ Bar lunch 80p–£2.90 Tea 50p–95p Dinner £5.35 Wine £3.90 Last dinner 8pm

★★ ***Hotel Roseland*** Warren Rd ☎(0803) 24614 Central plan **29** *C2*
Closed Nov–Apr
This hotel is in an elevated position overlooking the beach.

28rm(12➡) ₿

CTV 6⌂ Disco twice wkly

♧ ☐ Last dinner 8pm

VS

★★ **Shedden Hall** ☎(0803) 22964 Central plan **30** *C2*
Closed Nov–Mar
Family-run holiday hotel with a pleasant garden, on rising ground overlooking Torbay.

27rm(16➡14⋒)(4fb) 1⊟ CTV in 7 bedrooms ® sB&B£8.50–£12 dB&B£17–£22 dB&B➡⋒£19–£30 ₿

CTV 27P ✽ ≋ (heated)

V ♧ ☐ Bar lunch 45p–£1.90 Tea fr35p Dinner £7 Wine £3.65 Last dinner 8pm

Credit cards 1 3

★★ **Sunray** Aveland Rd, Babbacombe ☎(0803) 38285 District plan **55**
Closed Xmas
Situated near shops and sea front in Babbacombe.

22rm(13➡5⋒)(2fb) CTV available in bedrooms sB&B£9–£10 sB&B➡⋒£10–£11 dB&B£18–£20 dB&B➡⋒£19–£21 ₿

CTV 15P 1⌂ Disco wkly Live music and dancing wkly

▤ English & French ♧ ☐ Bar lunch fr90p Tea 60p Dinner £5–£6 Wine £4.20 Last dinner 8pm

Credit cards 1 3

★★ **Sydore** Meadfoot Rd ☎(0803) 24758 Central plan **32** *F2*
This villa in its own grounds is near town centre and harbour.

14rm(3➡)(3fb) CTV in 3 bedrooms TV in 10 bedrooms sB&B£7–£8.50 sB&B➡£8–£9.50 dB&B£14–£17 dB&B➡£16–£19 ₿

CTV 25P ✽ ⌂ *xmas*

V Lunch £3.50 Tea fr75p Dinner fr£4.75 Wine £3 Last dinner 7.30pm

VS

★★ ***Templestowe*** Tor Church Rd ☎(0803) 25145 Central plan **33** *C3*
Closed Jan & Feb
Holiday hotel, personally supervised by the resident owners, close to the beach and the town centre.

93rm(45➡2⋒) CTV available in bedrooms

Lift ☾ CTV 60P ≋ (heated) ⚲ (hard) ⌂

V ♧ ☐ Last dinner 8pm

Credit cards 1 3

★★ **Vernon Court** Warren Rd ☎(0803) 22676 Central plan **35** *C2*
Closed Nov–Mar
In superb, commanding position offering panoramic views over Torbay and the sea.

19rm(12➡2⋒)(5fb) TV in all bedrooms ® ✈ ✻ sB&B£9–£13 sB&B➡⋒£9.50–£16.50 dB&B£18–£26 dB&B➡⋒£19–£33 ₿

CTV 9P ⛟ ✽ nc3yrs

✻ Dinner £6 Wine £4 Last dinner 8pm

VS

★★ **Viscount** St Albans Rd, Babbacombe ☎(0803) 37444 District plan **56**
Closed Nov–mid Apr
Large villa situated just off main road.

20rm(6➡⋒)(3fb) TV in all bedrooms ® sB&B£10–£15 dB&B£20–£30 dB&B➡⋒£25–£35 ₿

CTV 20P ≋ (heated) nc3yrs

V ♧ ☐ ✻ Bar lunch £1.25–£2 Tea £1.25–£2 High Tea £4–£5 Dinner £6–£8 Wine £3.70 Last dinner 8pm

★ **Ashley Rise** 18 Babbacombe Rd, Babbacombe ☎(0803) 37282 District plan **38**
RS Nov–Mar (except Xmas)
Detached, modern hotel on the main Babbacombe road into Torquay, near the sea front and the shops.

29rm(1➡3⋒)(8fb) ® ✻ sB&B£9.75–£11.50 dB&B£18–£25.20 dB&B➡⋒£22–£29.20

CTV 14P 3⌂ Live music and dancing 3 nights wkly *xmas*

♧ ☐ Bar lunch £1.50 Tea £1 Dinner £5 Wine £3.50 Last dinner 7pm

★ **Carlton** Falkland Rd ☎(0803) 27666 Central plan **6** *B3*
Closed 22 Oct–30 Mar
Sea views can be enjoyed from this hotel.

35rm(12➡)(17fb) ✻ sB&B£7.50–£11.75 dB&B£15–£23.50 dB&B➡£17.50–£33.50 ₿

CTV 26P ✽ ≋ (heated) Disco Fri (Jun–Sep) Live music and dancing Mon & Fri Cabaret alternate Suns ⌂

V✿☕✱Lunch fr£3.45 Tea fr40p High Tea fr£1.50 Dinner fr£4.60 Wine £3.85 Last dinner 7.30pm
VS

★**Fairmount House** Herbert Rd, Chelston ☎(0803) 605446 District plan **44**
Closed 5 Nov–Jan
Quiet, well-appointed hotel, with personal service.
7rm(2➡3⋔)(3fb)Ⓡ sB&B£9–£10.25 dB&B£18–£20.50 dB&B➡⋔£20.50–£23
Unlicensed CTV 8P ⌂
▣English & Continental ✿Bar lunch £1.75–£4 Dinner £4.75–£5.50 Last dinner 7.30pm
Credit card [3] **VS**

★**Penrhyn** Cary Park, Babbacombe ☎(0803) 37385 District plan **54**
Closed Dec & Jan
Two adjoining villas have been linked by a new reception area in this hotel which overlooks the Park gardens.
20rm(5➡7⋔)(5fb)Ⓡ sB&B£8–£11 sB&B➡⋔£9.50–£12.50 dB&B£16–£22 dB&B➡⋔£19–£25 B
CTV 19P ✽
✿☕Lunch £2–£3 Tea £1–£1.50 Dinner £5 Wine £4 Last dinner 8.30pm

★**Shelley Court** Croft Rd ☎(0803) 25642 Central plan **31** *C3*
Closed Nov–Feb (except Xmas)
Attractive, villa-style hotel with a new extension, set in its own grounds, overlooking Abbey Sands.
29rm(1➡13⋔)(1fb) sB&B £8.05–£9.20 sB&B➡⋔£9.20–£10.35 dB&B£16.10–£18.40 dB&B➡⋔£18.40–£20.70 B
CTV 18P ✽ Disco twice wkly Cabaret wkly *xmas*
V✿☕Bar lunch £1–£2 Tea 35p–75p Wine £3.75 Last dinner 7.30pm
VS

★***Woodland Park*** Babbacombe Rd, Babbacombe ☎(0803) 38043 District plan **57** Closed Nov–Mar
Colour-washed villa in the Babbacombe area, near the shops and the clifftops.
18rm(5➡)
CTV 15P 🚗
V✿☕Last dinner 7.30pm
Credit card [3] **VS**

✕**Cafè Old Vienna** 6 Lisburne Sq ☎(0803) 25861 Central plan **25A** *F3*
Lunch not served Sun
▣Austrian **V** 24 seats ✱Lunch 60p–£4&alc Dinner £10alc Wine £4.75 Last dinner 10pm 6P
Credit cards [1] [3]

✕**Green Mantle** 135 Babbacombe Rd ☎(0803) 34292 District plan **46A**
Lunch not served Mon–Sat Dinner not served Sun
▣French 20 seats ✱Lunch £3.85 Dinner £6.95–£9.65&alc Wine £4.10 Last dinner 10pm ⊘
Credit cards [2] [3] **VS**

✕**Lisburne** 7 Lisburne Sq ☎(0803) 26968 Central plan **23A** *F3*
Closed Sun Lunch not served Mon
▣French & German 24 seats ✱Lunch £2.50–£4&alc Dinner £12alc Wine £4.90 Last dinner 10pm 3P
Credit cards [1] [2] [3] [5] **VS**

TORRIDON
Highland *Ross & Cromarty*
Map **14** NG85

★★***Loch Torridon*** ☎(044 587) 242
Closed mid Oct–Apr
On the southern shores of Loch Torridon, looking across to Torridon village.
19rm(11➡) B
CTV 30P 🚗 ✽ ⌂
▣Scottish & French ✿☕Last dinner 9pm
Credit cards [1] [2] [3] [4] [5]

TORRINGTON, GREAT
Devon
Map **2** SS41

★★**Castle Hill** South St ☎(08052) 2339
Commercial and holiday hotel in a quiet situation on the edge of the town.
12rm(8➡2⋔)(1fb) CTV in all bedrooms ✱sB&B£12.73 sB&B➡⋔£14.23 dB&B£18.70 dB&B➡⋔£21.70 B
CTV 40P ✽ *xmas*
▣Mainly grills **V**✿☕Lunch £1.95–£3.25 Tea 50p–£1 High Tea £1–£1.95 Dinner £3.90–£9.25&alc Wine £3.60 Last dinner 8.45pm
Credit cards [1] [3] **VS**

TOTLAND BAY
Isle of Wight
Map **4** SZ38

★★**Country Garden** Church Hill ☎Freshwater (0983) 754521
Closed 25 & 26 Dec
Small friendly hotel with comfortable modern bedrooms.
16➡ CTV in all bedrooms Ⓡ sB&B➡⋔£17–£18 dB&B➡⋔£34–£36 B
32P 🚗 ✽ nc14yrs
▣French Lunch £5.50 Dinner £10.50&alc Wine £4.60 Last dinner 9.30pm
Credit cards [1] [2] [3] [5]

★★**Sentry Mead** ☎Freshwater (0983) 753212
Closed Nov–Feb (except Xmas)
Small, cosy, family-run hotel.
13rm(5➡)(2fb) ✱sB&B£13–£15 sB&B➡£15–£17 dB&B£26–£30 dB&B➡£30–£34
⊬CTV 12P ✽
▣English & French ✿☕Bar lunch £2–£4 Tea 60p–£1.50 Dinner £7.50–£9 Wine £3.50 Last dinner 8pm
Credit cards [1] [2] [3]

TOTNES
Devon
Map **3** SX86

★★★**Seymour** Bridgetown ☎(0803) 864686
Spacious hotel beside the River Dart.
29rm(19➡)(1fb) CTV in 3 bedrooms ✱sB&B£15 sB&B➡£17.50 dB&B£22.50 dB&B➡£28.60 B
☾ CTV 30P 4🚗 ♪ *xmas*
▣English & French **V**✿☕Lunch £5.65–£6.50&alc Tea 45p–65p High Tea £1.20–£2 Dinner £5.65–£6.50&alc Wine £3.55 Last dinner 10pm
Credit cards [1] [2] [3] [5]

★★**Royal Seven Stars** ☎(0803) 862125
Historical coaching inn situated in town centre.
18rm(8➡)(5fb) sB&B£17.50–£18.50 sB&B➡£21–£22 dB&B£26–£28 dB&B➡£32–£34 B
CTV 25P Live music and dancing Sat Cabaret Sat *xmas*
✿Lunch £5–£5.50 Dinner £8.25–£8.50 Wine £4.90 Last dinner 9.30pm
Credit cards [1] [3] [5]
See advert on page 642

✕✕***Elbow Room*** ☎(0803) 863480
A former cider press, this is now an attractive, cottage-style restaurant in a quiet position on the edge of the town.
Dinner not served Sun & Mon (except Public hols)
▣International 30 seats Last dinner 9.30pm
Credit cards [2] [3]

✕✕**Ffoulkes** 30 High St ☎(0803) 863853
An attractive, double-fronted, terraced restaurant.
Dinner not served Sun
▣French **V** 60 seats Lunch £5alc Dinner £9.50alc Wine £4.50 Last dinner 9.45pm ⊘
Credit cards [1] [2] [3] [5]

TOTON
Nottinghamshire
Map **8** SK53

✕✕**Grange Farm** ☎Long Eaton (06076) 69426
Old stone farmhouse with traditional décor including porcelain figures in a display cabinet.
Closed Sun & Public hols
V 180 seats ✱Lunch £5.25alc Dinner £7.50alc Wine £3.75 Last dinner 9pm 150P Live music and dancing Sat
Credit cards [1] [3] [5]

TREARDDUR BAY
Gwynedd
Map **6** SH27

★★★**Beach** (Best Western) ☎(0407) 860332 Telex no 61529
Prominent hotel with extensive facilities, including a special health clinic, set back from the beach.
26rm(21→5⋒) (2fb) CTV in 19 bedrooms TV in 7 bedrooms Ⓡ *sB&B→⋒£19.95 dB&B→⋒£32.90 B
200P squash sauna bath Disco 3 nights wkly
V ♡ ⊒ *Lunch £4–£6 Tea 75p–£2.50 High Tea 75p–£2.50 Dinner £4–£6&alc Wine £4.50 Last dinner 10.30pm
Credit cards 1 2 3 5

★★★**Trearddur Bay** ☎(0407) 860301 Telex no 61609
Impressive, three-storey hotel with its own helipad, close to the beach.
28rm(17→) Annexe: 12rm(4→) (4fb) TV in 22 bedrooms CTV in 6 bedrooms Ⓡ sB&B£16–£20 sB&B→£20.50–£21.50 dB&B£29–£35 dB&B→£36–£40 B
☾ CTV 200P ✽ ⊡ (heated) *xmas*
V ♡ ⊒ Lunch £3.50–£4.50&alc Tea fr75p High Tea 75p–£2.50 Dinner £6.65&alc Wine £5.50
Last dinner 9.30pm
Credit cards 1 2 3 5

★★***Seacroft*** Ravenspoint Rd ☎(0407) 860348
Two-storey hotel near the beach.
6rm(1→2⋒) ★
CTV 35P ✽ nc3yrs
English & French ♡ Last dinner 9.15pm

TREBETHERICK
Cornwall
Map **2** SW97

★★**St Moritz** (Inter-Hotels) ☎(020886) 2242
Comfortable family hotel near beach.
50→ (5fb) CTV available in bedrooms sB&B→£16–£19 dB&B→£30–£36 B
CTV 200P ✽ Disco wkly ⌂ *xmas*
V ♡ ⊒ Lunch £4–£4.50 Tea 35p–£1.25 Dinner £7–£7.50 Wine £4.50 Last dinner 8.30pm
Credit cards 1 2 3 5

★***Fore Dore*** ☎(020886) 3471
Closed Nov–Mar
11rm
CTV 10P ✽
♡ ⊒ Last dinner 8.30pm

TREGARON
Dyfed
Map **3** SN65

★**Talbot** ☎(09744) 208
Closed Oct–Mar
14rm(4→) Ⓡ sB&B fr£11 sB&B→ fr£11 dB&B£20 dB&B→£20
TV
♡ Lunch fr£4.75 Dinner fr£7.50 Wine £2.75 Last dinner 9pm

TRELIGHTS
Cornwall
Map **2** SW97

★★**Long Cross** ☎Port Isaac (020888) 243 Closed mid Oct–19 Apr RS Oct
Fine Victorian house standing in 3 acres of gardens, with panoramic views of the North Cornwall coast.
16rm(4→4⋒) (8fb) 1 *sB&B£8.63 sB&B→⋒£10.92 dB&B£17.26 dB&B→⋒£21.84
CTV 50P ✽
♡ *Bar lunch 40p–£1.85 Dinner £4 Wine £2.75 Last dinner 8pm

TREMADOG
Gwynedd
Map **6** SH54

★★**Madoc** ☎Porthmadog (0766) 2021
Early 19th-century inn with oak beams and a granite fireplace.
22rm(2⋒) (4fb) sB&B fr£14 sB&B⋒ fr£15.75 dB&B fr£26 dB&B⋒ fr£27.75 B
CTV 14P 4 ✽ ⌂ *xmas*
V ♡ ⊒ Lunch £4–£4.50 Tea 60p–£1.20 High Tea £1.40–£2.50 Dinner £5.50alc Wine £3.25 Last dinner 9pm
Credit card 1 3

TREVONE
Cornwall
Map **2** SW87

★**Trevone Bay** (off B3276) ☎Padstow (0841) 520243
Closed Oct–Apr
Small family hotel with good sea views.
15rm (3fb) sB&B£8.05–£8.80 dB&B£16.10–£17.60
CTV 12P ⌂
♡ ⊒ Bar lunch £1–£3 Tea 70p Dinner £6 Wine £3.40
Last dinner 7.30pm

TREYARNON BAY
Cornwall
Map **2** SW87

★★**Waterbeach** St Merryn ☎Padstow (0841) 520292 Closed Nov–Apr
Comfortable, personally run, family holiday hotel in a peaceful setting, 200 yards from the beach.
16rm(7→) (2fb) ★ sB&B£19.75 dB&B£37.50 dB&B→£39.50
CTV 35P 6 ✽ (hard) ⌂
♡ ⊒ Bar lunch £2.50alc Tea 75p Dinner £8.25 Wine £4.50
Last dinner 8.30pm
Credit cards 1 3

TRING
Hertfordshire
Map **4** SP91

★★**Rose and Crown (Henekeys)** High St (Trusthouse Forte) ☎(044282) 4071
Built by a Rothschild in the early 20th century, this hotel is in the style of a Tudor coaching house.
16rm(8→) (2fb) CTV in all bedrooms Ⓡ sB&B£26 dB&B£36.50 dB&B→£41 B
CTV 30P *xmas*
Mainly grills ♡ Last dinner 9.30pm
Credit cards 1 2 3 4 5

T

TROON
Strathclyde *Ayrshire*
Map **10** NS33

★★★★**Marine** (Scottish Highland) ☎(0292) 314444 Telex no 778215
Victorian, red sandstone, traditional golfing hotel overlooking two golf courses and offering a choice of three restaurants.
70➡ (5fb) CTV in 70 bedrooms ® *sB&B➡£32 dB&B➡£54 B
Lift ☾ CTV 100P 5🚗 CFA ✽ 🎾(hard) billiards
English & French V ✿ ☕ *Lunch £5.50&alc Dinner £9.50–£11&alc Wine £4.75 Last dinner 10.30pm
Credit cards 1 2 3 4 5 VS

★★★*L* **Sun Court** Crosbie Rd ☎(0292) 312727
Spacious former home of a wealthy industrialist, overlooking the sea, the facilities incorporate a Real Tennis Court.
20rm(18➡) (2fb) CTV in all bedrooms sB&B£26 sB&B➡£29 dB&B£40 dB&B➡£44 B
CTV 70P ✽ 🎾(hard) squash
Scottish, French & Italian ✿ Lunch fr£7&alc Dinner fr£10&alc Wine £4 Last dinner 9.30pm
S% Credit cards 1 2

★★**Ardneil** St Meddans St ☎(0292) 311611
Closed 1 Jan
Popular busy hotel with friendly atmosphere and home cooking.
9rm(3➡) (2fb) CTV in 3 bedrooms ® sB&B£13 sB&B➡£15.50 dB&B£22 dB&B➡£27
CTV 45P ✽
✿ ☕ Bar lunch £2.80–£4.50 Tea £1.50 High Tea £3.95–£5.50 Dinner fr£7.25 Wine £3.70 Last dinner 8.30pm

★★**Craiglea** South Beach ☎(0292) 311366
Family run resort hotel on seafront.
22rm(11➡1⋒) (2fb) CTV in 12 bedrooms ® sB&B£17.50–£19.50 sB&B➡⋒£19.50–£21.50 dB&B£30–£33 dB&B➡⋒£32–£35 B
CTV 14P Live music and dancing Sat *xmas*
V ✿ ☕ Lunch £5–£6.50&alc Tea 40p–£1 High Tea £3.95–£5 Dinner £7.50–£8.50&alc Wine £4.50 Last dinner 8.45pm
Credit cards 1 2 3 5

★★*L* **Piersland Lodge** Craigend Rd ☎(0292) 314747
A listed historic building in Tudor style with open fires, wood panelling and carvings.
12rm(5➡7⋒) CTV in 9 bedrooms ® ★ sB&B➡⋒£17.50 dB&B➡⋒£28 B
CTV 150P ✽ 🎾 sauna bath Live music and dancing Fri & Sun *xmas*
French & Italian V ✿ ☕ Lunch £3.30alc Tea 55p alc High Tea £3alc Dinner £8.25&alc Wine £3.50 Last dinner 9pm
S% Credit cards 1 3 5 VS

★★**South Beach** South Beach Rd ☎(0292) 312033
RS Nov–Apr
Large, white painted hotel, close to the seafront and offering good value accommodation and food.
29rm(6➡) (2fb) CTV in 7 bedrooms ® *sB&B£12 sB&B➡£15.50 dB&B£24 dB&B➡⋒£29.50
CTV 40P ✽ billiards
✿ ☕ *Lunch £2.50–£5.50&alc Tea 75p–£1.75&alc High Tea £3.25–£5.25&alc Dinner £7.45&alc Wine £3.25 Last dinner 8pm
Credit cards 1 2 3 VS

✕✕**L'Auberge de Provence** (Marine Hotel) Crosbie Rd ☎(0292) 314444
Closed Sun & Mon Lunch not served
French V 50 seats *Dinner £10–£15&alc Wine £7 Last dinner 10.30pm 100P bedrooms available Live music and dancing Sat
Credit cards 1 2 3 4 5

TROWBRIDGE
Wiltshire
Map **3** ST85

★*B* **Hilbury Court** Hilperton Rd ☎(02214) 2949
Closed 25 Dec–1 Jan
12rm(4➡) (2fb) CTV in all bedrooms ® ★ sB&B£15 sB&B➡£17 dB&B£27 dB&B➡£29
CTV 20P ✽
✿ ☕ Bar lunch 75p–£2.50 Tea 60p Dinner £6 Wine £4.10 Last dinner 7.30pm
Credit cards 1 3

★**Polebarn House** Polebarn Rd ☎(02214) 65624 Telex no 444337
Clean simply furnished hotel in grade II listed building.
10rm(2⋒) (2fb) CTV in all bedrooms sB&B£18 sB&B⋒£19.50 dB&B£25 dB&B⋒£27 B
TV 12P Disco 3 nights wkly
English & French V ✿ Lunch £8alc High Tea £2alc Dinner £8alc Wine £4.25 Last dinner 9pm
Credit cards 1 2 3

TRURO
Cornwall
Map **2** SW84

★★★**Royal** Lemon St ☎(0872) 70345
RS Xmas
Commercial and tourist hotel in central situation with modern bedrooms.
34➡ (3fb) CTV in all bedrooms ® sB&B➡£18.50–£22 dB&B➡£35–£38 B
☾ CTV 20P 14🚗 CFA
✿ ☕ Lunch £3.95–£4.20 Tea 55p–75p Dinner £3.95–£4.20&alc Last dinner 9pm
Credit cards 1 3

★★**Brookdale** Tregoll's Rd ☎(0872) 73513
Small, professional hotel convenient for the city and touring in the area.
31rm(5➡7⋒) Annexe: 18rm(5➡3⋒) CTV in all bedrooms ® sB&B fr£20 sB&B➡⋒ fr£26 dB&B fr£32 dB&B➡⋒ fr£42 B
50P 10🚗
English & Italian V ✿ ☕ Lunch £3.50–£5 Tea fr60p Dinner £7.50–£9 Wine £4 →

T

Last dinner 8.45pm
Credit cards 1 2 3 5

★★**Carlton** Falmouth Rd ☎(0872) 72450
Closed 22 Dec–6 Jan
Small hotel on the Falmouth road, close to the city centre.
25rm(3⇌8⋒)(3fb) CTV in 25 bedrooms sB&B£13.96 sB&B⇌⋒£15.96 dB&B£22.50 dB&B⇌⋒£27 B
30P
V ♡ ☕ Dinner £4.85&alc Wine £3.60 Last dinner 8pm
Credit cards 1 3 VS

TUNBRIDGE WELLS (ROYAL)
Kent
Map **5** TQ53
★★★ *L* **Spa** Mount Ephraim ☎(0892) 20331 Telex no 957188
Well-run hotel with good compact bedrooms and skilful cooking.
70rm(68⇌2⋒)(4fb) CTV in all bedrooms ®sB&B⇌⋒£37.50–£40 dB&B⇌⋒£52–£56 B
Lift ☾ 100P 4⌂ CFA ✽ ⛳ (hard) xmas
English & French V ♡ ☕ Lunch £8.50–£9&alc Tea £1.25–£2 High Tea £3.50–£4 Dinner £9.50–£10&alc Wine £6.50 Last dinner 9.30pm
Credit cards 1 2 3 4 5 VS

★★**Calverley** Crescent Rd ☎(0892) 26455 Telex no 95395
Well managed hotel with spacious bedrooms and providing friendly service.
43rm(21⇌2⋒)(2fb) CTV in 20 bedrooms sB&B fr£16 sB&B⇌⋒ fr£19 dB&B fr£28 dB&B⇌⋒ fr£31 B
Lift ☾ CTV 34P ✽

T

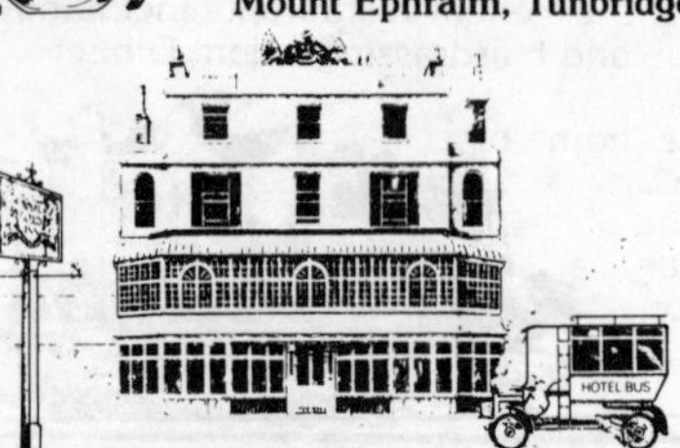
HOTEL BUS

✻Lunch fr£4.50 Tea fr60p Dinner fr£5.50&alc Wine £3.50 Last dinner 8.30pm
Credit cards 1 2 3 5 VS

★★**Royal Wells Inn** Mount Ephraim ☎(0892) 23414
Closed 25 Dec
Comfortable, old fashioned hotel with high standard of cooking.
15→ 2 CTV in all bedrooms sB&B→£18 dB&B→£28.60 B
CTV 20P
English & French V Lunch £5.50–£8&alc Dinner £8–£12&alc Wine £4.10 Last dinner 9.30pm
Credit cards 1 3 5 VS

★★*L* **Wellington** Mount Ephraim (ExecHotel) ☎(0892) 42911 Telex no 23152
The Victorian atmosphere here is combined with friendly service.
68rm(32→5) (3fb) 2 CTV in 8 bedrooms sB&B fr£14 sB&B→ fr£18.50 dB&B fr£26 dB&B→ fr£32 B
Lift ☾ CTV 25P CFA ✻ sauna bath *xmas*
Bar lunch £1.25–£5 Tea fr£1 High Tea £2.50 Dinner fr£7 Last dinner 9pm
Credit cards 1 2 3 5 VS

★**Russell** 80 London Rd (Minotel) ☎(0892) 44833
Friendly hotel, personally run by proprietor and being modernised.
21rm(5→10) (4fb) CTV in all bedrooms sB&B fr£15.50 sB&B→ fr£24 dB&B fr£28 dB&B→ fr£34
CTV 16P
English & French V Lunch £4–£7.50 Tea 60p–£2 Dinner fr£7.50&alc Wine £3.50 Last dinner 9pm
Credit cards 1 2 3 5

✕***La Vieille Auberge*** 9–11 Langton Rd ☎(0892) 21575
Popular roadside restaurant and wine bar with friendly, attentive, service.
Closed Mon
French & Swiss 60 seats Last dinner 10pm
Credit cards 1 2 3 5

TURNBERRY
Strathclyde *Ayrshire*
Map **10** NS20

★★★★*L* ***Turnberry*** ☎(06553) 202 Telex no 777779
Spacious Edwardian hotel overlooking championship golf courses. Beautifully appointed rooms and high standard of food.
124rm(116→8) CTV in all bedrooms B
Lift ☾ CTV 125P CFA ✻ (heated) 18 (hard) billiards sauna bath Live music and dancing Sat
French V Last dinner 9.30pm
Credit cards 1 2 3 4 5

TURVEY
Bedfordshire
Map **4** SP95

★★**Laws** ☎(023 064) 213
RS Xmas
Nicely appointed hotel with good restaurant.
5rm(4→1) TV in all bedrooms ® sB&B→ £24.50 dB&B→ £38.50
CTV 50P ✻ nc8yrs
English & French V Lunch £9.50alc Dinner £9.50alc Wine £4.50 Last dinner 9pm (10pm Fri & Sat)
Credit cards 1 3 VS

TUTBURY
Staffordshire
Map **8** SK22

★★★**Ye Olde Dog and Partridge** High St ☎Burton-on-Trent (0283) 813030
Closed 25, 26 Dec & 1 Jan
Remarkable 15th-century timbered inn with elegant period décor.
3rm(1→) Annexe: 14rm(12→2) 3 CTV in all bedrooms ® sB&B fr£20 sB&B→ fr£32 dB&B fr£26 dB&B→ fr£38

→

T

☾ 100P ⇌ ✽ Live music nightly nc6yrs
▣ English & French V ♆ Lunch fr£6.50&alc Dinner £6–£7&alc Wine £3.90 Last dinner 9.45pm
Credit cards 1 2 3

TUXFORD
Nottinghamshire
Map **8** SK77

★★ *L* ***Newcastle Arms*** ☎ (0777) 870208
73rm(6⇌2⋔) TV in 8 bedrooms CTV in 5 bedrooms
150P ⇌ ✽
▣ English & French ♆ ⊐ Last dinner 9.30pm
Credit cards 1 2 3 5

TWEEDSMUIR
Borders *Peeblesshire*
Map **11** NT12

★★ **Crook Inn** ☎ (08997) 272
Roadside hotel in rural upper Tweed Valley.
8rm(5⇌1⋔)(1fb) Ⓡ sB&B£15.80–£16.80 sB&B⇌⋔£16.80–£17.80 dB&B£29.60–£31.60 dB&B⇌⋔£31.60–£33.60 Ɓ
CTV 50P 3⌂ ⇌ ✽ ♪
▣ Scottish & French ♆ ⊐ Bar lunch £3.25alc High Tea £3.95 Dinner £8.25–£10.25&alc Wine £4.75 Last dinner 8.45pm

TWICKENHAM
Gt London
London plan **5** B2 (page 422)

✕ **Quincey's** 34 Church St ☎ 01-892 6366
Closed Sun & Public hols Lunch not served Sat
▣ English & French 26 seats ✱ Lunch £9alc Dinner £9alc Wine £4.60 Last dinner 10.45pm ⊅
S% Credit cards 1 2 3 5

TYNEMOUTH
Tyne and Wear
Map **12** NZ36

★★★ **Grand** Grand Pde ☎ North Shields (0632) 572106
Predominantly a commercial hotel in pleasant sea front location.
39rm(33⇌)(3fb) CTV in all bedrooms Ⓡ ✱ sB&B fr£19.50 sB&B⇌ fr£27 dB&B fr£32 dB&B⇌ fr£35 Ɓ
Lift ☾ CTV CFA Disco 3 nights wkly *xmas*
▣ International V ♆ ⊐ ✱ Lunch fr£4.50&alc Tea fr40p High Tea fr£1.95 Dinner fr£6.35&alc Wine £4.50 Last dinner 10pm
Credit cards 1 2 3 5 **VS**

★★ **Park** Grand Pde ☎ Newcastle (0632) 571406
RS Xmas & New Year
28rm(26⇌2⋔)(4fb) CTV in all bedrooms Ⓡ ✱ sB&B£11.50–£16 sB&B⇌⋔£11.50–£28 dB&B£23 dB&B⇌⋔£23–£33 Ɓ
☾ 500P Live music and dancing Wed
V ♆ ✱ Lunch £3.95–£5.25&alc Dinner £5.25–£7.25&alc Wine £4.90 Last dinner 10pm
Credit cards 1 2 3 5 **VS**

TYNET
Grampian *Banffshire*
Map **15** NJ36

★★ **Mill Motel** (Minotel) ☎ Clochan (05427) 233
Converted mill whose modern facilities blend well with the original features.
16rm(13⇌3⋔)(1fb) CTV in all bedrooms Ⓡ sB&B⇌⋔£18.50 dB&B⇌⋔£34 Ɓ
120P Live music and dancing Wed & Sat
V ♆ ⊐ Lunch £3–£3.50 Tea £1–£1.50 High Tea £2.50–£5 Dinner £7–£9 Wine £3 Last dinner 8.30pm
Credit cards 1 2 5

TYTHERLEIGH
Devon
Map **3** ST30

✕ ***Tytherleigh Arms*** ☎ South Chard (0460) 20214

T

Dinner not served Sun
▤English, French & Italian 40 seats Last dinner 9.30pm 75P
Credit cards 1 3

TYWYN
Gwynedd
Map **6** SH50

★★**Corbett Arms** Corbett Sq ☎(0654) 710264
26rm(10➡)(3fb) CTV in 3 bedrooms Ⓡ
✻sB&B£14.50 sB&B➡£16.50 dB&B£29 dB&B➡£33 Ᵽ
CTV 60P 10🚗✻ xmas
Lunch £3.75–£4.25 Tea 45p High Tea £1.95–£2.50 Dinner £5.25&alc Wine £4.50 Last dinner 8.45pm
Credit cards 1 2 3 5

★***Gorlan*** Marine Pde ☎(0654) 710404
Holiday hotel on sea front.
8rm Ᵽ
CTV 2P
▤English & French **V** Last dinner 9.30pm

UIG
Isle of Skye, Highland *Inverness-shire*
Map **13** NG36

★★**Uig** ☎(047 042) 205
Closed 8 Oct–14 Apr RS 14–30 Apr
Well appointed family run hotel overlooking Uig Bay.
12rm(6➡6⋒) Annexe: 9rm(4➡5⋒)(2fb)
Ⓡ sB&B➡⋒£15–£24 dB&B➡⋒£30–£48 Ᵽ
20P✻ nc12yrs
V Bar lunch £2–£2.50 Tea 70p–£1.10 High Tea £3–£4 Dinner £8–£9 Last dinner 8pm
Credit cards 1 2 3 5

★**Ferry Inn** ☎(047 042) 242
Closed 1 & 2 Jan RS Nov–Mar
Stone house set back from the road with views over the bay and the harbour.
6rm(1➡)(2fb) Ⓡ sB&B£12–£20 dB&B£20–£21 dB&B➡£22–£25 Ᵽ
CTV 12P
V Bar lunch 70p–£3&alc Dinner £4.50–£6 Wine £3.20 Last dinner 8.30pm

UIST (NORTH), ISLE OF
Western Isles *Inverness-shire*
See **Lochmaddy**

UIST (SOUTH), ISLE OF
Western Isles *Inverness-shire*
See **Lochboisdale**

ULLAPOOL
Highland *Ross & Cromarty*
Map **14** NH19
See also **Leckmelm**

☆☆☆**Ladbroke** North Rd (on A835) (Ladbroke) ☎(0854) 2314 Closed Nov–Mar
Modern, low-rise complex standing on the main north road.
60➡(24fb) TV in all bedrooms Ⓡ
✻sB➡£21.50 dB➡£30 (room only) Ᵽ
☾ CTV 120P✻ sauna bath
✻Dinner £8.50 Last dinner 9pm
Credit cards 1 2 3 5

★★ ***BL Ceilidh Place*** West Argyle St ☎(0854) 2103
Closed Nov–Mar
A friendly and informal hotel offering varied entertainment.
26rm(8➡)
30P✻ Live music and dancing twice wkly Cabaret twice wkly
V
Last dinner mdnt

★★ ***L Harbour Lights*** Garve Rd ☎(0854) 2222 Closed Nov
22rm(9➡6⋒) TV in 2 bedrooms Ⓡ
CTV 25P✻
▤Mainly grills **V** Last dinner 8.30pm
Credit cards 1 5

★***Ferry Boat Inn*** Shore St ☎(0854) 2366
Closed Dec–Feb
A small, friendly, family run hotel in pleasant shore location.
11rm
TV
▤Seafood Last dinner 9pm
Credit card 1

ULLSWATER
Cumbria
See **Glenridding, Patterdale, Pooley Bridge** and **Watermillock**

ULVERSTON
Cumbria
Map **7** SD27

★★***Lonsdale House*** Daltongate ☎(0229) 52598 Closed Xmas
Originally built as an 18th-century town house, it has now been converted into a family-run hotel.
22rm(14➡) CTV in 14 bedrooms Ⓡ
CTV 40P✻
▤French **V** Last dinner 8.30pm
Credit cards 1 2

★★**Sefton House** Queen St ☎(0229) 52190
11rm(2➡5⋒) CTV in 8 bedrooms Ⓡ★
sB&B£16 sB&B➡⋒£21.50 dB&B£29 dB&B➡⋒£35 Ᵽ
CTV 3P
Lunch £3alc Tea 35palc Dinner £7.25alc Wine £3.75 Last dinner 9pm
Credit cards 1 3

★**Railway** Princes St ☎(0229) 52208
A small hotel near the sea and the 2,000 acres of Birkrigg Common.
8rm(2fb) Ⓡ sB&B£13.50–£14 dB&B£22–£24 Ᵽ
CTV 40P 3🚗
Lunch £3.50alc Dinner £5.50alc Wine £3.70 Last dinner 9pm
VS

UMBERLEIGH
Devon
Map **2** SS62

★★ ***B*Rising Sun Inn** (Wessex Taverns) ☎High Bickington (0769) 60447
Closed Nov–Feb
6rm(4➡) Annexe: 2rm Ⓡ sB&B fr£16 sB&B➡fr£19 dB&B fr£30 dB&B➡fr£36
CTV 24P 2🚗
Bar lunch 50p–£1.30 Dinner £7–£8 Wine £3.75 Last dinner 8.30pm
Credit cards 1 3

U

UNDERBARROW
Cumbria
Map **7** SD49

✕✕Greenriggs Country House Hotel
☎Crosthwaite (04488) 387

Charming country house hotel with open fires.

Closed Sun & Jan Lunch not served

European 40 seats Dinner £10.50 Wine £3.30 Last dinner 8pm 30P bedrooms available

UPHALL
Lothian *West Lothian*
Map **11** NT07

★★★ *B* Houstoun House
☎Broxburn (0506) 853831 Telex no 727148
Closed 1–3 Jan

Historic baronial tastefully furnished and extended. Fine restaurant and very extensive wine list.

30rm(27➡3⋒) (1fb) 10 CTV in all bedrooms sB&B➡⋒£33–£43 dB&B➡⋒£44–£60
☾ 100P ✽ ⚑18

Scottish & French Lunch £9–£12 Tea 75p Dinner £13–£15 Wine £4 Last dinner 9.30pm

Credit cards 1 2 5

UPHOLLAND
Lancashire
Map **7** SD50

★★Holland Hall 6 Lafford Ln ☎(0695) 624426
RS Bank Holidays

10rm(4➡6⋒) 1 CTV in all bedrooms Ⓡ sB&B➡⋒£16–£20 dB&B➡⋒£25–£29 B

☾ 250P ✽ ⚑18 Disco Fri, Sat & Sun *xmas*

English & French **V** Lunch £5.50–£5.95&alc Tea 90p–£1.80 High Tea £1.50–£2.75 Dinner £6.50–£6.95&alc Wine £4.75 Last dinner 10pm

Credit cards 1 2 3 5 **VS**

UPLYME
Devon
Map **3** SY39

★★★ *H* Devon Lyme Rd (Best Western)
☎Lyme Regis (02974) 3231

Closed Nov–mid Mar

Former 16th-century monastery which has been converted into a relaxing hotel.

21➡ B

CTV 30P ✽ (heated)

English & French
Last dinner 8.30pm

Credit cards 1 2 3

UPPER SLAUGHTER
Gloucestershire
Map **4** SP12

★★★ *L* Lords of the Manor
☎Bourton-on-the-Water (0451) 20243 Telex no 83147

Comfortable 17th-century manor house hotel in 7½ acres of grounds.

15rm(14➡1⋒) 2 Ⓡ sB&B➡⋒£30 dB&B➡⋒£60 Continental breakfast B

CTV 25P ✽ *xmas*

Lunch £6alc Dinner £9.50alc Wine £5.25 Last dinner 9.30pm

Credit cards 1 2 3 5

UPPINGHAM
Leicestershire
Map **4** SP89

★★★Falcon High St ☎(0572) 823535
Closed 25 Dec–30 Jan

Former coaching inn situated in the centre of this attractive old town.

26rm(14➡2⋒) (2fb) 1 CTV in all bedrooms sB&B£25 sB&B➡⋒£30 dB&B£35 dB&B➡⋒£40 B

☾ 30P 2

English & Continental Lunch £7alc Tea £1.50alc Dinner £8alc Wine £5 Last dinner 9.45pm

S% Credit cards 1 2 3 4 5

★Central 16 High St West (Minotel)
☎(0572) 822352

12rm(4➡) (2fb) CTV in 1 bedroom Ⓡ sB&B£14 sB&B➡£18 dB&B£20.50 dB&B➡£25 B

CTV ✽

V Lunch £3.95–£4.95&alc Tea 60p High Tea £2.50–£3&alc Dinner £3.95–£6&alc Wine £3.10 Last dinner 9.30pm

Credit cards 1 2 3 5

UPTON NOBLE
Somerset
Map **3** ST73

✕Lamb Inn ☎(074985) 308
Closed Mon

60 seats ✻Lunch £3alc Dinner £7.50alc Wine £3.95 Last dinner 9.30pm 50P

UPTON ON SEVERN
Hereford & Worcester
Map **3** SO84

★★White Lion High St ☎(06846) 2551
Closed 23 Dec–5 Jan

Town-centre hotel with a Georgian façade which is popular with tourists.

10rm(8➡) CTV in all bedrooms Ⓡ sB&B£26 sB&B➡£28 dB&B£35.50 dB&B➡£37.50

20P

English & French **V** Lunch £7.50&alc Dinner £7.50&alc Wine £3.50 Last dinner 9.30pm

Credit card 1

USK
Gwent
Map **3** SO30

★★Glen-yr-Afon Pontypool Rd
☎(02913) 2302

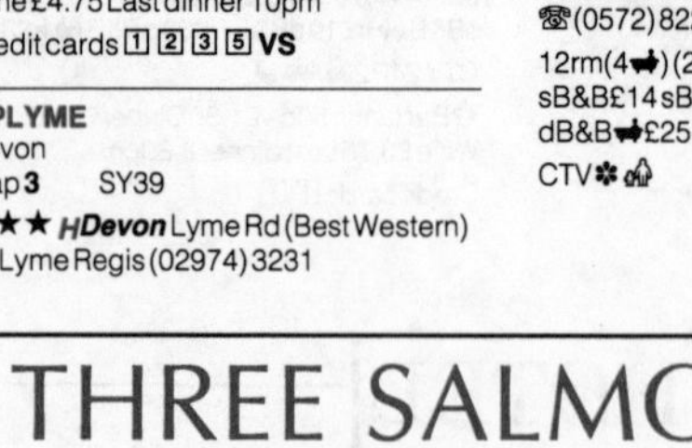

Elegant country house style hotel with attractive library. Good home cooked food.

15rm(1➡11⋒) (3fb) CTV in 1 bedroom TV in 1 bedroom sB&B£18.40 sB&B➡⋒£20.70 dB&B£24.15 dB&B➡⋒£26.45 B

CTV 40P 1 ✽

Lunch £5.75–£8&alc Tea £1 Dinner £6.75–£11.50&alc Wine £4.95 Last dinner 8pm

★★Three Salmons Bridge St ☎(02913) 2133
RS 24–26 Dec

Comfortable, well-appointed hotel.

13rm(10➡2⋒) Annexe: 18rm(16➡1⋒)

U

(2fb) 2⊟ CTV in all bedrooms ® *sB&B£19 sB&B⇌⋒ £23 dB&B⇌⋒ £29 B̶

60P ♿

⊟ Welsh & International ♔ *Lunch £5.95&alc Dinner £5.95&alc Wine £4.50 Last dinner 9.30pm

Credit cards 1 3

❀✕ **Mr Midgley's** Bridge St ☎(02913) 2459

(Rosette awarded for dinner only.)

Attractive cottage-style restaurant.

⊟ French **V** 28 seats Lunch £2.25–£15&alc Tea £2 High Tea £2 Dinner £15&alc Wine £4.50 Last dinner 9.30pm

S% Credit cards 1 2 3 5 **VS**

UTTOXETER
Staffordshire
Map **7** SK03

★★★ **White Hart** Carter St ☎(08893) 2437

A 16th-century coaching inn, where the Dutch linen-fold panelling is of particular interest.

16rm(8⇌3⋒) (2fb) CTV in 8 bedrooms ® *sB&B£20.75 sB&B⇌⋒ £23.80 dB&B£27.70 dB&B⇌⋒ £31.25 B̶

CTV 120P

V ♔ ⊐ *Lunch £7alc Tea £1.50–£2 High Tea £2.50–£3.50 Dinner £8.50alc Wine £4.75 Last dinner 10pm

S% Credit cards 1 2 3 5 **VS**

UXBRIDGE
Gt London
Map **4** TQ08

✕✕✕ ***Giovanni's*** Denham Lodge, Oxford Rd ☎(0895) 31568

Attractively situated restaurant surrounded by landscaped gardens.

Closed Sun Lunch not served Sat

⊟ Italian 100 seats Last dinner 10.30pm 30P

Credit cards 1 2 3 4 5

At **Hillingdon** (2m NE A40)

☆☆☆ **Master Brewer Motel** Western Av (A40) ☎(0895) 51199

64⇌⋒ 200P

VENTNOR
Isle of Wight
Map **4** SZ57

★★★ **Royal** Belgrave Rd (Trusthouse Forte) ☎(0983) 852186

Closed mid Nov–Feb

Well-appointed hotel overlooking the sea, with many outdoor facilities.

55⇌ (3fb) CTV in all bedrooms ® sB&B⇌£32.50 dB&B⇌£51.50 B̶

Lift ☾ (summer) 56P CFA ✽ ⇌ (heated)

♔ ⊐ Last dinner 9pm

Credit cards 1 2 3 4 5

★★★ ***H* Ventnor Towers** Madeira Rd (Exec Hotel) ☎(0983) 852277

Clifftop hotel, with comfortable lounges, set in grounds accommodating many outdoor sports.

30rm(17⇌4⋒) (4fb) CTV available in bedrooms sB&B£16.50–£18.50 sB&B⇌⋒ £17.50–£19.50 dB&B£33–£37 dB&B⇌⋒ £35–£39 B̶

CTV 40P 1 ⇌ ✽ ⇌ (heated) ⁄ (hard) *xmas*

♔ ⊐ Lunch £5&alc Tea 40p Dinner £7.50&alc Wine £3.50 Last dinner 9pm

S% Credit cards 1 2 3 5 **VS**

★★ **Bonchurch Manor** Bonchurch (1m E) ☎(0983) 852868

Closed Jan

Peaceful hotel with distant views of the sea.

11rm(7⇌3⋒) (2fb) CTV in all bedrooms ® sB&B⇌⋒ £17 dB&B⇌⋒ £34 B̶

10P ✽ (heated) nc4yrs *xmas*

Lunch £5.50 Dinner £9.50&alc Wine £3.80 Last dinner 9pm

Credit cards 1 2 3 5

★★ ***Metropole*** Esplanade ☎(0983) 852181

Closed Nov–Mar (except Xmas)

Privately owned resort hotel on sea front. →

V

40rm(11→12⋒) ⊟
Lift CTV 16P CFA sauna bath
▣English & Continental ♁ ⊒ Last dinner 8pm
Credit cards 1 3 5 VS

★★♛ ***BL* Winterbourne** Bonchurch (1m E) ☎(0983) 852535
Closed 6 Nov–Jan
Wonderfully situated hotel in four acres of splendid gardens that slope down to the sea. Elegant interiors.
13rm(10→) Annexe: 6→ (2fb) CTV in all bedrooms sB&B£19.25 sB&B→£24.20 dB&B£38.50 dB&B→£48.40 ⊟
CTV 22P ✽ ≏ (heated) nc7yrs
▣English & French ♁ ⊒ Lunch £6.35 Tea 45p–90p Dinner £10.25 Wine £4 Last dinner 9pm
Credit cards 1 2 3 5

★**Horseshoe Bay** Shore Rd, Bonchurch (1m E) ☎(0983) 852487
Closed Jan–Feb
This hotel has good bedrooms and fine views over Bonchurch Bay.
6rm(3→) Ⓡ sB&B£8–£11 dB&B£16–£24 dB&B→£18–£28
CTV 8P nc8yrs
V ♁ ⊒ Lunch £2.50–£5 Dinner £5–£8&alc Wine £2.80 Last dinner 9pm
Credit cards 1 3 5

★♛ ***L* Madeira Hall** Trinity Rd ☎(0983) 852624
Closed mid Oct–mid Mar
Beautifully situated hotel with Dickens associations. Good leisure facilities.
12rm(3→1⋒) (4fb) sB&B£11.50–£14.50 sB&B→⋒£14.50 dB&B£22–£28 dB&B→⋒£28 ⊟
CTV 12P ✽ ≏ (heated)
♁ Lunch £2.30–£4 Dinner £4–£5 Wine £3.50 Last dinner 7.15pm
Credit cards 1 3 VS

VERYAN
Cornwall
Map **2** SW93

★★★***L* Nare** ☎Truro (0872) 501279
On National Trust headland overlooking Gerrans Bay.
34rm(18→10⋒) Annexe: 3→ (7fb) CTV available in bedrooms Ⓡ sB&B£10.50–£23 sB&B→⋒£12–£25 dB&B£24–£48 dB&B→⋒£28–£54
CTV 120P 5 ✽ ≏ (heated) (hard) billiards sauna bath *xmas*
▣English & Continental V ♁ ⊒ Bar lunch £1–£4.50 Tea £1.50alc Dinner £10alc Wine £2.85 Last dinner 9.15pm
Credit cards 1 2 3 5

★★**Elerkey House** ☎Truro (0872) 501261
Closed 6 Oct–19 Apr
Small country hotel in this picturesque old Cornish village.
9rm(3→) (3fb) CTV in 3 bedrooms Ⓡ sB&B£12–£13.50 dB&B£24–£27 dB&B→£28–£31.75 ⊟
CTV 12P ✽ nc6yrs
♁ Lunch £1–£2.50 Dinner £7 Wine £4 Last dinner 7.30pm

✕**Treverbyn House** Pendower Rd ☎Truro (0872) 501201
A tiny, personally-run restaurant, in a picturesque setting, and offering predominantly home cooking.
Closed Nov–Feb Lunch not served
▣French V 20 seats Tea fr£1.30 Dinner £8.50 Wine £3.85 Last dinner 8.15pm 9P bedrooms available

VIRKIE
Shetland
Map **16** HU31

★***Meadowvale*** ☎Sumburgh (0950) 60240
Modern timber-clad, two-storey building, near the sea and overlooking Sumburgh Airport.
11rm(3⋒)
CTV 25P
♁ ⊒ Last dinner 8pm

WADDESDON
Buckinghamshire
Map **4** SP71

★**White Lion** High St ☎ Aylesbury (0296) 651227
A fairly simple public house near National Trust property.
7rm sB&B£11 dB&B£20
CTV 40P ⛟ ✽
♔ Lunch £3.35–£5.65&alc Dinner fr£3.35–£5.65&alc Wine £3 Last dinner 8.30pm
Credit card ③

WADEBRIDGE
Cornwall
Map **2** SW97

★★**Molesworth Arms** Molesworth St (Minotel) ☎ (020881) 2055
RS 25 Dec
Original 16th-century inn, comfortably furnished and offering a relaxed atmosphere.
13rm(8⇌) (2fb) Ⓡ sB&B£11 sB&B⇌£12.50 dB&B£19 dB&B⇌£21
CTV 50P 4⌂ nc8yrs
V ♔ ☕ Lunch £6.50&alc Dinner £6.50&alc Wine £3.60 Last dinner 9.30pm
Credit cards ① ③

WADHURST
East Sussex
Map **5** TQ63

❀★★♣**Spindlewood** Wallcrouch ☎ Ticehurst (0580) 200430
Closed Xmas
Small family run hotel with well maintained gardens.
10rm(7⇌1⋒) (1fb) ✱ *sB&B⇌⋒£19–£21 dB&B⇌⋒£35–£45 B
CTV 50P ⛟ ✽ ᑭ(hard)
▣ English & French V ♔ ☕ *Lunch £7.50–£8.50&alc Tea 65p–75p Dinner £7.50–£8.50&alc Wine £4.70 Last dinner 9pm
Credit cards ① ③

WAKEFIELD
West Yorkshire
Map **8** SE32

☆☆☆☆**Post House** Queen's Dr, Ossett (Trusthouse Forte) ☎ (0924) 276388 Telex no 55407
Well designed modern hotel with coffee shop and restaurant.
96⇌ (16fb) CTV in all bedrooms Ⓡ sB&B⇌£42 dB&B⇌£54 B
Lift ☾ CTV 140P CFA ✽
♔ ☕ Last dinner 10.30pm
Credit cards ① ② ③ ④ ⑤

★★★**Stoneleigh** Doncaster Rd ☎ (0924) 369461
A row of Victorian, stone built terraced houses have been converted into this modern hotel.
27rm(12⇌9⋒) CTV in all bedrooms Ⓡ ✱ sB&B£19–£23.75 sB&B⇌⋒£20–£31 dB&B⇌⋒£30–£43.50 B
☾ CTV 64P ⛟
▣ English, French & Italian ♔ ☕ Lunch £5.25–£6.25&alc Tea 60p Dinner £8–£9&alc Wine £5.25 Last dinner 10pm
Credit cards ① ③

★★★**Swallow** Queens St (Swallow) ☎ (0924) 372111
Closed 26 Dec–2 Jan
Modern, tower block hotel in the town centre.
64rm(56⇌8⋒) CTV in all bedrooms Ⓡ sB&B⇌⋒ £34.50 dB&B⇌⋒ £46 B
Lift ☾ ⊬ 60P CFA
▣ English & Continental ♔ ☕ Lunch fr£5.95&alc Tea fr50p Dinner fr£6.95&alc Wine £4.85 Last dinner 9.30pm
Credit cards ① ② ③ ⑤

★★★**Walton Hall** Walton (3m SE off B6378) ☎ (0924) 257911
Picturesquely set on an island in the middle of a lake, this 18th-century mansion has been converted into a hotel and leisure centre.
25⇌ 1▤ CTV in all bedrooms Ⓡ ✱ *sB&B⇌£31.75 dB&B⇌£42 B
☾ CTV 150P 4⌂ ✽ ▭(heated) ⌡ squash billiards sauna bath Disco wkly ⌂ *xmas*
▣ English & French V ♔ ☕ *Lunch fr£6.25&alc Tea fr60p High Tea fr£4.50 Dinner £6.75&alc Last dinner 10pm
S% Credit cards ① ② ③ ⑤

★***Sandal Court*** 108 Barnsley Rd ☎ (0924) 258725
12rm(1⇌) CTV in 1 bedroom Ⓡ ✱ B
CTV 20P
♔ ☕ Last dinner 9.30pm
Credit cards ① ③

WALBERSWICK
Suffolk
Map **5** TM47

★★**Anchor** ☎ Southwold (0502) 722112
The gabled, mock-Tudor exterior of this hotel gives way to the Scandinavian-style lounge and dining room, while there are also chalets in a garden setting.
6rm(2⇌) Annexe: 10rm(8⇌) (2fb) CTV in 14 bedrooms Ⓡ *sB&B£14.75–£15.95 dB&B£29.50–£31.90 dB&B⇌£33.50–£35.90 B
CTV 60P ✽ ⌂
♔ ☕ Lunch £5.25–£6.40 Tea fr55p Dinner £6.95–£8.10 Wine £4.65 Last dinner 8.30pm
Credit cards ① ② ③ ⑤

WALBERTON
West Sussex
Map **4** SU90

★★★***Avisford Park*** Yapton Ln ☎ Yapton (0243) 551215
Georgian manor house set in parkland with many leisure facilities.
80⇌ CTV in all bedrooms Ⓡ B
☾ 200P CFA ✽ ⩦(heated) ᑭ(grass) squash billiards Live music and dancing Sat ⌂
V Last dinner 9.30pm
Credit cards ① ② ③ **VS**

WALL
Northumberland
Map **12** NY96

★★***Hadrian*** ☎ Humshaugh (043481) 232
Creeper clad inn richly furnished with antiques, bedrooms simple and clean.
8rm
CTV 40P 4⌂ ✽
▣ English & Continental ♔
Last dinner 9.45pm

WALLASEY
Merseyside
Map **7** SJ29

★★**Grove House** Grove Rd (Porter) ☎ 051-639 3947 Telex no 837921
14rm (1fb) CTV in all bedrooms Ⓡ sB&B£12–£21 dB&B£22–£31 B
☾ 18P ✽ ⌂ *xmas*
▣ English & French V ♔ Lunch fr£5&alc Dinner fr£6&alc Wine £5 Last dinner 9.30pm
Credit cards ① ② ③ ⑤ **VS**

★**Belvidere** Seabank Rd, New Brighton ☎ 051-639 8145
30rm(5⇌) (2fb) sB&B£11.25 sB&B⇌£13.50 dB&B£19.50 dB&B⇌£25
☾ CTV 40P 3⌂ ✽
▣ English & French V ♔ ☕ Lunch £2.50–£5.50 Tea fr75p Dinner £3–£11 Wine £3.25 Last dinner 9.30pm

WALLINGFORD
Oxfordshire
Map **4** SU68

★★**George** High St (Kingsmead) ☎ (0491) 36665
Timbered and gabled Tudor inn with a courtyard and garden at the back.
18rm(7⇌2⋒) (1fb) CTV in all bedrooms Ⓡ sB&B£23.50 sB&B⇌⋒£30 dB&B£35 dB&B⇌⋒£39 B
80P ⛟ Live music Wed *xmas*
▣ English & French V ♔ ☕ Lunch £6.75&alc Tea 55p Dinner £6.75&alc Wine £5.25 Last dinner 10.30pm
Credit cards ① ② ③ ④ ⑤

★★*L* **Shillingford Bridge** Shillingford (2m N A329) ☎ Warborough (086732) 8567 Telex no 837763 SBH
Closed Xmas
Hotel with spacious rooms, modern bedrooms, and public rooms overlooking the Thames.
28rm(19⇌8⋒) (2fb) 1▤ CTV in all bedrooms Ⓡ sB&B⇌⋒ fr£30 dB&B⇌⋒ fr£42

→

W

100P ✽ ≈ (heated) ♪ squash Live music and dancing Sat Cabaret Sat ⌂

V ♧ ▭ Lunch fr£8&alc Tea fr£1.25 Dinner fr£8&alc Wine £5.50 Last dinner 10pm

Credit cards 1 2 3 5

WALLSEND
Tyne & Wear
Map **12** NZ26

☆☆☆**Newcastle Moat House** Coast Rd (Queens Moat) ☎ Newcastle upon Tyne (0632) 628989 Telex no 53583
Closed Xmas & New Year

Spacious modern hotel with comfortable bedrooms.

172 ⇌ (6fb) CTV in all bedrooms ® sB&B ⇌ £15–£34 dB&B ⇌ £19–£39 B

Lift ☾ ⚡ 500P CFA ✽ Sauna bath Live music Sat

▣ French ♧ ▭ ✻ Lunch fr£6.75 Tea fr£1.25 Dinner fr£6.75&alc Wine £4.75 Last dinner 9.45pm

Credit cards 1 2 3 4 5 **VS**

WALSALL
West Midlands
Map **7** SP09
See also **Barr, Great**

★★★ ***B*** **Barons Court** Walsall Rd, Walsall Wood (3m NE A461) (Best Western) ☎ Brownhills (0543) 376543
Telex no 338212

A bustling, popular hotel, located on the outskirts of the town.

76 ⇌ ⋒ (5fb) 21 ▤ CTV in all bedrooms ® ✈ sB&B ⇌ ⋒ £28–£30 dB&B ⇌ ⋒ £37–£39 B

Lift ☾ 180P CFA Live music and dancing Sat ⌂ *xmas*

▣ English & French V ♧ ▭ Lunch £3.75–£5.95&alc Tea fr70p Dinner fr£6.95&alc Wine £4.50 Last dinner 9.45pm

S% Credit cards 1 2 3 4 5 **VS**

★★★**Fairlawns** 178 Little Aston Rd, Aldridge (3m NE A454) ☎ Aldridge (0922) 55122 Telex no 339873

30rm (19 ⇌ 11 ⋒) CTV in all bedrooms ® ✈ sB&B ⇌ ⋒ £28.50 dB&B ⇌ ⋒ £35

☾ 50P ✽

▣ French ♧ ▭ Lunch £5–£5.50&alc Tea £2 Dinner £7–£7.50&alc Wine £5 Last dinner 10pm

Credit cards 1 2 3 5 **VS**

☆☆☆**Walsall Crest** Birmingham Rd (Crest) ☎ (0922) 33555 Telex no 335479
RS Xmas

Modern hotel close to busy motorway junctions.

106 ⇌ CTV in all bedrooms ®
✻ sB ⇌ fr£32 dB ⇌ fr£40 (room only) B

Lift ☾ ⚡ 300P CFA ♪ (hard) Live music and dancing Mon–Fri Cabaret Mon–Fri

▣ International V ♧ ▭ ✻ Lunch fr£4.50–£6.95&alc Tea 60p Dinner £8.50–£9.50&alc Last dinner 9.45pm

Credit cards 1 2 3 4 5 **VS**

★★**County** Birmingham Rd (Queens Moat) ☎ (0922) 32323
Closed Xmas

Extended and modernised house with a Tudor façade, now a commercial businessman's hotel.

47rm (11 ⇌ 3 ⋒) (1fb) CTV in all bedrooms ® sB&B £19–£23 sB&B ⇌ ⋒ £19–£27 dB&B £23–£34 dB&B ⇌ ⋒ £23–£35 B

☾ 35P

▣ English & French V ♧ Lunch fr£4.80&alc Dinner £6.50&alc Wine £4.20 Last dinner 9.45pm

Credit cards 1 2 3 5 **VS**

★★***Royal*** Ablewell St ☎ (0922) 24555

36rm (4 ⇌) TV in all bedrooms B

Lift ☾ 30P Disco Wed

▣ French ♧ ▭ Last dinner 8.45pm

Credit cards 1 2 3 5

WALSHFORD
North Yorkshire
Map **8** SE45

❀ ✕✕✕ **Bridge Inn** (Byron Room) Great North Rd ☎ Wetherby (0937) 62345

W

One of the most beautiful restaurants in Britain, serving cuisine of a very high standard.

Closed Mon Dinner not served Sun

▣English & French 70 seats Lunch £6.50&alc Dinner £9.95&alc Wine £5.95 Last dinner 9pm 100P

S% Credit cards ① ② ③ ⑤

WALTHAM, GREAT
Essex
Map **5** TL61

✕✕**Windmill** ☎Chelmsford (0245) 360292

Small country pub with Victorian atmosphere, offering good traditional English fare.

Closed Sun & Public hols Lunch not served Sat

▣International

40 seats Lunch £12alc Dinner £15alc Wine £4.90 Last dinner 9.30pm 100P

S% Credit cards ① ③

WALTON-ON-THAMES
Surrey
London plan **5** A1 (page 422)

✕***La Bussola*** 32a High St ☎(0932) 244889

Grotto style restaurant with Italian cuisine.

Lunch not served Sat Dinner not served Sun

▣Continental **V** 65 seats Last dinner 10.45pm

Credit cards ① ③

WALTON ON THE HILL
Surrey
Map **4** TQ25

❀✕✕**Ebenezer Cottage** 36 Walton St ☎Tadworth (073781) 3166

Early 16th-century cottage restaurant offering traditional English food in a number of period styled dining rooms.

Closed Mon Dinner not served Sun

✻Dinner £14.85 Wine £5.95 Last dinner 9.30pm

Credit cards ① ② ③ ⑤

WAMPHRAY
Dumfries & Galloway *Dumfriesshire*
Map **11** NY19

★*H* **Red House** ☎Johnstone Bridge (05764) 214

Closed 16 Nov–Etr

Small, comfortable hotel set in its own grounds, in a pleasant rural setting, with friendly owner and staff.

6rm Ⓡ sB&B fr £12.45 dB&B fr £24.90

CTV 20P

♔Lunch fr £4.15 High Tea fr £4.15 Dinner fr £6.25 Wine £4.60 Last dinner 7.30pm

Credit card ⑤ **VS**

WANSFORD
Cambridgeshire
Map **4** TL09

★★**Haycock** ☎Stamford (0780) 782223

Rebuilt in 1632, this former posting house contains a brew house, cock fighting loft and an Elizabethan granary.

28rm (15➡2⋒) 4⊟ CTV in all bedrooms sB&B fr £20.50 sB&B➡⋒ £39 dB&B fr £34 dB&B➡⋒ £43 Ᵽ

☾ 300P ✽

♔ ▭ ✻Wine £5.80 Last dinner 10.30pm

S% Credit cards ① ② ③ ⑤

WANTAGE
Oxfordshire
Map **4** SU48

★★**Bear** Market Pl ☎(02357) 66366

Comfortable hotel with well-equipped bedrooms and beautifully appointed restaurant.

26rm (13➡4⋒) (1fb) CTV in 26 bedrooms Ⓡ ✶ sB&B £20.50 sB&B➡⋒ £29.50 dB&B £30.50 dB&B➡⋒ £39.50 Ᵽ

Lift CTV ⚐ *xmas*

♔ ▭ ✻Lunch £5.50–£6.50 Tea fr £1.50 Dinner £8–£12alc Wine £4.95 Last dinner 9.45pm

Credit cards ① ② ③ ⑤

WARE
Hertfordshire
Map **5** TL31

☆☆☆**Ware Moat House** Baldock St (Queens Moat) ☎(0920) 5011

Modern, two-storey brick hotel with good car parking.

50rm (44➡6⋒) CTV in all bedrooms Ⓡ sB&B➡⋒ £30 dB&B➡⋒ £40 Ᵽ

Lift ☾ CTV 100P

▣English & French ♔Lunch fr £6.50&alc Tea fr 50p Dinner fr £6.50&alc Wine £4.70 Last dinner 9.30pm

Credit cards ① ② ③ ⑤

✕**Ben's Brasserie** 14 High St ☎(0920) 68383

A very popular, modern, town centre Brasserie with good home cooking and friendly service.

Dinner not served Sun

▣English & French 45 seats Last dinner 10.30pm

VS

WAREHAM
Dorset
Map **3** SY98

❀★★★*HB* **Priory** Church Green ☎(09295) 2772

(Rosette awarded for dinner only.)

15rm (11➡4⋒) 1⊟ CTV in all bedrooms ✶ sB&B➡⋒ £24–£32 dB&B➡⋒ £35–£55 Ᵽ

Lift 20P 2⌂ ✽ ♪ Live music Sat *xmas*

▣English & French **V** ♔ ▭ Lunch £5.95–£7.95 Tea £1.50–£2.50&alc High Tea £3.50–£5 Dinner £10.50–£12.50&alc Wine £4.75 Last dinner 9.45pm

Credit cards ① ② ③ ⑤

★★**Worgret Manor** ☎(09295) 2957

Closed Xmas

Quiet Georgian hotel with modern extension.

12rm (3⋒) (4fb) TV in 2 bedrooms Ⓡ sB&B £13.50–£16.50 sB&B⋒ £15.50–£18.50 dB&B £26–£30.50 dB&B⋒ £30–£35 Ᵽ

CTV 35P ✽

▣English & French **V** ♔ ▭ Lunch £6.50–£6.75&alc Dinner £6.50–£6.75&alc Wine £5 Last dinner 9.15pm

Credit cards ① ② ③ ⑤ **VS**

★**Black Bear** 14 South St ☎(09295) 3280

An 18th-century coaching inn with simple bedrooms situated in the town centre.

12rm (1➡) (3fb) TV in all bedrooms ✶ sB&B £11.50–£12.50 dB&B £22–£24 dB&B➡ £24–£26

CTV 4P

♔ ▭ Lunch £1–£4.25 Tea 75p Dinner £10alc Wine £3.90 Last dinner 9.15pm

Credit cards ① ③

✕**Old Granary** The Quay ☎(09295) 2010

V 75 seats ✻Lunch £1.80–£4.20&alc Tea 80p–£1.50 Dinner £7.95&alc Wine £3.95 Last dinner 9.30pm bedrooms available

Credit cards ① ② ③ ⑤ **VS**

✕**Olivers** West St ☎(09295) 6164

Closed 2wks May, 2wks Nov & Mon Lunch not served

▣French 36 seats Dinner £8.50alc Wine £4.75 Last dinner 10.30pm ⚐

S% Credit cards ② ③ ⑤

WARK
Northumberland
Map **12** NY87

★**Battlesteads** ☎Bellingham (0660) 30209

A pleasant village inn with charm and character conveyed by the proprietors.

6rm sB&B £12 dB&B £24 Ᵽ

CTV 50P ✽

▣Mainly grills **V** ♔ Bar lunch £1.20–£6 High Tea £3.50–£4 Dinner £4.50–£8&alc Wine £2.75 Last dinner 9pm

W

WARMINSTER
Wiltshire
Map **3** ST84

★★★

❀★★★★ **BISHOPSTROW HOUSE, WARMINSTER**
Boreham Rd (2m SE A36) ☎(0985) 212312
Closed 3 wks Jan

This is one of the more opulent Georgian country houses rivalling most in the elegance of its décor, comfort of the furniture and quality of the antiques, paintings and objets d'art. The bedrooms are equally well adorned with fine furniture as well as the modern features now demanded in hotels. They have beautiful soft furnishings and the bathrooms have smart Italian tiles. There is some seating in the hall, as well as a charming morning room and a most elegant drawing room for comfortable relaxation.
The dining room, sparkling with polished silver and glass, has an elegant conservatory extension which has been done in keeping with the proportions of the house and floored with Italian marble. With the arrival of a new chef, either three or four course meals are provided with sensible choice. The chef generally follows the modern school of cooking and has achieved a great success, so that we now feel justified in awarding a rosette for high quality and enjoyability. Afternoon tea deserves special mention too.

The house stands in 27 acres of peaceful grounds with a tunnel under the main road leading to the section with its river frontage where there is also an interesting pillared temple. The owners and their manager have imbued the staff with the right spirit so that one immediately feels welcome and cossetted. Such qualities cost money of course, but our members think it good value.
15➡ (2fb) 1⊞ CTV in all bedrooms sB&B➡ fr£38 dB&B➡ £46.60
Continental breakfast ⊟
30P 2⌂ ✱ (hard) ♩ nc3yrs
xmas
⊟ French Lunch £12.50–£13.50 Tea £3 Dinner £15–£16 Wine £6.50 Last dinner 9.30pm
Credit cards 1 2 3

★★**Old Bell** Market Pl ☎(0985) 216611
Contrasting colour-washed brick building in the centre of Warminster with a colonnaded arcade front, and double doors leading to an inner courtyard.
16rm(9➡1⋒) (2fb) CTV in 16 bedrooms Ⓡ sB&B£17 sB&B➡⋒ £21 dB&B£24 dB&B➡⋒ £30 ⊟
20P
V ♡ Lunch £5alc Dinner £5alc Wine £5.25 Last dinner 10.30pm
Credit cards 1 2 3 5

WARREN ROW
Berkshire
Map **4** SU88

✕✕**Warrener** ☎Littlewick Green (062882) 2803
A pub-restaurant introducing Swedish cuisine.
Closed Mon Lunch not served Tue–Fri
⊟ French & Swedish 30 seats ✱Lunch £13.25alc Dinner £13.25alc Wine £5.25 Last dinner 10.15pm
S% Credit cards 3 5

WARRINGTON
Cheshire
Map **7** SJ68

★★**Patten Arms** Parker St (Greenall Whitley) ☎(0925) 36602 Telex no 629462
Closed Xmas
Tall brick-built hotel with a modern extension, close to the railway station and the town centre.
43rm(29➡14⋒) (2fb) CTV in all bedooms Ⓡ sB&B➡⋒ £28–£29 dB&B➡⋒ £36–£37 ⊟
☾ 20P 5⌂
⊟ English & French V ♡ ☐ Lunch fr£3 Tea 55p Dinner £6&alc Wine £5.75 Last dinner 9.30pm
Credit cards 1 2 3 5 VS

★**Ribblesdale** Balmoral Rd, Grappenhall ☎(0925) 601197
Closed Xmas & New Year
14rm(4➡) (2fb) 1⊞ CTV in 4 bedrooms Ⓡ sB&B£14–£15 sB&B➡ £20–£22 dB&B£20–£24 dB&B➡ £26–£28 ⊟
CTV 30P
♡ Bar lunch £2.50–£6 Dinner £6–£7&alc Wine £4.50 Last dinner 9pm
Credit cards 1 3

★**Rockfield** 3 Alexandra Rd, Grappenhall (1¾m SE off A50) ☎(0925) 62898
A detached Edwardian house set in a quiet residential area of Warrington.
7rm(3➡) Annexe: 8rm(2➡) CTV in all bedrooms Ⓡ ✱ sB&B£15.60 sB&B➡ £19.60 dB&B£25 dB&B➡ £28.60
CTV 20P
V ✱ Dinner £6.75&alc Wine £4 Last dinner 8.30pm
Credit cards 1 3

WARWICK
Warwickshire
Map **4** SP26

☆☆☆☆**Ladbroke** Longbridge Rbt (junc A41/A46/A429) (Ladbroke) ☎(0926) 499555 Telex no 312468

A modern hotel on the outskirts of Warwick on the A46.

131➡⋔ (6fb) CTV in all bedrooms Ⓡ *sB➡⋔ fr£35 dB➡⋔ fr£45 (room only) B

Lift ☾ 195P ✽ (heated)

V ♡ *Lunch fr£6.50 Dinner fr£8.50 Last dinner 10pm

Credit cards 1 2 3 5

★★**Crown** Coventry Rd ☎(0926) 492087

An 18th-century, former coaching inn, with pillared entrance porch.

12rm(1➡) (3fb) sB&B£10 dB&B£20 dB&B➡£25

CTV 12P

V ♡ Lunch £5 Dinner £5 Wine £4 Last dinner 9pm

Credit cards 1 3

★★**Lord Leycester** Jury St ☎(0926) 491481

Central hotel on a busy road through Warwick.

44rm(24➡6⋔) (3fb) CTV in all bedrooms sB&B£18.35 sB&B➡⋔£23.10 dB&B£32.55 dB&B➡⋔£34.65 B

☾ 50P *xmas*

V ♡ Lunch £4&alc Tea 75p High Tea £1.75 Dinner £6.25&alc Wine £4.10 Last dinner 9.30pm

Credit cards 1 2 3 5 **VS**

★★**Warwick Arms** High St ☎(0926) 492759

RS 25 Dec–1 Jan

A busy hotel in the centre of Warwick dating back to 1591.

29rm(7➡9⋔) (4fb) CTV in all bedrooms Ⓡ sB&B£15 sB&B➡⋔£16.50 dB&B£27.25 dB&B➡⋔£30.25 B

CTV

English & French V ♡ Lunch £5 Tea 85p High Tea £3.25–£4 Dinner £5.95–£6.25&alc Wine £4.55 Last dinner 10pm

Credit cards 1 2 3 5

★★**Woolpack** Market Pl (Charrington) ☎(0926) 496191

Closed 25 Dec–2 Jan

A busy, commercial hotel, next to Warwick Museum, dating back to 1510.

29rm(9➡7⋔) (2fb) CTV in all bedrooms Ⓡ *sB&B£12.50–£14 sB&B➡⋔£17–£21 dB&B£20–£24 dB&B➡⋔£24–£32 B

☾

English & Italian ♡ *Bar lunch £1.30–£2.30 Dinner £6–£8&alc Wine £2.65 Last dinner 9.15pm

S% Credit cards 1 2 3

XXX ***Westgate Arms*** Bowling Green St ☎(0926) 492362

Large, white hotel, with a traditional restaurant that overlooks the garden and surrounding countryside.

Closed Sun & Public hols

English & French 75 seats Last dinner 10.30pm 50P

XX ***Aylesford*** High St ☎(0926) 492799

Closed Sun & Public hols Dinner not served Mon

Continental 80 seats Last dinner 10pm

Credit cards 1 2 3 5

XX **Randolph's** Coten End ☎(0926) 491292

A delightful French restaurant on the Leamington rd.

Closed Xmas & Sun Lunch not served

French 30 seats Dinner £12.50alc Wine £4.95

Credit cards 1 3 **VS**

WASDALE HEAD

Cumbria

Map **11** NY10

★★**Wasdale Head Inn**

☎Wasdale (09406) 229

Closed 7 Nov–27 Dec

10rm(8➡2⋔) (2fb) Ⓡ sB&B➡⋔£15.42–£17.57 dB&B➡⋔£30.84–£35.14

50P ✽

V ♡ Bar lunch £3.12–£5.43&alc Tea 54p High Tea £3.12–£5.43&alc Dinner £8.86 Last dinner 8pm

Credit cards 1 3

WASHINGBOROUGH

Lincolnshire

Map **8** TF07

★★**Washingborough Hall** Church Hill (Minotel) ☎Lincoln (0522) 790340

12rm(5➡3⋔) (1fb) 1 CTV in all bedrooms Ⓡ sB&B➡⋔£18 dB&B£22 dB&B➡⋔£26 B

CTV 50P ✽

International ♡ Lunch £4.50alc Tea 50p alc Dinner £7.50alc Wine £4 Last dinner 9.30pm

Credit cards 1 3

WASHINGTON

Tyne & Wear

Map **12** NZ35

★★★**George Washington** Stone Cellar Rd, District 12 (Best Western) ☎091-417 2626 Telex no 537748

70rm(68➡2⋔) (51fb) CTV in all bedrooms Ⓡ sB&B➡⋔£24–£39.50 dB&B➡⋔£28–£42.95 B

☾ # 170P CFA ✽ (heated) 18 squash Billiards sauna bath *xmas*

French ♡ Bar lunch £1.50–£4.50 Tea £2–£3 Dinner £7.95–£8.95&alc Wine £4.85 Last dinner 9.30pm

Credit cards 1 2 3 5

☆☆☆**Post House** (Trusthouse Forte) ☎091-416 2264 Telex no 537574

Conveniently situated post house close to A1(M) with spacious bedrooms and recently updated public rooms.

145➡ (68fb) CTV in all bedrooms Ⓡ sB&B➡£38 dB&B➡£50.50 B

Lift ☾ 198P CFA 3

♡ Last dinner 10pm

Credit cards 1 2 3 4 5

WATCHET

Somerset

Map **3** ST04

★★ ***HBL* Downfield** St Decuman's Rd ☎(0984) 31267

A pleasant, detached Victorian house in well tended gardens overlooking the harbour. Mrs Bermann is very hospitable and the drawing room is attractive and relaxing, while the spacious bedrooms →

W

are comfortable and well appointed. Honest food is served in the pleasant dining room, and light meals are available in the Hunter's Tavern.
6rm(2⇌4⋒)(2fb) CTV in all bedrooms ® sB&B⇌⋒ £21.85–£22.95 dB&B⇌⋒ £34.50–£35.50 B
20P ✽ U ⌂ *xmas*
English, French & German V ♔ ☐ Lunch £5.75–£7.50 Tea £1.20–£1.50 Dinner £7.50–£8.50 Wine £4.45 Last dinner 9.30pm
Credit cards 1 2 3 5 VS

WATERBEACH
West Sussex
Map **4** SU80
★★★**Richmond Arms** ☏ Chichester (0243) 775537
A modernised hotel in a peaceful, rural situation.
18rm(13⇌)(1fb) CTV in all bedrooms ® sB&B £21–£25 sB&B⇌⋒ £25–£28 dB&B £28–£30 dB&B⇌⋒ £32–£36 B
✽ 60P CFA *xmas*
English & French ♔ ☐ Lunch £3.50–£4.65&alc Tea fr55p High Tea fr£3.50 Dinner £5.80–£6.25&alc Wine £2.75 Last dinner 9.30pm
Credit cards 1 2 3 5

WATERGATE BAY
Cornwall
Map **2** SW86

★★**Tregurrian** ☏ St Mawgan (06374) 280
Closed Oct–Apr
A family-run hotel, close to the beach.
28rm(15⋒)(10fb) sB&B £9–£13.75 sB&B⋒ £11.75–£17 dB&B £18–£27.50 dB&B⋒ £22–£31.50 B
CTV 22P ✽ (heated) nc2yrs
♔ ☐ Bar lunch fr50p&alc Tea fr38p Dinner fr£4.50 Wine £3.28
Credit cards 1 3 VS

★**Cleavelands** ☏ St Mawgan (06374) 273
Closed Oct–Etr
Family holiday hotel near the beach.
28rm(8⇌1⋒)(6fb) ✱ sB&B £10–£14 sB&B⇌⋒ £11.50–£15.50 dB&B £20–£28 dB&B⇌⋒ £23–£31
☾ CTV 38P Cabaret twice wkly ⌂
♔ ☐ Lunch £2–£3 Tea 60p–£1.20 Dinner £4.50–£6 Wine £3.30 Last dinner 7.45pm

WATERHOUSES
Staffordshire
Map **7** SK05
✕ ***Olde Beams*** Leek Rd ☏ (05386) 254
Closed Mon, 1wk Jan Dinner not served Sun
English & French V 40 seats Last dinner 10pm 18P
Credit card 3

WATERMILLOCK
Cumbria
Map **12** NY42
★★★ ***HBL* Leeming House** Ullswater (Prestige) ☏ Pooley Bridge (08536) 444
Closed Jan & Feb
This elegant 1847 manor house is set in 20 acres of landscaped gardens on the edge of Ullswater, with breathtaking views of the fells. It is a comfortable, elegant hotel with spacious lounges, a delightful Regency-style dining room and individual, very well appointed bedrooms. Mr and Mrs Fitzpatrick provide a most tranquil and relaxing atmosphere here.
18rm(16⇌2⋒) 1 ✱ sB&B £33.75 sB&B⇌⋒ £33.75 dB&B £67.50 dB&B⇌⋒ £67.50 B
CTV 40P ✽ nc8yrs *xmas*
English & French V ♔ ☐ ✱ Lunch £6.32 Tea £3.45 Dinner £16.67 Wine £4.51 Last dinner 9pm
Credit cards 1 2 3 5

★ ***HL* Old Church** ☏ Pooley Bridge (08536) 204
Closed Jan–Mar RS Nov–Dec
An 18th-century country house built on the site of a 12th-century church.
12rm(7⇌)(1fb) sB&B £16 sB&B⇌ £20

dB&B£32 dB&B➡£40
CTV 30P ⊜✽ ♪
🅴 English & French ♡ ☕ Dinner £9.75
Wine £4.25 Last dinner 8.30pm

WATFORD
Hertfordshire
Map **4** TQ19

☆☆☆**Caledonian** St Albans Rd
☎(0923) 29212
Modern, busy, commercial hotel with modest bedrooms.
86➡⋒ CTV in all bedrooms Ⓡ
✱sB&B➡⋒£28.50 dB&B➡⋒£35 🅱
Lift ☾ 12P CFA *xmas*
🅴 English & French ♡ ☕ ✱Lunch £2.15&alc Tea 65p Dinner £7.25&alc Wine £4.89 Last dinner 9.30pm
Credit cards 1 2 3 5

✕**Flower Drum** 16 Market St ☎(0923) 26711
A well-appointed, pleasant restaurant with extensive menus.
Closed 24 & 25 Dec
🅴 Pekinese & Szechwan **V** 80 seats Lunch £4–£8.70&alc Dinner £8–£10.50&alc Wine £4.70 Last dinner 11.30pm ⚑
Credit cards 1 2 3 5

At **Bushey** (2m SE A41)
☆☆☆**Ladbroke** (& Conference centre)
Elton Way, Watford Bypass (A41) (Ladbroke) ☎(0923) 35881
175➡⋒ 400P

☆☆**Spider's Web Motel** Watford Bypass
☎01-950 6211
104➡ 300P

WEEDON
Northamptonshire
Map **4** SP65

★★**Crossroads** ☎(0327) 40354 Telex no 311165
Closed Xmas
28rm(25➡)(3fb) 1🛏 CTV in all bedrooms Ⓡ ✱ sB&B£25 sB&B➡£30 dB&B£32 dB&B➡£38 🅱
100P✽
V ♡ ☕ Lunch £9alc Tea £1 High Tea £3.50 Dinner £9alc Wine £5.25 Last dinner 10.30pm
Credit cards 1 2 3 5 **VS**

WELLESBOURNE
Warwickshire
Map **4** SP25

★★**Kings Head** (Minotel) ☎Stratford-upon-Avon (0789) 840206
A country inn, in the centre of this small village.
10rm(2➡2⋒)(2fb) Ⓡ sB&B£13–£17 sB&B➡⋒£18–£22 dB&B£18–£24 dB&B➡⋒£25–£30 🅱
CTV 40P Live music & dancing Fri
V ♡ Lunch fr£6alc Dinner fr£5.50&alc Wine £5 Last dinner 9pm
Credit cards 1 2 3

WELLINGBOROUGH
Northamptonshire
Map **4** SP86

★★★**Hind** Sheep St (Queens Moat)
☎(0933) 222827
32➡(1fb) 1🛏 CTV in all bedrooms Ⓡ
sB&B➡⋒£29.90–£33.35
dB&B➡⋒£39.10–£42.55 🅱
☾ 16P 3🏠 CFA
🅴 English & Continental ♡ ☕ Lunch £4.95–£5.25&alc Tea 55–60p Dinner £6.95–£7.25&alc Wine £4.65 Last dinner 9.30pm
Credit cards 1 2 3 4 5 **VS**

★***Columbia*** 19 Northampton Rd
☎(0933) 222094
Closed 21 Dec–6 Jan
34rm ✱ 🅱
CTV 12P sauna bath
🅴 Mainly grills ♡ ☕ Last dinner 7.45pm

★***B* High View** 156 Midland Rd ☎(0933) 226060
Friendly, mainly commercial, family-run hotel close to the town centre. →

W

17rm(6➡⋒)(2fb) CTV in 2 bedrooms sB&B£14.95 sB&B➡⋒£24 dB&B£18.95 dB&B➡⋒£29

CTV 8P ✽

Lunch £5.50alc Dinner £5.50alc Wine £2.85 Last dinner 7.30pm

Credit cards 1 2 3 5

WELLINGTON
Shropshire
Map **7** SJ61
See Telford

WELLINGTON
Somerset
Map **3** ST12

★★ ***Beam Bridge*** Sampford Arundel (2½m SW A38) ☎ Greenham (0823) 672223

6rm(4➡2⋒) CTV in all bedrooms Ⓡ B

100P nc4yrs

English & Continental ♡ Last dinner 9.30pm

Credit cards 1 2 3 5

WELLS
Somerset
Map **3** ST54

★★★ ***B*** **Swan** Sadler St (Best Western) ☎ (0749) 78877 Telex no 449658

Partly 16th-century and partly Victorian building which overlooks the West Front of the cathedral.

27rm(20➡5⋒)(1fb) 6 CTV in all bedrooms sB&B➡⋒ fr£25.50 dB&B➡⋒ fr£40 B

20P CFA *xmas*

English, French & Italian V ♡ Lunch fr£6.75 Tea fr70p Dinner fr£7.95 Wine £5 Last dinner 9.30pm

Credit cards 1 2 3 4 5 VS

★★ ***H*** **Crown** Market Pl ☎ (0749) 73457

Hospitable, traditional hotel of great character, near cathedral.

14rm(8➡1⋒)(2fb) 4 CTV in all bedrooms Ⓡ ✽sB&B£21.50 sB&B➡⋒£23.50 dB&B£34 dB&B➡⋒£37 B

10P Squash nc5yrs *xmas*

English & French ♡ ✽Lunch £7.95 Dinner £7.95&alc Wine £4.50 Last dinner 9.30pm

Credit cards 1 2 3 5 VS

★★ ***White Hart*** Sadler St ☎ (0749) 72056

Closed Xmas Day

A central, business and touring hotel with busy bars and a first floor lounge.

10rm(2➡1⋒) Annexe: 5➡ Ⓡ B

CTV 12P 4

V ♡ Last dinner 8.30pm

Credit cards 1 3

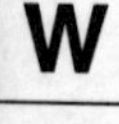

★ **Ancient Gate House** Sadler St ☎ (0749) 72029

11rm(1➡2⋒)(1fb) 6 CTV in 2 bedrooms sB&B£13–£14

sB&B➡⋒£18–£20 dB&B£22–£24 dB&B➡⋒£27–£30 B

CTV

English & Italian V ♡ Lunch £2.20–£4.80&alc Dinner £7.60&alc Wine £3.95 Last dinner 10pm

Credit cards 1 2 3 5 VS

★ ***King Charles*** High St ☎ (0749) 73920

6rm(1➡) Ⓡ B

CTV

Mainly grills ♡ Last dinner 9.45pm

Credit cards 1 3

★ ***H*** **Worth House** Worth (2m W B3139) ☎ (0749) 72041

Closed Dec–Feb (except Xmas)

A small, informally run hotel, a few miles from the centre of Wells.

8rm(2➡1⋒)(2fb) Ⓡ sB&B£12–£14 sB&B➡⋒£14–£16 dB&B£20–£24 dB&B➡⋒£24–£28

CTV 18P nc3yrs

V Wine £3.85 Last dinner 8pm

WELLS-NEXT-THE-SEA
Norfolk
Map **9** TF94

★ **Crown** The Buttlands ☎ Fakenham (0328) 710209

15rm (2fb) sB&B fr£15 dB&B fr£30 B

CTV 12P

English & French ♡ Bar lunch £4.50 Tea fr£1.20 High Tea £3.50alc Dinner £10–£12.50 Wine £5.15 Last dinner 9pm

Credit cards 2 3 5

WELSHPOOL
Powys
Map **7** SJ20

★★ **Royal Oak** ☎ (0938) 2217

Situated in the town centre is this red brick, early Victorian hotel.

25rm(8➡4⋒)(1fb) 1 ✽sB&B£13–£14 sB&B➡⋒£16.50–£17.50 dB&B£26.50–£27.50 dB&B➡⋒£29–£32 B

☾ CTV 80P 2

V ♡ ✽Lunch fr£4.74 Tea fr75p High Tea fr£2.75 Dinner fr£5.75&alc Wine £3.50 Last dinner 9pm

Credit cards 1 2 3 VS

★ **Garth Derwen** Buttington (2½m NE A458) ☎ Trewern (093874) 238

Closed mid Dec–mid Jan

Small, family run, red brick Victorian hotel with good home cooking.

8rm(5⋒)(4fb) 1 sB&B£11.50–£15 sB&B⋒£13–£15 dB&B£19–£26 dB&B⋒£22–£26 B

CTV 20P ✽

V ♡ Lunch fr£2.65&alc Tea £1.15 Dinner £4.95&alc Wine £3.45 Last dinner 7.30pm

Credit card 1 VS

WELWYN
Hertfordshire
Map **4** TL21

☆☆ **Clock Motel** ☎ (043871) 6911

This hotel has some newly built, well equipped bedrooms.

72rm(68➡4⋒)(1fb) CTV in all bedrooms Ⓡ sB&B➡⋒£24.95 dB&B➡⋒£32.95 B

CTV CFA Live music and dancing Sat Cabaret Sat ♿

English & Continental V ♡ Lunch fr£3.95 Tea fr£2.25 Dinner fr£3.95 Wine £4.95 Last dinner 10pm

S% Credit cards 1 2 3 5

WELWYN GARDEN CITY
Hertfordshire
Map **4** TL21

☆☆☆ **Crest** Homestead Ln (Crest) ☎ (07073) 24336 Telex no 261523

58rm(51➡7⋒) CTV in all bedrooms Ⓡ ✽sB➡⋒ fr£33.50 dB➡⋒ fr£43 (room only) B

Lift ☾ 50P CFA

International V ♡ ✽Bar lunch £2.80–£3.20 Dinner fr£8.25&alc Wine £5.95 Last dinner 9.30pm

Credit cards 1 2 3 4 5 VS

WEMBLEY
Gt London
London plan **5** *B4* (page 422)

☆☆☆☆ ***Wembley International*** Empire Way ☎ 01-902 8839 Telex no 24837

Modern, conveniently located, well appointed hotel.

320➡ CTV in all bedrooms Ⓡ B

Lift ☾ 200P CFA

International V ♡ Last dinner 10pm

Credit cards 1 2 3 4 5

WENTBRIDGE (nr Pontefract)
West Yorkshire
Map **8** SE41

★★★ ***H*** **Wentbridge House** ☎ Pontefract (0977) 620444

A converted country mansion with pleasant, well-kept grounds, and situated in a quiet village.

17rm(10➡7⋒) Annexe: 3rm 1 CTV in all bedrooms ✽sB&B fr£19.50 sB&B➡⋒ fr£28 dB&B fr£21.50 dB&B➡⋒ fr£35.50 Continental breakfast B

120P 4 ✽ ♿

English & French ♡ ✽Lunch £7.25&alc Tea fr65p Dinner £7alc Wine £5.85 Last dinner 9.30pm

Credit cards 1 2 3 5

WEOBLEY
Hereford & Worcester
Map **3** SO45

★★ **Red Lion** ☎ (05445) 220

A 14th-century timbered inn situated in the village centre.

7rm(2➡5⋒) CTV in all bedrooms sB&B➡⋒ fr£26 dB&B➡⋒ fr£33 B

70P 🚗 ✽
V ♔ Bar lunch £2–£6alc Dinner £10–£20alc Wine £5.50 Last dinner 9pm
Credit cards 1 2 3 5 **VS**

WEST BAY
Dorset
See **Bridport**

WEST BEXINGTON
Dorset
Map **3** SY58
★★**Manor** ☎ Burton Bradstock (0308) 897785
The original manor house of a quiet hamlet in rural Dorset, a short distance from the sea.
14rm(2➡) (1fb) CTV in 11 bedrooms TV in 1 bedroom Ⓡ sB&B£17–£19 sB&B➡£19.50–£21 dB&B£34–£38 dB&B➡£39–£42 B
22P 4🏠 🚗 ✽ nc10yrs *xmas*
🍴English & European **V** ♔ Bar lunch £1.50–£2.95&alc Dinner £6.50&alc Wine £3.30 Last dinner 9.30pm
Credit cards 1 3

WEST BROMWICH
West Midlands
Map **7** SP09
See also Barr, Great
☆☆☆**West Bromwich Moat House**
Birmingham Rd (Queens Moat)
☎021-553 6111 Telex no 336232
Birmingham District plan **34**
A typical, modern, purpose-built hotel by junction 1 of the M5.
180➡⋒ CTV in all bedrooms Ⓡ sB&B➡⋒£32.50 dB&B➡⋒£44.85 B
Lift ☾ ## 200P CFA ✽
🍴English & Continental **V** ♔ ☕ Lunch fr£6.95&alc Tea fr55p Dinner fr£6.95&alc Wine £5.20 Last dinner 9.45pm
Credit cards 1 2 3 5 **VS**

WESTBURY
Wiltshire
Map **3** ST85
★★**Lopes Arms** Market Pl ☎(0373) 822403

Weobley

This black and white building dates from the 14th century, and is situated near the parish church.
8rm(1⋒) (1fb) TV available in bedrooms Ⓡ sB&B£14 sB&B⋒£15 dB&B£20 dB&B⋒£22
CTV 12P
V ♔ *Lunch £1.50–£6.50&alc Dinner £4.50&alc Wine £3.20 Last dinner 9.30pm
VS

WEST CHILTINGTON
West Sussex
Map **4** TQ01
★★**Roundabout** Monkmead Ln (1¾m S) (Best Western) ☎(07983) 3838
Closed 2–16 Jan
Quiet Tudor style hotel with compact well furnished bedrooms.
21rm(18➡5⋒) (2fb) 4▭ CTV in all bedrooms Ⓡ sB&B➡⋒£24.75–£26.50 dB&B➡⋒£39.75–£43.50 B
50P 🚗 ✽ nc3yrs *xmas*
🍴English & French **V** ♔ ☕ Lunch £6.75 Tea £1.75 Dinner £8.25–£8.50 Wine £4.95 Last dinner 9pm
S% Credit cards 1 2 3 4

WESTCLIFF-ON-SEA
Essex
See **Southend-on-Sea**

WESTERHAM
Kent
Map **5** TQ45
✕✕✕**Ristorante Montmorency**
Quebec Sq ☎(0959) 62139
A house of Elizabethan origin providing well prepared Italian cuisine.
Closed Mon Dinner not served Sun
🍴French & Italian 46 seats *Lunch £14alc Dinner fr£8.25&alc Wine £7.65 Last dinner 11pm
Credit cards 1 2 3 5

WESTGATE-ON-SEA
Kent
Map **5** TR37
★★**Ivyside** 25 Sea Rd ☎Thanet (0843) 31082
Sea-front hotel with extensive recreational and leisure facilities.
55rm(23➡30⋒) (50fb) CTV in 30 bedrooms TV in 25 bedrooms Ⓡ sB&B➡⋒£14–£18 dB&B➡⋒£28–£36 B
☾ ⊁ CTV 40P CFA ✽ ▭ & ⛴ (heated) squash billiards sauna bath Disco twice wkly Live music and dancing wkly 🏠 *xmas*
🍴English & French **V** ♔ ☕ Lunch fr£5&alc Tea fr65p High Tea fr£1.50 Dinner £7.50&alc Wine £4 Last dinner 9pm
S% Credit cards 1 3
See advert on page 660

WEST HARTLEPOOL
Cleveland
See Hartlepool

WESTHILL
Grampian *Aberdeenshire*
Map **15** NJ80
☆☆☆**Westhill Inn** ☎ Aberdeen (0224) 740388 Telex no 739925
Modern, custom-built hotel, just off the A944, within a developing area 6m west of Aberdeen.
39➡ Annexe: 14rm(6➡8⋒) (2fb) CTV in all bedrooms Ⓡ *sB&B➡⋒£23–£25 dB&B➡⋒£29.50–£32 B
Lift ☾ CTV 250P CFA sauna bath
V ♔ ☕ *Lunch £4.25&alc Tea 45p Dinner fr£6.25&alc Last dinner 10pm
Credit cards 1 2 3 4 5 **VS**

WEST HUNTSPILL
Somerset
Map **3** ST34
✕✕**Huntspill Villa** 82 Main Rd
☎Burnham on Sea (0278) 782291
Closed Sun & Mon
V 46 seats Lunch £10–£14alc Dinner £10–£14alc Wine £5.50 Last dinner 9.45pm 20P bedrooms available
Credit cards 1 2 3 5 **VS**

W

WEST LULWORTH
Dorset
See Lulworth

WEST MERSEA
Essex
Map **5** TM01

✕✕**Le Roannals** 42 High St
☎Colchester (0206) 383922
Small, modern French restaurant, personally run by Jean Claude and Lynda Blanchin.
Closed Mon Dinner not served Sun
▣English & French **V** 45 seats ✱Lunch £5.25–£5.80&alc Dinner £8.50alc Wine £4.10 Last dinner 10pm 14P⚟
Credit cards ① ② ③ ⑤

✕**Le Champenois** (Blackwater Hotel)
20–22 Church Rd ☎(0206) 383338
Traditional French hospitality is combined with a homely atmosphere and personal service.
Lunch not served Tue Dinner not served Sun
▣English & French **V** 42 seats Lunch £5.80–£8.60 Tea fr£1.30 Dinner fr£7.50&alc Wine £4.55 Last dinner 10.30pm 20P bedrooms available
Credit cards ① ③ **VS**

WESTON
Shropshire
Map **7** SJ52

★★★*H* **Hawkstone Park** (Best Western) ☎Lee Brockhurst (093924) 611
43➡ Annexe: 16➡ (6fb) CTV in all bedrooms Ⓡ sB&B➡£24–£28 dB&B➡£35–£42 Ᵽ
☾ CTV 300P CFA ✽ ≋ ⚑18 ⚲(grass) ⚲ billiards sauna bath ⌂ *xmas* ♿
✿ ▭ Lunch £5.25 Tea £1.75 High Tea £4.50 Dinner £7.25 Wine £4.50 Last dinner 9.30pm
Credit cards ① ② ③ ⑤

WESTONBIRT
Gloucestershire
Map **3** ST89
See also Tetbury

★★★**Hare & Hounds** (Best Western)
☎(066 688) 233
A traditional country hotel in 9 acres of grounds close to the magnificent Arboretum.
23rm(19➡) (2fb) CTV in all bedrooms Ⓡ sB&B£19 sB&B➡£26–£32 dB&B£36 dB&B➡£40–£45 Ᵽ
50P 9⌂ ✽ ⚲(hard) squash ⌂ *xmas*
✿ ▭ Lunch £4.50–£7&alc Tea 65p&alc Dinner £8.50–£9.50&alc Wine £4 Last dinner 9pm
S% Credit cards ① ② ③

WESTON-ON-THE-GREEN
Oxfordshire
Map **4** SP51

★★★**Weston Manor** (Best Western)
☎Bletchington (0869) 50621
A 14th-century manor house with many historical associations, standing in its own grounds.
16rm(13➡) Annexe: 6rm(4➡) (3fb) 2▣ CTV in all bedrooms Ⓡ sB&B£27–£30 sB&B➡£33–£38 dB&B£38 dB&B➡£45–£60 Ᵽ
CTV 100P ✽ ≋(heated) squash ⌂ *xmas*
▣English & French ✿ ▭ Lunch £4–£6.50 Tea 60p Dinner £9–£10.95&alc Wine £5.95 Last dinner 9pm
S% Credit cards ① ② ③ ⑤

WESTON-SUPER-MARE
Avon
Map **3** ST36

★★★*L* **Grand Atlantic** Beach Rd (Trusthouse Forte) ☎(0934) 26543
Well appointed comfortable hotel with attractive garden.
79➡ (2fb) CTV in all bedrooms Ⓡ sB&B➡£33.50 dB&B➡£57.50 Ᵽ
Lift ☾ CTV 150P CFA ✽ ≋(heated) ⚲(hard) ⌂
✿ ▭ Last dinner 9pm
Credit cards ① ② ③ ④ ⑤

★★★*H* **Royal Pier** Birnbeck Rd
☎(0934) 26644 Closed Nov–mid Mar

Traditional holiday and business hotel, in a quiet situation by the sea.
48rm(23⇨)(2fb) CTV available in bedrooms ® sB&B fr£15 sB&B⇨ fr£17 dB&B fr£30 dB&B⇨ fr£34 B
Lift ☾ 30P billiards
Lunch £4.50–£5.45 Tea fr65p Dinner fr£7 Wine £4.55 Last dinner 8.30pm
Credit cards 1 3

★★ ***Grand Panorama*** 57 South Rd ☎(0934) 24980 RS Oct–May
23rm(11⇨) CTV available in bedrooms
CTV 16P nc5yrs
English & French V Last dinner 8pm

★★ ***H* Rozel** Madeira Cove ☎(0934) 21361
Large, traditional family-owned and run holiday and business hotel on the seafront.
58rm(32⇨3⋒)(32fb) CTV in all bedrooms ® sB&B £15–£18 sB&B⇨⋒ £16–£19 dB&B £28–£34 dB&B⇨⋒ £30–£36 B
Lift ☾ 25P 60 CFA (heated) sauna bath Live music and dancing twice wkly *xmas*
English & French Lunch £3.75–£4.25 Tea 50p–75p Dinner £4.50–£5.25 Wine £3.75 Last dinner 8pm
Credit cards 1 2 3

★ ***Monte Bello*** 48 Knightstone Rd ☎(0934) 22303
Closed 8 Oct–Xmas & Jan–Etr
Seasonal holiday hotel, which is privately owned and run and overlooks the sea.
32rm(8⋒)
Lift CTV nc3yrs
Last dinner 7pm
Credit card 3

✕✕ **Sands** 17 Beach Rd ☎(0934) 414414
French V 100 seats Lunch £4.50&alc Tea £1 Dinner £8alc Wine £4 Last dinner 11pm 50P Live music and dancing Mon–Sat
Credit cards 1 2 3 5

WESTON TURVILLE
Buckinghamshire
Map **4** SP81

★★ **Five Bells** 40 Main St ☎Stoke Mandeville (029 661) 3131
Modernised 19th-century inn with well appointed bedrooms.
16rm CTV in all bedrooms
P
Last dinner 10pm
Credit cards 1 3 VS

WEST RUNTON
Norfolk
Map **9** TG14

★★★ ***Links Country Park*** (Best Western) ☎(026375) 691
A popular golfing and tourist hotel in open country above the village.
34rm(20⇨14⋒) CTV in all bedrooms ® B
Lift ☾ 100P CFA
English & French V Last dinner 9.30pm
Credit cards 1 2 3 5

✕✕ ***Mirabelle*** Station Rd ☎(026375) 396
Closed Mon & 1st 2wks Nov Dinner not served Sun (Nov–Mar)
Continental V 50 seats Last dinner 9pm 25P
Credit cards 1 2 3 5

WESTWARD HO!
Devon
Map **2** SS42

★★ **Buckleigh Grange** Buckleigh Rd ☎Bideford (02372) 4468
Closed Nov–Etr
Comfortable family-run holiday hotel in a quiet situation.
12rm(2⇨2⋒)(6fb) sB&B £10.25–£11.30 sB&B⇨⋒ £13.25–£14.30 dB&B £20.50–£22.60 dB&B⇨⋒ £26.50–£28.60 B →

W

CTV 20P ✽ ⛳(grass)
♥ Bar lunch £2–£3.50 Dinner £5–£7 Wine £2.50 Last dinner 7pm

WEST WEMYSS
Fife
Map **11** NT39
✕✕ ***Belvedere Hotel*** Coxstalls
☎ Kirkcaldy (0592) 54167
A small hotel in a quiet coastal village overlooking the old harbour.
Dinner not served Sun
▣ Scottish & French **V** 60 seats Last dinner 10pm 35P bedrooms available
Credit cards 1 2 3

WEST WITTON
North Yorkshire
Map **7** SE08
★★**Wensleydale Heifer Inn**
☎ Wensleydale (0969) 22322
A 17th-century village inn on the main road through this Dales village.
9rm(5⇌4⋒) Annexe: 7rm(1⇌3⋒) (1fb) 1▭ CTV in all bedrooms Ⓡ sB&B£12–£15 sB&B⇌⋒ £16.25–£20 dB&B£20–£25 dB&B⇌⋒ £22.50–£32 B
30P
V ♥ Bar lunch £2alc Dinner £9.50alc Wine £5.85 Last dinner 10pm
Credit cards 1 3 **VS**

WEST WOODBURN
Northumberland
Map **12** NY88
★**Fox & Hounds** ☎ Bellingham (0660) 60210
An 18th-century roadside inn with a modern dining room where home cooking is provided.
10rm (2fb) sB&B£9–£10 dB&B£17.50–£19.50
CTV 30P
V ♥ ☐ Bar lunch 70p–£1.50 Tea 35p alc Dinner £3.95–£4.50 Last dinner 8pm

WETHERAL
Cumbria
Map **12** NY45
★★★ ***HBL*** **Crown** (Best Western)
☎ (0228) 61888
Originally an 18th century farmhouse but now completely modernised, this hotel retains much character and charm. The comfortable bedrooms are tastefully furnished and well equipped; the Conservatory Restaurant provides cuisine of a high standard and there are good sports and conference facilities.
50rm(48⇌2⋒) (4fb) 1▭ CTV in all bedrooms Ⓡ sB&B⇌⋒ £34–£38 dB&B⇌⋒ £48–£50 B
☾ CTV 70P 1 ⌂ CFA ✽ squash billiards sauna bath *xmas*
▣ English & French **V** ♥ ☐ ✻ Lunch £4.95–£8&alc Dinner £8.25–£10&alc Wine £4.45 Last dinner 9.30pm
Credit cards 1 2 3 5 **VS**

★★**Killoran** The Green ☎ (0228) 60200
Built in the late 1800s as a country residence, this hotel retains much of its original atmosphere.
10rm(4⋒) (2fb) TV in all bedrooms Ⓡ ✻ sB&B£12.50 sB&B⋒ £13.50 dB&B£25 dB&B⋒ £27 B
CTV 40P ⚑ ✽
♥ ☐ ✻ Bar lunch £1.20–£1.70 Tea fr 75p Dinner £7 Wine £3.75 Last dinner 8.45pm
Credit cards 1 3 **VS**

✕**Fantails** ☎ (0228) 60239
Closed Feb Lunch not served 1 Nov–1 Apr
▣ English & French **V** 70 seats ✻ Lunch £3.25–£7.50&alc Dinner £3.25–£7.50&alc Wine £4.45 Last dinner 9.30pm 25P
Credit cards 1 2 3 4 5 **VS**

WETHERBY
West Yorkshire
Map **8** SE44
☆☆☆**Ladbroke Wetherby** (junc A1/A58) (Ladbroke) ☎ (0937) 63881
Closed Xmas

W

Modern hotel with good facilities, bars and restaurants.

73➡ CTV in 70 bedrooms Ⓡ ✱sB➡£34 dB➡£42 (room only) ₿

☾ 114P ✽

🎞 International ♔ ✱Lunch fr£6.50 Dinner fr£8.50 Last dinner 10pm

Credit cards 1 2 3 4 5

✕✕✕**Cardinal** 16 Bank St ☎(0937) 62751

Closed Mon Lunch not served

🎞 French **V** 50 seats ✱Dinner £10.50alc Wine £4.75 Last dinner 10.30pm 8P

Credit cards 1 2 3 5

✕✕✕**Linton Spring** Sicklinghall Rd ☎(0937) 65353

Elegant mansion in attractive grounds serving traditional and international dishes.

Closed Mon & 1st 2wks Jan Lunch not served Sat Dinner not served Sun

🎞 English & French **V** 100 seats Lunch £5.95 Dinner £10.75alc Wine £4.95 Last dinner 9.30pm 60P Disco Tue–Sat

Credit cards 1 2 3 5 **VS**

WETHERINGSETT
Suffolk
Map **5** TM16

★★🏠**Wetheringsett Manor** ☎Mendlesham (04494) 545

9rm (5➡2⋒) (2fb) CTV in all bedrooms Ⓡ sB&B£22 sB&B➡⋒£28 dB&B£30 dB&B➡⋒£34–£37.50 ₿

100P 6🚘🚫✽ *xmas*

♔ ☕ Lunch £12–£16alc Tea 80p alc Dinner £12–£16alc Wine £5.15 Last dinner 9pm

Credit cards 1 3

WETHERSFIELD
Essex
Map **5** TL73

✕**Rudi's** Village Green ☎Great Dunmow (0371) 850723

Closed 1st 2wks Jan & Mon Dinner not served Sun

🎞 Austrian & French **V** 52 seats ✱Lunch £5.50&alc Dinner £8–£11alc Wine £3.90 Last dinner 9.30pm 10P Live music last Fri in mth

WEYBOURNE
Norfolk
Map **9** TG14

★★*HL* **Maltings** ☎(026370) 275

Formerly a manor, malting house and dairy, this original Norfolk flintstone house dates from the 16th century.

22rm (15➡2⋒) 1🛏 CTV in all bedrooms sB&B£22–£25 sB&B➡⋒£25–£27 dB&B£40–£44 dB&B➡⋒£45–£49 ₿

70P 🚫 *xmas*

🎞 English & French ♔ ☕ Lunch fr£7.50&alc Tea fr70p Dinner £10&alc Last dinner 9pm

S% Credit cards 1 2 3 5

✕✕**Gasche's Swiss** ☎(026370) 220

Friendly, family atmosphere in village cottage restaurant.

Closed Mon Dinner not served Sun

🎞 English & Continental **V** 65 seats ✱Lunch £6.95&alc Dinner £11.95&alc Wine £3.75 Last dinner 9pm 40P

Credit cards 2 3 5 **VS**

WEYBRIDGE
Surrey
Map **4** TQ06

★★★*L* **Oatlands Park** 146 Oatlands Dr (North) ☎(0932) 47242 Telex no 915123

Georgian/Victorian building in splendid large grounds.

147rm (94➡) (5fb) 1🛏 CTV in all bedrooms Ⓡ ✱sB&B£22 sB&B➡£30 dB&B£35 dB&B➡£43 ₿

Lift ☾ 80P CFA 40🚘✽ 🏊 ⛳ 🎾(hard) squash *xmas*

🎞 English & French ♔ ☕ ✱Lunch £6&alc Tea £2.50 Dinner £7.25&alc Wine £4.75 Last dinner 9.30pm

Credit cards 1 2 3 4 5 **VS**

W

★★★**Ship Thistle** Monument Green (Thistle) ☎(0932) 48364 Telex no 894271 Closed Xmas

Quiet Tudor style tourist hotel.

39➡⋒ CTV in all bedrooms ✻sB➡£37–£40 dB➡£45–£48 (room only) B

☾ ⚟ 65P CFA ✿ Live music & dancing Tue–Sat

English & French ▭ Lunch £7.50&alc Dinner £7.50–£9&alc Last dinner 9.30pm

Credit cards 1 2 3 4 5 **VS**

✕✕**Casa Romana** 2 Temple Hall, Monument Hill ☎(0932) 43470

Long established, flamboyant Italian restaurant with imaginative and authentic cooking.

Closed Mon & Xmas Lunch not served Sat

Italian **V** 70 seats Lunch £4.95&alc Wine £4.95 Last dinner 10.45pm 20P

Credit cards 1 2 3 4

WEYMOUTH
Dorset
Map **3** SY67

★★**Crown** 51–52 St Thomas St ☎(0305) 785695 RS Xmas

An imposing brick hotel with ornamental stone embellishments, close to the harbour and shops and a short distance from the sea.

79rm(44➡5⋒)(12fb) sB&B£14–£17 sB&B➡⋒£15–£18 dB&B£23–£26 dB&B➡⋒£26–£30 B

Lift ☾ CTV 9 CFA Live music and dancing 3 nights wkly Cabaret wkly

V Lunch £1.75–£6.50 Dinner £5–£6.50 Wine £3.50 Last dinner 8pm

Credit cards 1 3

★★**Golden Lion** St Edmonds Street ☎(0305) 786778

A colour-washed building with a large golden lion over the entrance, this hotel is located in the town centre near the harbour.

19rm(1➡) sB&B£12.08–£13.65 dB&B£24.15–£27.30 dB&B➡£26.25–£29.40 B

CTV

English & Italian ✻Lunch £2.50–£3.50 Dinner £3.25–£4.25 Wine £3.50 Last dinner 8pm

Credit cards 1 3

★★**Kingswood** 55 Rodwell Rd ☎(0305) 784926

Attractive colour-washed hotel supervised by resident owners.

14rm(2➡)(3fb) Ⓡ sB&B£10.50–£12.50 sB&B➡£12.50–£14.50 dB&B£19–£21 dB&B➡£21–£23

CTV 24P ✿ Disco wkly

V ▭ Lunch £2–£2.50&alc Tea £1.25–£1.50 Dinner £3–£3.50&alc Wine £3.50 Last dinner 8.30pm

Credit cards 1 2 3 5

★★**Old York** 55 The Esplanade ☎(0305) 786558 Closed Xmas

A seafront hotel in a Georgian style terraced development.

10⋒(2fb) ✻sB&B⋒£16–£18.50 dB&B⋒£26–£33 B

Lift CTV

V Lunch £2.50–£6&alc Dinner £3–£8&alc Wine £3.50 Last dinner 10.30pm

★★**Hotel Prince Regent** 139 The Esplanade ☎(03057) 71313 Closed Xmas

Victorian hotel on the seafront opposite the pier.

50rm(25➡)(11fb) CTV in 25 bedrooms ✻sB&B£16.75–£18.25 sB&B➡£20.75–£22.25 dB&B£31.50–£34.50 dB&B➡£35.50–£38.50 B

Lift ☾ CTV 2P 2 CFA Live music and dancing wkly in summer Cabaret wkly in summer

▭ ✻Lunch £4.45&alc Tea fr 55p Dinner £5.20&alc Wine £3.30 Last dinner 8.30pm

Credit cards 1 2 3 5

★★**Rembrandt** 12 Dorchester Rd ☎(0305) 786253

A brick building with a modern extension and good restaurant.

26rm(5➡)(6fb) CTV in 4 bedrooms TV in 22 bedrooms sB&B£12.65 sB&B➡£16.10 dB&B£25.30 dB&B➡£32.20

CTV 50P (heated) Live music and dancing twice wkly *xmas*

V ▭ Lunch fr £4.60 Tea 25p Dinner £5.75&alc Wine £3.60 Last dinner 9.30pm

Credit cards 1 3 5

★★**Hotel Rex** 29 The Esplanade ☎(03057) 73485

The hotel has a terraced Georgian façade and offers views across Weymouth Bay.

20rm(13➡7⋒)(3fb) CTV in all bedrooms sB&B➡⋒£17–£20 dB&B➡⋒£29–£36 B

Lift ☾ CTV 8

V ▭ Lunch £3–£7&alc Tea 50p–£1 Dinner £3.50–£8&alc Wine £3.50 Last dinner 10.30pm

Credit cards 1 3

★★**Streamside** 29 Preston Rd ☎Preston (0305) 833121

19rm(8➡1⋒)(6fb) CTV available in bedrooms sB&B£16.75–£18.75 sB&B➡⋒£20.12–£25.30 dB&B£28.75–£32.75 dB&B➡⋒£31.75–£34

CTV 40P Disco Fri Live music and dancing Sat

English & French **V** ▭ Bar lunch £3–£5 Tea £1.20–£1.50 Dinner £7.50&alc Wine £3.80 Last dinner 7.45pm

Credit cards 1 2 3 5

★**Bay View** 35 The Esplanade ☎(0305) 782083 RS Xmas

This hotel is near the Pavilion and the harbour and has magnificent views across Weymouth Bay.

10rm(6⋒)(2fb) CTV in all bedrooms sB&B£8.50 sB&B⋒£12 dB&B£15–£17 dB&B⋒£17.50–£20

CTV

Bar lunch £1–£3 Dinner £4&alc Wine £3 Last dinner 5pm

Credit cards 1 3 **VS**

W

✕**Sea Cow Bistro** Custom House Quay ☎(0305) 783524
Closed Sun (winter) Lunch not served Sun
English & Continental 120 seats Lunch £3.95–£5.25 Dinner £4.55–£5.95&alc Wine £3.90 Last dinner 10.15pm
Credit cards 1 3

WHIMPLE
Devon
Map **3** SY09
★★ *HBL* **Woodhayes** ☎(0404) 822237
Closed Jan
This delightful small Georgian Country House stands in its own tidy gardens and orchard in a peaceful locality near the pretty village of Whimple. Over recent years the house has been tastefully refurbished to provide comfortable public rooms including a well appointed dining room, and good bedrooms containing television, radio, telephone, flowers and magazines. Excellent standards of hospitality by the proprietor will ensure the comfort of their guests.
6 CTV in all bedrooms
*sB&B £22.50–£30 dB&B £35–£45
20P 4 ✽ nc12yrs
English & Continental Lunch £9 Tea £2 Dinner £14 Wine £6.25 Last dinner 8pm
S% Credit cards 1 2 3 5

WHIPPINGHAM
Isle of Wight
Map **4** SZ59
★★ **Padmore House** Beatrice Av ☎Cowes (0983) 293210 Closed Xmas
Friendly, well-appointed, Queen Anne style hotel set in Medina Valley.
11rm(6 1) CTV in all bedrooms Ⓡ sB&B £18.50 sB&B £21 dB&B £30 dB&B £41
30P ✽
English & French V *Lunch £5.75–£6.75 Tea 75p Dinner £8.50–£11 Wine £4.90 Last dinner 9.30pm
Credit cards 1 2 3 5

WHITBY
North Yorkshire
Map **8** NZ81
★★ ***Royal*** West Cliff ☎(0947) 602234
RS Oct–Mar
An imposing building overlooking the harbour, and the Abbey.
135rm(22 44) Ⓡ
Lift ☾ CTV
International **V** Last dinner 8pm
Credit cards 1 2 3 5

★★ **Saxonville** Ladysmith Av (off Argyle Rd) ☎(0947) 602631
Closed Nov–Apr
A conversion from four town houses, near the North Promenade.
22rm(2 4) (2fb) Ⓡ sB&B £13.25–£14.75 dB&B £26.50–£29.50 dB&B £30.50–£33.50
CTV 20P nc4yrs
V Lunch £3.75–£4.50 Dinner £6.25–£6.75&alc Wine £4.20 Last dinner 8pm
Credit cards 1 2 3 **VS**

★★ **Sneaton Hall** Sneaton (3m S B1416) ☎(0947) 605929
8rm(3 3) (1fb) Ⓡ sB&B £9–£12.50 dB&B £18–£25 dB&B £20–£27
CTV 15P ✽
V Lunch £4.50alc Tea £1.25alc Dinner £6.25&alc Wine £3 Last dinner 8.30pm
VS

★ **Marvic** White Point Rd ☎(0947) 602400
Closed Oct–Mar
A two-storey building near the West Cliffs.
26rm(2) (5fb) sB&B £11 dB&B £22 dB&B £24
CTV 50P
Lunch fr£4 Tea fr£1.50 Dinner fr£6 Last dinner 7.15pm
VS

★ **White House** Upgang Ln, West Cliff ☎(0947) 602098 Closed Nov–Feb
This Victorian farmhouse was converted into the present hotel in the 1920s.
11rm(3) (2fb) Ⓡ sB&B £10 dB&B £20 dB&B £22
CTV 50P ✽ Disco wkly Live music and dancing wkly
Lunch £2–£3 Dinner £5–£6 Wine £3 Last dinner 7.30pm

WHITCHURCH
Hereford & Worcester
Map **3** SO51
★ ***Doward*** Crockers Ash ☎Symonds Yat (0600) 890267
A privately run hotel in an elevated position with extensive panoramic views.
6rm(1) Annexe: 8rm TV in 5 bedrooms Ⓡ
CTV 90P ✽
French **V** Last dinner 9pm
Credit card 3

WHITCHURCH
Shropshire
Map **7** SJ54
See also Redbrook, Clwyd, Wales
★★★ **Terrick Hall** (off A49 NE town centre) ☎(0948) 3584
Busy hotel close to a golf course and sporting facilities.
10 (1fb) CTV in all bedrooms Ⓡ *sB&B £20.35 dB&B £27.50
50P ✽ (hard) squash billiards Disco Wed–Sat
Lunch £3.95&alc Dinner £6.50&alc Wine £4.75 Last dinner 9.30pm
Credit cards 1 2 3 5

★★ **Dodington Lodge** Dodington ☎(0948) 2539
A family-run friendly little hotel, near the A41 on the southern edge of town.
9rm(3) (2fb) sB&B £11.50 sB&B £15.50 dB&B £21 dB&B £25
CTV 40P ✽
English & French Lunch £5.50–£6&alc Tea fr£2.25 Dinner £6&alc Wine £3.90 Last dinner 9pm
Credit cards 1 3 **VS**

W

★★Redbrook Hunting Lodge
Wrexham Rd
(See **Redbrook**, Clwyd)

WHITEBRIDGE
Highland *Inverness-shire*
Map **14** NH41

★★Whitebridge (Minotel) ☎ Gorthleck (04563) 226
Closed Jan RS Nov, Dec & Feb
12rm(3⇌5⋒)(3fb) CTV in all bedrooms ® sB&B£11–£12 sB&B⇌⋒£12.95–£14 dB&B£22–£24 dB&B⇌⋒£25.90–£28 Ⓑ
30P 2⌂ ✽
Lunch fr£5 Tea £1.50–£2 High Tea £4.50–£5 Dinner £7–£7.25&alc Wine £3 Last dinner 8pm
Credit cards 1 2 3 5 VS

WHITEBROOK
Gwent
Map **3** SO50

★★ *H* Crown at Whitebrook (Exec Hotel) ☎ Monmouth (0600) 860254
Charming small hotel with attractive bedrooms.
8rm(6⇌2⋒) sB&B⇌⋒£18 dB&B⇌⋒£38 Ⓑ
40P ✽
French Lunch £13alc Tea 65p alc Dinner £13alc Wine £4.50 Last dinner 10pm
Credit cards 1 2 3 5 VS

WHITEHAVEN
Cumbria
Map **11** NX91

★★Chase Corkickle ☎ (0946) 3656
14rm(1⇌3⋒)(1fb) CTV in all bedrooms ® sB&B£16.25 sB&B⇌⋒£19 dB&B£23 dB&B⇌⋒£26 Ⓑ
40P ✽ Live music and dancing twice wkly
V Lunch £3.50–£8 Dinner £3.80–£9 Wine £3.50 Last dinner 9pm
Credit cards 1 3

★★ *L* Roseneath Country House Low Moresby (3m NE off A595) ☎ (0946) 61572
Closed Xmas Day
Georgian country house occupying an elevated position with views towards the Solway Coast.
6rm(4⇌) Annexe: 3⇌ CTV in 4 bedrooms TV in 4 bedrooms ✱ sB&B fr£15 sB&B⇌ fr£22.50 dB&B fr£28.50 dB&B⇌ fr£31.50 Ⓑ
15P ✽
V ✱ Dinner £8.50alc Wine £3.90 Last dinner 9pm
Credit cards 1 2 3 5 VS

★★Waverley Tangier St ☎ (0946) 4337
24rm(3⇌1⋒) TV in 15 bedrooms sB&B£15–£17 sB&B⇌⋒£18.50–£20 dB&B£24–£26 dB&B⇌⋒£26–£28
CTV 16P
V Lunch fr£5 Dinner £5.50–£7.50 Wine £3.20 Last dinner 8.45pm
Credit cards 1 2 3 VS

WHITENESS
Shetland
Map **16** HU44

★Westing's Wormadale ☎ Gott (059584) 242
Modern hotel with a popular grill restaurant, with panoramic views from its hillside position.
9rm(6⋒)(2fb) CTV in all bedrooms ® sB&B fr£21.50 dB&B⋒£28.75 Ⓑ
CTV 20P
Lunch £2.25–£5.50 Tea 75p–£1.50 High Tea £3.50–£5 Dinner £6.95&alc Wine £4.50 Last dinner 9.30pm
Credit card 1 VS

WHITE RODING
Essex
Map **5** TL51

✕House of Edward Bear ☎ (027976) 260
Closed Sun–Tue
International 38 seats ✱ Dinner fr£9 Last dinner 9.30pm

WHITING BAY
Isle of Arran, Strathclyde *Bute*
Map **10** NS02

★Cameronia ☎ (07707) 254
A two-storey, red-sandstone house on a main road, close to the sea and the beach.
8rm TV available on request ® sB&B£9–£12.50 dB&B£18–£25 Ⓑ
CTV 8P *xmas*
Bar lunch £1.10–£3 Dinner £1.10–£10&alc Wine £3.95 Last dinner 10pm

WHITLEY BAY
Tyne & Wear
Map **12** NZ37

★★Ambassador South Pde ☎ (0632) 531218
28rm(13⇌)(2fb) CTV in all bedrooms sB&B£15–£20 sB&B⇌£20–£28 dB&B£25–£30 dB&B⇌£30–£38 Ⓑ
☾ ## CTV 16P 2⌂ Disco twice wkly
French V Lunch £4–£5&alc Tea 80p–£2 High Tea £2–£4 Dinner £7&alc Wine £5 Last dinner 9.45pm
Credit cards 1 3

★★Croglin South Pde (Minotel) ☎ (0632) 523317
Closed Xmas Day RS 26 Dec
50rm(18⇌)(12fb) CTV in all bedrooms ® sB&B£16 sB&B⇌£22 dB&B⇌£28 Ⓑ
☾ CTV 16P
European Lunch £6alc Tea 80p alc Dinner £6alc Wine £4.80 Last dinner 9.30pm
Credit cards 1 5 VS

★★Holmedale Park Av ☎ (0632) 513903
22rm(5⇌)(1fb) CTV in 5 bedrooms TV in 9 bedrooms ✱ sB&B£10.60–£11.60 sB&B⇌£17.50–£18.50 dB&B£16.55–£18 dB&B⇌£23.55–£25
CTV 10P Disco Sat
✱ Dinner £4–£7.50&alc Wine £3.16 Last dinner 9.45pm
S% Credit cards 1 2 3 VS

★ *Manuels* 51–52 Esplanade ☎ (0632) 533010
11rm(6⇌⋒) CTV in 7 bedrooms Ⓑ

W

CTV 15P
Last dinner 10pm
Credit cards 1 2 3

★**Newquay** 50–54 South Pde (0632) 532211
16rm(2) CTV in 2 bedrooms TV in 14 bedrooms B
CTV 18P Disco nightly
Last dinner 8pm
Credit cards 1 3 5

WHITSTABLE
Kent
Map **5** TR16

★★**Marine** Marine Pde, Tankerton (1m E) (0227) 272672
A comfortable, traditional, well-run hotel, facing the sea.
20rm(16) sB&B£23.50–£25.50 sB&B £26–£28 dB&B £42–£46 B
CTV 15P 3 billiards
Lunch £4.50–£5&alc Tea 50p Dinner £6.50–£7&alc Wine £5 Last dinner 8.15pm
Credit cards 1 3 **VS**

XX**Giovanni's** 49–55 Canterbury Rd (0227) 273034
Modern, friendly restaurant, personally supervised by the proprietor.
Closed Mon
French & Italian **V** 85 seats *Lunch fr£4.50&alc Dinner fr£6.50&alc Wine £4.50 Last dinner 10.45pm 20P
S% Credit cards 1 2 3 5

XX**Windmill** Borstal Hill (0227) 272866
Closed Sun Lunch not served Sat
English & French **V** 40 seats *Lunch fr£4.50&alc Dinner fr£6.50&alc Wine £4.50 Last dinner 10.30pm 30P bedrooms available
S% Credit cards 1 2 3 5

X**Le Pousse Bedaine** 101 Tankerton Rd, Tankerton (1m E) (0227) 272056
A small French restaurant with a well balanced interesting menu, featuring chalkboard special, and a set menu gastronomique.

Closed Sun Lunch not served
French **V** 40 seats *Dinner £6.65&alc Wine £4.35 Last dinner 11pm Live music Fri & alternate Sat
S% Credit cards 1 2 3 5

WHITTINGTON
Shropshire
Map **7** SJ33

★**Ye Olde Boot Inn** (Frederic Robinson) Oswestry (0691) 662250
7rm (1fb) sB&B fr£10 dB&B fr£20 B
CTV 100P
V Lunch fr£4 Dinner fr£4&alc Wine £3.20 Last dinner 10pm

WHITTINGTON
Staffordshire
Map **7** SO88

XX***Whittington Inn*** (on A449) Kinver (038483) 2110
Closed Sun & Mon Lunch not served Sat
French 80 seats Last dinner 10pm 300P
Credit cards 2 3 5

WHITTLE-LE-WOODS
Lancashire
Map **7** SD52

★★★ *B* **Shaw Hill Golf & Country Club** Preston Rd Chorley (02572) 69221
Elegant Georgian mansion in rolling parkland with own golf course. Stylishly furnished. High standard of French cuisine.
9 (5fb) CTV in all bedrooms R sB&B £30 dB&B £50 B
150P billiards sauna bath Live music and dancing Fri & Sat *xmas*
French Lunch fr£6.50&alc Tea fr90p High Tea fr£1.50 Dinner fr£6.50&alc Wine £3 Last dinner 10pm
Credit cards 1 2 3 5

WHITTLESEY
Cambridgeshire
Map **4** TL29

XX**Falcon** Paradise Ln
Peterborough (0733) 203247
English, French & Italian **V** 70 seats Lunch £4.50–£11&alc Dinner £4.50–£11&alc Wine £4 Last dinner 10pm 35P bedrooms available
Credit cards 1 2 3 5 **VS**

WHITWELL-ON-THE-HILL
North Yorkshire
Map **8** SE76

★★ *L* **Whitwell Hall** (Exec Hotel) (065381) 551
11rm(5 6) Annexe: 9rm(4 5) 1 CTV available in bedrooms R sB&B £21–£24.15 dB&B £36.75–£49 B
50P (hard) nc 12yrs *xmas*
Dinner £13 Wine £4.95 Last dinner 8.30pm
Credit cards 1 2 3 5

WICK
Highland *Caithness*
Map **15** ND35

☆☆☆**Ladbroke** Riverside (Ladbroke) (0955) 3344
48 (6fb) CTV in all bedrooms R *sB fr£27 dB fr£38 (room only) B
20P Live music and dancing wkly
V *Lunch fr£6.50 Dinner fr£8.50 Last dinner 9pm
Credit cards 1 2 3 5

★★**Station** Bridge St (0955) 4545
A grey stone Victorian hotel, standing on the banks of the River Wick in the town centre.
54rm(2 22) (4fb) CTV in 28 bedrooms R sB&B £9.20 sB&B £13.80 dB&B £18.40 dB&B £27.60 B
Lift CTV 50P Disco 4 nights wkly Live music and dancing twice wkly
English & French **V** Lunch £4.60 Tea £1.50 High Tea £3.80–£6.20 Dinner £9 Wine £3.90 Last dinner 9pm
Credit cards 1 2 3 4 5

W

WICKEN
(Milton Keynes, Bucks)
Northamptonshire
Map **4** SP73

★★**Wicken Country** Cross Tree Rd ☎(090857) 239

16rm(4➡3⋒) (1fb) CTV in all bedrooms sB&B£25 sB&B➡⋒£27 dB&B£32 dB&B➡⋒£35 B

40P 4 ✽ (heated) (hard)

English & Continental Lunch £6.50&alc Tea £1–£2 Dinner £6.50&alc Wine £5.15 Last dinner 9.45pm

Credit cards 1 2 3 **VS**

WICKHAM
Hampshire
Map **4** SU51

❀★★ *B* **Old House** ☎(0329) 833049 Closed 10 days Xmas, 10 days Etr & 2wks Jul/Aug

A quiet, elegant house, furnished with antiques and having comfortable bedrooms.

10rm(8➡) (4fb) CTV in 6 bedrooms ✱sB&B➡£32 dB&B➡£45

CTV 12P

French **V** ✱Lunch £13.50alc Dinner £13.50alc Wine £5.75 Last dinner 9.30pm

S% Credit cards 1 3

WIDEMOUTH BAY
Cornwall
Map **2** SS20

★★**Trelawny** Marine Drive ☎(028 885) 328 Closed Oct–mid Apr

A small, friendly hotel overlooking Widemouth Bay.

10rm (3fb) sB&B£8.50–£10 dB&B£17–£20 B

CTV 30P ✽

✱Bar lunch 95p–£2.95 Tea 50p High Tea £1 Dinner £3.50–£5 Wine £3.25 Last dinner 7.30pm

VS

★**Brocksmoor** ☎(028 885) 207 Closed Oct–Mar

Country-house style single-storey hotel with spacious lawns and a putting green.

10rm(1➡) (6fb) sB&B£9 dB&B£18 dB&B➡£20

CTV 20P ✽ nc3yrs

Bar lunch 95p–£4.75 Tea 50p–£1.25 Dinner £5 Wine £1.80 Last dinner 6pm

WIDMERPOOL
Nottinghamshire
Map **8** SK62

✕ ***Pullman Inn*** ☎Kinoulton (09497) 300

Converted railway station with a restaurant on the platform. The railway is used as a test track.

Lunch not served Sat Dinner not served Sun

English & French 56 seats Last dinner 10pm 200P

Credit cards 1 2 3 5

WIDNES
Cheshire
Map **7** SJ58

★★**Hillcrest** 75 Cronton Ln ☎051-424 1616 Telex no 627098

46➡⋒ CTV in 40 bedrooms TV in 6 bedrooms Ⓡ sB&B➡⋒£18.50–£22 dB&B➡⋒£30

☾ 200P

V Lunch £10alc Dinner fr£4.75&alc Wine £4.70 Last dinner 10pm

Credit cards 1 2 3 5

WIGAN
Gt Manchester
Map **7** SD50

★★★**Brocket Arms** Mesnes Rd ☎(0942) 46283

A large hotel, close to the town centre.

27rm(25➡2⋒) CTV in all bedrooms Ⓡ ✱sB&B➡⋒£23 dB&B➡⋒£36 B

☾ 60P

V ✱Lunch £7.50alc Dinner £7.50alc Wine £3.15 Last dinner 9.30pm

Credit cards 1 2 3 5 **VS**

★★**Bel-Air** 236 Wigan Ln ☎(0942) 41410

12rm(11➡1⋒) (2fb) CTV in all bedrooms sB&B➡£17.95 dB&B➡£23.95

CTV 10P

English & French **V** Lunch £6alc Dinner £7.50alc Wine £3.90 Last dinner 9pm

Credit cards 1 3

★★***Bellingham*** 149 Wigan Ln ☎(0942) 43893

A commercial hotel, off the A49 on the north side of town.

16rm(1➡10⋒) CTV in all bedrooms Ⓡ B

CTV 25P ✽

Last dinner 9pm

Credit cards 1 2 3 5

At **Standish** (4m NW A49)

☆☆☆**Cassinellis Almond Brook Motor Inn** Almond Brook Rd ☎(0257) 425588

43➡ Annexe: 20⋒ 300P

WIGHT, ISLE OF
Map **4**

Refer to location atlas (Map **4**) for details of places with A.A. appointed hotels and restaurants.

WIGTON
Cumbria
Map **11** NY24

★★**Greenhill Lodge** Red Dial (2m S off A595) ☎(0965) 43304

Converted 17th-century mansion standing in 10 acres of grounds off the A595.

8rm(1➡) (2fb) 2 TV in all bedrooms Ⓡ sB&B£15 sB&B➡£17.50 dB&B£22.50 dB&B➡£27.50 B

120P ✽

English & French Lunch £4.50–£5.50 Tea £1.75–£2 High Tea £5 Dinner £7.50&alc Wine £4.20 Last dinner 9pm

Credit cards 1 3

★★***Kildare*** High St ☎(0965) 42182

A sandstone building opposite the church in the centre of this small market town.

8rm(1➡) TV in 4 bedrooms Ⓡ

CTV 7P billiards

Last dinner 9pm

Credit cards 1 3 5

WILLERBY
Humberside
Map **8** TA03

★★★**Willerby Manor** Well Ln ☎Hull (0482) 652616 Telex no 52629

RS Xmas

An extended private residence standing in its own well-kept gardens.

41rm(27➡14⋒) CTV in all bedrooms Ⓡ sB&B➡⋒£30.75 dB&B➡⋒ fr£45 B

☾ # 200P CFA

French ✱Lunch £6&alc Dinner £5.50&alc Wine £4.55 Last dinner 9.30pm

Credit cards 1 2 3 5

WILLITON
Somerset
Map **3** ST04

❀★★**White House** Long St ☎(0984) 32306 Closed Nov–13 May

A privately owned and run, holiday hotel.

8rm(2➡) Annexe: 5rm(4➡) sB&B£18.30 sB&B➡£20 dB&B£32 dB&B➡£34.60 B

CTV 21P

English & French Dinner £11.50 Wine £4.50 Last dinner 8.30pm

WILMCOTE
Warwickshire
Map **4** SP15

★★**Swan House** ☎Stratford-upon-Avon (0789) 67030

11rm(3➡) CTV in all bedrooms Ⓡ sB&B£16.50 dB&B£27.50 dB&B➡£30.80 B

45P *xmas*

English & French **V** Lunch £3.95–£7.50 Dinner £7.50–£12.50&alc Wine £4.80 Last dinner 9.30pm

Credit cards 1 2 3 **VS**

WILMINGTON
Devon
Map **3** SY29

★★ *HL* **Home Farm** ☎(040 483) 278 Closed 29 Dec–early Mar

Delightful, cottage style hotel, with good food served in pleasant restaurant.

9rm(5➡)Annexe:5rm(2⋒)(1fb)
*sB&B£14.50–£16 sB&B➡£17.50–£20 dB&B£25–£29 dB&B➡£29–£34 ⊟
CTV 20P ✽ *xmas*
French V Lunch £4.50alc Tea 75p High Tea £3alc Dinner £8.50&alc Wine £2.30 Last dinner 9pm
Credit cards 1 3 VS

WILMSLOW
Cheshire
Map **7** SJ88
✕✕**Mandarin** Parsonage Green ☎(0625) 524096
Popular friendly Chinese restaurant with good range of oriental dishes and 7-course banquet dinner.
Closed 25 & 26 Dec
Chinese V 85 seats *Lunch £2–£2.50&alc Dinner £6.50alc Wine £4 Last dinner 11.30pm 25P
Credit card 3

WILTON
Wiltshire
Map **4** SU03
★★**Pembroke Arms** ☎Salisbury (0722) 743127
Mellow, brick, creeper-clad building close to historic Wilton House.
8rm(2fb) sB&B£14–£16.50 dB&B£27 ⊟
CTV 40P 1 Disco Sat
English & French Lunch £5alc Tea £60p Dinner £8alc Wine £4 Last dinner 9.45pm
S% Credit cards 1 3

WIMBORNE MINSTER
Dorset
Map **4** SZ09
★★★**King's Head** The Square (Trusthouse Forte) ☎(0202) 880101
Comfortable, attractive town centre hotel.
28rm(12➡) CTV in all bedrooms Ⓡ sB&B£33 sB&B➡£35.50 dB&B£45.50 dB&B➡£52.50 ⊟
Lift CTV 25P *xmas*
Last dinner 9.15pm
Credit cards 1 2 3 4 5

✕✕*Old Town House* 9 Church St ☎(0202) 888227
Lunch not served
French 40 seats Last dinner 10pm
Credit card 3

At **Ferndown** (4m E junc A31/A348)
☆☆**Coach House Motel** Tricketts Cross (junc A31/A348) ☎(0202) 871222
44⋒ 220P

WINCANTON
Somerset
Map **3** ST72
★★**Dolphin** High St ☎(0963) 32215
Stone-built, single-storey terraced building with lattice windows and a courtyard.
10rm(4➡)(2⋒)(2fb) Ⓡ sB&B£16.50 sB&B➡£19 dB&B£31 dB&B➡£34 ⊟
CTV 30P ✽ *xmas*
English & French V Lunch £4 Tea fr45p Dinner £5&alc Wine £4.25 Last dinner 10pm
Credit cards 1 VS

★★*H* **Holbrook House** Castle Cary Rd ☎(0963) 32377
Large country house dating from 1685, set in wooded grounds.
20rm(8➡2⋒)(4fb) sB&B£15–£16 sB&B➡⋒£17–£18 dB&B£30–£32 dB&B➡⋒£34–£36 ⊟
CTV 30P 4 ✽ (heated) (hard & grass) squash *xmas*
Lunch £4–£5.25&alc Tea 75p High Tea £3.50–£4 Dinner £7alc Wine £3.95 Last dinner 8.30pm
Credit cards 1 2 3

WINCHCOMBE
Gloucestershire
Map **4** SP02
✕✕**Wesley House** High St ☎(0242) 602366
A country town restaurant with sound cooking and efficient service.
Closed Mon Dinner not served Sun
English & French V 50 seats Lunch £3–£6.50&alc Dinner £9&alc Wine £4.95 Last dinner 10pm
Credit cards 1 2 3 4 5 VS

WINCHELSEA
East Sussex
Map **5** TQ91
✕**Manna Plat** Mill Rd ☎(07976) 317
Friendly restaurant built above a 13th-century wine cellar.
Lunch not served Tue Dinner not served Sun
20 seats *Lunch fr£5.95&alc Dinner fr£5.95&alc Wine £4.60 Last dinner 9.30pm
S%

WINCHESTER
Hampshire
Map **4** SU42
★★★★**Wessex** Paternoster Row (Trusthouse Forte) ☎(0962) 61611 Telex no 47419
Modern two-storey brick building in the Cathedral precincts.
94rm(91➡3⋒) CTV in all bedrooms Ⓡ sB&B➡⋒£45.50 dB&B➡⋒£59 ⊟
Lift ☾ 40 CFA *xmas*
Last dinner 10pm
Credit cards 1 2 3 4 5

★★★*BL* ***Lainston House*** Sparsholt (3m NW off A272) (Prestige) ☎(0962) 63588 Telex no 477375
Renovated early 17th-century house of great historic interest and strong Swiss influence, set in 63 acres of grounds.
11rm(10➡⋒) Annexe: 17➡⋒ CTV in all bedrooms
☾ 90P ✽
Swiss Last dinner 10.30pm
Credit cards 1 2 3

★★**Westacre** Sleepers Hill ☎(0962) 68403
Hotel in landscaped gardens has colourful bar and dining room and spacious bedrooms. →

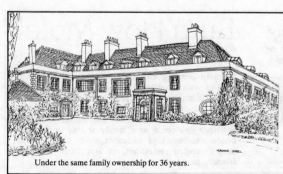

W

19rm(8➡)(2fb) sB&B£15–£20 sB&B➡£20–£25 dB&B£25–£30 dB&B➡£30–£35 B

CTV 60P ✽ Live music and dancing 3 nights wkly

English & Hungarian ♆ ☕ Lunch £1.50–£2.50&alc Tea £1–£1.50 High Tea £1.50–£2.50 Dinner £5&alc Wine £4 Last dinner 9.45pm

S%

✕✕Splinters 9 Great Minster St ☎(0962) 64004

Simple bistro style restaurant with good French and English cuisine.

Closed Sun

French 42 seats Lunch £6.50&alc Dinner £12.50alc Wine £4.55 Last dinner 10.30pm

S% Credit cards 1 2 3 4 5

WINDERMERE
Cumbria
Map **7** SD49
(See plan)

★★★★Old England Bowness-on-Windermere (Trusthouse Forte) ☎(09662) 2444 Telex no 65194 Plan **21** *A2*

Large, rambling four-storey hotel by the waterside, with fine views of the lake and the fells.

82➡(5fb) CTV in all bedrooms Ⓡ sB&B➡£42 dB&B➡£60 B

Lift ☾ 60P CFA ✽ (heated) *xmas*

♆ ☕ Last dinner 9.30pm

Credit cards 1 2 3 4 5

★★★Beech Hill Cartmel Fell (Prince of Wales) ☎(09662) 2137 Telex no 67415 Plan **2** *B1*

This hotel overlooking Lake Windermere has many leisure facilities including a floating dock.

46rm(36➡⋔)(7fb) CTV in all bedrooms Ⓡ sB&B➡⋔£32.50–£36 dB&B➡⋔£48–£52 B

☾ 50P CFA ✽ (heated) sauna bath Disco Fri & Sat *xmas*

V ♆ ☕ Bar lunch £2–£3.50 Tea 65p–£3.50 Dinner £6.60–£7.50&alc Wine £4.20 Last dinner 9pm

Credit cards 1 2 3 5

★★★Belsfield Bowness (Trusthouse Forte) ☎(09662) 2448 Telex no 65238 Plan **3** *B2*

Large hotel with good views offering well appointed bedrooms and spacious lounges.

64rm(36➡21⋔)(2fb) CTV in all bedrooms Ⓡ sB&B£29.50 sB&B➡⋔£37.50 dB&B£47 dB&B➡⋔£54.50 B

Lift ☾ 80P CFA ✽ (heated) *xmas*

♆ ☕ Last dinner 9.15pm

Credit cards 1 2 3 4 5

★★★Burn How Motel Back Belsfield Rd, Bowness ☎(09662) 6226 Plan **5** *B1*

Closed Jan

Hotel offers very spacious modern chalet style accommodation.

18➡⋔(10fb) 4 CTV in all bedrooms Ⓡ sB&B➡⋔£20–£25 dB&B➡⋔£32–£38 Continental breakfast

26P ✽ *xmas* ♿

English & French ♆ Bar lunch £2.50alc Dinner £8.50&alc Wine £4.90 Last dinner 9.15pm

Credit card 2 5 **VS**

★★★Hydro Helm Rd, Bowness (Mount Charlotte) ☎(09662) 4455 Telex no 65196 Plan **13** *B2*

Modernised Victorian hotel overlooking Lake Windermere, with views of the Langdale Pikes.

96rm(86➡10⋔) CTV in all bedrooms Ⓡ sB&B➡⋔£27 dB&B➡⋔£40 B

Lift ☾ 100P CFA

♆ ☕ Lunch £5.50–£5.75 Dinner £7–£7.25 Wine £5.75 Last dinner 8.30pm

Credit cards 1 2 3 5 **VS**

W

★★★ HL **Langdale Chase**
☎Ambleside (0966) 32201 Plan **15** *B5*
Large Victorian building in extensive grounds which descend to the lake shore.
35rm(25⇌7⋒) (5fb) 1⊟ CTV in all bedrooms Ⓡ *sB&B£24 sB&B⇌⋒£27.50 dB&B£46 dB&B⇌⋒£56 ⊟
☾ CTV 50P ✽ ⚲(grass) *xmas*
English & Continental V ♧ ⊒ *Lunch fr£6.25 Tea 65p–£3 Dinner fr£10.95 Wine £3.50 Last dinner 8.45pm
Credit cards 1 2 3 5

★★★ **Low Wood** (3m N A591)
☎Ambleside (0966) 33338 Telex no 65273 Plan **18** *B5* RS Nov–Mar
One of the original coaching inns, visited by John Ruskin as a boy of twelve. It stands on the northern banks of Lake Windermere, with spacious lawns and garden extending by the lake side.
148rm(68⇌10⋒) (15fb) CTV in 20 bedrooms Ⓡ sB&B£14–£16.95 sB&B⇌⋒£18.65–£21.95 dB&B£28–£33.90 dB&B⇌⋒£37.30–£43.90
☾ CTV 200P CFA ✽
English & French V ♧ ⊒ Lunch £2.50–£4 Tea £1.50 Dinner £8.50&alc Wine £3.50 Last dinner 10pm
Credit cards 1 2 3 5 **VS**

★★★ **Priory** Rayrigg Rd, Bowness
☎(09662) 4377 Plan **23** *A5*
The grounds of this hotel include a lakeside frontage with a jetty for the hotel's power-boat.
15rm(13⇌2⋒) (1fb) CTV in all bedrooms Ⓡ sB&B⇌⋒ fr£20 dB&B⇌⋒ fr£40 ⊟
Lift ☾ 50P ✽ billiards Disco Sat nc7yrs *xmas*
English & French V ♧ ⊒ Lunch £4.50 Tea 60p–£2.50 High Tea £4 Dinner fr£6.50 Wine £4.50 Last dinner 8.45pm
Credit cards 1 2 3 5

★★★ BL **Wild Boar** Crook (2½m S of Windermere on B5284 Crook road) (Best Western) ☎(09662) 5225 Plan **31** *D1*
A converted 17th-century house, situated 2m from Bowness in a setting of woodlands and fell slopes.
38rm(33⇌5⋒) (2fb) 2⊟ CTV in all bedrooms Ⓡ sB&B⇌⋒£22.90–£25 dB&B⇌⋒£45.80–£50 ⊟
CTV 60P 2⌂ CFA ✽ Live music and dancing Sat (Oct–Mar) *xmas*
English & French V ♧ ⊒ Lunch £6.50&alc Tea £1.50 Dinner £11&alc Wine £3.50 Last dinner 8.45pm
Credit cards 1 2 3 5 **VS**

★★ **Bordriggs Country House** Longtail Hill, Bowness ☎(09662) 3567 Plan **4** *B1*
Closed 2wks winter
Small friendly hotel in well tended gardens.
11rm(10⇌1⋒) Annexe: 1⇌ (3fb) CTV in all bedrooms sB&B⇌⋒£15.50 dB&B⇌⋒£31 ⊟
→

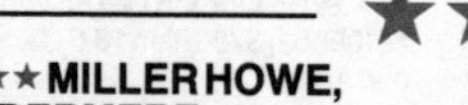

❀❀★★ MILLER HOWE, WINDERMERE

Rayrigg Rd ☎(09662) 2536
Plan **19** *A5*
Closed 5–31 Dec
(Rosette awarded for dinner only.)

If ever a hotel-keeper stamped his personality on a hotel it is John Tovey. To begin with he chose a spectacular situation on the edge of the lake with stunning views over it and the fells. He furnished it in exuberant style with many adornments and then staffed it with a group of young people whom he imbued with the idea that guests come first. Finally he fulfilled himself in his catering, providing innovative food that has earned him an international reputation. Indeed, it may be said that dinner is the main event of the day, and undoubtedly reflects John Tovey's theatrical past. Whet your appetite with an aperitif in one of the four comfortable lounges (there is no bar) and wait for the performance to start. You will be asked to choose your wine before being called to the dining room, when the lights are dimmed and you are then served, banquet-style, a five course dinner, that you will certainly remember. There is no choice until the puddings, but the meal is well balanced. Nor are the other meals to be ignored; you come down to a Buck's Fizz before the hearty breakfast, fine packed lunches are available and hearty afternoon teas are traditional. Naturally there is a fine wine list to complement the food. The bedrooms are beautifully furnished with lovely soft furnishings and they are provided with lots of extras for your convenience, among them hair-dryers, trouser press, books, magazines and games. As we have said, the staff have the right ideas, and their friendly attentions contribute to your enjoyment of this unique hotel. Our members enjoy it as much as ever and enthuse about its considerable virtues.

13rm(11⇌2⋒) 1⊟ CTV available in bedrooms sB&B⇌⋒ fr£60(incl dinner) dB&B⇌⋒£88–£130 (incl dinner) ⊟
60P ✽ nc12yrs
♧ ⊒ Tea fr£2.50 Dinner fr£16.50 Wine £4.50 Last dinner 8.30pm
S% Credit cards 2 5 **VS**

CTV 14P ✽ (heated) *xmas*

V Dinner £6.50–£8.50&alc Wine £3.25 Last dinner 5pm

★★**Burnside** Bowness (Trusthouse Forte) ☎(09662) 2211
Plan **6** *D1* Closed 2 Jan–2 Mar

Offering sweeping views of Lake Windermere and the surrounding hills, this hotel is set in 5 acres of its own gardens and woodland.

33rm(11→17⋒) (7fb) CTV in all bedrooms ® sB&B£26 sB&B→⋒£32.50 dB&B£41 dB&B→⋒£48 B

CTV 50P ✽ *xmas*

Last dinner 9pm

Credit cards 1 2 3 4 5

★★***Ellerthwaite Lodge*** New Rd ☎(09662) 5115 Plan **9** *C4*
Closed mid Nov–Mar

10→⋒ CTV in all bedrooms ® B

10P ✽

Last dinner 8pm

★★**Grey Walls** Elleray Rd ☎(09662) 3741 Plan **10** *B5* Closed Nov–Feb

Comfortable hotel with modernised bedrooms, personally supervised by resident proprietors.

18rm(4→11⋒) (3fb) CTV available in bedrooms ® sB&B→⋒£14.45 dB&B£27.50 dB&B→⋒£28.90 B

19P 4 ✽

V Bar lunch £1 Tea 60p–£1 Dinner £7.50–£8.50&alc Wine £4.25 Last dinner 8pm

Credit cards 1 2 5

★★***HB*Hideaway** Phoenix Way ☎(09662) 3070 Plan **11** *B5*

Comfortable family hotel, in a secluded situation.

11rm(5→6⋒) (3fb) 3 CTV in all buildings sB&B→⋒£10–£15 dB&B→⋒£20–£30 B

CTV 15P ✽

British & Continental V Bar lunch £1–£4 Tea 50p–£2 Dinner £8 Wine £4 Last dinner 8pm

VS

★★ ***BL*Holbeck Ghyll** Holbeck Ln ☎Ambleside (0966) 32375 Plan **12** *B5*
Closed Nov–Jan RS Feb

12rm(8→) (3fb) 1 CTV in 1 bedroom sB&B fr£12 dB&B fr£22 dB&B→ fr£27 B

CTV 12P ✽

Tea fr50p Dinner fr£8 Last dinner 8pm

★★ ***HB*Lindeth Fell** Bowness ☎(09662) 3286 Plan **16** *B1* Closed Nov–mid Apr

13rm(6→7⋒) (3fb) CTV in 11 bedrooms TV in 2 bedrooms ® sB&B→⋒ fr£19.95 dB&B→⋒ fr£39.90

CTV 20P ✽ (grass) nc5yrs

English & French V Dinner fr£9.95 Wine £2.95 Last dinner 7pm

Credit cards 1 2 3 5

★★ ***HBL*Linthwaite** Bowness ☎(09662) 3688 Plan **17** *B1*
Closed Nov–19 Apr

This family-run country house is comfortable, warm, friendly and peaceful. Good wholesome cooking from fresh, local produce is provided at dinner and the resident proprietors continually work to improve facilities and services.

11→ (2fb) CTV in all bedrooms
✽sB&B→£20 dB&B→£40

20P ✽ nc8yrs

English & French ✽Tea £1 Dinner £7.50 Wine £4
Last dinner 8pm

★★***Mortal Man*** Troutbeck (2½m N off A592) ☎Ambleside (0966) 33193
Plan **20** *B5*
Closed mid Nov–mid Feb

Old lakeland inn, built in 1689, originally known as the White House.

15rm(9→⋒) ®

CTV 20P ✽ nc5yrs

Last dinner 8pm

★★***H*Royal** Bowness (Best Western) ☎(09662) 3045 Plan **26** *B2*

A 16th-century hotel, once known as the White Lion, but renamed the Royal after a visit by Queen Adelaide in 1840. There is a secluded garden.

29rm(25→4⋒) (5fb) 1 CTV in all bedrooms ® sB&B→⋒£16.20–£21.40 dB&B→⋒£32.40–£42.80 B

20P 5 Live music and dancing Thu *xmas*

English & French Lunch £2.50–£4&alc Tea £1.50 Dinner £9&alc Wine £3.50 Last dinner 10.30pm

Credit cards 1 2 3 4 5 **VS**

Windermere

1 Applegarth ★
2 Beech Hill ★★★
3 Belsfield ★★★
4 Bordriggs Country House ★★
5 Burn How Motel ★★★
6 Burnside ★★
7 Cranleigh ★
9 Ellerthwaite Lodge ★★
10 Grey Walls ★★
11 Hideaway ★★
12 Holbeck Ghyll ★★
13 Hydro ★★★
14 Knoll ★
15 Langdale Chase ★★★
16 Lindeth Fell ★★
17 Linthwaite ★★
18 Low Wood ★★★
19 Miller Howe ❀❀★★
20 Mortal Man ★★
21 Old England ★★★★
22 Porthole Eating House ❀✕
23 Priory ★★★
24 Ravensworth ★
25 Roger's ✕
26 Royal ★★
27 St Martins ★★
28 La Silhouette ✕
29 Sun ★★
30 White Lodge ★
31 Wild Boar ★★★
32 Willowsmere ★

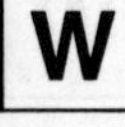

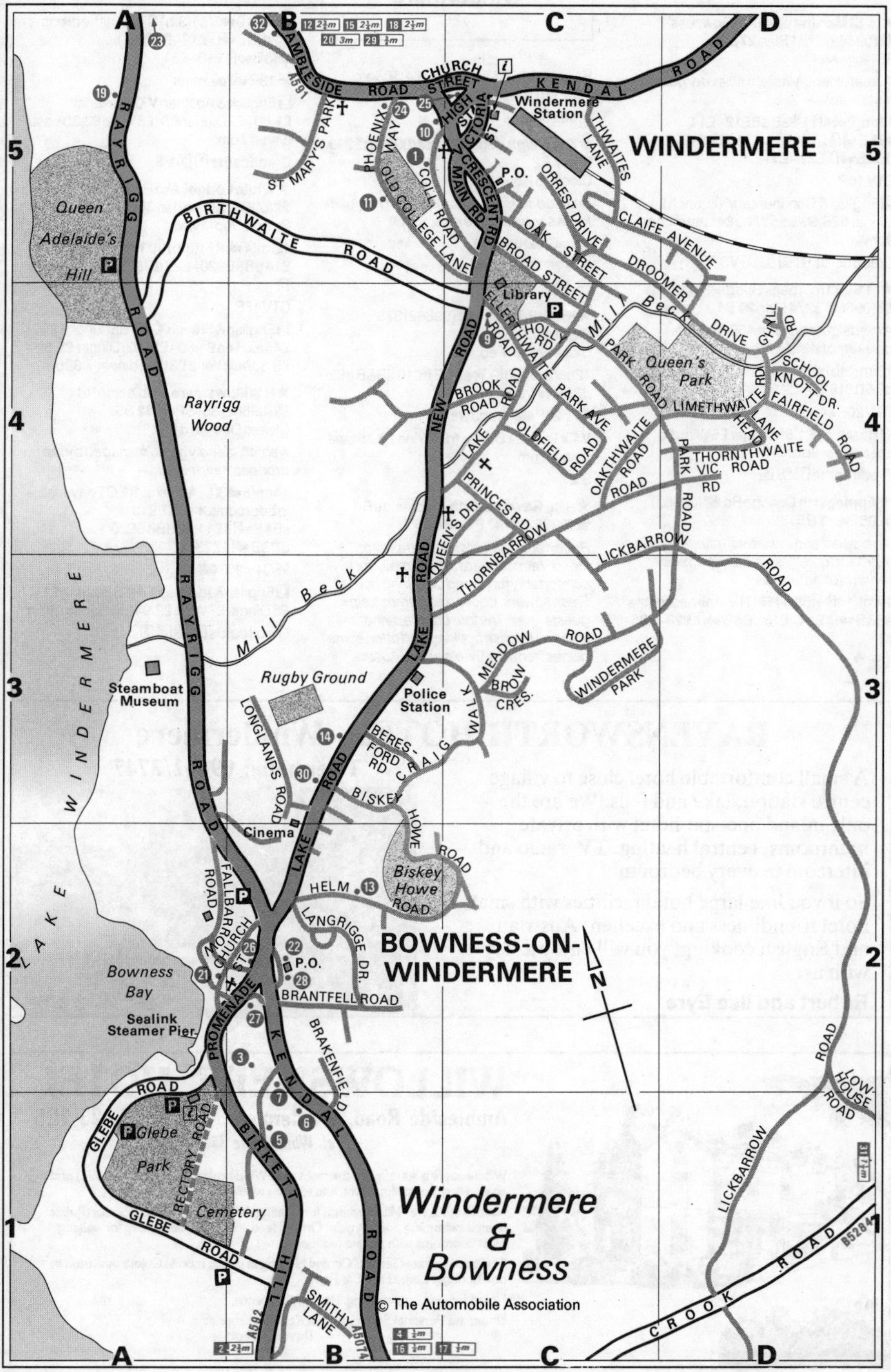

Windermere & Bowness

WINDERMERE

BOWNESS-ON-WINDERMERE

A B C D

5 4 3 2 1

Queen Adelaide's Hill
Rayrigg Wood
Lake Windermere
Steamboat Museum
Rugby Ground
Police Station
Cinema
Biskey Howe
Bowness Bay
Sealink Steamer Pier
Glebe Park
Cemetery
Queen's Park
Windermere Station
Library
P.O.
Mill Beck

Ambleside Road
Church Street
Kendal Road
High St
Victoria St
Crescent Rd
Main Rd
Phoenix Way
St Mary's Park
Coll. Road
Old College Lane
Birthwaite Road
Rayrigg Road
Thwaites Lane
Orrest Drive
Oak Street
Broad Street
Claife Avenue
Droomer Drive
Ghyll Rd
Ellerthwaite Road
Holly Rd
Mill Park Road
Ellerthwaite Park Ave
Brook Road
Lake Road
New Road
Oldfield Road
Limethwaite Road
School Knott Dr.
Fairfield Road
Head Lane
Thornthwaite Road
Oakthwaite Road
Park Road
Vic. Rd
Princes Rd
Queen's Dr.
Thornbarrow Road
Lickbarrow Road
Meadow Road
Windermere Park
Brow Cres.
Craig Walk
Beresford Rd
Biskey Howe Road
Longlands Road
Helm Road
Langrigge Dr.
Fallbarrow Road
Church St
Promenade
Brantfell Road
Brakenfield
Glebe Road
Rectory Road
Birkett Hill
Smithy Lane
Low House Road
Crook Road

A591 A592 A5074 B5284

12 2¾m 15 2½m 18 2½m 20 3m 29 ½m
2 2¾m
4 ½m 16 ½m 17 ½m
31 1½m

N

© The Automobile Association

W

★★**St Martins** Lake Rd, Bowness ☎(09662) 3731 Plan **27** *B2*
RS Nov–Mar
A small, friendly hotel with a very good restaurant.
17rm(2⇌4⋒) *sB&B£12–£14 sB&B⇌⋒£14–£16 dB&B£25–£27 dB&B⇌⋒£29–£31
CTV 10P
English & Continental **V** Lunch £4 Dinner fr£6.50&alc Wine £4 Last dinner 9pm
Credit cards 1 2 3 5 **VS**

★★**Sun** Troutbeck Bridge (3m N) ☎(09662) 3274 Plan **29** *B5*
A roadside inn by the A591, on the outskirts of Windermere.
10rm (3fb) sB&B£11–£12.50 dB&B£19.10–£21
CTV 20P *xmas*
Bar lunch £1.60 Dinner £5 Wine £5 Last dinner 9pm
Credit cards 1 3 5

★**Applegarth** College Rd ☎(09662) 3206 Plan **1** *B5*
An elegant and individual mansion, built in 1890 and quietly situated within easy reach of all amenities.
14rm(14⋒) (5fb) 1 CTV in all bedrooms sB&B⇌⋒£14–£16 dB&B⇌⋒£23–£25
15P

V Lunch £4.50&alc Dinner £4.50&alc Wine £5 Last dinner 10pm
Credit card 3

★***Cranleigh*** Kendal Rd ☎(09662) 3293 Plan **7** *B2*
Closed 6 Nov–14 Mar
Situated in peaceful surroundings, close to the shops and the lake.
11rm(3⇌) ®
CTV 7P nc5yrs
Last dinner 7pm

★**Knoll** Bowness ☎(09662) 3756 Plan **14** *B3*
Closed Nov–Feb
12rm(3⇌) (2fb) sB&B fr£10 dB&B fr£20 dB&B⇌ fr£24
CTV 20P nc3yrs
V Tea fr£1 Dinner fr£7 Wine £2.75 Last dinner 7pm
S%

★***HBL*** **Ravensworth** Ambleside Rd ☎(09662) 3747 Plan **24** *B5*
Robert and Ilse Eyre provide a warm, friendly atmosphere in this small, but comfortably furnished Lakeland house. Fresh flowers, books and games help guests relax. The four course dinner features English cooking and often some dishes from Mrs Eyre's native Austria.

13rm(10⇌3⋒) (3fb) CTV in all bedrooms ®sB&B⇌⋒£12–£15.50 dB&B⇌⋒£18–£31
13P *xmas*
English & Austrian **V** Bar lunch £1.50–£2 Dinner £7–£8 Wine £3.30 Last dinner 7pm
Credit cards 1 3 **VS**

★**White Lodge** Lake Rd, Bowness ☎(09662) 3624 Plan **30** *B3*
Closed Dec–Feb
12rm(4⇌4⋒) (3fb) ® sB&B⇌⋒£12–£14 dB&B£20–£23 dB&B⇌⋒£23–£25
CTV 16P
English & French Bar lunch £2–£4&alc Tea £1.50–£3&alc Dinner £5.50–£6.50&alc Wine £3 Last dinner 7.30pm

★***H*** **Willowsmere** Ambleside Rd ☎(09662) 3575 Plan **32** *B5*
Closed Dec–mid Mar
A small, friendly hotel, managed by the proprietor and his family.
14rm(5⇌3⋒) Annexe: 1⋒ CTV available in bedrooms *sB&B£10 sB&B⇌⋒£11.50 dB&B£20 dB&B⇌⋒£23
CTV 20P
English & Austrian *Bar lunch £1–£5 Dinner £7 Wine £2.94 Last dinner 8pm
Credit cards 1 2 3 5

WILLOWSMERE HOTEL

W

❀✕**Porthole Eating House** 3 Ash St, Bowness ☎(09662) 2793 Plan **22** *B2*
(Rosette awarded for dinner only.)
Closed Tue & Dec–mid Feb Lunch not served
French & Italian **V** 38 seats ✱Dinner £11alc Wine £5 Last dinner 10.30pm
Credit cards 1 2 3 **VS**

✕**Rogers** 4 High St ☎(09662) 4954 Plan **25** *C5*
Closed Sun Lunch not served Mon Dinner not served Mon (Jan–Apr)
French **V** 24 seats Lunch £5.95alc Dinner £9.50alc Wine £5.50 Last dinner 10pm
Credit cards 1 2 3 5 **VS**

✕**La Silhouette** Ash St, Bowness ☎(09662) 5663 Plan **28** *B2*
An intimate and comfortable French restaurant situated in the centre of Bowness.
Lunch not served
French 36 seats ✱Dinner £10alc Wine £3.95 Last dinner 10.30pm
Credit cards 2 5

WINDSOR
Berkshire
Map **4** SU97
See also Datchet

★★★★ *BL* **Oakley Court** Windsor Rd, Water Oakley (2m W A308)
☎Maidenhead (0628) 74141
Old country house mansion, built 1858, set in 35 acres of grounds beside river.
63➡ Annexe: 27➡ (19fb) CTV in all bedrooms sB&B➡£44 dB&B➡£55
☾ 100P ✽ *xmas*
✱Lunch fr£9.50 Dinner fr£15 Wine £6.25 Last dinner 8.30pm

★★★**Castle** High St (Trusthouse Forte) ☎(07535) 51011 Telex no 849220
Modernised Georgian style hotel with large bedrooms, comfortable bar and restaurant.
85➡ (12fb) CTV in all bedrooms Ⓡ sB&B➡£48.50 dB&B➡£59 B
Lift ☾ 90P CFA *xmas*
Last dinner 9.45pm
Credit cards 1 2 3 4 5

✕✕**Don Peppino** 30 Thames St ☎(07535) 60081
Hospitable Italian restaurant with well prepared specialities and reasonable wine list.
Closed Sun & 25–26 Dec
European 78 seats ✱Lunch £7.30&alc Dinner fr£7.30&alc Wine £4.60 Last dinner 11pm
Credit cards 1 2 3 5 **VS**

✕✕ ***Winsor's Peking*** 14 High St ☎(07535) 64942
Pekinese 100 seats Last dinner 11.15pm Disco Fri–Sat Live music Tue–Thu
Credit cards 1 2 3 4 5

WINSFORD
Somerset
Map **3** SS93

★★ *L* **Royal Oak Inn** ☎(064385) 232
Attractive, well-appointed, thatched, beamed inn with open fires.
7rm(5➡) Annexe: 5➡ CTV in 8 bedrooms sB&B£21 sB&B➡£23.50 dB&B£36 dB&B➡£40 B
CTV 14P 3 *xmas*
English & French Lunch £5.50–£7.50 Tea £1–£1.50 Dinner £11.50–£15.50 Wine £4.50 Last dinner 9.30pm
Credit cards 1 2 3 5

WISBECH
Cambridgeshire
Map **5** TF40

★★**Rose & Crown** Market Pl (Best Western) ☎(0945) 583187
20rm(15➡) (2fb) CTV in all bedrooms Ⓡ sB&B fr£19.95 sB&B➡ fr£26.25 dB&B fr£32 dB&B➡ fr£39 B →

CTV 12P *xmas*

V ♔ Lunch £6alc Dinner £8alc Wine £3.95 Last dinner 9pm

Credit cards 1 2 3 5

★★**White Lion** South Brink ☎ (0945) 584813

Once a coaching inn, this modernised hotel is centrally situated and overlooks the River Nene.

18rm(8➡3⋒)(1fb) CTV in all bedrooms Ⓡ sB&B£17 sB&B➡⋒£20 dB&B£27.50 dB&B➡⋒£30.50 B

25P

English & French ♔ ☕ Lunch £4.95–£5.95&alc Tea 50p–60p Dinner £4.95–£5.95&alc Wine £4.35 Last dinner 9pm

Credit cards 1 3 5 **VS**

WISHAW
Strathclyde *Lanarkshire*
Map **11** NS75
See also Motherwell

★**Coltness** Coltness Rd (Ind Coope) ☎ Cambusnethan (0698) 381616

Small, modern purpose-built hotel, situated on the outskirts of town.

12rm 1⊟ Ⓡ sB&B fr£15.68 dB&B fr£25.30 B

CTV 120P Live music and dancing twice wkly

Scottish & European ♔ ☕ ✱ Lunch £4.50alc Dinner £7alc Wine £3.35 Last dinner 9pm

Credit cards 1 2 3 5

WISHAW
Warwickshire
Map **7** SP19

★★★★**Belfry** Lichfield Rd (A446) (Greenall Whitley) ☎ Curdworth (0675) 70301 Telex no 338848

A busy hotel linked with national golf centre.

76➡⋒(4fb) 4⊟ CTV in all bedrooms Ⓡ sB&B➡⋒£31–£33 dB&B➡⋒£45–£49 B

CTV 2000P CFA ✿ Disco twice wkly

English & French **V** ♔ ☕ ✱ Lunch £6.50 Tea 50p–£1.50 Dinner £7.50–£9&alc Wine £4.50 Last dinner 10pm

Credit cards 1 2 3 5 **VS**

★★★**Moxhull Hall** Holly Ln (Exec Hotel) ☎ 021-329 2056

11rm(6➡5⋒)(2fb) CTV in all bedrooms Ⓡ sB&B➡⋒£23.50 dB&B➡⋒£29.50 B

60P ✿

English & French **V** ♔ Lunch £5.95 Dinner £5.95&alc Wine £4.25 Last dinner 10pm

Credit cards 1 2 3 5 **VS**

WITCHINGHAM, GREAT (Lenwade)
Norfolk
Map **9** TG01

★★ *BL* **Lenwade House** ☎ (060544) 288

14rm(9➡5⋒)(2fb) CTV in all bedrooms Ⓡ sB➡⋒£23.60 dB➡⋒£35 (room only) B

CTV 40P ✿ (heated) (grass) squash nc5yrs *xmas*

English & French **V** ♔ Lunch fr£4.95 Dinner fr£5.95 Wine £3.50 Last dinner 9pm

Credit cards 1 2 3 5

WITHAM
Essex
Map **5** TL81

☆☆ ***Rivenhall Motor Inn*** Rivenhall End ☎ (0376) 516969 Telex no 99414
Closed 26–30 Dec RS wknds

This hotel's modern bedrooms complement its smart restaurant and bars.

43rm(41➡1⋒) CTV in all bedrooms Ⓡ

100P squash

French ♔ ☕ Last dinner 9.30pm

Credit cards 1 2 3 5

WITHERIDGE
Devon
Map **3** SS81

★★ ***Mitre*** 2 The Square ☎ Tiverton (0884) 860395

Hospitable inn with good bar, restaurant and neat bedrooms.

10rm

CTV 10P

English & Continental ♔ Last dinner 9.30pm

WITHYPOOL
Somerset
Map **3** SS83

★★ *B* **Royal Oak Inn** ☎ Exford (064383) 236
Closed Xmas

Comfortable well appointed inn with good bars and restaurant.

8rm(2➡2⋒)(1fb) CTV in 6 bedrooms Ⓡ sB&B£16.50 sB&B➡⋒£19.50 dB&B£33 dB&B➡⋒£36

20P nc10yrs

English & French **V** ♔ ☕ Bar lunch 70p–£3.50 Tea 35p–£1.50 Dinner £10&alc Wine £5.25 Last dinner 9pm

Credit cards 1 2 3 5

★ *HB* **Westerclose Country House** ☎ Exford (064383) 302
Closed Dec–Feb

Small, privately owned and run hotel in extensive grounds which include stables.

10rm(6➡)(3fb) 1⊟ sB&B£15.50 sB&B➡£16.60 dB&B£30 dB&B➡£32

CTV 20P 2 ✿

♔ ☕ Lunch fr£4 Tea fr60p Dinner £7.50 Wine £3.50

WIVELISCOMBE
Somerset
Map **3** ST02

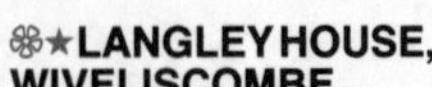

★ LANGLEY HOUSE, WIVELISCOMBE

Langley Marsh (1m N on unclass rd) ☎ (0984) 23318
Closed Nov–Feb

(Rosette awarded for dinner only)

Francis and Rosalind McCulloch are the owners of this small hotel, situated just outside the town amidst the lovely, rolling Somerset countryside. Three acres of attractive and beautifully maintained gardens add to its charm, and they include a vegetable plot that provides fresh produce for the kitchen. The latter is the domain of Mrs McCulloch and earns our rosette award by her enterprising use of good raw materials. Our members tell us of the delicious five course dinners which are sufficiently generous to satisfy the heartiest appetite. One sits down at a set time – banquet style – and there is no choice until the puddings. Mr McCulloch looks after the service as well as the rest of the front of the house with aplomb, aided by the friendly waitress.

The nicely appointed, beamed dining room, the little bar and the comfortable sitting room, are all attractively furnished and decorated,

enabling you to enjoy a very relaxing stay here. The bedrooms are individually decorated with great charm and contain a welcoming miniature of sherry. 'A delightful hotel with a country house atmosphere and informal but friendly and homely service' say our appreciative members, and at affordable prices too!

6rm(3➡2⋒) 1⊟ CTV in all rooms Ⓡ sB&B➡⋒£19.75 dB&B➡⋒£33.70 B

10P 4 ✿ nc7yrs

French Lunch £10 Tea £5 Dinner £9.20–£13.20 Wine £5.40 Last dinner 8.30pm

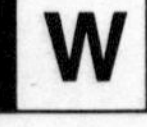

WIVENHOE
Essex
Map **5** TM02

✕**Smugglers** 47 High St ☎(020622) 3582
Closed Sun Lunch not served Mon (except Parties)
Continental **V** 38 seats Last dinner 10.30pm 4P

WOBURN
Bedfordshire
Map **4** SP93

★★★**Bedford Arms** George St (Kingsmead) ☎(052 525) 441 Telex no 825205
Tastefully modernised Georgian coaching inn, with stables and a modern wing, situated near the Abbey and the wildlife park.
55 (4fb) 1 CTV in all bedrooms Ⓡ *sB&B £37.50–£44 dB&B £42–£48 B
☾ 80P 2 CFA Live music and dancing Fri *xmas*
English & French **V** Lunch £7.30 Tea fr90p High Tea fr£1.50 Dinner £7.30–£8.50 Wine £5.25 Last dinner 10.30pm
Credit cards 1 2 3 5 **VS**

WOKINGHAM
Berkshire
Map **4** SU86

★★★**St Annes Manor** London Rd ☎(0734) 784427
20rm (19 1) (2fb) 1 CTV in all bedrooms Ⓡ *sB&B £27.25–£43 dB&B £33.25–£53 B
☾ 100P 2 CFA
V Lunch £6.50–£7&alc Tea £2 Dinner £8–£8.50&alc Wine £4.85 Last dinner 9.45pm
Credit cards 1 2 3 4 5 **VS**

WOLF'S CASTLE
Dyfed
Map **2** SM92

✕✕**Wolfscastle Country Hotel** ☎Treffgarne (043 787) 225
Closed Xmas
International **V** 50 seats Lunch £6alc Dinner £7.75&alc Wine £3.75 Last dinner 9.30pm 50P bedrooms available Live music wkly Live music & dancing mthly
Credit cards 1 3

WOLVERHAMPTON
West Midlands
Map **7** SO99

★★★**Connaught** Tettenhall Rd ☎(0902) 24433 Telex no 338490
Bustling hotel which caters for functions and dances.
70rm CTV in all bedrooms *sB&B fr£18 sB&B fr£23.50 dB&B fr£27 dB&B fr£32.50 B
Lift ☾ CTV 70P CFA sauna bath *xmas*
French **V** *Lunch £3.50 Tea 75p Dinner £5.50 Wine £3.60 Last dinner 10pm
Credit cards 1 2 5

★★★**Goldthorn** Penn Rd ☎(0902) 29216 Closed Xmas Day & Boxing Day
68rm (60 1) Annexe: 16rm (8 4) (2fb) CTV in 72 bedrooms TV in 12 bedrooms Ⓡ sB&B £22.43 sB&B £31.63 dB&B £32.78 dB&B £40.25
☾ 100P CFA
V *Lunch £6.45&alc Tea 80p Dinner £5.95–£7.25&alc Wine £4.20 Last dinner 9.30pm
Credit cards 1 3

★★★**Mount** Mount Rd, Tettenhall Wood (2½m W off A454) (Embassy) ☎(0902) 752055 RS 25 & 26 Dec
62rm (45 1) CTV in all bedrooms Ⓡ sB&B £22 sB&B £31 dB&B £32 dB&B £39.50 B
☾ 250P CFA Live music and dancing Sat →

W

English & French **V** Lunch £6.60 Dinner £7.70 Wine £4.75 Last dinner 9.30pm
Credit cards 1 2 3 5

★★★**Park Hall** Park Dr, Goldthorn Park (2m S off A459) (Embassy) ☎(0902) 331121 RS Xmas
Once the home of the Earl of Dudley, this is now a modernised hotel.
57rm(49) CTV in all bedrooms Ⓡ sB&B£22 sB&B£28.50 dB&B£31 dB&B£37
☾ 400P CFA ✽ Live music and dancing Sat
V Lunch £5 Dinner £7.80 Wine £4.50 Last dinner 9.45pm
Credit cards 1 2 3

★★**Fox** School St (Wolverhampton & Dudley) ☎(0902) 21680
29 CTV in all bedrooms Ⓡ ✱sB&B£13.50–£18 dB&B£20–£24
25P
✱Lunch fr£3.50&alc Dinner £5.50alc Wine £3.75 Last dinner 9.30pm
Credit cards 1 3 **VS**

★★**Ravensholt** Summerfield Rd (Wolverhampton & Dudley) ☎(0902) 24140
Situated in a quiet area close to the brewery.
17rm(12) Annexe: 12rm(7 1) (3fb) Ⓡ ✱sB&B£13.50 sB&B£14.50 dB&B£20 dB&B£22
CTV 40P
✱Lunch £3.75–£6.50&alc Dinner £4.50–£6.95&alc Wine £3.75 Last dinner 8.45pm
Credit cards 1 3 **VS**

★★**York** 138–140 Tettenhall Rd ☎(0902) 758211
Very busy, small but popular, personally-run hotel.
16rm(5 3) (1fb) CTV in all bedrooms Ⓡ ✱sB&B£14–£19.50 sB&B£14–£23.50 dB&B£25–£29 dB&B£25–£33
40P
English & French **V** ✱Lunch £3.25 Tea 75p Dinner £6.95&alc Wine £4 Last dinner 9.30pm
VS

★**Wulfrun** 37 Piper's Row ☎(0902) 24017
Small, individually-run hotel on a busy town-centre junction.
14rm sB&B£9.50 dB&B£18
CTV
Lunch £2.50–£5 Dinner £3–£6 Wine £3.75 Last dinner 8pm
Credit cards 1 3 **VS**

WOODBRIDGE
Suffolk
Map **5** TM24

★★★**Melton Grange** ☎(03943) 4147
Spacious, fully-modernised country mansion set in 11 acres of grounds on the outskirts of Woodbridge.
38rm(35) (3fb) CTV in all bedrooms Ⓡ sB&B£23 sB&B£23 dB&B£32.75
CTV 100P ✽ Live music and dancing Sat *xmas*
English & French **V** Lunch £5.50–£7 Tea 50p Dinner £6.50–£7.50&alc Wine £2
Last dinner 9.15pm
Credit cards 1 2 3 5

★★★ *L* **Seckford Hall** ☎(03943) 5678
Closed 25 Dec
Large, well-preserved brick built, Elizabethan house, converted by Sir Ralph Harwood.
24rm(23) 4 CTV in all bedrooms Ⓡ sB&B£29.50–£32 sB&B£32–£35 dB&B£45 dB&B£48
100P 3 ✽
V Lunch £7 Dinner £11.50alc Wine £4.95 Last dinner 9.30pm
Credit cards 1 2 3 5

★★**Crown** Thorofare (Trusthouse Forte) ☎(03943) 4242
Centrally situated, fully-modernised old coaching inn, parts of which date back to 1532.
15rm Annexe: 10 (10fb) CTV in all bedrooms Ⓡ sB&B£33 sB&B£35.50 dB&B£40.50 dB&B£52.50
30P *xmas*
Last dinner 9pm
Credit cards 1 2 3 4 5

✕✕ ***Le Provencal*** 42 Market Hill ☎(03943) 5726
Closed Sun, Mon, 1–25 Sep Lunch not served
French **V** 30 seats Last dinner 10.30pm

✕✕ ***Town House*** 13 Market Hill ☎(03943) 2957
Closed Mon Dinner not served Sun
English & French 52 seats Last dinner 10pm bedrooms available
Credit cards 1 2 3

WOODFORD BRIDGE
Devon
Map **2** SS31

★★★ ***HBL* Woodford Bridge** ☎Milton Damerel (040926) 481
An attractive, thatched, white-washed building in well tended gardens, this hotel offers every comfort. Lounges and bar have a cosy atmosphere and the attractive dining room serves excellent food. A superb range of sports and conference facilities are offered and the grounds contain 9 luxury cottage suites.
16rm(5 4) Annexe: 9 (1fb) CTV in 9 bedrooms ✱sB&B£16–£20 sB&B£18.40–£23 dB&B£32–£40 dB&B£39.20–£49
CTV 200P ✽ (heated) (hard) squash sauna bath Disco Sat *xmas*
English & French **V** Lunch £6.50 Tea 80p Dinner £10&alc Wine £4.60 Last dinner 8.45pm
VS

WOODFORD BRIDGE
Gt London
London plan **5** *F5* (page 423)

★★★ *L* **Prince Regent** ☎01-504 7635
Tastefully furnished hotel with modern, well-equipped bedrooms and an enterprising restaurant.
10rm CTV in all bedrooms Ⓡ ✱sB&B£34 dB&B£44
☾ 100P *xmas*
English, French & Italian **V** ✱Lunch £4.95–£10.95&alc Tea 75p High Tea £3.75 Dinner £10&alc Wine £4.95 Last dinner 10.30pm
Credit cards 1 2 3 4 5

WOODFORD GREEN
Gt London
London plan **5** *F5* (page 423)

☆☆☆**Woodford Moat House** Oak Hill (Queens) ☎01-505 4511
Modern hotel with good restaurant and pleasant service.
99rm CTV in all bedrooms Ⓡ sB&B£37 dB&B£46
Lift ☾ 150P CFA
Continental Lunch £7.50&alc Tea 65p Dinner £7.50&alc Wine £4.85 Last dinner 10.15pm
Credit cards 1 2 3 5 **VS**

WOODHALL SPA
Lincolnshire
Map **8** TF16

★★ ***B* Golf** The Broadway (Best Western) ☎(0526) 53535
Large, detached, late-Victorian building with mock Tudor frontage, in its own grounds.
55rm(18 12) (2fb) CTV in all bedrooms Ⓡ sB&B£20 sB&B£23 dB&B£32 dB&B£38
☾ 100P ✽ (hard) Disco Sat *xmas*
English & European **V** Lunch £6.25&alc Tea £1.25 Dinner £8&alc Wine £5 Last dinner 9.15pm
Credit cards 1 2 3 5 **VS**

WOODHOUSE EAVES
Leicestershire
Map **8** SK51

✕✕**The Cottage in the Wood** Maplewell Rd ☎(0509) 890318

Closed Mon Lunch not served Sat Dinner not served Sun

English & French 75 seats Lunch £4.50–£10alc Dinner £6.95&alc Wine £4.65 Last dinner 9.30pm 15P

Credit cards 1 2 3 5 **VS**

XX Ye Olde Bull's Head ☎(0509) 890255

Closed Mon Dinner not served Sun

English, French & Italian **V** 65 seats Lunch £4.50&alc Dinner £4.50&alc Last dinner 9.45pm 150P

Credit cards 1 2 3

Woodhouse Eaves — Woodlands

WOODLANDS
Hampshire
Map **4** SU31

★★ **Busketts Lawn** 174 Woodlands Rd ☎Ashurst (042129) 2272

Victorian house in woodland setting with all modern facilities.

15rm(2⇌6⋒) (3fb) CTV in all bedrooms Ⓡ sB&B£16–£17 sB&B⇌⋒£17–£18 dB&B£29–£34 dB&B⇌⋒£29–£34 Ⓑ

Lift CTV 50P ✽ ⩳(heated) 𝒫(hard) Live music and dancing wkly ⌂ *xmas*

English & Continental **V** ♡ ☐ Lunch £5–£6 Tea 60p–£1.80 High Tea £1.50–£3 Dinner £7–£7.75 Wine £5 Last dinner 8pm

S% Credit cards 1 2 3 5

★★ **Woodlands Lodge** Bartley Rd ☎Ashurst (042 129) 2257

Closed Nov–Jan

One of the original Forest Lodges with gardens and paddocks, quietly situated in the New Forest.

11rm(7⇌1⋒) (1fb) CTV in all bedrooms ✱ sB&B£13–£15 sB&B⇌£16–£18 dB&B£26–£30 dB&B⇌£32–£36 Ⓑ →

W

40P 🐕 ❄
Wine £3.95
Last dinner 8pm
Credit cards 1 2 3 5 **VS**

WOODSTOCK
Oxfordshire
Map **4** SP41

★★★ *B* **Bear** Park St (Porter) ☎ (0993) 811511 Telex no 837921
Charming and historic old inn with bedrooms around the courtyard.
31rm (25➡1🚿) Annexe: 13rm (10➡) (4fb) 2🛏 CTV in all bedrooms sB fr£28.05 sB➡🚿 fr£43.45 dB fr£52.80 dB➡🚿 fr£68.20 (room only) 🅱
☾ 30P CFA *xmas* ♿
🍴 English & French **V** 🍴 ☕ Lunch fr£8.75 Dinner fr£9.35 Wine £5.80 Last dinner 10pm
S% Credit cards 1 2 3 5 **VS**

★★ **King's Arms** ☎ (0993) 811412
Busy, tourist hotel offering modest accommodation.
8rm (2fb) CTV in all bedrooms Ⓡ sB&B£18–£20 dB&B£26–£30 🅱
CTV
🍴 ☕ Lunch £3.75–£4.50 Tea £1.45–£1.60 High Tea £3.75–£4.50 Dinner £5–£6 Wine £5.25 Last dinner 10pm
Credit cards 1 2 3 5

★★ **Marlborough Arms** Oxford St (Best Western) ☎ (0993) 811227
Partly 16th-century coaching inn called the George Inn in Scott's 'Woodstock'.
15rm (6➡1🚿) (1fb) CTV in all bedrooms Ⓡ sB&B£16 dB&B£30 dB&B➡🚿 £36 🅱
20P
V 🍴 ☕ Lunch £4–£5.50 Tea 90p–£1.50

W

Dinner £7.50–£9&alc Wine £4.75 Last dinner 9pm

Credit cards 1 2 3 5

WOODY BAY
Devon
Map **3** SS64

★★ *H* **Woody Bay** ☎ Parracombe (05983) 264

Pleasant, family-run holiday hotel in a woodland setting, high on the coast.

14rm(8➡1⋒) (1fb) 2▣ sB&B£15–£17 sB&B➡⋒£17–£19 dB&B£30–£34 dB&B➡⋒£34–£38 B

CTV 24P ✈ *xmas*

▣ English & French V ✿ ▭ Bar lunch 75p–£3.25 Tea 35p–£1 High Tea £2 Dinner £6.50&alc Wine £4.25 Last dinner 9.30pm

Credit cards 1 2 3 5 V$

WOOLACOMBE
Devon
Map **2** SS44

★★★ *HL* **Narracott Grand** ☎ (0271) 870418
Closed Jan

Large, traditional, privately-owned and run holiday hotel with good facilities and in a central position.

100rm(94➡6⋒) (66fb) CTV in all bedrooms ® sB&B➡⋒£16.50–£31.50 (incl dinner) dB&B➡⋒£33–£63 (incl dinner)

Lift ☾ CTV 50P 60🚗 CFA ✈ ▭ (heated) squash sauna bath Disco and Live music and dancing 6 nights wkly ⌂ *xmas*

V ✿ ▭ Tea 75p High Tea £2.50 Dinner £6.50 Wine £3.50 Last dinner 9pm

Credit cards 1 3

★★★ *H* **Watersmeet** ☎ (0271) 870333
Closed mid Oct–Apr

Traditional holiday hotel with a country house atmosphere in a superb situation.

36rm(17➡1⋒) (5fb) ✱ sB&B£19–£23 sB&B➡⋒£21–£25 dB&B£38–£46 dB&B➡⋒£42–£50 B

CTV 30P 20🚗 ✈ ✽ ≈ (heated) ⚲ (grass) Disco wkly Live music and dancing wkly ⌂

▣ English, French & Continental V ✿ ▭ Lunch £7.25–£8.50 Tea 55p Dinner £8.75–£10 Last dinner 8.30pm

S% Credit card 5

★★★ **Woolacombe Bay** South St ☎ (0271) 870388 Closed Xmas–19 Apr

Well-appointed, privately owned hotel in a prime situation whose many facilities ideally cater for family holidays.

48➡ (33fb) CTV in all bedrooms ®

*sB&B➡£18.98–£37.73 dB&B➡£37.95–£72.45

Lift ☾ CTV 70P CFA ✈ ✽ ▭ & ≈ (heated) ⚑ ⚲ (hard) squash billiards sauna bath Disco and Live music and dancing 6 nights wkly ⌂

V ✿ ▭ *Lunch £5.50&alc Tea 75p High Tea £3 Dinner £8&alc Wine £3.50 Last dinner 9pm

Credit cards 1 3

★★ **Atlantic** Sunnyside Rd ☎ (0271) 870469 Closed Oct–19 Apr

Comfortable, friendly, privately-owned holiday hotel, overlooking the village and bay.

12rm(8➡2⋒) (8fb) ® sB&B£11–£16 sB&B➡£13–£18 dB&B£22–£32 dB&B➡£25–£35

CTV 12P Disco wkly

✿ ▭ Dinner £5.50&alc Wine £4.50 Last dinner 7.30pm

VS

★★ *HB* **Beach** The Esplanade ☎ (0271) 870449 Closed Oct–19 Apr

Well-appointed, privately owned and personally-run holiday hotel.

35rm(22➡) (17fb) ® sB&B£10.50–£16.50 sB&B➡⋒£12.50–£20 dB&B£21–£33 dB&B➡⋒£25–£40

⊁ CTV 28P 3🚗 ▭ (heated) Disco twice wkly Live music and dancing twice wkly ⌂

→

Watersmeet Hotel

W

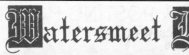

✿⊒ Bar lunch 75p–£4.50alc Tea 40p–80p Dinner £6.50–£8.50 Wine £4.50 Last dinner 8pm

★★**B Little Beach** The Esplanade (Minotel) ☎(0271) 870398 Closed Nov–Jan

Small holiday and business hotel close to the beach.

10rm(4→4⋒)(2fb) sB&B£11.25–£13.25 sB&B→⋒£16.25–£18.25 dB&B→⋒£22.50–£32 B

CTV 6P ⊜ sauna bath

✿ Bar lunch £3.50alc Tea 50p alc Dinner £7.75alc Wine £3.85 Last dinner 8pm

S% Credit cards 1 3 **VS**

★★***Sands*** Bay View Rd ☎(0271) 870550 Closed Oct–Apr

Spanish-style stucco building in a quiet road overlooking the sea and the beach.

24rm(4→2⋒)

CTV 19P 1⌂ ⊜ ⌂

✿⊒ Last dinner 8.15pm

★★**Whin Bay** Bay View Rd ☎(0271) 870475 Closed Nov–Feb RS Mar

Quiet holiday hotel overlooking sea.

17rm(4→11⋒)(17fb) ® sB&B→⋒£11–£13.50 dB&B→⋒£22–£27 B

CTV 16P ⊜ U ⌂

Bar lunch £1.40–£3.50 Dinner fr£6&alc Wine £2.40 Last dinner 8pm

Credit cards 1 3

★***HB* Crossways** The Esplanade ☎(0271) 870395 Closed Oct–Feb

Small, comfortable, holiday hotel, personally run by the owners.

8rm(3⋒)(4fb) sB&B£9–£12.50 sB&B⋒£10.50–£13.75 dB&B£18–£25 dB&B⋒£21–£27.50

CTV 9P

✿ Last dinner 6pm

VS

★**Headlands** Beach Rd ☎(0271) 870320 Closed 30 Oct–Mar

Family-run small hotel, specialising in family holidays.

11rm(1→2⋒)(5fb) 1⊟ sB&B£9–£13.50 sB&B→⋒£10.50–£14.75 dB&B£18–£27 dB&B→⋒£20.50–£29.50 B

CTV 15P ⌂

✿⊒ Bar lunch 60p–£2.20 Tea 50p High Tea £1.80 Dinner £4.75 Wine £3.65 Last dinner 7pm

S% Credit card 3 **VS**

★**Sunnyside** Sunnyside Rd ☎(0271) 870267 Closed mid Sep–mid May

Pleasant family holiday hotel in a quiet position.

17rm(2→)(4fb) sB&B£10–£13 sB&B→£11.50–£14.50 dB&B£20–£26 dB&B→£23–£29

CTV 12P ✽ Disco wkly ⌂

Dinner £5–£6 Wine £3 Last dinner 7.15pm

WOOLER
Northumberland
Map **12** NT92

★★**Tankerville Arms** Cottage Rd ☎(0668) 81581

17rm(4→1⋒)(2fb) B

CTV 90P ✽ ⌂

▣ English & French **V** ✿⊒ Lunch £4.50–£5 Dinner £6.50–£7.50&alc Wine £3.75 Last dinner 9pm

★**Ryecroft** Ryecroft Way ☎(0668) 81459 Closed Xmas

A friendly, comfortable hotel offering sound, home made cuisine.

11rm(3fb) ® ✻sB&B fr£11 dB&B fr£21 B

CTV 20P ⊜

✿⊒ Bar lunch fr£1 Tea fr40p Dinner fr£7.50 Wine £3.95 Last dinner 8pm

WOOLFARDISWORTHY
Devon
Map **2** SS32

★★**Manor House** (Exec Hotel) ☎Clovelly (02373) 380

7rm(6→1⋒)(6fb) TV in all bedrooms ✶ sB&B→⋒£12–£16 dB&B→⋒£24–£32 B

CTV 16P ✽ *xmas*

▣ French ✿⊒ Lunch £5alc Tea 50palc Dinner £8.50&alc Wine £3.90 Last dinner 9.30pm

Credit card 3 **VS**

WOOLVERTON
Somerset
Map **3** ST75

★★***H* Woolverton House** ☎Frome (0373) 830415 Closed Jan

Comfortable small country hotel offering food and relaxed atmosphere.

5rm(4→) Annexe: 3→(1fb) CTV in 5 bedrooms TV in 3 bedrooms ® sB&B→£23–£26 dB&B→£31–£36 Continental breakfast B

20P ⊜ ✽

▣ English & French ✿⊒ Bar lunch £5alc Tea 50p alc Dinner £9alc Wine £4.20 Last dinner 9pm

Credit cards 1 2 3 5 **VS**

WOOTTON WAWEN
Warwickshire
Map **4** SP16

✕***Ye Olde Bull's Head*** ☎Henley-in-Arden (05642) 2511

Dinner not served Sun & Mon

54 seats Last dinner 10pm 60P

Credit cards 1 2 3

WORCESTER
Hereford & Worcester
Map **3** SO85

★★★**Giffard** High St (Trusthouse Forte) ☎(0905) 27155 Telex no 338869

Modern, purpose-built hotel in the centre of Worcester.

104→ CTV in all bedrooms ® sB&B→£41 dB&B→£53 B

Lift ☾ CFA ⚑

✿⊒ Last dinner 9.45pm

Credit cards 1 2 3 4 5

★★***Diglis*** Riverside ☎(0905) 353518 Closed Xmas RS Sun

Old hotel on banks of River Severn.

W

15rm(3➡2⋒)
CTV 60P ✽ ♪
Last dinner 8.45pm
Credit card 1

★★**Star** Foregate St (Wolverhampton & Dudley) ☎(0905) 24308
Town-centre hotel, popular with business people.
38rm(20➡)(3fb) CTV in all bedrooms Ⓡ
✻sB&B£12–16.50 sB&B➡⋒£18–£22
dB&B£20–£26.50 dB&B➡⋒£24–£32 Ɓ
Lift ☾ CTV 80P
Bar lunch 95p–£2.75 Dinner £5.50alc Wine £3.75 Last dinner 9.45pm
Credit cards 1 3 **VS**

★★**Ye Olde Talbot** Friar St ☎(0905) 23573
Modern commercial hotel in the city centre.
13rm(1➡)(1fb) CTV in all bedrooms
✻sB&B£17 sB&B➡£22 dB&B£28
dB&B➡£32 Ɓ
CTV
Mainly grills ✻Lunch £5.50 Dinner £5.50alc Wine £3.85 Last dinner 10.30pm
Credit cards 1 2 3 5

★**Park House** 12 Droitwich Rd ☎(0905) 21816
Small, family-run hotel close to the city centre.
6rm(2fb) sB&B£10.50 dB&B£18 Ɓ
CTV 8P
English & Continental Lunch £4 Dinner £4.45–£4.90 Wine £3.50 Last dinner 7.30pm
VS

★***Talbot*** 8–10 Barbourne Rd ☎(0905) 21206
14rm
CTV 40P
Last dinner 10pm

✕✕**Brown's** The Old Cornmill, South Quay ☎(0905) 26263
An imaginatively modernised cornmill by the river.
Closed Xmas & New Year Closed Sun Lunch not served Sat
75 seats Lunch £10.94alc Dinner £14.24alc Wine £5.50 Last dinner 9.30pm
S% Credit cards 1 2 3

✕✕**King Charles II** New St ☎(0905) 22449
Closed Sun & Mon, 1st 3wks Aug, Xmas & New Year & Public hols
English, French & Italian 45 seats
✻Lunch £6.50&alc Dinner £8.50&alc Wine £5 Last dinner 9.30pm
Credit cards 1 2 3

✕**Purbani Tandoori** 27 The Tything ☎(0905) 27402
Indian **V** 80 seats ✻Lunch fr£1.87&alc Dinner £6.75alc Wine £3.75 Last dinner mdnt 5P
S% Credit cards 1 2 3 5 **VS**

WORKINGTON
Cumbria
Map **11** NX92

★★★**Cumberland Arms** Belle Isle St ☎(0900) 64401 Closed Xmas Day
Commercial, recently modernised hotel opposite the railway station.
29➡⋒(1fb) CTV in all bedrooms Ⓡ
✻sB&B➡⋒£22 dB&B➡⋒£27 Ɓ
Lift ☾ CTV 60P
V Lunch £2.25–£3.30&alc Tea 70p–£1.50 High Tea £2–£2.50 Dinner £2.25–£3.50&alc Wine £4.35 Last dinner 9.30pm
Credit cards 1 2 3 5

★★★***Westland*** Braithwaite Rd ☎(0900) 4544
A modern hotel, 2m outside Workington, just off the A595.
50rm(30➡⋒)
☾ CTV 200P ✽ Live music and dancing wkly
French Last dinner 10pm

★★***Beckstone*** Harrington ☎Harrington (0946) 831666
Formerly the local rectory, this hotel has been well modernised.
7rm(3➡3⋒) CTV in all bedrooms Ⓡ Ɓ
CTV 100P ✽
V Last dinner 9.30pm

★★***H Clifton*** Great Clifton ☎(0900) 64616
Modernised 18th century farmhouse that retains much original character.
14➡ CTV in all bedrooms Ⓡ
CTV 60P 3
V Last dinner 9.30pm
Credit cards 1 3 5

★★**Crossbarrow Motel** Little Clifton (3m E on A595) ☎(0900) 61443
A purpose-built complex with modern functional bedrooms.
37rm(29➡8⋒)(3fb) CTV in all bedrooms
✻sB&B➡⋒£19.20–£20.90
dB&B➡⋒£28–£33.75
50P ✽
Lunch £1.50–£6 Dinner £5–£8 Wine £4 Last dinner 8.30pm

★★**Green Dragon** Portland Sq ☎(0900) 3803
11rm(1➡) ✻sB&B£13.50
sB&B➡£15.50 dB&B fr£25 dB&B➡ fr£27
CTV
Lunch £1.25–£2.25 Dinner £5.95–£6.95 Last dinner 8.30pm

WORMIT
Fife
Map **11** NO32

★★**Sandford Hill** ☎Newport-on-Tay (0382) 541802
Closed New Years Day
Country house hotel with modern bedroom extension.
15rm(13➡)(2fb) CTV in all bedrooms Ⓡ
sB&B£21 sB&B➡£24.70 dB&B£33.60
dB&B➡£39 Ɓ
CTV 50P ✽ (hard)
Scottish & Continental **V** Lunch £5.15–£6.85&alc Tea 55p High Tea £4–£6&alc Dinner £8.55–£9&alc Wine £6 Last dinner 9.30pm
Credit cards 1 2 3 5

WORPLESDON
Surrey
Map **4** SU95

★★**Worplesdon Place** Perry Hill ☎(0483) 232407 Telex no 859500
Set in 5 acres, this hotel offers good quality cooking and traditional service.
15rm(9➡)(2fb) CTV in all bedrooms
sB&B£18 sB&B➡£23 dB&B£28
dB&B➡£32
100P ✽
French **V** Lunch £5.50&alc Tea £1.20 Dinner £6.50&alc Wine £4.70 Last dinner 10pm
S% Credit cards 1 2 3 5

WORTHING
West Sussex
Map **4** TQ10

★★★***L Beach*** Marine Pde ☎(0903) 34001
Victorian hotel with extremely comfortable lounge.
89rm(68➡9⋒)(2fb) CTV in all bedrooms
✻sB&B➡⋒£21–£25
dB&B➡⋒£33.60–£40 Ɓ
Lift ☾ 55P CFA nc8yrs *xmas*
Lunch £6&alc Tea fr£1.25 Dinner £7.50&alc Wine £4.50 Last dinner 8.45pm
Credit cards 1 2 3 4 5 **VS**
See advert on page 684

★★★**Berkeley** Marine Pde (North) ☎(0903) 31122
Seafront hotel with spacious lounge areas.
97rm(38➡3⋒) CTV in all bedrooms
sB&B£13.23–£15.66 sB&B➡⋒£16.47–£19.44 dB&B£23.22–£28.08
dB&B➡⋒£29.70–£35.64 Ɓ
Lift ☾ 30P Live music and dancing wkly
✻Lunch fr£5.50 Dinner fr£6 Last dinner 8pm
Credit cards 1 2 3 5 **VS**

★★★**Chatsworth** The Steyne ☎(0903) 36103 Telex no 877046
The hotel has an attractive Georgian frontage, and is situated in a terrace overlooking Steyne gardens and the sea. →

93rm(76➡3⋒)(7fb) CTV in all bedrooms ®✱sB&B£19 sB&B➡£24 dB&B fr£30 dB&B➡£40 Ⓑ

Lift ☾ CFA ✗ billiards *xmas*

English & Continental ✪ ☕ ✱Lunch £5.25&alc Tea 65p Dinner £5.95&alc Last dinner 9.15pm

Credit cards 1 3 **VS**

★★★**Eardley** Marine Pde ☎(0903) 34444 Telex no 877046

Modernised Victorian sea front terraced house.

83rm(53➡4⋒) CTV in all bedrooms ® sB&B£20–£21 sB&B➡⋒£24–£26 dB&B£32–£34 dB&B➡⋒£40–£46 Ⓑ

Lift ☾ 20P CFA *xmas*

V ✪ ☕ Lunch £5.35–£5.80 Tea 75p–85p Dinner £5.95–£6.50&alc Wine £4.25 Last dinner 9.30pm

Credit cards 1 3 **VS**

★★★**Warnes** Marine Pde (Best Western) ☎(0903) 35222 Telex no 877046

Closed 1–9 Jan

Georgian-style hotel overlooking the sea.

70rm(48➡7⋒)(2fb) CTV in all bedrooms ®✱sB&B£15 sB&B➡⋒£20–£25 dB&B£30 dB&B➡⋒£36–£38 Ⓑ

Lift ☾ CTV 30P 2🚗 CFA billiards *xmas*

✪ ☕ Lunch £5.75–£7&alc Tea 60p Dinner £7&alc Wine £4.90 Last dinner 8.30pm

Credit cards 1 2 3 5

★★***Ardington*** Steyne Gdns ☎(0903) 30451 Closed Xmas

Pleasantly situated hotel facing Steyne Gardens, close to the promenade and the shopping centre.

51rm(37→⋒) CTV in all bedrooms Ⓡ B
☾
Last dinner 8.15pm
Credit cards 1 3

★★ ***Beechwood Hall*** Park Crescent, Wykeham Rd ☎(0903) 32872
Regency period house set in own wooded grounds.
18rm(3→1⋒) CTV in 8 bedrooms B
CTV 60P ✽
V Last dinner 8pm
Credit cards 1 2 3 5 **VS**

★★ **Kingsway** Marine Pde ☎(0903) 37542
Sea front hotel with luxurious lounges and good home cooking.
30rm(18→2⋒) (2fb) CTV in 18 bedrooms Ⓡ sB&B£15–£19 sB&B→⋒£19–£22 dB&B£24–£28 dB&B→⋒£28–£37 B
Lift 6P xmas
Lunch £5&alc Tea 75p Dinner £6&alc Wine £4.40 Last dinner 8.30pm
Credit cards 1 2 3 5

✕✕ ***Paragon Continental*** 9–10 Brunswick Rd ☎(0903) 33367
Italian run international restaurant with good personal service.
Dinner not served Sun
English & French 40 seats Last dinner 10.15pm
Credit cards 1 2 3 4 5

WOTTON-UNDER-EDGE
Gloucestershire
Map **3** ST79
★★ **Swan** Market St ☎ Dursley (0453) 842329
A comfortable hotel with good bedroom facilities.
28rm(21→1⋒) (2fb) CTV in all bedrooms sB£24 sB→⋒£28 dB£28 dB→⋒£33 (room only) B
Live music and dancing Sat
Cosmopolitan V Lunch £9.50–£17.50&alc Dinner £12.50&alc Last dinner 10.15pm
Credit cards 1 2 3 4 5

WRAFTON
Devon
Map **2** SS43
✕✕ ***Poyers Farm*** ☎ Braunton (0271) 812149
Late 16th-century converted farm cottage with ships timbers and a thatched roof.
Closed last 2wks Oct Lunch not served Mon–Sat Dinner not served Sun
English & Continental 52 seats Last dinner 9.30pm 26P bedrooms available
Credit cards 2 3

WRELTON
North Yorkshire
Map **8** SE78
✕ **Huntsman** ☎ Pickering (0751) 72530
A converted farmhouse providing international menu in friendly homely surroundings.
Closed Mon, 2wks Feb & 2wks Oct Dinner not served Sun
45 seats Lunch £3.20–£8.50 Dinner £7.50–£15 Last dinner 9.30pm P bedrooms available

WREXHAM
Clwyd
Map **7** SJ34
☆☆☆ **Crest** High St/Yorke St (Crest) ☎(0978) 353431 Telex no 61674
Modern hotel, situated in the town centre.
80→ CTV in all bedrooms Ⓡ sB→ fr£29.50 dB→ fr£39.50 (room only) B
Lift ☾ 85P 24 CFA
English & International V ✽ Lunch fr£3.50–£5.50 Tea 60p–70p Dinner £6–£8.25 Wine £5.50 Last dinner 9.30pm
Credit cards 1 2 3 4 5 **VS**

WROTHAM HEATH
Kent
Map **5** TQ65
○ **Post House** (At junct M26/M20/A20) (Trusthouse Forte) ☎01-567 3444
120→ (Due to be opened Mar 1984)

WROXHAM
Norfolk
Map **9** TG31
★★ **Broads** Station Rd ☎(06053) 2869
19rm(10→) (3fb) Ⓡ sB&B£12 sB&B→£13.50 dB&B£20.50 dB&B→£22.50 B
CTV 18P
✽ Lunch £3alc Tea 50p High Tea £1.50alc Dinner £5alc Wine £3.10 Last dinner 9pm

★★ **Hotel Wroxham** Broads Centre, Hoveton ☎(06053) 2061
18rm(14→) (2fb) CTV in all bedrooms Ⓡ ✽ sB&B£16 sB&B→£23 dB&B£27 dB&B→£33 B
60P Live music and dancing Sat
V ✽ Lunch £5.25&alc Tea fr55p Dinner £5.50&alc Wine £4.90 Last dinner 9.30pm
Credit cards 1 2 3 5 **VS**

WROXTON
Oxfordshire
Map **4** SP44
★★ **Wroxton House** (Porter) ☎ Wroxton St Mary (029 573) 482
Beautifully appointed hotel with a formal restaurant.
12rm(7→2⋒) Annexe: 3rm (2fb) CTV in all bedrooms Ⓡ sB&B fr£25 sB&B→⋒ fr£38.50 dB&B fr£40.70 dB&B→⋒ fr£50.60 B
50P ✽ xmas
English & French V Lunch £5.75 Dinner £7 Wine £5 Last dinner 10pm
S% Credit cards 1 2 3 5 **VS**

WYE
Kent
Map **5** TR04
✕✕ ***Wife of Bath*** ☎(0233) 812540
Small cottage restaurant with low-ceilinged rooms hung with modern paintings.
Closed Sun, Mon & 25 Dec–1 Jan
French V 50 seats Last dinner 10pm 15P

W

WYKEHAM (nr Scarborough)
North Yorkshire
Map **8** SE98
★★ ***Downe Arms*** ☎ Scarborough (0723) 862471 Telex no 527192
6rm
Lift CTV 200P 4🏠 ✽
English & French ♡ ☕ Last dinner 8pm
Credit cards 1 2 3 5

WYMONDHAM
Norfolk
Map **5** TG10
★★ **Abbey** Church St ☎ (0953) 602148
Small, modernised hotel, part of which dates from the late 16th century, in a quiet location near Wymondham Abbey.
31rm(21→1⋒) (4fb) CTV in all bedrooms Ⓡ sB&B fr£12.50 sB&B→⋒ £15.50–£16.50 dB&B fr£23 dB&B→⋒ £26–£27 B
Lift ☾ 4P 3🏠
V ♡ ☕ Lunch £2.45–£3.20 Tea 65p–£1.20 High Tea £2.50–£3.50 Dinner £4.85–£5 Last dinner 8.30pm
S% Credit cards 1 2 3 5

❀ ✕ **Bullen's** 16 Damgate St ☎ (0953) 603533
Tiny homely cottage restaurant offering honest cooking using fresh produce.
Closed Sun & Mon Lunch not served
V 24 seats ✻ Dinner £9.65 Wine £3.70 Last dinner 8.30pm
Credit cards 1 3

WYRE PIDDLE
Hereford & Worcester
Map **3** SO94
★ ***HL*** **Avonside** Main Rd ☎ Pershore (0386) 552654
Closed mid Dec–mid Jan
Small, family-run hotel on the banks of the River Avon.
7rm(6→1⋒) (4fb) CTV in all bedrooms sB&B→⋒ £25–£32 dB&B→⋒ £32–£40 B
CTV 80P ✽ (heated) nc5yrs
V ♡ ☕ Bar lunch £1.80–£3.80 Tea fr£1 Dinner fr£7.75&alc Wine £5.50 Last dinner 8pm

YARCOMBE
Devon
Map **3** ST20
★★ ***Yarcombe Inn*** ☎ Upottery (040486) 218
A thatched building dating from the 14th century.
6rm Ⓡ ✱ B
CTV 18P
English & French ♡ Last dinner 9.30pm
Credit card 3

YARM
Cleveland
Map **8** NZ41
✕✕ ***Santoro*** 47 High St ☎ Eaglescliffe (0642) 781305
Closed Sun & Public hols
French & Italian 42 seats Last dinner 10.15pm P
Credit cards 3 5

YARMOUTH
Isle of Wight
Map **4** SZ38
Yarmouth telephone numbers due to change during the currency of this guide.
★★ **Bugle** The Square (Whitbread) ☎ (0983) 760272 RS Nov–Mar
Small, friendly inn with pleasant modern rooms and comfortable bedrooms.
10rm(2→2⋒) (1fb) ✱ sB&B fr£16 sB&B→⋒ fr£17.50 dB&B fr£28 dB&B→⋒ fr£33
CTV 15P
English & French ♡ Lunch fr£5 Dinner fr£7 Wine £4.75 Last dinner 9.30pm
Credit cards 1 2 3 5

★★ **George** Quay St ☎ (0983) 760331
Small hotel near Yarmouth Pier, dating from Charles II's time.
24rm(8→) (2fb) TV available in bedrooms sB&B £12–£20 sB&B→ £20–£40 dB&B £24–£40 dB&B→ £40–£60 B
4P 6🏠 ✽ Live music and dancing Sat (out of season) *xmas*
♡ ☕ Lunch £5.25–£5.95 Tea 75p–£1.50 Dinner £8.25–£8.95 Wine £3.95 Last dinner 9pm
Credit cards 1 2 3 4 5

YARMOUTH, GREAT
Norfolk
Map **5** TG50
★★★ **Carlton** Marine Parade South (Mount Charlotte) ☎ (0493) 55234 Telex no 97249
96rm(64→10⋒) CTV in all bedrooms sB&B→⋒ £31.50 dB&B→⋒ £45 B
Lift ☾ CTV 30P CFA
English & French V ♡ ☕ Lunch £5.75–£6 Dinner £8.75–£9 Wine £5 Last dinner 9.30pm
Credit cards 1 2 3 5 **VS**

★★★ ***BL*** **Cliff** Gorleston-on-Sea (2m S A12) ☎ (0493) 662179
29rm(19→2⋒) (5fb) CTV in all bedrooms sB&B fr£19 sB&B→⋒ fr£24 dB&B fr£33 dB&B→⋒ fr£42 B
☾ CTV 70P ✽ Live music and dancing Fri Cabaret Fri *xmas*
V ♡ ☕ Lunch fr£5.70&alc Tea fr55p Dinner fr£7&alc Wine £4.20 Last dinner 9pm
Credit cards 1 2 3 **VS**

★★★ **Sandringham** 74–75 Marine Pde ☎ (0493) 52427
24→⋒ (2fb) CTV in all bedrooms sB&B→⋒ £26.50 dB&B→⋒ £35.65 B
☾ CTV P 10🏠
English & French V ♡ ☕ Lunch £5–£7.50&alc Tea £1.50 High Tea £1.50 Dinner £8–£8.50&alc Wine £3.95 Last dinner 11.30pm
Credit cards 1 2 3 5

★★ **Burlington** North Dr ☎ (0493) 4568
Closed Nov–Mar
33rm(15→8⋒) (8fb) CTV in 15 bedrooms Ⓡ ✱ sB&B £16–£18 sB&B→⋒ £18–£22 dB&B £24–£28 dB&B→⋒ £30–£34 B
Lift CTV 30P CFA (heated) sauna bath Live music and dancing twice wkly *xmas*
English & French V ♡ ☕ Lunch £4.50–

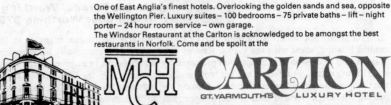

£5 Tea 50p–60p Dinner £6.50–£7.50 Wine £3.50 Last dinner 8pm

Credit cards 1 3

★★**Imperial** North Dr ☎(0493) 51113 45rm(26⇌11⋔)(11fb) CTV in all bedrooms ® *sB&B£19.50–£22.50 sB&B⇌⋔£22.50–£25.50 dB&B£23.50–£32 dB&B⇌⋔£29.50–£38 ⊟

Lift ☾ CTV 50P CFA *xmas*

English & French V Lunch £6.95&alc Tea £1.50 Dinner £8.95&alc Wine £5 Last dinner 9.30pm

Credit cards 1 2 3 4 5

★**Marine View** North Dr ☎(0493) 2879 50rm(1⇌12⋔) *sB&B£17.50–£18.50 sB&B⇌⋔£18.50–£19.50 dB&B£21–£23 dB&B⇌⋔£23–£25

Lift CTV 25P *xmas*

*Lunch £3.50 Dinner £4 Last dinner 7.30pm

YATTENDON

Berkshire

Map **4** SU57

★★*H* **Royal Oak** ☎Hermitage (0635) 201325 Closed Xmas Day

Very hospitable 16th-century inn with oak beams and log fires.

5⇌ CTV in all bedrooms sB&B⇌£30 dB&B⇌£45 ⊟

30P

English & French V Lunch £9.50alc Dinner £9.50alc Wine £3.75 Last dinner 9.30pm

Credit cards 1 2 3 5

YELDHAM, GREAT

Essex

Map **5** TL73

✕✕**White Hart** ☎(0787) 237250

Skilful cooking and good presentation are features of this medieval restaurant in extensive gardens.

English & French V 80 seats Lunch £12alc Dinner £14alc Wine £4.95 Last dinner 9.30pm 50P

Credit cards 1 2 3 4 5

YELVERTON

Devon

Map **2** SX56

★★★*L* **Moorland Links** (Forest Dale) ☎(0822) 852245

Purpose built hotel dating from 1935, in well kept grounds, offering rural views.

23⇌(2fb) CTV in all bedrooms sB&B⇌£27.50–£28.75 dB&B⇌£34–£36 ⊟

150P CFA *xmas*

V Lunch £5.25–£6.95 Dinner £7.95–£9.50 Wine £4.35 Last dinner 10pm

Credit cards 1 2 3 5 **VS**

★***Retreat*** Tavistock Rd ☎(082 285) 2099

Small congenial quiet hotel.

9rm(1⇌1⋔) ⊟

CTV 40P 4

Last dinner 9pm

YEOVIL

Somerset

Map **3** ST51

★★★*B* **Manor Crest** Hendford (Crest) ☎(0935) 23116 Telex no 46580

Convenient well run town centre hotel.

42rm(40⇌2⋔) CTV in all bedrooms ® sB&B⇌⋔ fr£31.50 dB&B⇌⋔ fr£39.50 ⊟

Lift ☾ 100P CFA

Mainly grills V *Lunch £6.35&alc Tea 65p–£1.15 Dinner fr£8.35&alc Wine £5.25 Last dinner 10pm

Credit cards 1 2 3 4 5 **VS**

★**Preston** Preston Rd ☎(0935) 74400

Privately owned and family run small hotel, on the edge of town.

7rm(3⇌⋔)(1fb) CTV in all bedrooms *sB&B£12.50 sB&B⇌⋔£14.50 dB&B£20 dB&B⇌£22

40P 6

*Lunch £3.50–£4.50 Tea 50p–75p Dinner £4.80–£5.50 Wine £2.20 Last dinner 8.30pm

Credit cards 1 3

✕✕**Little Barwick House** (2m S off A37) ☎(0935) 23902

Closed Sun & Xmas Lunch not served Mon

English & French V 30 seats *Bar lunch £5alc Dinner £10alc Wine £4.30 Last dinner 9.30pm 30P bedrooms available

S% Credit cards 1 2 3 5 **VS**

YORK

North Yorkshire

Map **8** SE65

★★★★***Royal York*** Station Rd ☎(0904) 53681 Telex no 57912

Massive railway palace in its own grounds, within sight of York Minster.

129rm(94⇌17⋔) CTV in all bedrooms

Lift ☾ 100P CFA

English & French Last dinner 9.30pm

Credit cards 1 2 3 4 5

☆☆☆☆**Viking** North St (Queens) ☎(0904) 59822 Telex no 57937

187rm(177⇌10⋔)(7fb) CTV in all bedrooms ® *sB&B⇌⋔£38–£39.50 dB&B⇌⋔£52.50–£55.50 ⊟

Lift ☾ 55 CFA *xmas*

V *Lunch fr£7.25 Tea fr70p High Tea fr£1.85 Dinner £7.25 Wine £4.80 Last dinner 11pm

Credit cards 1 2 3 4 5

★★★**Chase** Tadcaster Rd ☎(0904) 707171 Telex no 57582

Closed 24 & 25 Dec

Large traditional hotel with two bedroom wings recently refurbished.

80rm(59⇌15⋔)(2fb) CTV in all bedrooms sB&B£25 sB&B⇌⋔£28.50 dB&B£40 dB&B⇌⋔£46 ⊟

Lift ☾ CTV 100P 12 CFA Disco Sat (out of season) Live music and dancing Sat (out of season)

English, French & Italian V Lunch £5&alc Tea fr80p Dinner £9&alc Wine £4.50 Last dinner 8.45pm

Credit cards 1 2 3 5 **VS**

★★★**Dean Court** Duncombe Pl (Best Western) ☎(0904) 25082 Telex no 57577

Converted merchants' houses near Minster.

→

York

35rm(33⇌2⋒) CTV in all bedrooms ✱ sB&B⇌⋒£30–£33 B
Lift ☾ ## 10P ⇌ *xmas*
V ♧ ⊡ Lunch £6.50 Tea £1.50–£3.50 Dinner £10 Wine £5.12 Last dinner 9pm
Credit cards 1 2 3 4 5

★★★ *L* Fairfield Manor Shipton Rd, Skelton ☎(0904) 25621
Closed 3–11 Jan
Early Georgian mansion 3m north of York on the A19.
25rm(20⇌5⋒) (2fb) 2 ⊟ CTV in all bedrooms ® ✱ sB&B⇌⋒£26–£30 dB&B⇌⋒£36–£40 B
50P ✽ nc5yrs *xmas*
English & French V ♧ ⊡ Lunch £5.25&alc Tea £2.25 High Tea £3.25 Dinner £7.25&alc Last dinner 9.30pm
Credit cards 1 2 3 5

★★★ Ladbroke Abbey Park The Mount (Ladbroke) ☎(0904) 58301 Telex no 57993
84rm(80⇌) (6fb) CTV in all bedrooms ® sB&B⇌fr£33.25 dB&B⇌fr£46.50 B
Lift ☾ CTV 12P 21 ⌂ CFA Live music and dancing Sat
♧ ⊡ ✱ Lunch fr£6 Dinner fr£8.50 Last dinner 9.30pm
Credit cards 1 2 3 5

☆☆☆ Post House Tadcaster Rd (Trusthouse Forte) ☎(0904) 707921 Telex no 57798
Standing in lawns and gardens on the outskirts of the city, close to the racecourse.
147⇌ (40fb) CTV in all bedrooms ® sB&B⇌£42 dB&B⇌£56.50 B
Lift ☾ 180P CFA *xmas*
♧ ⊡ Last dinner 10pm
Credit cards 1 2 3 4 5

★★ Abbot's Mews 6 Marygate Ln, Bootham ☎(0904) 34866
This hotel near the city centre was converted from a coachman's cottage and stables.
15rm(1⇌14⋒) Annexe: 11rm(3⇌8⋒) (2fb) CTV in all bedrooms sB&B⇌⋒£20–£30 dB&B⇌⋒£30–£44
20P ⇌ ✽ Live music and dancing 4 nights wkly Cabaret 4 nights wkly *xmas*
International V ♧ ⊡ Lunch £4.50–£5.50 Tea fr90p Dinner fr£10 Wine £5.50 Last dinner 9.30pm
Credit cards 1 2 3 5

★★ Ashcroft 294 Bishopthorpe Rd ☎(0904) 59286
Closed Xmas & New Year
Large but quiet house with restful atmosphere and good home cooking.
12rm (2fb) CTV in all bedrooms sB&B fr£13 dB&B fr£26 B
CTV 40P ✽
♧ ⊡ Lunch fr£3.50 Tea fr£1.75 High Tea fr£3.50 Dinner £4.95–£6.10 Wine £3.45 Last dinner 7.45pm
Credit cards 1 3 VS

★★ Beechwood Close Shipton Rd ☎(0904) 58378 Closed Xmas Day
A detached house on the A19, in the suburb of Clifton.
12rm(1⇌1⋒) (3fb) CTV available in bedrooms ✱ sB&B£13.50–£13.75 dB&B£27–£27.50 dB&B⇌⋒£29–£29.50 B
⊬ CTV 36P ⇌
♧ ⊡ Lunch £3.50 Tea 50p–£1.50 Dinner £6–£7.50 Wine £4.20 Last dinner 9pm
Credit cards 1 3

★★ Disraeli's 140 Acomb Rd ☎(0904) 781181
Closed 1wk Xmas
9rm(6⇌) (3fb) CTV in all bedrooms ® ✱ sB&B£19.50 sB&B⇌£24.50 dB&B£33.50 dB&B⇌£39.50 B
CTV 32P ⇌
English & French V ♧ ⊡ Lunch fr£3.95 Tea fr50p High Tea fr£2.25 Dinner fr£6.95 Wine £3.69 Last dinner 10pm
Credit cards 1 2 3 5

★★ Hudson's 60 Bootham ☎(0904) 21267
Closed 24–26 Dec
13rm(6⇌7⋒) (3fb) 1 ⊟ CTV in all bedrooms ✱ sB&B⇌⋒£15–£18 dB&B⇌⋒£29–£39.50 B
14P 40 ⌂
V ♧ ⊡ Lunch £3.50–£4 Tea £1–£1.50 Dinner £4.80–£9.50&alc Wine £4.25 Last dinner 9.30pm
Credit card 1 2 3 5

★★ Kilima 129 Holgate Rd (Inter-Hotels) ☎(0904) 58844
15rm(11⇌4⋒) (1fb) CTV in all bedrooms ® ✱ sB&B⇌⋒£17–£24 dB&B⇌⋒£30–£36 B
25P *xmas*
International V ♧ ⊡ Lunch fr£4.50&alc Tea fr£1 Dinner fr£5.50&alc Wine £4.50 Last dinner 10pm
Credit cards 1 2 3 5 VS

★★ Sheppard 63 Blossom St ☎(0904) 20500
Closed 26 Dec
Four-storey town hotel, dating from 1834, on the A64.
20rm(13⇌7⋒) (3fb) 2 ⊟ CTV in all bedrooms ® ✱ sB&B⋒£15–£17.50 sB&B⇌£19–£22.50 dB&B⋒£20–£25 dB&B⇌£25–£32 B
☾ ⊬ CTV 10P 3 ⌂
English, French & Italian ♧ ⊡ ✱ Bar lunch £1–£2.50alc Dinner £5–£8alc Wine £3.95 Last dinner 9.30pm
Credit cards 1 3 VS

★★ *H* Town House 100–104 Holgate Rd ☎(0904) 36171
Closed 24 Dec–1 Jan
Friendly, hospitable hotel with well appointed accommodation.
23rm(11⇌6⋒) (5fb) CTV in all bedrooms sB&B£13.75 sB&B⇌⋒£19.75 dB&B£25 dB&B⇌⋒£29.50 B
21P
V ♧ ⊡ Lunch £4.50 Tea 70p Dinner £6&alc Wine £4.30 Last dinner 9.30pm
Credit cards 1 2 3 5 VS

★ Newington 147 Mount Vale ☎(0904) 25173
Four town houses have been suitably converted to form this hotel on the A1036 (South) approach road into the city. →

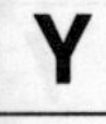
Y

Abbots Mews Hotel ★★

Marygate Lane, Bootham, York Y03 7DE

Telephone: 34866 & 22395

ABBOTS MEWS
HOTEL

Luxury hotel in the city centre only a few minutes walk from York Minster. All rooms with private bathrooms, colour TV, radio and telephone. Restaurant serving à la carte and table d'hôte meals every evening. Music and dancing, licensed bar. Car park. Solarium. Credit cards and cheques welcomed. Enquire about reduced winter rates. Conferences, functions and weddings quoted for.

Relax in our
POOL
Enjoy the Hotel's
heated
Swimming Pool

Relax

AND ENJOY YOUR STAY IN

•YORK•

Relax in our
SAUNA
Take advantage of the Hotel's Sauna

Close to the racecourse, within walking distance of the city centre.

Double, single and family rooms. Private car park.

NEWINGTON HOTEL. TEL: (0904) 25173

Please write for colour brochure to dept. A1:, **147 MOUNT VALE, YORK YO2 2DU**

The Town House Hotel

100-104 Holgate Road, York YO2 4BB
Telephone: 0904 36171

A fine example of early Victorian town houses, an ideal family run hotel for the tourist, holidaymaker or businessman. First class cuisine and an excellent selection of wines which will compliment your stay with us. The Town House is a short walk from the city centre, Yorks' famous Minster and other historical landmarks. The Racecourse is also close by. Please ask for our colour leaflet.

★★ AA

Y

29rm(2➡4⋒) Annexe: 17rm(1➡5⋒) (3fb) CTV in all bedrooms ✱sB&B£11.95 sB&B➡⋒£15.95 dB&B£20.70 dB&B➡⋒£28 B

Lift CTV 32P ▭ (heated) sauna bath Disco Sat *xmas*

V ♔ ▭ ✱Lunch £3.95–£7.50&alc Tea 45p Dinner £5.95&alc Wine £3.95 Last dinner 8.30pm

Credit cards 1 2 3 **VS**

★**Riverside Lodge** 292 Bishopthorpe Rd ☎(0904) 56464

22rm(9➡) (3fb) CTV in all bedrooms ® ★ ✱sB&B£12–£13 sB&B➡£18.50–£19 dB&B£22–£24 dB&B➡£28–£30 B 52P ✽

International **V** ♔ ▭ ✱Bar lunch £1.50–£2.50 Tea 70p–£1 Dinner £6–£8 Wine £4.30 Last dinner 8pm

Credit cards 1 3

✕✕✕**Tanglewood** Malton Rd (6m NE on A64) ☎Flaxton Moor (090486) 318

Closed Mon Dinner not served Sun

English & French **V** 90 seats Bar lunch £5–£6.50&alc Dinner £12–£14alc Wine £6.95 Last dinner 9.45pm 60P

Credit cards 1 3

✕✕**Staircase** 53 Micklegate ☎(0904) 22238

Restaurant with nightclub on premises.

Closed 1–14 Jan Dinner not served Sun Lunch not served except for private bookings.

French **V** 60 seats Dinner £9alc Wine £4.20 Last dinner 10pm 20P

Credit cards 1 2 3 5

✕**Jeeves** 39 Tanner Row ☎(0904) 59622

Closed Sun, Mon (Oct–Mar), Last wk Aug–1st wk Sep & 23 Dec–2 Jan

French 40 seats ✱Dinner £9.75–£15 Wine £5.50 Last dinner 10pm

S% Credit cards 1 2 5

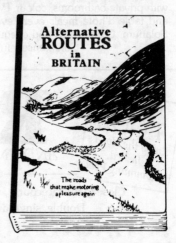

Y

cut along here

Report Form 1984

You are invited to help the AA by commenting on the hotels, motels, and restaurants you have visited.

To: The Automobile Association,
Hotel and Information Services Department,
9th Floor,
Fanum House,
Basingstoke,
Hampshire,
RG21 2EA

Name of establishment

Town	County

Date of visit

Did you find:	above expectation	satisfactory	below expectation
Hospitality and Service			
Bedroom Accommodation			
Public areas			
Meals			

Do you agree with with the classification or recommendation?	**YES**	**NO**
May we quote your name when taking up any complaint with the hotel/restaurant?	**YES**	**NO**
Did you take up your complaint with the manager at the time of your visit?	**YES**	**NO**

Name

Address

Date	Membership no.

Signature

Further copies of this form can be obtained from any AA office

Additional remarks

For office use:

Head office action	**Regional office action**
Acknowledged	Inspected by
Recorded	Date
Action	
File	
Inspect	

cut along here

AA Money-off voucher scheme

Listed below are those establishments who have agreed to participate in this scheme.

Abberley
Elms

Aberdeen
Caledonian Thistle
Dee Motel
Holiday Inn Bucksburn
Light of Bengal
Stakis Royal Darroch
Tree Tops Crest

Aberdeen Airport
Skean Dhu Dyce

Aberdour
Fairways

Aberdovey
Harbour
Trefeddian

Aberfoyle
Forest Hills

Abergavenny
Llanwenarth Arms

Aberlour
Aberlour

Abersoch
Abersoch Harbour
Porth Tocyn

Aberystwyth
Belle Vue Royal
Seabank

Aboyne
Huntley Arms

Achnasheen
Ledgowan Lodge

Aldbourne
Raffles

Aldeburgh
Wentworth

Alnmouth
Saddle
Schooner

Alnwick
White Swan

Alston
Lovelady Shield Country House
Lowbyer Manor

Alton
Leathern Bottle
Swan

Altrincham
Bowdon
George & Dragon

Alveley
Mill

Alveston
Alveston House

Ambleside
Nanny Brow Country House
Regent
Rothey Manor
Skelwith Bridge
Vale View
Waterhead
White Lion

Amersham
Kings Arms
Lam's Garden

Ammanford
Mill at Glynhir

Annan
Queensberry Arms

Appleby
Appleby Manor
Tufton Arms

Ardelve
Loch Duich

Arden
Lomond Castle

Ardeonaig
Ardeonaig

Ardfern
Galley of Lorne

Arinagour
Isle of Coll

Arundel
Norfolk Arms

Ashburton
Dartmoor Motel

Ashby-de-la-Zouch
Royal Crest

Ashford (Kent)
Eastwell Manor

Ashford (Surrey)
Terrazza

Ashton-under-Lyne
York House

Aultbea
Drumchork Lodge

Aviemore
Badenoch
Stakis Coylumbridge
Strathspey Thistle

Ayr
Belleisle
Fouter's Bistro
Stakis Ayr

Aysgarth
Palmer Flatt

Babell
Black Lion Inn

Bagshot
Pennyhill Park

Ballachulish
Ballachulish

Bamburgh
Sunningdale
Victoria

Banavie
Moorings

Banbury
Banbury Moat House

Banchory
Banchory Lodge
Burnett Arms
Tor-na-Coille

Banff
The County

Bangor
British
Ty Uchaf

Bardon Mill
Bowes
Vallum Lodge

Bar Hill
Cunard Cambridgeshire

Barmouth
Lion
Marwyn
Plas Mynach
Royal

Barnard Castle
Kings Head

Barnsley
Ardsley House

Barnstaple
Downrew House

Barnt Green
Barnt Green Inn & Restaurant

Barrhead
Dalmeny Park

Barry
Mount Sorrel

Barton
Barton Grange

Basildon
Crest

Basingstoke
Crest

Bath
Old Mill
Pratts
Rajpoot Tandoori

Bawtry
Crown

Beachley
Old Ferry

Beaconsfield
Crest

Bearsden
Stakis Burnbrae

Beattock
Old Brig Inn

Beauly
Priory

Beaumaris
Bulkeley Arms
Henllys Hall

Beddgelert
Bryn Eglwys

Beeley
Devonshire Arms

Bellingham
Riverdale Hall

Bembridge
Highbury

Benllech Bay
Bay Court
Glanrafon

Berkeley Road
Prince of Wales

Berwick-upon-Tweed
Castle
Kings Arms
Turret House

Betws-y-Coed
Craig-y-Dderwen Country House
Fairy Glen
Park Hill

Bexley
Crest

Beverley
Tickton Grange

Biddenden
Ye Maydes

Bideford
Riversford
Rosskerry
Yeoldon House

Bigbury-on-Sea
Henley

Biggleswade
Crown

Bilbrook
Bilbrook Lawns

Birkenhead
Bowler Hat
Riverhill

Birmingham
Hotel Annabelle
Apollo
Bristol Court
Grand
Holiday Inn
New Imperial
Plough & Harrow
Royal Angus Thistle
Strathallan Thistle
Wheatsheaf

Birmingham (National Exhibition Centre)
Arden Motel

Bishop Auckland
Binchester Hall

Blackburn
Saxon Inn

Blackpool
Chequers
Claremont
Cliffs
Gables Balmoral
Kimberley
New Clifton
Revill's
Savoy

Blackwood
Maes Manor

Blairgowrie
Golf View
Rosemount Golf

Blairlogie
Blairlogie House

Blakeney
Old Severn Bridge

Blanchland
Lord Crewe Arms

Bleadney
Stradlings

Blickling
Buckinghamshire Arms

Bloxham
Olde School

Blyth
Fourways

Boat-of-Garten
Craigard

Bodmin
Allegro

Bognor Regis
Lyndhurst
Royal
Royal Norfolk

Bollington
Belgrade

Bolton
Crest
Pack Horse

Bonnyrigg
Dalhousie Castle

Bontddu
Bontddu Hall

Bootle
Park

Boroughbridge
Crown

Borrowash
Wilmot Arms

Bosham
Millstream

Botallack
Count House

Botesdale
Crown Hill House

Bouley Bay
Water's Edge

Bournemouth
Anglo-Swiss
Avonmore
Boote's
Chinehurst
Cliff End
County
Hotel Courtlands
Crest
Durley Dean
Durley Grange
Durlaston Court
Embassy
Fircroft
Grange
Grosvenor
Heathlands
Highcliff
Langtry Manor
La Taverna
Manor House
Pinehurst
Queens
Sun Court
Tralee
Ullswater
Winterbourne
Winter Gardens
Yenton

Bovey Tracey
Blenheim
Edgemoor
Prestbury Country House

Bradford
Novotel Bradford
Stakis Norfolk Gardens

Bradworthy
Lake Villa

Brae
Busta House

Braemar
Invercauld Arms

Braithwaite
Ivy House

Brampton
Farlam Hall
Howard Arms

Bransgore
Harrow Lodge Country House

Branston
Moor Lodge

Brechfa
Ty Mawr Country House Hotel

Brecon
Lansdowne

Bridestowe
White Hart Inn

Bridge-of-Cally
Bridge of Cally

Bridge of Earn
Moncrieffe Arms

Bridgnorth
Falcon

Bridgwater
Old Vicarage
Royal Clarence

Bridlington
Expanse

Bridport
Haddon House

Brightlingsea
Jacobe's Hall

Brighton
Alexandra
Granville
La Marinade
Le Grandgousier
Old Ship
Royal Albion
St Catherines Lodge
Sackville
Vogue

Bristol
Avon Gorge
Crest
Grand
Redwood Lodge

Broad Haven
Rosehill Country

Broadstairs
Castlemere

Broadway
Broadway

Brockenhurst
Carey Manor Motor
Cloud
Forest Park

Brome
Brome Grange Motel

Bromsgrove
Grafton Manor

Broughton
Greenmantle

Bruton
Clogs

Buckfastleigh
Bossell House

Buckland-in-the-Moor
Buckland Hall

Bucklow Hill
Swan

Bude
Camelot
Flexbury Lodge
Penarvor
St Margarets

Burgh Heath
Pickard Motor

Burley
Burley Manor
Moorhill
White Buck

Burnham-on-Crouch
Ye Olde White Harte

Burnham-on-Sea
Royal Clarence

Burnley
Rosehill House

Burpham
Burpham Country

Burrington
Northcote Manor

Burton Bradstock
Burton Cliff

Bury
Normandie

Bushey
Spiders Web Motel

Buttermere
Bridge

Buxton
Leewood

Caersws
Maesmawr Hall

Callander
Lubnaig

Calstock
Boot Inn

Cambridge
Arundel House
Garden House

Cannock
Hollies
Roman Way

Canonbie
Riverside Inn

Canterbury
Slatters

Capel Curig
Ty'n-y-Coed

Cardiff
Crest
Inn on the Avenue
Park
Le Provencal
Riverside

Carlisle
Crest
Crown & Mitre
Cumbrian Thistle

Carnforth
Royal Station

Carnoustie
Carlogie House
Glencoe

Cartmel
Aynsome Manor
Grammar

Castle Donington
Priest House Inn

Castle Douglas
Imperial
Kings Arms

Castleton
Moorlands

Catterick Bridge
Bridge House

Chagford
Easton Court
Great Tree
Teignworthy
Three Crowns

Charlecote
Charlecote Pheasant Country

Charnock Richard
Hunters Lodge Motel

Cheadle Hulme
Cheshire Tandoori

Chedington
Chedington Court

Cheltenham
Hotel de la Bere
Golden Valley Thistle
Lilleybrook Aparthotel
Wyastone

Chenies
Bedford Arms Thistle

Chepstow
Castle View

Chester
Chester Grosvenor
Courtyard
Plantation Inn
Rowton Hall

Chiddingfold
Crown Inn

Chiddingstone
Castle Inn

Chideock
Clock House

Chilgrove
White Horse Inn

Chillington
Oddicombe House

Chilton Polden
Wilton Farm House

Chipping Norton
Crown & Cushion

Chirnside
Chirnside Country House

Christchurch
Fishermans Haunt
Kings Arms Crest
Waterford Lodge

Church Stretton
Stretton Hall

Cirencester
Corinium Court
Kings Head
Stratton House

Clachan Seil
Willowburn

Clacton-on-Sea
Kings Cliff

Clavering
Cricketers

Clawton
Court Barn Country House

Cleeve Hill
Malvern View

Cleish
Nivingston House

Cleobury Mortimer
Redfern

Clitheroe
Roefield

Clumber Park
Normanton Inn

Coatham Mundeville
Hall Garth

Cockermouth
Globe
Wordsworth

Colchester
Rose & Crown
Wm Scraggs

Coleford
Lambsquay

Coleshill
Swan

Colwyn Bay
Ashmount
Edelweiss
Hotel 70°
Lyndale
Marine
Norfolk House
Raynham
West Point
Whitehall

Colyton
Old Bakehouse

Combe Martin
Britannia
Delve's

Comrie
Comrie
Royal

Connel
Falls of Lora

Contin
Craigdarroch Lodge

Conwy
Castle Bank

Corby
Grosvenor

Cornhill-on-Tweed
Tillmouth Park

Corsham
Methuen Arms
Rudloe Park
Stagecoach
Weavers Loft

Cossington
Cossington Mill

Cottingham
Hunting Lodge

Covenham
Mill House

Coventry
Beechwood
Chace Crest
Crest
Novotel Coventry

Cowfold
St Peter Cottage

Crackington Haven
Coombe Barton

Crafthole
Whitsand Bay

Crail
Croma

Cranbrook
Kennel Holt
Willesley

Crantock
Fairbank

Crathorne
Crathorne Hall

Crediton
Coombe House Country

Criccieth
Caerwylan
George IV
Plas Gwyn

Crieff
George
Gwydyr House
Murray Park
Star

Crocketford
Galloway Arms

Cromer
Hotel-de-Paris
West Parade

Crooklands
Crooklands

Crudwell
Mayfield House

Cumnor
Bear and Ragged Staff

Cupar
Ostlers Close

Dalry
Lochinvar

Dalston
Dalston Hall

Dalwhinnie
Loch Ericht

Daresbury
Lord Daresbury

Darlington
Kings Head

Dartmouth
Royal Castle
Royle House

Darwen
Whitehall

Dawlish
Charlton House
Langstone Cliff

Deddington
Holcombe

Dedham
Dedham Vale
Le Talbooth
Maison Talbooth

Denbigh
Bull

Derby
Crest
International
Pennine

Dingwall
Royal

Dirleton
Open Arms

Doddiscombsleigh
Nobody Inn

Dolwyddelan
Plas Hall

Doncaster
Regent

Dorchester
Kings Arms

Dorking
Punch Bowl Motor

Dornoch
Burghfield House
Dornoch Castle

Douglas
Boncomptie's
Woodbourne

Dover
White Cliffs

Down Thomas
Langdon Court

Draycott
Tudor Court

Droitwich
Château Impney
Raven

Drumnadrochit
Polmaily House

Drymen
Buchanan Arms

Dudley
Station
Ward Arms

Dumfries
Station

Dunblane
Stakis Dunblane Hydro

Dundee
Angus Thistle
Invercarse

Dundonnell
Dundonnell

Dunfermline
Brucefield
King Malcolm Thistle

Dunkeld
Atholl Arms

Dunmow, Great
Starr

Dunoon
Argyll
Royal Marine

Dunstable
Old Palace Lodge

Dunster
Exmoor House

Duntulm
Duntulm

Duror
Stewart

Eastbourne
Chatsworth
Imperial
Lansdowne
Mansion House
New Wilmington
Princes
Sandhurst

East Kilbride
Stuart Thistle

Eastleigh
Crest

Edinburgh
Barnton Thistle
Bruntsfield
Crest
Donmaree
Handsel
Harp
Iona
Kalpna
King James Thistle
L'Auberge
Murrayfield
Oratava
Shamiana
Stakis Commodore

Edzell
Central

Egham
Runnymede

Eglwysfach
Ynyshir Hall

Elgin
Eight Acres
Enrico's

Ermington
Ermewood House

Erskine
Crest Hotel – Erskine Bridge

Esher
Haven

Ettrickbridge
Ettrickshaws

Evesham
Evesham

Exeter
Buckerell Lodge
Edgerton Park
Imperial
Red House
Rougemont
Trood Country House

Exford
Crown

Exmouth
Barn
Royal Beacon

Fairford
Hyperion

Falkirk
Pierre's
Stakis Park

Falmouth
Carthion
Crill House
Green Lawns
Melville
Park Grove
Pendower
Penmere Manor
St Michaels
Somerdale
Suncourt

Farnham
Trevena House

Faugh
String of Horses Inn

Faversham
Read's

Felixstowe
North Sea
Orwell Moat House

Ferndown
Coach House Motel

Fishguard
Fishguard Bay
Manor House

Fittleworth
Swan

Flamborough
Timoneer Country Manor

Fleet (Dorset)
Moonfleet Manor

Fleet (Hants)
Lismoyne

Flichity
Grouse & Trout

Folkestone
Chilworth Court

Fordingbridge
Hourglass
Three Lions Inn

Forsinard
Forsinard

Fort Augustus
Caledonian
Lovat Arms

Fort William
Alexandra
Grand
Highland
Imperial
Milton
Stag's Head

Fossebridge
Fossebridge Inn

Fowey
Marina

Fownhope
Green Man

Freshwater
Albion
Farringford

Fressingfield
Fox & Goose

Freuchie
Lomond

Frinton-on-Sea
Maplin
Rock

Frome
Portway

Gairloch
Creag Mhor

Garstang
Crofters

Garve
Garve
Inchbae Lodge

Gatehouse of Fleet
Murray Arms

Gatwick Airport
Chequers Thistle
Crest
Gatwick Moat House
Goffs Park
Saxon Inn Gatwick

Gaunts Earthcott
Manor House Restaurant & Junk Shop

Giffnock
MacDonald Thistle
Stakis Redhurst

Gifford
Tweeddale Arms

Gisburn
Stirk House

Glasgow
Crest Hotel Glasgow City
Le Provencal
Sherbrooke
Stakis Grosvenor
Stakis Ingram
Stakis Pond
Tinto Firs Thistle

Glasgow Airport
Ardgowan
Glynhill
Stakis Normandy
Stakis Watermill

Glastonbury
George & Pilgrim
No 3 Magdaline Street

Glencarse
Newton House

Glenlivet
Minmore House

Glenridding
Glenridding

Glenshee
Dalmunzie

Gloucester
Bowden Hall
Crest
Tara

Glyn Ceiriog
Glyn Valley

Goathland
Whitfield House

Golant
Cormorant

Golspie
Golf Links

Gosport
Anglesey

Goudhurst
Goudhurst

Gourock
Stakis Gantock

Grange-over-Sands
Grange
Methven

Grantown-on-Spey
Ben Mhor
Coppice
Dunvegan
Garth

Grasmere
Grasmere Red Lion
Michael's Nook
Prince of Wales
Ravenswood
White Moss House
Wordsworth

Greenock
Tontine

Greta Bridge
Morritt Arms

Gretna
Gretna Chase
Royal Stewart Motel

Grimsby
Crest
Humber Royal Crest

Grizedale
Ormandy

Gullane
Greywalls

Hackness
Hackness Grange Country

Halifax
Yorkshireman

Hamble
Beth's

Handforth
Belfry

Harlow
Saxon Motor Inn

Harome
Star Inn

Harpenden
Harpenden Moat House

Harrogate
Britania Lodge
Fern
Gables
Hospitality Inn
Russell
Hotel St George
Wessex

Harrow
Old Etonian

Harrow Weald
Grims Dyke Country

Hartlepool
Staincliffe

Haslemere
Fourteen Petworth Road
Georgian
L'Auberge de France
Lythe Hill

Hatch Beauchamp
Farthings Country House

Hathersage
Hathersage Inn

Hawick
Kirklands

Hawkhurst
Tudor Arms

Hawkshead
Tarn Mows

Haydon Bridge
Anchor

Haytor
Hayor Inn
Bel Alp

Helensburgh
Commodore

Helland Bridge
Tredethy Country

Helston
Angel Hotel

Hemel Hempstead
Hemel Hempstead Moat House

Henley-on-Thames
Hamlyn's

Hereford
Graftonbury

Hethersett
Park Farm

Hexam
County
Royal

High Easter
The Punch Bowl

High Offley
Royal Oak

High Wycombe
Crest

Hogsthorpe
Belmont

Holkham
Victoria

Hollingbourne
Great Danes

Holmes Chapel
Yellow Broom

Holywell Green
Rock Inn

Honiton
Deer Park

Hook
Raven Hotel

Hope
House of Anton

Hope Cove
Lantern Lodge

Horsforth
Low Hall

Horton
French Partridge

Hounslow
Master Robert

How Caple
How Caple Grange

Howden
Bowmans

Hull
Crest Hotel Hull-City
Crest Hotel–Humber Bridge

Hurstpierpoint
Barrons

Hythe
Stade Court

Ilfracombe
Carlton
Torrs
Tracy House

Ilkley
Box Tree
Sabera

Ilminster
Horton Cross
Shrubbery

Inverness
Culloden House
Cummings
Drumossie
Glen Mhor
Palace
Queensgate
Station

Invershin
Invershin

Ipswich
Belstead Brook
Ipswich Moat House

Isle of Whithorn
Queens Arms

Isle Ornsay
Kinloch Lodge
Hotel Eilean Iarmain

Jevington
Hungry Monk

Kegworth
Yew Lodge

Kelso
Queens Head

Kendal
Castle Dairy
County Thistle

Kenilworth
De Montfort
Diments
Kenilworth Moat House
Ristorante Portofino

Kennford
Fairwinds

Kentallen
Ardsheal House

Kerne Bridge
Castle View

Keswick
Chaucer House
Derwentwater
Lairbeck
Queens
Red House
Underscar

Kettering
George

Kettlewell
Racehorses

Kidderminster
Gainsborough House
Granary
Stone Manor

Kilchrenan
Ardanaiseig
Taychreggan

Kildrummy
Kildrummy Castle

Killiecrankie
Killiecrankie

Killin
Falls of Dochart
Killin
Morenish Lodge

Kilmarnock
Caesar's

Kinbuck
Cromlix House

Kinclaven
Ballathie House

Kingham
Mill House & Restaurant

Kingsbridge
Buckland-Tout-Saints
Kings Arms
Kingsbridge Motel
Rockwood

King's Lynn
Mildenhall

Kingsteignton
Thatchers

Kingswinford
Summerhill House

Kington
Burton

Kingussie
Osprey

Kinloch Rannoch
Loch Rannoch

Kinross
Green

Kintbury
Dundas Arms

Kirkby Fleetham
Kirkby Fleetham Hall

Kirkbymoorside
George & Dragon

Kirkby Stephen
Kings Arms

Kirkcolm
Knocknassie House

Kirk Langley
Meynell Arms

Kirkwall
Foveran

Kirkwhelpington
Knowesgate

Knaresborough
Mitre

Knightwick
Talbot

Knock
Toravaig House

Knowle
Greswolde Arms

Knowsley
Crest Hotel East Lancs Road

Knutsford
Rose & Crown

Kyle of Lochalsh
Lochalsh

Lairg
Sutherland Arms

Lamlash
Carraig Mhor

Lampeter
Black Lion Royal
Falcondale

Lamphey
Court

Langbank
Gleddoch House

Langholm
Eskdale

Langland Bay
Langland Court

Langstone
New Inn Motel

Largs
Elderslie

Lastingham
Lastingham Grange

Launceston
White Hart

Leamington Spa
Chesford Park
Park

Lechlade
Trout

Ledbury
Verzons

Leeds
Merrion
Stakis Windmill

Leeming Bar
White Rose

Leicester
Rowans

Leighton Buzzard
Cross Keys
Swan

Leintwardine
Lion

Leominster
Talbot

Lerwick
Lerwick Thistle

Letham
Fernie Castle

Letterfinlay
Letterfinlay Lodge

Lewes
Shelleys

Lichfield
Angel Croft

Lifton
Arundell Arms
Lifton Cottage

Limpsfield
Old Lodge

Lincoln
Grand

Liskeard
Country Castle

Little Weighton
Rowley Manor

Liverpool
Atlantic Tower Thistle
Crest Hotel Liverpool-City
Grange
Green Park
Holiday Inn

Lizard
Lizard

Llanarmon Dyffryn Ceriog
Hand

Llanbedrog
Bryn Derwen

Llanberis
Dol Peris
Gallt-y-Glyn

Llandeilo
Cawdor Arms

Llandovery
Picton Court

Llandrindod Wells
Hotel Commodore

Llandudno
Bodysgallen Hall
Bromwell Court
Fairhaven
Gogarth Abbey
Gwesty Leamore
Headlands
Hilbre Court
Imperial
Min-y-Don
Ormescliffe
Osborne
Ravenhurst
Richmond
Sunnymede
Tan-Lan

Llanfyllin
Bodfach Hall

Llangadog
Plas Glansevin

Llangollen
Hand

Llanrwst
Gwesty Plas Maenan
Meadowsweet

Llanwnda
Stables

Llanwrtyd Wells
Neuadd Arms

Lochawe
Carraig-Thura

Lochcarron
Lochcarron

Lochearnhead
Craigroyston House

Lochinver
Culag

Lockerbie
Dryfesdale

London Postal Districts
E1 Tower Thistle
EC2 Great Eastern Hotel
NW1 Harewood
NW3 Charles Bernard
NW8 Lords Rendezvous
SE1 South of the Border
SE13 Curry Centre
SW1 Lafayette
Lowndes
Royal Horseguards Thistle
Royal Westminster Thistle
SW3 Brasserie St Quentin
Chelsea Rendezvous
Don Luigi's
SW5 London International
SW7 Forum Hotel London
SW8 Chez Nico
SW13 Barnabys
W1 Au Jardin des Gourmet's
Churchill
Clifton-Ford
Gaylord
Kerzenstruberl
Lee Ho Fook
May Fair
Mount Royal
Piccadilly
Rathbone
Regent Crest
Selfridge Thistle
Terrazza
Verrey's
Washington
White Tower
W2 Central Park
Chez Franco
Hospitality Inn
W6 Cunard International
W8 Kensington Palace Thistle
Siam
W9 Didier
W11 La Jardnere
La Pomme d'Amour
W12 Shireen
W13 Maxims Chinese
W14 Royal Kensington
WC1 Bedford Corner
Bloomsbury Crest
Kites Chinese
Les Halles
London Ryan
Royal Scot Thistle
WC2 Chez Solange
L'Opera
Terrazza-Est
Thomas-de-Quincey's

Longhorsley
Linden Hall

Long Melford
Crown Inn

Lossiemouth
Stotfield

Lostwithiel
Carotel Motel

Loughborough
Cedars

Lower Slaughter
Manor

Low Row
Punch Bowl

Ludlow
Feathers
Overton Grange
Penny Anthony

Ludwell
Grove House

Luss
Inverbeg Inn

Luton
Chiltern
Crest Hotel – Luton
Strathmore Thistle

Lydford
Lydford House
Manor Inn

Lyme Regis
Alexandra
Beuna Vista
Royal Lion
Tudor House

Lyndhurst
Lyndhurst Park
Parkhill House
Pikes Hill Forest Lodge

Lynmouth
Bath
Shelley's Cottage

Lynton
Chough's Nest
Crown
Neubia House
Sandrock
Seawood

Lytham St Annes
Chadwick
Hotel Glendower
Grand Crest
Lindum

Macduff
Deveron House
The Fife Arms

Maidenhead
Crest

Malham
Buck Inn

Mallaig
Marine
West Highland

Malmesbury
Old Bell

Malvern, Great
Abbey
Beauchamp
Broomhill
Cotford

Malvern Wells
The Cottage in the Wood
Holdfast Cottage

Manchester
Portland Thistle
Simpsons
Truffles

Marazion
Cutty Sark

Margate
Walpole Bay

Market Harborough
Grove Motel

Markyate
Hertfordshire Moat House

Martinhoe
Old Rectory Hotel

Martock
White Hart

Maryport
Waverley

Masham
Jervaulix Hall

Mawgan Porth
Tredragon

Mawnan Smith
Dionysus Greek
Meudou
Trelawne

Maypool
Firwood Country

Measham
The Measham Inn (formerly Chequers Hotel)

Melksham
Kings Arms
Mr Bumbles

Melling
Melling Hall

Melrose
Burt's

Melton Mowbray
Harboro'

Mendham
Sir Alfred Munnings

Mere
Old Ship

Mere Brow
Crab & Lobster

Meriden
Manor

Merthyr Tydfil
Castle

Mevagissey
Spa

Middle Wallop
Fifehead Manor

Milford Haven
Sir Benfro

Milford-on-Sea
Mill House

Milngavie
Black Bull Thistle
Gavin's Mill

Milton
Milton Manor

Milton Keynes
Cock

Minehead
Beaconwood
Northfield
Hotel Remuera

Minster Lovell
Old Swan

Modbury
Modbury Inn
Modbury Pippin

Moffat
Moffat House

Monmouth
Kings Head
White Swan

Montrose
Park

Morar
Morar

Morecambe
Clarendon
Elms

Moreton-in-Marsh
Manor House

Mousehole
Lobster Pot

Muir-of-Ord
Ord House

Mullion
Polurrian

Musselburgh
Drummore
Pittencrieff

Nairn
Golf View

Nantwich
Alvaston Hall
Churche's Mansion
Rookery Hall

Narberth
Plas-Hyfryd

Narborough
Charnwood

Neath
The Castle
Cimla Court Motel

Newark on Trent
Ram
Robin Hood

Newbridge, Cornwall
Enzo

Newbridge on Wye
New Inn

Newcastle-under-Lyme
Crest

Newcastle-upon-Tyne
Avon
County Thistle
Crest Newcastle
Gosforth Park
Michelangelo
Northumbria
Ristorante Roma
Royal Turks Head Thistle
Swallow

Newcastle-upon-Tyne Airport
Stakis Airport

Newent
Soutters

Newgate Street
Ponsbourne

New Grimsby
New Inn

Newmarket
Bedford Lodge
Newmarket Moat House
Rosery Country House

Newport (Gwent)
Westgate

Newport (Salop)
Royal Victoria

Newquay
Atlantic
Beachcroft
Bewdley
Hotel Bristol
Cedars
Cross Mount
Edgcumbe
Kilbirnie
Pine Lodge
Porth Veor Manor House
Trebarwith
Trevone
Waters Edge

Newton Abbot
Queens

Newton Ferrers
Court House

Newton Stewart
Galloway Arms

Norman Cross
Crest

Northampton
Saxon Inn
Westone Moat House

North Berwick
Nether Abbey
Point Garry

Northophall Village
Chequers

North Petherton
Walnut Tree Inn

North Stoke
Springs

Norwich
Maids Head
Castle

Nottingham
Bestwood Lodge
Moulin Rouge
Stakis Victoria
Strathdon Thistle

Nuneaton
Chase

Nunnington
Ryedale Lodge

Oakham
George
Hambleton Hall
Rutland Angler

Oban
Alexandra
Caledonian

Oldbury
Jonathan's

Oldham
Bower

Ombersley
Crown & Sandys Arms

Onich
Creag Dhu

Orton
Gilded Apple

Otterburn
Percy Arms

Oulton
Crest

Oxford
Restaurant Elizabeth
Isis
Opium Den
Oxford Moat House

Padstow
Old Custom House Inn

Paignton
Luigis
Redcliffe
Seaford

Painswick
Painswick

Pandy
Park

Parkgate
Parkgate

Peebles
Dilkusha
Venlaw Castle

Pembroke
Coach House Inn

Penarth
Caprice
Glendale
Walton House

Pencraig
Pencraig Court

Pennal
Llugwy
Talgarth Hall

Penzance
Higher Faugan
Mount Prospect
Sea & Horses

Pershore
The Angel Inn
Manor House

Perth
Lovat
Stakis City Mills

Peterborough
Saxon Inn

Peterlee
Norseman

Petty France
Petty France

Pickering
Forest & Vale

Piddletrenthide
Old Bakehouse

Pillaton
Weary Friar

Pitlochry
Airdaniar
Burnside
Craigard
Craigvrack
Pine Trees
Pitlochry Hydro
Scotlands

Plymouth
Astor
Elfordleigh
Grosvenor
Highlands
Khyber
Merchantman
Novotel Plymouth

Pocklington
Feathers

Polkerris
Rashleigh Inn

Polmont
Inchyra Grange

Polperro
Kitchen
Polmary

Ponterwyd
Dyffryn Castell

Poole
Hospitality Inn
Isabel's
Mansion House
Warehouse

Port Appin
Airds

Port Gaverne
Port Gaverne

Porthcawl
Seaways

Portland
Portland Heights

Portloe
Lugger

Portree
Rosedale

Portscatho
Gerrans Bay
Roseland House
Rosevine

Portsmouth
Crest

Ocean
Royal Beach

Port William
Corsemalzie House

Powfoot
Powfoot Golf

Praa Sands
Prah Sands

Preston
Crest
French Bistro

Prestwick
North Beach

Pulborough
Chequers

Putsborough
Putsborough Sands

Queensferry (South)
Forth Bridges Moat House
Hawes Inn

Ramsbury
Bell

Rangeworthy
Rangeworthy Court

Ratho
Bridge Inn

Ravenglass
Pennington Arms

Ravenscar
Raven Hall

Redruth
Penventon

Retford (East)
West Retford

Rhayader
Elan Valley

Rhu
Rosslea Hall

Richmond upon Thames
Red Lion Chinese

Ripon
Ripon Spa
Unicorn

Rishworth
Royal

Robin Hood's Bay
Grosvenor

Rochdale
Midway

Rochester (Kent)
Crest

Rochester (Northumberland)
Redesdale Arms

Rock
St Enodoc

Rosedale Abbey
White Horse Farm

Rosemarkie
Marine

Ross on Wye
Pengethley
Rosswyn

Rosudgeon
Rosudgeon

Rotherham
Carlton Park

Rothesay
St Ebba

Rothley
Red Lion
Rothley Court

Rowardennan
Rowardennan

Ruan High Lanes
Hundred Houses
Pendower
Pendower Beach House

Rugby
Three Horse Shoes

Rugeley
Eaton Lodge

Runcorn
Crest

Rushyford
Eden Arms

Rutherglen
Stakis Burnside

Rye
Monastery

Saffron Walden
Saffron

St Agnes
Rose-in-Vale

St Albans
Noke Thistle
St Michael's Manor

St Andrews
Grange Inn
Rufflets
St Andrews
Scores

St Austell
Boscundle Manor
Clifden

Pier House
Porthavallen
White Hart

St Clements Bay
Ambassadeur
Shakespeare Hotel & Restaurant

St Columb Major
Old Rectory Hotel & Country Club

St Combs
Tufted Duck

St Davids
Old Cross
St Non's
Warpool Court

St Helens
Hay Loft

St Helier
Hotel Savoy

St Ives
Boskerris
Carbis Bay
Dunmar
Garrack
Karenza
Ocean Breezes
The Outrigger
Pedn-Olva
Tregenna Castle

St Keyne
Old Rectory

St Margaret's Hope
Creel

St Mawes
Idle Rocks
St Mawes
Ship & Castle

St Mawgan
Dalswinton Country House

St Mellons
St Mellons Hotel & Country Club

St Peter Port
Dunchoille
Le Nautique
Old Government House

St Saviour (Guernsey)
L'Atlantique

St Saviour (Jersey)
Longueville Manor

Salcombe
Bolt Head
Knowle
Marine
Sunny Cliff
Wells

Salisbury
Cathedral
Cranes
Old Bell Inn

Sandbach
Saxon Cross Motel

Sanderstead
Selsdon Park

Sandown
Melville Hall

Sanquhar
Nithsdale

Sandyhills
The Granary

Scalasaig
Colonsay

Scarborough
Brookland
Holbeck Hall
Lanterna Ristorante
Norbreck
Royal
St Nicholas
Southlands

Scole
Scole Inn

Scotch Corner
Scotch Corner

Scunthorpe
Royal

Seahouses
Beach House
St Aidans

Seaview
Seaview

Seavington St Mary
The Pheasant

Selkirk
Heatherlie Hill

Selmeston
Corins

Sennen
Tregiffian

Shaftesbury
Royal Chase

Shanklin
Luccombe Hall
Melbourne Ardenlea

Sheffield
Dore
Mosborough Hall
Royal Victoria

Shepton Mallet
Bowlish House

Sherborne
Saffron House

Shifnal
Park House

Shipham
Penscot Farmhouse

Shrewsbury
Ainsworth's Radbrook Hall
Penny Farthing

Sidmouth
Abbeydale
Applegarth
Fortfield
Riviera
Royal York & Faulkener

Simonsbath
Simonsbath House

Skelmorlie
Manor Park

Skinflats
Dutch Inn

Smallways
The A66 Motel

Southampton
Olivers
Southampton Moat House
Southampton Park

South Brent
Glazebrook House

Southend-on-Sea
Balmoral
Roslin

South Godstone
La Bonne Auberge

South Mimms
Crest

Southport
Metropole
Prince of Wales

South Shields
Sea

Southwold
Crown
Dutch Barn
Swan

South Zeal
Oxenham Arms

Spey Bay
Spey Bay

Stafford
Garth
Romaline
Vine

Staines
Pack Horse

Stalisfield Green
Plough Inn

Stamford
Lady Anne's

Steppingley
French Horn

Stewarton
Chapeltoun House

Stirling
Heritage
Hollybank
Stakis Station
Terraces

Stockport
Belgrade
Wycliffe Villa

Stockton-on-Tees
Billingham Arms
Golden Eagle Thistle
Parkmore
Stonyroyd

Stoke-on-Trent
Haydon House
Stakis Grand

Stone
Brooms

Stonehaven
Commodore

Stornoway
Caberfeidh
Seaforth

Stourbridge
Bell
Talbot

Stourport-on-Severn
Swan

Stow-on-the-Wold
King's Arms
Old Stocks
Rafters
Royalist
Unicorn Crest

Stratford upon Avon
Falcon
Grosvenor House
Marlowe's

Strathblane
Kirkhouse Inn

Strathdon
Colquhonnie

Strathpeffer
Brunstane Lodge
Dunraven Lodge

Streatley
Swan

Street
Wessex

Streetly
Parson & Clerk Motel

Strete
The Laughing Monk

Stroud
Alpine Lodge
The Bear of Rodborough
Burleigh Court

Sunbury-on-Thames
Castle

Sunderland
Seaburn

Sutton
Partners 23

Sutton Coldfield
Le Bon Viveur
Moor Hall
Sutton Court

Swanage
Grosvenor
Malverns
The Pines
Sefton

Swansea
Llwyn Helyg
Windsor Lodge

Sway
White Rose

Swindon
Blunsdon House
Crest

Tain
Royal

Talsarnau
Maes Y Neuadd

Tal-Y-Bont
Lodge

Tal-Y-Llyn
Tynycornel

Tarbert (Harris, Isle of, Western Isles)
Harris

Tarbert (Strathclyde)
Bruce

Tarporley
Willington Hall

Taunton
St Quintin
Quorum

Taynuilt
Polfearn

Tebay
Tebay Mountain Lodge

Teeside Airport
St George Hotel

Teignmouth
Bay
Belvedere
Glendaragh
London
Minadab

Telford
Buckatree Hall
White House

Tenby
Atlantic
Croft

Tetbury
Close
Restaurant Hubbits

Tewkesbury
Bell
Royal Hop Pole Crest
Tewkesbury Park Golf & Country Club

Thorne
Belmont

Thornhill
Buccleuch & Queensberry
Trigony House

Thornton
Cottage

Thornton Watlass
Buck Inn

Thorpe (Dovedale)
Izaak Walton

Thorverton
Berribridge House

Thrapston
Bridge

Three Legged Cross
Capercaizie

Tintagel
Atlantic View
Bossiney House

Tintern
Wye Valley

Titchwell
Manor

Tiverton
Tiverton Motel

Todwick
Red Lion

Tomintoul
Richmond Arms

Torquay
Albaston
Hotel Balmoral
Bancourt
Belgrave
Bowden Close
Brigantine Motor
Bute Court
Carlton
Chelston Tower
Devonshire
Fairmount House
Fonthill
Gleneagles
Grand
Green Mantle
Gresham Court
Homers
Hunsdon Lea
Kistor
Lansdowne
Lisburne
Livermead Cliff
Livermead House
Meadfoot Bay
Nethway
Orestone House
Overmead
Palm Court
Palace
Hotel Roseland
Shelley Court
Sydore
Toorak
Vernon Court
Woodland Park

Torrington, Great
Castle Hill

Troon
Marine
Piersland Lodge
South Beach

Truro
Carlton

Tunbridge Wells
Calverley
Royal Wells Inn
Spa
Wellington

Turvey
Laws

Tynemouth
Grand
Park

Ulverston
Railway

Upholland
Holland Hall

Usk
Mr Midgleys

Uttoxeter
White Hart

Ventnor
Madeira Hall
Metropole
Ventnor Towers

Walberton
Avisford Park

Wallasey
Grove House

Wallsend
Newcastle Moat House

Walsall
Barons Court
County
Fairlawns
Walsall Crest

Wamphray
Redhouse House

Ware
Ben's Brasserie

Wareham
Old Granary
Worgret Manor

Warrington
Patten Arms

Warwick
Lord Leycester
Randolph's

Watchet
Downfield

Watergate Bay
Tregurrian

Weedon
Crossroads

Wellingborough
Hind

Wells
Ancient Gate House
Crown
Swan

Welshpool
Garth Derwen
Royal Oak

Welwyn Garden City
Crest

Weobley
Red Lion

West Bromwich
West Bromwich Moat House

Westbury
Lopes Arms

Westhill
Westhill Inn

West Huntspill
Huntspill Villa

West Mersea
Le Champenois

Weston Turville
Five Bells

West Witton
Wensleydale Heifer Inn

Wetheral
Crown
Fantails
Killoran

Wetherby
Linton Spring

Weybourne
Gasche's Swiss

Weybridge
Oatlands Park
Ship

Weymouth
Bay View

Whitby
Marvic
Saxonville
Sneaton Hall

Whitchurch (Salop)
Dodington Lodge

Whitebridge
Whitebridge

Whitebrook
Crown at Whitebrook

Whitehaven
Roseneath Country House
Waverley

Whiteness
Westings

Whitley Bay
Croglin
Holmedale

Whitstable
Marine

Whittlesey
Falcon

Wicken
Wicken Country

Widemouth Bay
Trelawny

Wigan
Brocket Arms

Wilmcote
Swan House

Wilmington
Home Farm

Wincanton
Dolphin

Winchcombe
Wesley House

Windermere
Burn How Motel
Hideaway
Hydro
Low Wood
Miller Howe
Porthole Eating House
Ravensworth
Roger's
Royal
St Martin's
Wild Boar

Windsor
Don Peppino

Wisbech
White Lion

Wishaw
Belfry
Moxhull Hall

Woburn
Bedford Arms

Wokingham
St Annes Manor

Wolverhampton
Fox
Ravensholt
Wulfrun
York

Woodford Bridge
Woodford Bridge

Woodford Green
Woodford Moat House

Woodhall Spa
Golf

Woodhouse Eaves
The Cottage in the Wood

Woodlands
Woodlands Lodge

Woodstock
Bear

Woody Bay
Woody Bay

Woolacombe
Atlantic
Crossways
Headlands
Little Beach

Woolfardisworthy
Manor House

Woolverton
Woolverton House

Worcester
Park House
Purbani Tandoori
Star

Worthing
Beach
Beechwood Hall
Berkeley
Chatsworth
Eardley

Wrexham
Crest

Wroxham
Hotel Wroxham

Wroxton
Wroxton House

Yarmouth, Great
Carlton
Cliff

Yelverton
Moorland Links

Yeovil
Little Barwick House
Manor

York
Ashcroft
Chase
Kilima
Newington
Sheppard
Town House

Hotels and Restaurants with Subjective Awards

Hotels and restaurants are eligible for a number of subjective awards: *Merit Awards* are used to denote particular aspects of an hotel's operation which are considered to be significantly above the standard implied by the star classification granted. Three aspects of the hotel are assessed for these awards.

H Hospitality, friendliness and service
B Bedrooms
L Lounges, bars and public areas.

The award of *Red Stars* is the ultimate accolade, and is awarded to hotels which are outstanding in all respects.

Rosettes are awarded to hotels and restaurants where our inspectors considered the food was of a particularly high standard.

For further details of these awards see pages 10–11.

England

AVON			
Bath	★★★★	Royal Crescent	*H B L*
	★★★	Priory	❀ **Red Stars**
	✕✕✕	Hole in the Wall	❀
Bristol	★★★★	Grand	– *B* –
	☆☆☆☆	Ladbroke Dragonara	– – *L*
Freshford	★★★🌳	Homewood Park	❀*H B L*
Hunstrete	★★★🌳	Hunstrete House	❀ **Red Stars**
Lympsham	★★🌳	Batch Farm	*H* – *L*
Shipham	★★🌳	Daneswood House	*H* – –
Thornbury	★★★🌳	Thornbury Castle	❀ **Red Stars**
Weston-super-Mare	★★★	Royal Pier	*H* – –
	★★★	Grand Atlantic	– – *L*
	★★	Rozel	*H* – –
BEDFORDSHIRE			
Flitton	✕	White Hart	❀– – –
BERKSHIRE			
Bray	✕✕✕✕	Waterside	❀❀❀– – –
Elcot	★★	Elcot Park	– *B* –
Kintbury	✕✕	Dundas Arms	❀– – –
Maidenhead	★★★	Fredrick's	❀– – –
Shinfield	✕✕	Milton Sandford	❀– – –
Slough	☆☆☆☆	Holiday Inn	– *B* –
Sonning	★★★	White Hart	*H* – –
Streatley	★★★	Swan	– – *L*
Windsor	★★★★	Oakley Court	– *B L*
Yattendon	★★	Royal Oak	*H* – –
BUCKINGHAMSHIRE			
Aston Clinton	★★★	Bell Inn	❀ **Red Stars**
Marlow	★★★★	Compleat Angler	– *B L*
CAMBRIDGESHIRE			
Ely	✕	Old Fire Engine House	❀– – –
Six Mile Bottom	★★★🌳	Swynford Paddocks	– *B* –
CHESHIRE			
Chester	★★★★	Chester Grosvenor	**Red Stars**
Handforth (Manchester Airport)	★★★★	Belfry	❀*H* – –
Mottram St Andrews	★★★	Mottram Hall	– *B* –
Nantwich	★★★🌳	Rookery Hall	❀ **Red Stars**
Parkgate	★★	Ship	– *B* –
Tarporley	★★🌳	Willington Hall	– *B* –
CLEVELAND			
Hartlepool	★★	Grand	– *B* –
Stockton-on-Tees	★★	Parkmore	– *B* –
CORNWALL			
Bude	★★	Burn Court	*H* – –
	★	Penarvor	– – *L*

Place	Classification	Hotel/Restaurant	Awards
Cawsand	★★	Criterion	– – L
Constantine Bay	★★★	Treglos	H – L
Crafthole	★	Whitsand Bay	H – –
Falmouth	★★★🌲	Penmere Manor	H B –
	★★★	St Michael's	H – –
	★★	Carthion	H – L
	★★	Crill House	– B –
Fowey	★★	Marina	H – –
Golant	★★	Cormorant	H – L
Harlyn Bay	★	Polmark	– – L
Helford	XX	Riverside	❀ – –
Helland Bridge	★★★🌲	Tredethy	H – –
Helston	★🌲	Nansloe Manor	– – L
Lamorna Cove	★★★🌲	Lamorna Cove	H – L
	★★🌲	Menwinnion	– – L
Liskeard	★★🌲	Country Castle	H L
Lizard	★★	Housel Bay	– – L
Looe	★★★	Hannafore Point	– – L
	★★	Klymiarven	– – L
Mawgan Porth	★★	Tredragon	H – –
Mount Hawke	★	Tregarthen Cottage	H – L
Mousehole	★★	Lobster Pot	H – –
Newquay	★★★	Bristol	H – L
	★★★	Edgcumbe	H – L
	★★★	Glendorgal	– – L
	★★★	Riviera	– – L
	★★★	Trebarwith	– – L
	★★★	Windsor	– – L
	★★	Cross Mount	H – L
	★★	Whipsiddery	H – L
Pendoggett	★★	Cornish Arms	H – –
Penzance	★★★🌲	Higher Faugan	H – L
	★	Southern Comfort	H – –
Perranporth	★	Beach Dunes	H
Port Gaverne	★★	Port Gaverne	– – L
Portloe	★★	Lugger	H B –
Portscatho	★★	Gerrans Bay	H – L
Rosudgeon	★★	Rosudgeon	H – –
Ruan High Lanes	★★🌲	Polsue Manor	H – –
St Buryan	★	Trevervyn	H – –
St Columb Major	★★	Old Rectory	H – –
St Ives	★★★	Garrack	H – –
	★★	Boskerris	H – L
	★	Ocean Breezes	H – –
St Keyne	★★🌲	Old Rectory	– – L
St Mawes	★★★	Tresanton	**Red Stars**
St Mellion	☆☆☆	St Mellion	– – L
Sennen	★★	Tregiffian	– – L
Talland Bay	★★★🌲	Talland Bay	– – L
Tintagel	★★	Atlantic View	H – –
Veryan	★★★	Nare	– – L
CUMBRIA			
Alston	★★🌲	Lovelady Shield	H – L
Ambleside	★★★	Rothay Manor	❀H B L
	★★	Kirkstone Foot	H B L
	★★	Wateredge	– – L
	★	Nanny Brow	H – L
Bassenthwaite	★★🌲	Overwater Hall	H – L
	★★	Pheasant Inn	– – L
Borrowdale	★★★★	Lodore Swiss	**Red Stars**
	★★	Borrowdale	H B L
Brampton	★★🌲	Farlam Hall	❀ **Red Stars**
	★★	Tarn End	❀ –
Cartmel	★★	Aynsome Manor	– B –
Crosby-on-Eden	★★🌲	Crosby Lodge	H – –
Faugh	★★★	String of Horses	– B –
Grange (in-Borrowdale)	★★	Gates Country House	– – L
Grange-over-Sands	★★	Graythwaite Manor	– – L
	★	Methven	H – –
Grasmere	★★★🌲	Michael's Nook	❀H B L
	★★★	Swan	– B L
	★★	Oak Bank	H – –
	★★	Ravenswood	– B –
	★	White Moss House	❀ **Red Stars**

Kendal	✕	Castle Dairy	❀ – – –
Keswick	★★	Grange	– B L
	★★	Underscar	H – L
	★	Crow Park	– B –
Longtown	★🌲	March Bank	H – –
Penrith	★★	George	H – –
Pooley Bridge	★★★🌲	Sharrow Bay	❀❀ **Red Stars**
Temple Sowerby	★★	Temple Sowerby House	– B L
Watermillock	★★★🌲	Leeming House	H B L
	★🌲	Old Church	H – L
Wetheral	★★★	Crown	H B L
Whitehaven	★★🌲	Roseneath	– – L
Windermere	★★★🌲	Langdale Chase	H – L
	★★★	Wild Boar	– B L
	★★	Hideaway	H B –
	★★🌲	Holbeck Ghyll	– B L
	★★🌲	Lindeth Fell	H B L
	★★🌲	Linthwaite	H B L
	★★	Miller Howe	❀❀ **Red Stars**
	★★	Royal	H – –
	★	Ravensworth	H B L
	★	Willowsmere	H – –
	✕	Porthole Eating House	❀ – – –
Workington	★★	Clifton	H – –
DERBYSHIRE			
Bakewell	★	Milford House	H – –
Baslow	★★★	Cavendish	– B L
Derby	★★	Clarendon	H – –
Draycott	★★★	Tudor Court	H – L
Matlock	★★★🌲	Riber Hall	– B –
Thorpe (Dovedale)	★★★	Peveril of the Peak	– B –
DEVON			
Ashburton	★★🌲	Holne Chase	H – –
Barnstaple	★★🌲	Downrew House	**Red Stars**
Bovey Tracey	★★	Coombe Cross	– – L
	★★🌲	Prestbury Country House	H B L
	★	Redacre	– – L
Bradworthy	★	Lake Villa	H B –
Chagford	★★★🌲	Gidleigh Park	❀ **Red Stars**
	★★★🌲	Great Tree	H B –
	★★★🌲	Mill End	H – L
	★★★🌲	Teignworthy House	❀ H – –
	★	Easton Court	– B L
Clawton	★★🌲	Court Barn	H – L
Dartmouth	✕✕	Carved Angel	❀ – – –
Ermington	★★	Ermewood House	H B –
Exeter	★★★	Buckerell Lodge	H – –
	★★★	Gipsy Hill	– B L
Gittisham	★★🌲	Combe House	❀ **Red Stars**
Gulworthy	✕✕✕	Horn of Plenty	❀ – – –
Haytor	★★🌲	Bel Alp	H – –
Heddon's Mouth	★★🌲	Heddon's Gate	H B L
Holbeton	★★★🌲	Alston Hall	– – L
Honiton	★★★🌲	Deer Park	H – L
Hope Cove	★★	Lantern Lodge	H – L
Horns Cross	★★🌲	Foxdown Manor	– B L
Ilfracombe	★★	Imperial	– – L
Kennford	★★	Fairwinds	– B –
Kingsbridge	★★🌲	Buckland-Tout-Saints	**Red Stars**
Lydford	★🌲	Lydford House	H – –
Lynton	★★★	Lynton Cottage	H – L
	★★	Crown	– B –
	★★	Rockvale	H B –
	★	Chough's Nest	– B –
	★🌲	Combe Park	H – L
	★	Seawood	– B L
Martinhoe	★🌲	Old Rectory	H B L
Mary Tavy	★🌲	Moorland Hall	H – –
Moretonhampstead	★★🌲	Glebe House	H – –
Newton Ferrers	★★🌲	Court House	H – –
Ottery St Mary	★★★	Salston	H – –
Paignton	★★★	Redcliffe	H – –
Plymouth	☆☆☆☆	Holiday Inn	– – L

Hotels and Restaurants with Subjective Awards

Town	Classification	Hotel/Restaurant	Awards
Plymouth	★★★	Astor	– – L
	✕	Chez Nous	❀– – –
Putsborough	★★★	Putsborough Sands	H – –
Salcombe	★★★★	Marine	H – L
	★★★	Salcombe	H – –
	★★★	Tides Reach	❀H B L
	★★	Castle Point	H – –
	★★	Soar Mill Cove	H – –
	★★	South Sands	H – –
	★	Wells	H – –
Saunton	★★★★	Saunton Sands	H – –
Sidmouth	★★★★	Victoria	H – L
	★★★	Riviera	H – –
	★★★	Westcliff	H – –
	★★	Littlecourt	H – –
Stoke Gabriel	★★♣	Gabriel Court	H – –
Teignmouth	★★	Venn Farm Country House	H – –
Thurlestone	★★★	Thurlestone	H – L
	★★	Furzey Close	H – –
Torquay	★★★	Devonshire	H – –
	★★★	Homers	H B L
	★★★	Kistor	H – L
	★★★	Livermead Cliff	H – L
	★★★	Livermead House	H – L
	★★★	Toorak	H – L
	★★	Ardmore	H – –
	★★	Balmoral	– – L
	★★	Orestone House	H B –
Umberleigh	★★	Rising Sun	– B –
Uplyme	★★★	Devon	H – –
Whimple	★★♣	Woodhayes	H B L
Wilmington	★★	Home Farm	H – L
Woodford Bridge	★★★	Woodford Bridge	❀H B L
Woody Bay	★★	Woody Bay	H – –
Woolacombe	★★★	Narracott Grand	H – L
	★★★	Watersmeet	H – –
	★★	Beach	H B –
	★★	Little Beach	– B –
	★	Crossways	H B –
Yelverton	★★★	Moorland Links	– – L
DORSET			
Bournemouth & Boscombe	★★★★★	Royal Bath	– – L
	★★★	Burley Court	H – –
	★★★	Cliffside	H – –
	★★★	Grosvenor	– – L
	★★★	Langtry Manor	– B –
	★★★	Pavilion	H – –
	★★	Hinton Firs	– – L
	★★	Tralee	– – L
Lyme Regis	★★★	Mariners	H – –
Poole	★★★★	Hospitality Inn	H – –
	★★	Sea Witch	H – –
Sturminster Newton	✕✕	Plumber Manor	❀– – –
Swanage	★★★	Pines	H – –
	★	Sefton	H – –
Wareham	★★★	Priory	❀H B –
CO DURHAM			
Bishop Auckland	★★	Park Head	H B –
Coatham Mundeville	★★★♣	Hall Garth	– – L
Middleton-in-Teesdale	★★	Teesdale	– B –
Romaldkirk	★★	Rose & Crown	– B –
ESSEX			
Braintree	★★	White Hart	– B –
Chesterford, Great	★★	Crown House	H – –
Coggeshall	★★★	White Hart	H – –
Dedham	★★★♣	Maison Talbooth (& Le Talbooth)	❀ **Red Stars**
	★★	Dedham Vale	– B –
Dunmow, Great	★★	Saracens Head	– – L
	★★	Starr	❀– – –
Frinton-on-Sea	★★	Maplin	H – –
	★	Rock	H – –
Saffron Walden	★	Saffron	H – –

GLOUCESTERSHIRE

Town	Rating	Hotel / Restaurant	Awards
Amberley	★★	Amberley Inn	H – –
Berkeley Road	★★	Prince of Wales	– B –
Bibury	★★★	Swan	– – L
	★★🌳	Bibury Court	– – L
Blockley	★★	Lower Brook House	❀ – – –
Buckland	★★★🌳	Buckland Manor	❀ H B L
Chalford	★★	Springfield House	H – –
Cheltenham	★★★	De La Bere	– – L
	★★★🌳	Greenway	❀ Red Stars
	★★★	Wyastone	– B –
Chipping Campden	★★	King's Arms	❀ – – –
Cirencester	★★★★	King's Head	H – –
	★★★	Stratton House	– – L
Cleeve Hill	★★	Rising Sun	– B –
	XXX	Malvern View	❀ – – –
Coleford	★🌳	Lambsquay	H – –
Fairford	★	Hyperion House	H B –
Gloucester	☆☆☆	Crest	– B –
	★★★	Tara	– B –
Lower Slaughter	★★★🌳	Manor	– B L
Moreton-in-Marsh	★★★	Manor House	– B –
	XXX	Lambs	❀ – – –
Northleach	X	Country Friends	❀ – – –
Painswick	★★★	Painswick	H B L
Stinchcombe	★★🌳	Stinchcombe Manor Country House	– B –
Stow-on-the-Wold	★★	Old Stocks	H – –
	★★	Unicorn	– B –
	X	Rafters	❀ – – –
Stroud	★★★	Burleigh Court	H – –
Tetbury	★★★	Close	❀ H – –
Tewkesbury	☆☆☆	Tewkesbury Park	– B –
	★	Tudor House	– B –
Upper Slaughter	★★★🌳	Lords of the Manor	– – L

HAMPSHIRE

Town	Rating	Hotel / Restaurant	Awards
Alton	★★	Grange	H – –
Beaulieu	★★★	Montagu Arms	– – L
Bransgore	★★★🌳	Harrow Lodge	H – –
Grayshott	X	Woods	❀ – – –
Hayling Island	★★	Newtown House	H – L
Lymington	★★★🌳	Passford House	H – L
	★★	Stanwell House	– B –
	X	Limpets	❀ – – –
Lyndhurst	★★★🌳	Parkhill	– – L
	★	Forest Point	H – –
Middle Wallop	★★	Fifehead Manor	– – L
New Milton	★★★★🌳	Chewton Glen	❀❀ Red Stars
Portsmouth & Southsea	☆☆☆☆	Holiday Inn	– B L
Southampton	X	Golden Palace	❀ – – –
Wickham	★★	Old House	❀ – B –
Winchester	★★★🌳	Lainston House	– B L

HEREFORD & WORCESTER

Town	Rating	Hotel / Restaurant	Awards
Abberley	★★★🌳	Elms	❀ Red Stars
Broadway	★★★★	Lygon Arms	Red Stars
	★★★	Broadway	H – –
	★★★	Dormy House	H B –
	★★🌳	Collin House	H B –
Bromsgrove	XXX	Grafton Manor	❀ – – –
Corse Lawn	XXX	Corse Lawn House	❀ – – –
Droitwich	★★★★	Château Impney	H – –
Hereford	★★	Merton	– B –
Malvern, Great	★★	Cotford	H – –
	★★	Walmer Lodge	❀ – – –
Malvern Wells	★★★🌳	Cottage in the Wood	– – L
	XX	Croque en Bouche	❀ – – –
Much Birch	★★★	Pilgrim House	– B –
Ross-on-Wye	★★★	Chase	H – –
	★★★	Pengethley	H – –
	★★★	Royal	H – –
Worcester	XX	Brown's	❀ – – –
Wyre Piddle	★	Avonside	H – L

HERTFORDSHIRE			
Harpenden	★★★	Glen Eagle	*H* – –
Newgate Street	★★★	Ponsbourne	– – *L*
St Albans	✕	La Province	❀– – –
HUMBERSIDE			
Flamborough	★★	Timoneer Country Manor	– *B* –
KENT			
Ashford	★★★★♜	Eastwell Manor	– *B* *L*
Cranbrook	★★♜	Kennel Holt	– *B* *L*
Dover	☆☆☆	Dover Motel	*H* – –
Faversham	✕✕	Read's	❀– – –
Goudhurst	★★	Star & Eagle	– *B* –
Hollingbourne	★★★	Great Danes	– – *L*
Igtham	✕✕	Town House	❀– – –
Ramsgate	★★	Savoy	*H* – –
Tunbridge Wells (Royal)	★★★	Spa	– – *L*
	★★	Wellington	– – *L*
Whitstable	★★	Marine	– – *L*
	✕	Le Pousse Bedaine	❀– – –
LANCASHIRE			
Hurst Green	★★	Shireburn Arms	– *B* –
Lancaster	☆☆☆	Post House	– – *L*
Lytham St Annes	★★★	Grand	– *B* –
Whittle-le-Woods	★★★	Shaw Hill Golf & Country Club	– *B* –
LEICESTERSHIRE			
Lyddington	★★	Marquis of Exeter	– – *L*
Melton Mowbray	★★★	George	*H* *B* –
Oakham	★★★♜	Hambleton Hall	❀ **Red Stars**
Rothley	★★★	Rothley Court	– – *L*
LINCOLNSHIRE			
Lincoln	★★	Castle	– *B* –
	★★	Grand	*H* – –
	✕	White's	❀– – –
Market Rasen	★★	Limes	*H* – –
Woodhall Spa	★★	Golf	– *B* –
LONDON (POSTAL DISTRICTS)			
EC1	✕	Bubbs	❀– – –
EC2	✕✕✕	Le Poulbot	❀❀– – –
EC4	✕	Le Gamin	❀– – –
N1	✕✕✕	Carriers	❀– – –
NW3	☆☆☆☆	Holiday Inn	– *B* *L*
SW1	★★★★★	Berkeley	**Red Stars**
	★★★★★	Hyatt Carlton Tower (Chelsea Room)	❀– – –
	★★★★★	Hyde Park	– *B* –
	★★★★★	Sheraton Park Tower	– *B* –
	★★★★	Goring	**Red Stars**
	☆☆☆☆	Holiday Inn Chelsea	– – *L*
	★★★	Lowndes	– *B* –
	★★★	Royal Horseguards	– – *L*
	★	Ebury Court	**Red Star**
	✕✕	Ken Lo's Memories of China	❀– – –
	✕✕	Mijanou	❀– – –
	✕✕	Pomegranates	❀– – –
	✕✕	Salloos	❀– – –
SW3	★★★★	Capital	❀ **Red Stars**
	★★★	Basil Street	– – *L*
	✕✕	Tante Claire	❀❀– – –
	✕✕	Daphne's	❀– – –
	✕✕	English Garden	❀– – –
	✕✕	English House	❀– – –
	✕	Ma Cuisine	❀– – –
	✕✕✕	Waltons	❀– – –
	✕	Dan's	❀– – –
SW7	✕✕	Shezan	❀– – –
SW8	✕✕	Chez Nico	❀❀– – –
	✕✕	Alonso's	❀– – –
	✕✕	L'Arlequin	❀– – –
W1	★★★★★	Claridge's	**Red Stars**

Location	Classification	Name	Rosettes	Awards
	★★★★★	Connaught	❀❀	Red Stars
	★★★★★	Dorchester (Terrace Room)	❀❀❀	Red Stars
	★★★★★	Grosvenor House		– – L
	★★★★★	Hilton International		– – L
	★★★★★	Inn on the Park		– B L
	★★★★★	Inter-Continental		– – L
	★★★★★	Ritz		– – L
	★★★★	Athanaeum		Red Stars
	★★★★	Brown's	❀	– – L
	☆☆☆☆	Holiday Inn		– B L
	★★★★	Park Lane		– – L
	★★★	Chesterfield		H B –
	★★★	New Berners		– B –
	★★	Bryanston Court		H – –
	✕✕✕✕	Le Gavroche	❀❀❀	– – –
	✕	Chuen Cheng Ku	❀	– – –
	✕✕	Gay Hussar	❀	– – –
	✕✕	Odins	❀	– – –
W2	★★★★	Royal Lancaster		– – L
W11	✕✕✕	Leiths	❀	– – –
	✕✕	Chez Moi	❀	– – –
WC2	★★★★★	Savoy		Red Stars
	★★★★	Waldorf		– – L
	✕✕✕	Boulestin	❀	– – –
	✕✕✕✕	Inigo Jones	❀	– – –
	✕✕	Interlude de Tabaillau	❀	– – –
	✕✕	Poons (King St)	❀	– – –
	✕	Poons (Leicester St)	❀	– – –
LONDON, GREATER				
Heathrow Airport	☆☆☆☆	Holiday Inn		– B –
	☆☆☆☆	Sheraton		– – L
Richmond upon Thames	✕✕	Lichfields	❀	– – –
Surbiton	✕✕	Chez Max	❀	– – –
Woodford Bridge	★★	Prince Regent		– – L
MANCHESTER, GREATER				
Altrincham	★★★	Bowdon		H – –
Bolton	★★★ (country house)	Egerton House		– B –
Bury	✕✕	Normandie	❀	– – –
Manchester	✕✕	Isola Bella	❀	– – –
	✕	Yang Sing	❀	– – –
MERSEYSIDE				
Birkenhead	★★★	Bowler Hat		– B –
	★★	Riverhill		H – –
Liverpool	☆☆☆☆	Holiday Inn		– B –
NORFOLK				
Aldborough	✕✕	Old Red Lion	❀	– – –
Brockdish	✕✕	Sheriff House	❀	– – –
Bunwell	★★ (country house)	Bunwell Manor		– B L
Burnham Market	✕	Fishes	❀	– – –
Grimston	★★★ (country house)	Congham Hall	❀	H B L
Shipdham	★★	Shipdham Place		– B L
Thetford	★★★	Bell		– B L
Titchwell	★★	Manor		H B L
Witchingham, Great	★★ (country house)	Lenwade House		– B L
Wymondham	✕	Bullens	❀	– – –
Yarmouth, Great	★★	Cliff		– B L
NORTHAMPTONSHIRE				
Horton	✕✕	French Partridge	❀	– – –
Wellingborough	★	High View		– B –
NORTHUMBERLAND				
Cornhill-on-Tweed	★★★ (country house)	Tillmouth Park		– – L
Hexham	★★	County		H B L
Longhorsley	★★★★	Linden Hall		– B L
Seahouses	★★	Dunes		– – L
NOTTINGHAMSHIRE				
Nottingham	★★★	Bestwood Lodge		– – L
	★★★	North Lodge		– – L

Town	Classification	Hotel / Restaurant	Rosettes	H	B	L
Retford (East)	★★★	West Retford		–	B	L
Tuxford	★★	Newcastle Arms		–	–	L
OXFORDSHIRE						
Abingdon	★★	Upper Reaches		–	B	–
Horton-cum-Studley	★★★🌳	Studley Priory	❀	–	–	–
North Stoke	★★★	Springs		H	–	L
Oxford	✕✕	Les Quat'Saisons	❀❀	–	–	–
	✕✕✕	Elizabeth	❀	–	–	–
	✕	Wrens	❀	–	–	–
Thame	★★★	Spread Eagle		H	–	–
Wallingford	★★	Shillingford Bridge		–	–	L
Woodstock	★★★	Bear		–	B	–
SHROPSHIRE						
Ludlow	★★★	Feathers		H	B	–
Oswestry	★★🌳	Sweeney Hall		–	–	L
Shifnal	★★★	Park House		H	–	–
Telford	★★★	Buckatree Hall		–	B	–
	☆☆☆	Telford Hotel Golf & Country Club		–	B	–
Weston	★★★	Hawkestone Park		H	–	–
SOMERSET						
Bilbrook	★★	Dragon House	**Red Stars**			
Bridgwater	★★	Royal Clarence		–	–	L
Burnham-on-Sea	★★	Dunstan House		–	B	–
Castle Cary	★★	George		–	B	–
Crewkerne	★★	Old Parsonage		H	B	–
Dulverton	★★★🌳	Carnarvon Arms		H	–	L
	★★🌳	Three Acres		H	–	–
Dunster	★★★	Luttrell Arms		H	–	–
	★★	Exmoor House		H	–	L
Exford	★★	Crown		–	B	–
Hatch Beauchamp	★★	Farthings		H	B	L
Minehead	★★★	Benares		H	–	–
	★★★	Northfield		H	–	L
	★★	Remuera		H	–	L
	★★	Winsor		–	–	L
	★★🌳	Woodcombe Lodge		H	–	–
	★	Kingsway		H	–	–
	★	Mentone		H	–	–
North Petherton	★★	Walnut Tree		–	B	–
Porlock Weir	★★	Cottage		H	–	–
Simonsbath	★★🌳	Simonsbath House	**Red Stars**			
Ston Easton	★★★🌳	Ston Easton Park	❀ **Red Stars**			
Taunton	★★★★	Castle	❀	H	–	–
Watchet	★★	Downfield		H	B	L
Wells	★★★	Swan		–	B	–
	★★	Crown		H	–	–
	★	Worth House		H	–	–
Williton	★★	White House	❀	–	–	–
Wincanton	★★🌳	Holbrook House		H	–	–
Winsford	★★	Royal Oak		–	–	L
Withypool	★★	Royal Oak		–	B	–
	★🌳	Wester Close		H	B	–
Wiveliscombe	★	Langley House	❀ **Red Stars**			
Woolverton	★★	Woolverton House		H	–	–
Yeovil	★★★	Manor Crest		–	B	–
STAFFORDSHIRE						
Burton-on-Trent	★★	Brookhouse Inn		H	B	–
Newcastle Under Lyme	★	Denesfield		H	–	–
Stone	★★★	Crown		–	B	–
SUFFOLK						
Bury St Edmunds	★★★	Angel		–	B	L
Fressingfield	✕	Fox and Goose	❀	–	–	–
Ipswich	★★★	Belstead Brook		–	B	–
	★★★	Marlborough	❀	H	B	–
Lavenham	★★★	Swan		–	–	L
Needham Market	★★	Limes		–	B	–
Woodbridge	★★★🌳	Seckford Hall		–	–	L
SURREY						
Ashtead	✕	Snooty Fox	❀	–	–	–

Burgh Heath	☆☆	Pickard Motor	– B –
Churt	★★★	Frensham Pond	– – L
Dorking	★★★	Burford Bridge	– – L
Farnham	★★★	Bush	– – L
Haslemere	✕	Morels	❀– – –
Staines	★★	Pack Horse	– – L
Walton on the Hill	✕✕	Ebenezer Cottage	❀– – –
Weybridge	★★★	Oatlands Park	– – L

SUSSEX, EAST & WEST

Alfriston (E)	★★★	Star Inn	– – L
Ashington (W)	★★	Mill House	H – –
Battle (E)	★★★♣	Netherfield Place	– B L
Bognor Regis (W)	★★★	Royal Norfolk	– B –
	★	Lyndhurst	H – –
Bosham (W)	★★	Millstream	– B –
Brighton & Hove (E)	★★★	Courtlands	– B –
Chilgrove (W)	✕✕	White Horse Inn	❀– – –
Climping (W)	★★★♣	Bailiffscourt	– B L
Cuckfield (W)	★★★	Ockenden Manor	– B –
Eastbourne (E)	★★★★	Queens	H – –
	★★★	Imperial	– – L
	★★★	Lansdowne	– – L
	★★	Farrar's	H – –
East Grinstead (W)	★★★♣	Gravetye Manor	❀ **Red Stars**
Pulborough (W)	✕	Stane Street Hollow	❀– – –
Rottingdean (E)	★★	White Horse	– B –
Rushlake Green (E)	★★★♣	Priory Country House	**Red Stars**
Selmeston (E)	✕	Corins	❀– – –
Stone Cross (E)	★★★♣	Glyndley Manor	– – L
Storrington (W)	✕✕✕	Manleys	❀– – –
Thakeham (W)	★★★♣	Little Thakeham	– B L
Wadhurst (E)	★★♣	Spindlewood	❀– – –
Worthing (W)	★★★	Beach	– – L

TYNE & WEAR

Newcastle upon Tyne	★★★★	Gosforth Park	– B –
Seaton Burn	☆☆☆☆	Holiday Inn	– B –

WARWICKSHIRE

Billesley	★★★♣	Billesley Manor	– B L
Ettington	★★♣	Chase	❀H B –
Kenilworth	✕✕	Diments	❀– – –
Leamington Spa	★★♣	Mallory Court	❀ **Red Stars**
	★	Lansdowne	H B –
Stratford-upon-Avon	★★★★	Hilton	– – L
	★★★★	Welcombe	H – –

WEST MIDLANDS

Birmingham	☆☆☆☆	Holiday Inn	– B –
	★★★★	Plough & Harrow	❀– B –
	✕✕	Rajdoot	❀– – –
Coventry	★★★	Chace	– B –
Dorridge	★★	Forest	– B –
Knowle	★★	Greswolde Arms	– B –
Oldbury	✕✕	Jonathans'	❀– – –
Walsall	★★★	Barons Court	– B –

WILTSHIRE

Barford St Martin	✕✕	Michel's	❀– – –
Castle Combe	★★★♣	Manor House	– – L
Corsham	★★	Rudloe Park	– B –
Malmesbury	★★★♣	Whatley Manor	H – L
	★★★	Old Bell	H – –
Melksham	★★★	Beechfield House	❀– B –
Salisbury	★★	Old Bell Inn	❀H – –
	✕	Cranes	❀– – –
Swindon	★★★★	Blunsdon House	H – –
Trowbridge	★	Hilbury Court	– B –
Warminster	★★★♣	Bishopstrow House	❀ **Red Stars**

YORKSHIRE (NORTH, SOUTH & WEST)

Barnsley (S)	★★	Queens	– B –
Bolton Abbey (N)	★★★	Devonshire Arms	– – L
Boroughbridge (N)	★★★	Crown	H B L

Location	Classification	Establishment			
Brompton by Sawdon (N)	✕	Brompton Forge	❀–	–	–
Crathorne (N)	★★★★	Crathorne	–	–	L
Cullingworth (W)	★★★	Five Flags	–	B	–
Doncaster (S)	★★	Regent	–	B	–
Fadmoor (N)	✕	Plough Inn	❀–	–	–
Hackness (N)	★★★🌲	Hackness Grange	H	–	–
Halifax (W)	★★★	Holdsworth House	–	B	L
Harrogate (N)	★★★	Studley	–	B	–
	★★	Hotel Italia	–	–	L
	★	Gables	H	B	–
	✕✕	Number Six	❀–	–	–
Helmsley (N)	★★★	Black Swan	–	B	L
Holywell Green (W)	★★	Rock Inn	–	B	–
Hovingham (N)	★★	Worsley Arms	–	–	L
Ilkley (W)	★	Grove	–	B	–
	✕✕✕	Box Tree	❀❀–	–	–
Kildwick (W)	★★★	Kildwick Hall	H	B	–
Kirkby Fleetham (N)	★★★🌲	Kirkby Fleetham Hall	H	B	–
Kirkby Moorside (N)	★★	George and Dragon	–	B	–
Markington (N)	★★★🌲	Hob Green	–	B	L
Masham (N)	★★🌲	Jervaulx Hall	H	–	–
Pool in Wharfedale (W)	✕✕✕	Pool Court	❀–	–	–
Ravenscar (N)	★★	Raven Hall	H	–	–
Rotherham (S)	☆☆☆☆	Carlton Park	–	–	L
Scarborough (N)	★★★★	Royal	–	B	–
	★★🌲	Wrea Head	–	–	L
	★	Dorchester	H	–	–
Walshford (N)	✕✕✕	Bridge Inn (Byron Room)	❀–	–	–
Wentbridge (W)	★★★🌲	Wentbridge House	H	–	–
Whitwell-on-the-Hill (N)	★★🌲	Whitwell Hall	–	–	L
York (N)	★★★	Fairfield Manor	–	–	L
	★	Town House	H	–	–

ISLES OF SCILLY

Location	Classification	Establishment			
Old Grimsby, Tresco	★★★	Island	❀H	–	–

ISLE OF WIGHT

Location	Classification	Establishment			
Bembridge	★★🌲	Elm Country	–	B	L
	★★	Highbury	Red Stars		
Freshwater	★★★	Albion	H	–	–
St Helens	✕	Hayloft	❀–	–	–
St Lawrence	★★	Rocklands	H	–	–
Ventnor	★★★	Ventnor Towers	H	–	–
	★★★🌲	Winterbourne	–	B	L
	★🌲	Madeira Hall	–	–	L

Channel Islands

Location	Classification	Establishment			
Archirondel, Jersey	★★	Les Arches	–	B	–
Bouley Bay, Jersey	★★★★	Water's Edge	H	–	L
St Brelade, Jersey	★★★★	Hotel L'Horizon (Star Grill)	❀–	–	–
	★★★★	La Place	–	B	L
	★★★	Chateau Valeuse	❀–	–	–
St Clement's Bay, Jersey	★★★	Ambassadeur	–	–	L
St Helier, Jersey	★★★★	Grand (Victoria's)	❀–	–	L
	★★★	Pomme D'Or	–	B	L
	★★	Savoy	–	–	L
	✕✕	Mauro's	❀–	–	–
St Lawrence, Jersey	★★★	Little Grove	H	B	–
St Martin, Guernsey	★★★	Ronnie Ronalde's	H	–	–
St Peter Port, Guernsey	★★★	La Frégate	❀–	–	–
	★★	Dunchoille	–	–	L
St Saviour, Jersey	★★★★🌲	Longueville Manor	❀ Red Stars		
Sark	✕✕	Aval du Creux Hotel	❀–	–	–

Wales

CLWYD

Location	Classification	Establishment			
Colwyn Bay	★★★	Norfolk House	H	–	L
	☆☆☆	Hotel 70°	❀–	–	L
	★	St Enoch's	–	–	L
Glyn Ceiriog	★	Glyn Valley	H	–	–
Llanarmon Dyffryn Ceriog	★★★	Hand	H	–	–

	★★	West Arms		–	–	L
Llangollen	★★	Tyn-y-Wern		–	–	L
DYFED						
Ammanford	★★	Mill at Glynhir		–	B	–
Crugybar	★★🌳	Glanrannel Park		H	–	–
Eglwysfach	★★★🌳	Ynyshir Hall	❀	–	–	–
Gwbert-on-Sea	★★★	Cliff		–	–	L
Lampeter	★★	Falcondale		H	B	–
Letterston	★★	Brynawelon		–	B	–
Llandeilo	★★	Cawdor Arms		–	B	L
Llangadog	★★🌳	Plas Glansevin		H	–	–
Pembroke	★★	Old King's Arms		–	B	–
Pontargothi	★★	Cothi Bridge		H	–	–
St David's	★★★🌳	Warpool Court		–	B	–
Tenby	★★	Atlantic		H	–	–
GLAMORGAN (MID, SOUTH & WEST)						
Bridgend (M)	☆☆☆	Heronston		–	B	–
Cardiff (S)	★★★★	Park		–	B	–
	✕	Gibsons	❀	–	–	–
Porthcawl (M)	★★	Maid of Sker		–	B	–
	★	Brentwood		–	B	–
Swansea (W)	★	Windsor Lodge		H	B	–
GWENT						
Abergavenny	★★	Llanwenarth Arms		–	B	–
Chepstow	★★	Castle View		H	–	–
Llandewi Skirrid	✕	Walnut Tree	❀	–	–	–
Newport	★★★★	Celtic Manor		–	B	L
Usk	✕	Mr Midgley's	❀	–	–	–
Whitebrook	★★🌳	Crown at Whitebrook	❀	H	–	–
GWYNEDD						
Aberdovey	★★★🌳	Plas Penhelig		–	B	L
Abersoch	★★★🌳	Porth Tocyn	❀	H	–	L
Bangor	★★	Ty-Uchaf		–	–	L
	★★	Telford		H	–	–
Beaumaris	★★	Bishopgate House		H	–	–
Beddgelert	★🌳	Bryn Eglwys		H	–	–
Bontddu	★★★	Bontddu Hall		H	–	L
Llanbedr	★★	Ty Mawr		H	–	–
Llanbedrog	★★	Bryn Derwen		–	B	–
Llanberis	★★	Gallt-y-Glyn		H	–	–
Llandudno	★★★🌳	Bodysgallen Hall		**Red Stars**		
	★★★	Empire		–	–	L
	★★★	St George's		–	–	L
	★★	Bromwell Court		–	B	–
	★★	St Tudno		H	B	L
	★	Fairhaven		–	B	–
	★	Min-y-Don		H	–	–
	★	Sunnymede		–	–	L
Llanrwst	★★★🌳	Gwesty Plas Maenan		–	–	L
Llanwnda	☆☆☆	Stables		–	B	–
Pennal	★★★	Plas Talgarth Hall		–	B	–
	★★🌳	Llugwy		–	–	L
Red Wharf Bay	★	Min-y-Don		–	–	L
Roewen	★🌳	Tir-y-Coed		–	B	L
Tal-y-Bont	☆☆	Lodge	❀	–	–	–
Tal-y-Llyn	★	Minffordd		H	B	–
POWYS						
Builth Wells	★★🌳	Caer Beris Manor		H	–	–
Crickhowell	★★🌳	Gliffaes		H	–	L
	★	Bear		H	–	–
Glasbury on Wye	★★	Llwynaubach Lodge		H	–	–
Hay on Wye	★	Old Black Lion		–	B	–
Llanfyllin	★★🌳	Bodfach Hall		–	B	L
Llangurig	★	Glan Severn Arms		–	–	L
Llangynog	★	New Inn		H	–	–
Presteigne	★★	Radnorshire Arms		–	–	L
Three Cocks	★★	Three Cocks	❀	H	–	–

Scotland

BORDERS			
Broughton	★★	Greenmantle	H – –
Dryburgh	★★★⌂	Dryburgh Abbey	– – L
Melrose	★★	Burt's	– – L
Peebles	★★⌂	Cringletie House	H – L
CENTRAL			
Callander	★★★⌂	Roman Camp	– B L
	★	Lubnaig	– B L
	★	Bridgend House	H – L
Falkirk	✕	Pierre's	❀ – –
Kinbuck	★★★⌂	Cromlix House	❀H B L
Lochearnhead	★	Craigroyston House	– – L
Strathblane	★★★	Country Club	– B –
DUMFRIES AND GALLOWAY			
Canonbie	✕	Riverside	❀– – –
Crocketford	★★	Galloway Arms	H – –
Eskdalemuir	★★	Hart Manor	H – –
Gatehouse of Fleet	★★★	Murray Arms	– – L
Moffat	★★	Beechwood	❀H B –
Newton Stewart	★★★⌂	Kirroughtree	– B L
Portpatrick	★★⌂	Knockinaam Lodge	❀ **Red Stars**
Port William	★★★⌂	Corsemalzie House	– B L
Rockcliffe	★★★⌂	Barons Craig	– – L
Stranraer	★★★	North West Castle Hotel	– – L
Wamphray	★	Red House	H – –
FIFE			
Anstruther	✕✕	Cellar	❀– – –
Dunfermline	★★★	Keavil House	– B –
Elie	★★	Golf	H – L
Peat Inn	✕✕	Peat Inn	❀– – –
St Andrews	★★★	Rufflets	H – L
Letham	★★★⌂	Fernie Castle	– B L
GRAMPIAN			
Aberdeen	☆☆☆☆	Holiday Inn Bucksburn	– B –
	☆☆☆	Royal Darroch	– B –
	☆☆☆☆	Skean Dhu, Altens	– B –
Aberdeen Airport	☆☆☆☆	Skean Dhu	– B –
Aboyne	★★	Birse Lodge	H B –
Ballater	★★	Craigard	H – –
	★★	Darroch Learg	H – L
Banchory	★★★⌂	Banchory Lodge	**Red Stars**
Banff	★★	County	H – L
	★	Fife Lodge	– B –
Cullen	★★★	Seafield Arms	– – L
Drybridge	✕✕	Old Monastery	❀– – –
Forres	★★	Royal	– B –
Glenlivet	★★	Minmore House	– – L
Kildrummy	★★★⌂	Kildrummy Castle	H B L
Newburgh	★★	Udny Arms	❀– B L
Peterhead	☆☆☆	Waterside Inn	– B –
Rothes	★★★⌂	Rothes Glen	– – L
HIGHLAND			
Achnasheen	★★⌂	Ledgowan Lodge	H – –
Ardelve	★	Loch Duich	❀H – L
Arisaig	★★★⌂	Arisaig House	❀H B L
Aviemore	★★	Lynwig	H – –
Balmacara	★★	Balmacara	H – L
Banavie	★★	Moorings	H – L
Cromarty	★★	Royal	H – –
Daviot	★★	Meallmore Lodge	H – –
Drumnadrochit	★★⌂	Polmaily House	H B L
Dulnain Bridge	★★⌂	Muckrach Lodge	❀H – –
	★★	Skye of Curr	H B L
Duntulm	★★	Duntulm	– – L
Duror	★★	Stewart	– – L
Fort Augustus	★★	Lovat Arms	H – –
Fort William	★★★★⌂	Inverlochy Castle	❀❀ **Red Stars**
Glenborrodale	★★⌂	Glenborrodale Castle	– B L
	★★	Clan Morrison	– B –

Harlosh	★	Harlosh	H	–	–
Invergarry	★★🌲	Glengarry Castle	–	–	L
Inverness	★★★★🌲	Culloden House	H	B	L
	★★★	Kingsmill	H	B	L
	★★🌲	Dunain Park	❀ **Red Stars**		
Invershin	★★	Invershin	H	–	–
Kentallen	★★🌲	Ardsheal House	❀H	B	L
Kincraig	★★	Ossian	H	–	–
Kingussie	★	Osprey	❀H	–	–
	★	Columba	❀H	–	–
Knock	★★	Toravaig House	H	–	–
Laggan Bridge	★	Monadhliath	H	–	–
Letterfinlay	★★	Letterfinlay Lodge	H	–	L
Muir of Ord	★★🌲	Ord House	–	–	L
	★★	Ord Arms	–	B	–
Nairn	★★	Clifton	❀H	B	L
Nethy Bridge	★★★	Nethy Bridge	H	–	–
Newtonmore	★	Ard na Coille	H	–	–
Onich	★★	Creag Dhu	–	–	L
Plockton	★	Haven	H	–	L
Rosemarkie	★★	Marine	H	–	L
Shieldaig	★	Tigh an Eilean	–	B	–
Skeabost Bridge (Isle of Skye)	★★★🌲	Skeabost House	–	–	L
Strathpeffer	★	Holly Lodge	❀H	–	L
Talladale	★	Loch Maree	H	–	–
Ullapool	★★★	Harbour Lights	–	B	L
	★★	Ceilidh Place	–	B	L
LOTHIAN					
Bonnyrigg	★★★★🌲	Dalhousie Castle	H	B	L
Dirleton	★★★	Open Arms	H	B	L
Dunbar	★★	Bayswell	H	–	–
Edinburgh	★★★★	Caledonian	–	–	L
	★★★	Howard	–	–	L
	★★★	Roxburghe	H	B	L
	★★★	Donmaree	–	–	L
	✕	Shamiana	❀–	–	–
Gorebridge	★	Auld Toll	–	–	L
Gullane	★★★🌲	Greywalls	❀ **Red Stars**		
	✕	La Potinière	❀–	–	–
Humbie	★★★🌲	Johnstounburn House	H	B	L
North Berwick	★★★	Marine	–	–	L
Uphall	★★★🌲	Houstoun House	–	B	–
SHETLAND					
Brae	★★★🌲	Busta House	H	B	L
STRATHCLYDE					
Arden	★★★	Lomond Castle	–	B	–
Ardentinny	★★	Ardentinny	H	–	–
Arduaine	★★★	Loch Melfort	H	–	L
Ayr	★★★	Pickwick	H	–	–
	★★	Marine Court	–	–	L
Barrhead	✕✕	Dalmeny Park	❀–	–	–
Bothwell	★★	Silvertrees	–	B	–
Clachan-Seil	★	Willowburn	❀–	–	–
Connel	★★	Ossians	–	–	L
Cove	★★	Knockderry	H	B	–
Craighouse	★★	Jura	–	–	–
Crinan	★★★	Crinan	–	–	L
Dunoon	★★	Firpark	–	B	L
Gigha, Isle of	★★	Gigha	H	–	L
Glasgow	☆☆☆☆	Holiday Inn	–	B	L
	★★★★	Stakis Grosvenor	–	–	L
	★★★	Tinto Firs	–	B	–
	★★	Ewington	H	–	–
	✕✕	The Buttery	❀–	–	–
	✕✕	Poachers	❀–	–	–
Helensburgh	☆☆☆	Commodore	–	B	L
Kilchrenan	★★★🌲	Ardanaiseig	❀ **Red Stars**		
	★★★🌲	Taychreggan	–	–	L
Knipoch	★★★	Knipoch	–	B	L
Langbank	★★★🌲	Gleddoch House	–	B	L
Ledaig	★★★🌲	Isle of Eriska	**Red Stars**		
Lochawe	★★	Carraig-Thura	–	–	L

Town	Rating	Hotel	Awards
Oban	★★★	Alexandra	– – L
	★★	Lancaster	– – L
Port Appin	★★	Airds	❀ Red Stars
Port Ellen	★★	Dower House	H – –
Rhu	★★★	Rosslea Hall	– – L
	★	Ardencaple	– – L
Rothesay	★	Ardmory House	H – –
Scalasaig	★	Colonsay	H – –
Skelmorlie	★★★🌲	Manor Park	– B L
Stewarton	★★★🌲	Chapeltoun House	❀ Red Stars
Tarbert	★	West Loch	❀– – –
Troon	★★★	Sun Court	– – L
	★★	Piersland Lodge	– – L
Turnberry	★★★★	Turnberry	– – L
TAYSIDE			
Auchterarder	★★★★★	Gleneagles	– – L
Auchterhouse	★★★🌲	Old Mansion House	❀H B –
Blairgowrie	★★🌲	Kinloch House	❀H – –
Bridge of Cally	★	Bridge of Cally	❀H B L
Clova	★★🌲	Rottal Lodge	H B –
Crieff	★★	Murray Park	– B –
	★	Gwydyr	– B –
Dunkeld	★★★🌲	Dunkeld House	– – L
Edzell	★★	Panmure Arms	– B –
Glencarse	★★	Newton House	H – –
Glenshee	★★🌲	Dalmunzie	H – L
Killiecrankie	★★	Killiecrankie	H – L
Kinclaven	★★★🌲	Ballathie House	– B L
Kirkmichael	★★	Log Cabin	H – –
Meigle	★★🌲	Kings of Kinloch	H – –
Pitlochry	★★★	Atholl Palace	– – L
	★★	Burnside	H – L
	★★	Birchwood	– B –
	★★	Craigard	– – L
Scone	★★★🌲	Balcraig House	❀H B L
Strathtummel	★★🌲	Port-an-Eilean	– B –

Country-house hotels 🌲

Quiet, often secluded hotels are listed below. At an AA country-house hotel you should be assured of a restful night, together with a relaxed, informal atmosphere and personal welcome. On the other hand, some of the facilities may differ from those to be found in purpose-built, urban hotels of the same star rating.

It should be noted that not all rurally situated hotels are AA country-house hotels, neither are AA country-house hotels always located in an isolated situation.

See appropriate entry in gazetteer for other details, including merit awards where these apply.

England

AVON

Bath	★★★	Combe Grove
Freshford	❀★★★	Homewood Park
Hunstrete	❀★★★	Hunstrete House
Lympsham	★★	Batch Farm
Rangeworthy	★	Rangeworthy Court
Sidcot	★★	Sidcot
Thornbury	★★★	Thornbury Castle

CAMBRIDGESHIRE

Six Mile Bottom	★★★	Swynford Paddocks

CHESHIRE

Nantwich	❀★★★	Rookery Hall
Tarporley	★★	Willington Hall

CLEVELAND

Loftus	★★★	Grinkle Park

CORNWALL

Falmouth	★★★	Penmere Manor
Helland Bridge	★★★	Tredethy Country
Helston	★	Nansloe Manor Country
Lamorna Cove	★★★	Lamorna Cove
	★★	Menwinnion
Liskeard	★★	Country Castle
Mawnan Smith	★★★	Meudon
Newquay	★★	Porth Veor Manor House
Penzance	★★★	Higher Faugen
Portscatho	★★	Roseland House
Ruan High Lanes	★★	Polsue Manor
St Agnes	★★	Rose in Vale
St Keyne	★★	Old Rectory
St Wenn	★	Wenn Manor
Talland Bay	★★★	Talland Bay

CUMBRIA

Alston	★★	Lovelady Shield
Ambleside	★	Nanny Brow
Appleby	★★★	Appleby Manor
Bassenthwaite	★★★★	Armathwaite Hall
	★★	Overwater Hall
Brampton	❀★★	Farlam Hall
Crosby-on-Eden	★★	Crosby Lodge
Dalston	★★★	Dalston Hall
Grasmere	❀★★★	Michael's Nook
Hawkshead	★★★	Tarn Hows
Keswick	★★	Red House
	★★	Underscar
Levens	★★	Heaves
Longtown	★	March Bank
Pooley Bridge	❀❀★★★	Sharrow Bay
Thornthwaite	★★	Thwaite Howe
	★★	Woodend
Watermillock	★★★	Leeming House
	★	Old Church
Whitehaven	★★	Roseneath
Windermere	★★★	Langdale Chase
	★★	Holbeck Ghyll
	★★	Lindeth Fell
	★★	Linthwaite

DERBYSHIRE

Matlock	★★★	Riber Hall

DEVON

Ashburton	★★	Holne Chase
Barnstaple	★★	Downrew House
Bideford	★★	Yeoldon House
Bovey Tracey	★★	Edgemoor
	★★	Prestbury
Buckland in the Moor	★★	Buckland Hall
Burrington	★★★	Northcote Manor
Chagford	❀★★★	Gidleigh Park
	★★★	Great Tree
	★★★	Mill End
	❀★★★	Teignworthy
Clawton	★★	Court Barn
Combeinteignhead	★★	Netherton House
Down Thomas	★★	Langdon Court
Exeter	★★	Trood
Fairy Cross	★★★	Portledge
Gittisham	❀★★	Combe House
Haytor	★★	Bel Alp
Heddon's Mouth	★★	Heddon's Gate
Holbeton	★★★	Alston Hall
Honiton	★★★	Deer Park
Horns Cross	★★	Foxdown Manor
Kingsbridge	★★	Buckland-Tout-Saints
Lydford	★	Lydford House
Lynmouth	★★	Beacon
Lynton	★	Combe Park
Martinhoe	★	Old Rectory
Mary Tavy	★	Moorland Hall
Monkleigh	★★	Beaconside
Newton Ferrers	★★	Court House
North Huish	★★	Brookdale
Sidmouth	★★	Brownlands
South Brent	★	Glazebrook House
Sticklepath	★★	Skaigh House
Stoke Gabriel	★★	Gabriel Court
Teignmouth	★★	Venn Farm Country House
Whimple	★★	Woodhayes

DORSET

Bridport	★	Little Wych Country House
Charmouth	★★	Fernhill
Chedington	★★★	Chedington Court
Fleet	★★	Moonfleet Manor
Milton Abbas	★★	Milton Manor
Milton-on-Stour	★★★	Milton Lodge
Studland	★★	Manor House

ESSEX

Dedham	❀★★★	Maison Talbooth

GLOUCESTERSHIRE

Bibury	★★	Bibury Court
Buckland	❀★★★	Buckland Manor
Cheltenham	★★★	Greenway
Coleford	★	Lambsquay
Lower Slaughter	★★★	Manor
Stinchcombe	★★	Stinchcombe Manor
Stroud	★★	Burleigh Court
Upper Slaughter	★★★	Lords of the Manor

HAMPSHIRE

Bransgore	★★★	Harrow Lodge
Burley	★★★	Burley Manor
	★★★	Moorhill
Lymington	★★★	Passford House
Lyndhurst	★★★	Parkhill House
New Milton	❀❀★★★★	Chewton Glen
Winchester	★★★	Lainston House
Woodlands	★★	Woodlands Lodge

HEREFORD & WORCESTER

Abberley	❀★★★	Elms
Broadway	★★	Collin House
Malvern Wells	★★★	Cottage-in-the-Wood

Place	Rating	Hotel
Malvern Wells	★	Holdfast Cottage
Pencraig	★★	Pencraig Court
Ross-on-Wye	★★	Chasedale
	★★	Walford House
Symonds Yat (West)	★★	Wye Rapids

HUMBERSIDE

Place	Rating	Hotel
Driffield, Great	★★	Wold House
Little Weighton	★★★	Rowley Manor

ISLE OF WIGHT

Place	Rating	Hotel
Bembridge	★★	Elm Country
Ventnor	★★	Winterbourne
	★	Madeira Hall
Whippingham	★★	Padmore House

KENT

Place	Rating	Hotel
Ashford	★★★★	Eastwell Manor
Cranbrook	★★	Kennel Holt

LEICESTERSHIRE

Place	Rating	Hotel
Oakham	❀★★★	Hambleton Hall

MANCHESTER, GREATER

Place	Rating	Hotel
Bolton	★★★	Egerton House

NORFOLK

Place	Rating	Hotel
Bunwell	★★	Bunwell Manor
Grimston	❀★★★	Congham Hall
Witchingham, Great	★★	Lenwade House

NORTHUMBERLAND

Place	Rating	Hotel
Allendale	★★	Ashleigh
Cornhill-on-Tweed	★★★	Tillmouth Park
Otterburn	★★	Otterburn Tower

OXFORDSHIRE

Place	Rating	Hotel
Horton-cum-Studley	❀★★★	Studley Priory

SHROPSHIRE

Place	Rating	Hotel
Church Stretton	★★★	Stretton Hall
Oswestry	★★	Sweeney Hall

SOMERSET

Place	Rating	Hotel
Brent Knoll	★	Woodlands
Dulverton	★★★	Carnarvon Arms
	★★	Three Acres
Evercreech	★★	Glen
Holford	★★	Alfoxton Park
	★★	Combe House
Minehead	★★	Woodcombe Lodge
Shapwick	★★	Shapwick House
Simonsbath	★★	Simonsbath House
Ston Easton	❀★★★	Ston Easton Park
Wincanton	★★	Holbrook House
Withypool	★	Westerclose

SUFFOLK

Place	Rating	Hotel
Brome	★★	Oaksmere
Wetheringsett	★★	Wetheringsett Manor
Woodbridge	★★★	Seckford Hall

SURREY

Place	Rating	Hotel
Bagshot	★★★★	Pennyhill Park
Farnham	★★	Trevena House

SUSSEX, EAST

Place	Rating	Hotel
Battle	★★★	Netherfield Place
Hastings	★★★	Beauport Park
Rushlake Green	★★★	Priory
Stone Cross	★★★	Glyndley Manor
Wadhurst	❀★★	Spindlewood

SUSSEX, WEST

Place	Rating	Hotel
Climping	★★★	Baliffscourt
Cuckfield	★★	Hilton Park
East Grinstead	❀★★★	Gravetye Manor
Thakeham	★★★	Little Thakeham
	★★	Abingworth Hall

WARWICKSHIRE

Place	Rating	Hotel
Billesley	★★★	Billesley Manor
Ettington	❀★★	Chase
Leamington Spa (Royal)	❀★★	Mallory Court
Rugby	★★★	Clifton Court
Wishaw	★★★	Moxhull Hall

WILTSHIRE

Place	Rating	Hotel
Castle Combe	★★★	Manor House
Limpley Stoke	★★★	Cliffe
Malmesbury	★★★	Whatley Manor
Warminster	❀★★★	Bishopstrow House

YORKSHIRE, NORTH

Place	Rating	Hotel
Crathorne	★★★★	Crathorne Hall
Hackness	★★★	Hackness Grange
Kirkby Fleetham	★★★	Kirkby Fleetham Hall
Lastingham	★★	Lastingham Grange
Masham	★★	Jervaulx Hall
Monk Fryston	★★★	Monk Fryston Hall
Scarborough	★★	Wrea Head
Whitwell-on-the-Hill	★★	Whitwell Hall

YORKSHIRE, WEST

Place	Rating	Hotel
Wentbridge	★★★	Wentbridge House

Channel Islands

JERSEY

Place	Rating	Hotel
St Saviour	❀★★★★	Longueville Manor

Wales

DYFED

Place	Rating	Hotel
Aberystwyth	★★★	Conrah
Crugybar	★★	Glanrannell Park
Eglwysfach	★★★	Ynyshir Hall

Lamphey	★★★	Court
Llandovery	★★	Llanfair Grange
	★	Picton Court
Llangadog	★★	Plas Glansevin
Llanstephan	★★	Mansion House
Pembroke Dock	☆☆☆	Cleddau Bridge
St Davids	★★★	Warpool Court

GWYNEDD

Aberdovey	★★★	Plas Penhelig
Abersoch	❀★★★	Porth Tocyn
Barmouth	★★	Plas Mynach
Beddgelert	★	Bryn Eglwys
Criccieth	★★★	Bron Eifion
	★★	Parciau Manor
Dolwyddelan	★★★	Plas Hall
Llanbedr	★★	Cae Nest Hall
Llandudno	★★★	Bodysgallen Hall
Llanrwst	★★★	Gwesty-Plas Maenan
Pennal	★★	Llugwy Hall
Roewen	★	Tir-y-Coed
Talsarnau	★★	Maes-y-Neuadd

POWYS

Builth Wells	★★	Caer Beris Manor
Crickhowell	★★	Gliffaes
Llanfyllin	★★	Bodfach Hall
Llangammarch Wells	★★★	Lake

Scotland

BORDERS

Chirnside	★★	Chirnside
Dryburgh	★★★	Dryburgh Abbey
Ettrick Bridge	★★	Ettrickshaws
Peebles	★★	Cringletie House
	★★	Venlaw Castle

CENTRAL

Callander	★★★	Roman Camp
Kinbuck	❀★★★	Cromlix House

DUMFRIES & GALLOWAY

Auchencairn	★★★	Balcary Bay
Borgue	★★	Senwick House
Collin	★★★	Rockhall
Crossmichael	★★	Culgruff House
Monk Fryston	★★★	Monk Fryston Hall
Newton Stewart	★★★	Kirroughtree
Portpatrick	❀★★	Knockinaam Lodge
Port William	★★★	Corsemalzie House
Rockcliffe	★★★	Barons Craig
Thornhill	★★	Trigony House

FIFE

Glenrothes	★★★	Balgeddie House
Letham	★★★	Fernie Castle

GRAMPIAN

Banchory	★★★	Banchory Lodge
	★★★	Raemoir
Huntly	★★	Castle
Kildrummy	★★★	Kildrummy Castle
Rothes	★★★	Rothes Glen

HIGHLAND

Achnasheen	★★	Ledgowan Lodge
Arisaig	❀★★★	Arisaig House
Drumnadrochit	★★	Polmaily House
Dulnain Bridge	❀★★	Muckrach Lodge
Fort William	❀❀★★★★	Inverlochy Castle
Glenborrodale	★★	Glenborrodale Castle
Invergarry	★★	Glengarry Castle
Inverness	★★★★	Culloden House
	❀★★	Dunain Park
Invershin	★★	Aultnagar Lodge
Isle of Ornsay, (Isle of Skye)	★★	Kinloch Lodge
Kentallen	❀★★	Ardsheal House
Lechmelm	★	Tir Aluinn
Muir of Ord	★★	Ord House
Nairn	★★★★	Newton
Skeabost Bridge (Isle of Skye)	★★★	Skeabost House
Torridon	★★	Loch Torridon

LOTHIAN

Bonnyrigg	★★★★	Dalhousie Castle
Gullane	❀★★★	Greywalls
Humbie	★★★	Johnstounburn House
Uphall	★★★	Houstoun House

SHETLAND

Brae	★★★	Busta House

STRATHCLYDE

Hollybush	★★★	Hollybush House
Kilchrenan	❀★★★	Ardanaiseig
	★★★	Taychreggan
Langbank	★★★	Gleddoch House
Ledaig	★★★	Isle of Eriska
Skelmorlie	★★★	Manor Park
Stewarton	❀★★★	Chapletoun House
Tarbert (Loch Fyne)	★★★	Stonefield Castle

TAYSIDE

Alyth	★★★	Lands of Loyal
Auchterhouse	❀★★★	Old Mansion House
Blairgowrie	❀★★	Kinloch House
Clova	★★	Rottal Lodge
Dunkeld	★★★	Dunkeld House
Glenshee (Spital of)	★★	Dalmunzie
Kinclaven	★★★	Ballathie House
Meigle	★★	Kings of Kinloch
Pitlochry	★★	Pine Trees
Scone	❀★★★	Balcraig House
	★★★	Murrayshall House
Strathtummel	★★	Port-an-Eilean

Hotels with conference facilities

For those planning business seminars or conferences the list below gives hotels able to accommodate at least 40 guests in rooms with private bath or shower, one or more conference rooms seating a minimum of 40 people at tables and a dining room for delegates.

The following facilities are also available or can be arranged or supplied: a conference office with telephones, syndicate rooms, amplifying equipment, a speaker's rostrum, secretarial services and audio-visual aids.

The abbreviation **T** indicates that the hotel has telex, while **MLT** means that it can arrange multi-language translation.

See appropriate entry in gazetteer for other details, including merit awards where these apply.

England

AVON

- Alveston ☆☆☆ Post House **TMLT**
- ★★ Alveston House **TMLT**
- Bath ★★★★ Francis **TMLT**
- ☆☆☆☆ Ladbroke Beaufort **TMLT**
- ★★★ Lansdowne Grove **MLT**
- ★★★ Redcar **TMLT**
- ★★★ Royal York
- Blagdon ★★★ Mendip
- Bristol ☆☆☆☆ Crest **TMLT**
- ★★★★ Grand **TMLT**
- ☆☆☆☆ Holiday Inn **TMLT**
- ☆☆☆☆ Ladbroke Dragonara **TMLT**
- ☆☆☆☆ Unicorn **TMLT**
- ★★★ Avon Gorge **T**
- ☆☆☆ Redwood Lodge **T**
- ★★ St Vincent's Rocks **MLT**
- Weston-super-Mare ★★★ Grand Atlantic
- ★★ Rozel

BEDFORDSHIRE

- Bedford ★★★ Bedford Moat House **TMLT**
- ★★ Bedford Swan
- Luton ☆☆☆☆ Chiltern **TMLT**
- ☆☆☆☆ Strathmore Thistle **T**
- ☆☆☆ Crest Hotel– Luton **MLT**
- Woburn ★★★ Bedford Arms **TMLT**

BERKSHIRE

- Ascot ☆☆☆☆ Berystede **T**
- Maidenhead ☆☆☆☆ Crest **TMLT**
- Newbury ★★★ Chequers **TMLT**
- Reading ☆☆☆ Post House **TMLT**
- ★★ Ship **MLT**
- Slough ☆☆☆☆ Holiday Inn **TMLT**
- Windsor ★★★ Castle **T**
- Wokingham ★★★ St Annes Manor

BUCKINGHAMSHIRE

- Beaconsfield ☆☆☆☆ Bellhouse **TMLT**
- Gerrards Cross ★★★ Bull **MLT**
- High Wycombe ☆☆☆ Crest
- Marlow ★★★★ Compleat Angler **T**

CAMBRIDGESHIRE

- Bar Hill ☆☆☆☆ Cunard Cambridgeshire **T**
- Cambridge ★★★★ University Arms **T**
- ★★★ Gonville
- Norman Cross ☆☆☆ Crest **TMLT**
- Peterborough ★★★ Bull
- ☆☆☆ Saxon Inn Motor **TMLT**

CHESHIRE

- Backford Cross ☆☆☆ Ladbroke (& Conferencentre) **T**
- Chester ★★★★ Chester Grosvenor **TMLT**
- ☆☆☆ Abbots Well Inn **T MLT**
- ★★★ Blossoms **T**
- ★★★ Mollington Banastre **TMLT**
- ☆☆☆ Post House **TMLT**
- Crewe ★★★ Crewe Arms
- Daresbury ★★★ Lord Daresbury **T**
- Disley ★★★ Moorside **T**
- Handforth ❀★★★ Belfry **T**
- Lymm ★★ Lymm **MLT**
- Mottram St Andrew ★★★ Mottram Hall **TMLT**
- Nantwich ★★ Alvaston Hall
- Runcorn ☆☆☆ Crest **TMLT**
- Sandbach ☆☆☆ Saxon Cross **T**

CLEVELAND

- Middlesbrough ☆☆☆☆ Ladbroke Dragonara (& Conferencentre) **TMLT**
- ☆☆☆ Blue Bell Motor Inn **MLT**

	☆☆☆	Marton Way **MLT**
	★★★	Marton
Redcar	☆☆☆	Royal York **MLT**
Stockton-on-Tees	☆☆☆☆	Swallow **TMLT**
	★★★	Billingham Arms Thistle **TMLT**
	☆☆☆	Golden Eagle Thistle **MLT**
	☆☆☆	Post House **TMLT**

CORNWALL

Bude	★★★	Strand
Constantine Bay	★★★	Treglos
Falmouth	★★★	Falmouth **T**
	★★★	Green Lawns
	★★★	Hotel St Michaels **T**
Launceston	★★	White Hart
Mawnan Smith	★★★	Meudon **TMLT**
Mullion	★★★	Polurrian
Newquay	★★★	Atlantic
	★★★	Barrowfield **MLT**
	★★★	Hotel Bristol **TMLT**
	★★★	Hotel Mordros
	★★★	Hotel Riviera **T**
	★★	Great Western **TMLT**
St Ives	★★★	Tregenna Castle **T**
St Mellion	☆☆☆	St Mellion **MLT**
Truro	★★★	Royal

CUMBRIA

Carlisle	☆☆☆	Crest **MLT**
	★★★	Crown and Mitre **TMLT**
	★★★	Cumbrian Thistle **T**
	★★★	Swallow Hilltop **TMLT**
Glenridding	★★★	Ullswater **T**
Grange-over-Sands	★★★	Cumbria Grand **TMLT**
	★★	Grange **T**
Grasmere	★★★	Grasmere Red Lion
	★★★	Prince of Wales
Kendal	★★★	Woolpack Inn **T**
Keswick	★★★	Royal Oak **MLT**
Wetheral	★★★	Crown **MLT**
Windermere	★★★★	Old England **TMLT**
	★★★	Beech Hill **TMLT**
	★★★	Belsfield **TMLT**
	★★★	Hydro **TMLT**
	★★★	Low Wood **TMLT**
	★★★	Wild Boar **MLT**

DERBYSHIRE

Buxton	★★★	Leewood **MLT**
	★★★	Palace **MLT**
Chesterfield	★★★	Chesterfield
Derby	★★★	Midland **MLT**
	★★★	Pennine **T**
Long Eaton	☆☆☆	Novotel Nottingham **TMLT**
Matlock	★★★	New Bath **TMLT**
Sandiacre	☆☆☆	Post House **TMLT**
South Normanton	☆☆☆☆	Swallow
Thorpe (Dovedale)	★★★	Peveril of the Peak **MLT**

DEVON

Bideford	★★★	Durrant House
Dawlish	★★★	Langstone Cliff
Exeter	☆☆☆	Devon Motel **MLT**
	★★★	Rougemont **TMLT**
	★★★	Royal Clarence
Exmouth	★★★	Devoncourt **MLT**
	★★★	Imperial
	★★★	Royal Beacon **MLT**
	★★	Grand **TMLT**
Fairy Cross	★★★♜	Portledge
Honiton	★★★♜	Deer Park **MLT**
Lifton	★★★	Arundell Arms
Lynmouth	★★★	Tors
Ottery St Mary	★★★	Salston **T**
Paignton	★★★	Palace
	★★★	Redcliffe
Plymouth	☆☆☆☆	Holiday Inn
	★★★	Astor
	☆☆☆	Mayflower Post House
	☆☆☆	Novotel Plymouth **T**
	★★★	Strathmore
Salcombe	★★★★	Marine
	❀★★★	Tides Reach
Saunton	★★★★	Saunton Sands **MLT**
Sidmouth	★★★★	Victoria **MLT**
	★★★	Belmont
	★★★	Fortfield **MLT**
Thurlestone	★★★	Thurlestone
Tiverton	☆☆☆	Tiverton Motel
Torquay	★★★★★	Imperial **TMLT**
	★★★★	Grand **TMLT**
	★★★★	Palace **TMLT**
	★★★	Belgrave **MLT**
	★★★	Corbyn Head **TMLT**
	★★★	Kistor **MLT**
	★★★	Lincombe Hall
	★★★	Livermead Cliff **TMLT**
	★★★	Nepaul **MLT**
	★★★	Rainbow House **TMLT**
	★★★	Toorak
Woolacombe	★★★	Narracott Grand
	★★★	Woolacombe Bay **MLT**
Yelverton	★★★	Moorland Links

DORSET

Bournemouth	★★★★★	Royal Bath **TMLT**
	★★★★	East Cliff Court **MLT**
	★★★★	Highcliff **TMLT**
	★★★★	Marsham Court **MLT**
	★★★★	Palace Court **MLT**
	★★★	Anglo-Swiss **TMLT**
	★★★	Angus
	★★★	Chine **MLT**
	★★★	Cliff End **MLT**
	★★★	Cliffside **MLT**
	★★★	Hotel Courtlands **T**
	☆☆☆	Crest **TMLT**
	★★★	Durley Dean **MLT**
	★★★	Durley Hall **MLT**
	★★★	Durlston Court **TMLT**
	★★★	East Anglia **MLT**
	★★★	Embassy **MLT**
	★★★	Heathlands
	★★★	Ladbroke Savoy **TMLT**
	★★★	Pavillion
	★★★	Queens
	★★★	Wessex **TMLT**
	★★★	White Hermitage **MLT**
	★★	Fircroft **MLT**
	★★	Tralee
Christchurch	★★★	King's Arms Crest
Ferndown	★★★★	Dormy **MLT**
	☆☆	Coach House Motel **T**
Poole	★★★★	Hospitality Inn **TMLT**
	★★★	Sandbanks **MLT**
Portland	☆☆☆	Portland Heights **TMLT**
Sherborne	☆☆☆	Post House **TMLT**
Swanage	★★★	Grosvenor
	★★★	Pine's
Weymouth	★★	Crown
	★★	Hotel Prince Regent

CO DURHAM

Chester-le-Street	★★★	Lumley Castle **MLT**
Darlington	★★★★	Blackwell Grange Moat House **T**
	★★★	King's Head **MLT**
Durham	★★★★	Royal County **TMLT**
	★★★	Three Tuns **MLT**
Rushyford	★★★	Eden Arms **TMLT**
Tees-side Airport	★★★	St George

ESSEX

Basildon	☆☆☆	Crest **TMLT**
Brentwood	☆☆☆	Post House **TMLT**
Bulphan	☆☆	Ye Olde Plough House Motel **MLT**
Epping	☆☆☆	Post House **T**
Harlow	☆☆☆	Saxon Motor Inn **TMLT**
Marks Tey	☆☆☆	Marks Tey **T**
North Stifford	☆☆☆	Stifford Moat House
Southend-on-Sea	☆☆☆	Airport Moat House **MLT**

GLOUCESTERSHIRE

Cheltenham	☆☆☆☆	Golden Valley Thistle **TMLT**
	★★★★	Queen's **T**
	★★★	Carlton
	★★★	Hotel De la Bere **T**
	★★★	Lilleybrook Aparthotel
Cirencester	★★★★	King's Head **TMLT**
Gloucester	☆☆☆	Crest **TMLT**
Mickleton	★★	Three Ways **MLT**
Stroud	★★★	Bear of Rodborough **MLT**
Tewkesbury	★★★	Bell **MLT**
	★★★	Royal Hop Pole Crest **MLT**
	☆☆☆	Tewkesbury Park Golf & Country Club **T**

HAMPSHIRE

Alton	☆☆☆	Swan **MLT**
Ampfield	☆☆☆	Potters Heron
Basingstoke	☆☆☆	Crest
	☆☆☆	Ladbroke (& Conferencentre) **TMLT**
Brockenhurst	★★★	Ladbroke Balmer Lawn **TMLT**
Farnborough	☆☆☆	Queen's **TMLT**
Hayling Island	☆☆☆☆	Post House **TMLT**
Hook	☆☆	Raven **MLT**
Lymington	★★★	Passford House
Lyndhurst	★★★	Crown **MLT**
	★★★	Lyndhurst Park **TMLT**
New Milton	❀❀★★★★	Chewton Glen **TMLT**
Portsmouth & Southsea	☆☆☆☆	Holiday Inn **TMLT**
	☆☆☆	Crest **TMLT**
	★★★	Pendragon **TMLT**
	★★★	Royal Beach **T**
Romsey	★★★	White Horse **MLT**
Shedfield	☆☆☆	Meon Valley **T**
Southampton	★★★★	Polygon **T**
	★★★	Dolphin **TMLT**
	☆☆☆	Post House **TMLT**
	★★★	Southampton Moat House **TMLT**
	★★★	Southampton Park **T**
Winchester	★★★★	Wessex **TMLT**

HEREFORD & WORCESTER

Broadway	★★★★	Lygon Arms **TMLT**
	★★★	Dormy House **TMLT**
Bromsgrove	★★★	Perry Hall
Droitwich	★★★★	Château Impney **TMLT**
	★★★★	Raven **T**
Hereford	★★★	Green Dragon **T**
Kidderminster	★★★★	Stone Manor **TMLT**
	★★★	Gainsborough House **T**
Malvern, Great	★★★	Abbey **TMLT**
	★★★	Foley Arms **T**
Ross-on-Wye	★★★	Chase
	★★★	Wye **T**
Stourport-on-Seven	★★★	Mount Olympus **T**
Worcester	★★★	Giffard **TMLT**

HERTFORDSHIRE

Boreham Wood	☆☆☆	Elstree Moat House **MLT**
Bushey	☆☆☆	Ladbroke (& Conferencentre) **TMLT**
	☆☆	Spider's Web Motel **TMLT**
Harpenden	★★★	Glen Eagle **TMLT**
Hemel Hempstead	☆☆☆	Post House **TMLT**
Hitchin	★★★	Blakemore **TMLT**
Markyate	☆☆☆	Hertfordshire Moat House
St Albans	☆☆☆	Noke Thistle
	★★★	Sopwell House **MLT**
South Mimms	☆☆☆	Crest **TMLT**
Stevenage	☆☆☆	Grampian **T**
	☆☆☆	Roebuck Inn **T**
Watford	☆☆☆	Caledonian
Welwyn	☆☆	Clock Motel **MLT**
Welwyn Garden City	☆☆☆	Crest **MLT**

HUMBERSIDE

Grimsby	☆☆☆☆	Humber Royal Crest **TMLT**
	☆☆☆	Crest **TMLT**
Hull	☆☆☆	Crest Hotel Hull–City **TMLT**
Laceby	★★	Oaklands Hotel & Country Club
North Ferriby	☆☆☆	Crest Hotel Hull–Humber Bridge **TMLT**
Scunthorpe	★★	Royal **MLT**
Willerby	★★★	Willerby Manor **TMLT**

ISLE OF WIGHT

Shanklin	★★★	Cliff Tops **T**
Ventnor	★★★	Royal
	★★	Metropole

KENT

Ashford	★★★	Spearpoint **TMLT**
Canterbury	★★★	Chaucer
Dover	☆☆☆☆	Holiday Inn **T**
Folkestone	★★	Chilworth Court **MLT**
Hollingbourne	★★★	Great Danes **TMLT**
Hythe	★★★★	Hotel Imperial **TMLT**
	★★★	Stade Court **TMLT**
Larkfield	☆☆☆	Larkfield
Ramsgate	★★	San Clu
Shorne	☆☆☆	Inn on the Lake **MLT**
Southborough	★★	Hand & Sceptre **MLT**
Tonbridge	★★	Rose & Crown
Tunbridge Wells (Royal)	★★★	Spa **TMLT**
	★★	Wellington **T**
Westgate-on-Sea	★★	Ivyside **MLT**

LANCASHIRE

Barton	★★★	Barton Grange **TMLT**
Blackburn	★★★	Saxon Inn **TMLT**
Blackpool	★★★	Clifton **TMLT**
	★★★	Savoy
	★★	Claremont **MLT**
	★★	Gables Balmoral **T**
Charnock Richard	☆☆	Hunters Lodge Motel
Clitheroe	★★	Roefield
Gisburn	★★★	Stirk House **TMLT**
Leyland	☆☆☆☆	Ladbroke **TMLT**
Lytham St Annes	★★★★	Clifton Arms **T**
	★★★	Grand **TMLT**
	★★	Chadwick
	★★	Fernlea **T**
	★★	St Ives
	★	Lindum **TMLT**
Morecambe	★★★	Elms
Preston	☆☆☆	Crest **TMLT**
	☆☆☆	Tickled Trout **TMLT**
	☆☆☆	Trafalgar **T**

LEICESTERSHIRE

Leicester	★★★★	Grand
	☆☆☆☆	Holiday Inn **TMLT**
	★★★	Belmont **T**
	☆☆☆	Centre **TMLT**
	★★★	Leicestershire Moat House
	☆☆☆	Post House **TMLT**
Loughborough	★★★	Kings Head
Market Harborough	★★	Grove Motel
Measham	☆☆	Measham Inn
Rothley	★★★	Rothley Court

LINCOLNSHIRE

Grantham	★★★	George **TMLT**

Lincoln	★★★★	White Hart **T**
	★★★	Eastgate Post House **T**
Stamford	★★★	George **TMLT**

LONDON POSTAL DISTRICTS

W1	★★★★★	Churchill **TMLT**
W1	❀❀❀★★★★★	Dorchester **TMLT**
W1	★★★★★	Grosvenor House **TMLT**
W1	★★★★★	Hilton International **TMLT**
SW1	❀★★★★★	Hyatt Carlton Tower **TMLT**
SW1	★★★★★	Hyde Park **TMLT**
W1	★★★★★	Inn on the Park **TMLT**
W1	★★★★★	Inter-Continenal **TMLT**
W8	★★★★★	Royal Garden **TMLT**
WC2	★★★★★	Savoy **TMLT**
SW1	★★★★★	Sheraton Park Tower **TMLT**
W1	★★★★	Athenaeum **TMLT**
W1	★★★★	Britannia **TMLT**
W1	❀★★★★	Brown's **TMLT**
SW1	★★★★	Cavendish **TMLT**
NW3	☆☆☆☆	Clive **TMLT**
W1	★★★★	Cumberland **TMLT**
W6	☆☆☆☆	Cunard International
SW7	★★★★	Gloucester **T**
NW4	☆☆☆☆	Hendon Hall **TMLT**
W11	☆☆☆☆	Hilton International Kensington **TMLT**
W1	☆☆☆☆	Holiday Inn **TMLT**
SW1	☆☆☆☆	Holiday Inn Chelsea **TMLT**
W8	★★★★	Kensington Close **T**
W8	★★★★	Kensington Palace Thistle **T**
NW8	☆☆☆☆	Ladbroke Westmorland **TMLT**
W2	☆☆☆☆	London Embassy **TMLT**
SW5	☆☆☆☆	London International **TMLT**
W1	★★★★	London Marriott
W8	☆☆☆☆	London Tara **TMLT**
W1	★★★★	Park Lane **TMLT**
W1	★★★★	Piccadilly **TMLT**
W1	★★★★	Portman Inter-Continental **TMLT**
W1	☆☆☆☆	Regent Crest **TMLT**
W2	★★★★	Royal Lancaster **TMLT**
SW1	☆☆☆☆	Royal Westminster Thistle **TMLT**
WC1	★★★★	Hotel Russell **TMLT**
W1	★★★★	Selfridge Thistle **TMLT**
E1	★★★★	Tower Thistle **TMLT**
WC2	★★★★	Waldorf **TMLT**
W1	★★★★	Westbury **TMLT**
NW1	☆☆☆☆	White House
SW5	★★★	Barkston **TMLT**
SW3	★★★	Basil Street **T**
W1	★★★	Berners **TMLT**
WC1	☆☆☆	Bloomsbury Crest **TMLT**
W5	☆☆☆	Carnarvon **T**
W1	★★★	Clifton Ford **TMLT**
W2	★★★	Coburg **T**
W2	☆☆☆	Hospitality Inn
W1	★★★	Mount Royal
W2	★★★	Park Court **TMLT**
SW1	★★★	Royal Horseguards Thistle **TMLT**
W14	☆☆☆	Royal Kensington
WC1	☆☆☆	Royal Scot Thistle **TMLT**
NW7	☆☆☆	TraveLodge **T**
W1	★★★	Washington **TMLT**
WC1	★★	Cora **TMLT**
SE11	★★	London Park **TMLT**
W1	★★	Regent Palace

LONDON, GREATER

Bromley	★★★	Bromley Court **TMLT**
Croydon	☆☆☆	Aerodrome **TMLT**
Enfield	★★★	Royal Chace **TMLT**
Hadley Wood	★★★★	West Lodge Park **MLT**
Heathrow Airport	☆☆☆☆	Ariel **T**
	☆☆☆☆	Excelsior **TMLT**
	☆☆☆☆	Heathrow Penta **TMLT**
	☆☆☆☆	Holiday Inn **T**
	☆☆☆☆	Sheraton – Heathrow **TMLT**
	☆☆☆	Post House **TMLT**
	★★★	Skyway **TMLT**
Hillingdon	☆☆☆	Master Brewer Motel
Hornchurch	☆☆☆	Ladbroke (& Conferencentre) **TMLT**
Richmond upon Thames	★★★	Richmond Hill **TMLT**
Sanderstead	★★★★	Selsdon Park **TMLT**

Wembley ☆☆☆☆ Wembley International **TMLT**
Woodford Green ☆☆☆ Woodford Moat House **MLT**

MANCHESTER, GREATER

Altrincham ☆☆☆ Ashley
★★★ Bowdon
☆☆☆ Cresta Court **TMLT**
Bolton ☆☆☆ Crest **TMLT**
★★★ Last Drop **TMLT**
★★★ Pack Horse **T**
Bramhall ☆☆☆ Bramhall Moat House
Manchester ★★★★ Grand **TMLT**
★★★★ Hotel Piccadilly **TMLT**
★★★★ Portland Thistle **TMLT**
☆☆☆ Post House **TMLT**
Manchester Airport ☆☆☆☆ Excelsior **TMLT**
★★★ Valley Lodge **TMLT**
Oldham ★★★ Bower **TMLT**
Standish ☆☆☆ Cassinellis Almond Brook Inn Motor **TMLT**
Stockport ★★★ Alma Lodge
★★★ Belgrade **T**

MERSEYSIDE

Birkenhead ★★★ Bowler Hat **TMLT**
Bootle ★★★ Park **T**
Haydock ☆☆☆☆ Post House **T**
Knowsley ☆☆☆ Crest Hotel East Lancs Road
Liverpool ★★★★ Atlantic Tower Thistle **TMLT**
☆☆☆☆ Holiday Inn **TMLT**
★★★★ St George's **TMLT**
☆☆☆ Crest Hotel Liverpool – City **TMLT**
★★ Bradford **TMLT**
★★ Shaftesbury
St Helens ☆☆☆ Fleece **T**
Southport ★★★★ Prince of Wales **TMLT**
★★★ Royal Clifton **TMLT**
Thornton Hough ★★★ Thornton Hall

MIDLANDS, WEST

Barr, Great ☆☆☆ Post House **TMLT**
Birmingham ★★★★ Albany **TMLT**
☆☆☆☆ Holiday Inn **TMLT**
★★★★ Midland **TMLT**
☆☆☆☆ Strathallan Thistle **TMLT**
☆☆☆ Apollo **TMLT**
☆☆☆ Birmingham International
★★★ Grand **TMLT**
★★★ Royal Angus Thistle **TMLT**
Birmingham Airport ★★★★ Excelsior **TMLT**
Birmingham (National Exhibition Centre) ★★ Arden Motel **T**
Coventry ☆☆☆☆ Crest **TMLT**
★★★★ De Vere **TMLT**
★★★★ Hotel Leofric **TMLT**
☆☆☆ Novotel Coventry **TMLT**
☆☆☆ Post House **TMLT**
Meriden ★★★ Manor **TMLT**
Solihull ★★★ St John's **TMLT**
Sutton Coldfield ★★★★ Penns Hall **TMLT**
★★★ Moor Hall **MLT**
Walsall ★★★ Barons Court **TMLT**
☆☆☆ Walsall Crest **MLT**
West Bromwich ☆☆☆ West Bromwich Moat House **T**
Wolverhampton ★★★ Connaught **T**
★★★ Goldthorn
★★★ Mount
★★★ Park Hall

NORFOLK

Barnham Broom ★★★ Barnham Broom Golf & Country Club **TMLT**
Blakeney ★★★ Blakeney
Cromer ★★ Hotel de Paris
King's Lynn ★★★ Duke's Head **T**
Mundesley-on-Sea ★★★ Continental
Norwich ★★★ Lansdowne **MLT**
★★★ Maid's Head **T**
☆☆☆ Hotel Norwich **TMLT**
☆☆☆ Post House **TMLT**
★★★ Sprowston Hall **MLT**
★★ Castle **TMLT**
West Runton ★★★ Links Country Park **MLT**
Yarmouth, Great ★★★ Carlton **TMLT**
★★ Burlington
★★ Imperial

NORTHAMPTONSHIRE

Corby ★★★ Grosvenor **T**
Crick ☆☆☆☆ Post House **TMLT**
Northampton ★★★ Grand
★★★ Saxon Inn **T**
★★★ Weston Moat House **MLT**
Oundle ★★ Talbot **MLT**
Wellingborough ★★★ Hind **MLT**

NOTTINGHAMSHIRE

Barnby Moor ★★★ Ye Olde Bell
Newark-on-Trent ★★ Robin Hood **MLT**
Nottingham ★★★★ Albany **TMLT**
★★★ George **T**
★★★ Strathdon Thistle **TMLT**
Retford (East) ★★★ West Retford **T**

Southwell	★★★	Saracen's Head **MLT**

OXFORDSHIRE

Banbury	★★★★	Whately Hall **TMLT**
	★★★	Banbury Moat House
Milton Common	★★	Belfry **T**
Oxford	★★★★	Randolph **T**
	★★★	Ladbroke Linton Lodge **TMLT**
	☆☆☆	Oxford Moat House **TMLT**
	☆☆☆	TraveLodge **T**
	★★	Eastgate **MLT**
Woodstock	★★★	Bear **TMLT**

SHROPSHIRE

Ludlow	★★★	Feathers **T**
Shrewsbury	★★★	Ainsworth's Radbrook Hall
	★★★	Lion **TMLT**
	★★★	Lord Hill
	★★★	Prince Rupert **T**
Weston	★★★	Hawkstone Park

SOMERSET

Frome	☆☆☆	Mendip Lodge **T**
Ilminster	★★★	Horton Cross **TMLT**
Street	☆☆☆	Wessex
Taunton	❀★★★	Castle **TMLT**
	★★★	County **T**
Wells	★★★	Swan **TMLT**
Yeovil	★★★	Manor Crest **TMLT**

STAFFORDSHIRE

Haywood, Great	☆☆	Coach & Horses
Lichfield	★★★	George **MLT**
Newcastle-under-Lyme	★★★	Clayton Lodge **MLT**
	☆☆☆	Crest **TMLT**
Stafford	☆☆☆	Tillington Hall **T**
	★★	Swan
Stoke-on-Trent	★★★★	North Stafford **TMLT**
	★★★	Stakis Grand
Tamworth	★★	Castle **TMLT**

SUFFOLK

Bury St Edmunds	★★★	Angel **T**
Felixstowe	★★★★	Orwell Moat House
Ipswich	★★★	Belstead Brook **TMLT**
	☆☆☆	Ipswich Moat House **TMLT**
	☆☆☆	Post House **TMLT**
Newmarket	★★★	Newmarket Moat House
	★★	Rutland Arms
Sudbury	★★★	Mill **TMLT**

SURREY

Burgh Heath	☆☆	Pickard Motor **TMLT**
Camberley	★★★	Frimley Hall **T**
Cobham	☆☆☆	Ladbroke Seven Hills (& Conferencentre) **TMLT**
Dorking	★★★★	Burford Bridge **T**
Farnham	★★★	Bush **MLT**
Guildford	★★★	Angel **MLT**
Haslemere	★★★	Lythe Hill **TMLT**
Shepperton	☆☆☆	Shepperton Moat House **TMLT**
Weybridge	★★★	Oatlands Park **TMLT**
	★★★	Ship Thistle **TMLT**

SUSSEX, EAST

Brighton & Hove	★★★★	Dudley **T**
	★★★★	Grand **TMLT**
	★★★	Alexandra **TMLT**
	★★★	Courtlands **TMLT**
	★★★	Old Ship **TMLT**
	★★★	Royal Albion **TMLT**
	★★	Langfords **T**
	★★	St Catherine's Lodge **MLT**
Eastbourne	★★★★★	Grand **TMLT**
	★★★★	Cavendish **TMLT**
	★★★★	Queen's **TMLT**
	★★★	Chatsworth
	★★★	Cumberland
	★★★	Imperial
	★★★	Lansdowne
	★★★	Mansion
	★★★	Princes **MLT**
	★★★	Sandhurst **MLT**
	★★★	Wish Tower
Lewes	★★★	Shelleys **MLT**

SUSSEX, WEST

Bognor Regis	★★★	Royal Norfolk **MLT**
Chichester	★★★	Chichester Lodge **MLT**
	★★★	Dolphin & Anchor
East Grinstead	★★★	Felbridge Hotel & Health Club **TMLT**
Gatwick Airport	☆☆☆☆	Copthorne **TMLT**
	☆☆☆☆	Gatwick Hilton International **TMLT**
	☆☆☆☆	Gatwick Penta **TMLT**
	☆☆☆	Chequers Thistle **TMLT**
	☆☆☆	Crest
	☆☆☆	Gatwick Moat House **TMLT**
	★★★	George **TMLT**
	★★★	Goffs Park **T**
	☆☆☆	Post House **TMLT**

	☆☆☆	Saxon Inn Gatwick **TMLT**
Horsham	★★	Ye Olde King's Head **MLT**
Midhurst	★★★	Spread Eagle
Walberton	★★★	Avisford Park **MLT**
Waterbeach	★★★	Richmond Arms **TMLT**
Worthing	★★★	Beach **MLT**
	★★★	Chatsworth **TMLT**
	★★★	Eardley **T**
	★★★	Warnes **T**

TYNE & WEAR

Gateshead	☆☆☆	Five Bridges **TMLT**
Newcastle upon Tyne	★★★★	Gosforth Park Thistle **TMLT**
	★★★	County Thistle **TMLT**
	★★★	Imperial **TMLT**
	☆☆☆	Newcastle Crest **TMLT**
	★★★	Royal Turks Head Thistle
	☆☆☆	Swallow **T**
Newcastle upon Tyne Airport	☆☆☆	Stakis Airport **MLT**
Seaton Burn	☆☆☆☆	Holiday Inn **TMLT**
Sunderland	★★★	Seaburn **MLT**
Tynemouth	★★★	Grand **MLT**
Wallsend	☆☆☆	Newcastle Moat House **TMLT**
Washington	★★★	George Washington **TMLT**
	☆☆☆	Post House **TMLT**

WARWICKSHIRE

Brandon	★★★	Brandon Hall **T**
Kenilworth	★★★★	De Montfort **TMLT**
Leamington Spa (Royal)	★★★	Falstaff
	★★★	Manor House **TMLT**
	★★★	Regent **MLT**
Rugby	★★★	Three Horse Shoes **TMLT**
Stratford-upon-Avon	★★★★	Hilton **TMLT**
	★★★★	Shakespeare **T**
	★★★★	Welcome
	★★★	Alveston Manor **T**
	★★★	Arden **T**
	★★★	Falcon **TMLT**
	★★★	Grosvenor House **T**
	★★★	Swan's Nest **T**
	★★★	White Swan
Warwick	☆☆☆☆	Ladbroke **T**
	★★	Lord Leycester

WILTSHIRE

Corsham	☆☆	Stagecoach **MLT**
Limpley Stoke	★★	Limpley Stoke **MLT**
Salisbury	★★★	Rose & Crown **MLT**
	★★	Red Lion
Swindon	★★★★	Blunsdon House **T**
	★★★	Goddard Arms **MLT**
	☆☆☆	Post House **TMLT**
	★★★	Wiltshire **TMLT**

YORKSHIRE, NORTH

Bedale	☆☆☆	Motel Leeming
Harrogate	★★★★	Crown **TMLT**
	★★★★	Hotel Majestic **T**
	★★★★	Old Swan **TMLT**
	★★★	Cairn **T**
	★★★	Hospitality Inn
	★★★	Hotel St George **TMLT**
	★★	Fernlea **T**
Lumby	★★★	Selby Fork **TMLT**
Ripon	★★★	Ripon Spa **TMLT**
Scarborough	★★★★	Crown **TMLT**
	★★★★	Royal **TMLT**
	★★★	St Nicholas **TMLT**
	★★	Brooklands **MLT**
	★★	Esplanade
	★★	Norbreck
	★★	Southlands
Scotch Corner	★★★	Scotch Corner
York	★★★★	Royal Station **T**
	☆☆☆☆	Viking **TMLT**
	★★★	Chase **MLT**
	★★★	Ladbroke Abbey Park **T**
	☆☆☆	Post House **TMLT**

YORKSHIRE, SOUTH

Barnsley	★★	Queens **MLT**
Bawtry	★★★	Crown **MLT**
Doncaster	★★★	Danum
	★★★	Earl of Doncaster **TMLT**
Rotherham	☆☆☆☆	Carlton Park **TMLT**
Sheffield	★★★★	Grosvenor House **TMLT**
	★★★★	Hallan Tower Post House **TMLT**
	★★★	Royal Victoria **MLT**
	★★★	Hotel St George **T**
	★★	Rutland **T**

YORKSHIRE, WEST

Bingley	★★★	Bankfield **MLT**
Bradford	★★★	Victoria **TMLT**
Bramhope	☆☆☆	Post House **TMLT**
Garforth	☆☆☆	Ladbroke (& Conferencentre) **TMLT**
Halifax	★★★	Holdsworth House
Huddersfield	★★★	George
	☆☆☆	Ladbroke (& Conferencentre) **T**
Ilkley	★★★	Craiglands **TMLT**
Leeds	☆☆☆☆	Ladbroke Dragonara **TMLT**

Leeds	★★★★	Queen's **TMLT**
	★★★	Merrion **TMLT**
	★★★	Hotel Metropole **T**
Wakefield	☆☆☆☆	Post House **TMLT**
	★★★	Swallow **MLT**
Wetherby	☆☆☆	Ladbroke Wetherby

Isle of Man

Castletown	★★★	Golf Links **T**

Channel Islands

GUERNSEY

St Martin	★★★	Ronnie Ronalde's
	★★★	St Margarets Lodge **MLT**
St Peter Port	★★★★	Duke of Richmond **TMLT**
	★★★★	Old Government House **TMLT**
	★★★	Royal **TMLT**

JERSEY

Archirondel	★★	Les Arches **TMLT**
Bouley Bay	★★★★	Water's Edge **TMLT**
St Brelade	★★★★	Atlantic **T**
	❀★★★★	Hotel l'Horizon **T**
	★★★★	La Place **TMLT**
St Helier	❀★★★★	Grand **TMLT**
	★★★★	Hotel La Plage **T**
	★★★	Ommaroo **TMLT**
	★★★	Pomme d'Or **TMLT**
St Peter	★★★★	Mermaid **TMLT**

Wales

CLWYD

Colwyn Bay	❀☆☆☆	Hotel 70° **T**
Llangollen	★★★	Hand **TMLT**
Llanrhaedr	★★★	Bryn Morfydd
Northophall	★★★	Chequers **T**
Ruthin	★★★	Ruthin Castle **TMLT**
Wrexham	☆☆☆	Crest **MLT**

DYFED

Carmarthen	★★★	Ivy Bush Royal **T**
Fishguard	★★★	Fishguard Bay
Gwbert-on-Sea	★★★	Cliff **T**
Lamphey	★★★	Court **MLT**
Llanelli	★★★	Stradey Park **T**
Saundersfoot	★★★	St Bride's **TMLT**
Tenby	★★★	Imperial **T**
	★★	Atlantic

GLAMORGAN, MID

Bridgend	☆☆☆☆	Heronston **T**

GLAMORGAN, SOUTH

Barry	★★★	International **MLT**
Cardiff	☆☆☆☆	Inn on the Avenue **T**
	★★★★	Park **TMLT**
	☆☆☆	Crest **TMLT**
	☆☆☆	Post House **TMLT**
	★★★	Royal **MLT**
St Mellons	★★	St Mellons Hotel & Country Club

GLAMORGAN, WEST

Port Talbot	☆☆☆	Aberafon **T**
Swansea	☆☆☆☆	Dragon **T**

GWENT

Cwmbran	★★★	Hotel Commodore **TMLT**
Monmouth	★★★	King's Head
Newport	☆☆☆	Ladbroke (& Conferencentre) **TMLT**
	★★	Westgate **T**

GWYNEDD

Bangor	★★★	British
Llandudno	★★★	Empire **T**
	★★★	Imperial **MLT**
	★★★	Marine **T**
	★★★	St George's **T**
	★★	Esplanade **MLT**
	★★	Ormescliffe

POWYS

Llandrindod Wells	★★	Hotel Commodore

Scotland

BORDERS

Peebles	★★★	Peebles Hydro **TMLT**
	★★★	Tontine

CENTRAL

Dunblane	★★★	Stakis Dunblane Hydro **TMLT**
Falkirk	☆☆☆	Stakis Park
Polmont	★★★	Inchyra Grange **T**
Stirling	★★★	Golden Lion
	★★	King Robert **MLT**

DUMFRIES & GALLOWAY

Portpatrick	★★	Portpatrick **TMLT**
Stranraer	★★★	North West Castle **T**

FIFE

Dunfermline	★★★	King Malcolm Thistle
St Andrews	★★★	St Andrews Golf **TMLT**

GRAMPIAN

Aberdeen	☆☆☆☆	Holiday Inn Bucksburn **T**
	☆☆☆☆	Skean Dhu Altens **TMLT**
	★★★	Tree Tops Crest **TMLT**
	☆☆	Dee Motel **TMLT**

Aberdeen Airport	☆☆☆☆	Holiday Inn Aberdeen Airport **TMLT**
	☆☆☆☆	Skean Dhu Aberdeen Airport **TMLT**
	☆☆☆	Skean Dhu Dyce **TMLT**
Elgin	☆☆☆	Eight Acres
Ellon	☆☆☆	Ladbroke **TMLT**
Newburgh	❀★★	Udny Arms **T**
Peterhead	☆☆☆	Waterside Inn **T**
Westhill	☆☆☆	Westhill Inn **MLT**

HIGHLAND

Aviemore	☆☆☆☆	Stakis Coylumbridge **TMLT**
	☆☆☆	Badenoch **MLT**
	☆☆☆	Strathspey Thistle **TMLT**
Boat of Garten	★★★	Boat **MLT**
Fort William	☆☆☆	Ladbroke
Inverness	☆☆☆	Caledonian **TMLT**
	★★★	Kingsmill **TMLT**
	☆☆☆	Ladbroke (& Conferencentre) **T**
	★★	Drumossie **TMLT**
	★★	Queensgate **TMLT**
Nairn	★★★★	Golf View **TMLT**
	★★★	Windsor
Nethy Bridge	★★★	Nethybridge **T**
Wick	☆☆☆	Ladbroke

LOTHIAN

Bonnyrigg	★★★★	Dalhousie Castle **TMLT**
Edinburgh	★★★★	Caledonian **TMLT**
	★★★★	George **TMLT**
	☆☆☆☆	Ladbroke Dragonara **TMLT**
	☆☆☆☆	Royal Scot **T**
	★★★	Barnton Thistle **TMLT**
	★★★	Bruntsfield
	★★★	Carlton
	☆☆☆	Crest **TMLT**
	★★★	Howard **TMLT**
	☆☆☆	King James Thistle **TMLT**
	★★★	Old Waverley **T**
	★★★	Oratava **TMLT**
	☆☆☆	Post House **TMLT**
	★★★	Roxburghe **TMLT**
	☆☆	Stakis Commodore **TMLT**
Musselburgh	☆☆	Drummore **TMLT**
North Berwick	★★★	Marine **T**

STRATHCLYDE

Ayr	☆☆☆	Caledonian **MLT**
Blackwaterfoot (Isle of Arran)	★★	Kinloch **T**
East Kilbride	☆☆☆	Bruce **T**
Erskine	☆☆☆☆	Crest Hotel Erskine Bridge **MLT**
Giffnock	★★★	Macdonald Thistle **TMLT**
Glasgow	★★★★	Albany
	★★★	Bellahouston **TMLT**
	☆☆☆	Crest Hotel Glasgow–City **TMLT**
	☆☆☆	Stakis Ingram **TMLT**
Glasgow Airport	★★★★	Excelsior **T**
	☆☆☆☆	Stakis Normandy **TMLT**
	★★★	Dean Park **TMLT**
	★★★	Glynhill **TMLT**
Gourock	☆☆☆	Stakis Gantock **T**
Kilmarnock	☆☆☆	Howard Park **MLT**
Ledaig	★★★	Isle of Eriska
Motherwell	★★★	Garrion
Troon	★★★★	Marine
Turnberry	★★★★	Turnberry **T**

TAYSIDE

Auchterarder	★★★★★	Gleneagles **TMLT**
Blairgowrie	★★	Angus **TMLT**
Dundee	★★★	Angus Thistle **TMLT**
	★★	Tay **T**
Kinclaven	★★★	Ballathie House **T**
Kinross	★★★	Green **TMLT**
Montrose	★★★	Park **T**
Perth	★★★	Isle of Skye **MLT**
	☆☆☆	Stakis City Mills
	★★	Salutation **TMLT**
Pitlochry	★★★	Atholl Palace **T**
	★★★	Green Park
	★★★	Scotland's

Western Isles

ISLE OF LEWIS

Stornoway	★★★	Caberfeidh
	★★★	Seaforth

Special facilities for children

(For details of the specific facilities provided see page 13. For other details, including merit awards where applicable, see appropriate gazetteer entry.)

England

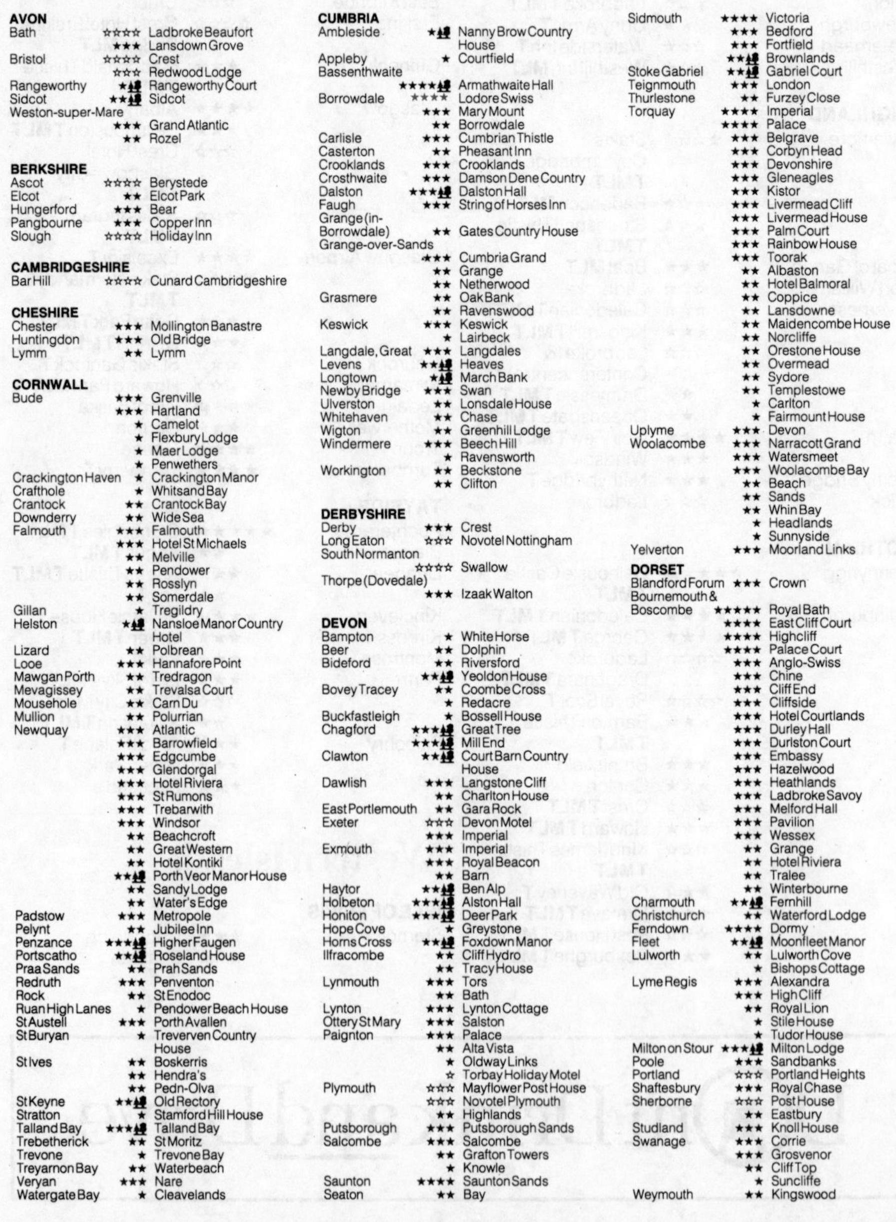

AVON

Bath	☆☆☆☆	Ladbroke Beaufort
	★★★	Lansdown Grove
Bristol	☆☆☆☆	Crest
	☆☆☆	Redwood Lodge
Rangeworthy	★	Rangeworthy Court
Sidcot	★★	Sidcot
Weston-super-Mare	★★★	Grand Atlantic
	★★	Rozel

BERKSHIRE

Ascot	☆☆☆☆	Berystede
Elcot	★★	Elcot Park
Hungerford	★★★	Bear
Pangbourne	★★★	Copper Inn
Slough	☆☆☆☆	Holiday Inn

CAMBRIDGESHIRE

Bar Hill	☆☆☆☆	Cunard Cambridgeshire

CHESHIRE

Chester	★★★	Mollington Banastre
Huntingdon	★★★	Old Bridge
Lymm	★★	Lymm

CORNWALL

Bude	★★★	Grenville
	★★★	Hartland
	★	Camelot
	★	Flexbury Lodge
	★	Maer Lodge
	★	Penwethers
Crackington Haven	★	Crackington Manor
Crafthole	★	Whitsand Bay
Crantock	★★	Crantock Bay
Downderry	★★	Wide Sea
Falmouth	★★★	Falmouth
	★★★	Hotel St Michaels
	★★★	Melville
	★★	Pendower
	★★	Rosslyn
	★★	Somerdale
Gillan	★	Tregildry
Helston	★	Nansloe Manor Country Hotel
Lizard	★★	Polbrean
Looe	★★★	Hannafore Point
Mawgan Porth	★★	Tredragon
Mevagissey	★★	Trevalsa Court
Mousehole	★★	Carn Du
Mullion	★★	Polurrian
Newquay	★★★	Atlantic
	★★★	Barrowfield
	★★★	Edgcumbe
	★★★	Glendorgal
	★★★	Hotel Riviera
	★★★	St Rumons
	★★★	Trebarwith
	★★★	Windsor
	★★	Beachcroft
	★★	Great Western
	★★	Hotel Kontiki
	★★	Porth Veor Manor House
	★★	Sandy Lodge
	★★	Water's Edge
Padstow	★★★	Metropole
Pelynt	★★	Jubilee Inn
Penzance	★★★	Higher Faugen
Portscatho	★★	Roseland House
Praa Sands	★★	Prah Sands
Redruth	★★★	Penventon
Rock	★★	St Enodoc
Ruan High Lanes	★	Pendower Beach House
St Austell	★★★	Porth Avallen
St Buryan	★	Treverven Country House
St Ives	★★	Boskerris
	★★	Hendra's
	★★	Pedn-Olva
St Keyne	★★	Old Rectory
Stratton	★	Stamford Hill House
Talland Bay	★★★	Talland Bay
Trebetherick	★★	St Moritz
Trevone	★	Trevone Bay
Treyarnon Bay	★★	Waterbeach
Veryan	★★★	Nare
Watergate Bay	★	Cleavelands

CUMBRIA

Ambleside	★	Nanny Brow Country House
Appleby	★	Courtfield
Bassenthwaite	★★★★	Armathwaite Hall
Borrowdale	★★★★	Lodore Swiss
	★★★	Mary Mount
	★★	Borrowdale
Carlisle	★★★	Cumbrian Thistle
Casterton	★★	Pheasant Inn
Crooklands	★★★	Crooklands
Crosthwaite	★★★	Damson Dene Country
Dalston	★★★	Dalston Hall
Faugh	★★★	String of Horses Inn
Grange (in-Borrowdale)	★★	Gates Country House
Grange-over-Sands	★★★	Cumbria Grand
	★★	Grange
	★★	Netherwood
Grasmere	★★	Oak Bank
	★★	Ravenswood
Keswick	★★★	Keswick
	★	Lairbeck
Langdale, Great	★★★	Langdales
Levens	★★	Heaves
Longtown	★	March Bank
Newby Bridge	★★★	Swan
Ulverston	★★	Lonsdale House
Whitehaven	★★	Chase
Wigton	★★	Greenhill Lodge
Windermere	★★★	Beech Hill
	★	Ravensworth
Workington	★★	Beckstone
	★★	Clifton

DERBYSHIRE

Derby	★★★	Crest
Long Eaton	☆☆☆	Novotel Nottingham
South Normanton	☆☆☆☆	Swallow
Thorpe (Dovedale)	★★★	Izaak Walton

DEVON

Bampton	★	White Horse
Beer	★★	Dolphin
Bideford	★★	Riversford
	★★	Yeoldon House
Bovey Tracey	★★	Coombe Cross
	★	Redacre
Buckfastleigh	★	Bossell House
Chagford	★★★	Great Tree
	★★★	Mill End
Clawton	★★	Court Barn Country House
Dawlish	★★★	Langstone Cliff
	★★	Charlton House
East Portlemouth	★★	Gara Rock
Exeter	☆☆☆	Devon Motel
	★★★	Imperial
Exmouth	★★★	Imperial
	★★★	Royal Beacon
	★★	Barn
Haytor	★★	Ben Alp
Holbeton	★★★	Alston Hall
Honiton	★★★	Deer Park
Hope Cove	★	Greystone
Horns Cross	★★	Foxdown Manor
Ilfracombe	★★	Cliff Hydro
	★★	Tracy House
Lynmouth	★★★	Tors
	★★	Bath
Lynton	★★★	Lynton Cottage
Ottery St Mary	★★★	Salston
Paignton	★★★	Palace
	★★	Alta Vista
	★	Oldway Links
	☆	Torbay Holiday Motel
Plymouth	☆☆☆	Mayflower Post House
	☆☆☆	Novotel Plymouth
	★★	Highlands
Putsborough	★★★	Putsborough Sands
Salcombe	★★★	Salcombe
	★★	Grafton Towers
	★	Knowle
Saunton	★★★★	Saunton Sands
Seaton	★★	Bay
Sidmouth	★★★★	Victoria
	★★★	Bedford
	★★★	Fortfield
	★★	Brownlands
Stoke Gabriel	★★	Gabriel Court
Teignmouth	★★★	London
Thurlestone	★★	Furzey Close
Torquay	★★★★	Imperial
	★★★★	Palace
	★★★	Belgrave
	★★★	Corbyn Head
	★★★	Devonshire
	★★★	Gleneagles
	★★★	Kistor
	★★★	Livermead Cliff
	★★★	Livermead House
	★★★	Palm Court
	★★★	Rainbow House
	★★★	Toorak
	★★	Albaston
	★★	Hotel Balmoral
	★★	Coppice
	★★	Lansdowne
	★★	Maidencombe House
	★★	Norcliffe
	★★	Orestone House
	★★	Overmead
	★★	Sydore
	★★	Templestowe
	★	Carlton
	★	Fairmount House
Uplyme	★★★	Devon
Woolacombe	★★★	Narracott Grand
	★★★	Watersmeet
	★★★	Woolacombe Bay
	★★	Beach
	★★	Sands
	★★	Whin Bay
	★	Headlands
	★	Sunnyside
Yelverton	★★★	Moorland Links

DORSET

Blandford Forum	★★★	Crown
Bournemouth & Boscombe	★★★★★	Royal Bath
	★★★★	East Cliff Court
	★★★★	Highcliff
	★★★★	Palace Court
	★★★	Anglo-Swiss
	★★★	Chine
	★★★	Cliff End
	★★★	Cliffside
	★★★	Hotel Courtlands
	★★★	Durley Hall
	★★★	Durlston Court
	★★★	Embassy
	★★★	Hazelwood
	★★★	Heathlands
	★★★	Ladbroke Savoy
	★★★	Melford Hall
	★★★	Pavilion
	★★★	Wessex
	★★	Grange
	★★	Hotel Riviera
	★★	Tralee
	★★	Winterbourne
Charmouth	★★	Fernhill
Christchurch	★★	Waterford Lodge
Ferndown	★★★★	Dormy
Fleet	★★	Moonfleet Manor
Lulworth	★★	Lulworth Cove
	★	Bishops Cottage
Lyme Regis	★★★	Alexandra
	★★★	High Cliff
	★★	Royal Lion
	★	Stile House
	★	Tudor House
Milton on Stour	★★★	Milton Lodge
Poole	★★★	Sandbanks
Portland	☆☆☆	Portland Heights
Shaftesbury	★★★	Royal Chase
Sherborne	☆☆☆	Post House
	★★	Eastbury
Studland	★★★	Knoll House
Swanage	★★★	Corrie
	★★★	Grosvenor
	★★	Cliff Top
	★	Suncliffe
Weymouth	★★	Kingswood

CO DURHAM
Chester-le-Street ★★★ Lumley Castle
Coatham Mundeville ★★★ Hall Garth
Durham ★★★ Bowburn Hall
Sedgefield ★★★ Hardwick Hall

ESSEX
Brentwood ★★★★ Brentwood Moat House
Bulphan ☆☆ Ye Olde Plough House Motel
Chelmsford ★★★ South Lodge
Darlington ☆☆☆☆ Blackwell Grange Moat House
Frinton-on-Sea ★★★ Frinton Lodge
★ Rock
Southend-on-Sea ★★ Roslin

GLOUCESTERSHIRE
Cirencester ★★★ Stratton House
Fairford ★★★ Bull
Gloucester ★★★ Bowden Hall
Mickleton ★★★ Three Ways
Newport ☆☆ Newport Towers Motel
Painswick ★★★ Painswick
Stow-on-the-Wold ★★ Fosse Manor
Stroud ★★ Burleigh Court
Westonbirt ★★★ Hare & Hounds

HAMPSHIRE
Avon ★★ Tyrells Ford Country House
Brockenhurst ★★★ Careys Manor Motor
★★★ Forest Park
★★★ Ladbroke Balmer Lawn
★★ Watersplash
Burley ★★★ Burley Manor
★★ Moorhill
Emsworth ★★ Brookfield
Fordingbridge ★★ Ashburn
Hayling Island ★★ Newtown House
Lymington ★★★ Passford House
Lyndhurst ★★★ Lyndhurst Park
Middle Wallop ★★ Fifehead Manor
Southampton ☆☆☆ Post House
Wickham ★★ Old House
Woodlands ★★ Busketts Lawn

HEREFORD & WORCESTER
Colwall ★★ Colwall Park
Crossway Green ★ Mitre Oak
Droitwich ★ St Andrews House
Evesham ★★★ Evesham Hotel
How Caple ★★★ How Caple Grange
Kerne Bridge ★★ Castle View
Kidderminster ★★★★ Stone Manor
Malvern, Great ★★ Thornbury
Ross-on-Wye ★★★ Chase
★★★ Wye
Whitchurch ★★ Doward

HERTFORDSHIRE
Bishop's Stortford ★★★ Foxley
Bushey ☆☆ Spiders Web Motel
Harpenden ★★★ Glen Eagle
Newgate Street ★★★ Ponsbourne
St Albans ★★★ Sopwell House
Stevenage ☆☆☆ Stevenage Moat House

HUMBERSIDE
Beverley ★★★ Tickton Grange
Bridlington ★★★ Expanse
★★ Monarch
Laceby ★★ Oaklands Hotel & Country Club

ISLE OF WIGHT
Bembridge ★★ Elm Country
St Lawrence ★★★ Rocklands
Ventnor ★★★ Royal
★★★ Ventnor Towers

KENT
Dover ☆☆☆ Dover Motel
★★ Cliffe Court
Folkestone ★★ Chilworth Court
Hythe ★★★★ Hotel Imperial
Margate ★★ Walpole Bay
Ramsgate ★★ San Clu
Sittingbourne ★★ Coniston
Tunbridge Wells (Royal) ★★★ Spa
Westgate-on-Sea ★★ Ivyside

LANCASHIRE
Blackpool ★★ Chequers
Burnley ★★ Rosehill House
Darwen ★★★ Whitehall
Hornby ★★ Castle
Lancaster ☆☆☆☆ Post House
Lytham St Annes ★★ Chadwick
★★ St Ives
Morecambe ★★★ Elms
Preston ★★★ Broughton Park House

LEICESTERSHIRE
Leicester ★★★ Belmont
Melton Mowbray ★★★ Harboro
Uppingham ★ Central

LINCOLNSHIRE
Market Rasen ★★ Limes
Skegness ★★ Country
Stamford ★★★ George
★★ Lady Anne's
Tetford ★ White Hart
Washingborough ★★ Washingborough Hall

LONDON, GREATER
Harrow Weald ★★★ Grim's Dyke Country
Heathrow Airport ☆☆☆☆ Holiday Inn
☆☆☆ Berkeley Arms
Sanderstead ★★★★ Selsdon Park
Woodford Bridge ★★★ Prince Regent

MANCHESTER, GREAT
Altrincham ☆☆ Pelican
Bramhall ☆☆☆ Bramhall Moat House

MIDLANDS, WEST
Birmingham ★★ Bristol Court
Coventry ☆☆☆ Novotel Coventry
Solihull ☆☆ Fleming's
Walsall ★★★ Barons Court
Wolverhampton ★★★ Mount
★★★ Park Hall
★★ York

MERSEYSIDE
Southport ★★★★ Prince of Wales
★★★ Royal Clifton
Thornton Hough ★★★ Thornton Hall
Wallasey ★★ Grove House

NORFOLK
Bunwell ★★ Bunwell Manor
Cromer ★★★ Colne House
Harleston ★★ Swan
Hethersett ★★ Park Farm
Hunstanton ★★ Le Strange Arms
★ Wash & Tope
King's Lynn ★ Stuart House
Mundesley-on-Sea ★★★ Continental
Sheringham ★★ Beaumaris
★ Two Lifeboats
Titchwell ★★ Manor
West Runton ★★★ Links Country Park
Yarmouth, Great ★★★ Cliff
★★★ Imperial

NORTHAMPTONSHIRE
Crick ☆☆☆☆ Post House
Marston Trussell ★★ Sun Inn
Oundle ★★ Talbot
Wicken ★★ Wicken Country

NORTHUMBERLAND
Bellingham ★★ Riverdale Hall
Berwick-on-Tweed ★★★ Turret House
★ Queens Head
Blanchland ★★ Lord Crewe Arms
Chollerford ★★★ George
Cornhill-on-Tweed ★★ Collingwood Arms
Longhorsley ★★★★ Linden Hall
Seahouses ★★ Olde Ship
Wooler ★★ Tankerville Arms

NOTTINGHAMSHIRE
Eastwood ★ Sun Inn
Nottingham ★★★ North Lodge
Retford (East) ★★★ West Retford

OXFORDSHIRE
Deddington ★★ Holcombe
Milton Common ★★ Belfry
Wallingford ★★ Shillingford Bridge
Weston-on-the-Green ★★★ Weston Manor
Wroxton ★★ Wroxton House

SCILLY, ISLES OF
Tresco, New Grimsby ★ New Inn
Old Grimsby ❀★★★ Island

SHROPSHIRE
Church Stretton ★★★ Long Mynd
Ludlow ★★ Overton Grange
Shifnal ★★★ Park House
Weston ★★ Hawkstone Park

SOMERSET
Dulverton ★★★ Carnarvon Arms
Dunster ★★ Exmoor House
Ilminster ★★★ Horton Cross
★★ Shrubbery
Minehead ★★★ Beach
Montacute ★★ King's Arms Inn
Shipham ★★ Daneswood House
★ Penscot Farmhouse
Watchet ★★ Downfield
Wincanton ★★ Dolphin
Withypool ★ Westerclose Country House

STAFFORDSHIRE
Haywood, Great ☆☆ Coach & Horses
Longnor ★★ Crewe & Harpur
Newcastle-under-Lyne ★ Deansfield
Stafford ☆☆☆ Tillington Hall
Tamworth ★★ Castle

SUFFOLK
Brome ☆☆ Brome Grange Motel
Ipswich ★★★ Belstead Brook
☆☆☆ Ipswich Moat House
Newmarket ★★ Bedford Lodge
Walberswick ★★ Anchor

SURREY
Bagshot ★★★★ Pennyhill Park
★ Cricketers (Henekey's)
Cobham ☆☆☆ Ladbroke Seven Hills
Esher ★ Haven
Haslemere ★★★ Lythe Hill
Seale ☆☆☆ Hog's Back

SUSSEX, EAST
Brighton & Hove ★★★★ Dudley
★★★ Alexandra
★★★ Courtlands
★★★ Old Ship
★★ St Catherine's Lodge
Eastbourne ★★★★★ Grand
★★★★ Cavendish
★★★★ Queens
★★★ Sandhurst

SUSSEX, WEST
Bognor Regis ★★★ Royal Norfolk
★★ Clarehaven
★ Black Mill House
★ Lyndhurst
Chichester ★★★ Chichester Lodge
Cuckfield ★★ Hilton Park
Thakeham ★★ Abingworth Hall
Walberton ★★★ Avisford Park
Worthing ★★★ Warnes

TYNE & WEAR
Newcastle upon Tyne ★★★★ Gosforth Park
Washington ★★★ George Washington

WARWICKSHIRE
Brandon ★★★ Brandon Hall
Charlecote ☆☆☆ Charlecote Pheasant Country
Eathorpe ★★ Eathorpe Park
Princethorpe ★★ Woodhouse
Stratford-upon-Avon ★★★ Arden
Warwick ☆☆☆☆ Ladbroke
Wishaw ★★★ Moxhull Hall

WILTSHIRE
Corsham ★★★ Rudloe Park
★★ Methuen Arms
☆☆ Stagecoach
Swindon ★★★★ Blunsdon House
★★★ Crest

YORKSHIRE, NORTH
Aysgarth ★ Palmer Flatt
Harrogate ★★★★ Hotel Majestic
★★★ Cairn
Lastingham ★★ Lastingham Grange
Ravenscar ★★ Raven Hall
Ripon ★★★ Ripon Spa
Scarborough ★★★★ Holbeck Hall
★★★★ Royal
★★★ St Nicholas
★★ Esplanade
★★ Wrea Head Country
★★ Norbreck
Settle ★★★ Falcon Manor
Threshfield ★★★ Wilson Arms
York ★★★★ Royal York
★★★ Chase

YORKSHIRE, SOUTH
- Bawtry ★★★ Crown
- Rotherham ★★ Brentwood

YORKSHIRE, WEST
- Bradford ☆☆☆ Novotel Bradford
- Garforth ☆☆☆ Ladbroke
- Halifax ★★★ Holdsworth House
- Holywell Green ★★ Rock Inn
- Ilkley ★★★ Craiglands
-   ★★ Greystones
- Rishworth ★★ Royal
- Wakefield ★★★ Walton Hall

Channel Islands

GUERNSEY
- Fermain Bay ★★★ La Chalet
-   ★★ La Favorita
- St Martin ★★★ Bella Luce
-   ★★★ St Margarets Lodge
- St Peter Port ★★★★ Old Government House
-   ★★ Dunchoille
-   ★★ Grange Lodge

JERSEY
- Bouley Bay ★★★★ Waters Edge
- Portelet Bay ★★★★ Portelet
- St Helier ★★★ Ommaroo
-   ★★ Mountview
- St Peter ★★★★ Mermaid

Wales

CLWYD
- Abergele ★★ Kinmel Manor
- Colwyn Bay ★ Edelweiss
-   ★ West Point
- Glyn Ceiriog ★★ Plas Owen
- Llangollen ★★★ Bryn Howel
- Llanrhaedr ★★★ Bryn Morfydd
- Redbrook ★★ Redbrook Hunting Lodge

DYFED
- Aberporth ★★ Hotel Penrallt
- Crugybar ★★⌂ Glanrannel Park
- Gwbert-on-Sea ★★★ Cliff
- Haverfordwest ★★ Pembroke House
- Lamphey ★★★⌂ Court
- Milton ★★ Milton Manor
- Narberth ★★ Plas Hyfryd
- Pembroke ★★ Coach House Inn
- Pembroke Dock ★★★⌂ Cleddau Bridge
- St Davids ★★★⌂ Warpool Court
- Tenby ★★★ Imperial
-   ★★ Fourcroft
-   ★★ Royal Lion

GLAMORGAN, MID
- Porthcawl ★★ Maid of Sker

GLAMORGAN, WEST
- Neath ★★ Cimla Court Motel

GWENT
- Blackwood ★★★ Maes Manor
- Cwmbran ★★★ Hotel Commodore
- Pandy ★★ Park

GWYNEDD
- Abersoch ★★ Deucoch
- Beaumaris ★★ Henllys Hall
- Beddgelert ★⌂ Bryn Eglwys
- Betws-y-Coed ★★ Craig-y-Dderwen Country House
-   ☆☆ Waterloo Motel
- Conwy ★★★ Sychnant Pass
- Deganwy ★★ Bryn Cregin
- Dolwyddelan ★★ Elen's Castle
- Fairbourne ★★ Springfield
- Llanbedrog ★★ Brynderwen
- Llanberis ★★ Gallt-y-Glyn
-   ★ Dol Peris
- Llandudno ★★ Ormescliffe
-   ★ Tan-Lan
- Llanfairpwllgwyngyll ★★ Carreg Bran Country
- Llanrwst ★★ Eagles
- Nefyn ★★ Nanhoron Arms
-   ★ Caeau Capel
- Pennal ★★★ Talgarth Hall
-   ★★ Llugwy Hall Country House
- Penrhyndeudraeth ★ Brynllydan
- Tremadog ★★ Madoc
- Tywyn ★★ Corbett Arms

POWYS
- Brecon ★★ Castle of Brecon
- Builth Wells ★★⌂ Caer Beris Manor
-   ★ Pencerrig Country House
- Caersws ★★ Maesmawr Hall
- Crickhowell ★★★⌂ Gliffaes
- Llandrindod Wells ★★ Hotel Commodore
- Llangammarch Wells ★★★⌂ Lake
- Llanwrtyd Wells ★ Neuadd Arms
- Rhayader ★★ Elan Valley
- Welshpool ★ Garth Derwen

Scotland

BORDERS
- Broughton ★★ Greenmantle
- Dryburgh ★★★⌂ Dryburgh Abbey
- Peebles ★★★ Peebles Hydro

CENTRAL
- Callander ★★★⌂ Roman Camp
- Kinbuck ✿★★★⌂ Cromlix House
- Strathblane ★★★ Country Club
-   ★★ Kirkhouse Inn

DUMFRIES & GALLOWAY
- Auchencairn ★★★⌂ Balcary Bay
- Beattock ★★ Auchen Castle
- Crocketford ★★ Galloway Arms
- Gatehouse of Fleet ★★★ Murray Arms
- Johnstone Bridge ★★ Dinwoodie Lodge
- Kirkcolm ★★ Knocknassie House
- Moniaive ★ Craigdarroch Arms
- Newton Stewart ★★ Creebridge House
-   ★★ Galloway Arms
- Portpatrick ★★★ Fernhill
-   ★★ Braefield House
-   ★★ Portpatrick

FIFE
- Crail ★ Croma
- Elie ★★ Golf
- St Andrews ★★★ Rufflets

GRAMPIAN
- Aboyne ★★ Balnacoil House
-   ★★ Huntley Arms
- Ballater ★★ Craigard
- Banchory ★★★⌂ Banchory Lodge
-   ★★★⌂ Raemoir
-   ★★★ Tor-na-Coille
-   ★★ Burnett Arms
- Banff ☆☆☆ Banff Springs
-   ★ Dounemount
-   ★ Fife Lodge
- Cullen ★★ Cullen Bay
- Glenlivet ★★ Minmore House
- Kelso ★★★ Ednam House
-   ★ Queens Head
- Kildrummy ★★★⌂ Kildrummy Castle
- Monymusk ★★ Grant Arms
- Potarch ★ Potarch
- Stonehaven ★★ St Leonards
- Tomintoul ★★ Richmond Arms

HIGHLAND
- Aviemore ☆☆☆ Post House
-   ☆☆☆ Strathspey Thistle
- Ballachulish ★★★ Ballachulish
- Boat of Garten ★★ Craigard
- Bonar Bridge ★★ Caledonian
- Brora ★★ Royal Marine
- Contin ★★ Craigdarroch Lodge
- Cromarty ★★ Royal
- Dalwhinnie ★★ Loch Ericht
- Dingwall ★★ Royal
- Dornoch ★★ Burghfield House
- Duror ★★ Stewart
- Gairloch ★★★ Gairloch
- Glenborrodale ★★★ Clan Morrison
- Grantown ★★ Garth
- Inverness ★★★ Kingsmills
-   ★★ Drumossie
-   ★ Redcliffe
- Invershin ★★⌂ Aultnager Lodge
- Lairg ★★★ Sutherland Arms
- Letterfinlay ★★★ Letterfinlay Lodge
- Lochinver ★★★ Culag
- Morar ★★★ Morar
- Nairn ★★★★ Golf View
-   ★★★ Royal Marine
-   ★★★ Windsor
-   ★★ Alton Burn
- Nethy Bridge ★★★ Nethy Bridge
- Newtonmore ★★ Main's
-   ★ Ard-na-Coille
- Roy Bridge ★★ Glenspean
- Skeabost Bridge, Isle of Skye ★★★⌂ Skeabost House
- Torridon ★★⌂ Loch Torridon

LOTHIAN
- Aberlady ★★ Kilspindie House
- Bonnyrigg ★★★★⌂ Dalhousie Castle
- Edinburgh ☆☆☆☆ Royal Scot
-   ★★★ Howard
- Humbie ★★★⌂ Johnstounburn House
- North Berwick ★★ Nether Abbey

SHETLAND
- Whiteness ★ Westings

STRATHCLYDE
- Arden ★★★ Lomond Castle
- Ardentinny ★★ Ardentinny
- Arduaine ★★★ Loch Melfort
- Ayr ★★★ Savoy Park
-   ★★ Balgarth
- Barrhead ✿★★ Dalmeny Park
- Blackwaterfoot, Isle of Arran ★★ Kinloch
- Carradale ★★ Carradale
- Connel ★★ Falls of Lora
-   ★★ Lochnell Arms
- Dunoon ★★ Argyll
- Glasgow ★★★ Bellahouston
- Greenock ★★★ Tontine
- Hollybush ★★⌂ Hollybush House
- Inverary ★ Fernpoint
- Kilcreggan ★★ Kilcreggan
- Kilmory ★★ Lagg
- Kirkoswald ★ Kirkton Jean's
- Lanark ★★ Cartland Bridge
- Langbank ★★★⌂ Gleddoch House
- Largs ★★ Elderslie
-   ★★ St Helens
- Luss ★★ Colquhoun Arms
- Port Ellen (Isle of Islay) ★ Dower
- Portsonachan ★★ Portsonachan
- Prestwick ★★ Queens
-   ★★ St Nicholas
- Rhu ★★★ Rosslea Hall
- Rosebank ★★★ Popinjay
- Rothesay ★ Ardmory House
- Strathaven ★ Strathaven
- Tarbert ★★★⌂ Stonefield Castle
- Troon ★★★ Sun Court
-   ★★ South Beach
- Turnberry ★★★★ Turnberry

TAYSIDE
- Auchterarder ★★★★★ Gleneagles
- Carnoustie ★★ Carlogie House
- Crieff ★★ Murray Park
- Dundee ☆☆☆ Swallow
- Edzell ★★★ Glen Esk
-   ★★ Panmure Arms
- Fearnan ★ Tigh-an-Loan
- Glencarse ★★ Newton House
- Killiecrankie ★★ Killiecrankie
- Kinclaven ★★★⌂ Ballathie House
- Kinross ★★★ Green
- Kirkmichael ★★ Log Cabin
- Logierait ★ Logierait
- Montrose ★★★ Park
- Perth ★★ Queens
-   ★ County
- Pitlochry ★★★ Pitlochry Hydro
-   ★★ Burnside
- St Fillans ★★ Drummond Arms

WESTERN ISLES
- Stornoway (Isle of Lewis) ★★★ Caberfeidh
- Tarbert (Isle of Harris) ★★ Harris

Overseas Offices of the British Tourist Authority

Australia

British Tourist Authority
171 Clarence St.
Sydney
N.S.W.
2000
T: 29-8627

Austria

British Tourist Authority
Wiedner Hauptstrasse 5/8
1040 Wien
(0222) 65 03 76

Belgium

British Tourist Authority
Rue de la Montagne 52 Bergstraat,
B2
1000 Brussels
T: 02/511.43.90

Brazil

British Tourist Authority
Avenida Ipiranga 318-A,
12° Andar, conj 1201
01046 São Paulo
=SP
T: 257-1834

Canada

British Tourist Authority
94 Cumberland Street, Suite 600
Toronto,
Ontario
M5R 3N3
T: (416) 925-6326

British Tourist Authority
409 Granville Street
Vancouver, British Columbia
T: (604) 669-2414

Denmark

Det Britiske Turistkontor
Møntergade 3
DK-1116 København
T: (01) 12 07 93

France

British Tourist Authority
6 Place Vendôme
75001 Paris
T: 296 47 60

Germany

British Tourist Authority
Neue Mainzer Str. 22
6000 Frankfurt am Main 1
T: (0611) 236428/29

Italy

British Tourist Authority
Via S. Eufemia 5
00187 Roma
T: 678.4998 or 678.5548

Japan

British Tourist Authority
Tokyo Club Building
3-2-6 Kasumigaseki, Chiyoda-ku
Tokyo 100
T: (03) 581-3603

Mexico

British Tourist Authority
Edificio Alber
Paseo de la Reforma 332-5 Piso
06600 Mexico DF
T: 533 63757

Netherlands

British Tourist Authority
(Written enquiries only)
Leidseplein 5
1017 PR Amsterdam
T: (020) 23.46.67

Netherlands

British Travel Centre
(Personal callers only)
Leidseplein 23
Amsterdam

New Zealand

British Tourist Authority
Box 3655
Wellington

Singapore

British Tourist Authority
14 Collyer Quay 05-05
Singapore Rubber House
Singapore 0104
T: Singapore 2242966/7

South Africa

British Tourist Authority 7th Floor
JBS Building
107 Commissioner Street
Johannesburg 2000
PO Box 6256
T: 29 67 70

Spain

British Tourist Authority
Torre de Madrid 6/4
Plaza de España
Madrid 13 España
T. 241 13 96

Sweden

British Tourist Authority
For visitors: Malmskillnadsg 42
1st Floor
For Mail: Box 7293
S-10390 Stockholm
T: 08-21 24 44

Switzerland

British Tourist Authority
Limmatquai 78 8001 Zurich
T: 01/47 42 77 or 47 42 97

USA Chicago

British Tourist Authority
John Hancock Center Suite 3320
875 N. Michigan Avenue
Chicago Illinois 60611
T: (312) 787-0490

USA Dallas

British Tourist Authority
Plaza of the Americas
750 North Tower LB346
Dallas Texas 75201
T: (214) 748-2279

USA Los Angeles

British Tourist Authority
612 South Flower Street
Los Angeles CA 90017
T: (213) 623-8196

USA New York

British Tourist Authority
40 West 57th Street
New York N.Y. 10019
T: (212) 581-4700

The National Grid

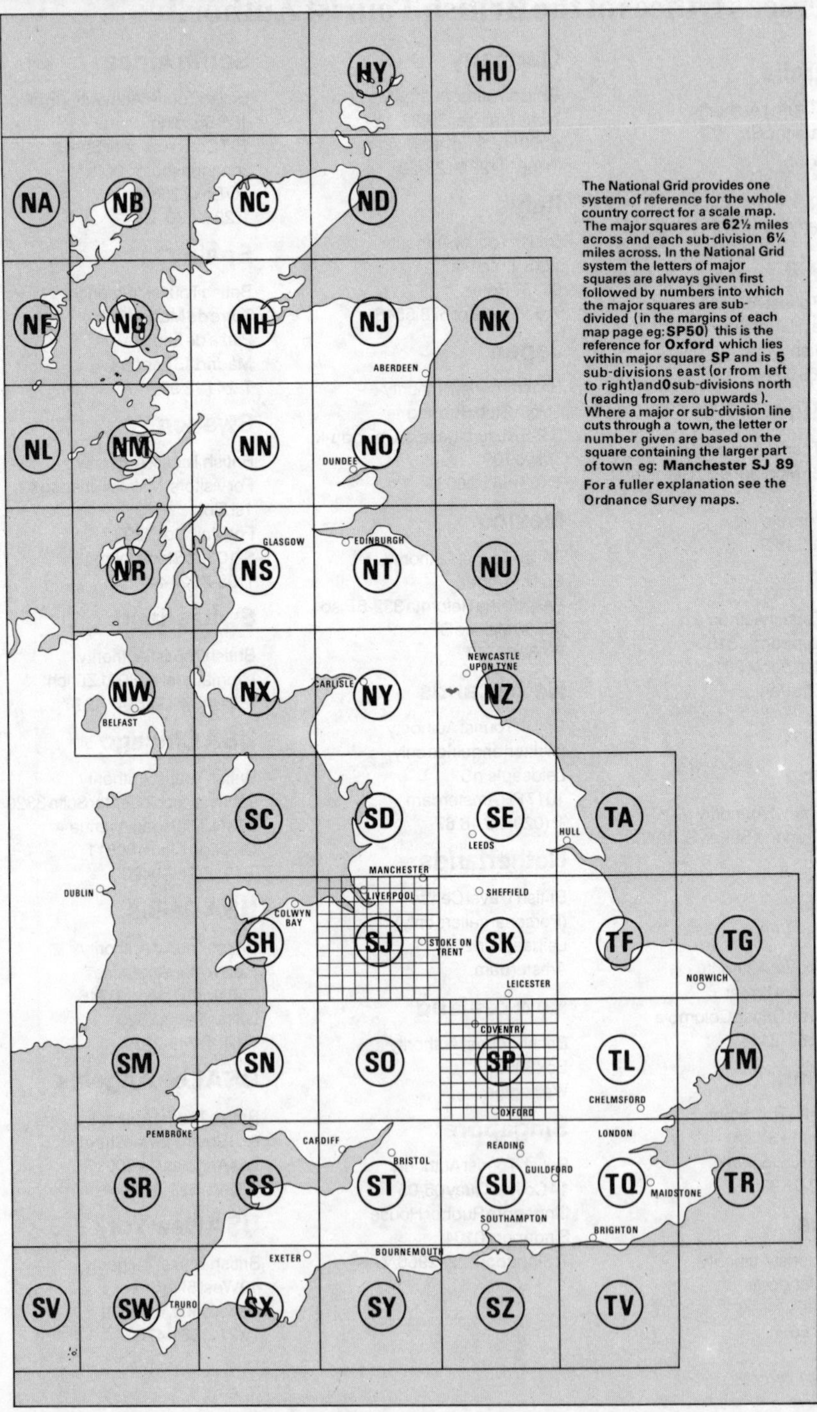

HY
HU
NA
NB
NC
ND
NF
NG
NH
NJ
NK
ABERDEEN
NL
NM
NN
NO
DUNDEE
GLASGOW
EDINBURGH
NR
NS
NT
NU
NEWCASTLE UPON TYNE
CARLISLE
NW
NX
NY
NZ
BELFAST
SC
SD
SE
TA
HULL
LEEDS
MANCHESTER
DUBLIN
LIVERPOOL
SHEFFIELD
COLWYN BAY
SH
SJ
STOKE ON TRENT
SK
TF
TG
NORWICH
LEICESTER
COVENTRY
SM
SN
SO
SP
TL
TM
CHELMSFORD
OXFORD
PEMBROKE
CARDIFF
LONDON
READING
BRISTOL
GUILDFORD
SR
SS
ST
SU
TQ
MAIDSTONE
TR
SOUTHAMPTON
BRIGHTON
EXETER
BOURNEMOUTH
SV
SW
TRURO
SX
SY
SZ
TV

The National Grid provides one system of reference for the whole country correct for a scale map. The major squares are 62½ miles across and each sub-division 6¼ miles across. In the National Grid system the letters of major squares are always given first followed by numbers into which the major squares are sub-divided (in the margins of each map page eg: **SP50**) this is the reference for **Oxford** which lies within major square **SP** and is **5** sub-divisions east (or from left to right) and **0** sub-divisions north (reading from zero upwards). Where a major or sub-division line cuts through a town, the letter or number given are based on the square containing the larger part of town eg: **Manchester SJ 89**

For a fuller explanation see the Ordnance Survey maps.

Key to Atlas

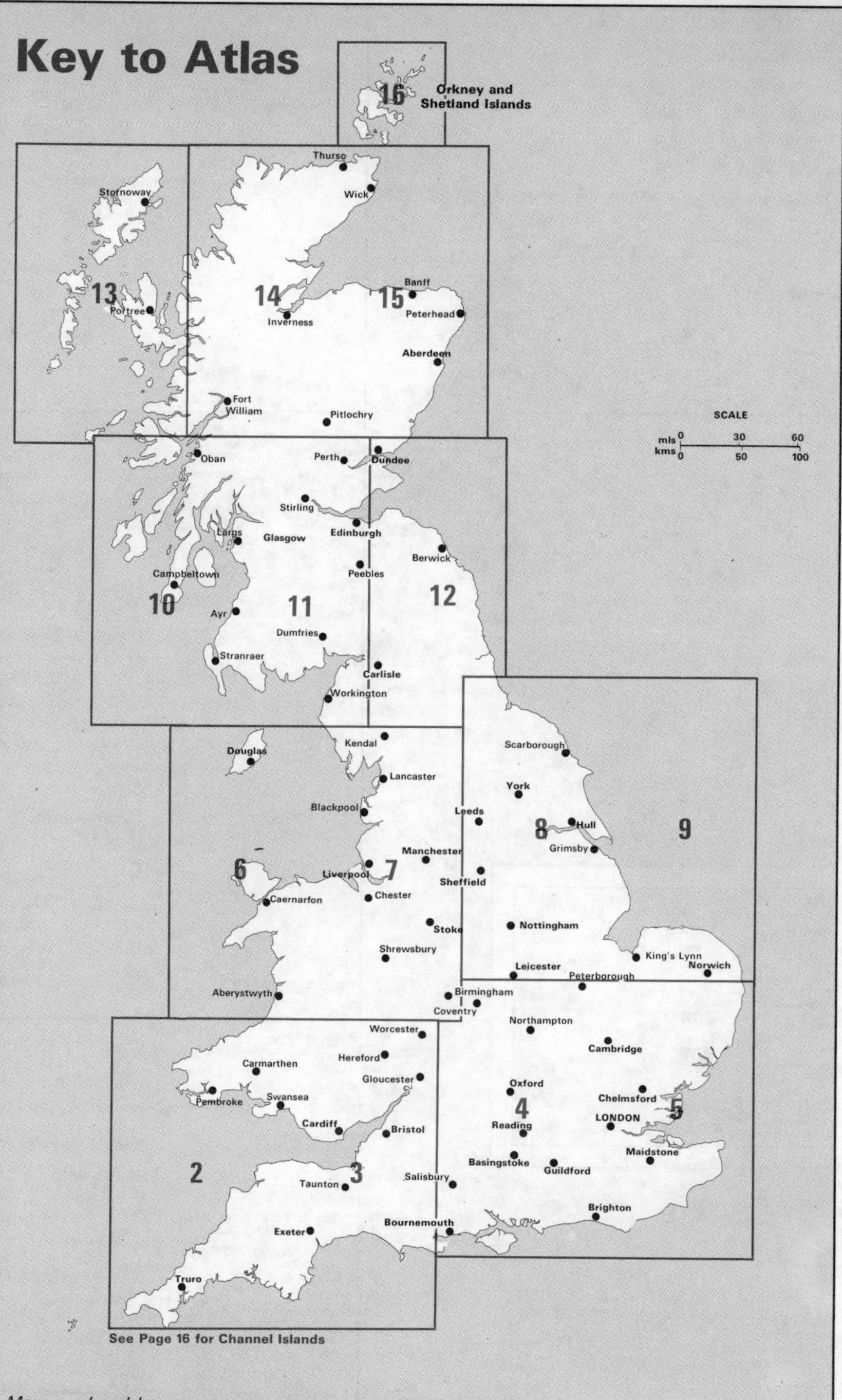

16
Orkney and
Shetland Islands
13
14
15
Thurso
Wick
Stornoway
Banff
Peterhead
Portree
Inverness
Aberdeen
Fort
William
Pitlochry
Oban
Perth
Dundee
Stirling
Edinburgh
Largs
Glasgow
Berwick
Peebles
Campbeltown
10
11
12
Ayr
Dumfries
Stranraer
Carlisle
Workington
Kendal
Douglas
Lancaster
Scarborough
York
Blackpool
Leeds
Hull
8
9
Grimsby
Manchester
6
Liverpool
7
Sheffield
Caernarfon
Chester
Stoke
Nottingham
Shrewsbury
King's Lynn
Norwich
Leicester
Peterborough
Aberystwyth
Birmingham
Coventry
Northampton
Worcester
Cambridge
Hereford
Carmarthen
Gloucester
Oxford
Chelmsford
Pembroke
Swansea
4
LONDON
5
Cardiff
Bristol
Reading
Maidstone
Basingstoke
Guildford
2
3
Taunton
Salisbury
Brighton
Bournemouth
Exeter
Truro
SCALE
mls 0 30 60
kms 0 50 100

See Page 16 for Channel Islands

Maps produced by
The AA Cartographic Department (Publications Division), Fanum House, Basingstoke, Hampshire RG21 2EA

This atlas is for location purposes Only: see Member's Handbook for current road and AA road services information

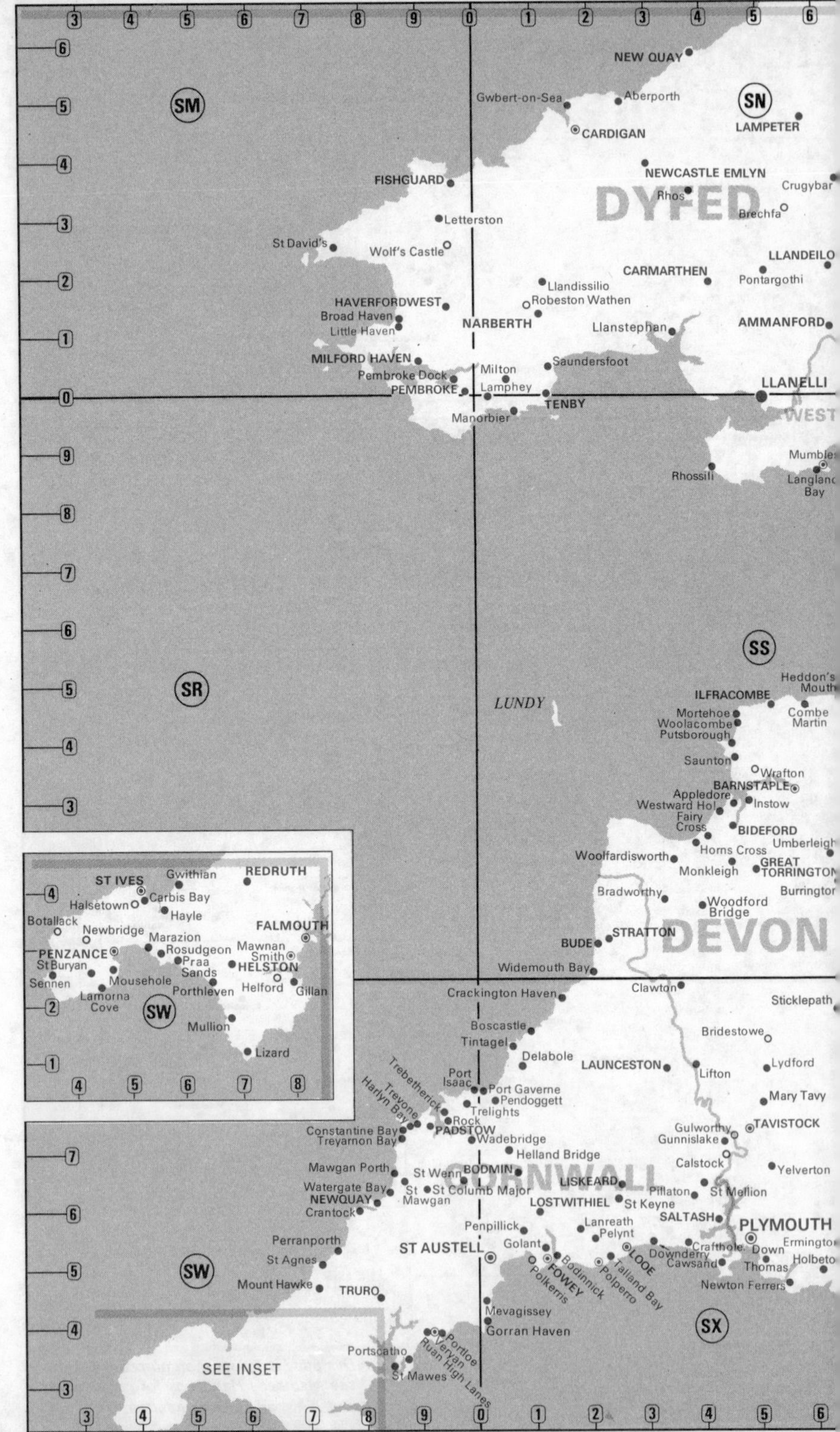
SM
SN
SR
SS
SW
SX
DYFED
DEVON
CORNWALL
WEST
NEW QUAY
Gwbert-on-Sea
Aberporth
CARDIGAN
LAMPETER
NEWCASTLE EMLYN
Crugybar
FISHGUARD
Rhos
Brechfa
Letterston
St David's
Wolf's Castle
LLANDEILO
CARMARTHEN
Pontargothi
Llandissilio
HAVERFORDWEST
Robeston Wathen
Broad Haven
Little Haven
NARBERTH
Llanstephan
AMMANFORD
MILFORD HAVEN
Saundersfoot
Milton
Pembroke Dock
PEMBROKE
Lamphey
TENBY
LLANELLI
Manorbier
Mumbles
Rhossili
Langland Bay
LUNDY
Heddon's Mouth
ILFRACOMBE
Combe Martin
Mortehoe
Woolacombe
Putsborough
Saunton
Wrafton
BARNSTAPLE
Appledore
Westward Ho!
Instow
Fairy Cross
BIDEFORD
Horns Cross
Umberleigh
Woolfardisworth
GREAT TORRINGTON
Monkleigh
Bradworthy
Burrington
Woodford Bridge
STRATTON
BUDE
Widemouth Bay
Clawton
Crackington Haven
Sticklepath
Boscastle
Bridestowe
Tintagel
Delabole
LAUNCESTON
Lydford
Lifton
Port Isaac
Port Gaverne
Mary Tavy
Trebetherick
Trevone
Harlyn Bay
Pendoggett
Trelights
Rock
PADSTOW
Constantine Bay
Treyarnon Bay
Wadebridge
Gulworthy
TAVISTOCK
Gunnislake
Helland Bridge
Calstock
Mawgan Porth
BODMIN
St Wenn
Yelverton
Watergate Bay
St Mawgan
St Columb Major
LISKEARD
NEWQUAY
LOSTWITHIEL
Pillaton
St Mellion
Crantock
St Keyne
SALTASH
Penpillick
Lanreath
Pelynt
PLYMOUTH
Perranporth
ST AUSTELL
Golant
LOOE
Downderry
Crafthole
Down Thomas
Ermington
St Agnes
Cawsand
Holbeton
FOWEY
Bodinnick
Polkerris
Polperro
Talland Bay
Newton Ferrers
Mount Hawke
TRURO
Mevagissey
Gorran Haven
Portloe
Veryan
Ruan High Lanes
Portscatho
St Mawes
SEE INSET
ST IVES
Gwithian
REDRUTH
Halsetown
Carbis Bay
Hayle
Botallack
Newbridge
Marazion
FALMOUTH
PENZANCE
Rosudgeon
Mawnan Smith
St Buryan
Praa Sands
HELSTON
Sennen
Mousehole
Porthleven
Helford
Gillan
Lamorna Cove
Mullion
Lizard

For continuation pages refer to numbered arrows

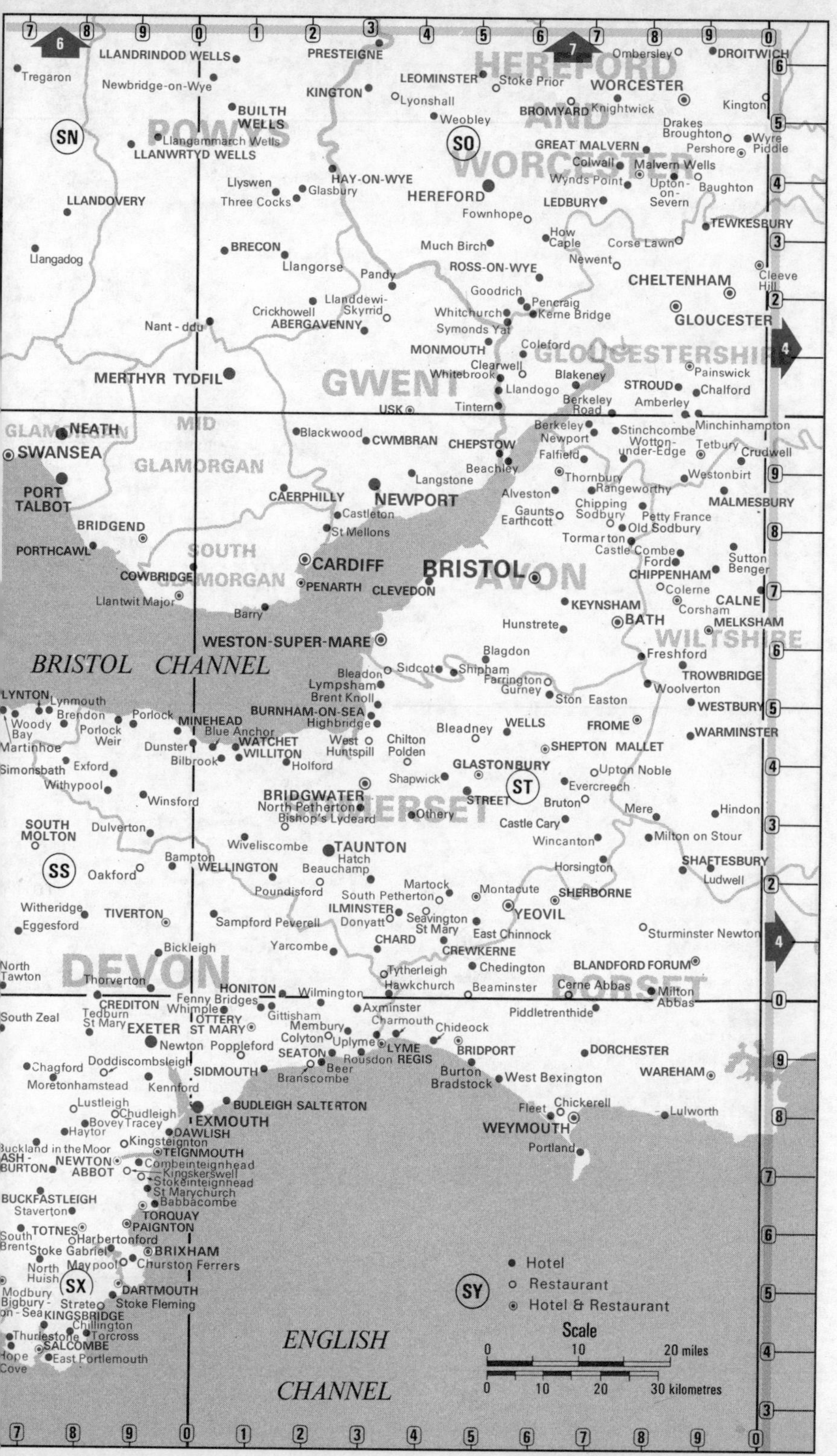

HEREFORD AND WORCESTER
POWYS
GWENT
GLOUCESTERSHIRE
WEST GLAMORGAN
MID GLAMORGAN
SOUTH GLAMORGAN
AVON
WILTSHIRE
SOMERSET
DEVON
DORSET
SN
SO
SS
ST
SX
SY
Tregaron
LLANDRINDOD WELLS
Newbridge-on-Wye
BUILTH WELLS
Llangammarch Wells
LLANWRTYD WELLS
LLANDOVERY
Llangadog
PRESTEIGNE
KINGTON
LEOMINSTER
Stoke Prior
Lyonshall
Weobley
Llyswen
Glasbury
Three Cocks
HAY-ON-WYE
HEREFORD
Fownhope
BRECON
Llangorse
Much Birch
ROSS-ON-WYE
Pandy
Llanddewi-Skyrrid
Crickhowell
ABERGAVENNY
Nant-ddu
Goodrich
Whitchurch
Symonds Yat
Pencraig
Kerne Bridge
MONMOUTH
Coleford
Clearwell
Whitebrook
Llandogo
Tintern
USK
MERTHYR TYDFIL
Ombersley
DROITWICH
WORCESTER
BROMYARD
Knightwick
Kington
Drakes Broughton
Wyre Piddle
Pershore
GREAT MALVERN
Colwall
Malvern Wells
Wynds Point
Upton-on-Severn
Baughton
LEDBURY
How Caple
Corse Lawn
TEWKESBURY
Newent
Cleeve Hill
CHELTENHAM
GLOUCESTER
Painswick
Blakeney
STROUD
Chalford
Berkeley Road
Amberley
Minchinhampton
Berkeley
Newport
Stinchcombe
Wotton-under-Edge
Tetbury
Crudwell
Falfield
Thornbury
Westonbirt
Rangeworthy
Alveston
Gaunts Earthcott
Chipping Sodbury
Petty France
MALMESBURY
Old Sodbury
Tormarton
Castle Combe
Ford
Sutton Benger
CHIPPENHAM
Colerne
Corsham
CALNE
MELKSHAM
KEYNSHAM
BATH
Hunstrete
Freshford
TROWBRIDGE
Woolverton
WESTBURY
WARMINSTER
NEATH
SWANSEA
PORT TALBOT
Blackwood
CWMBRAN
CHEPSTOW
Beachley
Langstone
CAERPHILLY
NEWPORT
Castleton
St Mellons
BRIDGEND
PORTHCAWL
CARDIFF
PENARTH
BRISTOL
CLEVEDON
COWBRIDGE
Llantwit Major
Barry
WESTON-SUPER-MARE
BRISTOL CHANNEL
Bleadon
Sidcot
Shipham
Blagdon
Farrington Gurney
Ston Easton
Lympsham
Brent Knoll
BURNHAM-ON-SEA
Highbridge
West Huntspill
Chilton Polden
Bleadney
WELLS
FROME
SHEPTON MALLET
GLASTONBURY
Upton Noble
Shapwick
Evercreech
STREET
Bruton
Hindon
Mere
Castle Cary
Wincanton
Milton on Stour
SHAFTESBURY
Ludwell
Horsington
SHERBORNE
YEOVIL
Montacute
Martock
South Petherton
Seavington St Mary
ILMINSTER
Donyatt
East Chinnock
CHARD
CREWKERNE
Sturminster Newton
Chedington
BLANDFORD FORUM
Tytherleigh
Hawkchurch
Beaminster
Cerne Abbas
Milton Abbas
Piddletrenthide
DORCHESTER
WAREHAM
Lulworth
LYNTON
Lynmouth
Brendon
Woody Bay
Martinhoe
Porlock
Porlock Weir
MINEHEAD
Blue Anchor
Dunster
WATCHET
WILLITON
Bilbrook
Holford
Simonsbath
Exford
Withypool
Winsford
BRIDGWATER
North Petherton
Bishop's Lydeard
Othery
SOUTH MOLTON
Dulverton
Wiveliscombe
TAUNTON
Hatch Beauchamp
Bampton
WELLINGTON
Oakford
Poundisford
Witheridge
TIVERTON
Eggesford
Sampford Peverell
Bickleigh
Yarcombe
North Tawton
Thorverton
CREDITON
HONITON
Fenny Bridges
Whimple
Wilmington
Axminster
South Zeal
Tedburn St Mary
EXETER
OTTERY ST MARY
Gittisham
Membury
Charmouth
Chideock
Colyton
Uplyme
LYME REGIS
BRIDPORT
Newton Poppleford
SEATON
Rousdon
Beer
Branscombe
Burton Bradstock
West Bexington
Chagford
Doddiscombsleigh
SIDMOUTH
Moretonhamstead
Kennford
Lustleigh
Chudleigh
Bovey Tracey
Haytor
BUDLEIGH SALTERTON
EXMOUTH
DAWLISH
Fleet
Chickerell
WEYMOUTH
Portland
Buckland in the Moor
ASHBURTON
NEWTON ABBOT
Kingsteignton
TEIGNMOUTH
Combeinteignhead
Kingskerswell
Stokeinteignhead
St Marychurch
Babbacombe
BUCKFASTLEIGH
Staverton
TORQUAY
PAIGNTON
TOTNES
Harbertonford
South Brent
Stoke Gabriel
BRIXHAM
Churston Ferrers
North Huish
Maypool
Modbury
DARTMOUTH
Bigbury-on-Sea
Strete
Stoke Fleming
KINGSBRIDGE
Chillington
Thurlestone
Torcross
SALCOMBE
Hope Cove
East Portlemouth
ENGLISH CHANNEL
Hotel
Restaurant
Hotel & Restaurant
Scale
0 10 20 miles
0 10 20 30 kilometres

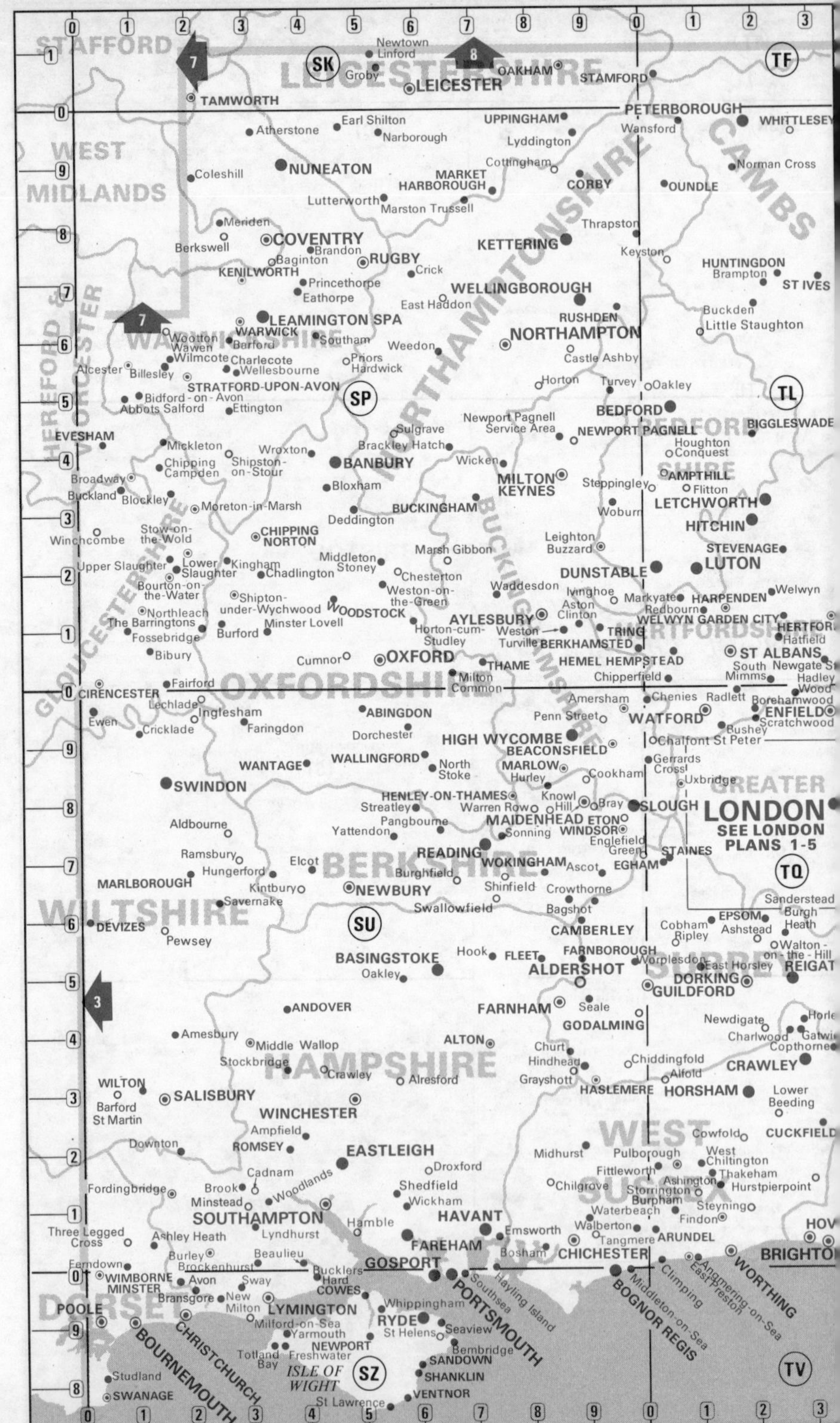

STAFFORD
LEICESTERSHIRE
Newtown Linford
Groby
LEICESTER
OAKHAM
STAMFORD
TAMWORTH
PETERBOROUGH
Wansford
WHITTLESEY
Earl Shilton
Atherstone
Narborough
UPPINGHAM
Lyddington
WEST MIDLANDS
CAMBS
Norman Cross
Coleshill
NUNEATON
Cottingham
MARKET HARBOROUGH
CORBY
OUNDLE
Lutterworth
Marston Trussell
Meriden
Berkswell
COVENTRY
Brandon
Baginton
RUGBY
Crick
Thrapston
KETTERING
Keyston
KENILWORTH
HUNTINGDON
Brampton
ST IVES
Princethorpe
Eathorpe
WELLINGBOROUGH
East Haddon
HEREFORD & WORCESTER
Buckden
Little Staughton
LEAMINGTON SPA
WARWICK
RUSHDEN
WARWICKSHIRE
Wootton Wawen
Barford
Southam
NORTHAMPTON
Weedon
Castle Ashby
Wilmcote
Charlecote
Wellesbourne
Priors Hardwick
NORTHAMPTONSHIRE
Alcester
Billesley
STRATFORD-UPON-AVON
Horton
Turvey
Oakley
Bidford-on-Avon
Abbots Salford
Ettington
BEDFORD
Sulgrave
Newport Pagnell Service Area
NEWPORT PAGNELL
BEDFORDSHIRE
BIGGLESWADE
EVESHAM
Mickleton
Wroxton
Brackley Hatch
Houghton Conquest
Chipping Campden
Shipston-on-Stour
BANBURY
Wicken
AMPTHILL
Broadway
MILTON KEYNES
Steppingley
Flitton
Buckland
Blockley
Bloxham
LETCHWORTH
Moreton-in-Marsh
BUCKINGHAM
Woburn
Deddington
HITCHIN
Winchcombe
Stow-on-the-Wold
CHIPPING NORTON
Leighton Buzzard
STEVENAGE
Marsh Gibbon
Middleton Stoney
BUCKINGHAMSHIRE
Upper Slaughter
Lower Slaughter
Kingham
Chadlington
Chesterton
DUNSTABLE
LUTON
Bourton-on-the-Water
Weston-on-the-Green
Waddesdon
Ivinghoe
Markyate
HARPENDEN
Welwyn
GLOUCESTERSHIRE
Shipton-under-Wychwood
WOODSTOCK
Aston Clinton
Redbourn
WELWYN GARDEN CITY
Northleach
AYLESBURY
HERTFORDSHIRE
HERTFORD
The Barringtons
Minster Lovell
Horton-cum-Studley
Weston Turville
TRING
Hatfield
Fossebridge
Burford
BERKHAMSTED
Bibury
Cumnor
OXFORD
THAME
HEMEL HEMPSTEAD
ST ALBANS
South Mimms
Newgate St
Milton Common
Chipperfield
Hadley Wood
CIRENCESTER
Fairford
OXFORDSHIRE
Amersham
Chenies
Radlett
Borehamwood
Lechlade
ENFIELD
Ewen
Inglesham
ABINGDON
Penn Street
WATFORD
Bushey
Scratchwood
Cricklade
Faringdon
Dorchester
HIGH WYCOMBE
Chalfont St Peter
BEACONSFIELD
WALLINGFORD
Gerrards Cross
WANTAGE
North Stoke
MARLOW
Hurley
Cookham
Uxbridge
SWINDON
GREATER LONDON
HENLEY-ON-THAMES
Knowl Hill
Streatley
Warren Row
Bray
SLOUGH
LONDON
SEE LONDON PLANS 1-5
Aldbourne
Pangbourne
MAIDENHEAD
ETON
WINDSOR
Yattendon
Sonning
Englefield Green
Ramsbury
READING
STAINES
Elcot
BERKSHIRE
WOKINGHAM
Ascot
EGHAM
Hungerford
Burghfield
MARLBOROUGH
Shinfield
Crowthorne
Kintbury
NEWBURY
Sanderstead
Savernake
Swallowfield
Bagshot
Burgh Heath
WILTSHIRE
EPSOM
DEVIZES
Cobham
Ashstead
Ripley
CAMBERLEY
Pewsey
Walton-on-the-Hill
Hook
FLEET
FARNBOROUGH
Worplesdon
East Horsley
BASINGSTOKE
ALDERSHOT
SURREY
REIGATE
Oakley
DORKING
GUILDFORD
FARNHAM
Seale
ANDOVER
GODALMING
Newdigate
Horley
Amesbury
Charlwood
Gatwick
ALTON
Copthorne
Middle Wallop
Churt
Hindhead
Chiddingfold
Stockbridge
HAMPSHIRE
CRAWLEY
Crawley
Alresford
Grayshott
Alfold
WILTON
HASLEMERE
HORSHAM
Lower Beeding
Barford St Martin
SALISBURY
WINCHESTER
WEST SUSSEX
Ampfield
Cowfold
CUCKFIELD
Downton
ROMSEY
EASTLEIGH
Midhurst
Pulborough
West Chiltington
Cadnam
Droxford
Fittleworth
Thakeham
Woodlands
Ashington
Fordingbridge
Brook
Shedfield
Chilgrove
Storrington
Hurstpierpoint
Minstead
Wickham
Burpham
Steyning
Waterbeach
SOUTHAMPTON
Hamble
HAVANT
Findon
Three Legged Cross
Ashley Heath
Lyndhurst
Emsworth
Walberton
ARUNDEL
HOVE
FAREHAM
Tangmere
Burley
Beaulieu
Bosham
CHICHESTER
BRIGHTON
Ferndown
Brockenhurst
GOSPORT
WORTHING
WIMBORNE MINSTER
Avon
Sway
Bucklers Hard
Southsea
Hayling Island
Middleton-on-Sea
Climping
East Preston
Angmering-on-Sea
COWES
PORTSMOUTH
BOGNOR REGIS
DORSET
Bransgore
New Milton
LYMINGTON
Whippingham
POOLE
Milford-on-Sea
RYDE
Seaview
BOURNEMOUTH
CHRISTCHURCH
Yarmouth
St Helens
NEWPORT
Bembridge
Totland Bay
Freshwater
SANDOWN
Studland
ISLE OF WIGHT
SHANKLIN
SWANAGE
St Lawrence
VENTNOR
SK
TF
SP
TL
SU
TQ
SZ
TV

For continuation pages refer to numbered arrows

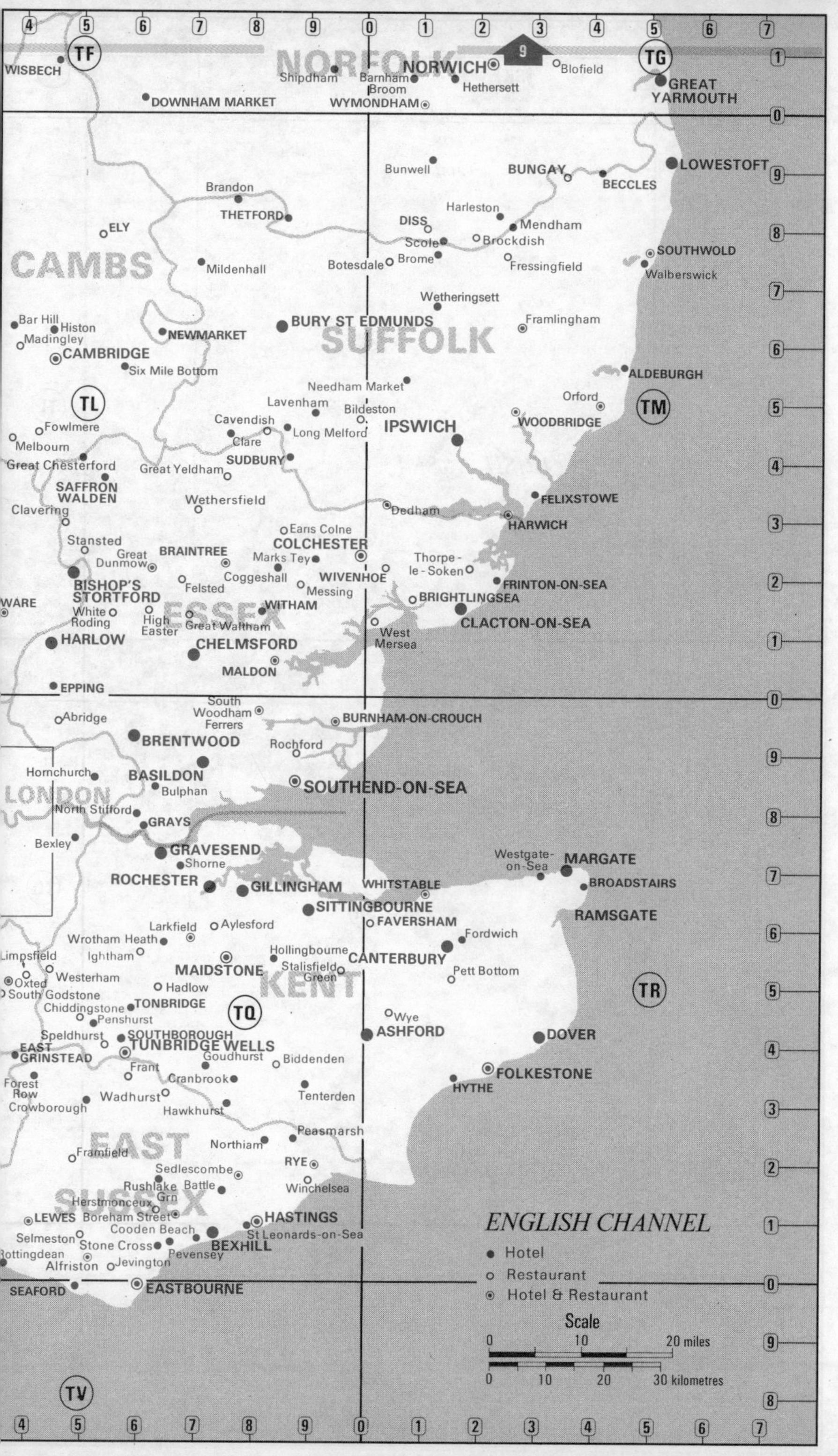
NORFOLK
9
TF
TG
WISBECH
Shipdham
Barnham Broom
NORWICH
Hethersett
Blofield
GREAT YARMOUTH
DOWNHAM MARKET
WYMONDHAM
Bunwell
BUNGAY
LOWESTOFT
BECCLES
Brandon
THETFORD
Harleston
ELY
DISS
Mendham
Scole
Brockdish
SOUTHWOLD
CAMBS
Mildenhall
Botesdale
Brome
Fressingfield
Walberswick
Wetheringsett
Bar Hill
Histon
Madingley
NEWMARKET
BURY ST EDMUNDS
Framlingham
CAMBRIDGE
SUFFOLK
Six Mile Bottom
ALDEBURGH
Needham Market
TL
Lavenham
Bildeston
Orford
TM
Cavendish
WOODBRIDGE
Fowlmere
Clare
Long Melford
IPSWICH
Melbourn
SUDBURY
Great Chesterford
Great Yeldham
SAFFRON WALDEN
Wethersfield
FELIXSTOWE
Clavering
Dedham
HARWICH
Earls Colne
Stansted
COLCHESTER
Great Dunmow
BRAINTREE
Marks Tey
Thorpe-le-Soken
BISHOP'S STORTFORD
Coggeshall
WIVENHOE
FRINTON-ON-SEA
Felsted
Messing
BRIGHTLINGSEA
WARE
White Roding
High Easter
ESSEX
Great Waltham
WITHAM
CLACTON-ON-SEA
West Mersea
HARLOW
CHELMSFORD
MALDON
EPPING
South Woodham Ferrers
Abridge
BURNHAM-ON-CROUCH
BRENTWOOD
Rochford
Hornchurch
BASILDON
LONDON
Bulphan
SOUTHEND-ON-SEA
North Stifford
GRAYS
Bexley
GRAVESEND
Shorne
Westgate-on-Sea
MARGATE
ROCHESTER
GILLINGHAM
WHITSTABLE
BROADSTAIRS
SITTINGBOURNE
RAMSGATE
Larkfield
Aylesford
FAVERSHAM
Wrotham Heath
Fordwich
Limpsfield
Ightham
Hollingbourne
MAIDSTONE
Stalisfield Green
CANTERBURY
Oxted
Westerham
Pett Bottom
South Godstone
Hadlow
KENT
TR
TONBRIDGE
Chiddingstone
TQ
Penshurst
Wye
Speldhurst
SOUTHBOROUGH
ASHFORD
DOVER
EAST GRINSTEAD
TUNBRIDGE WELLS
Goudhurst
Biddenden
Frant
FOLKESTONE
Forest Row
Cranbrook
Crowborough
Wadhurst
Tenterden
HYTHE
Hawkhurst
EAST
Peasmarsh
Northiam
Framfield
RYE
Sedlescombe
Rushlake Grn
Battle
Winchelsea
SUSSEX
Herstmonceux
LEWES
Boreham Street
HASTINGS
ENGLISH CHANNEL
Cooden Beach
Selmeston
Stone Cross
St Leonards-on-Sea
Rottingdean
Pevensey
BEXHILL
Alfriston
Jevington
Hotel
Restaurant
SEAFORD
EASTBOURNE
Hotel & Restaurant
Scale
0
10
20 miles
0
10
20
30 kilometres
TV

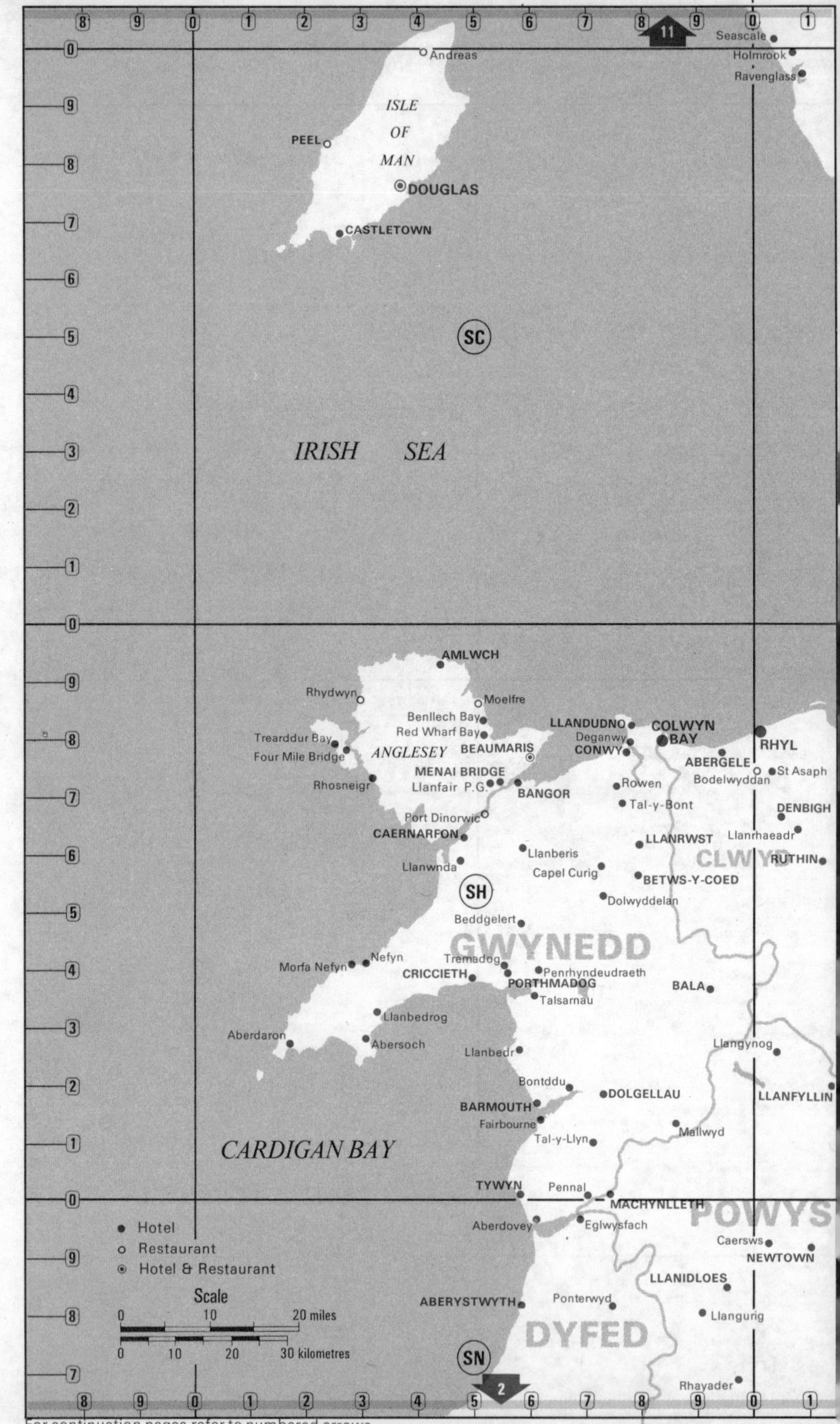
Seascale
Holmrook
Ravenglass
Andreas
ISLE OF MAN
PEEL
DOUGLAS
CASTLETOWN
SC
IRISH SEA
AMLWCH
Rhydwyn
Moelfre
Benllech Bay
Red Wharf Bay
Trearddur Bay
Four Mile Bridge
ANGLESEY
BEAUMARIS
MENAI BRIDGE
Llanfair P.G.
Rhosneigr
BANGOR
LLANDUDNO
Deganwy
CONWY
COLWYN BAY
RHYL
ABERGELE
St Asaph
Bodelwyddan
Rowen
Tal-y-Bont
DENBIGH
Llanrhaeadr
Port Dinorwic
CAERNARFON
LLANRWST
CLWYD
RUTHIN
Llanberis
Llanwnda
Capel Curig
BETWS-Y-COED
SH
Dolwyddelan
Beddgelert
GWYNEDD
Nefyn
Morfa Nefyn
Tremadog
CRICCIETH
Penrhyndeudraeth
PORTHMADOG
Talsarnau
BALA
Llanbedrog
Aberdaron
Abersoch
Llanbedr
Llangynog
Bontddu
DOLGELLAU
BARMOUTH
Fairbourne
LLANFYLLIN
Mallwyd
Tal-y-Llyn
CARDIGAN BAY
TYWYN
Pennal
MACHYNLLETH
POWYS
Aberdovey
Eglwysfach
Caersws
NEWTOWN
Hotel
Restaurant
Hotel & Restaurant
LLANIDLOES
Scale
0 10 20 miles
0 10 20 30 kilometres
ABERYSTWYTH
Ponterwyd
Llangurig
DYFED
SN
Rhayader
11
2

For continuation pages refer to numbered arrows

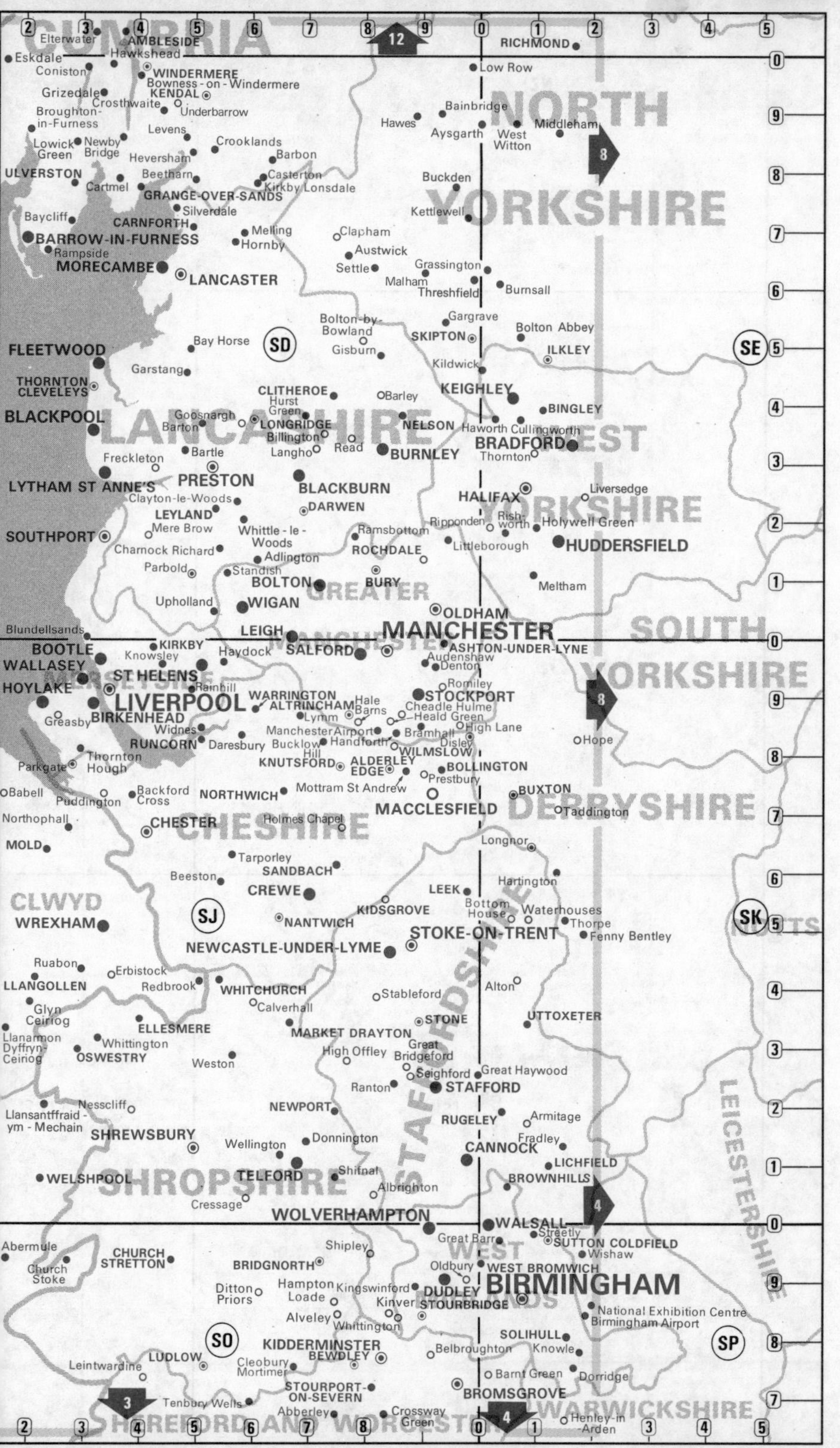

CUMBRIA
Elterwater
AMBLESIDE
Hawkshead
Eskdale
Coniston
WINDERMERE
Bowness-on-Windermere
KENDAL
Grizedale
Crosthwaite
Underbarrow
Broughton-in-Furness
Levens
Lowick Green
Newby Bridge
Heversham
Crooklands
Barbon
ULVERSTON
Cartmel
Beetham
Casterton
Kirkby Lonsdale
GRANGE-OVER-SANDS
Silverdale
Baycliff
CARNFORTH
Melling
Hornby
BARROW-IN-FURNESS
Rampside
MORECAMBE
LANCASTER
RICHMOND
Low Row
NORTH
YORKSHIRE
Bainbridge
Hawes
Aysgarth
West Witton
Middleham
Buckden
Kettlewell
Clapham
Austwick
Settle
Grassington
Malham
Threshfield
Burnsall
Gargrave
Bolton-by-Bowland
SKIPTON
Bolton Abbey
Gisburn
Kildwick
ILKLEY
Bay Horse
SD
SE
FLEETWOOD
Garstang
THORNTON CLEVELEYS
CLITHEROE
Hurst Green
Barley
KEIGHLEY
BINGLEY
BLACKPOOL
LANCASHIRE
Goosnargh
Barton
LONGRIDGE
Billington
NELSON
Haworth
Cullingworth
BRADFORD
WEST
Freckleton
Bartle
Langho
Read
BURNLEY
Thornton
PRESTON
BLACKBURN
HALIFAX
Liversedge
LYTHAM ST ANNE'S
Clayton-le-Woods
DARWEN
YORKSHIRE
LEYLAND
Mere Brow
Whittle-le-Woods
Ramsbottom
Ripponden
Rishworth
Holywell Green
SOUTHPORT
Littleborough
HUDDERSFIELD
Charnock Richard
Adlington
ROCHDALE
Parbold
Standish
BOLTON
BURY
GREATER
Meltham
Upholland
WIGAN
OLDHAM
Blundellsands
LEIGH
MANCHESTER
SOUTH
BOOTLE
KIRKBY
Haydock
SALFORD
ASHTON-UNDER-LYNE
WALLASEY
Knowsley
Audenshaw
Denton
YORKSHIRE
HOYLAKE
MERSEYSIDE
ST HELENS
Rainhill
Romiley
LIVERPOOL
WARRINGTON
ALTRINCHAM
Hale Barns
STOCKPORT
Cheadle Hulme
Greasby
BIRKENHEAD
Lymm
Heald Green
Widnes
Manchester Airport
Bramhall
High Lane
RUNCORN
Daresbury
Bucklow Hill
Handforth
Disley
Hope
Parkgate
Thornton Hough
KNUTSFORD
WILMSLOW
ALDERLEY EDGE
BOLLINGTON
Prestbury
Babell
Puddington
Backford Cross
NORTHWICH
Mottram St Andrew
BUXTON
Northophall
MACCLESFIELD
DERBYSHIRE
Taddington
CHESTER
Holmes Chapel
CHESHIRE
MOLD
Longnor
Tarporley
Beeston
SANDBACH
Hartington
CLWYD
CREWE
LEEK
SJ
Bottom House
Waterhouses
WREXHAM
KIDSGROVE
Thorpe
SK
NOTTS
NANTWICH
STOKE-ON-TRENT
Fenny Bentley
NEWCASTLE-UNDER-LYME
STAFFORDSHIRE
Ruabon
Erbistock
LLANGOLLEN
Redbrook
WHITCHURCH
Alton
Stableford
Glyn Ceiriog
Calverhall
STONE
UTTOXETER
Llanarmon Dyffryn-Ceiriog
ELLESMERE
MARKET DRAYTON
Whittington
OSWESTRY
High Offley
Great Bridgeford
Weston
Seighford
Great Haywood
Ranton
STAFFORD
LEICESTERSHIRE
Nesscliff
NEWPORT
Llansantffraid-ym-Mechain
RUGELEY
Armitage
SHREWSBURY
Donnington
Fradley
Wellington
CANNOCK
LICHFIELD
TELFORD
Shifnal
BROWNHILLS
WELSHPOOL
SHROPSHIRE
Albrighton
Cressage
WOLVERHAMPTON
WALSALL
Streetly
Abermule
Great Barr
SUTTON COLDFIELD
Shipley
WEST
Wishaw
CHURCH STRETTON
Church Stoke
BRIDGNORTH
Oldbury
WEST BROMWICH
Ditton Priors
Hampton Loade
Kingswinford
DUDLEY
BIRMINGHAM
MIDLANDS
Kinver
STOURBRIDGE
National Exhibition Centre
Birmingham Airport
Alveley
Whittington
SO
KIDDERMINSTER
SOLIHULL
SP
LUDLOW
BEWDLEY
Belbroughton
Knowle
Leintwardine
Cleobury Mortimer
Barnt Green
Dorridge
STOURPORT-ON-SEVERN
BROMSGROVE
Tenbury Wells
HEREFORD AND WORCESTER
WARWICKSHIRE
Abberley
Crossway Green
Henley-in-Arden
12
8
8
4
3
4

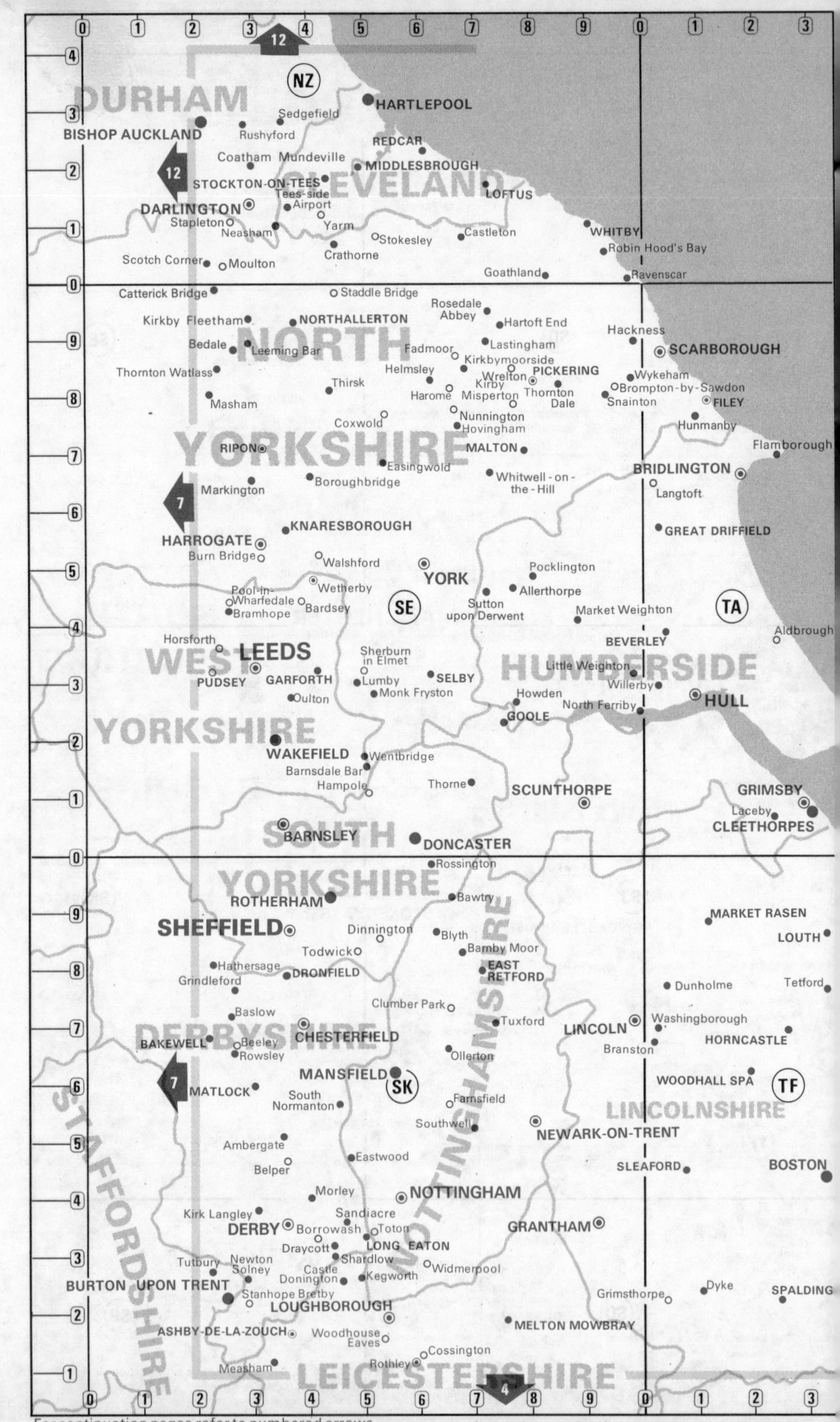

12
NZ
DURHAM
HARTLEPOOL
BISHOP AUCKLAND
Sedgefield
Rushyford
REDCAR
Coatham Mundeville
MIDDLESBROUGH
12
STOCKTON-ON-TEES
CLEVELAND
LOFTUS
Tees-side Airport
DARLINGTON
Stapleton
Yarm
Neasham
Stokesley
Castleton
WHITBY
Robin Hood's Bay
Crathorne
Scotch Corner
Moulton
Goathland
Ravenscar
Catterick Bridge
Staddle Bridge
Rosedale Abbey
Kirkby Fleetham
NORTHALLERTON
Hartoft End
Hackness
NORTH
Bedale
Leeming Bar
Lastingham
SCARBOROUGH
Fadmoor
Kirkbymoorside
Thornton Watlass
Helmsley
Wrelton
PICKERING
Wykeham
Kirby Misperton
Thornton Dale
Brompton-by-Sawdon
Thirsk
Harome
Snainton
FILEY
Masham
Nunnington
Coxwold
Hovingham
Hunmanby
YORKSHIRE
RIPON
MALTON
Flamborough
Easingwold
BRIDLINGTON
Whitwell-on-the-Hill
Markington
Boroughbridge
Langtoft
7
KNARESBOROUGH
GREAT DRIFFIELD
HARROGATE
Burn Bridge
Walshford
YORK
Pocklington
Pool-in-Wharfedale
Wetherby
Allerthorpe
Bramhope
Bardsey
SE
Sutton upon Derwent
Market Weighton
TA
Aldbrough
Horsforth
BEVERLEY
WEST
LEEDS
Sherburn in Elmet
HUMBERSIDE
Little Weighton
PUDSEY
GARFORTH
Lumby
SELBY
Willerby
Monk Fryston
Howden
Oulton
HULL
North Ferriby
GOOLE
YORKSHIRE
WAKEFIELD
Wentbridge
Barnsdale Bar
Hampole
Thorne
SCUNTHORPE
GRIMSBY
Laceby
CLEETHORPES
SOUTH
BARNSLEY
DONCASTER
Rossington
YORKSHIRE
ROTHERHAM
Bawtry
MARKET RASEN
SHEFFIELD
Dinnington
Blyth
LOUTH
Todwick
Barnby Moor
Hathersage
EAST RETFORD
DRONFIELD
Grindleford
Dunholme
Tetford
Clumber Park
Baslow
Tuxford
LINCOLN
Washingborough
DERBYSHIRE
CHESTERFIELD
HORNCASTLE
BAKEWELL
Beeley
Rowsley
Ollerton
Branston
MANSFIELD
SK
WOODHALL SPA
TF
7
MATLOCK
South Normanton
Farnsfield
LINCOLNSHIRE
STAFFORDSHIRE
Southwell
NEWARK-ON-TRENT
NOTTINGHAMSHIRE
Ambergate
Eastwood
SLEAFORD
BOSTON
Belper
Morley
NOTTINGHAM
Kirk Langley
Sandiacre
DERBY
Borrowash
Toton
GRANTHAM
Draycott
LONG EATON
Tutbury
Newton Solney
Shardlow
Castle Donington
Widmerpool
Kegworth
BURTON UPON TRENT
Stanhope Bretby
Grimsthorpe
Dyke
SPALDING
LOUGHBOROUGH
ASHBY-DE-LA-ZOUCH
MELTON MOWBRAY
Woodhouse Eaves
Cossington
Rothley
Measham
LEICESTERSHIRE
4

For continuation pages refer to numbered arrows

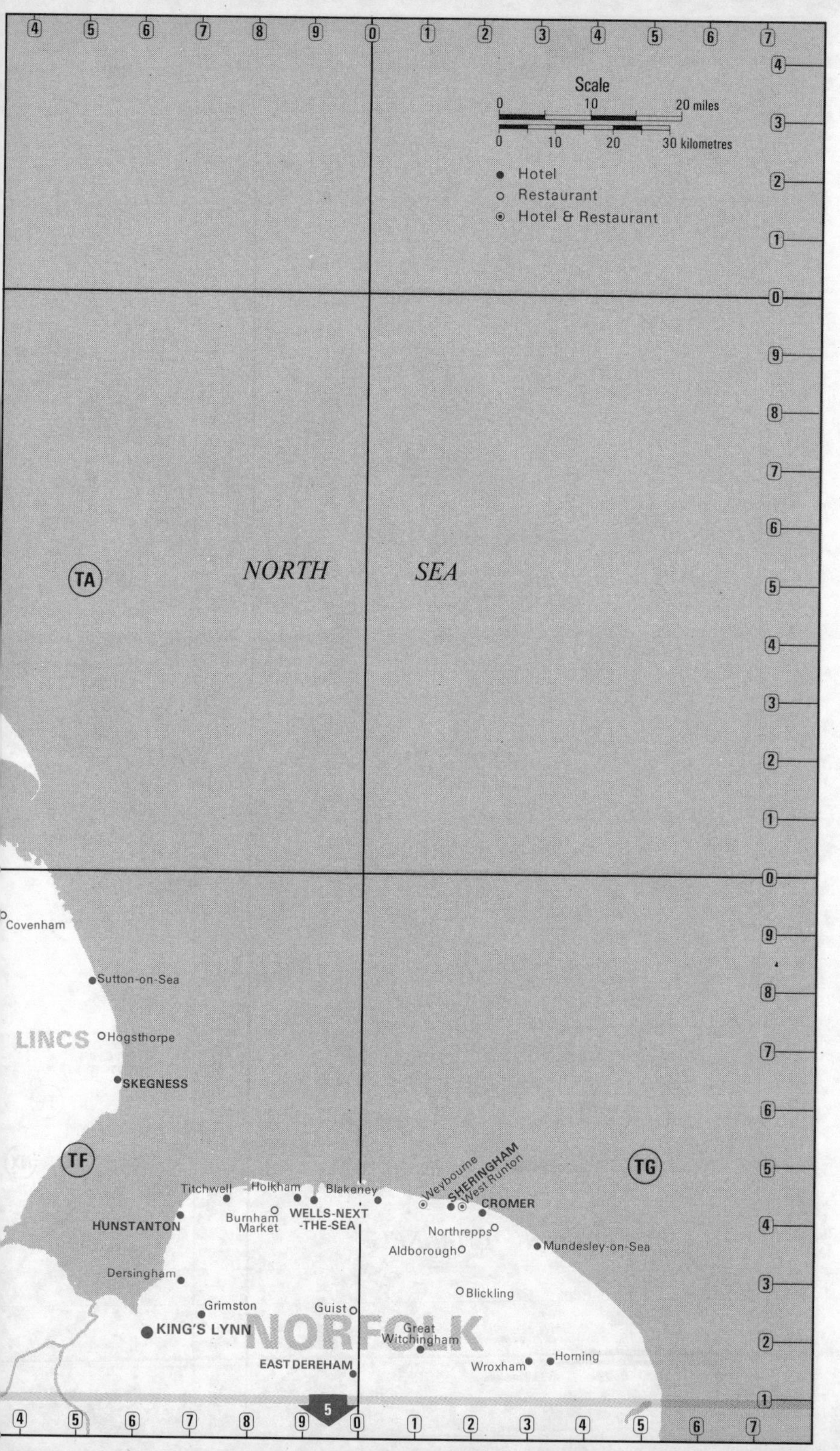
Scale
0
10
20 miles
0
10
20
30 kilometres
Hotel
Restaurant
Hotel & Restaurant
NORTH
SEA
TA
TF
TG
Covenham
Sutton-on-Sea
LINCS
Hogsthorpe
SKEGNESS
Titchwell
Holkham
Blakeney
Weybourne
SHERINGHAM
West Runton
CROMER
HUNSTANTON
Burnham Market
WELLS-NEXT-THE-SEA
Northrepps
Aldborough
Mundesley-on-Sea
Dersingham
Blickling
Grimston
Guist
KING'S LYNN
NORFOLK
Great Witchingham
Horning
Wroxham
EAST DEREHAM
5

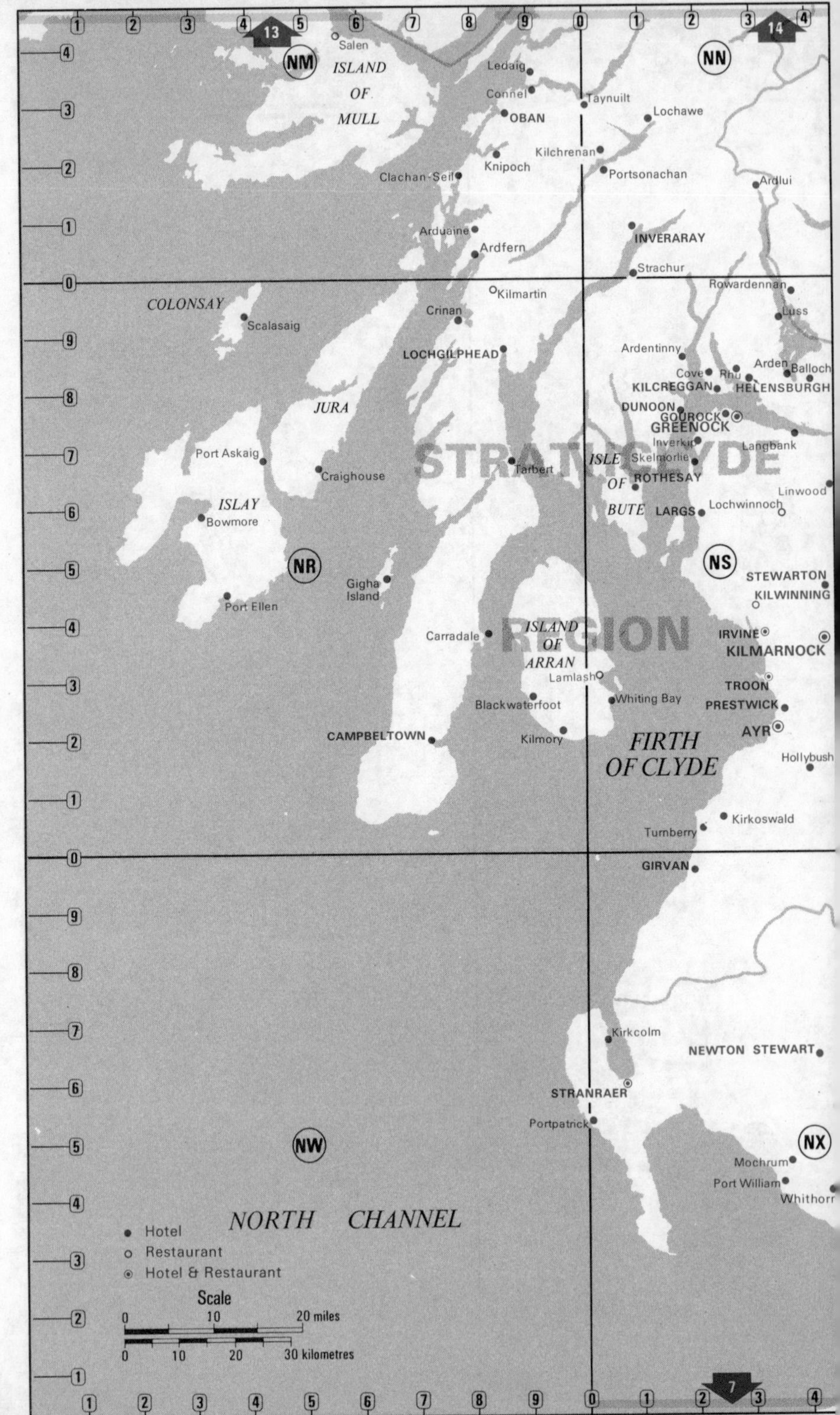
13
14
7
NM
NN
NR
NS
NW
NX
ISLAND OF MULL
Salen
Ledaig
Connel
Taynuilt
OBAN
Lochawe
Kilchrenan
Knipoch
Portsonachan
Clachan-Seil
Ardlui
Arduaine
Ardfern
INVERARAY
Strachur
Rowardennan
Kilmartin
COLONSAY
Scalasaig
Crinan
Luss
LOCHGILPHEAD
Ardentinny
Cove
Rhu
Arden
Balloch
KILCREGGAN
HELENSBURGH
DUNOON
GOUROCK
GREENOCK
JURA
Inverkip
Langbank
Port Askaig
STRATHCLYDE
Tarbert
ISLE OF BUTE
Skelmorlie
ROTHESAY
Craighouse
Linwood
ISLAY
Bowmore
LARGS
Lochwinnoch
STEWARTON
KILWINNING
Gigha Island
Port Ellen
Carradale
ISLAND OF ARRAN
REGION
IRVINE
KILMARNOCK
Lamlash
TROON
Blackwaterfoot
Whiting Bay
PRESTWICK
AYR
CAMPBELTOWN
Kilmory
FIRTH OF CLYDE
Hollybush
Kirkoswald
Turnberry
GIRVAN
Kirkcolm
NEWTON STEWART
STRANRAER
Portpatrick
Mochrum
Port William
Whithorn
NORTH CHANNEL
Hotel
Restaurant
Hotel & Restaurant
Scale
0
10
20 miles
0
10
20
30 kilometres

For continuation pages refer to numbered arrows

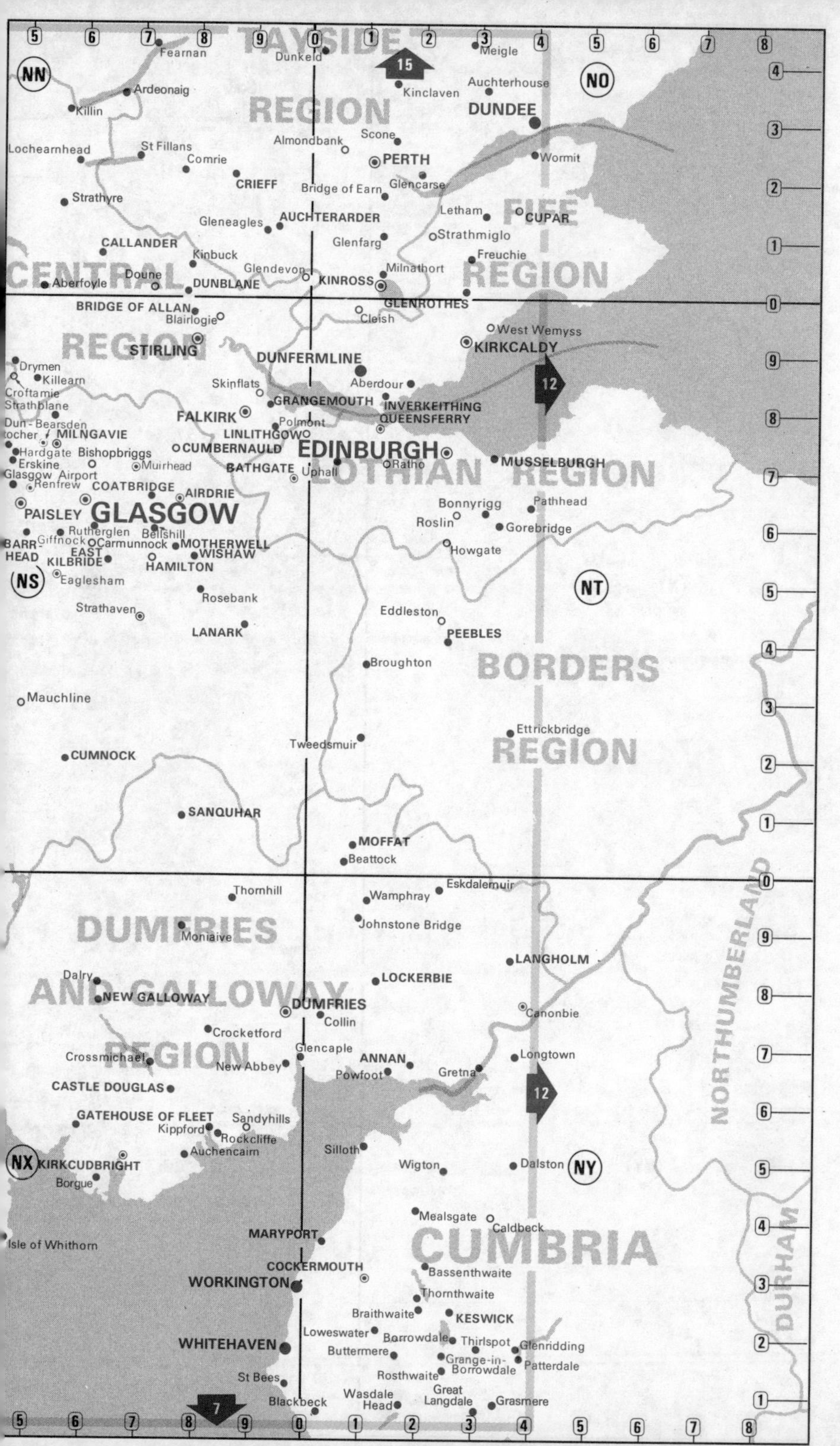

NN
NO
NS
NT
NX
NY
TAYSIDE REGION
CENTRAL REGION
FIFE REGION
LOTHIAN REGION
BORDERS REGION
DUMFRIES AND GALLOWAY REGION
CUMBRIA
NORTHUMBERLAND
DURHAM
15
12
12
7
Fearnan
Dunkeld
Meigle
Ardeonaig
Kinclaven
Auchterhouse
Killin
DUNDEE
Lochearnhead
St Fillans
Almondbank
Scone
Comrie
PERTH
Wormit
CRIEFF
Bridge of Earn
Glencarse
Strathyre
Gleneagles
AUCHTERARDER
Letham
CUPAR
Strathmiglo
Glenfarg
CALLANDER
Freuchie
Kinbuck
Glendevon
Milnathort
Doune
KINROSS
Aberfoyle
DUNBLANE
GLENROTHES
BRIDGE OF ALLAN
Blairlogie
Cleish
West Wemyss
STIRLING
KIRKCALDY
Drymen
DUNFERMLINE
Killearn
Skinflats
Aberdour
Croftamie
Strathblane
GRANGEMOUTH
INVERKEITHING
FALKIRK
QUEENSFERRY
Dun - Bearsden
tocher
MILNGAVIE
Polmont
LINLITHGOW
Hardgate
Bishopbriggs
CUMBERNAULD
EDINBURGH
MUSSELBURGH
Erskine
Muirhead
BATHGATE
Uphall
Ratho
Glasgow Airport
Renfrew
COATBRIDGE
AIRDRIE
Bonnyrigg
Pathhead
PAISLEY
GLASGOW
Roslin
Gorebridge
Rutherglen
Bellshill
Giffnock
Carmunnock
MOTHERWELL
BARR HEAD
EAST KILBRIDE
WISHAW
Howgate
HAMILTON
Eaglesham
Rosebank
Strathaven
Eddleston
LANARK
PEEBLES
Broughton
Mauchline
Ettrickbridge
Tweedsmuir
CUMNOCK
SANQUHAR
MOFFAT
Beattock
Thornhill
Eskdalemuir
Wamphray
Moniaive
Johnstone Bridge
LANGHOLM
Dalry
LOCKERBIE
NEW GALLOWAY
DUMFRIES
Canonbie
Collin
Crocketford
Glencaple
Crossmichael
ANNAN
Longtown
New Abbey
Powfoot
Gretna
CASTLE DOUGLAS
GATEHOUSE OF FLEET
Sandyhills
Kippford
Rockcliffe
Auchencairn
Silloth
KIRKCUDBRIGHT
Wigton
Dalston
Borgue
Mealsgate
Caldbeck
Isle of Whithorn
MARYPORT
COCKERMOUTH
Bassenthwaite
WORKINGTON
Thornthwaite
Braithwaite
KESWICK
Loweswater
Borrowdale
Thirlspot
Glenridding
WHITEHAVEN
Buttermere
Grange-in-Borrowdale
Patterdale
Rosthwaite
St Bees
Wasdale Head
Great Langdale
Grasmere
Blackbeck

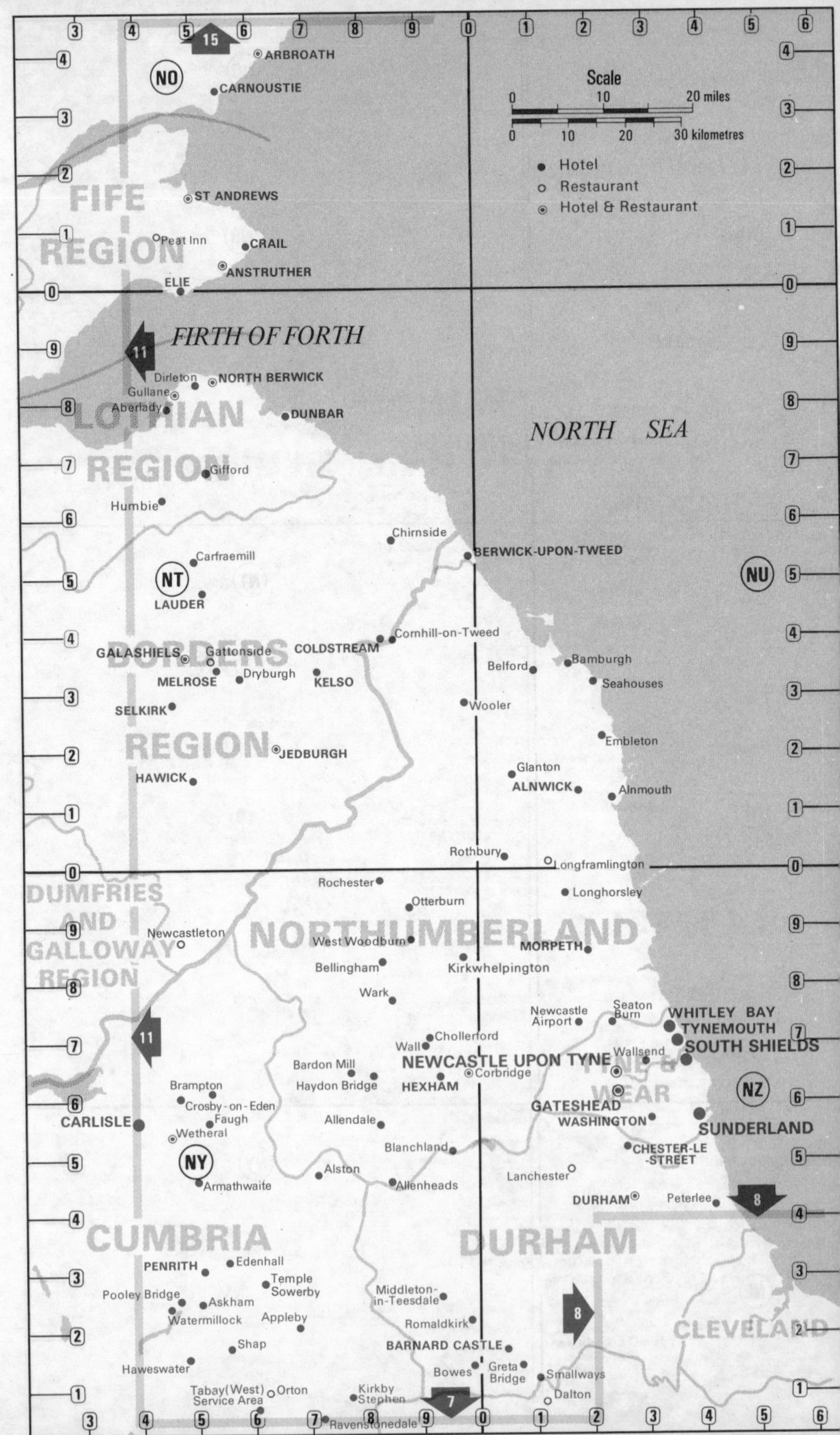
ARBROATH
NO
CARNOUSTIE
Scale
0 10 20 miles
0 10 20 30 kilometres
Hotel
Restaurant
Hotel & Restaurant
FIFE REGION
ST ANDREWS
Peat Inn
CRAIL
ANSTRUTHER
ELIE
FIRTH OF FORTH
Dirleton
NORTH BERWICK
Gullane
Aberlady
LOTHIAN REGION
DUNBAR
NORTH SEA
Gifford
Humbie
Chirnside
BERWICK-UPON-TWEED
Carfraemill
NT
NU
LAUDER
Cornhill-on-Tweed
BORDERS REGION
GALASHIELS
Gattonside
COLDSTREAM
MELROSE
Dryburgh
KELSO
Belford
Bamburgh
Seahouses
SELKIRK
Wooler
Embleton
JEDBURGH
HAWICK
Glanton
ALNWICK
Alnmouth
Rothbury
Longframlington
DUMFRIES AND GALLOWAY REGION
Rochester
Longhorsley
Otterburn
NORTHUMBERLAND
Newcastleton
West Woodburn
MORPETH
Bellingham
Kirkwhelpington
Wark
Newcastle Airport
Seaton Burn
WHITLEY BAY
TYNEMOUTH
SOUTH SHIELDS
Chollerford
Wall
Wallsend
NEWCASTLE UPON TYNE
Bardon Mill
Corbridge
Haydon Bridge
HEXHAM
TYNE & WEAR
NZ
Brampton
Crosby-on-Eden
GATESHEAD
WASHINGTON
CARLISLE
Faugh
Allendale
SUNDERLAND
Wetheral
Blanchland
CHESTER-LE-STREET
NY
Alston
Lanchester
Armathwaite
Allenheads
DURHAM
Peterlee
CUMBRIA
DURHAM
PENRITH
Edenhall
Temple Sowerby
Pooley Bridge
Askham
Middleton-in-Teesdale
Watermillock
Appleby
Romaldkirk
CLEVELAND
Shap
BARNARD CASTLE
Haweswater
Bowes
Greta Bridge
Smallways
Tabay (West) Service Area
Orton
Kirkby Stephen
Dalton
Ravenstonedale
15
11
8
7

For continuation pages refer to numbered arrows

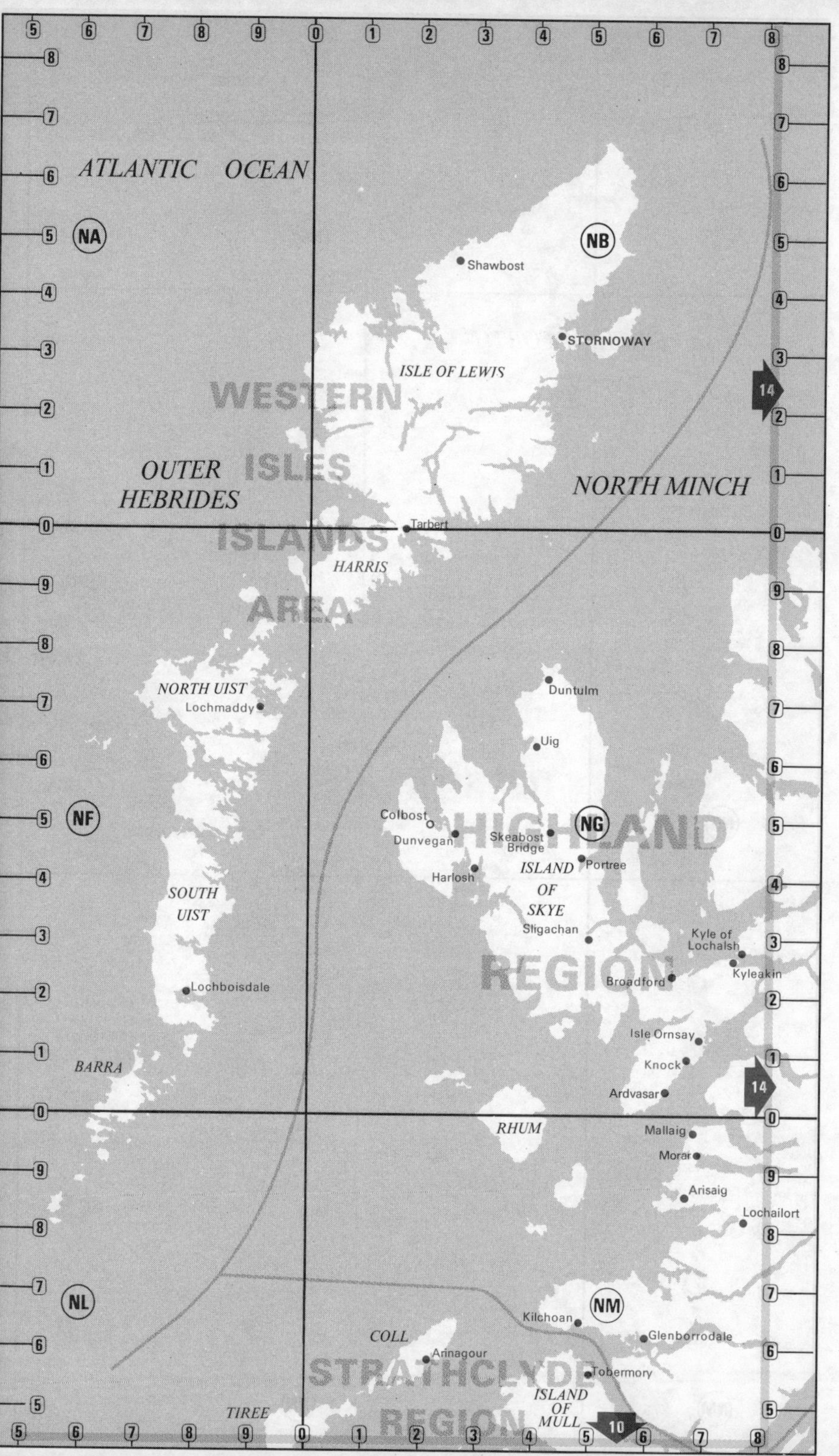
ATLANTIC OCEAN
NA
NB
Shawbost
STORNOWAY
ISLE OF LEWIS
WESTERN
ISLES
ISLANDS
AREA
OUTER
HEBRIDES
NORTH MINCH
14
Tarbert
HARRIS
NORTH UIST
Lochmaddy
Duntulm
Uig
NF
Colbost
Dunvegan
Skeabost
Bridge
NG
HIGHLAND
Portree
Harlosh
ISLAND
OF
SKYE
Sligachan
SOUTH
UIST
Kyle of
Lochalsh
Kyleakin
REGION
Broadford
Lochboisdale
Isle Ornsay
Knock
BARRA
Ardvasar
14
RHUM
Mallaig
Morar
Arisaig
Lochailort
NL
NM
Kilchoan
Glenborrodale
COLL
Arinagour
STRATHCLYDE
REGION
Tobermory
ISLAND
OF
MULL
TIREE
10

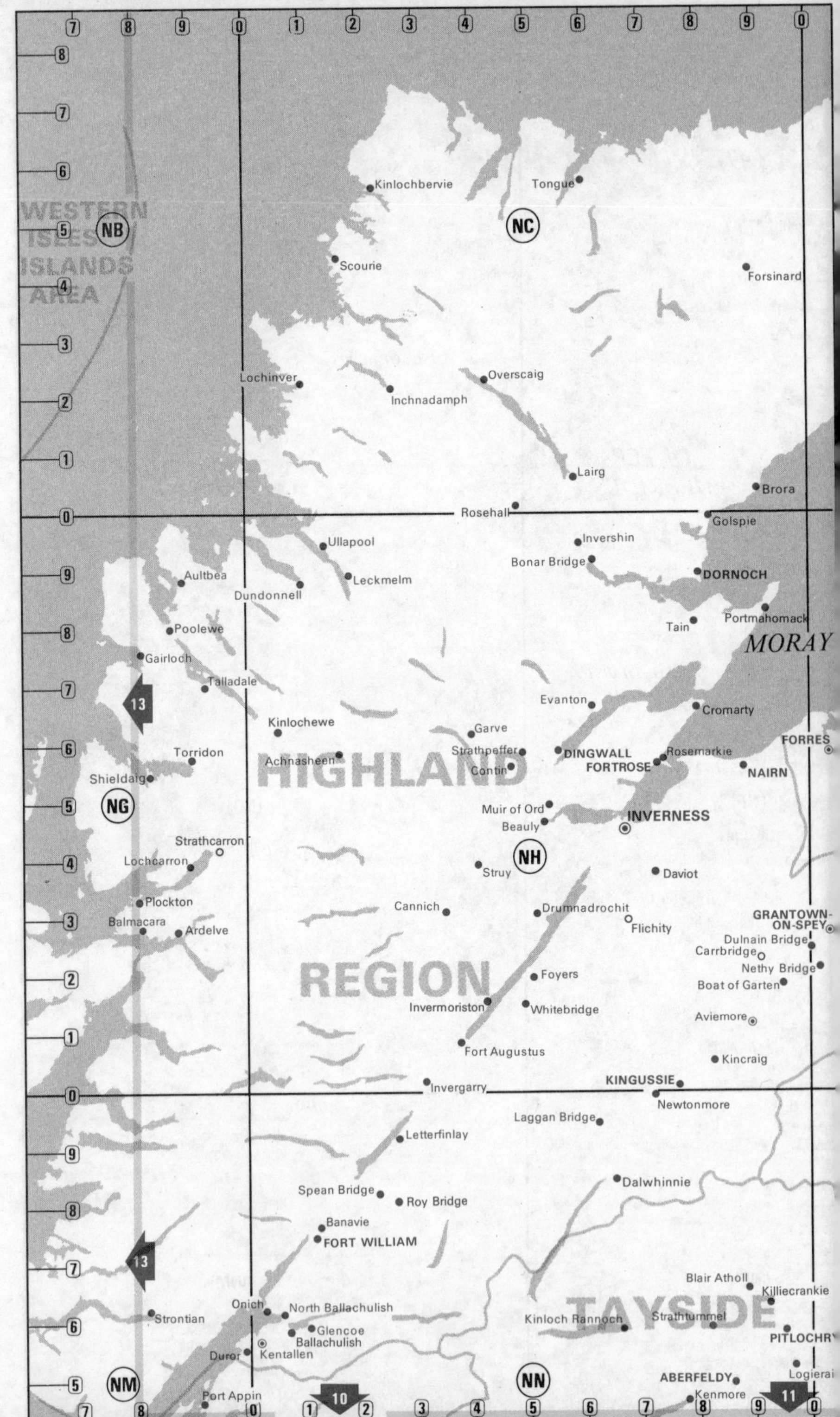
WESTERN ISLES ISLANDS AREA
NB
NC
NG
NH
NM
NN
HIGHLAND REGION
TAYSIDE
MORAY
Kinlochbervie
Tongue
Scourie
Forsinard
Lochinver
Overscaig
Inchnadamph
Lairg
Brora
Rosehall
Golspie
Ullapool
Invershin
Bonar Bridge
Aultbea
Leckmelm
Dundonnell
DORNOCH
Portmahomack
Tain
Poolewe
Gairloch
Talladale
Evanton
Cromarty
Kinlochewe
Garve
FORRES
Torridon
Achnasheen
Strathpeffer
DINGWALL
Rosemarkie
Contin
FORTROSE
NAIRN
Shieldaig
Muir of Ord
Beauly
INVERNESS
Strathcarron
Lochcarron
Struy
Daviot
Plockton
Cannich
Drumnadrochit
Flichity
Balmacara
Ardelve
GRANTOWN-ON-SPEY
Dulnain Bridge
Carrbridge
Nethy Bridge
Foyers
Boat of Garten
Invermoriston
Whitebridge
Aviemore
Fort Augustus
Kincraig
KINGUSSIE
Invergarry
Newtonmore
Laggan Bridge
Letterfinlay
Dalwhinnie
Spean Bridge
Roy Bridge
Banavie
FORT WILLIAM
Blair Atholl
Killiecrankie
Onich
North Ballachulish
Strontian
Glencoe
Ballachulish
Kinloch Rannoch
Strathtummel
PITLOCHRY
Duror
Kentallen
Logierait
ABERFELDY
Kenmore
Port Appin
13
10
11

For continuation pages refer to numbered arrows